# PETERSON'S
# COMPETITIVE COLLEGES

# 1995–1996

## Fourteenth Edition

Peterson's

Princeton, New Jersey

Visit Peterson's Education Center on the Internet
(World Wide Web) at http://www.petersons.com

Copyright © 1995 by Peterson's Guides, Inc.

Previous editions © 1981, 1982, 1983, 1984, 1985,
1986, 1987, 1988, 1989, 1990, 1991, 1992, 1993,
1994

Competitive Colleges is a registered trademark of
Peterson's Guides, Inc.

ISSN 0887-0152
ISBN 1-56079-480-1

Printed in the United States of America

10   9   8   7   6   5   4   3   2   1

# CONTENTS

# CHOOSING THE RIGHT COLLEGE FROM AMONG AMERICA'S BEST

Since the publication of its first edition in the spring of 1981, the purpose of Peterson's *Competitive Colleges* has been to help broaden the horizons of students like you: competitive students whose educational careers have been marked by academic or some other kind of distinction or achievement. As a competitive student, you have special needs when it comes to choosing the right college. You've excelled at what you do and you want to go on excelling. You need an educational environment that will push you, test you, help you break beyond the limits of your current potential. You require a college that "fits" exactly right, one that will help you develop your particular talents, skills, and experiences into what you uniquely can become.

Our experience at Peterson's, and that of hundreds of guidance counselors at high schools around the country, is that the search for the "right" college has perhaps never been more difficult than it is at the moment. It has always been true that, when it comes to understanding their options for college, students—especially competitive students—are often, at first, extremely limited in their thinking. It might be a worthwhile exercise for you to compile a list of the colleges mentioned whenever you and your friends discuss where you might apply. You'll probably find that everyone's list of colleges is very much alike—and strikingly narrow. With a few notable exceptions determined by the region in which you live, your specific interests, or your parents' particular alma maters, your list and those of your friends will probably include the Ivy League and a handful of other nationally known colleges and universities.

This is not surprising. Until you start to do some research, the only source of information you have about college is popular mythology, sometimes in the form of media stories but more often in the statements of enthusiastic teachers or well-intentioned relatives. Popular mythology does no real harm when it's corrected with accurate information, and it even serves the useful function of helping you begin to think. It is limiting, however; and it's often connected with a genuine misunderstanding about how the college admission process works—the same misunderstanding that is at the root of all the anxiety that competitive students frequently experience as they go about the business of applying to college.

What makes this situation especially difficult now and what concerns us at Peterson's, as well as many of our colleagues in the college admission and guidance communities, is the growing national tendency to institutionalize popular mythology in the guise of a college guide. It's one thing for your Uncle Joe to think that the only physics programs worth their salt are at MIT and Georgia Tech or for the students in your Advanced Placement class to think that their lives won't be meaningful unless they go to Harvard, Yale, or Princeton. It's quite another thing for "guides" to make such proclamations. Yet many do, with

colleges elaborately categorized and aligned in rank order and titles proclaiming that the colleges on the list are the "best this," the "most selective that," the "top 100," or the "most something else for your money."

But ask yourself: How should the quality of a college be measured? On its financial resources? Its faculty-student ratio? Its library holdings? The number of jobs students were offered by graduation? The number of articles and books published by professors? What would quality mean to you? To your best friend? To the captain of the debating team? To the star of your senior play? To the president of the science club? Quality cannot be assigned numbers and toted up for ranking. Judging a college is much harder than that. If close faculty interaction is important to you, you have to choose a college where the faculty value teaching. This may be indicated by the faculty-student ratio or the number of undergraduate courses taught by faculty. If you want to do research with some professors, you need a college where a lot is going on at the graduate level or where there is a strong commitment to undergraduate research of a high level. In this case, the number of undergraduate courses taught by professors and the faculty-student ratio probably won't be relevant.

We can leave it to the statisticians and philosophers to prove that the subjective opinion of millions of people is still subjective and that the division of a number of books by a number of students is more or less useless except in certain rigidly defined circumstances. The point is that every college or university is different, each having its own unique mission, standards, and characteristics, and you are different from all other applicants. No formula or set of statistics can adequately measure what goes on at a college. Thus, no college can be compared to any other college except in single quantifiable measures. College X may have a larger endowment than College Y. But College Y has more books and more faculty members than College X. Which is the better college? You can compare books, or endowments, or numbers of faculty members, but you can't add them up, and there's no such thing as a total of all these.

There are numbers you want to look at as you search for a college, but they have nothing to do with ranking and can't be prescribed by anyone other than you. If you love language, you might be interested in the percentage of students who scored high on the verbal section of their SATs or in the existence of programs in creative and expository writing, with graduates achieving success in related fields. If you've gotten addicted to the Internet, the number of computers on campus could be important, along with information about access to those computers in offices, libraries, and dorm rooms. Scholars might want to know what percent of the student body goes on to graduate school after receiving a bachelor's degree. If you'll need help paying for college, the amount of financial aid a college typically awards is a very important figure. The list of potentially interesting numbers is large, but you're the only one who can make up that list for you—out of your own needs and aspirations.

The editors of Peterson's *Competitive Colleges* ask you to reject the idea that artificial rankings are useful in the college admission process. We want you to think clearly and honestly about yourself and what you want from your college experience. We do make an assumption that the most influential factor in determining your experience on campus is the other students you will find there. Therefore, in selecting colleges for inclusion in this book, our focus has been on the competitiveness of the admission environment at those institutions, as evidenced by the quality of the students applying each year. The colleges selected for this book routinely attract and admit an above-average share of the nation's high-achieving students.

Good colleges typically take great care in admitting their student bodies. For them, the annual project of selecting the entering class is as Bill Fitzsimmons, Dean of Undergraduate Admission and Financial Aid at Harvard University, describes it: a process of "sculpting" the best possible class from the pool of qualified applicants. This is only in part a process of reviewing transcripts and standardized test scores. The goal of an admission committee is to bring together a community of students who can learn from one another, each one bringing particular talents, skills, and experiences that will contribute to the development of all the others.

We think you should adopt a similar approach in your attempt to find the "right" college. Construct your first—and broadest—list of possible colleges by looking at the other students on campus. Look not only for students with academic and extracurricular interests similar to yours but for students whose experiences will open up new worlds for you. Then, it's time to pay attention to the rest of the information we provide—class size, the number of computers on campus, library holdings, etc.—in terms of how this information suits your own unique needs. It's at this point only—and for you only—that it's appropriate to rank colleges. That's what this book is all about: helping you to discover the right college for you.

Best of luck in your search!

Michael Ditchkofsky
Director of Higher Education Services

*Peterson's would like to acknowledge the thoughtful contributions of the following reviewers: Francis D. Fergusson, President, Vassar College; David Johnson, Chancellor, University of Minnesota, Morris; Judith Rodin, President, University of Pennsylvania; and David P. Roselle, President, University of Delaware.*

# UNDERSTANDING THE COLLEGE ADMISSION PROCESS

## by Ted Spencer, Director of Admissions at the University of Michigan

The process you are about to begin, that of choosing a college, can be very challenging, sometimes frustrating, but is most often rewarding. As Director of Admissions at a large, selective university, I would like to provide some basic information about the admission process that should help you get into the college of your choice. Although each competitive college or university has its own distinctive qualities and goals, the process of applying to them is strikingly similar. The following will give you the basic information you need to know to help you plan and apply to college.

## Gathering Information

How do you get the information you need to choose a college? The fact that you are reading this article means that you have already found one of the many college information resources available today. Although colleges publish volumes of information about themselves that they are willing to mail or give out in person, another way to find out about them is through the numerous guides available, such as Peterson's *Competitive Colleges*. The major difference between the college-published brochures and the guides or handbooks is that the college information is meant to present the most appealing picture of a school and is perhaps, then, a little less objective. As a student seeking information about college, you should try to review both the information provided in the guides and handbooks and the information sent by the colleges. Your goal should be to use all of the available literature to assist you in developing your list of the top five or ten colleges in which you are interested.

Chances are, however, that if you are a top student and you have taken either the PSAT (Preliminary Scholastic Assessment Test), SAT I (Scholastic Assessment Test), ACT (American College Testing) Examination, PACT (Preliminary American College Testing) Examination, or AP (Advanced Placement) Test, you will receive a great deal of material directly from many colleges and universities. Colleges purchase lists of names of students taking these exams and then screen the list for students they think will be most successful at their institutions. This results in the sending of material that is often tailored to your particular interests. Some colleges will also automatically mail course catalogs, posters, departmental brochures and pamphlets, as well as videocassettes. If you do not receive this information but would like a sample, write or call that particular college.

My advice to students is to take a look at the materials you receive and then let them help you decide (if you don't already know) about the type of college you would like to attend. Even if you already have an idea about the type of college you plan to attend, allow the materials to help you narrow your list of top schools by comparing key facts and characteristics.

## OTHER HELPFUL SOURCES

Published information about colleges, printed by the colleges, is certainly an important way to narrow your choices. But there are at least five other means of learning more about colleges and universities:

- *High School Counselors.* Although most high school counselors are overburdened, they have established positive relationships with the college representatives in your state as well as with out-of-state universities where large numbers of their students apply. As you attempt to gain more information while narrowing your choice of colleges, the high school counselor can give you a fairly accurate assessment of colleges to which you will have the best chance of gaining admission.
- *Parents.* Because most prospective students and their parents are at that stage in life in which they view the same issues in different ways, students tend to be reluctant to ask parents' opinions about college choices. However, you may find that parents are very helpful because they often are actively gathering information about the colleges that they feel are best suited for you. And not only do they gather information—you can be sure that they have thoroughly read the piles of literature that colleges have mailed to you. Ask your parents questions about what they have read and also about the colleges from which they graduated. As alumni of schools on your list, parents can be a very valuable resource.
- *College Day/Night/Fairs Visitation.* One of the best ways to help narrow your college choices is to meet with a person representing a college while they are visiting your area or high school. In fact, most admission staff spend a good portion of the fall and late spring visiting high schools and attending college fairs. In some cases, colleges will bring along students, faculty, and alumni. Before attending one of these sessions, you should prepare a list of questions you would like to ask the representatives. Most students want to know about five major areas: academic preparation, the admission process, financial aid, social life, and job preparation. Most college representatives can be extremely helpful in addressing these questions as well as the many others that you may have. It is then up to you to decide if their answers fit your criteria of the college you are seeking.
- *Alumni.* For many schools, alumni are a very important part of their admission process. In some cases, alumni conduct interviews and even serve as surrogate admis-

sion officers, particularly when admission office staff cannot travel. As recent graduates, they can talk about their own experience and can give balance to the materials you have received from the college or university.

- *Campus Visit.* Finally, try to schedule a campus visit as part of your information-gathering process. By the time you begin thinking about a campus visit, you should have narrowed down your college shopping list. Hopefully your short list of colleges will have met your personal and educational goals. Before deciding which schools to visit, you should sort the materials into piles of "definitely not interested," "definitely interested," or "could be interested." Next, in an effort to make sure that the reality lives up to the printed viewbook, you should schedule a visit and see firsthand what the college is really like. Most colleges and universities provide daily campus tours to both prospective and admitted students. The tours for prospective students are generally set up to help you answer questions about the following: class size and student-to-teacher ratio; size of the library, residence halls, and computer centers; registration and faculty advising; and retention, graduation rates, and career placement planning. Since the tours may not cover everything you came prepared to ask about, be sure to ask questions of as many staff, students, and faculty members as possible before leaving the campus.

## The Admission Process

### ADMISSION CRITERIA

Perhaps one of the greatest areas of frustration for students and their parents is the admission process. After you go through the process of selecting a college or narrowing your choices to a few schools, the admission process now focuses on you—your academic record and skills—and judgment will be passed on these pieces of information for admission to a particular school. One of the first things you should find out, then, about each college on your priority list is what it takes to get in, or the admission criteria:

1. Does the college or university require standardized tests—the ACT or SAT I? Do they prefer one or the other, or will they accept either?
2. Do they require SAT II Subject Tests and, if so, which ones?
3. Are Advanced Placement scores accepted and, if so, what are the minimums needed?
4. In terms of grades and class rank, what is the profile of a typical entering student?
5. What is the application deadline and how long will it take to find out if you have been admitted?

It is also important to find out which type of admission notification system the college uses—rolling or deferred admission. On a rolling system, you find out your status within several weeks after applying; with the deferred system, notification is generally made in the spring. For the most part, public universities and colleges use rolling admission and private colleges generally use delayed notification.

### THE APPLICATION

The application is the primary vehicle used to introduce yourself to the admission office. As with any introduction, you should try to make a good first impression. The first thing you should do in presenting your application is to find out what the college or university wants from you. This means you should read the application carefully to learn the following:

1. Must the application be typed, or can you print it?
2. Is there an application fee and, if so, how much is it?
3. Is there a deadline and, if so, when is it?
4. What standardized tests are required?
5. Is an essay required?
6. Is an interview required?
7. Can you send letters of recommendation?
8. How long will it take to find out the admission decision?
9. What other things can you do to improve your chances of admission?

My advice is to submit your application early. It does not guarantee admission, but it is much better than submitting it late or near the deadline. Also, don't assume that colleges using rolling admission will always have openings close to their deadlines. Regardless of when you submit it, make sure that the application is legible and that all the information requested is provided.

### TRANSCRIPTS

While all of the components of the application are extremely important in the admission process, perhaps the single most important item is your transcript because it tells: (1) what courses you took; (2) which courses were college-preparatory and challenging; (3) class rank; and (4) grades and test scores.

- *Required Course Work.* Generally speaking, most colleges look at the high school transcript to see if the applicant followed a college-preparatory track while in high school. So, if you have taken four years of English, math, natural science, social sciences, and foreign language, you are on the right track. Many selective colleges require a minimum of four years of English; three years each of math, natural science, and social science; and two years of a foreign language. It is also true that some selective colleges believe students who are interested in majoring in math and science need more than the minimum requirements in those areas.
- *Challenging Courses.* As college admission staff members continue to evaluate your transcript, they also look to see how demanding your course load has been during high school. If the high school offered Advanced Placement or Honors courses, the expectation of most selective colleges is that students will have taken at least seven or more Honors classes or four or more AP courses during their four years in high school. However, if you do elect to take challenging courses, it is also important that you make good grades in those courses. Quite often, students ask, "If I take Honors and AP courses and get a 'C,' does that count more than getting a 'B' or higher in a strictly

college-prep course?" It's a difficult question to answer, because too many C's and B's can outweigh mostly A's. On the other hand, students who take the more challenging courses will be better prepared to take the more rigorous courses in college. Consequently, many colleges will give extra consideration when making their selections to the students who take the more demanding courses.

• *Transcript Trends.* Because the courses you take in high school are such a critical part of the college decision-making process, your performance in those courses indicates to colleges whether you are following an upward or downward trend. Beginning with the ninth grade, admission staff look at your transcript to see if you have started to develop good academic habits. In general, when colleges review your performance in the ninth grade, they are looking to see if you are in the college-preparatory track.

By sophomore year, students should begin choosing more demanding courses and become more involved in extracurricular activities. This will show that are beginning to learn how to balance your academic and extracurricular commitments. Many admission officers consider sophomore year to be the most critical and telling year for the student's future success.

The junior year is perhaps the second-most-important year in high school. The grades you earn and the courses you take will help to reinforce the trend you began in your sophomore year. At the end of your junior year, many colleges will know enough about the type of student you are to make their admission decision.

The upward and positive trend must continue, however, during your senior year. Many selective schools do not use senior grades in making their admission decisions. However, almost all do review the final transcript, so your last year needs to show a strong performance to the end. The research shows that students who finish their senior year with strong grades will start their freshman year in college with strong grades.

## The Application Review Process

### WHAT'S NEXT?

At this point, you have done all you can do. So you might as well sit back and relax, if that's possible, and wait for the letters to come in the mail. Hopefully, if you've evaluated all the college materials you were sent earlier and you prepared your application carefully and sent it to several colleges, you will be admitted to either your first, second, or third choice. It may help your peace of mind, however, to know what happens to your application after the materials have been submitted.

Once your application is received by the admission office, it is usually processed through the mailroom and then reviewed, in most cases by noncounseling staff, to determine if you have completed the application properly. If items are missing, you will receive a letter of notification identifying additional information that must be provided. Be sure to send any additional or missing information the

college requests back to them as soon as possible. Once your application is complete, it is then ready for the decision process.

### READER REVIEW

The process by which the decision is finalized varies from school to school. Most of the private colleges and universities use a system where each application is read by at least two or more admission staff members. In some cases, faculty members are also used as additional readers. If all of the readers agree on the decision, a letter is sent. Under this system, if the readers do not agree, the application will be reviewed by a committee or may be forwarded to an associate dean, dean, or director of admission for the final decision. One advantage to this process is that each applicant is reviewed by several people, thereby eliminating bias.

### COMMITTEE REVIEW

At some universities, a committee reviews every application. Under that system, a committee member is assigned a number of applications to present. It is that member's responsibility to prepare background information on each applicant and then present the file to the committee for discussion and a vote. In this process, every applicant is voted on.

### COUNSELOR REVIEW

The review process that many selective public institutions use is one in which the counselor responsible for a particular school or geographical territory makes the final decision. In this case, the counselor who makes the admission decision is also the one who identified and recruited the student, thereby lending a more personal tone to the process.

### COMPUTER-GENERATED REVIEW

Many large state universities that process nearly 20,000 applications a year have developed computer-generated guidelines to admit their applicants. If applicants meet the required GPA and test scores, they are immediately notified of the decision.

Once the decisions are made using one of these methods, colleges use a variety of ways to notify students. Again, the common methods used are early action or early decision, rolling admission, and deferred admission.

## A Word of Advice

When you start the admission process, do so with the idea of exploring as many college opportunities as you can. From the very beginning, avoid focusing on just one college or, for that matter, type of college. Look at private, public, large, small, highly selective, selective—in short, a variety of colleges and universities. Take advantage of every available resource, including students, parents, counselors, and college materials, in order to help identify the colleges that will be a great fit for you.

Finally, the most important thing you can do is to build a checklist of what you want out of the college experience and then match your list with one of the many wonderful colleges and universities just waiting for you to enroll.

# PAYING FOR COLLEGE

## by Don Betterton, Director of Financial Aid at Princeton University

Regardless of which college a student chooses, higher education requires a major investment of time, energy, and money. By taking advantage of a variety of available resources, most students can bring the education that is right for them within reach.

## A Note of Encouragement

While there is no denying that the cost of education at a competitive college can be high, it is important to recognize that, although the rate of increase in costs in the last ten years has outpaced gains in family income, there are more options available to pay for college than ever before.

Many families find it is economically wise to spread costs out over a number of years by borrowing money for college. Although increases in federal student aid funding have fallen short of college cost increases, there remains a significant amount of government money, both federal and state, available to students. Moreover, colleges themselves have expanded their own student aid efforts considerably. In spite of rapidly increasing costs, most competitive colleges are still able to provide financial aid to all admitted students with demonstrated need.

In addition, many colleges have developed ways to assist families who are not eligible for need-based assistance. These include an increasing number of merit scholarships as well as various forms of parental loans. There also are a number of organizations that give merit awards based on a student's academic record, talent, or special characteristics. Thus, regardless of your family's income, if you are academically qualified and knowledgeable about the many different sources of aid, you should be able to attend the college of your choice.

## Estimating Costs

If you have not yet settled on specific colleges and you would like to begin early financial planning, estimate a budget. Based on actual 1994–95 charges, we can estimate 1995–96 expenses at a typical competitive college as follows: tuition and fees, about $16,500; room and board, about $6,000; and an allowance for books and miscellaneous expenses, about $1,700. Thus a rough budget (excluding travel expenses) for the year is $24,200.

## Identifying Resources

There are essentially four sources of funds you can use to pay for college:

1. Money from your parents
2. Need-based scholarships or grants from a college or outside organization
3. Your own contribution from savings, loans, and jobs
4. Assistance unrelated to demonstrated financial need.

All of these are considered by the financial aid office, and the aid "package" given to a student after the parental contribution has been determined usually consists of a combination of scholarships, loans, and campus work.

### THE PARENTAL CONTRIBUTION

The financial aid policies of most colleges are based on the assumption that parents should contribute as much as they reasonably can to the educational expenses of their children. The amount of this contribution varies greatly, but almost every family is expected to pay something.

Because there is no limit on aid eligibility based solely on income, the best rule of thumb is *apply for financial aid if there is any reasonable doubt about your ability to meet college costs*. Since it is generally true that applying for financial aid does not affect a student's chances of being admitted, any candidate for admission should apply for aid if his or her family feels they will be unable to pay the entire cost of attendance.

Application for aid is made by completing the Free Application for Federal Student Aid (FAFSA). In addition, many competitive colleges will require you to also file the Financial Aid Form (FAF), since they need more detailed information to award their own funds. (Note: The FAF will be replaced by the "Profile" for 1996–97.) The financial aid section of a college's admission information booklet will tell you which financial aid application is required, when it should be filed, and whether a separate aid form of the college's own design is also necessary.

Colleges use the same national system to determine the parental contribution. This process, called "need analysis," examines income, assets, the number of family members, the number attending college, unusual expenses, and other variables that affect a family's financial strength.

You can estimate how much your parents might be asked to contribute for college by consulting the chart on page 10. (Keep in mind that the actual parental contribution is determined on campus by a financial aid officer, using the national system as a guideline.) A more detailed analysis is furnished as part of Peterson's Financial Aid Service, a comprehensive software program that provides a personalized method of judging parental ability to pay for college expenses and gives details on college, government, and private student aid sources. It can be found in many high school guidance offices.

Competitive colleges that also require the FAF (soon to be the "Profile") will have at their disposal information that they will analyze in addition to what is reported on the FAFSA. The net result of this further examination (for example, adding the value of the family home to the equation) will usually increase the expected parental contribution compared to the national system.

### Parental Borrowing

Some families who are judged to have sufficient resources to be able to finance their children's college costs find that lack of cash at any moment prevents them from paying college bills without difficulty. Other families prefer to use less current income by extending their payments over more than four years. In both instances, these families rely on borrowing to assist with college payments. Each year parental loans become a more important form of college financing.

The Federal PLUS program, part of the Federal Family Education Loan Program, is designed to help both aid and non-aid families and allows parents to pay a greater share of educational costs by borrowing at a reasonable interest rate, with the backing of the federal government. The 8–9 percent loans are available primarily from banks that offer Federal Stafford Student Loans. Many competitive colleges, state governments, and commercial lenders also have their own parental loan programs patterned along the lines of FPLUS. For more information about parental loans, contact a college financial aid office or your state higher education department.

A number of competitive colleges have developed their own parental loan programs with interest rates somewhat below those of the Federal PLUS program. A college's financial aid material will explain the terms of such loans.

### NEED-BASED SCHOLARSHIP OR GRANT ASSISTANCE

Need-based aid is primarily available from colleges themselves and federal and state governments. It is not necessary for a student to apply directly for a particular scholarship at a college; the financial aid office will match an eligible applicant with the appropriate fund.

The Federal Pell Grant is by far the largest single form of federal student assistance; an estimated 5 million students receive awards annually. Families with incomes of up to $25,000 (possibly higher in some cases) may be eligible for grants ranging from $250 to $2,400.

For state scholarships, students should check with the department of higher education about eligibility requirements.

Aid applicants are expected to apply directly to outside organizations for any scholarships for which they may be eligible. It is particularly important to apply for a Federal Pell Grant and a state scholarship. Application for both Pell and state scholarships is made by checking the appropriate box on the FAFSA. (Aid recipients are required to notify the college financial aid office about outside awards, as colleges take into consideration grants from all sources before assigning scholarships from their own funds.)

### THE STUDENT'S OWN CONTRIBUTION

All undergraduates, not only those who apply for financial aid, can assume responsibility for meeting a portion of their college expenses by borrowing, working during the academic year and the summer, and contributing a portion of their savings. Colleges require aid recipients to provide a "self-help" contribution before awarding scholarship money because they believe students should pay a reasonable share of their own educational costs.

### Student Loans

Many students will be able to borrow to help pay for college. Colleges administer three loans (all backed by the federal government): the Federal Subsidized and Unsubsidized Stafford Student Loans and the Federal Perkins Loan. Students must demonstrate financial need to be eligible for either the Subsidized Stafford Student Loan or the Perkins Loan.

Note: Starting in 1994–95, there is a new federal student borrowing option called Direct Loans. Colleges have the option to choose to participate in either the Stafford or Direct Loan program. As far as the student is concerned, the loan terms are essentially the same.

### Summer Employment

All students, whether or not they are receiving financial aid, should plan to work during the summer months. Students can be expected to save from $800 to $1,800 before their freshman year and $1,400 to $2,300 each summer while enrolled in college. It is worthwhile for a student to begin working while in high school to increase the chance of finding summer employment during college vacations.

### Term-Time Employment

Colleges have student employment offices that find jobs for students during the school year. Aid recipients on work-study receive priority in placement, but once they have been assisted, non-aid students are helped as well. Some jobs relate closely to academic interests; others should be viewed as a source of income rather than intellectual stimulation. A standard 8- to 12-hour-per-week job does not normally interfere with academic work or extracurricular activities and results in approximately $1,400 to $2,100 in earnings during the year.

### Student Savings

Student assets accumulated prior to starting college are available to help pay college bills. Student savings should be divided by four and a set amount earmarked for college each year. This source can often be quite substantial, particularly when families have accumulated large sums in the student's name (or in a trust fund with the student as the beneficiary) to gain a tax advantage. Federal tax codes are now more restrictive in this area, and parents should be aware of current rules before deciding how to set aside money for college.

### AID NOT REQUIRING NEED AS AN ELIGIBILITY CRITERION

There are scholarships available to students whether or not they are eligible for need-based financial aid. Awards based on merit are given by certain state scholarship programs, and National Merit Scholarship winners usually receive a $2,000 stipend regardless of family financial circumstances. Scholarships and prizes are also awarded by community organizations and other local groups. In addition, some parents receive tuition payments for their children as employment benefits. Most colleges offer merit scholarships to a limited group of highly qualified applicants. The selection of recipients for such awards depends on unusual talent in a specific area or on overall academic excellence. To find out more about qualifying for a merit scholarship, see your high school guidance counselor or consult a scholarship guide, such as Keeslar's *Financial Aid for Higher Education* and Peterson's *Paying Less for College*. (Students should be very careful about investing in computer-based scholarship searches that *promise* positive results.)

The Reserve Officers' Training Corps sponsors an extensive scholarship program that pays for tuition and books and provides $150 per month. The Army, Air Force, and Navy/Marine Corps have ROTC units at many colleges. High school guidance offices have brochures describing ROTC application procedures. For comprehensive information about financial aid programs sponsored by the military, see Peterson's *How the Military Will Help You Pay for College* (second edition).

## A SIMPLE METHOD FOR ESTIMATING FAMILY CONTRIBUTION IN 1995–96

The chart that follows will enable parents to make an approximation of the yearly amount the national financial aid need analysis system will expect them to pay for college in academic year 1995–96.

To use the chart, you need to work with your income, assets, and size of your family. Read the instructions below and enter the proper amounts in the spaces provided.

1. Parents' total 1994 income before taxes

    A. Adjusted gross income (equivalent to tax return entry; use actual or estimated) _____A

    B. Nontaxable income (Social Security benefits, child support, welfare, etc.) _____B

    Total Income: A + B _____①

2. Parents' total assets

    C. Total of cash, savings, and checking accounts _____C

    D. Total value of investments (stocks, bonds, real estate other than home, etc.) _____D

    Total Assets: C + D _____②

3. Family size (include student, parents, other dependent children, and other dependents) _____③

Now find the figures on the chart that correspond to your entries in ①, ②, and ③ to determine your approximate expected parental contribution, interpolating as necessary. (If there will be more than one family member in college half-time or more during 1995–96, divide the result by the number in college. This figure represents an approximate expected parental contribution for each person in college.)

# APPROXIMATE EXPECTED PARENTAL CONTRIBUTION FOR 1995–1996

| | ASSETS▼ | $ 20,000 | 30,000 | 40,000 | 50,000 | 60,000 | 70,000 | 80,000 | 90,000 | 100,000 |
|---|---|---|---|---|---|---|---|---|---|---|
| | | | | | **INCOME BEFORE TAXES** | | | | | |
| | **$ 20,000** | | | | | | | | | |
| FAMILY SIZE | 3 | $ 400 | 2,000 | 3,900 | 6,700 | 9,500 | 12,400 | 15,300 | 18,300 | 21,200 |
| | 4 | 0 | 1,300 | 3,000 | 5,400 | 8,300 | 11,200 | 14,100 | 17,100 | 20,000 |
| | 5 | 0 | 700 | 2,300 | 4,300 | 7,100 | 10,100 | 13,000 | 15,900 | 18,900 |
| | 6 | 0 | 100 | 1,600 | 3,300 | 5,800 | 8,800 | 11,700 | 14,600 | 17,600 |
| | **$ 30,000** | | | | | | | | | |
| FAMILY SIZE | 3 | $ 400 | 2,000 | 3,900 | 6,700 | 9,500 | 12,400 | 15,300 | 18,300 | 21,200 |
| | 4 | 0 | 1,300 | 3,000 | 5,400 | 8,300 | 11,200 | 14,100 | 17,100 | 20,000 |
| | 5 | 0 | 700 | 2,300 | 4,300 | 7,100 | 10,100 | 13,000 | 15,900 | 18,900 |
| | 6 | 0 | 100 | 1,600 | 3,300 | 5,800 | 8,800 | 11,700 | 14,600 | 17,600 |
| | **$ 40,000** | | | | | | | | | |
| FAMILY SIZE | 3 | $ 500 | 2,000 | 3,900 | 6,800 | 9,500 | 12,500 | 15,400 | 18,300 | 21,300 |
| | 4 | 0 | 1,400 | 3,000 | 5,400 | 8,300 | 11,200 | 14,200 | 17,100 | 20,100 |
| | 5 | 0 | 800 | 2,300 | 4,300 | 7,200 | 10,100 | 13,100 | 16,000 | 18,900 |
| | 6 | 0 | 100 | 1,600 | 3,300 | 5,900 | 8,800 | 11,800 | 14,700 | 17,600 |
| | **$ 50,000** | | | | | | | | | |
| FAMILY SIZE | 3 | $ 700 | 2,300 | 4,300 | 7,300 | 10,100 | 13,000 | 16,000 | 18,900 | 21,800 |
| | 4 | 100 | 1,600 | 3,400 | 6,000 | 8,900 | 11,800 | 14,700 | 17,700 | 20,600 |
| | 5 | 0 | 1,000 | 2,300 | 4,800 | 7,800 | 10,700 | 13,600 | 16,600 | 19,500 |
| | 6 | 0 | 400 | 1,900 | 3,700 | 6,500 | 9,400 | 12,300 | 15,300 | 18,200 |
| | **$ 60,000** | | | | | | | | | |
| FAMILY SIZE | 3 | $ 1,000 | 2,600 | 4,800 | 7,900 | 10,700 | 13,600 | 16,500 | 19,500 | 22,400 |
| | 4 | 400 | 1,900 | 3,700 | 6,500 | 9,400 | 12,400 | 15,300 | 18,300 | 21,200 |
| | 5 | 0 | 1,300 | 2,900 | 5,300 | 8,300 | 11,200 | 14,200 | 17,100 | 20,100 |
| | 6 | 0 | 600 | 2,100 | 4,100 | 7,000 | 10,000 | 12,900 | 15,800 | 18,800 |
| | **$ 80,000** | | | | | | | | | |
| FAMILY SIZE | 3 | $ 1,500 | 3,200 | 5,800 | 9,000 | 11,800 | 14,700 | 17,600 | 20,600 | 23,500 |
| | 4 | 900 | 2,500 | 4,600 | 7,700 | 10,600 | 13,500 | 16,400 | 19,400 | 22,300 |
| | 5 | 300 | 1,800 | 3,600 | 6,400 | 9,400 | 12,400 | 15,300 | 18,200 | 21,200 |
| | 6 | 0 | 1,100 | 2,700 | 5,000 | 8,200 | 11,100 | 14,000 | 17,000 | 19,900 |
| | **$100,000** | | | | | | | | | |
| FAMILY SIZE | 3 | $ 2,100 | 4,000 | 6,900 | 10,200 | 12,900 | 15,800 | 18,800 | 21,700 | 24,700 |
| | 4 | 1,400 | 3,100 | 5,500 | 8,800 | 11,700 | 14,600 | 17,600 | 20,500 | 23,400 |
| | 5 | 800 | 2,400 | 4,400 | 7,500 | 10,600 | 13,500 | 16,400 | 19,400 | 22,300 |
| | 6 | 100 | 1,700 | 3,400 | 6,100 | 9,300 | 12,200 | 15,100 | 18,100 | 21,000 |
| | **$120,000** | | | | | | | | | |
| FAMILY SIZE | 3 | $ 2,600 | 4,900 | 8,000 | 11,300 | 14,000 | 17,000 | 19,900 | 22,800 | 25,800 |
| | 4 | 2,000 | 3,800 | 6,700 | 9,900 | 12,800 | 15,800 | 18,700 | 21,600 | 24,600 |
| | 5 | 1,400 | 3,000 | 5,400 | 8,700 | 11,700 | 14,600 | 17,600 | 20,500 | 23,400 |
| | 6 | 600 | 2,200 | 4,200 | 7,200 | 10,400 | 13,300 | 16,300 | 19,200 | 22,200 |
| | **$140,000** | | | | | | | | | |
| FAMILY SIZE | 3 | $ 3,300 | 5,900 | 9,200 | 12,400 | 15,200 | 18,100 | 21,000 | 24,000 | 26,900 |
| | 4 | 2,500 | 4,700 | 7,800 | 11,100 | 14,000 | 16,900 | 19,800 | 22,800 | 25,700 |
| | 5 | 1,900 | 3,700 | 6,500 | 9,800 | 12,800 | 15,800 | 18,700 | 21,600 | 24,600 |
| | 6 | 1,200 | 2,800 | 5,100 | 8,300 | 11,500 | 14,500 | 17,400 | 20,300 | 23,300 |

# HOW TO FIND WHAT YOU WANT IN A COLLEGE DESCRIPTION

Each of the 361 schools in the main section of this book has a single-page description that follows a uniform structure so you can easily compare colleges. The description shown here is typical.

---

# ILLINOIS WESLEYAN UNIVERSITY

Bloomington, Illinois • Suburban setting • Private • Independent • Coed

Illinois Wesleyan, located midway between Chicago and St. Louis on a 60-acre landscaped campus, enrolls 1,800 students from more than 30 states and 35 countries. IWU offers a liberal arts curriculum and professional programs in a College of Fine Arts and a 4-year School of Nursing. Many students double major in different fields. A $24-million Center for Natural Science Learning and Research will open in fall 1995. A $15-million athletics, recreation, and wellness center opened in fall 1994. The student-faculty ratio is 13:1, and about 70% of students graduate in 4 years, compared to the national average of 46% in 6 years.

## Academics

IWU offers a liberal arts curriculum and core academic program. It awards bachelor's **degrees**. Challenging opportunities include advanced placement, accelerated degree programs, self-designed majors, an honors program, and Sigma Xi. Special programs include internships, summer session for credit, off-campus study, study abroad, and Army ROTC.

The most popular **majors** include business, biology/biological sciences, and English. A complete listing of majors at IWU appears in the Majors Index beginning on page 380.

The **faculty** at IWU has 150 full-time teachers, 92% with terminal degrees. 89% of the faculty serve as student advisers. The student-faculty ratio is 13:1, and the average class size in required courses is 16.

## Computers on Campus

Students are not required to have a computer. 340 **computers** available in the computer center, special labs, classrooms, the library, and dormitories provide access to e-mail and on-line services. Staffed computer lab on campus provides training in the use of computers and software.

The **library** has 203,202 books, 107,892 microform titles, and 1,045 subscriptions.

## Campus Life

There are 60 active **organizations** on campus, including a drama/theater group and student-run newspaper and radio station. 30% of eligible men and 30% of eligible women are members of 6 national **fraternities** and 5 national **sororities**. Student **safety services** include student/administration security committee, late night transport/escort service, 24-hour emergency telephone alarm devices, and 24-hour patrols by trained security personnel.

IWU is a member of the NCAA (Division III). **Intercollegiate sports** include baseball (m), basketball (m, w), cross-country running (m, w), football (m), golf (m), sailing (m, w), soccer (m, w), softball (w), swimming and diving (m, w), tennis (m, w), track and field (m, w), volleyball (w).

## Applying

IWU requires an essay, a high school transcript, and SAT I or ACT. It recommends 3 years of high school math and science, 3 years of high school foreign language, 3 recommendations, and a campus interview. Early, deferred, and midyear entrance are possible, with rolling admissions and continuous processing to 3/1 for financial aid. **Contact:** Mr. James R. Ruoti, Dean of Admissions, 1312 North Park Street, Bloomington, IL 61702-2900, 309-556-3031 or toll-free 800-332-2498; fax 309-556-3411.

### GETTING IN LAST YEAR
2,886 applied
54% were accepted
33% enrolled (517)
54% from top tenth of their h.s. class
28% had SAT verbal scores over 600
60% had SAT math scores over 600
79% had ACT scores over 26
4% had SAT verbal scores over 700
16% had SAT math scores over 700
31% had ACT scores over 30
24 National Merit Scholars

### THE STUDENT BODY
1,855 undergraduates
From 32 states and territories,
 31 other countries
83% from Illinois
52% women, 48% men
3% African Americans
1% Native Americans
1% Hispanics
4% Asian Americans
3% international students

### AFTER FRESHMAN YEAR
88% returned for sophomore year
71% got a degree within 4 years
75% got a degree within 5 years
76% got a degree within 6 years

### AFTER GRADUATION
29% pursued further study (16% arts and
 sciences, 3% medicine, 2% business)
28 corporations, 17 government agencies, 47
 nonprofit organizations recruited on campus

### WHAT YOU WILL PAY
Tuition and fees $15,510
Room and board $4290
65% receive need-based financial aid
 averaging $6226
20% receive non-need financial aid averaging
 $4283

---

On page 12 you will find an outline of a description that summarizes what you will learn from each area of the page. For instance, if you are looking for some idea of who your classmates will be, check the section at the bottom of the page and look at **GETTING IN LAST YEAR** and **THE STUDENT BODY**. Money matters appear in **WHAT YOU WILL PAY**. You get the idea. . . .

But what about majors? They're in the Majors Index following the Arts Colleges and Conservatories section of the book. You'll also find many other indexes to help you find the school you want. See page 432 for more details.

# UNIVERSITY NAME

Location • Setting • Affiliation • Affiliation • Coed?

> Most schools have chosen to submit a brief message in order to highlight special programs or opportunities that are available or to more fully explain their particular commitment to higher education. That message appears in this box.

 ## Academics

You'll find discussions of key study and learning topics in this section of each page:

- Curriculum and courses
- Degrees awarded
- Most popular majors
- Faculty
- Class size

 ## Computers on Campus

You'll discover information about:

- Computer resources, including purchase plans and training

- Network, e-mail, and on-line services
- Library facilities

 ## Campus Life

Here's where you'll get the story on:

- Organizations, activities, and student participation
- Fraternities and sororities
- Safety provisions
- Sports

 ## Applying

What you'll need to get in:

- Documents, high school courses, and standard tests required
- GPA minimum
- Interviews
- Deadlines
- Main contact name, address, phone, and fax

## The statistical picture for each school:

**GETTING IN LAST YEAR**
- Number who applied
- Percent accepted
- Percent enrolled
- Percent h.s. achievers
- Average GPA
- SAT I/ACT performance
- Number of National Merit Scholars
- Number of senior class presidents
- Number of valedictorians

**THE STUDENT BODY**
- How many students on campus and number who are undergrads
- Where they come from
- Percentage from in-state
- Who they are:
  —Men and women
  —Ethnic makeup
  —International students

**AFTER FRESHMAN YEAR**
- How many come back
- How many graduate within 4 years
- How many graduate within 5 years
- How many graduate within 6 years

**AFTER GRADUATION**
- Percentage pursuing further study and breakdown of 3 most popular fields
- Percentage with job offers within 3 months
- How many companies recruit on campus
- Major academic awards won by students

**WHAT YOU WILL PAY**
- Tuition and fees
- Room and board
- Percent getting aid
- Average need-based and non-need aid

# AGNES SCOTT COLLEGE

Decatur, Georgia • Urban setting • Private • Independent-Religious • Women

▶ The 4 facets of an Agnes Scott education—liberal arts curriculum, small size, private funding, and all-female environment—provide the best life preparation. The liberal education offered by Agnes Scott prepares students to realize their potential within their families, their friendships, and the global community. At Agnes Scott, education is a collaborative enterprise through which students develop the critical intelligence to challenge conventional wisdom, to evaluate evidence, to construct new hypotheses, and to reach conclusions. A comparable value in terms of academic quality, individual attention, financial strength, and a student-governed honor system cannot be found at any other college.

## Academics

Agnes Scott offers a liberal arts curriculum and core academic program; more than half of graduate courses are open to undergraduates. It awards bachelor's and master's **degrees**. Challenging opportunities include advanced placement, accelerated degree programs, self-designed majors, tutorials, and Phi Beta Kappa. Special programs include internships, off-campus study, study abroad, and Naval and Air Force ROTC.

The most popular **majors** include English, psychology, and economics. A complete listing of majors at Agnes Scott appears in the Majors Index beginning on page 380.

The **faculty** at Agnes Scott has 66 full-time graduate and undergraduate teachers, 99% with terminal degrees. 94% of the faculty serve as student advisers. The student-faculty ratio is 8:1, and the average class size in required courses is 13.

## Computers on Campus

Students are not required to have a computer. Student rooms are linked to a campus network. 110 **computers**

available in the computer center, computer labs, the learning resource center, Collaborative Learning Center, writing lab, classrooms, the library, and dormitories provide access to e-mail and on-line services. Staffed computer lab on campus (open 24 hours a day) provides training in the use of computers and software.

The 2 **libraries** have 193,924 books, 24,898 microform titles, and 774 subscriptions. They are connected to 2 national **on-line** catalogs.

## Campus Life

There are 39 active **organizations** on campus, including a drama/theater group and student-run newspaper. Student **safety services** include late night transport/escort service, 24-hour emergency telephone alarm devices, and 24-hour patrols by trained security personnel.

Agnes Scott is a member of the NCAA (Division III). **Intercollegiate sports** include basketball, cross-country running, soccer, softball, tennis, volleyball.

## Applying

Agnes Scott requires an essay, a high school transcript, 1 recommendation, and SAT I or ACT. It recommends 3 years of high school math and science, 2 years of high school foreign language, an interview, and 3 SAT II Subject Tests. Early, deferred, and midyear entrance are possible, with a 3/1 deadline and continuous processing to 3/15 for financial aid. **Contact:** Ms. Stephanie Balmer, Acting Director of Admission, 141 East College Avenue, Decatur, GA 30030-3797, 404-638-6285 or toll-free 800-868-8602; fax 404-638-6414.

---

### GETTING IN LAST YEAR
406 applied
88% were accepted
43% enrolled (153)
45% from top tenth of their h.s. class
3.42 average high school GPA
22% had SAT verbal scores over 600
26% had SAT math scores over 600
3% had SAT verbal scores over 700
4% had SAT math scores over 700

### THE STUDENT BODY
Total 594, of whom 568
   are undergraduates
From 32 states and territories,
   12 other countries

57% from Georgia
100% women
14% African Americans
1% Native Americans
3% Hispanics
3% Asian Americans
3% international students

### AFTER FRESHMAN YEAR
73% returned for sophomore year
56% got a degree within 4 years
59% got a degree within 5 years
60% got a degree within 6 years

### AFTER GRADUATION
37% pursued further study (24% arts and
   sciences, 6% law, 4% medicine)
21 corporations, 2 government agencies, 2
   nonprofit organizations recruited on campus
1 Fulbright scholar

### WHAT YOU WILL PAY
Tuition and fees $13,095
Room and board $5450
68% receive need-based financial aid
   averaging $5225
46% receive non-need financial aid averaging
   $6127

# ALBERT A. LIST COLLEGE, JEWISH THEOLOGICAL SEMINARY OF AMERICA

New York, New York • Urban setting • Private • Independent-Religious • Coed

▶ The Albert A. List College of Jewish Studies of the Jewish Theological Seminary offers students an opportunity to earn 2 bachelor's degrees simultaneously. Students pursue one degree in a specific major of Jewish study at List College and another in the liberal arts major of their choice at Columbia University's School of General Studies or Barnard College. In small classes, students receive personal attention from faculty members, while they enjoy the warm, supportive community at List College and the exciting, diverse campus life at Columbia or Barnard.

##  Academics

JTS offers an interdisciplinary Jewish studies curriculum and core academic program; more than half of graduate courses are open to undergraduates. It awards bachelor's, master's, and doctoral **degrees** (double bachelor's with Barnard College, Columbia University (NY). Challenging opportunities include advanced placement, self-designed majors, tutorials, Freshmen Honors College, an honors program, and a senior project. Special programs include summer session for credit, off-campus study, and study abroad.

The most popular **majors** include biblical studies, history, and philosophy. A complete listing of majors at JTS appears in the Majors Index beginning on page 380.

The **faculty** at JTS has 55 full-time graduate and undergraduate teachers, 100% with terminal degrees. 12% of the faculty serve as student advisers. The student-faculty ratio is 5:1, and the average class size in required courses is 25.

##  Computers on Campus

Students are not required to have a computer. Student rooms are linked to a campus network. 20 **computers** available in classrooms, the library, and student rooms provide access to e-mail and on-line services.

The **library** has 271,000 books, 9,100 microform titles, and 720 subscriptions.

##  Campus Life

Active **organizations** on campus include drama/theater group. 90% of students participate in student government elections. Student **safety services** include late night transport/escort service, 24-hour patrols by trained security personnel, and electronically operated dormitory entrances.

This institution has no intercollegiate sports.

##  Applying

JTS requires an essay, a high school transcript, 3 years of high school math and science, 2 recommendations, SAT I or ACT, and SAT II: Writing Test. It recommends some high school foreign language, an interview, and a minimum high school GPA of 3.0. Early, deferred, and midyear entrance are possible, with a 2/15 deadline and continuous processing to 3/1 for financial aid. **Contact:** Ms. Marci Harris Blumenthal, Director of Admissions, Room 614 Schiff, 3080 Broadway, New York, NY 10027-4649, 212-678-8832; fax 212-678-8947.

---

### GETTING IN LAST YEAR
78 applied
64% were accepted
54% enrolled (27)
25% from top tenth of their h.s. class
3.6 average high school GPA
40% had SAT verbal scores over 600
40% had SAT math scores over 600
100% had ACT scores over 26
0% had SAT verbal scores over 700
5% had SAT math scores over 700
20% had ACT scores over 30
2 National Merit Scholars
3 valedictorians

### THE STUDENT BODY
Total 476, of whom 99
  are undergraduates
From 21 states and territories,
  2 other countries
25% from New York
55% women, 45% men
0% African Americans
0% Native Americans
1% Hispanics
0% Asian Americans
3% international students

### AFTER FRESHMAN YEAR
99% returned for sophomore year

### AFTER GRADUATION
80% pursued further study

### WHAT YOU WILL PAY
Tuition and fees $7120
Room only $3640
50% receive need-based financial aid
  averaging $12,000
15% receive non-need financial aid averaging
  $6000

# ALBERTSON COLLEGE

Caldwell, Idaho • Small-town setting • Private • Independent • Coed

Students seeking the academic rigor and intellectual diversity of a competitive liberal arts experience will feel at home at Albertson. An inviting 44-acre campus is situated at the gateway to the Pacific Northwest, surrounded by outdoor opportunities in mountains, wild rivers, deserts, and forests. The urban culture of Boise is readily accessible (20 minutes away). Students choose Albertson for its quality of teaching, easy access to faculty, and informal, residential lifestyle. Ninety-two percent of applicants to medical school have been accepted over the past 3 decades. Prelaw acceptance is similarly high. Albertson has produced 7 Rhodes Scholars—2 in the last 5 years.

 ## Academics

Albertson offers a broad-based liberal arts curriculum and core academic program. It awards bachelor's **degrees**. Challenging opportunities include advanced placement, accelerated degree programs, self-designed majors, tutorials, an honors program, and a senior project. Special programs include internships, summer session for credit, off-campus study, and study abroad.

The most popular **majors** include biology/biological sciences, business, and elementary education. A complete listing of majors at Albertson appears in the Majors Index beginning on page 380.

The **faculty** at Albertson has 62 full-time teachers, 85% with terminal degrees. 100% of the faculty serve as student advisers. The student-faculty ratio is 11:1.

 ## Computers on Campus

Students are not required to have a computer. 120 **computers** available in the computer center, computer labs, academic buildings, the library, and dormitories. Staffed computer lab on campus.

The 2 **libraries** have 161,489 books, 45,940 microform titles, and 792 subscriptions.

 ## Campus Life

There are 40 active **organizations** on campus, including a drama/theater group and student-run newspaper. 20% of eligible men and 15% of eligible women are members of 2 national **fraternities**, 1 national **sorority**, 1 local fraternity, and 2 local sororities. Student **safety services** include late night transport/escort service, 24-hour emergency telephone alarm devices, 24-hour patrols by trained security personnel, and student patrols.

Albertson is a member of the NAIA. **Intercollegiate sports** (some offering scholarships) include baseball (m), basketball (m), skiing (cross-country) (m, w), skiing (downhill) (m, w), soccer (m, w), tennis (w), volleyball (w).

 ## Applying

Albertson requires an essay, a high school transcript, 1 recommendation, and SAT I or ACT. It recommends 3 years of high school math and science, 2 years of high school foreign language, an interview, and a minimum high school GPA of 2.0. Early, deferred, and midyear entrance are possible, with rolling admissions and continuous processing to 2/15 for financial aid. **Contact:** Mr. Dennis P. Berguall, Dean of Admissions, 2112 Cleveland Boulevard, Caldwell, ID 83605-4494, 208-459-5305 or toll-free 800-AC-IDAHO; fax 208-454-2077.

### GETTING IN LAST YEAR
601 applied
87% were accepted
36% enrolled (188)
36% from top tenth of their h.s. class
3.49 average high school GPA
14% had SAT verbal scores over 600
41% had SAT math scores over 600
45% had ACT scores over 26
5% had SAT verbal scores over 700
6% had SAT math scores over 700
18% had ACT scores over 30
5 National Merit Scholars

### THE STUDENT BODY
646 undergraduates
From 15 states and territories,
  12 other countries
70% from Idaho
52% women, 48% men
1% Native Americans
1% Hispanics
1% Asian Americans
5% international students

### AFTER FRESHMAN YEAR
71% returned for sophomore year
46% got a degree within 5 years

### AFTER GRADUATION
13 corporations, 7 government agencies, 2
  nonprofit organizations recruited on campus

### WHAT YOU WILL PAY
Tuition and fees $14,317
Room and board $3075
67% receive need-based financial aid
  averaging $4400
10% receive non-need financial aid averaging
  $4400

# ALBION COLLEGE

Albion, Michigan • Small-town setting • Private • Independent-Religious • Coed

Albion believes that a liberal arts education that provides practical career preparation is the ideal educational experience. To enhance that experience, opportunities for experiential learning include study in 21 countries, internships, and opportunities to undertake research with professors. Albion is a member of the Undergraduate Science Group, composed of 50 prestigious liberal arts colleges that have distinguished themselves in science education and research. Each year, an average of 25 Albion seniors attend medical school—an 87% acceptance rate in the past 5 years (52% nationally). Albion also ranks in the top 8% of 867 private undergraduate colleges in the number of alumni who are corporate executives.

 **Academics**

Albion offers a core academic program. It awards bachelor's **degrees**. Challenging opportunities include advanced placement, self-designed majors, tutorials, an honors program, a senior project, Phi Beta Kappa, and Sigma Xi. Special programs include internships, summer session for credit, off-campus study, and study abroad.

The most popular **majors** include economics, biology/biological sciences, and English. A complete listing of majors at Albion appears in the Majors Index beginning on page 380.

The **faculty** at Albion has 110 full-time teachers, 98% with terminal degrees. 81% of the faculty serve as student advisers. The student-faculty ratio is 13:1, and the average class size in required courses is 21.

 **Computers on Campus**

Students are not required to have a computer. 120 **computers** available in the computer center, computer labs, academic buildings, classrooms, the library, and dormitories provide access to the main academic computer, off-campus computing facilities, e-mail, and on-line services. Staffed computer lab on campus provides training in the use of computers and software.

The **library** has 286,600 books, 19,403 microform titles, and 920 subscriptions. It is connected to 5 national **on-line** catalogs.

 **Campus Life**

There are 104 active **organizations** on campus, including a drama/theater group and student-run newspaper and radio station. 45% of eligible men and 44% of eligible women are members of 6 national **fraternities** and 6 national **sororities**. Student **safety services** include late night transport/escort service, 24-hour emergency telephone alarm devices, 24-hour patrols by trained security personnel, student patrols, and electronically operated dormitory entrances.

Albion is a member of the NCAA (Division III). **Intercollegiate sports** include baseball (m), basketball (m, w), cross-country running (m, w), field hockey (w), football (m), golf (m, w), lacrosse (m, w), soccer (m, w), softball (w), swimming and diving (m, w), tennis (m, w), track and field (m, w), volleyball (m, w).

 **Applying**

Albion requires a high school transcript, 1 recommendation, and SAT I or ACT. Early, deferred, and midyear entrance are possible, with rolling admissions and continuous processing to 3/1 for financial aid. **Contact:** Dr. Frank Bonta, Dean of Admissions, 616 East Michigan, Albion, MI 49224-1831, 517-629-0321 or toll-free 800-858-6770; fax 517-629-0509.

## GETTING IN LAST YEAR
1,510 applied
93% were accepted
31% enrolled (433)
39% from top tenth of their h.s. class
3.4 average high school GPA
20% had SAT verbal scores over 600
39% had SAT math scores over 600
41% had ACT scores over 26
2% had SAT verbal scores over 700
11% had SAT math scores over 700
13% had ACT scores over 30
11 National Merit Scholars
22 valedictorians

## THE STUDENT BODY
1,641 undergraduates
From 29 states and territories,
  15 other countries
81% from Michigan
50% women, 50% men
3% African Americans
1% Hispanics
3% Asian Americans
2% international students

## AFTER FRESHMAN YEAR
82% returned for sophomore year

## AFTER GRADUATION
35% pursued further study (20% arts and sciences, 6% law, 5% medicine)
25 corporations, 1 government agency, 1 nonprofit organization recruited on campus

## WHAT YOU WILL PAY
Tuition and fees $14,910
Room and board $4826
59% receive need-based financial aid averaging $8219
22% receive non-need financial aid averaging $8254

# ALBRIGHT COLLEGE

Reading, Pennsylvania • Suburban setting • Private • Independent-Religious • Coed

Historically strong in the sciences and committed to the liberal arts, Albright College offers programs that are rigorous, flexible, and practical. A Methodist-affiliated institution that stresses the importance of values in education, Albright encourages its students to grow spiritually, socially, and culturally in an atmosphere of academic freedom. Albright's innovative Alpha Program gives students the intellectual space to investigate before choosing an area of concentration. This openness prepares them to accepts the challenge of lifelong learning. An excellence in academic and preprofessional courses, well integrated with cocurricular programs, is the distinguishing hallmark of the Albright experience.

## Academics

Albright offers a core academic program. It awards bachelor's **degrees**. Challenging opportunities include advanced placement, accelerated degree programs, self-designed majors, tutorials, an honors program, and a senior project. Special programs include internships, summer session for credit, off-campus study, and Army and Air Force ROTC.

The most popular **majors** include business, biology/biological sciences, and psychology. A complete listing of majors at Albright appears in the Majors Index beginning on page 380.

The **faculty** at Albright has 64 full-time teachers, 92% with terminal degrees. 100% of the faculty serve as student advisers. The student-faculty ratio is 12:1, and the average class size in required courses is 18.

## Computers on Campus

Students are not required to have a computer. 225 **computers** available in the computer center, computer labs, labs in classroom buildings, classrooms, the library, the student center, and dormitories provide access to the main academic computer, off-campus computing facilities, and e-mail. Staffed computer lab on campus provides training in the use of computers and software.

The **library** has 184,833 books, 10,081 microform titles, and 700 subscriptions. It is connected to 7 national **on-line** catalogs.

## Campus Life

There are 70 active **organizations** on campus, including a drama/theater group and student-run newspaper and radio station. 90% of students participate in student government elections. 25% of eligible men and 27% of eligible women are members of 5 national **fraternities** and 4 national **sororities**. Student **safety services** include late night transport/escort service, 24-hour emergency telephone alarm devices, 24-hour patrols by trained security personnel, student patrols, and electronically operated dormitory entrances.

Albright is a member of the NCAA (Division III). **Intercollegiate sports** include badminton (w), baseball (m), basketball (m, w), cross-country running (m, w), field hockey (w), football (m), golf (m, w), ice hockey (m), lacrosse (m), rugby (m), soccer (m), softball (w), swimming and diving (m, w), tennis (m, w), track and field (m, w), volleyball (w), wrestling (m).

## Applying

Albright requires an essay, a high school transcript, 2 years of high school foreign language, 2 recommendations, and SAT I or ACT. It recommends 3 years of high school math and science, an interview, and 3 SAT II Subject Tests. Early, deferred, and midyear entrance are possible, with a 2/15 deadline and continuous processing to 3/1 for financial aid. **Contact:** Ms. S. Elizabeth VanVelsor, Director of Admissions, Reading, PA 19612-5234, 610-921-7512 or toll-free 800-252-1856; fax 610-921-7530.

### GETTING IN LAST YEAR
1,000 applied
88% were accepted
34% enrolled (295)
21% from top tenth of their h.s. class
3.08 average high school GPA
4% had SAT verbal scores over 600
18% had SAT math scores over 600
38% had ACT scores over 26
0% had SAT verbal scores over 700
2% had SAT math scores over 700
0% had ACT scores over 30

### THE STUDENT BODY
1,072 undergraduates
From 24 states and territories,
    17 other countries
60% from Pennsylvania
52% women, 48% men
4% African Americans
1% Native Americans
2% Hispanics
3% Asian Americans
4% international students

### AFTER FRESHMAN YEAR
85% returned for sophomore year
66% got a degree within 4 years

70% got a degree within 5 years
71% got a degree within 6 years

### AFTER GRADUATION
32% pursued further study (12% arts and
    sciences, 9% law, 5% business)
25 corporations, 3 government agencies, 3
    nonprofit organizations recruited on campus

### WHAT YOU WILL PAY
Tuition and fees $15,795
Room and board $4400
73% receive need-based financial aid
    averaging $6976
12% receive non-need financial aid averaging
    $8569

# ALFRED UNIVERSITY

Alfred, New York • Rural setting • Private • Independent • Coed

▶ Alfred is undertaking an unprecedented building campaign. In 1992, the University dedicated the $6.2-million Scholes Library of Ceramics, the largest library in the United States dedicated to the study of ceramics. The $5.6-million College of Business F. W. Olin Foundation building was dedicated in 1993, and the $10-million Powell Campus Center was dedicated in 1994. In addition, a $6-million performing arts center will be completed by early 1995.

## Academics

Alfred offers a core academic program; fewer than half of graduate courses are open to undergraduates. It awards bachelor's, master's, and doctoral **degrees**. Challenging opportunities include advanced placement, accelerated degree programs, self-designed majors, an honors program, a senior project, and Sigma Xi. Special programs include cooperative education, internships, summer session for credit, off-campus study, study abroad, and Army ROTC.

The most popular **majors** include art/fine arts, business, and psychology. A complete listing of majors at Alfred appears in the Majors Index beginning on page 380.

The **faculty** at Alfred has 160 full-time graduate and undergraduate teachers, 87% with terminal degrees. 70% of the faculty serve as student advisers. The student-faculty ratio is 12:1, and the average class size in required courses is 18.

## Computers on Campus

Students are not required to have a computer. 400 **computers** available in the computer center, computer labs, the learning resource center, academic departments, the library, and dormitories.

The 2 **libraries** have 323,234 books, 92,643 microform titles, and 1,300 subscriptions.

## Campus Life

There are 74 active **organizations** on campus, including a drama/theater group and student-run newspaper and radio station. 30% of eligible men and 15% of eligible women are members of 5 national **fraternities**, 1 national **sorority**, 2 local fraternities, and 3 local sororities. Student **safety services** include late night transport/escort service, 24-hour emergency telephone alarm devices, and student patrols.

Alfred is a member of the NCAA (Division III). **Intercollegiate sports** include basketball (m, w), cross-country running (m, w), equestrian sports (m, w), football (m), golf (m, w), lacrosse (m, w), skiing (downhill) (m, w), soccer (m, w), softball (w), swimming and diving (m, w), tennis (m, w), track and field (m), volleyball (w).

## Applying

Alfred requires an essay, a high school transcript, 1 recommendation, SAT I or ACT, SAT II: Writing Test, and in some cases 3 years of high school math and science and an interview. It recommends 3 years of high school math and science, some high school foreign language, and an interview. Early, deferred, and midyear entrance are possible, with a 2/15 deadline and continuous processing to 4/1 for financial aid. **Contact:** Ms. Laurie Richer, Acting Director of Admissions, Alumni Hall, Alfred, NY 14802-1232, 607-871-2115 or toll-free 800-541-9229; fax 607-871-2198.

### GETTING IN LAST YEAR
1,732 applied
82% were accepted
34% enrolled (479)
39% from top tenth of their h.s. class
3.2 average high school GPA
20% had SAT verbal scores over 600
49% had SAT math scores over 600
60% had ACT scores over 26
5% had SAT verbal scores over 700
14% had SAT math scores over 700
11% had ACT scores over 30
25 National Merit Scholars
17 class presidents
49 valedictorians

### THE STUDENT BODY
Total 2,326, of whom 1,830
  are undergraduates
From 33 states and territories,
  21 other countries
69% from New York
44% women, 56% men
5% African Americans
1% Native Americans
2% Hispanics
2% Asian Americans
2% international students

### AFTER FRESHMAN YEAR
90% returned for sophomore year

### AFTER GRADUATION
35% pursued further study (15% engineering, 7% arts and sciences, 7% business)
40 corporations, 8 government agencies, 1 nonprofit organization recruited on campus

### WHAT YOU WILL PAY
Tuition and fees $16,972
Room and board $5406
Need-based financial aid averages $8500
Non-need financial aid averages $7500

# ALLEGHENY COLLEGE

Meadville, Pennsylvania • Small-town setting • Private • Independent-Religious • Coed

One of America's oldest colleges, Allegheny stands out today for the breadth of the skills and understandings consistently developed in its students: superior professional capabilities, from writing to leadership to problem solving; skills for managing everyday life; important social abilities; talents for responsible citizenship; and values clarification. Students are actively engaged in learning through small and dynamic classes, hands-on laboratories, original research projects, and collaborations with faculty. All students complete a substantial creative or research project in the senior year, proving their abilities to complete a major assignment, work independently, analyze and synthesize, and write and speak persuasively.

##  Academics

Allegheny offers a multidisciplinary curriculum and core academic program. It awards bachelor's **degrees**. Challenging opportunities include advanced placement, accelerated degree programs, self-designed majors, tutorials, a senior project, and Phi Beta Kappa. Special programs include internships, summer session for credit, off-campus study, study abroad, and Army ROTC.

The most popular **majors** include English, economics, and psychology. A complete listing of majors at Allegheny appears in the Majors Index beginning on page 380.

The **faculty** at Allegheny has 156 full-time teachers, 94% with terminal degrees. 100% of the faculty serve as student advisers. The student-faculty ratio is 11:1, and the average class size in required courses is 15.

##  Computers on Campus

Students are not required to have a computer. Student rooms are linked to a campus network. 300 **computers** available in computer labs, academic buildings, and the library provide access to off-campus computing facilities, e-mail, and on-line services. Staffed computer lab on campus (open 24 hours a day) provides training in the use of computers and software.

The 3 **libraries** have 401,188 books, 197,388 microform titles, and 1,176 subscriptions. They are connected to 4 national **on-line** catalogs.

##  Campus Life

There are 108 active **organizations** on campus, including a drama/theater group and student-run newspaper and radio station. 45% of students participate in student government elections. 30% of eligible men and 35% of eligible women are members of 6 national **fraternities** and 5 national **sororities**. Student **safety services** include late night transport/escort service, 24-hour emergency telephone alarm devices, 24-hour patrols by trained security personnel, student patrols, and electronically operated dormitory entrances.

Allegheny is a member of the NCAA (Division III). **Intercollegiate sports** include baseball (m), basketball (m, w), cross-country running (m, w), fencing (m, w), football (m), golf (m), ice hockey (m), lacrosse (m, w), rugby (m), skiing (downhill) (m, w), soccer (m, w), softball (w), swimming and diving (m, w), tennis (m, w), track and field (m, w), volleyball (m, w).

##  Applying

Allegheny requires an essay, a high school transcript, 2 recommendations, and SAT I or ACT. It recommends 3 years of high school math and science, 2 years of high school foreign language, an interview, and 2 SAT II Subject Tests. Early, deferred, and midyear entrance are possible, with a 2/15 deadline and continuous processing to 2/15 for financial aid. **Contact:** Ms. Gayle Pollock, Director of Admissions, Park Avenue, Meadville, PA 16335, 814-332-4351 or toll-free 800-521-5293; fax 814-337-0988.

### GETTING IN LAST YEAR
2,684 applied
73% were accepted
24% enrolled (475)
44% from top tenth of their h.s. class
16% had SAT verbal scores over 600
40% had SAT math scores over 600
47% had ACT scores over 26
1% had SAT verbal scores over 700
5% had SAT math scores over 700
12% had ACT scores over 30
1 National Merit Scholar
30 class presidents
20 valedictorians

### THE STUDENT BODY
1,809 undergraduates
From 38 states and territories,
 24 other countries
56% from Pennsylvania
51% women, 49% men
3% African Americans
1% Native Americans
1% Hispanics
2% Asian Americans
3% international students

### AFTER FRESHMAN YEAR
87% returned for sophomore year
65% got a degree within 4 years
73% got a degree within 5 years
74% got a degree within 6 years

### AFTER GRADUATION
32% pursued further study (19% arts and
 sciences, 7% law, 3% medicine)

### WHAT YOU WILL PAY
Tuition and fees $17,340
Room and board $4440
75% receive need-based financial aid
 averaging $9093
45% receive non-need financial aid averaging
 $5262

# ALMA COLLEGE

Alma, Michigan • Small-town setting • Private • Independent-Religious • Coed

Alma's undergraduates thrive on challenging academic programs in a supportive, small-college atmosphere. The College is committed to a value-added liberal arts curriculum with opportunities for one-on-one research and publication with faculty whose first priority is teaching. Students enjoy small classes in modern facilities, including the new $7-million Heritage Center for the Performing Arts. Alma College offers excellent preparation for professional careers in business, law, medicine, the arts, and a wide range of other fields.

 **Academics**

Alma offers an interdisciplinary curriculum and core academic program. It awards bachelor's **degrees**. Challenging opportunities include advanced placement, accelerated degree programs, self-designed majors, tutorials, an honors program, a senior project, and Phi Beta Kappa. Special programs include internships, summer session for credit, off-campus study, study abroad, and Army ROTC.

The most popular **majors** include business, biology/biological sciences, and physical fitness/human movement. A complete listing of majors at Alma appears in the Majors Index beginning on page 380.

The **faculty** at Alma has 83 full-time teachers, 89% with terminal degrees. 95% of the faculty serve as student advisers. The student-faculty ratio is 14:1, and the average class size in required courses is 22.

 **Computers on Campus**

Students are not required to have a computer. 397 **computers** available in the computer center, computer labs, the research center, faculty offices, classrooms, the library, and dormitories provide access to the main academic computer, off-campus computing facilities, e-mail, and on-line services. Staffed computer lab on campus provides training in the use of computers and software.

The **library** has 202,600 books, 30,900 microform titles, and 1,125 subscriptions. It is connected to 4 national **on-line** catalogs.

 **Campus Life**

There are 128 active **organizations** on campus, including a drama/theater group and student-run newspaper and radio station. 40% of eligible men and 40% of eligible women are members of 4 national **fraternities**, 3 national **sororities**, 1 local fraternity, and 1 local sorority. Student **safety services** include 24-hour emergency telephone alarm devices and 24-hour patrols by trained security personnel.

Alma is a member of the NCAA (Division III). **Intercollegiate sports** include baseball (m), basketball (m, w), cross-country running (m, w), football (m), golf (m, w), soccer (m, w), softball (w), swimming and diving (m, w), tennis (m, w), track and field (m, w), volleyball (w).

 **Applying**

Alma requires a high school transcript, 2 recommendations, SAT I or ACT, a minimum high school GPA of 2.0, and in some cases a campus interview. It recommends an essay, 3 years of high school math and science, and 2 years of high school foreign language. Early, deferred, and midyear entrance are possible, with rolling admissions and continuous processing to 3/1 for financial aid. **Contact:** Mr. John Seveland, Vice President for Enrollment and Student Affairs, 614 West Superior Street, Alma, MI 48801-1599, 517-463-7139 or toll-free 800-321-ALMA.

---

**GETTING IN LAST YEAR**

1,154 applied
89% were accepted
36% enrolled (368)
42% from top tenth of their h.s. class
3.5 average high school GPA
51% had ACT scores over 26
8% had ACT scores over 30
3 National Merit Scholars

**THE STUDENT BODY**

1,404 undergraduates
From 20 states and territories,
12 other countries

95% from Michigan
55% women, 45% men
1% African Americans
1% Native Americans
1% Hispanics
2% Asian Americans
1% international students

**AFTER FRESHMAN YEAR**

86% returned for sophomore year
57% got a degree within 4 years
72% got a degree within 5 years

**AFTER GRADUATION**

27% pursued further study (11% arts and
sciences, 6% business, 4% law)
90% had job offers within 3 months
15 corporations, 4 government agencies, 6
nonprofit organizations recruited on campus

**WHAT YOU WILL PAY**

Tuition and fees $12,695
Room and board $4552
74% receive need-based financial aid
averaging $4288
25% receive non-need financial aid averaging
$5908

# AMERICAN UNIVERSITY

Washington, D.C. • Suburban setting • Private • Independent-Religious • Coed

▶ Students who believe the world can be a better place, and want to lead their peers in making it a better place, should be at The American University. That is because the University's mission, unique in higher education, is to turn ideas into service by emphasizing the liberal arts and sciences and connecting them to the issues of contemporary public affairs.

##  Academics

AU offers a liberal arts curriculum and core academic program. It awards associate, bachelor's, master's, doctoral, and first professional **degrees**. Challenging opportunities include advanced placement, self-designed majors, an honors program, a senior project, and Sigma Xi. Special programs include cooperative education, internships, summer session for credit, off-campus study, study abroad, and Army and Air Force ROTC.

The most popular **majors** include international studies, communication, and political science/government. A complete listing of majors at AU appears in the Majors Index beginning on page 380.

The **faculty** at AU has 570 full-time graduate and undergraduate teachers, 92% with terminal degrees. The student-faculty ratio is 14:1.

##  Computers on Campus

Students are not required to have a computer. 500 **computers** available in the computer center, labs, and the student center provide access to the main academic computer, off-campus computing facilities, e-mail, and on-line services.

Staffed computer lab on campus (open 24 hours a day) provides training in the use of computers and software.

The 2 **libraries** have 580,000 books and 2,900 subscriptions.

##  Campus Life

There are 80 active **organizations** on campus, including a drama/theater group and student-run newspaper and radio station. 25% of eligible men and 25% of eligible women are members of 7 national **fraternities** and 7 national **sororities**. Student **safety services** include late night transport/escort service, 24-hour emergency telephone alarm devices, 24-hour patrols by trained security personnel, and electronically operated dormitory entrances.

AU is a member of the NCAA (Division I). **Intercollegiate sports** (some offering scholarships) include basketball (m, w), cross-country running (m, w), field hockey (w), golf (m), lacrosse (m), soccer (m, w), swimming and diving (m, w), tennis (m, w), volleyball (w), wrestling (m).

##  Applying

AU requires an essay, a high school transcript, 3 years of high school math, 2 years of high school foreign language, 3 recommendations, SAT I or ACT, and a minimum high school GPA of 2.0. It recommends 3 years of high school science, an interview, 3 SAT II Subject Tests, and a minimum high school GPA of 3.0. Early, deferred, and midyear entrance are possible, with a 2/1 deadline and continuous processing to 3/1 for financial aid. **Contact:** Ms. Marcelle D. Heerschap, Director of Admissions, 4400 Massachusetts Avenue, NW, Washington, DC 20016-8001, 202-885-6000; fax 202-885-6014.

---

### GETTING IN LAST YEAR
4,597 applied
78% were accepted
29% enrolled (1,025)
35% from top tenth of their h.s. class
3.3 average high school GPA
28% had SAT verbal scores over 600
46% had SAT math scores over 600
3% had SAT verbal scores over 700
8% had SAT math scores over 700
22 National Merit Scholars

### THE STUDENT BODY
Total 11,708, of whom 4,926
  are undergraduates
From 53 states and territories,
  110 other countries
6% from District of Columbia
59% women, 41% men
7% African Americans
1% Native Americans
4% Hispanics
5% Asian Americans
12% international students

### AFTER FRESHMAN YEAR
86% returned for sophomore year
62% got a degree within 4 years
68% got a degree within 5 years
69% got a degree within 6 years

### WHAT YOU WILL PAY
Tuition and fees $16,144
Room and board $6420
Need-based financial aid averages $3748

# AMHERST COLLEGE

Amherst, Massachusetts • Small-town setting • Private • Independent • Coed

Amherst seeks talented students who have demonstrated their passion for learning along with a willingness to be involved in the world around them. With its dynamic, dedicated faculty, Amherst is a lively intellectual and cultural community in which students are active members; small classes and a wide variety of extracurricular offerings provide many opportunities for exploration. An open curriculum with majors ranging from neuroscience to women's and gender studies allows students substantial freedom to pursue their goals.

## Academics

Amherst College offers an open curriculum and no core academic program. It awards bachelor's **degrees**. Challenging opportunities include self-designed majors, an honors program, a senior project, Phi Beta Kappa, and Sigma Xi. Special programs include off-campus study and study abroad.

The most popular **majors** include English, political science/government, and economics. A complete listing of majors at Amherst College appears in the Majors Index beginning on page 380. The **faculty** at Amherst College has 163 full-time teachers, 77% with terminal degrees. 100% of the faculty serve as student advisers. The student-faculty ratio is 9:1, and the average class size in required courses is 22.

## Computers on Campus

Students are not required to have a computer. Student rooms are linked to a campus network. 75 **computers** available in the computer center, academic departments,

the library, and dormitories provide access to e-mail. Staffed computer lab on campus.

The 7 **libraries** have 786,345 books, 417,618 microform titles, and 4,530 subscriptions.

## Campus Life

There are 100 active **organizations** on campus, including a drama/theater group and student-run newspaper and radio station. 65% of students participate in student government elections. Student **safety services** include late night transport/escort service and electronically operated dormitory entrances.

Amherst College is a member of the NCAA (Division III). **Intercollegiate sports** include baseball (m), basketball (m, w), crew (m, w), cross-country running (m, w), equestrian sports (m, w), field hockey (w), football (m), golf (m, w), ice hockey (m, w), lacrosse (m, w), rugby (m, w), sailing (m, w), skiing (downhill) (m, w), soccer (m, w), softball (w), squash (m, w), swimming and diving (m, w), tennis (m, w), track and field (m, w), volleyball (m, w), water polo (m, w).

## Applying

Amherst College requires an essay, a high school transcript, 3 years of high school math, 3 recommendations, SAT I or ACT, and 3 SAT II Subject Tests. It recommends 4 years of high school math, 3 years of high school science, and 3 years of high school foreign language. Early and deferred entrance are possible, with a 12/31 deadline and a 2/1 priority date for financial aid. **Contact:** Ms. Jane E. Reynolds, Dean of Admission, Route 116, South Pleasant Street, Amherst, MA 01002, 413-542-2328; fax 413-542-2040.

---

### GETTING IN LAST YEAR

4,823 applied
20% were accepted
43% enrolled (418)
83% from top tenth of their h.s. class
70% had SAT verbal scores over 600
83% had SAT math scores over 600
23% had SAT verbal scores over 700
43% had SAT math scores over 700

### THE STUDENT BODY

1,608 undergraduates
From 50 states and territories, 29 other countries
12% from Massachusetts
45% women, 55% men
7% African Americans
1% Native Americans
8% Hispanics
11% Asian Americans
3% international students

### AFTER FRESHMAN YEAR

98% returned for sophomore year

### AFTER GRADUATION

28% pursued further study (12% arts and sciences, 7% law, 7% medicine)
56 corporations, 2 government agencies, 7 nonprofit organizations recruited on campus
2 Fulbright scholars

### WHAT YOU WILL PAY

Tuition and fees $20,052
Room and board $5300
42% receive need-based financial aid averaging $15,326

# Auburn University

Auburn, Alabama • Small-town setting • Public • State-supported • Coed

▶ Auburn University strives continuously to provide outstanding, economically accessible instruction to its undergraduate, graduate, and professional students, with programs in agriculture, life sciences, engineering, architecture, pharmacy, and veterinary medicine being especially well known. Auburn has been identified as 1 of 20 institutions with the most alumni serving as CEOs of Fortune 500 and Service 500 industries and is among the top 10 in providing NASA astronauts. Yet, despite the diversity of offerings and the emphasis on academic excellence, Auburn is best known for its friendliness, with a welcoming small-town environment and activities for every interest.

 **Academics**

Auburn offers a sciences and humanities curriculum and core academic program; fewer than half of graduate courses are open to undergraduates. It awards bachelor's, master's, doctoral, and first professional **degrees**. Challenging opportunities include advanced placement, accelerated degree programs, an honors program, a senior project, and Sigma Xi. Special programs include cooperative education, internships, summer session for credit, study abroad, and Army, Naval, and Air Force ROTC.

The most popular **majors** include finance/banking, mechanical engineering, and psychology. A complete listing of majors at Auburn appears in the Majors Index beginning on page 380.

The **faculty** at Auburn has 1,172 full-time graduate and undergraduate teachers, 89% with terminal degrees. The student-faculty ratio is 16:1.

 **Computers on Campus**

Students are not required to have a computer. 600 **computers** available in computer labs, the library, and dormitories provide access to the main academic computer and e-mail. Staffed computer lab on campus (open 24 hours a day).

The 3 **libraries** have 2.2 million books, 2.9 million microform titles, and 19,636 subscriptions. They are connected to 13 national **on-line** catalogs.

 **Campus Life**

There are 300 active **organizations** on campus, including a drama/theater group and student-run newspaper and radio station. 18% of eligible men and 30% of eligible women are members of 29 national **fraternities** and 17 national **sororities**. Student **safety services** include late night transport/escort service, 24-hour emergency telephone alarm devices, 24-hour patrols by trained security personnel, and electronically operated dormitory entrances.

Auburn is a member of the NCAA (Division I). **Intercollegiate sports** (some offering scholarships) include baseball (m), basketball (m, w), cross-country running (m, w), football (m), golf (m, w), gymnastics (w), soccer (w), softball (w), swimming and diving (m, w), tennis (m, w), track and field (m, w), volleyball (w).

 **Applying**

Auburn requires a high school transcript, 3 years of high school math, SAT I or ACT, a minimum high school GPA of 2.0, and in some cases a minimum high school GPA of 3.0. It recommends 3 years of high school science and 1 year of high school foreign language. Early, deferred, and midyear entrance are possible, with a 9/1 deadline and continuous processing to 4/17 for financial aid. **Contact:** Dr. Charles F. Reeder, Director of Admissions, 202 Mary Martin Hall, Auburn University, AL 36849-0001, 334-844-4080 or toll-free 800-392-8051 (in-state).

---

### GETTING IN LAST YEAR
8,032 applied
90% were accepted
44% enrolled (3,199)
24% from top tenth of their h.s. class
3.2 average high school GPA
14% had SAT verbal scores over 600
43% had SAT math scores over 600
30% had ACT scores over 26
1% had SAT verbal scores over 700
9% had SAT math scores over 700
8% had ACT scores over 30
22 National Merit Scholars

### THE STUDENT BODY
Total 21,226, of whom 18,106
   are undergraduates
From 53 states and territories,
   46 other countries
63% from Alabama
46% women, 54% men
6% African Americans
1% Native Americans
1% Hispanics
1% Asian Americans
1% international students

### AFTER FRESHMAN YEAR
85% returned for sophomore year
32% got a degree within 4 years
60% got a degree within 5 years
69% got a degree within 6 years

### AFTER GRADUATION
30% pursued further study (10% business, 6% arts and sciences, 4% engineering)
450 corporations, 20 government agencies, 5 nonprofit organizations recruited on campus
2 Fulbright scholars

### WHAT YOU WILL PAY
Resident tuition and fees $2100
Nonresident tuition and fees $6300
Room only $1410
32% receive need-based financial aid averaging $1046
26% receive non-need financial aid averaging $1838

# AUGUSTANA COLLEGE

Rock Island, Illinois • Urban setting • Private • Independent-Religious • Coed

Augustana College seeks to develop in students the characteristics of liberally educated persons: clarity of thought and expression, curiosity, fair-mindedness, appreciation for the arts and cultural diversity, intellectual honesty, and a considered set of personal values and commitments. Students combine exploration of the arts, sciences, and humanities with in-depth study in their major field(s), guided by an excellent, committed faculty; they grow personally and socially through participation in wide extracurricular and cocurricular opportunities on one of the most beautiful campuses in the country. Special features include innovative interdisciplinary first-year course sequences, foreign study, and internships—both domestic and international.

## Academics

Augie offers a liberal arts and sciences curriculum and core academic program. It awards bachelor's **degrees**. Challenging opportunities include advanced placement, tutorials, Freshmen Honors College, an honors program, a senior project, and Phi Beta Kappa. Special programs include cooperative education, internships, summer session for credit, and study abroad.

The most popular **majors** include business, biology/biological sciences, and English. A complete listing of majors at Augie appears in the Majors Index beginning on page 380.

The **faculty** at Augie has 134 full-time teachers, 86% with terminal degrees. 92% of the faculty serve as student advisers. The student-faculty ratio is 12:1, and the average class size in required courses is 20.

## Computers on Campus

Students are not required to have a computer. Student rooms are linked to a campus network. 205 **computers** available in the computer center, computer labs, the learning resource center, all classroom buildings, classrooms, the library, and dormitories provide access to the main academic computer, off-campus computing facilities, e-mail, and on-line services. Staffed computer lab on campus provides training in the use of computers and software.

The 4 **libraries** have 239,774 books, 7,571 microform titles, and 1,561 subscriptions. They are connected to 7 national **on-line** catalogs.

## Campus Life

There are 150 active **organizations** on campus, including a drama/theater group and student-run newspaper and radio station. 33% of students participate in student government elections. 38% of eligible men and 38% of eligible women are members of 7 local **fraternities** and 6 local **sororities**. Student **safety services** include late night transport/escort service, 24-hour emergency telephone alarm devices, and 24-hour patrols by trained security personnel.

Augie is a member of the NCAA (Division III). **Intercollegiate sports** include baseball (m), basketball (m, w), cross-country running (m, w), football (m), golf (m), soccer (m, w), softball (w), swimming and diving (m, w), tennis (m, w), track and field (m, w), volleyball (w), wrestling (m).

## Applying

Augie requires a high school transcript, SAT I or ACT, and in some cases an essay, 2 recommendations, and an interview. It recommends 3 years of high school math and science and 1 year of high school foreign language. Early, deferred, and midyear entrance are possible, with rolling admissions and continuous processing to 4/1 for financial aid. **Contact:** Mr. Martin Sauer, Director of Admissions, 820 38th Street, Rock Island, IL 61201-2296, 309-794-7341 or toll-free 800-798-8100; fax 309-794-7431.

### GETTING IN LAST YEAR
1,777 applied
92% were accepted
33% enrolled (543)
36% from top tenth of their h.s. class
3.5 average high school GPA
41% had ACT scores over 26
12% had ACT scores over 30
26 valedictorians

### THE STUDENT BODY
2,054 undergraduates
From 30 states and territories, 24 other countries

81% from Illinois
58% women, 42% men
3% African Americans
1% Native Americans
2% Hispanics
2% Asian Americans
3% international students

### AFTER FRESHMAN YEAR
81% returned for sophomore year
69% got a degree within 4 years
73% got a degree within 5 years
74% got a degree within 6 years

### AFTER GRADUATION
33% pursued further study (18% arts and sciences, 5% medicine, 4% law)
75 corporations, 7 government agencies, 20 nonprofit organizations recruited on campus

### WHAT YOU WILL PAY
Tuition and fees $14,064
Room and board $4257
81% receive need-based financial aid averaging $6264
71% receive non-need financial aid averaging $4084

# AUGUSTANA COLLEGE

Sioux Falls, South Dakota • Urban setting • Private • Independent-Religious • Coed

The Augustana College curriculum creates a learning environment with educational bookends. First-year students take New Student Seminar, a course that facilitates a positive transition to the College community and ends with the Capstone course. This team-taught class stimulates seniors to recognize the relationship of their college studies to central issues of human existence. Augustana was recently named a "top 10 regional liberal arts college" and a "best value" by *U.S. News & World Report*. Sioux Falls continues to be recognized as one of America's top 10 cities by *Money* magazine. This partnership affords a stimulating learning environment and opportunities for internships and employment.

 **Academics**

Augustana offers a core academic program; fewer than half of graduate courses are open to undergraduates. It awards associate, bachelor's, and master's **degrees**. Challenging opportunities include advanced placement, accelerated degree programs, self-designed majors, tutorials, an honors program, and a senior project. Special programs include cooperative education, internships, summer session for credit, off-campus study, and study abroad.

The most popular **majors** include biology/biological sciences, education, and business. A complete listing of majors at Augustana appears in the Majors Index beginning on page 380.

The **faculty** at Augustana has 124 full-time undergraduate teachers, 68% with terminal degrees. 100% of the faculty serve as student advisers. The student-faculty ratio is 13:1, and the average class size in required courses is 30.

 **Computers on Campus**

Students are not required to have a computer. 78 **computers** available in the computer center, computer labs, academic departments, classrooms, the library, the student center, and dormitories provide access to e-mail. Staffed computer lab on campus.

The 2 **libraries** have 233,440 books, 58,635 microform titles, and 943 subscriptions. They are connected to 1 national **on-line** catalog.

 **Campus Life**

There are 70 active **organizations** on campus, including a drama/theater group and student-run newspaper and radio station. 60% of students participate in student government elections. 25% of eligible men and 30% of eligible women are members of 1 local **fraternity** and 1 local **sorority**. Student **safety services** include 18-hour patrols by trained security personnel, late night transport/escort service, 24-hour emergency telephone alarm devices, and electronically operated dormitory entrances.

Augustana is a member of the NCAA (Division II). **Intercollegiate sports** (some offering scholarships) include baseball (m), basketball (m, w), cross-country running (m, w), football (m), softball (w), tennis (m, w), track and field (m, w), volleyball (w), wrestling (m).

 **Applying**

Augustana requires a high school transcript, 2 recommendations, minimum 2.5 GPA, ACT, and in some cases an essay and SAT I. It recommends 3 years of high school math and science, some high school foreign language, and an interview. Early, deferred, and midyear entrance are possible, with rolling admissions and continuous processing to 3/1 for financial aid. **Contact:** Mr. Robert A. Preloger, Assistant to the President/Dean of Enrollment, 2001 South Summit, Sioux Falls, SD 57197, 605-336-5516 or toll-free 800-727-2844; fax 605-336-5518.

## GETTING IN LAST YEAR
- 1,027 applied
- 91% were accepted
- 41% enrolled (381)
- 21% from top tenth of their h.s. class
- 3.43 average high school GPA
- 34% had ACT scores over 26
- 8% had ACT scores over 30
- 2 National Merit Scholars

## THE STUDENT BODY
- Total 1,667, of whom 1,624 are undergraduates
- From 39 states and territories, 12 other countries
- 53% from South Dakota
- 65% women, 35% men
- 1% African Americans
- 1% Native Americans
- 1% Hispanics
- 3% international students

## AFTER FRESHMAN YEAR
- 79% returned for sophomore year
- 49% got a degree within 4 years
- 57% got a degree within 5 years
- 58% got a degree within 6 years

## AFTER GRADUATION
- 20% pursued further study (5% business, 4% arts and sciences, 4% law)
- 65% had job offers within 3 months

## WHAT YOU WILL PAY
Tuition and fees $11,115
Room and board $3358

# AUSTIN COLLEGE

Sherman, Texas • Suburban setting • Private • Independent-Religious • Coed

▶ During the commencement address given to classmates at Austin College, a senior student stated, "I came to Austin College so that I could see the world . . . and I did." Students at Austin see first a beautifully landscaped tree-lined campus where learning extends far beyond the 65-acre campus and where meaningful and lasting relationships are made with faculty, administration, and peers. Austin may be the oldest college in Texas still operating under its original charter, but there is a newness reflected in its campus and programs that gives perspective and meaning to the global world in which its students will live their lives.

## 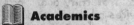 Academics

AC offers an interdisciplinary curriculum and core academic program. It awards bachelor's and master's **degrees**. Challenging opportunities include advanced placement, accelerated degree programs, self-designed majors, tutorials, and an honors program. Special programs include internships, summer session for credit, off-campus study, and study abroad.

The most popular **majors** include psychology, biology/biological sciences, and business. A complete listing of majors at AC appears in the Majors Index beginning on page 380.

The **faculty** at AC has 85 full-time graduate and undergraduate teachers, 97% with terminal degrees. 100% of the faculty serve as student advisers. The student-faculty ratio is 13:1.

## 🖥 Computers on Campus

Students are not required to have a computer. Student rooms are linked to a campus network. 125 **computers** available in the computer center, computer labs, the research center, psychology department, social science lab, classrooms, the library, and dormitories provide access to e-mail. Staffed computer lab on campus (open 24 hours a day) provides training in the use of computers and software.

The **library** has 408,276 books, 148,569 microform titles, and 1,739 subscriptions. It is connected to 5 national **on-line** catalogs.

##  Campus Life

There are 35 active **organizations** on campus, including a drama/theater group and student-run newspaper. 49% of students participate in student government elections. 28% of eligible men and 30% of eligible women are members of 8 local **fraternities** and 6 local **sororities**. Student **safety services** include late night transport/escort service, 24-hour emergency telephone alarm devices, 24-hour patrols by trained security personnel, and electronically operated dormitory entrances.

AC is a member of the NAIA. **Intercollegiate sports** include baseball (m), basketball (m, w), football (m), golf (m), soccer (m), swimming and diving (m, w), tennis (m, w), track and field (m, w), volleyball (w).

## 🎓 Applying

AC requires an essay, a high school transcript, 3 years of high school math and science, 2 recommendations, SAT I or ACT, and in some cases an interview. It recommends 2 years of high school foreign language and an interview. Early, deferred, and midyear entrance are possible, with a 2/1 deadline and continuous processing to 3/15 for financial aid. **Contact:** Mr. Jay Evans, Senior Associate Director of Admissions, 900 North Grand Avenue, Suite 6N, Sherman, TX 75090-4440, 903-813-3000 or toll-free 800-442-5363; fax 903-813-3198.

---

### GETTING IN LAST YEAR

918 applied
85% were accepted
35% enrolled (271)
42% from top tenth of their h.s. class
16% had SAT verbal scores over 600
32% had SAT math scores over 600
38% had ACT scores over 26
3% had SAT verbal scores over 700
8% had SAT math scores over 700
9% had ACT scores over 30
7 National Merit Scholars

### THE STUDENT BODY

Total 1,152, of whom 1,095 are undergraduates

From 20 states and territories,
14 other countries
91% from Texas
54% women, 46% men
4% African Americans
1% Native Americans
10% Hispanics
6% Asian Americans
2% international students

### AFTER FRESHMAN YEAR

74% returned for sophomore year
58% got a degree within 4 years
67% got a degree within 5 years

### AFTER GRADUATION

38% pursued further study (20% arts and sciences, 6% business, 6% medicine)
40% had job offers within 3 months
10 corporations recruited on campus

### WHAT YOU WILL PAY

Tuition and fees $12,195
Room and board $4524
63% receive need-based financial aid averaging $4281
27% receive non-need financial aid averaging $2755

# BABSON COLLEGE

Wellesley, Massachusetts • Suburban setting • Private • Independent • Coed

Babson is committed to being an international leader in management education. Through a balanced and rigorous program of management and liberal arts courses, the College educates students who are capable of initiating, managing, and implementing change. With an enrollment of approximately 1,600 undergraduates, Babson offers students the opportunity to participate in class discussions and other activities. Through more than 50 organizations and clubs and 30 student-run businesses, students play a role in shaping campus life. Babson's 450-acre residential campus is located 14 miles west of Boston, where students can take advantage of many social and career exploration opportunities.

## Academics

Babson offers a business, management, liberal arts curriculum and core academic program. It awards bachelor's and master's **degrees**. Challenging opportunities include advanced placement, accelerated degree programs, self-designed majors, tutorials, Freshmen Honors College, an honors program, and a senior project. Special programs include internships, summer session for credit, off-campus study, study abroad, and Army ROTC.

The most popular **majors** include marketing/retailing/merchandising, economics, and finance/banking. A complete listing of majors at Babson appears in the Majors Index beginning on page 380.

The **faculty** at Babson has 126 full-time graduate and undergraduate teachers, 90% with terminal degrees. 50% of the faculty serve as student advisers. The average class size in required courses is 27.

## Computers on Campus

Students are not required to have a computer. 120 **computers** available in the computer center, computer labs, the library, and dormitories provide access to the main academic computer, e-mail, and on-line services. Staffed computer lab on campus (open 24 hours a day) provides training in the use of computers and software.

The **library** has 120,942 books, 345,947 microform titles, and 1,400 subscriptions. It is connected to 8 national **on-line** catalogs.

## Campus Life

There are 56 active **organizations** on campus, including a drama/theater group and student-run newspaper. 12% of eligible men and 8% of eligible women are members of 4 national **fraternities** and 2 national **sororities**. Student **safety services** include late night transport/escort service, 24-hour emergency telephone alarm devices, 24-hour patrols by trained security personnel, and electronically operated dormitory entrances.

Babson is a member of the NCAA (Division III). **Intercollegiate sports** include baseball (m), basketball (m, w), cross-country running (m, w), field hockey (w), golf (m), ice hockey (m), lacrosse (m, w), rugby (m), sailing (m, w), skiing (downhill) (m, w), soccer (m, w), softball (w), squash (m, w), swimming and diving (m, w), tennis (m, w), volleyball (m, w).

## Applying

Babson requires an essay, a high school transcript, 3 years of high school math, 1 recommendation, SAT I or ACT, and 2 SAT II Subject Tests. It recommends 4 years of high school math, 3 years of high school science, 2 years of high school foreign language, and an interview. Early, deferred, and midyear entrance are possible, with a 2/1 deadline and 2/1 for financial aid. **Contact:** Dr. Charles Nolan, Dean of Undergraduate Admission, Office of Undergraduate Admission, Mustard Hall, Babson Park, MA 02157-0310, 617-239-5522 or toll-free 800-488-3696; fax 617-239-4006.

**GETTING IN LAST YEAR**
2,144 applied
51% were accepted
37% enrolled (404)
29% from top tenth of their h.s. class
4% had SAT verbal scores over 600
45% had SAT math scores over 600
0% had SAT verbal scores over 700
7% had SAT math scores over 700
3 valedictorians

**THE STUDENT BODY**
Total 3,263, of whom 1,631
   are undergraduates
From 41 states and territories,
   71 other countries

41% from Massachusetts
38% women, 62% men
2% African Americans
0% Native Americans
3% Hispanics
4% Asian Americans
16% international students

**AFTER FRESHMAN YEAR**
88% returned for sophomore year
80% got a degree within 4 years
84% got a degree within 5 years
85% got a degree within 6 years

**AFTER GRADUATION**
5% pursued further study (3% law)
75% had job offers within 3 months
215 corporations, 4 government agencies
   recruited on campus

**WHAT YOU WILL PAY**
Tuition and fees $17,260
Room and board $6985
49% receive need-based financial aid
   averaging $8649
4% receive non-need financial aid averaging
   $5000

# BALDWIN-WALLACE COLLEGE

Berea, Ohio • Suburban setting • Private • Independent-Religious • Coed

Founded in 1845, Baldwin-Wallace was among the first colleges to admit students without regard to race or gender. That spirit of inclusiveness and innovation continues today. The academic program, rooted in the liberal arts, yet balanced by abundant opportunities for career exploration and application, is designed to prepare students to make a living . . . and a life worth living. It's a program committed to quality and distinguished by a personalized approach to learning that celebrates each student. "Quality education with a personal touch" is more than a slogan at B-W. It's a statement of purpose. It's who Baldwin-Wallace is.

##  Academics

B-W offers a liberal arts curriculum and core academic program. It awards bachelor's and master's **degrees**. Challenging opportunities include advanced placement, accelerated degree programs, self-designed majors, tutorials, an honors program, and a senior project. Special programs include internships, summer session for credit, off-campus study, study abroad, and Army and Air Force ROTC.

The most popular **majors** include business and education. A complete listing of majors at B-W appears in the Majors Index beginning on page 380.

The **faculty** at B-W has 154 full-time undergraduate teachers, 75% with terminal degrees. 100% of the faculty serve as student advisers. The student-faculty ratio is 18:1, and the average class size in required courses is 25.

##  Computers on Campus

Students are not required to have a computer. 490 **computers** available in the computer center, computer labs, all academic buildings, the library, and dormitories. Staffed computer lab on campus provides training in the use of computers and software.

The 2 **libraries** have 230,000 books, 102,865 microform titles, and 950 subscriptions.

##  Campus Life

There are 40 active **organizations** on campus, including a drama/theater group and student-run newspaper and radio station. 38% of eligible men and 38% of eligible women are members of 5 national **fraternities** and 7 national **sororities**. Student **safety services** include late night transport/escort service, 24-hour emergency telephone alarm devices, 24-hour patrols by trained security personnel, student patrols, and electronically operated dormitory entrances.

B-W is a member of the NCAA (Division III). **Intercollegiate sports** include baseball (m), basketball (m, w), cross-country running (m, w), football (m), golf (m), soccer (m, w), softball (w), swimming and diving (m, w), tennis (m, w), track and field (m, w), volleyball (w), wrestling (m).

##  Applying

B-W requires an essay, a high school transcript, 1 recommendation, and SAT I or ACT. It recommends 3 years of high school math and science, 2 years of high school foreign language, and an interview. Deferred and midyear entrance are possible, with rolling admissions and continuous processing to 5/1 for financial aid. **Contact:** Mrs. Julie Baker, Director of Undergraduate Admission, 275 Eastland Road, Berea, OH 44017-2088, 216-826-2222.

## GETTING IN LAST YEAR

1,703 applied
85% were accepted
44% enrolled (642)
25% from top tenth of their h.s. class
3.2 average high school GPA
8% had SAT verbal scores over 600
30% had SAT math scores over 600
22% had ACT scores over 26
1% had SAT verbal scores over 700
3% had SAT math scores over 700
3% had ACT scores over 30
14 valedictorians

## THE STUDENT BODY

Total 4,716, of whom 4,105
    are undergraduates
From 32 states and territories,
    19 other countries
90% from Ohio
60% women, 40% men
5% African Americans
0% Native Americans
2% Hispanics
1% Asian Americans
2% international students

## AFTER FRESHMAN YEAR

85% returned for sophomore year
59% got a degree within 4 years
65% got a degree within 5 years
66% got a degree within 6 years

## AFTER GRADUATION

12% pursued further study (4% business, 3% arts and sciences, 2% law)
45 corporations, 5 government agencies, 11 nonprofit organizations recruited on campus

## WHAT YOU WILL PAY

Tuition and fees $11,580
Room and board $4410
74% receive need-based financial aid averaging $5447
Non-need financial aid averages $3219

# Bard College

Annandale-on-Hudson, New York • Rural setting • Private • Independent • Coed

Bard is a place to think. Its rural setting on 600 acres within the historic Hudson River Valley affords the safety and serenity conducive to serious academic study. Proximity to New York City, 90 miles to the south, provides innumerable opportunities. Typical Bard students are multitalented. The 10:1 student-faculty ratio encourages tailored programs; students develop many interests while completing specific majors. Classes are small, engaging, and rigorous. Writing and original work are emphasized across the disciplines. An Arts Division supports creative expression. About 13% of the 1,000 undergraduates are international students representing some 48 countries; students attend from all U.S. states.

 **Academics**

Bard offers a writing-intensive interdisciplinary curriculum and core academic program. It awards bachelor's and master's **degrees**. Challenging opportunities include advanced placement, accelerated degree programs, self-designed majors, tutorials, and a senior project. Special programs include internships, off-campus study, and study abroad.

The most popular **majors** include social science, art/fine arts, and literature. A complete listing of majors at Bard appears in the Majors Index beginning on page 380.

The **faculty** at Bard has 92 full-time undergraduate teachers, 95% with terminal degrees. 100% of the faculty serve as student advisers. The student-faculty ratio is 10:1, and the average class size in required courses is 15.

 **Computers on Campus**

Students are not required to have a computer. 90 **computers** available in the computer center, computer labs, the research center, academic departments, and the library provide access to e-mail. Staffed computer lab on campus provides training in the use of computers and software.

The 4 **libraries** have 260,000 books, 8,502 microform titles, and 745 subscriptions. They are connected to 3 national **on-line** catalogs.

 **Campus Life**

There are 60 active **organizations** on campus, including a drama/theater group and student-run newspaper and radio station. Student **safety services** include late night transport/escort service, 24-hour emergency telephone alarm devices, 24-hour patrols by trained security personnel, student patrols, and electronically operated dormitory entrances.

Bard is a member of the NCAA (Division III) and NAIA. **Intercollegiate sports** include basketball (m), cross-country running (m, w), fencing (m, w), soccer (m, w), squash (m, w), tennis (m, w), volleyball (m, w).

 **Applying**

Bard requires an essay, a high school transcript, 3 recommendations, and in some cases a campus interview. It recommends 4 years of high school math and science, 3 years of high school foreign language, a campus interview, SAT I or ACT, SAT II Subject Tests, and a minimum high school GPA of 3.0. Early, deferred, and midyear entrance are possible, with a 1/31 deadline and a 3/15 priority date for financial aid. **Contact:** Ms. Mary Backlund, Director of Admissions, Annandale Road, Annandale-on-Hudson, NY 12504, 914-758-7472.

---

### GETTING IN LAST YEAR
2,000 applied
43% were accepted
36% enrolled (310)
50% from top tenth of their h.s. class
3.3 average high school GPA

### THE STUDENT BODY
Total 1,148, of whom 1,023
  are undergraduates
From 50 states and territories,
  48 other countries
25% from New York
51% women, 49% men
8% African Americans

1% Native Americans
5% Hispanics
5% Asian Americans
12% international students

### AFTER FRESHMAN YEAR
89% returned for sophomore year
77% got a degree within 4 years
78% got a degree within 5 years
79% got a degree within 6 years

### AFTER GRADUATION
60% pursued further study (45% arts and
  sciences, 5% law, 3% medicine)
25 corporations, 10 government agencies, 45
  nonprofit organizations recruited on campus

### WHAT YOU WILL PAY
Tuition and fees $19,819
Room and board $6206
68% receive need-based financial aid
  averaging $11,285
3% receive non-need financial aid averaging
  $18,522

# BARNARD COLLEGE

New York, New York • Urban setting • Private • Independent • Women

Barnard is a small, select liberal arts college for women. Its superb faculty, about half of whom are women, are not only leading scholars but also accessible, dedicated teachers. Barnard's unique affiliation with Columbia University, which is just across the street, gives students a vast selection of courses and extracurricular activities, Division I athletic competition, and a fully coeducational social life. Adding immeasurably to a Barnard education is its location in New York City, where students have access to hundreds of internships and unparalleled cultural, intellectual, and social resources.

 ## Academics

Barnard offers a liberal arts and sciences curriculum and core academic program. It awards bachelor's **degrees**. Challenging opportunities include advanced placement, accelerated degree programs, self-designed majors, tutorials, an honors program, a senior project, Phi Beta Kappa, and Sigma Xi. Special programs include internships, off-campus study, and study abroad.

The most popular **majors** include English, political science/government, and psychology. A complete listing of majors at Barnard appears in the Majors Index beginning on page 380.

The **faculty** at Barnard has 162 full-time teachers, 93% with terminal degrees. 100% of the faculty serve as student advisers. The student-faculty ratio is 10:1, and the average class size in required courses is 21.

 ## Computers on Campus

Students are not required to have a computer. 120 **computers** available in the computer center, computer labs, classrooms, the library, the student center, and dormitories provide access to the main academic computer, off-campus computing facilities, e-mail, and on-line services. Staffed computer lab on campus provides training in the use of computers and software.

The **library** has 169,514 books, 13,994 microform titles, and 710 subscriptions.

 ## Campus Life

There are 80 active **organizations** on campus, including a drama/theater group and student-run newspaper and radio station. Student **safety services** include late night transport/escort service, 24-hour emergency telephone alarm devices, and 24-hour patrols by trained security personnel.

Barnard is a member of the NCAA (Division I). **Intercollegiate sports** include archery, basketball, crew, cross-country running, fencing, soccer, swimming and diving, tennis, track and field, volleyball.

 ## Applying

Barnard requires an essay, a high school transcript, 3 years of high school math, 3 recommendations, SAT I or ACT, and 3 SAT II Subject Tests (including SAT II: Writing Test). It recommends 3 years of high school science, 3 years of high school foreign language, and an interview. Early, deferred, and midyear entrance are possible, with a 1/15 deadline and 2/1 for financial aid. **Contact:** Ms. Doris Davis, Director of Admissions, 11 Milbank Hall, New York, NY 10027-6598, 212-854-2014; fax 212-854-6220.

## GETTING IN LAST YEAR
2,734 applied
49% were accepted
42% enrolled (558)
51% from top tenth of their h.s. class
3.66 average high school GPA
54% had SAT verbal scores over 600
67% had SAT math scores over 600
78% had ACT scores over 26
6% had SAT verbal scores over 700
18% had SAT math scores over 700
17% had ACT scores over 30
10 National Merit Scholars

## THE STUDENT BODY
2,274 undergraduates
From 52 states and territories,
   29 other countries
39% from New York
100% women
4% African Americans
1% Native Americans
5% Hispanics
26% Asian Americans
4% international students

## AFTER FRESHMAN YEAR
95% returned for sophomore year
81% got a degree within 4 years
85% got a degree within 5 years
87% got a degree within 6 years

## AFTER GRADUATION
35% pursued further study

## WHAT YOU WILL PAY
Tuition and fees $18,646
Room and board $8124
60% receive need-based financial aid
   averaging $12,620

# BATES COLLEGE

Lewiston, Maine • Suburban setting • Private • Independent • Coed

▶ Bates is the first coeducational college in New England and among the oldest such institutions in the nation. On principle, all organizations on campus are open to all students; there have never been fraternities or sororities at Bates. Another attraction is the opportunity to live in Maine, a state with unsurpassed landscape, distinctive architecture, an interesting diversity of people, and a strong sense of living history. Graduates of Bates often leave subtly changed by their 4 years in this special place.

 ## Academics

Bates offers a liberal arts curriculum and core academic program. It awards bachelor's **degrees**. Challenging opportunities include advanced placement, accelerated degree programs, self-designed majors, tutorials, an honors program, a senior project, and Phi Beta Kappa. Special programs include internships, off-campus study, and study abroad.

The most popular **majors** include English, political science/government, and psychology. A complete listing of majors at Bates appears in the Majors Index beginning on page 380.

The **faculty** at Bates has 150 full-time teachers, 96% with terminal degrees. 100% of the faculty serve as student advisers. The student-faculty ratio is 11:1, and the average class size in required courses is 15.

 ## Computers on Campus

Students are not required to have a computer. Student rooms are linked to a campus network. 280 **computers** available in the computer center, computer labs, the research center, the learning resource center, classroom buildings, classrooms, and the library provide access to the main academic computer, off-campus computing facilities, e-mail, and on-line services. Staffed computer lab on campus (open 24 hours a day) provides training in the use of computers and software.

The **library** has 585,041 books, 277,784 microform titles, and 1,848 subscriptions. It is connected to 7 national **on-line** catalogs.

 ## Campus Life

There are 60 active **organizations** on campus, including a drama/theater group and student-run newspaper and radio station. Student **safety services** include late night transport/escort service, 24-hour emergency telephone alarm devices, 24-hour patrols by trained security personnel, and student patrols.

Bates is a member of the NCAA (Division III). **Intercollegiate sports** include badminton (m, w), baseball (m), basketball (m, w), crew (m, w), cross-country running (m, w), equestrian sports (m, w), fencing (m, w), field hockey (w), football (m), golf (m, w), ice hockey (m, w), lacrosse (m, w), rugby (m, w), sailing (m, w), skiing (cross-country) (m, w), skiing (downhill) (m, w), soccer (m, w), softball (w), squash (m, w), swimming and diving (m, w), tennis (m, w), track and field (m, w), volleyball (m, w), water polo (m, w).

 ## Applying

Bates requires an essay, a high school transcript, and 3 recommendations. It recommends 3 years of high school math and science, some high school foreign language, and an interview. Early, deferred, and midyear entrance are possible, with a 1/15 deadline and 2/10 for financial aid. **Contact:** Mr. Wylie L. Mitchell, Dean of Admissions, 23 Campus Avenue, Lewiston, ME 04240-6028, 207-786-6000; fax 207-786-6025.

---

**GETTING IN LAST YEAR**
3,594 applied
34% were accepted
36% enrolled (448)
54% from top tenth of their h.s. class
50% had SAT verbal scores over 600
80% had SAT math scores over 600
4% had SAT verbal scores over 700
23% had SAT math scores over 700

**THE STUDENT BODY**
1,562 undergraduates
From 47 states and territories,
   31 other countries

13% from Maine
51% women, 49% men
3% African Americans
0% Native Americans
1% Hispanics
4% Asian Americans
3% international students

**AFTER FRESHMAN YEAR**
93% returned for sophomore year
81% got a degree within 4 years
88% got a degree within 5 years

**AFTER GRADUATION**
111 corporations, 14 government agencies,
   22 nonprofit organizations recruited on
   campus
1 Fulbright scholar

**WHAT YOU WILL PAY**
Comprehensive fee $25,180
54% receive need-based financial aid
   averaging $12,974

# BAYLOR UNIVERSITY

Waco, Texas • Urban setting • Private • Independent-Religious • Coed

▶ *U.S. News & World Report, Money* magazine, and the *National Review College Guide* each named Baylor one of the nation's top universities. Proud of its Christian heritage, Baylor emphasizes teaching, scholarly attention to discovery, and service to others. With a low student-professor ratio, Baylor offers a more intimate, relationship-based education than is found in most major universities. Baylor operates a $64-million financial aid program and assists almost 70% of its students with loans, grants, scholarships, and campus work-study jobs. Baylor's academic quality, accessibility, and affordability make it an exceptional value in higher education today.

 **Academics**

Baylor offers an interdisciplinary curriculum and core academic program; fewer than half of graduate courses are open to undergraduates. It awards bachelor's, master's, doctoral, and first professional **degrees**. Challenging opportunities include advanced placement, accelerated degree programs, self-designed majors, an honors program, a senior project, Phi Beta Kappa, and Sigma Xi. Special programs include internships, summer session for credit, study abroad, and Air Force ROTC.

A complete listing of majors at Baylor appears in the Majors Index beginning on page 380.

The **faculty** at Baylor has 599 full-time graduate and undergraduate teachers, 73% with terminal degrees. The student-faculty ratio is 18:1, and the average class size in required courses is 30.

 **Computers on Campus**

Students are not required to have a computer. 634 **computers** available in the computer center, computer labs, the learning resource center, all major academic buildings, the library, and dormitories.

The 9 **libraries** have 1.5 million books, 12,466 microform titles, and 10,561 subscriptions. They are connected to 5 national **on-line** catalogs.

 **Campus Life**

Active **organizations** on campus include drama/theater group and student-run newspaper and radio station. 17% of students participate in student government elections. 20% of eligible men and 25% of eligible women are members of 13 national **fraternities**, 12 national **sororities**, 2 local fraternities, and 1 local sorority. Student **safety services** include bicycle patrols by campus police, late night transport/escort service, 24-hour emergency telephone alarm devices, 24-hour patrols by trained security personnel, and electronically operated dormitory entrances.

Baylor is a member of the NCAA (Division I). **Intercollegiate sports** (some offering scholarships) include badminton (m, w), baseball (m), basketball (m, w), cross-country running (m, w), football (m), golf (m, w), lacrosse (m, w), sailing (m, w), soccer (m, w), softball (w), tennis (m, w), track and field (m, w), volleyball (m, w).

 **Applying**

Baylor requires an essay, a high school transcript, and SAT I or ACT. It recommends 3 years of high school math and science, some high school foreign language, recommendations, and a campus interview. Early, deferred, and midyear entrance are possible, with rolling admissions and continuous processing to 3/1 for financial aid. **Contact:** Mr. Ramiro Peña, Office of Recruitment, PO Box 97056, Waco, TX 76798, 817-755-3435 or toll-free 800-BAYLOR U.

---

### GETTING IN LAST YEAR
12% had SAT verbal scores over 600
39% had SAT math scores over 600
30% had ACT scores over 26
2% had SAT verbal scores over 700
9% had SAT math scores over 700
6% had ACT scores over 30
59 National Merit Scholars

### THE STUDENT BODY
Total 12,240, of whom 10,373
  are undergraduates
From 52 states and territories,
  67 other countries
77% from Texas
56% women, 44% men
5% African Americans
1% Native Americans
7% Hispanics
4% Asian Americans
2% international students

### AFTER FRESHMAN YEAR
84% returned for sophomore year

### WHAT YOU WILL PAY
Tuition and fees $7560
Room and board $4035
Need-based financial aid averages $829
Non-need financial aid averages $1957

---

# BELLARMINE COLLEGE

Louisville, Kentucky • Suburban setting • Private • Independent-Religious • Coed

A wealth of opportunity awaits students at Bellarmine College's 120-acre campus, nestled in one of Louisville's most desirable neighborhoods. The small class size makes it easy to get to know professors and other students. Students can study in one of the 37 countries participating in the foreign exchange program. More than 50 student organizations are active on campus. Students can participate in a multitude of internship programs, which have served as a stepping stone to full-time positions. Bellarmine graduates work in leadership capacities with Fortune 500 companies both in the Louisville region and nationwide.

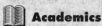
## Academics

Bellarmine offers a liberal arts curriculum and core academic program; a few graduate courses are open to undergraduates. It awards bachelor's and master's **degrees**. Challenging opportunities include advanced placement, Freshmen Honors College, an honors program, and a senior project. Special programs include internships, summer session for credit, off-campus study, study abroad, and Army and Air Force ROTC.

The most popular **majors** include business, accounting, and nursing. A complete listing of majors at Bellarmine appears in the Majors Index beginning on page 380.

The **faculty** at Bellarmine has 90 full-time graduate and undergraduate teachers, 82% with terminal degrees. 100% of the faculty serve as student advisers. The student-faculty ratio is 13:1, and the average class size in required courses is 18.

## Computers on Campus

Students are not required to have a computer. 80 **computers** available in the computer center, computer labs, and classrooms. Staffed computer lab on campus provides training in the use of computers and software.

The 2 **libraries** have 117,358 books and 614 subscriptions. They are connected to 1 national **on-line** catalog.

## Campus Life

Active **organizations** on campus include a drama/theater group and student-run newspaper. 20% of eligible men are members of 1 national **fraternity**. Student **safety services** include 24-hour emergency telephone alarm devices and 24-hour patrols by trained security personnel.

Bellarmine is a member of the NCAA (Division II). **Intercollegiate sports** (some offering scholarships) include baseball (m), basketball (m, w), cross-country running (m, w), field hockey (w), golf (m, w), soccer (m, w), softball (w), tennis (m, w), track and field (m, w), volleyball (w).

## Applying

Bellarmine requires an essay, a high school transcript, 3 years of high school math, recommendations, minimum 2.5 high school GPA, and SAT I or ACT. It recommends 3 years of high school science, 2 years of high school foreign language, and an interview. Early, deferred, and midyear entrance are possible, with an 8/1 deadline and continuous processing to 3/15 for financial aid. **Contact:** Mr. Timothy A. Sturgeon, Associate Dean of Admissions, 2001 Newburg Road, Louisville, KY 40205-0671, 502-452-8131 or toll-free 800-274-4723; fax 502-456-1844.

---

**GETTING IN LAST YEAR**
730 applied
90% were accepted
52% enrolled (343)
30% from top tenth of their h.s. class
3.35 average high school GPA
26% had ACT scores over 26
5% had ACT scores over 30

**THE STUDENT BODY**
Total 2,411, of whom 1,865
  are undergraduates
From 20 states and territories,
  14 other countries

80% from Kentucky
58% women, 42% men
2% African Americans
0% Native Americans
1% Hispanics
1% Asian Americans
1% international students

**AFTER FRESHMAN YEAR**
75% returned for sophomore year
51% got a degree within 4 years
56% got a degree within 5 years
57% got a degree within 6 years

**AFTER GRADUATION**
23% pursued further study (9% business, 5% arts and sciences, 5% law)
42 corporations, 5 government agencies, 8 nonprofit organizations recruited on campus

**WHAT YOU WILL PAY**
Tuition and fees $8940
Room and board $2950
70% receive need-based financial aid averaging $1817
30% receive non-need financial aid averaging $2896

# BELMONT UNIVERSITY

Nashville, Tennessee • Urban setting • Private • Independent-Religious • Coed

Belmont University students receive an education that revolves around the spirit of the individual. Focusing on academic excellence and continuous improvement, the University recognizes students as central to its mission as it dedicates itself to providing students from diverse backgrounds with an academically challenging education in a Christian community. The University's vision is to be a premier teaching university that brings together the best of liberal arts and professional education in a consistently caring Christian environment. Values that fulfill this vision encourage students as well as University leadership to be honest, treat every person with respect, and listen and learn from everyone.

 **Academics**

Belmont offers a core academic program. It awards associate, bachelor's, and master's **degrees**. Challenging opportunities include advanced placement, accelerated degree programs, and an honors program. Special programs include cooperative education, internships, summer session for credit, study abroad, and Army, Naval, and Air Force ROTC.

The most popular **majors** include music business, accounting, and elementary education. A complete listing of majors at Belmont appears in the Majors Index beginning on page 380.

The **faculty** at Belmont has 150 full-time undergraduate teachers, 67% with terminal degrees. 100% of the faculty serve as student advisers. The student-faculty ratio is 14:1, and the average class size in required courses is 20.

## Computers on Campus

Students are not required to have a computer. Student rooms are linked to a campus network. 200 **computers** available in the computer center, computer labs, academic departments, and the library provide access to the main academic computer and e-mail. Staffed computer lab on campus provides training in the use of computers and software.

The **library** has 155,000 books, 10,000 microform titles, and 1,100 subscriptions. It is connected to 2 national **on-line** catalogs.

 **Campus Life**

Active **organizations** on campus include drama/theater group and student-run newspaper. Belmont has 2 local **fraternities** and 2 local **sororities**. Student **safety services** include late night transport/escort service and electronically operated dormitory entrances.

Belmont is a member of the NAIA. **Intercollegiate sports** (some offering scholarships) include baseball (m), basketball (m, w), cross-country running (m, w), golf (m, w), soccer (m), softball (w), tennis (m, w), track and field (m, w), volleyball (w).

## Applying

Belmont requires a high school transcript, SAT I or ACT, a minimum high school GPA of 2.0, and in some cases an interview. It recommends 3 years of high school math, some high school foreign language, and SAT II Subject Tests. Early, deferred, and midyear entrance are possible, with an 8/2 deadline and continuous processing to 3/15 for financial aid. **Contact:** Dr. Kathryn Baugher, Dean of Admissions, 1900 Belmont Boulevard, Nashville, TN 37212-3757, 615-385-6785.

### GETTING IN LAST YEAR

78% were accepted
45% enrolled (395)
31% from top tenth of their h.s. class
3.0 average high school GPA
13% had SAT verbal scores over 600
17% had SAT math scores over 600
33% had ACT scores over 26
0% had SAT verbal scores over 700
1% had SAT math scores over 700
4% had ACT scores over 30
3 National Merit Scholars

### THE STUDENT BODY

Total 2,961, of whom 2,617
 are undergraduates
From 45 states and territories,
 44 other countries
70% from Tennessee
58% women, 42% men
3% African Americans
0% Native Americans
1% Hispanics
1% Asian Americans
5% international students

### AFTER FRESHMAN YEAR

66% returned for sophomore year
40% got a degree within 4 years
43% got a degree within 5 years
45% got a degree within 6 years

### AFTER GRADUATION

15% pursued further study (6% business, 4% arts and sciences, 1% dentistry)

### WHAT YOU WILL PAY

Tuition and fees $8050
Room and board $3486
Non-need financial aid averages $1000

# BELOIT COLLEGE

Beloit, Wisconsin • Small-town setting • Private • Independent • Coed

▶ The process of finding one's own direction is far too personal an adventure to be standardized. At Beloit College, there is no lengthy list of requirements, no rigid formula for choosing a major, no mold or stereotype in which one is expected to fit. Students can invent themselves at Beloit. Beloit's job—its commitment—is to provide students with resources that will allow them to develop to the fullest, starting with an extraordinary faculty in which even the most senior professors serve as advisers and mentors to first-year students and upperclassmen alike.

 ## Academics

Beloit offers a core academic program; more than half of graduate courses are open to undergraduates. It awards bachelor's and master's **degrees**. Challenging opportunities include advanced placement, self-designed majors, tutorials, a senior project, and Phi Beta Kappa. Special programs include internships, summer session for credit, off-campus study, and study abroad.

The most popular **majors** include business, anthropology, and literature. A complete listing of majors at Beloit appears in the Majors Index beginning on page 380.

The **faculty** at Beloit has 87 full-time undergraduate teachers, 95% with terminal degrees. 100% of the faculty serve as student advisers. The student-faculty ratio is 11:1, and the average class size in required courses is 16.

 ## Computers on Campus

Students are not required to have a computer. 115 **computers** available in the computer center, computer labs, the library, the student center, and dormitories provide access to off-campus computing facilities, e-mail, and on-line services. Staffed computer lab on campus provides training in the use of computers and software.

The **library** has 235,438 books, 1,295 microform titles, and 937 subscriptions. It is connected to 12 national **on-line** catalogs.

 ## Campus Life

Active **organizations** on campus include drama/theater group and student-run newspaper and radio station. 25% of eligible men and 11% of eligible women are members of 4 national **fraternities** and 2 local **sororities**. Student **safety services** include late night transport/escort service, 24-hour emergency telephone alarm devices, and 24-hour patrols by trained security personnel.

Beloit is a member of the NCAA (Division III). **Intercollegiate sports** include baseball (m), basketball (m, w), cross-country running (m, w), fencing (m, w), football (m), golf (m), ice hockey (m), lacrosse (m, w), soccer (m, w), softball (w), swimming and diving (m, w), tennis (m, w), track and field (m, w), volleyball (w).

 ## Applying

Beloit requires an essay, a high school transcript, SAT I or ACT, and in some cases 1 recommendation and a campus interview. It recommends 3 years of high school math and science, 2 years of high school foreign language, and an interview. Early, deferred, and midyear entrance are possible, with rolling admissions and continuous processing to 4/15 for financial aid. **Contact:** Mr. Alan G. McIvor, Vice President of Enrollment Services, 700 College Street, Beloit, WI 53511-5596, 608-363-2500 or toll-free 800-356-0751 (out-of-state).

---

### GETTING IN LAST YEAR

1,406 applied
74% were accepted
29% enrolled (300)
30% from top tenth of their h.s. class
3.3 average high school GPA
34% had SAT verbal scores over 600
36% had SAT math scores over 600
53% had ACT scores over 26
3% had SAT verbal scores over 700
8% had SAT math scores over 700
17% had ACT scores over 30

### THE STUDENT BODY

Total 1,256, of whom 1,246
    are undergraduates
From 47 states and territories,
    52 other countries
23% from Wisconsin
57% women, 43% men
3% African Americans
1% Native Americans
2% Hispanics
3% Asian Americans
10% international students

### AFTER FRESHMAN YEAR

92% returned for sophomore year
52% got a degree within 4 years
64% got a degree within 5 years
65% got a degree within 6 years

### AFTER GRADUATION

38% pursued further study (17% arts and
    sciences, 7% business, 7% law)
45 corporations, 15 government agencies, 25
    nonprofit organizations recruited on campus

### WHAT YOU WILL PAY

Tuition and fees $16,474
Room and board $3616
69% receive need-based financial aid
    averaging $8133
15% receive non-need financial aid averaging
    $3740

# BENNINGTON COLLEGE

Bennington, Vermont • Small-town setting • Private • Independent • Coed

A Bennington education imparts more than a body of knowledge or an excellent liberal arts education. It imparts an approach to life--the belief that the way to get things done is to do them. The College was founded more than 6 decades ago on the premise that people learn best by pursuing that which most interests them and by working closely with teachers who are themselves actively engaged in their interests. Self-directedness is central; the power of the Bennington experience has everything to do with the empowerment of the student, and the result is lifelong confidence, adaptability, and independence of mind.

 **Academics**

Bennington offers an interdisciplinary curriculum and core academic program. It awards bachelor's and master's **degrees**. Challenging opportunities include self-designed majors, tutorials, and a senior project. Special programs include internships, off-campus study, and study abroad.

The most popular **majors** include literature, interdisciplinary studies, and theater arts/drama. A complete listing of majors at Bennington appears in the Majors Index beginning on page 380.

The **faculty** at Bennington has 48 full-time graduate and undergraduate teachers, 59% with terminal degrees. 100% of the faculty serve as student advisers. The student-faculty ratio is 7:1.

 **Computers on Campus**

Student rooms are linked to a campus network. 21 **computers** available in the computer center, computer labs, media center, and classrooms provide access to the main academic computer and e-mail. Staffed computer lab on campus provides training in the use of computers and software.

The 5 **libraries** have 114,689 books, 6,075 microform titles, and 580 subscriptions. They are connected to 1 national **on-line** catalog.

 **Campus Life**

There are 15 active **organizations** on campus, including a drama/theater group and student-run newspaper and radio station. 90% of students participate in student government elections. Student **safety services** include late night transport/escort service and 24-hour patrols by trained security personnel. **Intercollegiate sports** include soccer (m, w).

 **Applying**

Bennington requires an essay, a high school transcript, 2 recommendations, an interview, guidance counselor recommendation and family statement, and SAT I or ACT. It recommends 3 years of high school math and science and 3 years of high school foreign language. Early, deferred, and midyear entrance are possible, with a 1/15 deadline and continuous processing to 3/1 for financial aid. **Contact:** Ms. Elena Ruocco Bachrach, Dean of Admissions, Bennington, VT 05201-9993, 802-442-6349 or toll-free 800-833-6845.

## GETTING IN LAST YEAR
469 applied
59% were accepted
33% enrolled (93)
27% from top tenth of their h.s. class
3.5 average high school GPA
48% had SAT verbal scores over 600
45% had SAT math scores over 600
64% had ACT scores over 26
11% had SAT verbal scores over 700
6% had SAT math scores over 700
32% had ACT scores over 30
8 National Merit Scholars

## THE STUDENT BODY
Total 458, of whom 373
   are undergraduates
From 39 states and territories,
   17 other countries
6% from Vermont
60% women, 40% men
1% African Americans
0% Native Americans
4% Hispanics
1% Asian Americans
10% international students

## AFTER FRESHMAN YEAR
80% returned for sophomore year
60% got a degree within 6 years

## AFTER GRADUATION
2 nonprofit organizations recruited on campus

## WHAT YOU WILL PAY
Comprehensive fee $25,800
78% receive need-based financial aid
   averaging $13,500
23% receive non-need financial aid averaging
   $5400

# BERRY COLLEGE

Mount Berry, Georgia • Small-town setting • Private • Independent • Coed

Berry College is an independent, coeducational college with fully accredited arts, sciences, and professional programs as well as specialized graduate programs in education and business administration. The College serves humanity by inspiring and educating students regardless of their economic status and emphasizes a comprehensive educational program committed to high academic standards, Christian values, and practical work experiences. The campus is an unusually beautiful environment with approximately 28,000 acres of land. Fields, forests, lakes, and mountains provide scenic beauty in a protected natural setting. The College is located in Rome, Georgia, 65 miles northwest of Atlanta and 65 miles south of Chattanooga.

##  Academics

Berry offers a core academic program; fewer than half of graduate courses are open to undergraduates. It awards bachelor's and master's **degrees**. Challenging opportunities include advanced placement, accelerated degree programs, self-designed majors, an honors program, and a senior project. Special programs include cooperative education, internships, summer session for credit, and study abroad.

The most popular **majors** include business, education, and psychology. A complete listing of majors at Berry appears in the Majors Index beginning on page 380.

The **faculty** at Berry has 90 full-time graduate and undergraduate teachers, 86% with terminal degrees. 100% of the faculty serve as student advisers. The student-faculty ratio is 17:1.

##  Computers on Campus

Students are not required to have a computer. 96 **computers** available in the computer center, classroom labs, and the library. Staffed computer lab on campus provides training in the use of computers and software.

The **library** has 150,755 books, 389,454 microform titles, and 1,280 subscriptions.

##  Campus Life

There are 60 active **organizations** on campus, including a drama/theater group and student-run newspaper. Student **safety services** include late night transport/escort service, 24-hour emergency telephone alarm devices, and 24-hour patrols by trained security personnel.

Berry is a member of the NAIA. **Intercollegiate sports** (some offering scholarships) include baseball (m), basketball (m, w), crew (m, w), cross-country running (m, w), equestrian sports (m, w), golf (m), rugby (m), soccer (m, w), tennis (m, w), track and field (m, w).

## Applying

Berry requires a high school transcript, 3 years of high school math and science, 2 years of high school foreign language, and SAT I or ACT. Early, deferred, and midyear entrance are possible, with rolling admissions and continuous processing to 4/1 for financial aid. **Contact:** Mr. George Gaddie, Dean of Admissions, Hermann Hall, Mount Berry, GA 30149-0159, 706-236-2215 or toll-free 800-237-7942.

### GETTING IN LAST YEAR
1,917 applied
78% were accepted
32% enrolled (483)
32% from top tenth of their h.s. class
3.41 average high school GPA
16% had SAT verbal scores over 600
23% had SAT math scores over 600
36% had ACT scores over 26
2% had SAT verbal scores over 700
3% had SAT math scores over 700
9% had ACT scores over 30
1 National Merit Scholar

### THE STUDENT BODY
Total 1,876, of whom 1,725
  are undergraduates

From 29 states and territories,
  27 other countries
81% from Georgia
62% women, 38% men
2% African Americans
0% Native Americans
1% Hispanics
1% Asian Americans
1% international students

### AFTER FRESHMAN YEAR
74% returned for sophomore year
37% got a degree within 4 years
51% got a degree within 5 years
52% got a degree within 6 years

### AFTER GRADUATION
31% pursued further study (4% business, 2%
  arts and sciences, 1% dentistry)
30 corporations, 40 government agencies
  recruited on campus

### WHAT YOU WILL PAY
Tuition and fees $8614
Room and board $3891
Need-based financial aid averages $3132
Non-need financial aid averages $2245

# BETHEL COLLEGE

St. Paul, Minnesota • Suburban setting • Private • Independent-Religious • Coed

▶ Bethel College is a Christian learning community whose goal is to foster an effective academic program and to create a supportive environment for the development of growing persons. Learning at Bethel promotes self-knowledge, appreciation of intellectual and cultural heritage, critical thinking, creative communication of ideas, and lifelong learning. Christian faith is viewed as relevant to all facets of knowledge and experience and is integrated throughout the curriculum. What makes Bethel outstanding are its excellent students, expert faculty, and dedicated staff. Bethel is committed to providing a high-quality liberal arts education to prepare tomorrow's leaders to make a difference in their community, the church, and the world.

 ## Academics

Bethel offers a core academic program. It awards associate, bachelor's, and master's **degrees**. Challenging opportunities include advanced placement, self-designed majors, Freshmen Honors College, an honors program, and a senior project. Special programs include internships, summer session for credit, off-campus study, study abroad, and Army, Naval, and Air Force ROTC.

The most popular **majors** include education, nursing, and business. A complete listing of majors at Bethel appears in the Majors Index beginning on page 380.

The **faculty** at Bethel has 111 full-time undergraduate teachers, 66% with terminal degrees. The student-faculty ratio is 15:1.

 ## Computers on Campus

Students are not required to have a computer. 100 **computers** available in the computer center, computer labs, the learning resource center, dormitories, and student rooms provide access to the main academic computer and off-campus computing facilities.

The **library** has 129,000 books and 640 subscriptions.

 ## Campus Life

Active **organizations** on campus include drama/theater group and student-run newspaper and radio station. Student **safety services** include late night transport/escort service, 24-hour emergency telephone alarm devices, student patrols, and electronically operated dormitory entrances.

Bethel is a member of the NCAA (Division III). **Intercollegiate sports** include baseball (m), basketball (m, w), cross-country running (m, w), football (m), golf (m), ice hockey (m), soccer (m, w), softball (w), tennis (m, w), track and field (m, w), volleyball (w).

 ## Applying

Bethel requires an essay, a high school transcript, 2 recommendations, SAT I or ACT, PSAT, and in some cases an interview. It recommends 3 years of high school math and science and an interview. Early, deferred, and midyear entrance are possible, with rolling admissions and continuous processing to 4/15 for financial aid. **Contact:** Mr. John C. Lassen, Director of Admissions, 3900 Bethel Drive, St. Paul, MN 55112-6999, 612-638-6242 or toll-free 800-255-8706.

---

### GETTING IN LAST YEAR
992 applied
90% were accepted
54% enrolled (481)
26% from top tenth of their h.s. class
13% had SAT verbal scores over 600
33% had SAT math scores over 600
38% had ACT scores over 26
0% had SAT verbal scores over 700
5% had SAT math scores over 700
7% had ACT scores over 30

### THE STUDENT BODY
Total 2,208, of whom 2,109 are undergraduates
67% from Minnesota
59% women, 41% men
1% African Americans
1% Native Americans
1% Hispanics
2% Asian Americans
1% international students

### AFTER FRESHMAN YEAR
74% returned for sophomore year

### WHAT YOU WILL PAY
Tuition and fees $11,700
Room and board $4220

# BIRMINGHAM-SOUTHERN COLLEGE

Birmingham, Alabama • Urban setting • Private • Independent-Religious • Coed

▶ The College continues to be recognized as one of the nation's leading liberal arts colleges by *National Review, U.S. News & World Report,* and *Money* magazine. Special features of the curriculum are the Interim Term and the Honors Program, as well as undergraduate research, the Leadership Studies Program, service learning opportunities, and international study programs. The Interim Term (January) provides an opportunity for independent study, foreign and domestic trips, and internships with government and private organizations. The College has been recognized for its outstanding track record of graduate admission to medical, law, and graduate schools and job placement.

 **Academics**

Birmingham-Southern offers a liberal arts curriculum and core academic program; a few graduate courses are open to undergraduates. It awards bachelor's and master's **degrees**. Challenging opportunities include advanced placement, accelerated degree programs, self-designed majors, tutorials, an honors program, a senior project, and Phi Beta Kappa. Special programs include internships, summer session for credit, off-campus study, study abroad, and Army and Air Force ROTC.

The most popular **majors** include business, biology/biological sciences, and English. A complete listing of majors at Birmingham-Southern appears in the Majors Index beginning on page 380.

The **faculty** at Birmingham-Southern has 98 full-time graduate and undergraduate teachers, 90% with terminal degrees. 100% of the faculty serve as student advisers. The student-faculty ratio is 13:1, and the average class size in required courses is 20.

 **Computers on Campus**

Students are not required to have a computer. Student rooms are linked to a campus network. 114 **computers**

available in the computer center, computer labs, the learning resource center, classroom buildings, classrooms, the library, and dormitories provide access to the main academic computer, off-campus computing facilities, e-mail, and on-line services. Staffed computer lab on campus (open 24 hours a day) provides training in the use of computers and software.

The **library** has 190,922 books, 30,950 microform titles, and 855 subscriptions. It is connected to 1 national **on-line** catalog.

 **Campus Life**

There are 70 active **organizations** on campus, including a drama/theater group and student-run newspaper. 60% of eligible men and 60% of eligible women are members of 6 national **fraternities** and 6 national **sororities**. Student **safety services** include late night transport/escort service, 24-hour emergency telephone alarm devices, 24-hour patrols by trained security personnel, and electronically operated dormitory entrances.

Birmingham-Southern is a member of the NAIA. **Intercollegiate sports** (some offering scholarships) include baseball (m), basketball (m), soccer (m, w), tennis (m, w).

 **Applying**

Birmingham-Southern requires an essay, a high school transcript, 3 years of high school math and science, recommendations, SAT I or ACT, a minimum high school GPA of 2.0, and in some cases an interview. It recommends some high school foreign language. Early, deferred, and midyear entrance are possible, with a 5/1 deadline and continuous processing to 3/31 for financial aid. **Contact:** Mr. Robert Dortch, Vice President of Admissions Services, 900 Arkadelphia Road, Birmingham, AL 35254, 205-226-4686 or toll-free 800-523-5793; fax 205-226-4627.

---

**GETTING IN LAST YEAR**
695 applied
80% were accepted
51% enrolled (283)
39% from top tenth of their h.s. class
3.29 average high school GPA
25% had SAT verbal scores over 600
39% had SAT math scores over 600
75% had ACT scores over 26
1% had SAT verbal scores over 700
5% had SAT math scores over 700
18% had ACT scores over 30
7 National Merit Scholars

**THE STUDENT BODY**
Total 1,583, of whom 1,501
   are undergraduates

From 22 states and territories,
   13 other countries
77% from Alabama
57% women, 43% men
13% African Americans
0% Native Americans
0% Hispanics
3% Asian Americans
1% international students

**AFTER FRESHMAN YEAR**
90% returned for sophomore year
69% got a degree within 4 years
70% got a degree within 5 years

**AFTER GRADUATION**
42% pursued further study (21% arts and
   sciences, 7% law, 6% medicine)
44 corporations, 4 government agencies, 5
   nonprofit organizations recruited on campus

**WHAT YOU WILL PAY**
Tuition and fees $11,780
Room and board $3850
60% receive need-based financial aid
   averaging $1500
30% receive non-need financial aid averaging
   $4000

# BOSTON COLLEGE

Chestnut Hill, Massachusetts • Suburban setting • Private • Independent-Religious • Coed

The Jesuit philosophy of education emphasizes firm grounding in the liberal arts, service to others, and the cultivation of leaders. Ten Presidential Scholars in each freshman class receive a half-tuition scholarship irrespective of need, with funding available to meet full demonstrated need. These students, selected from the top 1% of the early action applicant pool, participate in the most rewarding intellectual experience offered at the College.

##  Academics

BC offers a core academic program; more than half of graduate courses are open to undergraduates. It awards bachelor's, master's, doctoral, and first professional **degrees** (also offers continuing education program with significant enrollment not reflected in profile). Challenging opportunities include advanced placement, accelerated degree programs, self-designed majors, tutorials, Freshmen Honors College, an honors program, and Phi Beta Kappa. Special programs include internships, summer session for credit, off-campus study, study abroad, and Army, Naval, and Air Force ROTC.

The most popular **majors** include English, finance/banking, and political science/government. A complete listing of majors at BC appears in the Majors Index beginning on page 380.

The **faculty** at BC has 604 full-time graduate and undergraduate teachers, 95% with terminal degrees. 100% of the faculty serve as student advisers. The student-faculty ratio is 15:1.

##  Computers on Campus

Students are not required to have a computer. Student rooms are linked to a campus network. 200 **computers** available in the computer center, computer labs, the learning resource center, classrooms, and the library provide access to the main academic computer, off-campus computing facilities, e-mail, and on-line services. Staffed computer lab on campus provides training in the use of computers and software.

The **library** has 1.4 million books, 2.4 million microform titles, and 15,075 subscriptions.

##  Campus Life

There are 140 active **organizations** on campus, including a drama/theater group and student-run newspaper and radio station. Student **safety services** include late night transport/escort service, 24-hour emergency telephone alarm devices, 24-hour patrols by trained security personnel, and electronically operated dormitory entrances.

BC is a member of the NCAA (Division I). **Intercollegiate sports** (some offering scholarships) include baseball (m), basketball (m, w), crew (m, w), cross-country running (m, w), fencing (m, w), field hockey (w), football (m), golf (m, w), ice hockey (m, w), lacrosse (m, w), rugby (m, w), sailing (m, w), skiing (downhill) (m, w), soccer (m, w), softball (w), squash (m, w), swimming and diving (m, w), tennis (m, w), track and field (m, w), volleyball (w), water polo (m), wrestling (m).

##  Applying

BC requires an essay, a high school transcript, 2 recommendations, SAT I or ACT, and 3 SAT II Subject Tests (including SAT II: Writing Test). It recommends 4 years of high school math, 3 years of high school science, 4 years of high school foreign language, and an interview. Early, deferred, and midyear entrance are possible, with a 1/10 deadline and a 2/1 priority date for financial aid. **Contact:** Mr. John L. Mahoney Jr., Director of Undergraduate Admission, 140 Commonwealth Avenue, Lyons Hall 120, Chestnut Hill, MA 02167-9991, 617-552-3100.

---

### GETTING IN LAST YEAR

15,522 applied
41% were accepted
35% enrolled (2,250)
35% had SAT verbal scores over 600
75% had SAT math scores over 600
3% had SAT verbal scores over 700
21% had SAT math scores over 700
7 National Merit Scholars

### THE STUDENT BODY

Total 14,698, of whom 9,079
 are undergraduates
From 51 states and territories,
 86 other countries

30% from Massachusetts
53% women, 47% men
3% African Americans
5% Hispanics
7% Asian Americans
4% international students

### AFTER FRESHMAN YEAR

93% returned for sophomore year

### AFTER GRADUATION

26% pursued further study (9% arts and sciences, 8% law, 5% business)

279 corporations, 3 government agencies, 4
 nonprofit organizations recruited on campus
1 Fulbright scholar

### WHAT YOU WILL PAY

Tuition and fees $17,103
Room and board $6960
49% receive need-based financial aid
 averaging $8604
19% receive non-need financial aid averaging
 $14,628

---

# BOSTON UNIVERSITY

Boston, Massachusetts • Urban setting • Private • Independent • Coed

The Spirit of Boston University is in the possibilities:*The excitement of living and learning in one of the world's greatest cities*With students from more than 130 countries, the most culturally diverse student body in the United States*The challenge of the honors curriculum in the College of Liberal Arts*An internship with Westpac Bank in Sydney, writing for a magazine in Paris, researching stories for the BBC, studying small business in Moscow, or . . . .

 **Academics**

Boston University offers a conjunction of a liberal arts curriculum with professional opportunities and core academic program; more than half of graduate courses are open to undergraduates. It awards bachelor's, master's, doctoral, and first professional **degrees**. Challenging opportunities include advanced placement, accelerated degree programs, self-designed majors, tutorials, Freshmen Honors College, an honors program, a senior project, Phi Beta Kappa, and Sigma Xi. Special programs include cooperative education, internships, summer session for credit, off-campus study, study abroad, and Army, Naval, and Air Force ROTC.

The most popular **majors** include business, social science, and communication. A complete listing of majors at Boston University appears in the Majors Index beginning on page 380.

The **faculty** at Boston University has 1,717 full-time graduate and undergraduate teachers, 81% with terminal degrees. 95% of the faculty serve as student advisers. The student-faculty ratio is 9:1.

 **Computers on Campus**

Students are not required to have a computer. Student rooms are linked to a campus network. 500 **computers** available in the computer center, computer labs, the research center, the learning resource center, academic departments, the library, and dormitories provide access to the main academic computer, off-campus computing facilities, e-mail, and on-line services. Staffed computer lab on campus provides training in the use of computers and software.

The 24 **libraries** have 1.9 million books and 28,795 subscriptions.

 **Campus Life**

There are 300 active **organizations** on campus, including a drama/theater group and student-run newspaper and radio station. 30% of students participate in student government elections. 5% of eligible men and 8% of eligible women are members of 9 national **fraternities** and 9 national **sororities**. Student **safety services** include security personnel at dormitory entrances, late night transport/escort service, 24-hour emergency telephone alarm devices, 24-hour patrols by trained security personnel, and electronically operated dormitory entrances.

Boston University is a member of the NCAA (Division I). **Intercollegiate sports** (some offering scholarships) include archery (m, w), badminton (m, w), baseball (m), basketball (m, w), crew (m, w), cross-country running (m, w), equestrian sports (m, w), fencing (m, w), field hockey (w), football (m), golf (m, w), gymnastics (m, w), ice hockey (m, w), lacrosse (m, w), rugby (m), sailing (m, w), skiing (downhill) (m, w), soccer (m, w), softball (m, w), swimming and diving (m, w), table tennis (m, w), tennis (m, w), track and field (m, w), volleyball (m, w), water polo (m, w), weight lifting (m, w), wrestling (m).

 **Applying**

Boston University requires an essay, a high school transcript, 4 years of high school math and science, 2 recommendations, SAT I or ACT, a minimum high school GPA of 2.0, and in some cases a campus interview, audition, portfolio, and SAT II Subject Tests (including SAT II: Writing Test). It recommends 3 years of high school foreign language and a minimum high school GPA of 3.0. Early, deferred, and midyear entrance are possible, with a 1/15 deadline and continuous processing to 3/1 for financial aid. **Contact:** Ms. Debra Kocar, Associate Director, Admissions Reception Center, 121 Bay State Road, Boston, MA 02215, 617-353-2300.

---

### GETTING IN LAST YEAR
21,874 applied
63% were accepted
27% enrolled (3,728)
45% from top tenth of their h.s. class
26% had SAT verbal scores over 600
52% had SAT math scores over 600
3% had SAT verbal scores over 700
13% had SAT math scores over 700
39 National Merit Scholars
76 valedictorians

### THE STUDENT BODY
Total 28,664, of whom 14,590
    are undergraduates
From 54 states and territories,
    135 other countries
27% from Massachusetts
55% women, 45% men
4% African Americans
6% Hispanics
15% Asian Americans
12% international students

### AFTER FRESHMAN YEAR
85% returned for sophomore year
71% got a degree within 6 years

### WHAT YOU WILL PAY
Tuition and fees $19,700
Room and board $7100
52% receive need-based financial aid
    averaging $10,437
11% receive non-need financial aid averaging
    $10,515

# BOWDOIN COLLEGE

Brunswick, Maine • Small-town setting • Private • Independent • Coed

---

▶ Public health care in Europe, South Asian art, the effects of cognitive style on learning, gender and labor in Israeli kibbutzes, prison reform—these are some of the topics students are studying in classes and independently at Bowdoin. Bowdoin offers one of the most demanding and exciting academic programs in the country, preparing students to become leaders in their academic and professional fields and in their communities. Located just 3 miles from the ocean but 25 minutes from Maine's largest city, Bowdoin balances extremely challenging academics with an active but informal setting, creating a distinctive personality among the nation's top schools.

##  Academics

Bowdoin offers a liberal arts curriculum and core academic program. It awards bachelor's **degrees**. Challenging opportunities include advanced placement, accelerated degree programs, self-designed majors, tutorials, and Phi Beta Kappa. Special programs include off-campus study, study abroad, and Army ROTC.

The most popular **majors** include political science/government, history, and economics. A complete listing of majors at Bowdoin appears in the Majors Index beginning on page 380.

The **faculty** at Bowdoin has 137 full-time teachers, 88% with terminal degrees. 100% of the faculty serve as student advisers. The student-faculty ratio is 11:1.

##  Computers on Campus

Students are not required to have a computer. 127 **computers** available in the computer center, computer labs, the research center, academic departments, and the library provide access to the main academic computer, e-mail, and on-line services. Staffed computer lab on campus (open 24 hours a day) provides training in the use of computers and software.

The 5 **libraries** have 827,974 books and 2,049 subscriptions. They are connected to 5 national **on-line** catalogs.

##  Campus Life

There are 56 active **organizations** on campus, including a drama/theater group and student-run newspaper and radio station. 50% of students participate in student government elections. Bowdoin has 8 coed fraternities. Student **safety services** include late night transport/escort service, 24-hour emergency telephone alarm devices, 24-hour patrols by trained security personnel, and student patrols.

Bowdoin is a member of the NCAA (Division III). **Intercollegiate sports** include baseball (m), basketball (m, w), cross-country running (m, w), field hockey (w), football (m), golf (m, w), ice hockey (m, w), lacrosse (m, w), sailing (m, w), skiing (cross-country) (m, w), skiing (downhill) (m, w), soccer (m, w), softball (w), squash (m, w), swimming and diving (m, w), tennis (m, w), track and field (m, w), volleyball (w).

##  Applying

Bowdoin requires an essay, a high school transcript, and 3 recommendations. It recommends 4 years of high school math, 3 years of high school science, 4 years of high school foreign language, and an interview. Early and deferred entrance are possible, with a 1/15 deadline and a 3/1 priority date for financial aid. **Contact:** Dr. Richard E. Steele, Dean of Admissions, College Street, Brunswick, ME 04011-2546, 207-725-3190; fax 207-725-3003.

---

### GETTING IN LAST YEAR
3,662 applied
30% were accepted
39% enrolled (431)
80% from top tenth of their h.s. class
58% had SAT verbal scores over 600
88% had SAT math scores over 600
8% had SAT verbal scores over 700
30% had SAT math scores over 700

### THE STUDENT BODY
1,489 undergraduates
From 50 states and territories,
   26 other countries
14% from Maine
51% women, 49% men
2% African Americans
1% Native Americans
2% Hispanics
8% Asian Americans
3% international students

### AFTER FRESHMAN YEAR
93% returned for sophomore year

### AFTER GRADUATION
17% pursued further study (10% arts and
   sciences, 4% law)
29 corporations, 10 nonprofit organizations
   recruited on campus
5 Fulbright scholars

### WHAT YOU WILL PAY
Tuition and fees $19,355
Room and board $5885
36% receive need-based financial aid
   averaging $18,280

# BRADLEY UNIVERSITY

Peoria, Illinois • Urban setting • Private • Independent • Coed

## Academics

Bradley offers a core academic program. It awards bachelor's and master's **degrees**. Challenging opportunities include advanced placement, accelerated degree programs, self-designed majors, tutorials, and an honors program. Special programs include cooperative education, internships, summer session for credit, study abroad, and Army ROTC.

A complete listing of majors at Bradley appears in the Majors Index beginning on page 380.

The **faculty** at Bradley has 310 full-time graduate and undergraduate teachers, 80% with terminal degrees. 78% of the faculty serve as student advisers. The student-faculty ratio is 15:1.

## Computers on Campus

Students are not required to have a computer. Student rooms are linked to a campus network. 1,246 **computers** available in the computer center, computer labs, classrooms, the library, the student center, and dormitories provide access to e-mail and on-line services.

The **library** has 531,744 books, 26,268 microform titles, and 1,833 subscriptions.

## Campus Life

There are 220 active **organizations** on campus, including a drama/theater group and student-run news-paper and radio station. 43% of eligible men and 34% of eligible women are members of 18 national **fraternities** and 11 national **sororities**. Student **safety services** include late night transport/escort service, 24-hour emergency telephone alarm devices, 24-hour patrols by trained security personnel, and electronically operated dormitory entrances.

Bradley is a member of the NCAA (Division I). **Intercollegiate sports** (some offering scholarships) include baseball (m), basketball (m, w), cross-country running (m, w), golf (m, w), ice hockey (m), soccer (m), softball (w), swimming and diving (m, w), table tennis (m, w), tennis (m, w), volleyball (w).

## Applying

Bradley requires a high school transcript, SAT I or ACT, a minimum high school GPA of 2.0, and in some cases 3 years of high school math and science. It recommends an essay, some high school foreign language, recommendations, an interview, and a minimum high school GPA of 3.0. Early and deferred entrance are possible, with rolling admissions and continuous processing to 3/1 for financial aid. **Contact:** Mr. Gary Bergman, Executive Director of Enrollment Management, 100 Swords Hall, Peoria, IL 61625-0002, 309-677-1000 or toll-free 800-447-6460.

---

### GETTING IN LAST YEAR
3,879 applied
90% were accepted
30% enrolled (1,046)
30% from top tenth of their h.s. class
24% had SAT verbal scores over 600
54% had SAT math scores over 600
38% had ACT scores over 26
6% had SAT verbal scores over 700
16% had SAT math scores over 700
8% had ACT scores over 30
53 National Merit Scholars

### THE STUDENT BODY
Total 5,882, of whom 5,061
   are undergraduates
From 45 states and territories,
   43 other countries
76% from Illinois
52% women, 48% men
6% African Americans
0% Native Americans
4% Hispanics
3% Asian Americans
1% international students

### AFTER FRESHMAN YEAR
80% returned for sophomore year

### AFTER GRADUATION
15% pursued further study
183 corporations, 14 government agencies, 3
   nonprofit organizations recruited on campus
2 Fulbright scholars

### WHAT YOU WILL PAY
Tuition and fees $10,938
Room and board $4440
55% receive need-based financial aid
   averaging $2095
32% receive non-need financial aid averaging
   $2395

# BRANDEIS UNIVERSITY

Waltham, Massachusetts • Suburban setting • Private • Independent • Coed

The National Center for Complex Systems was formed for the purpose of studying large, complex systems, with the brain and intelligence as the systems of greatest interest. Together, faculty and students from biology, biochemistry, chemistry, computer science, experimental psychology, linguistics, cognitive science, and physics are conducting ground-breaking research on the brain's cognitive processes. Brandeis offers a number of merit-based scholarships for especially talented individuals from throughout the United States and for some international students. These scholarships are awarded to incoming freshmen who demonstrate exceptional scholarly achievement and promise. Awards cover up to 75% of tuition and are renewable annually.

 **Academics**

Brandeis offers an interdisciplinary curriculum and core academic program; fewer than half of graduate courses are open to undergraduates. It awards bachelor's, master's, and doctoral **degrees**. Challenging opportunities include advanced placement, self-designed majors, tutorials, a senior project, and Phi Beta Kappa. Special programs include internships, summer session for credit, off-campus study, and Army and Air Force ROTC.

The most popular **majors** include political science/government, English, and psychology. A complete listing of majors at Brandeis appears in the Majors Index beginning on page 380.

The **faculty** at Brandeis has 358 full-time graduate and undergraduate teachers, 97% with terminal degrees. 90% of the faculty serve as student advisers. The student-faculty ratio is 8:1, and the average class size in required courses is 18.

 **Computers on Campus**

Students are not required to have a computer. Student rooms are linked to a campus network. 100 **computers**

available in the computer center, computer labs, the research center, the learning resource center, science library, classrooms, the library, the student center, and dormitories provide access to off-campus computing facilities, e-mail, on-line services, and educational software. Staffed computer lab on campus provides training in the use of computers and software.

The 3 **libraries** have 960,000 books, 841,906 microform titles, and 7,052 subscriptions. They are connected to 13 national **on-line** catalogs.

 **Campus Life**

There are 130 active **organizations** on campus, including a drama/theater group and student-run newspaper and radio station. 35% of students participate in student government elections. Student **safety services** include late night transport/escort service, 24-hour emergency telephone alarm devices, 24-hour patrols by trained security personnel, and electronically operated dormitory entrances.

Brandeis is a member of the NCAA (Division III). **Intercollegiate sports** include baseball (m), basketball (m, w), crew (m, w), cross-country running (m, w), fencing (m, w), field hockey (w), golf (m), ice hockey (m), lacrosse (m), rugby (m, w), sailing (m, w), skiing (cross-country) (m, w), soccer (m, w), softball (w), swimming and diving (m, w), tennis (m, w), track and field (m, w), volleyball (w), water polo (m, w).

 **Applying**

Brandeis requires an essay, a high school transcript, 3 years of high school foreign language, 2 recommendations, ACT or SAT I and 3 SAT II Subject Tests. It recommends 3 years of high school math and science, an interview, and a minimum high school GPA of 3.0. Early, deferred, and midyear entrance are possible, with a 2/1 deadline and a 2/15 priority date for financial aid. **Contact:** Mr. David L. Gould, Dean of Admissions, 415 South Street, Waltham, MA 02254-9110, 617-736-3500 or toll-free 800-622-0622 (out-of-state); fax 617-736-3536.

---

**GETTING IN LAST YEAR**
4,321 applied
68% were accepted
27% enrolled (788)
48% from top tenth of their h.s. class
8 National Merit Scholars

**THE STUDENT BODY**
Total 4,008, of whom 2,877
   are undergraduates
From 51 states and territories,
   65 other countries
25% from Massachusetts

53% women, 47% men
4% African Americans
0% Native Americans
3% Hispanics
9% Asian Americans
5% international students

**AFTER FRESHMAN YEAR**
89% returned for sophomore year
77% got a degree within 4 years
79% got a degree within 5 years
80% got a degree within 6 years

**AFTER GRADUATION**
39% pursued further study (13% law, 11% arts and sciences, 9% medicine)
27 corporations, 1 government agency, 6 nonprofit organizations recruited on campus

**WHAT YOU WILL PAY**
Tuition and fees $19,830
Room and board $6750
54% receive need-based financial aid averaging $13,509
8% receive non-need financial aid averaging $9362

# BRIGHAM YOUNG UNIVERSITY

Provo, Utah • Suburban setting • Private • Independent-Religious • Coed

BYU, sponsored by the Church of Jesus Christ of Latter-day Saints, offers a range of resources and opportunities, including an extensive study-abroad program. Students choose from over 277 fields in 10 colleges and pursue more than 150 extracurricular activities. The admission process is rigorous. The committee considers academic achievements, extracurricular strengths, and personal qualities. Students likely to benefit from BYU possess a high degree of self-discipline and enthusiasm for learning. BYU ranks in the top 15 among institutions that have National Merit Scholars. Students come from all 50 states and nearly 100 countries and bring a diversity of backgrounds and ideas.

 ## Academics

BYU offers an interdisciplinary curriculum and core academic program; fewer than half of graduate courses are open to undergraduates. It awards bachelor's, master's, doctoral, and first professional **degrees**. Challenging opportunities include advanced placement, accelerated degree programs, self-designed majors, Freshmen Honors College, an honors program, a senior project, and Sigma Xi. Special programs include cooperative education, internships, summer session for credit, study abroad, and Army and Air Force ROTC.

The most popular **majors** include business, elementary education, and English. A complete listing of majors at BYU appears in the Majors Index beginning on page 380.

The **faculty** at BYU has 1,374 full-time graduate and undergraduate teachers, 80% with terminal degrees. The student-faculty ratio is 29:1, and the average class size in required courses is 38.

 ## Computers on Campus

Students are not required to have a computer. 1,800 **computers** available in the computer center, computer labs, the research center, the learning resource center, classrooms, the library, the student center, and dormitories provide access to e-mail and on-line services. Staffed computer lab on campus.

The 4 **libraries** have 2.3 million books, 2.2 million microform titles, and 18,067 subscriptions.

 ## Campus Life

Active **organizations** on campus include drama/theater group and student-run newspaper and radio station. 19% of students participate in student government elections. Student **safety services** include 24-hour emergency telephone alarm devices and 24-hour patrols by trained security personnel.

BYU is a member of the NCAA (Division I). **Intercollegiate sports** (some offering scholarships) include baseball (m), basketball (m, w), cross-country running (m, w), field hockey (w), football (m), golf (m, w), gymnastics (m, w), skiing (downhill) (m, w), soccer (m), softball (w), swimming and diving (m, w), tennis (m, w), track and field (m, w), volleyball (m, w), wrestling (m).

 ## Applying

BYU requires an essay, a high school transcript, 1 recommendation, an interview, ACT, and a minimum high school GPA of 3.0. It recommends 3 years of high school math and science and 2 years of high school foreign language. Early and midyear entrance are possible, with a 2/15 deadline and continuous processing to 3/1 for financial aid. **Contact:** Mr. Erlend D. Peterson, Dean of Admissions and Records, A-183 Abraham Smoot Building, Provo, UT 84602-1001, 801-378-2539.

---

### GETTING IN LAST YEAR
6,988 applied
76% were accepted
83% enrolled (4,404)
54% from top tenth of their h.s. class
3.66 average high school GPA
65% had ACT scores over 26
24% had ACT scores over 30
120 National Merit Scholars

### THE STUDENT BODY
Total 30,413, of whom 27,507
  are undergraduates
From 53 states and territories,
  98 other countries

31% from Utah
50% women, 50% men
1% African Americans
1% Native Americans
2% Hispanics
3% Asian Americans
5% international students

### AFTER FRESHMAN YEAR
89% returned for sophomore year
19% got a degree within 4 years
39% got a degree within 5 years
51% got a degree within 6 years

### AFTER GRADUATION
15% pursued further study
84% had job offers within 3 months
2 Fulbright scholars

### WHAT YOU WILL PAY
Tuition and fees $2340
Room and board $3580
2% receive need-based financial aid averaging
  $1379
19% receive non-need financial aid averaging
  $1614

# BROWN UNIVERSITY

Providence, Rhode Island • Urban setting • Private • Independent • Coed

---

Brown is a university/college with a renowned faculty that teaches students in both the undergraduate college and the graduate school. The unique, nonrestrictive curriculum allows students freedom in selecting their courses, and they may choose their concentration from 83 areas, complete a double major, or pursue an independent concentration. The 140-acre campus is set in a residential neighborhood (National Historic District) and features state-of-the-art computing facilities and an athletics complex. A real sense of community exists on campus, as every student has an academic adviser, and there are several peer counselors in the residence halls.

 **Academics**

Brown offers a liberal arts curriculum and no core academic program; all graduate courses are open to undergraduates. It awards bachelor's, master's, doctoral, and first professional **degrees**. Challenging opportunities include advanced placement, accelerated degree programs, self-designed majors, tutorials, a senior project, Phi Beta Kappa, and Sigma Xi. Special programs include internships, summer session for credit, off-campus study, study abroad, and Army ROTC.

The most popular **majors** include biology/biological sciences, history, and English. A complete listing of majors at Brown appears in the Majors Index beginning on page 380.

The **faculty** at Brown has 538 full-time graduate and undergraduate teachers, 98% with terminal degrees. 70% of the faculty serve as student advisers. The student-faculty ratio is 9:1.

 **Computers on Campus**

Students are not required to have a computer. Student rooms are linked to a campus network. 400 **computers** available in the computer center, computer labs, the learning resource center, the library, the student center, and dormitories provide access to e-mail and on-line services. Staffed computer lab on campus provides training in the use of computers and software.

The 7 **libraries** have 2.5 million books, 1 million microform titles, and 15,090 subscriptions.

 **Campus Life**

There are 240 active **organizations** on campus, including a drama/theater group and student-run newspaper and radio station. 43% of students participate in student government elections. 12% of eligible men and 2% of eligible women are members of 11 national **fraternities**, 2 national **sororities**, and 1 coed fraternity. Student **safety services** include late night transport/escort service, 24-hour emergency telephone alarm devices, and 24-hour patrols by trained security personnel.

Brown is a member of the NCAA (Division I). **Intercollegiate sports** include baseball (m), basketball (m, w), crew (m, w), cross-country running (m, w), fencing (m, w), field hockey (w), football (m), golf (m, w), gymnastics (w), ice hockey (m, w), lacrosse (m, w), rugby (m, w), sailing (m, w), skiing (cross-country) (m, w), skiing (downhill) (m, w), soccer (m, w), softball (w), squash (m, w), swimming and diving (m, w), tennis (m, w), track and field (m, w), volleyball (m, w), water polo (m, w), wrestling (m).

**Applying**

Brown requires an essay, a high school transcript, 3 years of high school math and science, 3 years of high school foreign language, 2 recommendations, SAT I or ACT, and 3 SAT II Subject Tests. Early and deferred entrance are possible, with a 1/1 deadline and 1/1 for financial aid. **Contact:** Mr. Michael Goldberger, Director of Admission, Box 1876, Providence, RI 02912, 401-863-2378; fax 401-863-9300.

---

## GETTING IN LAST YEAR

13,222 applied
22% were accepted
49% enrolled (1,428)
80% from top tenth of their h.s. class
67% had SAT verbal scores over 600
86% had SAT math scores over 600
87% had ACT scores over 26
19% had SAT verbal scores over 700
47% had SAT math scores over 700
44% had ACT scores over 30
75 National Merit Scholars

## THE STUDENT BODY

Total 7,801, of whom 6,127
    are undergraduates

From 52 states and territories,
    63 other countries
3% from Rhode Island
52% women, 48% men
6% African Americans
1% Native Americans
5% Hispanics
15% Asian Americans
7% international students

## AFTER FRESHMAN YEAR

97% returned for sophomore year
80% got a degree within 4 years
92% got a degree within 5 years
93% got a degree within 6 years

## AFTER GRADUATION

26% pursued further study (9% medicine, 8%
    arts and sciences, 8% law)
175 corporations, 50 government agencies,
    75 nonprofit organizations recruited on
    campus
1 Rhodes, 2 Marshall, 14 Fulbright scholars

## WHAT YOU WILL PAY

Tuition and fees $20,028
Room and board $5926
32% receive need-based financial aid
    averaging $11,115

# BRYN MAWR COLLEGE

Bryn Mawr, Pennsylvania • Suburban setting • Private • Independent • Women

▶ Bryn Mawr, founded in 1885 to offer women the challenging education then available only to men, remains a place where women succeed beyond all stereotypical notions of "suitability." Women major in the sciences and mathematics 3 to 5 times more often than the national average (29 times the national average in physics), and Bryn Mawr ranks first in the nation in the percentage of undergraduates who earn a Ph.D. in the humanities and fourth in all fields. Close relationships with faculty members praised for their teaching and known for their scholarship foster an education that is active and enjoyable.

##  Academics

Bryn Mawr offers a liberal arts and sciences curriculum and core academic program; fewer than half of graduate courses are open to undergraduates. It awards bachelor's, master's, and doctoral **degrees**. Challenging opportunities include advanced placement, accelerated degree programs, self-designed majors, tutorials, an honors program, and Sigma Xi. Special programs include summer session for credit, off-campus study, study abroad, and Army, Naval, and Air Force ROTC.

The most popular **majors** include English, history, and political science/government. A complete listing of majors at Bryn Mawr appears in the Majors Index beginning on page 380.

The **faculty** at Bryn Mawr has 151 full-time graduate and undergraduate teachers, 99% with terminal degrees. 20% of the faculty serve as student advisers. The student-faculty ratio is 9:1, and the average class size in required courses is 16.

##  Computers on Campus

Students are not required to have a computer. Student rooms are linked to a campus network. 150 **computers**

available in the computer center, computer labs, the library, the student center, and dormitories provide access to the main academic computer, e-mail, and on-line services. Staffed computer lab on campus provides training in the use of computers and software.

The 5 **libraries** have 949,714 books, 117,240 microform titles, and 1,974 subscriptions. They are connected to 5 national **on-line** catalogs.

##  Campus Life

There are 95 active **organizations** on campus, including a drama/theater group and student-run newspaper and radio station. Student **safety services** include late night transport/escort service, 24-hour emergency telephone alarm devices, 24-hour patrols by trained security personnel, and electronically operated dormitory entrances.

Bryn Mawr is a member of the NCAA (Division III). **Intercollegiate sports** include badminton, basketball, cross-country running, fencing, field hockey, lacrosse, rugby, sailing, soccer, swimming and diving, tennis, track and field, volleyball.

##  Applying

Bryn Mawr requires an essay, a high school transcript, 3 years of high school math, 3 years of high school foreign language, 3 recommendations, SAT I, and 3 SAT II Subject Tests (including SAT II: Writing Test). It recommends 3 years of high school science, an interview, and ACT. Early, deferred, and midyear entrance are possible, with a 1/15 deadline and 1/15 for financial aid. **Contact:** Ms. Elizabeth G. Vermey, Director of Admissions, Ely House, Bryn Mawr, PA 19010-2899, 610-526-5152; fax 610-526-7471.

---

### GETTING IN LAST YEAR
1,583 applied
54% were accepted
38% enrolled (329)
71% from top tenth of their h.s. class
60% had SAT verbal scores over 600
63% had SAT math scores over 600
14% had SAT verbal scores over 700
13% had SAT math scores over 700

### THE STUDENT BODY
Total 1,778, of whom 1,158
 are undergraduates
From 49 states and territories,
 44 other countries

11% from Pennsylvania
100% women
5% African Americans
1% Native Americans
4% Hispanics
17% Asian Americans
12% international students

### AFTER FRESHMAN YEAR
96% returned for sophomore year
74% got a degree within 4 years
84% got a degree within 5 years
85% got a degree within 6 years

### AFTER GRADUATION
45% pursued further study (20% arts and
 sciences, 10% law, 4% medicine)
34 corporations, 5 government agencies, 15
 nonprofit organizations recruited on campus
3 Fulbright scholars

### WHAT YOU WILL PAY
Tuition and fees $18,725
Room and board $6750
48% receive need-based financial aid
 averaging $12,692

---

# BUCKNELL UNIVERSITY

Lewisburg, Pennsylvania • Small-town setting • Private • Independent • Coed

Since 1846, scholars have come together at Bucknell to ask questions and explore answers. Bucknell professors enjoy national reputations, and Bucknell students are known for their intelligence and vitality. Together, they explore a wide-ranging curriculum that includes the arts, humanities, social sciences, education, business administration, and engineering. Beginning with first-year foundation seminars, students and faculty learn to respect each other through lively classroom discussions and through collaboration in research and scholarly papers. In the supportive atmosphere of Bucknell, each person makes full use of the present and finds exciting possibilities for the future.

##  Academics

Bucknell offers no core academic program; fewer than half of graduate courses are open to undergraduates. It awards bachelor's and master's **degrees**. Challenging opportunities include advanced placement, accelerated degree programs, self-designed majors, an honors program, a senior project, Phi Beta Kappa, and Sigma Xi. Special programs include internships, summer session for credit, off-campus study, study abroad, and Army ROTC.

The most popular **majors** include business, economics, and biology/biological sciences. A complete listing of majors at Bucknell appears in the Majors Index beginning on page 380.

The **faculty** at Bucknell has 245 full-time graduate and undergraduate teachers, 96% with terminal degrees. 80% of the faculty serve as student advisers. The student-faculty ratio is 13:1, and the average class size in required courses is 20.

##  Computers on Campus

Students are not required to have a computer. Student rooms are linked to a campus network. 800 **computers** available in the computer center, computer labs, classrooms, the library, and dormitories provide access to the main academic computer, e-mail, and on-line services. Staffed computer lab on campus provides training in the use of computers and software.

The **library** has 563,080 books, 636,900 microform titles, and 2,400 subscriptions. It is connected to 2 national **on-line** catalogs.

##  Campus Life

There are 100 active **organizations** on campus, including a drama/theater group and student-run newspaper and radio station. 45% of eligible men and 50% of eligible women are members of 12 national **fraternities**, 8 national **sororities**, 2 local fraternities, and 2 local sororities. Student **safety services** include late night transport/escort service, 24-hour emergency telephone alarm devices, and 24-hour patrols by trained security personnel.

Bucknell is a member of the NCAA (Division I). **Intercollegiate sports** include baseball (m), basketball (m, w), crew (m, w), cross-country running (m, w), field hockey (w), football (m), golf (m), ice hockey (m), lacrosse (m, w), riflery (m, w), rugby (m, w), sailing (m, w), skiing (cross-country) (m, w), soccer (m, w), softball (w), swimming and diving (m, w), tennis (m, w), track and field (m, w), volleyball (m, w), water polo (m), wrestling (m).

##  Applying

Bucknell requires an essay, a high school transcript, 3 years of high school math, some high school foreign language, recommendations, and SAT I. It recommends 3 years of high school science and an interview. Early, deferred, and midyear entrance are possible, with a 1/1 deadline and a 2/1 priority date for financial aid. **Contact:** Mr. Mark D. Davies, Dean of Admissions, Freas Hall, Lewisburg, PA 17837, 717-524-1101; fax 717-524-3760.

---

### GETTING IN LAST YEAR
6,399 applied
59% were accepted
24% enrolled (899)
49% from top tenth of their h.s. class
3.4 average high school GPA
20% had SAT verbal scores over 600
71% had SAT math scores over 600
1% had SAT verbal scores over 700
18% had SAT math scores over 700
4 National Merit Scholars
20 class presidents
29 valedictorians

### THE STUDENT BODY
Total 3,528, of whom 3,301
  are undergraduates

From 42 states and territories,
  22 other countries
33% from Pennsylvania
49% women, 51% men
2% African Americans
1% Native Americans
2% Hispanics
3% Asian Americans
2% international students

### AFTER FRESHMAN YEAR
94% returned for sophomore year
85% got a degree within 4 years
88% got a degree within 5 years
89% got a degree within 6 years

### AFTER GRADUATION
26% pursued further study (13% arts and
  sciences, 5% law, 4% engineering)
65% had job offers within 3 months
127 corporations, 4 government agencies, 13
  nonprofit organizations recruited on campus

### WHAT YOU WILL PAY
Tuition and fees $19,470
Room and board $4925
60% receive need-based financial aid
  averaging $12,573

# BUENA VISTA COLLEGE

Storm Lake, Iowa • Small-town setting • Private • Independent-Religious • Coed

Buena Vista College's students are given the opportunity to excel due to a student-professor ratio of 14:1, sophisticated technology and facilities, innovative academic programs, and career and graduate school placement services. Students can view the world through exchange programs with schools in Japan and Taiwan and January Interim programs in Europe, Australia, and other countries. They meet national and international leaders and performers on campus through the Academic & Cultural Events Series. Located in America's heartland, Buena Vista's lakeside campus offers a peaceful environment in a progressive college town.

## Academics

BV offers an interdisciplinary curriculum and core academic program. It awards bachelor's **degrees**. Challenging opportunities include advanced placement, accelerated degree programs, self-designed majors, tutorials, an honors program, and a senior project. Special programs include internships, summer session for credit, off-campus study, and study abroad.

The most popular **majors** include business, education, and science. A complete listing of majors at BV appears in the Majors Index beginning on page 380.

The **faculty** at BV has 70 full-time teachers, 65% with terminal degrees. 100% of the faculty serve as student advisers. The student-faculty ratio is 14:1, and the average class size in required courses is 25.

## Computers on Campus

Students are not required to have a computer. 300 **computers** available in the computer center, computer labs, the learning resource center, mass communication building, media center, classrooms, the library, the student center, and dormitories provide access to the main academic computer, e-mail, and on-line services. Staffed computer lab on campus provides training in the use of computers and software.

The **library** has 135,214 books, 273 microform titles, and 1,130 subscriptions. It is connected to 1 national **on-line** catalog.

## Campus Life

There are 40 active **organizations** on campus, including a drama/theater group and student-run newspaper and radio station. Student **safety services** include late night transport/escort service, 24-hour emergency telephone alarm devices, and electronically operated dormitory entrances.

BV is a member of the NCAA (Division III). **Intercollegiate sports** include baseball (m), basketball (m, w), cross-country running (m, w), football (m), golf (m, w), softball (w), swimming and diving (m, w), tennis (m, w), track and field (m, w), volleyball (w), wrestling (m).

## Applying

BV requires a high school transcript, 1 recommendation, SAT I or ACT, and in some cases an essay and an interview. It recommends 3 years of high school math and science, some high school foreign language, and a minimum high school GPA of 3.0. Early, deferred, and midyear entrance are possible, with a 6/1 deadline and continuous processing to 4/20 for financial aid. **Contact:** Mr. Mike Frantz, Director of Admissions, 610 West Fourth Street, Storm Lake, IA 50588-1798, 712-749-2235 or toll-free 800-383-9600; fax 712-749-2037.

---

### GETTING IN LAST YEAR

1,141 applied
86% were accepted
33% enrolled (321)
26% from top tenth of their h.s. class
3.2 average high school GPA
49% had ACT scores over 26
4% had ACT scores over 30
16 class presidents
21 valedictorians

### THE STUDENT BODY

1,085 undergraduates
From 19 states and territories,
 11 other countries

76% from Iowa
51% women, 49% men
1% African Americans
1% Hispanics
1% Asian Americans
4% international students

### AFTER FRESHMAN YEAR

73% returned for sophomore year
53% got a degree within 4 years
56% got a degree within 5 years
57% got a degree within 6 years

### AFTER GRADUATION

16% pursued further study (7% arts and
 sciences, 4% medicine, 3% law)
80% had job offers within 3 months
21 corporations, 5 government agencies, 2
 nonprofit organizations recruited on campus

### WHAT YOU WILL PAY

Tuition and fees $13,306
Room and board $3797
Need-based financial aid averages $1483
Non-need financial aid averages $5510

# BUTLER UNIVERSITY

Indianapolis, Indiana • Urban setting • Private • Independent • Coed

Nearly 4,000 students attend Butler University, an independent university composed of a college of liberal arts and sciences and 4 professional colleges. Founded in 1855, Butler offers large-university opportunities in a small-college atmosphere. Undergraduates choose from more than 60 majors while still enjoying the personal attention of a low student-faculty ratio. Butler combines a strong liberal arts foundation with practical education and career-minded professional programs and also offers an active student life program featuring over 70 student organizations.

 **Academics**

Butler offers an interdisciplinary curriculum and core academic program; fewer than half of graduate courses are open to undergraduates. It awards bachelor's and master's **degrees**. Challenging opportunities include advanced placement, accelerated degree programs, self-designed majors, tutorials, an honors program, and Sigma Xi. Special programs include cooperative education, internships, summer session for credit, off-campus study, study abroad, and Army and Air Force ROTC.

The most popular **majors** include pharmacy/pharmaceutical sciences, biology/biological sciences, and elementary education. A complete listing of majors at Butler appears in the Majors Index beginning on page 380.

The **faculty** at Butler has 223 full-time graduate and undergraduate teachers, 81% with terminal degrees. 90% of the faculty serve as student advisers. The student-faculty ratio is 13:1; average class size in required courses is 22.

 **Computers on Campus**

Students are not required to have a computer. 200 **computers** available in the computer center, labs, classrooms, the library, and dormitories provide access to the main academic computer and e-mail. Staffed computer lab on campus provides training in the use of computers and software.

The **library** has 286,112 books, 235,280 microform titles, and 2,903 subscriptions. It is connected to 1 national **on-line** catalog.

 **Campus Life**

There are 73 active **organizations** on campus, including a drama/theater group and student-run newspaper and radio station. 26% of eligible men and 22% of eligible women are members of 8 national **fraternities** and 9 national **sororities**. Student **safety services** include late night transport/escort service, 24-hour emergency telephone alarm devices, 24-hour patrols by trained security personnel, and electronically operated dormitory entrances.

Butler is a member of the NCAA (Division I). **Intercollegiate sports** (some offering scholarships) include baseball (m), basketball (m, w), crew (m, w), cross-country running (m, w), football (m), golf (m), lacrosse (m), soccer (m, w), softball (w), swimming and diving (m, w), tennis (m, w), track and field (m, w), volleyball (w).

 **Applying**

Butler requires an essay, a high school transcript, 3 years of high school math, 2 years of high school foreign language, SAT I or ACT, and in some cases 3 years of high school science, a campus interview, and audition. It recommends SAT II Subject Tests. Early, deferred, and midyear entrance are possible, with an 8/15 deadline and continuous processing to 3/1 for financial aid. **Contact:** Ms. Carroll Davis, Dean of Admission, 4600 Sunset Avenue, Indianapolis, IN 46208-3485, 317-283-9255 or toll-free 800-972-2882.

---

## GETTING IN LAST YEAR

2,332 applied
87% were accepted
35% enrolled (710)
37% from top tenth of their h.s. class
3.3 average high school GPA
9% had SAT verbal scores over 600
35% had SAT math scores over 600
61% had ACT scores over 26
1% had SAT verbal scores over 700
6% had SAT math scores over 700
16% had ACT scores over 30
9 National Merit Scholars
32 valedictorians

## THE STUDENT BODY

Total 3,758, of whom 2,830
 are undergraduates

From 38 states and territories,
 31 other countries
66% from Indiana
59% women, 41% men
6% African Americans
0% Native Americans
1% Hispanics
2% Asian Americans
1% international students

## AFTER FRESHMAN YEAR

84% returned for sophomore year
44% got a degree within 4 years
62% got a degree within 5 years
65% got a degree within 6 years

## AFTER GRADUATION

20% pursued further study (9% arts and
 sciences, 5% law, 2% business)
50% had job offers within 3 months
65 corporations, 4 government agencies, 2
 nonprofit organizations recruited on campus

## WHAT YOU WILL PAY

Tuition and fees $13,130
Room and board $4420
49% receive need-based financial aid
 averaging $4200
44% receive non-need financial aid averaging
 $5800

# CALIFORNIA INSTITUTE OF TECHNOLOGY

Pasadena, California • Suburban setting • Private • Independent • Coed

A student attending the California Institute of Technology says, "Why did I come to Caltech? I think that maybe I was born in the wrong time. There aren't any big blank spaces left on the maps, there aren't even any really fuzzy spots. I want to be able to explore places that no one has ever been to before. I want to see things that haven't been seen before. So I've come to Caltech to become an astronomer, and to look into the depths of space and time, where people aren't, and see what really is."

 **Academics**

Caltech offers a science and math curriculum and core academic program; all graduate courses are open to undergraduates. It awards bachelor's, master's, and doctoral **degrees**. Challenging opportunities include self-designed majors, tutorials, and Sigma Xi. Special programs include internships, off-campus study, study abroad, and Army and Air Force ROTC.

The most popular **majors** include engineering and applied sciences, physical sciences, and biochemistry. A complete listing of majors at Caltech appears in the Majors Index beginning on page 380.

The **faculty** at Caltech has 295 graduate and undergraduate teachers, 100% with terminal degrees. The student-faculty ratio is 3:1.

 **Computers on Campus**

Students are not required to have a computer. 500 **computers** available in the computer center, computer labs, the research center, the library, the student center, dormitories, and student rooms. Staffed computer lab on campus (open 24 hours a day).

The 11 **libraries** have 487,000 books and 6,370 subscriptions.

 **Campus Life**

Active **organizations** on campus include drama/theater group and student-run newspaper. Student **safety services** include late night transport/escort service, 24-hour emergency telephone alarm devices, and 24-hour patrols by trained security personnel.

Caltech is a member of the NCAA (Division III). **Intercollegiate sports** include basketball (m), cross-country running (m, w), fencing (m, w), football (m), golf (m, w), ice hockey (m), sailing (m, w), soccer (m, w), swimming and diving (m, w), tennis (m, w), track and field (m, w), volleyball (w), water polo (m, w), wrestling (m).

 **Applying**

Caltech requires an essay, a high school transcript, 4 years of high school math, 3 recommendations, SAT I, and 3 SAT II Subject Tests (including SAT II: Writing Test). It recommends 3 years of high school science. Early and deferred entrance are possible, with a 1/1 deadline and a 2/1 priority date for financial aid. **Contact:** Ms. Charlene Liebau, Director of Admissions, 1201 East California Boulevard, Pasadena, CA 91125-0001, 818-395-6341 or toll-free 800-568-8324; fax 818-683-3026.

### GETTING IN LAST YEAR
2,012 applied
25% were accepted
46% enrolled (231)
100% from top tenth of their h.s. class
84% had SAT verbal scores over 600
100% had SAT math scores over 600
21% had SAT verbal scores over 700
93% had SAT math scores over 700
30 National Merit Scholars

### THE STUDENT BODY
Total 1,929, of whom 918
   are undergraduates
From 46 states and territories,
   30 other countries
35% from California
26% women, 74% men
2% African Americans
0% Native Americans
6% Hispanics
30% Asian Americans
8% international students

### AFTER FRESHMAN YEAR
94% returned for sophomore year

### AFTER GRADUATION
61% pursued further study (34% arts and
   sciences, 20% engineering, 4% medicine)
129 corporations, 1 government agency
   recruited on campus
1 Fulbright scholar

### WHAT YOU WILL PAY
Tuition and fees $16,905
Room and board $5051
65% receive need-based financial aid
   averaging $12,500
10% receive non-need financial aid averaging
   $9400

# CALVIN COLLEGE

Grand Rapids, Michigan • Suburban setting • Private • Independent-Religious • Coed

Calvin College is a place where knowledge and faith can grow—where students prepare to take their individual place in God's world. On Calvin's spacious campus, students, faculty, and staff form a community of supportive, committed people who savor the joyful task of serving God through intellectual curiosity, spirited interaction, and conscientious work. Nearly 4,000 students from throughout the U.S. and many other countries have found Calvin to be an ideal place for thinking, questing people who are committed to a lifetime of service in today's world.

## Academics

Calvin offers a Christ-centered liberal arts curriculum and core academic program; fewer than half of graduate courses are open to undergraduates. It awards bachelor's and master's **degrees**. Challenging opportunities include advanced placement, self-designed majors, tutorials, Freshmen Honors College, an honors program, and a senior project. Special programs include cooperative education, internships, summer session for credit, off-campus study, and study abroad.

The most popular **majors** include education, business, and engineering (general). A complete listing of majors at Calvin appears in the Majors Index beginning on page 380.

The **faculty** at Calvin has 230 full-time graduate and undergraduate teachers, 80% with terminal degrees. 96% of the faculty serve as student advisers. The student-faculty ratio is 15:1, and the average class size in required courses is 24.

## Computers on Campus

Students are not required to have a computer. 291 **computers** available in the computer center, computer labs, the research center, the library, the student center, and dormitories provide access to the main academic computer, off-campus computing facilities, e-mail, and on-line services. Staffed computer lab on campus.

The **library** has 635,000 books, 476,000 microform titles, and 2,800 subscriptions.

## Campus Life

There are 32 active **organizations** on campus, including a drama/theater group and student-run newspaper and radio station. Student **safety services** include crime prevention programs, crime alert bulletins, late night transport/escort service, 24-hour patrols by trained security personnel, and student patrols.

Calvin is a member of the NCAA (Division III). **Intercollegiate sports** include baseball (m), basketball (m, w), cross-country running (m, w), golf (m, w), ice hockey (m), lacrosse (m), soccer (m, w), softball (w), swimming and diving (m, w), tennis (m, w), track and field (m, w), volleyball (m, w).

## Applying

Calvin requires an essay, a high school transcript, 1 recommendation, SAT I or ACT, and a minimum high school GPA of 2.0. It recommends 3 years of high school math and science, 2 years of high school foreign language, and an interview. Early, deferred, and midyear entrance are possible, with rolling admissions and continuous processing to 2/15 for financial aid. **Contact:** Mr. Thomas E. McWhertor, Director of Admissions, 3201 Burton Street, SE, Grand Rapids, MI 49546-4388, 616-957-6106 or toll-free 800-668-0122.

### GETTING IN LAST YEAR

1,731 applied
96% were accepted
56% enrolled (938)
28% from top tenth of their h.s. class
3.35 average high school GPA
18% had SAT verbal scores over 600
35% had SAT math scores over 600
41% had ACT scores over 26
3% had SAT verbal scores over 700
11% had SAT math scores over 700
10% had ACT scores over 30
20 National Merit Scholars
48 valedictorians

### THE STUDENT BODY

Total 3,793, of whom 3,609 are undergraduates
From 49 states and territories, 28 other countries
53% from Michigan
55% women, 45% men
1% African Americans
1% Native Americans
1% Hispanics
2% Asian Americans
9% international students

### AFTER FRESHMAN YEAR

79% returned for sophomore year
41% got a degree within 4 years
56% got a degree within 5 years
58% got a degree within 6 years

### AFTER GRADUATION

22% pursued further study (14% arts and sciences, 2% engineering, 2% theology)
41 corporations, 1 government agency, 43 nonprofit organizations recruited on campus

### WHAT YOU WILL PAY

Tuition and fees $10,230
Room and board $3710
65% receive need-based financial aid averaging $2500
25% receive non-need financial aid averaging $1070

# CARLETON COLLEGE

Northfield, Minnesota • Small-town setting • Private • Independent • Coed

Carleton, a residential coeducational liberal arts college, is located about 35 miles south of Minneapolis–St. Paul. About 75% of Carleton students enter graduate or professional school within 5 years of graduation. Carleton ranks first of all liberal arts colleges in the number of graduates who earned PhDs in the laboratory sciences from 1986 and 6th in the number who earned PhDs in all fields. Two thirds of Carleton students choose to spend at least one term on an off-campus program for academic credit. A new Center for Mathematics and Computing opened in 1993, and a new biology teaching and research facility will open in 1995.

## Academics

Carleton offers a liberal arts curriculum and core academic program. It awards bachelor's **degrees**. Challenging opportunities include advanced placement, accelerated degree programs, self-designed majors, a senior project, Phi Beta Kappa, and Sigma Xi. Special programs include off-campus study and study abroad.

The most popular **majors** include English, history, and political science/government. A complete listing of majors at Carleton appears in the Majors Index beginning on page 380.

The **faculty** at Carleton has 146 full-time teachers, 96% with terminal degrees. 100% of the faculty serve as student advisers. The student-faculty ratio is 11:1, and the average class size in required courses is 17.

## Computers on Campus

Students are not required to have a computer. 163 **computers** available in the computer center, computer labs, the research center, the learning resource center, labs, academic buildings, classrooms, and the library provide access to the main academic computer, off-campus computing facilities, and e-mail. Staffed computer lab on campus (open 24 hours a day) provides training in the use of software.

The 2 **libraries** have 502,770 books, 18,465 microform titles, and 1,505 subscriptions.

## Campus Life

Active **organizations** on campus include drama/theater group and student-run newspaper and radio station. 40% of students participate in student government elections. Student **safety services** include late night transport/escort service, 24-hour emergency telephone alarm devices, 24-hour patrols by trained security personnel, and student patrols.

Carleton is a member of the NCAA (Division III). **Intercollegiate sports** include baseball (m), basketball (m, w), cross-country running (m, w), fencing (m, w), field hockey (w), football (m), golf (m, w), gymnastics (w), ice hockey (m), lacrosse (m), rugby (m, w), skiing (cross-country) (m, w), skiing (downhill) (m, w), soccer (m, w), softball (w), swimming and diving (m, w), tennis (m, w), track and field (m, w), volleyball (m, w), water polo (m), wrestling (m).

## Applying

Carleton requires an essay, a high school transcript, 3 years of high school math, 3 recommendations, and SAT I or ACT. It recommends 3 years of high school science, 2 years of high school foreign language, an interview, and 3 SAT II Subject Tests. Early and deferred entrance are possible, with a 2/1 deadline and a 2/15 priority date for financial aid. **Contact:** Mr. Paul Thiboutot, Dean of Admissions, 100 South College Street, Northfield, MN 55057-4001, 507-663-4190 or toll-free 800-995-2275; fax 507-663-4526.

---

### GETTING IN LAST YEAR
2,782 applied
57% were accepted
33% enrolled (524)
70% from top tenth of their h.s. class
61% had SAT verbal scores over 600
79% had SAT math scores over 600
82% had ACT scores over 26
18% had SAT verbal scores over 700
35% had SAT math scores over 700
48% had ACT scores over 30
94 National Merit Scholars
59 valedictorians

### THE STUDENT BODY
1,754 undergraduates
From 53 states and territories, 21 other countries
22% from Minnesota
50% women, 50% men
3% African Americans
1% Native Americans
4% Hispanics
9% Asian Americans
1% international students

### AFTER FRESHMAN YEAR
94% returned for sophomore year
84% got a degree within 4 years
89% got a degree within 5 years
90% got a degree within 6 years

### AFTER GRADUATION
29% pursued further study (20% arts and sciences, 5% law, 3% medicine)
60% had job offers within 3 months
30 corporations, 7 government agencies, 13 nonprofit organizations recruited on campus
1 Fulbright scholar

### WHAT YOU WILL PAY
Tuition and fees $20,379
Room and board $4125
59% receive need-based financial aid averaging $9641
8% receive non-need financial aid averaging $977

# CARNEGIE MELLON UNIVERSITY

Pittsburgh, Pennsylvania • Urban setting • Private • Independent • Coed

When asked what impresses them most about Carnegie Mellon, students give different answers. For some, it is the University's pioneering research efforts. For others, it is the creative spirit embodied at Carnegie Mellon. Others appreciate the way the University fosters its students' ability to take smart risks and succeed. But the one thing that impresses everyone who comes to Carnegie Mellon is the way this University and its people thrive on challenge. At Carnegie Mellon, students are challenged to perform academically and to stretch their understanding of and channel their knowledge into groundbreaking applications in their fields.

## Academics

CMU offers an interdisciplinary professional liberal arts and sciences curriculum and core academic program; fewer than half of graduate courses are open to undergraduates. It awards bachelor's, master's, and doctoral **degrees**. Challenging opportunities include advanced placement, accelerated degree programs, self-designed majors, an honors program, a senior project, Phi Beta Kappa, and Sigma Xi. Special programs include cooperative education, internships, summer session for credit, off-campus study, study abroad, and Army, Naval, and Air Force ROTC.

The most popular **majors** include electrical engineering, industrial administration, and architecture. A complete listing of majors at CMU appears in the Majors Index beginning on page 380.

The **faculty** at CMU has 549 full-time undergraduate teachers, 91% with terminal degrees. The student-faculty ratio is 9:1, and the average class size in required courses is 21.

## Computers on Campus

Students are not required to have a computer. Student rooms are linked to a campus network. 343 **computers**

available in the computer center, the library, the student center, and dormitories provide access to e-mail and on-line services. Staffed computer lab on campus (open 24 hours a day) provides training in the use of computers and software.

The 3 **libraries** have 852,241 books, 756,985 microform titles, and 3,889 subscriptions. They are connected to 9 national **on-line** catalogs.

## Campus Life

Active **organizations** on campus include drama/theater group and student-run newspaper and radio station. 20% of students participate in student government elections. 25% of eligible men and 14% of eligible women are members of 12 national **fraternities** and 4 national **sororities**. Student **safety services** include late night transport/escort service and electronically operated dormitory entrances.

CMU is a member of the NCAA (Division III). **Intercollegiate sports** include baseball (m), basketball (m, w), crew (m, w), cross-country running (m, w), fencing (m, w), football (m), golf (m), ice hockey (m), lacrosse (m, w), riflery (m), rugby (m), skiing (cross-country) (m, w), soccer (m, w), swimming and diving (m, w), tennis (m, w), track and field (m, w), volleyball (m, w).

## Applying

CMU requires an essay, a high school transcript, 1 recommendation, SAT I or ACT, 3 SAT II Subject Tests, and in some cases 4 years of high school math and science, portfolio, audition, and SAT II: Writing Test. It recommends 2 years of high school foreign language and an interview. Early, deferred, and midyear entrance are possible, with a 2/1 deadline and continuous processing to 2/15 for financial aid. **Contact:** Mr. Michael Steidel, Director of Admissions, Warner Hall, Room 101, Pittsburgh, PA 15213-3891, 412-268-2082; fax 412-268-7838.

### GETTING IN LAST YEAR
8,644 applied
59% were accepted
23% enrolled (1,164)
71% from top tenth of their h.s. class
3.43 average high school GPA
41% had SAT verbal scores over 600
81% had SAT math scores over 600
7% had SAT verbal scores over 700
44% had SAT math scores over 700
65 valedictorians

### THE STUDENT BODY
Total 7,141, of whom 4,437
    are undergraduates

From 52 states and territories,
    44 other countries
29% from Pennsylvania
32% women, 68% men
4% African Americans
1% Native Americans
3% Hispanics
15% Asian Americans
10% international students

### AFTER FRESHMAN YEAR
90% returned for sophomore year
56% got a degree within 4 years
62% got a degree within 5 years
73% got a degree within 6 years

### AFTER GRADUATION
28% pursued further study (8% engineering,
    7% arts and sciences, 6% business)
159 corporations, 2 government agencies, 3
    nonprofit organizations recruited on campus
2 Fulbright scholars

### WHAT YOU WILL PAY
Tuition and fees $18,000
Room and board $5680
57% receive need-based financial aid
    averaging $9212
27% receive non-need financial aid averaging
    $5277

# CARROLL COLLEGE

Helena, Montana • Small-town setting • Private • Independent-Religious • Coed

 Carroll College offers students an outstanding liberal arts education through diverse curricula, impressive facilities, and dedicated, student-oriented faculty. Carroll's superb student-faculty ratio ensures modest class sizes and a personalized education for each student. Independent studies and cooperative education programs provide opportunities to customize students' academic progress in professional surroundings. Carroll's students and faculty regularly receive national honors for their accomplishments, including Truman and Fulbright scholarships. Carroll lies midway between Glacier and Yellowstone National Parks, surrounded by world-class skiing, fishing, and wilderness areas. Together, Carroll College and Montana's capital city provide an ideal setting in which to live and learn.

## Academics

Carroll offers a core academic program. It awards associate and bachelor's **degrees**. Challenging opportunities include advanced placement, accelerated degree programs, self-designed majors, tutorials, Freshmen Honors College, an honors program, and a senior project. Special programs include cooperative education, internships, summer session for credit, and study abroad.

The most popular **majors** include business, elementary education, and biology/biological sciences. A complete listing of majors at Carroll appears in the Majors Index beginning on page 380.

The **faculty** at Carroll has 70 full-time teachers, 53% with terminal degrees. 100% of the faculty serve as student advisers. The student-faculty ratio is 13:1, and the average class size in required courses is 19.

## Computers on Campus

Students are not required to have a computer. 75 **computers** available in the computer center, the learning resource center, the library, and dormitories. Staffed computer lab on campus provides training in the use of computers and software.

The **library** has 94,000 books, 25,000 microform titles, and 562 subscriptions.

## Campus Life

There are 37 active **organizations** on campus, including a drama/theater group and student-run newspaper and radio station. Student **safety services** include late night transport/escort service.

Carroll is a member of the NAIA. **Intercollegiate sports** (some offering scholarships) include basketball (m, w), football (m), swimming and diving (m, w), volleyball (w).

## Applying

Carroll requires an essay, a high school transcript, 1 recommendation, SAT I or ACT, a minimum high school GPA of 2.0, and in some cases a campus interview. It recommends 3 years of high school math and science, 2 years of high school foreign language, an interview, and a minimum high school GPA of 3.0. Early, deferred, and midyear entrance are possible, with a 7/1 deadline and continuous processing to 3/1 for financial aid. **Contact:** Ms. Candace A. Cain, Director of Admission, North Benton Avenue, Helena, MT 59625-0002, 406-447-4384 or toll-free 800-99-ADMIT.

### GETTING IN LAST YEAR
709 applied
92% were accepted
45% enrolled (292)
25% from top tenth of their h.s. class
3.33 average high school GPA
5% had SAT verbal scores over 600
24% had SAT math scores over 600
27% had ACT scores over 26
0% had SAT verbal scores over 700
3% had SAT math scores over 700
4% had ACT scores over 30
11 valedictorians

### THE STUDENT BODY
1,438 undergraduates
From 29 states and territories,
 17 other countries
70% from Montana
63% women, 37% men
1% African Americans
2% Native Americans
2% Hispanics
1% Asian Americans
6% international students

### AFTER FRESHMAN YEAR
75% returned for sophomore year

### AFTER GRADUATION
40% pursued further study (12% arts and sciences, 8% law, 7% medicine)
9 corporations, 4 government agencies, 2 nonprofit organizations recruited on campus

### WHAT YOU WILL PAY
Tuition and fees $8940
Room and board $3810
83% receive need-based financial aid averaging $1685
71% receive non-need financial aid averaging $3631

# CASE WESTERN RESERVE UNIVERSITY

Cleveland, Ohio • Urban setting • Private • Independent • Coed

▶ Case Western Reserve admits students based on overall academic and personal qualities, not on an intended major. With superb programs in arts and sciences, engineering, and management, students can determine what major is suitable for them after they have learned about it. Only CWRU's Bachelor of Science in Nursing program requires a declared major at the time of application.

 **Academics**

CWRU offers a quantitative, analytic, and communication skills curriculum and core academic program. It awards bachelor's, master's, doctoral, and first professional **degrees**. Challenging opportunities include advanced placement, accelerated degree programs, self-designed majors, tutorials, an honors program, a senior project, Phi Beta Kappa, and Sigma Xi. Special programs include cooperative education, internships, summer session for credit, off-campus study, and Army and Air Force ROTC.

The most popular **majors** include mechanical and electrical engineering and biology/biological sciences. A complete listing of majors at CWRU appears in the Majors Index beginning on page 380.

The **faculty** at CWRU has 1,850 full-time graduate and undergraduate teachers, 95% with terminal degrees. 85% of the faculty serve as student advisers. The student-faculty ratio is 8:1; average class size in required courses is 35.

 **Computers on Campus**

Students are not required to have a computer. Student rooms are linked to a campus network. 200 **computers** available across campus and in dormitories provide access to the main academic computer, off-campus computing facilities, e-mail, on-line services, and software library. Staffed computer lab on campus provides training in the use of computers and software.

The 7 **libraries** have 1.9 million books and 13,819 subscriptions. They are connected to 5 national **on-line** catalogs.

 **Campus Life**

There are 100 active **organizations** on campus, including a drama/theater group and student-run newspaper and radio station. 5% of students participate in student government elections. 40% of eligible men and 20% of eligible women are members of 17 national **fraternities**, 4 national **sororities**, and 1 local sorority. Student **safety services** include crime prevention programs, late night transport/escort service, 24-hour emergency telephone alarm devices, 24-hour patrols by trained security personnel, student patrols, and electronically operated dormitory entrances.

CWRU is a member of the NCAA (Division III). **Intercollegiate sports** include archery (m, w), baseball (m), basketball (m, w), crew (m, w), cross-country running (m, w), fencing (m, w), football (m), golf (m), ice hockey (m, w), lacrosse (m, w), soccer (m, w), swimming and diving (m, w), tennis (m, w), track and field (m, w), volleyball (m, w), wrestling (m).

 **Applying**

CWRU requires an essay, a high school transcript, 3 years of high school math, 1 recommendation, SAT I or ACT, and in some cases 3 SAT II Subject Tests. It recommends 3 years of high school science, 2 years of high school foreign language, an interview, and 3 SAT II Subject Tests. Early, deferred, and midyear entrance are possible, with a 2/1 deadline and continuous processing to 2/1 for financial aid. **Contact:** Mr. William T. Conley, Dean of Undergraduate Admissions, Tomlinson Hall, 10900 Euclid Avenue, Cleveland, OH 44106, 216-368-4450; fax 216-368-5111.

## GETTING IN LAST YEAR
4,075 applied
81% were accepted
22% enrolled (735)
73% from top tenth of their h.s. class
41% had SAT verbal scores over 600
78% had SAT math scores over 600
84% had ACT scores over 26
7% had SAT verbal scores over 700
38% had SAT math scores over 700
46% had ACT scores over 30
82 National Merit Scholars
81 valedictorians

## THE STUDENT BODY
Total 9,569, of whom 3,658 are undergraduates

From 50 states and territories, 39 other countries
62% from Ohio
43% women, 57% men
7% African Americans
1% Native Americans
2% Hispanics
11% Asian Americans
7% international students

## AFTER FRESHMAN YEAR
91% returned for sophomore year
41% got a degree within 4 years
65% got a degree within 5 years
70% got a degree within 6 years

## AFTER GRADUATION
35% pursued further study (13% arts and sciences, 9% engineering, 9% medicine)
43% had job offers within 3 months
138 corporations, 3 government agencies, 2 nonprofit organizations recruited on campus
1 Fulbright scholar

## WHAT YOU WILL PAY
Tuition and fees $15,826
Room and board $4500
57% receive need-based financial aid averaging $6688
70% receive non-need financial aid averaging $8054

# CATHOLIC UNIVERSITY OF AMERICA

Washington, D.C. • Urban setting • Private • Independent-Religious • Coed

The Catholic University of America, situated on 154 residential tree-lined acres in Washington, D.C., offers the beauty of a traditional collegiate campus and the excitement of the nation's capital. The national university of the Catholic Church, CUA has built its foundation from a time-honored liberal arts tradition. CUA has become a valuable resource for employers looking to fill top internships. Undergraduates work in congressional offices, executive agencies, professional organizations, research institutes, lobbying groups, and media organizations. Overseas programs include internships with the British and Irish parliaments.

 ## Academics

CUA offers a liberal studies curriculum and core academic program; fewer than half of graduate courses are open to undergraduates. It awards bachelor's, master's, doctoral, and first professional **degrees**. Challenging opportunities include advanced placement, accelerated degree programs, self-designed majors, tutorials, Freshmen Honors College, an honors program, a senior project, Phi Beta Kappa, and Sigma Xi. Special programs include internships, summer session for credit, off-campus study, study abroad, and Army, Naval, and Air Force ROTC.

The most popular **majors** include nursing, political science/government, and architecture. A complete listing of majors at CUA appears in the Majors Index beginning on page 380.

The **faculty** at CUA has 374 full-time graduate and undergraduate teachers, 95% with terminal degrees. The student-faculty ratio is 9:1, and the average class size in required courses is 27.

 ## Computers on Campus

Students are not required to have a computer. 200 **computers** available in the computer center, computer labs, the learning resource center, classrooms, the library, and dormitories provide access to the main academic computer, off-campus computing facilities, e-mail, and on-line services. Staffed computer lab on campus provides training in the use of computers and software.

The 8 **libraries** have 1.4 million books, 1.1 million microform titles, and 9,310 subscriptions. They are connected to 4 national **on-line** catalogs.

 ## Campus Life

There are 120 active **organizations** on campus, including a drama/theater group and student-run newspaper and radio station. 33% of students participate in student government elections. 1% of eligible men and 1% of eligible women are members of 1 national **fraternity**, 1 national **sorority**, and 1 local sorority. Student **safety services** include late night transport/escort service, 24-hour emergency telephone alarm devices, 24-hour patrols by trained security personnel, and electronically operated dormitory entrances.

CUA is a member of the NCAA (Division III). **Intercollegiate sports** include baseball (m), basketball (m, w), cross-country running (m, w), field hockey (w), football (m), soccer (m, w), softball (w), swimming and diving (m, w), tennis (m, w), track and field (m, w), volleyball (w).

 ## Applying

CUA requires an essay, a high school transcript, 3 years of high school math, 2 years of high school foreign language, 1 recommendation, SAT I or ACT, 3 SAT II Subject Tests, and in some cases an interview. It recommends 3 years of high school science. Early, deferred, and midyear entrance are possible, with a 2/15 deadline and 1/15 for financial aid. **Contact:** Mr. David R. Gibson, Dean of Admissions and Financial Aid, Cardinal Station, Washington, DC 20064, 202-319-5305 or toll-free 800-673-2772 (out-of-state); fax 202-319-6533.

---

### GETTING IN LAST YEAR
2,079 applied
82% were accepted
30% enrolled (505)
24% from top tenth of their h.s. class
3.1 average high school GPA
19% had SAT verbal scores over 600
30% had SAT math scores over 600
40% had ACT scores over 26
1% had SAT verbal scores over 700
7% had SAT math scores over 700
13% had ACT scores over 30

### THE STUDENT BODY
Total 6,128, of whom 2,364
  are undergraduates

From 45 states and territories,
  76 other countries
3% from District of Columbia
55% women, 45% men
7% African Americans
0% Native Americans
5% Hispanics
4% Asian Americans
10% international students

### AFTER FRESHMAN YEAR
85% returned for sophomore year
67% got a degree within 4 years
75% got a degree within 5 years

### AFTER GRADUATION
30% pursued further study
87% had job offers within 3 months
23 corporations, 13 government agencies, 5
  nonprofit organizations recruited on campus
4 Fulbright scholars

### WHAT YOU WILL PAY
Tuition and fees $14,252
Room and board $6408
58% receive need-based financial aid
  averaging $4235
48% receive non-need financial aid averaging
  $5140

# CEDARVILLE COLLEGE

Cedarville, Ohio • Rural setting • Private • Independent-Religious • Coed

Commitment to Christ and achievement characterize the education Cedarville offers. All students and faculty members testify to personal faith in Christ. A Bible minor complements every major, and relevant daily chapels encourage spiritual growth. Over 150 local and worldwide ministries provide avenues for outreach. Cedarville teams consistently finish among top universities in national academic competitions, and national, regional, and local graduate schools recruit students pursuing any of the College's 80 academic programs. The College has been recognized nationally for its pervasive and innovative campuswide computer network. Reasonable costs and financial aid make Cedarville affordable to committed Christian students aspiring to be competent professionals.

 **Academics**

Cedarville offers a biblically-integrated comprehensive liberal arts curriculum and core academic program. It awards associate and bachelor's **degrees**. Challenging opportunities include advanced placement, accelerated degree programs, an honors program, and a senior project. Special programs include internships, summer session for credit, study abroad, and Army and Air Force ROTC.

The most popular **majors** include elementary education, business, and communication. A complete listing of majors at Cedarville appears in the Majors Index beginning on page 380.

The **faculty** at Cedarville has 130 full-time teachers, 64% with terminal degrees. 100% of the faculty serve as student advisers. The student-faculty ratio is 18:1, and the average class size in required courses is 38.

 **Computers on Campus**

Students are not required to have a computer. Student rooms are linked to a campus network. 1,200 **computers**

available in the computer center, computer labs, academic buildings, the library, dormitories, and student rooms. Staffed computer lab on campus provides training in the use of computers and software.

The **library** has 120,454 books, 1,918 microform titles, and 1,030 subscriptions. It is connected to 1 national **on-line** catalog.

 **Campus Life**

Active **organizations** on campus include drama/theater group and student-run newspaper and radio station. Student **safety services** include late night transport/escort service, 24-hour emergency telephone alarm devices, 24-hour patrols by trained security personnel, and student patrols.

Cedarville is a member of the NAIA. **Intercollegiate sports** (some offering scholarships) include baseball (m), basketball (m, w), cross-country running (m, w), golf (m), soccer (m), softball (w), tennis (m, w), track and field (m, w), volleyball (w).

 **Applying**

Cedarville requires an essay, a high school transcript, 2 recommendations, SAT I or ACT, a minimum high school GPA of 3.0, and in some cases an interview. It recommends 3 years of high school math and science and 2 years of high school foreign language. Early, deferred, and midyear entrance are possible, with rolling admissions and continuous processing to 3/1 for financial aid. **Contact:** Mr. Roscoe F. Smith, Associate Director of Admissions, PO Box 601, Cedarville, OH 45314-0601, 513-766-7700 or toll-free 800-CEDARVILLE.

---

### GETTING IN LAST YEAR
1,437 applied
77% were accepted
53% enrolled (591)
26% from top tenth of their h.s. class
3.42 average high school GPA
13% had SAT verbal scores over 600
26% had SAT math scores over 600
36% had ACT scores over 26
2% had SAT verbal scores over 700
5% had SAT math scores over 700
9% had ACT scores over 30
6 National Merit Scholars
61 valedictorians

### THE STUDENT BODY
2,378 undergraduates
From 48 states and territories,
   12 other countries
38% from Ohio
56% women, 44% men
1% African Americans
1% Native Americans
1% Hispanics
1% Asian Americans
1% international students

### AFTER FRESHMAN YEAR
82% returned for sophomore year
47% got a degree within 4 years

53% got a degree within 5 years
54% got a degree within 6 years

### AFTER GRADUATION
18% pursued further study (13% arts and
   sciences, 2% business, 1% law)
28 corporations, 4 government agencies, 36
   nonprofit organizations recruited on campus

### WHAT YOU WILL PAY
Tuition and fees $7470
Room and board $4410
52% receive need-based financial aid
   averaging $1027
22% receive non-need financial aid averaging
   $1138

# CENTENARY COLLEGE OF LOUISIANA

Shreveport, Louisiana • Suburban setting • Private • Independent-Religious • Coed

Centenary College of Louisiana, a 65-acre campus of Georgian architecture, gardens, and shaded groves, is more than a beautiful campus. It is a community of students and faculty members who are serious about learning. The Centenary College education supports students in their quest for success in advanced study, their personal lives, and their careers. The curriculum is designed to provide broad-based and integrated general knowledge, depth in the chosen major, oral and written communication skills, and computer skills. The Centenary experience also includes commitment to service-based learning, career exploration through an internship, and living and learning in another culture.

 **Academics**

Centenary offers a liberal arts core curriculum and core academic program; a few graduate courses are open to undergraduates. It awards bachelor's and master's **degrees**. Challenging opportunities include advanced placement, accelerated degree programs, self-designed majors, tutorials, an honors program, and a senior project. Special programs include internships, summer session for credit, off-campus study, study abroad, and Army ROTC.

The most popular **majors** include business, biology/biological sciences, and education. A complete listing of majors at Centenary appears in the Majors Index beginning on page 380.

The **faculty** at Centenary has 65 full-time graduate and undergraduate teachers, 94% with terminal degrees. 95% of the faculty serve as student advisers. The student-faculty ratio is 11:1, and the average class size in required courses is 11.

 **Computers on Campus**

Students are not required to have a computer. 150 **computers** available in the computer center, computer labs, biology labs, chemistry labs, business center, the library, and dormitories provide access to e-mail and on-line services. Staffed computer lab on campus provides training in the use of computers and software.

The 2 **libraries** have 168,000 books and 923 subscriptions.

 **Campus Life**

There are 14 active **organizations** on campus, including a drama/theater group and student-run newspaper and radio station. 39% of students participate in student government elections. 24% of eligible men and 24% of eligible women are members of 4 national **fraternities** and 2 national **sororities**. Student **safety services** include late night transport/escort service, 24-hour emergency telephone alarm devices, 24-hour patrols by trained security personnel, and electronically operated dormitory entrances.

Centenary is a member of the NCAA (Division I). **Intercollegiate sports** (some offering scholarships) include baseball (m), basketball (m), cross-country running (m, w), golf (m), gymnastics (w), riflery (m, w), soccer (m), softball (w), tennis (m, w), volleyball (w).

 **Applying**

Centenary requires an essay, a high school transcript, recommendations, an interview, and SAT I or ACT. It recommends 3 years of high school math and science, some high school foreign language, and 3 SAT II Subject Tests. Early, deferred, and midyear entrance are possible, with rolling admissions and continuous processing to 3/15 for financial aid. **Contact:** Dr. Dorothy Bird Gwin, Dean of Enrollment Management, 2911 Centenary Boulevard, Shreveport, LA 71134-1188, 318-869-5131.

---

**GETTING IN LAST YEAR**
517 applied
93% were accepted
44% enrolled (211)
33% from top tenth of their h.s. class
3.48 average high school GPA
15% had SAT verbal scores over 600
28% had SAT math scores over 600
41% had ACT scores over 26
2% had SAT verbal scores over 700
3% had SAT math scores over 700
16% had ACT scores over 30

**THE STUDENT BODY**
Total 1,014, of whom 796
    are undergraduates

From 22 states and territories,
    10 other countries
57% from Louisiana
56% women, 44% men
8% African Americans
1% Native Americans
1% Hispanics
2% Asian Americans
4% international students

**AFTER FRESHMAN YEAR**
66% returned for sophomore year
43% got a degree within 4 years
55% got a degree within 5 years
57% got a degree within 6 years

**AFTER GRADUATION**
33% pursued further study (13% arts and
    sciences, 10% business, 3% law)
31 corporations recruited on campus

**WHAT YOU WILL PAY**
Tuition and fees $9250
Room and board $3490
48% receive need-based financial aid
    averaging $1093
34% receive non-need financial aid averaging
    $2482

# CENTRAL COLLEGE

Pella, Iowa • Small-town setting • Private • Independent-Religious • Coed

Whether studying ancient art in China, researching Mayan villages in Mexico, or delivering meals to homeless people in Chicago, Central College students get their education in the ultimate outdoor classroom. With 8 foreign-study programs and several off-campus learning projects to choose from, this 143-year-old liberal arts college produces students with a "WorldWise" perspective.

## Academics

Central College offers a liberal studies curriculum emphasizing cross-cultural experience and communication skills and core academic program. It awards bachelor's **degrees**. Challenging opportunities include advanced placement, self-designed majors, tutorials, Freshmen Honors College, an honors program, and a senior project. Special programs include internships, summer session for credit, off-campus study, and study abroad.

The most popular **majors** include business, elementary education, and liberal arts/general studies. A complete listing of majors at Central College appears in the Majors Index beginning on page 380.

The **faculty** at Central College has 88 full-time teachers, 90% with terminal degrees. 98% of the faculty serve as student advisers. The student-faculty ratio is 14:1, and the average class size in required courses is 24.

## Computers on Campus

Students are not required to have a computer. 228 **computers** available in the computer center, computer labs, academic buildings, and the library provide access to the main academic computer and e-mail.

The 3 **libraries** have 178,325 books, 52,940 microform titles, and 944 subscriptions. They are connected to 2 national **on-line** catalogs.

## Campus Life

There are 58 active **organizations** on campus, including a drama/theater group and student-run newspaper and radio station. 35% of students participate in student government elections. 12% of eligible men and 4% of eligible women are members of 4 local **fraternities** and 2 local **sororities**. Student **safety services** include late night transport/escort service, student patrols, and electronically operated dormitory entrances.

Central College is a member of the NCAA (Division III). **Intercollegiate sports** include baseball (m), basketball (m, w), cross-country running (m, w), football (m), golf (m, w), soccer (m), softball (w), tennis (m, w), track and field (m, w), volleyball (w), wrestling (m).

## Applying

Central College requires a high school transcript, SAT I or ACT, and in some cases an essay, 3 recommendations, and an interview. It recommends 3 years of high school math and science, 2 years of high school foreign language, and an interview. Early, deferred, and midyear entrance are possible, with rolling admissions and continuous processing to 1/1 for financial aid. **Contact:** Mr. Eric Sickler, Vice President of Admission and Marketing, 812 University Street, Pella, IA 50219-1999, 515-628-5285 or toll-free 800-458-5503; fax 515-628-5316.

---

### GETTING IN LAST YEAR
1,319 applied
85% were accepted
30% enrolled (337)
35% from top tenth of their h.s. class
3.47 average high school GPA
40% had ACT scores over 26
6% had ACT scores over 30

### THE STUDENT BODY
1,452 undergraduates
From 39 states and territories,
   20 other countries
76% from Iowa

57% women, 43% men
1% African Americans
0% Native Americans
3% Hispanics
2% Asian Americans
3% international students

### AFTER FRESHMAN YEAR
74% returned for sophomore year
62% got a degree within 4 years
67% got a degree within 5 years
68% got a degree within 6 years

### AFTER GRADUATION
15% pursued further study (8% arts and
   sciences, 5% medicine, 2% business)
22% had job offers within 3 months
37 corporations, 4 government agencies, 3
   nonprofit organizations recruited on campus

### WHAT YOU WILL PAY
Tuition and fees $11,079
Room and board $3660
81% receive need-based financial aid
   averaging $5328
12% receive non-need financial aid averaging
   $3737

# CENTRE COLLEGE

Danville, Kentucky • Small-town setting • Private • Independent • Coed

At Centre College, students are within a short drive of Cincinnati and Louisville. But once they have learned about the Norton Center for the Arts, some hardly ever leave campus. After a challenging lab in biology or an intense discussion in government, a short walk across campus takes students to another world—a world of dance with Mikhail Baryshnikov or music with the St. Louis Orchestra or hot rock 'n' roll with Wolfman Jack. Art and drama majors can just take an elevator down from the art studios for sculpting and glass-blowing, or run the flight of stairs up from the massive production areas used for student drama productions.

## Academics

Centre offers an interdisciplinary curriculum and core academic program. It awards bachelor's **degrees**. Challenging opportunities include advanced placement, self-designed majors, tutorials, a senior project, and Phi Beta Kappa. Special programs include internships, summer session for credit, off-campus study, study abroad, and Army and Air Force ROTC.

The most popular **majors** include economics, English, and history. A complete listing of majors at Centre appears in the Majors Index beginning on page 380.

The **faculty** at Centre has 80 full-time teachers, 94% with terminal degrees. 100% of the faculty serve as student advisers. The student-faculty ratio is 11:1, and the average class size in required courses is 16.

## Computers on Campus

Students are not required to have a computer. Student rooms are linked to a campus network. 80 **computers** available in the computer center, computer labs, classroom buildings, the library, the student center, and dormitories provide access to e-mail. Staffed computer lab on campus (open 24 hours a day) provides training in the use of computers and software.

The 2 **libraries** have 180,000 books, 48,362 microform titles, and 900 subscriptions.

## Campus Life

There are 66 active **organizations** on campus, including a drama/theater group and student-run newspaper. 65% of eligible men and 55% of eligible women are members of 6 national **fraternities** and 3 national **sororities**. Student **safety services** include late night transport/escort service, 24-hour emergency telephone alarm devices, 24-hour patrols by trained security personnel, and electronically operated dormitory entrances.

Centre is a member of the NCAA (Division III). **Intercollegiate sports** include baseball (m), basketball (m, w), cross-country running (m, w), field hockey (w), football (m), golf (m, w), soccer (m, w), swimming and diving (m, w), tennis (m, w), track and field (m, w), volleyball (w).

## Applying

Centre requires an essay, a high school transcript, 3 years of high school math, 1 recommendation, 2 years of high school social studies, SAT I or ACT, and a minimum high school GPA of 2.0. It recommends 4 years of high school math and science, 2 years of high school foreign language, a campus interview, SAT II Subject Tests, and a minimum high school GPA of 3.0. Early, deferred, and midyear entrance are possible, with a 3/1 deadline and continuous processing to 3/1 for financial aid. **Contact:** Mr. Thomas B. Martin, Executive Director of Enrollment Management, 600 West Walnut Street, Danville, KY 40422-1394, 606-238-5350 or toll-free 800-423-6236.

### GETTING IN LAST YEAR
992 applied
90% were accepted
29% enrolled (255)
58% from top tenth of their h.s. class
3.6 average high school GPA
22% had SAT verbal scores over 600
42% had SAT math scores over 600
60% had ACT scores over 26
0% had SAT verbal scores over 700
7% had SAT math scores over 700
9% had ACT scores over 30
9 National Merit Scholars
25 valedictorians

### THE STUDENT BODY
955 undergraduates
From 33 states and territories,
  4 other countries
65% from Kentucky
51% women, 49% men
3% African Americans
0% Native Americans
1% Hispanics
2% Asian Americans
1% international students

### AFTER FRESHMAN YEAR
86% returned for sophomore year

### AFTER GRADUATION
35% pursued further study (19% arts and
  sciences, 7% law, 4% medicine)
50 corporations, 10 government agencies, 5
  nonprofit organizations recruited on campus
1 Fulbright scholar

### WHAT YOU WILL PAY
Tuition and fees $12,200
Room and board $4140
55% receive need-based financial aid
  averaging $3065
46% receive non-need financial aid averaging
  $3122

# CHRISTENDOM COLLEGE

Front Royal, Virginia • Small-town setting • Private • Independent-Religious • Coed

### Academics

Christendom offers a core academic program. It awards bachelor's **degrees**. Challenging opportunities include advanced placement, accelerated degree programs, and a senior project. Special programs include internships, summer session for credit, and study abroad.

A complete listing of majors at Christendom appears in the Majors Index beginning on page 380.

The **faculty** at Christendom has 13 full-time teachers, 70% with terminal degrees. 66% of the faculty serve as student advisers. The student-faculty ratio is 10:1, and the average class size in required courses is 25.

### Computers on Campus

Students are not required to have a computer. 9 **computers** available in the computer center.

The **library** has 40,000 books, 724 microform titles, and 274 subscriptions. It is connected to 1 national **on-line** catalog.

### Campus Life

There are 15 active **organizations** on campus, including a drama/theater group. Student **safety services** include late night transport/escort service and 24-hour emergency telephone alarm devices. **Intercollegiate sports** include basketball (m, w).

### Applying

Christendom requires an essay, a high school transcript, 2 recommendations, and SAT I or ACT. It recommends 3 years of high school math and science, some high school foreign language, an interview, and a minimum high school GPA of 3.0. Early and midyear entrance are possible, with an 8/15 deadline and continuous processing to 4/1 for financial aid. **Contact:** Mr. John Ciskanik, Director of Admissions, 2101 Shenandoah Shores Road, Front Royal, VA 22630-5149, 703-636-2900 ext. 290 or toll-free 800-877-5456; fax 703-636-1655.

## GETTING IN LAST YEAR
98 applied
76% were accepted
66% enrolled (49)
45% from top tenth of their h.s. class
3.52 average high school GPA
42% had SAT verbal scores over 600
29% had SAT math scores over 600
67% had ACT scores over 26
9% had SAT verbal scores over 700
16% had SAT math scores over 700
9% had ACT scores over 30

## THE STUDENT BODY
173 undergraduates
From 41 states and territories,
 3 other countries
30% from Virginia
65% women, 35% men
1% African Americans
0% Native Americans
4% Hispanics
2% Asian Americans
2% international students

## AFTER FRESHMAN YEAR
77% returned for sophomore year

## WHAT YOU WILL PAY
Tuition and fees $8880
Room and board $3600
52% receive need-based financial aid
 averaging $1641
24% receive non-need financial aid averaging
 $3679

# CHRISTIAN BROTHERS UNIVERSITY

Memphis, Tennessee • Urban setting • Private • Independent-Religious • Coed

Christian Brothers University is located in the center of the friendly Southern city of Memphis, Tennessee. Its beautiful 70-acre campus encourages a true sense of excellence and achievement that comes with the history and the tradition of the Christian Brothers. CBU offers a 15:1 student-faculty ratio and is known for the high academic caliber of its students and the caring commitment of its faculty. At Christian Brothers University, students "dream no little dreams." Outstanding acceptance rates for medical and law school students, along with a graduate placement rate of 96%, ensure that CBU's graduates are prepared for the future.

 **Academics**

CBU offers a liberal arts curriculum and core academic program. It awards bachelor's and master's **degrees**. Challenging opportunities include advanced placement, accelerated degree programs, tutorials, an honors program, and a senior project. Special programs include cooperative education, internships, summer session for credit, off-campus study, and Army, Naval, and Air Force ROTC.

The most popular **majors** include accounting, electrical engineering, and business. A complete listing of majors at CBU appears in the Majors Index beginning on page 380.

The **faculty** at CBU has 106 full-time undergraduate teachers, 75% with terminal degrees. 90% of the faculty serve as student advisers. The student-faculty ratio is 15:1, and the average class size in required courses is 17.

 **Computers on Campus**

Students are not required to have a computer. 250 **computers** available in the computer center, computer labs, classrooms, and the library provide access to the main academic computer, e-mail, and on-line services. Staffed computer lab on campus provides training in the use of computers and software.

The **library** has 91,830 books, 4,000 microform titles, and 582 subscriptions.

 **Campus Life**

There are 35 active **organizations** on campus, including a drama/theater group and student-run newspaper. 25% of eligible men and 25% of eligible women are members of 4 national **fraternities**, 3 national **sororities**, 1 local fraternity, 2 local sororities, and 25 social clubs. Student **safety services** include late night transport/escort service, 24-hour emergency telephone alarm devices, 24-hour patrols by trained security personnel, and student patrols.

CBU is a member of the NAIA. **Intercollegiate sports** (some offering scholarships) include baseball (m), basketball (m, w), cross-country running (m, w), golf (m), soccer (m, w), softball (w), tennis (m, w), volleyball (w).

 **Applying**

CBU requires an essay, a high school transcript, ACT, a minimum high school GPA of 2.0, and in some cases 2 recommendations. It recommends 3 years of high school math and science, some high school foreign language, an interview, SAT I, and a minimum high school GPA of 3.0. Early and midyear entrance are possible, with a 7/1 deadline and continuous processing to 4/1 for financial aid. **Contact:** Mr. Michael Dausch, Dean of Admissions, 650 East Parkway South, Memphis, TN 38104-5581, 901-722-0205 ext. 210 or toll-free 800-288-7576.

---

### GETTING IN LAST YEAR
857 applied
75% were accepted
48% enrolled (310)
21% from top tenth of their h.s. class
3.0 average high school GPA
39% had ACT scores over 26
8% had ACT scores over 30

### THE STUDENT BODY
Total 1,710, of whom 1,406
   are undergraduates
From 35 states and territories,
   19 other countries

77% from Tennessee
46% women, 54% men
15% African Americans
1% Native Americans
1% Hispanics
3% Asian Americans
4% international students

### AFTER FRESHMAN YEAR
81% returned for sophomore year
52% got a degree within 5 years

### AFTER GRADUATION
22% pursued further study (8% arts and
   sciences, 7% business, 7% law)
50 corporations recruited on campus

### WHAT YOU WILL PAY
Tuition and fees $10,120
Room and board $3340
69% receive need-based financial aid
   averaging $4203
31% receive non-need financial aid averaging
   $2500

# CLAREMONT MCKENNA COLLEGE

Claremont, California • Suburban setting • Private • Independent • Coed

As part of the Claremont Colleges (including Harvey Mudd, Pitzer, Pomona, and Scripps), CMC offers the "best of both worlds." All 5,000 students share facilities, cross-campus registration, and cooperative extracurricular opportunities, enabling CMC to provide the advantages of a medium-sized university with the benefits of a smaller college. With a commitment to preparing students for responsible leadership, CMC recognizes that environmental concerns are among the most important issues facing leaders today. The introduction of a new CMC major, The Environment, Economics and Politics, coincided with the opening of the $16.5-million Keck Science Center in 1992.

 ## Academics

CMC offers a public affairs and liberal arts curriculum and core academic program. It awards bachelor's **degrees**. Challenging opportunities include advanced placement, accelerated degree programs, self-designed majors, tutorials, an honors program, a senior project, Phi Beta Kappa, and Sigma Xi. Special programs include internships, off-campus study, study abroad, and Army, Naval, and Air Force ROTC.

The most popular **majors** include economics, political science/government, and psychology. A complete listing of majors at CMC appears in the Majors Index beginning on page 380.

The **faculty** at CMC has 103 full-time teachers, 99% with terminal degrees. 100% of the faculty serve as student advisers. The student-faculty ratio is 9:1.

 ## Computers on Campus

Students are not required to have a computer. Student rooms are linked to a campus network. 40 **computers** available in the computer center, computer labs, the learning resource center, research institutes, classrooms, and the library provide access to the main academic computer, off-campus computing facilities, e-mail, and on-line services. Staffed computer lab on campus.

The 4 **libraries** have 1.9 million books, 1.2 million microform titles, and 6,100 subscriptions. They are connected to 11 national **on-line** catalogs.

 ## Campus Life

There are 280 active **organizations** on campus, including a drama/theater group and student-run newspaper and radio station. 69% of students participate in student government elections. Student **safety services** include late night transport/escort service, 24-hour emergency telephone alarm devices, 24-hour patrols by trained security personnel, student patrols, and electronically operated dormitory entrances.

CMC is a member of the NCAA (Division III). **Intercollegiate sports** include badminton (m, w), baseball (m), basketball (m, w), cross-country running (m, w), football (m), golf (m, w), lacrosse (m, w), rugby (m, w), skiing (downhill) (m, w), soccer (m, w), softball (w), swimming and diving (m, w), tennis (m, w), track and field (m, w), volleyball (m, w), water polo (m, w).

 ## Applying

CMC requires an essay, a high school transcript, 3 years of high school math, 2 years of high school foreign language, 2 recommendations, and SAT I or ACT. It recommends 3 years of high school science, a campus interview, and 3 SAT II Subject Tests. Early, deferred, and midyear entrance are possible, with a 1/15 deadline and a 2/1 priority date for financial aid. **Contact:** Mr. Richard C. Vos, Vice President/Dean of Admission and Financial Aid, 890 Columbia Avenue, Claremont, CA 91711-3901, 909-621-8088.

## GETTING IN LAST YEAR

2,066 applied
42% were accepted
27% enrolled (232)
71% from top tenth of their h.s. class
3.83 average high school GPA
57% had SAT verbal scores over 600
81% had SAT math scores over 600
78% had ACT scores over 26
9% had SAT verbal scores over 700
32% had SAT math scores over 700
35% had ACT scores over 30
16 National Merit Scholars
13 class presidents
18 valedictorians

## THE STUDENT BODY

877 undergraduates
From 40 states and territories,
    21 other countries
62% from California
42% women, 58% men
6% African Americans
1% Native Americans
10% Hispanics
20% Asian Americans
4% international students

## AFTER FRESHMAN YEAR

92% returned for sophomore year
78% got a degree within 4 years
81% got a degree within 5 years

## AFTER GRADUATION

46% pursued further study (13% arts and
    sciences, 11% law, 8% engineering)
80 corporations, 7 government agencies, 36
    nonprofit organizations recruited on campus

## WHAT YOU WILL PAY

Tuition and fees $17,140
Room and board $6010
57% receive need-based financial aid
    averaging $9669
7% receive non-need financial aid averaging
    $2643

# CLARKSON UNIVERSITY

Potsdam, New York • Small-town setting • Private • Independent • Coed

Clarkson is a blend of vivid contrasts—high-powered academics in a cooperative and friendly community, technically oriented students who enjoy people, and a location that serves as a gateway to outdoor recreation and activities of 4 other colleges within a 10-mile radius. Clarkson's students are described as smart, hard-working, outgoing, energized, team players; the academic programs as rigorous, relevant, flexible, and nationally respected; the teachers as demanding, approachable, concerned, accomplished, and inspiring. Clarkson alumni, students, and faculty share an exceptionally strong bond and the lifetime benefits that come from a global network of personal and professional ties.

## Academics

Clarkson offers a core academic program. It awards bachelor's, master's, and doctoral **degrees**. Challenging opportunities include advanced placement, accelerated degree programs, self-designed majors, and Sigma Xi. Special programs include cooperative education, summer session for credit, off-campus study, study abroad, and Army and Air Force ROTC.

The most popular **majors** include civil engineering, mechanical engineering, and electrical engineering. A complete listing of majors at Clarkson appears in the Majors Index beginning on page 380.

The **faculty** at Clarkson has 160 full-time graduate and undergraduate teachers, 96% with terminal degrees. The student-faculty ratio is 15:1.

## Computers on Campus

Students are required to have a computer. PCs are provided. 2,471 **computers** available in the computer center,

computer labs, the learning resource center, classrooms, the library, the student center, and dormitories provide access to the main academic computer, off-campus computing facilities, e-mail, and on-line services.

The **library** has 219,948 books, 264,777 microform titles, and 2,835 subscriptions.

## Campus Life

Active **organizations** on campus include drama/theater group and student-run newspaper and radio station. 23% of eligible men and 28% of eligible women are members of 11 national **fraternities**, 3 national **sororities**, and 5 local fraternities. Student **safety services** include late night transport/escort service, 24-hour emergency telephone alarm devices, 24-hour patrols by trained security personnel, and electronically operated dormitory entrances.

Clarkson is a member of the NCAA (Division III). **Intercollegiate sports** (some offering scholarships) include baseball (m), basketball (m, w), cross-country running (m, w), golf (m, w), ice hockey (m), lacrosse (m, w), skiing (cross-country) (m), skiing (downhill) (m, w), soccer (m, w), swimming and diving (m, w), tennis (m, w), volleyball (w).

## Applying

Clarkson requires a high school transcript, 3 years of high school math, 1 recommendation, SAT I or ACT, and in some cases 3 years of high school science. It recommends a campus interview and SAT II Subject Tests. Early and deferred entrance are possible, with a 3/15 deadline and a 2/15 priority date for financial aid. **Contact:** Mr. Robert Croot, Executive Director of Undergraduate Admission, Holcroft House, Potsdam, NY 13699-5557, 315-268-6463 or toll-free 800-527-6577 (in-state), 800-527-6578 (out-of-state); fax 315-268-7647.

### GETTING IN LAST YEAR

2,241 applied
39% from top tenth of their h.s. class
3.0 average high school GPA
24% had SAT verbal scores over 600
60% had SAT math scores over 600
5% had SAT verbal scores over 700
14% had SAT math scores over 700
6 National Merit Scholars
11 valedictorians

### THE STUDENT BODY

Total 2,601, of whom 2,246
  are undergraduates

From 35 states and territories,
  27 other countries
67% from New York
23% women, 77% men
2% African Americans
1% Native Americans
2% Hispanics
2% Asian Americans
4% international students

### AFTER FRESHMAN YEAR

85% returned for sophomore year
64% got a degree within 4 years
72% got a degree within 5 years
73% got a degree within 6 years

### AFTER GRADUATION

17% pursued further study (6% arts and
  sciences, 5% engineering, 4% business)
106 corporations recruited on campus

### WHAT YOU WILL PAY

Tuition and fees $16,283
Room and board $5580
90% receive need-based financial aid
  averaging $4852
Non-need financial aid averages $4748

# CLARK UNIVERSITY

Worcester, Massachusetts • Urban setting • Private • Independent • Coed

A teaching and research institution founded in 1887, Clark University has a history of academic excellence and innovation. Clark was the location for Sigmund Freud's famous lectures on psychoanalysis and was home to Robert Goddard, father of the space age, and A. A. Michelson, the first American awarded a Nobel Prize in Science. Clark's most recent innovation is the Fifth Year Free B.A./M.A. Program, which allows students to earn their bachelor's and master's degrees in only five years with the fifth year completely tuition-free. Close student-faculty interaction, a strong sense of community, and an international student body make Clark an ideal choice.

## Academics

Clark offers a liberal arts and sciences curriculum and core academic program; more than half of graduate courses are open to undergraduates. It awards bachelor's, master's, doctoral, and first professional **degrees**. Challenging opportunities include advanced placement, accelerated degree programs, self-designed majors, tutorials, an honors program, a senior project, and Phi Beta Kappa. Special programs include internships, summer session for credit, off-campus study, study abroad, and Army and Air Force ROTC.

The most popular **majors** include psychology, political science/government, and business. A complete listing of majors at Clark appears in the Majors Index beginning on page 380.

The **faculty** at Clark has 170 full-time graduate and undergraduate teachers, 99% with terminal degrees. 100% of the faculty serve as student advisers. The student-faculty ratio is 11:1.

## Computers on Campus

Students are not required to have a computer. Student rooms are linked to a campus network. 100 **computers**

available in the computer center, computer labs, academic buildings and departments, classrooms, and the library provide access to the main academic computer, off-campus computing facilities, e-mail, and on-line services. Staffed computer lab on campus provides training in the use of software.

The 5 **libraries** have 528,000 books, 14,400 microform titles, and 1,909 subscriptions.

## Campus Life

There are 74 active **organizations** on campus, including a drama/theater group and student-run newspaper and radio station. Student **safety services** include late night transport/escort service, 24-hour emergency telephone alarm devices, 24-hour patrols by trained security personnel, student patrols, and electronically operated dormitory entrances.

Clark is a member of the NCAA (Division III). **Intercollegiate sports** include baseball (m), basketball (m, w), crew (m, w), cross-country running (m, w), field hockey (w), golf (m), lacrosse (m), soccer (m, w), softball (w), swimming and diving (m, w), tennis (m, w), volleyball (w).

## Applying

Clark requires an essay, a high school transcript, SAT I or ACT, and SAT II: Writing Test. It recommends 3 years of high school math and science, 2 years of high school foreign language, 2 recommendations, an interview, 2 SAT II Subject Tests, and a minimum high school GPA of 3.0. Early, deferred, and midyear entrance are possible, with a 2/1 deadline and continuous processing to 2/1 for financial aid. **Contact:** Mr. Richard W. Pierson, Dean of Admissions, Admissions House, 950 Main Street, Worcester, MA 01610-1477, 508-793-7431.

---

**GETTING IN LAST YEAR**
2,634 applied
73% were accepted
25% enrolled (483)
30% from top tenth of their h.s. class
3.03 average high school GPA

**THE STUDENT BODY**
Total 2,670, of whom 1,890
   are undergraduates
From 38 states and territories,
   70 other countries
34% from Massachusetts

57% women, 43% men
3% African Americans
3% Hispanics
4% Asian Americans
17% international students

**AFTER FRESHMAN YEAR**
83% returned for sophomore year

**AFTER GRADUATION**
28% pursued further study (14% arts and
   sciences, 6% business, 4% law)

21 corporations, 7 government agencies, 34
   nonprofit organizations recruited on campus
3 Fulbright scholars

**WHAT YOU WILL PAY**
Tuition and fees $17,940
Room and board $4300
63% receive need-based financial aid
   averaging $10,200
Non-need financial aid averages $5000

---

# CLEMSON UNIVERSITY

Clemson, South Carolina • Small-town setting • Public • State-supported • Coed

Recently cited by *Money* magazine as one of the nation's best honors programs among state universities, Clemson's Calhoun College is designed for academically talented, highly motivated students who are naturally inquisitive and dedicated to the life of the mind. The honors experience includes a core of interdisciplinary seminars for freshmen and sophomores and independent research projects for juniors and seniors. Housing for 300 Calhoun scholars is available in Holmes Hall, located in the heart of Clemson's beautiful campus.

##  Academics

Clemson offers a core academic program; more than half of graduate courses are open to undergraduates. It awards bachelor's, master's, and doctoral **degrees**. Challenging opportunities include advanced placement, accelerated degree programs, an honors program, and Sigma Xi. Special programs include cooperative education, internships, summer session for credit, study abroad, and Army and Air Force ROTC.

The most popular **majors** include business, finance/banking, and marketing/retailing/merchandising. A complete listing of majors at Clemson appears in the Majors Index beginning on page 380.

The **faculty** at Clemson has 1,189 full-time graduate and undergraduate teachers, 87% with terminal degrees. The student-faculty ratio is 18:1, and the average class size in required courses is 31.

##  Computers on Campus

Students are not required to have a computer. 1,000 **computers** available in the computer center, academic buildings, and the library provide access to the main academic computer and on-line services. Staffed computer lab on campus (open 24 hours a day) provides training in the use of computers and software.

The 2 **libraries** have 1.4 million books and 7,114 subscriptions.

##  Campus Life

There are 260 active **organizations** on campus, including a drama/theater group and student-run newspaper and radio station. 15% of eligible men and 26% of eligible women are members of 20 national **fraternities** and 14 national **sororities**. Student **safety services** include late night transport/escort service, 24-hour emergency telephone alarm devices, and 24-hour patrols by trained security personnel.

Clemson is a member of the NCAA (Division I). **Intercollegiate sports** (some offering scholarships) include baseball (m), basketball (m, w), bowling (m, w), crew (m, w), cross-country running (m, w), equestrian sports (m, w), fencing (m, w), field hockey (w), football (m), golf (m, w), gymnastics (m, w), lacrosse (m), rugby (m, w), sailing (m, w), skiing (cross-country) (m, w), skiing (downhill) (m, w), soccer (m, w), swimming and diving (m, w), table tennis (m, w), tennis (m, w), track and field (m, w), volleyball (m, w), weight lifting (m, w), wrestling (m).

##  Applying

Clemson requires a high school transcript, 3 years of high school math, 2 years of high school foreign language, SAT I or ACT, and in some cases SAT II Subject Tests. It recommends an essay, 3 years of high school science, recommendations, an interview, and SAT II Subject Tests. Early, deferred, and midyear entrance are possible, with rolling admissions and continuous processing to 3/1 for financial aid. **Contact:** Dr. Michael Heintze, Director of Admissions, 105 Sikes Hall, PO Box 345124, Clemson, SC 29634, 803-656-2287; fax 803-656-0622.

---

### GETTING IN LAST YEAR
8,263 applied
70% were accepted
41% enrolled (2,371)
34% from top tenth of their h.s. class
9% had SAT verbal scores over 600
34% had SAT math scores over 600
1% had SAT verbal scores over 700
6% had SAT math scores over 700
24 National Merit Scholars

### THE STUDENT BODY
Total 16,296, of whom 12,302
   are undergraduates

From 51 states and territories,
   71 other countries
73% from South Carolina
45% women, 55% men
9% African Americans
1% Native Americans
1% Hispanics
1% Asian Americans
1% international students

### AFTER FRESHMAN YEAR
85% returned for sophomore year

### AFTER GRADUATION
29% pursued further study
269 corporations, 10 government agencies
   recruited on campus
1 Fulbright scholar

### WHAT YOU WILL PAY
Resident tuition and fees $3086
Nonresident tuition and fees $8166
Room and board $3744
40% receive need-based financial aid
   averaging $3600
18% receive non-need financial aid averaging
   $2350

# COE COLLEGE

Cedar Rapids, Iowa • Urban setting • Private • Independent-Religious • Coed

At Coe College, students can walk out of their door on any day of the week and into a $5-million fitness center. Or they can walk into a beautiful library that, at a touch of a key, gives them access to libraries throughout the world. Students also have access to an electron microscope that they actually get to use. At Coe, students can experiment, perform, create, research—and, in the process, plant the seeds of a brilliant career in science, history, business, or the arts.

##  Academics

Coe offers a liberal arts for life curriculum and core academic program. It awards bachelor's and master's **degrees**. Challenging opportunities include advanced placement, accelerated degree programs, self-designed majors, tutorials, Freshmen Honors College, an honors program, a senior project, and Phi Beta Kappa. Special programs include internships, summer session for credit, off-campus study, study abroad, and Army ROTC.

The most popular **majors** include business, psychology, and biology/biological sciences. A complete listing of majors at Coe appears in the Majors Index beginning on page 380.

The **faculty** at Coe has 86 full-time graduate and undergraduate teachers, 87% with terminal degrees. 100% of the faculty serve as student advisers. The student-faculty ratio is 12:1, and the average class size in required courses is 16.

##  Computers on Campus

Students are not required to have a computer. 100 **computers** available in the computer center, computer labs, and the library provide access to the main academic computer, off-campus computing facilities, e-mail, and on-line services. Staffed computer lab on campus provides training in the use of computers and software.

The 2 **libraries** have 183,591 books, 35,744 microform titles, and 916 subscriptions. They are connected to 1 national **on-line** catalog.

##  Campus Life

There are 60 active **organizations** on campus, including a drama/theater group and student-run newspaper. 50% of students participate in student government elections. 25% of eligible men and 25% of eligible women are members of 4 national **fraternities** and 3 national **sororities**. Student **safety services** include late night transport/escort service, 24-hour emergency telephone alarm devices, and 24-hour patrols by trained security personnel.

Coe is a member of the NCAA (Division III). **Intercollegiate sports** include baseball (m), basketball (m, w), cross-country running (m, w), football (m), golf (m, w), soccer (m, w), softball (w), swimming and diving (m, w), tennis (m, w), track and field (m, w), volleyball (w), wrestling (m).

##  Applying

Coe requires an essay, a high school transcript, 1 recommendation, and SAT I or ACT. It recommends 3 years of high school math and science, 2 years of high school foreign language, an interview, minimum 2.5 GPA, and 2 SAT II Subject Tests. Early, deferred, and midyear entrance are possible, with a 3/1 deadline and continuous processing to 3/1 for financial aid. **Contact:** Mr. Michael White, Dean of Admissions and Financial Aid, 1220 1st Avenue, NE, Cedar Rapids, IA 52402-5070, 319-399-8500 or toll-free 800-332-8404; fax 319-399-8816.

## GETTING IN LAST YEAR

892 applied
79% were accepted
42% enrolled (295)
29% from top tenth of their h.s. class
3.35 average high school GPA
22% had SAT verbal scores over 600
33% had SAT math scores over 600
35% had ACT scores over 26
2% had SAT verbal scores over 700
10% had SAT math scores over 700
12% had ACT scores over 30
1 National Merit Scholar
16 valedictorians

## THE STUDENT BODY

Total 1,343, of whom 1,304
  are undergraduates
From 35 states and territories,
  20 other countries
57% from Iowa
56% women, 44% men
3% African Americans
1% Native Americans
2% Hispanics
2% Asian Americans
5% international students

## AFTER FRESHMAN YEAR

81% returned for sophomore year
62% got a degree within 4 years
64% got a degree within 5 years
66% got a degree within 6 years

## AFTER GRADUATION

24% pursued further study (13% arts and
  sciences, 5% business, 4% law)
50% had job offers within 3 months
65 corporations, 10 government agencies, 5
  nonprofit organizations recruited on campus

## WHAT YOU WILL PAY

Tuition and fees $14,050
Room and board $4390
75% receive need-based financial aid
  averaging $5760
10% receive non-need financial aid averaging
  $2800

# COLBY COLLEGE

Waterville, Maine • Small-town setting • Private • Independent • Coed

Colby, located on a 714-acre campus in central Maine, is among the oldest and most respected colleges in the nation. Colby pioneered the January Program of intensive study, has been a leader in study-abroad programs (70% of all Colby students now study in another country at some point in their college careers), and was among the first colleges to integrate computers into its academic programs. Colby's 1,650 students enjoy an 11:1 student-faculty ratio, and close interaction between the two groups is the norm rather than the exception. Colby's academic program is enhanced by a variety of extracurricular offerings.

 ## Academics

Colby offers a liberal arts curriculum and core academic program. It awards bachelor's **degrees**. Challenging opportunities include advanced placement, self-designed majors, tutorials, an honors program, a senior project, and Phi Beta Kappa. Special programs include internships, off-campus study, study abroad, and Army ROTC.

The most popular **majors** include English, biology/biological sciences, and economics. A complete listing of majors at Colby appears in the Majors Index beginning on page 380.

The **faculty** at Colby has 137 full-time teachers, 99% with terminal degrees. 100% of the faculty serve as student advisers. The student-faculty ratio is 11:1, and the average class size in required courses is 17.

 ## Computers on Campus

Students are not required to have a computer. Student rooms are linked to a campus network. 150 **computers** available in the computer center, computer labs, the research center, the learning resource center, science complex, classrooms, and the library provide access to the main academic computer, off-campus computing facilities, e-mail, and on-line services. Staffed computer lab on campus (open 24 hours a day) provides training in the use of computers and software.

The 3 **libraries** have 488,000 books, 266,000 microform titles, and 2,710 subscriptions. They are connected to 3 national **on-line** catalogs.

 ## Campus Life

There are 90 active **organizations** on campus, including a drama/theater group and student-run newspaper and radio station. 60% of students participate in student government elections. No national or local **fraternities** or **sororities**. Student **safety services** include late night transport/escort service, 24-hour emergency telephone alarm devices, and 24-hour patrols by trained security personnel.

Colby is a member of the NCAA (Division III). **Intercollegiate sports** include baseball (m), basketball (m, w), crew (m, w), cross-country running (m, w), field hockey (w), football (m), golf (m, w), ice hockey (m, w), lacrosse (m, w), rugby (m, w), sailing (m, w), skiing (cross-country) (m, w), skiing (downhill) (m, w), soccer (m, w), softball (w), squash (m, w), swimming and diving (m, w), tennis (m, w), track and field (m, w), volleyball (m, w), water polo (m, w).

 ## Applying

Colby requires an essay, a high school transcript, 2 recommendations, and SAT I or ACT. It recommends 3 years of high school math and science, 3 years of high school foreign language, an interview, and SAT II Subject Tests. Early, deferred, and midyear entrance are possible, with a 1/15 deadline and a 2/1 priority date for financial aid. **Contact:** Mr. Parker J. Beverage, Dean of Admissions and Financial Aid, 150 Mayflower Hill Drive, Waterville, ME 04901, 207-872-3168 or toll-free 800-723-3032.

### GETTING IN LAST YEAR

3,413 applied
41% were accepted
31% enrolled (434)
67% from top tenth of their h.s. class
43% had SAT verbal scores over 600
72% had SAT math scores over 600
75% had ACT scores over 26
4% had SAT verbal scores over 700
20% had SAT math scores over 700
28% had ACT scores over 30
13 valedictorians

### THE STUDENT BODY

1,650 undergraduates
From 47 states and territories,
    43 other countries
12% from Maine
55% women, 45% men
3% African Americans
1% Native Americans
3% Hispanics
4% Asian Americans
6% international students

### AFTER FRESHMAN YEAR

96% returned for sophomore year
93% got a degree within 4 years

97% got a degree within 5 years
98% got a degree within 6 years

### AFTER GRADUATION

17% pursued further study (13% arts and sciences, 3% law, 1% medicine)
26 corporations, 3 government agencies, 10 nonprofit organizations recruited on campus

### WHAT YOU WILL PAY

Tuition and fees $19,830
Room and board $5590
40% receive need-based financial aid averaging $11,875

# COLGATE UNIVERSITY

Hamilton, New York • Rural setting • Private • Independent • Coed

When the Roper Organization asked graduates from 1980–92 "What most influenced your decision to attend Colgate," the key factor—cited on 90% of their responses—was academic reputation. Asked "how well Colgate measured up to your expectations academically," 97% of those graduates responded positively. Faculty initiative has given the college a rich mix of learning opportunities. But there is more to Colgate, including 70 student organizations, athletics and recreation at all levels, and one of the most beautiful campuses in the country.

##  Academics

Colgate offers an interdisciplinary curriculum and core academic program; all graduate courses are open to undergraduates. It awards bachelor's and master's **degrees**. Challenging opportunities include advanced placement, self-designed majors, tutorials, an honors program, a senior project, and Phi Beta Kappa. Special programs include off-campus study and study abroad.

The most popular **majors** include English, history, and political science/government. A complete listing of majors at Colgate appears in the Majors Index beginning on page 380.

The **faculty** at Colgate has 198 full-time undergraduate teachers, 98% with terminal degrees. 100% of the faculty serve as student advisers. The student-faculty ratio is 11:1, and the average class size in required courses is 22.

##  Computers on Campus

Students are not required to have a computer. 260 **computers** available in the computer center, computer labs, the learning resource center, various academic departments, classrooms, the library, and the student center.

The 2 **libraries** have 530,000 books and 2,450 subscriptions. They are connected to 5 national **on-line** catalogs.

##  Campus Life

There are 70 active **organizations** on campus, including a drama/theater group and student-run newspaper and radio station. 37% of eligible men and 25% of eligible women are members of 8 national **fraternities**, 4 national **sororities**, and 1 local fraternity. Student **safety services** include late night transport/escort service, 24-hour emergency telephone alarm devices, 24-hour patrols by trained security personnel, student patrols, and electronically operated dormitory entrances.

Colgate is a member of the NCAA (Division I). **Intercollegiate sports** include basketball (m, w), crew (m, w), cross-country running (m, w), field hockey (w), football (m), golf (m), ice hockey (m, w), lacrosse (m, w), rugby (m, w), sailing (m, w), skiing (downhill) (m, w), soccer (m, w), softball (w), squash (m, w), swimming and diving (m, w), tennis (m, w), track and field (m, w), volleyball (m, w), water polo (m, w).

##  Applying

Colgate requires an essay, a high school transcript, 3 years of high school math, 3 years of high school foreign language, 3 recommendations, SAT I, ACT, or 5 SAT II Subject Tests (including SAT II: Writing Test and math subject test). It recommends 4 years of high school science and an interview. Early, deferred, and midyear entrance are possible, with a 1/15 deadline and a 2/1 priority date for financial aid. **Contact:** Mr. Gary L. Ross, Director of Admission, 13 Oak Drive, Hamilton, NY 13346-1386, 315-824-7401; fax 315-824-7544.

---

### GETTING IN LAST YEAR
5,322 applied
51% were accepted
32% enrolled (862)
56% from top tenth of their h.s. class
30% had SAT verbal scores over 600
74% had SAT math scores over 600
65% had ACT scores over 26
2% had SAT verbal scores over 700
18% had SAT math scores over 700
15% had ACT scores over 30

### THE STUDENT BODY
Total 2,759, of whom 2,746
   are undergraduates

From 46 states and territories,
   35 other countries
33% from New York
51% women, 49% men
4% African Americans
1% Native Americans
3% Hispanics
5% Asian Americans
2% international students

### AFTER FRESHMAN YEAR
92% returned for sophomore year
85% got a degree within 4 years
88% got a degree within 5 years
89% got a degree within 6 years

### AFTER GRADUATION
29% pursued further study (14% arts and
   sciences, 7% law, 5% medicine)
38 corporations, 2 government agencies, 2
   nonprofit organizations recruited on campus
1 Fulbright scholar

### WHAT YOU WILL PAY
Tuition and fees $19,655
Room and board $5055
65% receive need-based financial aid
   averaging $13,610

# COLLEGE OF INSURANCE

New York, New York • Urban setting • Private • Independent • Coed

The College of Insurance is a fully accredited institution that is sponsored by over 300 companies in the insurance and financial services industry. The College of Insurance is centrally located in the heart of the financial district, within walking distance of the World Trade Center, SoHo, Chinatown, and the South Street Seaport. The College is housed in an award-winning, self-contained building with dormitories on the top 4 floors. The College of Insurance offers qualified students the opportunity to participate in a unique cooperative work-study program.

##  Academics

College of Insurance offers a core academic program. It awards associate, bachelor's, and master's **degrees**. Challenging opportunities include advanced placement and a senior project. Special programs include cooperative education and summer session for credit.

The most popular **majors** include insurance and actuarial science. A complete listing of majors at College of Insurance appears in the Majors Index beginning on page 380.

The **faculty** at College of Insurance has 22 full-time undergraduate teachers, 25% with terminal degrees. The student-faculty ratio is 12:1.

##  Computers on Campus

Students are not required to have a computer. 16 **computers** available in computer labs.

The **library** has 95,426 books and 359 subscriptions.

##  Campus Life

Active **organizations** on campus include drama/theater group and student-run newspaper. College of Insurance has 1 national **fraternity**. Student **safety services** include 24-hour emergency telephone alarm devices and 24-hour patrols by trained security personnel. **Intercollegiate sports** include bowling (m, w).

##  Applying

College of Insurance requires a high school transcript, 3 years of high school math, an interview, and SAT I or ACT. It recommends an essay and recommendations. Early, deferred, and midyear entrance are possible, with a 5/1 deadline and continuous processing to 6/1 for financial aid. **Contact:** Ms. Theresa C. Marro, Director of Admissions, 101 Murray Street, New York, NY 10007-2165, 212-815-9232 or toll-free 800-356-5146.

---

**GETTING IN LAST YEAR**
185 applied
59% were accepted
71% enrolled (78)
35% from top tenth of their h.s. class
7% had SAT verbal scores over 600
68% had SAT math scores over 600
0% had SAT verbal scores over 700
30% had SAT math scores over 700

**THE STUDENT BODY**
Total 2,388, of whom 2,199
   are undergraduates
80% from New York
52% women, 48% men
13% African Americans
10% Hispanics
8% Asian Americans
10% international students

**AFTER FRESHMAN YEAR**
97% returned for sophomore year

**WHAT YOU WILL PAY**
Tuition and fees $11,480
Room and board $7648
Need-based financial aid averages $2329
Non-need financial aid averages $5779

# COLLEGE OF SAINT BENEDICT

*Coordinate with Saint John's University*

Saint Joseph, Minnesota • Small-town setting • Private • Independent-Religious • Women

The College of Saint Benedict and Saint John's University are liberal arts colleges in the Catholic university tradition. Their mission is to foster learning, leadership, and wisdom for a lifetime. This is achieved through a unified curriculum stressing open inquiry, intellectual challenge, cooperative scholarship, and artistic creativity; an emphasis on the personal growth of women and men through separate residence halls, student development programming, athletics, and leadership opportunities; an experience of Benedictine values, including the formation of community built on respect for individual persons; and an entry into a heritage of leadership and service.

##  Academics

St. Ben's offers an interdisciplinary curriculum and core academic program. It awards bachelor's **degrees**. Challenging opportunities include advanced placement, self-designed majors, tutorials, an honors program, and a senior project. Special programs include internships, off-campus study, study abroad, and Army ROTC.

The most popular **majors** include education, nursing, and business. A complete listing of majors at St. Ben's appears in the Majors Index beginning on page 380.

The **faculty** at St. Ben's has 130 full-time teachers, 80% with terminal degrees. 100% of the faculty serve as student advisers. The student-faculty ratio is 14:1, and the average class size in required courses is 21.

##  Computers on Campus

Students are not required to have a computer. 250 **computers** available in the computer center, computer labs, faculty offices, academic and administration buildings, classrooms, the library, the student center, and dormitories provide access to the main academic computer, e-mail, and on-line services. Staffed computer lab on campus provides training in the use of computers and software.

The 2 **libraries** have 509,000 books, 97,000 microform titles, and 1,700 subscriptions. They are connected to 5 national **on-line** catalogs.

##  Campus Life

There are 80 active **organizations** on campus, including a drama/theater group and student-run newspaper and radio station. Student **safety services** include late night transport/escort service, 24-hour emergency telephone alarm devices, 24-hour patrols by trained security personnel, and electronically operated dormitory entrances.

St. Ben's is a member of the NCAA (Division III). **Intercollegiate sports** include basketball, crew, cross-country running, golf, lacrosse, rugby, skiing (cross-country), skiing (downhill), soccer, softball, swimming and diving, tennis, track and field, volleyball.

##  Applying

St. Ben's requires an essay, a high school transcript, SAT I or ACT, and in some cases recommendations. It recommends 3 years of high school math and science, 2 years of high school foreign language, an interview, and a minimum high school GPA of 3.0. Early, deferred, and midyear entrance are possible, with rolling admissions and continuous processing to 8/15 for financial aid. **Contact:** Ms. Mary Milbert, Director of Admissions, 37 South College Avenue, Saint Joseph, MN 56374, 612-363-5308 or toll-free 800-544-1489; fax 612-363-6099.

---

### GETTING IN LAST YEAR
969 applied
89% were accepted
57% enrolled (488)
34% from top tenth of their h.s. class
3.5 average high school GPA
9% had SAT verbal scores over 600
26% had SAT math scores over 600
29% had ACT scores over 26
1% had SAT verbal scores over 700
5% had SAT math scores over 700
8% had ACT scores over 30
5 National Merit Scholars

### THE STUDENT BODY
1,796 undergraduates
From 37 states and territories,
   36 other countries
84% from Minnesota
100% women
1% African Americans
1% Native Americans
1% Hispanics
2% Asian Americans
2% international students

### AFTER FRESHMAN YEAR
86% returned for sophomore year
57% got a degree within 4 years
65% got a degree within 5 years
66% got a degree within 6 years

### AFTER GRADUATION
25% pursued further study (10% arts and
   sciences, 5% business, 5% law)
60% had job offers within 3 months
100 corporations, 8 government agencies, 11
   nonprofit organizations recruited on campus

### WHAT YOU WILL PAY
Tuition and fees $12,335
Room and board $4221
72% receive need-based financial aid
   averaging $4211
14% receive non-need financial aid averaging
   $2625

---

# COLLEGE OF ST. SCHOLASTICA

Duluth, Minnesota • Suburban setting • Private • Independent-Religious • Coed

---

▶ St. Scholastica attracts bright, lively students who bring to the campus a love of learning, exploring, and contributing. When they graduate, they take with them an excellent academic experience combining the liberal arts with career preparation, memories of a close-knit and supportive community, and a readiness to accept important responsibilities in their careers and communities. The College encourages students to visit its 160-acre campus overlooking Lake Superior.

## Academics

St. Scholastica offers a core academic program; a few graduate courses are open to undergraduates. It awards bachelor's and master's **degrees**. Challenging opportunities include advanced placement, self-designed majors, tutorials, an honors program, and a senior project. Special programs include internships, summer session for credit, off-campus study, study abroad, and Army and Air Force ROTC.

The most popular **majors** include nursing, business, and health services administration. A complete listing of majors at St. Scholastica appears in the Majors Index beginning on page 380.

The **faculty** at St. Scholastica has 124 full-time graduate and undergraduate teachers, 70% with terminal degrees. 100% of the faculty serve as student advisers. The student-faculty ratio is 11:1, and the average class size in required courses is 15.

## Computers on Campus

Students are not required to have a computer. 100 **computers** available in computer labs, classrooms, the library, and dormitories provide access to e-mail. Staffed computer lab on campus provides training in the use of computers and software.

The 2 **libraries** have 122,169 books, 9,767 microform titles, and 800 subscriptions. They are connected to 1 national **on-line** catalog.

## Campus Life

There are 40 active **organizations** on campus, including a drama/theater group and student-run newspaper. 20% of students participate in student government elections. Student **safety services** include student door monitor at night, late night transport/escort service, 24-hour emergency telephone alarm devices, 24-hour patrols by trained security personnel, and electronically operated dormitory entrances.

St. Scholastica is a member of the NCAA (Division III) and NAIA. **Intercollegiate sports** include baseball (m), basketball (m, w), cross-country running (m, w), ice hockey (m), soccer (m, w), softball (w), volleyball (w).

## Applying

St. Scholastica requires an essay, a high school transcript, SAT I or ACT, and in some cases an interview and a minimum high school GPA of 2.0. It recommends 3 years of high school math and science, some high school foreign language, recommendations, a campus interview, and PSAT. Early, deferred, and midyear entrance are possible, with rolling admissions and continuous processing to 3/15 for financial aid. **Contact:** Ms. Rebecca Urbanski-Junkert, Vice President for Admissions and Student Financial Planning, 1200 Kenwood Avenue, Duluth, MN 55811-4199, 218-723-6046 or toll-free 800-447-5444; fax 218-723-6290.

---

### GETTING IN LAST YEAR
723 applied
88% were accepted
44% enrolled (283)
30% from top tenth of their h.s. class
0% had SAT verbal scores over 600
0% had SAT math scores over 600
33% had ACT scores over 26
0% had SAT verbal scores over 700
0% had SAT math scores over 700
6% had ACT scores over 30

### THE STUDENT BODY
Total 1,849, of whom 1,588
   are undergraduates

From 23 states and territories,
   5 other countries
88% from Minnesota
71% women, 29% men
1% African Americans
2% Native Americans
1% Hispanics
1% Asian Americans
1% international students

### AFTER FRESHMAN YEAR
70% returned for sophomore year
34% got a degree within 4 years
48% got a degree within 5 years
49% got a degree within 6 years

### AFTER GRADUATION
19% pursued further study (17% arts and
   sciences, 1% law, 1% medicine)
2 corporations recruited on campus

### WHAT YOU WILL PAY
Tuition and fees $11,919
Room and board $3696
85% receive need-based financial aid
   averaging $2200
22% receive non-need financial aid averaging
   $1326

# COLLEGE OF THE HOLY CROSS

Worcester, Massachusetts • Suburban setting • Private • Independent-Religious • Coed

In a college world of shrinking resources and growing class enrollments, Holy Cross continues to fully support and refine its 150-year-old mission as a completely undergraduate Jesuit liberal arts college. An example of that commitment to open intellectual discourse is the popular First Year Program. Every one of the course offerings is taught by a faculty member, and the average class size is 19 students. The Jesuit nature of the community ensures that all its members recognize the importance of service to others and the need for social justice in daily affairs.

##  Academics

Holy Cross offers a liberal arts curriculum and core academic program. It awards bachelor's **degrees**. Challenging opportunities include advanced placement, accelerated degree programs, self-designed majors, tutorials, an honors program, Phi Beta Kappa, and Sigma Xi. Special programs include internships, off-campus study, study abroad, and Army, Naval, and Air Force ROTC.

The most popular **majors** include English, political science/government, and history. A complete listing of majors at Holy Cross appears in the Majors Index beginning on page 380.

The **faculty** at Holy Cross has 213 full-time teachers, 92% with terminal degrees. 100% of the faculty serve as student advisers. The student-faculty ratio is 13:1, and the average class size in required courses is 19.

##  Computers on Campus

Students are not required to have a computer. Student rooms are linked to a campus network. 130 **computers** available in the computer center, computer labs, the research center, science center, psychology labs, and the library provide access to the main academic computer, off-campus computing facilities, and e-mail. Staffed computer lab on campus (open 24 hours a day) provides training in the use of computers and software.

The 3 **libraries** have 501,347 books, 463 microform titles, and 2,180 subscriptions. They are connected to 9 national **on-line** catalogs.

##  Campus Life

There are 75 active **organizations** on campus, including a drama/theater group and student-run newspaper and radio station. 42% of students participate in student government elections. Student **safety services** include late night transport/escort service, 24-hour emergency telephone alarm devices, 24-hour patrols by trained security personnel, and electronically operated dormitory entrances.

Holy Cross is a member of the NCAA (Division I). **Intercollegiate sports** include baseball (m), basketball (m, w), crew (m, w), cross-country running (m, w), fencing (m, w), field hockey (w), football (m), golf (m), ice hockey (m, w), lacrosse (m, w), rugby (m, w), sailing (m, w), soccer (m, w), softball (w), swimming and diving (m, w), tennis (m, w), track and field (m, w), volleyball (m, w), water polo (m, w).

##  Applying

Holy Cross requires an essay, a high school transcript, 2 recommendations, SAT I or ACT, and 3 SAT II Subject Tests (including SAT II: Writing Test). It recommends 3 years of high school math and science, some high school foreign language, and an interview. Early, deferred, and midyear entrance are possible, with a 2/1 deadline and continuous processing to 2/1 for financial aid. **Contact:** Ms. Ann Bowe McDermott, Director of Admissions, 1 College Street, Worcester, MA 01610, 508-793-2443.

## GETTING IN LAST YEAR
3,859 applied
46% were accepted
38% enrolled (672)
58% from top tenth of their h.s. class
33% had SAT verbal scores over 600
59% had SAT math scores over 600
2% had SAT verbal scores over 700
14% had SAT math scores over 700
5 National Merit Scholars
39 valedictorians

## THE STUDENT BODY
2,720 undergraduates
From 46 states and territories, 13 other countries
41% from Massachusetts
52% women, 48% men
4% African Americans
0% Native Americans
3% Hispanics
2% Asian Americans
1% international students

## AFTER FRESHMAN YEAR
96% returned for sophomore year
92% got a degree within 4 years
93% got a degree within 5 years

## AFTER GRADUATION
24% pursued further study (8% arts and sciences, 7% law, 5% business)
60 corporations, 2 government agencies, 3 nonprofit organizations recruited on campus
5 Fulbright scholars

## WHAT YOU WILL PAY
Tuition and fees $18,355
Room and board $6300
63% receive need-based financial aid averaging $9291
Non-need financial aid averages $18,000

# COLLEGE OF WILLIAM AND MARY

Williamsburg, Virginia • Small-town setting • Public • State-supported • Coed

The College of William and Mary, chartered in 1693, is the second-oldest college in the United States and is known as the "alma mater of a nation." The College was first among American universities to have an interscholastic fraternity, Phi Beta Kappa, and an honor system. Committed to the principles of a liberal arts education, this "public ivy" offers undergraduate degrees in the arts and sciences. William and Mary's distinguished faculty is equally dedicated to the pursuit of research and teaching. Freshman seminars allow maximum interaction with faculty members beginning with a student's first semester.

## Academics

William and Mary offers a liberal arts and sciences curriculum and core academic program; fewer than half of graduate courses are open to undergraduates. It awards bachelor's, master's, doctoral, and first professional **degrees**. Challenging opportunities include advanced placement, accelerated degree programs, self-designed majors, tutorials, an honors program, a senior project, Phi Beta Kappa, and Sigma Xi. Special programs include summer session for credit, study abroad, and Army ROTC.

The most popular **majors** include business, biology/biological sciences, and English. A complete listing of majors at William and Mary appears in the Majors Index beginning on page 380.

The **faculty** at William and Mary has 534 full-time graduate and undergraduate teachers, 92% with terminal degrees. 30% of the faculty serve as student advisers.

## Computers on Campus

Students are not required to have a computer. Student rooms are linked to a campus network. 275 **computers** available in computer labs, classroom buildings, the library, and dormitories provide access to the main academic computer, off-campus computing facilities, e-mail, and on-line services. Staffed computer lab on campus (open 24 hours a day) provides training in the use of computers and software.

The 10 **libraries** have 1.2 million books, 1.8 million microform titles, and 10,414 subscriptions. They are connected to 24 national **on-line** catalogs.

## Campus Life

There are 196 active **organizations** on campus, including a drama/theater group and student-run newspaper and radio station. 35% of students participate in student government elections. 40% of eligible men and 45% of eligible women are members of 17 national **fraternities** and 13 national **sororities**. Student **safety services** include late night transport/escort service, 24-hour emergency telephone alarm devices, 24-hour patrols by trained security personnel, student patrols, and electronically operated dormitory entrances.

William and Mary is a member of the NCAA (Division I). **Intercollegiate sports** (some offering scholarships) include baseball (m), basketball (m, w), cross-country running (m, w), fencing (m, w), field hockey (w), football (m), golf (m, w), gymnastics (m, w), lacrosse (w), soccer (m, w), swimming and diving (m, w), tennis (m, w), track and field (m, w), volleyball (w).

## Applying

William and Mary requires an essay, a high school transcript, SAT I or ACT, SAT II: Writing Test, and in some cases a campus interview. It recommends 4 years of high school math and science, 4 years of high school foreign language, 1 recommendation, and 3 SAT II Subject Tests. Early, deferred, and midyear entrance are possible, with a 1/15 deadline and a 2/15 priority date for financial aid. **Contact:** Ms. Virginia Carey, Dean of Admission, Richmond Road, Williamsburg, VA 23187-8795, 804-221-4223.

---

### GETTING IN LAST YEAR
7,638 applied
40% were accepted
41% enrolled (1,256)
69% from top tenth of their h.s. class
48% had SAT verbal scores over 600
70% had SAT math scores over 600
67% had ACT scores over 26
9% had SAT verbal scores over 700
24% had SAT math scores over 700
59% had ACT scores over 30
46 National Merit Scholars
78 valedictorians

### THE STUDENT BODY
Total 7,547, of whom 5,359
    are undergraduates
From 50 states and territories,
    47 other countries
66% from Virginia
56% women, 44% men
7% African Americans
1% Native Americans
2% Hispanics
7% Asian Americans
2% international students

### AFTER FRESHMAN YEAR
92% returned for sophomore year

### AFTER GRADUATION
39% pursued further study (15% law, 12%
    arts and sciences, 6% medicine)
163 corporations recruited on campus
1 Fulbright scholar

### WHAT YOU WILL PAY
Resident tuition and fees $4556
Nonresident tuition and fees $13,468
Room and board $4298
30% receive need-based financial aid
    averaging $3353
28% receive non-need financial aid averaging
    $3007

# THE COLLEGE OF WOOSTER

Wooster, Ohio • Small-town setting • Private • Independent-Religious • Coed

▶ Wooster's curriculum provides students the breadth that is to be found in hundreds of course offerings and the depth that comes from 36 majors and programs of study. Small classes and an accessible faculty committed to teaching undergraduates ensure individual attention for every student. A first-year seminar links advising with teaching in a small seminar setting, while senior-year students work one-on-one with a faculty member on an Independent Study Project, a concept that was introduced into Wooster's curriculum almost 50 years ago. Wooster is one of the very few colleges that allow every student this opportunity for independent research and thought.

##  Academics

Wooster offers an interdisciplinary curriculum and core academic program. It awards bachelor's **degrees**. Challenging opportunities include advanced placement, self-designed majors, a senior project, Phi Beta Kappa, and Sigma Xi. Special programs include internships, summer session for credit, and study abroad.

The most popular **majors** include history, English, and chemistry. A complete listing of majors at Wooster appears in the Majors Index beginning on page 380.

The **faculty** at Wooster has 119 full-time teachers, 95% with terminal degrees. 95% of the faculty serve as student advisers. The student-faculty ratio is 12:1.

##  Computers on Campus

Students are not required to have a computer. Student rooms are linked to a campus network. 150 **computers** available in the computer center, computer labs, academic departments, classrooms, the library, dormitories, and student rooms provide access to the main academic computer and e-mail. Staffed computer lab on campus (open 24 hours a day) provides training in the use of computers and software.

The **library** has 650,538 books, 258,478 microform titles, and 1,254 subscriptions.

##  Campus Life

Active **organizations** on campus include drama/theater group and student-run newspaper and radio station. 24% of eligible men and 17% of eligible women are members of 7 local **fraternities**, 5 local **sororities**, and eating clubs, coed fraternity. Student **safety services** include late night transport/escort service.

Wooster is a member of the NCAA (Division III). **Intercollegiate sports** include baseball (m), basketball (m, w), cross-country running (m, w), field hockey (w), football (m), golf (m), ice hockey (m), lacrosse (m, w), soccer (m, w), swimming and diving (m, w), tennis (m, w), track and field (m, w), volleyball (m, w).

##  Applying

Wooster requires an essay, a high school transcript, 2 recommendations, and SAT I or ACT. It recommends 3 years of high school math and science, some high school foreign language, and an interview. Early and deferred entrance are possible, with a 2/15 deadline and a 2/15 priority date for financial aid. **Contact:** Dr. W. A. Hayden Schilling, Dean of Admissions, 1101 North Bever Street, Wooster, OH 44691, 216-263-2270 or toll-free 800-877-9905; fax 216-263-2594.

### GETTING IN LAST YEAR
1,854 applied
90% were accepted
27% enrolled (445)
57% from top tenth of their h.s. class
23% had SAT verbal scores over 600
37% had SAT math scores over 600
52% had ACT scores over 26
2% had SAT verbal scores over 700
8% had SAT math scores over 700
19% had ACT scores over 30
12 National Merit Scholars

### THE STUDENT BODY
1,644 undergraduates
From 45 states and territories,
   48 other countries
41% from Ohio
51% women, 49% men
6% African Americans
1% Native Americans
1% Hispanics
1% Asian Americans
7% international students

### AFTER FRESHMAN YEAR
86% returned for sophomore year
66% got a degree within 4 years

### AFTER GRADUATION
50 corporations, 5 government agencies, 5 nonprofit organizations recruited on campus

### WHAT YOU WILL PAY
Tuition and fees $16,240
Room and board $4690
Need-based financial aid averages $10,000
Non-need financial aid averages $3000

# THE COLORADO COLLEGE

Colorado Springs, Colorado • Suburban setting • Private • Independent • Coed

At Colorado College, students study a liberal arts and sciences curriculum on a distinctive class schedule called the Block Plan. The year is divided into eight 3½-week segments (blocks) in which students take only one course and professors teach only one course during a segment. With no other academic obligations, students devote all their attention and time to one class. They do not have to juggle 4 different homework assignments or rush off to other classes. Courses can take place in environments most suited to learning the subject. Implemented in 1970, the Block Plan emphasizes active participation and "hands-on" learning.

## Academics

CC offers an interdisciplinary curriculum and core academic program. It awards bachelor's and master's **degrees** (master's in education only). Challenging opportunities include advanced placement, self-designed majors, tutorials, an honors program, a senior project, and Phi Beta Kappa. Special programs include internships, summer session for credit, study abroad, and Army ROTC.

The most popular **majors** include English, biology/biological sciences, and economics. A complete listing of majors at CC appears in the Majors Index beginning on page 380.

The **faculty** at CC has 155 full-time undergraduate teachers, 95% with terminal degrees. 100% of the faculty serve as student advisers. The student-faculty ratio is 12:1, and the average class size in required courses is 15.

## Computers on Campus

Students are not required to have a computer. 190 **computers** available in the computer center, computer labs, academic buildings, the library, the student center, and dormitories provide access to the main academic computer, off-campus computing facilities, e-mail, and on-line services. Staffed computer lab on campus (open 24 hours a day) provides training in the use of computers and software.

The **library** has 480,000 books, 20,000 microform titles, and 1,600 subscriptions. It is connected to 1 national **on-line** catalog.

## Campus Life

There are 60 active **organizations** on campus, including a drama/theater group and student-run newspaper and radio station. 20% of eligible men and 20% of eligible women are members of 4 national **fraternities** and 4 national **sororities**. Student **safety services** include whistle program, late night transport/escort service, 24-hour emergency telephone alarm devices, 24-hour patrols by trained security personnel, and electronically operated dormitory entrances.

CC is a member of the NCAA (Division III). **Intercollegiate sports** (some offering scholarships) include basketball (m, w), cross-country running (m, w), field hockey (m, w), football (m), ice hockey (m, w), lacrosse (m, w), rugby (m), soccer (m, w), softball (w), squash (m, w), swimming and diving (m, w), tennis (m, w), track and field (m, w), volleyball (w).

## Applying

CC requires an essay, a high school transcript, 3 recommendations, and SAT I or ACT. It recommends 3 years of high school math and science and some high school foreign language. Early and deferred entrance are possible, with a 1/15 deadline and a 2/15 priority date for financial aid. **Contact:** Mr. Terrance K. Swenson, Dean of Admission and Financial Aid, 14 East Cache La Poudre, Colorado Springs, CO 80903-3294, 719-389-6344 or toll-free 800-542-7214; fax 719-389-6816.

### GETTING IN LAST YEAR

3,265 applied
55% were accepted
30% enrolled (536)
47% from top tenth of their h.s. class
36% had SAT verbal scores over 600
63% had SAT math scores over 600
96% had ACT scores over 26
4% had SAT verbal scores over 700
16% had SAT math scores over 700
71% had ACT scores over 30
11 National Merit Scholars
34 valedictorians

### THE STUDENT BODY

Total 1,933, of whom 1,904
  are undergraduates

From 51 states and territories,
  23 other countries
28% from Colorado
52% women, 48% men
2% African Americans
1% Native Americans
5% Hispanics
4% Asian Americans
2% international students

### AFTER FRESHMAN YEAR

90% returned for sophomore year
70% got a degree within 4 years
79% got a degree within 5 years
80% got a degree within 6 years

### AFTER GRADUATION

30% pursued further study (16% arts and
  sciences, 5% law, 5% medicine)
17 corporations, 1 government agency, 10
  nonprofit organizations recruited on campus

### WHAT YOU WILL PAY

Tuition and fees $17,142
Room and board $4310
50% receive need-based financial aid
  averaging $9000

# COLORADO SCHOOL OF MINES

Golden, Colorado • Small-town setting • Public • State-supported • Coed

▶ CSM is a western school — not a typical college or university located in the West. The social atmosphere is informal and friendly, and the academic atmosphere is competitive but not cutthroat. Founded as a school of mining and geology, today CSM offers much more. From interdisciplinary, nontraditional programs in civil, electrical, and mechanical engineering to economics to environmental chemistry to chemical engineering, CSM students can choose from 14 study areas. Because CSM emphasizes hands-on experience and practical application, students prepare for their careers from their first days as freshmen.

##  Academics

CSM offers an engineering and applied science curriculum and no core academic program; fewer than half of graduate courses are open to undergraduates. It awards bachelor's, master's, and doctoral **degrees**. Challenging opportunities include advanced placement, accelerated degree programs, an honors program, a senior project, and Sigma Xi. Special programs include cooperative education, summer session for credit, study abroad, and Army and Air Force ROTC.

The most popular **majors** include engineering (general), chemical engineering, and computer science. A complete listing of majors at CSM appears in the Majors Index beginning on page 380.

The **faculty** at CSM has 175 full-time undergraduate teachers, 95% with terminal degrees. 90% of the faculty serve as student advisers. The student-faculty ratio is 14:1, and the average class size in required courses is 35.

##  Computers on Campus

Students are not required to have a computer. 250 **computers** available in the computer center, computer labs, the research center, classroom buildings, the library, the student center, and dormitories provide access to the main academic computer, e-mail, and on-line services. Staffed computer lab on campus provides training in the use of computers and software.

The **library** has 356,000 books, 2,000 microform titles, and 2,500 subscriptions.

##  Campus Life

Active **organizations** on campus include drama/theater group and student-run newspaper. 25% of eligible men and 25% of eligible women are members of 7 national **fraternities** and 2 national **sororities**. Student **safety services** include 24-hour emergency telephone alarm devices and 24-hour patrols by trained security personnel.

CSM is a member of the NCAA (Division II). **Intercollegiate sports** (some offering scholarships) include baseball (m), basketball (m, w), cross-country running (m, w), football (m), golf (m, w), lacrosse (m), rugby (m), soccer (m), softball (w), swimming and diving (m, w), tennis (m, w), track and field (m, w), volleyball (w), wrestling (m).

##  Applying

CSM requires a high school transcript, 4 years of high school math, 3 years of high school science, SAT I or ACT, and in some cases recommendations and an interview. It recommends some high school foreign language. Early, deferred, and midyear entrance are possible, with a 6/1 deadline and continuous processing to 3/1 for financial aid. **Contact:** Mr. A. William Young, Director of Enrollment Management, Twin Towers-1811 Elm Street, Golden, CO 80401-1887, 303-273-3220 ext. 3227 or toll-free 800-245-1060 (in-state), 800-446-9488 (out-of-state); fax 303-273-3165.

---

### GETTING IN LAST YEAR
1,515 applied
81% were accepted
39% enrolled (480)
65% from top tenth of their h.s. class
3.75 average high school GPA
12% had SAT verbal scores over 600
80% had SAT math scores over 600
79% had ACT scores over 26
1% had SAT verbal scores over 700
10% had SAT math scores over 700
20% had ACT scores over 30

### THE STUDENT BODY
Total 3,146, of whom 2,207
   are undergraduates
From 51 states and territories,
   69 other countries
69% from Colorado
25% women, 75% men
2% African Americans
1% Native Americans
6% Hispanics
4% Asian Americans
10% international students

### AFTER FRESHMAN YEAR
85% returned for sophomore year

### AFTER GRADUATION
15% pursued further study (8% engineering,
   4% arts and sciences, 1% business)
79% had job offers within 3 months
78 corporations, 1 government agency
   recruited on campus

### WHAT YOU WILL PAY
Resident tuition and fees $4760
Nonresident tuition and fees $13,498
Room and board $4400
70% receive need-based financial aid
   averaging $4500
15% receive non-need financial aid averaging
   $3500

# COLORADO STATE UNIVERSITY

Fort Collins, Colorado • Urban setting • Public • State-supported • Coed

Colorado State's scenic location, at the base of the Rocky Mountain foothills, provides the perfect background for intellectual and personal growth. Students describe the University as providing them with "an academically challenging and rigorous curriculum in a supportive environment," a place where they can feel at ease to be themselves and encouraged to develop their own unique talents. In addition to nearly 100 programs of study, special academic opportunities also include the popular study-abroad program, a challenging honors program, and ROTC. Colorado State students graduate with the confidence that their education will make a difference.

 **Academics**

Colorado State offers an interdisciplinary curriculum and core academic program. It awards bachelor's, master's, doctoral, and first professional **degrees**. Challenging opportunities include advanced placement, accelerated degree programs, self-designed majors, an honors program, a senior project, Phi Beta Kappa, and Sigma Xi. Special programs include cooperative education, internships, summer session for credit, study abroad, and Army and Air Force ROTC.

The most popular **majors** include business, social science, and physical fitness/human movement. A complete listing of majors at Colorado State appears in the Majors Index beginning on page 380.

The **faculty** at Colorado State has 1,001 full-time undergraduate teachers, 87% with terminal degrees. 100% of the faculty serve as student advisers. The student-faculty ratio is 21:1.

 **Computers on Campus**

Students are not required to have a computer. Student rooms are linked to a campus network. 3,500 **computers** available in the computer center, computer labs, the research center, the learning resource center, classrooms, the library, the student center, and dormitories provide access to the main academic computer, off-campus computing facilities, e-mail, and on-line services. Staffed computer lab on campus provides training in the use of computers and software.

The 4 **libraries** have 1.8 million books, 1.6 million microform titles, and 20,000 subscriptions.

 **Campus Life**

There are 300 active **organizations** on campus, including a drama/theater group and student-run newspaper and radio station. 14% of eligible men and 14% of eligible women are members of 22 national **fraternities** and 14 national **sororities**. Student **safety services** include late night transport/escort service, 24-hour emergency telephone alarm devices, 24-hour patrols by trained security personnel, student patrols, and electronically operated dormitory entrances.

Colorado State is a member of the NCAA (Division I). **Intercollegiate sports** (some offering scholarships) include basketball (m, w), cross-country running (m, w), football (m), golf (m, w), softball (w), swimming and diving (w), tennis (m, w), track and field (m, w), volleyball (w).

 **Applying**

Colorado State requires a high school transcript, 3 years of high school math and science, 4 years of high school English, and SAT I or ACT. It recommends an essay, 2 years of high school foreign language, recommendations, and an interview. Deferred and midyear entrance are possible, with a 7/1 deadline and continuous processing to 3/1 for financial aid. **Contact:** Ms. Mary Ontiveros, Director of Admissions, Administration Building, Fort Collins, CO 80523, 970-491-6909; fax 970-491-7799.

**GETTING IN LAST YEAR**
8,478 applied
73% were accepted
37% enrolled (2,295)
27% from top tenth of their h.s. class
3.47 average high school GPA
9% had SAT verbal scores over 600
28% had SAT math scores over 600
37% had ACT scores over 26
0% had SAT verbal scores over 700
4% had SAT math scores over 700
7% had ACT scores over 30

**THE STUDENT BODY**
Total 21,461, of whom 17,800 are undergraduates

From 56 states and territories, 51 other countries
75% from Colorado
50% women, 50% men
2% African Americans
1% Native Americans
5% Hispanics
3% Asian Americans
1% international students

**AFTER FRESHMAN YEAR**
81% returned for sophomore year
20% got a degree within 4 years
28% got a degree within 5 years

**AFTER GRADUATION**
150 corporations, 10 government agencies, 1 nonprofit organization recruited on campus

**WHAT YOU WILL PAY**
Resident tuition and fees $2709
Nonresident tuition and fees $8997
Room and board $4180
52% receive need-based financial aid averaging $825
22% receive non-need financial aid averaging $1012

# COLORADO TECHNICAL COLLEGE

Colorado Springs, Colorado • Suburban setting • Private • Proprietary • Coed

Colorado Tech's mission is to provide a superior, college-level, career-oriented education. By teaching real-world, state-of-the-practice programs in selected technical fields, Colorado Tech serves the needs of students for employment and advancement in industry and the needs of industry for highly qualified, technically oriented professionals at the associate, bachelor's, master's, and doctoral levels.

## Academics

Colorado Tech offers a core academic program. It awards associate, bachelor's, master's, and doctoral **degrees**. Challenging opportunities include advanced placement, accelerated degree programs, tutorials, an honors program, and a senior project. Special programs include cooperative education, internships, summer session for credit, study abroad, and Army ROTC.

The most popular **majors** include electronics engineering technology, computer science, and electrical engineering. A complete listing of majors at Colorado Tech appears in the Majors Index beginning on page 380.

The **faculty** at Colorado Tech has 32 full-time graduate and undergraduate teachers, 47% with terminal degrees. 22% of the faculty serve as student advisers. The student-faculty ratio is 13:1, and the average class size in required courses is 22.

## Computers on Campus

Students are not required to have a computer. 117 **computers** available in computer labs, the library, and the student center. Staffed computer lab on campus provides training in the use of computers and software.

The **library** has 12,300 books, 30 microform titles, and 331 subscriptions. It is connected to 8 national **on-line** catalogs.

## Campus Life

There are 6 active **organizations** on campus, including a drama/theater group. Student **safety services** include 24-hour emergency telephone alarm devices.

This institution has no intercollegiate sports.

## Applying

Colorado Tech requires SAT I or ACT, and in some cases an essay, a high school transcript, 2 recommendations, and ASSET tests in English and math. It recommends 3 years of high school math and science, an interview, and a minimum high school GPA of 3.0. Deferred and midyear entrance are possible, with rolling admissions and continuous processing to 10/1 for financial aid. **Contact:** Mr. John Richardson, Undergraduate Admissions Advisor/Mentor, 4435 North Chestnut Street, Colorado Springs, CO 80907-3896, 719-598-0200; fax 719-598-3740.

---

### GETTING IN LAST YEAR
217 applied
92% were accepted
85% enrolled (170)
42% from top tenth of their h.s. class
3.45 average high school GPA
35% had SAT verbal scores over 600
27% had SAT math scores over 600
50% had ACT scores over 26
5% had SAT verbal scores over 700
2% had SAT math scores over 700
10% had ACT scores over 30

### THE STUDENT BODY
Total 1,413, of whom 1,026
   are undergraduates
98% from Colorado
18% women, 82% men
6% African Americans
1% Native Americans
5% Hispanics
3% Asian Americans
2% international students

### AFTER FRESHMAN YEAR
42% returned for sophomore year

### AFTER GRADUATION
5% pursued further study (3% business, 2% engineering)
50 corporations, 10 government agencies recruited on campus

### WHAT YOU WILL PAY
Tuition and fees $5985
40% receive need-based financial aid averaging $4000
60% receive non-need financial aid averaging $2000

# COLUMBIA COLLEGE

New York, New York • Urban setting • Private • Independent • Coed

Located in the world's most international city, Columbia College, Columbia University's undergraduate liberal arts school, offers to a diverse student body a broad and solid foundation coupled with more advanced study in specific departments. More than 50 majors and interdisciplinary studies are available, and joint-degree programs take full advantage of the University's graduate and professional schools. The pace and excitement of New York color all aspects of life on campus, but students nevertheless feel a part of a small college community; the College is the Ivy League's smallest liberal arts school.

## Academics

Columbia offers a Western civilization curriculum and core academic program; fewer than half of graduate courses are open to undergraduates. It awards bachelor's **degrees**. Challenging opportunities include advanced placement, self-designed majors, an honors program, a senior project, and Phi Beta Kappa. Special programs include summer session for credit, off-campus study, and study abroad.

The most popular **majors** include English, history, and political science/government. A complete listing of majors at Columbia appears in the Majors Index beginning on page 380.

The **faculty** at Columbia has 521 full-time teachers, 99% with terminal degrees. The student-faculty ratio is 7:1, and the average class size in required courses is 25.

## Computers on Campus

Students are not required to have a computer. Student rooms are linked to a campus network. 400 **computers** available in the computer center, the library, and dormitories provide access to the main academic computer, e-mail, and on-line services. Staffed computer lab on campus provides training in the use of computers and software.

The 21 **libraries** have 6 million books, 4 million microform titles, and 59,000 subscriptions.

## Campus Life

Active **organizations** on campus include drama/theater group and student-run newspaper and radio station. 18% of eligible men and 8% of eligible women are members of 12 national **fraternities** and 7 national **sororities**. Student **safety services** include 24-hour ID check at door, late night transport/escort service, 24-hour emergency telephone alarm devices, and 24-hour patrols by trained security personnel.

Columbia is a member of the NCAA (Division I). **Intercollegiate sports** include archery (m, w), badminton (m, w), baseball (m), basketball (m, w), crew (m, w), cross-country running (m, w), equestrian sports (m, w), fencing (m, w), field hockey (w), football (m), golf (m), ice hockey (m), lacrosse (m, w), racquetball (m, w), riflery (m, w), rugby (m, w), sailing (m, w), skiing (cross-country) (m, w), soccer (m, w), softball (w), squash (m), swimming and diving (m, w), table tennis (m, w), tennis (m, w), track and field (m, w), volleyball (m, w), water polo (m), weight lifting (m), wrestling (m).

## Applying

Columbia requires an essay, a high school transcript, 2 recommendations, SAT I or ACT, and 3 SAT II Subject Tests (including SAT II: Writing Test). It recommends 3 years of high school math and science, 3 years of high school foreign language, and an interview. Early and deferred entrance are possible, with a 1/1 deadline and 2/1 for financial aid. **Contact:** Ms. Drusilla Blackman, Dean of Undergraduate Admissions and Financial Aid, 212 Hamilton Hall, New York, NY 10027, 212-854-2522; fax 212-854-1209.

---

**GETTING IN LAST YEAR**
7,860 applied
25% were accepted
45% enrolled (872)
76% from top tenth of their h.s. class

**THE STUDENT BODY**
3,518 undergraduates
From 52 states and territories,
   36 other countries
19% from New York
49% women, 51% men

9% African Americans
1% Native Americans
9% Hispanics
20% Asian Americans
5% international students

**AFTER FRESHMAN YEAR**
96% returned for sophomore year
80% got a degree within 4 years
90% got a degree within 6 years

**AFTER GRADUATION**
312 corporations, 15 government agencies,
   24 nonprofit organizations recruited on
   campus

**WHAT YOU WILL PAY**
Tuition and fees $19,068
Room and board $6664
53% receive need-based financial aid
   averaging $10,852

# COLUMBIA UNIVERSITY, SCHOOL OF ENGINEERING AND APPLIED SCIENCE

New York, New York • Urban setting • Private • Independent • Coed

Located in the world's most international city, Columbia University's undergraduate School of Engineering and Applied Science (SEAS) offers to a diverse student body a solid and basic foundation coupled with more advanced study in specific departments; 17 engineering disciplines are offered, and joint-degree programs take full advantage of the University's other divisions, both undergraduate and graduate. The pace and excitement of New York color all aspects of life on campus, but, with under 1,000 undergraduates in SEAS, students feel part of a small-college community. Housing is guaranteed for 4 years.

## Academics

Columbia SEAS offers a core academic program. It awards bachelor's, master's, and doctoral **degrees**. Challenging opportunities include advanced placement, accelerated degree programs, tutorials, and an honors program. Special programs include internships, summer session for credit, and study abroad.

The most popular **majors** include computer science, electrical engineering, and mechanical engineering. A complete listing of majors at Columbia SEAS appears in the Majors Index beginning on page 380.

The **faculty** at Columbia SEAS has 93 full-time undergraduate teachers, 100% with terminal degrees. The average class size in required courses is 30.

## Computers on Campus

Students are not required to have a computer. Student rooms are linked to a campus network. 400 **computers** available in the computer center, computer labs, engineering departments, the library, and dormitories provide access to the main academic computer, e-mail, and on-line services.

Staffed computer lab on campus provides training in the use of computers and software.

The 21 **libraries** have 6 million books, 4 million microform titles, and 59,000 subscriptions.

## Campus Life

Active **organizations** on campus include drama/theater group and student-run newspaper and radio station. 7% of eligible men and 2% of eligible women are members of 12 national **fraternities**, 7 national **sororities**, 6 local fraternities, 2 local sororities, and 6 coed social clubs. Student **safety services** include 24-hour ID check at door, late night transport/escort service, 24-hour emergency telephone alarm devices, and 24-hour patrols by trained security personnel.

Columbia SEAS is a member of the NCAA (Division I). **Intercollegiate sports** include archery (m, w), baseball (m), basketball (m, w), crew (m, w), cross-country running (m, w), fencing (m, w), field hockey (w), football (m), golf (m), racquetball (m, w), soccer (m, w), swimming and diving (m, w), tennis (m, w), track and field (m, w), volleyball (w), water polo (m), weight lifting (m), wrestling (m).

## Applying

Columbia SEAS requires an essay, a high school transcript, 4 years of high school math, 3 years of high school science, 2 recommendations, SAT I or ACT, and 3 SAT II Subject Tests (including SAT II: Writing Test). It recommends 2 years of high school foreign language and an interview. Early and deferred entrance are possible, with a 1/1 deadline and 2/1 for financial aid. **Contact:** Ms. Drusilla Blackman, Dean of Undergraduate Admissions and Financial Aid, 212 Hamilton Hall, New York, NY 10027, 212-854-2522; fax 212-854-1209.

### GETTING IN LAST YEAR
1,384 applied
48% were accepted
40% enrolled (268)
70% from top tenth of their h.s. class

### THE STUDENT BODY
996 undergraduates
From 38 states and territories,
  23 other countries
42% from New York

19% women, 81% men
4% African Americans
0% Native Americans
5% Hispanics
46% Asian Americans
11% international students

### AFTER FRESHMAN YEAR
89% returned for sophomore year
84% got a degree within 4 years

### AFTER GRADUATION
41% pursued further study
312 corporations, 15 government agencies,
  24 nonprofit organizations recruited on
  campus

### WHAT YOU WILL PAY
Tuition and fees $19,025
Room and board $7000
60% receive need-based financial aid
  averaging $7994

# CONCORDIA COLLEGE

Moorhead, Minnesota • Suburban setting • Private • Independent-Religious • Coed

The academic program is distinguished by its blending of liberal arts and career preparation. Both on-campus academic offerings and an extensive off-campus cooperative education program aid students in meeting career goals. The campus community is best known for its friendliness and warmth, exhibited by mutual respect between students and faculty. One of the largest colleges in the Midwest, Concordia may also be one of the "Best Buys." As a result of extraordinary donor support, the College has a reputation for outstanding faculty and strong academic programs yet has maintained a tuition rate several thousand dollars below comparable colleges.

 **Academics**

Concordia College offers a liberal arts/career preparation curriculum and core academic program. It awards bachelor's **degrees**. Challenging opportunities include advanced placement, tutorials, Freshmen Honors College, an honors program, and a senior project. Special programs include cooperative education, internships, summer session for credit, off-campus study, study abroad, and Army and Air Force ROTC.

The most popular **majors** include business, communication, and elementary education. A complete listing of majors at Concordia College appears in the Majors Index beginning on page 380.

The **faculty** at Concordia College has 200 full-time teachers, 68% with terminal degrees. The student-faculty ratio is 15:1, and the average class size in required courses is 22.

 **Computers on Campus**

Students are not required to have a computer. 106 **computers** available in computer labs, classrooms, the library,

and dormitories provide access to the main academic computer, off-campus computing facilities, e-mail, and on-line services. Staffed computer lab on campus provides training in the use of computers and software.

The **library** has 270,031 books, 34,648 microform titles, and 1,500 subscriptions.

 **Campus Life**

There are 30 active **organizations** on campus, including a drama/theater group and student-run newspaper and radio station. 40% of students participate in student government elections. 5% of eligible men and 5% of eligible women are members of 3 local **fraternities** and 3 local **sororities**. Student **safety services** include late night transport/ escort service, 24-hour patrols by trained security personnel, and student patrols.

Concordia College is a member of the NCAA (Division III). **Intercollegiate sports** include baseball (m), basketball (m, w), cross-country running (m, w), football (m), golf (m, w), ice hockey (m), soccer (m, w), softball (w), tennis (m, w), track and field (m, w), volleyball (w), wrestling (m).

 **Applying**

Concordia College requires a high school transcript, 2 recommendations, and SAT I or ACT. It recommends 3 years of high school math and science, 2 years of high school foreign language, and an interview. Early, deferred, and midyear entrance are possible, with rolling admissions and continuous processing for financial aid. **Contact:** Mr. Lee E. Johnson, Director of Admissions, 901 8th Street South, Moorhead, MN 56562, 218-299-3004; fax 218-299-3947.

---

**GETTING IN LAST YEAR**

2,110 applied
86% were accepted
45% enrolled (821)
28% from top tenth of their h.s. class
15% had SAT verbal scores over 600
32% had SAT math scores over 600
32% had ACT scores over 26
0% had SAT verbal scores over 700
9% had SAT math scores over 700
8% had ACT scores over 30
8 National Merit Scholars

**THE STUDENT BODY**

2,970 undergraduates
From 38 states and territories,
   33 other countries
62% from Minnesota
60% women, 40% men
1% African Americans
1% Native Americans
1% Hispanics
2% Asian Americans
4% international students

**AFTER FRESHMAN YEAR**

76% returned for sophomore year
61% got a degree within 4 years
66% got a degree within 5 years

**AFTER GRADUATION**

20% pursued further study (8% arts and
   sciences, 4% medicine, 2% business)
35 corporations recruited on campus
2 Fulbright scholars

**WHAT YOU WILL PAY**

Tuition and fees $10,720
Room and board $3280
72% receive need-based financial aid
   averaging $3095

# CONNECTICUT COLLEGE

New London, Connecticut • Suburban setting • Private • Independent • Coed

A traditionally high level of meaningful student involvement in College decision-making, coupled with a student-run honor code, enhance the development of responsibility and community interdependence. The Center for International Studies and the Liberal Arts provides powerful preparation for global understanding and leadership. The new science, athletic, and student centers add to the already superb facilities available for both intellectual and personal growth. The Centers for Arts and Technology and Conservation Biology and Environmental Studies, paid science internships, and the Freshman Focus integrated studies program are representative of the many innovations of a faculty dedicated to preparing students for the new world order of the 21st century.

##  Academics

Connecticut offers a core academic program. It awards bachelor's and master's **degrees**. Challenging opportunities include advanced placement, accelerated degree programs, self-designed majors, tutorials, an honors program, a senior project, and Phi Beta Kappa. Special programs include internships, summer session for credit, off-campus study, and study abroad.

The most popular **majors** include history, political science/government, and English. A complete listing of majors at Connecticut appears in the Majors Index beginning on page 380.

The **faculty** at Connecticut has 156 full-time undergraduate teachers, 94% with terminal degrees. 100% of the faculty serve as student advisers. The student-faculty ratio is 11:1, and the average class size in required courses is 17.

##  Computers on Campus

Students are not required to have a computer. Student rooms are linked to a campus network. 145 **computers** available in the computer center, computer labs, science building, art, dance and music studio, Winthrop Annex, and the library provide access to off-campus computing facilities, e-mail, and on-line services. Staffed computer lab on campus (open 24 hours a day) provides training in the use of computers and software.

The 2 **libraries** have 456,706 books, 259,101 microform titles, and 2,161 subscriptions.

##  Campus Life

There are 75 active **organizations** on campus, including a drama/theater group and student-run newspaper and radio station. Student **safety services** include late night transport/escort service, 24-hour emergency telephone alarm devices, 24-hour patrols by trained security personnel, and electronically operated dormitory entrances.

Connecticut is a member of the NCAA (Division III). **Intercollegiate sports** include basketball (m, w), crew (m, w), cross-country running (m, w), equestrian sports (m, w), fencing (m, w), field hockey (w), golf (m, w), ice hockey (m, w), lacrosse (m, w), rugby (m, w), sailing (m, w), skiing (downhill) (m, w), soccer (m, w), squash (m, w), swimming and diving (m, w), tennis (m, w), track and field (m, w), volleyball (w).

##  Applying

Connecticut requires an essay, a high school transcript, 2 recommendations, ACT, and 3 SAT II Subject Tests (including SAT II: Writing Test). It recommends 3 years of high school math and science, 3 years of high school foreign language, and an interview. Early and deferred entrance are possible, with a 1/15 deadline and a 2/1 priority date for financial aid. **Contact:** Ms. Claire K. Matthews, Dean of Admissions and Planning, 270 Mohegan Avenue, New London, CT 06320-4196, 203-439-2200; fax 203-439-4301.

### GETTING IN LAST YEAR
3,100 applied
49% were accepted
30% enrolled (455)
42% from top tenth of their h.s. class

### THE STUDENT BODY
Total 1,919, of whom 1,604
   are undergraduates
From 45 states and territories,
   48 other countries
29% from Connecticut
57% women, 43% men

4% African Americans
1% Native Americans
2% Hispanics
2% Asian Americans
11% international students

### AFTER FRESHMAN YEAR
91% returned for sophomore year
87% got a degree within 4 years
88% got a degree within 5 years

### AFTER GRADUATION
22% pursued further study (13% arts and
   sciences, 4% law, 3% medicine)
93 corporations, 3 government agencies, 43
   nonprofit organizations recruited on campus

### WHAT YOU WILL PAY
Tuition and fees $18,950
Room and board $6300
54% receive need-based financial aid
   averaging $12,498

# COOPER UNION FOR THE ADVANCEMENT OF SCIENCE AND ART

New York, New York • Urban setting • Private • Independent • Coed

> Each of Cooper Union's schools—Art, Architecture, Engineering—adheres strongly to preparation for its profession within a design-centered, problem-solving philosophy of education in a tuition-free environment. A rigorous curriculum and group projects reinforce this unique atmosphere in higher education and are factors in *Money* magazine's decision to name Cooper Union "In a Class by Itself."

##  Academics

Cooper Union offers a world civilization and English literature curriculum and core academic program; all graduate courses are open to undergraduates. It awards bachelor's and master's **degrees**. Challenging opportunities include advanced placement, self-designed majors, tutorials, an honors program, and a senior project. Special programs include internships, summer session for credit, and off-campus study.

The most popular **majors** include art/fine arts, architecture, and electrical engineering. A complete listing of majors at Cooper Union appears in the Majors Index beginning on page 380.

The **faculty** at Cooper Union has 60 full-time graduate and undergraduate teachers, 40% with terminal degrees. 100% of the faculty serve as student advisers. The student-faculty ratio is 7:1, and the average class size in required courses is 19.

##  Computers on Campus

Students are not required to have a computer. 160 **computers** available in the computer center, computer labs, the research center, the learning resource center, the library, and dormitories provide access to the main academic computer, off-campus computing facilities, e-mail, and on-line services. Staffed computer lab on campus provides training in the use of computers and software.

The **library** has 97,000 books, 4,700 microform titles, and 370 subscriptions.

##  Campus Life

There are 20 active **organizations** on campus, including a drama/theater group and student-run newspaper. 53% of students participate in student government elections. 30% of eligible men and 20% of eligible women are members of 3 national **fraternities** and 2 national **sororities**. Student **safety services** include 24-hour emergency telephone alarm devices, 24-hour patrols by trained security personnel, and electronically operated dormitory entrances. **Intercollegiate sports** include basketball (m), tennis (m, w).

##  Applying

Cooper Union requires a high school transcript, SAT I or ACT, a minimum high school GPA of 2.0, and in some cases an essay, 3 years of high school math and science, 3 recommendations, portfolio, home test, and 2 SAT II Subject Tests. It recommends a minimum high school GPA of 3.0. Early and deferred entrance are possible, with 4/15 for financial aid. **Contact:** Mr. Richard Bory, Dean of Admissions and Records, 30 Cooper Square, New York, NY 10003-7120, 212-353-4120; fax 212-353-4343.

---

**GETTING IN LAST YEAR**
2,304 applied
13% were accepted
65% enrolled (199)
80% from top tenth of their h.s. class
3.2 average high school GPA

**THE STUDENT BODY**
Total 1,064, of whom 960
 are undergraduates
From 37 states and territories,
 12 other countries
67% from New York

35% women, 65% men
7% African Americans
1% Native Americans
8% Hispanics
26% Asian Americans
9% international students

**AFTER FRESHMAN YEAR**
88% returned for sophomore year
55% got a degree within 4 years
73% got a degree within 5 years

**AFTER GRADUATION**
55% pursued further study (40% engineering,
 6% law, 5% arts and sciences)
70% had job offers within 3 months
30 corporations, 4 government agencies
 recruited on campus
1 Fulbright scholar

**WHAT YOU WILL PAY**
Tuition and fees $400
Room only $4900
43% receive need-based financial aid
 averaging $2470

# CORNELL COLLEGE

Mount Vernon, Iowa • Small-town setting • Private • Independent-Religious • Coed

Since its founding in 1853, Cornell College has maintained a strong commitment to excellence in the liberal arts. Nearly 2 decades ago, the College adopted a distinctive and innovative academic calendar called One-Course-At-A-Time, which divides the traditional academic year into 9 terms, each three and a half weeks long, with a 4-day break between terms. More than 50 courses are available to students each term. Cornell's experience with single-course study now indicates that it can maximize the effect of a liberal arts education by allowing students and professors to focus their efforts exclusively on each course.

 **Academics**

Cornell offers no core academic program. It awards bachelor's **degrees**. Challenging opportunities include advanced placement, accelerated degree programs, self-designed majors, tutorials, a senior project, and Phi Beta Kappa. Special programs include internships, off-campus study, and study abroad.

The most popular **majors** include business economics, English, and history. A complete listing of majors at Cornell appears in the Majors Index beginning on page 380.

The **faculty** at Cornell has 76 full-time teachers, 80% with terminal degrees. 100% of the faculty serve as student advisers. The student-faculty ratio is 13:1, and the average class size in required courses is 16.

 **Computers on Campus**

Students are not required to have a computer. 175 **computers** available in the computer center, computer labs, classroom buildings, the library, the student center, and dormitories.

The 2 **libraries** have 181,500 books, 615 microform titles, and 600 subscriptions.

 **Campus Life**

There are 71 active **organizations** on campus, including a drama/theater group and student-run newspaper and radio station. 35% of eligible men and 35% of eligible women are members of 7 local **fraternities**, 6 local **sororities**, and 1 coed fraternity. Student **safety services** include late night transport/escort service, 24-hour emergency telephone alarm devices, and 24-hour patrols by trained security personnel.

Cornell is a member of the NCAA (Division III). **Intercollegiate sports** include baseball (m), basketball (m, w), cross-country running (m, w), football (m), golf (m), ice hockey (m), soccer (m, w), softball (w), swimming and diving (m, w), tennis (m, w), track and field (m, w), volleyball (m, w), wrestling (m).

 **Applying**

Cornell requires an essay, a high school transcript, 1 recommendation, and SAT I or ACT. It recommends 3 years of high school math and science, some high school foreign language, and an interview. Early, deferred, and midyear entrance are possible, with a 3/1 deadline and continuous processing to 3/1 for financial aid. **Contact:** Mr. Kevin Crockett, Dean of Admissions and Enrollment Management, 600 First Street West, Mount Vernon, IA 52314-1098, 319-895-4477 or toll-free 800-747-1112 (out-of-state); fax 319-895-4451.

## GETTING IN LAST YEAR
1,436 applied
93% were accepted
27% enrolled (355)
34% from top tenth of their h.s. class
3.43 average high school GPA
27% had SAT verbal scores over 600
40% had SAT math scores over 600
53% had ACT scores over 26
3% had SAT verbal scores over 700
7% had SAT math scores over 700
13% had ACT scores over 30

## THE STUDENT BODY
1,133 undergraduates
From 44 states and territories,
 15 other countries
28% from Iowa
58% women, 42% men
3% African Americans
1% Native Americans
2% Hispanics
3% Asian Americans
2% international students

## AFTER FRESHMAN YEAR
72% returned for sophomore year
65% got a degree within 4 years

## AFTER GRADUATION
35% pursued further study
7 corporations, 8 government agencies, 16 nonprofit organizations recruited on campus

## WHAT YOU WILL PAY
Tuition and fees $15,373
Room and board $4323
Need-based financial aid averages $7659

# CORNELL UNIVERSITY

Ithaca, New York • Small-town setting • Private • Independent • Coed

Ezra Cornell created a university that offered instruction to all who were qualified, regardless of race or gender; welcomed rich and poor; and encouraged students to choose their own programs. Cornell is still a place where a wide variety of students engage in discovery in a curriculum that is unequaled in interdisciplinary breadth.

##  Academics

Cornell offers no core academic program; fewer than half of graduate courses are open to undergraduates. It awards bachelor's, master's, doctoral, and first professional **degrees**. Challenging opportunities include advanced placement, self-designed majors, tutorials, an honors program, a senior project, Phi Beta Kappa, and Sigma Xi. Special programs include cooperative education, internships, summer session for credit, off-campus study, study abroad, and Army, Naval, and Air Force ROTC.

The most popular **majors** include biology/biological sciences, economics, and political science/government. A complete listing of majors at Cornell appears in the Majors Index beginning on page 380.

The **faculty** at Cornell has 1,520 full-time graduate and undergraduate teachers, 96% with terminal degrees. The student-faculty ratio is 8:1, and the average class size in required courses is 55.

##  Computers on Campus

Students are not required to have a computer. Student rooms are linked to a campus network. **Computers** available in various locations on campus provide access to the main academic computer, off-campus computing facilities, e-mail, and on-line services. Staffed computer lab on campus provides training in the use of computers and software.

The 16 **libraries** have 5.7 million books and 62,332 subscriptions. They are connected to 2 national **on-line** catalogs.

##  Campus Life

There are 400 active **organizations** on campus, including a drama/theater group and student-run newspaper and radio station. 25% of students participate in student government elections. 34% of eligible men and 32% of eligible women are members of 46 national **fraternities**, 16 national **sororities**, 1 local fraternity, and 2 local sororities. Student **safety services** include late night transport/escort service, 24-hour emergency telephone alarm devices, 24-hour patrols by trained security personnel, and electronically operated dormitory entrances.

Cornell is a member of the NCAA (Division I). **Intercollegiate sports** include baseball (m), basketball (m, w), bowling (m, w), crew (m, w), cross-country running (m, w), equestrian sports (m, w), fencing (w), field hockey (w), football (m), golf (m), gymnastics (w), ice hockey (m, w), lacrosse (m, w), riflery (m, w), sailing (m, w), skiing (cross-country) (m, w), skiing (downhill) (m, w), soccer (m, w), softball (w), squash (m, w), swimming and diving (m, w), table tennis (m, w), tennis (m, w), track and field (m, w), volleyball (m, w), water polo (m, w), wrestling (m).

##  Applying

Cornell requires an essay, a high school transcript, 3 years of high school math, 1 recommendation, SAT I or ACT, and in some cases 3 years of high school science, 3 years of high school foreign language, a campus interview, and SAT II: Writing Test. Early, deferred, and midyear entrance are possible, with a 1/1 deadline and a 2/15 priority date for financial aid. **Contact:** Ms. Nancy Meislahn, Director of Admissions, 410 Thurston Avenue, Ithaca, NY 14850, 607-255-5241; fax 607-255-0659.

---

### GETTING IN LAST YEAR
20,076 applied
33% were accepted
47% enrolled (3,103)
83% from top tenth of their h.s. class
53% had SAT verbal scores over 600
87% had SAT math scores over 600
9% had SAT verbal scores over 700
47% had SAT math scores over 700
53 National Merit Scholars

### THE STUDENT BODY
Total 18,811, of whom 13,228
   are undergraduates
From 56 states and territories,
   78 other countries

43% from New York
47% women, 53% men
4% African Americans
1% Native Americans
6% Hispanics
16% Asian Americans
6% international students

### AFTER FRESHMAN YEAR
95% returned for sophomore year
82% got a degree within 4 years
90% got a degree within 5 years
93% got a degree within 6 years

### AFTER GRADUATION
32% pursued further study (13% arts and
   sciences, 8% medicine, 6% law)
450 corporations, 25 government agencies,
   25 nonprofit organizations recruited on
   campus
1 Marshall, 7 Fulbright scholars

### WHAT YOU WILL PAY
Tuition and fees $19,066
Room and board $6238
48% receive need-based financial aid
   averaging $9240

# CREIGHTON UNIVERSITY

Omaha, Nebraska • Urban setting • Private • Independent-Religious • Coed

> With the revitalization of its scholarship program, Creighton provides even greater support for qualified students to attend. A high percentage of incoming students are working toward acceptance into Creighton's professional schools of medicine, dentistry, pharmacy, or law or into professional programs of occupational and physical therapy. Creighton students receive admission preference in these programs.

##  Academics

Creighton offers a values-centered, globalized curriculum and core academic program; a few graduate courses are open to undergraduates. It awards associate, bachelor's, master's, doctoral, and first professional **degrees**. Challenging opportunities include advanced placement, accelerated degree programs, tutorials, an honors program, and a senior project. Special programs include internships, summer session for credit, study abroad, and Army and Air Force ROTC.

The most popular **majors** include finance/banking, psychology, and biology/biological sciences. A complete listing of majors at Creighton appears in the Majors Index beginning on page 380.

The **faculty** at Creighton has 640 full-time graduate and undergraduate teachers, 88% with terminal degrees. 80% of the faculty serve as student advisers. The student-faculty ratio is 14:1, and the average class size in required courses is 35.

##  Computers on Campus

Students are not required to have a computer. Student rooms are linked to a campus network. 250 **computers** available in the computer center, College of Business Administration computer center, English composition lab, academic buildings, the library, and dormitories. Staffed computer lab on campus provides training in the use of computers and software.

The 3 **libraries** have 713,250 books, 287,561 microform titles, and 9,859 subscriptions. They are connected to 10 national **on-line** catalogs.

##  Campus Life

There are 100 active **organizations** on campus, including a drama/theater group and student-run newspaper. 31% of eligible men and 29% of eligible women are members of 7 national **fraternities** and 6 national **sororities**. Student **safety services** include late night transport/escort service, 24-hour emergency telephone alarm devices, 24-hour patrols by trained security personnel, student patrols, and electronically operated dormitory entrances.

Creighton is a member of the NCAA (Division I). **Intercollegiate sports** (some offering scholarships) include baseball (m), basketball (m, w), crew (m, w), cross-country running (m, w), fencing (m, w), golf (m, w), ice hockey (m), lacrosse (m), rugby (m), sailing (m, w), soccer (m, w), softball (w), swimming and diving (m, w), tennis (m, w), volleyball (w).

##  Applying

Creighton requires a high school transcript, 1 recommendation, SAT I or ACT, and a minimum high school GPA of 2.0. It recommends 3 years of high school math and science and some high school foreign language. Deferred and midyear entrance are possible, with rolling admissions and continuous processing to 4/1 for financial aid. **Contact:** Mr. Howard J. Bachman, Assistant Vice President for Enrollment Management, 2500 California Plaza, Omaha, NE 68178-0001, 402-280-2703; fax 402-280-2685.

---

### GETTING IN LAST YEAR

3,308 applied
91% were accepted
27% enrolled (824)
29% from top tenth of their h.s. class
3.30 average high school GPA
40% had ACT scores over 26
10% had ACT scores over 30

### THE STUDENT BODY

Total 6,341, of whom 4,094
   are undergraduates
From 45 states and territories,
   48 other countries
36% from Nebraska

53% women, 47% men
3% African Americans
1% Native Americans
3% Hispanics
5% Asian Americans
3% international students

### AFTER FRESHMAN YEAR

81% returned for sophomore year
57% got a degree within 4 years
64% got a degree within 5 years
66% got a degree within 6 years

### AFTER GRADUATION

41% pursued further study (10% law, 10% medicine, 7% arts and sciences)
75% had job offers within 3 months
99 corporations, 5 government agencies, 5 nonprofit organizations recruited on campus
1 Fulbright scholar

### WHAT YOU WILL PAY

Tuition and fees $10,964
Room and board $4372
53% receive need-based financial aid averaging $1795
33% receive non-need financial aid averaging $3450

# DARTMOUTH COLLEGE

Hanover, New Hampshire • Rural setting • Private • Independent • Coed

> Dartmouth's blending of university resources with a college's focus on undergraduate education offers small classes, outstanding research facilities, and remarkable opportunities for collaboration between faculty and students. A wide range of resources support a variety of academic, social, cultural, and extracurricular pursuits on the campus. All of this takes place within a small community that is almost entirely devoted to education.

##  Academics

Dartmouth offers an interdisciplinary curriculum and core academic program; more than half of graduate courses are open to undergraduates. It awards bachelor's, master's, and doctoral **degrees**. Challenging opportunities include advanced placement, accelerated degree programs, self-designed majors, tutorials, an honors program, a senior project, Phi Beta Kappa, and Sigma Xi. Special programs include internships, summer session for credit, off-campus study, study abroad, and Army ROTC.

The most popular **majors** include political science/government, history, and engineering (general). A complete listing of majors at Dartmouth appears in the Majors Index beginning on page 380.

The **faculty** at Dartmouth has 334 full-time undergraduate teachers, 98% with terminal degrees. 75% of the faculty serve as student advisers. The student-faculty ratio is 11:1.

##  Computers on Campus

Students are required to have a computer. Purchase options are available. Student rooms are linked to a campus network. 6,000 **computers** available in the computer center, computer labs, the research center, the learning resource center, academic departments, classrooms, the library, the student center, dormitories, and student rooms. Staffed computer lab on campus (open 24 hours a day) provides training in the use of computers and software.

The 8 **libraries** have 2 million books, 1.6 million microform titles, and 19,000 subscriptions.

##  Campus Life

There are 290 active **organizations** on campus, including a drama/theater group and student-run newspaper and radio station. 45% of eligible men and 40% of eligible women are members of 9 national **fraternities**, 3 national **sororities**, 8 local fraternities, 5 local sororities, and 4 coed fraternities. Student **safety services** include late night transport/escort service, 24-hour emergency telephone alarm devices, 24-hour patrols by trained security personnel, and student patrols.

Dartmouth is a member of the NCAA (Division I). **Intercollegiate sports** include baseball (m), basketball (m, w), crew (m, w), cross-country running (m, w), equestrian sports (m, w), fencing (m, w), field hockey (w), football (m), golf (m, w), gymnastics (m), ice hockey (m, w), lacrosse (m, w), riflery (m, w), rugby (m, w), sailing (m, w), skiing (cross-country) (m, w), skiing (downhill) (m, w), soccer (m, w), softball (w), squash (m, w), swimming and diving (m, w), tennis (m, w), track and field (m, w), volleyball (m, w), water polo (m, w), wrestling (m).

##  Applying

Dartmouth requires an essay, a high school transcript, SAT I or ACT, and 3 SAT II Subject Tests. It recommends 3 years of high school math and science, some high school foreign language, and an interview. Early and deferred entrance are possible, with a 1/1 deadline and 2/1 for financial aid. **Contact:** Mr. Karl M. Furstenberg, Dean of Admissions and Financial Aid, 6016 McNutt Hall, Hanover, NH 03755, 603-646-2875; fax 603-646-1216.

---

### GETTING IN LAST YEAR
9,521 applied
23% were accepted
48% enrolled (1,057)
90% from top tenth of their h.s. class
74% had SAT verbal scores over 600
89% had SAT math scores over 600
23% had SAT verbal scores over 700
55% had SAT math scores over 700
53 National Merit Scholars
185 valedictorians

### THE STUDENT BODY
Total 5,300, of whom 4,287
 are undergraduates
From 52 states and territories,
 54 other countries
3% from New Hampshire
46% women, 54% men
7% African Americans
3% Native Americans
5% Hispanics
10% Asian Americans
7% international students

### AFTER FRESHMAN YEAR
98% returned for sophomore year

### AFTER GRADUATION
24% pursued further study (8% arts and
 sciences, 8% law, 6% medicine)
1 Rhodes, 1 Fulbright scholar

### WHAT YOU WILL PAY
Tuition and fees $19,650
Room and board $6069
Need-based financial aid averages $14,660

# DAVID LIPSCOMB UNIVERSITY

Nashville, Tennessee • Urban setting • Private • Independent-Religious • Coed

Since 1891, Lipscomb University has offered high-quality courses of study combined with Christian values essential to successful living. More than 100 major programs of study are offered. Lipscomb's 21st-century campuswide fiber-optic network provides PC connections in every dorm room, dorm lobby lab, and many other locations for Internet access to resources worldwide. Lipscomb University is a beautiful, quiet place with a special atmosphere that encourages learning. Nashville is one of the most exciting cities in the South. Its wide range of cultural and career opportunities enhances the academic program and each student's potential for employment following graduation.

##  Academics

Lipscomb University offers a core academic program; more than half of graduate courses are open to undergraduates. It awards bachelor's and master's **degrees**. Challenging opportunities include advanced placement, accelerated degree programs, self-designed majors, tutorials, an honors program, and a senior project. Special programs include internships, summer session for credit, study abroad, and Army and Air Force ROTC.

The most popular **majors** include business, (pre)medicine sequence, and education. A complete listing of majors at Lipscomb University appears in the Majors Index beginning on page 380.

The **faculty** at Lipscomb University has 100 full-time undergraduate teachers, 75% with terminal degrees. 100% of the faculty serve as student advisers. The student-faculty ratio is 16:1, and the average class size in required courses is 20.

##  Computers on Campus

Students are not required to have a computer. Student rooms are linked to a campus network. 280 **computers** available in the computer center, computer labs, the learning resource center, business center, classrooms, the library, and dormitories provide access to the main academic computer, off-campus computing facilities, e-mail, and on-line services. Staffed computer lab on campus provides training in the use of computers and software.

The 2 **libraries** have 196,391 books and 904 subscriptions.

##  Campus Life

There are 50 active **organizations** on campus, including a drama/theater group and student-run newspaper and radio station. 19% of eligible men and 17% of eligible women are members of 7 local **fraternities** and 8 local **sororities**. Student **safety services** include late night transport/escort service, 24-hour emergency telephone alarm devices, 24-hour patrols by trained security personnel, and electronically operated dormitory entrances.

Lipscomb University is a member of the NAIA. **Intercollegiate sports** (some offering scholarships) include baseball (m), basketball (m, w), cross-country running (m, w), golf (m), soccer (m), tennis (m, w), volleyball (w).

##  Applying

Lipscomb University requires a high school transcript, 3 years of high school math and science, 2 years of high school foreign language, 2 recommendations, SAT I or ACT, and a minimum high school GPA of 2.0. It recommends an essay and an interview. Early and midyear entrance are possible, with rolling admissions and continuous processing to 4/15 for financial aid. **Contact:** Mrs. Cyndi Butler, Director of Admissions, 3901 Granny White Pike, Nashville, TN 37204-3951, 615-269-1000 ext. 1776 or toll-free 800-333-4358; fax 615-269-1804.

---

### GETTING IN LAST YEAR
1,206 applied
92% were accepted
50% enrolled (557)
30% from top tenth of their h.s. class
3.2 average high school GPA
7% had SAT verbal scores over 600
23% had SAT math scores over 600
27% had ACT scores over 26
1% had SAT verbal scores over 700
4% had SAT math scores over 700
8% had ACT scores over 30
3 National Merit Scholars

### THE STUDENT BODY
Total 2,432, of whom 2,322
  are undergraduates
From 41 states and territories,
  28 other countries
63% from Tennessee
55% women, 45% men
5% African Americans
1% Native Americans
1% Hispanics
1% Asian Americans
2% international students

### AFTER FRESHMAN YEAR
80% returned for sophomore year
35% got a degree within 4 years
51% got a degree within 5 years
54% got a degree within 6 years

### WHAT YOU WILL PAY
Tuition and fees $6885
Room and board $3290
Need-based financial aid averages $1031
Non-need financial aid averages $1210

# DAVIDSON COLLEGE

Davidson, North Carolina • Small-town setting • Private • Independent-Religious • Coed

Davidson College is one of the nation's premier academic institutions, a college of the liberal arts and sciences respected for its intellectual vigor, the high quality of its faculty and students, and the achievements of its alumni. It is distinguished by its strong honor system, close interaction between professors and students, an environment that encourages both intellectual growth and community service, and a commitment to international education. Davidson places great value on student participation in extracurricular activities, intercollegiate athletics, and intramural sports. The College has a strong regional identity, which includes traditions of civility and mutual respect, and has historic ties to the Presbyterian Church.

 ## Academics

Davidson College offers a core academic program. It awards bachelor's **degrees**. Challenging opportunities include advanced placement, self-designed majors, tutorials, an honors program, a senior project, and Phi Beta Kappa. Special programs include off-campus study, study abroad, and Army and Air Force ROTC.

The most popular **majors** include history, English, and psychology. A complete listing of majors at Davidson College appears in the Majors Index beginning on page 380.

The **faculty** at Davidson College has 137 full-time teachers, 99% with terminal degrees. 100% of the faculty serve as student advisers. The student-faculty ratio is 12:1.

 ## Computers on Campus

Students are not required to have a computer. 138 **computers** available in the computer center, computer labs, the research center, academic buildings, classrooms, and the library. Staffed computer lab on campus provides training in the use of computers and software.

The 2 **libraries** have 407,402 books, 60,259 microform titles, and 2,672 subscriptions. They are connected to 2 national **on-line** catalogs.

 ## Campus Life

There are 100 active **organizations** on campus, including a drama/theater group and student-run newspaper and radio station. 55% of eligible men and 65% of eligible women are members of 7 national **fraternities** and 3 women's eating houses. Student **safety services** include late night transport/escort service, 24-hour emergency telephone alarm devices, 24-hour patrols by trained security personnel, and electronically operated dormitory entrances.

Davidson College is a member of the NCAA (Division I). **Intercollegiate sports** (some offering scholarships) include baseball (m), basketball (m, w), crew (m, w), cross-country running (m, w), fencing (m, w), field hockey (w), football (m), golf (m), lacrosse (m, w), rugby (m), sailing (m, w), soccer (m, w), swimming and diving (m, w), tennis (m, w), track and field (m, w), volleyball (m, w), water polo (m, w), wrestling (m).

 ## Applying

Davidson College requires an essay, a high school transcript, 3 years of high school math, 2 years of high school foreign language, 4 recommendations, and SAT I or ACT. It recommends 3 years of high school science, a campus interview, and 3 SAT II Subject Tests. Early and deferred entrance are possible, with a 1/15 deadline and 2/15 for financial aid. **Contact:** Dr. Nancy Cable Wells, Dean of Admission and Financial Aid, 405 North Main Street, Davidson, NC 28036-1719, 704-892-2231 or toll-free 800-768-0380; fax 704-892-2016.

## GETTING IN LAST YEAR

2,724 applied
37% were accepted
45% enrolled (451)
77% from top tenth of their h.s. class
50% had SAT verbal scores over 600
85% had SAT math scores over 600
6% had SAT verbal scores over 700
29% had SAT math scores over 700
30 National Merit Scholars
50 valedictorians

## THE STUDENT BODY

1,614 undergraduates
From 46 states and territories, 29 other countries
22% from North Carolina
47% women, 53% men
3% African Americans
1% Hispanics
4% Asian Americans
3% international students

## AFTER FRESHMAN YEAR

96% returned for sophomore year
82% got a degree within 4 years
86% got a degree within 5 years

## AFTER GRADUATION

43% pursued further study (20% arts and sciences, 11% medicine, 5% business)
35 corporations, 2 government agencies, 15 nonprofit organizations recruited on campus
3 Fulbright scholars

## WHAT YOU WILL PAY

Tuition and fees $18,626
Room and board $5364
32% receive need-based financial aid averaging $9475
30% receive non-need financial aid averaging $6500

# DEEP SPRINGS COLLEGE

Deep Springs, California • Rural setting • Private • Independent • Men

Founded in 1917, Deep Springs College lies in an isolated desert valley of California, 1 hour from the nearest town. Its enrollment is limited to 26 students, each of whom receives a full scholarship, valued at $38,092, covering tuition, room, and board. The students, whose SAT scores average over 1450, engage in a rigorous academic program, govern themselves (including admissions and curriculum decisions), and participate in the operation of the school-owned cattle and organic alfalfa ranch. After 2 or 3 years, they transfer to other schools, often Brown, Cornell, Harvard, or Stanford, to complete their studies.

 **Academics**

DS offers a liberal arts and sciences curriculum and no core academic program. It awards associate **degrees**. Challenging opportunities include tutorials and an honors program. Special programs include summer session for credit and study abroad.

The **faculty** at DS has 3 full-time teachers, 100% with terminal degrees. 100% of the faculty serve as student advisers. The student-faculty ratio is 4:1, and the average class size in required courses is 6.

 **Computers on Campus**

Students are not required to have a computer. 12 **computers** available in the computer center, the library, and dormitories.

The **library** has 26,000 books and 50 subscriptions.

 **Campus Life**

Active **organizations** on campus include drama/theater group and student-run radio station.

This institution has no intercollegiate sports.

 **Applying**

DS requires an essay, a high school transcript, a campus interview, SAT I, and 2 SAT II Subject Tests. It recommends 2 years of high school foreign language. Early entrance is possible, with an 11/15 deadline. **Contact:** Dr. Sherwin Howard, President, HC 72, Box 45001, Dyer, NV 89010-9803, 619-872-2000.

---

**GETTING IN LAST YEAR**
210 applied
8% were accepted
88% enrolled (14)
100% from top tenth of their h.s. class
100% had SAT verbal scores over 600
100% had SAT math scores over 600
92% had SAT verbal scores over 700
90% had SAT math scores over 700

**THE STUDENT BODY**
26 undergraduates
From 17 states and territories,
  0 other countries
3% from California
100% men
0% African Americans
0% Native Americans
0% Hispanics
0% Asian Americans
0% international students

**AFTER FRESHMAN YEAR**
92% returned for sophomore year

**WHAT YOU WILL PAY**
Comprehensive fee $0

# DENISON UNIVERSITY

Granville, Ohio • Small-town setting • Private • Independent • Coed

Denison University, a 4-year independent coeducational liberal arts college located in Granville, Ohio, has achieved a national reputation for its curricular innovation and faculty/student research opportunities. Its 1,800 students choose from 36 academic and 9 preprofessional programs available or design their own majors while living on the beautiful 1,200-acre hillside campus. A national college, Denison attracts students from 41 states and 29 other countries. Two magnificent new facilities, the F. W. Olin Science Hall and the Mitchell Recreation and Athletics Center, are evidence of the success of a recently completed $70-million capital campaign and the loyalty of Denison's nearly 23,000 alumni.

## Academics

Denison offers a core academic program. It awards bachelor's **degrees**. Challenging opportunities include advanced placement, self-designed majors, tutorials, an honors program, a senior project, Phi Beta Kappa, and Sigma Xi. Special programs include internships, off-campus study, and study abroad.

The most popular **majors** include economics, history, and English. A complete listing of majors at Denison appears in the Majors Index beginning on page 380.

The **faculty** at Denison has 153 full-time teachers, 98% with terminal degrees. 98% of the faculty serve as student advisers. The student-faculty ratio is 11:1, and the average class size in required courses is 19.

## Computers on Campus

Students are not required to have a computer. 160 **computers** available in the computer center, computer labs, the learning resource center, all academic departments, the library, and dormitories.

The **library** has 315,243 books, 62,608 microform titles, and 1,191 subscriptions.

## Campus Life

There are 118 active **organizations** on campus, including a drama/theater group and student-run newspaper and radio station. 32% of eligible men and 46% of eligible women are members of 10 national **fraternities** and 8 national **sororities**. Student **safety services** include late night transport/escort service, 24-hour emergency telephone alarm devices, 24-hour patrols by trained security personnel, and electronically operated dormitory entrances.

Denison is a member of the NCAA (Division III). **Intercollegiate sports** include baseball (m), basketball (m, w), crew (m), cross-country running (m, w), equestrian sports (m, w), field hockey (w), football (m), golf (m), ice hockey (m), lacrosse (m, w), riflery (m, w), rugby (m, w), sailing (m, w), skiing (downhill) (m, w), soccer (m, w), softball (w), squash (m, w), swimming and diving (m, w), tennis (m, w), track and field (m, w), volleyball (w).

## Applying

Denison requires an essay, a high school transcript, 2 recommendations, and SAT I or ACT. It recommends 3 years of high school math and science, 3 years of high school foreign language, an interview, and SAT II Subject Tests. Early and deferred entrance are possible, with a 2/1 deadline and a 3/1 priority date for financial aid. **Contact:** Ms. Stuart Oremus, Director of Admissions, Box H, Granville, OH 43023, 614-587-6627 or toll-free 800-DENISON.

---

### GETTING IN LAST YEAR
2,449 applied
84% were accepted
25% enrolled (508)
36% from top tenth of their h.s. class
14% had SAT verbal scores over 600
30% had SAT math scores over 600
64% had ACT scores over 26
1% had SAT verbal scores over 700
5% had SAT math scores over 700
22% had ACT scores over 30
10 National Merit Scholars
35 valedictorians

### THE STUDENT BODY
1,834 undergraduates
From 40 states and territories,
   29 other countries
39% from Ohio
53% women, 47% men
4% African Americans
0% Native Americans
2% Hispanics
2% Asian Americans
2% international students

### AFTER FRESHMAN YEAR
79% returned for sophomore year
73% got a degree within 4 years
77% got a degree within 5 years
78% got a degree within 6 years

### AFTER GRADUATION
19% pursued further study (10% arts and
   sciences, 4% law, 2% medicine)
31 corporations, 2 government agencies, 5
   nonprofit organizations recruited on campus
1 Fulbright scholar

### WHAT YOU WILL PAY
Tuition and fees $17,720
Room and board $4720
44% receive need-based financial aid
   averaging $11,649
24% receive non-need financial aid averaging
   $6499

# DEPAUL UNIVERSITY

Chicago, Illinois • Urban setting • Private • Independent-Religious • Coed

▶ DePaul is an urban university offering over 100 undergraduate and graduate programs. A private Catholic institution founded by the Vincentian order in 1898, today DePaul reflects a wide diversity of ethnic, religious, and economic backgrounds. DePaul students study in a great city with unlimited opportunities for professional experience before graduation. Students are active participants in projects and organizations working to meet the needs of the city. DePaul continues to emphasize teaching ability as a priority for faculty selection.

## Academics

DePaul offers an interdisciplinary curriculum and core academic program; fewer than half of graduate courses are open to undergraduates. It awards bachelor's, master's, doctoral, and first professional **degrees**. Challenging opportunities include advanced placement, accelerated degree programs, self-designed majors, tutorials, Freshmen Honors College, an honors program, and a senior project. Special programs include internships, summer session for credit, study abroad, and Army ROTC.

The most popular **majors** include social science, accounting, and finance/banking. A complete listing of majors at DePaul appears in the Majors Index beginning on page 380.

The **faculty** at DePaul has 1,149 graduate and undergraduate teachers, 88% with terminal degrees. 89% of the faculty serve as student advisers. The student-faculty ratio is 13:1, and the average class size in required courses is 25.

## Computers on Campus

Students are not required to have a computer. 850 **computers** available in the computer center, labs throughout the four campuses, classrooms, the library, the student center,

and dormitories provide access to the main academic computer. Staffed computer lab on campus provides training in the use of computers and software.

The 4 **libraries** have 659,605 books, 298,899 microform titles, and 16,804 subscriptions. They are connected to 10 national **on-line** catalogs.

## Campus Life

There are 85 active **organizations** on campus, including a drama/theater group and student-run newspaper and radio station. 10% of students participate in student government elections. 3% of eligible men and 3% of eligible women are members of 3 national **fraternities** and 2 national **sororities**. Student **safety services** include late night transport/escort service, 24-hour emergency telephone alarm devices, 24-hour patrols by trained security personnel, and electronically operated dormitory entrances.

DePaul is a member of the NCAA (Division I). **Intercollegiate sports** (some offering scholarships) include basketball (m, w), cross-country running (m, w), golf (m), riflery (m, w), soccer (m), softball (w), tennis (m, w), track and field (m, w), volleyball (w).

## Applying

DePaul requires a high school transcript, 1 recommendation, SAT I or ACT, a minimum high school GPA of 2.0, and in some cases an interview, audition, and a minimum high school GPA of 3.0. It recommends 3 years of high school math and science, 2 years of high school foreign language, SAT II Subject Tests, and a minimum high school GPA of 3.0. Early, deferred, and midyear entrance are possible, with an 8/15 deadline and continuous processing to 4/1 for financial aid. **Contact:** Ms. Ellen Cohen, Director of Undergraduate Admission, 1 East Jackson Boulevard, Chicago, IL 60604-2287, 312-362-8300 or toll-free 800-4DE-PAUL (out-of-state); fax 312-362-5322.

### GETTING IN LAST YEAR

5,107 applied
72% were accepted
33% enrolled (1,209)
31% from top tenth of their h.s. class
3.4 average high school GPA
16% had SAT verbal scores over 600
33% had SAT math scores over 600
54% had ACT scores over 26
1% had SAT verbal scores over 700
7% had SAT math scores over 700
9% had ACT scores over 30

### THE STUDENT BODY

Total 16,747, of whom 10,113
  are undergraduates

From 50 states and territories,
  56 other countries
75% from Illinois
59% women, 41% men
10% African Americans
1% Native Americans
13% Hispanics
7% Asian Americans
1% international students

### AFTER FRESHMAN YEAR

82% returned for sophomore year
50% got a degree within 4 years
60% got a degree within 5 years
65% got a degree within 6 years

### AFTER GRADUATION

900 corporations, 60 government agencies,
  50 nonprofit organizations recruited on
  campus
1 Fulbright scholar

### WHAT YOU WILL PAY

Tuition and fees $11,214
Room and board $4458
Need-based financial aid averages $2450
Non-need financial aid averages $3000

# DEPAUW UNIVERSITY

Greencastle, Indiana • Small-town setting • Private • Independent-Religious • Coed

DePauw University provides a traditional liberal arts education complemented by one of the largest internship programs in the nation. There are extensive internship opportunities in business, science, and news media as well as in professional and not-for-profit organizations nationally and internationally. Honors programs are offered in classics, management, media, and science. DePauw offers large university facilities but small classes. Ample opportunities are available for students to personalize education and engage in collaborative research with professors. There are extensive opportunities for international study. More than half of DePauw's students volunteer for community service locally, nationally, and internationally each year.

 **Academics**

DePauw offers a liberal arts curriculum and core academic program. It awards bachelor's **degrees**. Challenging opportunities include advanced placement, self-designed majors, tutorials, an honors program, a senior project, Phi Beta Kappa, and Sigma Xi. Special programs include internships, off-campus study, study abroad, and Army and Air Force ROTC.

The most popular **majors** include communication, political science/government, and economics. A complete listing of majors at DePauw appears in the Majors Index beginning on page 380.

The **faculty** at DePauw has 150 full-time teachers, 90% with terminal degrees. 91% of the faculty serve as student advisers. The student-faculty ratio is 11:1, and the average class size in required courses is 17.

 **Computers on Campus**

Students are not required to have a computer. 212 **computers** available in the computer center, computer labs, the learning resource center, the library, and dormitories provide access to e-mail and on-line services. Staffed computer lab on campus.

The 3 **libraries** have 276,470 books, 35,303 microform titles, and 1,201 subscriptions. They are connected to 4 national **on-line** catalogs.

 **Campus Life**

There are 65 active **organizations** on campus, including a drama/theater group and student-run newspaper and radio station. 80% of eligible men and 71% of eligible women are members of 15 national **fraternities** and 9 national **sororities**. Student **safety services** include late night transport/escort service, 24-hour emergency telephone alarm devices, and 24-hour patrols by trained security personnel.

DePauw is a member of the NCAA (Division III). **Intercollegiate sports** include baseball (m), basketball (m, w), crew (m, w), cross-country running (m, w), fencing (m, w), field hockey (w), football (m), golf (m, w), sailing (m, w), soccer (m, w), softball (m, w), swimming and diving (m, w), tennis (m, w), track and field (m, w), volleyball (w).

 **Applying**

DePauw requires an essay, a high school transcript, 3 years of high school math and science, 1 recommendation, and SAT I or ACT. It recommends 2 years of high school foreign language, a campus interview, and a minimum high school GPA of 3.0. Early, deferred, and midyear entrance are possible, with a 2/15 deadline and continuous processing to 2/15 for financial aid. **Contact:** Mr. David Murray, Dean of Admissions and Associate Provost, 101 East Seminary Street, Greencastle, IN 46135-1772, 317-658-4006 or toll-free 800-447-2495; fax 317-658-4007.

---

### GETTING IN LAST YEAR
2,218 applied
83% were accepted
35% enrolled (641)
48% from top tenth of their h.s. class
26% had SAT verbal scores over 600
55% had SAT math scores over 600
52% had ACT scores over 26
2% had SAT verbal scores over 700
15% had SAT math scores over 700
14% had ACT scores over 30

### THE STUDENT BODY
2,042 undergraduates
From 47 states and territories,
  20 other countries

41% from Indiana
55% women, 45% men
8% African Americans
1% Native Americans
3% Hispanics
2% Asian Americans
2% international students

### AFTER FRESHMAN YEAR
90% returned for sophomore year
72% got a degree within 4 years
78% got a degree within 5 years
79% got a degree within 6 years

### AFTER GRADUATION
27% pursued further study (12% arts and
  sciences, 6% law, 4% medicine)
65% had job offers within 3 months
47 corporations, 3 government agencies
  recruited on campus

### WHAT YOU WILL PAY
Tuition and fees $15,475
Room and board $5245
44% receive need-based financial aid
  averaging $7880
40% receive non-need financial aid averaging
  $5525

# DICKINSON COLLEGE

Carlisle, Pennsylvania • Suburban setting • Private • Independent • Coed

A commitment to international education pervades Dickinson's liberal arts program. Its nationally recognized international study centers in Europe, Africa, and Asia and its related on-campus choices foster astute international understanding and open attractive career opportunities in the rapidly evolving global community. Dickinson has pioneered in developing innovative "hands-on" introductory physics, chemistry, and mathematics courses taught in a workshop format. It also has an established and distinguished reputation for sending graduates on to business and law. One tenth of its alumni are practicing attorneys; many others are active in the corporate and business world as top executives.

 **Academics**

Dickinson offers a liberal arts curriculum with international education thrust and core academic program. It awards bachelor's **degrees**. Challenging opportunities include advanced placement, accelerated degree programs, self-designed majors, tutorials, an honors program, a senior project, and Phi Beta Kappa. Special programs include internships, summer session for credit, off-campus study, study abroad, and Army ROTC.

The most popular **majors** include political science/government, English, and history. A complete listing of majors at Dickinson appears in the Majors Index beginning on page 380.

The **faculty** at Dickinson has 184 teachers, 99% with terminal degrees. 100% of the faculty serve as student advisers. The student-faculty ratio is 10:1, and the average class size in required courses is 15.

 **Computers on Campus**

Students are not required to have a computer. Student rooms are linked to a campus network. 450 **computers** available in the computer center, computer labs, classroom buildings, classrooms, the library, the student center, and dormitories provide access to the main academic computer, off-campus computing facilities, e-mail, and on-line services. Staffed computer lab on campus (open 24 hours a day) provides training in the use of computers and software.

The **library** has 409,266 books, 161,374 microform titles, and 1,707 subscriptions.

 **Campus Life**

There are 136 active **organizations** on campus, including a drama/theater group and student-run newspaper and radio station. 38% of eligible men and 32% of eligible women are members of 8 national **fraternities**, 4 national **sororities**, 1 local fraternity, and 1 local sorority. Student **safety services** include late night transport/escort service, 24-hour emergency telephone alarm devices, 24-hour patrols by trained security personnel, student patrols, and electronically operated dormitory entrances.

Dickinson is a member of the NCAA (Division III). **Intercollegiate sports** include baseball (m), basketball (m, w), cross-country running (m, w), equestrian sports (m, w), fencing (m, w), field hockey (w), football (m), golf (m), ice hockey (m), lacrosse (m, w), sailing (m, w), skiing (downhill) (m, w), soccer (m, w), softball (w), squash (m, w), swimming and diving (m, w), tennis (m, w), track and field (m, w), volleyball (m, w), wrestling (m).

 **Applying**

Dickinson requires an essay, a high school transcript, 3 years of high school math and science, 2 years of high school foreign language, and 2 recommendations. It recommends an interview. Early, deferred, and midyear entrance are possible, with a 2/20 deadline and a 2/15 priority date for financial aid. **Contact:** Mr. R. Russell Shunk, Dean of Admissions, PO Box 1773, Carlisle, PA 17013-2896, 717-245-1231.

---

### GETTING IN LAST YEAR
3,034 applied
83% were accepted
21% enrolled (519)
37% from top tenth of their h.s. class
16% had SAT verbal scores over 600
32% had SAT math scores over 600
1% had SAT verbal scores over 700
5% had SAT math scores over 700
8 class presidents
10 valedictorians

### THE STUDENT BODY
1,875 undergraduates
From 48 states and territories,
  37 other countries
41% from Pennsylvania
57% women, 43% men
1% African Americans
1% Native Americans
2% Hispanics
3% Asian Americans
1% international students

### AFTER FRESHMAN YEAR
86% returned for sophomore year
84% got a degree within 4 years
86% got a degree within 5 years

### AFTER GRADUATION
20% pursued further study (9% arts and sciences, 5% law, 3% business)
23 corporations, 2 government agencies, 6 nonprofit organizations recruited on campus

### WHAT YOU WILL PAY
Tuition and fees $18,825
Room and board $5000
63% receive need-based financial aid averaging $9656
Non-need financial aid averages $459

# DRAKE UNIVERSITY

Des Moines, Iowa • Suburban setting • Private • Independent • Coed

Drake University offers students the best of both worlds: a sound liberal arts education complemented by professional and preprofessional programs. Drake's faculty members are dedicated to teaching. From their first introductory classes through the most advanced classes in their majors, students are taught by full-time faculty members who are master teachers. Drake University is a national leader in the use of computers and educational technology. Every residence hall room is equipped with a Power Mac computer, a printer, and software. Students can retrieve library information and access national and international information networks, such as the Internet, from their residence hall rooms.

 **Academics**

Drake offers a liberal arts curriculum with professional and pre-professional programs and no core academic program; all graduate courses are open to undergraduates. It awards bachelor's, master's, doctoral, and first professional **degrees**. Challenging opportunities include advanced placement, accelerated degree programs, self-designed majors, an honors program, a senior project, and Phi Beta Kappa. Special programs include cooperative education, internships, summer session for credit, off-campus study, study abroad, and Army and Air Force ROTC.

The most popular **majors** include pharmacy/pharmaceutical sciences, advertising, and marketing/retailing/merchandising. A complete listing of majors at Drake appears in the Majors Index beginning on page 380.

The **faculty** at Drake has 278 full-time undergraduate teachers, 93% with terminal degrees. 100% of the faculty serve as student advisers. The student-faculty ratio is 16:1, and the average class size in required courses is 41.

 **Computers on Campus**

Students are not required to have a computer. Student rooms are linked to a campus network. 900 **computers** available in the computer center, computer labs, academic buildings, classrooms, the library, the student center, dormitories, and student rooms provide access to the main academic computer, e-mail, and on-line services. Staffed computer lab on campus.

The 2 **libraries** have 580,000 books and 2,400 subscriptions. They are connected to 1 national **on-line** catalog.

 **Campus Life**

Active **organizations** on campus include drama/theater group and student-run newspaper and radio station. 35% of eligible men and 28% of eligible women are members of 11 national **fraternities** and 10 national **sororities**. Student **safety services** include late night transport/escort service, 24-hour emergency telephone alarm devices, 24-hour patrols by trained security personnel, and electronically operated dormitory entrances.

Drake is a member of the NCAA (Division I). **Intercollegiate sports** (some offering scholarships) include baseball (m), basketball (m, w), crew (m, w), cross-country running (m, w), football (m), golf (m), ice hockey (m), lacrosse (m), rugby (m), soccer (m, w), softball (w), swimming and diving (m, w), tennis (m, w), track and field (m, w), volleyball (m, w).

 **Applying**

Drake requires a high school transcript, recommendations, SAT I or ACT, a minimum high school GPA of 2.0, and in some cases 3 years of high school math and science. It recommends an essay, 2 years of high school foreign language, and an interview. Early, deferred, and midyear entrance are possible, with rolling admissions and continuous processing to 3/1 for financial aid. **Contact:** Mr. Thomas F. Willoughby, Director of Admission, 2507 University Avenue, Des Moines, IA 50311-4516, 515-271-3181 or toll-free 800-44 DRAKE; fax 515-271-2831.

## GETTING IN LAST YEAR

2,175 applied
93% were accepted
37% enrolled (750)
37% from top tenth of their h.s. class
3.42 average high school GPA
26% had SAT verbal scores over 600
11% had SAT math scores over 600
53% had ACT scores over 26
8% had SAT verbal scores over 700
1% had SAT math scores over 700
17% had ACT scores over 30
7 National Merit Scholars
52 valedictorians

## THE STUDENT BODY

Total 5,954, of whom 3,918
    are undergraduates
From 46 states and territories,
    48 other countries
30% from Iowa
55% women, 45% men
4% African Americans
1% Native Americans
3% Hispanics
4% Asian Americans
5% international students

## AFTER FRESHMAN YEAR

80% returned for sophomore year

## AFTER GRADUATION

15% pursued further study (4% arts and
    sciences, 4% law, 3% business)
93% had job offers within 3 months
78 corporations recruited on campus

## WHAT YOU WILL PAY

Tuition and fees $13,420
Room and board $4570
55% receive need-based financial aid
    averaging $1900

# DREW UNIVERSITY

Madison, New Jersey • Suburban setting • Private • Independent-Religious • Coed

A small school on a forested campus 30 miles from Manhattan, Drew offers inspired undergraduate teaching supported by an advanced voice, data, and video network, with an emphasis on the issues that affect a global society. Studying in an international center for the arts, commerce, government, communications, and science, Drew students engage in challenging internships and have an outstanding record of career and graduate/professional school placement in these fields. Extensive off-campus and study abroad opportunities further educate Drew students to help shape the world of the future.

##  Academics

Drew offers a liberal arts curriculum; more than half of graduate courses are open to undergraduates. It awards bachelor's, master's, doctoral, and first professional **degrees**. Challenging opportunities include advanced placement, self-designed majors, an honors program, a senior project, and Phi Beta Kappa. Special programs include internships, summer session for credit, off-campus study, study abroad, and Army ROTC.

The most popular **majors** include political science/government, psychology, and English. A complete listing of majors at Drew appears in the Majors Index beginning on page 380.

The **faculty** at Drew has 124 full-time graduate and undergraduate teachers, 91% with terminal degrees. 100% of the faculty serve as student advisers. The student-faculty ratio is 11:1, and the average class size in required courses is 18.

##  Computers on Campus

Students are required to have a computer. PCs are provided. 2,200 **computers** available in the computer center,

computer labs, the library, and dormitories provide access to the main academic computer, e-mail, and on-line services. Staffed computer lab on campus provides training in the use of computers and software.

The **library** has 437,493 books, 294,018 microform titles, and 2,006 subscriptions. It is connected to 1 national **on-line** catalog.

##  Campus Life

Active **organizations** on campus include drama/theater group and student-run newspaper and radio station. Student **safety services** include late night transport/escort service, 24-hour emergency telephone alarm devices, 24-hour patrols by trained security personnel, and electronically operated dormitory entrances.

Drew is a member of the NCAA (Division III). **Intercollegiate sports** include baseball (m), basketball (m, w), cross-country running (m, w), equestrian sports (m, w), fencing (m, w), field hockey (w), lacrosse (m, w), soccer (m, w), softball (w), swimming and diving (m, w), tennis (m, w).

##  Applying

Drew requires an essay, a high school transcript, 2 recommendations, and SAT I or ACT. It recommends 3 years of high school math and science, 2 years of high school foreign language, an interview, and 3 SAT II Subject Tests. Early, deferred, and midyear entrance are possible, with a 2/15 deadline and 3/1 for financial aid. **Contact:** Mr. Roberto Noya, Dean of Admissions for the College of Liberal Arts, 36 Madison Avenue, Madison, NJ 07940-1493, 201-408-3739; fax 201-408-3939.

## GETTING IN LAST YEAR

2,274 applied
76% were accepted
18% enrolled (318)
47% from top tenth of their h.s. class
32% had SAT verbal scores over 600
54% had SAT math scores over 600
5% had SAT verbal scores over 700
17% had SAT math scores over 700
11 National Merit Scholars

## THE STUDENT BODY

Total 2,047, of whom 1,319
  are undergraduates
From 38 states and territories,
  12 other countries

59% from New Jersey
61% women, 39% men
4% African Americans
0% Native Americans
5% Hispanics
7% Asian Americans
2% international students

## AFTER FRESHMAN YEAR

90% returned for sophomore year
67% got a degree within 4 years
72% got a degree within 5 years
73% got a degree within 6 years

## AFTER GRADUATION

24% pursued further study (13% arts and
  sciences, 8% law, 2% medicine)
72 corporations, 3 government agencies, 2
  nonprofit organizations recruited on campus

## WHAT YOU WILL PAY

Tuition and fees $18,942
Room and board $5616
55% receive need-based financial aid
  averaging $7151
19% receive non-need financial aid averaging
  $5296

# DRURY COLLEGE

Springfield, Missouri • Urban setting • Private • Independent • Coed

Preparation for the future is an advantage Drury graduates have. Students learn from full-time faculty in small-class settings with a university curriculum. Science students are co-researchers with professors, communication majors learn in the regional PBS affiliate located on campus, and architecture students are part of a national model for combining liberal arts and architecture. The Drury experience works: nearly 96% of graduates are employed or select from more than one graduate school in which to continue their education. The Drury liberal arts education helps students achieve their goals.

 **Academics**

Drury offers a core academic program It awards bachelor's and master's **degrees**. Challenging opportunities include advanced placement, accelerated degree programs, Freshmen Honors College, an honors program, and a senior project. Special programs include internships, summer session for credit, off-campus study, study abroad, and Army ROTC.

The most popular **majors** include business, communication, and behavioral sciences. A complete listing of majors at Drury appears in the Majors Index beginning on page 380.

The **faculty** at Drury has 86 full-time undergraduate teachers, 95% with terminal degrees. 75% of the faculty serve as student advisers. The student-faculty ratio is 14:1, and the average class size in required courses is 20.

 **Computers on Campus**

Students are not required to have a computer. Student rooms are linked to a campus network. 91 **computers** available in the computer center, computer labs, the research center, the learning resource center, academic departments, classrooms, the library, and the student center provide access to the main academic computer, off-campus computing facilities, e-mail, and on-line services. Staffed computer lab on campus provides training in the use of computers and software.

The 2 **libraries** have 165,000 books, 212 microform titles, and 953 subscriptions.

 **Campus Life**

There are 48 active **organizations** on campus, including a drama/theater group and student-run newspaper and radio station. 40% of eligible men and 40% of eligible women are members of 4 national **fraternities** and 4 national **sororities**. Student **safety services** include late night transport/escort service, 24-hour emergency telephone alarm devices, 24-hour patrols by trained security personnel, student patrols, and electronically operated dormitory entrances.

Drury is a member of the NCAA (Division II). **Intercollegiate sports** (some offering scholarships) include basketball (m), golf (m), soccer (m, w), swimming and diving (m, w), tennis (m, w), volleyball (w).

 **Applying**

Drury requires an essay, a high school transcript, 1 recommendation, and SAT I or ACT. It recommends 3 years of high school math and science, 1 year of high school foreign language, and a campus interview. Early and deferred entrance are possible, with rolling admissions and continuous processing to 2/15 for financial aid. **Contact:** Mr. Michael Thomas, Director of Admissions, Burnham Hall, Springfield, MO 65802-3791, 417-873-7879; fax 417-873-7529.

---

**GETTING IN LAST YEAR**
749 applied
87% were accepted
47% enrolled (306)
32% from top tenth of their h.s. class
3.4 average high school GPA
44% had ACT scores over 26
16% had ACT scores over 30

**THE STUDENT BODY**
Total 1,377, of whom 1,233
   are undergraduates
From 30 states and territories,
   23 other countries
80% from Missouri
54% women, 46% men
1% African Americans
0% Native Americans
1% Hispanics
1% Asian Americans
4% international students

**AFTER FRESHMAN YEAR**
84% returned for sophomore year
54% got a degree within 5 years
57% got a degree within 6 years

**AFTER GRADUATION**
29% pursued further study (15% arts and
   sciences, 5% medicine, 3% business)

**WHAT YOU WILL PAY**
Tuition and fees $9002
Room and board $3522

# UNIVERSITY

...olina • Suburban setting • Private • Independent-Religious • Coed

...academic program. It awards bachelor's, master's, doctoral, and first professional **degrees**. Challenging opportunities include advanced placement, accelerated degree programs, self-designed majors, tutorials, an honors program, a senior project, Phi Beta Kappa, and Sigma Xi. Special programs include internships, summer session for credit, off-campus study, study abroad, and Army, Naval, and Air Force ROTC.

The most popular **majors** include biology/biological sciences, history, and political science/government. A complete listing of majors at Duke appears in the Majors Index beginning on page 380.

The **faculty** at Duke has 2,046 full-time graduate and undergraduate teachers, 97% with terminal degrees. The student-faculty ratio is 11:1.

and radio station. 35% of eligible men and 40% of eligible women are members of 21 national **fraternities** and 13 national **sororities**. Student **safety services** include late night transport/escort service, 24-hour emergency telephone alarm devices, 24-hour patrols by trained security personnel, and electronically operated dormitory entrances.

Duke is a member of the NCAA (Division I). **Intercollegiate sports** (some offering scholarships) include badminton (m, w), baseball (m), basketball (m, w), crew (m, w), cross-country running (m, w), equestrian sports (m, w), fencing (m, w), field hockey (m, w), football (m, w), golf (m, w), ice hockey (m, w), lacrosse (m, w), racquetball (m, w), rugby (m, w), sailing (m, w), skiing (cross-country) (m, w), skiing (downhill) (m, w), soccer (m, w), softball (m, w), swimming and diving (m, w), tennis (m, w), track and field (m, w), volleyball (m, w), water polo (m, w), wrestling (m).

## Computers on Campus

Students are not required to have a computer. Student rooms are linked to a campus network. 800 **computers** available in the computer center, computer labs, academic buildings, classrooms, the library, and dormitories provide access to the main academic computer, e-mail, and on-line services. Staffed computer lab on campus (open 24 hours a day) provides training in the use of computers and software.

The 11 **libraries** have 4.2 million books, 1.9 million microform titles, and 32,732 subscriptions.

## Campus Life

There are 300 active **organizations** on campus, including a drama/theater group and student-run newspaper

## Applying

Duke requires an essay, a high school transcript, 3 recommendations, SAT I or ACT, SAT II: Writing Test, and in some cases 3 SAT II Subject Tests. It recommends 3 years of high school math and science, 3 years of high school foreign language, an interview, audition tape for applicants with outstanding dance, dramatic, or musical talent; slides of artwork, and a minimum high school GPA of 3.0. Early, deferred, and midyear entrance are possible, with a 1/2 deadline and a 2/1 priority date for financial aid. **Contact:** Mr. Christoph Guttentag, Director of Admissions, 2138 Campus Drive, Durham, NC 27708-0586, 919-684-3214; fax 919-681-8941.

---

### GETTING IN LAST YEAR
14,324 applied
30% were accepted
40% enrolled (1,719)
90% from top tenth of their h.s. class
64% had SAT verbal scores over 600
86% had SAT math scores over 600
94% had ACT scores over 26
14% had SAT verbal scores over 700
45% had SAT math scores over 700
69% had ACT scores over 30

### THE STUDENT BODY
Total 11,352, of whom 6,144 are undergraduates

From 52 states and territories, 39 other countries
14% from North Carolina
47% women, 53% men
9% African Americans
1% Native Americans
4% Hispanics
11% Asian Americans
2% international students

### AFTER FRESHMAN YEAR
99% returned for sophomore year
93% got a degree within 4 years
95% got a degree within 5 years
96% got a degree within 6 years

### AFTER GRADUATION
38% pursued further study (12% medicine, 11% law, 10% arts and sciences)
155 corporations, 45 government agencies, 50 nonprofit organizations recruited on campus
1 Rhodes, 1 Marshall, 13 Fulbright scholars

### WHAT YOU WILL PAY
Tuition and fees $19,995
Room and board $6320
40% receive need-based financial aid averaging $12,716
4% receive non-need financial aid averaging $12,617

# EARLHAM COLLEGE

Richmond, Indiana • Small-town setting • Private • Independent-Religious • Coed

Along with exceptionally strong programs in such traditional areas as literature, psychology, and premedical study, the College leads in curricular innovation and multidisciplinary offerings. As examples, Peace and Global Studies, Human Development and Social Relations, Women's Studies, Japanese Studies, and African and African-American Studies are among the many less traditional and popular majors at Earlham. Two thirds of Earlham undergraduates live and study abroad before graduation, compared to less than 1% of all college students. They choose from 20 College programs that include opportunities in Kenya, Mexico, Jerusalem, and Japan as well as in several European countries.

##  Academics

Earlham offers a liberal arts curriculum and core academic program. It awards bachelor's **degrees**. Challenging opportunities include advanced placement, accelerated degree programs, self-designed majors, tutorials, a senior project, and Phi Beta Kappa. Special programs include internships, off-campus study, and study abroad.

The most popular **majors** include biology/biological sciences, English, and psychology. A complete listing of majors at Earlham appears in the Majors Index beginning on page 380.

The **faculty** at Earlham has 78 full-time teachers, 80% with terminal degrees. 100% of the faculty serve as student advisers. The student-faculty ratio is 12:1, and the average class size in required courses is 25.

##  Computers on Campus

Students are not required to have a computer. 115 **computers** available in the computer center, classroom buildings, and the library provide access to the main academic computer, e-mail, and on-line services. Staffed computer lab on campus (open 24 hours a day) provides training in the use of computers and software.

The 3 **libraries** have 347,054 books, 177,921 microform titles, and 1,255 subscriptions. They are connected to 1 national **on-line** catalog.

##  Campus Life

There are 50 active **organizations** on campus, including a drama/theater group and student-run newspaper and radio station. 40% of students participate in student government elections. Student **safety services** include late night transport/escort service, 24-hour emergency telephone alarm devices, and 24-hour patrols by trained security personnel.

Earlham is a member of the NCAA (Division III) and NAIA. **Intercollegiate sports** include baseball (m), basketball (m, w), cross-country running (m, w), field hockey (w), football (m), lacrosse (w), soccer (m, w), tennis (m, w), track and field (m, w), volleyball (m, w).

##  Applying

Earlham requires an essay, a high school transcript, 3 years of high school math, 2 years of high school foreign language, 2 recommendations, and SAT I or ACT. It recommends 3 years of high school science and a campus interview. Early, deferred, and midyear entrance are possible, with a 2/15 deadline and continuous processing to 3/1 for financial aid. **Contact:** Mr. Robert L. deVeer, Dean of Admissions, National Road West, Richmond, IN 47374, 317-983-1600 or toll-free 800-327-5426; fax 317-983-1560.

### GETTING IN LAST YEAR

1,190 applied
77% were accepted
30% enrolled (272)
37% from top tenth of their h.s. class
32% had SAT verbal scores over 600
32% had SAT math scores over 600
48% had ACT scores over 26
5% had SAT verbal scores over 700
6% had SAT math scores over 700
10% had ACT scores over 30
4 National Merit Scholars

### THE STUDENT BODY

982 undergraduates
From 42 states and territories,
  15 other countries
21% from Indiana
56% women, 44% men
9% African Americans
0% Native Americans
1% Hispanics
5% Asian Americans
4% international students

### AFTER FRESHMAN YEAR

83% returned for sophomore year
66% got a degree within 4 years
71% got a degree within 5 years

### AFTER GRADUATION

36% pursued further study (25% arts and
  sciences, 5% medicine, 4% law)
50% had job offers within 3 months
52 corporations, 15 government agencies, 55
  nonprofit organizations recruited on campus

### WHAT YOU WILL PAY

Tuition and fees $16,152
Room and board $4191
65% receive need-based financial aid
  averaging $9415
Non-need financial aid averages $2995

# ECKERD COLLEGE

St. Petersburg, Florida • Suburban setting • Private • Independent-Religious • Coed

The Eckerd campus is a peaceful, tropical setting bordering Tampa Bay and the Gulf of Mexico. Students feel very secure in the suburban environment, while having easy access to the cultural, social, and recreational opportunities of the Tampa Bay metropolitan area. Classes are small. Independent study and study-abroad experiences are encouraged. Almost all students live on campus, where a sense of community flourishes. Students enjoy a great deal of freedom in their social lives and in the design of their academic programs. Volunteer service is extensive, since the Eckerd Honor Code encourages students to be "givers" rather than "takers."

##  Academics

Eckerd offers an interdisciplinary curriculum and core academic program. It awards bachelor's **degrees**. Challenging opportunities include advanced placement, accelerated degree programs, self-designed majors, tutorials, an honors program, a senior project, and Sigma Xi. Special programs include internships, summer session for credit, off-campus study, study abroad, and Army and Air Force ROTC.

The most popular **majors** include international business, business, and psychology. A complete listing of majors at Eckerd appears in the Majors Index beginning on page 380.

The **faculty** at Eckerd has 90 full-time teachers, 92% with terminal degrees. 100% of the faculty serve as student advisers. The student-faculty ratio is 12:1, and the average class size in required courses is 25.

##  Computers on Campus

Students are not required to have a computer. Student rooms are linked to a campus network. 350 **computers** available in the computer center, computer labs, the learning resource center, and the library provide access to the main academic computer, off-campus computing facilities, e-mail, and on-line services. Staffed computer lab on campus provides training in the use of computers and software.

The 2 **libraries** have 144,000 books, 14,000 microform titles, and 1,000 subscriptions. They are connected to 2 national **on-line** catalogs.

##  Campus Life

There are 70 active **organizations** on campus, including a drama/theater group and student-run newspaper and radio station. 50% of students participate in student government elections. Student **safety services** include late night transport/escort service, 24-hour emergency telephone alarm devices, 24-hour patrols by trained security personnel, and electronically operated dormitory entrances.

Eckerd is a member of the NCAA (Division II). **Intercollegiate sports** (some offering scholarships) include baseball (m), basketball (m, w), cross-country running (m, w), golf (m), sailing (m, w), soccer (m, w), softball (w), swimming and diving (m, w), tennis (m, w), volleyball (m, w).

##  Applying

Eckerd requires an essay, a high school transcript, 3 years of high school math and science, 2 years of high school foreign language, 1 recommendation, and SAT I or ACT. It recommends an interview, SAT II Subject Tests, and a minimum high school GPA of 3.0. Early, deferred, and midyear entrance are possible, with rolling admissions and continuous processing to 3/1 for financial aid. **Contact:** Dr. Richard R. Hallin, Dean of Admissions, 4200 54th Avenue, South, St. Petersburg, FL 33711, 813-864-8331 or toll-free 800-456-9009; fax 813-866-2304.

---

### GETTING IN LAST YEAR
1,524 applied
77% were accepted
31% enrolled (363)
35% from top tenth of their h.s. class
3.20 average high school GPA
18% had SAT verbal scores over 600
34% had SAT math scores over 600
50% had ACT scores over 26
4% had SAT verbal scores over 700
6% had SAT math scores over 700
15% had ACT scores over 30
7 National Merit Scholars
15 class presidents
20 valedictorians

### THE STUDENT BODY
1,387 undergraduates
From 49 states and territories,
   55 other countries
30% from Florida
51% women, 49% men
3% African Americans
1% Native Americans
4% Hispanics
2% Asian Americans
11% international students

### AFTER FRESHMAN YEAR
78% returned for sophomore year
57% got a degree within 4 years
63% got a degree within 5 years
64% got a degree within 6 years

### AFTER GRADUATION
45% pursued further study (16% arts and
   sciences, 15% business, 6% law)
75 corporations, 45 government agencies, 25
   nonprofit organizations recruited on campus
1 Fulbright scholar

### WHAT YOU WILL PAY
Tuition and fees $15,520
Room and board $4080
67% receive need-based financial aid
   averaging $6500
13% receive non-need financial aid averaging
   $6200

# ELIZABETHTOWN COLLEGE

Elizabethtown, Pennsylvania • Small-town setting • Private • Independent-Religious • Coed

Elizabethtown College aims to develop sound intellectual judgment, keen moral sensitivity, and an appreciation for beauty in the world. Its educational process fosters the capacity for independent thought and commitment to personal integrity. In keeping with its tradition, the College affirms the values of peace, justice, and human dignity, as it strives to achieve a distinctive blend of the liberal arts and professional studies. This union of the world of spirit and the world of work is expressed in the College motto, "Educate for Service."

 **Academics**

E-town offers an interdisciplinary curriculum and core academic program. It awards bachelor's **degrees**. Challenging opportunities include advanced placement, accelerated degree programs, and a senior project. Special programs include internships, summer session for credit, off-campus study, and study abroad.

The most popular **majors** include business, education, and communication. A complete listing of majors at E-town appears in the Majors Index beginning on page 380.

The **faculty** at E-town has 106 full-time teachers, 72% with terminal degrees. 97% of the faculty serve as student advisers. The student-faculty ratio is 14:1, and the average class size in required courses is 18.

 **Computers on Campus**

Students are not required to have a computer. Student rooms are linked to a campus network. 80 **computers** available in computer labs, classrooms, and the library provide access to the main academic computer, off-campus computing facilities, and e-mail. Staffed computer lab on campus provides training in the use of computers and software.

The 2 **libraries** have 158,357 books, 652 microform titles, and 1,129 subscriptions. They are connected to 2 national **on-line** catalogs.

 **Campus Life**

There are 50 active **organizations** on campus, including a drama/theater group and student-run newspaper and radio station. No national or local **fraternities** or **sororities**. Student **safety services** include self-defense workshops, crime prevention program, late night transport/escort service, 24-hour emergency telephone alarm devices, 24-hour patrols by trained security personnel, and student patrols.

E-town is a member of the NCAA (Division III). **Intercollegiate sports** include baseball (m), basketball (m, w), cross-country running (m, w), field hockey (w), golf (m), soccer (m, w), softball (w), swimming and diving (m, w), tennis (m, w), track and field (m, w), volleyball (m, w), wrestling (m).

 **Applying**

E-town requires an essay, a high school transcript, 2 recommendations, SAT I or ACT, a minimum high school GPA of 2.0, and in some cases a campus interview. It recommends 3 years of high school math and science, 2 years of high school foreign language, a campus interview, and a minimum high school GPA of 3.0. Early, deferred, and midyear entrance are possible, with rolling admissions and continuous processing to 4/1 for financial aid. **Contact:** Mr. Ronald D. Potier, Director of Admissions, 1 Alpha Drive, Elizabethtown, PA 17022-2298, 717-361-1400.

## GETTING IN LAST YEAR

2,438 applied
76% were accepted
25% enrolled (473)
36% from top tenth of their h.s. class
9% had SAT verbal scores over 600
29% had SAT math scores over 600
38% had ACT scores over 26
1% had SAT verbal scores over 700
3% had SAT math scores over 700
5% had ACT scores over 30

## THE STUDENT BODY

1,818 undergraduates
From 19 states and territories,
  19 other countries
62% from Pennsylvania
64% women, 36% men
2% African Americans
0% Native Americans
1% Hispanics
2% Asian Americans
2% international students

## AFTER FRESHMAN YEAR

85% returned for sophomore year

## AFTER GRADUATION

17% pursued further study
20 corporations, 1 government agency, 2
  nonprofit organizations recruited on campus
1 Rhodes scholar

## WHAT YOU WILL PAY

Tuition and fees $14,590
Room and board $4450
60% receive need-based financial aid
  averaging $5316
32% receive non-need financial aid averaging
  $3908

# EMORY UNIVERSITY

Atlanta, Georgia • Suburban setting • Private • Independent-Religious • Coed

Emory seeks students who have met the high standards of an academically challenging program. An extensive review of each applicant helps the Admission Committee to understand and appreciate each student's record, including exemplary academic performance, special talents, involvements, interests, and demonstrated interest in attending Emory. The committee is attentive to the difficulty of the curriculum, the many variations in high school grading systems and the opportunities schools provide their students, and recommendations and standardized test scores.

## Academics

Emory offers a broad-based liberal arts curriculum and core academic program; a few graduate courses are open to undergraduates. It awards bachelor's, master's, doctoral, and first professional **degrees**. Challenging opportunities include advanced placement, accelerated degree programs, tutorials, an honors program, a senior project, Phi Beta Kappa, and Sigma Xi. Special programs include internships, summer session for credit, off-campus study, study abroad, and Naval ROTC.

The most popular **majors** include psychology, biology/biological sciences, and political science/government. A complete listing of majors at Emory appears in the Majors Index beginning on page 380.

The **faculty** at Emory has 1,748 full-time graduate and undergraduate teachers, 98% with terminal degrees. 100% of the faculty serve as student advisers. The student-faculty ratio is 10:1, and the average class size in required courses is 30.

## Computers on Campus

Students are not required to have a computer. Student rooms are linked to a campus network. 483 **computers** available in the computer center, computer labs, law school, theological school buildings, the library, the student center, and dormitories provide access to the main academic computer, off-campus computing facilities, e-mail, and on-line services. Staffed computer lab on campus (open 24 hours a day) provides training in the use of computers and software.

The 7 **libraries** have 2.2 million books and 23,555 subscriptions. They are connected to 27 national **on-line** catalogs.

## Campus Life

There are 200 active **organizations** on campus, including a drama/theater group and student-run newspaper and radio station. 33% of eligible men and 33% of eligible women are members of 12 national **fraternities** and 10 national **sororities**. Student **safety services** include late night transport/escort service, 24-hour emergency telephone alarm devices, 24-hour patrols by trained security personnel, and student patrols.

Emory is a member of the NCAA (Division III). **Intercollegiate sports** include badminton (m, w), baseball (m), basketball (m, w), bowling (m, w), crew (m, w), cross-country running (m, w), fencing (m, w), field hockey (w), golf (m), ice hockey (m), lacrosse (m), racquetball (m, w), rugby (m), sailing (m, w), soccer (m, w), swimming and diving (m, w), tennis (m, w), track and field (m, w), volleyball (m, w), wrestling (m).

## Applying

Emory requires an essay, a high school transcript, 3 years of high school math and science, some high school foreign language, 1 recommendation, and SAT I or ACT. It recommends SAT II Subject Tests and a minimum high school GPA of 3.0. Early and deferred entrance are possible, with a 1/15 deadline and continuous processing to 2/15 for financial aid. **Contact:** Mr. Daniel C. Walls, Dean of Admissions, Boisfeuillet Jones Center–Office of Admissions, Atlanta, GA 30322-1100, 404-727-6036 or toll-free 800-727-6036.

### GETTING IN LAST YEAR
9,654 applied
49% were accepted
25% enrolled (1,200)
76% from top tenth of their h.s. class
3.7 average high school GPA
39% had SAT verbal scores over 600
80% had SAT math scores over 600
70% had ACT scores over 26
5% had SAT verbal scores over 700
23% had SAT math scores over 700
41% had ACT scores over 30
56 National Merit Scholars

### THE STUDENT BODY
Total 10,800, of whom 5,100
 are undergraduates

From 51 states and territories,
 44 other countries
19% from Georgia
54% women, 46% men
9% African Americans
0% Native Americans
3% Hispanics
11% Asian Americans
2% international students

### AFTER FRESHMAN YEAR
91% returned for sophomore year
90% got a degree within 4 years
92% got a degree within 5 years
94% got a degree within 6 years

### AFTER GRADUATION
66% pursued further study (24% arts and
 sciences, 22% law, 18% medicine)
1 Fulbright scholar

### WHAT YOU WILL PAY
Tuition and fees $17,832
Room and board $5998
46% receive need-based financial aid
 averaging $10,841
15% receive non-need financial aid averaging
 $9653

# EUGENE LANG COLLEGE, NEW SCHOOL FOR SOCIAL RESEARCH

New York, New York • Urban setting • Private • Independent • Coed

Eugene Lang College offers students of diverse backgrounds the opportunity to design their own program of study within one of 5 interdisciplinary concentrations in the social sciences and the humanities. Students discuss and debate issues in small seminar courses that are never larger than 15 students. They enrich their programs with internships in a wide variety of areas, such as media and publishing, community service, and education, and they can pursue a dual degree at one of the University's 5 other divisions. The Greenwich Village location means all the cultural treasures of the city—museums, libraries, dance, music, and theater—are literally at one's doorstep.

 ## Academics

Lang College offers an interdisciplinary, multicultural curriculum and no core academic program. It awards bachelor's **degrees**. Challenging opportunities include advanced placement, accelerated degree programs, self-designed majors, tutorials, and a senior project. Special programs include internships, summer session for credit, off-campus study, and study abroad.

The most popular **majors** include creative writing, theater arts/drama, and interdisciplinary studies. A complete listing of majors at Lang College appears in the Majors Index beginning on page 380.

The **faculty** at Lang College has 13 full-time teachers, 77% with terminal degrees. 100% of the faculty serve as student advisers. The average class size in required courses is 12.

 ## Computers on Campus

Students are not required to have a computer. 223 **computers** available in the computer center, the learning resource center, and writing center provide access to the main academic computer and e-mail. Staffed computer lab on campus provides training in the use of computers and software.

The 3 **libraries** have 155,000 books, 65,000 microform titles, and 700 subscriptions.

 ## Campus Life

There are 10 active **organizations** on campus, including a drama/theater group and student-run newspaper. 62% of students participate in student government elections. Student **safety services** include 24-hour desk attendants in dormitories and electronically operated dormitory entrances.

This institution has no intercollegiate sports.

 ## Applying

Lang College requires an essay, a high school transcript, 2 recommendations, an interview, SAT I, ACT or 4 SAT II Subject Tests, a minimum high school GPA of 2.0. It recommends 3 years of high school math and science, 2 years of high school foreign language, and a minimum high school GPA of 3.0. Early, deferred, and midyear entrance are possible, with a 2/1 deadline and continuous processing to 4/1 for financial aid. **Contact:** Ms. Jennifer Fondiller, Director of Admissions, 65 West 11th Street, New York, NY 10011-8601, 212-229-5665; fax 212-229-5355.

## GETTING IN LAST YEAR

261 applied
77% were accepted
38% enrolled (77)
51% from top tenth of their h.s. class
28% had SAT verbal scores over 600
17% had SAT math scores over 600
4% had SAT verbal scores over 700
0% had SAT math scores over 700

## THE STUDENT BODY

363 undergraduates
From 26 states and territories,
   12 other countries
42% from New York
70% women, 30% men
7% African Americans
0% Native Americans
10% Hispanics
3% Asian Americans
8% international students

## AFTER FRESHMAN YEAR

80% returned for sophomore year

## AFTER GRADUATION

50% pursued further study
85% had job offers within 3 months

## WHAT YOU WILL PAY

Tuition and fees $14,960
Room only $5170
68% receive need-based financial aid
   averaging $7117

# FAIRFIELD UNIVERSITY

Fairfield, Connecticut • Suburban setting • Private • Independent-Religious • Coed

Founded by the Jesuits in 1942, Fairfield is a comprehensive university and a close-knit community located in southern Connecticut. The University offers challenging programs in 3 undergraduate divisions: the College of Arts and Sciences and the Schools of Business and Nursing. Faculty and students are encouraged to participate in the larger community and in programs abroad through service and academic activities. Most of all, Fairfield serves the wider community by educating its students to be socially aware and morally responsible. The well-rounded Fairfield education is complemented by extensive extracurricular activities and Division I sports. Fairfield invites prospective students to visit its campus.

## Academics

Fairfield University offers a core academic program; fewer than half of graduate courses are open to undergraduates. It awards bachelor's and master's **degrees**. Challenging opportunities include advanced placement, tutorials, Freshmen Honors College, an honors program, a senior project, and Phi Beta Kappa. Special programs include internships, summer session for credit, off-campus study, and study abroad.

The most popular **majors** include English, biology/biological sciences, and nursing. A complete listing of majors at Fairfield University appears in the Majors Index beginning on page 380.

The **faculty** at Fairfield University has 200 full-time graduate and undergraduate teachers. 90% of the faculty serve as student advisers. The student-faculty ratio is 16:1, and the average class size in required courses is 24.

## Computers on Campus

Students are not required to have a computer. Student rooms are linked to a campus network. 140 **computers** available in the computer center, computer labs, classroom buildings, and the library provide access to the main academic computer and e-mail. Staffed computer lab on campus (open 24 hours a day) provides training in the use of computers and software.

The **library** has 310,000 books, 433,800 microform titles, and 1,797 subscriptions. It is connected to 5 national **on-line** catalogs.

## Campus Life

Active **organizations** on campus include drama/theater group and student-run newspaper and radio station. 65% of students participate in student government elections. Student **safety services** include late night transport/escort service, 24-hour emergency telephone alarm devices, 24-hour patrols by trained security personnel, and electronically operated dormitory entrances.

Fairfield University is a member of the NCAA (Division I). **Intercollegiate sports** (some offering scholarships) include baseball (m), basketball (m, w), cross-country running (m, w), field hockey (w), golf (m), ice hockey (m), lacrosse (m), soccer (m, w), softball (w), swimming and diving (m, w), tennis (m, w), volleyball (w).

## Applying

Fairfield University requires a high school transcript, 3 years of high school math and science, 2 years of high school foreign language, rank in upper 40% of high school class, minimum 2.5 GPA for transfers from two-year colleges, SAT I or ACT, a minimum high school GPA of 2.0, and in some cases 4 years of high school math and science. It recommends recommendations, an interview, and SAT II Subject Tests. Early and deferred entrance are possible, with a 3/1 deadline and 2/15 for financial aid. **Contact:** Mr. David Flynn, Dean of Admission, North Benson Road, Fairfield, CT 06430-7524, 203-254-4100; fax 203-254-4199.

### GETTING IN LAST YEAR
4,596 applied
76% were accepted
23% enrolled (795)
23% from top tenth of their h.s. class
2.85 average high school GPA
11% had SAT verbal scores over 600
34% had SAT math scores over 600
1% had SAT verbal scores over 700
4% had SAT math scores over 700
1 National Merit Scholar
19 class presidents

### THE STUDENT BODY
Total 4,969, of whom 2,901
   are undergraduates
From 37 states and territories,
   22 other countries
32% from Connecticut
52% women, 48% men
2% African Americans
0% Native Americans
4% Hispanics
4% Asian Americans
1% international students

### AFTER FRESHMAN YEAR
89% returned for sophomore year

### AFTER GRADUATION
20% pursued further study (8% arts and sciences, 4% law, 4% medicine)
45% had job offers within 3 months
75 corporations, 1 government agency, 3 nonprofit organizations recruited on campus
3 Fulbright scholars

### WHAT YOU WILL PAY
Tuition and fees $15,310
Room and board $6200
Need-based financial aid averages $6890
Non-need financial aid averages $3920

# FISK UNIVERSITY

Nashville, Tennessee • Urban setting • Private • Independent-Religious • Coed

---

Fisk University is a private liberal arts institution. Since its founding in 1966, Fisk has stood as a proud symbol of achievement—the first historically black college granted a chapter of Phi Beta Kappa honor society. Students are encouraged to extend themselves and to broaden their perspectives by participating in a number of academic programs, including the exchange program and the study-abroad program. The University of Ghana has been added to the list of participating institutions. New scientific facilities are under way that will provide more opportunities for students to engage in meaningful research.

## Academics

Fisk offers a core academic program. It awards bachelor's and master's **degrees**. Challenging opportunities include advanced placement, self-designed majors, an honors program, and Phi Beta Kappa. Special programs include cooperative education, internships, off-campus study, and Army and Air Force ROTC.

The most popular **majors** include business, chemistry, and psychology. A complete listing of majors at Fisk appears in the Majors Index beginning on page 380.

The **faculty** at Fisk has 71 full-time undergraduate teachers, 75% with terminal degrees. The student-faculty ratio is 10:1, and the average class size in required courses is 30.

## Computers on Campus

Students are not required to have a computer. **Computers** available in the computer center, computer labs, and the library provide access to the main academic computer. Staffed computer lab on campus provides training in the use of computers and software.

The **library** has 197,000 books, 5,670 microform titles, and 330 subscriptions.

## Campus Life

Active **organizations** on campus include drama/theater group and student-run newspaper and radio station. 25% of eligible men and 35% of eligible women are members of 4 national **fraternities** and 4 national **sororities**. Student **safety services** include late night transport/escort service and 24-hour patrols by trained security personnel.

Fisk is a member of the NCAA (Division III). **Intercollegiate sports** include baseball (m), basketball (m, w), cross-country running (m, w), golf (m), tennis (m, w), track and field (m, w), volleyball (w).

## Applying

Fisk requires an essay, a high school transcript, 2 recommendations, and medical history. It recommends 3 years of high school math, some high school foreign language, SAT I or ACT, and SAT II Subject Tests. Early and midyear entrance are possible, with a 6/15 deadline and continuous processing to 4/1 for financial aid. **Contact:** Mr. Harrison F. DeShields Jr., Director of Admissions and Records, 1000 17th Avenue North, Nashville, TN 37208-3051, 615-329-8665 or toll-free 800-443-FISK.

---

### GETTING IN LAST YEAR
1,980 applied
47% were accepted
38% enrolled (350)
15% from top tenth of their h.s. class

### THE STUDENT BODY
Total 872, of whom 839
  are undergraduates
From 41 states and territories,
  11 other countries

10% from Tennessee
72% women, 28% men
98% African Americans
1% Native Americans
1% Hispanics
0% Asian Americans
11% international students

### AFTER FRESHMAN YEAR
69% returned for sophomore year

### AFTER GRADUATION
58% pursued further study (15% law, 15% medicine, 10% business)
35 corporations, 15 government agencies, 5 nonprofit organizations recruited on campus

### WHAT YOU WILL PAY
Tuition and fees $6550
Room and board $3690
Need-based financial aid averages $2100
Non-need financial aid averages $4286

# FLORIDA INSTITUTE OF TECHNOLOGY

Melbourne, Florida • Small-town setting • Private • Independent • Coed

Florida Tech is among the leaders in integrating engineering curricula, research faculty, and students. The new $8-million advanced engineering complex scheduled to break ground in the summer of 1995 will enable both the College of Engineering and the University to broaden the education and research initiatives beyond the classroom walls to provide lifelong learning opportunities for industry and students.

## Academics

Florida Tech offers a core academic program; fewer than half of graduate courses are open to undergraduates. It awards bachelor's, master's, and doctoral **degrees**. Challenging opportunities include advanced placement, accelerated degree programs, tutorials, a senior project, and Sigma Xi. Special programs include cooperative education, internships, summer session for credit, off-campus study, study abroad, and Army ROTC.

The most popular **majors** include biology/biological sciences, aerospace sciences, and mechanical engineering. A complete listing of majors at Florida Tech appears in the Majors Index beginning on page 380.

The **faculty** at Florida Tech has 199 full-time graduate and undergraduate teachers, 87% with terminal degrees. 100% of the faculty serve as student advisers. The student-faculty ratio is 12:1.

## Computers on Campus

Students are not required to have a computer. 400 **computers** available in the computer center, computer labs, and the library provide access to the main academic computer, off-campus computing facilities, e-mail, and on-line services.

Staffed computer lab on campus provides training in the use of software.

The **library** has 264,626 books, 184,285 microform titles, and 1,700 subscriptions.

## Campus Life

There are 60 active **organizations** on campus, including a drama/theater group and student-run newspaper and radio station. 8% of eligible men and 10% of eligible women are members of 9 national **fraternities**, 3 national **sororities**, and 1 local fraternity. Student **safety services** include late night transport/escort service, 24-hour emergency telephone alarm devices, 24-hour patrols by trained security personnel, and electronically operated dormitory entrances.

Florida Tech is a member of the NCAA (Division II). **Intercollegiate sports** (some offering scholarships) include baseball (m), basketball (m, w), crew (m, w), cross-country running (m, w), fencing (m, w), riflery (m, w), sailing (m, w), soccer (m), softball (w), tennis (m, w), volleyball (m, w).

## Applying

Florida Tech requires an essay, a high school transcript, 4 years of high school math, SAT I or ACT, a minimum high school GPA of 2.0, and in some cases 3 years of high school science. It recommends some high school foreign language, recommendations, an interview, and a minimum high school GPA of 3.0. Early, deferred, and midyear entrance are possible, with rolling admissions and continuous processing to 2/15 for financial aid. **Contact:** Mr. Gregg A. Meyer, Dean of Admissions, 150 West University Boulevard, Melbourne, FL 32901-6988, 407-768-8000 ext. 8030 or toll-free 800-348-4636 (in-state), 800-888-4348 (out-of-state); fax 407-723-9468.

### GETTING IN LAST YEAR
2,171 applied
80% were accepted
22% enrolled (390)
43% from top tenth of their h.s. class
3.42 average high school GPA
12% had SAT verbal scores over 600
49% had SAT math scores over 600
2% had SAT verbal scores over 700
11% had SAT math scores over 700
1 National Merit Scholar

### THE STUDENT BODY
Total 4,564, of whom 1,881
   are undergraduates
From 50 states and territories,
   70 other countries
38% from Florida
31% women, 69% men
3% African Americans
1% Native Americans
6% Hispanics
3% Asian Americans
22% international students

### AFTER FRESHMAN YEAR
75% returned for sophomore year
31% got a degree within 4 years
51% got a degree within 5 years

### AFTER GRADUATION
24% pursued further study (8% arts and
   sciences, 8% business, 3% engineering)
29% had job offers within 3 months
21 corporations, 13 government agencies
   recruited on campus

### WHAT YOU WILL PAY
Tuition and fees $14,535
Room and board $4140
73% receive need-based financial aid
   averaging $1327
Non-need financial aid averages $3575

# FLORIDA STATE UNIVERSITY

Tallahassee, Florida • Suburban setting • Public • State-supported • Coed

Florida State University is one of the nation's most popular universities, enrolling students from all 50 states and over 100 countries. Its diverse student population participates in a Liberal Studies Program that has been nationally recognized for its effectiveness in fostering a spirit of free inquiry into humane values and for developing strong written analytical skills. Home of the National High Magnetic Field Laboratory, the Supercomputer Computations Institute, and other internationally acclaimed research centers, Florida State is one of only 88 institutions in the Research I category as classified by the Carnegie Foundation for the Advancement of Teaching. FSU invites students to explore the state of their future, Florida State University.

 **Academics**

Florida State offers a liberal studies curriculum and core academic program; fewer than half of graduate courses are open to undergraduates. It awards associate, bachelor's, master's, doctoral, and first professional **degrees**. Challenging opportunities include advanced placement, accelerated degree programs, an honors program, a senior project, Phi Beta Kappa, and Sigma Xi. Special programs include cooperative education, internships, summer session for credit, off-campus study, study abroad, and Army, Naval, and Air Force ROTC.

The most popular **majors** include biology/biological sciences and psychology. A complete listing of majors at Florida State appears in the Majors Index beginning on page 380.

The **faculty** at Florida State has 1,435 full-time graduate and undergraduate teachers, 87% with terminal degrees.

 **Computers on Campus**

Students are not required to have a computer. Student rooms are linked to a campus network. 650 **computers**

available in the computer center, computer labs, classrooms, the library, the student center, and dormitories provide access to the main academic computer, off-campus computing facilities, and e-mail. Staffed computer lab on campus provides training in the use of computers and software.

The 7 **libraries** have 2 million books, 4.2 million microform titles, and 18,498 subscriptions.

 **Campus Life**

There are 290 active **organizations** on campus, including a drama/theater group and student-run newspaper and radio station. 20% of eligible men and 20% of eligible women are members of 25 national **fraternities** and 19 national **sororities**. Student **safety services** include late night transport/escort service, 24-hour emergency telephone alarm devices, 24-hour patrols by trained security personnel, and electronically operated dormitory entrances.

Florida State is a member of the NCAA (Division I). **Intercollegiate sports** (some offering scholarships) include baseball (m), basketball (m, w), cross-country running (m, w), football (m), golf (m, w), soccer (w), softball (w), swimming and diving (m, w), tennis (m, w), track and field (m, w), volleyball (w).

 **Applying**

Florida State requires a high school transcript, 3 years of high school math and science, 2 years of high school foreign language, SAT I or ACT, and in some cases audition. It recommends a minimum high school GPA of 3.0. Early entrance is possible, with a 3/1 deadline and continuous processing to 3/1 for financial aid. **Contact:** Ms. Janice Finney, Associate Director of Admissions, Office of Admissions, FSU University Center, Tallahassee, FL 32306-1009, 904-644-6200 ext. 31.

---

**GETTING IN LAST YEAR**
13,412 applied
74% were accepted
33% enrolled (3,323)
43% from top tenth of their h.s. class
12% had SAT verbal scores over 600
37% had SAT math scores over 600
36% had ACT scores over 26
1% had SAT verbal scores over 700
5% had SAT math scores over 700
8% had ACT scores over 30
40 National Merit Scholars

**THE STUDENT BODY**
Total 29,630, of whom 22,202 are undergraduates
From 51 states and territories, 101 other countries
80% from Florida
57% women, 43% men
9% African Americans
6% Hispanics
2% Asian Americans
1% international students

**AFTER FRESHMAN YEAR**
86% returned for sophomore year

**WHAT YOU WILL PAY**
Resident tuition and fees $1798
Nonresident tuition and fees $6700
Room and board $4285
Need-based financial aid averages $1278
Non-need financial aid averages $1842

# FORDHAM UNIVERSITY

New York, New York • Urban setting • Private • Independent-Religious • Coed

Fordham University has been helping students educate themselves for more than 150 years. It has encouraged young people to explore the world's knowledge, to examine its ideas, to question its truths, to engage their own minds, and to value others. The process is enhanced by a powerful setting: New York City. The Jesuit ideals of learning are served not only by the range of experience the city offers but also by the examples of excellence it provides. Combining the resources of an excellent, caring faculty and a great city, the University aims to prepare students for satisfying and productive lives.

##  Academics

Fordham offers a liberal arts-oriented curriculum in the Jesuit tradition and core academic program; fewer than half of graduate courses are open to undergraduates. It awards bachelor's, master's, doctoral, and first professional **degrees.** Challenging opportunities include advanced placement, accelerated degree programs, self-designed majors, tutorials, Freshmen Honors College, an honors program, a senior project, Phi Beta Kappa, and Sigma Xi. Special programs include internships, summer session for credit, off-campus study, study abroad, and Army, Naval, and Air Force ROTC.

The most popular **majors** include business, communication, and English. A complete listing of majors at Fordham appears in the Majors Index beginning on page 380.

The **faculty** at Fordham has 528 full-time graduate and undergraduate teachers, 97% with terminal degrees. 30% of the faculty serve as student advisers. The student-faculty ratio is 17:1, and the average class size in required courses is 24.

##  Computers on Campus

Students are not required to have a computer. 230 **computers** available in the computer center, computer labs, the research center, classrooms, and the library. Staffed computer lab on campus (open 24 hours a day) provides training in the use of computers and software.

The 5 **libraries** have 1.6 million books, 1.9 million microform titles, and 9,968 subscriptions.

##  Campus Life

There are 130 active **organizations** on campus, including a drama/theater group and student-run newspaper and radio station. Student **safety services** include late night transport/escort service, 24-hour emergency telephone alarm devices, 24-hour patrols by trained security personnel, student patrols, and electronically operated dormitory entrances.

Fordham is a member of the NCAA (Division I). **Intercollegiate sports** (some offering scholarships) include baseball (m), basketball (m, w), crew (m, w), cross-country running (m, w), equestrian sports (m, w), football (m), golf (m), ice hockey (m), lacrosse (m, w), riflery (m, w), rugby (m), soccer (m, w), softball (w), squash (m), swimming and diving (m, w), tennis (m, w), track and field (m, w), volleyball (w), water polo (m), wrestling (m).

##  Applying

Fordham requires an essay, a high school transcript, 3 years of high school math, 1 recommendation, SAT I or ACT, and in some cases a campus interview. It recommends 3 years of high school science, 2 years of high school foreign language, an interview, SAT II Subject Tests, and a minimum high school GPA of 3.0. Early, deferred, and midyear entrance are possible, with a 2/1 deadline and continuous processing to 2/1 for financial aid. **Contact:** Mr. John W. Buckley, Director of Admissions, Dealy Hall, Room 115, New York, NY 10458, 718-817-4000 or toll-free 800-FORDHAM; fax 718-367-9404.

## GETTING IN LAST YEAR
4,272 applied
68% were accepted
36% enrolled (1,051)
31% from top tenth of their h.s. class
3.2 average high school GPA
15% had SAT verbal scores over 600
28% had SAT math scores over 600
2% had SAT verbal scores over 700
6% had SAT math scores over 700

## THE STUDENT BODY
Total 14,423, of whom 5,740 are undergraduates
From 42 states and territories, 50 other countries

66% from New York
55% women, 45% men
6% African Americans
0% Native Americans
15% Hispanics
5% Asian Americans
2% international students

## AFTER FRESHMAN YEAR
92% returned for sophomore year
76% got a degree within 4 years
78% got a degree within 5 years
81% got a degree within 6 years

## AFTER GRADUATION
25% pursued further study (10% law, 8% arts and sciences, 6% business)
85% had job offers within 3 months
300 corporations recruited on campus
2 Fulbright scholars

## WHAT YOU WILL PAY
Tuition and fees $14,109
Room and board $6905
90% receive need-based financial aid averaging $6800
10% receive non-need financial aid averaging $6800

# FRANKLIN AND MARSHALL COLLEGE

Lancaster, Pennsylvania • Suburban setting • Private • Independent • Coed

> Franklin & Marshall is an institution that typifies the concept of liberal learning. Whether the course is in theater or physics, classes are small, engagement is high, and discussion dominates over lecture. Beginning with the First Year Seminar, students at Franklin & Marshall are repeatedly invited to participate actively in intellectual investigation at a high level. Graduates consistently testify to the quality of an F&M education as mental preparation for life.

##  Academics

F & M offers a core academic program. It awards bachelor's **degrees**. Challenging opportunities include advanced placement, accelerated degree programs, self-designed majors, tutorials, a senior project, Phi Beta Kappa, and Sigma Xi. Special programs include internships, summer session for credit, off-campus study, and Army ROTC.

The most popular **majors** include political science/government, business, and English. A complete listing of majors at F & M appears in the Majors Index beginning on page 380.

The **faculty** at F & M has 149 full-time teachers, 98% with terminal degrees. 100% of the faculty serve as student advisers. The student-faculty ratio is 11:1, and the average class size in required courses is 19.

##  Computers on Campus

Students are not required to have a computer. Student rooms are linked to a campus network. 70 **computers** available in the computer center, computer labs, academic departments, classrooms, and the library provide access to the main academic computer, off-campus computing facilities, e-mail, and on-line services. Staffed computer lab on campus provides training in the use of computers and software.

The 2 **libraries** have 366,000 books, 258,978 microform titles, and 1,692 subscriptions. They are connected to 26 national **on-line** catalogs.

##  Campus Life

There are 120 active **organizations** on campus, including a drama/theater group and student-run newspaper and radio station. 70% of students participate in student government elections. 40% of eligible men and 30% of eligible women are members of 9 national **fraternities** and 3 national **sororities**. Student **safety services** include residence hall security, late night transport/escort service, 24-hour emergency telephone alarm devices, 24-hour patrols by trained security personnel, and electronically operated dormitory entrances.

F & M is a member of the NCAA (Division III). **Intercollegiate sports** include badminton (m, w), baseball (m), basketball (m, w), crew (m, w), cross-country running (m, w), fencing (m, w), field hockey (w), football (m), golf (m, w), ice hockey (m), lacrosse (m, w), rugby (m, w), soccer (m, w), softball (w), squash (m, w), swimming and diving (m, w), tennis (m, w), track and field (m, w), volleyball (m, w), wrestling (m).

##  Applying

F & M requires an essay, a high school transcript, 2 recommendations, and in some cases SAT I or ACT and SAT II: Writing Test. It recommends 4 years of high school math, 3 years of high school science, 3 years of high school foreign language, and an interview. Early, deferred, and midyear entrance are possible, with a 2/1 deadline and a 2/1 priority date for financial aid. **Contact:** Mr. Peter W. VanBuskirk, Dean of Admissions, College Avenue, Lancaster, PA 17604-3003, 717-291-3953; fax 717-291-4389.

### GETTING IN LAST YEAR
3,308 applied
66% were accepted
23% enrolled (500)
50% from top tenth of their h.s. class
28% had SAT verbal scores over 600
62% had SAT math scores over 600
57% had ACT scores over 26
2% had SAT verbal scores over 700
16% had SAT math scores over 700
10% had ACT scores over 30
20 valedictorians

### THE STUDENT BODY
1,834 undergraduates
From 40 states and territories, 37 other countries
35% from Pennsylvania
47% women, 53% men
3% African Americans
0% Native Americans
4% Hispanics
8% Asian Americans
7% international students

### AFTER FRESHMAN YEAR
94% returned for sophomore year
74% got a degree within 4 years
77% got a degree within 5 years

### AFTER GRADUATION
32% pursued further study (10% arts and sciences, 7% medicine, 6% law)
43% had job offers within 3 months
61 corporations, 1 government agency, 3 nonprofit organizations recruited on campus
1 Fulbright scholar

### WHAT YOU WILL PAY
Comprehensive fee $24,940
51% receive need-based financial aid averaging $12,529
8% receive non-need financial aid averaging $4574

# FURMAN UNIVERSITY

Greenville, South Carolina • Suburban setting • Private • Independent • Coed

As a leading liberal arts college, Furman University is committed to helping students become responsible citizens and intellectual leaders. Furman students come from a wide range of backgrounds and share a desire to be part of an academic environment in which they are challenged to do their best intellectually and creatively. Outside the classroom, programs such as a volunteer service corps give students a chance to assist the less fortunate. The result is a caring community of scholars, where students and faculty work together to discover just how exciting the educational process can be.

 **Academics**

Furman offers a core academic program; a few graduate courses are open to undergraduates. It awards bachelor's and master's **degrees**. Challenging opportunities include advanced placement, accelerated degree programs, self-designed majors, tutorials, a senior project, and Phi Beta Kappa. Special programs include cooperative education, internships, summer session for credit, study abroad, and Army ROTC.

The most popular **majors** include political science/government, biology/biological sciences, and physical fitness/human movement. A complete listing of majors at Furman appears in the Majors Index beginning on page 380.

The **faculty** at Furman has 188 full-time undergraduate teachers, 93% with terminal degrees. 100% of the faculty serve as student advisers. The student-faculty ratio is 12:1, and the average class size in required courses is 20.

 **Computers on Campus**

Students are not required to have a computer. Student rooms are linked to a campus network. 207 **computers** available in the computer center, computer labs, academic buildings, classrooms, and the library provide access to the main academic computer, off-campus computing facilities, e-mail, and on-line services. Staffed computer lab on campus.

The 2 **libraries** have 360,404 books and 1,557 subscriptions. They are connected to 3 national **on-line** catalogs.

 **Campus Life**

There are 128 active **organizations** on campus, including a drama/theater group and student-run newspaper and radio station. 38% of students participate in student government elections. 35% of eligible men and 35% of eligible women are members of 9 national **fraternities** and 8 national **sororities**. Student **safety services** include late night transport/escort service, 24-hour emergency telephone alarm devices, 24-hour patrols by trained security personnel, student patrols, and electronically operated dormitory entrances.

Furman is a member of the NCAA (Division I). **Intercollegiate sports** (some offering scholarships) include baseball (m), basketball (m, w), crew (m, w), cross-country running (m, w), fencing (m, w), football (m), golf (m, w), soccer (m, w), softball (w), tennis (m, w), track and field (m, w), volleyball (m, w), weight lifting (m, w).

 **Applying**

Furman requires an essay, a high school transcript, 3 years of high school math and science, some high school foreign language, and SAT I or ACT. It recommends recommendations. Early and midyear entrance are possible, with a 2/1 deadline and continuous processing to 2/15 for financial aid. **Contact:** Mr. J. Carey Thompson, Director of Admissions, 3300 Poinsett Highway, Greenville, SC 29613, 803-294-2034; fax 803-294-3127.

## GETTING IN LAST YEAR

2,609 applied
77% were accepted
32% enrolled (647)
50% from top tenth of their h.s. class
22% had SAT verbal scores over 600
51% had SAT math scores over 600
46% had ACT scores over 26
3% had SAT verbal scores over 700
11% had SAT math scores over 700
14% had ACT scores over 30

## THE STUDENT BODY

Total 2,663, of whom 2,448 are undergraduates

From 40 states and territories, 18 other countries
31% from South Carolina
54% women, 46% men
4% African Americans
0% Native Americans
1% Hispanics
2% Asian Americans
1% international students

## AFTER FRESHMAN YEAR

85% returned for sophomore year
75% got a degree within 4 years
81% got a degree within 5 years
82% got a degree within 6 years

## AFTER GRADUATION

36% pursued further study (24% arts and sciences, 4% medicine, 3% law)
55% had job offers within 3 months
60 corporations, 3 government agencies, 2 nonprofit organizations recruited on campus
1 Rhodes scholar

## WHAT YOU WILL PAY

Tuition and fees $13,574
Room and board $4048
65% receive need-based financial aid averaging $4700
16% receive non-need financial aid averaging $4000

# GEORGETOWN COLLEGE

Georgetown, Kentucky • Small-town setting • Private • Independent-Religious • Coed

▶ Georgetown College distinguishes itself from many other small liberal arts colleges across the nation by offering a combination of a rigorous and respected academic program, a wealth of opportunities for leadership and involvement in extracurricular activities, and a strong commitment to Christian values and principles. While there is no shortage of schools that possess any one of these characteristics, institutions that combine any two of these qualities are less common. By placing all three side by side at unique levels and combinations, Georgetown provides a special framework that fosters intellectual, social, and spiritual growth.

 ## Academics

Georgetown offers a traditional liberal arts curriculum and core academic program. It awards bachelor's and master's **degrees**. Challenging opportunities include advanced placement, accelerated degree programs, self-designed majors, tutorials, and a senior project. Special programs include cooperative education, internships, summer session for credit, off-campus study, study abroad, and Army and Air Force ROTC.

The most popular **majors** include business, elementary education, and English. A complete listing of majors at Georgetown appears in the Majors Index beginning on page 380.

The **faculty** at Georgetown has 73 full-time undergraduate teachers, 74% with terminal degrees. 93% of the faculty serve as student advisers. The student-faculty ratio is 15:1, and the average class size in required courses is 25.

 ## Computers on Campus

Students are not required to have a computer. 45 **computers** available in the computer center, classrooms, and the library provide access to the main academic computer, off-campus computing facilities, and e-mail. Staffed computer lab on campus provides training in the use of computers and software.

The **library** has 125,851 books and 1,044 subscriptions.

 ## Campus Life

There are 50 active **organizations** on campus, including a drama/theater group and student-run newspaper and radio station. 33% of eligible men and 29% of eligible women are members of 4 national **fraternities**, 3 national **sororities**, and 1 local fraternity. Student **safety services** include late night transport/escort service and 24-hour patrols by trained security personnel.

Georgetown is a member of the NAIA. **Intercollegiate sports** (some offering scholarships) include baseball (m), basketball (m, w), cross-country running (m, w), football (m), golf (m), soccer (m, w), softball (w), tennis (m, w), volleyball (w).

 ## Applying

Georgetown requires an essay, a high school transcript, SAT I or ACT, and in some cases recommendations. It recommends 3 years of high school math and science and some high school foreign language. Midyear entrance is possible, with rolling admissions and continuous processing to 4/1 for financial aid. **Contact:** Mr. Garvel Kindrick, Director of Admissions, 400 East College Street, Georgetown, KY 40324-1696, 502-863-8009 or toll-free 800-788-9985; fax 502-868-8888.

### GETTING IN LAST YEAR
868 applied
90% were accepted
45% enrolled (354)
32% from top tenth of their h.s. class
3.35 average high school GPA
25% had ACT scores over 26
5% had ACT scores over 30

### THE STUDENT BODY
Total 1,405, of whom 1,136
   are undergraduates
From 25 states and territories,
   10 other countries

79% from Kentucky
54% women, 46% men
3% African Americans
0% Native Americans
0% Hispanics
0% Asian Americans
2% international students

### AFTER FRESHMAN YEAR
68% returned for sophomore year
33% got a degree within 4 years
42% got a degree within 5 years
48% got a degree within 6 years

### AFTER GRADUATION
38% pursued further study (10% business, 9% theology, 5% arts and sciences)

### WHAT YOU WILL PAY
Tuition and fees $8050
Room and board $3950
90% receive need-based financial aid
   averaging $1300
8% receive non-need financial aid averaging
   $2170

# GEORGETOWN UNIVERSITY

Washington, D.C. • Urban setting • Private • Independent-Religious • Coed

---

Georgetown's founder, John Carroll, in the spirit of revolution in 1789, saw his academy as an attempt to define the boundaries of American education. Georgetown, the oldest Catholic university in the United States, includes 5 undergraduate schools, a graduate school, and professional schools of law and medicine. It fosters a spirit of inquiry and innovation as it brings the values of the liberal arts tradition to bear on current issues. The resources of Washington, DC, provide a rich complement to the historic village of Georgetown. Students from all 50 states and more than 100 other countries find at Georgetown a unique national and international character.

 **Academics**

Georgetown offers a core academic program; fewer than half of graduate courses are open to undergraduates. It awards bachelor's, master's, doctoral, and first professional **degrees**. Challenging opportunities include advanced placement, self-designed majors, tutorials, an honors program, a senior project, Phi Beta Kappa, and Sigma Xi. Special programs include internships, summer session for credit, off-campus study, study abroad, and Army, Naval, and Air Force ROTC.

The most popular **majors** include political science/government and English. A complete listing of majors at Georgetown appears in the Majors Index beginning on page 380.

The **faculty** at Georgetown has 1,346 full-time graduate and undergraduate teachers, 90% with terminal degrees. 35% of the faculty serve as student advisers.

## Computers on Campus

Students are not required to have a computer. 300 **computers** available in the computer center, computer labs, and the library.

The 4 **libraries** have 2 million books, 170,000 microform titles, and 24,763 subscriptions. They are connected to 5 national **on-line** catalogs.

 **Campus Life**

There are 100 active **organizations** on campus, including a drama/theater group and student-run newspaper and radio station. Student **safety services** include late night transport/escort service, 24-hour emergency telephone alarm devices, 24-hour patrols by trained security personnel, and electronically operated dormitory entrances.

Georgetown is a member of the NCAA (Division I). **Intercollegiate sports** (some offering scholarships) include baseball (m), basketball (m, w), crew (m, w), cross-country running (m, w), field hockey (w), football (m), golf (m), ice hockey (m), lacrosse (m, w), rugby (m), sailing (m, w), soccer (m, w), swimming and diving (m, w), tennis (m, w), track and field (m, w), volleyball (w).

## Applying

Georgetown requires an essay, a high school transcript, 2 recommendations, an interview, and SAT I or ACT. It recommends 3 years of high school math and science, some high school foreign language, and 3 SAT II Subject Tests. Early and deferred entrance are possible, with a 1/10 deadline and continuous processing to 2/1 for financial aid. **Contact:** Mr. Charles A. Deacon, Dean of Undergraduate Admissions, 57th and O Streets, NW, Washington, DC 20057, 202-687-3600; fax 202-687-5084.

---

### GETTING IN LAST YEAR
12,652 applied
24% were accepted
47% enrolled (1,449)
71% from top tenth of their h.s. class
58% had SAT verbal scores over 600
78% had SAT math scores over 600
85% had ACT scores over 26
11% had SAT verbal scores over 700
29% had SAT math scores over 700
45% had ACT scores over 30
204 class presidents
110 valedictorians

### THE STUDENT BODY
Total 12,617, of whom 6,378
  are undergraduates
From 52 states and territories,
  116 other countries
3% from District of Columbia
51% women, 49% men
7% African Americans
1% Native Americans
6% Hispanics
8% Asian Americans
10% international students

### AFTER FRESHMAN YEAR
95% returned for sophomore year

### AFTER GRADUATION
25% pursued further study (12% arts and
  sciences, 8% law, 3% medicine)
165 corporations, 7 government agencies, 2
  nonprofit organizations recruited on campus
2 Marshall, 9 Fulbright scholars

### WHAT YOU WILL PAY
Tuition and fees $18,417
Room and board $5992
45% receive need-based financial aid
  averaging $11,340
10% receive non-need financial aid averaging
  $12,421

# THE GEORGE WASHINGTON UNIVERSITY

Washington, D.C. • Urban setting • Private • Independent • Coed

▶ GW's challenging academic programs are based on a strong curriculum, specialized majors, and interconnections between scholarly theory and experiential education. Programs at GW include a Science Scholars Program in chemistry/physics, a University Honors Program, a 7-year integrated B.A./M.D. program, combined 5-year B.A./M.A. or B.A./M.S. programs, and integrated engineering/law or engineering/medicine programs, all with individual scholarships. Additional scholarships range from $2500 to $15,000.

 **Academics**

GW offers a core academic program; fewer than half of graduate courses are open to undergraduates. It awards associate, bachelor's, master's, doctoral, and first professional **degrees**. Challenging opportunities include advanced placement, accelerated degree programs, self-designed majors, tutorials, an honors program, a senior project, Phi Beta Kappa, and Sigma Xi. Special programs include cooperative education, internships, summer session for credit, off-campus study, study abroad, and Army, Naval, and Air Force ROTC.

The most popular **majors** include international studies, business, and biology/biological sciences. A complete listing of majors at GW appears in the Majors Index beginning on page 380.

The **faculty** at GW has 1,403 full-time graduate and undergraduate teachers, 93% with terminal degrees. The student-faculty ratio is 14:1, and the average class size in required courses is 30.

 **Computers on Campus**

Students are not required to have a computer. Student rooms are linked to a campus network. 550 **computers** available in the computer center, computer labs, classrooms, the library, the student center, and dormitories provide access to the main academic computer, e-mail, and on-line services. Staffed computer lab on campus (open 24 hours a day) provides training in the use of computers and software.

The 3 **libraries** have 1.7 million books, 2 million microform titles, and 14,129 subscriptions. They are connected to 6 national **on-line** catalogs.

 **Campus Life**

There are 230 active **organizations** on campus, including a drama/theater group and student-run newspaper and radio station. 30% of students participate in student government elections. 16% of eligible men and 12% of eligible women are members of 13 national **fraternities** and 8 national **sororities**. Student **safety services** include student community service aides, late night transport/escort service, 24-hour emergency telephone alarm devices, 24-hour patrols by trained security personnel, and electronically operated dormitory entrances.

GW is a member of the NCAA (Division I). **Intercollegiate sports** (some offering scholarships) include baseball (m), basketball (m, w), crew (m, w), cross-country running (m, w), golf (m), gymnastics (w), soccer (m, w), swimming and diving (m, w), tennis (m, w), volleyball (w), water polo (m).

 **Applying**

GW requires an essay, a high school transcript, 2 recommendations, SAT I or ACT, and in some cases 3 years of high school math, 2 years of high school science required for some; minimum 2.5 GPA for transfer students, and 3 SAT II Subject Tests. It recommends 2 years of high school foreign language and SAT II: Writing Test. Early, deferred, and midyear entrance are possible, with a 12/1 deadline and continuous processing to 2/1 for financial aid. **Contact:** Mr. Frederic A. Siegel, Director of Undergraduate Admissions, Office of Undergraduate Admissions, Washington, DC 20052, 202-994-6054 or toll-free 800-447-3765; fax 202-994-0325.

---

**GETTING IN LAST YEAR**
9,681 applied
59% were accepted
27% enrolled (1,568)
40% from top tenth of their h.s. class
30% had SAT verbal scores over 600
51% had SAT math scores over 600
69% had ACT scores over 26
4% had SAT verbal scores over 700
10% had SAT math scores over 700
22% had ACT scores over 30
70 National Merit Scholars
34 valedictorians

**THE STUDENT BODY**
Total 19,298, of whom 6,192
  are undergraduates

From 54 states and territories,
  93 other countries
11% from District of Columbia
52% women, 48% men
7% African Americans
1% Native Americans
4% Hispanics
11% Asian Americans
10% international students

**AFTER FRESHMAN YEAR**
87% returned for sophomore year
59% got a degree within 4 years
67% got a degree within 5 years
69% got a degree within 6 years

**AFTER GRADUATION**
21% pursued further study (11% arts and sciences, 5% law, 3% business)
79 corporations, 9 government agencies, 1 nonprofit organization recruited on campus
2 Fulbright scholars

**WHAT YOU WILL PAY**
Tuition and fees $18,170
Room and board $5598
46% receive need-based financial aid averaging $16,191
27% receive non-need financial aid averaging $9363

# GEORGIA INSTITUTE OF TECHNOLOGY

Atlanta, Georgia • Urban setting • Public • State-supported • Coed

▶ Georgia Tech is ranked as the third-best educational value in the nation according to *U.S. News & World Report*; is one of the top 10 engineering graduate programs in the U.S.; has the largest voluntary cooperative education program in the U.S.; enrolls the highest percentage of National Merit Scholars and the second-highest percentage of National Achievement Scholars among publicly supported U.S. institutions; ranks first in the total number of all degrees awarded in engineering; and ranks first in the total number of women engineers graduated.

 **Academics**

Georgia Tech offers a core academic program; fewer than half of graduate courses are open to undergraduates. It awards bachelor's, master's, and doctoral **degrees**. Challenging opportunities include advanced placement, accelerated degree programs, self-designed majors, tutorials, an honors program, a senior project, and Sigma Xi. Special programs include cooperative education, internships, summer session for credit, off-campus study, study abroad, and Army, Naval, and Air Force ROTC.

The most popular **majors** include electrical engineering, mechanical engineering, and business. A complete listing of majors at Georgia Tech appears in the Majors Index beginning on page 380.

The **faculty** at Georgia Tech has 630 full-time graduate and undergraduate teachers, 92% with terminal degrees. The student-faculty ratio is 20:1.

 **Computers on Campus**

Students are not required to have a computer. 5,000 **computers** available in the computer center, academic buildings, the library, the student center, and dormitories.

The 2 **libraries** have 1.8 million books and 11,524 subscriptions. They are connected to 5 national **on-line** catalogs.

 **Campus Life**

There are 250 active **organizations** on campus, including a drama/theater group and student-run newspaper and radio station. 30% of eligible men and 26% of eligible women are members of 32 national **fraternities** and 8 national **sororities**. Student **safety services** include late night transport/escort service, 24-hour emergency telephone alarm devices, 24-hour patrols by trained security personnel, student patrols, and electronically operated dormitory entrances.

Georgia Tech is a member of the NCAA (Division I). **Intercollegiate sports** (some offering scholarships) include baseball (m), basketball (m, w), cross-country running (m, w), football (m), golf (m), ice hockey (m), lacrosse (m), rugby (m), softball (w), swimming and diving (m), tennis (m, w), track and field (m, w), volleyball (w).

 **Applying**

Georgia Tech requires a high school transcript, 4 years of high school math, 3 years of high school science, 2 years of high school foreign language, SAT I, and in some cases ACT. Early and midyear entrance are possible, with a 2/1 deadline and continuous processing to 3/1 for financial aid. **Contact:** Ms. Deborah Smith, Director of Admissions, 225 North Avenue, NW, Atlanta, GA 30332-0320, 404-894-4154; fax 404-853-9163.

**GETTING IN LAST YEAR**
7,875 applied
59% were accepted
38% enrolled (1,763)
90% from top tenth of their h.s. class
3.6 average high school GPA
30% had SAT verbal scores over 600
87% had SAT math scores over 600
4% had SAT verbal scores over 700
39% had SAT math scores over 700
109 National Merit Scholars

**THE STUDENT BODY**
Total 12,901, of whom 9,213 are undergraduates

From 52 states and territories, 67 other countries
26% women, 74% men
9% African Americans
1% Native Americans
4% Hispanics
11% Asian Americans

**AFTER FRESHMAN YEAR**
83% returned for sophomore year
28% got a degree within 4 years
60% got a degree within 5 years

**AFTER GRADUATION**
20% pursued further study

**WHAT YOU WILL PAY**
Resident tuition and fees $2343
Nonresident tuition and fees $5034
Room and board $4686
Need-based financial aid averages $1200
Non-need financial aid averages $1400

# GEORGIA SOUTHERN UNIVERSITY

Statesboro, Georgia • Small-town setting • Public • State-supported • Coed

 **Academics**

Georgia Southern offers a liberal arts curriculum and core academic program. It awards associate, bachelor's, master's, and doctoral **degrees**. Challenging opportunities include advanced placement, an honors program, a senior project, and Sigma Xi. Special programs include cooperative education, internships, summer session for credit, study abroad, and Army ROTC.

The most popular **majors** include early childhood education, marketing/retailing/merchandising, and finance/banking. A complete listing of majors at Georgia Southern appears in the Majors Index beginning on page 380.

The **faculty** at Georgia Southern has 590 full-time undergraduate teachers. The student-faculty ratio is 24:1, and the average class size in required courses is 30.

 **Computers on Campus**

Students are not required to have a computer. 275 **computers** available in the computer center, computer labs, the learning resource center, the library, and dormitories.

The **library** has 451,292 books and 3,511 subscriptions.

 **Campus Life**

Active **organizations** on campus include drama/theater group and student-run newspaper and radio station. 25% of eligible men and 21% of eligible women are members of 16 national **fraternities** and 11 national **sororities**. Student **safety services** include residence hall security, late night transport/escort service, 24-hour emergency telephone alarm devices, 24-hour patrols by trained security personnel, student patrols, and electronically operated dormitory entrances.

Georgia Southern is a member of the NCAA (Division I). **Intercollegiate sports** (some offering scholarships) include baseball (m), basketball (m, w), cross-country running (m, w), fencing (m, w), football (m), golf (m), rugby (m), sailing (m), soccer (m, w), softball (m, w), swimming and diving (m, w), tennis (m, w), volleyball (m, w).

 **Applying**

Georgia Southern requires a high school transcript, 3 years of high school math and science, 2 years of high school foreign language, proof of immunization, and SAT I or ACT. Early entrance is possible, with an 8/1 deadline and continuous processing to 4/15 for financial aid. **Contact:** Dr. Dale Wasson, Director of Admissions, Rosenwald Boulevard, Sweetheart Circle, Statesboro, GA 30460-8100, 912-681-5531; fax 912-681-0081.

---

**GETTING IN LAST YEAR**
8,445 applied
73% were accepted
63% enrolled (3,880)
2% had SAT verbal scores over 600
6% had SAT math scores over 600
1% had SAT verbal scores over 700
1% had SAT math scores over 700

**THE STUDENT BODY**
Total 14,138, of whom 11,155
   are undergraduates
From 50 states and territories,
   67 other countries
88% from Georgia
54% women, 46% men
19% African Americans
1% Native Americans
1% Hispanics
1% Asian Americans
1% international students

**AFTER FRESHMAN YEAR**
74% returned for sophomore year

**AFTER GRADUATION**
80 corporations recruited on campus
1 Fulbright scholar

**WHAT YOU WILL PAY**
Resident tuition and fees $1797
Nonresident tuition and fees $4641
Room and board $3285
Need-based financial aid averages $1100
Non-need financial aid averages $1050

# GETTYSBURG COLLEGE

Gettysburg, Pennsylvania • Small-town setting • Private • Independent • Coed

## Academics

Gettysburg College offers an interdisciplinary curriculum and core academic program. It awards bachelor's **degrees**. Challenging opportunities include advanced placement, accelerated degree programs, self-designed majors, an honors program, and Phi Beta Kappa. Special programs include internships, off-campus study, and study abroad.

The most popular **majors** include business, political science/government, and psychology. A complete listing of majors at Gettysburg College appears in the Majors Index beginning on page 380.

The **faculty** at Gettysburg College has 154 full-time teachers, 95% with terminal degrees. 100% of the faculty serve as student advisers. The student-faculty ratio is 12:1, and the average class size in required courses is 20.

## Computers on Campus

Students are not required to have a computer. Student rooms are linked to a campus network. 250 **computers** available in the computer center, computer labs, the learning resource center, the library, the student center, and dormitories provide access to the main academic computer, off-campus computing facilities, e-mail, and on-line services. Staffed computer lab on campus (open 24 hours a day) provides training in the use of computers and software.

The **library** has 340,000 books, 35,000 microform titles, and 1,350 subscriptions.

## Campus Life

There are 60 active **organizations** on campus, including a drama/theater group and student-run newspaper and radio station. 55% of eligible men and 45% of eligible women are members of 11 national **fraternities** and 5 national **sororities**. Student **safety services** include late night transport/escort service, 24-hour emergency telephone alarm devices, 24-hour patrols by trained security personnel, and electronically operated dormitory entrances.

Gettysburg College is a member of the NCAA (Division III). **Intercollegiate sports** include baseball (m), basketball (m, w), cross-country running (m, w), field hockey (w), football (m), golf (m, w), lacrosse (m, w), rugby (m), soccer (m, w), softball (w), swimming and diving (m, w), tennis (m, w), track and field (m, w), volleyball (w), wrestling (m).

## Applying

Gettysburg College requires an essay, a high school transcript, 1 recommendation, SAT I or ACT, and a minimum high school GPA of 2.0. It recommends 3 years of high school math and science, some high school foreign language, a campus interview, 3 SAT II Subject Tests, and a minimum high school GPA of 3.0. Early, deferred, and midyear entrance are possible, with a 2/15 deadline and continuous processing to 2/15 for financial aid. **Contact:** Mr. Delwin K. Gustafson, Dean of Admissions, Eisenhower House, Gettysburg, PA 17325-1411, 717-337-6100 or toll-free 800-431-0803; fax 717-337-6145.

### GETTING IN LAST YEAR
3,398 applied
76% were accepted
24% enrolled (609)
40% from top tenth of their h.s. class
3.5 average high school GPA
17% had SAT verbal scores over 600
40% had SAT math scores over 600
2% had SAT verbal scores over 700
5% had SAT math scores over 700

### THE STUDENT BODY
1,950 undergraduates
From 40 states and territories,
 25 other countries
25% from Pennsylvania
50% women, 50% men
3% African Americans
1% Native Americans
2% Hispanics
3% Asian Americans
2% international students

### AFTER FRESHMAN YEAR
90% returned for sophomore year
79% got a degree within 4 years
80% got a degree within 5 years

### AFTER GRADUATION
31% pursued further study (11% arts and
 sciences, 7% law, 5% business)

### WHAT YOU WILL PAY
Tuition and fees $20,054
Room and board $4100
51% receive need-based financial aid
 averaging $10,600

# GMI ENGINEERING & MANAGEMENT INSTITUTE

Flint, Michigan • Suburban setting • Private • Independent • Coed

GMI Engineering & Management Institute is an independent college established in 1919 that operates on a unique 5-year, fully cooperative plan of education. Students alternate 12-week academic terms on campus with 12-week terms of paid work experience with their co-op employer. Affiliated employers are located in 43 states and several countries; 70% of students are able to live at home during work sessions.

##  Academics

GMI offers a core academic program; a few graduate courses are open to undergraduates. It awards bachelor's and master's **degrees**. Challenging opportunities include advanced placement, an honors program, and a senior project. Special programs include cooperative education, internships, and study abroad.

The most popular **majors** include mechanical engineering, electrical engineering, and manufacturing engineering. A complete listing of majors at GMI appears in the Majors Index beginning on page 380.

The **faculty** at GMI has 150 full-time undergraduate teachers, 75% with terminal degrees. 50% of the faculty serve as student advisers. The student-faculty ratio is 13:1.

##  Computers on Campus

Students are not required to have a computer. 300 **computers** available in the computer center, labs, and classrooms provide access to the main academic computer, off-campus computing facilities, e-mail, and on-line services. Staffed computer lab on campus (open 24 hours a day) provides training in the use of computers and software.

The **library** has 62,000 books, 27,000 microform titles, and 877 subscriptions.

##  Campus Life

Active **organizations** on campus include drama/theater group and student-run newspaper and radio station. 65% of eligible men and 60% of eligible women are members of 14 national **fraternities** and 6 national **sororities**. Student **safety services** include 24-hour emergency telephone alarm devices, 24-hour patrols by trained security personnel, and electronically operated dormitory entrances. **Intercollegiate sports** include ice hockey (m), soccer (m), volleyball (m).

##  Applying

GMI requires a high school transcript, 3 years of high school math and science, 1 recommendation, SAT I or ACT, and a minimum high school GPA of 3.0. It recommends some high school foreign language and 2 SAT II Subject Tests. Deferred and midyear entrance are possible, with rolling admissions and continuous processing to 3/30 for financial aid. **Contact:** Mr. Phillip D. Lavender, Director of Admissions, 1700 West Third Avenue, Flint, MI 48504-4898, 810-762-7865 or toll-free 800-955-4464; fax 810-762-9837.

### GETTING IN LAST YEAR
1,748 applied
76% were accepted
42% enrolled (559)
50% from top tenth of their h.s. class
3.44 average high school GPA
14% had SAT verbal scores over 600
68% had SAT math scores over 600
57% had ACT scores over 26
1% had SAT verbal scores over 700
16% had SAT math scores over 700
15% had ACT scores over 30

### THE STUDENT BODY
Total 3,258, of whom 2,395
    are undergraduates
From 46 states and territories,
    14 other countries
48% from Michigan
19% women, 81% men
5% African Americans
1% Native Americans
2% Hispanics
7% Asian Americans
4% international students

### AFTER FRESHMAN YEAR
91% returned for sophomore year
2% got a degree within 4 years
64% got a degree within 5 years
73% got a degree within 6 years

### AFTER GRADUATION
6% pursued further study
30 corporations recruited on campus

### WHAT YOU WILL PAY
Tuition and fees $11,730
Room and board $3462
Need-based financial aid averages $1570
Non-need financial aid averages $2054

# GOSHEN COLLEGE

Goshen, Indiana • Small-town setting • Private • Independent-Religious • Coed

Goshen College is dedicated to the development of informed, articulate, sensitive, responsible Christians. As a ministry of the Mennonite Church, Goshen seeks to integrate Christian values with educational and professional life. As a community of faith and learning, Goshen strives to foster personal, intellectual, spiritual, and social growth. The College views education as a moral activity that produces servant leaders for the church and the world. Goshen has attracted national attention for its groundbreaking international education program and for providing an above-average education for a below-average price.

 **Academics**

Goshen offers a Christian development curriculum and core academic program. It awards bachelor's **degrees**. Challenging opportunities include advanced placement, accelerated degree programs, self-designed majors, tutorials, and a senior project. Special programs include cooperative education, internships, summer session for credit, off-campus study, and study abroad.

The most popular **majors** include business, nursing, and elementary education. A complete listing of majors at Goshen appears in the Majors Index beginning on page 380.

The **faculty** at Goshen has 85 full-time teachers, 63% with terminal degrees. 90% of the faculty serve as student advisers. The student-faculty ratio is 13:1, and the average class size in required courses is 25.

 **Computers on Campus**

Students are not required to have a computer. Student rooms are linked to a campus network. 80 **computers**

available in the computer center, computer labs, and dormitories provide access to the main academic computer, e-mail, and on-line services. Staffed computer lab on campus (open 24 hours a day) provides training in the use of computers and software.

The 2 **libraries** have 115,000 books, 100 microform titles, and 860 subscriptions. They are connected to 2 national **on-line** catalogs.

 **Campus Life**

There are 20 active **organizations** on campus, including a drama/theater group and student-run newspaper and radio station. Student **safety services** include night security and 24-hour emergency telephone alarm devices.

Goshen is a member of the NAIA. **Intercollegiate sports** (some offering scholarships) include basketball (m, w), cross-country running (m, w), golf (m), soccer (m, w), softball (w), tennis (m, w), track and field (m, w), volleyball (w).

 **Applying**

Goshen requires a high school transcript, 1 recommendation, and SAT I or ACT. It recommends 3 years of high school math and science, some high school foreign language, and an interview. Early, deferred, and midyear entrance are possible, with rolling admissions and continuous processing to 3/1 for financial aid. **Contact:** Ms. Martha Lehman, Director of Admissions, 1700 South Main Street, Goshen, IN 46526-4794, 219-535-7535 or toll-free 800-348-7422 (out-of-state); fax 219-535-7609.

## GETTING IN LAST YEAR
485 applied
91% were accepted
48% enrolled (211)
26% from top tenth of their h.s. class
3.27 average high school GPA
10% had SAT verbal scores over 600
22% had SAT math scores over 600
1% had SAT verbal scores over 700
7% had SAT math scores over 700
5 National Merit Scholars

## THE STUDENT BODY
1,011 undergraduates
From 41 states and territories,
  29 other countries

47% from Indiana
54% women, 46% men
3% African Americans
0% Native Americans
4% Hispanics
1% Asian Americans
10% international students

## AFTER FRESHMAN YEAR
90% returned for sophomore year
50% got a degree within 4 years
64% got a degree within 5 years
68% got a degree within 6 years

## AFTER GRADUATION
39% pursued further study (15% arts and
  sciences, 10% medicine, 5% business)
8 corporations, 20 nonprofit organizations
  recruited on campus

## WHAT YOU WILL PAY
Tuition and fees $9900
Room and board $3760
69% receive need-based financial aid
  averaging $1118
76% receive non-need financial aid averaging
  $1218

# GOUCHER COLLEGE

Baltimore, Maryland • Suburban setting • Private • Independent • Coed

At Goucher, the traditional concept of the liberal arts is expanded to encompass a global perspective and an interdisciplinary way of thinking about the world. In typically small classes, Goucher professors approach education as a collaborative process between students and teachers; they take time to know the students and how they learn. As active participants in their own education, students are encouraged to tailor their course of study to their individual interests; some even create their own majors. Life at Goucher is shaped by a rigorous academic experience and a strong sense of community to which everyone contributes.

 ## Academics

Goucher offers an interdisciplinary curriculum and core academic program. It awards bachelor's and master's **degrees**. Challenging opportunities include advanced placement, accelerated degree programs, self-designed majors, tutorials, an honors program, a senior project, and Phi Beta Kappa. Special programs include internships, off-campus study, study abroad, and Army ROTC.

The most popular **majors** include English, education, and psychology. A complete listing of majors at Goucher appears in the Majors Index beginning on page 380.

The **faculty** at Goucher has 84 full-time undergraduate teachers, 90% with terminal degrees. 100% of the faculty serve as student advisers. The student-faculty ratio is 9:1, and the average class size in required courses is 11.

 ## Computers on Campus

Students are not required to have a computer. 100 **computers** available in the computer center, academic buildings, and the library.

The **library** has 279,000 books, 9,330 microform titles, and 1,114 subscriptions. It is connected to 1 national **on-line** catalog.

 ## Campus Life

There are 43 active **organizations** on campus, including a drama/theater group and student-run newspaper. Student **safety services** include late night transport/escort service and electronically operated dormitory entrances.

Goucher is a member of the NCAA (Division III). **Intercollegiate sports** include basketball (m, w), cross-country running (m, w), equestrian sports (m, w), fencing (m, w), field hockey (w), lacrosse (m, w), soccer (m, w), swimming and diving (m, w), tennis (m, w), volleyball (w).

 ## Applying

Goucher requires an essay, a high school transcript, 3 years of high school math, 2 years of high school foreign language, 3 recommendations, SAT I or ACT, and a minimum high school GPA of 2.0. It recommends 3 years of high school science, an interview, 3 SAT II Subject Tests, and a minimum high school GPA of 3.0. Early, deferred, and midyear entrance are possible, with a 2/1 deadline and continuous processing to 2/15 for financial aid. **Contact:** Ms. Elise Seraydarian, Director of Admissions, 1021 Dulaney Valley Road, Baltimore, MD 21204-2794, 410-337-6100 or toll-free 800-638-4278; fax 410-337-6123.

### GETTING IN LAST YEAR
1,168 applied
70% were accepted
31% enrolled (256)
37% from top tenth of their h.s. class
3.27 average high school GPA
24% had SAT verbal scores over 600
28% had SAT math scores over 600
3% had SAT verbal scores over 700
8% had SAT math scores over 700
2 National Merit Scholars
6 valedictorians

### THE STUDENT BODY
Total 1,130, of whom 1,031 are undergraduates
From 40 states and territories, 18 other countries
49% from Maryland
66% women, 34% men
9% African Americans
0% Native Americans
3% Hispanics
4% Asian Americans
3% international students

### AFTER FRESHMAN YEAR
88% returned for sophomore year

### AFTER GRADUATION
30% pursued further study (17% arts and sciences, 5% medicine, 4% business)
18 corporations recruited on campus
1 Fulbright scholar

### WHAT YOU WILL PAY
Tuition and fees $15,688
Room and board $6174
48% receive need-based financial aid averaging $8300
40% receive non-need financial aid averaging $8300

# GRINNELL COLLEGE

Grinnell, Iowa • Small-town setting • Private • Independent • Coed

Grinnell may seem like many distinguished liberal arts colleges. But, like the students it attracts, Grinnell is marked by an unusual blend of individualism, academic rigor, informality, innovation, and social justice. Free from core requirements, students design programs that fulfill their own educational needs. Intimate class settings allow faculty to become both mentors and lifelong friends. Grinnellians feel empowered in and out of the classroom. Residential life is largely self-governing; opinions are not only heard, but treasured. Encouraged to share their distinct perspectives, students from nearly 50 states and more than 40 countries make Grinnell an international haven in America's heartland.

 **Academics**

Grinnell College offers an open curriculum and no core academic program. It awards bachelor's **degrees**. Challenging opportunities include advanced placement, self-designed majors, tutorials, and Phi Beta Kappa. Special programs include internships, off-campus study, and study abroad.

The most popular **majors** include economics, English, and history. A complete listing of majors at Grinnell College appears in the Majors Index beginning on page 380.

The **faculty** at Grinnell College has 140 full-time teachers, 96% with terminal degrees. 89% of the faculty serve as student advisers. The student-faculty ratio is 10:1.

 **Computers on Campus**

Students are not required to have a computer. 365 **computers** available in the computer center, science building,

Carnegie Hall, classrooms, the library, and dormitories provide access to the main academic computer, off-campus computing facilities, e-mail, and on-line services. Staffed computer lab on campus provides training in the use of computers and software.

The 3 **libraries** have 363,916 books, 7,830 microform titles, and 2,453 subscriptions. They are connected to 5 national **on-line** catalogs.

 **Campus Life**

There are 106 active **organizations** on campus, including a drama/theater group and student-run newspaper and radio station. 55% of students participate in student government elections. Student **safety services** include late night transport/escort service.

Grinnell College is a member of the NCAA (Division III). **Intercollegiate sports** include baseball (m), basketball (m, w), cross-country running (m, w), football (m), golf (m, w), soccer (m, w), softball (w), swimming and diving (m, w), tennis (m, w), track and field (m, w), volleyball (w).

 **Applying**

Grinnell College requires an essay, a high school transcript, 3 years of high school math, 2 recommendations, and SAT I or ACT. It recommends 3 years of high school science, 3 years of high school foreign language, and an interview. Early and deferred entrance are possible, with a 2/1 deadline and continuous processing to 2/1 for financial aid. **Contact:** Mr. Vincent Cuseo, Director of Admission, Mears Cottage, Grinnell, IA 50112-0807, 515-269-3600 or toll-free 800-247-0113 (in-state); fax 515-269-4800.

## GETTING IN LAST YEAR

1,843 applied
64% were accepted
28% enrolled (337)
64% from top tenth of their h.s. class
64% had SAT verbal scores over 600
81% had SAT math scores over 600
89% had ACT scores over 26
10% had SAT verbal scores over 700
29% had SAT math scores over 700
49% had ACT scores over 30
26 National Merit Scholars
32 valedictorians

## THE STUDENT BODY

1,295 undergraduates
From 50 states and territories,
   42 other countries
14% from Iowa
55% women, 45% men
4% African Americans
0% Native Americans
3% Hispanics
4% Asian Americans
10% international students

## AFTER FRESHMAN YEAR

93% returned for sophomore year
76% got a degree within 4 years
82% got a degree within 5 years
83% got a degree within 6 years

## AFTER GRADUATION

24% pursued further study
12 corporations, 15 nonprofit organizations
   recruited on campus
1 Fulbright scholar

## WHAT YOU WILL PAY

Tuition and fees $16,062
Room and board $4618
68% receive need-based financial aid
   averaging $10,211
15% receive non-need financial aid averaging
   $5571

# GROVE CITY COLLEGE

Grove City, Pennsylvania • Small-town setting • Private • Independent-Religious • Coed

Grove City is a nationally acclaimed 4-year private college emphasizing strong academics, solid traditional values, and a sensible price. Outstanding scholars and leaders in education, science, and international affairs visit Grove City College each year. The College's magnificent Pew Fine Arts Center houses facilities for theater, music, dance, photography, and the visual arts. The state-of-the-art Technological Learning Center provides a high-quality computer center for student use. Over 100 student organizations on campus offer opportunities for a wide variety of cocurricular activities, and an NCAA Division III sports program, with excellent facilities, provides great intercollegiate competition for men and women.

## Academics

Grove City offers a Western civilization curriculum and core academic program. It awards bachelor's **degrees**. Challenging opportunities include advanced placement, self-designed majors, and a senior project. Special programs include internships and summer session for credit.

The most popular **majors** include business, elementary education, and accounting. A complete listing of majors at Grove City appears in the Majors Index beginning on page 380.

The **faculty** at Grove City has 108 full-time teachers, 66% with terminal degrees. 65% of the faculty serve as student advisers. The student-faculty ratio is 20:1, and the average class size in required courses is 56.

## Computers on Campus

Students are required to have a computer. PCs are provided. 150 **computers** available in the computer center, engineering labs, science building, and the library provide access to the main academic computer and e-mail. Staffed computer lab on campus provides training in the use of computers and software.

The **library** has 169,000 books, 244,000 microform titles, and 1,200 subscriptions.

## Campus Life

There are 123 active **organizations** on campus, including a drama/theater group and student-run newspaper and radio station. 30% of eligible men and 50% of eligible women are members of 8 local **fraternities** and 8 local **sororities**. Student **safety services** include monitored women's dormitory entrances, late night transport/escort service, 24-hour emergency telephone alarm devices, 24-hour patrols by trained security personnel, student patrols, and electronically operated dormitory entrances.

Grove City is a member of the NCAA (Division III). **Intercollegiate sports** include baseball (m), basketball (m, w), cross-country running (m, w), football (m), golf (m, w), soccer (m, w), softball (w), swimming and diving (m, w), tennis (m, w), track and field (m, w), volleyball (w).

## Applying

Grove City requires an essay, a high school transcript, 2 recommendations, and SAT I or ACT. It recommends 3 years of high school math and science, 3 years of high school foreign language, and a campus interview. Early, deferred, and midyear entrance are possible, with a 2/15 deadline and a 5/1 priority date for financial aid. **Contact:** Mr. Jeffrey C. Mincey, Director of Admissions, 100 Campus Drive, Grove City, PA 16127-2104, 412-458-2100.

---

### GETTING IN LAST YEAR

2,505 applied
47% were accepted
52% enrolled (607)
54% from top tenth of their h.s. class
3.7 average high school GPA
22% had SAT verbal scores over 600
58% had SAT math scores over 600
80% had ACT scores over 26
1% had SAT verbal scores over 700
12% had SAT math scores over 700
20% had ACT scores over 30
7 National Merit Scholars
32 valedictorians

### THE STUDENT BODY

2,280 undergraduates
From 42 states and territories,
   20 other countries
63% from Pennsylvania
49% women, 51% men
1% African Americans
0% Native Americans
1% Hispanics
1% Asian Americans
1% international students

### AFTER FRESHMAN YEAR

88% returned for sophomore year
74% got a degree within 4 years
79% got a degree within 5 years

### AFTER GRADUATION

17% pursued further study (10% arts and
   sciences, 3% law, 2% business)
60 corporations, 3 government agencies
   recruited on campus

### WHAT YOU WILL PAY

Tuition and fees $5224
Room and board $3048
36% receive need-based financial aid
   averaging $1411
33% receive non-need financial aid averaging
   $2565

---

# GUILFORD COLLEGE

Greensboro, North Carolina • Suburban setting • Private • Independent-Religious • Coed

---

In each of the last 2 years the majority of graduating seniors have chosen the same 2 adjectives to describe Guilford: friendly and challenging. Although students work hard, they have solid, friendly relationships with faculty members who support the students in their course work. The College continues to believe that it is important for students to strike a balance between their studies and activities. Guilford students tend to be aware, concerned, issue oriented, open minded, and supportive of each other.

 ## Academics

Guilford offers an area distribution and interdisciplinary curriculum and core academic program. It awards bachelor's **degrees**. Challenging opportunities include advanced placement, accelerated degree programs, self-designed majors, tutorials, an honors program, and a senior project. Special programs include internships, summer session for credit, off-campus study, study abroad, and Army and Air Force ROTC.

The most popular **majors** include business, English, and criminal justice. A complete listing of majors at Guilford appears in the Majors Index beginning on page 380.

The **faculty** at Guilford has 89 full-time teachers, 86% with terminal degrees. 100% of the faculty serve as student advisers. The student-faculty ratio is 14:1, and the average class size in required courses is 17.

 ## Computers on Campus

Students are not required to have a computer. Student rooms are linked to a campus network. 150 **computers** available in the computer center, computer labs, the learn-ing resource center, classroom buildings, the library, the student center, and dormitories provide access to the main academic computer and e-mail. Staffed computer lab on campus provides training in the use of computers and software.

The **library** has 191,382 books, 55 microform titles, and 1,217 subscriptions. It is connected to 6 national **on-line** catalogs.

 ## Campus Life

There are 42 active **organizations** on campus, including a drama/theater group and student-run newspaper and radio station. 62% of students participate in student government elections. Student **safety services** include late night transport/escort service, 24-hour emergency telephone alarm devices, 24-hour patrols by trained security personnel, and student patrols.

Guilford is a member of the NCAA (Division III). **Intercollegiate sports** include baseball (m), basketball (m, w), football (m), golf (m), lacrosse (m, w), rugby (m, w), soccer (m, w), tennis (m, w), volleyball (w).

 ## Applying

Guilford requires an essay, a high school transcript, 3 years of high school math, 2 years of high school foreign language, 1 recommendation, SAT I or ACT, and a minimum high school GPA of 2.0. It recommends 3 years of high school science, an interview, SAT II Subject Tests, and a minimum high school GPA of 3.0. Early, deferred, and midyear entrance are possible, with a 2/1 deadline and continuous processing to 3/1 for financial aid. **Contact:** Mr. Alton Newell, Dean of Admission, 5800 West Friendly Avenue, Greensboro, NC 27410-4173, 910-316-2124 or toll-free 800-992-7759; fax 910-316-2954.

---

### GETTING IN LAST YEAR

1,305 applied
81% were accepted
31% enrolled (328)
29% from top tenth of their h.s. class
3.24 average high school GPA
22% had SAT verbal scores over 600
33% had SAT math scores over 600
38% had ACT scores over 26
3% had SAT verbal scores over 700
4% had SAT math scores over 700
9% had ACT scores over 30
6 valedictorians

### THE STUDENT BODY

1,187 undergraduates
From 43 states and territories, 30 other countries
35% from North Carolina
52% women, 48% men
6% African Americans
1% Native Americans
2% Hispanics
1% Asian Americans
4% international students

### AFTER FRESHMAN YEAR

77% returned for sophomore year
47% got a degree within 4 years
56% got a degree within 5 years
58% got a degree within 6 years

### AFTER GRADUATION

22% pursued further study (15% arts and sciences, 3% law, 2% medicine)
60 corporations, 10 government agencies, 60 nonprofit organizations recruited on campus

### WHAT YOU WILL PAY

Tuition and fees $13,610
Room and board $5160
52% receive need-based financial aid averaging $5820
24% receive non-need financial aid averaging $2450

---

# GUSTAVUS ADOLPHUS COLLEGE

St. Peter, Minnesota • Small-town setting • Private • Independent-Religious • Coed

Gustavus Adolphus College is a national liberal arts college committed to high-quality teaching, the liberal arts and sciences, and its Lutheran heritage. Innovation in the classroom is demonstrated through the 4-1-4 calendar, 2 core curricula, the Writing Across the Curriculum program, and one of the most progressive undergraduate research programs in the country. Cost is made affordable through the Guaranteed Cost Plan, Partners in Scholarship Award for research mentoring, and the new government direct loan program. Excellent facilities include Olin Hall for physics, mathematics, and computer science; Confer Hall for humanities; and Lund Center for physical education, athletics, and health.

## Academics

Gustavus offers a liberal arts curriculum and core academic program. It awards bachelor's **degrees**. Challenging opportunities include advanced placement, accelerated degree programs, self-designed majors, tutorials, an honors program, a senior project, Phi Beta Kappa, and Sigma Xi. Special programs include cooperative education, internships, summer session for credit, off-campus study, study abroad, and Army ROTC.

The most popular **majors** include biology/biological sciences, psychology, and political science/government. A complete listing of majors at Gustavus appears in the Majors Index beginning on page 380.

The **faculty** at Gustavus has 164 full-time teachers, 81% with terminal degrees. 100% of the faculty serve as student advisers. The student-faculty ratio is 13:1, and the average class size in required courses is 22.

## Computers on Campus

Students are not required to have a computer. 200 **computers** available in the computer center, computer labs, classrooms, and the library provide access to e-mail. Staffed computer lab on campus provides training in the use of computers and software.

The 5 **libraries** have 233,000 books, 30,000 microform titles, and 1,200 subscriptions. They are connected to 5 national **on-line** catalogs.

## Campus Life

There are 85 active **organizations** on campus, including a drama/theater group and student-run newspaper and radio station. 60% of students participate in student government elections. 20% of eligible men and 25% of eligible women are members of 6 local **fraternities** and 6 local **sororities**. Student **safety services** include late night transport/escort service, 24-hour emergency telephone alarm devices, 24-hour patrols by trained security personnel, and electronically operated dormitory entrances.

Gustavus is a member of the NCAA (Division III). **Intercollegiate sports** include baseball (m), basketball (m, w), cross-country running (m, w), football (m), golf (m, w), gymnastics (w), ice hockey (m), soccer (m, w), softball (w), swimming and diving (m, w), tennis (m, w), track and field (m, w), volleyball (w).

## Applying

Gustavus requires an essay, a high school transcript, 2 recommendations, and SAT I or ACT. It recommends 3 years of high school math and science, some high school foreign language, and an interview. Early, deferred, and midyear entrance are possible, with a 4/1 deadline and continuous processing to 4/1 for financial aid. **Contact:** Mr. Mark Anderson, Director of Admissions, 800 College Avenue, St. Peter, MN 56082-1498, 507-933-7676 or toll-free 800-GUSTAVU(S).

### GETTING IN LAST YEAR

1,828 applied
79% were accepted
42% enrolled (604)
37% from top tenth of their h.s. class
28% had SAT verbal scores over 600
49% had SAT math scores over 600
48% had ACT scores over 26
4% had SAT verbal scores over 700
19% had SAT math scores over 700
15% had ACT scores over 30
18 National Merit Scholars

### THE STUDENT BODY

2,334 undergraduates
From 43 states and territories,
   22 other countries
72% from Minnesota
54% women, 46% men
2% African Americans
0% Native Americans
1% Hispanics
3% Asian Americans
2% international students

### AFTER FRESHMAN YEAR

88% returned for sophomore year
74% got a degree within 4 years
77% got a degree within 5 years
78% got a degree within 6 years

### AFTER GRADUATION

36% pursued further study (13% arts and
   sciences, 7% business, 5% law)
25 corporations, 5 government agencies, 10
   nonprofit organizations recruited on campus

### WHAT YOU WILL PAY

Tuition and fees $14,195
Room and board $3600
68% receive need-based financial aid
   averaging $8267
6% receive non-need financial aid averaging
   $5000

# HAMILTON COLLEGE

Clinton, New York • Rural setting • Private • Independent • Coed

Hamilton College is situated in the hills overlooking the Mohawk Valley in central New York State on a picturesque campus of more than 1,000 acres. Facilities include the new Schambach Center for the Performing Arts, fully equipped scientific laboratories, a library with more than 470,000 volumes, and a computer center with microcomputers for student use. One of America's oldest colleges, Hamilton has remained small and is committed solely to undergraduate education. The favorable student-faculty ratio assures each of Hamilton's students small classes and access to professors.

## Academics

Hamilton offers a liberal arts curriculum and core academic program. It awards bachelor's **degrees**. Challenging opportunities include advanced placement, accelerated degree programs, self-designed majors, tutorials, a senior project, Phi Beta Kappa, and Sigma Xi. Special programs include internships, off-campus study, study abroad, and Army and Air Force ROTC.

The most popular **majors** include political science/government, history, and economics. A complete listing of majors at Hamilton appears in the Majors Index beginning on page 380.

The **faculty** at Hamilton has 176 full-time teachers, 98% with terminal degrees. 100% of the faculty serve as student advisers. The student-faculty ratio is 10:1.

## Computers on Campus

Students are not required to have a computer. Student rooms are linked to a campus network. 150 **computers** available in the computer center, reading/writing center, the library, and the student center provide access to e-mail and on-line services. Staffed computer lab on campus provides training in the use of computers.

The 4 **libraries** have 495,048 books, 888 microform titles, and 2,801 subscriptions. They are connected to 8 national **on-line** catalogs.

## Campus Life

There are 80 active **organizations** on campus, including a drama/theater group and student-run newspaper and radio station. 43% of eligible men and 6% of eligible women are members of 6 national **fraternities**, 3 local **sororities**, and 1 private society. Student **safety services** include student safety program, late night transport/escort service, and 24-hour patrols by trained security personnel.

Hamilton is a member of the NCAA (Division III). **Intercollegiate sports** include baseball (m), basketball (m, w), crew (m, w), cross-country running (m, w), fencing (m, w), field hockey (w), football (m), golf (m, w), ice hockey (m, w), lacrosse (m, w), rugby (m, w), sailing (m, w), skiing (downhill) (m, w), soccer (m, w), softball (w), squash (m, w), swimming and diving (m, w), tennis (m, w), track and field (m, w), volleyball (m, w).

## Applying

Hamilton requires an essay, a high school transcript, 1 recommendation, sample of expository prose, and SAT I or ACT. It recommends 3 years of high school math and science, 3 years of high school foreign language, an interview, and 3 SAT II Subject Tests. Early and deferred entrance are possible, with a 1/15 deadline and 2/1 for financial aid. **Contact:** Mr. Douglas C. Thompson, Dean of Admission, 198 College Hill Road, Clinton, NY 13323-1218, 315-859-4421 or toll-free 800-843-2655; fax 315-859-4457.

---

### GETTING IN LAST YEAR

3,472 applied
54% were accepted
26% enrolled (481)
44% from top tenth of their h.s. class
21% had SAT verbal scores over 600
56% had SAT math scores over 600
3% had SAT verbal scores over 700
9% had SAT math scores over 700
12 valedictorians

### THE STUDENT BODY

1,664 undergraduates
From 43 states and territories,
   44 other countries
46% from New York
46% women, 54% men
4% African Americans
0% Native Americans
3% Hispanics
4% Asian Americans
6% international students

### AFTER FRESHMAN YEAR

100% returned for sophomore year
84% got a degree within 4 years
87% got a degree within 5 years
88% got a degree within 6 years

### AFTER GRADUATION

20% pursued further study (8% arts and
   sciences, 6% law, 5% medicine)

### WHAT YOU WILL PAY

Tuition and fees $19,700
Room and board $5050
55% receive need-based financial aid
   averaging $10,630

---

# HAMLINE UNIVERSITY

St. Paul, Minnesota • Urban setting • Private • Independent-Religious • Coed

▶ When it comes to education, Hamline students want the best. They want a school with an excellent academic reputation (membership in Phi Beta Kappa; the Hamline Plan, an award-winning curriculum) that provides interaction with professors (12:1 student-faculty ratio). They want the best of living in a metropolitan area (Minneapolis and St. Paul) and a safe, friendly environment (a residential campus). They want a liberal arts experience and a career advantage (internship opportunities). Hamline brings these qualities together and assures students that they may finish their degrees in four years, or the fifth year is tuition-free.

 ## Academics

Hamline offers a goal-directed, interdisciplinary curriculum and core academic program; fewer than half of graduate courses are open to undergraduates. It awards bachelor's, master's, and first professional **degrees**. Challenging opportunities include advanced placement, self-designed majors, tutorials, an honors program, a senior project, and Phi Beta Kappa. Special programs include cooperative education, internships, summer session for credit, off-campus study, study abroad, and Air Force ROTC.

The most popular **majors** include psychology, political science/government, and English. A complete listing of majors at Hamline appears in the Majors Index beginning on page 380.

The **faculty** at Hamline has 126 full-time graduate and undergraduate teachers, 96% with terminal degrees. 100% of the faculty serve as student advisers. The student-faculty ratio is 12:1, and the average class size in required courses is 18.

 ## Computers on Campus

Students are not required to have a computer. 170 **computers** available in the computer center, computer labs, the research center, the learning resource center, science building, classrooms, the library, the student center, and dormitories provide access to the main academic computer, e-mail, and on-line services. Staffed computer lab on campus provides training in the use of computers and software.

The 2 **libraries** have 312,345 books, 101,234 microform titles, and 3,453 subscriptions. They are connected to 3 national **on-line** catalogs.

 ## Campus Life

There are 75 active **organizations** on campus, including a drama/theater group and student-run newspaper. 5% of eligible men and 5% of eligible women are members of 2 national **fraternities** and 2 local **sororities**. Student **safety services** include late night transport/escort service, 24-hour emergency telephone alarm devices, 24-hour patrols by trained security personnel, and electronically operated dormitory entrances.

Hamline is a member of the NCAA (Division III). **Intercollegiate sports** include baseball (m), basketball (m, w), cross-country running (m, w), football (m), gymnastics (w), ice hockey (m), soccer (m, w), softball (w), swimming and diving (m, w), tennis (m, w), track and field (m, w), volleyball (w).

 ## Applying

Hamline requires an essay, a high school transcript, 2 recommendations, and SAT I or ACT. It recommends 3 years of high school math and science, 2 years of high school foreign language, and an interview. Early and deferred entrance are possible, with rolling admissions and continuous processing to 4/15 for financial aid. **Contact:** Dr. W. Scott Friedhoff, Dean of Undergraduate Admissions, 833 Snelling Avenue, St. Paul, MN 55104-1284, 612-641-2207 or toll-free 800-753-9753; fax 612-641-2458.

## GETTING IN LAST YEAR

1,056 applied
82% were accepted
41% enrolled (355)
34% from top tenth of their h.s. class
3.4 average high school GPA
31% had SAT verbal scores over 600
56% had SAT math scores over 600
43% had ACT scores over 26
4% had SAT verbal scores over 700
11% had SAT math scores over 700
10% had ACT scores over 30
5 National Merit Scholars

## THE STUDENT BODY

Total 2,698, of whom 1,491 are undergraduates
From 42 states and territories, 34 other countries
72% from Minnesota
56% women, 44% men
3% African Americans
1% Native Americans
2% Hispanics
5% Asian Americans
3% international students

## AFTER FRESHMAN YEAR

82% returned for sophomore year
54% got a degree within 5 years
57% got a degree within 6 years

## AFTER GRADUATION

24% pursued further study (12% arts and sciences, 5% law, 2% business)
41 corporations, 1 government agency, 2 nonprofit organizations recruited on campus

## WHAT YOU WILL PAY

Tuition and fees $13,412
Room and board $4193
76% receive need-based financial aid averaging $6575
7% receive non-need financial aid averaging $2468

# HAMPDEN-SYDNEY COLLEGE

Hampden-Sydney, Virginia • Rural setting • Private • Independent-Religious • Men

The spirit of Hampden-Sydney lies in its sense of community and its preservation of tradition. Honor and civility inform the life of the College. Challenged by the curriculum, students can get help when they need it because classes are small. The greatest advantage of small-college life is that everyone can be involved. Athletics, debating, publications, fraternity life—all are part of the educational process. Many students enjoy hunting, fishing, camping, and hiking. The total experience at the College produces a man well-suited for the challenges of a job, the demands of social service, and the pleasure of personal endeavors.

 ## Academics

Hampden–Sydney offers a liberal arts curriculum and core academic program. It awards bachelor's **degrees**. Challenging opportunities include advanced placement, accelerated degree programs, tutorials, an honors program, a senior project, Phi Beta Kappa, and Sigma Xi. Special programs include internships, summer session for credit, off-campus study, study abroad, and Army ROTC.

The most popular **majors** include economics, history, and political science/government. A complete listing of majors at Hampden–Sydney appears in the Majors Index beginning on page 380.

The **faculty** at Hampden–Sydney has 65 full-time teachers, 87% with terminal degrees. 90% of the faculty serve as student advisers. The student-faculty ratio is 13:1, and the average class size in required courses is 19.

 ## Computers on Campus

Students are not required to have a computer. Student rooms are linked to a campus network. 140 **computers** available in the computer center, computer labs, classrooms, the library, and dormitories provide access to the main academic computer. Staffed computer lab on campus provides training in the use of computers and software.

The **library** has 200,570 books, 39,800 microform titles, and 835 subscriptions. It is connected to 2 national **on-line** catalogs.

 ## Campus Life

There are 27 active **organizations** on campus, including a drama/theater group and student-run newspaper and radio station. 75% of students participate in student government elections. 50% of eligible undergraduates are members of 12 national **fraternities**. Student **safety services** include 24-hour emergency telephone alarm devices and 24-hour patrols by trained security personnel.

Hampden–Sydney is a member of the NCAA (Division III). **Intercollegiate sports** include baseball, basketball, cross-country running, fencing, football, golf, lacrosse, rugby, soccer, tennis, water polo, wrestling.

 ## Applying

Hampden–Sydney requires an essay, a high school transcript, 3 years of high school math, 2 years of high school foreign language, 2 recommendations, and SAT I or ACT. It recommends 3 years of high school science, a campus interview, SAT II Subject Tests, and a minimum high school GPA of 2.0. Early and midyear entrance are possible, with a 3/1 deadline and continuous processing to 3/1 for financial aid. **Contact:** Mr. Robert H. Jones, Senior Vice President/Dean of Admissions, College Road, Hampden-Sydney, VA 23943-0667, 804-223-6120 or toll-free 800-755-0733 (in-state); fax 804-223-6346.

### GETTING IN LAST YEAR
865 applied
75% were accepted
46% enrolled (299)
20% from top tenth of their h.s. class
3.0 average high school GPA
12% had SAT verbal scores over 600
37% had SAT math scores over 600
2% had SAT verbal scores over 700
4% had SAT math scores over 700
7 class presidents
5 valedictorians

### THE STUDENT BODY
970 undergraduates
From 28 states and territories,
 6 other countries
53% from Virginia
100% men
3% African Americans
0% Native Americans
1% Hispanics
1% Asian Americans
1% international students

### AFTER FRESHMAN YEAR
78% returned for sophomore year
64% got a degree within 4 years
71% got a degree within 5 years

### AFTER GRADUATION
18% pursued further study (8% arts and
 sciences, 6% law, 2% business)
32 corporations, 13 government agencies, 5
 nonprofit organizations recruited on campus

### WHAT YOU WILL PAY
Tuition and fees $13,628
Room and board $5238
48% receive need-based financial aid
 averaging $7353
27% receive non-need financial aid averaging
 $5483

# HAMPSHIRE COLLEGE

Amherst, Massachusetts • Rural setting • Private • Independent • Coed

---

▶ Hampshire's motto, *Non Satis Scire:* To Know is Not Enough, grew out of a sense that the College must offer students more than factual knowledge; it must also endow students with the tools to *use* knowledge and the moral commitment to make a difference in the world. The College believes the central task of liberal education is to help young men and women learn to live their adult lives fully and well in a society of intense change, immense opportunity, and great hazards. Hampshire's constant intellectual goal is to enlarge the capability of each student to conduct his or her own education.

 ## Academics

Hampshire offers an individually-designed curriculum and core academic program. It awards bachelor's **degrees**. Challenging opportunities include accelerated degree programs, self-designed majors, and a senior project. Special programs include internships, off-campus study, and Army ROTC.

The most popular **majors** include art/fine arts, psychology, and theater arts/drama. A complete listing of majors at Hampshire appears in the Majors Index beginning on page 380.

The **faculty** at Hampshire has 92 full-time teachers, 81% with terminal degrees. 100% of the faculty serve as student advisers. The student-faculty ratio is 11:1.

 ## Computers on Campus

Students are not required to have a computer. Student rooms are linked to a campus network. 60 **computers** available in the computer center, computer labs, Adele Simmons Hall, Cole Science Center, and the library provide access to the main academic computer and e-mail. Staffed computer lab on campus provides training in the use of computers and software.

The **library** has 111,000 books, 400 microform titles, and 800 subscriptions. It is connected to 1 national **on-line** catalog.

 ## Campus Life

There are 80 active **organizations** on campus, including a drama/theater group and student-run newspaper. Student **safety services** include late night transport/escort service, 24-hour emergency telephone alarm devices, 24-hour patrols by trained security personnel, and student patrols. **Intercollegiate sports** include baseball (m), basketball (m, w), equestrian sports (m, w), soccer (m, w), volleyball (m, w).

 ## Applying

Hampshire requires an essay, a high school transcript, and 2 recommendations. It recommends an interview. Early, deferred, and midyear entrance are possible, with a 2/1 deadline and continuous processing to 2/15 for financial aid. **Contact:** Ms. Audrey Smith, Director of Admissions, West Street, Amherst, MA 01002, 413-582-5471; fax 413-582-5631.

---

**GETTING IN LAST YEAR**
1,319 applied
80% were accepted
29% enrolled (302)
19% from top tenth of their h.s. class
3.0 average high school GPA

**THE STUDENT BODY**
1,086 undergraduates
From 49 states and territories,
   28 other countries
16% from Massachusetts
57% women, 43% men
3% African Americans
1% Native Americans
4% Hispanics
3% Asian Americans
4% international students

**AFTER FRESHMAN YEAR**
84% returned for sophomore year
42% got a degree within 4 years
62% got a degree within 5 years
64% got a degree within 6 years

**WHAT YOU WILL PAY**
Tuition and fees $20,670
Room and board $5475
55% receive need-based financial aid
   averaging $10,770
1% receive non-need financial aid averaging
   $3800

# HARDING UNIVERSITY

Searcy, Arkansas • Small-town setting • Private • Independent-Religious • Coed

Located in the beautiful foothills of the Ozark Mountains, Harding is one of America's more highly regarded private universities. At Harding, students build lifetime friendships and, upon graduation, are highly recruited. Harding's Christian environment and challenging academic program develop students who can compete and succeed. Whether on the main campus or in the international studies program in Italy, Greece, or England, Harding is a caring and serving family. From Missouri flood relief to working with orphans in Haiti or farmers in Kenya, each year hundreds of Harding students serve others worldwide.

 **Academics**

Harding offers an interdisciplinary curriculum and core academic program; more than half of graduate courses are open to undergraduates. It awards bachelor's and master's **degrees**. Challenging opportunities include advanced placement, accelerated degree programs, self-designed majors, tutorials, Freshmen Honors College, an honors program, and a senior project. Special programs include cooperative education, internships, summer session for credit, study abroad, and Army ROTC.

The most popular **majors** include business, elementary education, and communication. A complete listing of majors at Harding appears in the Majors Index beginning on page 380.

The **faculty** at Harding has 185 full-time undergraduate teachers, 70% with terminal degrees. 98% of the faculty serve as student advisers. The student-faculty ratio is 16:1, and the average class size in required courses is 30.

 **Computers on Campus**

Students are not required to have a computer. Student rooms are linked to a campus network. 275 **computers** available in the computer center, computer labs, the learning resource center, classrooms, and the library provide access to the main academic computer, off-campus computing facilities, and e-mail. Staffed computer lab on campus (open 24 hours a day) provides training in the use of computers and software.

The 2 **libraries** have 325,820 books, 182,333 microform titles, and 1,812 subscriptions. They are connected to 10 national **on-line** catalogs.

 **Campus Life**

There are 52 active **organizations** on campus, including a drama/theater group and student-run newspaper and radio station. 40% of students participate in student government elections. 85% of eligible men and 80% of eligible women are members of 20 local **fraternities**, 20 local **sororities**, and social clubs. Student **safety services** include 24-hour patrols by trained security personnel.

Harding is a member of the NCAA (Division II). **Intercollegiate sports** (some offering scholarships) include baseball (m), basketball (m, w), cross-country running (m, w), football (m), golf (m), tennis (m, w), track and field (m, w), volleyball (w).

 **Applying**

Harding requires a high school transcript, 3 years of high school math and science, 2 recommendations, an interview, and SAT I or ACT. It recommends 2 years of high school foreign language. Early, deferred, and midyear entrance are possible, with a 7/1 deadline and continuous processing to 3/1 for financial aid. **Contact:** Mr. Mike Williams, Director of Admissions, Box 2255, Searcy, AR 72149-0001, 501-279-4407 or toll-free 800-477-4407; fax 501-279-4865.

---

**GETTING IN LAST YEAR**
1,628 applied
66% were accepted
81% enrolled (867)
30% from top tenth of their h.s. class
3.3 average high school GPA
44% had ACT scores over 26
14% had ACT scores over 30
17 National Merit Scholars
40 valedictorians

**THE STUDENT BODY**
Total 3,817, of whom 3,375
   are undergraduates
From 50 states and territories,
   32 other countries

27% from Arkansas
52% women, 48% men
5% African Americans
1% Native Americans
2% Hispanics
1% Asian Americans
5% international students

**AFTER FRESHMAN YEAR**
77% returned for sophomore year
50% got a degree within 4 years
53% got a degree within 5 years
54% got a degree within 6 years

**AFTER GRADUATION**
30% pursued further study (10% arts and
   sciences, 6% business, 6% theology)
97% had job offers within 3 months
105 corporations, 30 government agencies,
   16 nonprofit organizations recruited on
   campus

**WHAT YOU WILL PAY**
Tuition and fees $6450
Room and board $3750
60% receive need-based financial aid
   averaging $500
35% receive non-need financial aid averaging
   $1000

# HARVARD UNIVERSITY

Cambridge, Massachusetts • Urban setting • Private • Independent • Coed

▶ Harvard and Radcliffe, the coeducational undergraduate colleges of Harvard University, offer a curriculum of 3,000 courses, the world's largest university library, a state-of-the-art Science Center, art museums, athletic facilities, and an intimate housing system. Distinction and diversity are the hallmarks of the experience. Students come from all 50 states and other countries and from all educational, ethnic, and economic backgrounds. Students choose from over 40 academic fields and pursue more than 250 different extracurricular activities. The admission process is rigorous. The committee considers academic achievement, extracurricular strengths, and personal qualities. Harvard and Radcliffe offer need-based financial aid.

##  Academics

Harvard offers a liberal arts curriculum and core academic program. It awards bachelor's, master's, doctoral, and first professional **degrees**. Challenging opportunities include advanced placement, accelerated degree programs, self-designed majors, tutorials, an honors program, a senior project, Phi Beta Kappa, and Sigma Xi. Special programs include summer session for credit, off-campus study, and Army, Naval, and Air Force ROTC.

The most popular **majors** include political science/government, literature, and economics. A complete listing of majors at Harvard appears in the Majors Index beginning on page 380.

The **faculty** at Harvard has 1,990 full-time graduate and undergraduate teachers, 100% with terminal degrees. 50% of the faculty serve as student advisers. The student-faculty ratio is 8:1.

##  Computers on Campus

Students are not required to have a computer. Student rooms are linked to a campus network. **Computers** available in the computer center, computer labs, the research center, classrooms, the libra[...] rooms provide access to th[...] e-mail, and on-line service[...] campus.

The 91 **libraries** have 12.6 mill[...] microform titles, and 96,357 subscriptions.

##  Campus Life

There are 250 active **organizations** on campus, including a drama/theater group and student-run newspaper and radio station. 99% of eligible men and 99% of eligible women are members of "House" system. Student **safety services** include required and optional safety courses, late night transport/escort service, 24-hour emergency telephone alarm devices, 24-hour patrols by trained security personnel, and electronically operated dormitory entrances.

Harvard is a member of the NCAA (Division I). **Intercollegiate sports** include baseball (m), basketball (m, w), crew (m, w), cross-country running (m, w), fencing (m, w), field hockey (w), football (m), golf (m, w), ice hockey (m, w), lacrosse (m, w), sailing (m, w), skiing (cross-country) (m, w), skiing (downhill) (m, w), soccer (m, w), softball (w), squash (m, w), swimming and diving (m, w), tennis (m, w), track and field (m, w), volleyball (m, w), water polo (m, w), wrestling (m).

##  Applying

Harvard requires an essay, a high school transcript, 2 recommendations, an interview, SAT I or ACT, and 3 SAT II Subject Tests. It recommends 4 years of high school math, 3 years of high school science, 3 years of high school foreign language, and 4 years of high school English, 3 years of high school history. Early and deferred entrance are possible, with a 1/1 deadline and a 2/15 priority date for financial aid. **Contact:** Office of Admissions and Financial Aid, Byerly Hall, 8 Garden Street, Cambridge, MA 02138, 617-495-1551.

---

### GETTING IN LAST YEAR

15,261 applied
14% were accepted
75% enrolled (1,619)
90% from top tenth of their h.s. class
405 National Merit Scholars
487 valedictorians

### THE STUDENT BODY

Total 18,694, of whom 6,799 are undergraduates
From 53 states and territories, 94 other countries

16% from Massachusetts
41% women, 59% men
7% African Americans
1% Native Americans
8% Hispanics
18% Asian Americans
7% international students

### AFTER FRESHMAN YEAR

97% returned for sophomore year
93% got a degree within 4 years
97% got a degree within 5 years

### AFTER GRADUATION

28% pursued further study
6 Rhodes, 5 Marshall, 30 Fulbright scholars

### WHAT YOU WILL PAY

Tuition and fees $19,186
Room and board $6410
45% receive need-based financial aid averaging $11,700

# HARVEY MUDD COLLEGE

Claremont, California • Suburban setting • Private • Independent • Coed

Harvey Mudd College is a school of math, science, and engineering, with nearly a third of the course work in the humanities and social sciences. As one of the 6 Claremont Colleges, Harvey Mudd offers access to classes, social opportunities, and facilities at the other colleges—all within easy walking distance of one another. The student body of approximately 650 works closely with faculty. Last year, over $2 million of undergraduate research was conducted. Students may work directly with a professor or participate in a clinic whereby a team of students solves real-world problems for high-tech companies.

## Academics

Harvey Mudd offers a science/engineering-oriented curriculum and core academic program. It awards bachelor's and master's **degrees**. Challenging opportunities include advanced placement, self-designed majors, tutorials, and a senior project. Special programs include off-campus study, study abroad, and Army and Air Force ROTC.

The most popular **majors** include engineering (general), physics, and chemistry. A complete listing of majors at Harvey Mudd appears in the Majors Index beginning on page 380.

The **faculty** at Harvey Mudd has 69 full-time undergraduate teachers, 100% with terminal degrees. 100% of the faculty serve as student advisers. The student-faculty ratio is 8:1, and the average class size in required courses is 20.

## Computers on Campus

Students are not required to have a computer. Student rooms are linked to a campus network. 100 **computers** available in the computer center, computer labs, and the library provide access to the main academic computer, off-campus computing facilities, e-mail, and on-line services. Staffed computer lab on campus (open 24 hours a day) provides training in the use of computers and software.

The 2 **libraries** have 1.8 million books, 1.2 million microform titles, and 5,922 subscriptions.

## Campus Life

Active **organizations** on campus include drama/theater group and student-run newspaper and radio station. Student **safety services** include late night transport/escort service and 24-hour patrols by trained security personnel.

Harvey Mudd is a member of the NCAA (Division III). **Intercollegiate sports** include baseball (m), basketball (m, w), cross-country running (m, w), football (m), golf (m), soccer (m, w), softball (w), swimming and diving (m, w), tennis (m, w), track and field (m, w), volleyball (w), water polo (m).

## Applying

Harvey Mudd requires an essay, a high school transcript, 4 years of high school math, 3 years of high school science, 3 recommendations, SAT I, and 3 SAT II Subject Tests (including SAT II: Writing Test). It recommends 2 years of high school foreign language and an interview. Early and deferred entrance are possible, with a 2/1 deadline and a 2/1 priority date for financial aid. **Contact:** Ms. Patricia Coleman, Dean of Admission, 301 East 12th Street, Kingston Hall, Claremont, CA 91711-5994, 909-621-8011.

### GETTING IN LAST YEAR

1,388 applied
40% were accepted
30% enrolled (169)
100% from top tenth of their h.s. class
76% had SAT verbal scores over 600
100% had SAT math scores over 600
26% had SAT verbal scores over 700
87% had SAT math scores over 700
68 National Merit Scholars

### THE STUDENT BODY

Total 648, of whom 635
 are undergraduates
From 42 states and territories,
 13 other countries
48% from California
26% women, 74% men
1% African Americans
1% Native Americans
5% Hispanics
22% Asian Americans
2% international students

### AFTER FRESHMAN YEAR

87% returned for sophomore year
75% got a degree within 4 years
82% got a degree within 5 years
83% got a degree within 6 years

### AFTER GRADUATION

63% pursued further study (39% arts and
 sciences, 24% engineering, 1% medicine)
85% had job offers within 3 months
35 corporations, 7 government agencies
 recruited on campus

### WHAT YOU WILL PAY

Tuition and fees $17,696
Room and board $6690
75% receive need-based financial aid
 averaging $10,947

# HAVERFORD COLLEGE

Haverford, Pennsylvania • Suburban setting • Private • Independent • Coed

---

Haverford College, located 10 miles west of Center City Philadelphia, is situated on a 216-acre arboretum. Founded by the Society of Friends in 1833, Haverford offers a rigorous study of the liberal arts. Students also take pride in the Honor Code, begun in 1897. The community's commitment to service is exemplified by the large percentage of students involved in volunteer activities. Haverford's commitment to academic excellence is underscored by the fact that 80% of graduates enroll in graduate school within 5 years of graduation. Prospective students are encouraged to experience the many dimensions of Haverford by visiting the campus.

##  Academics

Haverford offers a liberal arts curriculum and core academic program. It awards bachelor's **degrees**. Challenging opportunities include advanced placement, accelerated degree programs, self-designed majors, tutorials, a senior project, and Phi Beta Kappa. Off-campus study is a special program.

The most popular **majors** include biology/biological sciences, history, and English. A complete listing of majors at Haverford appears in the Majors Index beginning on page 380.

The **faculty** at Haverford has 97 full-time teachers, 98% with terminal degrees. 100% of the faculty serve as student advisers. The student-faculty ratio is 10:1, and the average class size in required courses is 19.

##  Computers on Campus

Students are not required to have a computer. Student rooms are linked to a campus network. 171 **computers** available in the computer center, the learning resource center, clusters throughout campus, classrooms, the library, and dormitories provide access to the main academic computer, off-campus computing facilities, e-mail, and on-line services. Staffed computer lab on campus provides training in the use of computers and software.

The 6 **libraries** have 400,000 books, 72,000 microform titles, and 1,265 subscriptions. They are connected to 4 national **on-line** catalogs.

##  Campus Life

There are 50 active **organizations** on campus, including a drama/theater group and student-run newspaper and radio station. 45% of students participate in student government elections. Student **safety services** include late night transport/escort service, 24-hour emergency telephone alarm devices, and 24-hour patrols by trained security personnel.

Haverford is a member of the NCAA (Division III). **Intercollegiate sports** include baseball (m), basketball (m, w), cross-country running (m, w), fencing (m, w), field hockey (w), lacrosse (m, w), soccer (m, w), softball (w), squash (m, w), tennis (m, w), track and field (m, w), volleyball (w), wrestling (m).

##  Applying

Haverford requires an essay, a high school transcript, 3 years of high school math, 3 years of high school foreign language, 2 recommendations, SAT I, and 3 SAT II Subject Tests. It recommends 3 years of high school science and an interview. Early and deferred entrance are possible, with a 1/15 deadline and 1/31 for financial aid. **Contact:** Ms. Delsie Phillips, Director of Admissions, 370 Lancaster Avenue, Haverford, PA 19041-1392, 610-896-1350; fax 610-896-1338.

---

### GETTING IN LAST YEAR

2,466 applied
39% were accepted
33% enrolled (314)
75% from top tenth of their h.s. class
64% had SAT verbal scores over 600
88% had SAT math scores over 600
15% had SAT verbal scores over 700
37% had SAT math scores over 700

### THE STUDENT BODY

1,109 undergraduates
From 46 states and territories,
   33 other countries

16% from Pennsylvania
49% women, 51% men
5% African Americans
5% Hispanics
9% Asian Americans
3% international students

### AFTER FRESHMAN YEAR

98% returned for sophomore year
86% got a degree within 4 years
92% got a degree within 5 years

### AFTER GRADUATION

25% pursued further study (14% arts and
   sciences, 7% medicine, 3% law)
30 corporations, 2 government agencies, 20
   nonprofit organizations recruited on campus

### WHAT YOU WILL PAY

Tuition and fees $19,015
Room and board $6235
45% receive need-based financial aid
   averaging $13,902

---

# HENDRIX COLLEGE

Conway, Arkansas • Suburban setting • Private • Independent-Religious • Coed

## Academics

Hendrix offers a Western civilization curriculum and core academic program. It awards bachelor's **degrees**. Challenging opportunities include advanced placement, self-designed majors, tutorials, an honors program, and a senior project. Special programs include internships, study abroad, and Army ROTC.

The most popular **majors** include biology/biological sciences, psychology, and economics. A complete listing of majors at Hendrix appears in the Majors Index beginning on page 380.

The **faculty** at Hendrix has 70 full-time teachers, 100% with terminal degrees. 100% of the faculty serve as student advisers. The student-faculty ratio is 14:1, and the average class size in required courses is 18.

## Campus Life

Active **organizations** on campus include drama/theater group and student-run newspaper and radio station. Student **safety services** include late night transport/escort service, 24-hour patrols by trained security personnel, and electronically operated dormitory entrances.

Hendrix is a member of the NCAA (Division III). **Intercollegiate sports** include baseball (m), basketball (m, w), cross-country running (m, w), golf (m), rugby (m), soccer (m, w), swimming and diving (m, w), tennis (m, w), track and field (m, w), volleyball (w).

## Computers on Campus

Students are not required to have a computer. 45 **computers** available in the computer center, terminal room, and the library provide access to the main academic computer, e-mail, and on-line services. Staffed computer lab on campus (open 24 hours a day) provides training in the use of computers and software.

The **library** has 195,000 books, 143,608 microform titles, and 586 subscriptions.

## Applying

Hendrix requires an essay, a high school transcript, SAT I or ACT, and in some cases 1 recommendation and a campus interview. It recommends 3 years of high school math and science and 1 year of high school foreign language. Early, deferred, and midyear entrance are possible, with rolling admissions and continuous processing to 4/1 for financial aid. **Contact:** Ms. Caroline Kelsey, Vice President of Enrollment, 1601 Harkrider Street, Conway, AR 72032, 501-450-1362 or toll-free 800-277-9017.

### GETTING IN LAST YEAR
743 applied
90% were accepted
45% enrolled (299)
49% from top tenth of their h.s. class
3.45 average high school GPA
31% had SAT verbal scores over 600
29% had SAT math scores over 600
57% had ACT scores over 26
2% had SAT verbal scores over 700
8% had SAT math scores over 700
18% had ACT scores over 30
15 National Merit Scholars

### THE STUDENT BODY
941 undergraduates
From 29 states and territories,
   17 other countries
77% from Arkansas
53% women, 47% men
6% African Americans
0% Native Americans
1% Hispanics
2% Asian Americans
3% international students

### AFTER FRESHMAN YEAR
84% returned for sophomore year

### AFTER GRADUATION
50% pursued further study (20% arts and
   sciences, 8% medicine, 7% law)
16 corporations, 1 nonprofit organization
   recruited on campus
1 Fulbright scholar

### WHAT YOU WILL PAY
Tuition and fees $8928
Room and board $3225
Need-based financial aid averages $2311
Non-need financial aid averages $2329

# HILLSDALE COLLEGE

Hillsdale, Michigan • Small-town setting • Private • Independent • Coed

Located in south-central Michigan, Hillsdale College provides a value-based liberal arts education grounded in the Judeo-Christian heritage and the traditions of the Western world. The refusal of government funding is what makes Hillsdale unique. The College's fierce independence is critical to the level and type of educational excellence Hillsdale is able to provide.

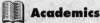

## Academics

Hillsdale offers a great books and Western civilization curriculum and core academic program. It awards bachelor's **degrees**. Challenging opportunities include advanced placement, accelerated degree programs, tutorials, an honors program, and a senior project. Special programs include internships, summer session for credit, study abroad, and Army, Naval, and Air Force ROTC.

The most popular **majors** include business, English, and education. A complete listing of majors at Hillsdale appears in the Majors Index beginning on page 380.

The **faculty** at Hillsdale has 80 full-time teachers, 82% with terminal degrees. 95% of the faculty serve as student advisers. The student-faculty ratio is 12:1, and the average class size in required courses is 21.

## Computers on Campus

Students are not required to have a computer. 150 **computers** available in the computer center, computer labs, the research center, the learning resource center, classrooms, the library, and dormitories provide access to the main academic computer, off-campus computing facilities, e-mail, and on-line services. Staffed computer lab on campus provides training in the use of computers and software.

The 4 **libraries** have 175,000 books, 20,000 microform titles, and 1,800 subscriptions.

## Campus Life

There are 38 active **organizations** on campus, including a drama/theater group and student-run newspaper. 50% of eligible men and 50% of eligible women are members of 5 national **fraternities** and 4 national **sororities**. Student **safety services** include late night transport/escort service, 24-hour emergency telephone alarm devices, 24-hour patrols by trained security personnel, and electronically operated dormitory entrances.

Hillsdale is a member of the NCAA (Division II) and NAIA. **Intercollegiate sports** (some offering scholarships) include baseball (m), basketball (m, w), cross-country running (m, w), equestrian sports (w), football (m), golf (m), ice hockey (m), lacrosse (m), softball (w), swimming and diving (w), tennis (m, w), track and field (m, w), volleyball (w).

## Applying

Hillsdale requires an essay, a high school transcript, 1 recommendation, SAT I or ACT, a minimum high school GPA of 3.0, and in some cases a campus interview. It recommends 3 years of high school math and science, 2 years of high school foreign language, and SAT II Subject Tests. Early and midyear entrance are possible, with rolling admissions and continuous processing to 3/15 for financial aid. **Contact:** Mr. Jeffrey S. Lantis, Director of Admissions, 33 College Street, Hillsdale, MI 49242-1298, 517-437-7341 ext. 2327; fax 517-437-3923.

---

### GETTING IN LAST YEAR

1,090 applied
79% were accepted
39% enrolled (339)
36% from top tenth of their h.s. class
3.43 average high school GPA
33% had SAT verbal scores over 600
35% had SAT math scores over 600
39% had ACT scores over 26
4% had SAT verbal scores over 700
7% had SAT math scores over 700
13% had ACT scores over 30
6 National Merit Scholars
25 valedictorians

### THE STUDENT BODY

1,160 undergraduates
From 41 states and territories,
    10 other countries
55% from Michigan
52% women, 48% men
1% international students

### AFTER FRESHMAN YEAR

92% returned for sophomore year
74% got a degree within 4 years
76% got a degree within 5 years
77% got a degree within 6 years

### AFTER GRADUATION

23% pursued further study (7% arts and
    sciences, 4% business, 4% law)
66% had job offers within 3 months
37 corporations, 4 government agencies, 2
    nonprofit organizations recruited on campus

### WHAT YOU WILL PAY

Tuition and fees $11,300
Room and board $4700
60% receive need-based financial aid
    averaging $4500
10% receive non-need financial aid averaging
    $4500

---

# HIRAM COLLEGE

Hiram, Ohio • Rural setting • Private • Independent-Religious • Coed

Hiram's academic calendar is unique among colleges and universities. Each 15-week semester is divided into 12-week and 3-week terms. During the 3-week term students take only one course, which is studied inclusively. Hiram supplements classroom study through career-oriented internships and an extensive and distinctive study-abroad program that takes Hiram students all over the world. More than 40% of Hiram students participate, and all courses are taught by Hiram faculty and are a regular part of the curriculum. In August 1995, Hiram will open a new $7.2-million library.

## Academics

Hiram offers a core academic program. It awards bachelor's **degrees**. Challenging opportunities include advanced placement, accelerated degree programs, self-designed majors, tutorials, a senior project, and Phi Beta Kappa. Special programs include internships, summer session for credit, and study abroad.

A complete listing of majors at Hiram appears in the Majors Index, beginning on page 380.

The **faculty** at Hiram has 81 full-time teachers, 95% with terminal degrees. 100% of the faculty serve as student advisers. The student-faculty ratio is 12:1, and the average class size in required courses is 16.

## Computers on Campus

Students are not required to have a computer. Student rooms are linked to a campus network. 150 **computers** available in the computer center, computer labs, the learning resource center, academic buildings, classrooms, the library, the student center, and dormitories provide access to the main academic computer, off-campus computing facilities, and e-mail. Staffed computer lab on campus (open 24 hours a day) provides training in the use of computers and software.

The **library** has 170,598 books, 80,829 microform titles, and 939 subscriptions.

## Campus Life

There are 50 active **organizations** on campus, including a drama/theater group and student-run newspaper and radio station. Student **safety services** include late night transport/escort service, 24-hour emergency telephone alarm devices, 24-hour patrols by trained security personnel, and electronically operated dormitory entrances.

Hiram is a member of the NCAA (Division III). **Intercollegiate sports** include baseball (m), basketball (m, w), cross-country running (m, w), equestrian sports (m, w), football (m), golf (m, w), rugby (m, w), sailing (m, w), soccer (m, w), softball (w), swimming and diving (m, w), tennis (m, w), track and field (m, w), volleyball (w).

## Applying

Hiram requires an essay, a high school transcript, 2 recommendations, and SAT I or ACT. It recommends 3 years of high school math and science, 2 years of high school foreign language, and a campus interview. Early and deferred entrance are possible, with a 4/15 deadline and a 3/1 priority date for financial aid. **Contact:** Mr. Gary G. Craig, Dean of Admissions, Rodefer House, Hiram, OH 44234-0096, 216-569-5169 or toll-free 800-362-5280; fax 216-569-5944.

## GETTING IN LAST YEAR

790 applied
77% were accepted
35% enrolled (212)
40% from top tenth of their h.s. class
3.4 average high school GPA
27% had SAT verbal scores over 600
31% had SAT math scores over 600
66% had ACT scores over 26
2% had SAT verbal scores over 700
8% had SAT math scores over 700
15% had ACT scores over 30

## THE STUDENT BODY

847 undergraduates
From 21 states and territories,
  8 other countries
80% from Ohio
51% women, 49% men
6% African Americans
0% Native Americans
1% Hispanics
1% Asian Americans

### AFTER FRESHMAN YEAR

84% returned for sophomore year
70% got a degree within 4 years
73% got a degree within 5 years

## AFTER GRADUATION

30% pursued further study
15 corporations recruited on campus

## WHAT YOU WILL PAY

Tuition and fees $14,337
Room and board $4560
95% receive need-based financial aid
  averaging $8108
36% receive non-need financial aid averaging
  $4795

# HOBART COLLEGE

*Coordinate with William Smith College*

Geneva, New York • Small-town setting • Private • Independent-Religious • Men

▶ Hobart and William Smith Colleges together offer the best features of conventionally coeducational colleges: all classes and many residences are coed and students share all campus facilities and social activities. At the same time, each College maintains its own student government, athletic program, and dean's office. Through this coordinate-college system, men and women have equal opportunities for leadership and visibility. Small classes, a dedicated faculty, and extensive opportunities for independent study and off-campus study contribute to a climate that is academically rigorous and strongly supportive. Students balance academics with involvement in over 60 clubs and athletics ranging from intramurals to intercollegiate varsity competition.

 **Academics**

Hobart offers an interdisciplinary curriculum and core academic program. It awards bachelor's **degrees**. Challenging opportunities include advanced placement, accelerated degree programs, self-designed majors, tutorials, an honors program, a senior project, and Phi Beta Kappa. Special programs include internships, off-campus study, and study abroad.

The most popular **majors** include English, economics, and psychology. A complete listing of majors at Hobart appears in the Majors Index beginning on page 380.

The **faculty** at Hobart has 142 full-time teachers, 98% with terminal degrees. 95% of the faculty serve as student advisers. The student-faculty ratio is 13:1, and the average class size in required courses is 20.

 **Computers on Campus**

Students are not required to have a computer. Student rooms are linked to a campus network. 146 **computers** available in the computer center, computer labs, the research center, the learning resource center, honors room, classrooms, and the library provide access to the main academic computer, off-campus computing facilities, e-mail, and on-line services. Staffed computer lab on campus provides training in the use of computers and software.

The 2 **libraries** have 312,000 books, 42,000 microform titles, and 1,860 subscriptions. They are connected to 3 national **on-line** catalogs.

 **Campus Life**

There are 60 active **organizations** on campus, including a drama/theater group and student-run newspaper and radio station. 19% of eligible undergraduates are members of 7 national **fraternities**. Student **safety services** include late night transport/escort service, 24-hour emergency telephone alarm devices, and 24-hour patrols by trained security personnel.

Hobart is a member of the NCAA (Division III). **Intercollegiate sports** include basketball, crew, cross-country running, football, golf, ice hockey, lacrosse, rugby, sailing, skiing (downhill), soccer, squash, tennis.

**Applying**

Hobart requires an essay, a high school transcript, 3 years of high school math, 2 years of high school foreign language, 2 recommendations, and SAT I or ACT. It recommends 3 years of high school science, an interview, and SAT II Subject Tests. Early and deferred entrance are possible, with a 2/15 deadline and a 2/15 priority date for financial aid. **Contact:** Ms. Mara O'Laughlin, Director of Admission, 639 South Main Street, Geneva, NY 14456-3397, 315-781-3622 or toll-free 800-852-2256; fax 315-781-3914.

---

**GETTING IN LAST YEAR**
1,568 applied
67% were accepted
22% enrolled (235)
24% from top tenth of their h.s. class
12% had SAT verbal scores over 600
36% had SAT math scores over 600
39% had ACT scores over 26
1% had SAT verbal scores over 700
5% had SAT math scores over 700
10% had ACT scores over 30

**THE STUDENT BODY**
919 undergraduates
From 41 states and territories,
   24 other countries

49% from New York
0% women, 100% men
4% African Americans
1% Native Americans
4% Hispanics
2% Asian Americans
3% international students

**AFTER FRESHMAN YEAR**
90% returned for sophomore year
71% got a degree within 4 years
78% got a degree within 5 years
79% got a degree within 6 years

**AFTER GRADUATION**
24% pursued further study (17% arts and
   sciences, 4% law, 2% medicine)
98 corporations, 23 government agencies,
   108 nonprofit organizations recruited on
   campus

**WHAT YOU WILL PAY**
Tuition and fees $19,480
Room and board $5841
58% receive need-based financial aid
   averaging $11,007
1% receive non-need financial aid averaging
   $10,000

# HOFSTRA UNIVERSITY

Hempstead, New York • Suburban setting • Private • Independent • Coed

Founded in 1935 and young by many standards, Hofstra University has grown to be recognized both nationally and internationally by its resources, academic offerings, accreditations, conferences, and cultural events. Focused on undergraduate education, Hofstra places great emphasis on the role of the student in the life of the University. Students are assigned an adviser prior to arrival on campus—a mentor throughout 4 years of study. Students have easy access to the theater and cultural life of New York City yet have a learning environment on Long Island on a 238-acre campus that is also an accredited arboretum and museum.

## Academics

Hofstra offers an interdisciplinary curriculum and core academic program; fewer than half of graduate courses are open to undergraduates. It awards bachelor's, master's, doctoral, and first professional **degrees**. Challenging opportunities include advanced placement, accelerated degree programs, self-designed majors, tutorials, an honors program, a senior project, and Phi Beta Kappa. Special programs include internships, summer session for credit, study abroad, and Army and Air Force ROTC.

The most popular **majors** include accounting, marketing/retailing/merchandising, and psychology. A complete listing of majors at Hofstra appears in the Majors Index beginning on page 380.

The **faculty** at Hofstra has 404 full-time graduate and undergraduate teachers, 90% with terminal degrees. 100% of the faculty serve as student advisers. The student-faculty ratio is 16:1, and the average class size in required courses is 26.

## Computers on Campus

Students are not required to have a computer. 300 **computers** available in the computer center, computer labs, the library, the student center, and dormitories. Staffed computer lab on campus.

The **library** has 1.3 million books, 30,098 microform titles, and 7,017 subscriptions.

## Campus Life

There are 100 active **organizations** on campus, including a drama/theater group and student-run newspaper and radio station. 16% of eligible men and 15% of eligible women are members of 9 national **fraternities**, 5 national **sororities**, 5 local fraternities, and 4 local sororities. Student **safety services** include security booths at each residence hall, late night transport/escort service, 24-hour emergency telephone alarm devices, 24-hour patrols by trained security personnel, and student patrols.

Hofstra is a member of the NCAA (Division I). **Intercollegiate sports** (some offering scholarships) include baseball (m), basketball (m, w), cross-country running (m, w), field hockey (w), golf (m, w), lacrosse (m, w), soccer (m, w), softball (w), tennis (m, w), volleyball (w), wrestling (m).

## Applying

Hofstra requires a high school transcript, 2 years of high school foreign language, 1 recommendation, SAT I or ACT, and in some cases an essay and a campus interview. It recommends 3 years of high school math and science and SAT II Subject Tests. Early, deferred, and midyear entrance are possible, with rolling admissions and continuous processing to 5/1 for financial aid. **Contact:** Ms. Mary Beth Carey, Dean of Admissions, 100 Hofstra University, Hempstead, NY 11550-1090, 516-463-6700 or toll-free 800-HOFSTRA; fax 516-560-7660.

### GETTING IN LAST YEAR
7,357 applied
78% were accepted
22% enrolled (1,278)
21% from top tenth of their h.s. class
3.0 average high school GPA
6% had SAT verbal scores over 600
23% had SAT math scores over 600
51% had ACT scores over 26
1% had SAT verbal scores over 700
3% had SAT math scores over 700
16% had ACT scores over 30

### THE STUDENT BODY
Total 11,545, of whom 7,662 are undergraduates

From 40 states and territories, 71 other countries
84% from New York
53% women, 47% men
5% African Americans
1% Native Americans
5% Hispanics
5% Asian Americans
4% international students

### AFTER FRESHMAN YEAR
80% returned for sophomore year
50% got a degree within 4 years
64% got a degree within 5 years
67% got a degree within 6 years

### AFTER GRADUATION
150 corporations, 10 government agencies, 12 nonprofit organizations recruited on campus

### WHAT YOU WILL PAY
Tuition and fees $11,710
Room and board $5920
70% receive need-based financial aid averaging $2375
Non-need financial aid averages $3532

# HOPE COLLEGE

Holland, Michigan • Small-town setting • Private • Independent-Religious • Coed

Hope College's special niche in American higher education is influenced considerably by a blend of two important characteristics: an outright recognition as one of America's premier liberal arts colleges and, as a Christian college, an openness and freedom of inquiry that are supportive of students who wrestle with significant questions of faith and life. Hope is recognized as a leader for its collaborative research efforts conducted by students and professors. Students who desire a partnership relationship with their college professors will find the academic climate at Hope both stimulating and affirming.

 **Academics**

Hope offers a discipline-oriented curriculum and core academic program. It awards bachelor's **degrees**. Challenging opportunities include advanced placement, self-designed majors, tutorials, a senior project, Phi Beta Kappa, and Sigma Xi. Special programs include internships, summer session for credit, off-campus study, and study abroad.

The most popular **majors** include business, biology/biological sciences, and chemistry. A complete listing of majors at Hope appears in the Majors Index beginning on page 380.

The **faculty** at Hope has 179 full-time teachers, 89% with terminal degrees. 95% of the faculty serve as student advisers. The student-faculty ratio is 13:1, and the average class size in required courses is 35.

 **Computers on Campus**

Students are not required to have a computer. 260 **computers** available in the computer center, computer labs, the research center, classrooms, the library, the student center, and dormitories provide access to e-mail.

The 2 **libraries** have 300,000 books, 178,924 microform titles, and 1,494 subscriptions. They are connected to 7 national **on-line** catalogs.

 **Campus Life**

There are 55 active **organizations** on campus, including a drama/theater group and student-run newspaper and radio station. 9% of eligible men and 10% of eligible women are members of 6 local **fraternities** and 6 local **sororities**. Student **safety services** include late night transport/escort service, 24-hour emergency telephone alarm devices, 24-hour patrols by trained security personnel, and electronically operated dormitory entrances.

Hope is a member of the NCAA (Division III). **Intercollegiate sports** include baseball (m), basketball (m, w), cross-country running (m, w), football (m), golf (m, w), lacrosse (m), soccer (m, w), softball (w), swimming and diving (m, w), tennis (m, w), track and field (m, w), volleyball (m, w).

 **Applying**

Hope requires an essay, a high school transcript, 3 years of high school math, SAT I or ACT, and in some cases 1 recommendation. It recommends 3 years of high school science, 2 years of high school foreign language, and an interview. Early, deferred, and midyear entrance are possible, with rolling admissions and continuous processing to 3/1 for financial aid. **Contact:** Office of Admissions, 69 East 10th Street, Holland, MI 49422-9000, 616-395-7850 or toll-free 800-968-7850; fax 616-395-7130.

---

### GETTING IN LAST YEAR

1,670 applied
89% were accepted
46% enrolled (679)
34% from top tenth of their h.s. class
3.5 average high school GPA
16% had SAT verbal scores over 600
43% had SAT math scores over 600
43% had ACT scores over 26
2% had SAT verbal scores over 700
11% had SAT math scores over 700
6% had ACT scores over 30
16 National Merit Scholars
37 valedictorians

### THE STUDENT BODY

2,825 undergraduates
From 40 states and territories,
   34 other countries
79% from Michigan
57% women, 43% men
1% African Americans
0% Native Americans
2% Hispanics
2% Asian Americans
3% international students

### AFTER FRESHMAN YEAR

90% returned for sophomore year

### AFTER GRADUATION

28% pursued further study (15% arts and
   sciences, 4% medicine, 3% law)
50 corporations, 1 government agency, 4
   nonprofit organizations recruited on campus
1 Marshall scholar

### WHAT YOU WILL PAY

Tuition and fees $12,359
Room and board $4190
60% receive need-based financial aid
   averaging $3288
26% receive non-need financial aid averaging
   $3647

# HOUGHTON COLLEGE

Houghton, New York • Rural setting • Private • Independent-Religious • Coed

Since 1883 Houghton College has provided an educational experience that integrates high academic quality with the Christian faith. Offering 40 majors and programs, the College has received widespread national recognition. Located on a scenic 1,300-acre campus in the countryside of western New York, the college operates an equestrian center in addition to its modern residential, academic, and recreational facilities. Houghton attracts 1,200 academically talented students annually from across the U.S. and around the world. A comprehensive financial aid program benefits more than 90% of the current student body. Numerous off-campus and study-abroad programs are available.

 **Academics**

Houghton offers an interdisciplinary curriculum and core academic program. It awards associate and bachelor's **degrees**. Challenging opportunities include advanced placement, tutorials, an honors program, and a senior project. Special programs include internships, summer session for credit, off-campus study, and Army ROTC.

The most popular **majors** include elementary education, business, and psychology. A complete listing of majors at Houghton appears in the Majors Index beginning on page 380.

The **faculty** at Houghton has 64 full-time teachers, 71% with terminal degrees. 82% of the faculty serve as student advisers. The student-faculty ratio is 15:1, and the average class size in required courses is 21.

 **Computers on Campus**

Students are not required to have a computer. 130 **computers** available in the computer center, computer labs, divisional offices, the library, and dormitories. Staffed computer lab on campus provides training in the use of computers and software.

The **library** has 220,000 books, 5,000 microform titles, and 822 subscriptions.

 **Campus Life**

There are 50 active **organizations** on campus, including a drama/theater group and student-run newspaper and radio station. 40% of students participate in student government elections. Student **safety services** include late night transport/escort service, 24-hour patrols by trained security personnel, and electronically operated dormitory entrances.

Houghton is a member of the NAIA. **Intercollegiate sports** (some offering scholarships) include basketball (m, w), cross-country running (m, w), field hockey (w), soccer (m, w), track and field (m, w), volleyball (w).

 **Applying**

Houghton requires an essay, a high school transcript, 1 recommendation, pastoral recommendation, and SAT I or ACT. It recommends 3 years of high school math, some high school foreign language, and an interview. Early, deferred, and midyear entrance are possible, with an 8/1 deadline and continuous processing to 3/15 for financial aid. **Contact:** Mr. Timothy R. Fuller, Vice President for Alumni and Admissions, PO Box 128, Houghton, NY 14744, 716-567-9353 or toll-free 800-777-2556; fax 716-567-9522.

## GETTING IN LAST YEAR
1,021 applied
81% were accepted
43% enrolled (354)
31% from top tenth of their h.s. class
3.36 average high school GPA
23% had SAT verbal scores over 600
27% had SAT math scores over 600
29% had ACT scores over 26
3% had SAT verbal scores over 700
7% had SAT math scores over 700
7% had ACT scores over 30
17 valedictorians

## THE STUDENT BODY
1,332 undergraduates
From 38 states and territories,
  20 other countries
61% from New York
61% women, 39% men
2% African Americans
1% Native Americans
1% Hispanics
1% Asian Americans
5% international students

### AFTER FRESHMAN YEAR
88% returned for sophomore year
62% got a degree within 4 years
64% got a degree within 5 years
66% got a degree within 6 years

## AFTER GRADUATION
21% pursued further study (8% arts and
  sciences, 4% theology, 3% business)
46 nonprofit organizations recruited on
  campus

## WHAT YOU WILL PAY
Tuition and fees $10,300
Room and board $3550
86% receive need-based financial aid
  averaging $2753
6% receive non-need financial aid averaging
  $2758

# ILLINOIS COLLEGE

Jacksonville, Illinois • Small-town setting • Private • Independent-Religious • Coed

Founded in 1829, Illinois College was the first college in Illinois to award the baccalaureate degree. The College is recognized as a best buy in education and was recently designated Bachelor of Arts 1 by the Carnegie Classification System. Illinois College offers a Phi Beta Kappa education at an annual tuition of $8050. As a premier liberal arts college, the College's goal is to prepare young women and men for a lifetime of learning and a place among the leadership of the community. The campus is a blend of historic New England charm and state-of-the-art computer-based learning facilities.

 **Academics**

IC offers a core academic program. It awards bachelor's **degrees**. Challenging opportunities include advanced placement, accelerated degree programs, a senior project, and Phi Beta Kappa. Special programs include internships, summer session for credit, and study abroad.

The most popular **majors** include business and computer science. A complete listing of majors at IC appears in the Majors Index beginning on page 380.

The **faculty** at IC has 63 full-time teachers, 78% with terminal degrees. 87% of the faculty serve as student advisers. The student-faculty ratio is 15:1, and the average class size in required courses is 23.

 **Computers on Campus**

Students are not required to have a computer. 77 **computers** available in the computer center and computer labs.

Staffed computer lab on campus provides training in the use of computers and software.

The **library** has 135,000 books, 111 microform titles, and 620 subscriptions.

 **Campus Life**

There are 37 active **organizations** on campus, including a drama/theater group and student-run newspaper. 35% of eligible men and 35% of eligible women are members of 7 Greek literary societies. Student **safety services** include night security patrol, late night transport/escort service, 24-hour emergency telephone alarm devices, and electronically operated dormitory entrances.

IC is a member of the NCAA (Division III). **Intercollegiate sports** include baseball (m), basketball (m, w), cross-country running (m, w), football (m), golf (m), soccer (m, w), softball (w), tennis (m, w), track and field (m, w), volleyball (w), wrestling (m).

 **Applying**

IC requires a high school transcript, 2 recommendations, SAT I or ACT, and in some cases an essay. It recommends 3 years of high school math and science and an interview. Early and midyear entrance are possible, with an 8/15 deadline and continuous processing to 5/1 for financial aid. **Contact:** Mr. Gale Vaughn, Director of Enrollment, 1101 West College Avenue, Jacksonville, IL 62650-2299, 217-245-3030; fax 217-245-3034.

## GETTING IN LAST YEAR
919 applied
87% were accepted
38% enrolled (306)
25% from top tenth of their h.s. class
3.4 average high school GPA
15% had SAT verbal scores over 600
43% had SAT math scores over 600
25% had ACT scores over 26
0% had SAT verbal scores over 700
0% had SAT math scores over 700
4% had ACT scores over 30
3 National Merit Scholars
12 valedictorians

## THE STUDENT BODY
986 undergraduates
From 15 states and territories,
  6 other countries
94% from Illinois
52% women, 48% men
1% African Americans
1% Native Americans
1% Hispanics
2% Asian Americans
1% international students

## AFTER FRESHMAN YEAR
78% returned for sophomore year
39% got a degree within 4 years
50% got a degree within 5 years
51% got a degree within 6 years

## AFTER GRADUATION
20% pursued further study (5% business, 4% law, 3% dentistry)
85% had job offers within 3 months

## WHAT YOU WILL PAY
Tuition and fees $8600
Room and board $4000
72% receive need-based financial aid averaging $1199
60% receive non-need financial aid averaging $1976

# ILLINOIS INSTITUTE OF TECHNOLOGY

Chicago, Illinois • Urban setting • Private • Independent • Coed

Located in the heart of Chicago, one of the world's great cities, IIT is an ideal place to study architecture, design, business, engineering, science, premed, and prelaw. Cutting edge programs include architectural engineering, financial markets, trading, and manufacturing management. IIT students get jobs! Ninety-three percent of 1994 graduates were placed in jobs or graduate school by fall. Faculty members are first-rate and accessible. Nobel Laureate Leon Lederman teaches freshman physics. Research, internship, and co-op opportunities abound. Athletics, clubs, and the recreational opportunities offered by a bowling alley and radio station are popular. On-campus housing is guaranteed. Financial aid makes IIT affordable.

## Academics

IIT offers a core academic program. It awards bachelor's, master's, doctoral, and first professional **degrees**. Challenging opportunities include advanced placement, accelerated degree programs, self-designed majors, an honors program, and Sigma Xi. Special programs include cooperative education, internships, summer session for credit, study abroad, and Army, Naval, and Air Force ROTC.

The most popular **majors** include electrical engineering, mechanical engineering, and architecture. A complete listing of majors at IIT appears in the Majors Index beginning on page 380.

The **faculty** at IIT has 276 full-time undergraduate teachers, 90% with terminal degrees. The student-faculty ratio is 10:1, and the average class size in required courses is 21.

## Computers on Campus

Students are not required to have a computer. Student rooms are linked to a campus network. 250 **computers**

available in the computer center, computer labs, the learning resource center, academic buildings, classrooms, the library, and dormitories provide access to the main academic computer and e-mail. Staffed computer lab on campus provides training in the use of computers and software.

The 5 **libraries** have 400,000 books, 175,500 microform titles, and 750 subscriptions.

## Campus Life

There are 75 active **organizations** on campus, including a drama/theater group and student-run newspaper and radio station. 15% of eligible men and 10% of eligible women are members of 9 national **fraternities**, 1 national **sorority**, and 1 local sorority. Student **safety services** include late night transport/escort service, 24-hour emergency telephone alarm devices, 24-hour patrols by trained security personnel, and electronically operated dormitory entrances.

IIT is a member of the NAIA. **Intercollegiate sports** (some offering scholarships) include baseball (m), basketball (m, w), cross-country running (m, w), softball (w), swimming and diving (m, w), volleyball (m, w).

## Applying

IIT requires an essay, a high school transcript, 3 years of high school math, 1 recommendation, and SAT I or ACT. It recommends 3 years of high school science, an interview, and SAT II Subject Tests. Early and deferred entrance are possible, with a 3/15 deadline and continuous processing to 3/15 for financial aid. **Contact:** Dr. Carole N. Snow, Dean of Admission and Financial Aid, 10 West 33rd Street, Room 101, Chicago, IL 60616, 312-567-3025 or toll-free 800-572-1587 (in-state), 800-448-2329 (out-of-state); fax 312-567-8828.

### GETTING IN LAST YEAR

1,736 applied
67% were accepted
38% enrolled (436)
40% from top tenth of their h.s. class
3.51 average high school GPA
13% had SAT verbal scores over 600
53% had SAT math scores over 600
66% had ACT scores over 26
1% had SAT verbal scores over 700
13% had SAT math scores over 700
11% had ACT scores over 30

### THE STUDENT BODY

Total 7,157, of whom 2,546
 are undergraduates

From 40 states and territories,
 75 other countries
62% from Illinois
25% women, 75% men
13% African Americans
0% Native Americans
8% Hispanics
13% Asian Americans
10% international students

### AFTER FRESHMAN YEAR

77% returned for sophomore year
26% got a degree within 4 years
49% got a degree within 5 years
53% got a degree within 6 years

### AFTER GRADUATION

18% pursued further study (6% engineering,
 3% arts and sciences, 1% business)
90% had job offers within 3 months
96 corporations recruited on campus

### WHAT YOU WILL PAY

Tuition and fees $14,600
Room and board $4520
58% receive need-based financial aid
 averaging $6348
36% receive non-need financial aid averaging
 $4045

# ILLINOIS WESLEYAN UNIVERSITY

Bloomington, Illinois • Suburban setting • Private • Independent • Coed

Illinois Wesleyan, located midway between Chicago and St. Louis on a 60-acre landscaped campus, enrolls 1,800 students from more than 30 states and 35 countries. IWU offers a liberal arts curriculum and professional programs in a College of Fine Arts and a 4-year School of Nursing. Many students double major in different fields. A $24-million Center for Natural Science Learning and Research will open in fall 1995. A $15-million athletics, recreation, and wellness center opened in fall 1994. The student-faculty ratio is 13:1, and about 70% of students graduate in 4 years, compared to the national average of 46% in 6 years.

## Academics

IWU offers a liberal arts curriculum and core academic program. It awards bachelor's **degrees**. Challenging opportunities include advanced placement, accelerated degree programs, self-designed majors, an honors program, and Sigma Xi. Special programs include internships, summer session for credit, off-campus study, study abroad, and Army ROTC.

The most popular **majors** include business, biology/biological sciences, and English. A complete listing of majors at IWU appears in the Majors Index beginning on page 380.

The **faculty** at IWU has 150 full-time teachers, 92% with terminal degrees. 89% of the faculty serve as student advisers. The student-faculty ratio is 13:1, and the average class size in required courses is 16.

## Computers on Campus

Students are not required to have a computer. 340 **computers** available in the computer center, special labs, classrooms, the library, and dormitories provide access to e-mail and on-line services. Staffed computer lab on campus provides training in the use of computers and software.

The **library** has 203,202 books, 107,892 microform titles, and 1,045 subscriptions.

## Campus Life

There are 60 active **organizations** on campus, including a drama/theater group and student-run newspaper and radio station. 30% of eligible men and 30% of eligible women are members of 6 national **fraternities** and 5 national **sororities**. Student **safety services** include student/administration security committee, late night transport/escort service, 24-hour emergency telephone alarm devices, and 24-hour patrols by trained security personnel.

IWU is a member of the NCAA (Division III). **Intercollegiate sports** include baseball (m), basketball (m, w), cross-country running (m, w), football (m), golf (m), sailing (m, w), soccer (m, w), softball (w), swimming and diving (m, w), tennis (m, w), track and field (m, w), volleyball (w).

## Applying

IWU requires an essay, a high school transcript, and SAT I or ACT. It recommends 3 years of high school math and science, 3 years of high school foreign language, 3 recommendations, and a campus interview. Early, deferred, and midyear entrance are possible, with rolling admissions and continuous processing to 3/1 for financial aid. **Contact:** Mr. James R. Ruoti, Dean of Admissions, 1312 North Park Street, Bloomington, IL 61702-2900, 309-556-3031 or toll-free 800-332-2498; fax 309-556-3411.

### GETTING IN LAST YEAR

2,886 applied
54% were accepted
33% enrolled (517)
54% from top tenth of their h.s. class
28% had SAT verbal scores over 600
60% had SAT math scores over 600
79% had ACT scores over 26
4% had SAT verbal scores over 700
16% had SAT math scores over 700
31% had ACT scores over 30
24 National Merit Scholars

### THE STUDENT BODY

1,855 undergraduates
From 32 states and territories,
   31 other countries
83% from Illinois
52% women, 48% men
3% African Americans
1% Native Americans
1% Hispanics
4% Asian Americans
3% international students

### AFTER FRESHMAN YEAR

88% returned for sophomore year
71% got a degree within 4 years
75% got a degree within 5 years
76% got a degree within 6 years

### AFTER GRADUATION

29% pursued further study (16% arts and
   sciences, 3% medicine, 2% business)
28 corporations, 17 government agencies, 47
   nonprofit organizations recruited on campus

### WHAT YOU WILL PAY

Tuition and fees $15,510
Room and board $4290
65% receive need-based financial aid
   averaging $6226
20% receive non-need financial aid averaging
   $4283

# IOWA STATE UNIVERSITY OF SCIENCE AND TECHNOLOGY

Ames, Iowa • Suburban setting • Public • State-supported • Coed

> ▶ Iowa State offers all the advantages of a major university along with the friendliness and warmth of a residential campus. Iowa State's students are exceptional academically, diverse racially and culturally, and active socially. Iowa State has been recognized for the exemplary out-of-class experiences offered to its students, including student organizations, intramural sports, residence halls, fraternities, sororities, and a multitude of arts and recreational activities.

## Academics

Iowa State offers no core academic program; fewer than half of graduate courses are open to undergraduates. It awards bachelor's, master's, doctoral, and first professional **degrees**. Challenging opportunities include advanced placement, accelerated degree programs, self-designed majors, tutorials, Freshmen Honors College, an honors program, a senior project, Phi Beta Kappa, and Sigma Xi. Special programs include cooperative education, internships, summer session for credit, off-campus study, study abroad, and Army, Naval, and Air Force ROTC.

The most popular **majors** include elementary education, mechanical engineering, and finance/banking. A complete listing of majors at Iowa State appears in the Majors Index beginning on page 380.

The **faculty** at Iowa State has 1,590 full-time graduate and undergraduate teachers, 88% with terminal degrees. The student-faculty ratio is 18:1, and the average class size in required courses is 30.

## Computers on Campus

Students are not required to have a computer. Student rooms are linked to a campus network. 1,500 **computers** available across campus, and dormitories provide access to the main academic computer, off-campus computing facilities, e-mail, and on-line services. Staffed computer lab on campus provides training in the use of computers and software.

The 2 **libraries** have 2.1 million books, 2.6 million microform titles, and 22,000 subscriptions. They are connected to 20 national **on-line** catalogs.

## Campus Life

Active **organizations** on campus include a drama/theater group and student-run newspaper and radio station. 8% of students participate in student government elections. 15% of eligible men and 15% of eligible women are members of 35 national **fraternities**, 20 national **sororities**, and 1 local fraternity. Student **safety services** include late night transport/escort service, 24-hour emergency telephone alarm devices, 24-hour patrols by trained security personnel, and student patrols.

Iowa State is a member of the NCAA (Division I). **Intercollegiate sports** (some offering scholarships) include baseball (m), basketball (m, w), cross-country running (m, w), football (m), golf (m, w), gymnastics (w), softball (w), swimming and diving (m, w), tennis (w), track and field (m, w), volleyball (w), wrestling (m).

## Applying

Iowa State requires a high school transcript, 3 years of high school math and science, rank in upper half of high school class or achievement of a satisfactory combination of high school rank and ACT/SAT I scores, SAT I or ACT, and in some cases 2 years of high school foreign language. It recommends 2 years of high school foreign language. Early, deferred, and midyear entrance are possible, with rolling admissions and continuous processing to 3/1 for financial aid. **Contact:** Mr. Phil Caffrey, Assistant Director for Freshman Admissions, 314 Alumni Hall, Ames, IA 50011-2010, 515-294-5836 or toll-free 800-262-3810; fax 515-294-6106.

### GETTING IN LAST YEAR
8,950 applied
87% were accepted
43% enrolled (3,356)
26% from top tenth of their h.s. class
3.34 average high school GPA
12% had SAT verbal scores over 600
36% had SAT math scores over 600
37% had ACT scores over 26
1% had SAT verbal scores over 700
12% had SAT math scores over 700
10% had ACT scores over 30
57 National Merit Scholars
124 valedictorians

### THE STUDENT BODY
Total 24,728, of whom 20,312 are undergraduates

From 53 states and territories, 84 other countries
76% from Iowa
43% women, 57% men
3% African Americans
0% Native Americans
2% Hispanics
2% Asian Americans
6% international students

### AFTER FRESHMAN YEAR
81% returned for sophomore year
22% got a degree within 4 years
56% got a degree within 5 years
64% got a degree within 6 years

### AFTER GRADUATION
18% pursued further study (9% arts and sciences, 2% business, 2% engineering)
691 corporations, 49 government agencies, 31 nonprofit organizations recruited on campus
1 Rhodes, 1 Fulbright scholar

### WHAT YOU WILL PAY
Resident tuition and fees $2574
Nonresident tuition and fees $8192
Room and board $3386
61% receive need-based financial aid averaging $785
18% receive non-need financial aid averaging $1587

# JAMES MADISON UNIVERSITY

Harrisonburg, Virginia • Small-town setting • Public • State-supported • Coed

James Madison University has been described as the "Ultimate University." It is a close-knit community that possesses a unique atmosphere for living and learning. The special kind of spirit on campus emphasizes excellence in all aspects of a student's life. Students are challenged both inside and outside the classroom by talented and caring faculty and staff and by other JMU students who are friendly, diverse, and actively involved in their own educations. A beautiful campus, supportive environment, and strong commitment to students' preparation for the 21st century combine to make JMU a distinctive institution.

##  Academics

JMU offers a major concentration/liberal studies curriculum and core academic program; fewer than half of graduate courses are open to undergraduates. It awards bachelor's and master's **degrees**. Challenging opportunities include advanced placement, accelerated degree programs, Freshmen Honors College, an honors program, a senior project, and Sigma Xi. Special programs include internships, summer session for credit, study abroad, and Army ROTC.

The most popular **majors** include psychology, English, and political science/government. A complete listing of majors at JMU appears in the Majors Index beginning on page 380.

The **faculty** at JMU has 520 full-time graduate and undergraduate teachers, 81% with terminal degrees. 6% of the faculty serve as student advisers. The student-faculty ratio is 18:1, and the average class size in required courses is 24.

##  Computers on Campus

Students are not required to have a computer. Student rooms are linked to a campus network. 445 **computers** available in the computer center, computer labs, academic buildings, classrooms, the library, and dormitories. Staffed computer lab on campus (open 24 hours a day) provides training in the use of computers and software.

The 2 **libraries** have 352,160 books, 1.3 million microform titles, and 2,312 subscriptions.

##  Campus Life

There are 218 active **organizations** on campus, including a drama/theater group and student-run newspaper and radio station. 15% of students participate in student government elections. 18% of eligible men and 19% of eligible women are members of 18 national **fraternities** and 12 national **sororities**. Student **safety services** include late night transport/escort service, 24-hour emergency telephone alarm devices, 24-hour patrols by trained security personnel, student patrols, and electronically operated dormitory entrances.

JMU is a member of the NCAA (Division I). **Intercollegiate sports** (some offering scholarships) include archery (m, w), baseball (m), basketball (m, w), cross-country running (m, w), fencing (w), field hockey (w), football (m), golf (m, w), gymnastics (m, w), lacrosse (w), soccer (m, w), swimming and diving (m, w), tennis (m, w), track and field (m, w), volleyball (w), wrestling (m).

##  Applying

JMU requires an essay, a high school transcript, English proficiency for foreign students, SAT I or ACT, a minimum high school GPA of 2.0, and in some cases some high school foreign language. It recommends 3 years of high school math and science. Early and midyear entrance are possible, with a 1/15 deadline and a 2/15 priority date for financial aid. **Contact:** Mrs. Roxie Shabazz, Director of Admissions, Office of Admissions, Harrisonburg, VA 22807, 703-568-6147.

---

### GETTING IN LAST YEAR
11,712 applied
53% were accepted
37% enrolled (2,289)
15% had SAT verbal scores over 600
47% had SAT math scores over 600
1% had SAT verbal scores over 700
6% had SAT math scores over 700

### THE STUDENT BODY
Total 11,539, of whom 10,152
  are undergraduates
From 45 states and territories,
  39 other countries

73% from Virginia
54% women, 46% men
7% African Americans
1% Native Americans
1% Hispanics
3% Asian Americans
1% international students

### AFTER FRESHMAN YEAR
92% returned for sophomore year
60% got a degree within 4 years
80% got a degree within 5 years
82% got a degree within 6 years

### AFTER GRADUATION
18% pursued further study (3% arts and
  sciences, 2% business, 2% law)
133 corporations, 16 government agencies, 1
  nonprofit organization recruited on campus

### WHAT YOU WILL PAY
Resident tuition and fees $3900
Nonresident tuition and fees $7994
Room and board $4544
35% receive need-based financial aid
  averaging $3900
24% receive non-need financial aid averaging
  $12,538

---

# JOHN CARROLL UNIVERSITY

University Heights, Ohio • Suburban setting • Private • Independent-Religious • Coed

Carroll, founded in 1886, is one of 28 Catholic colleges and universities operated in the United States by the Society of Jesus. In the Jesuit tradition of leadership, faith, and service, John Carroll provides its students with a rigorous education rooted in the liberal arts and focused on questions of moral and ethical values. John Carroll offers more than 85 student organizations, community volunteer service opportunities, and academic honor societies to foster leadership activities outside the classroom.

 **Academics**

Carroll offers a well-rounded Jesuit core curriculum and core academic program; fewer than half of graduate courses are open to undergraduates. It awards bachelor's and master's **degrees**. Challenging opportunities include advanced placement, accelerated degree programs, self-designed majors, tutorials, an honors program, and a senior project. Special programs include cooperative education, internships, summer session for credit, off-campus study, study abroad, and Army ROTC.

The most popular **majors** include communication, psychology, and marketing/retailing/merchandising. A complete listing of majors at Carroll appears in the Majors Index beginning on page 380.

The **faculty** at Carroll has 213 full-time undergraduate teachers, 89% with terminal degrees. 100% of the faculty serve as student advisers. The student-faculty ratio is 15:1, and the average class size in required courses is 21.

 **Computers on Campus**

Students are not required to have a computer. Student rooms are linked to a campus network. 126 **computers** available across the campus, and in dormitories provide access to the main academic computer, off-campus computing facilities, e-mail, and on-line services. Staffed computer lab on campus provides training in the use of computers and software.

The **library** has 549,618 books, 169,804 microform titles, and 1,691 subscriptions. It is connected to 6 national **on-line** catalogs.

 **Campus Life**

There are 87 active **organizations** on campus, including a drama/theater group and student-run newspaper and radio station. 55% of students participate in student government elections. 32% of eligible men and 35% of eligible women are members of 12 local **fraternities** and 7 local **sororities**. Student **safety services** include late night transport/escort service, 24-hour emergency telephone alarm devices, and 24-hour patrols by trained security personnel.

Carroll is a member of the NCAA (Division III). **Intercollegiate sports** include baseball (m), basketball (m, w), cross-country running (m, w), football (m), golf (m), ice hockey (m), lacrosse (m, w), rugby (m, w), sailing (m, w), skiing (cross-country) (m, w), skiing (downhill) (m, w), soccer (m, w), softball (w), swimming and diving (m, w), tennis (m, w), track and field (m, w), volleyball (m, w), wrestling (m).

 **Applying**

Carroll requires a high school transcript, 3 years of high school math, 2 years of high school foreign language, 1 recommendation, and SAT I or ACT. It recommends an essay, 3 years of high school science, a campus interview, and SAT II Subject Tests. Early, deferred, and midyear entrance are possible, with rolling admissions and continuous processing to 3/1 for financial aid. **Contact:** Ms. Laryn Runco, Director of Admission, 20700 North Park Boulevard, University Heights, OH 44118-4581, 216-397-4294; fax 216-397-4256.

---

### GETTING IN LAST YEAR
2,299 applied
90% were accepted
38% enrolled (791)
27% from top tenth of their h.s. class
3.23 average high school GPA
13% had SAT verbal scores over 600
42% had SAT math scores over 600
25% had ACT scores over 26
1% had SAT verbal scores over 700
7% had SAT math scores over 700
4% had ACT scores over 30
7 National Merit Scholars
23 valedictorians

### THE STUDENT BODY
Total 4,342, of whom 3,469
   are undergraduates

From 31 states and territories,
   15 other countries
65% from Ohio
51% women, 49% men
4% African Americans
0% Native Americans
1% Hispanics
3% Asian Americans
1% international students

### AFTER FRESHMAN YEAR
84% returned for sophomore year
63% got a degree within 4 years
75% got a degree within 5 years
76% got a degree within 6 years

### AFTER GRADUATION
27% pursued further study (20% arts and
   sciences, 5% law, 2% medicine)
65% had job offers within 3 months
175 corporations, 10 government agencies,
   40 nonprofit organizations recruited on
   campus

### WHAT YOU WILL PAY
Tuition and fees $12,390
Room and board $5550
Need-based financial aid averages $3211
Non-need financial aid averages $2941

# JOHNS HOPKINS UNIVERSITY

Baltimore, Maryland • Urban setting • Private • Independent • Coed

The School of Arts and Sciences and the Whiting School of Engineering are the heart of a small but unusually diverse coeducational university. Johns Hopkins was founded in 1876 as the first true American university on the European research university model. With a favorable student-faculty ratio, most classes are small and give students an excellent opportunity for advanced studies and creative investigation.

 **Academics**

Johns Hopkins offers an interdisciplinary curriculum and no core academic program; all graduate courses are open to undergraduates. It awards bachelor's, master's, and doctoral **degrees**. Challenging opportunities include advanced placement, accelerated degree programs, self-designed majors, tutorials, a senior project, Phi Beta Kappa, and Sigma Xi. Special programs include cooperative education, internships, summer session for credit, off-campus study, study abroad, and Army and Air Force ROTC.

The most popular **majors** include biology/biological sciences, biomedical engineering, and international studies. A complete listing of majors at Johns Hopkins appears in the Majors Index beginning on page 380.

The **faculty** at Johns Hopkins has 361 full-time graduate and undergraduate teachers, 99% with terminal degrees. 70% of the faculty serve as student advisers. The student-faculty ratio is 10:1, and the average class size in required courses is 35.

 **Computers on Campus**

Students are not required to have a computer. Student rooms are linked to a campus network. 180 **computers** available across campus, and in dormitories provide access to the main academic computer, off-campus computing facilities, e-mail, and on-line services. Staffed computer lab on campus provides training in the use of computers and software.

The 7 **libraries** have 3.1 million books, 1.8 million microform titles, and 20,000 subscriptions.

 **Campus Life**

Active **organizations** on campus include a drama/theater group and student-run newspaper and radio station. 55% of students participate in student government elections. 30% of eligible men and 25% of eligible women are members of 13 national **fraternities** and 5 national **sororities**. Student **safety services** include late night transport/escort service, 24-hour emergency telephone alarm devices, 24-hour patrols by trained security personnel, student patrols, and electronically operated dormitory entrances.

Johns Hopkins is a member of the NCAA (Division III). **Intercollegiate sports** (some offering scholarships) include baseball (m), basketball (m, w), crew (m, w), cross-country running (m, w), fencing (m, w), field hockey (w), football (m), golf (m), ice hockey (m), lacrosse (m, w), riflery (m, w), rugby (m), soccer (m, w), squash (w), swimming and diving (m, w), tennis (m, w), track and field (m, w), volleyball (w), water polo (m, w), wrestling (m).

 **Applying**

Johns Hopkins requires an essay, a high school transcript, 1 recommendation, SAT I or ACT, and 3 SAT II Subject Tests (including SAT II: Writing Test). It recommends an interview and 3 years of high school math, science, and foreign language. Early and deferred entrance are possible, with a 1/1 deadline and a 2/1 priority date for financial aid. **Contact:** Mr. Paul White, Director of Undergraduate Admissions, 3400 North Charles Street, Baltimore, MD 21218-2699, 410-516-8171.

## GETTING IN LAST YEAR
7,695 applied
43% were accepted
29% enrolled (952)
75% from top tenth of their h.s. class
3.8 average high school GPA
63% had SAT verbal scores over 600
91% had SAT math scores over 600
91% had ACT scores over 26
8% had SAT verbal scores over 700
46% had SAT math scores over 700
48% had ACT scores over 30
38 National Merit Scholars
64 valedictorians

## THE STUDENT BODY
Total 4,812, of whom 3,421
   are undergraduates
From 52 states and territories,
   36 other countries
13% from Maryland
38% women, 62% men
6% African Americans
1% Native Americans
3% Hispanics
22% Asian Americans
5% international students

## AFTER FRESHMAN YEAR
93% returned for sophomore year
83% got a degree within 4 years
86% got a degree within 5 years

## AFTER GRADUATION
67% pursued further study (28% medicine, 14% arts and sciences, 10% business)
41% had job offers within 3 months
87 corporations, 9 government agencies, 7 nonprofit organizations recruited on campus
11 Fulbright scholars

## WHAT YOU WILL PAY
Tuition and fees $19,700
Room and board $7050
45% receive need-based financial aid averaging $10,250

# JUNIATA COLLEGE

Huntingdon, Pennsylvania • Small-town setting • Private • Independent • Coed

Interest in study-abroad opportunities at Juniata is at an all-time high. More than 20% of Juniata's most recent junior class spent 1 semester or the entire academic year living and learning in another country. From traditional study-abroad locations, such as England, France, Germany, and Spain, to nontraditional study-abroad locations, such as China, Ecuador, Greece, Japan, and Mexico, Juniata students earn academic credit and broaden their intellectual, cultural, and personal capacities. Study-abroad candidates who are in good academic standing as sophomores may apply for these opportunities. At Juniata, the greatest classroom is the world.

## Academics

Juniata offers an interdisciplinary curriculum and core academic program. It awards bachelor's **degrees**. Challenging opportunities include advanced placement, accelerated degree programs, self-designed majors, tutorials, and a senior project. Special programs include internships, summer session for credit, off-campus study, and study abroad.

The most popular **majors** include business, education, and natural sciences. A complete listing of majors at Juniata appears in the Majors Index beginning on page 380.

The **faculty** at Juniata has 75 full-time teachers, 92% with terminal degrees. 100% of the faculty serve as student advisers. The student-faculty ratio is 13:1, and the average class size in required courses is 30.

## Computers on Campus

Students are not required to have a computer. 90 **computers** available in the computer center, computer labs, academic buildings, and the library provide access to the main academic computer and e-mail. Staffed computer lab on campus provides training in the use of computers and software.

The **library** has 129,809 books, 9,435 microform titles, and 895 subscriptions.

## Campus Life

There are 75 active **organizations** on campus, including a drama/theater group and student-run newspaper and radio station. Student **safety services** include late night transport/escort service, 24-hour emergency telephone alarm devices, and 24-hour patrols by trained security personnel.

Juniata is a member of the NCAA (Division III). **Intercollegiate sports** include baseball (m), basketball (m, w), cross-country running (m, w), field hockey (w), football (m), golf (m), lacrosse (m), rugby (m), skiing (downhill) (m), soccer (m, w), softball (w), swimming and diving (m, w), tennis (m, w), track and field (m, w), volleyball (m, w), wrestling (m).

## Applying

Juniata requires an essay, a high school transcript, 2 years of high school foreign language, 1 recommendation, SAT I or ACT, and in some cases an interview. It recommends 3 years of high school math and science, a campus interview, and SAT II Subject Tests. Early, deferred, and midyear entrance are possible, with a 3/1 deadline and continuous processing to 3/1 for financial aid. **Contact:** Mr. Carlton E. Surbeck III, Director of Admissions, 1700 Moore Street, Huntingdon, PA 16652-2119, 814-643-4310 ext. 420 or toll-free 800-526-1970; fax 814-643-3620.

### GETTING IN LAST YEAR
954 applied
86% were accepted
32% enrolled (258)
36% from top tenth of their h.s. class
3.1 average high school GPA
10% had SAT verbal scores over 600
28% had SAT math scores over 600
29% had ACT scores over 26
0% had SAT verbal scores over 700
2% had SAT math scores over 700
3% had ACT scores over 30

### THE STUDENT BODY
1,068 undergraduates
From 28 states and territories,
 13 other countries
70% from Pennsylvania
51% women, 49% men
1% African Americans
0% Native Americans
1% Hispanics
1% Asian Americans
2% international students

### AFTER FRESHMAN YEAR
97% returned for sophomore year
79% got a degree within 4 years
80% got a degree within 5 years

### AFTER GRADUATION
34% pursued further study (20% arts and
 sciences, 5% law, 5% medicine)
70% had job offers within 3 months

### WHAT YOU WILL PAY
Tuition and fees $14,850
Room and board $4460
Need-based financial aid averages $4492
Non-need financial aid averages $4156

# KALAMAZOO COLLEGE

Kalamazoo, Michigan • Suburban setting • Private • Independent • Coed

A Kalamazoo College education prepares students to better understand, live successfully within, and provide enlightened leadership to a richly diverse and increasingly complex world. The College is nationally recognized for its "Kalamazoo Plan," which includes on-campus immersion in the liberal arts and sciences, a meaningful career internship, a senior individualized project, and study abroad. Over 85% of Kalamazoo students choose to study abroad at one of the College's centers in Africa, Asia, Europe, and Latin America. Kalamazoo students graduate with excellent academic qualifications and impressive hands-on experiences that prepare them for success in graduate programs and careers.

## Academics

K-College offers a liberal arts/sciences curriculum and core academic program. It awards bachelor's **degrees**. Challenging opportunities include advanced placement, tutorials, a senior project, Phi Beta Kappa, and Sigma Xi. Special programs include cooperative education, internships, summer session for credit, off-campus study, study abroad, and Army ROTC.

The most popular **majors** include economics, biology/biological sciences, and psychology. A complete listing of majors at K-College appears in the Majors Index beginning on page 380.

The **faculty** at K-College has 91 full-time teachers, 93% with terminal degrees. 95% of the faculty serve as student advisers. The student-faculty ratio is 12:1, and the average class size in required courses is 17.

## Computers on Campus

Students are not required to have a computer. 70 **computers** available in the computer center, computer labs, and classrooms provide access to e-mail and on-line services. Staffed computer lab on campus (open 24 hours a day).

The **library** has 309,111 books, 18,348 microform titles, and 1,338 subscriptions. It is connected to 5 national **on-line** catalogs.

## Campus Life

There are 36 active **organizations** on campus, including a drama/theater group and student-run newspaper and radio station. Student **safety services** include late night transport/escort service, 24-hour emergency telephone alarm devices, and electronically operated dormitory entrances.

K-College is a member of the NCAA (Division III). **Intercollegiate sports** include baseball (m), basketball (m, w), cross-country running (m, w), football (m), golf (m, w), soccer (m, w), softball (w), swimming and diving (m, w), tennis (m, w), volleyball (w).

## Applying

K-College requires an essay, a high school transcript, 2 recommendations, and SAT I or ACT. It recommends 3 years of high school math and science, some high school foreign language, an interview, and a minimum high school GPA of 3.0. Early, deferred, and midyear entrance are possible, with a 2/15 deadline and continuous processing to 2/15 for financial aid. **Contact:** Ms. Teresa M. Lahti, Dean of Admission, Mandelle Hall, Kalamazoo, MI 49006-3295, 616-337-7166 or toll-free 800-253-3602; fax 616-337-7390.

### GETTING IN LAST YEAR
1,274 applied
93% were accepted
29% enrolled (337)
42% from top tenth of their h.s. class
3.52 average high school GPA
29% had SAT verbal scores over 600
59% had SAT math scores over 600
66% had ACT scores over 26
3% had SAT verbal scores over 700
17% had SAT math scores over 700
21% had ACT scores over 30
12 National Merit Scholars
11 valedictorians

### THE STUDENT BODY
1,241 undergraduates
From 38 states and territories, 18 other countries
70% from Michigan
54% women, 46% men
3% African Americans
1% Native Americans
1% Hispanics
6% Asian Americans
4% international students

### AFTER FRESHMAN YEAR
87% returned for sophomore year
61% got a degree within 4 years
66% got a degree within 5 years
68% got a degree within 6 years

### AFTER GRADUATION
30% pursued further study (18% arts and sciences, 5% law, 4% medicine)
5 corporations, 1 government agency recruited on campus

### WHAT YOU WILL PAY
Tuition and fees $16,249
Room and board $5094
54% receive need-based financial aid averaging $5546
45% receive non-need financial aid averaging $4390

# KENTUCKY WESLEYAN COLLEGE

Owensboro, Kentucky • Suburban setting • Private • Independent-Religious • Coed

 **Academics**

Kentucky Wesleyan offers a broad cultural curriculum and core academic program. It awards associate and bachelor's **degrees**. Challenging opportunities include advanced placement, tutorials, and a senior project. Special programs include internships, off-campus study, and study abroad.

The most popular **majors** include nursing, business, and criminal justice. A complete listing of majors at Kentucky Wesleyan appears in the Majors Index beginning on page 380.

The **faculty** at Kentucky Wesleyan has 51 full-time teachers, 70% with terminal degrees. 100% of the faculty serve as student advisers. The student-faculty ratio is 11:1, and the average class size in required courses is 25.

 **Computers on Campus**

Students are not required to have a computer. Student rooms are linked to a campus network. 50 **computers** available in the computer center, computer labs, faculty offices, classrooms, the library, and dormitories provide access to the main academic computer and e-mail. Staffed computer lab on campus.

The **library** has 93,940 books, 347 microform titles, and 453 subscriptions. It is connected to 1 national **on-line** catalog.

 **Campus Life**

There are 21 active **organizations** on campus, including a drama/theater group and student-run newspaper and radio station. Kentucky Wesleyan has 3 national **fraternities** and 2 national **sororities**. Student **safety services** include 12-hour patrols by trained security personnel and late night transport/escort service.

Kentucky Wesleyan is a member of the NCAA (Division II). **Intercollegiate sports** (some offering scholarships) include baseball (m), basketball (m, w), football (m), golf (m, w), soccer (m, w), softball (w), tennis (m, w), volleyball (w).

 **Applying**

Kentucky Wesleyan requires a high school transcript, minimum 2.25 GPA, SAT I or ACT, and in some cases recommendations and an interview. It recommends an essay, 3 years of high school math and science, and 2 years of high school foreign language. Early, deferred, and midyear entrance are possible, with rolling admissions and continuous processing to 3/1 for financial aid. **Contact:** Ms. Gloria Smith Kunik, Director of Enrollment Services, 3000 Frederica Street, Owensboro, KY 42302-1039, 502-926-3111 ext. 143 or toll-free 800-999-0592; fax 502-926-3196.

## GETTING IN LAST YEAR

482 applied
92% were accepted
35% enrolled (154)
20% from top tenth of their h.s. class
3.0 average high school GPA
2% had SAT verbal scores over 600
4% had SAT math scores over 600
24% had ACT scores over 26
0% had SAT verbal scores over 700
2% had SAT math scores over 700
3% had ACT scores over 30
2 valedictorians

## THE STUDENT BODY

740 undergraduates
From 29 states and territories,
  5 other countries
77% from Kentucky
58% women, 42% men
3% African Americans
0% Native Americans
0% Hispanics
1% Asian Americans
1% international students

### AFTER FRESHMAN YEAR

60% returned for sophomore year

## AFTER GRADUATION

54% pursued further study (35% arts and sciences, 9% business, 4% medicine)

## WHAT YOU WILL PAY

Tuition and fees $8200
Room and board $4150
63% receive need-based financial aid averaging $750
51% receive non-need financial aid averaging $3800

# KENYON COLLEGE

Gambier, Ohio • Rural setting • Private • Independent • Coed

---

▶ Ranked in the top 30 undergraduate colleges for academic reputation, Kenyon is also one of only a handful of colleges included on 3 "Top 50" lists: whose graduates earn Ph.D.s in the sciences or humanities, whose graduates are major corporate executives, and whose students study abroad. Students cite quality of teaching, accessibility of faculty, and a strong sense of community as reasons they chose Kenyon. Half of the classes have 15 or fewer students. A campus-wide computer network links the campus to information sources worldwide. Kenyon's 800-acre campus set in the quintessential college town has been described as one of the most beautiful in the country.

## Academics

Kenyon offers a liberal arts and sciences curriculum and core academic program. It awards bachelor's **degrees**. Challenging opportunities include advanced placement, self-designed majors, tutorials, an honors program, a senior project, and Phi Beta Kappa. Special programs include internships, off-campus study, and study abroad.

The most popular **majors** include English, history, and psychology. A complete listing of majors at Kenyon appears in the Majors Index beginning on page 380.

The **faculty** at Kenyon has 113 full-time teachers, 96% with terminal degrees. 100% of the faculty serve as student advisers. The student-faculty ratio is 10:1, and the average class size in required courses is 18.

## Computers on Campus

Students are not required to have a computer. Student rooms are linked to a campus network. 165 **computers** available in the computer center, computer labs, the research center, classrooms, the library, dormitories, and student rooms provide access to the main academic computer, off-campus computing facilities, e-mail, and on-line services.

Staffed computer lab on campus provides training in the use of computers and software.

The **library** has 411,479 books, 329,962 microform titles, and 1,265 subscriptions. It is connected to 4 national **on-line** catalogs.

## Campus Life

There are 99 active **organizations** on campus, including a drama/theater group and student-run newspaper and radio station. 33% of students participate in student government elections. 25% of eligible men and 2% of eligible women are members of 7 national **fraternities**, 1 local fraternity, 2 local **sororities**, and 2 co-ed social clubs. Student **safety services** include late night transport/escort service, 24-hour emergency telephone alarm devices, 24-hour patrols by trained security personnel, and student patrols.

Kenyon is a member of the NCAA (Division III). **Intercollegiate sports** include baseball (m), basketball (m, w), cross-country running (m, w), field hockey (w), football (m), golf (m, w), lacrosse (m, w), soccer (m, w), swimming and diving (m, w), tennis (m, w), track and field (m, w), volleyball (w).

## Applying

Kenyon requires an essay, a high school transcript, 3 years of high school math, 3 years of high school foreign language, 1 recommendation, SAT I or ACT, and a minimum high school GPA of 2.0. It recommends 4 years of high school math, 3 years of high school science, 4 years of high school foreign language, an interview, and a minimum high school GPA of 3.0. Early, deferred, and midyear entrance are possible, with a 2/15 deadline and 2/15 for financial aid. **Contact:** Mr. John W. Anderson, Dean of Admissions, Ransom Hall, Gambier, OH 43022-9623, 614-427-5776 or toll-free 800-848-2468; fax 614-427-2634.

---

### GETTING IN LAST YEAR
1,942 applied
79% were accepted
28% enrolled (434)
43% from top tenth of their h.s. class
3.52 average high school GPA
35% had SAT verbal scores over 600
53% had SAT math scores over 600
77% had ACT scores over 26
5% had SAT verbal scores over 700
10% had SAT math scores over 700
26% had ACT scores over 30
17 National Merit Scholars
16 class presidents
20 valedictorians

### THE STUDENT BODY
1,510 undergraduates
From 47 states and territories,
  25 other countries
26% from Ohio
53% women, 47% men
4% African Americans
1% Native Americans
2% Hispanics
4% Asian Americans
4% international students

### AFTER FRESHMAN YEAR
90% returned for sophomore year
83% got a degree within 4 years

87% got a degree within 5 years
88% got a degree within 6 years

### AFTER GRADUATION
20 corporations, 3 government agencies, 4 nonprofit organizations recruited on campus

### WHAT YOU WILL PAY
Tuition and fees $19,850
Room and board $3690
40% receive need-based financial aid averaging $10,502
5% receive non-need financial aid averaging $8538

# KNOX COLLEGE

Galesburg, Illinois • Small-town setting • Private • Independent • Coed

For more than 150 years, Knox College has offered students the chance to work closely with distinguished teachers. Knox provides a superior liberal arts program with special strengths in the sciences and creative arts. A college of exceptional diversity, Knox enjoys an open, easygoing campus culture that allows students to take charge of their own lives and to flourish; students can go anywhere with a Knox degree. Knox is eleventh among liberal arts colleges in the percentage of graduates who earn math/science PhDs and thirtieth in the percentage of graduates who become business executives.

 **Academics**

Knox offers an interdisciplinary curriculum and core academic program. It awards bachelor's **degrees**. Challenging opportunities include advanced placement, self-designed majors, tutorials, a senior project, Phi Beta Kappa, and Sigma Xi. Special programs include internships, off-campus study, and study abroad.

The most popular **majors** include English, political science/government, and biology/biological sciences. A complete listing of majors at Knox appears in the Majors Index beginning on page 380.

The **faculty** at Knox has 88 full-time teachers, 90% with terminal degrees. 70% of the faculty serve as student advisers. The student-faculty ratio is 12:1, and the average class size in required courses is 16.

 **Computers on Campus**

Students are not required to have a computer. Student rooms are linked to a campus network. 130 **computers** available in the computer center, computer labs, all academic buildings, classrooms, the library, and the student center provide access to the main academic computer, e-mail, and on-line services. Staffed computer lab on campus (open 24 hours a day) provides training in the use of computers and software.

The 3 **libraries** have 266,503 books, 94,968 microform titles, and 732 subscriptions. They are connected to 5 national **on-line** catalogs.

 **Campus Life**

There are 82 active **organizations** on campus, including a drama/theater group and student-run newspaper and radio station. 35% of eligible men and 15% of eligible women are members of 5 national **fraternities** and 2 national **sororities**. Student **safety services** include late night transport/escort service and 24-hour emergency telephone alarm devices.

Knox is a member of the NCAA (Division III). **Intercollegiate sports** include baseball (m), basketball (m, w), cross-country running (m, w), football (m), golf (m, w), soccer (m, w), softball (w), swimming and diving (m, w), tennis (m, w), track and field (m, w), volleyball (w), wrestling (m).

 **Applying**

Knox requires an essay, a high school transcript, 3 years of high school math and science, 2 recommendations, and SAT I or ACT. It recommends some high school foreign language and an interview. Early, deferred, and midyear entrance are possible, with a 2/15 deadline and continuous processing to 3/1 for financial aid. **Contact:** Mr. Paul Steenis, Director of Admissions, Admissions Office, Box K-148, Galesburg, IL 61401, 309-343-0112 ext. 123 or toll-free 800-678-KNOX; fax 309-343-5376.

## GETTING IN LAST YEAR

1,023 applied
83% were accepted
32% enrolled (275)
50% from top tenth of their h.s. class
33% had SAT verbal scores over 600
50% had SAT math scores over 600
55% had ACT scores over 26
5% had SAT verbal scores over 700
15% had SAT math scores over 700
20% had ACT scores over 30
12 National Merit Scholars
17 valedictorians

## THE STUDENT BODY

1,056 undergraduates
From 41 states and territories,
    33 other countries
57% from Illinois
54% women, 46% men
6% African Americans
1% Native Americans
2% Hispanics
4% Asian Americans
7% international students

### AFTER FRESHMAN YEAR

87% returned for sophomore year
69% got a degree within 4 years
73% got a degree within 5 years
74% got a degree within 6 years

## AFTER GRADUATION

36% pursued further study (24% arts and
    sciences, 7% medicine, 4% law)
12 corporations, 32 nonprofit organizations
    recruited on campus

## WHAT YOU WILL PAY

Tuition and fees $16,692
Room and board $4257
79% receive need-based financial aid
    averaging $8202
9% receive non-need financial aid averaging
    $5077

# LAFAYETTE COLLEGE

Easton, Pennsylvania • Suburban setting • Private • Independent-Religious • Coed

▶ Lafayette College has achieved a unique niche in American higher education: liberal arts and engineering programs in a small-college setting. Lafayette offers small classes, interdisciplinary first-year seminars, and student-faculty collaborative research on a residential campus located in eastern Pennsylvania close to New York and Philadelphia.

## Academics

Lafayette offers an interdisciplinary curriculum and core academic program. It awards bachelor's **degrees**. Challenging opportunities include advanced placement, accelerated degree programs, self-designed majors, tutorials, an honors program, Phi Beta Kappa, and Sigma Xi. Special programs include internships, summer session for credit, off-campus study, study abroad, and Army ROTC.

The most popular **majors** include biology/biological sciences, business economics, and psychology. A complete listing of majors at Lafayette appears in the Majors Index beginning on page 380.

The **faculty** at Lafayette has 180 full-time teachers, 92% with terminal degrees. 63% of the faculty serve as student advisers. The student-faculty ratio is 11:1, and the average class size in required courses is 18.

## Computers on Campus

Students are not required to have a computer. Student rooms are linked to a campus network. 250 **computers** available in the computer center, classroom buildings, the library, and dormitories provide access to the main academic computer, off-campus computing facilities, e-mail, and on-line services. Staffed computer lab on campus (open 24 hours a day) provides training in the use of computers and software.

The 2 **libraries** have 448,490 books and 1,839 subscriptions. They are connected to 5 national **on-line** catalogs.

## Campus Life

There are 95 active **organizations** on campus, including a drama/theater group and student-run newspaper and radio station. 25% of students participate in student government elections. 50% of eligible men and 70% of eligible women are members of 12 national **fraternities**, 6 national **sororities**, and 2 social dorms. Student **safety services** include late night transport/escort service, 24-hour emergency telephone alarm devices, 24-hour patrols by trained security personnel, student patrols, and electronically operated dormitory entrances.

Lafayette is a member of the NCAA (Division I). **Intercollegiate sports** include baseball (m), basketball (m, w), crew (m, w), cross-country running (m, w), equestrian sports (m, w), fencing (m, w), field hockey (w), football (m), golf (m), lacrosse (m, w), rugby (m, w), skiing (downhill) (m, w), soccer (m, w), softball (w), squash (m), swimming and diving (m, w), tennis (m, w), track and field (m, w), volleyball (w), weight lifting (m, w), wrestling (m).

## Applying

Lafayette requires an essay, a high school transcript, 3 years of high school math, 2 years of high school foreign language, and 1 recommendation. It recommends 3 years of high school science and an interview. Early and deferred entrance are possible, with a 1/15 deadline and continuous processing to 2/15 for financial aid. **Contact:** Dr. Gary Ripple, Director of Admissions, 118 Markle Hall, Easton, PA 18042-1798, 610-250-5100; fax 610-250-5355.

---

### GETTING IN LAST YEAR
4,084 applied
59% were accepted
23% enrolled (557)
37% from top tenth of their h.s. class
13% had SAT verbal scores over 600
53% had SAT math scores over 600
1% had SAT verbal scores over 700
9% had SAT math scores over 700
1 National Merit Scholar

### THE STUDENT BODY
2,219 undergraduates
From 39 states and territories,
   50 other countries
26% from Pennsylvania
45% women, 55% men
4% African Americans
1% Native Americans
2% Hispanics
3% Asian Americans
6% international students

### AFTER FRESHMAN YEAR
92% returned for sophomore year
83% got a degree within 4 years
86% got a degree within 5 years

### AFTER GRADUATION
25% pursued further study (12% arts and
   sciences, 6% law, 3% engineering)
99 corporations, 6 government agencies, 1
   nonprofit organization recruited on campus

### WHAT YOU WILL PAY
Tuition and fees $19,601
Room and board $6000
55% receive need-based financial aid
   averaging $11,173

---

# LAKE FOREST COLLEGE

Lake Forest, Illinois • Suburban setting • Private • Independent • Coed

The College is situated in the beautiful community of Lake Forest, Illinois' safest city, with a population of more than 5,000. Chicago is just 30 miles south of the campus, where students enhance their liberal arts education through the world-renowned resources of this great city. Over 80% of LFC students strengthen their education through domestic and international internships, practicums, and the College's extensive study-abroad program. On campus, the distinguished faculty offer students high-quality teaching and the unique opportunity to conduct independent research.

 **Academics**

Lake Forest offers a liberal arts curriculum and core academic program. It awards bachelor's and master's **degrees**. Challenging opportunities include advanced placement, accelerated degree programs, self-designed majors, tutorials, Freshmen Honors College, a senior project, Phi Beta Kappa, and Sigma Xi. Special programs include internships, summer session for credit, off-campus study, and study abroad.

The most popular **majors** include psychology, English, and business economics. A complete listing of majors at Lake Forest appears in the Majors Index beginning on page 380.

The **faculty** at Lake Forest has 77 full-time undergraduate teachers, 95% with terminal degrees. 100% of the faculty serve as student advisers. The student-faculty ratio is 10:1, and the average class size in required courses is 16.

 **Computers on Campus**

Students are not required to have a computer. Student rooms are linked to a campus network. 176 **computers**

available across campus, and dormitories provide access to the main academic computer, e-mail, and on-line services. Staffed computer lab on campus (open 24 hours a day) provides training in the use of computers and software.

The 2 **libraries** have 382,000 books, 120,000 microform titles, and 1,200 subscriptions.

 **Campus Life**

There are 46 active **organizations** on campus, including a drama/theater group and student-run newspaper and radio station. 60% of students participate in student government elections. 22% of eligible men and 19% of eligible women are members of 1 national **fraternity**, 3 local fraternities, and 3 local **sororities**. Student **safety services** include late night transport/escort service, 24-hour emergency telephone alarm devices, 24-hour patrols by trained security personnel, and student patrols.

Lake Forest is a member of the NCAA (Division III). **Intercollegiate sports** include baseball (m), basketball (m, w), cross-country running (m, w), football (m), ice hockey (m), lacrosse (m, w), sailing (m, w), soccer (m, w), softball (w), swimming and diving (m, w), tennis (m, w), volleyball (m, w), water polo (m).

**Applying**

Lake Forest requires an essay, a high school transcript, 2 recommendations, and SAT I or ACT. It recommends 3 years of high school math, 2 years of high school foreign language, and an interview. Early, deferred, and midyear entrance are possible, with a 3/1 deadline and continuous processing to 3/1 for financial aid. **Contact:** Mr. William G. Motzer Jr., Director of Admissions, 555 North Sheridan Road, Lake Forest, IL 60045-2399, 708-735-5000; fax 708-735-6291.

---

## GETTING IN LAST YEAR

1,110 applied
68% were accepted
30% enrolled (229)
29% from top tenth of their h.s. class
3.3 average high school GPA
16% had SAT verbal scores over 600
26% had SAT math scores over 600
39% had ACT scores over 26
2% had SAT verbal scores over 700
5% had SAT math scores over 700
7% had ACT scores over 30
1 National Merit Scholar
15 class presidents
4 valedictorians

## THE STUDENT BODY

Total 1,013, of whom 996
  are undergraduates
From 48 states and territories,
  30 other countries
34% from Illinois
52% women, 48% men
6% African Americans
1% Native Americans
4% Hispanics
4% Asian Americans
5% international students

## AFTER FRESHMAN YEAR

77% returned for sophomore year
63% got a degree within 4 years
68% got a degree within 5 years
69% got a degree within 6 years

## AFTER GRADUATION

22% pursued further study (7% law, 6% arts
  and sciences, 4% business)
70% had job offers within 3 months
46 corporations, 5 government agencies, 11
  nonprofit organizations recruited on campus

## WHAT YOU WILL PAY

Tuition and fees $17,110
Room and board $3970
67% receive need-based financial aid
  averaging $12,062
1% receive non-need financial aid averaging
  $10,809

# LA SALLE UNIVERSITY

Philadelphia, Pennsylvania • Suburban setting • Private • Independent-Religious • Coed

---

▶ La Salle University offers one of the country's most respected honors programs. Established in 1963 to meet the needs of La Salle's most gifted students, the program has become a national model and has been praised by the National Collegiate Honors Council for its "extraordinary record in terms of garnering Fulbright, Danforth and Marshall Fellowships." La Salle has been ranked among the nation's leading colleges by *U.S. News & World Report*, *Money* magazine, *Barron's*, and the *New York Times*.

 **Academics**

La Salle offers a core academic program; a few graduate courses are open to undergraduates. It awards associate, bachelor's, and master's **degrees**. Challenging opportunities include advanced placement, accelerated degree programs, self-designed majors, tutorials, Freshmen Honors College, an honors program, and a senior project. Special programs include cooperative education, internships, summer session for credit, off-campus study, study abroad, and Army, Naval, and Air Force ROTC.

The most popular **majors** include accounting, (pre)medicine sequence, and communication. A complete listing of majors at La Salle appears in the Majors Index beginning on page 380.

The **faculty** at La Salle has 228 full-time undergraduate teachers, 88% with terminal degrees. 80% of the faculty serve as student advisers. The student-faculty ratio is 14:1, and the average class size in required courses is 19.

 **Computers on Campus**

Students are not required to have a computer. 310 **computers** available in the computer center, computer labs, the research center, the learning resource center, classrooms, the library, and the student center.

The **library** has 347,000 books, 36,470 microform titles, and 1,650 subscriptions. It is connected to 3 national **on-line** catalogs.

 **Campus Life**

There are 115 active **organizations** on campus, including a drama/theater group and student-run newspaper and radio station. 15% of eligible men and 13% of eligible women are members of 8 national **fraternities**, 8 national **sororities**, 1 local fraternity, and 1 local sorority. Student **safety services** include late night transport/escort service, 24-hour emergency telephone alarm devices, 24-hour patrols by trained security personnel, student patrols, and electronically operated dormitory entrances.

La Salle is a member of the NCAA (Division I) and NAIA. **Intercollegiate sports** (some offering scholarships) include baseball (m), basketball (m, w), crew (m, w), cross-country running (m, w), field hockey (w), golf (m, w), soccer (m, w), softball (w), swimming and diving (m, w), tennis (m, w), track and field (m, w), volleyball (w), wrestling (m).

 **Applying**

La Salle requires an essay, a high school transcript, 3 years of high school math, 2 years of high school foreign language, and SAT I or ACT. It recommends recommendations, a campus interview, and SAT II Subject Tests. Early, deferred, and midyear entrance are possible, with an 8/15 deadline and continuous processing to 2/15 for financial aid. **Contact:** Mr. Christopher P. Lydon, Director of Undergraduate Admissions, 20th and Olney Avenue, Philadelphia, PA 19141-1199, 215-951-1500 or toll-free 800-382-1910; fax 215-951-1488.

---

### GETTING IN LAST YEAR

2,740 applied
73% were accepted
27% enrolled (535)
23% from top tenth of their h.s. class
15% had SAT verbal scores over 600
27% had SAT math scores over 600
4% had SAT verbal scores over 700
10% had SAT math scores over 700
3 National Merit Scholars
12 class presidents
9 valedictorians

### THE STUDENT BODY

Total 5,376, of whom 4,012
   are undergraduates
From 27 states and territories,
   25 other countries
68% from Pennsylvania
52% women, 48% men
10% African Americans
0% Native Americans
3% Hispanics
4% Asian Americans
2% international students

### AFTER FRESHMAN YEAR

91% returned for sophomore year
61% got a degree within 4 years
65% got a degree within 5 years

### AFTER GRADUATION

22% pursued further study
135 corporations, 25 government agencies,
   15 nonprofit organizations recruited on
   campus
1 Fulbright scholar

### WHAT YOU WILL PAY

Tuition and fees $12,515
Room and board $5120
80% receive need-based financial aid
   averaging $5200

---

# LAWRENCE UNIVERSITY

Appleton, Wisconsin • Small-town setting • Private • Independent • Coed

Lawrence University is committed to the development of intellect and talent, the acquisition of knowledge and understanding, and the cultivation of judgment and values. Its graduates earn Fulbrights, Watsons, Rhodes, and other prestigious fellowships for continuing their education beyond the undergraduate level. Every year, Lawrence students have the highest academic profile of any institution of higher learning in Wisconsin. Research opportunities with faculty members, an outstanding laser physics laboratory, an excellent conservatory of music offering a 5-year double-degree program, and especially strong interdisciplinary areas of study are among the most attractive programs available at Lawrence.

## Academics

Lawrence offers a core academic program. It awards bachelor's **degrees**. Challenging opportunities include advanced placement, self-designed majors, tutorials, an honors program, a senior project, and Phi Beta Kappa. Special programs include internships and study abroad.

The most popular **majors** include biology/biological sciences, English, and psychology. A complete listing of majors at Lawrence appears in the Majors Index beginning on page 380.

The **faculty** at Lawrence has 108 full-time teachers, 94% with terminal degrees. 100% of the faculty serve as student advisers. The student-faculty ratio is 11:1, and the average class size in required courses is 12.

## Computers on Campus

Students are not required to have a computer. Student rooms are linked to a campus network. 140 **computers** available in the computer center, computer labs, the learn-ing resource center, academic buildings, the library, and dormitories provide access to the main academic computer, off-campus computing facilities, and e-mail. Staffed computer lab on campus provides training in the use of computers and software.

The **library** has 332,121 books, 102,753 microform titles, and 1,328 subscriptions. It is connected to 3 national **on-line** catalogs.

## Campus Life

There are 120 active **organizations** on campus, including a drama/theater group and student-run newspaper. 40% of eligible men and 40% of eligible women are members of 5 national **fraternities** and 3 national **sororities**.

Lawrence is a member of the NCAA (Division III). **Intercollegiate sports** include baseball (m), basketball (m, w), crew (m, w), cross-country running (m, w), fencing (m, w), football (m), golf (m), ice hockey (m), lacrosse (m, w), rugby (w), soccer (m, w), softball (w), swimming and diving (m, w), tennis (m, w), track and field (m, w), volleyball (w), wrestling (m).

## Applying

Lawrence requires an essay, a high school transcript, 2 recommendations, audition for music majors, and SAT I or ACT. It recommends 3 years of high school math and science, 2 years of high school foreign language, and an interview. Early, deferred, and midyear entrance are possible, with a 2/1 deadline and continuous processing to 3/15 for financial aid. **Contact:** Mr. Steven T. Syverson, Dean of Admissions and Financial Aid, 706 East College Avenue, Appleton, WI 54912-0599, 414-832-6500 or toll-free 800-227-0982; fax 414-832-6782.

### GETTING IN LAST YEAR
1,499 applied
60% were accepted
31% enrolled (284)
39% from top tenth of their h.s. class
3.53 average high school GPA
38% had SAT verbal scores over 600
53% had SAT math scores over 600
59% had ACT scores over 26
6% had SAT verbal scores over 700
15% had SAT math scores over 700
27% had ACT scores over 30
7 National Merit Scholars
17 valedictorians

### THE STUDENT BODY
1,161 undergraduates
From 46 states and territories,
   47 other countries
39% from Wisconsin
54% women, 46% men
2% African Americans
1% Native Americans
2% Hispanics
3% Asian Americans
11% international students

### AFTER FRESHMAN YEAR
84% returned for sophomore year
65% got a degree within 4 years
74% got a degree within 5 years
75% got a degree within 6 years

### AFTER GRADUATION
27% pursued further study (20% arts and
   sciences, 3% law, 1% business)
10 corporations, 3 government agencies, 9
   nonprofit organizations recruited on campus

### WHAT YOU WILL PAY
Tuition and fees $17,253
Room and board $3891
Need-based financial aid averages $9238
Non-need financial aid averages $5299

# LEHIGH UNIVERSITY

Bethlehem, Pennsylvania • Suburban setting • Private • Independent • Coed

▶Lehigh University is a comprehensive national university located on a spectacular 1600-acre campus. The University comprises 3 undergraduate colleges—Arts and Sciences, Business and Economics, and Engineering and Applied Sciences; a graduate school; and a graduate-level College of Education. Since its founding in 1865, Lehigh's philosophy has been to prepare young people for a rewarding and successful life. The hallmarks of Lehigh are close student-faculty interaction and experiential learning both inside and outside the classroom.

## Academics

Lehigh offers an interdisciplinary curriculum and no core academic program; fewer than half of graduate courses are open to undergraduates. It awards bachelor's, master's, and doctoral **degrees**. Challenging opportunities include advanced placement, accelerated degree programs, self-designed majors, tutorials, an honors program, a senior project, Phi Beta Kappa, and Sigma Xi. Special programs include cooperative education, internships, summer session for credit, off-campus study, study abroad, and Army ROTC.

The most popular **majors** include mechanical engineering, civil engineering, and accounting. A complete listing of majors at Lehigh appears in the Majors Index beginning on page 380.

The **faculty** at Lehigh has 410 full-time graduate and undergraduate teachers, 98% with terminal degrees. The student-faculty ratio is 11:1, and the average class size in required courses is 29.

## Computers on Campus

Students are not required to have a computer. Student rooms are linked to a campus network. 500 **computers** available in the computer center, computer labs, the research center, the learning resource center, academic buildings, classrooms, the library, the student center, and dormitories provide access to the main academic computer, off-campus

computing facilities, e-mail, and on-line services. Staffed computer lab on campus (open 24 hours a day) provides training in the use of computers and software.

The 3 **libraries** have 1.1 million books, 1.7 million microform titles, and 10,510 subscriptions. They are connected to 9 national **on-line** catalogs.

## Campus Life

There are 130 active **organizations** on campus, including a drama/theater group and student-run newspaper and radio station. 48% of eligible men and 48% of eligible women are members of 28 national **fraternities** and 8 national **sororities**. Student **safety services** include late night transport/escort service, 24-hour emergency telephone alarm devices, 24-hour patrols by trained security personnel, student patrols, and electronically operated dormitory entrances.

Lehigh is a member of the NCAA (Division I). **Intercollegiate sports** (some offering scholarships) include baseball (m), basketball (m, w), crew (m, w), cross-country running (m, w), equestrian sports (m, w), field hockey (w), football (m, w), golf (m), gymnastics (w), ice hockey (m), lacrosse (m, w), riflery (m, w), rugby (m), sailing (m, w), skiing (downhill) (m, w), soccer (m, w), softball (w), squash (m), swimming and diving (m, w), tennis (m, w), track and field (m, w), volleyball (m, w), water polo (m), wrestling (m).

## Applying

Lehigh requires a high school transcript, 2 years of high school foreign language, 1 recommendation, graded writing sample, SAT I or ACT, and in some cases 4 years of high school math and 3 years of high school science. It recommends a campus interview. Early, deferred, and midyear entrance are possible, with a 2/15 deadline and a 2/15 priority date for financial aid. **Contact:** Mrs. Patricia G. Boig, Director of Admissions, 27 Memorial Drive West, Bethlehem, PA 18015-3094, 610-758-3100; fax 610-758-4361.

### GETTING IN LAST YEAR

6,521 applied
64% were accepted
26% enrolled (1,105)
40% from top tenth of their h.s. class
13% had SAT verbal scores over 600
57% had SAT math scores over 600
32% had ACT scores over 26
1% had SAT verbal scores over 700
14% had SAT math scores over 700
11% had ACT scores over 30
10 National Merit Scholars

### THE STUDENT BODY

Total 6,447, of whom 4,406
 are undergraduates

From 45 states and territories,
 44 other countries
33% from Pennsylvania
37% women, 63% men
3% African Americans
1% Native Americans
2% Hispanics
5% Asian Americans
4% international students

### AFTER FRESHMAN YEAR

90% returned for sophomore year
70% got a degree within 4 years
83% got a degree within 5 years
85% got a degree within 6 years

### AFTER GRADUATION

23% pursued further study (7% arts and
 sciences, 6% law, 5% engineering)
184 corporations, 44 government agencies
 recruited on campus

### WHAT YOU WILL PAY

Tuition and fees $19,650
Room and board $5440
52% receive need-based financial aid
 averaging $10,825

# Le Moyne College

Syracuse, New York • Suburban setting • Private • Independent-Religious • Coed

Le Moyne offers several scholarships: Presidential/Ignatian Scholarships are $20,000 merit awards distributed over 4 years. There are as many as 25 Presidential Scholarships; one Ignatian Scholarship is available for each Jesuit high school. Criteria include an A average, a minimum score of 1200 on the SAT or 29 on the ACT, and proven leadership skills. Leader Scholar Awards ($2000 per year) are merit awards for students who have high levels of academic and extracurricular achievement. All applicants are considered. Urban League Scholarships are awarded annually to qualified multicultural students. There are 4 Urban League (full need) awards, and all multicultural applicants are considered.

## Academics

Le Moyne offers a Western culture curriculum and core academic program. It awards bachelor's and master's **degrees**. Challenging opportunities include advanced placement, accelerated degree programs, an honors program, and a senior project. Special programs include internships, summer session for credit, off-campus study, and Army and Air Force ROTC.

The most popular **majors** include business, accounting, and psychology. A complete listing of majors at Le Moyne appears in the Majors Index beginning on page 380.

The **faculty** at Le Moyne has 129 full-time undergraduate teachers, 92% with terminal degrees. 62% of the faculty serve as student advisers. The student-faculty ratio is 15:1, and the average class size in required courses is 20.

## Computers on Campus

Students are not required to have a computer. Student rooms are linked to a campus network. 150 **computers**
available in the computer center, computer labs, the learning resource center, science center, the library, and dormitories provide access to the main academic computer, e-mail, and on-line services. Staffed computer lab on campus.

The **library** has 210,191 books, 293 microform titles, and 1,683 subscriptions. It is connected to 5 national **on-line** catalogs.

## Campus Life

There are 61 active **organizations** on campus, including a drama/theater group and student-run newspaper and radio station. 40% of students participate in student government elections. Student **safety services** include late night transport/escort service, 24-hour patrols by trained security personnel, and electronically operated dormitory entrances.

Le Moyne is a member of the NCAA (Division II). **Intercollegiate sports** (some offering scholarships) include baseball (m), basketball (m, w), cross-country running (m, w), golf (m), lacrosse (m, w), soccer (m, w), softball (w), swimming and diving (m, w), tennis (m, w), volleyball (w).

## Applying

Le Moyne requires a high school transcript, 3 years of high school math and science, 3 years of high school foreign language, 1 recommendation, SAT I or ACT, and in some cases an essay. It recommends an essay and an interview. Early, deferred, and midyear entrance are possible, with a 3/15 deadline and a 2/15 priority date for financial aid. **Contact:** Dr. Edwin B. Harris, Director of Admissions, Syracuse, NY 13214, 315-445-4300 or toll-free 800-333-4733.

---

### GETTING IN LAST YEAR
1,559 applied
79% were accepted
33% enrolled (404)
24% from top tenth of their h.s. class
3.5 average high school GPA
6% had SAT verbal scores over 600
27% had SAT math scores over 600
32% had ACT scores over 26
0% had SAT verbal scores over 700
3% had SAT math scores over 700
5% had ACT scores over 30
74 class presidents
28 valedictorians

### THE STUDENT BODY
Total 2,756, of whom 2,395
   are undergraduates

From 21 states and territories,
   6 other countries
93% from New York
57% women, 43% men
4% African Americans
1% Native Americans
3% Hispanics
2% Asian Americans
1% international students

### AFTER FRESHMAN YEAR
88% returned for sophomore year
73% got a degree within 4 years
78% got a degree within 5 years
79% got a degree within 6 years

### AFTER GRADUATION
29% pursued further study (20% arts and
   sciences, 3% business, 3% law)
50 corporations, 5 government agencies, 8
   nonprofit organizations recruited on campus

### WHAT YOU WILL PAY
Tuition and fees $11,360
Room and board $4840
70% receive need-based financial aid
   averaging $6000
24% receive non-need financial aid averaging
   $3264

# LETOURNEAU UNIVERSITY

Longview, Texas • Suburban setting • Private • Independent-Religious • Coed

---

▶ Set apart by a special "spirit of ingenuity," LeTourneau University continues to expand on the excellence and inventive zeal of its heritage. Always striving to excel, LeTourneau was the first evangelical Christian college to receive professional accreditation by the Accreditation Board for Engineering and Technology (ABET). The University provides solid programs in more than 40 majors, with special emphasis on aviation, business, engineering, and technology. Set in the beautiful pine woods and lakes of East Texas, the spacious contemporary campus is home to innovative students from virtually every state and more than 25 nations. At LeTourneau, "Faith brings us together, ingenuity sets us apart."

##  Academics

LeTourneau offers a core academic program. It awards associate, bachelor's, and master's **degrees** (freshman enrollment and application numbers below include students in the LeTourneau Education for Adult Professionals program). Challenging opportunities include advanced placement and a senior project. Special programs include cooperative education, internships, summer session for credit, and off-campus study.

The most popular **majors** include aviation technology, electrical engineering, and mechanical engineering. A complete listing of majors at LeTourneau appears in the Majors Index beginning on page 380.

The **faculty** at LeTourneau has 57 full-time graduate and undergraduate teachers, 75% with terminal degrees. 95% of the faculty serve as student advisers. The student-faculty ratio is 15:1, and the average class size in required courses is 16.

##  Computers on Campus

Students are not required to have a computer. 300 **computers** available in the computer center, computer labs, and the library provide access to on-line services. Staffed computer lab on campus.

The **library** has 83,577 books, 39,946 microform titles, and 1,156 subscriptions. It is connected to 3 national **on-line** catalogs.

##  Campus Life

There are 27 active **organizations** on campus, including a drama/theater group and student-run newspaper. 3% of eligible men are members of 5 local **fraternities**. Student **safety services** include late night transport/escort service, 24-hour emergency telephone alarm devices, 24-hour patrols by trained security personnel, and electronically operated dormitory entrances.

LeTourneau is a member of the NAIA. **Intercollegiate sports** (some offering scholarships) include baseball (m), basketball (m, w), cross-country running (m, w), soccer (m), track and field (m, w), volleyball (w).

##  Applying

LeTourneau requires an essay, a high school transcript, 2 recommendations, SAT I or ACT, a minimum high school GPA of 2.0, and in some cases 3 years of high school math and a campus interview. It recommends 3 years of high school science. Early, deferred, and midyear entrance are possible, with an 8/15 deadline and continuous processing to 2/15 for financial aid. **Contact:** Mr. Howard Wilson, Director of Admissions, 2100 South Mobberly, Longview, TX 75607-7001, 903-753-0231 ext. 240 or toll-free 800-759-8811; fax 903-237-2730.

---

### GETTING IN LAST YEAR
2,078 applied
76% were accepted
66% enrolled (1,052)
23% from top tenth of their h.s. class
3.31 average high school GPA
13% had SAT verbal scores over 600
32% had SAT math scores over 600
32% had ACT scores over 26
2% had SAT verbal scores over 700
5% had SAT math scores over 700
6% had ACT scores over 30
2 National Merit Scholars
5 valedictorians

### THE STUDENT BODY
Total 2,047, of whom 1,879 are undergraduates

From 48 states and territories, 27 other countries
67% from Texas
31% women, 69% men
4% African Americans
1% Native Americans
4% Hispanics
1% Asian Americans
3% international students

### AFTER FRESHMAN YEAR
68% returned for sophomore year
27% got a degree within 4 years
43% got a degree within 5 years
45% got a degree within 6 years

### AFTER GRADUATION
5% pursued further study (2% engineering, 1% business, 1% law)
90% had job offers within 3 months
15 corporations, 25 nonprofit organizations recruited on campus

### WHAT YOU WILL PAY
Tuition and fees $9550
Room and board $4430
77% receive need-based financial aid averaging $3180
14% receive non-need financial aid averaging $1945

# LEWIS & CLARK COLLEGE

Portland, Oregon • Suburban setting • Private • Independent • Coed

▶ Lewis & Clark College students are motivated, reflective, intellectually curious, adventurous, and politically, environmentally, and culturally aware . . . and busy! As fast as change occurs in today's world, Lewis & Clark believes students need a college experience that will make them versatile professionals and creative and ethical leaders, no matter what the endeavor. The College's liberal arts and sciences curriculum builds strong skills of analysis and communication, emphasizes international and cross-cultural learning, and fosters an informed respect for the environment. The classes are small, conducted in seminar style, and work, both written and oral, is scrutinized by faculty members whose first priority is teaching.

 ## Academics

L & C offers a liberal arts and sciences curriculum with an international focus and core academic program. It awards bachelor's, master's, and first professional **degrees**. Challenging opportunities include advanced placement, accelerated degree programs, self-designed majors, tutorials, an honors program, and a senior project. Special programs include internships, summer session for credit, off-campus study, and study abroad.

The most popular **majors** include English, psychology, and international studies. A complete listing of majors at L & C appears in the Majors Index beginning on page 380.

The **faculty** at L & C has 179 full-time graduate and undergraduate teachers, 93% with terminal degrees. 99% of the faculty serve as student advisers. The student-faculty ratio is 14:1, and the average class size in required courses is 21.

## 🖥 Computers on Campus

Students are not required to have a computer. Student rooms are linked to a campus network. 150 **computers** available in the computer center, computer labs, computer rooms, the library, and dormitories provide access to the main academic computer, off-campus computing facilities, and e-mail. Staffed computer lab on campus provides training in the use of computers and software.

The 2 **libraries** have 452,590 books, 280,455 microform titles, and 7,030 subscriptions. They are connected to 13 national **on-line** catalogs.

## 🌲 Campus Life

There are 60 active **organizations** on campus, including a drama/theater group and student-run newspaper and radio station. Student **safety services** include late night transport/escort service, 24-hour emergency telephone alarm devices, 24-hour patrols by trained security personnel, student patrols, and electronically operated dormitory entrances.

L & C is a member of the NAIA. **Intercollegiate sports** include baseball (m), basketball (m, w), crew (m, w), cross-country running (m, w), football (m), golf (m, w), lacrosse (m, w), rugby (m, w), sailing (m, w), skiing (cross-country) (m, w), skiing (downhill) (m, w), soccer (m, w), softball (w), swimming and diving (m, w), tennis (m, w), track and field (m, w), volleyball (m, w).

 ## Applying

L & C requires an essay, a high school transcript, 2 recommendations, SAT I or ACT or academic portfolio, a minimum high school GPA of 2.0, and in some cases individualized portfolio. It recommends 3 years of high school math and science, 2 years of high school foreign language, and an interview. Early, deferred, and midyear entrance are possible, with a 2/1 deadline and continuous processing to 2/15 for financial aid. **Contact:** Mr. Michael Sexton, Dean of Admissions and Student Financial Services, 0615 Southwest Palatine Hill Road, Portland, OR 97219-7879, 503-768-7040 or toll-free 800-444-4111 (out-of-state); fax 503-768-7055.

---

### GETTING IN LAST YEAR
2,992 applied
77% were accepted
22% enrolled (515)
36% from top tenth of their h.s. class
25% had SAT verbal scores over 600
39% had SAT math scores over 600
52% had ACT scores over 26
4% had SAT verbal scores over 700
9% had SAT math scores over 700
15% had ACT scores over 30
6 National Merit Scholars
25 valedictorians

### THE STUDENT BODY
Total 3,234, of whom 1,797
   are undergraduates

From 49 states and territories,
   44 other countries
29% from Oregon
55% women, 45% men
2% African Americans
1% Native Americans
3% Hispanics
11% Asian Americans
6% international students

### AFTER FRESHMAN YEAR
76% returned for sophomore year
60% got a degree within 4 years
70% got a degree within 5 years
71% got a degree within 6 years

### AFTER GRADUATION
20% pursued further study (10% arts and
   sciences, 3% business, 3% law)
33% had job offers within 3 months
74 corporations, 19 government agencies, 20
   nonprofit organizations recruited on campus

### WHAT YOU WILL PAY
Tuition and fees $15,800
Room and board $4790
55% receive need-based financial aid
   averaging $9411
15% receive non-need financial aid averaging
   $5385

# LINFIELD COLLEGE

McMinnville, Oregon • Small-town setting • Private • Independent-Religious • Coed

---

▶ Distinctive features of Linfield College include the opportunity for student research in the Science Division and Linfield Research Institute, the annual Oregon Nobel Laureate Symposium, award-winning theater and music programs, popular study-abroad programs, a new physical education/recreation complex, and nationally competitive athletic programs.

 **Academics**

Linfield offers a core academic program; fewer than half of graduate courses are open to undergraduates. It awards bachelor's and master's **degrees**. Challenging opportunities include advanced placement, accelerated degree programs, self-designed majors, an honors program, and a senior project. Special programs include internships, summer session for credit, off-campus study, study abroad, and Air Force ROTC.

The most popular **majors** include business, nursing, and liberal arts/general studies. A complete listing of majors at Linfield appears in the Majors Index beginning on page 380.

The **faculty** at Linfield has 122 full-time graduate and undergraduate teachers, 92% with terminal degrees. 76% of the faculty serve as student advisers. The student-faculty ratio is 13:1, and the average class size in required courses is 30.

 **Computers on Campus**

Students are not required to have a computer. Student rooms are linked to a campus network. 150 **computers** available in the computer center, computer labs, and dormitories provide access to e-mail. Staffed computer lab on campus provides training in the use of computers and software.

The 2 **libraries** have 128,705 books, 116,363 microform titles, and 1,029 subscriptions. They are connected to 4 national **on-line** catalogs.

 **Campus Life**

There are 20 active **organizations** on campus, including a drama/theater group and student-run newspaper and radio station. 46% of students participate in student government elections. 30% of eligible men and 30% of eligible women are members of 3 national **fraternities**, 2 national **sororities**, 1 local fraternity, and 1 local sorority. Student **safety services** include late night transport/escort service, 24-hour emergency telephone alarm devices, 24-hour patrols by trained security personnel, and student patrols.

Linfield is a member of the NAIA. **Intercollegiate sports** include baseball (m), basketball (m, w), cross-country running (m, w), football (m), golf (m), lacrosse (m), soccer (m, w), softball (w), swimming and diving (m, w), tennis (m, w), track and field (m, w), volleyball (w).

 **Applying**

Linfield requires an essay, a high school transcript, 2 recommendations, and SAT I or ACT. It recommends 3 years of high school math and science, some high school foreign language, and an interview. Early, deferred, and midyear entrance are possible, with a 2/15 deadline and continuous processing to 2/1 for financial aid. **Contact:** Mr. John W. Reed, Dean of Enrollment Services, 900 S. Baker Street, McMinnville, OR 97128-6894, 503-434-2213 or toll-free 800-640-2287; fax 503-434-2472.

---

**GETTING IN LAST YEAR**
1,689 applied
74% were accepted
30% enrolled (378)
47% from top tenth of their h.s. class
3.58 average high school GPA
14% had SAT verbal scores over 600
34% had SAT math scores over 600
46% had ACT scores over 26
4% had SAT verbal scores over 700
7% had SAT math scores over 700
13% had ACT scores over 30
6 National Merit Scholars

**THE STUDENT BODY**
Total 1,570, of whom 1,476
    are undergraduates
From 28 states and territories,
    34 other countries
63% from Oregon
52% women, 48% men
2% African Americans
1% Native Americans
2% Hispanics
5% Asian Americans
6% international students

**AFTER FRESHMAN YEAR**
73% returned for sophomore year

**AFTER GRADUATION**
15% pursued further study (8% arts and
    sciences, 2% business, 2% medicine)
120 corporations recruited on campus

**WHAT YOU WILL PAY**
Tuition and fees $13,490
Room and board $4210
75% receive need-based financial aid
    averaging $1848
Non-need financial aid averages $3474

---

# LOUISIANA STATE UNIVERSITY AND AGRICULTURAL AND MECHANICAL COLLEGE

Baton Rouge, Louisiana • Urban setting • Public • State-supported • Coed

Louisiana State University, the state's only Research University I under the Carnegie Foundation designation, is one of Louisiana's most selective and comprehensive institutions. Some students enjoy the traditional college experience, while others enhance their college programs by participating in Academic Program Abroad, National Student Exchange, and the Honors College. LSU's campus is listed among the 20 best campuses in America in Thomas A. Gaines's *The Campus as a Work of Art.*

## Academics

LSU offers a core academic program; fewer than half of graduate courses are open to undergraduates. It awards bachelor's, master's, doctoral, and first professional **degrees**. Challenging opportunities include advanced placement, self-designed majors, Freshmen Honors College, an honors program, a senior project, Phi Beta Kappa, and Sigma Xi. Special programs include cooperative education, internships, summer session for credit, off-campus study, study abroad, and Army, Naval, and Air Force ROTC.

The most popular **majors** include liberal arts/general studies, psychology, and accounting. A complete listing of majors at LSU appears in the Majors Index beginning on page 380.

The **faculty** at LSU has 1,210 full-time graduate and undergraduate teachers, 86% with terminal degrees. The student-faculty ratio is 19:1, and the average class size in required courses is 27.

## Computers on Campus

Students are not required to have a computer. 2,000 **computers** available in the computer center, computer labs, business, engineering colleges, the library, and dormitories provide access to the main academic computer, off-campus computing facilities, e-mail, and on-line services. Staffed computer lab on campus.

The 8 **libraries** have 2.8 million books and 14,537 subscriptions. They are connected to 10 national **on-line** catalogs.

## Campus Life

There are 194 active **organizations** on campus, including a drama/theater group and student-run newspaper and radio station. 10% of students participate in student government elections. 14% of eligible men and 14% of eligible women are members of 23 national **fraternities** and 14 national **sororities**. Student **safety services** include self-defense education, crime prevention programs, late night transport/escort service, 24-hour emergency telephone alarm devices, 24-hour patrols by trained security personnel, and electronically operated dormitory entrances.

LSU is a member of the NCAA (Division I). **Intercollegiate sports** (some offering scholarships) include baseball (m), basketball (m, w), cross-country running (m, w), football (m), golf (m, w), gymnastics (w), swimming and diving (m, w), tennis (m, w), track and field (m, w), volleyball (w).

## Applying

LSU requires a high school transcript, 3 years of high school math and science, 2 years of high school foreign language, minimum 2.3 high school GPA on high school requirements, SAT I or ACT, a minimum high school GPA of 2.0, and in some cases 1 recommendation. Early and midyear entrance are possible, with a 6/1 deadline and continuous processing to 5/1 for financial aid. **Contact:** Ms. Lisa Harris, Director of Admissions, Thomas Boyd Hall, Baton Rouge, LA 70803-3103, 504-388-1175.

---

### GETTING IN LAST YEAR
6,356 applied
84% were accepted
59% enrolled (3,155)
29% from top tenth of their h.s. class
3.04 average high school GPA
33% had ACT scores over 26
9% had ACT scores over 30
27 National Merit Scholars
93 valedictorians

### THE STUDENT BODY
Total 25,317, of whom 19,972 are undergraduates
From 52 states and territories, 101 other countries

88% from Louisiana
50% women, 50% men
8% African Americans
0% Native Americans
2% Hispanics
4% Asian Americans
3% international students

### AFTER FRESHMAN YEAR
77% returned for sophomore year
15% got a degree within 4 years
37% got a degree within 5 years
46% got a degree within 6 years

### AFTER GRADUATION
23% pursued further study
767 corporations, 16 government agencies, 69 nonprofit organizations recruited on campus
1 Rhodes, 2 Fulbright scholars

### WHAT YOU WILL PAY
Resident tuition and fees $2645
Nonresident tuition and fees $5945
Room and board $3310
35% receive non-need financial aid averaging $2829

# LOYOLA COLLEGE

Baltimore, Maryland • Suburban setting • Private • Independent-Religious • Coed

> Traditional academic standards are central to Jesuit education. Loyola's curriculum is rigorous, and the faculty's expectations for students are high. The aim is to challenge students and to try to develop their skills and abilities. Hard work is required for a good education, and Loyola is interested in admitting students who have been ambitious in their course selection in high school and who have shown that they can do well in academic work.

## Academics

Loyola offers a core academic program; fewer than half of graduate courses are open to undergraduates. It awards bachelor's, master's, and doctoral **degrees**. Challenging opportunities include advanced placement, an honors program, a senior project, and Phi Beta Kappa. Special programs include internships, summer session for credit, off-campus study, study abroad, and Army and Air Force ROTC.

A complete listing of majors at Loyola appears in the Majors Index beginning on page 380.

The **faculty** at Loyola has 222 full-time undergraduate teachers, 88% with terminal degrees. 90% of the faculty serve as student advisers. The student-faculty ratio is 14:1.

## Computers on Campus

Students are not required to have a computer. Student rooms are linked to a campus network. 168 **computers** available in the computer center, academic buildings, dormitories, and student rooms provide access to the main academic computer and e-mail. Staffed computer lab on campus (open 24 hours a day) provides training in the use of computers and software.

The **library** has 307,276 books, 38 microform titles, and 2,057 subscriptions. It is connected to 2 national **on-line** catalogs.

## Campus Life

Active **organizations** on campus include drama/theater group and student-run newspaper and radio station. Student **safety services** include late night transport/escort service, 24-hour emergency telephone alarm devices, 24-hour patrols by trained security personnel, student patrols, and electronically operated dormitory entrances.

Loyola is a member of the NCAA (Division I). **Intercollegiate sports** (some offering scholarships) include baseball (m), basketball (m, w), crew (m, w), cross-country running (m, w), field hockey (w), golf (m), ice hockey (m), lacrosse (m, w), rugby (m, w), sailing (m, w), soccer (m, w), swimming and diving (m, w), tennis (m, w), track and field (m, w), volleyball (m, w).

## Applying

Loyola requires an essay, a high school transcript, 3 years of high school math and science, 2 years of high school foreign language, SAT I, and in some cases 1 recommendation. It recommends an interview. Early and deferred entrance are possible, with a 2/1 deadline and continuous processing to 2/1 for financial aid. **Contact:** Mr. William Bossemeyer, Director of Admissions, 4501 North Charles Street, Baltimore, MD 21210-2699, 410-617-2000 ext. 2252 or toll-free 800-221-9107 Ext. 2252 (in-state); fax 410-617-2176.

---

### GETTING IN LAST YEAR
4,492 applied
68% were accepted
26% enrolled (798)
30% from top tenth of their h.s. class
3.3 average high school GPA
15% had SAT verbal scores over 600
41% had SAT math scores over 600
2% had SAT verbal scores over 700
7% had SAT math scores over 700

### THE STUDENT BODY
Total 6,169, of whom 3,194
  are undergraduates

From 36 states and territories,
  11 other countries
47% from Maryland
57% women, 43% men
3% African Americans
0% Native Americans
2% Hispanics
2% Asian Americans
2% international students

### AFTER FRESHMAN YEAR
91% returned for sophomore year

### AFTER GRADUATION
22% pursued further study (9% arts and
  sciences, 3% law, 2% business)
231 corporations recruited on campus

### WHAT YOU WILL PAY
Tuition and fees $13,500
Room and board $6300
41% receive need-based financial aid
  averaging $4880
Non-need financial aid averages $6100

# LOYOLA UNIVERSITY CHICAGO

Chicago, Illinois • Urban setting • Private • Independent-Religious • Coed

##  Academics

Loyola offers a core academic program. It awards bachelor's, master's, doctoral, and first professional **degrees** (also offers adult part-time program with significant enrollment not reflected in profile). Challenging opportunities include advanced placement, accelerated degree programs, an honors program, and Sigma Xi. Special programs include internships, summer session for credit, off-campus study, study abroad, and Army, Naval, and Air Force ROTC.

The most popular **majors** include psychology, biology/biological sciences, and communication. A complete listing of majors at Loyola appears in the Majors Index beginning on page 380.

The **faculty** at Loyola has 606 full-time graduate and undergraduate teachers, 93% with terminal degrees. The student-faculty ratio is 13:1, and the average class size in required courses is 19.

##  Campus Life

There are 136 active **organizations** on campus, including a drama/theater group and student-run newspaper and radio station. 8% of eligible men and 7% of eligible women are members of 6 national **fraternities** and 9 national **sororities**. Student **safety services** include late night transport/escort service, 24-hour emergency telephone alarm devices, 24-hour patrols by trained security personnel, and electronically operated dormitory entrances.

Loyola is a member of the NCAA (Division I) and NAIA. **Intercollegiate sports** (some offering scholarships) include basketball (m, w), cross-country running (m, w), golf (m, w), soccer (m, w), softball (w), track and field (m, w), volleyball (m, w).

##  Computers on Campus

Students are not required to have a computer. 318 **computers** available in the computer center, computer labs, academic buildings, the library, and dormitories provide access to the main academic computer, e-mail, and on-line services. Staffed computer lab on campus provides training in the use of computers and software.

The 4 **libraries** have 1.3 million books, 1.2 million microform titles, and 11,545 subscriptions.

##  Applying

Loyola requires a high school transcript and SAT I or ACT. It recommends an essay, 3 years of high school math and science, some high school foreign language, and an interview. Early and midyear entrance are possible, with a 4/1 deadline and continuous processing to 3/1 for financial aid. **Contact:** Mr. Robert Blust, Director of Admissions, 820 North Michigan Avenue, Chicago, IL 60611-2196, 312-915-6500 or toll-free 800-262-2373.

### GETTING IN LAST YEAR

3,457 applied
83% were accepted
39% enrolled (1,107)
32% from top tenth of their h.s. class
9% had SAT verbal scores over 600
27% had SAT math scores over 600
36% had ACT scores over 26
1% had SAT verbal scores over 700
4% had SAT math scores over 700
8% had ACT scores over 30
18 valedictorians

### THE STUDENT BODY

Total 13,806, of whom 8,106
   are undergraduates
From 50 states and territories,
   67 other countries
86% from Illinois

61% women, 39% men
5% African Americans
1% Native Americans
7% Hispanics
14% Asian Americans
1% international students

### AFTER FRESHMAN YEAR

83% returned for sophomore year
35% got a degree within 4 years
59% got a degree within 5 years
62% got a degree within 6 years

### AFTER GRADUATION

110 corporations, 35 government agencies
   recruited on campus
2 Fulbright scholars

### WHAT YOU WILL PAY

Tuition and fees $13,300
Room and board $5330
75% receive need-based financial aid
   averaging $3982
Non-need financial aid averages $4370

# LUTHER COLLEGE

Decorah, Iowa • Small-town setting • Private • Independent-Religious • Coed

A Phi Beta Kappa institution, Luther is one of the top colleges in the Midwest. Luther's 800-acre campus is noteworthy for its size, modern buildings, and natural beauty. The College offers more than 60 majors and preprofessional and certificate programs leading to the Bachelor of Arts degree. Of Luther's 156 full-time faculty members, 86% hold an earned doctorate or terminal degree. The 2,400-member student body comes from 36 states and 45 countries. Cocurricular activities include intercollegiate sports for men and women and 10 music ensembles. The College's strong academic program includes internship, professional semester, and extensive study-abroad opportunities.

## Academics

Luther offers a core academic program. It awards bachelor's **degrees**. Challenging opportunities include advanced placement, self-designed majors, tutorials, an honors program, a senior project, and Phi Beta Kappa. Special programs include internships, summer session for credit, and study abroad.

The most popular **majors** include biology/biological sciences, business, and elementary education. A complete listing of majors at Luther appears in the Majors Index beginning on page 380.

The **faculty** at Luther has 156 full-time teachers, 86% with terminal degrees. 100% of the faculty serve as student advisers. The student-faculty ratio is 13:1, and the average class size in required courses is 20.

## Computers on Campus

Students are not required to have a computer. 278 **computers** available in the computer center, all classroom buildings, classrooms, the library, and dormitories provide access to the main academic computer, off-campus computing facilities, e-mail, and on-line services. Staffed computer lab on campus provides training in the use of computers and software.

The **library** has 301,155 books, 21,000 microform titles, and 1,100 subscriptions.

## Campus Life

There are 81 active **organizations** on campus, including a drama/theater group and student-run newspaper and radio station. 14% of eligible men and 18% of eligible women are members of 1 national **fraternity**, 5 local fraternities, and 4 local **sororities**. Student **safety services** include door monitors, late night transport/escort service, 24-hour emergency telephone alarm devices, 24-hour patrols by trained security personnel, and electronically operated dormitory entrances.

Luther is a member of the NCAA (Division III). **Intercollegiate sports** include baseball (m), basketball (m, w), cross-country running (m, w), football (m), golf (m, w), soccer (m, w), softball (w), swimming and diving (m, w), tennis (m, w), track and field (m, w), volleyball (w), wrestling (m).

## Applying

Luther requires an essay, a high school transcript, 2 years of high school foreign language, 1 recommendation, 3 years of high school social science, and SAT I or ACT. It recommends 3 years of high school math and science and an interview. Early, deferred, and midyear entrance are possible, with a 6/1 deadline and continuous processing to 3/1 for financial aid. **Contact:** Dr. David Sallee, Dean for Enrollment Management, 700 College Drive, Decorah, IA 52101-1045, 319-387-1287 or toll-free 800-458-8437; fax 319-387-2159.

### GETTING IN LAST YEAR
1,789 applied
90% were accepted
39% enrolled (621)
38% from top tenth of their h.s. class
3.51 average high school GPA
18% had SAT verbal scores over 600
53% had SAT math scores over 600
49% had ACT scores over 26
4% had SAT verbal scores over 700
19% had SAT math scores over 700
15% had ACT scores over 30
14 National Merit Scholars
44 valedictorians

### THE STUDENT BODY
2,383 undergraduates
From 36 states and territories,
  45 other countries
39% from Iowa
60% women, 40% men
1% African Americans
1% Hispanics
2% Asian Americans
6% international students

### AFTER FRESHMAN YEAR
89% returned for sophomore year
67% got a degree within 4 years
74% got a degree within 5 years
76% got a degree within 6 years

### AFTER GRADUATION
21% pursued further study (11% arts and sciences, 3% medicine, 2% law)
57 corporations, 4 government agencies, 44 nonprofit organizations recruited on campus

### WHAT YOU WILL PAY
Tuition and fees $13,240
Room and board $3560
68% receive need-based financial aid averaging $2600
12% receive non-need financial aid averaging $2800

# LYON COLLEGE

Batesville, Arkansas • Small-town setting • Private • Independent-Religious • Coed

Lyon College is one of the nation's finest and most afford-able small liberal arts colleges. Founded in 1872 as Arkansas College, Lyon enrolls fewer than 1,000 students and maintains a low student-faculty ratio of 11:1. A hallmark of the academic program is a student-faculty research program, in part accounting for a near-perfect acceptance rate of Lyon students by graduate schools. Lyon students are attracted by the College's strong sense of community and many opportunities for involvement. A large endowment enables Lyon to offer an exceptional education at moderate cost and a strong scholarship and financial aid program.

## Academics

Lyon offers a liberal education curriculum and core academic program. It awards bachelor's **degrees**. Challenging opportunities include advanced placement, self-designed majors, tutorials, and a senior project. Special programs include cooperative education, internships, summer session for credit, and study abroad.

The most popular **majors** include psychology and biology/biological sciences. A complete listing of majors at Lyon appears in the Majors Index beginning on page 380.

The **faculty** at Lyon has 43 full-time teachers, 91% with terminal degrees. 100% of the faculty serve as student advisers. The student-faculty ratio is 11:1, and the average class size in required courses is 21.

## Computers on Campus

Students are not required to have a computer. 58 **comput-ers** available in the computer center, computer labs, the research center, the learning resource center, Smith Science Building, classrooms, the library, and the student center provide access to the main academic computer, off-campus computing facilities, e-mail, and on-line services. Staffed computer lab on campus provides training in the use of computers and software.

The **library** has 110,000 books, 6,165 microform titles, and 950 subscriptions. It is connected to 5 national **on-line** catalogs.

## Campus Life

There are 24 active **organizations** on campus, including a drama/theater group and student-run newspaper. 85% of students participate in student government elections. 21% of eligible men and 23% of eligible women are members of 2 national **fraternities**, 2 national **sororities**, 1 local fraternity, and 1 local sorority. Student **safety services** include late night transport/escort service, 24-hour emergency telephone alarm devices, and 24-hour patrols by trained security personnel.

Lyon is a member of the NAIA. **Intercollegiate sports** (some offering scholarships) include baseball (m), basketball (m, w), cross-country running (m, w), golf (m), soccer (m, w), tennis (m, w), volleyball (w).

## Applying

Lyon requires an essay, a high school transcript, 3 years of high school math and science, 1 year of high school foreign language, 4 years of English, 3 years of social science, and SAT I or ACT. It recommends 1 recommendation and an interview. Early, deferred, and midyear entrance are pos-sible, with rolling admissions and continuous processing to 4/1 for financial aid. **Contact:** Mr. Jonathan Stroud, Dean of Admissions and Financial Aid, 2300 Highland Drive, Batesville, AR 72503-2317, 501-698-4250 or toll-free 800-423-2542 (out-of-state); fax 501-698-4622.

---

### GETTING IN LAST YEAR

776 applied
41% were accepted
45% enrolled (145)
48% from top tenth of their h.s. class
3.43 average high school GPA
35% had SAT verbal scores over 600
35% had SAT math scores over 600
49% had ACT scores over 26
4% had SAT verbal scores over 700
4% had SAT math scores over 700
14% had ACT scores over 30

### THE STUDENT BODY

628 undergraduates
From 18 states and territories,
   4 other countries
82% from Arkansas
61% women, 39% men
5% African Americans
1% Native Americans
1% Hispanics
2% Asian Americans
1% international students

### AFTER FRESHMAN YEAR

70% returned for sophomore year
28% got a degree within 4 years
35% got a degree within 5 years

### AFTER GRADUATION

14% pursued further study (5% arts and
   sciences, 2% business, 2% law)
35% had job offers within 3 months
8 corporations, 7 government agencies, 4
   nonprofit organizations recruited on campus

### WHAT YOU WILL PAY

Tuition and fees $8764
Room and board $3922
72% receive need-based financial aid
   averaging $2141
24% receive non-need financial aid averaging
   $3686

# MACALESTER COLLEGE

St. Paul, Minnesota • Urban setting • Private • Independent-Religious • Coed

The intellectual partnering of distinguished faculty and talented students is at the core of Macalester's academic program. A $475-million endowment enables Macalester to support this interaction with top facilities and an 11:1 student-faculty ratio that will drop to 10:1 in the next few years. A residential, campus-centered college, Macalester is located in a historic and serene neighborhood several miles from the city centers of Minneapolis and St. Paul. Macalester students come from virtually every state and over 80 other countries; over half ranked in the top 10% of their high school class.

 **Academics**

Mac offers a core academic program. It awards bachelor's **degrees**. Challenging opportunities include advanced placement, self-designed majors, tutorials, an honors program, a senior project, and Phi Beta Kappa. Special programs include internships, off-campus study, study abroad, and Naval and Air Force ROTC.

The most popular **majors** include history, economics, and international studies. A complete listing of majors at Mac appears in the Majors Index beginning on page 380.

The **faculty** at Mac has 131 full-time teachers, 92% with terminal degrees. 100% of the faculty serve as student advisers. The student-faculty ratio is 11:1.

 **Computers on Campus**

Students are not required to have a computer. Student rooms are linked to a campus network. 350 **computers** available in the computer center, academic departments, the library, and dormitories provide access to the main academic computer, e-mail, and on-line services. Staffed computer lab on campus provides training in the use of computers and software.

The **library** has 351,891 books, 58,050 microform titles, and 1,449 subscriptions. It is connected to 5 national **on-line** catalogs.

 **Campus Life**

There are 80 active **organizations** on campus, including a drama/theater group and student-run newspaper and radio station. 32% of students participate in student government elections. Student **safety services** include late night transport/escort service, 24-hour emergency telephone alarm devices, 24-hour patrols by trained security personnel, and electronically operated dormitory entrances.

Mac is a member of the NCAA (Division III). **Intercollegiate sports** include baseball (m), basketball (m, w), crew (m, w), cross-country running (m, w), fencing (m, w), football (m), golf (m, w), ice hockey (m, w), rugby (m, w), skiing (cross-country) (m, w), soccer (m, w), softball (w), swimming and diving (m, w), tennis (m, w), track and field (m, w), volleyball (m, w), water polo (m, w), weight lifting (m, w).

 **Applying**

Mac requires an essay, a high school transcript, 3 recommendations, and SAT I or ACT. It recommends 3 years of high school math and science, 3 years of high school foreign language, a campus interview, and SAT II Subject Tests. Early and deferred entrance are possible, with a 1/15 deadline and a 2/8 priority date for financial aid. **Contact:** Mr. William M. Shain, Dean of Admissions, 1600 Grand Avenue, St. Paul, MN 55105-1899, 612-696-6357 or toll-free 800-231-7974; fax 612-696-6726.

### GETTING IN LAST YEAR

2,752 applied
58% were accepted
28% enrolled (452)
53% from top tenth of their h.s. class
60% had SAT verbal scores over 600
72% had SAT math scores over 600
84% had ACT scores over 26
11% had SAT verbal scores over 700
24% had SAT math scores over 700
42% had ACT scores over 30
41 National Merit Scholars

### THE STUDENT BODY

1,796 undergraduates
From 51 states and territories,
   83 other countries
24% from Minnesota
55% women, 45% men
4% African Americans
1% Native Americans
4% Hispanics
5% Asian Americans
10% international students

### AFTER FRESHMAN YEAR

89% returned for sophomore year
67% got a degree within 4 years
76% got a degree within 5 years
79% got a degree within 6 years

### AFTER GRADUATION

29% pursued further study (19% arts and
   sciences, 3% law, 3% medicine)
54 corporations, 4 government agencies, 13
   nonprofit organizations recruited on campus
1 Fulbright scholar

### WHAT YOU WILL PAY

Tuition and fees $16,010
Room and board $4774
70% receive need-based financial aid
   averaging $9168
5% receive non-need financial aid averaging
   $2380

# MARIETTA COLLEGE

Marietta, Ohio • Suburban setting • Private • Independent • Coed

Marietta College, a 4-year, private liberal arts college, has a long-standing history of academic excellence. Proud to have the 16th-oldest chapter of Phi Beta Kappa, Marietta is also consistently ranked among the top 10 by *U.S. News & World Report's Best Liberal Arts Colleges in the Midwest.* Approximately 1,350 students, representing 34 states and 6 other countries, can choose from over 30 majors. There is a 13:1 student-faculty ratio and a premier leadership program. Marietta students involve themselves in many clubs and organizations, including athletics, student government, radio and television stations, and the student newspaper.

##  Academics

Marietta offers an interdisciplinary curriculum and core academic program. It awards associate, bachelor's, and master's **degrees**. Challenging opportunities include advanced placement, accelerated degree programs, self-designed majors, tutorials, an honors program, a senior project, and Phi Beta Kappa. Special programs include internships, summer session for credit, off-campus study, and Army ROTC.

The most popular **majors** include business, communication, and education. A complete listing of majors at Marietta appears in the Majors Index beginning on page 380.

The **faculty** at Marietta has 85 full-time undergraduate teachers, 50% with terminal degrees. 80% of the faculty serve as student advisers. The student-faculty ratio is 13:1, and the average class size in required courses is 18.

##  Computers on Campus

Students are not required to have a computer. 150 **computers** available in the computer center, departmental labs, the library, and the student center. Staffed computer lab on campus provides training in the use of computers and software.

The **library** has 250,600 books, 28,384 microform titles, and 935 subscriptions.

##  Campus Life

There are 65 active **organizations** on campus, including a drama/theater group and student-run newspaper and radio station. 30% of eligible men and 35% of eligible women are members of 6 national **fraternities** and 4 national **sororities**. Student **safety services** include late night transport/escort service, 24-hour emergency telephone alarm devices, 24-hour patrols by trained security personnel, student patrols, and electronically operated dormitory entrances.

Marietta is a member of the NCAA (Division III). **Intercollegiate sports** include baseball (m), basketball (m, w), crew (m, w), football (m), golf (m), lacrosse (m), soccer (m, w), softball (w), tennis (m, w), volleyball (w).

##  Applying

Marietta requires an essay, a high school transcript, 3 years of high school math and science, 1 recommendation, SAT I or ACT, and a minimum high school GPA of 2.0. It recommends some high school foreign language, an interview, SAT II Subject Tests, and a minimum high school GPA of 3.0. Early, deferred, and midyear entrance are possible, with rolling admissions and continuous processing to 3/1 for financial aid. **Contact:** Mr. Dennis DePerro, Dean of Admission and Financial Aid, 215 Fifth Street, Marietta, OH 45750-4000, 614-374-4600 or toll-free 800-331-7896; fax 614-374-4896.

---

### GETTING IN LAST YEAR

1,414 applied
62% were accepted
34% enrolled (301)
12% from top tenth of their h.s. class
3.12 average high school GPA
8% had SAT verbal scores over 600
25% had SAT math scores over 600
32% had ACT scores over 26
0% had SAT verbal scores over 700
3% had SAT math scores over 700
4% had ACT scores over 30

### THE STUDENT BODY

Total 1,319, of whom 1,257
    are undergraduates
From 34 states and territories,
    6 other countries
60% from Ohio
48% women, 52% men
1% African Americans
1% Native Americans
1% Hispanics
1% Asian Americans
2% international students

### AFTER FRESHMAN YEAR

78% returned for sophomore year

### AFTER GRADUATION

14% pursued further study (9% arts and
    sciences, 3% law, 1% business)
17 corporations recruited on campus

### WHAT YOU WILL PAY

Tuition and fees $14,120
Room and board $3920
80% receive need-based financial aid
    averaging $8310
17% receive non-need financial aid averaging
    $2675

# MARLBORO COLLEGE

Marlboro, Vermont • Rural setting • Private • Independent • Coed

With about 270 students, Marlboro chooses to remain one of the smallest liberal arts colleges in the world as part of its commitment to keeping its 8:1 student-faculty ratio. Its intimate size is ideal for pursuing a personal approach to education and for building meaningful friendships. Such small size stimulates one-on-one relationships between students and faculty. At the heart of a Marlboro education is the Oxford-style tutorial system for upperclass students. Tutorials make it virtually impossible for any Marlboro student to fade into the background. The result is a community in which ideas are exchanged both in and out of the classroom.

## Academics

Marlboro College offers a self-designed, interdisciplinary curriculum and no core academic program. It awards bachelor's and master's **degrees**. Challenging opportunities include advanced placement, accelerated degree programs, self-designed majors, tutorials, an honors program, and a senior project. Special programs include internships, summer session for credit, and off-campus study.

A complete listing of majors at Marlboro appears in the Majors Index beginning on page 380.

The **faculty** at Marlboro College has 32 full-time undergraduate teachers, 57% with terminal degrees. 100% of the faculty serve as student advisers. The student-faculty ratio is 8:1, and the average class size in required courses is 8.

 **Computers on Campus**

Students are not required to have a computer. 15 **computers** available in the computer center. Staffed computer lab on campus (open 24 hours a day) provides training in the use of computers and software.

The **library** has 63,000 books, 4,500 microform titles, and 192 subscriptions. It is connected to 2 national **on-line** catalogs.

 **Campus Life**

There are 12 active **organizations** on campus, including a drama/theater group and student-run newspaper. Student **safety services** include late night transport/escort service and 24-hour emergency telephone alarm devices. **Intercollegiate sports** include skiing (cross-country) (m, w), skiing (downhill) (m, w), soccer (m, w), volleyball (m, w).

 **Applying**

Marlboro College requires an essay, a high school transcript, 1 recommendation, a campus interview, sample of expository prose, and SAT I or ACT. It recommends 3 years of high school math and science, some high school foreign language, SAT II Subject Tests, and a minimum high school GPA of 3.0. Early, deferred, and midyear entrance are possible, with rolling admissions and continuous processing to 3/1 for financial aid. **Contact:** Mr. Wayne R. Wood, Director of Admissions, South Road, Marlboro, VT 05344, 802-257-4333 ext. 237 or toll-free 800-343-0049 (out-of-state).

---

**GETTING IN LAST YEAR**
245 applied
90% were accepted
41% enrolled (91)

**THE STUDENT BODY**
270 undergraduates
From 35 states and territories,
  8 other countries

12% from Vermont
58% women, 42% men
1% African Americans
0% Native Americans
1% Hispanics
1% Asian Americans
6% international students

**AFTER FRESHMAN YEAR**
80% returned for sophomore year

**WHAT YOU WILL PAY**
Tuition and fees $18,670
Room and board $5960
75% receive need-based financial aid
  averaging $9000
Non-need financial aid averages $5000

# Marquette University

Milwaukee, Wisconsin • Urban setting • Private • Independent-Religious • Coed

Since 1881, Marquette University has challenged students to work toward reaching their potential in every facet of their lives. A Jesuit university, Marquette places emphasis on the liberal arts, Christian ideals, and humanistic concern for others. Nearly 95% of the faculty members hold the PhD or equivalent terminal degrees, and all are expected to teach and to do research. Marquette's diverse, residential student body hails from all 50 states and approximately 80 other countries. Marquette's campus is adjacent to downtown Milwaukee and 1 mile west of Lake Michigan.

 ## Academics

Marquette offers a core academic program. It awards associate, bachelor's, master's, doctoral, and first professional **degrees**. Challenging opportunities include advanced placement, accelerated degree programs, self-designed majors, tutorials, Freshmen Honors College, an honors program, Phi Beta Kappa, and Sigma Xi. Special programs include cooperative education, internships, summer session for credit, off-campus study, study abroad, and Army, Naval, and Air Force ROTC.

The most popular **majors** include mechanical engineering, accounting, and electrical engineering. A complete listing of majors at Marquette appears in the Majors Index beginning on page 380.

The **faculty** at Marquette has 569 full-time graduate and undergraduate teachers, 95% with terminal degrees. The student-faculty ratio is 15:1.

 ## Computers on Campus

Students are not required to have a computer. Student rooms are linked to a campus network. 800 **computers** available in the computer center, labs, clusters, the library, and dormitories. Staffed computer lab on campus (open 24 hours a day) provides training in the use of computers and software.

The 3 **libraries** have 1 million books, 362,178 microform titles, and 8,964 subscriptions. They are connected to 6 national **on-line** catalogs.

 ## Campus Life

There are 150 active **organizations** on campus, including a drama/theater group and student-run newspaper and radio station. 7% of eligible men and 7% of eligible women are members of 10 national **fraternities** and 9 national **sororities**. Student **safety services** include late night transport/escort service, 24-hour emergency telephone alarm devices, and 24-hour patrols by trained security personnel.

Marquette is a member of the NCAA (Division I). **Intercollegiate sports** (some offering scholarships) include baseball (m), basketball (m, w), crew (m, w), cross-country running (m, w), football (m), golf (m), ice hockey (m), lacrosse (m), riflery (m), rugby (m), sailing (m, w), skiing (downhill) (m, w), soccer (m, w), softball (w), swimming and diving (m, w), tennis (m, w), track and field (m, w), volleyball (m, w), wrestling (m).

 ## Applying

Marquette requires an essay, a high school transcript, SAT I or ACT, and in some cases 3 years of high school math. It recommends 3 years of high school science, 2 years of high school foreign language, and an interview. Rolling admissions and continuous processing to 3/1 for financial aid. **Contact:** Mr. David Buckholdt, Director of Enrollment Management, 615 North 11th Street, Milwaukee, WI 53201-1881, 414-288-7302 or toll-free 800-222-6544.

---

## GETTING IN LAST YEAR

5,806 applied
85% were accepted
32% enrolled (1,581)
37% from top tenth of their h.s. class
9% had SAT verbal scores over 600
39% had SAT math scores over 600
49% had ACT scores over 26
0% had SAT verbal scores over 700
6% had SAT math scores over 700
11% had ACT scores over 30
68 valedictorians

## THE STUDENT BODY

Total 10,749, of whom 7,690
  are undergraduates

From 55 states and territories,
  80 other countries
52% from Wisconsin
52% women, 48% men
4% African Americans
0% Native Americans
4% Hispanics
8% Asian Americans
5% international students

## AFTER FRESHMAN YEAR

85% returned for sophomore year
54% got a degree within 4 years
75% got a degree within 5 years
77% got a degree within 6 years

## AFTER GRADUATION

25% pursued further study (5% arts and
  sciences, 5% law, 4% engineering)
99 corporations, 1 government agency, 1
  nonprofit organization recruited on campus
1 Fulbright scholar

## WHAT YOU WILL PAY

Tuition and fees $11,760
Room and board $4930
Need-based financial aid averages $6500
Non-need financial aid averages $4030

# MARYVILLE UNIVERSITY OF SAINT LOUIS

St. Louis, Missouri • Suburban setting • Private • Independent • Coed

Maryville University of Saint Louis is committed to integrating the liberal arts with professional education by providing innovative and interactive programs with the business, education, health care, cultural, and arts communities it serves. Academic programs are grounded in the humanizing values and ideals that move and guide society—all in the spirit of the liberal arts. In addition, these programs provide opportunities for students to perfect their skills in settings beyond the classroom, gain self-confidence, and profit from the energy of experience.

##  Academics

Maryville offers an integrated professional liberal education curriculum and core academic program; fewer than half of graduate courses are open to undergraduates. It awards bachelor's and master's **degrees**. Challenging opportunities include advanced placement, accelerated degree programs, tutorials, Freshmen Honors College, an honors program, and a senior project. Special programs include cooperative education, internships, summer session for credit, off-campus study, study abroad, and Army ROTC.

The most popular **majors** include business, accounting, and nursing. A complete listing of majors at Maryville appears in the Majors Index beginning on page 380.

The **faculty** at Maryville has 85 full-time graduate and undergraduate teachers, 68% with terminal degrees. 100% of the faculty serve as student advisers. The student-faculty ratio is 12:1, and the average class size in required courses is 13.

##  Computers on Campus

Students are not required to have a computer. 225 **computers** available in the computer center, computer labs, career management, nursing, and housing offices, and the library provide access to the main academic computer. Staffed computer lab on campus.

The **library** has 144,680 books and 790 subscriptions.

##  Campus Life

There are 33 active **organizations** on campus, including a drama/theater group and student-run newspaper. 15% of students participate in student government elections. Student **safety services** include video/audio security system in residence halls, emergency "blue-light" phones throughout the campus, late night transport/escort service, 24-hour emergency telephone alarm devices, 24-hour patrols by trained security personnel, and electronically operated dormitory entrances.

Maryville is a member of the NCAA (Division III). **Intercollegiate sports** include baseball (m), basketball (m, w), cross-country running (m, w), golf (m), soccer (m, w), softball (w), tennis (m, w), volleyball (w).

##  Applying

Maryville requires a high school transcript, 3 years of high school math and science, SAT I or ACT, a minimum high school GPA of 2.0, and in some cases an essay, recommendations, a campus interview, and audition, portfolio. Early, deferred, and midyear entrance are possible, with rolling admissions and continuous processing to 2/1 for financial aid. **Contact:** Dr. Martha Wade, Dean of Admissions and Enrollment Management, Gander Hall, St. Louis, MO 63141-7299, 314-529-9350 or toll-free 800-627-9855; fax 314-542-9085.

## GETTING IN LAST YEAR

651 applied
75% were accepted
37% enrolled (180)
29% from top tenth of their h.s. class
3.22 average high school GPA
9% had SAT verbal scores over 600
32% had SAT math scores over 600
32% had ACT scores over 26
3% had SAT verbal scores over 700
3% had SAT math scores over 700
8% had ACT scores over 30
8 valedictorians

## THE STUDENT BODY

Total 3,425, of whom 2,859
   are undergraduates
From 16 states and territories,
   32 other countries
87% from Missouri
70% women, 30% men
4% African Americans
1% Hispanics
1% Asian Americans
6% international students

## AFTER FRESHMAN YEAR

78% returned for sophomore year
45% got a degree within 4 years
54% got a degree within 5 years

## WHAT YOU WILL PAY

Tuition and fees $9250
Room and board $4550
37% receive need-based financial aid
   averaging $2165
48% receive non-need financial aid averaging
   $2554

# MARY WASHINGTON COLLEGE

Fredericksburg, Virginia • Small-town setting • Public • State-supported • Coed

> Academic excellence, personal attention to students, outstanding value: together these terms best describe Mary Washington College. As Virginia's public college of the liberal arts and sciences, Mary Washington is distinctive. Its students come from throughout the country and the world to study on the beautiful, neoclassical campus, which is located in historic Fredericksburg, just 50 miles south of Washington, D.C. The College recently installed one of the nation's most advanced fiber-optic campus networks. Residence halls feature in-room phone and voice-mail service, full computer access, and video services. The College features a strong undergraduate research program and offers outstanding internship opportunities due to its convenient location.

 ## Academics

Mary Washington offers a writing-intensive liberal arts curriculum and core academic program. It awards bachelor's and master's **degrees**. Challenging opportunities include advanced placement, accelerated degree programs, self-designed majors, tutorials, a senior project, and Phi Beta Kappa. Special programs include cooperative education, internships, summer session for credit, and study abroad.

The most popular **majors** include business, psychology, and English. A complete listing of majors at Mary Washington appears in the Majors Index beginning on page 380.

The **faculty** at Mary Washington has 168 full-time undergraduate teachers, 85% with terminal degrees. 90% of the faculty serve as student advisers. The student-faculty ratio is 17:1, and the average class size in required courses is 25.

 ## Computers on Campus

Students are not required to have a computer. Student rooms are linked to a campus network. 110 **computers** available in the computer center, computer labs, and the library. Staffed computer lab on campus (open 24 hours a day).

The **library** has 337,990 books, 320,608 microform titles, and 1,381 subscriptions. It is connected to 5 national **on-line** catalogs.

 ## Campus Life

There are 85 active **organizations** on campus, including a drama/theater group and student-run newspaper and radio station. Student **safety services** include late night transport/escort service, 24-hour emergency telephone alarm devices, 24-hour patrols by trained security personnel, and electronically operated dormitory entrances.

Mary Washington is a member of the NCAA (Division III). **Intercollegiate sports** include baseball (m), basketball (m, w), crew (m, w), cross-country running (m, w), equestrian sports (m, w), field hockey (w), lacrosse (m, w), rugby (m, w), soccer (m, w), softball (w), swimming and diving (m, w), tennis (m, w), track and field (m, w), volleyball (m, w).

## Applying

Mary Washington requires an essay, a high school transcript, 3 years of high school math and science, 3 years of high school foreign language, and SAT I. It recommends 3 SAT II Subject Tests. Early, deferred, and midyear entrance are possible, with a 2/1 deadline and 3/1 for financial aid. **Contact:** Dr. Martin A. Wilder Jr., Vice President for Admissions and Financial Aid, 1301 College Avenue, Fredericksburg, VA 22401-5358, 703-899-4681 or toll-free 800-468-5614.

---

### GETTING IN LAST YEAR
4,267 applied
52% were accepted
32% enrolled (710)
40% from top tenth of their h.s. class
3.51 average high school GPA
21% had SAT verbal scores over 600
36% had SAT math scores over 600
7% had SAT verbal scores over 700
11% had SAT math scores over 700
4 National Merit Scholars
17 valedictorians

### THE STUDENT BODY
Total 3,489, of whom 3,439
   are undergraduates

From 40 states and territories,
   16 other countries
70% from Virginia
65% women, 35% men
5% African Americans
0% Native Americans
2% Hispanics
3% Asian Americans
1% international students

### AFTER FRESHMAN YEAR
92% returned for sophomore year
64% got a degree within 4 years
73% got a degree within 5 years
77% got a degree within 6 years

### AFTER GRADUATION
20% pursued further study
50 corporations, 41 government agencies, 42
   nonprofit organizations recruited on campus

### WHAT YOU WILL PAY
Resident tuition and fees $3206
Nonresident tuition and fees $7670
Room and board $4942
38% receive need-based financial aid
   averaging $1800
15% receive non-need financial aid averaging
   $1820

---

# MASSACHUSETTS INSTITUTE OF TECHNO

Cambridge, Massachusetts • Urban setting • Private • Independent • Coed

## Academics

MIT offers a science and technology-based general curriculum and core academic program; all graduate courses are open to undergraduates. It awards bachelor's, master's, and doctoral **degrees**. Challenging opportunities include advanced placement, accelerated degree programs, self-designed majors, tutorials, a senior project, Phi Beta Kappa, and Sigma Xi. Special programs include cooperative education, internships, summer session for credit, off-campus study, and Army, Naval, and Air Force ROTC.

The most popular **majors** include electrical engineering, mechanical engineering, and computer science. A complete listing of majors at MIT appears in the Majors Index beginning on page 380.

The **faculty** at MIT has 938 full-time graduate and undergraduate teachers, 99% with terminal degrees. 60% of the faculty serve as student advisers. The student-faculty ratio is 5:1.

## Computers on Campus

Students are not required to have a computer. Student rooms are linked to a campus network. 800 **computers** available in the computer center, computer labs, the research center, the learning resource center, academic buildings, classrooms, the library, the student center, dormitories, and student rooms provide access to the main academic computer, off-campus computing facilities, e-mail, and on-line services. Staffed computer lab on campus (open 24 hours a day) provides training in the use of computers and software.

The 23 **libraries** have 2.3 million books, 2 million microform titles, and 21,259 subscriptions. They are connected to 8 national **on-line** catalogs.

## Campus Life

There are 280 active **organi**... ing a drama/theater group and radio station. 35% of stu... government elections. 50% of ... eligible women are members of 20 national **fraternities**, 5 national **sororities**, 2 local fraternities, and social clubs. Student **safety services** include late night transport/escort service, 24-hour emergency telephone alarm devices, 24-hour patrols by trained security personnel, student patrols, and electronically operated dormitory entrances.

MIT is a member of the NCAA (Division III). **Intercollegiate sports** include baseball (m), basketball (m, w), crew (m, w), cross-country running (m, w), fencing (m, w), field hockey (w), football (m), golf (m), gymnastics (m, w), ice hockey (m, w), lacrosse (m, w), riflery (m, w), rugby (m, w), sailing (m, w), skiing (cross-country) (m, w), skiing (downhill) (m, w), soccer (m, w), softball (w), squash (m), swimming and diving (m, w), tennis (m, w), track and field (m, w), volleyball (m, w), water polo (m), wrestling (m).

## Applying

MIT requires an essay, a high school transcript, 2 recommendations, an interview, SAT I or ACT, and 3 SAT II Subject Tests. It recommends 4 years of high school math and science and 2 years of high school foreign language. Early and deferred entrance are possible, with a 1/1 deadline and a 1/13 priority date for financial aid. **Contact:** Mr. Michael C. Behnke, Director of Admissions, 77 Massachusetts Avenue, Room 3-107, Cambridge, MA 02139-4307, 617-253-4791; fax 617-258-8304.

---

### GETTING IN LAST YEAR

7,136 applied
30% were accepted
51% enrolled (1,095)
94% from top tenth of their h.s. class
75% had SAT verbal scores over 600
97% had SAT math scores over 600
98% had ACT scores over 26
24% had SAT verbal scores over 700
83% had SAT math scores over 700
85% had ACT scores over 30
252 valedictorians

### THE STUDENT BODY

Total 9,774, of whom 4,472 are undergraduates

From 53 states and territories, 74 other countries
8% from Massachusetts
36% women, 64% men
6% African Americans
1% Native Americans
9% Hispanics
28% Asian Americans
8% international students

### AFTER FRESHMAN YEAR

97% returned for sophomore year
80% got a degree within 4 years
89% got a degree within 5 years
90% got a degree within 6 years

### AFTER GRADUATION

55% pursued further study (25% arts and sciences, 20% engineering, 6% medicine)
35% had job offers within 3 months
385 corporations, 6 government agencies recruited on campus
3 Marshall, 2 Fulbright scholars

### WHAT YOU WILL PAY

Tuition and fees $20,100
Room and board $5975
54% receive need-based financial aid averaging $12,806

# [MESS]IAH COLLEGE

Pennsylvania • Small-town setting • Private • Independent-Religious • Coed

[Mes]siah College is a four-year, coeducational, Christian college of the arts and sciences. The main campus is located in Grantham, Pennsylvania, 10 miles southwest of Harrisburg, the state capital. Messiah College seeks to integrate faith and learning, providing strong academic emphasis in both the traditional liberal arts and professional programs of study. Approximately 2,300 students are currently pursuing undergraduate degrees in over 40 academic programs, including business, science, math, nursing, education, engineering, and other traditional liberal arts curricula. The College is accredited by the Middle States Association of Colleges and Schools. Both merit and need-based scholarships and grants are available for eligible students.

 **Academics**

Messiah College offers a core academic program. It awards bachelor's **degrees**. Challenging opportunities include advanced placement, accelerated degree programs, self-designed majors, an honors program, and a senior project. Special programs include internships, summer session for credit, off-campus study, and study abroad.

The most popular **majors** include business, natural sciences, and education. A complete listing of majors at Messiah College appears in the Majors Index beginning on page 380.

The **faculty** at Messiah College has 147 full-time teachers, 69% with terminal degrees. 100% of the faculty serve as student advisers. The student-faculty ratio is 18:1, and the average class size in required courses is 25.

 **Computers on Campus**

Students are not required to have a computer. Student rooms are linked to a campus network. 275 **computers** available in the computer center, computer labs, the research center, the learning resource center, classrooms, the library, and dormitories provide access to the main academic computer, off-campus computing facilities, e-mail, and on-line services. Staffed computer lab on campus provides training in the use of computers and software.

The **library** has 200,000 books, 5,000 microform titles, and 1,000 subscriptions.

 **Campus Life**

There are 58 active **organizations** on campus, including a drama/theater group and student-run newspaper and radio station. No national or local **fraternities** or **sororities**. Student **safety services** include late night transport/escort service, 24-hour emergency telephone alarm devices, and 24-hour patrols by trained security personnel.

Messiah College is a member of the NCAA (Division III). **Intercollegiate sports** include baseball (m), basketball (m, w), cross-country running (m, w), field hockey (w), golf (m), soccer (m, w), softball (w), tennis (m, w), track and field (m, w), volleyball (w), wrestling (m).

**Applying**

Messiah College requires an essay, a high school transcript, 2 recommendations, SAT I or ACT, and in some cases some high school foreign language. It recommends 3 years of high school math and science. Early and deferred entrance are possible, with rolling admissions and a 4/1 priority date for financial aid. **Contact:** Mr. Ron E. Long, Vice President for Communications, Old Main Building, Grantham, PA 17027, 717-691-6000 or toll-free 800-382-1349 (in-state), 800-233-4220 (out-of-state); fax 717-691-6025.

## GETTING IN LAST YEAR

1,877 applied
80% were accepted
40% enrolled (594)
32% from top tenth of their h.s. class
15% had SAT verbal scores over 600
32% had SAT math scores over 600
31% had ACT scores over 26
1% had SAT verbal scores over 700
7% had SAT math scores over 700
7% had ACT scores over 30
3 National Merit Scholars
39 valedictorians

## THE STUDENT BODY

2,320 undergraduates
From 39 states and territories, 21 other countries
52% from Pennsylvania
60% women, 40% men
3% African Americans
0% Native Americans
3% Hispanics
3% Asian Americans
1% international students

### AFTER FRESHMAN YEAR

86% returned for sophomore year
65% got a degree within 4 years
69% got a degree within 5 years
70% got a degree within 6 years

## AFTER GRADUATION

30% pursued further study (8% arts and sciences, 8% business, 4% medicine)
82 corporations, 5 government agencies, 32 nonprofit organizations recruited on campus

## WHAT YOU WILL PAY

Tuition and fees $10,384
Room and board $5070
Need-based financial aid averages $3750
Non-need financial aid averages $1300

# MIAMI UNIVERSITY

Oxford, Ohio • Small-town setting • Public • State-related • Coed

Miami has received national recognition for its emphasis on undergraduate education. Co-winner of the national 1994 Theodore M. Hesburgh Award for the program to enrich faculty teaching skills, Miami was also ranked 35th on a list of the 100 best buys in American higher education by *Money* magazine. Miami ranks 4th nationally for the number of students who study abroad each year, whether at their European Center or at universities around the world. Students are involved in the many opportunities for research projects with faculty, leadership development, and service projects, as well as in the school's more than 300 clubs and organizations.

##  Academics

Miami University offers a liberal arts curriculum and core academic program; more than half of graduate courses are open to undergraduates. It awards bachelor's, master's, and doctoral **degrees**. Challenging opportunities include advanced placement, accelerated degree programs, self-designed majors, tutorials, an honors program, a senior project, Phi Beta Kappa, and Sigma Xi. Special programs include cooperative education, internships, summer session for credit, off-campus study, study abroad, and Army, Naval, and Air Force ROTC.

The most popular **majors** include business, zoology, and accounting. A complete listing of majors at Miami University appears in the Majors Index beginning on page 380.

The **faculty** at Miami University has 767 full-time graduate and undergraduate teachers, 89% with terminal degrees. The student-faculty ratio is 17:1, and the average class size in required courses is 28.

##  Computers on Campus

Students are not required to have a computer. 700 **computers** available in the computer center, computer labs, the learning resource center, academic buildings, classrooms, the library, and dormitories provide access to the main academic computer, off-campus computing facilities, e-mail, and on-line services. Staffed computer lab on campus provides training in the use of computers and software.

The 4 **libraries** have 1.5 million books, 924,000 microform titles, and 11,850 subscriptions. They are connected to 5 national **on-line** catalogs.

##  Campus Life

There are 325 active **organizations** on campus, including a drama/theater group and student-run newspaper and radio station. 20% of students participate in student government elections. 31% of eligible men and 34% of eligible women are members of 28 national **fraternities** and 22 national **sororities**. Student **safety services** include late night transport/escort service, 24-hour emergency telephone alarm devices, 24-hour patrols by trained security personnel, and student patrols.

Miami University is a member of the NCAA (Division I). **Intercollegiate sports** (some offering scholarships) include archery (m, w), baseball (m), basketball (m, w), cross-country running (m, w), equestrian sports (m, w), fencing (m, w), field hockey (w), football (m), golf (m), gymnastics (m, w), ice hockey (m), lacrosse (m), racquetball (m, w), rugby (m), sailing (m, w), soccer (m, w), softball (w), swimming and diving (m, w), tennis (m, w), track and field (m, w), volleyball (m, w), wrestling (m).

##  Applying

Miami University requires a high school transcript, 3 years of high school math and science, 2 years of high school foreign language, and SAT I or ACT. It recommends an essay and 1 recommendation. Early and midyear entrance are possible, with a 1/31 deadline and continuous processing to 2/15 for financial aid. **Contact:** Dr. James S. McCoy, Assistant Vice President for Enrollment Services, Glos Admissions Center, Oxford, OH 45056, 513-529-2531.

### GETTING IN LAST YEAR
10,242 applied
72% were accepted
41% enrolled (3,039)
41% from top tenth of their h.s. class
13% had SAT verbal scores over 600
51% had SAT math scores over 600
54% had ACT scores over 26
1% had SAT verbal scores over 700
8% had SAT math scores over 700
12% had ACT scores over 30
53 class presidents

### THE STUDENT BODY
Total 15,882, of whom 14,014
  are undergraduates

From 48 states and territories,
  54 other countries
71% from Ohio
54% women, 46% men
3% African Americans
1% Native Americans
1% Hispanics
2% Asian Americans
1% international students

### AFTER FRESHMAN YEAR
90% returned for sophomore year
75% got a degree within 4 years
77% got a degree within 5 years
82% got a degree within 6 years

### AFTER GRADUATION
52% pursued further study (19% arts and
  sciences, 12% law, 9% business)
321 corporations, 5 government agencies, 10
  nonprofit organizations recruited on campus
1 Marshall scholar

### WHAT YOU WILL PAY
Resident tuition and fees $4612
Nonresident tuition and fees $9728
Room and board $3960
34% receive need-based financial aid
  averaging $1698
28% receive non-need financial aid averaging
  $2928

# Michigan State University

East Lansing, Michigan • Small-town setting • Public • State-supported • Coed

Dedicated to undergraduate education, Michigan State University, the nation's premier land-grant institution, offers 11 degree-granting colleges that support 150 academic programs of study, 350 student groups, 80 overseas study programs, a campus of unparalleled beauty, and Big Ten athletics—few institutions have it all. The Honors College offers enriched curricula in all majors, and 2 residential programs, Lyman Briggs School and James Madison College, integrate academic pursuits and living environment. Undergraduate research opportunities exist in majors ranging from advertising and biochemistry to criminal justice and engineering. Joint freshman admission programs are administered by the Colleges of Human Medicine and Veterinary Medicine.

 **Academics**

Michigan State offers a core academic program; fewer than half of graduate courses are open to undergraduates. It awards bachelor's, master's, doctoral, and first professional **degrees**. Challenging opportunities include advanced placement, self-designed majors, tutorials, Freshmen Honors College, an honors program, a senior project, Phi Beta Kappa, and Sigma Xi. Special programs include cooperative education, internships, summer session for credit, study abroad, and Army and Air Force ROTC.

The most popular **majors** include accounting, advertising, and psychology. A complete listing of majors at Michigan State appears in the Majors Index beginning on page 380.

The **faculty** at Michigan State has 2,432 full-time undergraduate teachers, 95% with terminal degrees.

 **Computers on Campus**

Students are not required to have a computer. 2,500 **computers** available in the computer center, computer labs, the library, the student center, and dormitories provide access to the main academic computer and e-mail. Staffed computer lab on campus.

The 15 **libraries** have 3.9 million books and 28,000 subscriptions.

 **Campus Life**

There are 400 active **organizations** on campus, including a drama/theater group and student-run newspaper and radio station. 8% of eligible men and 8% of eligible women are members of 31 national **fraternities** and 19 national **sororities**. Student **safety services** include self-defense workshops, late night transport/escort service, 24-hour emergency telephone alarm devices, and 24-hour patrols by trained security personnel.

Michigan State is a member of the NCAA (Division I). **Intercollegiate sports** (some offering scholarships) include baseball (m), basketball (m, w), cross-country running (m, w), equestrian sports (m, w), fencing (m), field hockey (w), football (m), golf (m, w), gymnastics (m, w), ice hockey (m), lacrosse (m), soccer (m), swimming and diving (m, w), tennis (m, w), track and field (m, w), volleyball (w), wrestling (m).

 **Applying**

Michigan State requires a high school transcript and SAT I or ACT. It recommends 3 years of high school math, 2 years of high school foreign language, 2 years of high school science, 4 years of high school English, and 3 years of high school social science. Deferred and midyear entrance are possible, with a 7/30 deadline and continuous processing for financial aid. **Contact:** Dr. William H. Turner, Director of Admissions, 250 Administration Building, East Lansing, MI 48824-1020, 517-355-8332.

---

### GETTING IN LAST YEAR
18,663 applied
85% were accepted
41% enrolled (6,403)
17% from top tenth of their h.s. class
3.28 average high school GPA
8% had SAT verbal scores over 600
28% had SAT math scores over 600
25% had ACT scores over 26
1% had SAT verbal scores over 700
6% had SAT math scores over 700
5% had ACT scores over 30

### THE STUDENT BODY
Total 40,254, of whom 31,056 are undergraduates
From 54 states and territories, 66 other countries
91% from Michigan
52% women, 48% men
8% African Americans
1% Native Americans
2% Hispanics
4% Asian Americans
2% international students

### AFTER FRESHMAN YEAR
86% returned for sophomore year
33% got a degree within 4 years
64% got a degree within 5 years
70% got a degree within 6 years

### WHAT YOU WILL PAY
Resident tuition and fees $4626
Nonresident tuition and fees $11,182
Room and board $3764
45% receive need-based financial aid averaging $1285
Non-need financial aid averages $2597

# MICHIGAN TECHNOLOGICAL UNIVERSITY

Houghton, Michigan • Small-town setting • Public • State-supported • Coed

▶ Michigan Tech is recognized as one of the nation's leading universities for undergraduate and graduate education in science and engineering. MTU's state-of-the-art campus is located near Lake Superior in Michigan's beautiful Upper Peninsula. For 4 consecutive years, Michigan Tech has received *Money* magazine's top 100 rating and has been rated by *U.S. News & World Report* as among the top 5 college buys in the Midwest. MTU is one of Michigan's 4 nationally recognized research universities.

##  Academics

Michigan Tech offers an interdisciplinary curriculum and core academic program; fewer than half of graduate courses are open to undergraduates. It awards associate, bachelor's, master's, and doctoral **degrees**. Challenging opportunities include advanced placement, self-designed majors, tutorials, a senior project, and Sigma Xi. Special programs include cooperative education, internships, summer session for credit, study abroad, and Army and Air Force ROTC.

The most popular **majors** include mechanical engineering, electrical engineering, and civil engineering. A complete listing of majors at Michigan Tech appears in the Majors Index beginning on page 380.

The **faculty** at Michigan Tech has 348 full-time graduate and undergraduate teachers, 74% with terminal degrees. 17% of the faculty serve as student advisers. The student-faculty ratio is 16:1, and the average class size in required courses is 26.

##  Computers on Campus

Students are not required to have a computer. 500 **computers** available in the computer center, computer labs, the research center, the learning resource center, classrooms, and dormitories provide access to e-mail. Staffed computer lab on campus provides training in the use of computers and software.

The **library** has 785,936 books, 415,801 microform titles, and 4,221 subscriptions. It is connected to 1 national **on-line** catalog.

##  Campus Life

There are 175 active **organizations** on campus, including a drama/theater group and student-run newspaper and radio station. 13% of eligible men and 16% of eligible women are members of 12 national **fraternities**, 4 national **sororities**, 4 local fraternities, 4 local sororities, and social clubs. Student **safety services** include late night transport/escort service, 24-hour emergency telephone alarm devices, and 24-hour patrols by trained security personnel.

Michigan Tech is a member of the NCAA (Division II). **Intercollegiate sports** (some offering scholarships) include basketball (m, w), cross-country running (m, w), football (m), ice hockey (m), skiing (cross-country) (m, w), swimming and diving (m, w), tennis (m, w), track and field (m, w), volleyball (w).

##  Applying

Michigan Tech requires a high school transcript, and in some cases 3 years of high school math. It recommends 3 years of high school science, some high school foreign language, an interview, SAT I or ACT, and SAT II Subject Tests. Deferred and midyear entrance are possible, with rolling admissions and 3/1 for financial aid. **Contact:** Mr. Joseph Galetto, Executive Director of Enrollment Management, 1400 Townsend Drive, Houghton, MI 49931-1295, 906-487-2319; fax 906-487-3343.

---

### GETTING IN LAST YEAR
2,484 applied
92% were accepted
45% enrolled (1,028)
41% from top tenth of their h.s. class
3.48 average high school GPA
14% had SAT verbal scores over 600
68% had SAT math scores over 600
50% had ACT scores over 26
2% had SAT verbal scores over 700
20% had SAT math scores over 700
14% had ACT scores over 30
15 National Merit Scholars
96 valedictorians

### THE STUDENT BODY
Total 6,460, of whom 5,776
 are undergraduates

From 43 states and territories,
 41 other countries
78% from Michigan
25% women, 75% men
2% African Americans
1% Native Americans
1% Hispanics
1% Asian Americans
4% international students

### AFTER FRESHMAN YEAR
85% returned for sophomore year
17% got a degree within 4 years
48% got a degree within 5 years
57% got a degree within 6 years

### AFTER GRADUATION
15% pursued further study
311 corporations, 10 government agencies, 2
 nonprofit organizations recruited on campus

### WHAT YOU WILL PAY
Resident tuition and fees $3636
Nonresident tuition and fees $8253
Room and board $3978
40% receive need-based financial aid
 averaging $908
31% receive non-need financial aid averaging
 $1846

---

# MIDDLEBURY COLLEGE

Middlebury, Vermont • Small-town setting • Private • Independent • Coed

Middlebury College is often described as an international university masquerading as a small liberal arts college in Vermont. The feeling of internationalism pervades the campus and its programs. Prominent international visitors are made available to students, including His Holiness the Dalai Lama joining students for lunch in the dining hall. The American Collegiate Consortium, the Geonomics Institute, and the Salzburg Seminar are 3 independent international programs that contribute to the international character of the College. Middlebury's student body includes students from 49 states and 70 countries. Its need-blind admission policy ensures equal opportunity for those who qualify for admission.

## Academics

Middlebury offers a core academic program. It awards bachelor's, master's, and doctoral **degrees**. Challenging opportunities include advanced placement, self-designed majors, and Phi Beta Kappa. Special programs include internships, off-campus study, study abroad, and Army ROTC.

The most popular **majors** include English, political science/government, and history. A complete listing of majors at Middlebury appears in the Majors Index beginning on page 380.

The **faculty** at Middlebury has 234 undergraduate teachers, 95% with terminal degrees. 100% of the faculty serve as student advisers. The student-faculty ratio is 11:1.

## Computers on Campus

Students are not required to have a computer. 150 **computers** available in the computer center, the library, the student center, and dormitories.

The 4 **libraries** have 703,262 books, 236,999 microform titles, and 2,006 subscriptions.

## Campus Life

There are 90 active **organizations** on campus, including a drama/theater group and student-run newspaper and radio station. Middlebury has 6 social houses, commons system. Student **safety services** include late night transport/escort service.

Middlebury is a member of the NCAA (Division III). **Intercollegiate sports** include baseball (m), basketball (m, w), cross-country running (m, w), field hockey (w), football (m), golf (m), ice hockey (m, w), lacrosse (m, w), skiing (cross-country) (m, w), skiing (downhill) (m, w), soccer (m, w), squash (w), swimming and diving (m, w), tennis (m, w), track and field (m, w).

## Applying

Middlebury requires an essay, a high school transcript, ACT or SAT I and 3 SAT II Subject Tests (including SAT II: Writing Test) or 5 SAT II Subject Tests (including SAT II: Writing Test). It recommends 4 years of high school math, 4 years of high school foreign language, recommendations, an interview, and 2 years of high school science. Early and deferred entrance are possible, with a 1/1 deadline and a 1/15 priority date for financial aid. **Contact:** Mr. Geoffrey Smith, Director of Admissions, 131 South Main, Middlebury, VT 05753-6000, 802-388-3711 ext. 2222.

---

**GETTING IN LAST YEAR**
3,871 applied
32% were accepted
40% enrolled (493)
63% from top tenth of their h.s. class

**THE STUDENT BODY**
1,940 undergraduates
From 49 states and territories,
 70 other countries
5% from Vermont

50% women, 50% men
2% African Americans
1% Native Americans
3% Hispanics
6% Asian Americans
9% international students

**AFTER FRESHMAN YEAR**
94% returned for sophomore year

**AFTER GRADUATION**
33% pursued further study
35 corporations, 4 government agencies, 2
 nonprofit organizations recruited on campus

**WHAT YOU WILL PAY**
Comprehensive fee $27,020
Need-based financial aid averages $13,963

# MILLIKIN UNIVERSITY

Decatur, Illinois • Suburban setting • Private • Independent-Religious • Coed

Millikin remains true to its founding mission of combining the liberal arts with professional education. Nearly every major offers opportunities for internships and other hands-on experience. Career planning services are readily available, and the placement rate of graduates is consistently above 95%. International study is available at more than 20 sites. With its combination of liberal arts and career preparation and a size that is small enough to be personal and large enough to offer diversity, Millikin offers the best of both worlds. The University is most often described as friendly and academically challenging.

##  Academics

Millikin offers an interdisciplinary curriculum and core academic program. It awards bachelor's **degrees**. Challenging opportunities include advanced placement, self-designed majors, tutorials, an honors program, and a senior project. Special programs include internships, summer session for credit, off-campus study, and study abroad.

The most popular **majors** include nursing, accounting, and biology/biological sciences. A complete listing of majors at Millikin appears in the Majors Index beginning on page 380.

The **faculty** at Millikin has 117 full-time teachers, 95% with terminal degrees. 100% of the faculty serve as student advisers. The student-faculty ratio is 14:1, and the average class size in required courses is 21.

##  Computers on Campus

Students are not required to have a computer. Student rooms are linked to a campus network. 115 **computers** available in the computer center, computer labs, the learning resource center, specialized labs, and the library provide access to e-mail and on-line services. Staffed computer lab on campus.

The **library** has 149,098 books, 24,014 microform titles, and 1,005 subscriptions. It is connected to 12 national **on-line** catalogs.

##  Campus Life

There are 78 active **organizations** on campus, including a drama/theater group and student-run newspaper and radio station. 32% of eligible men and 20% of eligible women are members of 7 national **fraternities** and 4 national **sororities**. Student **safety services** include late night transport/escort service, 24-hour emergency telephone alarm devices, 24-hour patrols by trained security personnel, and electronically operated dormitory entrances.

Millikin is a member of the NCAA (Division III). **Intercollegiate sports** include baseball (m), basketball (m, w), cross-country running (m, w), football (m), golf (m), soccer (m), softball (w), swimming and diving (m, w), tennis (m, w), track and field (m, w), volleyball (w), wrestling (m).

##  Applying

Millikin requires a high school transcript, 3 recommendations, SAT I or ACT, and a minimum high school GPA of 2.0. It recommends 3 years of high school math and science, 2 years of high school foreign language, and an interview. Deferred and midyear entrance are possible, with rolling admissions and continuous processing to 8/1 for financial aid. **Contact:** Mr. Lin Stoner, Dean of Admission, 1184 West Main Street, Decatur, IL 62522, 217-424-6210 or toll-free 800-373-7733; fax 217-424-3993.

---

### GETTING IN LAST YEAR
1,310 applied
92% were accepted
37% enrolled (443)
27% from top tenth of their h.s. class
3.1 average high school GPA
28% had SAT verbal scores over 600
24% had SAT math scores over 600
34% had ACT scores over 26
4% had SAT verbal scores over 700
1% had SAT math scores over 700
5% had ACT scores over 30
29 valedictorians

### THE STUDENT BODY
1,863 undergraduates
From 35 states and territories,
 6 other countries
87% from Illinois
59% women, 41% men
4% African Americans
1% Native Americans
1% Hispanics
1% Asian Americans
1% international students

### AFTER FRESHMAN YEAR
80% returned for sophomore year
60% got a degree within 4 years
64% got a degree within 5 years

### AFTER GRADUATION
22 corporations, 3 government agencies, 2
 nonprofit organizations recruited on campus

### WHAT YOU WILL PAY
Tuition and fees $12,001
Room and board $4378
82% receive need-based financial aid
 averaging $5890
9% receive non-need financial aid averaging
 $3792

# MILLSAPS COLLEGE

Jackson, Mississippi • Urban setting • Private • Independent-Religious • Coed

 **Academics**

Millsaps College offers an interdisciplinary curriculum and core academic program; a few graduate courses are open to undergraduates. It awards bachelor's and master's **degrees**. Challenging opportunities include advanced placement, tutorials, an honors program, a senior project, and Phi Beta Kappa. Special programs include internships, summer session for credit, off-campus study, study abroad, and Army ROTC.

The most popular **majors** include English, business, and biology/biological sciences. A complete listing of majors at Millsaps College appears in the Majors Index beginning on page 380.

The **faculty** at Millsaps College has 96 full-time graduate and undergraduate teachers, 87% with terminal degrees. 80% of the faculty serve as student advisers. The student-faculty ratio is 14:1, and the average class size in required courses is 16.

 **Computers on Campus**

Students are not required to have a computer. Student rooms are linked to a campus network. 125 **computers** available in the computer center, student labs, dormitories, and student rooms provide access to the main academic computer, off-campus computing facilities, e-mail, and on-line services. Staffed computer lab on campus (open 24 hours a day) provides training in the use of computers and software.

The **library** has 278,000 books, 20,000 microform titles, and 804 subscriptions. It is connected to 3 national **on-line** catalogs.

 **Campus Life**

Active **organizations** on campus include drama/theater group and student-run newspaper. 60% of students participate in student government elections. 62% of eligible men and 61% of eligible women are members of 6 national **fraternities** and 5 national **sororities**. Student **safety services** include late night transport/escort service, 24-hour emergency telephone alarm devices, 24-hour patrols by trained security personnel, student patrols, and electronically operated dormitory entrances.

Millsaps College is a member of the NCAA (Division III). **Intercollegiate sports** include baseball (m), basketball (m, w), cross-country running (m, w), football (m), golf (m), soccer (m, w), tennis (m, w), volleyball (w).

 **Applying**

Millsaps College requires an essay, a high school transcript, and SAT I or ACT. It recommends 3 years of high school math and science, some high school foreign language, recommendations, an interview, 4 years of high school English, and SAT II Subject Tests. Early, deferred, and midyear entrance are possible, with a 4/1 deadline and continuous processing to 3/1 for financial aid. **Contact:** Ms. Florence W. Hines, Director of Admissions, 1701 North State Street, Jackson, MS 39210-0001, 601-974-1050 or toll-free 800-352-1050; fax 601-974-1059.

## GETTING IN LAST YEAR
1,062 applied
84% were accepted
38% enrolled (336)
40% from top tenth of their h.s. class
3.25 average high school GPA
34% had SAT verbal scores over 600
22% had SAT math scores over 600
49% had ACT scores over 26
8% had SAT verbal scores over 700
1% had SAT math scores over 700
16% had ACT scores over 30
20 National Merit Scholars
35 class presidents
32 valedictorians

## THE STUDENT BODY
Total 1,437, of whom 1,313
  are undergraduates
From 30 states and territories,
  8 other countries
65% from Mississippi
52% women, 48% men
6% African Americans
1% Native Americans
1% Hispanics
1% Asian Americans
1% international students

## AFTER FRESHMAN YEAR
87% returned for sophomore year
58% got a degree within 4 years
64% got a degree within 5 years
65% got a degree within 6 years

## AFTER GRADUATION
42% pursued further study (18% arts and
  sciences, 9% law, 7% business)
80% had job offers within 3 months
110 corporations, 9 government agencies, 16
  nonprofit organizations recruited on campus
1 Fulbright scholar

## WHAT YOU WILL PAY
Tuition and fees $11,320
Room and board $4501
58% receive need-based financial aid
  averaging $9062
22% receive non-need financial aid averaging
  $5427

# MILLS COLLEGE

Oakland, California • Urban setting • Private • Independent • Women

Mills can change a woman's life. Recent highly publicized research has demonstrated why women in coed colleges aren't equal; the students who struck to keep Mills a women's college in 1990 already knew. Mills knows how to teach women. Even in their first year, students can discover the excitement of original hands-on research (most students don't experience this until graduate school). All Mills' resources are committed to women. Since half the professors at Mills are women, students have successful role models in every field. And internship opportunities provide wide career experience. When women graduate from Mills, they know they can succeed. And that confidence makes all the difference.

 **Academics**

Mills offers a multicultural and interdisciplinary curriculum and core academic program; more than half of graduate courses are open to undergraduates. It awards bachelor's and master's **degrees**. Challenging opportunities include advanced placement, accelerated degree programs, self-designed majors, tutorials, a senior project, and Phi Beta Kappa. Special programs include cooperative education, internships, and off-campus study.

The most popular **majors** include English, political, legal, and economic analysis, and communication. A complete listing of majors at Mills appears in the Majors Index beginning on page 380.

The **faculty** at Mills has 72 full-time graduate and undergraduate teachers, 99% with terminal degrees. The student-faculty ratio is 12:1, and the average class size in required courses is 15.

 **Computers on Campus**

Students are not required to have a computer. 122 **computers** available in the computer center, student lounge,

academic buildings, the library, the student center, and dormitories provide access to the main academic computer, off-campus computing facilities, e-mail, and on-line services. Staffed computer lab on campus provides training in the use of computers and software.

The 2 **libraries** have 210,802 books, 8,017 microform titles, and 738 subscriptions. They are connected to 4 national **on-line** catalogs.

 **Campus Life**

There are 40 active **organizations** on campus, including a drama/theater group and student-run newspaper. Student **safety services** include late night transport/escort service, 24-hour emergency telephone alarm devices, and 24-hour patrols by trained security personnel.

Mills is a member of the NCAA (Division III). **Intercollegiate sports** include basketball, crew, cross-country running, tennis, volleyball.

 **Applying**

Mills requires a high school transcript, 3 recommendations, essay or graded paper, SAT I, and in some cases ACT. It recommends 3 years of high school math and science, 2 years of high school foreign language, an interview, and 3 SAT II Subject Tests. Early, deferred, and midyear entrance are possible, with rolling admissions and a 2/15 priority date for financial aid. **Contact:** Ms. Genevieve Ann Flaherty, Dean, Admission and Financial Aid, 5000 MacArthur Boulevard, Oakland, CA 94613-1000, 510-430-2135 or toll-free 800-87-MILLS.

## GETTING IN LAST YEAR

602 applied
82% were accepted
29% enrolled (142)
26% from top tenth of their h.s. class
3.44 average high school GPA
25% had SAT verbal scores over 600
28% had SAT math scores over 600
58% had ACT scores over 26
3% had SAT verbal scores over 700
4% had SAT math scores over 700
0% had ACT scores over 30

## THE STUDENT BODY

Total 1,169, of whom 860
  are undergraduates
From 35 states and territories,
  12 other countries
76% from California
100% women
7% African Americans
1% Native Americans
7% Hispanics
9% Asian Americans
2% international students

## AFTER FRESHMAN YEAR

78% returned for sophomore year
66% got a degree within 4 years
69% got a degree within 5 years
70% got a degree within 6 years

## WHAT YOU WILL PAY

Tuition and fees $14,542
Room and board $6000
78% receive need-based financial aid
  averaging $8690
8% receive non-need financial aid averaging
  $4583

# MILWAUKEE SCHOOL OF ENGINEERING

Milwaukee, Wisconsin • Urban setting • Private • Independent • Coed

Oscar Werwath, a practicing engineer and a graduate of European technical schools, organized MSOE in 1903. He was the first to plan an American educational institution based on an applications-oriented curriculum. Leaders of business and industry cooperated in the college's development, and a close relationship was established that continues today. MSOE offers 13 bachelor's degrees, 2 associate degrees, 3 master's degrees, and 10 certificate programs. MSOE is located near the center of downtown Milwaukee, just a few blocks from the theater district and Lake Michigan and with easy access to Milwaukee's business and industrial centers and major cultural and artistic facilities.

##  Academics

MSOE offers a core academic program. It awards associate, bachelor's, and master's **degrees**. Challenging opportunities include advanced placement, an honors program, and a senior project. Special programs include internships, summer session for credit, study abroad, and Army and Air Force ROTC.

The most popular **majors** include electrical engineering, mechanical engineering, and architectural engineering. A complete listing of majors at MSOE appears in the Majors Index beginning on page 380.

The **faculty** at MSOE has 103 full-time graduate and undergraduate teachers, 35% with terminal degrees. The student-faculty ratio is 15:1, and the average class size in required courses is 25.

##  Computers on Campus

Students are not required to have a computer. 175 **computers** available in the computer center, computer labs, the learning resource center, labs, classrooms, the library, the student center, and dormitories provide access to the main academic computer, off-campus computing facilities, e-mail, and on-line services. Staffed computer lab on campus provides training in the use of computers and software.

The **library** has 60,000 books, 30 microform titles, and 529 subscriptions. It is connected to 3 national **on-line** catalogs.

##  Campus Life

There are 57 active **organizations** on campus, including a drama/theater group and student-run newspaper and radio station. 10% of eligible men and 15% of eligible women are members of 1 national **fraternity**, 1 national **sorority**, 4 local fraternities, and 1 local sorority. Student **safety services** include late night transport/escort service and 24-hour patrols by trained security personnel.

MSOE is a member of the NCAA (Division III). **Intercollegiate sports** include baseball (m), basketball (m, w), cross-country running (m, w), golf (m), ice hockey (m), soccer (m), softball (w), tennis (m, w), volleyball (w), wrestling (m).

##  Applying

MSOE requires an essay, a high school transcript, SAT I or ACT, and in some cases 3 years of high school science. It recommends 3 years of high school math, 1 recommendation, and an interview. Deferred and midyear entrance are possible, with rolling admissions and continuous processing to 3/15 for financial aid. **Contact:** Mr. T. Owen Smith, Dean of Admissions, Student Life and Campus Center, Milwaukee, WI 53202-3109, 414-277-7202 or toll-free 800-332-6763; fax 414-277-7475.

---

**GETTING IN LAST YEAR**
1,054 applied
98% were accepted
47% enrolled (483)
36% from top tenth of their h.s. class
3.2 average high school GPA
39% had ACT scores over 26
8% had ACT scores over 30

**THE STUDENT BODY**
Total 3,031, of whom 2,772
   are undergraduates

From 25 states and territories,
   27 other countries
75% from Wisconsin
15% women, 85% men
4% African Americans
1% Native Americans
2% Hispanics
2% Asian Americans
3% international students

**AFTER FRESHMAN YEAR**
74% returned for sophomore year

**AFTER GRADUATION**
8% pursued further study (5% engineering)
81 corporations, 4 government agencies, 1
   nonprofit organization recruited on campus

**WHAT YOU WILL PAY**
Tuition and fees $11,505
Room and board $3255
Need-based financial aid averages $1700
Non-need financial aid averages $3500

# MONMOUTH COLLEGE

Monmouth, Illinois • Small-town setting • Private • Independent-Religious • Coed

A school rich in traditions, Monmouth College was founded in 1853 by determined Presbyterian pioneers. Situated on 35 rolling acres in the heart of a quiet community, its campus features an appealing blend of stately old buildings and state-of-the-art facilities. Monmouth's commitment to providing a broad-based liberal arts education is reflected in a faculty totally dedicated to undergraduate teaching. A freshman seminar gives all students a firm foothold for pursuing their education, and a senior capstone course helps them solidify what they have learned. With an enrollment of just under 850, the College offers ample opportunities for individual leadership in curricular and extracurricular activities.

 **Academics**

Monmouth offers a core academic program. It awards bachelor's **degrees**. Challenging opportunities include advanced placement, self-designed majors, tutorials, an honors program, and a senior project. Special programs include internships, summer session for credit, off-campus study, and Army ROTC.

The most popular **majors** include business, education, and biology/biological sciences. A complete listing of majors at Monmouth appears in the Majors Index beginning on page 380.

The **faculty** at Monmouth has 50 full-time teachers, 90% with terminal degrees. 100% of the faculty serve as student advisers. The student-faculty ratio is 13:1, and the average class size in required courses is 18.

 **Computers on Campus**

Students are not required to have a computer. 103 **computers** available in the computer center, computer labs, classrooms, and the library provide access to the main academic computer, off-campus computing facilities, e-mail, and on-line services. Staffed computer lab on campus provides training in the use of computers and software.

The **library** has 240,000 books, 67,000 microform titles, and 800 subscriptions.

 **Campus Life**

Active **organizations** on campus include drama/theater group and student-run newspaper and radio station. 60% of students participate in student government elections. 40% of eligible men and 45% of eligible women are members of 3 national **fraternities** and 3 national **sororities**. Student **safety services** include night security and late night transport/escort service.

Monmouth is a member of the NCAA (Division III). **Intercollegiate sports** include baseball (m), basketball (m, w), cross-country running (m, w), football (m), soccer (m, w), softball (w), track and field (m, w), volleyball (w), wrestling (m).

 **Applying**

Monmouth requires a high school transcript, 3 years of high school math, SAT I or ACT, and in some cases an essay. It recommends 3 years of high school science, 2 years of high school foreign language, 2 recommendations, and an interview. Early, deferred, and midyear entrance are possible, with a 5/1 deadline and continuous processing to 4/30 for financial aid. **Contact:** Mr. Richard Valentine, Dean of Admissions, 700 East Broadway, Monmouth, IL 61462-1998, 309-457-2131 or toll-free 800-747-2687; fax 309-457-2141.

---

**GETTING IN LAST YEAR**
1,100 applied
77% were accepted
36% enrolled (309)
20% from top tenth of their h.s. class
3.1 average high school GPA
20% had ACT scores over 26
2% had ACT scores over 30
15 class presidents
8 valedictorians

**THE STUDENT BODY**
837 undergraduates
From 18 states and territories,
    13 other countries

89% from Illinois
54% women, 46% men
3% African Americans
0% Native Americans
2% Hispanics
1% Asian Americans
4% international students

**AFTER FRESHMAN YEAR**
74% returned for sophomore year
54% got a degree within 4 years
59% got a degree within 5 years
60% got a degree within 6 years

**AFTER GRADUATION**
35% pursued further study (17% business, 6% arts and sciences, 4% law)
90% had job offers within 3 months
26 corporations, 7 government agencies, 10 nonprofit organizations recruited on campus

**WHAT YOU WILL PAY**
Tuition and fees $13,660
Room and board $4200
66% receive need-based financial aid averaging $5624
37% receive non-need financial aid averaging $4833

# MOREHOUSE COLLEGE

Atlanta, Georgia • Urban setting • Private • Independent • Men

 ## Academics

Morehouse College offers a core academic program. It awards bachelor's **degrees**. Challenging opportunities include advanced placement, tutorials, an honors program, a senior project, and Phi Beta Kappa. Special programs include cooperative education, internships, summer session for credit, off-campus study, study abroad, and Army, Naval, and Air Force ROTC.

The most popular **majors** include biology/biological sciences, engineering (general), and political science/government. A complete listing of majors at Morehouse College appears in the Majors Index beginning on page 380.

The **faculty** at Morehouse College has 150 full-time teachers, 72% with terminal degrees. 100% of the faculty serve as student advisers. The student-faculty ratio is 17:1.

 ## Computers on Campus

Students are not required to have a computer. 325 **computers** available in the computer center, science building, writing skills lab, the library, and dormitories.

The **library** has 560,000 books, 110,000 microform titles, and 1,000 subscriptions.

 ## Campus Life

Active **organizations** on campus include drama/theater group and student-run newspaper. 3% of eligible undergraduates are members of 5 national **fraternities**. Student **safety services** include late night transport/escort service.

Morehouse College is a member of the NCAA (Division II). **Intercollegiate sports** (some offering scholarships) include basketball, cross-country running, football, swimming and diving, tennis, track and field.

 ## Applying

Morehouse College requires an essay, a high school transcript, 3 years of high school math, SAT I or ACT, a minimum high school GPA of 2.0, and in some cases recommendations and an interview. It recommends 3 years of high school science, some high school foreign language, and a minimum high school GPA of 3.0. Early, deferred, and midyear entrance are possible, with a 2/15 deadline and 4/1 for financial aid. **Contact:** Mr. Milford Green, Director of Admissions, 830 Westview Drive, Atlanta, GA 30314, 404-215-2632 or toll-free 800-992-0642; fax 404-659-6536.

### GETTING IN LAST YEAR

3,263 applied
57% were accepted
38% enrolled (704)
28% from top tenth of their h.s. class
3.0 average high school GPA
19% had SAT verbal scores over 600
25% had SAT math scores over 600
32% had ACT scores over 26
2% had SAT verbal scores over 700
4% had SAT math scores over 700
5% had ACT scores over 30
27 valedictorians

### THE STUDENT BODY

2,992 undergraduates
From 41 states and territories, 18 other countries
18% from Georgia
100% men
98% African Americans
2% international students

### AFTER FRESHMAN YEAR

85% returned for sophomore year

### AFTER GRADUATION

350 corporations, 30 government agencies, 5 nonprofit organizations recruited on campus

### WHAT YOU WILL PAY

Tuition and fees $8470
Room and board $5490
Need-based financial aid averages $4500
Non-need financial aid averages $1800

# MOUNT HOLYOKE COLLEGE

South Hadley, Massachusetts • Small-town setting • Private • Independent • Women

Located in a small town in the Connecticut River Valley of Massachusetts, Mount Holyoke College is a liberal arts college for women, the oldest of its kind in the United States. Believing that the ability to make sound decisions is one of the chief benefits of a liberal education, the College gives its students primary responsibility for planning and achieving their educational goals. To this end, it offers a high degree of independence and a wide range of opportunities, including all that come with membership in the Five College Consortium with Amherst, Hampshire, and Smith colleges and the University of Massachusetts.

## Academics

Mount Holyoke offers a core academic program. It awards bachelor's and master's **degrees**. Challenging opportunities include advanced placement, accelerated degree programs, self-designed majors, tutorials, an honors program, Phi Beta Kappa, and Sigma Xi. Special programs include internships, off-campus study, study abroad, and Army and Air Force ROTC.

The most popular **majors** include English, political science/government, and biology/biological sciences. A complete listing of majors at Mount Holyoke appears in the Majors Index beginning on page 380.

The **faculty** at Mount Holyoke has 181 full-time graduate and undergraduate teachers, 96% with terminal degrees. The student-faculty ratio is 9:1, and the average class size in required courses is 10.

## Computers on Campus

Students are not required to have a computer. 245 **computers** available in the computer center, classroom buildings, the library, and dormitories.

The 2 **libraries** have 623,336 books, 15,120 microform titles, and 1,811 subscriptions.

## Campus Life

There are 100 active **organizations** on campus, including a drama/theater group and student-run newspaper and radio station. Student **safety services** include late night transport/escort service, 24-hour emergency telephone alarm devices, 24-hour patrols by trained security personnel, and student patrols.

Mount Holyoke is a member of the NCAA (Division III). **Intercollegiate sports** include basketball, crew, cross-country running, equestrian sports, field hockey, golf, lacrosse, soccer, squash, swimming and diving, tennis, track and field, volleyball.

## Applying

Mount Holyoke requires an essay, a high school transcript, 3 years of high school math, 2 recommendations, an interview, SAT I and 3 SAT II Subject Tests (including SAT II: Writing Test) or ACT. It recommends 3 years of high school science and 4 years of high school foreign language. Early and deferred entrance are possible, with a 1/15 deadline and 2/1 for financial aid. **Contact:** Ms. Anita Smith, Director of Admissions, College Street, South Hadley, MA 01075-1414, 413-538-2023; fax 413-538-2409.

### GETTING IN LAST YEAR
1,991 applied
65% were accepted
35% enrolled (454)
53% from top tenth of their h.s. class
31% had SAT verbal scores over 600
44% had SAT math scores over 600
5% had SAT verbal scores over 700
8% had SAT math scores over 700

### THE STUDENT BODY
Total 1,925, of whom 1,911 are undergraduates
From 49 states and territories, 64 other countries
20% from Massachusetts
100% women
4% African Americans
1% Native Americans
4% Hispanics
8% Asian Americans
12% international students

### AFTER FRESHMAN YEAR
96% returned for sophomore year

### AFTER GRADUATION
25% pursued further study (10% arts and sciences, 6% law, 5% medicine)
2 Fulbright scholars

### WHAT YOU WILL PAY
Tuition and fees $19,435
Room and board $5700
Need-based financial aid averages $13,800

# Mount Union College

Alliance, Ohio • Suburban setting • Private • Independent-Religious • Coed

Mount Union College has established a reputation for producing successful graduates in a wide array of occupations. Founded in 1846 by Orville Nelson Hartshorn, the College was established as "a place committed to a lifetime of learning—where men and women would be educated with equal opportunity, where science would parallel the humanities, and where there would be no distinction due to race, color, or sex." These principles continue to guide the institution. Mount Union strives to provide the best education possible for each of its students so that its graduates have developed communication skills, critical thinking, a sensitivity to social responsibility, and a concern for human needs.

## Academics

Mount Union offers a core academic program. It awards bachelor's **degrees**. Challenging opportunities include advanced placement, accelerated degree programs, self-designed majors, tutorials, an honors program, and a senior project. Special programs include cooperative education, internships, summer session for credit, off-campus study, study abroad, and Army and Air Force ROTC.

The most popular **majors** include business, education, and accounting. A complete listing of majors at Mount Union appears in the Majors Index beginning on page 380.

The **faculty** at Mount Union has 80 full-time teachers, 80% with terminal degrees. 100% of the faculty serve as student advisers. The student-faculty ratio is 19:1, and the average class size in required courses is 25.

## Computers on Campus

Students are not required to have a computer. 130 **computers** available in personal computer lab. Staffed computer lab on campus.

The 3 **libraries** have 215,397 books, 29,523 microform titles, and 868 subscriptions. They are connected to 3 national **on-line** catalogs.

## Campus Life

There are 72 active **organizations** on campus, including a drama/theater group and student-run newspaper and radio station. 35% of eligible men and 35% of eligible women are members of 5 national **fraternities**, 4 national **sororities**, and 1 local sorority. Student **safety services** include 24-hour locked dormitory entrances with outside phone and 24-hour patrols by trained security personnel.

Mount Union is a member of the NCAA (Division III). **Intercollegiate sports** include baseball (m), basketball (m, w), cross-country running (m, w), football (m), golf (m), soccer (m, w), softball (w), swimming and diving (m, w), tennis (m, w), track and field (m, w), volleyball (w), wrestling (m).

## Applying

Mount Union requires an essay, a high school transcript, 1 recommendation, SAT I or ACT, and a minimum high school GPA of 2.0. It recommends 3 years of high school math and science, 2 years of high school foreign language, and a campus interview. Early, deferred, and midyear entrance are possible, with rolling admissions and continuous processing to 5/1 for financial aid. **Contact:** Mr. Greg King, Director of Admissions and Enrollment Management, 1972 Clark Avenue, Alliance, OH 44601-3929, 216-823-2590 or toll-free 800-334-6682 (in-state), 800-992-6682 (out-of-state); fax 216-821-0425.

**GETTING IN LAST YEAR**
1,529 applied
82% were accepted
43% enrolled (542)
25% from top tenth of their h.s. class
25% had ACT scores over 26
5% had ACT scores over 30

**THE STUDENT BODY**
1,481 undergraduates
From 22 states and territories,
   22 other countries

86% from Ohio
49% women, 51% men
4% African Americans
1% Native Americans
1% Hispanics
1% Asian Americans
5% international students

**AFTER FRESHMAN YEAR**
91% returned for sophomore year

**AFTER GRADUATION**
27% pursued further study (13% arts and
   sciences, 5% business, 4% law)
35 corporations recruited on campus

**WHAT YOU WILL PAY**
Tuition and fees $12,950
Room and board $3530
Need-based financial aid averages $5300

# MUHLENBERG COLLEGE

Allentown, Pennsylvania • Suburban setting • Private • Independent-Religious • Coed

Muhlenberg offers merit scholarships ranging in value from $1000 to $7000, renewable annually based on a 3.0 GPA. Last year, 50 students enrolled with a merit award. Merit recipients typically scored 1200 or better on the combined SAT and ranked in the top 10% of their high school classes. Two Honors Programs—Muhlenberg Scholar and Dana Associates—also carry an annual stipend.

 **Academics**

Muhlenberg offers an interdisciplinary curriculum and core academic program. It awards bachelor's **degrees**. Challenging opportunities include advanced placement, accelerated degree programs, self-designed majors, tutorials, an honors program, a senior project, and Phi Beta Kappa. Special programs include internships, summer session for credit, off-campus study, study abroad, and Army ROTC.

The most popular **majors** include biology/biological sciences, psychology, and English. A complete listing of majors at Muhlenberg appears in the Majors Index beginning on page 380.

The **faculty** at Muhlenberg has 115 full-time teachers, 86% with terminal degrees. 90% of the faculty serve as student advisers. The student-faculty ratio is 13:1, and the average class size in required courses is 24.

 **Computers on Campus**

Students are not required to have a computer. 100 **computers** available in the computer center, computer labs, and the library provide access to the main academic computer and e-mail. Staffed computer lab on campus provides training in the use of computers and software.

The **library** has 200,000 books, 437 microform titles, and 1,302 subscriptions. It is connected to 2 national **on-line** catalogs.

 **Campus Life**

There are 80 active **organizations** on campus, including a drama/theater group and student-run newspaper and radio station. 50% of eligible men and 40% of eligible women are members of 5 national **fraternities** and 4 national **sororities**. Student **safety services** include late night transport/escort service, 24-hour emergency telephone alarm devices, 24-hour patrols by trained security personnel, and electronically operated dormitory entrances.

Muhlenberg is a member of the NCAA (Division III). **Intercollegiate sports** include baseball (m), basketball (m, w), cross-country running (m, w), field hockey (w), football (m), golf (m), lacrosse (w), soccer (m, w), softball (w), tennis (m, w), track and field (m, w), volleyball (w), wrestling (m).

 **Applying**

Muhlenberg requires an essay, a high school transcript, 3 years of high school math, 2 years of high school foreign language, 2 recommendations, and SAT I or ACT. It recommends 3 years of high school science and a campus interview. Early, deferred, and midyear entrance are possible, with a 2/15 deadline and a 2/15 priority date for financial aid. **Contact:** Mr. Christopher Hooker-Haring, Dean of Admissions, 2400 Chew Street, Allentown, PA 18104-5586, 610-821-3200; fax 610-821-3234.

---

**GETTING IN LAST YEAR**
2,574 applied
71% were accepted
25% enrolled (462)
25% from top tenth of their h.s. class
3.3 average high school GPA
10% had SAT verbal scores over 600
37% had SAT math scores over 600
24% had ACT scores over 26
1% had SAT verbal scores over 700
6% had SAT math scores over 700
1% had ACT scores over 30
21 class presidents
6 valedictorians

**THE STUDENT BODY**
1,704 undergraduates
From 35 states and territories,
   12 other countries
31% from Pennsylvania
53% women, 47% men
2% African Americans
0% Native Americans
2% Hispanics
4% Asian Americans
2% international students

**AFTER FRESHMAN YEAR**
92% returned for sophomore year

**AFTER GRADUATION**
31% pursued further study (15% arts and
   sciences, 6% law, 5% medicine)
50 corporations, 1 government agency, 1
   nonprofit organization recruited on campus

**WHAT YOU WILL PAY**
Tuition and fees $17,550
Room and board $4720
Need-based financial aid averages $8200
Non-need financial aid averages $4500

# NEBRASKA WESLEYAN UNIVERSITY

Lincoln, Nebraska • Suburban setting • Private • Independent-Religious • Coed

A Nebraska Wesleyan education is driven by the differences among and within all students. Strong relationships with the faculty enable students to develop and refine interests, talents, and critical thinking and communication skills necessary to be competitive. Superior research facilities provide experience for students as early as their first year. The benefits of integrated advising, orientation, and career services are evident in Nebraska Wesleyan's high retention and graduate/professional school placement rates. Development of leadership skills is well within reach of all students through more than 80 honoraries, clubs, and organizations, and through service learning and local, national, and international volunteer opportunities.

 ## Academics

NWU offers a core academic program. It awards bachelor's **degrees**. Challenging opportunities include advanced placement and a senior project. Special programs include internships, summer session for credit, off-campus study, study abroad, and Army and Air Force ROTC.

The most popular **majors** include business, biology/biological sciences, and psychology. A complete listing of majors at NWU appears in the Majors Index beginning on page 380.

The **faculty** at NWU has 89 full-time teachers, 83% with terminal degrees. 84% of the faculty serve as student advisers. The student-faculty ratio is 13:1.

 ## Computers on Campus

Students are not required to have a computer. 170 **computers** available in the computer center, computer labs, the learning resource center, classrooms, the library, and dormitories.

The **library** has 174,553 books, 19 microform titles, and 768 subscriptions. It is connected to 2 national **on-line** catalogs.

 ## Campus Life

There are 80 active **organizations** on campus, including a drama/theater group and student-run newspaper. 38% of eligible men and 32% of eligible women are members of 5 national **fraternities**, 2 national **sororities**, and 1 local sorority. Student **safety services** include late night transport/escort service, 24-hour patrols by trained security personnel, and electronically operated dormitory entrances.

NWU is a member of the NCAA (Division III) and NAIA. **Intercollegiate sports** include baseball (m), basketball (m, w), cross-country running (m, w), football (m), golf (m, w), soccer (m, w), softball (w), tennis (m, w), track and field (m, w), volleyball (w).

 ## Applying

NWU requires a high school transcript, ACT, a minimum high school GPA of 2.0, and in some cases an essay and resumé of activities. It recommends some high school foreign language, recommendations, an interview, and SAT I. Early, deferred, and midyear entrance are possible, with a 3/15 deadline and continuous processing to 7/15 for financial aid. **Contact:** Mr. Ken Sieg, Director of Admissions, 5000 Saint Paul Avenue, Lincoln, NE 68504-2796, 402-465-2218 or toll-free 800-541-3818 (in-state); fax 402-465-2179.

## GETTING IN LAST YEAR
768 applied
93% were accepted
47% enrolled (337)
27% from top tenth of their h.s. class
33% had ACT scores over 26
6% had ACT scores over 30
2 National Merit Scholars
25 valedictorians

## THE STUDENT BODY
1,610 undergraduates
From 28 states and territories,
    10 other countries

93% from Nebraska
58% women, 42% men
2% African Americans
1% Native Americans
2% Hispanics
1% Asian Americans
1% international students

## AFTER FRESHMAN YEAR
80% returned for sophomore year
49% got a degree within 4 years
63% got a degree within 5 years
66% got a degree within 6 years

## AFTER GRADUATION
33 corporations, 1 government agency
    recruited on campus
1 Fulbright scholar

## WHAT YOU WILL PAY
Tuition and fees $9849
Room and board $3320
78% receive need-based financial aid
    averaging $2465
79% receive non-need financial aid averaging
    $1287

# NEW COLLEGE OF THE UNIVERSITY OF SOUTH FLORIDA

Sarasota, Florida • Suburban setting • Public • State-supported • Coed

 Descriptions such as highly rigorous, intellectually sophisticated, and innovative apply to New College and to the manner in which individuals are selected to become a part of the student body. Admission is rigorous; usually fewer than 35% of those who apply are admitted. A significant level of intellectual sophistication is required to successfully negotiate the admissions process; there are 5 writing samples required, including a graded paper. Innovativeness is also a central tenet in the selection process. Students are considered and notified on a rolling basis (an approach that is rare for highly selective colleges), and applicants are never put on a waiting list.

## Academics

New College of USF offers an interdisciplinary curriculum and no core academic program. It awards bachelor's **degrees**. Challenging opportunities include accelerated degree programs, self-designed majors, tutorials, an honors program, and a senior project. Special programs include internships, off-campus study, study abroad, and Army and Air Force ROTC.

The most popular **majors** include psychology, biology/biological sciences, and literature. A complete listing of majors at New College of USF appears in the Majors Index beginning on page 380.

The **faculty** at New College of USF has 55 full-time teachers, 95% with terminal degrees. 100% of the faculty serve as student advisers. The student-faculty ratio is 10:1, and the average class size in required courses is 18.

##  Computers on Campus

Students are not required to have a computer. 40 **computers** available in the computer center, natural sciences building, the library, and the student center provide access to e-mail. Staffed computer lab on campus provides training in the use of computers and software.

The **library** has 230,000 books, 400,000 microform titles, and 1,100 subscriptions. It is connected to 1 national **on-line** catalog.

##  Campus Life

Active **organizations** on campus include drama/theater group and student-run newspaper. Student **safety services** include late night transport/escort service, 24-hour emergency telephone alarm devices, and 24-hour patrols by trained security personnel.

This institution has no intercollegiate sports.

##  Applying

New College of USF requires an essay, a high school transcript, 3 years of high school math and science, 2 years of high school foreign language, 2 recommendations, graded writing sample, SAT I or ACT, and in some cases a campus interview. It recommends an interview and a minimum high school GPA of 3.0. Early and deferred entrance are possible, with rolling admissions and continuous processing to 2/1 for financial aid. **Contact:** Mr. David L. Anderson, Director of Admissions, 5700 North Tamiami Trail, Sarasota, FL 34243-2197, 813-359-4269.

### GETTING IN LAST YEAR
687 applied
40% were accepted
48% enrolled (131)
65% from top tenth of their h.s. class
3.81 average high school GPA
66% had SAT verbal scores over 600
71% had SAT math scores over 600
86% had ACT scores over 26
20% had SAT verbal scores over 700
22% had SAT math scores over 700
40% had ACT scores over 30
17 National Merit Scholars

### THE STUDENT BODY
555 undergraduates
From 40 states and territories,
   10 other countries
55% from Florida
53% women, 47% men
2% African Americans
0% Native Americans
5% Hispanics
6% Asian Americans
4% international students

### AFTER FRESHMAN YEAR
85% returned for sophomore year
50% got a degree within 4 years
60% got a degree within 5 years

### AFTER GRADUATION
31% pursued further study (28% arts and
   sciences, 3% law, 2% medicine)
10 corporations, 2 government agencies
   recruited on campus
1 Fulbright scholar

### WHAT YOU WILL PAY
Resident tuition and fees $2030
Nonresident tuition and fees $7913
Room and board $3717
65% receive need-based financial aid
   averaging $4029
15% receive non-need financial aid averaging
   $5400

# NEW JERSEY INSTITUTE OF TECHNOLOGY

Newark, New Jersey • Urban setting • Public • State-related • Coed

In 1993, the Albert Dorman Honors College was approved. The college is an expansion of the Honors Program, which is one of the leaders in technologically oriented honors education. The college strives to set a university-wide standard of excellence. Admission is highly selective. Most successful applicants rank in the top 10% of their high school, with SAT scores above 1250. Graduates are currently employed by leading corporations or are pursuing further education in such areas as law, medicine, science, engineering, and anthropology. Honors students receive a minimum $1300 scholarship.

 ## Academics

NJIT offers a technology and applied science curriculum and core academic program; a few graduate courses are open to undergraduates. It awards bachelor's, master's, and doctoral **degrees**. Challenging opportunities include advanced placement, self-designed majors, Freshmen Honors College, an honors program, a senior project, and Sigma Xi. Special programs include cooperative education, internships, summer session for credit, off-campus study, study abroad, and Air Force ROTC.

The most popular **majors** include electrical engineering, engineering technology, and mechanical engineering. A complete listing of majors at NJIT appears in the Majors Index beginning on page 380.

The **faculty** at NJIT has 329 full-time graduate and undergraduate teachers, 98% with terminal degrees. 60% of the faculty serve as student advisers. The student-faculty ratio is 13:1, and the average class size in required courses is 28.

 ## Computers on Campus

Students are not required to have a computer. Student rooms are linked to a campus network. 1,000 **computers**

available in the computer center, computer labs, the research center, the learning resource center, classrooms, the library, the student center, dormitories, and student rooms provide access to the main academic computer, off-campus computing facilities, e-mail, and on-line services. Staffed computer lab on campus provides training in the use of computers and software.

The 2 **libraries** have 204,471 books, 4,735 microform titles, and 1,271 subscriptions. They are connected to 2 national **on-line** catalogs.

 ## Campus Life

There are 20 active **organizations** on campus, including a drama/theater group and student-run newspaper and radio station. 18% of eligible men and 19% of eligible women are members of 11 national **fraternities**, 3 national **sororities**, 7 local fraternities, and 4 local sororities. Student **safety services** include late night transport/escort service, 24-hour emergency telephone alarm devices, 24-hour patrols by trained security personnel, and electronically operated dormitory entrances.

NJIT is a member of the NCAA (Division III). **Intercollegiate sports** include baseball (m), basketball (m, w), cross-country running (m), fencing (m, w), golf (m), soccer (m), softball (w), tennis (m, w), volleyball (m, w).

 ## Applying

NJIT requires a high school transcript, 4 years of high school math, SAT I, and 1 SAT II Subject Test. It recommends an essay and 3 years of high school science. Early and midyear entrance are possible, with a 4/1 deadline and continuous processing to 3/15 for financial aid. **Contact:** Ms. Kathy Kelly, Director of Admissions, Newark, NJ 07102-1982, 201-596-3300 or toll-free 800-222-NJIT (in-state); fax 201-802-1854.

---

### GETTING IN LAST YEAR

2,043 applied
68% were accepted
40% enrolled (550)
24% from top tenth of their h.s. class
9% had SAT verbal scores over 600
47% had SAT math scores over 600
1% had SAT verbal scores over 700
11% had SAT math scores over 700
3 valedictorians

### THE STUDENT BODY

Total 7,504, of whom 4,973
  are undergraduates

From 21 states and territories,
  42 other countries
93% from New Jersey
17% women, 83% men
13% African Americans
1% Native Americans
13% Hispanics
18% Asian Americans
4% international students

### AFTER FRESHMAN YEAR

80% returned for sophomore year

### AFTER GRADUATION

16% pursued further study (6% engineering,
  3% business, 2% arts and sciences)
65 corporations, 5 government agencies
  recruited on campus

### WHAT YOU WILL PAY

Resident tuition and fees $4980
Nonresident tuition and fees $9324
Room and board $5376
51% receive need-based financial aid
  averaging $2379
15% receive non-need financial aid averaging
  $1237

---

# NEW MEXICO INSTITUTE OF MINING AND TECHNOLOGY

Socorro, New Mexico • Small-town setting • Public • State-supported • Coed

New Mexico Tech is able to offer an exceptional education in science and engineering due in large part to its faculty. One recent graduate said, "Many of Tech's faculty are amazingly friendly, congenial, and humorous—characteristics cultivated by the informal Tech atmosphere. Here, students *know* professors. Most professors give their home phone numbers to students; they encourage questions. Tech's faculty and staff overall do an outstanding job of providing a good education." Faculty members bring research into their classrooms and employ students in their research labs; more than 50% of undergraduates work in research positions.

 **Academics**

New Mexico Tech offers a science and engineering curriculum and core academic program; fewer than half of graduate courses are open to undergraduates. It awards associate, bachelor's, master's, and doctoral **degrees**. Challenging opportunities include advanced placement, self-designed majors, tutorials, a senior project, and Sigma Xi. Special programs include cooperative education, internships, summer session for credit, off-campus study, and study abroad.

The most popular **majors** include environmental engineering, electrical engineering, and physics. A complete listing of majors at New Mexico Tech appears in the Majors Index beginning on page 380.

The **faculty** at New Mexico Tech has 101 full-time graduate and undergraduate teachers, 96% with terminal degrees. 90% of the faculty serve as student advisers. The student-faculty ratio is 13:1, and the average class size in required courses is 30.

 **Computers on Campus**

Students are not required to have a computer. Student rooms are linked to a campus network. 125 **computers** available in the computer center, computer labs, technical communications lab, most academic departments, and classrooms provide access to off-campus computing facilities, e-mail, and on-line services. Staffed computer lab on campus provides training in the use of computers and software.

The 2 **libraries** have 242,500 books, 177,500 microform titles, and 865 subscriptions. They are connected to 2 national **on-line** catalogs.

 **Campus Life**

There are 60 active **organizations** on campus, including a drama/theater group and student-run newspaper and radio station. 16% of students participate in student government elections. Student **safety services** include late night transport/escort service, 24-hour emergency telephone alarm devices, and 24-hour patrols by trained security personnel.

This institution has no intercollegiate sports.

 **Applying**

New Mexico Tech requires a high school transcript, 3 years of high school math and science, some high school foreign language, SAT I or ACT, a minimum high school GPA of 2.0, and in some cases 2 recommendations. It recommends an interview and SAT II Subject Tests. Early, deferred, and midyear entrance are possible, with an 8/1 deadline and continuous processing to 3/1 for financial aid. **Contact:** Ms. Louise E. Chamberlin, Director of Admissions, Brown Hall, Socorro, NM 87801, 505-835-5424 or toll-free 800-428-TECH.

## GETTING IN LAST YEAR

781 applied
76% were accepted
34% enrolled (202)
42% from top tenth of their h.s. class
3.3 average high school GPA
14% had SAT verbal scores over 600
29% had SAT math scores over 600
57% had ACT scores over 26
0% had SAT verbal scores over 700
0% had SAT math scores over 700
11% had ACT scores over 30
5 National Merit Scholars
5 valedictorians

## THE STUDENT BODY

Total 1,657, of whom 1,399 are undergraduates
From 50 states and territories, 34 other countries
80% from New Mexico
40% women, 60% men
1% African Americans
3% Native Americans
19% Hispanics
3% Asian Americans
3% international students

### AFTER FRESHMAN YEAR

65% returned for sophomore year
36% got a degree within 5 years
43% got a degree within 6 years

## AFTER GRADUATION

36% pursued further study (27% arts and sciences, 8% engineering, 1% medicine)
11 corporations, 2 government agencies, 2 nonprofit organizations recruited on campus

## WHAT YOU WILL PAY

Resident tuition and fees $1858
Nonresident tuition and fees $5932
Room and board $3426
31% receive need-based financial aid averaging $1678
37% receive non-need financial aid averaging $1565

# NEW YORK UNIVERSITY

New York, New York • Urban setting • Private • Independent • Coed

---

▶ NYU is one of the most distinguished private universities in the United States—a world-renowned research university devoted to scholarship, teaching, and learning. The preeminence of its faculty, the extraordinary range and quality of its resources, and its interaction with New York City offer undergraduates the opportunity to learn and grow in an intellectual environment. University facilities include one of the largest open-stack research libraries in the nation; institutes famous for research in applied mathematics, physics, and fine arts; foreign language and cultural centers offering lectures, films, and concerts; art galleries and exhibition spaces; and advanced computer and recreational facilities.

 **Academics**

NYU offers a core academic program; fewer than half of graduate courses are open to undergraduates. It awards associate, bachelor's, master's, doctoral, and first professional **degrees**. Challenging opportunities include advanced placement, self-designed majors, tutorials, Freshmen Honors College, an honors program, a senior project, Phi Beta Kappa, and Sigma Xi. Special programs include internships, summer session for credit, off-campus study, study abroad, and Air Force ROTC.

The most popular **major** is business. A complete listing of majors at NYU appears in the Majors Index beginning on page 380.

The **faculty** at NYU has 1,427 full-time graduate and undergraduate teachers, 99% with terminal degrees. The student-faculty ratio is 13:1, and the average class size in required courses is 30.

 **Computers on Campus**

Students are not required to have a computer. 859 **computers** available in the computer center, computer labs, classrooms, the library, the student center, and dormitories provide access to the main academic computer, e-mail, and on-line services. Staffed computer lab on campus provides training in the use of computers and software.

The 8 **libraries** have 3.6 million books, 3 million microform titles, and 29,244 subscriptions.

 **Campus Life**

There are 230 active **organizations** on campus, including a drama/theater group and student-run newspaper and radio station. 7% of eligible men and 6% of eligible women are members of 11 national **fraternities**, 3 national **sororities**, and 7 local sororities. Student **safety services** include 24-hour security in all residence halls, late night transport/escort service, 24-hour emergency telephone alarm devices, 24-hour patrols by trained security personnel, student patrols, and electronically operated dormitory entrances.

NYU is a member of the NCAA (Division III). **Intercollegiate sports** include basketball (m, w), cross-country running (m, w), fencing (m, w), golf (m), soccer (m, w), swimming and diving (m, w), tennis (m, w), track and field (m, w), volleyball (m, w), wrestling (m).

 **Applying**

NYU requires an essay, a high school transcript, 3 years of high school math and science, 2 years of high school foreign language, 1 recommendation, SAT I or ACT, a minimum high school GPA of 3.0, and in some cases a campus interview and SAT II Subject Tests. It recommends SAT II Subject Tests. Early, deferred, and midyear entrance are possible, with a 2/1 deadline and a 2/15 priority date for financial aid. **Contact:** Mr. Richard Avitabile, Director of Admissions, 22 Washington Square North, New York, NY 10012-1019, 212-998-4515; fax 212-995-4902.

---

### GETTING IN LAST YEAR
14,451 applied
52% were accepted
38% enrolled (2,865)
42% from top tenth of their h.s. class
3.5 average high school GPA
42 National Merit Scholars

### THE STUDENT BODY
Total 33,428, of whom 15,653
   are undergraduates
From 52 states and territories,
   120 other countries
63% from New York
59% women, 41% men

10% African Americans
0% Native Americans
8% Hispanics
19% Asian Americans
6% international students

### AFTER FRESHMAN YEAR
87% returned for sophomore year
65% got a degree within 4 years
71% got a degree within 5 years
72% got a degree within 6 years

### AFTER GRADUATION
80% pursued further study (38% arts and
   sciences, 24% law, 14% medicine)

88% had job offers within 3 months
400 corporations, 10 government agencies,
   50 nonprofit organizations recruited on
   campus
5 Fulbright scholars

### WHAT YOU WILL PAY
Tuition and fees $18,739
Room and board $7262
66% receive need-based financial aid
   averaging $6245
Non-need financial aid averages $4092

---

# NORTH CAROLINA STATE UNIVERSITY

Raleigh, North Carolina • Suburban setting • Public • State-supported • Coed

---

Students select NCSU for its strong programs, excellent reputation, location, low cost, and friendly atmosphere. Students like the excitement of a large campus and the opportunities it offers, such as cooperative education, study abroad, and extensive scholars programming. Each year hundreds of graduates are accepted into medical and law schools and other areas of professional study.

## 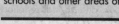 Academics

NC State offers a core academic program; fewer than half of graduate courses are open to undergraduates. It awards associate, bachelor's, master's, and doctoral **degrees**. Challenging opportunities include advanced placement, self-designed majors, tutorials, an honors program, a senior project, Phi Beta Kappa, and Sigma Xi. Special programs include cooperative education, internships, summer session for credit, off-campus study, study abroad, and Army, Naval, and Air Force ROTC.

The most popular **majors** include business, electrical engineering, and mechanical engineering. A complete listing of majors at NC State appears in the Majors Index beginning on page 380.

The **faculty** at NC State has 1,327 full-time graduate and undergraduate teachers, 91% with terminal degrees. 100% of the faculty serve as student advisers. The student-faculty ratio is 14:1, and the average class size in required courses is 32.

## Computers on Campus

Students are not required to have a computer. Student rooms are linked to a campus network. 3,700 **computers** available across campus and in dormitories provide access to the main academic computer, off-campus computing facilities, e-mail, and on-line services. Staffed computer lab on campus provides training in the use of computers and software.

The 5 **libraries** have 2 million books, 3.7 million microform titles, and 18,086 subscriptions. They are connected to 8 national **on-line** catalogs.

##  Campus Life

There are 300 active **organizations** on campus, including a drama/theater group and student-run newspaper and radio station. 30% of students participate in student government elections. 15% of eligible men and 18% of eligible women are members of 25 national **fraternities** and 10 national **sororities**. Student **safety services** include late night transport/escort service, 24-hour emergency telephone alarm devices, 24-hour patrols by trained security personnel, student patrols, and electronically operated dormitory entrances.

NC State is a member of the NCAA (Division I). **Intercollegiate sports** (some offering scholarships) include baseball (m), basketball (m, w), cross-country running (m, w), fencing (m, w), football (m), golf (m, w), gymnastics (m, w), ice hockey (m), lacrosse (m), racquetball (m, w), riflery (m, w), rugby (m, w), sailing (m, w), skiing (downhill) (m, w), soccer (m, w), swimming and diving (m, w), tennis (m, w), track and field (m, w), volleyball (m, w), water polo (m, w), weight lifting (m, w), wrestling (m).

##  Applying

NC State requires a high school transcript, 3 years of high school math and science, 2 years of high school foreign language, 4 years of high school English, 2 years of high school social studies, SAT I or ACT, SAT II Subject Test in math, and in some cases recommendations and an interview. It recommends an essay and a minimum high school GPA of 3.0. Early and midyear entrance are possible, with a 2/1 deadline and continuous processing to 3/1 for financial aid. **Contact:** Ms. Laura L. Huntley, Assistant Director of Admissions, Box 7103, 112 Peele Hall, Raleigh, NC 27695, 919-515-2434; fax 919-515-5039.

---

### GETTING IN LAST YEAR
11,150 applied
64% were accepted
50% enrolled (3,530)
49% from top tenth of their h.s. class
3.63 average high school GPA
17% had SAT verbal scores over 600
42% had SAT math scores over 600
2% had SAT verbal scores over 700
10% had SAT math scores over 700
34 National Merit Scholars
98 class presidents
375 valedictorians

### THE STUDENT BODY
Total 27,577, of whom 18,792
  are undergraduates

From 52 states and territories,
  92 other countries
82% from North Carolina
42% women, 58% men
12% African Americans
1% Native Americans
2% Hispanics
3% Asian Americans
4% international students

### AFTER FRESHMAN YEAR
93% returned for sophomore year
36% got a degree within 4 years
59% got a degree within 5 years
78% got a degree within 6 years

### AFTER GRADUATION
29% pursued further study (4% medicine, 3% law, 2% veterinary medicine)
60% had job offers within 3 months
559 corporations, 37 government agencies, 2 nonprofit organizations recruited on campus
2 Fulbright scholars

### WHAT YOU WILL PAY
Resident tuition and fees $1584
Nonresident tuition and fees $9110
Room and board $3540
44% receive need-based financial aid averaging $740
Non-need financial aid averages $3048

# NORTH CENTRAL COLLEGE

Naperville, Illinois • Suburban setting • Private • Independent-Religious • Coed

North Central College offers over 50 areas of concentration in preprofessional and liberal arts disciplines. Located 29 miles west of Chicago, in the Illinois Research and Development Corridor, NCC provides unlimited internship and career opportunities. A student-faculty ratio of 14:1 facilitates personalized study, while the Leadership, Ethics and Values Program provides a unique educational philosophy. Cocurricular opportunities include Model UN, performing arts, Students in Free Enterprise, student government, the radio station, campus ministry, and Division III varsity athletic programs. Ninety-four percent of freshman students receive some type of financial assistance.

## Academics

North Central offers a leadership curriculum and core academic program; more than half of graduate courses are open to undergraduates. It awards bachelor's and master's **degrees**. Challenging opportunities include advanced placement, accelerated degree programs, self-designed majors, tutorials, an honors program, and a senior project. Special programs include cooperative education, internships, summer session for credit, off-campus study, study abroad, and Army, Naval, and Air Force ROTC.

The most popular **majors** include business, broadcasting, and computer science. A complete listing of majors at North Central appears in the Majors Index beginning on page 380.

The **faculty** at North Central has 93 full-time graduate and undergraduate teachers, 86% with terminal degrees. 100% of the faculty serve as student advisers. The student-faculty ratio is 14:1, and the average class size in required courses is 19.

## Computers on Campus

Students are not required to have a computer. 110 **computers** available in the computer center, computer labs, the library, and dormitories.

The **library** has 113,647 books and 587 subscriptions. It is connected to 1 national **on-line** catalog.

## Campus Life

Active **organizations** on campus include drama/theater group and student-run newspaper and radio station. Student **safety services** include late night transport/escort service.

North Central is a member of the NCAA (Division III). **Intercollegiate sports** include baseball (m), basketball (m, w), cross-country running (m, w), football (m), golf (m, w), soccer (m), softball (w), swimming and diving (m, w), tennis (m, w), track and field (m, w), volleyball (w), wrestling (m).

## Applying

North Central requires a high school transcript, SAT I or ACT, a minimum high school GPA of 2.0, and in some cases an interview. It recommends an essay, 3 years of high school math and science, some high school foreign language, and recommendations. Early, deferred, and midyear entrance are possible, with rolling admissions and continuous processing to 7/1 for financial aid. **Contact:** Mr. Fred Schebor, Dean of Admission, 30 North Brainard Street, Naperville, IL 60566-7063, 708-420-3414.

---

### GETTING IN LAST YEAR
1,040 applied
83% were accepted
38% enrolled (325)
27% from top tenth of their h.s. class
13% had SAT verbal scores over 600
29% had SAT math scores over 600
38% had ACT scores over 26
0% had SAT verbal scores over 700
11% had SAT math scores over 700
4% had ACT scores over 30

### THE STUDENT BODY
Total 2,446, of whom 1,645 are undergraduates
From 24 states and territories, 8 other countries
81% from Illinois
54% women, 46% men
7% African Americans
5% Hispanics
3% Asian Americans
1% international students

### AFTER FRESHMAN YEAR
73% returned for sophomore year

### AFTER GRADUATION
12% pursued further study
1 Fulbright scholar

### WHAT YOU WILL PAY
Tuition and fees $11,838
Room and board $4398
Need-based financial aid averages $2671
Non-need financial aid averages $3288

# NORTHEAST MISSOURI STATE UNIVERSITY

Kirksville, Missouri • Small-town setting • Public • State-supported • Coed

---

Northeast has embraced the challenge of becoming an uncommon public university, where undergraduates are encouraged to succeed and are given the support to flourish. A Northeast education has as its foundation an extensive liberal arts and sciences curriculum in which dynamic classrooms advocate the acquisition of skills and knowledge. Cocurricular opportunities in undergraduate, research, student government, and performing arts allow talents to build upon that foundation. An added appeal is that students can afford to experience Northeast. Ranked by *1995 Money Guide* as the 5th-best buy nationally, Northeast has long supported the ideal of educational value.

 **Academics**

Northeast offers a liberal arts and sciences curriculum and core academic program; fewer than half of graduate courses are open to undergraduates. It awards bachelor's and master's **degrees**. Challenging opportunities include advanced placement, accelerated degree programs, an honors program, and a senior project. Special programs include internships, summer session for credit, off-campus study, study abroad, and Army ROTC.

The most popular **majors** include business, psychology, and biology/biological sciences. A complete listing of majors at Northeast appears in the Majors Index beginning on page 380.

The **faculty** at Northeast has 334 full-time graduate and undergraduate teachers, 76% with terminal degrees. 82% of the faculty serve as student advisers. The student-faculty ratio is 16:1, and the average class size in required courses is 23.

 **Computers on Campus**

Students are not required to have a computer. 950 **computers** available in computer labs, academic buildings, the library, and dormitories provide access to the main academic computer, e-mail, and on-line services. Staffed computer lab on campus provides training in the use of computers and software.

The 2 **libraries** have 383,419 books and 1,943 subscriptions. They are connected to 25 national **on-line** catalogs.

 **Campus Life**

There are 153 active **organizations** on campus, including a drama/theater group and student-run newspaper and radio station. 15% of students participate in student government elections. 28% of eligible men and 19% of eligible women are members of 17 national **fraternities**, 10 national **sororities**, and 1 local sorority. Student **safety services** include patrols by commissioned officers, late night transport/escort service, 24-hour emergency telephone alarm devices, 24-hour patrols by trained security personnel, and student patrols.

Northeast is a member of the NCAA (Division II). **Intercollegiate sports** (some offering scholarships) include baseball (m), basketball (m, w), cross-country running (m, w), equestrian sports (m, w), football (m), golf (m, w), rugby (m, w), soccer (m, w), softball (w), swimming and diving (m, w), tennis (m, w), track and field (m, w), volleyball (w), wrestling (m).

 **Applying**

Northeast requires an essay, a high school transcript, 3 years of high school math and science, 2 years of high school foreign language, SAT I or ACT, and in some cases recommendations. It recommends a minimum high school GPA of 3.0. Early, deferred, and midyear entrance are possible, with a 3/1 deadline and continuous processing to 4/30 for financial aid. **Contact:** Ms. Kathy Rieck, Dean of Admission and Records, 205 McClain Hall, Kirksville, MO 63501, 816-785-4114 or toll-free 800-892-7792 (in-state); fax 816-785-4181.

---

### GETTING IN LAST YEAR
5,676 applied
76% were accepted
36% enrolled (1,545)
36% from top tenth of their h.s. class
3.5 average high school GPA
53% had ACT scores over 26
19% had ACT scores over 30
17 National Merit Scholars
120 class presidents
99 valedictorians

### THE STUDENT BODY
Total 6,317, of whom 6,061
    are undergraduates

From 38 states and territories,
    54 other countries
69% from Missouri
57% women, 43% men
3% African Americans
1% Native Americans
1% Hispanics
2% Asian Americans
3% international students

### AFTER FRESHMAN YEAR
83% returned for sophomore year
58% got a degree within 4 years
63% got a degree within 5 years
64% got a degree within 6 years

### AFTER GRADUATION
40% pursued further study (28% arts and
    sciences, 5% business, 3% medicine)
115 corporations, 26 government agencies, 6
    nonprofit organizations recruited on campus
1 Fulbright scholar

### WHAT YOU WILL PAY
Resident tuition and fees $2722
Nonresident tuition and fees $4874
Room and board $3416
45% receive need-based financial aid
    averaging $793
59% receive non-need financial aid averaging
    $1648

---

# NORTHWESTERN COLLEGE

Orange City, Iowa • Rural setting • Private • Independent-Religious • Coed

 **Academics**

Northwestern offers a Western civilization and interdisciplinary curriculum and core academic program; fewer than half of graduate courses are open to undergraduates. It awards associate, bachelor's, and master's **degrees**. Challenging opportunities include advanced placement, accelerated degree programs, self-designed majors, an honors program, and a senior project. Special programs include cooperative education, internships, summer session for credit, off-campus study, and study abroad.

The most popular **majors** include business, elementary education, and biology/biological sciences. A complete listing of majors at Northwestern appears in the Majors Index beginning on page 380.

The **faculty** at Northwestern has 61 full-time undergraduate teachers, 70% with terminal degrees. 85% of the faculty serve as student advisers. The student-faculty ratio is 16:1, and the average class size in required courses is 30.

 **Computers on Campus**

Students are not required to have a computer. Student rooms are linked to a campus network. 175 **computers** available in the computer center, the learning resource center, Demco Business Center, Kresge Education Center, classrooms, the library, and dormitories. Staffed computer lab on campus provides training in the use of computers and software.

The 3 **libraries** have 108,000 books, 3,500 microform titles, and 500 subscriptions.

 **Campus Life**

There are 30 active **organizations** on campus, including a drama/theater group and student-run newspaper and radio station. 65% of students participate in student government elections. Student **safety services** include 24-hour emergency telephone alarm devices and electronically operated dormitory entrances.

Northwestern is a member of the NAIA. **Intercollegiate sports** (some offering scholarships) include baseball (m), basketball (m, w), cross-country running (m, w), football (m), golf (m, w), soccer (m, w), softball (w), tennis (m, w), track and field (m, w), volleyball (w), wrestling (m).

 **Applying**

Northwestern requires a high school transcript, 1 recommendation, and SAT I or ACT. It recommends 3 years of high school math and science and an interview. Deferred and midyear entrance are possible, with rolling admissions and continuous processing to 4/1 for financial aid. **Contact:** Mr. Ronald K. DeJong, Director of Admissions, 101 College Lane, Orange City, IA 51041-1996, 712-737-7000 or toll-free 800-747-4757 (in-state); fax 712-737-7247.

---

**GETTING IN LAST YEAR**

1,082 applied
90% were accepted
35% enrolled (342)
25% from top tenth of their h.s. class
3.2 average high school GPA
26% had ACT scores over 26
5% had ACT scores over 30

**THE STUDENT BODY**

Total 1,150, of whom 1,141
  are undergraduates
From 27 states and territories,
  15 other countries

65% from Iowa
57% women, 43% men
1% African Americans
1% Native Americans
1% Hispanics
1% Asian Americans
5% international students

**AFTER FRESHMAN YEAR**

69% returned for sophomore year
38% got a degree within 4 years
48% got a degree within 5 years
50% got a degree within 6 years

**AFTER GRADUATION**

16% pursued further study (7% theology, 3% medicine, 2% business)
80% had job offers within 3 months
5 corporations, 2 government agencies, 20 nonprofit organizations recruited on campus

**WHAT YOU WILL PAY**

Tuition and fees $9900
Room and board $3075
75% receive need-based financial aid averaging $2000
20% receive non-need financial aid averaging $2300

# NORTHWESTERN UNIVERSITY

Evanston, Illinois • Suburban setting • Private • Independent • Coed

Northwestern, on the shore of Lake Michigan just north of Chicago, combines the accessibility of 6 small colleges with the resources and opportunities of a major university. The College of Arts and Sciences, the Schools of Education and Social Policy, of Music, and of Speech; the Medill School of Journalism; and the McCormick School of Engineering and Applied Science offer a sound foundation in the liberal arts as an integral part of a student's education. Northwestern's 7,500 undergraduates come from all 50 states and a variety of backgrounds. Fifty percent are women, and approximately 26 percent are minority group members.

 ## Academics

Northwestern offers a core academic program; fewer than half of graduate courses are open to undergraduates. It awards bachelor's, master's, doctoral, and first professional **degrees**. Challenging opportunities include advanced placement, accelerated degree programs, self-designed majors, tutorials, an honors program, a senior project, Phi Beta Kappa, and Sigma Xi. Special programs include cooperative education, internships, summer session for credit, off-campus study, study abroad, and Army, Naval, and Air Force ROTC.

The most popular **majors** include economics, political science/government, and journalism. A complete listing of majors at Northwestern appears in the Majors Index beginning on page 380.

The **faculty** at Northwestern has 801 full-time undergraduate teachers, 100% with terminal degrees. 100% of the faculty serve as student advisers. The student-faculty ratio is 8:1, and the average class size in required courses is 25.

 ## Computers on Campus

Students are not required to have a computer. Student rooms are linked to a campus network. 250 **computers** available in the computer center, academic buildings, the library, the student center, and dormitories. Staffed computer lab on campus provides training in the use of computers and software.

The 11 **libraries** have 3.7 million books, 2.9 million microform titles, and 36,626 subscriptions. They are connected to 15 national **on-line** catalogs.

 ## Campus Life

There are 250 active **organizations** on campus, including a drama/theater group and student-run newspaper and radio station. 40% of eligible men and 39% of eligible women are members of 20 national **fraternities** and 12 national **sororities**. Student **safety services** include late night transport/escort service, 24-hour emergency telephone alarm devices, and electronically operated dormitory entrances.

Northwestern is a member of the NCAA (Division I). **Intercollegiate sports** (some offering scholarships) include baseball (m), basketball (m, w), fencing (w), field hockey (w), football (m), golf (m, w), soccer (m, w), softball (w), swimming and diving (m, w), tennis (m, w), volleyball (w), wrestling (m).

 ## Applying

Northwestern requires an essay, a high school transcript, 1 recommendation, SAT I or ACT, and in some cases audition for music majors and SAT II Subject Tests. It recommends 3 years of high school math and science, 2 years of high school foreign language, and an interview. Early, deferred, and midyear entrance are possible, with a 1/1 deadline and continuous processing to 2/15 for financial aid. **Contact:** Ms. Carol Lunkenheimer, Director of Admissions, 1801 Hinman Avenue, Evanston, IL 60208, 708-491-7271.

---

### GETTING IN LAST YEAR
13,515 applied
39% were accepted
36% enrolled (1,867)
82% from top tenth of their h.s. class
44% had SAT verbal scores over 600
78% had SAT math scores over 600
92% had ACT scores over 26
5% had SAT verbal scores over 700
34% had SAT math scores over 700
48% had ACT scores over 30
118 National Merit Scholars

### THE STUDENT BODY
Total 12,179, of whom 7,574
  are undergraduates
From 52 states and territories,
  27 other countries
25% from Illinois
50% women, 50% men
6% African Americans
1% Native Americans
2% Hispanics
17% Asian Americans
2% international students

### AFTER FRESHMAN YEAR
96% returned for sophomore year

### WHAT YOU WILL PAY
Tuition and fees $16,404
Room and board $5520
60% receive need-based financial aid
  averaging $8600

# OBERLIN COLLEGE

Oberlin, Ohio • Small-town setting • Private • Independent • Coed

As long as there has been an Oberlin, Oberlinians have been changing the world. Oberlin was the first coeducational school in the United States and a historic leader in educating African American students. Among primarily undergraduate institutions, Oberlin ranks first for the number of students who go on to earn PhD degrees. Its alumni, who include 3 Nobel laureates, are leaders in law, scientific and scholarly research, medicine, the arts, theology, communication, business, and government. Oberlin also offers a 5-year double-degree program, combining studies at the Conservatory of Music and the College of Arts and Sciences.

## Academics

Oberlin offers a liberal arts curriculum and core academic program. It awards bachelor's **degrees**. Challenging opportunities include advanced placement, self-designed majors, tutorials, an honors program, a senior project, Phi Beta Kappa, and Sigma Xi. Special programs include internships, off-campus study, and study abroad.

The most popular **majors** include English, biology/biological sciences, and history. A complete listing of majors at Oberlin appears in the Majors Index beginning on page 380.

The **faculty** at Oberlin has 176 full-time teachers, 95% with terminal degrees. 100% of the faculty serve as student advisers. The student-faculty ratio is 12:1.

## Computers on Campus

Students are not required to have a computer. Student rooms are linked to a campus network. 240 **computers** available in the computer center, classrooms, the library, the student center, and dormitories provide access to the main academic computer, off-campus computing facilities, e-mail, and on-line services.

The 4 **libraries** have 1.1 million books, 309,983 microform titles, and 2,636 subscriptions. They are connected to 6 national **on-line** catalogs.

## Campus Life

There are 100 active **organizations** on campus, including a drama/theater group and student-run newspaper and radio station. Student **safety services** include crime prevention programs, late night transport/escort service, 24-hour emergency telephone alarm devices, 24-hour patrols by trained security personnel, and electronically operated dormitory entrances.

Oberlin is a member of the NCAA (Division III). **Intercollegiate sports** include baseball (m), basketball (m, w), cross-country running (m, w), equestrian sports (m, w), fencing (m, w), field hockey (w), football (m), ice hockey (m), lacrosse (m, w), racquetball (m, w), rugby (m, w), soccer (m, w), softball (w), squash (m, w), swimming and diving (m, w), tennis (m, w), track and field (m, w), volleyball (m, w), water polo (m).

## Applying

Oberlin requires an essay, a high school transcript, 2 recommendations, and SAT I or ACT. It recommends 4 years of high school math, 3 years of high school science, 3 years of high school foreign language, an interview, and 3 SAT II Subject Tests. Early, deferred, and midyear entrance are possible, with a 1/15 deadline and continuous processing to 2/1 for financial aid. **Contact:** Ms. Debra Chermonte, Director of College Admissions, 101 North Professor Street, Oberlin, OH 44074, 216-775-8411 or toll-free 800-622-OBIE.

---

### GETTING IN LAST YEAR

3,887 applied
64% were accepted
32% enrolled (788)
52% from top tenth of their h.s. class
59% had SAT verbal scores over 600
69% had SAT math scores over 600
81% had ACT scores over 26
12% had SAT verbal scores over 700
20% had SAT math scores over 700
45% had ACT scores over 30
39 National Merit Scholars
26 valedictorians

### THE STUDENT BODY

2,744 undergraduates
From 51 states and territories,
  51 other countries
10% from Ohio
56% women, 44% men
8% African Americans
1% Native Americans
3% Hispanics
10% Asian Americans
5% international students

### AFTER FRESHMAN YEAR

88% returned for sophomore year

### AFTER GRADUATION

34% pursued further study
1 Marshall, 1 Fulbright scholar

### WHAT YOU WILL PAY

Tuition and fees $19,796
Room and board $5820
52% receive need-based financial aid
  averaging $11,080
5% receive non-need financial aid averaging
  $4499

# OCCIDENTAL COLLEGE

Los Angeles, California • Urban setting • Private • Independent • Coed

Occidental College offers abundant opportunities for students to live and learn within a community of scholars dedicated to providing leadership for an increasingly complex and global society. Since its founding in 1887, Occidental College has been committed to education in the best tradition of liberal arts. The College encourages a broad understanding of many fields of knowledge, erasing boundaries of subjects as one comes to realize the relationships among them and providing a foundation for lifelong learning. Students and faculty alike are willing to consider new ideas with an open mind and an enthusiasm for the ideals of multiculturalism that is the hallmark of the "Oxy" experience.

 **Academics**

Occidental offers an interdisciplinary curriculum and core academic program. It awards bachelor's and master's **degrees**. Challenging opportunities include advanced placement, self-designed majors, tutorials, an honors program, a senior project, and Phi Beta Kappa. Special programs include internships, summer session for credit, off-campus study, study abroad, and Army and Air Force ROTC.

The most popular **majors** include art/fine arts, English, and history. A complete listing of majors at Occidental appears in the Majors Index beginning on page 380.

The **faculty** at Occidental has 137 full-time undergraduate teachers, 96% with terminal degrees. 94% of the faculty serve as student advisers. The student-faculty ratio is 12:1, and the average class size in required courses is 12.

 **Computers on Campus**

Students are not required to have a computer. Student rooms are linked to a campus network. 100 **computers** available in the computer center, computer labs, the research center, the learning resource center, classrooms, the library, and dormitories provide access to e-mail. Staffed computer lab on campus.

The 3 **libraries** have 521,883 books, 254,689 microform titles, and 1,457 subscriptions. They are connected to 5 national **on-line** catalogs.

 **Campus Life**

There are 85 active **organizations** on campus, including a drama/theater group and student-run newspaper and radio station. 15% of eligible men and 15% of eligible women are members of 3 national **fraternities** and 3 local **sororities**. Student **safety services** include community policing services, late night transport/escort service, 24-hour emergency telephone alarm devices, 24-hour patrols by trained security personnel, student patrols, and electronically operated dormitory entrances.

Occidental is a member of the NCAA (Division III) and NAIA. **Intercollegiate sports** include badminton (m, w), baseball (m), basketball (m, w), cross-country running (m, w), equestrian sports (m, w), fencing (m, w), field hockey (w), football (m), golf (m, w), lacrosse (m, w), rugby (m), skiing (downhill) (m, w), soccer (m, w), softball (w), swimming and diving (m, w), tennis (m, w), track and field (m, w), volleyball (m, w), water polo (m, w).

 **Applying**

Occidental requires an essay, a high school transcript, 2 years of high school foreign language, 3 recommendations, and SAT I or ACT. It recommends 3 years of high school math and science, an interview, and SAT II Subject Tests. Early and deferred entrance are possible, with a 1/15 deadline and 2/1 for financial aid. **Contact:** Mr. David P. Morgan, Interim Dean of Admissions, 1600 Campus Road, Los Angeles, CA 90041-3392, 213-259-2700 or toll-free 800-825-5262; fax 213-259-2958.

## GETTING IN LAST YEAR

2,325 applied
59% were accepted
27% enrolled (375)
55% from top tenth of their h.s. class
17% had SAT verbal scores over 600
40% had SAT math scores over 600
1% had SAT verbal scores over 700
12% had SAT math scores over 700
6 National Merit Scholars
17 valedictorians

## THE STUDENT BODY

Total 1,604, of whom 1,563
    are undergraduates
From 48 states and territories,
    28 other countries
59% from California
53% women, 47% men
6% African Americans
1% Native Americans
18% Hispanics
17% Asian Americans
3% international students

## AFTER FRESHMAN YEAR

90% returned for sophomore year

## AFTER GRADUATION

52% pursued further study (30% arts and sciences, 6% business, 4% law)
29 corporations, 5 government agencies, 20 nonprofit organizations recruited on campus

## WHAT YOU WILL PAY

Tuition and fees $16,894
Room and board $5440
64% receive need-based financial aid averaging $7825
6% receive non-need financial aid averaging $6146

# OGLETHORPE UNIVERSITY

Atlanta, Georgia • Suburban setting • Private • Independent • Coed

It's not just the rigorous academic program, the small class discussions, and the motivating professors that make Oglethorpe different. It's the location—near the center of one of the country's most exciting, dynamic, international cities—Atlanta. A revamped honors program and a dynamic Urban Leadership Program are gaining much recognition from city leaders as Oglethorpe helps connect students to the rich resources of Atlanta. Internships are available in virtually every major and are very popular among the student body.

## Academics

Oglethorpe offers a primary sources curriculum and core academic program; more than half of graduate courses are open to undergraduates. It awards bachelor's and master's **degrees**. Challenging opportunities include advanced placement, accelerated degree programs, self-designed majors, tutorials, an honors program, and a senior project. Special programs include cooperative education, internships, summer session for credit, off-campus study, study abroad, and Army and Air Force ROTC.

The most popular **majors** include business, psychology, and accounting. A complete listing of majors at Oglethorpe appears in the Majors Index beginning on page 380.

The **faculty** at Oglethorpe has 45 full-time graduate and undergraduate teachers, 95% with terminal degrees. 100% of the faculty serve as student advisers. The student-faculty ratio is 10:1, and the average class size in required courses is 16.

## Computers on Campus

Students are not required to have a computer. 57 **computers** available in the computer center, computer labs, and the library. Staffed computer lab on campus.

The **library** has 106,820 books, 2 microform titles, and 760 subscriptions. It is connected to 1 national **on-line** catalog.

## Campus Life

There are 40 active **organizations** on campus, including a drama/theater group and student-run newspaper and radio station. 38% of eligible men and 25% of eligible women are members of 4 national **fraternities** and 2 national **sororities**. Student **safety services** include late night transport/escort service, 24-hour emergency telephone alarm devices, 24-hour patrols by trained security personnel, and student patrols.

Oglethorpe is a member of the NCAA (Division III). **Intercollegiate sports** include baseball (m), basketball (m, w), cross-country running (m, w), golf (m), soccer (m, w), tennis (m, w), track and field (m, w), volleyball (w).

## Applying

Oglethorpe requires a high school transcript, 3 years of high school math, 1 recommendation, SAT I or ACT, and in some cases an interview. It recommends 3 years of high school science, some high school foreign language, an interview, and minimum 2.5 GPA. Early, deferred, and mid-year entrance are possible, with an 8/1 deadline and continuous processing to 3/1 for financial aid. **Contact:** Mr. Dennis T. Matthews, Director of Admissions, 4484 Peachtree Road, NE, Atlanta, GA 30319-2797, 404-364-8307 or toll-free 800-428-4484 (out-of-state); fax 404-364-8500.

### GETTING IN LAST YEAR
830 applied
83% were accepted
32% enrolled (221)
55% from top tenth of their h.s. class
3.65 average high school GPA
31% had SAT verbal scores over 600
47% had SAT math scores over 600
73% had ACT scores over 26
4% had SAT verbal scores over 700
12% had SAT math scores over 700
30% had ACT scores over 30
2 class presidents
8 valedictorians

### THE STUDENT BODY
Total 1,280, of whom 1,222
  are undergraduates
From 31 states and territories,
  30 other countries
52% from Georgia
58% women, 42% men
4% African Americans
1% Native Americans
4% Hispanics
5% Asian Americans
7% international students

### AFTER FRESHMAN YEAR
80% returned for sophomore year
56% got a degree within 4 years
62% got a degree within 5 years
63% got a degree within 6 years

### AFTER GRADUATION
35% pursued further study (18% arts and
  sciences, 9% law, 5% business)
63% had job offers within 3 months
5 corporations, 1 government agency, 2
  nonprofit organizations recruited on campus

### WHAT YOU WILL PAY
Tuition and fees $12,960
Room and board $4500
65% receive need-based financial aid
  averaging $3644
82% receive non-need financial aid averaging
  $6387

# OHIO NORTHERN UNIVERSITY

Ada, Ohio • Small-town setting • Private • Independent-Religious • Coed

> National recognition, excellent facilities, superb teaching faculty, and a rich and diverse curriculum are some of the features that set ONU apart from other universities in the Midwest. But what truly makes Ohio Northern unique is the student body. It reflects the value of service to others, which is the product of the individual attention students receive from the faculty, staff, and administration of ONU.

##  Academics

Ohio Northern offers no core academic program. It awards bachelor's and first professional **degrees**. Challenging opportunities include advanced placement, tutorials, a senior project, and Sigma Xi. Special programs include cooperative education, internships, summer session for credit, study abroad, and Army and Air Force ROTC.

The most popular **majors** include pharmacy/pharmaceutical sciences, mechanical engineering, and elementary education. A complete listing of majors at Ohio Northern appears in the Majors Index beginning on page 380.

The **faculty** at Ohio Northern has 178 full-time graduate and undergraduate teachers, 79% with terminal degrees. 95% of the faculty serve as student advisers. The student-faculty ratio is 13:1, and the average class size in required courses is 24.

## Computers on Campus

Students are not required to have a computer. Student rooms are linked to a campus network. 281 **computers** available in the computer center, computer labs, academic buildings, the library, and dormitories provide access to the main academic computer, off-campus computing facilities, e-mail, and on-line services. Staffed computer lab on campus.

The 2 **libraries** have 407,928 books, 79,146 microform titles, and 4,390 subscriptions. They are connected to 1 national **on-line** catalog.

##  Campus Life

There are 25 active **organizations** on campus, including a drama/theater group and student-run newspaper and radio station. 30% of eligible men and 30% of eligible women are members of 8 national **fraternities** and 5 national **sororities**. Student **safety services** include late night transport/escort service, 24-hour emergency telephone alarm devices, 24-hour patrols by trained security personnel, and electronically operated dormitory entrances.

Ohio Northern is a member of the NCAA (Division III). **Intercollegiate sports** include baseball (m), basketball (m, w), cross-country running (m, w), football (m), golf (m), soccer (m, w), softball (w), swimming and diving (m, w), tennis (m, w), track and field (m, w), volleyball (w), wrestling (m).

##  Applying

Ohio Northern requires a high school transcript, 3 years of high school math, and SAT I or ACT. It recommends an essay, 3 years of high school science, 2 years of high school foreign language, recommendations, and a campus interview. Early, deferred, and midyear entrance are possible, with an 8/15 deadline and continuous processing to 5/1 for financial aid. **Contact:** Ms. Karen Condeni, Dean of Admissions and Financial Aid, Lehr Memorial Building, Ada, OH 45810, 419-772-2260; fax 419-772-2313.

## GETTING IN LAST YEAR

1,971 applied
89% were accepted
34% enrolled (588)
38% from top tenth of their h.s. class
3.4 average high school GPA
6% had SAT verbal scores over 600
27% had SAT math scores over 600
31% had ACT scores over 26
0% had SAT verbal scores over 700
6% had SAT math scores over 700
5% had ACT scores over 30
1 National Merit Scholar
38 valedictorians

## THE STUDENT BODY

Total 2,872, of whom 2,506 are undergraduates
From 35 states and territories, 20 other countries
85% from Ohio
47% women, 53% men
3% African Americans
1% Hispanics
1% Asian Americans
3% international students

## AFTER FRESHMAN YEAR

78% returned for sophomore year
30% got a degree within 4 years
61% got a degree within 5 years

## AFTER GRADUATION

29% pursued further study (8% arts and sciences, 3% law, 2% engineering)
61% had job offers within 3 months
46 corporations, 8 government agencies, 59 nonprofit organizations recruited on campus

## WHAT YOU WILL PAY

Tuition and fees $14,220
Room and board $4080
72% receive need-based financial aid averaging $6540
32% receive non-need financial aid averaging $5490

# OHIO STATE UNIVERSITY

Columbus, Ohio • Urban setting • Public • State-supported • Coed

More students choose Ohio State than any other single-campus university in the country. Ohio State offers nearly 200 major areas of study, more than 11,000 courses, and over 500 student organizations. As the state's leading center for teaching, research, and public service, it has the faculty, facilities, academic programs, and support services that few universities can match. Ohio State continues to attract a competitive student body, and its tuition costs and fees are also competitive.

##  Academics

Ohio State offers a core academic program; more than half of graduate courses are open to undergraduates. It awards associate, bachelor's, master's, doctoral, and first professional **degrees**. Challenging opportunities include advanced placement, accelerated degree programs, self-designed majors, tutorials, an honors program, a senior project, Phi Beta Kappa, and Sigma Xi. Special programs include cooperative education, internships, summer session for credit, off-campus study, study abroad, and Army, Naval, and Air Force ROTC.

The most popular **majors** include psychology and English. A complete listing of majors at Ohio State appears in the Majors Index beginning on page 380.

The **faculty** at Ohio State has 2,977 full-time graduate and undergraduate teachers, 95% with terminal degrees. The student-faculty ratio is 13:1, and the average class size in required courses is 24.

##  Computers on Campus

Students are not required to have a computer. 1,110 **computers** available in the computer center, computer labs, the research center, the learning resource center, labs,

the library, the student center, and dormitories provide access to e-mail. Staffed computer lab on campus.

The 51 **libraries** have 4.7 million books, 3.7 million microform titles, and 33,010 subscriptions. They are connected to 3 national **on-line** catalogs.

##  Campus Life

There are 550 active **organizations** on campus, including a drama/theater group and student-run newspaper and radio station. 10% of eligible men and 11% of eligible women are members of 35 national **fraternities** and 24 national **sororities**. Student **safety services** include late night transport/escort service, 24-hour emergency telephone alarm devices, 24-hour patrols by trained security personnel, and student patrols.

Ohio State is a member of the NCAA (Division I). **Intercollegiate sports** (some offering scholarships) include baseball (m), basketball (m, w), cross-country running (m, w), fencing (m, w), field hockey (w), football (m), golf (m, w), gymnastics (m, w), ice hockey (m), lacrosse (m), riflery (m, w), soccer (m, w), softball (w), swimming and diving (m, w), tennis (m, w), track and field (m, w), volleyball (m, w), wrestling (m).

##  Applying

Ohio State requires a high school transcript, 3 years of high school math, 2 years of high school foreign language, 2 years each of natural science and social science, 1 year of visual/performing arts, 4 years of English, and SAT I or ACT. It recommends 3 years of high school science and recommendations. Early and midyear entrance are possible, with a 2/15 deadline and a 2/15 priority date for financial aid. **Contact:** Ms. Stephanie Sanders, Information Center Manager, 3rd Floor, Lincoln Tower, Columbus, OH 43210, 614-292-3980; fax 614-292-4818.

---

### GETTING IN LAST YEAR
15,915 applied
91% were accepted
41% enrolled (5,968)
22% from top tenth of their h.s. class
10% had SAT verbal scores over 600
29% had SAT math scores over 600
26% had ACT scores over 26
1% had SAT verbal scores over 700
7% had SAT math scores over 700
7% had ACT scores over 30
93 National Merit Scholars
147 valedictorians

### THE STUDENT BODY
Total 49,542, of whom 36,166
 are undergraduates
From 53 states and territories,
 78 other countries
91% from Ohio
47% women, 53% men
7% African Americans
1% Native Americans
2% Hispanics
4% Asian Americans
3% international students

### AFTER FRESHMAN YEAR
77% returned for sophomore year
20% got a degree within 4 years
52% got a degree within 5 years
60% got a degree within 6 years

### WHAT YOU WILL PAY
Resident tuition and fees $3087
Nonresident tuition and fees $9315
Room and board $4532

# OHIO UNIVERSITY

Athens, Ohio • Small-town setting • Public • State-supported • Coed

Chartered in 1804, Ohio University symbolizes America's early commitment to higher education. Its historic campus provides a setting matched by only a handful of other universities in the country. Students choose Ohio University mainly because of its academic strength, but the beautiful setting and college-town atmosphere are also factors in their decision. Ohio University is the central focus of Athens, Ohio, located approximately 75 miles southeast of Columbus. The University encourages prospective students to come for a visit and experience its beauty and academic excellence.

## Academics

OU offers a core academic program. It awards associate, bachelor's, master's, doctoral, and first professional **degrees**. Challenging opportunities include advanced placement, accelerated degree programs, self-designed majors, an honors program, a senior project, Phi Beta Kappa, and Sigma Xi. Special programs include cooperative education, internships, summer session for credit, study abroad, and Army and Air Force ROTC.

The most popular **majors** include education and journalism. A complete listing of majors at OU appears in the Majors Index beginning on page 380.

The **faculty** at OU has 832 full-time graduate and undergraduate teachers, 88% with terminal degrees. 100% of the faculty serve as student advisers. The student-faculty ratio is 18:1, and the average class size in required courses is 22.

## Computers on Campus

Students are not required to have a computer. Student rooms are linked to a campus network. 903 **computers** available in the computer center, computer labs, classroom buildings, the library, and dormitories provide access to the main academic computer, off-campus computing facilities, e-mail, and on-line services. Staffed computer lab on campus (open 24 hours a day) provides training in the use of computers and software.

The **library** has 1.7 million books, 2.2 million microform titles, and 11,414 subscriptions. It is connected to 6 national **on-line** catalogs.

## Campus Life

There are 338 active **organizations** on campus, including a drama/theater group and student-run newspaper and radio station. 13% of eligible men and 17% of eligible women are members of 19 national **fraternities** and 12 national **sororities**. Student **safety services** include security lighting, late night transport/escort service, 24-hour emergency telephone alarm devices, 24-hour patrols by trained security personnel, and electronically operated dormitory entrances.

OU is a member of the NCAA (Division I). **Intercollegiate sports** (some offering scholarships) include baseball (m), basketball (m, w), cross-country running (m, w), equestrian sports (m, w), field hockey (w), football (m), golf (m), ice hockey (m), lacrosse (m, w), rugby (m, w), soccer (m, w), softball (w), swimming and diving (m, w), track and field (m, w), volleyball (m, w), water polo (m), weight lifting (m), wrestling (m).

## Applying

OU requires a high school transcript and SAT I or ACT. It recommends an essay, 3 years of high school math and science, 2 years of high school foreign language, 2 recommendations, and an interview. Early, deferred, and midyear entrance are possible, with a 3/1 deadline and continuous processing to 4/1 for financial aid. **Contact:** Mr. N. Kip Howard, Director of Admissions, 120 Chubb Hall, Athens, OH 45701, 614-593-4100; fax 614-593-0560.

### GETTING IN LAST YEAR
10,892 applied
78% were accepted
39% enrolled (3,314)
20% from top tenth of their h.s. class
3.2 average high school GPA
7% had SAT verbal scores over 600
20% had SAT math scores over 600
1% had SAT verbal scores over 700
3% had SAT math scores over 700
9 National Merit Scholars

### THE STUDENT BODY
Total 18,855, of whom 15,949
  are undergraduates

From 52 states and territories,
  100 other countries
88% from Ohio
54% women, 46% men
4% African Americans
1% Native Americans
1% Hispanics
1% Asian Americans
2% international students

### AFTER FRESHMAN YEAR
85% returned for sophomore year
60% got a degree within 4 years
65% got a degree within 5 years
70% got a degree within 6 years

### AFTER GRADUATION
28% pursued further study (13% arts and
  sciences, 5% business, 3% law)
1 Fulbright scholar

### WHAT YOU WILL PAY
Resident tuition and fees $3552
Nonresident tuition and fees $7629
Room and board $3963
Need-based financial aid averages $2458
Non-need financial aid averages $1982

# OHIO WESLEYAN UNIVERSITY

Delaware, Ohio • Small-town setting • Private • Independent-Religious • Coed

---

Ohio Wesleyan is one of the nation's most balanced selective liberal arts colleges. Students praise the faculty for their dedication to teaching and active encouragement in the classroom. Students balance their academic experience with strong participation in community service, athletics, and student government. Each year the University offers a speaker series and seminar classes that focus on a major public issue of concern (National Colloquium). Loren Pope, author of *Beyond the Ivy League*, says "Ohio Wesleyan has a much more diverse, cosmopolitan, and friendly student body than a lot of the selective east and west coast schools."

## Academics

Ohio Wesleyan offers an interdisciplinary curriculum and core academic program. It awards bachelor's **degrees**. Challenging opportunities include advanced placement, self-designed majors, tutorials, Freshmen Honors College, an honors program, a senior project, Phi Beta Kappa, and Sigma Xi. Special programs include internships, summer session for credit, off-campus study, and study abroad.

The most popular **majors** include business, biology/biological sciences, and political science/government. A complete listing of majors at Ohio Wesleyan appears in the Majors Index beginning on page 380.

The **faculty** at Ohio Wesleyan has 130 full-time teachers, 94% with terminal degrees. 95% of the faculty serve as student advisers. The student-faculty ratio is 13:1, and the average class size in required courses is 15.

## Computers on Campus

Students are not required to have a computer. Student rooms are linked to a campus network. 170 **computers** available in the computer center, academic departments, the library, and dormitories provide access to the main academic computer, e-mail, and on-line services. Staffed computer lab on campus provides training in the use of computers and software.

The 4 **libraries** have 480,000 books, 47,972 microform titles, and 1,060 subscriptions.

## Campus Life

There are 55 active **organizations** on campus, including a drama/theater group and student-run newspaper and radio station. 50% of students participate in student government elections. 40% of eligible men and 30% of eligible women are members of 11 national **fraternities** and 7 national **sororities**. Student **safety services** include late night transport/escort service, 24-hour emergency telephone alarm devices, 24-hour patrols by trained security personnel, and electronically operated dormitory entrances.

Ohio Wesleyan is a member of the NCAA (Division III). **Intercollegiate sports** include basketball (m, w), cross-country running (m, w), equestrian sports (m, w), field hockey (w), football (m), golf (m), lacrosse (m, w), rugby (m), sailing (m, w), soccer (m, w), swimming and diving (m, w), tennis (m, w), track and field (m, w), volleyball (w).

## Applying

Ohio Wesleyan requires an essay, a high school transcript, 3 years of high school math, 2 recommendations, and SAT I or ACT. It recommends 3 years of high school science, 3 years of high school foreign language, and an interview. Early, deferred, and midyear entrance are possible, with a 3/1 deadline and continuous processing to 3/1 for financial aid. **Contact:** Mr. Douglas C. Thompson, Dean of Admission, Slocum Hall, Delaware, OH 43015, 614-368-3020 or toll-free 800-922-8953; fax 614-368-3314.

---

### GETTING IN LAST YEAR

2,051 applied
85% were accepted
28% enrolled (481)
35% from top tenth of their h.s. class
3.4 average high school GPA
28% had SAT verbal scores over 600
45% had SAT math scores over 600
47% had ACT scores over 26
3% had SAT verbal scores over 700
13% had SAT math scores over 700
19% had ACT scores over 30
24 valedictorians

### THE STUDENT BODY

1,732 undergraduates
From 45 states and territories,
   44 other countries
50% from Ohio
51% women, 49% men
4% African Americans
1% Native Americans
1% Hispanics
2% Asian Americans
8% international students

### AFTER FRESHMAN YEAR

84% returned for sophomore year
68% got a degree within 4 years
71% got a degree within 5 years
73% got a degree within 6 years

### AFTER GRADUATION

30% pursued further study (7% medicine, 6% law, 5% arts and sciences)
65% had job offers within 3 months
20 corporations, 2 government agencies, 5 nonprofit organizations recruited on campus
1 Fulbright scholar

### WHAT YOU WILL PAY

Tuition and fees $17,569
Room and board $5876
55% receive need-based financial aid averaging $9507
21% receive non-need financial aid averaging $9770

---

# OKLAHOMA STATE UNIVERSITY

Stillwater, Oklahoma • Small-town setting • Public • State-supported • Coed

Oklahoma State University offers exceptional opportunities. An exciting Honors Program provides special honors sections, personal advising, priority class selection, and special housing. Selected freshmen become Research Scholars, working with faculty mentors on critical national projects in lasers, biotechnology, environmental sciences, manufacturing, public policy, and materials sciences. Engineering, accounting, mathematics, agricultural sciences and natural resources, music and performing arts, biological sciences, creative writing, and hotel and restaurant management are nationally recognized programs.

## Academics

OSU offers an interdisciplinary curriculum and core academic program; more than half of graduate courses are open to undergraduates. It awards bachelor's, master's, doctoral, and first professional **degrees**. Challenging opportunities include advanced placement, accelerated degree programs, self-designed majors, tutorials, an honors program, a senior project, and Sigma Xi. Special programs include cooperative education, internships, summer session for credit, off-campus study, study abroad, and Army and Air Force ROTC.

The most popular **majors** include education, management information systems, and marketing/retailing/merchandising. A complete listing of majors at OSU appears in the Majors Index beginning on page 380.

The **faculty** at OSU has 809 full-time graduate and undergraduate teachers, 88% with terminal degrees. The student-faculty ratio is 24:1, and the average class size in required courses is 46.

## Computers on Campus

Students are not required to have a computer. Student rooms are linked to a campus network. 800 **computers** available in the computer center, computer labs, labs, classrooms, the library, the student center, and dormitories provide access to the main academic computer, off-campus computing facilities, e-mail, and on-line services. Staffed computer lab on campus provides training in the use of computers and software.

The **library** has 1.7 million books, 2.8 million microform titles, and 16,130 subscriptions. It is connected to 4 national **on-line** catalogs.

## Campus Life

There are 265 active **organizations** on campus, including a student-run newspaper and radio station. 10% of students participate in student government elections. 17% of eligible men and 16% of eligible women are members of 25 national **fraternities** and 14 national **sororities**. Student **safety services** include late night transport/escort service, 24-hour emergency telephone alarm devices, 24-hour patrols by trained security personnel, and student patrols.

OSU is a member of the NCAA (Division I). **Intercollegiate sports** (some offering scholarships) include baseball (m), basketball (m, w), cross-country running (m, w), football (m), golf (m, w), softball (w), tennis (m, w), track and field (m, w), wrestling (m).

## Applying

OSU requires a high school transcript, 3 years of high school math, 4 years of high school English, 2 years each of high school history and science, SAT I or ACT, and a minimum high school GPA of 3.0. It recommends 2 years of high school foreign language. Early, deferred, and midyear entrance are possible, with rolling admissions and continuous processing to 3/1 for financial aid. **Contact:**, High School and College Relations, 104 Whitehurst Hall, Stillwater, OK 74078, 405-744-5358 or toll-free 800-233-5019 (in-state), 800-852-1255 (out-of-state); fax 405-744-5285.

### GETTING IN LAST YEAR
4,003 applied
96% were accepted
57% enrolled (2,177)
29% from top tenth of their h.s. class
3.42 average high school GPA
31% had ACT scores over 26
9% had ACT scores over 30
23 National Merit Scholars
250 valedictorians

### THE STUDENT BODY
Total 18,561, of whom 14,281
are undergraduates
From 50 states and territories,
100 other countries

84% from Oklahoma
46% women, 54% men
2% African Americans
7% Native Americans
2% Hispanics
2% Asian Americans
7% international students

### AFTER FRESHMAN YEAR
76% returned for sophomore year
16% got a degree within 4 years
38% got a degree within 5 years
47% got a degree within 6 years

### AFTER GRADUATION
65% had job offers within 3 months
265 corporations, 5 government agencies, 10
nonprofit organizations recruited on campus

### WHAT YOU WILL PAY
Resident tuition and fees $1843
Nonresident tuition and fees $5083
Room and board $3344
43% receive need-based financial aid
averaging $980
17% receive non-need financial aid averaging
$1315

# PACIFIC LUTHERAN UNIVERSITY

Tacoma, Washington • Suburban setting • Private • Independent-Religious • Coed

When Russia's international airline, Aeroflot, wanted to learn Western accounting systems, it sent 80 of its executives to Pacific Lutheran; when Israel needed a world authority on the Holocaust, a PLU history professor was chosen; when Chinese officials needed to know how to deal with social changes brought about by free enterprise, a PLU anthropology professor was consulted; and when Russia's universities wanted an economics text on market economics, they chose a text by a PLU economics professor. These and many other top-flight scholars teach undergraduates at PLU because teaching is their first love.

##  Academics

PLU offers a liberal arts curriculum and core academic program; fewer than half of graduate courses are open to undergraduates. It awards bachelor's and master's **degrees**. Challenging opportunities include advanced placement, accelerated degree programs, self-designed majors, tutorials, Freshmen Honors College, an honors program, and a senior project. Special programs include cooperative education, internships, summer session for credit, study abroad, and Army ROTC.

The most popular **majors** include business, education, and nursing. A complete listing of majors at PLU appears in the Majors Index beginning on page 380.

The **faculty** at PLU has 230 full-time graduate and undergraduate teachers, 85% with terminal degrees. 95% of the faculty serve as student advisers. The student-faculty ratio is 16:1.

##  Computers on Campus

Students are not required to have a computer. 200 **computers** available in the computer center, computer labs, science building, classrooms, the library, and dormitories provide access to the main academic computer, off-campus computing facilities, e-mail, and on-line services. Staffed computer lab on campus provides training in the use of computers and software.

The **library** has 320,382 books and 1,989 subscriptions. It is connected to 3 national **on-line** catalogs.

##  Campus Life

There are 55 active **organizations** on campus, including a drama/theater group and student-run newspaper and radio station. 20% of students participate in student government elections. Student **safety services** include late night transport/escort service, 24-hour emergency telephone alarm devices, 24-hour patrols by trained security personnel, and student patrols.

PLU is a member of the NAIA. **Intercollegiate sports** (some offering scholarships) include baseball (m), basketball (m, w), crew (m, w), cross-country running (m, w), football (m), golf (m, w), lacrosse (m, w), skiing (cross-country) (m, w), skiing (downhill) (m, w), soccer (m, w), softball (w), swimming and diving (m, w), tennis (m, w), track and field (m, w), volleyball (m, w), wrestling (m).

##  Applying

PLU requires an essay, a high school transcript, 2 years of high school foreign language, 2 recommendations, SAT I or ACT, and in some cases an interview. It recommends 3 years of high school math and science. Early, deferred, and midyear entrance are possible, with rolling admissions and continuous processing to 3/1 for financial aid. **Contact:** Mr. David Hawsey, Dean of Admissions and Enrollment Management, Administration Building, Room 115, Tacoma, WA 98447, 206-535-7151 or toll-free 800-274-6758.

### GETTING IN LAST YEAR
1,749 applied
83% were accepted
39% enrolled (566)
34% from top tenth of their h.s. class
3.51 average high school GPA
7% had SAT verbal scores over 600
26% had SAT math scores over 600
0% had SAT verbal scores over 700
3% had SAT math scores over 700
3 National Merit Scholars

### THE STUDENT BODY
Total 3,257, of whom 2,955
  are undergraduates
From 39 states and territories,
  23 other countries
69% from Washington
61% women, 39% men
2% African Americans
1% Native Americans
2% Hispanics
5% Asian Americans
4% international students

### AFTER FRESHMAN YEAR
79% returned for sophomore year
39% got a degree within 4 years
60% got a degree within 5 years
61% got a degree within 6 years

### AFTER GRADUATION
40 corporations, 10 government agencies, 10
  nonprofit organizations recruited on campus
2 Fulbright scholars

### WHAT YOU WILL PAY
Tuition and fees $13,312
Room and board $4488
69% receive need-based financial aid
  averaging $4214
13% receive non-need financial aid averaging
  $2785

# PENNSYLVANIA STATE UNIVERSITY
# UNIVERSITY PARK CAMPUS

State College, Pennsylvania • Small-town setting • Public • State-related • Coed

Recognized nationally as one of the finest public universities, Penn State offers its students a broad curriculum filled with opportunity and challenge. Foremost amongst those challenges is the University Scholars Program, a University-wide honors program. University Scholars enroll in small honors classes and seminars, work closely with honors advisers, conduct independent study and research projects, and complete honors theses and receive honors degrees. Computer accounts, registration priority, and extended library privileges support honors study. Students are encouraged to take advantage of the extensive study-abroad, externship, and internship programs.

 **Academics**

Penn State offers a core academic program. It awards associate, bachelor's, master's, and doctoral **degrees**. Challenging opportunities include advanced placement, self-designed majors, Freshmen Honors College, an honors program, a senior project, Phi Beta Kappa, and Sigma Xi. Special programs include cooperative education, internships, summer session for credit, study abroad, and Army, Naval, and Air Force ROTC.

The most popular **majors** include engineering (general), science, and business. A complete listing of majors at Penn State appears in the Majors Index beginning on page 380.

The **faculty** at Penn State has 1,868 full-time graduate and undergraduate teachers, 90% with terminal degrees. The student-faculty ratio is 18:1.

 **Computers on Campus**

Students are not required to have a computer. Student rooms are linked to a campus network. 2,817 **computers** available across campus and in dormitories provide access to the main academic computer, off-campus computing facilities, e-mail, and on-line services. Staffed computer lab on campus (open 24 hours a day) provides training in the use of computers and software.

The 8 **libraries** have 2.5 million books and 27,634 subscriptions.

 **Campus Life**

There are 400 active **organizations** on campus, including a drama/theater group and student-run newspaper and radio station. 20% of students participate in student government elections. 14% of eligible men and 17% of eligible women are members of 55 national **fraternities** and 25 national **sororities**. Student **safety services** include late night transport/escort service, 24-hour emergency telephone alarm devices, 24-hour patrols by trained security personnel, student patrols, and electronically operated dormitory entrances.

Penn State is a member of the NCAA (Division I). **Intercollegiate sports** (some offering scholarships) include baseball (m), basketball (m, w), cross-country running (m, w), equestrian sports (m, w), fencing (m, w), field hockey (w), football (m), golf (m, w), gymnastics (m, w), ice hockey (m), lacrosse (m, w), rugby (m, w), skiing (downhill) (m, w), soccer (m, w), softball (w), swimming and diving (m, w), table tennis (m), tennis (m, w), track and field (m, w), volleyball (m, w), water polo (m, w), weight lifting (m), wrestling (m).

 **Applying**

Penn State requires a high school transcript, 3 years of high school math and science, SAT I or ACT, and in some cases some high school foreign language. Midyear entrance is possible, with rolling admissions and continuous processing to 2/15 for financial aid. **Contact:** Dr. John J. Romano, Vice Provost for Enrollment Management and Administration, 201 Shields Building, University Park, PA 16802-1503, 814-865-5471.

---

**GETTING IN LAST YEAR**
19,527 applied
54% were accepted
35% enrolled (3,687)
45% from top tenth of their h.s. class
3.44 average high school GPA
15% had SAT verbal scores over 600
50% had SAT math scores over 600
2% had SAT verbal scores over 700
12% had SAT math scores over 700

**THE STUDENT BODY**
Total 38,294, of whom 31,496
   are undergraduates

From 52 states and territories
82% from Pennsylvania
44% women, 56% men
3% African Americans
1% Native Americans
2% Hispanics
5% Asian Americans
1% international students

**AFTER FRESHMAN YEAR**
93% returned for sophomore year

**AFTER GRADUATION**
66% had job offers within 3 months
712 corporations, 30 government agencies,
   11 nonprofit organizations recruited on
   campus
15 Fulbright scholars

**WHAT YOU WILL PAY**
Resident tuition and fees $5036
Nonresident tuition and fees $10,724
Room and board $3920

# PEPPERDINE UNIVERSITY

Malibu, California • Small-town setting • Private • Independent-Religious • Coed

## Academics

Pepperdine offers an interdisciplinary curriculum and core academic program. It awards bachelor's, master's, doctoral, and first professional **degrees**. The University is organized into four colleges: Seaver, the School of Law, the School of Business and Management, and the Graduate School of Education and Psychology. Seaver College is the undergraduate, residential, liberal arts school of the University and is committed to providing education of outstanding academic quality with particular attention to Christian values. Challenging opportunities include advanced placement, accelerated degree programs, self-designed majors, tutorials, an honors program, and a senior project. Special programs include internships, summer session for credit, study abroad, and Army, Naval, and Air Force ROTC.

The most popular **majors** include business, communication, and international studies. A complete listing of majors at Pepperdine appears in the Majors Index beginning on page 380.

The **faculty** at Pepperdine has 153 full-time undergraduate teachers, 99% with terminal degrees. 100% of the faculty serve as student advisers. The student-faculty ratio is 13:1, and the average class size in required courses is 17.

## Computers on Campus

Students are not required to have a computer. 292 **computers** available in the computer center, electronic classrooms, the library, the student center, and dormitories.

The 2 **libraries** have 422,277 books, 115,378 microform titles, and 3,083 subscriptions. They are connected to 3 national **on-line** catalogs.

## Campus Life

Active **organizations** on campus include drama/theater group and student-run newspaper and radio station. 25% of eligible men and 30% of eligible women are members of 6 local **fraternities** and 7 local **sororities**. Student **safety services** include late night transport/escort service and student patrols.

Pepperdine is a member of the NCAA (Division I). **Intercollegiate sports** (some offering scholarships) include baseball (m), basketball (m, w), cross-country running (m, w), golf (m, w), ice hockey (m), lacrosse (m), rugby (m), soccer (m, w), swimming and diving (w), tennis (m, w), volleyball (m, w), water polo (m).

## Applying

Pepperdine requires an essay, a high school transcript, 3 years of high school math, 2 recommendations, and SAT I or ACT. It recommends 3 years of high school science, 2 years of high school foreign language, an interview, and SAT II Subject Tests. Early and midyear entrance are possible, with a 2/1 deadline and continuous processing to 2/15 for financial aid. **Contact:** Mr. Paul Long, Dean of Admission, 24255 Pacific Coast Highway, Malibu, CA 90263-0001, 310-456-4392; fax 310-456-4861.

---

### GETTING IN LAST YEAR
3,390 applied
71% were accepted
26% enrolled (631)
85% from top tenth of their h.s. class
3.41 average high school GPA
13% had SAT verbal scores over 600
38% had SAT math scores over 600
40% had ACT scores over 26
1% had SAT verbal scores over 700
6% had SAT math scores over 700
9% had ACT scores over 30
3 National Merit Scholars

### THE STUDENT BODY
Total 7,264, of whom 2,661
  are undergraduates
From 51 states and territories,
  56 other countries
55% from California
57% women, 43% men
3% African Americans
1% Native Americans
7% Hispanics
6% Asian Americans
8% international students

### AFTER FRESHMAN YEAR
90% returned for sophomore year
67% got a degree within 4 years

### AFTER GRADUATION
52% pursued further study (21% business,
  18% arts and sciences, 8% law)
60 corporations, 5 government agencies, 7
  nonprofit organizations recruited on campus

### WHAT YOU WILL PAY
Tuition and fees $18,270
Room and board $6770
53% receive need-based financial aid
  averaging $7799
46% receive non-need financial aid averaging
  $3900

# PITZER COLLEGE

Claremont, California • Small-town setting • Private • Independent • Coed

A liberal arts college of 750 students, Pitzer offers close, personal attention within the university environment of The Claremont Colleges (which include Pomona, Scripps, Claremont McKenna, and Harvey Mudd colleges). Students may enroll at classes offered by any of the campuses and enjoy such shared resources as a major library, the $16.5-million Keck Science Center, theaters, recreational and competitive sports, and social activities. Pitzer's interdisciplinary and multicultural curriculum emphasizes self-direction and independent thought and provides a large number of community-service internship opportunities. Pitzer's award-winning study-abroad program provides intensive language and culture immersion in countries from Australia to Zimbabwe.

 ## Academics

Pitzer offers an interdisciplinary curriculum and core academic program. It awards bachelor's **degrees**. Challenging opportunities include advanced placement, self-designed majors, an honors program, a senior project, and Sigma Xi. Special programs include cooperative education, internships, off-campus study, and study abroad.

The most popular **majors** include psychology and English. A complete listing of majors at Pitzer appears in the Majors Index beginning on page 380.

The **faculty** at Pitzer has 60 full-time teachers, 99% with terminal degrees. 100% of the faculty serve as student advisers. The student-faculty ratio is 10:1.

 ## Computers on Campus

Students are not required to have a computer. 45 **computers** available in the computer center, computer labs, and the library. Staffed computer lab on campus provides training in the use of computers and software.

The **library** has 1.9 million books, 1 million microform titles, and 10,900 subscriptions. It is connected to 4 national **on-line** catalogs.

 ## Campus Life

Active **organizations** on campus include drama/theater group and student-run newspaper and radio station. 50% of students participate in student government elections. Student **safety services** include late night transport/escort service, 24-hour emergency telephone alarm devices, 24-hour patrols by trained security personnel, and electronically operated dormitory entrances.

Pitzer is a member of the NCAA (Division III). **Intercollegiate sports** include badminton (m, w), baseball (m), basketball (m, w), cross-country running (m, w), fencing (m, w), football (m), golf (m), soccer (m, w), softball (w), swimming and diving (m, w), tennis (m, w), track and field (m, w), volleyball (w), water polo (m), wrestling (m).

 ## Applying

Pitzer requires an essay, a high school transcript, 2 recommendations, and SAT I or ACT. It recommends 3 years of high school math and science, 2 years of high school foreign language, an interview, and 3 SAT II Subject Tests. Early, deferred, and midyear entrance are possible, with a 2/1 deadline and 2/1 for financial aid. **Contact:** Dr. Paul B. Ranslow, Dean of Admission and College Relations, 1050 North Mills Avenue, Claremont, CA 91711-6110, 909-621-8129.

---

### GETTING IN LAST YEAR

1,159 applied
60% were accepted
26% enrolled (180)
40% from top tenth of their h.s. class
3.4 average high school GPA
31% had SAT verbal scores over 600
29% had SAT math scores over 600
52% had ACT scores over 26
9% had SAT verbal scores over 700
8% had SAT math scores over 700
13% had ACT scores over 30

### THE STUDENT BODY

750 undergraduates
From 42 states and territories,
    26 other countries
42% from California
58% women, 42% men
7% African Americans
1% Native Americans
16% Hispanics
17% Asian Americans
10% international students

### AFTER FRESHMAN YEAR

90% returned for sophomore year
74% got a degree within 4 years
80% got a degree within 5 years

### AFTER GRADUATION

39% pursued further study (17% arts and
    sciences, 7% law, 6% business)
38% had job offers within 3 months
54 corporations, 20 government agencies, 55
    nonprofit organizations recruited on campus
2 Fulbright scholars

### WHAT YOU WILL PAY

Tuition and fees $19,132
Room and board $5900
38% receive need-based financial aid
    averaging $9500

---

# POLYTECHNIC UNIVERSITY, BROOKLYN CAMPUS

Brooklyn, New York • Urban setting • Private • Independent • Coed

 **Academics**

Polytechnic offers a core academic program; fewer than half of graduate courses are open to undergraduates. It awards bachelor's, master's, and doctoral **degrees**. Challenging opportunities include advanced placement, accelerated degree programs, tutorials, an honors program, a senior project, and Sigma Xi. Special programs include cooperative education, summer session for credit, and Army and Air Force ROTC.

The most popular **majors** include electrical engineering and mechanical engineering. A complete listing of majors at Polytechnic appears in the Majors Index beginning on page 380.

The **faculty** at Polytechnic has 168 full-time graduate and undergraduate teachers, 99% with terminal degrees. 10% of the faculty serve as student advisers. The student-faculty ratio is 15:1, and the average class size in required courses is 25.

 **Computers on Campus**

Students are not required to have a computer. Student rooms are linked to a campus network. 160 **computers** available in the computer center, computer labs, the research center, and the library provide access to the main academic computer, e-mail, and on-line services. Staffed computer lab on campus provides training in the use of computers and software.

The **library** has 192,738 books, 375 microform titles, and 1,762 subscriptions.

 **Campus Life**

There are 47 active **organizations** on campus, including a student-run newspaper. 50% of students participate in student government elections. 6% of eligible men are members of 3 national **fraternities**. Student **safety services** include 24-hour patrols by trained security personnel.

Polytechnic is a member of the NCAA (Division III). **Intercollegiate sports** include baseball (m), basketball (m), cross-country running (m, w), lacrosse (m), soccer (m), tennis (m, w), volleyball (w), wrestling (m).

 **Applying**

Polytechnic requires an essay, a high school transcript, 3 years of high school math and science, recommendations, and SAT I or ACT. It recommends some high school foreign language, an interview, and SAT II Subject Tests. Early, deferred, and midyear entrance are possible, with rolling admissions and continuous processing to 3/1 for financial aid. **Contact:** Mr. Peter Grant Jordan, Dean of Admissions, 6 Metrotech Center, Brooklyn, NY 11201-2990, 718-260-3100 or toll-free 800-POLYTECH; fax 718-260-3136.

---

**GETTING IN LAST YEAR**

800 applied
74% were accepted
34% enrolled (201)
67% from top tenth of their h.s. class
3.7 average high school GPA
11% had SAT verbal scores over 600
59% had SAT math scores over 600
3% had SAT verbal scores over 700
21% had SAT math scores over 700

**THE STUDENT BODY**

Total 2,187, of whom 1,122
  are undergraduates
From 23 states and territories,
  26 other countries
90% from New York
14% women, 86% men
11% African Americans
0% Native Americans
9% Hispanics
35% Asian Americans
7% international students

**AFTER FRESHMAN YEAR**

80% returned for sophomore year
29% got a degree within 4 years
47% got a degree within 5 years
50% got a degree within 6 years

**AFTER GRADUATION**

4% pursued further study
88% had job offers within 3 months
45 corporations, 5 government agencies
  recruited on campus
1 Fulbright scholar

**WHAT YOU WILL PAY**

Tuition and fees $16,450
Room and board $3610
Need-based financial aid averages $5405

# POLYTECHNIC UNIVERSITY, FARMINGDALE CAMPUS

Farmingdale, New York • Suburban setting • Private • Independent • Coed

## Academics

Polytech offers a core academic program; fewer than half of graduate courses are open to undergraduates. It awards bachelor's and master's **degrees**. Challenging opportunities include advanced placement, tutorials, an honors program, and a senior project. Special programs include cooperative education, summer session for credit, off-campus study, and Army and Air Force ROTC.

The most popular **majors** include electrical engineering, mechanical engineering, and aerospace engineering. A complete listing of majors at Polytech appears in the Majors Index beginning on page 380.

The **faculty** at Polytech has 168 full-time graduate and undergraduate teachers, 99% with terminal degrees. 10% of the faculty serve as student advisers. The student-faculty ratio is 15:1, and the average class size in required courses is 20.

## Computers on Campus

Students are not required to have a computer. Student rooms are linked to a campus network. 86 **computers** available in the computer center, computer labs, the research center, and the library provide access to the main academic computer, e-mail, and on-line services. Staffed computer lab on campus provides training in the use of computers and software.

The **library** has 192,738 books, 375 microform titles, and 1,762 subscriptions. It is connected to 1 national **on-line** catalog.

## Campus Life

There are 24 active **organizations** on campus, including a drama/theater group and student-run newspaper. 70% of students participate in student government elections. 15% of eligible men and 15% of eligible women are members of 1 national **fraternity**, 1 local fraternity, and 1 coed fraternity. Student **safety services** include 24-hour patrols by trained security personnel and electronically operated dormitory entrances.

Polytech is a member of the NCAA (Division III). **Intercollegiate sports** include baseball (m), basketball (m), cross-country running (m, w), lacrosse (m), soccer (m), tennis (m, w), volleyball (w), wrestling (m).

## Applying

Polytech requires an essay, a high school transcript, 3 years of high school math and science, recommendations, and SAT I or ACT. It recommends some high school foreign language, an interview, and SAT II Subject Tests. Early, deferred, and midyear entrance are possible, with rolling admissions and continuous processing to 3/1 for financial aid. **Contact:** Mr. Peter Grant Jordan, Dean of Admissions, Long Island Center, Main Building, Farmingdale, NY 11735-3995, 516-755-4200 or toll-free 800-POLYTECH; fax 516-755-4404.

---

### GETTING IN LAST YEAR
411 applied
77% were accepted
29% enrolled (93)
60% from top tenth of their h.s. class
3.6 average high school GPA
15% had SAT verbal scores over 600
65% had SAT math scores over 600
3% had SAT verbal scores over 700
12% had SAT math scores over 700

### THE STUDENT BODY
Total 655, of whom 358
  are undergraduates
From 8 states and territories,
  7 other countries
91% from New York
13% women, 87% men
4% African Americans

0% Native Americans
8% Hispanics
17% Asian Americans
2% international students

### AFTER FRESHMAN YEAR
80% returned for sophomore year
29% got a degree within 4 years
47% got a degree within 5 years
50% got a degree within 6 years

### AFTER GRADUATION
4% pursued further study
88% had job offers within 3 months
54 corporations, 5 government agencies
  recruited on campus

### WHAT YOU WILL PAY
Tuition and fees $16,450
Room and board $4280
Need-based financial aid averages $4936
Non-need financial aid averages $6587

# POMONA COLLEGE

Claremont, California • Suburban setting • Private • Independent • Coed

Pomona College is located in Claremont, California, 35 miles east of Los Angeles, and is the founding member of the Claremont Colleges. Recognized as one of the nation's premier liberal arts colleges, Pomona offers a comprehensive undergraduate curriculum and enrolls students from around the nation and across class and ethnicity. With financial resources among the strongest of any national liberal arts college, Pomona offers a broad range of physical and intellectual resources and opportunities, including an extensive study-abroad program. The community enjoys academic, cultural, and extracurricular activities usually found only at large universities, with all the benefits and advantages of a small college.

 ## Academics

Pomona offers a perception, analysis, and communication skills curriculum and core academic program. It awards bachelor's **degrees**. Challenging opportunities include advanced placement, self-designed majors, a senior project, Phi Beta Kappa, and Sigma Xi. Special programs include internships, off-campus study, and study abroad.

The most popular **majors** include biology/biological sciences, political science/government, and psychology. A complete listing of majors at Pomona appears in the Majors Index beginning on page 380.

The **faculty** at Pomona has 158 full-time teachers, 100% with terminal degrees. 100% of the faculty serve as student advisers. The student-faculty ratio is 9:1, and the average class size in required courses is 14.

 ## Computers on Campus

Students are not required to have a computer. Student rooms are linked to a campus network. 180 **computers** available in the computer center, computer labs, classroom buildings, classrooms, the library, the student center, and dormitories provide access to the main academic computer, off-campus computing facilities, and e-mail. Staffed computer lab on campus provides training in the use of computers and software.

The 4 **libraries** have 1.8 million books, 1 million microform titles, and 6,830 subscriptions. They are connected to 4 national **on-line** catalogs.

 ## Campus Life

There are 280 active **organizations** on campus, including a drama/theater group and student-run newspaper and radio station. 88% of students participate in student government elections. 8% of eligible men and 2% of eligible women are members of 3 local **fraternities** and 4 local coed fraternities. Student **safety services** include late night transport/escort service, 24-hour emergency telephone alarm devices, 24-hour patrols by trained security personnel, and electronically operated dormitory entrances.

Pomona is a member of the NCAA (Division III). **Intercollegiate sports** include baseball (m), basketball (m, w), cross-country running (m, w), football (m), golf (m), soccer (m, w), softball (w), swimming and diving (m, w), tennis (m, w), track and field (m, w), volleyball (w), water polo (m).

 ## Applying

Pomona requires an essay, a high school transcript, 3 years of high school math, 2 recommendations, SAT I or ACT, and a minimum high school GPA of 2.0. It recommends 3 years of high school science, 3 years of high school foreign language, an interview, portfolio or tapes for art and performing arts programs, and 3 SAT II Subject Tests. Early and deferred entrance are possible, with a 1/15 deadline and 2/11 for financial aid. **Contact:** Mr. Bruce Poch, Dean of Admissions, 333 North College Way, Claremont, CA 91711-6301, 909-621-8134; fax 909-621-8403.

## GETTING IN LAST YEAR
3,293 applied
32% were accepted
36% enrolled (379)
80% from top tenth of their h.s. class
77% had SAT verbal scores over 600
94% had SAT math scores over 600
92% had ACT scores over 26
18% had SAT verbal scores over 700
55% had SAT math scores over 700
58% had ACT scores over 30
30 National Merit Scholars
17 class presidents
45 valedictorians

## THE STUDENT BODY
1,382 undergraduates
From 46 states and territories,
  21 other countries
44% from California
48% women, 52% men
5% African Americans
1% Native Americans
12% Hispanics
21% Asian Americans
4% international students

## AFTER FRESHMAN YEAR
99% returned for sophomore year
88% got a degree within 4 years

89% got a degree within 5 years
90% got a degree within 6 years

## AFTER GRADUATION
35% pursued further study (20% arts and
  sciences, 6% law, 6% medicine)
93 corporations, 9 government agencies, 10
  nonprofit organizations recruited on campus
2 Fulbright scholars

## WHAT YOU WILL PAY
Tuition and fees $17,900
Room and board $7220
54% receive need-based financial aid
  averaging $13,700

# PRESBYTERIAN COLLEGE

Clinton, South Carolina • Small-town setting • Private • Independent-Religious • Coed

Presbyterian—with 33 national and international scholarship recipients in recent years, including a Rhodes scholar—provides an environment that nurtures the best and brightest. Students respect and live by a strong Honor Code and well over half volunteer for community service. Students also may study with PC's Service Learning Program or participate with the study-abroad programs available around the world. Six new buildings have been constructed recently, and a $5-million Mathematics and Social Science Center will open in 1995. A scholarship program for outstanding students is supported by one of the largest endowments per student in the region.

## Academics

Presbyterian College offers a vocational preparation within a strong liberal arts curriculum and core academic program. It awards bachelor's **degrees**. Challenging opportunities include advanced placement, accelerated degree programs, tutorials, Freshmen Honors College, an honors program, and a senior project. Special programs include internships, summer session for credit, off-campus study, study abroad, and Army ROTC.

The most popular **majors** include business, education, and biology/biological sciences. A complete listing of majors at Presbyterian College appears in the Majors Index beginning on page 380.

The **faculty** at Presbyterian College has 75 full-time teachers, 90% with terminal degrees. 99% of the faculty serve as student advisers. The student-faculty ratio is 15:1, and the average class size in required courses is 15.

## Computers on Campus

Students are not required to have a computer. 100 **computers** available in the computer center, computer labs,

academic buildings, classrooms, and the library provide access to the main academic computer, e-mail, and on-line services. Staffed computer lab on campus provides training in the use of computers and software.

The **library** has 143,000 books, 4,627 microform titles, and 810 subscriptions. It is connected to 3 national **on-line** catalogs.

## Campus Life

There are 90 active **organizations** on campus, including a drama/theater group and student-run newspaper and radio station. 44% of eligible men and 41% of eligible women are members of 6 national **fraternities**, 3 national **sororities**, and Women's Social Hall, Minority Social Club. Student **safety services** include late night transport/escort service, 24-hour emergency telephone alarm devices, 24-hour patrols by trained security personnel, and electronically operated dormitory entrances.

Presbyterian College is a member of the NCAA (Division II). **Intercollegiate sports** (some offering scholarships) include baseball (m), basketball (m, w), football (m), golf (m, w), riflery (m, w), soccer (m, w), tennis (m, w), track and field (m), volleyball (w).

## Applying

Presbyterian College requires an essay, a high school transcript, 3 years of high school math, 2 years of high school foreign language, 1 recommendation, SAT I or ACT, and a minimum high school GPA of 2.0. It recommends 3 years of high school science and an interview. Early, deferred, and midyear entrance are possible, with a 4/1 deadline and continuous processing to 3/1 for financial aid. **Contact:** Mr. Eddie G. Rogers, Associate Director of Admissions, South Broad Street, Clinton, SC 29325, 803-833-8228 or toll-free 800-476-7272; fax 803-833-8481.

### GETTING IN LAST YEAR
1,215 applied
78% were accepted
30% enrolled (281)
34% from top tenth of their h.s. class
3.2 average high school GPA
11% had SAT verbal scores over 600
29% had SAT math scores over 600
38% had ACT scores over 26
3% had SAT verbal scores over 700
3% had SAT math scores over 700
3% had ACT scores over 30
3 National Merit Scholars
14 class presidents
8 valedictorians

### THE STUDENT BODY
1,122 undergraduates
From 28 states and territories,
 9 other countries
46% from South Carolina
40% women, 60% men
5% African Americans
0% Native Americans
1% Hispanics
1% Asian Americans
1% international students

### AFTER FRESHMAN YEAR
93% returned for sophomore year
78% got a degree within 4 years
82% got a degree within 5 years
83% got a degree within 6 years

### AFTER GRADUATION
25% pursued further study (12% arts and
 sciences, 6% medicine, 3% business)
57% had job offers within 3 months
41 corporations, 1 government agency
 recruited on campus

### WHAT YOU WILL PAY
Tuition and fees $12,751
Room and board $3635
39% receive need-based financial aid
 averaging $3546
78% receive non-need financial aid averaging
 $2937

# PRINCETON UNIVERSITY

Princeton, New Jersey • Suburban setting • Private • Independent • Coed

 **Academics**

Princeton offers a core academic program. It awards bachelor's, master's, and doctoral **degrees**. Challenging opportunities include advanced placement, accelerated degree programs, self-designed majors, an honors program, Phi Beta Kappa, and Sigma Xi. Special programs include internships, off-campus study, and Army and Air Force ROTC.

The most popular **majors** include history, political science/government, and English. A complete listing of majors at Princeton appears in the Majors Index beginning on page 380.

The **faculty** at Princeton has 716 full-time undergraduate teachers, 99% with terminal degrees. The student-faculty ratio is 5:1.

 **Computers on Campus**

Students are not required to have a computer. 438 **computers** available in the computer center, computer labs, the research center, academic departments, classrooms, the library, and dormitories.

The 23 **libraries** have 5 million books, 3 million microform titles, and 30,000 subscriptions.

 **Campus Life**

Active **organizations** on campus include drama/theater group and student-run newspaper and radio station. 70%

of eligible men and 70% of eligible women are members of 11 eating clubs. Student **safety services** include late night transport/escort service, 24-hour emergency telephone alarm devices, 24-hour patrols by trained security personnel, and electronically operated dormitory entrances.

Princeton is a member of the NCAA (Division I) and NAIA. **Intercollegiate sports** include baseball (m), basketball (m, w), crew (m, w), cross-country running (m, w), fencing (m, w), field hockey (w), football (m), golf (m, w), ice hockey (m, w), lacrosse (m, w), soccer (m, w), softball (w), squash (m, w), swimming and diving (m, w), table tennis (m, w), tennis (m, w), track and field (m, w), volleyball (m, w), water polo (m, w), wrestling (m).

 **Applying**

Princeton requires an essay, a high school transcript, recommendations, SAT I, and in some cases SAT II Subject Tests. It recommends 4 years of high school math, 3 years of high school science, 4 years of high school foreign language, an interview, and 3 SAT II Subject Tests. Early and deferred entrance are possible, with a 1/2 deadline and 2/1 for financial aid. **Contact:** Mr. Fred A. Hargadon, Dean of Admission, West College, Princeton, NJ 08544-1019, 609-258-3060.

---

### GETTING IN LAST YEAR
14,363 applied
14% were accepted
57% enrolled (1,158)
90% from top tenth of their h.s. class
79% had SAT verbal scores over 600
94% had SAT math scores over 600
27% had SAT verbal scores over 700
63% had SAT math scores over 700

### THE STUDENT BODY
Total 6,444, of whom 4,538
    are undergraduates
From 52 states and territories,
    70 other countries
14% from New Jersey
43% women, 57% men
6% African Americans
1% Native Americans
6% Hispanics
10% Asian Americans
6% international students

### AFTER FRESHMAN YEAR
98% returned for sophomore year
87% got a degree within 4 years
94% got a degree within 5 years
95% got a degree within 6 years

### WHAT YOU WILL PAY
Tuition and fees $20,960
Room and board $6116
42% receive need-based financial aid
    averaging $11,416

---

# PROVIDENCE COLLEGE

Providence, Rhode Island • Urban setting • Private • Independent-Religious • Coed

Infused with the history, tradition, and learning of a 700-year-old Catholic teaching order, the Dominican Friars, Providence College offers a value-affirming environment where students are enriched through spiritual, social, physical, and cultural growth as well as through intellectual development. The faculty is noted for a strong commitment to teaching. A close student-faculty relationship allows for in-depth classwork, independent research projects, and detailed career exploration. While noted for the physical facilities and academic opportunities associated with larger universities, Providence also fosters personal growth through a spirited family-like atmosphere that encourages involvement in student activities and athletics.

##  Academics

Providence College offers a liberal arts curriculum and core academic program; all graduate courses are open to undergraduates. It awards associate, bachelor's, master's, and doctoral **degrees**. Challenging opportunities include advanced placement, self-designed majors, tutorials, an honors program, and a senior project. Special programs include internships, summer session for credit, study abroad, and Army ROTC.

The most popular **majors** include business, education, and English. A complete listing of majors at Providence College appears in the Majors Index beginning on page 380.

The **faculty** at Providence College has 260 full-time graduate and undergraduate teachers, 86% with terminal degrees. 98% of the faculty serve as student advisers. The student-faculty ratio is 14:1, and the average class size in required courses is 30.

##  Computers on Campus

Students are not required to have a computer. Student rooms are linked to a campus network. 144 **computers** available in the computer center and classrooms. Staffed computer lab on campus provides training in the use of computers and software.

The **library** has 307,655 books, 25,709 microform titles, and 1,894 subscriptions.

##  Campus Life

There are 64 active **organizations** on campus, including a drama/theater group and student-run newspaper and radio station. Student **safety services** include late night transport/escort service, 24-hour emergency telephone alarm devices, 24-hour patrols by trained security personnel, student patrols, and electronically operated dormitory entrances.

Providence College is a member of the NCAA (Division I). **Intercollegiate sports** (some offering scholarships) include baseball (m), basketball (m, w), cross-country running (m, w), field hockey (w), golf (m), ice hockey (m, w), lacrosse (m), racquetball (m, w), rugby (m, w), soccer (m, w), softball (w), swimming and diving (m, w), tennis (m, w), track and field (m, w), volleyball (w).

##  Applying

Providence College requires an essay, a high school transcript, SAT I or ACT, and in some cases 3 years of high school science. It recommends 3 years of high school math, 3 years of high school foreign language, recommendations, a campus interview, 3 SAT II Subject Tests, and a minimum high school GPA of 3.0. Early, deferred, and midyear entrance are possible, with a 2/1 deadline and a 2/15 priority date for financial aid. **Contact:** Mr. William DiBrienza, Dean of Admissions and Financial Aid, Eaton Street and River Avenue, Providence, RI 02918, 401-865-2535 or toll-free 800-721-6444 (in-state); fax 401-865-2826.

### GETTING IN LAST YEAR
4,820 applied
66% were accepted
27% enrolled (863)
21% from top tenth of their h.s. class
5% had SAT verbal scores over 600
25% had SAT math scores over 600
38% had ACT scores over 26
0% had SAT verbal scores over 700
3% had SAT math scores over 700
2% had ACT scores over 30
24 class presidents
18 valedictorians

### THE STUDENT BODY
Total 5,842, of whom 3,561
    are undergraduates
From 40 states and territories,
    14 other countries
14% from Rhode Island
55% women, 45% men
4% African Americans
0% Native Americans
3% Hispanics
2% Asian Americans
1% international students

### AFTER FRESHMAN YEAR
95% returned for sophomore year
11% got a degree within 4 years
92% got a degree within 5 years

### AFTER GRADUATION
32% pursued further study (12% arts and
    sciences, 8% law, 7% business)
80 corporations, 12 government agencies, 8
    nonprofit organizations recruited on campus

### WHAT YOU WILL PAY
Tuition and fees $14,525
Room and board $6200
64% receive need-based financial aid
    averaging $7250
4% receive non-need financial aid averaging
    $13,500

# PURDUE UNIVERSITY

West Lafayette, Indiana • Suburban setting • Public • State-supported • Coed

Located in the heart of the Midwest, Purdue University is a land-grant institution founded in 1869. Beginning with academic areas in agriculture and mechanics arts, Purdue now offers more than 200 programs that range from pharmacy and restaurant/hotel management to engineering and linguistics. Purdue students come from all 50 states and more than 70 countries. They bring to campus a diversity of backgrounds and ideas that complement their academic preparation. With its international reputation for academic excellence, highly regarded faculty, and competitive student body, Purdue offers more than just a college degree: it offers an educational experience for now and for the future.

##  Academics

Purdue offers no core academic program; fewer than half of graduate courses are open to undergraduates. It awards associate, bachelor's, master's, and doctoral **degrees**. Challenging opportunities include advanced placement, accelerated degree programs, self-designed majors, an honors program, a senior project, Phi Beta Kappa, and Sigma Xi. Special programs include cooperative education, internships, summer session for credit, study abroad, and Army, Naval, and Air Force ROTC.

The most popular **majors** include communication, electrical engineering, and mechanical engineering. A complete listing of majors at Purdue appears in the Majors Index beginning on page 380.

The **faculty** at Purdue has 2,103 full-time graduate and undergraduate teachers, 99% with terminal degrees. The student-faculty ratio is 17:1, and the average class size in required courses is 30.

##  Computers on Campus

Students are not required to have a computer. Student rooms are linked to a campus network. 2,000 **computers**
available in the computer center, computer labs, individual schools, the student center, and dormitories provide access to the main academic computer, e-mail, and on-line services. Staffed computer lab on campus.

The 16 **libraries** have 2.1 million books, 2.1 million microform titles, and 14,331 subscriptions.

##  Campus Life

There are 564 active **organizations** on campus, including a drama/theater group and student-run newspaper and radio station. 6% of students participate in student government elections. 20% of eligible men and 18% of eligible women are members of 46 national **fraternities**, 23 national **sororities**, and 1 local sorority. Student **safety services** include late night transport/escort service, 24-hour emergency telephone alarm devices, and student patrols.

Purdue is a member of the NCAA (Division I). **intercollegiate sports** (some offering scholarships) include archery (m, w), baseball (m), basketball (m, w), crew (m, w), cross-country running (m, w), equestrian sports (m, w), fencing (m, w), football (m), golf (m, w), gymnastics (m, w), ice hockey (m), lacrosse (m, w), racquetball (m, w), riflery (m, w), rugby (m, w), sailing (m, w), soccer (m, w), softball (w), squash (m, w), swimming and diving (m, w), table tennis (m, w), tennis (m, w), track and field (m, w), volleyball (m, w), water polo (m, w), wrestling (m).

##  Applying

Purdue requires a high school transcript, SAT I or ACT, and in some cases 3 years of high school math and science. It recommends 3 years of high school math and science and some high school foreign language. Early and midyear entrance are possible, with rolling admissions and continuous processing to 3/1 for financial aid. **Contact:** Office of Admissions, Schleman Hall, West Lafayette, IN 47907-1080, 317-494-1776.

| GETTING IN LAST YEAR | THE STUDENT BODY | AFTER FRESHMAN YEAR |
|---|---|---|
| 15,620 applied | Total 34,484, of whom 27,750 | 83% returned for sophomore year |
| 90% were accepted | are undergraduates | 30% got a degree within 4 years |
| 39% enrolled (5,486) | From 54 states and territories, | 61% got a degree within 5 years |
| 28% from top tenth of their h.s. class | 77 other countries | |
| 5% had SAT verbal scores over 600 | 73% from Indiana | **WHAT YOU WILL PAY** |
| 34% had SAT math scores over 600 | 43% women, 57% men | Resident tuition and fees $2884 |
| 38% had ACT scores over 26 | 4% African Americans | Nonresident tuition and fees $9556 |
| 0% had SAT verbal scores over 700 | 1% Native Americans | Room and board $4100 |
| 8% had SAT math scores over 700 | 2% Hispanics | 53% receive need-based financial aid |
| 10% had ACT scores over 30 | 4% Asian Americans | averaging $1200 |
| 39 National Merit Scholars | 2% international students | Non-need financial aid averages $4200 |
| 119 valedictorians | | |

# QUINCY UNIVERSITY

Quincy, Illinois • Small-town setting • Private • Independent-Religious • Coed

More students than ever are applying to Quincy University—and with good reason. Quincy University is the place to be. Personal attention is paramount throughout the student's education. Freshmen participate in the "First-Year Experience," a program designed to assist first-year students in their transition from high school to university life. This seminar format allows students to develop critical reading and writing skills, as well as to hone their oral communication and analytical thinking skills. Graduates realize the benefits of a Quincy University education, with over 93% being employed or continuing in graduate school within 90 days of graduation.

 **Academics**

Quincy University offers a liberal arts/career preparation curriculum and core academic program; all graduate courses are open to undergraduates. It awards associate, bachelor's, and master's **degrees**. Challenging opportunities include advanced placement, accelerated degree programs, self-designed majors, tutorials, Freshmen Honors College, an honors program, and a senior project. Special programs include internships and summer session for credit.

The most popular **majors** include business, elementary education, and accounting. A complete listing of majors at Quincy University appears in the Majors Index beginning on page 380.

The **faculty** at Quincy University has 71 full-time graduate and undergraduate teachers, 78% with terminal degrees. 100% of the faculty serve as student advisers. The student-faculty ratio is 12:1, and the average class size in required courses is 28.

 **Computers on Campus**

Students are not required to have a computer. Student rooms are linked to a campus network. 192 **computers**

available in the computer center, computer labs, honors houses, classrooms, the library, and dormitories provide access to the main academic computer, off-campus computing facilities, e-mail, and on-line services. Staffed computer lab on campus provides training in the use of computers and software.

The **library** has 229,742 books, 147,395 microform titles, and 645 subscriptions. It is connected to 7 national **on-line** catalogs.

 **Campus Life**

There are 41 active **organizations** on campus, including a drama/theater group and student-run newspaper and radio station. Student **safety services** include late night transport/escort service, 24-hour emergency telephone alarm devices, student patrols, and electronically operated dormitory entrances.

Quincy University is a member of the NCAA (Division II). **Intercollegiate sports** (some offering scholarships) include baseball (m), basketball (m, w), cross-country running (m, w), football (m), soccer (m, w), softball (w), tennis (m, w), volleyball (m, w).

 **Applying**

Quincy University requires a high school transcript, 1 recommendation, and SAT I or ACT. It recommends 3 years of high school math and science, some high school foreign language, an interview, and a minimum high school GPA of 2.0. Early, deferred, and midyear entrance are possible, with rolling admissions and continuous processing to 4/1 for financial aid. **Contact:** Mr. Frank Bevec, Director of Admissions, 1800 College Avenue, Quincy, IL 62301-2699, 217-222-8020 ext. 5215 or toll-free 800-688-4295; fax 217-228-5479.

## GETTING IN LAST YEAR
1,007 applied
81% were accepted
37% enrolled (302)
23% from top tenth of their h.s. class
3.2 average high school GPA
16% had SAT verbal scores over 600
27% had SAT math scores over 600
32% had ACT scores over 26
1% had SAT verbal scores over 700
4% had SAT math scores over 700
8% had ACT scores over 30
1 National Merit Scholar

## THE STUDENT BODY
Total 1,164, of whom 1,107
  are undergraduates
From 30 states and territories,
  11 other countries
68% from Illinois
49% women, 51% men
6% African Americans
1% Native Americans
2% Hispanics
2% Asian Americans
2% international students

## AFTER FRESHMAN YEAR
70% returned for sophomore year

## AFTER GRADUATION
21% pursued further study (11% arts and
  sciences, 4% business, 3% law)
93% had job offers within 3 months
10 corporations, 3 government agencies, 6
  nonprofit organizations recruited on campus

## WHAT YOU WILL PAY
Tuition and fees $10,310
Room and board $4140
81% receive need-based financial aid
  averaging $4584
68% receive non-need financial aid averaging
  $4099

# RANDOLPH-MACON WOMAN'S COLLEGE

Lynchburg, Virginia • Suburban setting • Private • Independent-Religious • Women

A singular education, self-awareness, and involvement—these are priorities at Randolph-Macon Woman's College. Students seize opportunities to study abroad, participate in internships, conduct original research with faculty members, become active in campus organizations, and volunteer in the community. They discover new interests. The supportive and engaging atmosphere fosters academic excellence and leadership potential, with 70% of all classes having 15 or fewer students. Contemporary facilities and advanced technology afford women a competitive edge for career prospects. The College provides a setting for learning and living that prepares women for meaningful personal and professional lives.

## Academics

R-MWC offers a liberal arts and sciences curriculum and core academic program. It awards bachelor's **degrees**. Challenging opportunities include advanced placement, accelerated degree programs, self-designed majors, an honors program, a senior project, and Phi Beta Kappa. Special programs include internships, summer session for credit, off-campus study, and study abroad.

The most popular **majors** include psychology, English, and political science/government. A complete listing of majors at R-MWC appears in the Majors Index beginning on page 380.

The **faculty** at R-MWC has 63 full-time teachers, 95% with terminal degrees. 100% of the faculty serve as student advisers. The student-faculty ratio is 9:1, and the average class size in required courses is 16.

## Computers on Campus

Students are not required to have a computer. Student rooms are linked to a campus network. 70 **computers** available in the computer center, computer labs, the research center, the learning resource center, multimedia rooms, classrooms, and the library provide access to the main academic computer, off-campus computing facilities, e-mail, and on-line services. Staffed computer lab on campus (open 24 hours a day).

The **library** has 165,300 books, 350 microform titles, and 855 subscriptions. It is connected to 3 national **on-line** catalogs.

## Campus Life

There are 30 active **organizations** on campus, including a drama/theater group. Student **safety services** include late night transport/escort service, 24-hour emergency telephone alarm devices, and 24-hour patrols by trained security personnel.

R-MWC is a member of the NCAA (Division III). **Intercollegiate sports** include basketball, equestrian sports, field hockey, lacrosse, soccer, softball, swimming and diving, tennis, volleyball.

## Applying

R-MWC requires an essay, a high school transcript, 2 recommendations, and SAT I or ACT. It recommends 3 years of high school math and science, 3 years of high school foreign language, an interview, and 2 SAT II Subject Tests. Early, deferred, and midyear entrance are possible, with a 3/1 deadline and continuous processing to 3/1 for financial aid. **Contact:** Ms. Jean H. Stewart, Director of Admissions, 2500 Rivermont Avenue, Lynchburg, VA 24503-1526, 804-947-8100 or toll-free 800-745- 7692 (in-state).

## GETTING IN LAST YEAR
580 applied
89% were accepted
38% enrolled (198)
36% from top tenth of their h.s. class
22% had SAT verbal scores over 600
25% had SAT math scores over 600
39% had ACT scores over 26
2% had SAT verbal scores over 700
4% had SAT math scores over 700
8% had ACT scores over 30
3 valedictorians

## THE STUDENT BODY
738 undergraduates
From 48 states and territories,
   20 other countries
37% from Virginia
100% women
5% African Americans
1% Native Americans
2% Hispanics
3% Asian Americans
5% international students

## AFTER FRESHMAN YEAR
73% returned for sophomore year
68% got a degree within 4 years
69% got a degree within 5 years

## AFTER GRADUATION
20% pursued further study (14% arts and
   sciences, 3% law, 2% medicine)

## WHAT YOU WILL PAY
Tuition and fees $14,090
Room and board $6110
54% receive need-based financial aid
   averaging $6175
Non-need financial aid averages $3964

# REED COLLEGE

Portland, Oregon • Suburban setting • Private • Independent • Coed

Reed's traditional, integrated curriculum provides a context for rigorous study, with a focus on individual responsibility and tolerance for different viewpoints. Students possess a high degree of self-discipline, intellectual curiosity, independence, and genuine enthusiasm for learning. One national survey of professors ranked Reed first in faculty commitment to teaching. Results show Reed ranks first among national undergraduate institutions in percentage of graduates earning PhDs. Reed has produced 30 Rhodes scholars since 1915, a number met by only one other liberal arts college. Graduates remember Reed as "a four-year-long debate" where they "learned how to learn."

 ## Academics

Reed offers a core academic program. It awards bachelor's and master's **degrees**. Challenging opportunities include advanced placement, accelerated degree programs, self-designed majors, tutorials, and Phi Beta Kappa. Special programs include off-campus study, study abroad, and Army ROTC.

The most popular **majors** include English, psychology, and biology/biological sciences. A complete listing of majors at Reed appears in the Majors Index beginning on page 380.

The **faculty** at Reed has 100 full-time graduate and undergraduate teachers, 81% with terminal degrees. 90% of the faculty serve as student advisers. The student-faculty ratio is 10:1, and the average class size in required courses is 15.

 ## Computers on Campus

Students are not required to have a computer. Student rooms are linked to a campus network. 140 **computers** available in the computer center, computer labs, various academic departments, and the library provide access to the main academic computer, off-campus computing facilities, e-mail, and on-line services. Staffed computer lab on campus (open 24 hours a day) provides training in the use of computers and software.

The 2 **libraries** have 375,516 books, 51,103 microform titles, and 1,727 subscriptions. They are connected to 72 national **on-line** catalogs.

 ## Campus Life

Active **organizations** on campus include drama/theater group and student-run newspaper and radio station. Student **safety services** include 24-hour emergency dispatch, late night transport/escort service, 24-hour emergency telephone alarm devices, 24-hour patrols by trained security personnel, student patrols, and electronically operated dormitory entrances. **Intercollegiate sports** include basketball (m), crew (m, w), fencing (m, w), rugby (m, w), sailing (m, w), skiing (cross-country) (m, w), skiing (downhill) (m, w), soccer (m, w).

 ## Applying

Reed requires an essay, a high school transcript, 2 recommendations, SAT I or ACT, and in some cases 3 SAT II Subject Tests. It recommends 3 years of high school math and science, some high school foreign language, an interview, 3 SAT II Subject Tests, and a minimum high school GPA of 3.0. Early, deferred, and midyear entrance are possible, with a 2/1 deadline and 3/1 for financial aid. **Contact:** Mr. Robert Mansueto, Dean of Admission, 3203 Southeast Woodstock Boulevard, Portland, OR 97202-8199, 503-777-7511 or toll-free 800-547-4750 (out-of-state).

## GETTING IN LAST YEAR

1,940 applied
70% were accepted
22% enrolled (302)
51% from top tenth of their h.s. class
3.65 average high school GPA
57% had SAT verbal scores over 600
69% had SAT math scores over 600
13% had SAT verbal scores over 700
21% had SAT math scores over 700
12 National Merit Scholars
15 valedictorians

## THE STUDENT BODY

Total 1,279, of whom 1,260 are undergraduates
From 47 states and territories, 23 other countries
15% from Oregon
51% women, 49% men
1% African Americans
1% Native Americans
3% Hispanics
9% Asian Americans
7% international students

## AFTER FRESHMAN YEAR

84% returned for sophomore year
41% got a degree within 4 years
61% got a degree within 5 years
63% got a degree within 6 years

## AFTER GRADUATION

57% pursued further study (36% arts and sciences, 7% law, 5% business)
31% had job offers within 3 months
2 Fulbright scholars

## WHAT YOU WILL PAY

Tuition and fees $20,110
Room and board $5490
45% receive need-based financial aid averaging $13,220

# RENSSELAER POLYTECHNIC INSTITUTE

Troy, New York • Suburban setting • Private • Independent • Coed

Rensselaer undergraduates have numerous opportunities to conduct research through the University-funded Undergraduate Research Program and to gain valuable job experience by participation in the Cooperative Education Program. Among successful Rensselaer graduates are Washington Roebling, chief engineer of the Brooklyn Bridge; Nancy Fitzroy, the first woman president of the American Society of Mechanical Engineers; and William Mow, founder of Bugle Boy Industries.

##  Academics

Rensselaer offers an interactive curriculum and core academic program; more than half of graduate courses are open to undergraduates. It awards bachelor's, master's, and doctoral **degrees**. Challenging opportunities include advanced placement, accelerated degree programs, tutorials, an honors program, a senior project, and Sigma Xi. Special programs include cooperative education, internships, summer session for credit, off-campus study, study abroad, and Army, Naval, and Air Force ROTC.

The most popular **majors** include mechanical engineering, electrical engineering, and computer science. A complete listing of majors at Rensselaer appears in the Majors Index beginning on page 380.

The **faculty** at Rensselaer has 348 full-time undergraduate teachers, 99% with terminal degrees. The student-faculty ratio is 12:1, and the average class size in required courses is 25.

##  Computers on Campus

Students are not required to have a computer. Student rooms are linked to a campus network. 618 **computers** available in the computer center, computer labs, academic buildings, classrooms, the library, and dormitories provide access to e-mail and on-line services. Staffed computer lab on campus (open 24 hours a day) provides training in the use of computers and software.

The 2 **libraries** have 430,000 books and 3,875 subscriptions. They are connected to 10 national **on-line** catalogs.

##  Campus Life

There are 114 active **organizations** on campus, including a drama/theater group and student-run newspaper and radio station. 40% of eligible men and 40% of eligible women are members of 29 national **fraternities**, 5 national **sororities**, 1 local fraternity, 1 local sorority, and 1 coed fraternity. Student **safety services** include campus foot patrols at night, late night transport/escort service, 24-hour emergency telephone alarm devices, 24-hour patrols by trained security personnel, and electronically operated dormitory entrances.

Rensselaer is a member of the NCAA (Division III). **Intercollegiate sports** (some offering scholarships) include baseball (m), basketball (m, w), crew (m, w), cross-country running (m, w), equestrian sports (m, w), fencing (m, w), field hockey (w), football (m), golf (m), ice hockey (m, w), lacrosse (m, w), racquetball (m, w), rugby (m), skiing (cross-country) (m, w), skiing (downhill) (m, w), soccer (m, w), softball (w), swimming and diving (m, w), tennis (m, w), track and field (m, w), volleyball (m, w), wrestling (m).

##  Applying

Rensselaer requires an essay, a high school transcript, 4 years of high school math, 3 years of high school science, 1 recommendation, SAT I or ACT, and in some cases 3 SAT II Subject Tests. It recommends some high school foreign language, a campus interview, and 3 SAT II Subject Tests. Early, deferred, and midyear entrance are possible, with a 1/15 deadline and a 2/15 priority date for financial aid. **Contact:** Ms. Teresa Duffy, Acting Dean of Admissions, Sage and Eaton Streets, Troy, NY 12180-3590, 518-276-6216 or toll-free 800-448-6562; fax 518-276-4072.

### GETTING IN LAST YEAR
4,823 applied
77% were accepted
27% enrolled (987)
56% from top tenth of their h.s. class
22% had SAT verbal scores over 600
75% had SAT math scores over 600
2% had SAT verbal scores over 700
28% had SAT math scores over 700
26 National Merit Scholars
63 valedictorians

### THE STUDENT BODY
Total 6,331, of whom 4,262
  are undergraduates

From 53 states and territories,
  70 other countries
37% from New York
22% women, 78% men
4% African Americans
1% Native Americans
5% Hispanics
14% Asian Americans
6% international students

### AFTER FRESHMAN YEAR
87% returned for sophomore year
49% got a degree within 4 years
69% got a degree within 5 years
72% got a degree within 6 years

### AFTER GRADUATION
56% had job offers within 3 months
223 corporations, 7 government agencies, 2
  nonprofit organizations recruited on campus

### WHAT YOU WILL PAY
Tuition and fees $18,025
Room and board $5976
Need-based financial aid averages $10,000
Non-need financial aid averages $6300

# RHODES COLLEGE

Memphis, Tennessee • Suburban setting • Private • Independent-Religious • Coed

▶ Rhodes offers something that is not found around most highly selective national liberal arts colleges—a big city. Memphis is a hub of commerce and culture with local theaters, touring Broadway shows, a symphony, concerts, professional sports, restaurants, and shops. There are also many opportunities for internships—60% of Rhodes' students gain internship experience during their 4 years. Rhodes is distinctive for its commitment to community service and for broad involvement by students in their own self-governance. Central to Rhodes is a completely student-run honor system.

 **Academics**

Rhodes offers a traditional liberal arts curriculum with an international emphasis and core academic program; fewer than half of graduate courses are open to undergraduates. It awards bachelor's and master's **degrees** (master's in accounting only). Challenging opportunities include advanced placement, accelerated degree programs, self-designed majors, tutorials, Freshmen Honors College, an honors program, a senior project, and Phi Beta Kappa. Special programs include internships, summer session for credit, off-campus study, study abroad, and Army and Air Force ROTC.

The most popular **majors** include English, biology/biological sciences, and international studies. A complete listing of majors at Rhodes appears in the Majors Index beginning on page 380.

The **faculty** at Rhodes has 114 full-time graduate and undergraduate teachers, 99% with terminal degrees, 100% serve as student advisers. The student-faculty ratio is 12:1, and the average class size in required courses is 17.

 **Computers on Campus**

Students are not required to have a computer. 110 **computers** available across campus provide access to the main academic computer, off-campus computing facilities, e-mail, and on-line services. Staffed computer lab on campus provides training in the use of computers and software.

The 4 **libraries** have 233,000 books, 6,300 microform titles, and 1,187 subscriptions. They are connected to 2 national **on-line** catalogs.

 **Campus Life**

There are 46 active **organizations** on campus, including a drama/theater group and student-run newspaper. 54% of eligible men and 57% of eligible women are members of 6 national **fraternities** and 7 national **sororities**. Student **safety services** include 24-hour monitored security cameras in parking areas, fenced campus with monitored access at night, late night transport/escort service, 24-hour emergency telephone alarm devices, 24-hour patrols by trained security personnel, and student patrols.

Rhodes is a member of the NCAA (Division III). **Intercollegiate sports** include baseball (m), basketball (m, w), cross-country running (m, w), equestrian sports (m, w), football (m), golf (m, w), lacrosse (m), rugby (m), soccer (m, w), swimming and diving (m, w), tennis (m, w), track and field (m, w), volleyball (w).

 **Applying**

Rhodes requires an essay, a high school transcript, 3 years of high school math, 2 years of high school foreign language, 2 recommendations, 2 years of high school science, and SAT I or ACT. It recommends an interview. Early, deferred, and midyear entrance are possible, with a 2/1 deadline and continuous processing to 3/1 for financial aid. **Contact:** Mr. David J. Wottle, Dean of Admissions and Financial Aid, 2000 North Parkway, Memphis, TN 38112-1690, 901-726-3700 or toll-free 800-844-5969 (out-of-state); fax 901-726-3719.

## GETTING IN LAST YEAR

2,270 applied
80% were accepted
23% enrolled (424)
55% from top tenth of their h.s. class
3.5 average high school GPA
33% had SAT verbal scores over 600
56% had SAT math scores over 600
70% had ACT scores over 26
5% had SAT verbal scores over 700
15% had SAT math scores over 700
28% had ACT scores over 30
18 National Merit Scholars
38 class presidents

## THE STUDENT BODY

Total 1,469, of whom 1,464
  are undergraduates

From 44 states and territories,
  19 other countries
34% from Tennessee
56% women, 44% men
4% African Americans
0% Native Americans
0% Hispanics
4% Asian Americans
3% international students

## AFTER FRESHMAN YEAR

89% returned for sophomore year
64% got a degree within 4 years
68% got a degree within 5 years
69% got a degree within 6 years

## AFTER GRADUATION

33% pursued further study (17% arts and
  sciences, 6% law, 5% medicine)
63% had job offers within 3 months
34 corporations, 6 government agencies, 3
  nonprofit organizations recruited on campus
1 Fulbright scholar

## WHAT YOU WILL PAY

Tuition and fees $15,358
Room and board $4768
43% receive need-based financial aid
  averaging $8110
25% receive non-need financial aid averaging
  $7116

# RICE UNIVERSITY

Houston, Texas • Urban setting • Private • Independent • Coed

Adjacent to the largest medical center in the country and the Houston museum district, Rice University offers students access to a wide range of educational and cultural opportunities. Much of Rice's distinctiveness stems from combining the characteristics of a relatively small liberal arts college with those of a true research university. In addition, the University maintains one of the few remaining honor systems in the country as well as a residential college system. Recognized as one of the best educational bargains in the country, Rice offers need-based assistance as well as athletic, academic, and minority scholarships.

##  Academics

Rice University offers an interdisciplinary curriculum and core academic program; more than half of graduate courses are open to undergraduates. It awards bachelor's, master's, doctoral, and first professional **degrees**. Challenging opportunities include advanced placement, accelerated degree programs, self-designed majors, an honors program, a senior project, Phi Beta Kappa, and Sigma Xi. Special programs include internships, summer session for credit, off-campus study, study abroad, and Army and Naval ROTC.

The most popular **majors** include political science/government, English, and history. A complete listing of majors at Rice University appears in the Majors Index beginning on page 380.

The **faculty** at Rice University has 422 full-time graduate and undergraduate teachers, 100% with terminal degrees. The student-faculty ratio is 9:1, and the average class size in required courses is 18.

##  Computers on Campus

Students are not required to have a computer. 200 **computers** available in the computer center, computer labs, academic department buildings, and dormitories.

The **library** has 1.8 million books, 1.8 million microform titles, and 13,100 subscriptions.

##  Campus Life

There are 80 active **organizations** on campus, including a drama/theater group and student-run newspaper and radio station. Student **safety services** include late night transport/escort service, 24-hour emergency telephone alarm devices, 24-hour patrols by trained security personnel, and electronically operated dormitory entrances.

Rice University is a member of the NCAA (Division I). **Intercollegiate sports** (some offering scholarships) include baseball (m), basketball (m, w), crew (m, w), cross-country running (m, w), football (m), golf (m), lacrosse (m), riflery (m, w), rugby (m), sailing (m, w), soccer (m, w), swimming and diving (m, w), tennis (m, w), track and field (m, w), volleyball (w).

## Applying

Rice University requires an essay, a high school transcript, 3 years of high school math, 2 years of high school foreign language, 2 recommendations, SAT I, 3 SAT II Subject Tests (including SAT II: Writing Test), and in some cases 3 years of high school science. It recommends an interview. Early and deferred entrance are possible, with a 1/2 deadline and continuous processing for financial aid. **Contact:** Mr. Ron W. Moss, Director of Admissions, MS 17, Houston, TX 77005, 713-527-4036 or toll-free 800-527-OWLS (out-of-state).

---

**GETTING IN LAST YEAR**
7,779 applied
22% were accepted
37% enrolled (620)
87% from top tenth of their h.s. class
75% had SAT verbal scores over 600
92% had SAT math scores over 600
34% had SAT verbal scores over 700
64% had SAT math scores over 700
240 National Merit Scholars

**THE STUDENT BODY**
Total 4,073, of whom 2,625 are undergraduates
From 52 states and territories, 32 other countries

48% from Texas
43% women, 57% men
6% African Americans
1% Native Americans
9% Hispanics
13% Asian Americans
2% international students

**AFTER FRESHMAN YEAR**
95% returned for sophomore year
66% got a degree within 4 years
85% got a degree within 5 years
87% got a degree within 6 years

**AFTER GRADUATION**
60% pursued further study (23% law, 15% arts and sciences, 9% business)
300 corporations recruited on campus
4 Fulbright scholars

**WHAT YOU WILL PAY**
Tuition and fees $10,775
Room and board $5725
20% receive need-based financial aid averaging $4191
35% receive non-need financial aid averaging $4016

# RIPON COLLEGE

Ripon, Wisconsin • Small-town setting • Private • Independent • Coed

Ripon College has an unrivaled commitment to the liberal arts and a dedicated teaching faculty to ensure its fulfillment. The traditional, residential nature of Ripon creates a distinctive academic and social community. This atmosphere offers the best educational value, and scholarship and financial aid programs represent the commitment to making Ripon affordable.

## Academics

Ripon offers a core academic program. It awards bachelor's **degrees**. Challenging opportunities include advanced placement, accelerated degree programs, self-designed majors, tutorials, a senior project, and Phi Beta Kappa. Special programs include internships, off-campus study, study abroad, and Army ROTC.

The most popular **majors** include history, English, and biology/biological sciences. A complete listing of majors at Ripon appears in the Majors Index beginning on page 380.

The **faculty** at Ripon has 69 full-time teachers. 100% of the faculty serve as student advisers. The student-faculty ratio is 10:1.

## Computers on Campus

Students are not required to have a computer. 140 **computers** available in the computer center, classrooms, the library, and dormitories.

The **library** has 157,780 books and 715 subscriptions.

## Campus Life

There are 80 active **organizations** on campus, including a drama/theater group and student-run newspaper and radio station. 65% of eligible men and 30% of eligible women are members of 3 national **fraternities**, 2 national **sororities**, 2 local fraternities, and 1 local sorority. Student **safety services** include late night transport/escort service, 24-hour emergency telephone alarm devices, student patrols, and electronically operated dormitory entrances.

Ripon is a member of the NCAA (Division III). **Intercollegiate sports** include baseball (m), basketball (m, w), cross-country running (m, w), fencing (m, w), football (m), golf (m), ice hockey (m, w), lacrosse (m, w), riflery (m, w), rugby (m), soccer (m, w), softball (w), swimming and diving (m, w), tennis (m, w), track and field (m, w), volleyball (m, w), wrestling (m).

## Applying

Ripon requires an essay, a high school transcript, 1 recommendation, SAT I or ACT, and a minimum high school GPA of 2.0. It recommends 3 years of high school math and science, some high school foreign language, and an interview. Early, deferred, and midyear entrance are possible, with a 3/15 deadline and continuous processing to 3/1 for financial aid. **Contact:** Mr. Paul J. Weeks, Vice President and Dean of Admission, 300 Seward Street, Ripon, WI 54971, 414-748-8102 or toll-free 800-947-4766.

---

**GETTING IN LAST YEAR**
609 applied
86% were accepted
41% enrolled (215)
25% from top tenth of their h.s. class
3.2 average high school GPA
30% had SAT verbal scores over 600
38% had SAT math scores over 600
35% had ACT scores over 26
3% had SAT verbal scores over 700
11% had SAT math scores over 700
10% had ACT scores over 30

**THE STUDENT BODY**
791 undergraduates
From 41 states and territories,
 17 other countries
55% from Wisconsin
50% women, 50% men
1% African Americans
1% Native Americans
2% Hispanics
2% Asian Americans
4% international students

**AFTER FRESHMAN YEAR**
91% returned for sophomore year

**AFTER GRADUATION**
30% pursued further study (23% arts and sciences, 5% medicine, 2% law)
75 corporations, 10 nonprofit organizations recruited on campus

**WHAT YOU WILL PAY**
Tuition and fees $15,390
Room and board $4100
75% receive need-based financial aid averaging $6100
10% receive non-need financial aid averaging $3100

# ROCHESTER INSTITUTE OF TECHNOLOGY

Rochester, New York • Suburban setting • Private • Independent • Coed

Respected internationally as a leader in career-oriented education, RIT has been setting an innovative pace since 1829. RIT offers outstanding teaching, a strong foundation in the liberal arts and sciences, modern classroom facilities, and work experience gained through the cooperative education program. Programs include microelectronic engineering, imaging science, film/video, biotechnology, international business. The programs of RIT's National Technical Institute for the Deaf (NTID) draw students from every state and more than 70 other countries.

##  Academics

RIT offers a humanities and social sciences curriculum and core academic program; fewer than half of graduate courses are open to undergraduates. It awards associate, bachelor's, master's, and doctoral **degrees**. Challenging opportunities include advanced placement, self-designed majors, tutorials, and a senior project. Special programs include cooperative education, internships, summer session for credit, off-campus study, study abroad, and Army, Naval, and Air Force ROTC.

The most popular **majors** include business, engineering (general), and engineering technology. A complete listing of majors at RIT appears in the Majors Index beginning on page 380.

The **faculty** at RIT has 640 full-time graduate and undergraduate teachers, 70% with terminal degrees. 90% of the faculty serve as student advisers. The student-faculty ratio is 12:1, and the average class size in required courses is 25.

## Computers on Campus

Students are not required to have a computer. Student rooms are linked to a campus network. 800 **computers** available across campus, and dormitories provide access to the main academic computer, off-campus computing facilities, e-mail, on-line services, and course registration and student account information. Staffed computer lab on campus provides training in the use of computers and software.

The **library** has 355,750 books, 220,168 microform titles, and 4,768 subscriptions. It is connected to 2 national **on-line** catalogs.

##  Campus Life

There are 75 active **organizations** on campus, including a drama/theater group and student-run newspaper and radio station. 10% of eligible men and 10% of eligible women are members of 15 national **fraternities** and 9 national **sororities**. Student **safety services** include late night transport/escort service, 24-hour emergency telephone alarm devices, 24-hour patrols by trained security personnel, and student patrols.

RIT is a member of the NCAA (Division III). **Intercollegiate sports** include baseball (m), basketball (m, w), crew (m, w), cross-country running (m, w), ice hockey (m, w), lacrosse (m, w), soccer (m, w), softball (w), swimming and diving (m, w), tennis (m, w), track and field (m, w), volleyball (m, w), wrestling (m).

##  Applying

RIT requires an essay, a high school transcript, SAT I or ACT, and in some cases 3 years of high school math and science, portfolio for art majors, a minimum high school GPA of 3.0. It recommends recommendations and an interview. Early, deferred, and midyear entrance are possible, with a 7/1 deadline and continuous processing to 3/15 for financial aid. **Contact:** Mr. Daniel Shelley, Director of Admissions, 60 Lomb Memorial Drive, Rochester, NY 14623-5604, 716-475-6631; fax 716-475-7424.

### GETTING IN LAST YEAR
5,026 applied
77% were accepted
36% enrolled (1,412)
25% from top tenth of their h.s. class
3.7 average high school GPA
11% had SAT verbal scores over 600
42% had SAT math scores over 600
55% had ACT scores over 26
1% had SAT verbal scores over 700
10% had SAT math scores over 700
10% had ACT scores over 30
15 National Merit Scholars

### THE STUDENT BODY
Total 12,250, of whom 10,286
   are undergraduates
From 50 states and territories,
   70 other countries
60% from New York
33% women, 67% men
5% African Americans
1% Native Americans
3% Hispanics
5% Asian Americans
4% international students

### AFTER FRESHMAN YEAR
86% returned for sophomore year
62% got a degree within 6 years

### AFTER GRADUATION
10% pursued further study
450 corporations, 15 government agencies, 5
   nonprofit organizations recruited on campus

### WHAT YOU WILL PAY
Tuition and fees $14,229
Room and board $5670
60% receive need-based financial aid
   averaging $5100
20% receive non-need financial aid averaging
   $3500

# ROCKHURST COLLEGE

Kansas City, Missouri • Urban setting • Private • Independent-Religious • Coed

Rockhurst College prides itself on teaching students not just what to think, but how to think. The Rockhurst method of critical questioning is based on the 450-year-old Jesuit tradition. Rockhurst's 35-acre campus in Kansas City's cultural district hosts a learning community characterized by close student-faculty interaction; highly ranked academic excellence in the liberal arts, management, and allied health; and an award-winning service learning program. Rockhurst prepares students for success after graduation: "Famous Rocks," as its distinguished alumni are known, serve in leadership roles throughout the nation in many fields. Rockhurst challenges prospective students to "climb the Rock" by visiting campus.

 **Academics**

Rockhurst offers an interdisciplinary curriculum and core academic program; fewer than half of graduate courses are open to undergraduates. It awards bachelor's and master's **degrees**. Challenging opportunities include advanced placement, accelerated degree programs, tutorials, Freshmen Honors College, an honors program, and a senior project. Special programs include cooperative education, internships, summer session for credit, off-campus study, study abroad, and Army ROTC.

The most popular **majors** include nursing, accounting, and psychology. A complete listing of majors at Rockhurst appears in the Majors Index beginning on page 380.

The **faculty** at Rockhurst has 132 full-time graduate and undergraduate teachers, 79% with terminal degrees. 70% of the faculty serve as student advisers. The student-faculty ratio is 11:1.

 **Computers on Campus**

Students are not required to have a computer. 300 **computers** available in the computer center, computer labs, classrooms, the library, and dormitories provide access to the main academic computer, e-mail, and on-line services. Staffed computer lab on campus provides training in the use of computers and software.

The **library** has 103,676 books, 112,261 microform titles, and 704 subscriptions. It is connected to 1 national **on-line** catalog.

 **Campus Life**

There are 43 active **organizations** on campus, including a drama/theater group and student-run newspaper and radio station. 50% of students participate in student government elections. 33% of eligible men and 35% of eligible women are members of 4 national **fraternities** and 2 national **sororities**. Student **safety services** include late night transport/escort service, 24-hour emergency telephone alarm devices, 24-hour patrols by trained security personnel, and electronically operated dormitory entrances.

Rockhurst is a member of the NAIA. **Intercollegiate sports** (some offering scholarships) include baseball (m), basketball (m, w), cross-country running (m, w), golf (m, w), soccer (m, w), tennis (m, w), volleyball (w).

 **Applying**

Rockhurst requires a high school transcript, 1 recommendation, and SAT I or ACT. It recommends 3 years of high school math and science, some high school foreign language, an interview, and 4 years of high school English, 2 years of high school social sciences, some high school fine arts. Early, deferred, and midyear entrance are possible, with a 6/30 deadline and continuous processing to 4/1 for financial aid. **Contact:** Ms. Barbara O'Connell, Director of Enrollment Services, 1100 Rockhurst Road, Kansas City, MO 64110-2561, 816-926-4100 or toll-free 800-842-6776; fax 816-926-4588.

## GETTING IN LAST YEAR

1,085 applied
87% were accepted
40% enrolled (373)
25% from top tenth of their h.s. class
7% had SAT verbal scores over 600
32% had SAT math scores over 600
31% had ACT scores over 26
0% had SAT verbal scores over 700
2% had SAT math scores over 700
7% had ACT scores over 30
10 valedictorians

## THE STUDENT BODY

Total 2,658, of whom 1,936 are undergraduates
From 23 states and territories, 6 other countries
77% from Missouri
61% women, 39% men
9% African Americans
1% Native Americans
5% Hispanics
2% Asian Americans
1% international students

## AFTER FRESHMAN YEAR

77% returned for sophomore year
52% got a degree within 4 years
61% got a degree within 5 years
62% got a degree within 6 years

## AFTER GRADUATION

23% pursued further study (10% medicine, 5% arts and sciences, 3% business)

## WHAT YOU WILL PAY

Tuition and fees $9730
Room and board $4000
Need-based financial aid averages $1919
Non-need financial aid averages $2900

# ROLLINS COLLEGE

Winter Park, Florida • Suburban setting • Private • Independent • Coed

Rollins is responding to the needs of today's student by combining a high-quality liberal arts education with a focus on developing postgraduate marketability. The Rollins Advantage Program (RAP) has 5 components: the professional development series, computer competency, business basics, leadership development, and experiential learning. Whether a student's plans include continuing with education or getting a job immediately after graduation, RAP is designed to give the edge in any competitive situation. A student can select a major in one of 28 different fields, combine studies with a minor in business, complete an internship, and develop leadership skills.

 ## Academics

Rollins offers a liberal arts curriculum and core academic program. It awards bachelor's and master's **degrees**. Challenging opportunities include advanced placement, accelerated degree programs, self-designed majors, tutorials, an honors program, a senior project, and Sigma Xi. Special programs include internships, off-campus study, and study abroad.

The most popular **majors** include psychology, economics, and English. A complete listing of majors at Rollins appears in the Majors Index beginning on page 380.

The **faculty** at Rollins has 145 full-time graduate and undergraduate teachers, 92% with terminal degrees. 91% of the faculty serve as student advisers. The student-faculty ratio is 12:1, and the average class size in required courses is 16.

 ## Computers on Campus

Students are not required to have a computer. 150 **computers** available in the computer center, computer labs, writing center, classrooms, the library, and dormitories provide access to the main academic computer, off-campus computing facilities, e-mail, and on-line services. Staffed computer lab on campus provides training in the use of computers and software.

The **library** has 263,658 books, 37,758 microform titles, and 1,554 subscriptions. It is connected to 3 national **on-line** catalogs.

 ## Campus Life

There are 54 active **organizations** on campus, including a drama/theater group and student-run newspaper and radio station. 50% of students participate in student government elections. 35% of eligible men and 35% of eligible women are members of 5 national **fraternities**, 5 national **sororities**, 1 local fraternity, and 1 local sorority. Student **safety services** include late night transport/escort service, 24-hour emergency telephone alarm devices, 24-hour patrols by trained security personnel, and electronically operated dormitory entrances.

Rollins is a member of the NCAA (Division II). **Intercollegiate sports** (some offering scholarships) include baseball (m), basketball (m, w), crew (m, w), cross-country running (m, w), golf (m, w), sailing (m, w), soccer (m, w), softball (w), tennis (m, w), volleyball (w).

 ## Applying

Rollins requires an essay, a high school transcript, 3 years of high school math, 1 recommendation, and SAT I or ACT. It recommends 3 years of high school science, 2 years of high school foreign language, an interview, and 3 SAT II Subject Tests. Early, deferred, and midyear entrance are possible, with a 2/15 deadline and continuous processing to 3/1 for financial aid. **Contact:** Mr. David Erdmann, Dean of Admissions and Student Financial Planning, 1000 Holt Avenue, Winter Park, FL 32789-4499, 407-646-2161; fax 407-646-2600.

---

### GETTING IN LAST YEAR
1,804 applied
71% were accepted
33% enrolled (417)
37% from top tenth of their h.s. class
15% had SAT verbal scores over 600
37% had SAT math scores over 600
34% had ACT scores over 26
2% had SAT verbal scores over 700
7% had SAT math scores over 700
5% had ACT scores over 30

### THE STUDENT BODY
Total 3,284, of whom 1,422
  are undergraduates

From 42 states and territories,
  24 other countries
40% from Florida
55% women, 45% men
3% African Americans
1% Native Americans
6% Hispanics
4% Asian Americans
4% international students

### AFTER FRESHMAN YEAR
88% returned for sophomore year
72% got a degree within 4 years
75% got a degree within 5 years

### AFTER GRADUATION
20% pursued further study (10% arts and
  sciences, 6% law, 2% business)
30 corporations, 3 government agencies, 7
  nonprofit organizations recruited on campus

### WHAT YOU WILL PAY
Tuition and fees $16,895
Room and board $5220
40% receive need-based financial aid
  averaging $8348
20% receive non-need financial aid averaging
  $5300

# ROSE-HULMAN INSTITUTE OF TECHNOLOGY

Terre Haute, Indiana • Rural setting • Private • Independent • Coed

 **Academics**

Rose-Hulman offers an engineering and science curriculum and core academic program; fewer than half of graduate courses are open to undergraduates. It awards bachelor's and master's **degrees**. Challenging opportunities include advanced placement, an honors program, and a senior project. Special programs include internships, off-campus study, study abroad, and Army and Air Force ROTC.

A complete listing of majors at Rose-Hulman appears in the Majors Index beginning on page 380.

The **faculty** at Rose-Hulman has 100 full-time undergraduate teachers, 95% with terminal degrees. 100% of the faculty serve as student advisers. The student-faculty ratio is 13:1, and the average class size in required courses is 24.

 **Computers on Campus**

Students are required to have a computer. Purchase options are available. Student rooms are linked to a campus network. 300 **computers** available in the computer center, computer labs, academic buildings, classrooms, the library, and the student center provide access to the main academic computer, off-campus computing facilities, e-mail, and on-line services. Staffed computer lab on campus (open 24 hours a day) provides training in the use of computers and software.

The **library** has 68,000 books and 392 subscriptions. It is connected to 2 national **on-line** catalogs.

 **Campus Life**

Active **organizations** on campus include drama/theater group and student-run newspaper and radio station. 40% of students participate in student government elections. 40% of eligible men are members of 8 national **fraternities**. Student **safety services** include 24-hour emergency telephone alarm devices and 24-hour patrols by trained security personnel.

Rose-Hulman is a member of the NCAA (Division III). **Intercollegiate sports** include baseball (m), basketball (m, w), cross-country running (m, w), football (m), golf (m), riflery (m, w), soccer (m), tennis (m), track and field (m, w), volleyball (w), wrestling (m).

 **Applying**

Rose-Hulman requires a high school transcript, 4 years of high school math, 1 recommendation, and SAT I. It recommends 3 years of high school science and ACT. Rolling admissions and a 3/1 priority date for financial aid. **Contact:** Mr. Charles G. Howard, Dean of Admissions, 5500 Wabash Avenue, Terre Haute, IN 47803-3920, 812-877-8213 or toll-free 800-552-0725 (in-state), 800-248-7448 (out-of-state); fax 812-877-3198.

**GETTING IN LAST YEAR**
3,293 applied
61% were accepted
18% enrolled (352)
65% from top tenth of their h.s. class
20% had SAT verbal scores over 600
82% had SAT math scores over 600
100% had ACT scores over 26
3% had SAT verbal scores over 700
31% had SAT math scores over 700
80% had ACT scores over 30
23 National Merit Scholars

**THE STUDENT BODY**
Total 1,420, of whom 1,320
　are undergraduates
From 41 states and territories,
　6 other countries
59% from Indiana
100% men
1% African Americans
1% Native Americans
1% Hispanics
2% Asian Americans
4% international students

**AFTER FRESHMAN YEAR**
74% returned for sophomore year

**AFTER GRADUATION**
20% pursued further study (12% engineering, 4% arts and sciences, 2% business)
180 corporations, 20 government agencies recruited on campus

**WHAT YOU WILL PAY**
Tuition and fees $14,300
Room and board $4400
Need-based financial aid averages $2000
Non-need financial aid averages $2000

# RUTGERS, THE STATE UNIVERSITY OF NEW JERSEY, COLLEGE OF ENGINEERING

Piscataway, New Jersey • Small-town setting • Public • State-supported • Coed

▶ The College of Engineering maintains 2 principal objectives: the sound technical and cultural education of its students and the advancement of knowledge through research. Its programs emphasize a thorough understanding of fundamental engineering principles, methods of analysis, and reasoning. The College offers 4-year degree programs in 8 major areas: applied sciences in engineering and bioresource, ceramic, chemical, civil, electrical, industrial, and mechanical engineering. In addition, students can specialize in areas such as aerospace, agricultural, biochemical, biomedical, computer, environmental, food, and packaging engineering.

 **Academics**

Rutgers, The State University of New Jersey, College of Engineering offers a core academic program. It awards bachelor's **degrees** (master of science, master of philosophy, and doctor of philosophy are offered through the Graduate School, New Brunswick). Challenging opportunities include advanced placement, self-designed majors, tutorials, an honors program, and a senior project. Special programs include internships, summer session for credit, off-campus study, study abroad, and Army and Air Force ROTC.

The most popular **majors** include electrical engineering, mechanical engineering, and civil engineering. A complete listing of majors at Rutgers, The State University of New Jersey, College of Engineering appears in the Majors Index beginning on page 380.

The **faculty** at Rutgers, The State University of New Jersey, College of Engineering has 132 full-time teachers, 95% with terminal degrees. The student-faculty ratio is 11:1, and the average class size in required courses is 42.

 **Computers on Campus**

Students are not required to have a computer. Student rooms are linked to a campus network. 750 **computers** available in the computer center, computer labs, the research center, the learning resource center, various locations on campus, classrooms, the library, the student center, dormitories,

and student rooms provide access to the main academic computer, off-campus computing facilities, e-mail, and on-line services. Staffed computer lab on campus (open 24 hours a day) provides training in the use of computers and software.

The 17 **libraries** have 4.4 million books, 2.7 million microform titles, and 19,025 subscriptions.

 **Campus Life**

There are 350 active **organizations** on campus, including a drama/theater group and student-run newspaper and radio station. 25% of students participate in student government elections. 5% of eligible men and 5% of eligible women are members of 24 national **fraternities**, 11 national **sororities**, 5 local fraternities, and 4 local sororities. Student **safety services** include late night transport/escort service, 24-hour emergency telephone alarm devices, 24-hour patrols by trained security personnel, student patrols, and electronically operated dormitory entrances.

Rutgers, The State University of New Jersey, College of Engineering is a member of the NCAA (Division I). **Intercollegiate sports** (some offering scholarships) include baseball (m), basketball (m, w), crew (m, w), cross-country running (m, w), fencing (m, w), field hockey (w), football (m), golf (m, w), gymnastics (w), lacrosse (m, w), soccer (m, w), softball (w), swimming and diving (m, w), tennis (m, w), track and field (m, w), volleyball (w), wrestling (m).

 **Applying**

Rutgers, The State University of New Jersey, College of Engineering requires a high school transcript, 4 years of high school math, 1 course each in chemistry and physics, SAT I or ACT, and in some cases 3 SAT II Subject Tests. Early and deferred entrance are possible, with a 1/15 deadline and continuous processing to 3/1 for financial aid. **Contact:** Dr. Elizabeth Mitchell, Assistant V.P. for University Undergraduate Admissions, PO Box 2101, New Brunswick, NJ 08903-2101, 908-445-3770; fax 908-445-0237.

---

**GETTING IN LAST YEAR**
3,172 applied
71% were accepted
23% enrolled (510)
41% from top tenth of their h.s. class
14% had SAT verbal scores over 600
82% had SAT math scores over 600
2% had SAT verbal scores over 700
27% had SAT math scores over 700
1 National Merit Scholar
9 valedictorians

**THE STUDENT BODY**
2,260 undergraduates
From 22 states and territories,
   36 other countries
86% from New Jersey
18% women, 82% men
7% African Americans
6% Hispanics
23% Asian Americans
6% international students

**WHAT YOU WILL PAY**
Resident tuition and fees $5011
Nonresident tuition and fees $9192
Room and board $4748
53% receive need-based financial aid
   averaging $1224
27% receive non-need financial aid averaging
   $2413

# RUTGERS, THE STATE UNIVERSITY OF NEW JERSEY, COLLEGE OF PHARMACY

Piscataway, New Jersey • Small-town setting • Public • State-supported • Coed

The College of Pharmacy is one of the most selective and competitive programs in the nation. The 5-year BS curriculum prepares students for practicing the profession of pharmacy in community pharmacies and hospitals as well as in the pharmaceutical industry. Students develop high levels of comprehension and professional problem-solving skills.

 **Academics**

Rutgers, The State University of New Jersey, College of Pharmacy offers a core academic program. It awards bachelor's and doctoral **degrees** (In addition to the master of science and doctor of philosophy degrees offered through the Graduate School, New Brunswick, a two year doctor of pharmacy degree (Pharm. D) is offered through the college of pharmacy). Challenging opportunities include advanced placement, tutorials, an honors program, and a senior project. Special programs include internships, summer session for credit, off-campus study, study abroad, and Army and Air Force ROTC.

A complete listing of majors at Rutgers, The State University of New Jersey, College of Pharmacy appears in the Majors Index, beginning on page 380.

The **faculty** at Rutgers, The State University of New Jersey, College of Pharmacy has 59 full-time graduate and undergraduate teachers, 95% with terminal degrees. The student-faculty ratio is 14:1, and the average class size in required courses is 45.

 **Computers on Campus**

Students are not required to have a computer. Student rooms are linked to a campus network. 750 **computers** available in the computer center, computer labs, the research center, the learning resource center, various locations on campus, classrooms, the library, the student center, dormitories, and student rooms provide access to the main academic computer, off-campus computing facilities, e-mail, and on-line services. Staffed computer lab on campus (open 24 hours a day) provides training in the use of computers and software.

The 17 **libraries** have 4.4 million books, 2.7 million microform titles, and 19,025 subscriptions.

 **Campus Life**

There are 350 active **organizations** on campus, including a drama/theater group and student-run newspaper and radio station. 5% of eligible men and 5% of eligible women are members of 24 national **fraternities**, 11 national **sororities**, 5 local fraternities, and 4 local sororities. Student **safety services** include late night transport/escort service, 24-hour emergency telephone alarm devices, 24-hour patrols by trained security personnel, student patrols, and electronically operated dormitory entrances.

Rutgers, The State University of New Jersey, College of Pharmacy is a member of the NCAA (Division I). **Intercollegiate sports** (some offering scholarships) include baseball (m), basketball (m, w), crew (m, w), cross-country running (m, w), fencing (m, w), field hockey (w), football (m), golf (m, w), gymnastics (w), lacrosse (m, w), soccer (m, w), softball (w), swimming and diving (m, w), tennis (m, w), track and field (m, w), volleyball (w), wrestling (m).

 **Applying**

Rutgers, The State University of New Jersey, College of Pharmacy requires a high school transcript, 3 years of high school math, 2 years of high school foreign language, 1 course each in biology and chemistry, SAT I or ACT, and in some cases 3 SAT II Subject Tests. Early and deferred entrance are possible, with a 1/15 deadline and continuous processing to 3/1 for financial aid. **Contact:** Dr. Elizabeth Mitchell, Assistant V.P. for University Undergraduate Admissions, Davidson Road, Piscataway, NJ 08855-0789, 908-445-3770; fax 908-445-0237.

## GETTING IN LAST YEAR

1,690 applied
32% were accepted
36% enrolled (198)
79% from top tenth of their h.s. class
19% had SAT verbal scores over 600
81% had SAT math scores over 600
1% had SAT verbal scores over 700
24% had SAT math scores over 700
1 National Merit Scholar
10 valedictorians

## THE STUDENT BODY

Total 938, of whom 889
 are undergraduates
From 14 states and territories,
 8 other countries
87% from New Jersey
64% women, 36% men
5% African Americans
8% Hispanics
39% Asian Americans
2% international students

## WHAT YOU WILL PAY

Resident tuition and fees $5011
Nonresident tuition and fees $9192
Room and board $4748
62% receive need-based financial aid
 averaging $1343
33% receive non-need financial aid averaging
 $2409

# RUTGERS, THE STATE UNIVERSITY OF NEW JERSEY, COOK COLLEGE

New Brunswick, New Jersey • Small-town setting • Public • State-supported • Coed

Cook College offers an extensive range of academic programs in the life, environmental, marine and coastal, and agricultural sciences. Students choose from 26 majors with nearly 59 more specialized options. While all programs are based on a strong foundation in the physical and biological sciences, the social and human dimensions of scientific practice form a special emphasis within the curriculum. Advanced technology centers offer exceptional facilities for independent research, allowing undergraduates the opportunity to turn scientific theory into practice. Cook College students graduate with the skill and confidence to pursue careers or advanced-degree programs.

## Academics

Rutgers, The State University of New Jersey, Cook College offers a core academic program. It awards bachelor's **degrees**. Challenging opportunities include advanced placement, self-designed majors, tutorials, an honors program, and a senior project. Special programs include cooperative education, internships, summer session for credit, off-campus study, study abroad, and Army and Air Force ROTC.

The most popular **majors** include environmental sciences, biology/biological sciences, and business economics. A complete listing of majors at Rutgers, The State University of New Jersey, Cook College appears in the Majors Index beginning on page 380.

The **faculty** at Rutgers, The State University of New Jersey, Cook College has 97 full-time teachers, 95% with terminal degrees. The student-faculty ratio is 16:1, and the average class size in required courses is 39.

## Computers on Campus

Students are not required to have a computer. Student rooms are linked to a campus network. 750 **computers** available in the computer center, computer labs, the research center, the learning resource center, various locations on campus, classrooms, the library, the student center, dormitories, and student rooms provide access to the main academic computer, off-campus computing facilities, e-mail, and on-line services. Staffed computer lab on campus (open 24 hours a day) provides training in the use of computers and software.

The 17 **libraries** have 4.4 million books, 2.7 million microform titles, and 19,025 subscriptions.

## Campus Life

There are 350 active **organizations** on campus, including a drama/theater group and student-run newspaper and radio station. 15% of students participate in student government elections. 5% of eligible men and 5% of eligible women are members of 24 national **fraternities**, 11 national **sororities**, 5 local fraternities, and 4 local sororities. Student **safety services** include late night transport/escort service, 24-hour emergency telephone alarm devices, 24-hour patrols by trained security personnel, student patrols, and electronically operated dormitory entrances.

Rutgers, The State University of New Jersey, Cook College is a member of the NCAA (Division I). **Intercollegiate sports** (some offering scholarships) include baseball (m), basketball (m, w), crew (m, w), cross-country running (m, w), fencing (m, w), field hockey (w), football (m), golf (m, w), gymnastics (w), lacrosse (m, w), soccer (m, w), softball (w), swimming and diving (m, w), tennis (m, w), track and field (m, w), volleyball (w), wrestling (m).

## Applying

Rutgers, The State University of New Jersey, Cook College requires a high school transcript, 3 years of high school math, SAT I or ACT, and in some cases 3 SAT II Subject Tests. It recommends 4 years of high school math. Early and deferred entrance are possible, with a 1/15 deadline and continuous processing to 3/1 for financial aid. **Contact:** Dr. Elizabeth Mitchell, Assistant V.P. for University Undergraduate Admissions, Davidson Road, New Brunswick, NJ 08903-2101, 908-445-3770; fax 908-445-0237.

| GETTING IN LAST YEAR | THE STUDENT BODY | WHAT YOU WILL PAY |
|---|---|---|
| 7,031 applied | 3,010 undergraduates | Resident tuition and fees $5032 |
| 60% were accepted | From 30 states and territories, | Nonresident tuition and fees $9213 |
| 14% enrolled (581) | 21 other countries | Room and board $4748 |
| 30% from top tenth of their h.s. class | 90% from New Jersey | 48% receive need-based financial aid |
| 12% had SAT verbal scores over 600 | 48% women, 52% men | averaging $1163 |
| 38% had SAT math scores over 600 | 5% African Americans | 22% receive non-need financial aid averaging |
| 1% had SAT verbal scores over 700 | 6% Hispanics | $1940 |
| 4% had SAT math scores over 700 | 10% Asian Americans | |
| 2 National Merit Scholars | 1% international students | |
| 5 valedictorians | | |

# RUTGERS, THE STATE UNIVERSITY OF NEW JERSEY, DOUGLASS COLLEGE

New Brunswick, New Jersey • Small-town setting • Public • State-supported • Women

▶Douglass is the largest women's college in the United States. It is dedicated to the development, advancement, and achievement of women in contemporary society and has the range of academic programs, research facilities, and social activities possible only in large coeducational universities. Douglass offers majors in the arts and sciences as well as several professional programs. Features include language and cultural residences, an alumnae career externship program, a math-science residence hall, and an honors program. The College is a national center for research, public service, and community outreach programs focusing on women and is the site of the University's model women's studies program.

##  Academics

Rutgers, The State University of New Jersey, Douglass College offers a core academic program. It awards bachelor's **degrees**. Challenging opportunities include advanced placement, self-designed majors, tutorials, an honors program, a senior project, and Phi Beta Kappa. Special programs include internships, summer session for credit, off-campus study, study abroad, and Army and Air Force ROTC.

The most popular **majors** include psychology, English, and communication. A complete listing of majors at Rutgers, The State University of New Jersey, Douglass College appears in the Majors Index beginning on page 380.

The **faculty** at Rutgers, The State University of New Jersey, Douglass College has 745 full-time teachers, 95% with terminal degrees. The student-faculty ratio is 17:1, and the average class size in required courses is 45.

##  Computers on Campus

Students are not required to have a computer. Student rooms are linked to a campus network. 750 **computers** available in the computer center, computer labs, the research center, the learning resource center, computer stations, classrooms, the library, the student center, dormitories, and student rooms provide access to the main academic computer, off-campus computing facilities, e-mail, and on-line services. Staffed computer lab on campus (open 24 hours a day) provides training in the use of computers and software.

The **library** has 4.4 million books, 2.7 million microform titles, and 19,025 subscriptions.

##  Campus Life

There are 350 active **organizations** on campus, including a drama/theater group and student-run newspaper and radio station. 5% of eligible undergraduates are members of 11 national **sororities** and 4 local sororities. Student **safety services** include late night transport/escort service, 24-hour emergency telephone alarm devices, 24-hour patrols by trained security personnel, student patrols, and electronically operated dormitory entrances.

Rutgers, The State University of New Jersey, Douglass College is a member of the NCAA (Division I). **Intercollegiate sports** (some offering scholarships) include basketball, crew, cross-country running, fencing, field hockey, golf, gymnastics, lacrosse, soccer, softball, swimming and diving, tennis, track and field, volleyball.

##  Applying

Rutgers, The State University of New Jersey, Douglass College requires a high school transcript, 3 years of high school math, 2 years of high school foreign language, 2 years of high school science, SAT I or ACT, and in some cases 3 SAT II Subject Tests. It recommends 4 years of high school math. Early and deferred entrance are possible, with a 1/15 deadline and continuous processing to 3/1 for financial aid. **Contact:** Dr. Elizabeth Mitchell, Assistant V.P. for University Undergraduate Admissions, PO Box 2101, New Brunswick, NJ 08903-2101, 908-445-3770; fax 908-445-0237.

---

### GETTING IN LAST YEAR

5,618 applied
65% were accepted
16% enrolled (582)
25% from top tenth of their h.s. class
10% had SAT verbal scores over 600
27% had SAT math scores over 600
2% had SAT verbal scores over 700
4% had SAT math scores over 700
3 National Merit Scholars
12 valedictorians

### THE STUDENT BODY

2,986 undergraduates
From 24 states and territories,
 19 other countries
93% from New Jersey
100% women
11% African Americans
7% Hispanics
14% Asian Americans
1% international students

### WHAT YOU WILL PAY

Resident tuition and fees $4611
Nonresident tuition and fees $8381
Room and board $4748
48% receive need-based financial aid
 averaging $1233
26% receive non-need financial aid averaging
 $1580

# RUTGERS, THE STATE UNIVERSITY OF NEW JERSEY, RUTGERS COLLEGE

New Brunswick, New Jersey • Small-town setting • Public • State-supported • Coed

Rutgers College is the eighth-oldest institution of higher learning in America, predating many of the Ivy League schools. Rutgers has always been dedicated to "the education of youth in the learned languages, liberal and useful arts and sciences." Times have changed, but the College's philosophy remains the same: to provide a broad liberal arts experience. Rutgers College students select a major and a minor from a full range of liberal arts and preprofessional subjects. General education requirements provide a mastery of writing and quantitative skills and an understanding of the natural and social sciences, humanities, and non-Western cultures.

 **Academics**

Rutgers, The State University of New Jersey, Rutgers College offers a core academic program. It awards bachelor's **degrees**. Challenging opportunities include advanced placement, self-designed majors, tutorials, an honors program, a senior project, Phi Beta Kappa, and Sigma Xi. Special programs include internships, summer session for credit, off-campus study, study abroad, and Army and Air Force ROTC.

The most popular **majors** include psychology, English, and political science/government. A complete listing of majors at Rutgers, The State University of New Jersey, Rutgers College appears in the Majors Index beginning on page 380.

The **faculty** at Rutgers, The State University of New Jersey, Rutgers College has 745 full-time teachers, 95% with terminal degrees. The student-faculty ratio is 17:1, and the average class size in required courses is 45.

 **Computers on Campus**

Students are not required to have a computer. Student rooms are linked to a campus network. 750 **computers** available in the computer center, computer labs, the research center, the learning resource center, various locations on campus, classrooms, the library, the student center, dormitories, and student rooms provide access to the main academic computer, off-campus computing facilities, e-mail, and on-line services. Staffed computer lab on campus (open 24 hours a day) provides training in the use of computers and software.

The 17 **libraries** have 4.4 million books, 2.7 million microform titles, and 19,025 subscriptions.

 **Campus Life**

There are 350 active **organizations** on campus, including a drama/theater group and student-run newspaper and radio station. 10% of students participate in student government elections. 5% of eligible men and 5% of eligible women are members of 24 national **fraternities**, 11 national **sororities**, 5 local fraternities, and 4 local sororities. Student **safety services** include late night transport/escort service, 24-hour emergency telephone alarm devices, 24-hour patrols by trained security personnel, student patrols, and electronically operated dormitory entrances.

Rutgers, The State University of New Jersey, Rutgers College is a member of the NCAA (Division I). **Intercollegiate sports** (some offering scholarships) include baseball (m), basketball (m, w), crew (m, w), cross-country running (m, w), fencing (m, w), field hockey (w), football (m), golf (m, w), gymnastics (w), lacrosse (m, w), soccer (m, w), softball (w), swimming and diving (m, w), tennis (m, w), track and field (m, w), volleyball (w), wrestling (m).

 **Applying**

Rutgers, The State University of New Jersey, Rutgers College requires a high school transcript, 3 years of high school math, 2 years of high school foreign language, 2 years of high school science, SAT I or ACT, and in some cases 3 SAT II Subject Tests. It recommends 4 years of high school math. Early and deferred entrance are possible, with a 1/15 deadline and continuous processing to 3/1 for financial aid. **Contact:** Dr. Elizabeth Mitchell, Assistant V.P. for University Undergraduate Admissions, Davidson Road, New Brunswick, NJ 08903-2101, 908-445-3770; fax 908-445-0237.

---

### GETTING IN LAST YEAR

16,684 applied
49% were accepted
23% enrolled (1,871)
46% from top tenth of their h.s. class
21% had SAT verbal scores over 600
60% had SAT math scores over 600
2% had SAT verbal scores over 700
17% had SAT math scores over 700
14 National Merit Scholars
29 valedictorians

### THE STUDENT BODY

8,908 undergraduates
From 40 states and territories,
   45 other countries
88% from New Jersey
50% women, 50% men
8% African Americans
11% Hispanics
16% Asian Americans
2% international students

### WHAT YOU WILL PAY

Resident tuition and fees $4646
Nonresident tuition and fees $8416
Room and board $4748
55% receive need-based financial aid
   averaging $1284
27% receive non-need financial aid averaging
   $2466

# ST. JOHN'S COLLEGE

Annapolis, Maryland • Small-town setting • Private • Independent • Coed

---

Great Books Program: St. John's offers an integrated liberal arts and sciences curriculum structured around seminar discussions of major works of Western civilization. These discussions are supported by tutorials in mathematics, music, language, and the physical sciences. Only original sources are read, and all classes are small discussion groups.

## Academics

St. John's offers a great books curriculum in works of Western civilization and core academic program. It awards bachelor's and master's **degrees**. Challenging opportunities include tutorials and a senior project. Special programs include off-campus study and study abroad.

A complete listing of majors at St. John's appears in the Majors Index beginning on page 380.

The **faculty** at St. John's has 56 full-time graduate and undergraduate teachers, 58% with terminal degrees. 100% of the faculty serve as student advisers. The student-faculty ratio is 8:1, and the average class size in required courses is 15.

## Computers on Campus

Students are not required to have a computer. 12 **computers** available in the computer center and the library. Staffed computer lab on campus provides training in the use of computers and software.

The 2 **libraries** have 96,158 books, 75 microform titles, and 126 subscriptions. They are connected to 1 national **on-line** catalog.

## Campus Life

There are 35 active **organizations** on campus, including a drama/theater group and student-run newspaper. Student **safety services** include late night transport/escort service, 24-hour emergency telephone alarm devices, 24-hour patrols by trained security personnel, and electronically operated dormitory entrances.

This institution has no intercollegiate sports.

## Applying

St. John's requires an essay, a high school transcript, 3 years of high school math, and 2 recommendations. It recommends 3 years of high school science, 2 years of high school foreign language, an interview, and SAT I or ACT. Early, deferred, and midyear entrance are possible, with rolling admissions and continuous processing to 2/15 for financial aid. **Contact:** Mr. John Christensen, Director of Admissions, PO Box 2800, Annapolis, MD 21404, 410-263-2371 ext. 222 or toll-free 800-727-9238.

---

### GETTING IN LAST YEAR
334 applied
84% were accepted
40% enrolled (113)
33% from top tenth of their h.s. class
58% had SAT verbal scores over 600
47% had SAT math scores over 600
13% had SAT verbal scores over 700
11% had SAT math scores over 700
2 National Merit Scholars

### THE STUDENT BODY
Total 477, of whom 395
   are undergraduates
From 45 states and territories,
   9 other countries

15% from Maryland
47% women, 53% men
2% African Americans
1% Native Americans
3% Hispanics
4% Asian Americans
6% international students

### AFTER FRESHMAN YEAR
84% returned for sophomore year
46% got a degree within 4 years
56% got a degree within 5 years
59% got a degree within 6 years

### AFTER GRADUATION
58% pursued further study (42% arts and
   sciences, 7% law, 6% medicine)
7% had job offers within 3 months
7 corporations, 3 government agencies, 5
   nonprofit organizations recruited on campus

### WHAT YOU WILL PAY
Tuition and fees $17,630
Room and board $5720
55% receive need-based financial aid
   averaging $10,124

# ST. JOHN'S COLLEGE

Santa Fe, New Mexico • Small-town setting • Private • Independent • Coed

St. John's College, founded in 1696, has 2 campuses in Santa Fe, New Mexico, and Annapolis, Maryland. Students may attend both campuses during their programs of study. The College awards Bachelor of Arts and Master of Arts degrees. The bachelor's program is a rigorous interdisciplinary curriculum based on the reading, study, and discussion of great books—literature, mathematics, philosophy, science, theology, political theory, psychology, economics—and works of music and art, through which the development of Western thought from ancient Greece to modern times is traced. Graduates are as likely to pursue a career in teaching as they are in medicine or law.

## Academics

St. John's offers a great books, interdisciplinary, arts and sciences curriculum and core academic program. It awards bachelor's and master's **degrees**. Challenging opportunities include tutorials and a senior project. Special programs include off-campus study and study abroad.

A complete listing of majors at St. John's appears in the Majors Index beginning on page 380.

The **faculty** at St. John's has 45 full-time undergraduate teachers, 60% with terminal degrees. 100% of the faculty serve as student advisers. The student-faculty ratio is 8:1, and the average class size in required courses is 15.

## Computers on Campus

Students are not required to have a computer. 9 **computers** available in the lab building and the library.

The **library** has 60,000 books and 160 subscriptions. It is connected to 1 national **on-line** catalog.

## Campus Life

Active **organizations** on campus include drama/theater group and student-run newspaper. No national or local **fraternities** or **sororities**. Student **safety services** include late night transport/escort service, 24-hour emergency telephone alarm devices, 24-hour patrols by trained security personnel, student patrols, and electronically operated dormitory entrances.

This institution has no intercollegiate sports.

## Applying

St. John's requires an essay, a high school transcript, 3 recommendations, and in some cases an interview. It recommends 3 years of high school math and science, 2 years of high school foreign language, an interview, and SAT I or ACT. Early, deferred, and midyear entrance are possible, with rolling admissions and continuous processing to 2/15 for financial aid. **Contact:** Mr. Larry Clendenin, Director of Admissions, 1160 Camino Cruz Blanca, Santa Fe, NM 87501-4599, 505-984-6060 or toll-free 800-331-5232 (out-of-state).

---

### GETTING IN LAST YEAR
290 applied
84% were accepted
43% enrolled (104)
19% from top tenth of their h.s. class
47% had SAT verbal scores over 600
48% had SAT math scores over 600
10% had SAT verbal scores over 700
19% had SAT math scores over 700
3 National Merit Scholars

### THE STUDENT BODY
Total 487, of whom 394
   are undergraduates
From 51 states and territories,
   7 other countries
11% from New Mexico

48% women, 52% men
1% African Americans
1% Native Americans
7% Hispanics
3% Asian Americans
2% international students

### AFTER FRESHMAN YEAR
85% returned for sophomore year
64% got a degree within 4 years
71% got a degree within 5 years

### AFTER GRADUATION
58% pursued further study (42% arts and
   sciences, 7% law, 6% medicine)
15 corporations, 25 government agencies, 4
   nonprofit organizations recruited on campus

### WHAT YOU WILL PAY
Tuition and fees $17,630
Room and board $5720
65% receive need-based financial aid
   averaging $9562

# SAINT JOHN'S UNIVERSITY

*Coordinate with College of Saint Benedict*

Collegeville, Minnesota • Rural setting • Private • Independent-Religious • Men

 **Academics**

St. John's offers an interdisciplinary curriculum and core academic program; fewer than half of graduate courses are open to undergraduates. It awards bachelor's and master's **degrees**. Challenging opportunities include advanced placement, self-designed majors, tutorials, an honors program, and a senior project. Special programs include internships, off-campus study, study abroad, and Army ROTC.

The most popular **majors** include business, biology/biological sciences, and accounting. A complete listing of majors at St. John's appears in the Majors Index beginning on page 380.

The **faculty** at St. John's has 135 full-time graduate and undergraduate teachers, 85% with terminal degrees. 100% of the faculty serve as student advisers. The student-faculty ratio is 14:1, and the average class size in required courses is 21.

 **Computers on Campus**

Students are not required to have a computer. 250 **computers** available in the computer center, computer labs, academic buildings, classrooms, the library, the student center, and dormitories provide access to the main academic computer, e-mail, on-line services, and campus network. Staffed computer lab on campus provides training in the use of computers and software.

The 3 **libraries** have 509,000 books, 97,000 microform titles, and 1,700 subscriptions. They are connected to 5 national **on-line** catalogs.

 **Campus Life**

There are 80 active **organizations** on campus, including a drama/theater group and student-run newspaper and radio station. Student **safety services** include late night transport/escort service and 24-hour emergency telephone alarm devices.

St. John's is a member of the NCAA (Division III) and NAIA. **Intercollegiate sports** include baseball, basketball, crew, cross-country running, football, golf, ice hockey, lacrosse, riflery, rugby, skiing (cross-country), skiing (downhill), soccer, swimming and diving, tennis, track and field, wrestling.

 **Applying**

St. John's requires an essay, a high school transcript, SAT I or ACT, and in some cases recommendations. It recommends 3 years of high school math and science, 2 years of high school foreign language, an interview, and a minimum high school GPA of 3.0. Early, deferred, and midyear entrance are possible, with rolling admissions and continuous processing to 3/1 for financial aid. **Contact:** Ms. Mary Milbert, Director of Admissions, The Great Hall, Collegeville, MN 56321, 612-363-2196 or toll-free 800-24 JOHNS; fax 612-363-2115.

## GETTING IN LAST YEAR

922 applied
83% were accepted
56% enrolled (430)
19% from top tenth of their h.s. class
3.4 average high school GPA
7% had SAT verbal scores over 600
31% had SAT math scores over 600
37% had ACT scores over 26
1% had SAT verbal scores over 700
8% had SAT math scores over 700
7% had ACT scores over 30
2 National Merit Scholars

## THE STUDENT BODY

Total 1,820, of whom 1,685
  are undergraduates
From 37 states and territories,
  34 other countries
78% from Minnesota
100% men
1% African Americans
1% Native Americans
1% Hispanics
2% Asian Americans
2% international students

## AFTER FRESHMAN YEAR

83% returned for sophomore year
61% got a degree within 4 years
69% got a degree within 5 years
70% got a degree within 6 years

## AFTER GRADUATION

25% pursued further study (10% arts and
  sciences, 5% business, 5% law)
60% had job offers within 3 months
100 corporations, 8 government agencies, 11
  nonprofit organizations recruited on campus

## WHAT YOU WILL PAY

Tuition and fees $12,335
Room and board $4081
70% receive need-based financial aid
  averaging $3075
8% receive non-need financial aid averaging
  $3100

# SAINT JOSEPH'S UNIVERSITY

Philadelphia, Pennsylvania • Suburban setting • Private • Independent-Religious • Coed

▶ Saint Joseph's, Philadelphia's Jesuit university, recently added 5 accelerated–degree programs in cooperation with Thomas Jefferson University's College of Allied Health. Students in diagnostic imaging, laboratory sciences, nursing, occupational therapy, and physical therapy have the opportunity to earn degrees from both institutions, giving them a distinct competitive advantage when entering the job market. In the field of physical therapy, students participate in a 6-year program leading to a bachelor's degree in biology and a bachelor's and master's degree in physical therapy. Other allied health sciences are 5-year programs leading to a bachelor's degree in biology and a bachelor's degree in the desired field.

##  Academics

SJU offers a core academic program; fewer than half of graduate courses are open to undergraduates. It awards associate, bachelor's, and master's **degrees**. Challenging opportunities include advanced placement, accelerated degree programs, self-designed majors, tutorials, an honors program, a senior project, and Sigma Xi. Special programs include cooperative education, internships, summer session for credit, off-campus study, study abroad, and Army, Naval, and Air Force ROTC.

The most popular **majors** include marketing/retailing/merchandising, food marketing, and psychology. A complete listing of majors at SJU appears in the Majors Index beginning on page 380.

The **faculty** at SJU has 156 full-time graduate and undergraduate teachers, 89% with terminal degrees. 100% of the faculty serve as student advisers. The student-faculty ratio is 16:1, and the average class size in required courses is 30.

##  Computers on Campus

Students are not required to have a computer. 215 **computers** available in the computer center, academic buildings, classrooms, the library, and dormitories provide access to e-mail. Staffed computer lab on campus.

The 2 **libraries** have 317,000 books, 711,677 microform titles, and 1,700 subscriptions. They are connected to 3 national **on-line** catalogs.

##  Campus Life

There are 57 active **organizations** on campus, including a drama/theater group and student-run newspaper and radio station. 25% of eligible men and 25% of eligible women are members of 4 national **fraternities** and 3 national **sororities**. Student **safety services** include 24-hour shuttle/escort service, late night transport/escort service, 24-hour emergency telephone alarm devices, 24-hour patrols by trained security personnel, and electronically operated dormitory entrances.

SJU is a member of the NCAA (Division I). **Intercollegiate sports** (some offering scholarships) include baseball (m), basketball (m, w), crew (m, w), cross-country running (m, w), field hockey (w), golf (m), lacrosse (m, w), soccer (m), softball (w), tennis (m, w), track and field (m, w).

##  Applying

SJU requires an essay, a high school transcript, 3 years of high school math, 2 years of high school foreign language, 1 recommendation, and SAT I or ACT. It recommends 3 years of high school science, a campus interview, and a minimum high school GPA of 2.0. Early, deferred, and midyear entrance are possible, with rolling admissions and a 3/1 priority date for financial aid. **Contact:** Mr. David Conway, Dean of Enrollment Management, 5600 City Avenue, Philadelphia, PA 19131-1376, 610-660-1300.

---

### GETTING IN LAST YEAR
2,733 applied
79% were accepted
33% enrolled (715)
39% from top tenth of their h.s. class
9% had SAT verbal scores over 600
19% had SAT math scores over 600
1% had SAT verbal scores over 700
3% had SAT math scores over 700

### THE STUDENT BODY
Total 6,771, of whom 3,626
  are undergraduates

From 28 states and territories,
  67 other countries
53% from Pennsylvania
55% women, 45% men
8% African Americans
0% Native Americans
2% Hispanics
2% Asian Americans
4% international students

### AFTER FRESHMAN YEAR
86% returned for sophomore year
66% got a degree within 4 years

75% got a degree within 5 years
79% got a degree within 6 years

### AFTER GRADUATION
21% pursued further study (6% arts and
  sciences, 6% business, 5% law)
93 corporations, 5 government agencies, 4
  nonprofit organizations recruited on campus
1 Fulbright scholar

### WHAT YOU WILL PAY
Tuition and fees $12,800
Room and board $6000

# ST. LAWRENCE UNIVERSITY

Canton, New York • Small-town setting • Private • Independent • Coed

St. Lawrence prepares students for life after college in all its dimensions. A tight-knit community prepares students for involvement in other communities after graduation. Eleven international study possibilities offer students the opportunity to succeed in an ever-smaller world. Distinguished environmental studies and outdoor education programs take advantage of the University's location and prepare the student to assume stewardship responsibilities for, as well as enjoyable use of, the earth. A program in the first year emphasizing writing, speaking, faculty attention, and how to handle independence helps students make the most of their college experiences.

 ## Academics

St. Lawrence offers an interdisciplinary/international curriculum and core academic program; fewer than half of graduate courses are open to undergraduates. It awards bachelor's and master's **degrees**. Challenging opportunities include advanced placement, self-designed majors, tutorials, an honors program, a senior project, and Phi Beta Kappa. Special programs include internships, summer session for credit, off-campus study, study abroad, and Air Force ROTC.

The most popular **majors** include economics, English, and political science/government. A complete listing of majors at St. Lawrence appears in the Majors Index beginning on page 380.

The **faculty** at St. Lawrence has 151 full-time undergraduate teachers, 95% with terminal degrees. 100% of the faculty serve as student advisers. The student-faculty ratio is 12:1, and the average class size in required courses is 16.

 ## Computers on Campus

Students are not required to have a computer. 600 **computers** available in the computer center, computer labs, the library, and dormitories.

The 3 **libraries** have 428,360 books and 2,177 subscriptions.

 ## Campus Life

There are 75 active **organizations** on campus, including a drama/theater group and student-run newspaper and radio station. 27% of eligible men and 34% of eligible women are members of 7 national **fraternities**, 4 national **sororities**, and 1 local sorority. Student **safety services** include late night transport/escort service, 24-hour emergency telephone alarm devices, and 24-hour patrols by trained security personnel.

St. Lawrence is a member of the NCAA (Division III). **Intercollegiate sports** include baseball (m), basketball (m, w), crew (m), cross-country running (m, w), equestrian sports (m, w), field hockey (w), football (m), ice hockey (m, w), lacrosse (m, w), rugby (m), skiing (cross-country) (m, w), skiing (downhill) (m, w), soccer (m, w), swimming and diving (m, w), tennis (m, w), track and field (m, w), volleyball (w).

 ## Applying

St. Lawrence requires an essay, a high school transcript, 3 years of high school math and science, 3 years of high school foreign language, 2 recommendations, SAT I or ACT, and 1 SAT II Subject Test. It recommends an interview and 2 SAT II Subject Tests. Early, deferred, and midyear entrance are possible, with a 2/1 deadline and 2/15 for financial aid. **Contact:** Mr. Joel Wincowski, Dean of Admissions and Financial Aid, Payson Hall, Admissions, Canton, NY 13617-1455, 315-379-5261; fax 315-379-5502.

---

### GETTING IN LAST YEAR

2,693 applied
71% were accepted
30% enrolled (574)
32% from top tenth of their h.s. class
11% had SAT verbal scores over 600
35% had SAT math scores over 600
0% had SAT verbal scores over 700
4% had SAT math scores over 700

### THE STUDENT BODY

Total 2,045, of whom 1,937
  are undergraduates
From 42 states and territories,
  21 other countries

49% from New York
52% women, 48% men
2% African Americans
1% Native Americans
2% Hispanics
2% Asian Americans
4% international students

### AFTER FRESHMAN YEAR

90% returned for sophomore year
77% got a degree within 4 years
79% got a degree within 5 years
81% got a degree within 6 years

### AFTER GRADUATION

24% pursued further study (10% arts and
  sciences, 4% law, 3% medicine)
30 corporations, 30 government agencies, 30
  nonprofit organizations recruited on campus

### WHAT YOU WILL PAY

Tuition and fees $18,845
Room and board $5730
66% receive need-based financial aid
  averaging $12,914
1% receive non-need financial aid averaging
  $10,000

# ST. LOUIS COLLEGE OF PHARMACY

St. Louis, Missouri • Urban setting • Private • Independent • Coed

▶ The St. Louis College of Pharmacy is located in the heart of St. Louis' central west-end medical community and is the oldest college of its type west of the Mississippi River. The College is a national leader in pharmacy education, offering an integration of pharmaceutical knowledge and skills with a sound preparation in the basic sciences and liberal arts. The College strives to improve the well-being of society by preparing students to lead useful and satisfying lives, to contribute and lead in their communities, and to advance the profession of pharmacy.

##  Academics

St. Louis College of Pharmacy offers a core academic program; more than half of graduate courses are open to undergraduates. It awards bachelor's and master's **degrees**. Challenging opportunities include advanced placement, tutorials, and a senior project. Special programs include internships, summer session for credit, study abroad, and Army and Air Force ROTC.

A complete listing of majors at St. Louis College of Pharmacy appears in the Majors Index beginning on page 380.

The **faculty** at St. Louis College of Pharmacy has 63 full-time graduate and undergraduate teachers. 64% of the faculty serve as student advisers. The student-faculty ratio is 12:1.

##  Computers on Campus

Students are not required to have a computer. Student rooms are linked to a campus network. 60 **computers**
available in computer labs, the library, and the student center provide access to the main academic computer, e-mail, and on-line services. Staffed computer lab on campus provides training in the use of computers and software.

The 4 **libraries** have 35,553 books and 465 subscriptions. They are connected to 2 national **on-line** catalogs.

##  Campus Life

There are 15 active **organizations** on campus, including a drama/theater group and student-run newspaper. 70% of eligible men and 65% of eligible women are members of 4 national **fraternities** and 1 national **sorority**. Student **safety services** include late night transport/escort service, 24-hour emergency telephone alarm devices, 24-hour patrols by trained security personnel, and electronically operated dormitory entrances.

St. Louis College of Pharmacy is a member of the NAIA. **Intercollegiate sports** include basketball (m), volleyball (w).

##  Applying

St. Louis College of Pharmacy requires an essay, a high school transcript, 3 years of high school math, ACT, and in some cases SAT I. It recommends 3 years of high school science, some high school foreign language, an interview, and a minimum high school GPA of 3.0. Midyear entrance is possible, with rolling admissions and continuous processing to 6/30 for financial aid. **Contact:** Ms. Lisa Boeschen, Director of Admissions, 4588 Parkview Place, St. Louis, MO 63110-1088, 314-367-8700 ext. 227; fax 314-367-2784.

---

### GETTING IN LAST YEAR
292 applied
84% were accepted
58% enrolled (143)
35% from top tenth of their h.s. class
3.5 average high school GPA
43% had ACT scores over 26
5% had ACT scores over 30
6 valedictorians

### THE STUDENT BODY
Total 829, of whom 779
 are undergraduates
From 15 states and territories,
 1 other country
43% from Missouri
62% women, 38% men
2% African Americans
0% Native Americans
1% Hispanics
6% Asian Americans
2% international students

### AFTER FRESHMAN YEAR
90% returned for sophomore year

### AFTER GRADUATION
6% pursued further study (2% arts and
 sciences, 2% business, 1% law)

### WHAT YOU WILL PAY
Tuition and fees $9770
Room and board $4350
Need-based financial aid averages $1250
Non-need financial aid averages $1500

# SAINT LOUIS UNIVERSITY

St. Louis, Missouri • Urban setting • Private • Independent-Religious • Coed

For more than 175 years, Saint Louis University has earned a reputation for excellence in education. In its history, Saint Louis has accomplished a list of firsts that makes it a true center of higher learning: first university west of the Mississippi; first Catholic college in the United States to have faculty in schools of philosophy, theology, medicine, law, and business; first federally certified air college (Parks College); and first free-standing European campus (Madrid, Spain) operated by an American university. Saint Louis's academic reputation is the foundation of its success today.

##  Academics

SLU offers a traditional liberal arts curriculum and core academic program; fewer than half of graduate courses are open to undergraduates. It awards associate, bachelor's, master's, doctoral, and first professional **degrees**. Challenging opportunities include advanced placement, accelerated degree programs, self-designed majors, tutorials, an honors program, a senior project, Phi Beta Kappa, and Sigma Xi. Special programs include internships, summer session for credit, off-campus study, study abroad, and Army and Air Force ROTC.

The most popular **majors** include business, political science/government, and communication. A complete listing of majors at SLU appears in the Majors Index beginning on page 380.

The **faculty** at SLU has 1,217 full-time graduate and undergraduate teachers, 96% with terminal degrees. 100% of the faculty serve as student advisers. The student-faculty ratio is 6:1, and the average class size in required courses is 35.

##  Computers on Campus

Students are not required to have a computer. 225 **computers** available in the computer center, computer labs, the learning resource center, academic buildings, and dormitories provide access to the main academic computer, off-campus computing facilities, and e-mail. Staffed computer lab on campus provides training in the use of computers and software.

The 4 **libraries** have 1.4 million books and 13,578 subscriptions.

##  Campus Life

There are 60 active **organizations** on campus, including a drama/theater group and student-run newspaper and radio station. 24% of students participate in student government elections. 16% of eligible men and 10% of eligible women are members of 9 national **fraternities** and 5 national **sororities**. Student **safety services** include late night transport/escort service, 24-hour emergency telephone alarm devices, 24-hour patrols by trained security personnel, and electronically operated dormitory entrances.

SLU is a member of the NCAA (Division I). **Intercollegiate sports** (some offering scholarships) include baseball (m), basketball (m, w), cross-country running (m, w), field hockey (w), golf (m), ice hockey (m), riflery (m, w), rugby (m), soccer (m), softball (w), swimming and diving (m, w), tennis (m, w), volleyball (w).

##  Applying

SLU requires a high school transcript, minimum 2.5 GPA, SAT I or ACT, and in some cases an essay. It recommends 3 years of high school math and science, some high school foreign language, recommendations, and an interview. Deferred and midyear entrance are possible, with rolling admissions and continuous processing to 4/1 for financial aid. **Contact:** Director of Undergraduate Admissions, 221 North Grand Boulevard, St. Louis, MO 63103-2097, 314-977-2500 or toll-free 800-758-4968 (out-of-state); fax 314-977-3874.

### GETTING IN LAST YEAR
3,725 applied
87% were accepted
34% enrolled (1,088)
30% from top tenth of their h.s. class
47% had ACT scores over 26
14% had ACT scores over 30
9 National Merit Scholars

### THE STUDENT BODY
Total 10,768, of whom 6,214
  are undergraduates
From 49 states and territories

55% from Missouri
53% women, 47% men
9% African Americans
1% Native Americans
2% Hispanics
4% Asian Americans
5% international students

### AFTER FRESHMAN YEAR
82% returned for sophomore year
44% got a degree within 4 years
59% got a degree within 5 years
61% got a degree within 6 years

### AFTER GRADUATION
99 corporations, 7 government agencies, 8
  nonprofit organizations recruited on campus
1 Fulbright scholar

### WHAT YOU WILL PAY
Tuition and fees $11,770
Room and board $4730
Need-based financial aid averages $4450
Non-need financial aid averages $5335

# SAINT MARY'S COLLEGE

Notre Dame, Indiana • Suburban setting • Private • Independent-Religious • Women

 ## Academics

Saint Mary's offers a core academic program. It awards bachelor's **degrees**. Challenging opportunities include advanced placement, self-designed majors, and a senior project. Special programs include internships, off-campus study, study abroad, and Army, Naval, and Air Force ROTC.

The most popular **majors** include business, English, and communication. A complete listing of majors at Saint Mary's appears in the Majors Index beginning on page 380.

The **faculty** at Saint Mary's has 115 full-time teachers, 95% with terminal degrees. 100% of the faculty serve as student advisers. The student-faculty ratio is 11:1, and the average class size in required courses is 17.

 ## Computers on Campus

Students are not required to have a computer. Student rooms are linked to a campus network. 103 **computers** available in the computer center, computer labs, the learning resource center, classroom buildings, the library, and dormitories provide access to the main academic computer, off-campus computing facilities, and e-mail. Staffed computer lab on campus (open 24 hours a day).

The **library** has 194,395 books, 5,746 microform titles, and 772 subscriptions.

 ## Campus Life

There are 75 active **organizations** on campus, including a drama/theater group and student-run newspaper. Student **safety services** include late night transport/escort service, 24-hour emergency telephone alarm devices, 24-hour patrols by trained security personnel, and electronically operated dormitory entrances.

Saint Mary's is a member of the NCAA (Division III). **Intercollegiate sports** include basketball, crew, fencing, gymnastics, sailing, skiing (downhill), soccer, softball, swimming and diving, tennis, track and field, volleyball.

 ## Applying

Saint Mary's requires an essay, a high school transcript, 3 years of high school math, 2 years of high school foreign language, 1 recommendation, SAT I or ACT, and 3 SAT II Subject Tests (including SAT II: Writing Test). It recommends 3 years of high school science and an interview. Early, deferred, and midyear entrance are possible, with a 3/1 deadline and continuous processing to 3/1 for financial aid. **Contact:** Ms. Mary Pat Nolan, Director of Admission, 116 LeMans Hall, Notre Dame, IN 46556, 219-284-4587.

### GETTING IN LAST YEAR
907 applied
84% were accepted
52% enrolled (393)
29% from top tenth of their h.s. class
3.47 average high school GPA
8% had SAT verbal scores over 600
21% had SAT math scores over 600
38% had ACT scores over 26
1% had SAT verbal scores over 700
1% had SAT math scores over 700
7% had ACT scores over 30
12 National Merit Scholars
5 class presidents
7 valedictorians

### THE STUDENT BODY
1,545 undergraduates
From 45 states and territories,
  20 other countries
20% from Indiana
100% women
1% African Americans
0% Native Americans
2% Hispanics
1% Asian Americans
2% international students

### AFTER FRESHMAN YEAR
90% returned for sophomore year
74% got a degree within 4 years
78% got a degree within 5 years
79% got a degree within 6 years

### AFTER GRADUATION
20% pursued further study (5% arts and sciences, 3% business, 3% law)
55 corporations, 46 nonprofit organizations recruited on campus

### WHAT YOU WILL PAY
Tuition and fees $13,419
Room and board $4627
Need-based financial aid averages $5760
Non-need financial aid averages $5000

# SAINT MARY'S COLLEGE OF CALIFORNIA

Moraga, California • Suburban setting • Private • Independent-Religious • Coed

It has been said that Saint Mary's College is "a classic example of a school committed to teaching students *how* to think rather than *what* to think." It is home to some of the "happiest students in the nation," has a safe and beautiful campus, and is a "good buy." Saint Mary's intimate academic community of 2,200 undergraduates is located 20 miles east of San Francisco. Operated and owned by the Christian Brothers, the College is committed to providing students with a comprehensive liberal arts education that includes reading and discussing the Great Books.

##  Academics

Saint Mary's offers a core academic program; a few graduate courses are open to undergraduates. It awards bachelor's and master's **degrees**. Challenging opportunities include advanced placement, self-designed majors, tutorials, an honors program, and a senior project. Special programs include internships, off-campus study, study abroad, and Army, Naval, and Air Force ROTC.

The most popular **majors** include business, biology/biological sciences, and communication. A complete listing of majors at Saint Mary's appears in the Majors Index beginning on page 380.

The **faculty** at Saint Mary's has 141 full-time undergraduate teachers, 91% with terminal degrees. 100% of the faculty serve as student advisers. The student-faculty ratio is 15:1, and the average class size in required courses is 20.

##  Computers on Campus

Students are not required to have a computer. 139 **computers** available in the computer center, computer labs, classrooms, and the library. Staffed computer lab on campus provides training in the use of computers and software.

The **library** has 179,485 books, 177,756 microform titles, and 1,097 subscriptions.

##  Campus Life

There are 32 active **organizations** on campus, including a drama/theater group and student-run newspaper and radio station. Student **safety services** include late night transport/escort service, 24-hour emergency telephone alarm devices, and 24-hour patrols by trained security personnel.

Saint Mary's is a member of the NCAA (Division I). **Intercollegiate sports** (some offering scholarships) include baseball (m), basketball (m, w), crew (m, w), cross-country running (m, w), football (m), golf (m), ice hockey (m), lacrosse (m, w), rugby (m), soccer (m, w), softball (w), tennis (m, w), volleyball (w).

##  Applying

Saint Mary's requires an essay, a high school transcript, 1 recommendation, SAT I or ACT, a minimum high school GPA of 2.0, and in some cases 3 years of high school science, an interview, and a minimum high school GPA of 3.0. It recommends 3 years of high school math, some high school foreign language, and a minimum high school GPA of 3.0. Early, deferred, and midyear entrance are possible, with a 3/1 deadline and continuous processing to 3/1 for financial aid. **Contact:** Mr. Michael Tressel, Director of Admissions, PO Box 4800, Moraga, CA 94575, 510-631-4224; fax 510-376-7193.

---

### GETTING IN LAST YEAR
2,554 applied
81% were accepted
24% enrolled (501)
39% from top tenth of their h.s. class
3.4 average high school GPA
7% had SAT verbal scores over 600
25% had SAT math scores over 600
1% had SAT verbal scores over 700
1% had SAT math scores over 700
1 National Merit Scholar

### THE STUDENT BODY
Total 4,247, of whom 2,144
   are undergraduates
From 36 states and territories,
   21 other countries
76% from California
54% women, 46% men
4% African Americans
1% Native Americans
13% Hispanics
9% Asian Americans
4% international students

### AFTER FRESHMAN YEAR
90% returned for sophomore year

### AFTER GRADUATION
35% pursued further study (10% business,
   10% law, 6% medicine)
75 corporations, 10 government agencies, 30
   nonprofit organizations recruited on campus

### WHAT YOU WILL PAY
Tuition and fees $13,432
Room and board $6270
55% receive need-based financial aid
   averaging $8332

---

# ST. MARY'S COLLEGE OF MARYLAND

St. Mary's City, Maryland • Rural setting • Public • State-supported • Coed

St. Mary's College of Maryland, with its distinctive identity as a public honors college, is emerging as one of the finest liberal arts and sciences colleges in the country. A lively academic atmosphere combines with the serene yet stunning natural beauty of a riverfront campus to create a challenging and memorable college experience for 1,300 students. Construction in recent years includes 40 town house student residences, a new library, and a new state-of-the-art science building. Newly opened are 40 additional town house residences, and both the student center and the gymnasium are scheduled for expansion soon.

##  Academics

St. Mary's offers a liberal arts and sciences curriculum and core academic program. It awards bachelor's **degrees**. Challenging opportunities include advanced placement, self-designed majors, tutorials, Freshmen Honors College, and a senior project. Special programs include internships, summer session for credit, off-campus study, and study abroad.

The most popular **majors** include economics, psychology, and biology/biological sciences. A complete listing of majors at St. Mary's appears in the Majors Index beginning on page 380.

The **faculty** at St. Mary's has 110 full-time teachers, 95% with terminal degrees. 85% of the faculty serve as student advisers. The student-faculty ratio is 13:1, and the average class size in required courses is 14.

##  Computers on Campus

Students are not required to have a computer. 95 **computers** available in the computer center, computer labs, the research center, and the library provide access to the main academic computer, off-campus computing facilities, e-mail, and on-line services. Staffed computer lab on campus provides training in the use of computers and software.

The **library** has 146,126 books, 32,213 microform titles, and 1,563 subscriptions. It is connected to 3 national **on-line** catalogs.

##  Campus Life

There are 46 active **organizations** on campus, including a drama/theater group and student-run newspaper and radio station. 33% of students participate in student government elections. Student **safety services** include late night transport/escort service, 24-hour emergency telephone alarm devices, 24-hour patrols by trained security personnel, student patrols, and electronically operated dormitory entrances.

St. Mary's is a member of the NCAA (Division III). **Intercollegiate sports** include baseball (m), basketball (m, w), crew (m, w), fencing (m, w), field hockey (w), golf (m, w), lacrosse (m, w), rugby (m), sailing (m, w), soccer (m, w), swimming and diving (m, w), tennis (m, w), volleyball (m, w), wrestling (m).

##  Applying

St. Mary's requires an essay, a high school transcript, 3 years of high school math, 2 years of high school foreign language, and SAT I or ACT. It recommends 3 years of high school science, 4 years of high school foreign language, 3 recommendations, and a campus interview. Early and midyear entrance are possible, with a 1/15 deadline and a 3/1 priority date for financial aid. **Contact:** Mr. Richard Edgar, Director of Admissions, Admissions Office, St. Mary's City, MD 20686, 301-862-0292 or toll-free 800-492-7181.

---

### GETTING IN LAST YEAR

1,227 applied
65% were accepted
38% enrolled (304)
3.4 average high school GPA
37% had SAT verbal scores over 600
60% had SAT math scores over 600
4% had SAT verbal scores over 700
12% had SAT math scores over 700
42 National Merit Scholars
11 valedictorians

### THE STUDENT BODY

1,376 undergraduates
From 35 states and territories,
  20 other countries

84% from Maryland
57% women, 43% men
10% African Americans
0% Native Americans
2% Hispanics
4% Asian Americans
1% international students

### AFTER FRESHMAN YEAR

87% returned for sophomore year
53% got a degree within 4 years
69% got a degree within 5 years
71% got a degree within 6 years

### AFTER GRADUATION

32% pursued further study (26% arts and
  sciences, 2% business, 2% law)
4 corporations, 1 nonprofit organization
  recruited on campus
1 Fulbright scholar

### WHAT YOU WILL PAY

Resident tuition and fees $5435
Nonresident tuition and fees $8735
Room and board $4970
16% receive need-based financial aid
  averaging $2025
50% receive non-need financial aid averaging
  $3000

# ST. NORBERT COLLEGE

De Pere, Wisconsin • Suburban setting • Private • Independent-Religious • Coed

Recognized nationally for its academic program, St. Norbert College provides students with the resources necessary to compete with the nation's best. With a faculty determined to provide the best possible instruction and advising, the College is committed to helping students achieve their goals. The College community, steeped in the values of the Norbertine tradition, encourages students to discover ways in which they can enrich their lives, society, and the world. Students considering St. Norbert are welcome to visit the campus, sit in on classes, and meet with faculty members.

##  Academics

St. Norbert offers a liberal arts and sciences curriculum and core academic program; a few graduate courses are open to undergraduates. It awards bachelor's and master's **degrees**. Challenging opportunities include advanced placement, accelerated degree programs, self-designed majors, tutorials, an honors program, and a senior project. Special programs include cooperative education, internships, summer session for credit, off-campus study, study abroad, and Army ROTC.

The most popular **majors** include business, communication, and elementary education. A complete listing of majors at St. Norbert appears in the Majors Index beginning on page 380.

The **faculty** at St. Norbert has 118 full-time undergraduate teachers, 75% with terminal degrees. 100% of the faculty serve as student advisers. The student-faculty ratio is 15:1, and the average class size in required courses is 25.

##  Computers on Campus

Students are not required to have a computer. Student rooms are linked to a campus network. 95 **computers** available in the computer center and the library provide access to the main academic computer, e-mail, and on-line services. Staffed computer lab on campus provides training in the use of computers and software.

The **library** has 170,551 books, 24,879 microform titles, and 852 subscriptions.

##  Campus Life

There are 65 active **organizations** on campus, including a drama/theater group and student-run newspaper and radio station. 30% of students participate in student government elections. 41% of eligible men and 57% of eligible women are members of 3 national **fraternities**, 1 national **sorority**, 2 local fraternities, 3 local sororities, and 13 social clubs. Student **safety services** include late night transport/escort service, 24-hour emergency telephone alarm devices, and 24-hour patrols by trained security personnel.

St. Norbert is a member of the NCAA (Division III). **Intercollegiate sports** include baseball (m), basketball (m, w), cross-country running (m, w), football (m), golf (m, w), ice hockey (m), soccer (m, w), softball (w), tennis (m, w), track and field (m, w), volleyball (w).

##  Applying

St. Norbert requires an essay, a high school transcript, 3 years of high school math, recommendations, and SAT I or ACT. It recommends 3 years of high school science, 2 years of high school foreign language, and an interview. Early, deferred, and midyear entrance are possible, with rolling admissions and continuous processing to 3/1 for financial aid. **Contact:** Mr. Craig Wesley, Dean of Admission, 100 Grant Street, Office of Admission, De Pere, WI 54115-2099, 414-337-3005 or toll-free 800-236-4878.

---

### GETTING IN LAST YEAR
1,300 applied
91% were accepted
42% enrolled (496)
31% from top tenth of their h.s. class
3.25 average high school GPA
30% had ACT scores over 26
5% had ACT scores over 30

### THE STUDENT BODY
Total 2,092, of whom 2,059 are undergraduates
From 27 states and territories, 11 other countries

71% from Wisconsin
57% women, 43% men
1% African Americans
1% Native Americans
1% Hispanics
1% Asian Americans
2% international students

### AFTER FRESHMAN YEAR
84% returned for sophomore year
70% got a degree within 4 years
74% got a degree within 5 years
74% got a degree within 6 years

### AFTER GRADUATION
18% pursued further study (15% arts and sciences, 1% business, 1% law)
34 corporations recruited on campus

### WHAT YOU WILL PAY
Tuition and fees $12,215
Room and board $4450
65% receive need-based financial aid averaging $4906
27% receive non-need financial aid averaging $3590

# ST. OLAF COLLEGE

Northfield, Minnesota • Small-town setting • Private • Independent-Religious • Coed

St. Olaf College strives to instill in its students the moral sensitivity and critical thinking necessary for knowledgeable and responsible citizenship of the world. An undergraduate residential institution of the Evangelical Lutheran Church in America, St. Olaf provides an education committed to the liberal arts, rooted in the Christian gospel, and incorporating a global perspective. Its nationally ranked science and mathematics departments, widely acclaimed international studies program, superb choral tradition, and competitive membership in the Minnesota Intercollegiate Athletic Conference are special features. St. Olaf has been widely recognized as one of America's leading colleges and as a "best buy" among the nation's liberal arts institutions.

 **Academics**

St. Olaf offers an interdisciplinary curriculum and core academic program. It awards bachelor's **degrees**. Challenging opportunities include advanced placement, accelerated degree programs, self-designed majors, tutorials, a senior project, and Phi Beta Kappa. Special programs include internships, summer session for credit, off-campus study, and study abroad.

The most popular **majors** include economics, mathematics, and English. A complete listing of majors at St. Olaf appears in the Majors Index beginning on page 380.

The **faculty** at St. Olaf has 276 full-time teachers, 75% with terminal degrees. 100% of the faculty serve as student advisers. The student-faculty ratio is 12:1, and the average class size in required courses is 21.

 **Computers on Campus**

Students are not required to have a computer. 380 **computers** available in the computer center, computer labs, all academic buildings, the library, and dormitories provide access to the main academic computer, e-mail, and on-line services. Staffed computer lab on campus (open 24 hours a day) provides training in the use of computers and software.

The 4 **libraries** have 435,735 books, 53,709 microform titles, and 1,586 subscriptions. They are connected to 1 national **on-line** catalog.

 **Campus Life**

There are 80 active **organizations** on campus, including a drama/theater group and student-run newspaper and radio station. 25% of students participate in student government elections. Student **safety services** include late night transport/escort service, 24-hour emergency telephone alarm devices, 24-hour patrols by trained security personnel, and electronically operated dormitory entrances.

St. Olaf is a member of the NCAA (Division III). **Intercollegiate sports** include baseball (m), basketball (m, w), cross-country running (m, w), football (m), golf (m, w), ice hockey (m), skiing (cross-country) (m, w), skiing (downhill) (m, w), soccer (m, w), softball (w), swimming and diving (m, w), tennis (m, w), track and field (m, w), volleyball (w), wrestling (m).

 **Applying**

St. Olaf requires an essay, a high school transcript, 2 recommendations, SAT I or ACT, PSAT, and a minimum high school GPA of 3.0. It recommends 3 years of high school math and science, 2 years of high school foreign language, and an interview. Early, deferred, and midyear entrance are possible, with rolling admissions and continuous processing to 3/1 for financial aid. **Contact:** Ms. Barbara Lundberg, Director of Admissions, 1520 St. Olaf Avenue, Northfield, MN 55057-1098, 507-646-3025 or toll-free 800-800-3025 (in-state); fax 507-646-3549.

---

### GETTING IN LAST YEAR
2,235 applied
76% were accepted
44% enrolled (752)
38% from top tenth of their h.s. class
3.5 average high school GPA
26% had SAT verbal scores over 600
45% had SAT math scores over 600
3% had SAT verbal scores over 700
10% had SAT math scores over 700
19 National Merit Scholars

### THE STUDENT BODY
2,958 undergraduates
From 39 states and territories,
   25 other countries

55% from Minnesota
58% women, 42% men
2% African Americans
1% Native Americans
1% Hispanics
4% Asian Americans
2% international students

### AFTER FRESHMAN YEAR
87% returned for sophomore year
75% got a degree within 4 years
81% got a degree within 5 years
82% got a degree within 6 years

### AFTER GRADUATION
29% pursued further study
19 corporations, 3 government agencies, 9
   nonprofit organizations recruited on campus
3 Fulbright scholars

### WHAT YOU WILL PAY
Tuition and fees $14,350
Room and board $3750
62% receive need-based financial aid
   averaging $5457
3% receive non-need financial aid averaging
   $3500

# SAMFORD UNIVERSITY

Birmingham, Alabama • Suburban setting • Private • Independent-Religious • Coed

Samford University is the largest private accredited university in Alabama, yet with 4,500 students, it is an ideal size. More than half the undergraduates reside on campus. Students from 43 states and 42 other countries enjoy a beautiful setting characterized by Georgian-Colonial architecture. The institution takes seriously its Christian heritage and is consistently listed in rankings of Southeastern institutions. Faculty members have earned degrees from more than 160 colleges and universities, with over 80% holding the terminal degree in their field. Excellent opportunity to "stretch" academically, socially, physically, and spiritually is provided, along with special opportunities in computer competency, in international experiences, and in externships.

 **Academics**

Samford offers a liberal arts curriculum and core academic program; a few graduate courses are open to undergraduates. It awards associate, bachelor's, master's, and first professional **degrees**. Challenging opportunities include advanced placement, accelerated degree programs, self-designed majors, an honors program, and a senior project. Special programs include cooperative education, internships, summer session for credit, off-campus study, study abroad, and Army and Air Force ROTC.

The most popular **majors** include liberal arts/general studies, pharmacy/pharmaceutical sciences, and business. A complete listing of majors at Samford appears in the Majors Index beginning on page 380.

The **faculty** at Samford has 256 full-time graduate and undergraduate teachers, 85% with terminal degrees. 60% of the faculty serve as student advisers. The student-faculty ratio is 14:1, and the average class size in required courses is 25.

 **Computers on Campus**

Students are not required to have a computer. 250 **computers** available in the computer center, business,

nursing, education, science, pharmacy, music schools, and the library provide access to e-mail. Staffed computer lab on campus provides training in the use of computers and software.

The 4 **libraries** have 512,051 books, 288,559 microform titles, and 1,644 subscriptions. They are connected to 2 national **on-line** catalogs.

 **Campus Life**

There are 110 active **organizations** on campus, including a drama/theater group and student-run newspaper and radio station. 30% of students participate in student government elections. 30% of eligible men and 30% of eligible women are members of 5 national **fraternities** and 7 national **sororities**. Student **safety services** include 24-hour patrols by trained security personnel and electronically operated dormitory entrances.

Samford is a member of the NCAA (Division I). **Intercollegiate sports** (some offering scholarships) include baseball (m), basketball (m), cross-country running (m, w), football (m), golf (m, w), softball (w), tennis (m, w), track and field (m, w), volleyball (w).

 **Applying**

Samford requires an essay, a high school transcript, 2 recommendations, SAT I or ACT, and a minimum high school GPA of 3.0. It recommends 3 years of high school math and science, some high school foreign language, and a campus interview. Early, deferred, and midyear entrance are possible, with rolling admissions and continuous processing to 3/1 for financial aid. **Contact:** Dr. Don Belcher, Dean of Admissions and Financial Aid, Samford Hall, Birmingham, AL 35229-0002, 205-870-2901 or toll-free 800-888-7218; fax 205-870-2171.

## GETTING IN LAST YEAR

1,516 applied
93% were accepted
42% enrolled (591)
30% from top tenth of their h.s. class
3.4 average high school GPA
8% had SAT verbal scores over 600
21% had SAT math scores over 600
36% had ACT scores over 26
1% had SAT verbal scores over 700
3% had SAT math scores over 700
9% had ACT scores over 30
11 National Merit Scholars
29 valedictorians

## THE STUDENT BODY

Total 4,571, of whom 3,236
  are undergraduates
51% from Alabama
62% women, 38% men
5% African Americans
0% Native Americans
1% Hispanics
1% Asian Americans
1% international students

## AFTER GRADUATION

70 corporations, 48 government agencies, 7 nonprofit organizations recruited on campus

## WHAT YOU WILL PAY

Tuition and fees $8236
Room and board $3654
Need-based financial aid averages $1500
Non-need financial aid averages $1500

# SANTA CLARA UNIVERSITY

Santa Clara, California • Suburban setting • Private • Independent-Religious • Coed

▶ Students who are interested in a strong academic program, a commitment to social justice, California weather and diversity, and a learning environment where professors know their students should consider Santa Clara University. In addition to the undergraduate divisions of arts and sciences, business, and engineering, special programs are offered in environmental studies, retail studies, studies abroad, and courses that incorporate community service. Santa Clara is looking for students who have taken solid, college-prep courses in high school and who are prepared to handle a rigorous collegiate program. The University also welcomes students who share a concern for and commitment to solving society's problems.

 **Academics**

Santa Clara offers an education of the whole person curriculum and core academic program. It awards bachelor's, master's, doctoral, and first professional **degrees**. Challenging opportunities include advanced placement, self-designed majors, tutorials, Freshmen Honors College, an honors program, a senior project, Phi Beta Kappa, and Sigma Xi. Special programs include cooperative education, internships, summer session for credit, and Army, Naval, and Air Force ROTC.

The most popular **majors** include finance/banking, psychology, and political science/government. A complete listing of majors at Santa Clara appears in the Majors Index beginning on page 380.

The **faculty** at Santa Clara has 353 full-time graduate and undergraduate teachers, 91% with terminal degrees. 100% of the faculty serve as student advisers. The student-faculty ratio is 14:1.

 **Computers on Campus**

Students are not required to have a computer. 327 **computers** available in the computer center, computer labs, classrooms, the library, and the student center provide access to the main academic computer and e-mail. Staffed computer lab on campus provides training in the use of computers and software.

The **library** has 593,593 books, 36,939 microform titles, and 5,763 subscriptions.

 **Campus Life**

There are 97 active **organizations** on campus, including a drama/theater group and student-run newspaper and radio station. 15% of eligible men and 16% of eligible women are members of 4 national **fraternities** and 3 national **sororities**. Student **safety services** include late night transport/escort service and 24-hour emergency telephone alarm devices.

Santa Clara is a member of the NCAA (Division I). **Intercollegiate sports** (some offering scholarships) include baseball (m), basketball (m, w), crew (m, w), cross-country running (m, w), golf (m), lacrosse (m), rugby (m), soccer (m, w), tennis (m, w), volleyball (m, w), water polo (m).

 **Applying**

Santa Clara requires an essay, a high school transcript, 3 years of high school math, 3 years of high school foreign language, 1 recommendation, SAT I or ACT, and in some cases 3 years of high school science. It recommends an interview. 2/1 deadline and continuous processing to 2/1 for financial aid. **Contact:** Mr. Daniel J. Saracino, Dean of Admissions, 500 El Camino Real, Santa Clara, CA 95053-0001, 408-554-4700; fax 408-554-5255.

---

**GETTING IN LAST YEAR**
- 4,667 applied
- 66% were accepted
- 29% enrolled (910)
- 39% from top tenth of their h.s. class
- 3.45 average high school GPA
- 12% had SAT verbal scores over 600
- 45% had SAT math scores over 600
- 1% had SAT verbal scores over 700
- 7% had SAT math scores over 700
- 6 National Merit Scholars
- 40 valedictorians

**THE STUDENT BODY**
Total 7,513, of whom 4,013 are undergraduates

From 48 states and territories, 81 other countries
- 67% from California
- 52% women, 48% men
- 3% African Americans
- 1% Native Americans
- 14% Hispanics
- 19% Asian Americans
- 4% international students

**AFTER FRESHMAN YEAR**
- 90% returned for sophomore year
- 70% got a degree within 4 years
- 81% got a degree within 5 years
- 83% got a degree within 6 years

**AFTER GRADUATION**
- 19% pursued further study (8% arts and sciences, 3% medicine, 2% business)
- 71% had job offers within 3 months
- 140 corporations, 5 government agencies, 19 nonprofit organizations recruited on campus

**WHAT YOU WILL PAY**
- Tuition and fees $13,584
- Room and board $5904
- 64% receive need-based financial aid averaging $6512
- 4% receive non-need financial aid averaging $11,994

# SARAH LAWRENCE COLLEGE

Bronxville, New York • Suburban setting • Private • Independent • Coed

A private coeducational liberal arts college founded in 1926, Sarah Lawrence is a lively community of students, scholars, and artists. Sarah Lawrence's innovative seminar/conference course structure makes it unique among other leading liberal arts colleges. Most of its courses are composed of two parts: the seminar, which is limited to 15 students, and the conference, which is a private biweekly meeting with the seminar professor. The freedom of the seminar allows for spirited discussion of classwork among a small number of students; conferences bring together professor and student to create individual projects that extend the seminar's texts, connecting them with the student's academic interests.

## Academics

Sarah Lawrence offers an interdisciplinary curriculum and core academic program; a few graduate courses are open to undergraduates. It awards bachelor's and master's **degrees**. Challenging opportunities include advanced placement, self-designed majors, and tutorials. Special programs include internships and study abroad.

The most popular **majors** include literature, creative writing, and psychology. A complete listing of majors at Sarah Lawrence appears in the Majors Index beginning on page 380.

The **faculty** at Sarah Lawrence has 165 full-time undergraduate teachers, 94% with terminal degrees. 100% of the faculty serve as student advisers. The student-faculty ratio is 6:1, and the average class size in required courses is 11.

## Computers on Campus

Students are not required to have a computer. 46 **computers** available in the computer center provide access to e-mail. Staffed computer lab on campus provides training in the use of computers and software.

The 3 **libraries** have 214,531 books, 14,843 microform titles, and 1,201 subscriptions. They are connected to 6 national **on-line** catalogs.

## Campus Life

There are 30 active **organizations** on campus, including a drama/theater group and student-run newspaper. 40% of students participate in student government elections.

No national or local **fraternities** or **sororities**. Student **safety services** include late night transport/escort service, 24-hour emergency telephone alarm devices, 24-hour patrols by trained security personnel, and electronically operated dormitory entrances. **Intercollegiate sports** include crew (m, w), equestrian sports (m, w), soccer (m), tennis (m, w), volleyball (w).

## Applying

Sarah Lawrence requires an essay, a high school transcript, 3 recommendations, SAT I, ACT or any 3 SAT II Subject Tests. It recommends 3 years of high school math and science, some high school foreign language, an interview, and a minimum high school GPA of 3.0. Early, deferred, and midyear entrance are possible, with a 2/1 deadline and 2/1 for financial aid. **Contact:** Mr. Bob Kinally, Acting Dean of Admissions, 1 Meadway, Bronxville, NY 10708, 914-395-2510 or toll-free 800-888-2858; fax 914-395-2668.

### GETTING IN LAST YEAR

1,248 applied
56% were accepted
37% enrolled (262)
57% from top tenth of their h.s. class
3.41 average high school GPA
40% had SAT verbal scores over 600
27% had SAT math scores over 600
8% had SAT verbal scores over 700
4% had SAT math scores over 700

### THE STUDENT BODY

Total 1,306, of whom 1,056 are undergraduates
From 53 states and territories, 26 other countries
24% from New York
72% women, 28% men
6% African Americans
1% Native Americans
5% Hispanics
5% Asian Americans
4% international students

### AFTER FRESHMAN YEAR

94% returned for sophomore year
75% got a degree within 4 years
75% got a degree within 5 years
80% got a degree within 6 years

### WHAT YOU WILL PAY

Tuition and fees $19,564
Room and board $6694

# SCRIPPS COLLEGE

Claremont, California • Suburban setting • Private • Independent • Women

From its founding in 1926 as one of the few institutions in the West dedicated to educating women for professional careers as well as personal intellectual growth, Scripps College has championed the qualities of mind and spirit described by its founder, newspaper entrepreneur and philanthropist Ellen Browning Scripps. While many colleges are now coeducational, Scripps continues as a women's college because it believes that having women at the core of its concerns provides the very best environment for intellectually ambitious women to learn from a distinguished teaching faculty and from each other. Scripps emphasizes a challenging liberal arts curriculum based on interdisciplinary humanistic studies.

##  Academics

Scripps offers a core academic program. It awards bachelor's **degrees**. Challenging opportunities include advanced placement, self-designed majors, tutorials, an honors program, and Phi Beta Kappa. Special programs include internships, off-campus study, study abroad, and Army and Air Force ROTC.

The most popular **majors** include psychology and biology/biological sciences. A complete listing of majors at Scripps appears in the Majors Index beginning on page 380.

The **faculty** at Scripps has 58 full-time teachers, 100% with terminal degrees. 100% of the faculty serve as student advisers. The student-faculty ratio is 9:1, and the average class size in required courses is 14.

##  Computers on Campus

Students are not required to have a computer. 40 **computers** available in the computer center, classrooms, and dormitories provide access to the main academic computer, off-campus computing facilities, and e-mail.

The 2 **libraries** have 1.9 million books, 1.1 million microform titles, and 6,800 subscriptions.

##  Campus Life

There are 200 active **organizations** on campus, including a drama/theater group and student-run newspaper and radio station. Student **safety services** include late night transport/escort service, 24-hour emergency telephone alarm devices, 24-hour patrols by trained security personnel, and electronically operated dormitory entrances.

Scripps is a member of the NCAA (Division III). **Intercollegiate sports** include basketball, cross-country running, golf, soccer, softball, swimming and diving, tennis, track and field, volleyball.

##  Applying

Scripps requires an essay, a high school transcript, 3 recommendations, graded writing sample, and SAT I or ACT. It recommends 4 years of high school math, 3 years of high school science, 3 years of high school foreign language, an interview, 3 SAT II Subject Tests, and a minimum high school GPA of 3.0. Early, deferred, and midyear entrance are possible, with a 2/1 deadline and a 2/1 priority date for financial aid. **Contact:** Ms. Mimi Tung, Director of Admission, 1030 Columbia Avenue, Claremont, CA 91711-3948, 909-621-8149; fax 909-621-8323.

### GETTING IN LAST YEAR
930 applied
78% were accepted
23% enrolled (167)
45% from top tenth of their h.s. class
3.55 average high school GPA
30% had SAT verbal scores over 600
47% had SAT math scores over 600
45% had ACT scores over 26
7% had SAT verbal scores over 700
10% had SAT math scores over 700
23% had ACT scores over 30
20 class presidents
7 valedictorians

### THE STUDENT BODY
608 undergraduates
From 37 states and territories,
   19 other countries
57% from California
100% women
4% African Americans
0% Native Americans
10% Hispanics
20% Asian Americans
5% international students

### AFTER FRESHMAN YEAR
85% returned for sophomore year
75% got a degree within 4 years

### AFTER GRADUATION
21% pursued further study (13% arts and
   sciences, 3% business, 3% law)
77 corporations, 14 government agencies, 19
   nonprofit organizations recruited on campus

### WHAT YOU WILL PAY
Tuition and fees $17,350
Room and board $7350
50% receive need-based financial aid
   averaging $11,966
7% receive non-need financial aid averaging
   $5606

# SHEPHERD COLLEGE

Shepherdstown, West Virginia • Small-town setting • Public • State-supported • Coed

---

Since Shepherd College is located only an hour's drive from the Baltimore and Washington Beltways, it offers numerous internships and co-op programs with government agencies, scientific research centers, and corporations in the area. It is also the home of the Center for the Study of the Civil War, the professional Equity Contemporary American Theater Festival, and the Russian American Center.

##  Academics

Shepherd offers a core academic program. It awards associate and bachelor's **degrees**. Challenging opportunities include advanced placement, accelerated degree programs, an honors program, and a senior project. Special programs include cooperative education, internships, summer session for credit, and Army and Air Force ROTC.

The most popular **majors** include business, education, and nursing. A complete listing of majors at Shepherd appears in the Majors Index beginning on page 380.

The **faculty** at Shepherd has 115 full-time teachers, 65% with terminal degrees. 100% of the faculty serve as student advisers. The student-faculty ratio is 15:1, and the average class size in required courses is 35.

##  Computers on Campus

Students are not required to have a computer. 202 **computers** available in the computer center, computer labs, the learning resource center, and the library provide access to the main academic computer, e-mail, and on-line services. Staffed computer lab on campus provides training in the use of computers and software.

The **library** has 255,336 books, 55,000 microform titles, and 958 subscriptions. It is connected to 4 national **on-line** catalogs.

##  Campus Life

There are 70 active **organizations** on campus, including a drama/theater group and student-run newspaper and radio station. 40% of students participate in student government elections. 25% of eligible men and 25% of eligible women are members of 5 national **fraternities** and 3 national **sororities**. Student **safety services** include late night transport/escort service, 24-hour emergency telephone alarm devices, 24-hour patrols by trained security personnel, and electronically operated dormitory entrances.

Shepherd is a member of the NCAA (Division II). **Intercollegiate sports** (some offering scholarships) include baseball (m), basketball (m, w), cross-country running (m, w), football (m), golf (m, w), soccer (m), softball (w), tennis (m, w), volleyball (w).

##  Applying

Shepherd requires an essay, a high school transcript, 3 years of high school math and science, 3 recommendations, and SAT I or ACT. It recommends 2 years of high school foreign language and a campus interview. Early, deferred, and midyear entrance are possible, with a 2/1 deadline and continuous processing to 3/1 for financial aid. **Contact:** Mr. Karl L. Wolf, Director of Admissions, McMurran Hall, Shepherdstown, WV 25443, 304-876-5212 or toll-free 800-344-5231; fax 304-876-3101.

---

**GETTING IN LAST YEAR**

1,600 applied
73% were accepted
50% enrolled (584)
21% had SAT verbal scores over 600
21% had SAT math scores over 600
20% had ACT scores over 26
1% had SAT verbal scores over 700
1% had SAT math scores over 700
2% had ACT scores over 30
6 National Merit Scholars
15 class presidents
20 valedictorians

**THE STUDENT BODY**

3,648 undergraduates
From 35 states and territories,
   10 other countries
72% from West Virginia
61% women, 39% men
6% African Americans
1% Native Americans
2% Hispanics
1% Asian Americans
1% international students

**AFTER FRESHMAN YEAR**

76% returned for sophomore year

**AFTER GRADUATION**

30% pursued further study
60% had job offers within 3 months
35 corporations, 15 government agencies, 50
   nonprofit organizations recruited on campus

**WHAT YOU WILL PAY**

Resident tuition and fees $2064
Nonresident tuition and fees $4694
Room and board $3820
39% receive non-need financial aid averaging
   $535

---

# SIENA COLLEGE

Loudonville, New York • Suburban setting • Private • Independent-Religious • Coed

Siena's top-flight faculty members call forth the best Siena students have to give, and the students do the same for them. Siena people are competitive but not at each other's expense. A caring network of faculty, friars, students, and staff ensures a complete education for each individual student. The curriculum includes 23 majors in 3 divisions—arts, science, and business. In addition, there are more than 15 preprofessional and special academic programs. Siena's 152-acre campus is located in Loudonville, a suburb of Albany, New York, the state capital.

 ## Academics

Siena offers a core academic program. It awards bachelor's **degrees**. Challenging opportunities include advanced placement, tutorials, an honors program, and a senior project. Special programs include internships, summer session for credit, off-campus study, and Army and Air Force ROTC.

The most popular **majors** include marketing/retailing/merchandising, accounting, and finance/banking. A complete listing of majors at Siena appears in the Majors Index beginning on page 380.

The **faculty** at Siena has 166 full-time teachers, 84% with terminal degrees. 100% of the faculty serve as student advisers. The student-faculty ratio is 16:1, and the average class size in required courses is 21.

 ## Computers on Campus

Students are not required to have a computer. 500 **computers** available in the computer center, computer labs, academic buildings, and classrooms provide access to the main academic computer and e-mail. Staffed computer lab on campus (open 24 hours a day) provides training in the use of computers and software.

The **library** has 251,080 books, 30,006 microform titles, and 1,654 subscriptions.

 ## Campus Life

There are 77 active **organizations** on campus, including a drama/theater group and student-run newspaper and radio station. Student **safety services** include call boxes in parking lots and on roadways, late night transport/escort service, 24-hour emergency telephone alarm devices, 24-hour patrols by trained security personnel, and electronically operated dormitory entrances.

Siena is a member of the NCAA (Division I). **Intercollegiate sports** (some offering scholarships) include baseball (m), basketball (m, w), cross-country running (m, w), equestrian sports (m, w), fencing (m, w), field hockey (w), football (m), golf (m), ice hockey (m), lacrosse (m, w), rugby (m), skiing (downhill) (m, w), soccer (m, w), tennis (m, w), track and field (m, w), volleyball (w).

 ## Applying

Siena requires an essay, a high school transcript, 3 years of high school math and science, 1 recommendation, SAT I or ACT, and in some cases a campus interview. It recommends 2 years of high school foreign language and SAT II Subject Tests. Early, deferred, and midyear entrance are possible, with a 3/1 deadline and continuous processing to 2/1 for financial aid. **Contact:** Ms. Katherine McCarthy, Dean of Admissions, 515 Loudon Road, Loudonville, NY 12211-1462, 518-783-2423 or toll-free 800-45-SIENA.

## GETTING IN LAST YEAR

2,943 applied
75% were accepted
29% enrolled (639)
19% from top tenth of their h.s. class
7% had SAT verbal scores over 600
28% had SAT math scores over 600
24% had ACT scores over 26
1% had SAT verbal scores over 700
4% had SAT math scores over 700
1% had ACT scores over 30

## THE STUDENT BODY

3,232 undergraduates
From 29 states and territories,
   11 other countries
83% from New York
53% women, 47% men
2% African Americans
1% Native Americans
2% Hispanics
2% Asian Americans
1% international students

## AFTER FRESHMAN YEAR

88% returned for sophomore year
72% got a degree within 4 years
79% got a degree within 5 years

## AFTER GRADUATION

31% pursued further study
95 corporations, 11 government agencies
   recruited on campus

## WHAT YOU WILL PAY

Tuition and fees $11,110
Room and board $5100
61% receive need-based financial aid
   averaging $3043
7% receive non-need financial aid averaging
   $4204

# SIMON'S ROCK COLLEGE OF BARD

Great Barrington, Massachusetts • Small-town setting • Private • Independent • Coed

▶ In fall 1993, Simon's Rock installed its own Internet node. Students now have free access to the system and individual accounts to use as they wish. The influence of this system on society in general and the College in particular is likely to be profound. William Gibson's *Neuromancer* has already made its way into the curriculum. The admissions office is keenly interested in applicants with network experience. Interested students should send electronic mail to brian@plato.simons-rock.edu for more information.

## Academics

Simon's Rock offers an interdisciplinary curriculum and core academic program. It awards associate and bachelor's **degrees**. Challenging opportunities include tutorials, an honors program, and a senior project. Special programs include internships, off-campus study, and study abroad.

A complete listing of majors at Simon's Rock appears in the Majors Index beginning on page 380.

The **faculty** at Simon's Rock has 34 full-time teachers, 100% with terminal degrees. 100% of the faculty serve as student advisers. The student-faculty ratio is 9:1, and the average class size in required courses is 12.

## Computers on Campus

Students are not required to have a computer. 20 **computers** available in the computer center, computer labs, the library, and dormitories provide access to off-campus computing facilities, e-mail, and on-line services. Staffed computer lab on campus provides training in the use of computers and software.

The **library** has 65,000 books, 140 microform titles, and 433 subscriptions. It is connected to 3 national **on-line** catalogs.

## Campus Life

Active **organizations** on campus include drama/theater group and student-run newspaper. Student **safety services** include late night transport/escort service, 24-hour patrols by trained security personnel, and electronically operated dormitory entrances.

Simon's Rock is a member of the NSCAA. **Intercollegiate sports** include basketball (m, w), soccer (m, w), tennis (m, w).

## Applying

Simon's Rock requires an essay, a high school transcript, 2 recommendations, a campus interview, parent application, SAT I or ACT, and PSAT. Early, deferred, and midyear entrance are possible, with a 6/15 deadline and continuous processing to 6/15 for financial aid. **Contact:** Mr. Brian R. Hopewell, Director of Admissions, 84 Alford Road, Great Barrington, MA 01230-9702, 413-528-0771 ext. 313 or toll-free 800-235-7186; fax 413-528-7334.

### GETTING IN LAST YEAR
267 applied
68% were accepted
75% enrolled (137)
42% had SAT verbal scores over 600
43% had SAT math scores over 600
7% had SAT verbal scores over 700
10% had SAT math scores over 700

### THE STUDENT BODY
318 undergraduates
From 39 states and territories,
 3 other countries

13% from Massachusetts
54% women, 46% men
4% African Americans
0% Native Americans
0% Hispanics
6% Asian Americans
1% international students

### AFTER FRESHMAN YEAR
72% returned for sophomore year

### AFTER GRADUATION
33% pursued further study (31% arts and
 sciences, 1% engineering, 1% medicine)
50% had job offers within 3 months

### WHAT YOU WILL PAY
Tuition and fees $18,900
Room and board $5620
68% receive need-based financial aid
 averaging $7964
13% receive non-need financial aid averaging
 $16,657

# SIMPSON COLLEGE

Indianola, Iowa • Small-town setting • Private • Independent-Religious • Coed

Simpson combines the best of a liberal arts education with outstanding career preparation and extracurricular programs. Activities range from an award-winning music program to nationally recognized NCAA Division III teams. Located 12 miles from Des Moines, Simpson offers the friendliness of a small town and the advantages of a metropolitan area. In fall 1993, Carver Science Center, named after Simpson's most distinguished alumnus, George Washington Carver, opened after a $9-million expansion. This state-of-the-art building provides new classrooms, offices, and research facilities for mathematics and computer science, biology, and physical and environmental sciences.

## Academics

Simpson offers a liberal arts curriculum and core academic program. It awards bachelor's **degrees**. Challenging opportunities include advanced placement, accelerated degree programs, self-designed majors, tutorials, Freshmen Honors College, an honors program, and a senior project. Special programs include cooperative education, internships, summer session for credit, off-campus study, and study abroad.

The most popular **majors** include business, education, and science. A complete listing of majors at Simpson appears in the Majors Index beginning on page 380.

The **faculty** at Simpson has 72 full-time teachers, 77% with terminal degrees. 93% of the faculty serve as student advisers. The student-faculty ratio is 13:1, and the average class size in required courses is 25.

## Computers on Campus

Students are not required to have a computer. 200 **computers** available in the computer center, computer labs, lounge areas in dorms, fraternities, the library, and dormitories provide access to the main academic computer, off-campus computing facilities, and e-mail. Staffed computer lab on campus provides training in the use of computers and software.

The **library** has 145,905 books, 100 microform titles, and 593 subscriptions. It is connected to 3 national **on-line** catalogs.

## Campus Life

There are 81 active **organizations** on campus, including a drama/theater group and student-run newspaper and radio station. 40% of students participate in student government elections. 36% of eligible men and 32% of eligible women are members of 3 national **fraternities**, 4 national **sororities**, and 1 local fraternity. Student **safety services** include late night transport/escort service, 24-hour emergency telephone alarm devices, 24-hour patrols by trained security personnel, student patrols, and electronically operated dormitory entrances.

Simpson is a member of the NCAA (Division III). **Intercollegiate sports** include baseball (m), basketball (m, w), cross-country running (m, w), football (m), golf (m, w), rugby (m), soccer (m, w), softball (w), swimming and diving (m, w), tennis (m, w), track and field (m, w), volleyball (w), wrestling (m).

## Applying

Simpson requires a high school transcript, 1 recommendation, and SAT I or ACT. It recommends 3 years of high school math and science, 3 years of high school foreign language, an interview, and rank in top half of graduating class. Early, deferred, and midyear entrance are possible, with rolling admissions and continuous processing to 4/20 for financial aid. **Contact:** Mr. John Kellogg, Vice President, Enrollment and Planning, 701 North C Street, Indianola, IA 50125-1297, 515-961-1624 or toll-free 800-362-2454; fax 515-961-1498.

---

**GETTING IN LAST YEAR**
917 applied
87% were accepted
31% enrolled (246)
27% from top tenth of their h.s. class
24% had ACT scores over 26
12% had ACT scores over 30

**THE STUDENT BODY**
1,613 undergraduates
From 18 states and territories,
    5 other countries
90% from Iowa
53% women, 47% men
2% African Americans

1% Native Americans
1% Hispanics
1% Asian Americans
1% international students

**AFTER FRESHMAN YEAR**
78% returned for sophomore year
55% got a degree within 4 years
62% got a degree within 5 years

**AFTER GRADUATION**
15% pursued further study (8% arts and
    sciences, 2% business, 2% law)
12 corporations, 3 government agencies, 5
    nonprofit organizations recruited on campus

**WHAT YOU WILL PAY**
Tuition and fees $11,355
Room and board $3980
87% receive need-based financial aid
    averaging $3461
13% receive non-need financial aid averaging
    $3860

# SKIDMORE COLLEGE

Saratoga Springs, New York • Small-town setting • Private • Independent • Coed

Skidmore College, located on a beautiful 850-acre campus, is a liberal arts college with a history of innovation and imagination. An interdisciplinary liberal studies curriculum challenges students to explore broadly. A rich cocurricular program provides further opportunities for personal growth and leadership. Among the largest majors are business, studio art, English, psychology, government, and biology/chemistry. A total of 2,150 students from 47 states and 20 countries live and learn in Skidmore's lively intellectual climate and beautiful campus surroundings.

## Academics

Skidmore College offers an interdisciplinary curriculum and core academic program. It awards bachelor's and master's **degrees**. Challenging opportunities include advanced placement, accelerated degree programs, self-designed majors, tutorials, a senior project, and Phi Beta Kappa. Special programs include internships, summer session for credit, off-campus study, study abroad, and Army and Air Force ROTC.

The most popular **majors** include business, English, and political science/government. A complete listing of majors at Skidmore College appears in the Majors Index beginning on page 380.

The **faculty** at Skidmore College has 195 full-time graduate and undergraduate teachers, 94% with terminal degrees. 100% of the faculty serve as student advisers. The student-faculty ratio is 11:1, and the average class size in required courses is 17.

## Computers on Campus

Students are not required to have a computer. Student rooms are linked to a campus network. 200 **computers**

available in the computer center, computer labs, classroom buildings, the library, the student center, and dormitories provide access to the main academic computer, e-mail, and on-line services. Staffed computer lab on campus (open 24 hours a day) provides training in the use of computers and software.

The 2 **libraries** have 410,000 books, 243,000 microform titles, and 1,700 subscriptions. They are connected to 8 national **on-line** catalogs.

## Campus Life

There are 80 active **organizations** on campus, including a drama/theater group and student-run newspaper and radio station. Student **safety services** include late night transport/escort service, 24-hour emergency telephone alarm devices, 24-hour patrols by trained security personnel, and electronically operated dormitory entrances.

Skidmore College is a member of the NCAA (Division III). **Intercollegiate sports** include baseball (m), basketball (m, w), crew (m, w), equestrian sports (m, w), field hockey (w), golf (m), ice hockey (m, w), lacrosse (m, w), skiing (downhill) (m, w), soccer (m, w), softball (w), swimming and diving (m, w), tennis (m, w), volleyball (w).

## Applying

Skidmore College requires an essay, a high school transcript, 3 years of high school math and science, 3 years of high school foreign language, 2 recommendations, and SAT I or ACT. It recommends an interview and 3 SAT II Subject Tests. Early, deferred, and midyear entrance are possible, with a 2/1 deadline and 2/1 for financial aid. **Contact:** Ms. Mary Lou Bates, Director of Admissions, North Broadway, Saratoga Springs, NY 12866-1632, 518-584-5000 ext. 2213.

---

### GETTING IN LAST YEAR
4,623 applied
61% were accepted
22% enrolled (613)
32% from top tenth of their h.s. class
24% had SAT verbal scores over 600
49% had SAT math scores over 600
59% had ACT scores over 26
2% had SAT verbal scores over 700
8% had SAT math scores over 700
3% had ACT scores over 30

### THE STUDENT BODY
Total 2,198, of whom 2,150
 are undergraduates

From 47 states and territories,
 20 other countries
33% from New York
60% women, 40% men
2% African Americans
1% Native Americans
5% Hispanics
3% Asian Americans
2% international students

### AFTER FRESHMAN YEAR
90% returned for sophomore year
69% got a degree within 4 years
76% got a degree within 5 years
78% got a degree within 6 years

### AFTER GRADUATION
25% pursued further study (14% arts and
 sciences, 7% law, 3% business)
50 corporations, 10 government agencies, 5
 nonprofit organizations recruited on campus
1 Fulbright scholar

### WHAT YOU WILL PAY
Tuition and fees $18,926
Room and board $5685
30% receive need-based financial aid
 averaging $11,963
19% receive non-need financial aid averaging
 $6000

# SMITH COLLEGE

Northampton, Massachusetts • Small-town setting • Private • Independent • Women

▶ Students choose Smith because it is one of the most outstanding and highly selective liberal arts colleges in the United States. From its founding in 1871, the College has been committed to helping women develop fully their intellects and talents by providing them with the highest quality undergraduate education. Smith has taken a progressive, expansive, and student-oriented view of its role as a liberal arts college. Each student has the freedom and responsibility to design a course of studies to fit her individual needs and interests, since there are no specific course requirements outside of a student's major.

##  Academics

Smith offers an open curriculum and no core academic program; a few graduate courses are open to undergraduates. It awards bachelor's, master's, and doctoral **degrees**. Challenging opportunities include advanced placement, accelerated degree programs, self-designed majors, tutorials, an honors program, a senior project, Phi Beta Kappa, and Sigma Xi. Special programs include internships, off-campus study, study abroad, and Army and Air Force ROTC.

The most popular **majors** include political science/government, art/fine arts, and psychology. A complete listing of majors at Smith appears in the Majors Index beginning on page 380.

The **faculty** at Smith has 268 full-time graduate and undergraduate teachers, 97% with terminal degrees. 100% of the faculty serve as student advisers. The student-faculty ratio is 10:1.

##  Computers on Campus

Students are not required to have a computer. 230 **computers** available in the computer center and resource centers, special needs computer room. Staffed computer lab on campus provides training in the use of computers and software.

The 4 **libraries** have 1.1 million books and 3,102 subscriptions. They are connected to 5 national **on-line** catalogs.

##  Campus Life

There are 93 active **organizations** on campus, including a drama/theater group and student-run newspaper and radio station. 30% of students participate in student government elections. Student **safety services** include late night transport/escort service, 24-hour emergency telephone alarm devices, and 24-hour patrols by trained security personnel.

Smith is a member of the NCAA (Division III). **Intercollegiate sports** include basketball, crew, cross-country running, equestrian sports, field hockey, lacrosse, skiing (downhill), soccer, softball, squash, swimming and diving, tennis, track and field, volleyball.

##  Applying

Smith requires an essay, a high school transcript, 2 recommendations, and SAT I or ACT. It recommends 3 years of high school math and science, 3 years of high school foreign language, an interview, and 3 SAT II Subject Tests. Early and deferred entrance are possible, with a 1/15 deadline and 2/1 for financial aid. **Contact:** Ms. Nanci Tessier, Director of Admissions, 7 College Lane, Northampton, MA 01063, 413-585-2500; fax 413-585-2527.

---

### GETTING IN LAST YEAR
2,908 applied
53% were accepted
42% enrolled (648)
58% from top tenth of their h.s. class
50% had SAT verbal scores over 600
54% had SAT math scores over 600
75% had ACT scores over 26
8% had SAT verbal scores over 700
10% had SAT math scores over 700
25% had ACT scores over 30
41 valedictorians

### THE STUDENT BODY
Total 3,036, of whom 2,537
  are undergraduates

From 52 states and territories,
  68 other countries
19% from Massachusetts
100% women
3% African Americans
1% Native Americans
4% Hispanics
13% Asian Americans
8% international students

### AFTER FRESHMAN YEAR
89% returned for sophomore year
83% got a degree within 4 years
86% got a degree within 5 years
87% got a degree within 6 years

### AFTER GRADUATION
25% pursued further study (13% arts and
  sciences, 3% law, 1% medicine)
41 corporations, 3 government agencies, 7
  nonprofit organizations recruited on campus
4 Fulbright scholars

### WHAT YOU WILL PAY
Tuition and fees $18,983
Room and board $6390
Need-based financial aid averages $12,015

# SOUTH DAKOTA SCHOOL OF MINES AND TECHNOLOGY

Rapid City, South Dakota • Suburban setting • Public • State-supported • Coed

---

South Dakota School of Mines and Technology is one of only a select few moderately sized, affordably priced universities that emphasize Bachelor of Science, Master of Science, and doctorate- level programs exclusively in the areas of engineering and science. This specialization enhances the School's national and international reputation for academic excellence, makes its graduates highly sought by industry, allows the School to furnish classrooms and laboratories with the latest in high-tech state-of-the-art scientific equipment, and provides a greater degree of fellowship among students, making it easy for students to study and work together in a group effort.

 **Academics**

SDSM & T offers a general curriculum and core academic program; fewer than half of graduate courses are open to undergraduates. It awards bachelor's, master's, and doctoral **degrees**. Challenging opportunities include advanced placement, self-designed majors, a senior project, and Sigma Xi. Special programs include cooperative education, summer session for credit, study abroad, and Army ROTC.

The most popular **majors** include mechanical engineering, computer science, and electrical engineering. A complete listing of majors at SDSM & T appears in the Majors Index beginning on page 380.

The **faculty** at SDSM & T has 102 full-time graduate and undergraduate teachers, 78% with terminal degrees. 69% of the faculty serve as student advisers. The student-faculty ratio is 16:1.

 **Computers on Campus**

Students are not required to have a computer. Student rooms are linked to a campus network. 130 **computers** available in the computer center, computer labs, classrooms, the library, the student center, and dormitories provide access to the main academic computer, off-campus computing facilities, e-mail, and on-line services. Staffed computer lab on campus provides training in the use of computers and software.

The 2 **libraries** have 155,886 books, 194,614 microform titles, and 959 subscriptions.

 **Campus Life**

Active **organizations** on campus include drama/theater group and student-run newspaper and radio station. 19% of eligible men and 21% of eligible women are members of 4 national **fraternities** and 2 national **sororities**. Student **safety services** include late night transport/escort service, 24-hour emergency telephone alarm devices, and 24-hour patrols by trained security personnel.

SDSM & T is a member of the NAIA. **Intercollegiate sports** (some offering scholarships) include basketball (m, w), cross-country running (m, w), football (m), tennis (m), track and field (m, w), volleyball (w).

 **Applying**

SDSM & T requires a high school transcript, 3 years of high school math and science, SAT I or ACT, and a minimum high school GPA of 2.0. It recommends some high school foreign language. Rolling admissions and continuous processing to 4/15 for financial aid. **Contact:** Mr. Chuck Colombe, Director of Admissions, 501 East Saint Joseph Street, Rapid City, SD 57701-3995, 605-394-2400 or toll-free 800-544-8162; fax 605-394-6721 ext. 2400.

---

### GETTING IN LAST YEAR
754 applied
79% were accepted
73% enrolled (436)
27% from top tenth of their h.s. class
43% had ACT scores over 26
9% had ACT scores over 30
2 National Merit Scholars
18 valedictorians

### THE STUDENT BODY
Total 2,463, of whom 2,226 are undergraduates
From 38 states and territories, 17 other countries

66% from South Dakota
33% women, 67% men
1% African Americans
2% Native Americans
1% Hispanics
1% Asian Americans
5% international students

### AFTER FRESHMAN YEAR
62% returned for sophomore year

### AFTER GRADUATION
13% pursued further study (7% engineering, 2% business, 2% medicine)

77% had job offers within 3 months
50 corporations, 5 government agencies, 3 nonprofit organizations recruited on campus

### WHAT YOU WILL PAY
Resident tuition and fees $3720
Nonresident tuition and fees $6319
Room and board $3120
56% receive need-based financial aid averaging $1134
22% receive non-need financial aid averaging $405

---

# SOUTHERN METHODIST UNIVERSITY

Dallas, Texas • Suburban setting • Private • Independent-Religious • Coed

SMU offers an education as individual as each of its students, with more than 70 majors in the humanities, sciences, business, engineering, and the arts. Small classes taught by full-time faculty members provide personal attention and mentoring opportunities. SMU offers more than 10 study-abroad programs and a summer campus near Taos, New Mexico. SMU's diverse student body represents all 50 states, many countries, and numerous faiths; 20% are members of minority groups. More than 69% of undergraduates receive financial assistance. SMU's park-like campus is just 5 miles north of downtown Dallas, a dynamic center of commerce and culture.

## Academics

SMU offers a liberal arts and professional curriculum and core academic program; fewer than half of graduate courses are open to undergraduates. It awards bachelor's, master's, doctoral, and first professional **degrees**. Challenging opportunities include advanced placement, self-designed majors, tutorials, an honors program, Phi Beta Kappa, and Sigma Xi. Special programs include cooperative education, internships, summer session for credit, study abroad, and Army and Air Force ROTC.

The most popular **majors** include business, psychology, and advertising. A complete listing of majors at SMU appears in the Majors Index beginning on page 380.

The **faculty** at SMU has 483 full-time graduate and undergraduate teachers, 87% with terminal degrees. The average class size in required courses is 24.

## Computers on Campus

Students are not required to have a computer. 300 **computers** available in the computer center, computer labs, the research center, the learning resource center, various locations on campus, classrooms, the library, the student center, and dormitories provide access to the main academic computer, off-campus computing facilities, and e-mail. Staffed computer lab on campus provides training in the use of computers and software.

The 8 **libraries** have 2.9 million books, 1.5 million microform titles, and 5,647 subscriptions. They are connected to 2 national **on-line** catalogs.

## Campus Life

There are 152 active **organizations** on campus, including a drama/theater group and student-run newspaper and radio station. 41% of eligible men and 48% of eligible women are members of 15 national **fraternities** and 11 national **sororities**. Student **safety services** include late night transport/escort service, 24-hour emergency telephone alarm devices, 24-hour patrols by trained security personnel, and electronically operated dormitory entrances.

SMU is a member of the NCAA (Division I). **Intercollegiate sports** (some offering scholarships) include basketball (m, w), cross-country running (m, w), football (m), golf (m, w), soccer (m, w), swimming and diving (m, w), tennis (m, w), track and field (m, w).

## Applying

SMU requires an essay, a high school transcript, 3 years of high school math and science, 2 years of high school foreign language, 1 recommendation, SAT I or ACT, and in some cases SAT II Subject Tests. Early, deferred, and midyear entrance are possible, with a 4/1 deadline and continuous processing to 1/15 for financial aid. **Contact:** Mr. Ron W. Moss, Director of Admission and Enrollment Management, 6425 Boaz Street, Dallas, TX 75275, 214-768-2058 or toll-free 800-323-0672.

---

### GETTING IN LAST YEAR
4,434 applied
81% were accepted
32% enrolled (1,164)
35% from top tenth of their h.s. class
3.2 average high school GPA

### THE STUDENT BODY
Total 9,014, of whom 5,247
  are undergraduates
From 50 states and territories,
  65 other countries

59% from Texas
52% women, 48% men
6% African Americans
6% Asian Americans
3% international students

### AFTER FRESHMAN YEAR
84% returned for sophomore year
54% got a degree within 4 years
67% got a degree within 5 years
69% got a degree within 6 years

### AFTER GRADUATION
150 corporations recruited on campus

### WHAT YOU WILL PAY
Tuition and fees $14,396
Room and board $5078
38% receive need-based financial aid
  averaging $3160
32% receive non-need financial aid averaging
  $5460

# Southwestern University

Georgetown, Texas • Suburban setting • Private • Independent-Religious • Coed

---

▶ Southwestern is a national liberal arts college recognized for a high-quality academic program and priced well below most comparable schools. In the past year, Southwestern accepted a chapter of Phi Beta Kappa, had a teacher named U.S. Professor of the Year, received a $6.5-million, state-of-the-art academic building from the F. W. Olin Foundation, and was selected to join the Southern Collegiate Athletic Association in Division III of the NCAA. Located north of Austin, SU offers a values-centered mission, a broad-based curriculum, and extensive study-abroad opportunities to its 1,200 students.

##  Academics

SU offers a liberal arts and sciences curriculum and core academic program. It awards bachelor's **degrees**. Challenging opportunities include advanced placement, accelerated degree programs, self-designed majors, tutorials, an honors program, a senior project, and Phi Beta Kappa. Special programs include internships, summer session for credit, and study abroad.

The most popular **majors** include business, psychology, and biology/biological sciences. A complete listing of majors at SU appears in the Majors Index beginning on page 380.

The **faculty** at SU has 91 full-time teachers, 92% with terminal degrees. 100% of the faculty serve as student advisers. The student-faculty ratio is 12:1, and the average class size in required courses is 19.

##  Computers on Campus

Students are not required to have a computer. 159 **computers** available in the computer center, computer labs, academic departments, the library, and dormitories provide access to the main academic computer, off-campus computing facilities, e-mail, and on-line services. Staffed computer lab on campus provides training in the use of computers and software.

The **library** has 261,353 books, 30,064 microform titles, and 1,391 subscriptions. It is connected to 3 national **on-line** catalogs.

##  Campus Life

There are 87 active **organizations** on campus, including a drama/theater group and student-run newspaper. 40% of students participate in student government elections. 31% of eligible men and 37% of eligible women are members of 4 national **fraternities** and 4 national **sororities**. Student **safety services** include late night transport/escort service, 24-hour emergency telephone alarm devices, 24-hour patrols by trained security personnel, and electronically operated dormitory entrances.

SU is a member of the NCAA (Division III). **Intercollegiate sports** include baseball (m), basketball (m, w), cross-country running (m, w), golf (m, w), soccer (m, w), tennis (m, w), volleyball (w).

##  Applying

SU requires an essay, a high school transcript, 1 recommendation, SAT I or ACT, and in some cases an interview. It recommends 4 years of high school math, 3 years of high school science, 2 years of high school foreign language, and an interview. Early, deferred, and midyear entrance are possible, with a 2/15 deadline and continuous processing to 3/1 for financial aid. **Contact:** Mr. John W. Lind, Vice President for Enrollment Management, University at Maple, Georgetown, TX 78626, 512-863-1202 or toll-free 800-252-3166; fax 512-863-5788.

---

### GETTING IN LAST YEAR
1,339 applied
71% were accepted
35% enrolled (336)
45% from top tenth of their h.s. class
3.4 average high school GPA
22% had SAT verbal scores over 600
46% had SAT math scores over 600
53% had ACT scores over 26
4% had SAT verbal scores over 700
8% had SAT math scores over 700
14% had ACT scores over 30
8 National Merit Scholars
26 class presidents
15 valedictorians

### THE STUDENT BODY
1,238 undergraduates
From 32 states and territories,
    18 other countries
86% from Texas
55% women, 45% men
2% African Americans
0% Native Americans
11% Hispanics
5% Asian Americans
2% international students

### AFTER FRESHMAN YEAR
85% returned for sophomore year
60% got a degree within 4 years
73% got a degree within 5 years

### AFTER GRADUATION
34% pursued further study (13% arts and
    sciences, 8% medicine, 6% law)
50% had job offers within 3 months
28 corporations, 39 government agencies, 13
    nonprofit organizations recruited on campus
1 Fulbright scholar

### WHAT YOU WILL PAY
Tuition and fees $11,850
Room and board $4675
61% receive need-based financial aid
    averaging $6832
9% receive non-need financial aid averaging
    $3230

---

# SPELMAN COLLEGE

Atlanta, Georgia • Urban setting • Private • Independent • Women

Located in Atlanta, Georgia, Spelman College is a historically black, privately endowed, 4-year, liberal arts college for women. Founded in 1881 as the Atlanta Baptist Female Seminary, Spelman today is one of America's top liberal arts colleges, providing academic excellence for women. Spelman's commitment to excellence is demonstrated by its dedicated and accessible faculty and low student-faculty ratio of 15:1, as well as by the outstanding success of students and alumnae.

 ## Academics

Spelman offers a core academic program. It awards bachelor's **degrees**. Challenging opportunities include advanced placement, accelerated degree programs, self-designed majors, an honors program, and a senior project. Special programs include internships, off-campus study, study abroad, and Army, Naval, and Air Force ROTC.

The most popular **majors** include psychology, economics, and English. A complete listing of majors at Spelman appears in the Majors Index beginning on page 380.

The **faculty** at Spelman has 134 full-time teachers, 78% with terminal degrees. 85% of the faculty serve as student advisers. The student-faculty ratio is 15:1.

 ## Computers on Campus

Students are not required to have a computer. 105 **computers** available in the computer center, academic buildings, classrooms, and the library. Staffed computer lab on campus provides training in the use of computers and software.

The **library** has 404,991 books, 69,750 microform titles, and 2,693 subscriptions.

 ## Campus Life

Active **organizations** on campus include drama/theater group and student-run newspaper. 61% of students participate in student government elections. 15% of eligible undergraduates are members of 4 national **sororities**. Student **safety services** include late night transport/escort service, 24-hour emergency telephone alarm devices, 24-hour patrols by trained security personnel, and electronically operated dormitory entrances. **Intercollegiate sports** include basketball, tennis, track and field, volleyball.

 ## Applying

Spelman requires an essay, a high school transcript, 2 recommendations, SAT I or ACT, and in some cases an interview. It recommends 3 years of high school math and science and 2 years of high school foreign language. Early and midyear entrance are possible, with a 2/1 deadline and continuous processing to 4/1 for financial aid. **Contact:** Ms. Victoria Valle, Director of Admissions and Orientation Services, 350 Spelman Lane, SW, Atlanta, GA 30314-4399, 404-681-3643 ext. 2188 or toll-free 800-982-2411 (out-of-state); fax 404-223-1449.

---

**GETTING IN LAST YEAR**
3,650 applied
38% were accepted
33% enrolled (448)
47% from top tenth of their h.s. class
7% had SAT verbal scores over 600
13% had SAT math scores over 600
27% had ACT scores over 26
1% had SAT verbal scores over 700
1% had SAT math scores over 700
3% had ACT scores over 30
10 National Merit Scholars
52 class presidents

**THE STUDENT BODY**
1,976 undergraduates
From 45 states and territories,
    21 other countries
21% from Georgia
100% women
98% African Americans
0% Native Americans
0% Hispanics
0% Asian Americans
2% international students

**AFTER FRESHMAN YEAR**
91% returned for sophomore year
61% got a degree within 4 years

72% got a degree within 5 years
74% got a degree within 6 years

**AFTER GRADUATION**
38% pursued further study
1 Marshall scholar

**WHAT YOU WILL PAY**
Tuition and fees $8024
Room and board $5565
Need-based financial aid averages $992
Non-need financial aid averages $2211

# STANFORD UNIVERSITY

Stanford, California • Suburban setting • Private • Independent • Coed

▶ Renowned for the quality of its faculty (12 Nobel laureates, 6 Pulitzer Prize winners, 14 MacArthur Prizes, 19 National Medal of Science winners), Stanford University is equally proud of its graduates, which include 72 Rhodes Scholars and 49 Marshall Scholars. Stanford students are both challenged and warmly supported by their faculty mentors, and share in an invigorating and open intellectual environment. Undergraduates are encouraged to undertake original research. The University fosters personal and intellectual growth in a residential setting, and admits students it believes will contribute to the sum of human knowledge and enrich human experience through the creative arts.

 **Academics**

Stanford offers a core academic program. It awards bachelor's, master's, doctoral, and first professional **degrees**. Challenging opportunities include advanced placement, accelerated degree programs, self-designed majors, tutorials, an honors program, a senior project, Phi Beta Kappa, and Sigma Xi. Special programs include internships, summer session for credit, off-campus study, study abroad, and Army, Naval, and Air Force ROTC.

The most popular **majors** include economics, history, and political science/government. A complete listing of majors at Stanford appears in the Majors Index beginning on page 380.

The **faculty** at Stanford has 1,428 full-time graduate and undergraduate teachers, 99% with terminal degrees. The student-faculty ratio is 10:1.

 **Computers on Campus**

Students are not required to have a computer. 1,000 **computers** available in the computer center, computer labs, computer clusters, classrooms center, and dormitories.

The 19 **libraries** have 6.4 mill microform titles, and 65,600 subscri

 **Campus Life**

There are 300 active **organizations** on campus, including a drama/theater group and student-run newspaper and radio station. 10% of eligible men and 10% of eligible women are members of 18 national **fraternities**, 8 national **sororities**, and 6 eating clubs. Student **safety services** include late night transport/escort service, 24-hour emergency telephone alarm devices, 24-hour patrols by trained security personnel, and electronically operated dormitory entrances.

Stanford is a member of the NCAA (Division I) and NAIA. **Intercollegiate sports** (some offering scholarships) include baseball (m), basketball (m, w), crew (m, w), cross-country running (m, w), equestrian sports (m, w), fencing (m, w), field hockey (m, w), football (m), golf (m, w), gymnastics (m, w), ice hockey (m, w), lacrosse (m, w), racquetball (m, w), rugby (m, w), sailing (m, w), skiing (cross-country) (m, w), skiing (downhill) (m, w), soccer (m, w), squash (m, w), swimming and diving (m, w), tennis (m, w), track and field (m, w), volleyball (m, w), water polo (m, w), wrestling (m).

 **Applying**

Stanford requires an essay, a high school transcript, 3 recommendations, and SAT I or ACT. It recommends 3 years of high school math and science, some high school foreign language, and SAT II Subject Tests. Early and deferred entrance are possible, with a 12/15 deadline and a 2/1 priority date for financial aid. **Contact:** Mr. John Bunnell, Associate Dean of Admissions, Old Union Building, Room 232, Stanford, CA 94305-9991, 415-723-2091; fax 415-725-2846.

---

**GETTING IN LAST YEAR**
14,609 applied
20% were accepted
55% enrolled (1,606)
91% from top tenth of their h.s. class
75% had SAT verbal scores over 600
90% had SAT math scores over 600
26% had SAT verbal scores over 700
62% had SAT math scores over 700

**THE STUDENT BODY**
Total 14,031, of whom 6,561
  are undergraduates

From 52 states and territories,
  57 other countries
45% from California
48% women, 52% men
8% African Americans
1% Native Americans
11% Hispanics
25% Asian Americans
5% international students

**AFTER FRESHMAN YEAR**
97% returned for sophomore year
76% got a degree within 4 years

91% got a degree within 5 years
93% got a degree within 6 years

**AFTER GRADUATION**
376 corporations, 8 government agencies, 20
  nonprofit organizations recruited on campus
1 Rhodes, 1 Marshall, 16 Fulbright scholars

**WHAT YOU WILL PAY**
Tuition and fees $18,669
Room and board $6796
Need-based financial aid averages $12,222

# UNIVERSITY OF NEW YORK
# BINGHAMTON

Binghamton, New York • Suburban setting • Public • State-supported • Coed

Mid-sized Binghamton University, in upstate New York's scenic southern tier, is known for the excellent teaching and solid research of its outstanding, accessible faculty. At Binghamton, challenging academic programs combine with virtually unlimited opportunities for student participation in all areas of campus life. More than 135 campus organizations offer activities for every interest. In a community that values excellence and independence, Binghamton students excel.

 **Academics**

Binghamton University offers a core academic program; fewer than half of graduate courses are open to undergraduates. It awards bachelor's, master's, and doctoral **degrees**. Challenging opportunities include advanced placement, self-designed majors, tutorials, an honors program, a senior project, and Phi Beta Kappa. Special programs include internships, summer session for credit, off-campus study, and study abroad.

The most popular **majors** include English, psychology, and biology/biological sciences. A complete listing of majors at Binghamton University appears in the Majors Index beginning on page 380.

The **faculty** at Binghamton University has 498 full-time graduate and undergraduate teachers, 95% with terminal degrees. 100% of the faculty serve as student advisers. The student-faculty ratio is 19:1.

 **Computers on Campus**

Students are not required to have a computer. Student rooms are linked to a campus network. 1,000 **computers** available in the computer center, computer labs, the learning resource center, the library, and dormitories provide access to the main academic computer, e-mail, and on-line services. Staffed computer lab on campus provides training in the use of computers and software.

The 3 **libraries** have 1.5 million books, 1.4 million microform titles, and 9,358 subscriptions.

 **Campus Life**

There are 135 active **organizations** on campus, including a drama/theater group and student-run newspaper and radio station. 15% of eligible men and 15% of eligible women are members of 18 national **fraternities** and 12 national **sororities**. Student **safety services** include late night transport/escort service, 24-hour emergency telephone alarm devices, 24-hour patrols by trained security personnel, and electronically operated dormitory entrances.

Binghamton University is a member of the NCAA (Division III). **Intercollegiate sports** include baseball (m), basketball (m, w), bowling (m), crew (m, w), cross-country running (m, w), equestrian sports (m, w), fencing (m, w), golf (m), lacrosse (m, w), racquetball (m, w), rugby (m, w), skiing (downhill) (m, w), soccer (m, w), softball (w), swimming and diving (m, w), tennis (m, w), track and field (m, w), volleyball (m, w), wrestling (m).

 **Applying**

Binghamton University requires an essay, a high school transcript, SAT I or ACT, and in some cases 3 years of high school math and science, some high school foreign language, and 1 recommendation. It recommends 3 years of high school math and science, some high school foreign language, and portfolio, audition. Early, deferred, and midyear entrance are possible, with a 2/15 deadline and continuous processing to 3/1 for financial aid. **Contact:** Mr. Geoffrey D. Gould, Director of Admissions, PO Box 6001, Binghamton, NY 13902-6001, 607-777-2171.

## GETTING IN LAST YEAR
15,314 applied
42% were accepted
28% enrolled (1,789)
55% from top tenth of their h.s. class
21% had SAT verbal scores over 600
61% had SAT math scores over 600
61% had ACT scores over 26
1% had SAT verbal scores over 700
14% had SAT math scores over 700
16% had ACT scores over 30

## THE STUDENT BODY
Total 12,088, of whom 9,314
   are undergraduates

From 28 states and territories,
   49 other countries
92% from New York
54% women, 46% men
6% African Americans
1% Native Americans
5% Hispanics
9% Asian Americans
2% international students

## AFTER FRESHMAN YEAR
93% returned for sophomore year
66% got a degree within 4 years
78% got a degree within 5 years
80% got a degree within 6 years

## AFTER GRADUATION
40% pursued further study (22% arts and
   sciences, 7% law, 5% business)
100 corporations recruited on campus
3 Fulbright scholars

## WHAT YOU WILL PAY
Resident tuition and fees $2961
Nonresident tuition and fees $6861
Room and board $5080
Need-based financial aid averages $700
Non-need financial aid averages $2300

# STATE UNIVERSITY OF NEW YORK AT BUFFALO

Buffalo, New York • Suburban setting • Public • State-supported • Coed

Students are invited to learn more about the University at Buffalo, New York's premier public research university—an academic community in which undergraduates can explore an exceptional range of possible futures with faculty and graduate students working on the leading edge in their fields. UB offers the most comprehensive selection of undergraduate and graduate programs in the State University of New York system. Students are encouraged to explore the possibilities, in a community of student and faculty scholars, among 30 programs in the arts and sciences and extensive offerings in the health sciences, management, engineering, architecture, nursing, medicine, and biomedical sciences and pharmacy.

## Academics

UB offers an interdisciplinary curriculum and core academic program. It awards bachelor's, master's, doctoral, and first professional **degrees**. Challenging opportunities include advanced placement, self-designed majors, tutorials, Freshmen Honors College, an honors program, a senior project, Phi Beta Kappa, and Sigma Xi. Special programs include internships, summer session for credit, off-campus study, study abroad, and Army ROTC.

The most popular **majors** include business, social science, and psychology. A complete listing of majors at UB appears in the Majors Index beginning on page 380.

The **faculty** at UB has 1,599 full-time graduate and undergraduate teachers, 97% with terminal degrees. The student-faculty ratio is 20:1, and the average class size in required courses is 20.

## Computers on Campus

Students are not required to have a computer. 750 **computers** available in the computer center, computer labs, academic buildings, the library, and dormitories provide access to the main academic computer, e-mail, and on-line services. Staffed computer lab on campus provides training in the use of computers and software.

The 8 **libraries** have 2.9 million books, 4.3 million microform titles, and 20,051 subscriptions.

## Campus Life

There are 150 active **organizations** on campus, including a drama/theater group and student-run newspaper and radio station. 8% of eligible men and 4% of eligible women are members of 18 national **fraternities**, 6 national **sororities**, 4 local fraternities, and 3 local sororities. Student **safety services** include late night transport/escort service.

UB is a member of the NCAA (Division I). **Intercollegiate sports** (some offering scholarships) include basketball (m, w), cross-country running (m, w), football (m), soccer (m, w), swimming and diving (m, w), tennis (m, w), track and field (m, w), volleyball (w), wrestling (m).

## Applying

UB requires a high school transcript, SAT I or ACT, and in some cases recommendations and portfolio, audition. It recommends 3 years of high school math and science and 3 years of high school foreign language. Early entrance is possible, with a 1/5 deadline and continuous processing to 3/15 for financial aid. **Contact:** Mr. Kevin M. Durkin, Director of Admissions, Capen Hall, Room 17, North Campus, Buffalo, NY 14260-1660, 716-645-6900; fax 716-645-6411.

### GETTING IN LAST YEAR
15,473 applied
60% were accepted
24% enrolled (2,263)
29% from top tenth of their h.s. class
3.3 average high school GPA
11% had SAT verbal scores over 600
46% had SAT math scores over 600
1% had SAT verbal scores over 700
9% had SAT math scores over 700

### THE STUDENT BODY
Total 24,943, of whom 16,411
   are undergraduates
From 32 states and territories,
   52 other countries

97% from New York
44% women, 56% men
7% African Americans
1% Native Americans
4% Hispanics
10% Asian Americans
2% international students

### AFTER FRESHMAN YEAR
86% returned for sophomore year
29% got a degree within 4 years
53% got a degree within 5 years
59% got a degree within 6 years

### AFTER GRADUATION
35% pursued further study
172 corporations, 21 government agencies,
   29 nonprofit organizations recruited on
   campus
3 Fulbright scholars

### WHAT YOU WILL PAY
Resident tuition and fees $3244
Nonresident tuition and fees $7144
Room and board $5024
60% receive need-based financial aid
   averaging $600
5% receive non-need financial aid averaging
   $1190

# STATE UNIVERSITY OF NEW YORK COLLEGE AT GENESEO

Geneseo, New York • Small-town setting • Public • State-supported • Coed

---

The *New York Times* cited Geneseo as "one of the nation's most selective, highly regarded colleges." This reputation is derived not only from the extraordinarily able students who enroll but also from the College's total dedication to a single mission: teaching undergraduates. Geneseo offers a personal atmosphere in which students, faculty, and staff are concerned about each other. Students have the opportunity to study with others who have demonstrated a seriousness of purpose and a high level of academic achievement. The Geneseo experience is created by a collegiate environment, small size, excellent curricular offerings, and idyllic location.

 **Academics**

Geneseo College offers an interdisciplinary curriculum and core academic program; a few graduate courses are open to undergraduates. It awards bachelor's and master's **degrees**. Challenging opportunities include advanced placement, tutorials, an honors program, and a senior project. Special programs include internships, summer session for credit, off-campus study, study abroad, and Army and Air Force ROTC.

The most popular **majors** include psychology, business, and education. A complete listing of majors at Geneseo College appears in the Majors Index beginning on page 380.

The **faculty** at Geneseo College has 251 full-time graduate and undergraduate teachers, 84% with terminal degrees. 95% of the faculty serve as student advisers. The student-faculty ratio is 19:1.

 **Computers on Campus**

Students are not required to have a computer. 700 **computers** available in the computer center, computer labs, academic departments, the library, the student center, and dormitories provide access to the main academic computer, e-mail, and on-line services. Staffed computer lab on campus provides training in the use of computers and software.

The 2 **libraries** have 521,558 books and 3,156 subscriptions.

 **Campus Life**

There are 175 active **organizations** on campus, including a drama/theater group and student-run newspaper and radio station. 10% of students participate in student government elections. 19% of eligible men and 15% of eligible women are members of 6 national **fraternities**, 4 national **sororities**, 4 local fraternities, and 6 local sororities. Student **safety services** include late night transport/escort service, 24-hour emergency telephone alarm devices, 24-hour patrols by trained security personnel, and student patrols.

Geneseo College is a member of the NCAA (Division III). **Intercollegiate sports** include basketball (m, w), crew (m, w), cross-country running (m, w), ice hockey (m), lacrosse (m, w), racquetball (m, w), rugby (m, w), soccer (m, w), softball (w), squash (m, w), swimming and diving (m, w), tennis (w), track and field (m, w), volleyball (m, w).

 **Applying**

Geneseo College requires an essay, a high school transcript, and SAT I or ACT. It recommends 4 years of high school math and science, 3 years of high school foreign language, recommendations, and a campus interview. Early, deferred, and midyear entrance are possible, with a 2/15 deadline and continuous processing to 2/15 for financial aid. **Contact:** Ms. Jill Conlon, Director of Admissions, Erwin Building, Geneseo, NY 14454-1401, 716-245-5571.

---

**GETTING IN LAST YEAR**
9,000 applied
53% were accepted
25% enrolled (1,198)
52% from top tenth of their h.s. class
17% had SAT verbal scores over 600
55% had SAT math scores over 600
1% had SAT verbal scores over 700
9% had SAT math scores over 700

**THE STUDENT BODY**
Total 5,754, of whom 5,357 are undergraduates
From 21 states and territories, 10 other countries

98% from New York
63% women, 37% men
2% African Americans
1% Native Americans
4% Hispanics
7% Asian Americans
1% international students

**AFTER FRESHMAN YEAR**
92% returned for sophomore year
65% got a degree within 4 years
76% got a degree within 5 years
77% got a degree within 6 years

**AFTER GRADUATION**
35% pursued further study
45% had job offers within 3 months
33 corporations, 5 government agencies, 3 nonprofit organizations recruited on campus

**WHAT YOU WILL PAY**
Resident tuition and fees $3083
Nonresident tuition and fees $6983
Room and board $4170
65% receive need-based financial aid averaging $2800
Non-need financial aid averages $758

# STATE UNIVERSITY OF NEW YORK COLLEGE OF ENVIRONMENTAL SCIENCE AND FORESTRY

Syracuse, New York • Urban setting • Public • State-supported • Coed

ESF is the only college in the country with academic programs focused exclusively on the natural environment. Located on a 12-acre site adjacent to Syracuse University, ESF's core academic programs in the basic sciences, environmental sciences, engineering, and landscape architecture are supplemented by the vast array of course offerings at SU. Students at this small, distinguished professional college with an international reputation will discover a world of opportunity in both ESF's and SU's academic, athletic, and social life.

 ## Academics

ESF offers an engineering, natural science and design curriculum and core academic program; fewer than half of graduate courses are open to undergraduates. It awards bachelor's, master's, and doctoral **degrees**. Challenging opportunities include advanced placement, an honors program, and a senior project. Special programs include internships, off-campus study, and Army and Air Force ROTC.

The most popular **majors** include environmental biology, landscape architecture/design, and environmental sciences. A complete listing of majors at ESF appears in the Majors Index beginning on page 380.

The **faculty** at ESF has 120 full-time undergraduate teachers, 88% with terminal degrees. 85% of the faculty serve as student advisers. The average class size in required courses is 25.

 ## Computers on Campus

Students are not required to have a computer. 100 **computers** available in the computer center, academic buildings, and the library. Staffed computer lab on campus provides training in the use of computers and software.

The 2 **libraries** have 114,398 books, 91,000 microform titles, and 1,767 subscriptions.

 ## Campus Life

There are 300 active **organizations** on campus, including a drama/theater group and student-run newspaper and radio station. 25% of eligible men and 25% of eligible women are members of 25 national **fraternities**, 13 national **sororities**, and 1 local fraternity. Student **safety services** include 24-hour emergency telephone alarm devices and 24-hour patrols by trained security personnel.

This institution has no intercollegiate sports.

 ## Applying

ESF requires an essay, a high school transcript, 4 years of high school math and science, and SAT I or ACT. It recommends recommendations and an interview. Early and deferred entrance are possible, with rolling admissions and continuous processing to 3/1 for financial aid. **Contact:** Ms. Susan Sanford, Associate Director of Admissions, 1 Forestry Drive, Syracuse, NY 13210-2779, 315-470-6600 or toll-free 800-777-7ESF; fax 315-470-6933.

### GETTING IN LAST YEAR

720 applied
18% were accepted
62% enrolled (80)
39% from top tenth of their h.s. class
3.5 average high school GPA
21% had SAT verbal scores over 600
53% had SAT math scores over 600
0% had SAT verbal scores over 700
14% had SAT math scores over 700

### THE STUDENT BODY

Total 1,787, of whom 1,169
  are undergraduates
From 13 states and territories,
  2 other countries
90% from New York
31% women, 69% men
3% African Americans
1% Native Americans
2% Hispanics
2% Asian Americans
1% international students

### AFTER FRESHMAN YEAR

90% returned for sophomore year

### AFTER GRADUATION

22 corporations, 1 government agency, 3
  nonprofit organizations recruited on campus

### WHAT YOU WILL PAY

Resident tuition and fees $2952
Nonresident tuition and fees $6852
Room and board $6790
Need-based financial aid averages $300
Non-need financial aid averages $2000

# STATE UNIVERSITY OF NEW YORK MARITIME COLLEGE

Throgs Neck, New York • Suburban setting • Public • State-supported • Coed

▶ Maritime is a coeducational 4-year college. Graduates may pursue on-shore careers in industry, government service, or the professions; careers at sea as civilian officers in the Merchant Marine; or careers in the Navy, Marine Corps, Coast Guard, Air Force, or NOAA. The College offers BS or BE degrees in engineering, business administration/marine transportation, naval architecture, meteorology, oceanography (environmental science), and a humanities concentration. Essential to the Maritime College curricula is the annual 2-month Summer Sea Term aboard the training ship *Empire State*, providing hands-on training to cadets who, under supervision, assume responsibility for the ship's operation in preparation for the U.S. Merchant Marine Officer's license.

 **Academics**

Maritime College offers a core academic program; fewer than half of graduate courses are open to undergraduates. It awards bachelor's and master's **degrees**. Challenging opportunities include advanced placement, tutorials, and a senior project. Special programs include internships, summer session for credit, study abroad, and Naval and Air Force ROTC.

The most popular **majors** include business, marine engineering, and electrical engineering. A complete listing of majors at Maritime College appears in the Majors Index beginning on page 380.

The **faculty** at Maritime College has 65 full-time undergraduate teachers. 81% of the faculty serve as student advisers. The student-faculty ratio is 14:1, and the average class size in required courses is 25.

 **Computers on Campus**

Students are not required to have a computer. 85 **computers** available in the computer center, student lounge, and the library provide access to the main academic computer.

The **library** has 79,083 books and 354 subscriptions. It is connected to 2 national **on-line** catalogs.

 **Campus Life**

Active **organizations** on campus include student-run newspaper. 4% of eligible men are members of 1 local **fraternity**. Student **safety services** include late night transport/escort service, 24-hour emergency telephone alarm devices, 24-hour patrols by trained security personnel, and student patrols.

Maritime College is a member of the NCAA (Division III). **Intercollegiate sports** include basketball (m, w), crew (m, w), cross-country running (m, w), ice hockey (m), lacrosse (m), riflery (m, w), rugby (m), sailing (m, w), soccer (m), swimming and diving (m, w), tennis (m, w), wrestling (m).

 **Applying**

Maritime College requires a high school transcript, 3 years of high school math and science, 1 recommendation, medical history, SAT I or ACT, and a minimum high school GPA of 2.0. It recommends an essay, some high school foreign language, an interview, and SAT II Subject Tests. Early, deferred, and midyear entrance are possible, with rolling admissions and continuous processing to 5/1 for financial aid. **Contact:** Mr. Peter Cooney, Director of Admissions and Financial Aid, 6 Pennyfield Avenue, Throgs Neck, NY 10465, 718-409-7220 or toll-free 800-654-1874 (in-state), 800-642-1874 (out-of-state); fax 718-409-7392.

---

### GETTING IN LAST YEAR

780 applied
58% were accepted
48% enrolled (217)
10% from top tenth of their h.s. class
3% had SAT verbal scores over 600
12% had SAT math scores over 600
0% had SAT verbal scores over 700
0% had SAT math scores over 700

### THE STUDENT BODY

Total 836, of whom 656
  are undergraduates
From 22 states and territories
72% from New York
10% women, 90% men
5% African Americans
1% Native Americans
6% Hispanics
5% Asian Americans
9% international students

### AFTER FRESHMAN YEAR

78% returned for sophomore year

### AFTER GRADUATION

3% pursued further study (2% engineering, 1% business)
47 corporations, 15 government agencies recruited on campus

### WHAT YOU WILL PAY

Resident tuition and fees $3086
Nonresident tuition and fees $6986
Room and board $4694
Need-based financial aid averages $3500
Non-need financial aid averages $1700

# STETSON UNIVERSITY

DeLand, Florida • Small-town setting • Private • Independent • Coed

Stetson expects students to make a difference, personally and professionally. The University believes students learn best how to do this by doing. Therefore, students may be found managing an investment portfolio of more than $1 million, operating a campus outlet for an international firm, or conducting biology research with pygmy rattlesnakes in a nearby wildlife preserve. Beyond the classroom, students practice social responsibility by building Habitat for Humanity houses and working with at-risk youngsters in Youth Motivators. With a strong emphasis on student-professor interaction and liberal learning, Stetson offers a total environment that supports students' development as mature, responsible adults.

## Academics

Stetson offers a comprehensive curriculum and core academic program; fewer than half of graduate courses are open to undergraduates. It awards bachelor's, master's, and first professional **degrees**. Challenging opportunities include advanced placement, accelerated degree programs, self-designed majors, an honors program, a senior project, and Phi Beta Kappa. Special programs include internships, summer session for credit, off-campus study, study abroad, and Army ROTC.

The most popular **majors** include business, education, and psychology. A complete listing of majors at Stetson appears in the Majors Index beginning on page 380.

The **faculty** at Stetson has 155 full-time undergraduate teachers, 90% with terminal degrees. 100% of the faculty serve as student advisers. The student-faculty ratio is 11:1, and the average class size in required courses is 20.

## Computers on Campus

Students are not required to have a computer. 120 **computers** available in the computer center, computer labs, the research center, science hall, classrooms, and the library. Staffed computer lab on campus.

The 3 **libraries** have 336,486 books, 6,532 microform titles, and 1,339 subscriptions. They are connected to 1 national **on-line** catalog.

## Campus Life

There are 80 active **organizations** on campus, including a drama/theater group and student-run newspaper and radio station. 35% of eligible men and 35% of eligible women are members of 6 national **fraternities** and 6 national **sororities**. Student **safety services** include late night transport/escort service, 24-hour emergency telephone alarm devices, and 24-hour patrols by trained security personnel.

Stetson is a member of the NCAA (Division I). **Intercollegiate sports** (some offering scholarships) include baseball (m), basketball (m, w), crew (m, w), cross-country running (m, w), golf (m, w), soccer (m, w), softball (w), tennis (m, w), volleyball (w).

## Applying

Stetson requires an essay, a high school transcript, 3 years of high school math and science, some high school foreign language, recommendations, and SAT I or ACT. It recommends an interview and SAT II Subject Tests. Early and midyear entrance are possible, with a 3/15 deadline and continuous processing to 3/15 for financial aid. **Contact:** Ms. Linda Glover, Dean of Admissions, Griffith Hall, DeLand, FL 32720-3781, 904-822-7100 or toll-free 800-688-0101; fax 904-822-8832.

## GETTING IN LAST YEAR

1,760 applied
85% were accepted
33% enrolled (485)
38% from top tenth of their h.s. class
3.47 average high school GPA
9% had SAT verbal scores over 600
29% had SAT math scores over 600
38% had ACT scores over 26
1% had SAT verbal scores over 700
4% had SAT math scores over 700
9% had ACT scores over 30

## THE STUDENT BODY

Total 2,883, of whom 1,999
    are undergraduates
From 36 states and territories,
    41 other countries
80% from Florida
58% women, 42% men
3% African Americans
1% Native Americans
4% Hispanics
2% Asian Americans
5% international students

## AFTER FRESHMAN YEAR

80% returned for sophomore year

## AFTER GRADUATION

40% pursued further study (9% business, 8% arts and sciences, 7% law)
34 corporations, 3 government agencies, 2 nonprofit organizations recruited on campus

## WHAT YOU WILL PAY

Tuition and fees $12,870
Room and board $4565
59% receive need-based financial aid
    averaging $3080
30% receive non-need financial aid averaging
    $4196

# STEVENS INSTITUTE OF TECHNOLOGY

Hoboken, New Jersey • Urban setting • Private • Independent • Coed

Stevens continues to enjoy an outstanding reputation among leaders in research and technology. The mission of Stevens is to sustain a community of individuals who are dedicated to the achievement of excellence and who share a vision related to engineering, management, and applied and pure science. Because of the distinctive approach of the Institute, success is a by-product of the Stevens education. Each undergraduate program—science, engineering, humanities, and computer science—calls for study in a variety of fields within and outside the discipline. This comprehensive approach prepares Stevens graduates with a thorough understanding of science and technology and their implications for society.

 ## Academics

Stevens offers a core academic program; more than half of graduate courses are open to undergraduates. It awards bachelor's, master's, and doctoral **degrees**. Challenging opportunities include advanced placement, accelerated degree programs, tutorials, Freshmen Honors College, an honors program, a senior project, and Sigma Xi. Special programs include cooperative education, internships, summer session for credit, off-campus study, study abroad, and Army and Air Force ROTC.

The most popular **majors** include electrical engineering, mechanical engineering, and civil engineering. A complete listing of majors at Stevens appears in the Majors Index beginning on page 380.

The **faculty** at Stevens has 133 full-time graduate and undergraduate teachers, 90% with terminal degrees. 50% of the faculty serve as student advisers. The student-faculty ratio is 9:1, and the average class size in required courses is 20.

 ## Computers on Campus

Students are required to have a computer. PCs are provided. Student rooms are linked to a campus network. 1,520 **computers** available in the computer center, computer labs, the research center, the learning resource center, the library, the student center, dormitories, and student rooms provide access to e-mail and on-line services. Staffed computer lab on campus provides training in the use of computers and software.

The **library** has 101,948 books, 20 microform titles, and 138 subscriptions.

 ## Campus Life

There are 50 active **organizations** on campus, including a drama/theater group and student-run newspaper and radio station. Stevens has 10 national **fraternities** and 3 national **sororities**. Student **safety services** include late night transport/escort service, 24-hour emergency telephone alarm devices, 24-hour patrols by trained security personnel, and electronically operated dormitory entrances.

Stevens is a member of the NCAA (Division III). **Intercollegiate sports** include archery (m, w), baseball (m, w), basketball (m), bowling (m), cross-country running (m), fencing (m, w), golf (m), lacrosse (m), rugby (m), sailing (m, w), skiing (cross-country) (m, w), skiing (downhill) (m, w), soccer (m, w), squash (m), tennis (m, w), volleyball (m, w), wrestling (m).

 ## Applying

Stevens requires a high school transcript, 4 years of high school math, 3 years of high school science, an interview, and SAT I. It recommends an essay, some high school foreign language, recommendations, and SAT II Subject Tests. Early and deferred entrance are possible, with a 3/1 deadline and continuous processing to 3/1 for financial aid. **Contact:** Mrs. Maureen P. Weatherall, Dean of Undergraduate Admissions and Financial Aid, Stevens Center, Hoboken, NJ 07030, 201-216-5194 or toll-free 800-458-5323; fax 201-216-8348.

---

### GETTING IN LAST YEAR
1,757 applied
69% were accepted
32% enrolled (389)
51% from top tenth of their h.s. class

### THE STUDENT BODY
Total 2,872, of whom 1,280
    are undergraduates
From 40 states and territories,
    20 other countries

55% from New Jersey
25% women, 75% men
6% African Americans
11% Hispanics
19% Asian Americans
10% international students

### AFTER FRESHMAN YEAR
85% returned for sophomore year

### AFTER GRADUATION
15% pursued further study (6% arts and
    sciences, 6% engineering, 1% dentistry)
102 corporations, 10 government agencies, 1
    nonprofit organization recruited on campus

### WHAT YOU WILL PAY
Tuition and fees $17,100
Room and board $5520
80% receive need-based financial aid
    averaging $5400
Non-need financial aid averages $3500

# SWARTHMORE COLLEGE

Swarthmore, Pennsylvania • Suburban setting • Private • Independent • Coed

Swarthmore is a selective college of liberal arts and engineering, located 11 miles southwest of Philadelphia. Founded as a coeducational institution in 1864, it is nonsectarian but reflects many traditions and values of its Quaker founders. Swarthmore's Honors Program provides an option to study in small seminars during the junior and senior years. The campus occupies over 330 acres of woodland and is officially designated an arboretum. A small school by deliberate policy, its enrollment is about 1,350, with a student-faculty ratio of about 9:1. It attracts students from 50 states and 39 overseas countries.

 ## Academics

Swarthmore offers a core academic program. It awards bachelor's **degrees**. Challenging opportunities include advanced placement, self-designed majors, tutorials, an honors program, Phi Beta Kappa, and Sigma Xi. Special programs include internships, off-campus study, study abroad, and Army, Naval, and Air Force ROTC.

The most popular **majors** include literature, economics, and biology/biological sciences. A complete listing of majors at Swarthmore appears in the Majors Index beginning on page 380.

The **faculty** at Swarthmore has 151 full-time teachers, 97% with terminal degrees. The student-faculty ratio is 9:1.

 ## Computers on Campus

Students are not required to have a computer. Student rooms are linked to a campus network. 100 **computers** available in the computer center, computer labs, the learning resource center, labs, and the library provide access to the main academic computer, off-campus ties, e-mail, and on-line services. Staffed computer campus provides training in the use of computers and software.

The 3 **libraries** have 800,000 books, 270,000 microform titles, and 2,343 subscriptions.

 ## Campus Life

There are 60 active **organizations** on campus, including a drama/theater group and student-run newspaper and radio station. 7% of eligible men are members of 1 national **fraternity** and 1 local fraternity. Student **safety services** include late night transport/escort service, 24-hour patrols by trained security personnel, and electronically operated dormitory entrances.

Swarthmore is a member of the NCAA (Division III). **Intercollegiate sports** include badminton (w), baseball (m), basketball (m, w), cross-country running (m, w), field hockey (w), football (m), golf (m), lacrosse (m, w), rugby (m, w), soccer (m, w), softball (w), swimming and diving (m, w), tennis (m, w), track and field (m, w), volleyball (m, w), wrestling (m).

 ## Applying

Swarthmore requires an essay, a high school transcript, 2 recommendations, SAT I or ACT, and 3 SAT II Subject Tests (including SAT II: Writing Test). It recommends 3 years of high school math and science, some high school foreign language, and an interview. Early and deferred entrance are possible, with a 1/1 deadline and a 2/1 priority date for financial aid. **Contact:** Office of Admissions, 500 College Avenue, Swarthmore, PA 19081-1397, 610-328-8300; fax 610-328-8673.

---

### GETTING IN LAST YEAR

3,349 applied
30% were accepted
33% enrolled (328)
87% from top tenth of their h.s. class
77% had SAT verbal scores over 600
88% had SAT math scores over 600
30% had SAT verbal scores over 700
50% had SAT math scores over 700
33 National Merit Scholars

### THE STUDENT BODY

1,320 undergraduates
From 53 states and territories,
  39 other countries
12% from Pennsylvania
51% women, 49% men
6% African Americans
0% Native Americans
5% Hispanics
10% Asian Americans
5% international students

### AFTER FRESHMAN YEAR

98% returned for sophomore year

### AFTER GRADUATION

31% pursued further study
50 corporations, 5 government agencies, 20
  nonprofit organizations recruited on campus
1 Marshall, 3 Fulbright scholars

### WHAT YOU WILL PAY

Tuition and fees $19,316
Room and board $6584
48% receive need-based financial aid
  averaging $13,027
2% receive non-need financial aid averaging
  $19,164

# SWEET BRIAR COLLEGE

Sweet Briar, Virginia • Rural setting • Private • Independent • Women

▶ Sweet Briar women take charge and revel in their accomplishments. This attitude helps graduates compete confidently in graduate school and in the corporate world as scientists and writers, lawyers and judges, and dancers and art historians. Sweet Briar attracts women who enjoy being involved not only in a first-rate academic program but also in meaningful activities outside the classroom. A hands-on, one-on-one approach to the sciences, a 4-year honors program, and superior study-abroad programs encourage bright students to excel. Sweet Briar students are taken seriously, and professors take an interest in their intellectual development and personal growth.

## Academics

Sweet Briar offers a core academic program. It awards bachelor's **degrees**. Challenging opportunities include advanced placement, accelerated degree programs, self-designed majors, tutorials, an honors program, a senior project, and Phi Beta Kappa. Special programs include internships, off-campus study, study abroad, and Army ROTC.

The most popular **majors** include psychology, political science/government, and English. A complete listing of majors at Sweet Briar appears in the Majors Index beginning on page 380.

The **faculty** at Sweet Briar has 68 full-time teachers, 94% with terminal degrees. 62% of the faculty serve as student advisers. The student-faculty ratio is 8:1, and the average class size in required courses is 12.

## Computers on Campus

Students are not required to have a computer. Student rooms are linked to a campus network. 100 **computers** available in the computer center, computer labs, the learning resource center, academic support center, classrooms, the library, and dormitories provide access to the main academic computer, off-campus computing facilities, e-mail, and on-line services. Staffed computer lab on campus (open 24 hours a day) provides training in the use of computers and software.

The 4 **libraries** have 230,000 books, 350,000 microform titles, and 1,133 subscriptions. They are connected to 4 national **on-line** catalogs.

## Campus Life

There are 43 active **organizations** on campus, including a drama/theater group and student-run newspaper and radio station. Student **safety services** include front gate security, late night transport/escort service, 24-hour patrols by trained security personnel, and electronically operated dormitory entrances.

Sweet Briar is a member of the NCAA (Division III). **Intercollegiate sports** include basketball, equestrian sports, fencing, field hockey, golf, lacrosse, soccer, softball, swimming and diving, tennis, volleyball.

## Applying

Sweet Briar requires an essay, a high school transcript, 3 years of high school math, 2 years of high school foreign language, 2 recommendations, 4 years of high school English, 3 years of high school social studies, 2 years of high school science, and SAT I or ACT. It recommends an interview and 3 SAT II Subject Tests. Early and deferred entrance are possible, with a 2/15 deadline and continuous processing to 3/1 for financial aid. **Contact:** Ms. Nancy E. Church, Executive Director of Admissions and Financial Aid, PO Box B, Sweet Briar, VA 24595, 804-381-6142 or toll-free 800-381-6142; fax 804-381-6152.

---

**GETTING IN LAST YEAR**
479 applied
89% were accepted
43% enrolled (184)
32% from top tenth of their h.s. class
3.2 average high school GPA
4 class presidents
8 valedictorians

**THE STUDENT BODY**
609 undergraduates
From 39 states and territories,
  15 other countries
26% from Virginia

100% women
6% African Americans
1% Native Americans
1% Hispanics
4% Asian Americans
4% international students

**AFTER FRESHMAN YEAR**
75% returned for sophomore year
66% got a degree within 6 years

**AFTER GRADUATION**
23% pursued further study (14% arts and
  sciences, 3% law, 1% business)

61% had job offers within 3 months
4 corporations, 2 government agencies
  recruited on campus

**WHAT YOU WILL PAY**
Tuition and fees $14,625
Room and board $6000
56% receive need-based financial aid
  averaging $6290
27% receive non-need financial aid averaging
  $5537

---

# SYRACUSE UNIVERSITY

Syracuse, New York • Urban setting • Private • Independent • Coed

---

Syracuse University strives to provide an enriching, high-quality educational experience. Faculty members encourage interaction through small classes and integrate research into teaching. A continued commitment to the liberal arts complements professional teaching in all schools and colleges. Students' individual needs are met through the University's enhanced system of orientation and advising, expanded use of introductory courses, and increased selection of minors. Syracuse students augment their course work with internships, travel-abroad opportunities, and a wide variety of extracurricular activities.

 **Academics**

SU offers a professional and liberal arts curriculum and core academic program. It awards bachelor's, master's, doctoral, and first professional **degrees**. Challenging opportunities include advanced placement, accelerated degree programs, self-designed majors, tutorials, an honors program, a senior project, Phi Beta Kappa, and Sigma Xi. Special programs include cooperative education, internships, summer session for credit, off-campus study, study abroad, and Army and Air Force ROTC.

The most popular **majors** include psychology, political science/government, and architecture. A complete listing of majors at SU appears in the Majors Index beginning on page 380.

The **faculty** at SU has 868 full-time graduate and undergraduate teachers, 83% with terminal degrees. 100% of the faculty serve as student advisers. The student-faculty ratio is 10:1, and the average class size in required courses is 18.

 **Computers on Campus**

Students are not required to have a computer. Student rooms are linked to a campus network. 700 **computers** available in the computer center, computer labs, academic buildings, classrooms, the library, the student center, and dormitories provide access to the main academic computer, off-campus computing facilities, and e-mail. Staffed computer lab on campus (open 24 hours a day) provides training in the use of computers and software.

The 7 **libraries** have 2.8 million books, 3.3 million microform titles, and 15,650 subscriptions. They are connected to 5 national **on-line** catalogs.

 **Campus Life**

There are 250 active **organizations** on campus, including a drama/theater group and student-run newspaper and radio station. 27% of eligible men and 21% of eligible women are members of 23 national **fraternities**, 19 national **sororities**, 2 local fraternities, and 2 local sororities. Student **safety services** include late night transport/escort service, 24-hour emergency telephone alarm devices, 24-hour patrols by trained security personnel, and electronically operated dormitory entrances.

SU is a member of the NCAA (Division I). **Intercollegiate sports** (some offering scholarships) include basketball (m, w), crew (m, w), cross-country running (m, w), field hockey (w), football (m), gymnastics (m), lacrosse (m), soccer (m), swimming and diving (m, w), tennis (w), track and field (m, w), volleyball (w), wrestling (m).

 **Applying**

SU requires an essay, a high school transcript, 3 years of high school math and science, 2 years of high school foreign language, 1 recommendation, SAT I or ACT, a minimum high school GPA of 2.0, and in some cases audition for drama and music majors, portfolio for art and architecture majors and a minimum high school GPA of 3.0. It recommends an interview. Early, deferred, and midyear entrance are possible, with a 2/1 deadline and 2/15 for financial aid. **Contact:** Office of Admissions, 201 Tolley Administration Building, Syracuse, NY 13244-0003, 315-443-3611.

---

**GETTING IN LAST YEAR**
10,020 applied
67% were accepted
38% enrolled (2,518)
33% from top tenth of their h.s. class
18% had SAT verbal scores over 600
39% had SAT math scores over 600
2% had SAT verbal scores over 700
9% had SAT math scores over 700
24 valedictorians

**THE STUDENT BODY**
Total 14,550, of whom 10,133 are undergraduates

From 54 states and territories, 66 other countries
41% from New York
50% women, 50% men
10% African Americans
1% Native Americans
5% Hispanics
6% Asian Americans
4% international students

**AFTER FRESHMAN YEAR**
88% returned for sophomore year
69% got a degree within 5 years

**AFTER GRADUATION**
20% pursued further study (7% business, 5% law, 3% engineering)
119 corporations, 70 government agencies, 3 nonprofit organizations recruited on campus
3 Fulbright scholars

**WHAT YOU WILL PAY**
Tuition and fees $15,510
Room and board $6290
60% receive need-based financial aid averaging $6500
10% receive non-need financial aid averaging $4500

---

# TAYLOR UNIVERSITY

Upland, Indiana • Rural setting • Private • Independent • Coed

▶ Taylor University seeks Christian scholars who wish to experience thoughtful and rigorous academic studies thoroughly integrated with biblical Christianity. It seeks students who will respond to a supportive campus community that expects responsible decision making in the context of Christian freedom. It seeks students who will endeavor to translate their 4-year experience into lifelong learning and ministering the redemptive love of Jesus Christ to a world in need. Taylor's president, Dr. Jay Kesler, and outstanding Christian faculty invite students to consider the call to become a part of Taylor's exceptional student body and begin their own Taylor tradition.

 ## Academics

Taylor University offers a core academic program. It awards associate and bachelor's **degrees**. Challenging opportunities include advanced placement, accelerated degree programs, self-designed majors, tutorials, an honors program, and a senior project. Special programs include internships, summer session for credit, off-campus study, and study abroad.

The most popular **majors** include business, elementary education, and psychology. A complete listing of majors at Taylor University appears in the Majors Index beginning on page 380.

The **faculty** at Taylor University has 113 full-time teachers, 67% with terminal degrees. 100% of the faculty serve as student advisers. The student-faculty ratio is 18:1, and the average class size in required courses is 30.

 ## Computers on Campus

Students are not required to have a computer. Student rooms are linked to a campus network. 169 **computers** available in computer labs, the learning resource center, the library, and dormitories provide access to the main academic computer, e-mail, and on-line services. Staffed computer lab on campus provides training in the use of computers and software.

The **library** has 159,127 books, 8,428 microform titles, and 720 subscriptions. It is connected to 10 national **on-line** catalogs.

 ## Campus Life

There are 30 active **organizations** on campus, including a drama/theater group and student-run newspaper and radio station. Student **safety services** include late night transport/escort service, 24-hour patrols by trained security personnel, and student patrols.

Taylor University is a member of the NAIA. **Intercollegiate sports** (some offering scholarships) include baseball (m), basketball (m, w), cross-country running (m, w), equestrian sports (m, w), football (m), golf (m), soccer (m, w), softball (w), tennis (m, w), track and field (m, w), volleyball (m, w).

 ## Applying

Taylor University requires an essay, a high school transcript, 3 years of high school math and science, 2 recommendations, and SAT I or ACT. It recommends 2 years of high school foreign language, an interview, and a minimum high school GPA of 3.0. Deferred and midyear entrance are possible, with rolling admissions and continuous processing to 3/1 for financial aid. **Contact:** Mr. Stephen R. Mortland, Director of Admissions, 500 West Reade Avenue, Upland, IN 46989-1001, 317-998-5134 or toll-free 800-882-3456.

---

### GETTING IN LAST YEAR
1,792 applied
60% were accepted
40% enrolled (431)
46% from top tenth of their h.s. class
3.4 average high school GPA
32% had SAT verbal scores over 600
35% had SAT math scores over 600
5% had SAT verbal scores over 700
7% had SAT math scores over 700
31 valedictorians

### THE STUDENT BODY
1,831 undergraduates
From 46 states and territories,
 18 other countries
31% from Indiana
52% women, 48% men
2% African Americans
1% Native Americans
1% Hispanics
3% Asian Americans
2% international students

### AFTER FRESHMAN YEAR
87% returned for sophomore year
55% got a degree within 4 years
70% got a degree within 5 years
73% got a degree within 6 years

### AFTER GRADUATION
12% pursued further study (6% arts and
 sciences, 3% theology, 2% medicine)
32% had job offers within 3 months
36 corporations, 6 government agencies, 44
 nonprofit organizations recruited on campus

### WHAT YOU WILL PAY
Tuition and fees $11,175
Room and board $4000
56% receive need-based financial aid
 averaging $1912
15% receive non-need financial aid averaging
 $1245

# TEXAS A&M UNIVERSITY

College Station, Texas • Suburban setting • Public • State-supported • Coed

▶An internationally acclaimed research university, Texas A&M is widely recognized for the strength of its undergraduate curricular and extracurricular programs. Expanding frontiers of knowledge, from the humanities and social sciences to business studies, science, and engineering, Texas A&M's distinguished faculty includes Pulitzer and Nobel prize recipients. An outstanding student body is attracted from 50 states and 100 countries to pursue degrees in over 150 fields of study. The University's 5,000-acre main campus is home to the cyclotron, supercomputer, visualization lab, art galleries, recreation centers, and fitness facilities. More than 700 recognized student organizations provide unparalleled opportunities for leadership development.

 ## Academics

Texas A&M offers an interdisciplinary core curriculum and core academic program; fewer than half of graduate courses are open to undergraduates. It awards bachelor's, master's, doctoral, and first professional **degrees**. Challenging opportunities include advanced placement, accelerated degree programs, tutorials, an honors program, and Sigma Xi. Special programs include cooperative education, internships, summer session for credit, off-campus study, study abroad, and Army, Naval, and Air Force ROTC.

The most popular **majors** include biomedical sciences, interdisciplinary studies, and psychology. A complete listing of majors at Texas A&M appears in the Majors Index beginning on page 380.

The **faculty** at Texas A&M has 1,946 full-time graduate and undergraduate teachers, 92% with terminal degrees. The student-faculty ratio is 20:1, and the average class size in required courses is 56.

 ## Computers on Campus

Students are not required to have a computer. Student rooms are linked to a campus network. 1,700 **computers** available in the computer center, computer labs, the research center, the learning resource center, various locations on campus, classrooms, the library, the student center, and dormitories provide access to the main academic computer, off-campus computing facilities, e-mail, and on-line services. Staffed computer lab on campus (open 24 hours a day) provides training in the use of computers and software.

The 4 **libraries** have 2.1 million books, 4.3 million microform titles, and 13,000 subscriptions. They are connected to 18 national **on-line** catalogs.

 ## Campus Life

There are 700 active **organizations** on campus, including a drama/theater group and student-run newspaper and radio station. 17% of students participate in student government elections. 9% of eligible men and 12% of eligible women are members of 29 national **fraternities** and 15 national **sororities**. Student **safety services** include late night transport/escort service, 24-hour emergency telephone alarm devices, 24-hour patrols by trained security personnel, and electronically operated dormitory entrances.

Texas A&M is a member of the NCAA (Division I). **Intercollegiate sports** (some offering scholarships) include baseball (m), basketball (m, w), cross-country running (m, w), football (m), golf (m, w), riflery (m, w), soccer (w), softball (w), swimming and diving (m, w), tennis (m, w), track and field (m, w), volleyball (w).

 ## Applying

Texas A&M requires a high school transcript, SAT I or ACT, and in some cases recommendations. It recommends 2 years of high school foreign language and 2 SAT II Subject Tests. Early, deferred, and midyear entrance are possible, with a 3/1 deadline and continuous processing to 4/1 for financial aid. **Contact:** Mr. Gary R. Engelgau, Office of Admissions and Records, 217 John J. Koldus Building, College Station, TX 77843-1265, 409-845-3741.

---

### GETTING IN LAST YEAR
15,243 applied
67% were accepted
59% enrolled (6,047)
49% from top tenth of their h.s. class
15% had SAT verbal scores over 600
46% had SAT math scores over 600
3% had SAT verbal scores over 700
11% had SAT math scores over 700
191 National Merit Scholars

### THE STUDENT BODY
Total 42,018, of whom 34,278
  are undergraduates

From 55 states and territories
92% from Texas
43% women, 57% men
3% African Americans
0% Native Americans
9% Hispanics
4% Asian Americans
2% international students

### AFTER FRESHMAN YEAR
85% returned for sophomore year
27% got a degree within 4 years
60% got a degree within 5 years
67% got a degree within 6 years

### AFTER GRADUATION
420 corporations, 175 government agencies,
  5 nonprofit organizations recruited on
  campus
2 Fulbright scholars

### WHAT YOU WILL PAY
Resident tuition and fees $1752
Nonresident tuition and fees $6042
Room and board $2200
Need-based financial aid averages $1305
Non-need financial aid averages $1820

---

# TEXAS CHRISTIAN UNIVERSITY

Fort Worth, Texas • Suburban setting • Private • Independent-Religious • Coed

More than 120 years ago, 2 young and courageous teachers defied the status quo and established a coeducational college new to the untamed American frontier. That dream has evolved into Texas Christian University, a premier university with global vision, educating students from every state and 60 countries. TCU offers an environment of discovery and intellectual challenge while providing support to foster academic success. There is also a tradition of friendliness at TCU! This atmosphere is further enhanced by the ready acceptance of all cultural, intellectual, religious, and artistic viewpoints. This diversity helps create a dynamic university community.

##  Academics

TCU offers an interdisciplinary curriculum and core academic program. It awards bachelor's, master's, doctoral, and first professional **degrees**. Challenging opportunities include advanced placement, accelerated degree programs, self-designed majors, tutorials, an honors program, Phi Beta Kappa, and Sigma Xi. Special programs include internships, summer session for credit, study abroad, and Army and Air Force ROTC.

The most popular **majors** include business, nursing, and psychology. A complete listing of majors at TCU appears in the Majors Index beginning on page 380.

The **faculty** at TCU has 323 full-time undergraduate teachers, 93% with terminal degrees. 76% of the faculty serve as student advisers. The student-faculty ratio is 14:1, and the average class size in required courses is 26.

##  Computers on Campus

Students are not required to have a computer. 350 **computers** available in the computer center, computer labs, writing center, academic buildings, the library, and dormitories provide access to the main academic computer, e-mail, and on-line services. Staffed computer lab on campus provides training in the use of computers and software.

The **library** has 760,732 books, 442,295 microform titles, and 3,765 subscriptions.

##  Campus Life

There are 212 active **organizations** on campus, including a drama/theater group and student-run newspaper and radio station. 29% of eligible men and 38% of eligible women are members of 8 national **fraternities**, 11 national **sororities**, 2 local fraternities, and 2 local sororities. Student **safety services** include late night transport/escort service, 24-hour emergency telephone alarm devices, 24-hour patrols by trained security personnel, student patrols, and electronically operated dormitory entrances.

TCU is a member of the NCAA (Division I). **Intercollegiate sports** (some offering scholarships) include baseball (m), basketball (m, w), cross-country running (m, w), football (m), golf (m, w), riflery (w), soccer (m, w), swimming and diving (m, w), tennis (m, w), track and field (m, w).

##  Applying

TCU requires an essay, a high school transcript, 3 years of high school math and science, 2 recommendations, SAT I or ACT, and a minimum high school GPA of 2.0. It recommends 2 years of high school foreign language, an interview, and a minimum high school GPA of 3.0. Early, deferred, and midyear entrance are possible, with a 2/15 deadline and continuous processing to 5/1 for financial aid. **Contact:** Ms. Sandra Ware, Associate Dean of Admissions, PO Box 32905, Fort Worth, TX 76129-0002, 817-921-7490 or toll-free 800-828-3764; fax 817-921-7333.

---

**GETTING IN LAST YEAR**
4,081 applied
73% were accepted
39% enrolled (1,168)
33% from top tenth of their h.s. class
9 National Merit Scholars

**THE STUDENT BODY**
Total 6,706, of whom 5,337
   are undergraduates
From 50 states and territories,
   68 other countries
71% from Texas

59% women, 41% men
4% African Americans
1% Native Americans
6% Hispanics
2% Asian Americans
3% international students

**AFTER FRESHMAN YEAR**
78% returned for sophomore year
40% got a degree within 4 years
58% got a degree within 5 years
59% got a degree within 6 years

**AFTER GRADUATION**
104 corporations, 81 government agencies,
   29 nonprofit organizations recruited on
   campus

**WHAT YOU WILL PAY**
Tuition and fees $9480
Room and board $3320
33% receive need-based financial aid
   averaging $3630
46% receive non-need financial aid averaging
   $4232

# THOMAS AQUINAS COLLEGE

Santa Paula, California • Rural setting • Private • Independent-Religious • Coed

▶ The College's curriculum is based on the Great Books, the original works of the principal philosophers, theologians, scientists, mathematicians, poets, and writers of Western civilization. This unique program attracts students of exceptional ability and diverse backgrounds to a community of learning. Conventional lectures are replaced by small seminars, tutorials, and laboratories in which faculty lead rigorous and lively conversations about classic works in the arts and sciences. The unified, required curriculum integrates the essential intellectual disciplines of a classical liberal education. The College's academic program and community life are guided by the philosophic and religious traditions of the Catholic Church.

 ## Computers on Campus

Students are not required to have a computer. 10 **computers** available in the library, the student center, and dormitories.

The **library** has 34,000 books and 40 subscriptions.

 ## Campus Life

There is 1 active **organization** on campus. Student **safety services** include 24-hour emergency telephone alarm devices and student patrols.

This institution has no intercollegiate sports.

 ## Academics

TAC offers a great books curriculum and core academic program. It awards bachelor's **degrees**. A senior project is a challenging opportunity. Study abroad is a special program.

A complete listing of majors at Thomas Aquinas appears in the Majors Index beginning on page 380.

The **faculty** at TAC has 22 full-time teachers, 73% with terminal degrees. 85% of the faculty serve as student advisers. The student-faculty ratio is 10:1, and the average class size in required courses is 16.

 ## Applying

TAC requires an essay, a high school transcript, 2 years of high school foreign language, 3 recommendations, SAT I or ACT, and in some cases an interview. It recommends 3 years of high school math and science. Early and deferred entrance are possible, with rolling admissions and continuous processing to 9/1 for financial aid. **Contact:** Mr. Thomas J. Susanka Jr., Director of Admissions, 10000 North Ojai Road, Santa Paula, CA 93060-9980, 805-525-4417 ext. 359 or toll-free 800-634-9797; fax 805-525-0620.

### GETTING IN LAST YEAR
120 applied
76% were accepted
75% enrolled (68)
41% from top tenth of their h.s. class
3.35 average high school GPA
43% had SAT verbal scores over 600
47% had SAT math scores over 600
53% had ACT scores over 26
13% had SAT verbal scores over 700
21% had SAT math scores over 700
24% had ACT scores over 30

### THE STUDENT BODY
221 undergraduates
From 36 states and territories,
    11 other countries
29% from California
46% women, 54% men
1% African Americans
0% Native Americans
3% Hispanics
2% Asian Americans
14% international students

### AFTER FRESHMAN YEAR
94% returned for sophomore year
70% got a degree within 4 years
72% got a degree within 5 years

### WHAT YOU WILL PAY
Tuition and fees $13,400
Room and board $5200
82% receive need-based financial aid
    averaging $8627

# TRANSYLVANIA UNIVERSITY

Lexington, Kentucky • Urban setting • Private • Independent-Religious • Coed

Today, in its 215th year, Transylvania is a distinguished liberal arts college enrolling nearly 1,000 students. A strong commitment to undergraduate teaching and small classes are among Transylvania's distinctive assets. Students repeatedly cite their personal relationships with faculty members as being among the most valuable aspects of their Transylvania experience. Transylvania's location in Lexington, at the heart of Kentucky's beautiful Bluegrass region, provides students with an exceptional range of cultural and recreational activities. Now in its third century, Transylvania is consistently ranked as one of the nation's top regional liberal arts colleges.

##  Academics

Transylvania offers an interdisciplinary liberal arts curriculum and core academic program. It awards bachelor's **degrees**. Challenging opportunities include advanced placement, accelerated degree programs, self-designed majors, and tutorials. Special programs include internships, summer session for credit, off-campus study, study abroad, and Army and Air Force ROTC.

The most popular **majors** include business, biology/biological sciences, and psychology. A complete listing of majors at Transylvania appears in the Majors Index beginning on page 380.

The **faculty** at Transylvania has 65 full-time teachers, 92% with terminal degrees. 100% of the faculty serve as student advisers. The student-faculty ratio is 13:1, and the average class size in required courses is 17.

##  Computers on Campus

Students are not required to have a computer. Student rooms are linked to a campus network. 210 **computers** available in the computer center, computer labs, the research center, the learning resource center, academic buildings, classrooms, the library, the student center, and dormitories provide access to the main academic computer, off-campus computing facilities, and e-mail. Staffed computer lab on campus provides training in the use of computers and software.

The **library** has 130,000 books, 64 microform titles, and 580 subscriptions. It is connected to 2 national **on-line** catalogs.

##  Campus Life

There are 43 active **organizations** on campus, including a drama/theater group and student-run newspaper and radio station. 60% of eligible men and 62% of eligible women are members of 4 national **fraternities** and 4 national **sororities**. Student **safety services** include late night transport/escort service, 24-hour emergency telephone alarm devices, and 24-hour patrols by trained security personnel.

Transylvania is a member of the NAIA. **Intercollegiate sports** (some offering scholarships) include baseball (m), basketball (m, w), cross-country running (m, w), field hockey (w), golf (m), soccer (m, w), softball (w), swimming and diving (m, w), tennis (m, w).

##  Applying

Transylvania requires an essay, a high school transcript, 3 years of high school math, 2 recommendations, minimum 2.25 GPA, SAT I or ACT, and in some cases an interview. It recommends 3 years of high school science, some high school foreign language, and an interview. Early, deferred, and midyear entrance are possible, with a 3/1 deadline and continuous processing to 3/15 for financial aid. **Contact:** Mr. Michael J. Suzo, Director of Admissions, 300 North Broadway, Lexington, KY 40508-1797, 606-233-8242 or toll-free 800-872-6798; fax 606-233-8797.

---

### GETTING IN LAST YEAR
799 applied
94% were accepted
34% enrolled (258)
55% from top tenth of their h.s. class
3.41 average high school GPA
17% had SAT verbal scores over 600
32% had SAT math scores over 600
60% had ACT scores over 26
2% had SAT verbal scores over 700
7% had SAT math scores over 700
25% had ACT scores over 30
8 National Merit Scholars
27 valedictorians

### THE STUDENT BODY
871 undergraduates
From 31 states and territories,
    13 other countries
80% from Kentucky
56% women, 44% men
2% African Americans
0% Native Americans
1% Hispanics
3% Asian Americans
1% international students

### AFTER FRESHMAN YEAR
79% returned for sophomore year
60% got a degree within 4 years
69% got a degree within 5 years
71% got a degree within 6 years

### AFTER GRADUATION
46% pursued further study (22% arts and
    sciences, 8% law, 7% medicine)
35% had job offers within 3 months
8 corporations, 2 government agencies, 3
    nonprofit organizations recruited on campus

### WHAT YOU WILL PAY
Tuition and fees $11,350
Room and board $4450
45% receive need-based financial aid
    averaging $6406
42% receive non-need financial aid averaging
    $5674

# TRENTON STATE COLLEGE

Trenton, New Jersey • Suburban setting • Public • State-supported • Coed

▶ Trenton State College is a highly selective institution that has received consistent national recognition for its commitment to quality. The College enrolls bright and creative students who contribute actively to campus life and to their own intellectual growth. They join a community of learners dedicated to the ideals of public service, excellence, diversity, and community. In a learning partnership with faculty, TSC students enhance their skills, expand their knowledge, and formulate the values and attitudes necessary to assume the responsibilities of an increasingly complex society. TSC graduates take their places as productive citizens and as future leaders in their professions.

 **Academics**

TSC offers an interdisciplinary curriculum and core academic program; fewer than half of graduate courses are open to undergraduates. It awards bachelor's and master's **degrees**. Challenging opportunities include advanced placement, accelerated degree programs, tutorials, an honors program, and a senior project. Special programs include internships, summer session for credit, off-campus study, study abroad, and Army and Air Force ROTC.

The most popular **majors** include elementary education, art/fine arts, and criminal justice. A complete listing of majors at TSC appears in the Majors Index beginning on page 380.

The **faculty** at TSC has 309 full-time undergraduate teachers, 83% with terminal degrees. 100% of the faculty serve as student advisers. The student-faculty ratio is 15:1, and the average class size in required courses is 14.

 **Computers on Campus**

Students are not required to have a computer. Student rooms are linked to a campus network. 420 **computers**

available in the computer center, computer labs, academic buildings, the library, and the student center. Staffed computer lab on campus provides training in the use of computers and software.

The **library** has 500,000 books, 200,000 microform titles, and 1,563 subscriptions. It is connected to 6 national **on-line** catalogs.

 **Campus Life**

There are 130 active **organizations** on campus, including a drama/theater group and student-run newspaper and radio station. 13% of students participate in student government elections. 14% of eligible men and 14% of eligible women are members of 11 national **fraternities**, 13 national **sororities**, 4 local fraternities, and 4 local sororities. Student **safety services** include late night transport/escort service, 24-hour emergency telephone alarm devices, 24-hour patrols by trained security personnel, and electronically operated dormitory entrances.

TSC is a member of the NCAA (Division III). **Intercollegiate sports** include baseball (m), basketball (m, w), cross-country running (m, w), field hockey (w), football (m), golf (m), lacrosse (w), soccer (m, w), softball (w), swimming and diving (m, w), tennis (m, w), track and field (m, w), wrestling (m).

 **Applying**

TSC requires an essay, a high school transcript, 3 years of high school math and science, SAT I, and in some cases an interview. It recommends 2 years of high school foreign language and recommendations. Early and deferred entrance are possible, with a 3/1 deadline and continuous processing to 4/15 for financial aid. **Contact:** Mr. Frank Cooper, Director of Admissions, Green Hall, Trenton, NJ 08650-4700, 609-771-2131 or toll-free 800-624-0967 (in-state).

---

**GETTING IN LAST YEAR**
5,484 applied
49% were accepted
40% enrolled (1,061)
60% from top tenth of their h.s. class
3.35 average high school GPA
17% had SAT verbal scores over 600
52% had SAT math scores over 600
2% had SAT verbal scores over 700
11% had SAT math scores over 700

**THE STUDENT BODY**
Total 6,981, of whom 5,984
 are undergraduates
From 23 states and territories,
 16 other countries

92% from New Jersey
60% women, 40% men
7% African Americans
1% Native Americans
4% Hispanics
4% Asian Americans
1% international students

**AFTER FRESHMAN YEAR**
95% returned for sophomore year

**AFTER GRADUATION**
13% pursued further study (4% arts and
 sciences, 3% law, 2% business)

250 corporations, 10 government agencies,
 20 nonprofit organizations recruited on
 campus

**WHAT YOU WILL PAY**
Resident tuition and fees $4012
Nonresident tuition and fees $6287
Room and board $5411
48% receive need-based financial aid
 averaging $500
36% receive non-need financial aid averaging
 $1500

# TRINITY COLLEGE

Hartford, Connecticut • Urban setting • Private • Independent • Coed

---

Trinity offers its students the distinctive combination of a beautiful hilltop campus in a thriving capital city. Students find hundreds of internship and volunteer opportunities and cultural or entertainment activities in Hartford. More than 50% pursue internships in business, politics, law, medicine, education, and the arts. Community Outreach, the organization that coordinates some 20 volunteer projects, involves more than 400 students in community service work annually. Long considered one of America's premier liberal arts colleges, Trinity is one of only a few such distinguished institutions that can provide its students with the rich opportunities available only in a major metropolitan area.

##  Academics

Trinity College offers a core academic program; more than half of graduate courses are open to undergraduates. It awards bachelor's and master's **degrees**. Challenging opportunities include advanced placement, accelerated degree programs, self-designed majors, tutorials, a senior project, and Phi Beta Kappa. Special programs include internships, summer session for credit, off-campus study, study abroad, and Army ROTC.

The most popular **majors** include English, economics, and political science/government. A complete listing of majors at Trinity College appears in the Majors Index beginning on page 380.

The **faculty** at Trinity College has 163 full-time undergraduate teachers, 98% with terminal degrees. 95% of the faculty serve as student advisers. The student-faculty ratio is 10:1.

##  Computers on Campus

Students are not required to have a computer. Student rooms are linked to a campus network. 150 **computers** available in the computer center, academic departments, and the library provide access to the main academic computer, off-campus computing facilities, and e-mail. Staffed computer lab on campus (open 24 hours a day).

The 3 **libraries** have 878,891 books, 284,789 microform titles, and 2,241 subscriptions.

##  Campus Life

There are 80 active **organizations** on campus, including a drama/theater group and student-run newspaper and radio station. 30% of students participate in student government elections. 33% of eligible men and 11% of eligible women are members of 8 national **fraternities** and 2 national **sororities**. Student **safety services** include late night transport/escort service, 24-hour emergency telephone alarm devices, and 24-hour patrols by trained security personnel.

Trinity College is a member of the NCAA (Division III). **Intercollegiate sports** include baseball (m), basketball (m, w), crew (m, w), cross-country running (m, w), equestrian sports (m, w), fencing (m, w), field hockey (w), football (m), golf (m), ice hockey (m), lacrosse (m, w), rugby (m, w), sailing (m, w), skiing (downhill) (m, w), soccer (m, w), softball (w), squash (m, w), swimming and diving (m, w), tennis (m, w), track and field (m, w), volleyball (m, w), water polo (m, w), wrestling (m).

##  Applying

Trinity College requires an essay, a high school transcript, 3 years of high school math, 2 years of high school foreign language, 3 recommendations, SAT I or ACT, and SAT II: Writing Test. It recommends 3 years of high school science and an interview. Early and deferred entrance are possible, with a 1/15 deadline and 2/1 for financial aid. **Contact:** Dr. David M. Borus, Dean of Admissions and Financial Aid, 300 Summit Street, Hartford, CT 06106-3100, 203-297-2180; fax 203-297-2287.

---

### GETTING IN LAST YEAR
3,009 applied
59% were accepted
27% enrolled (473)
45% from top tenth of their h.s. class
26% had SAT verbal scores over 600
59% had SAT math scores over 600
55% had ACT scores over 26
2% had SAT verbal scores over 700
10% had SAT math scores over 700
12% had ACT scores over 30

### THE STUDENT BODY
Total 2,146, of whom 1,961
 are undergraduates
From 49 states and territories,
 25 other countries
31% from Connecticut
50% women, 50% men
6% African Americans
0% Native Americans
4% Hispanics
5% Asian Americans
2% international students

### AFTER FRESHMAN YEAR
95% returned for sophomore year

### WHAT YOU WILL PAY
Tuition and fees $19,560
Room and board $5690
Need-based financial aid averages $13,500

---

# TRINITY UNIVERSITY

San Antonio, Texas • Urban setting • Private • Independent-Religious • Coed

Trinity University in San Antonio, Texas, isn't for everyone. A national leader in undergraduate education, Trinity seeks to enroll only gifted, motivated students who have excelled in high school and who wish to continue pursuing excellence in college. Through a highly selective admission policy, Trinity attracts academically gifted students interested in being active participants in their education. With the historic and multicultural resources of San Antonio, a beautiful hilltop campus, and one of the nation's largest per-student endowments, Trinity can offer the individual attention expected of a small school with much of the diversity of opportunity typical of a large research institution.

 **Academics**

Trinity offers a curriculum based on the six understandings and core academic program; a few graduate courses are open to undergraduates. It awards bachelor's and master's **degrees**. Challenging opportunities include advanced placement, accelerated degree programs, tutorials, and Phi Beta Kappa. Special programs include internships, summer session for credit, study abroad, and Air Force ROTC.

The most popular **majors** include business, economics, and English. A complete listing of majors at Trinity appears in the Majors Index beginning on page 380.

The **faculty** at Trinity has 224 full-time graduate and undergraduate teachers, 95% with terminal degrees. 95% of the faculty serve as student advisers. The student-faculty ratio is 10:1, and the average class size in required courses is 20.

 **Computers on Campus**

Students are not required to have a computer. 400 **computers** available in the computer center and the student center. Staffed computer lab on campus (open 24 hours a day).

The **library** has 760,675 books, 268,288 microform titles, and 2,485 subscriptions.

 **Campus Life**

Active **organizations** on campus include drama/theater group and student-run newspaper and radio station. 30% of eligible men and 33% of eligible women are members of 6 local **fraternities** and 6 local **sororities**. Student **safety services** include late night transport/escort service, 24-hour emergency telephone alarm devices, 24-hour patrols by trained security personnel, and student patrols.

Trinity is a member of the NCAA (Division III). **Intercollegiate sports** include baseball (m), basketball (m, w), cross-country running (m, w), football (m), golf (m), soccer (m, w), softball (w), swimming and diving (m, w), tennis (m, w), track and field (m, w), volleyball (m, w).

 **Applying**

Trinity requires an essay, a high school transcript, 3 years of high school math and science, 2 years of high school foreign language, recommendations, and SAT I or ACT. It recommends an interview. Early, deferred, and midyear entrance are possible, with a 2/1 deadline and a 2/1 priority date for financial aid. **Contact:** Dr. George Boyd, Director of Admissions, 715 Stadium Drive, San Antonio, TX 78212-7200, 210-736-7207 or toll-free 800-TRINITY.

## GETTING IN LAST YEAR

2,520 applied
79% were accepted
32% enrolled (637)
63% from top tenth of their h.s. class
3.8 average high school GPA
32% had SAT verbal scores over 600
66% had SAT math scores over 600
73% had ACT scores over 26
3% had SAT verbal scores over 700
16% had SAT math scores over 700
17% had ACT scores over 30
32 National Merit Scholars

## THE STUDENT BODY

Total 2,479, of whom 2,226 are undergraduates
From 50 states and territories, 21 other countries
63% from Texas
49% women, 51% men
2% African Americans
1% Native Americans
8% Hispanics
9% Asian Americans
3% international students

## AFTER FRESHMAN YEAR

85% returned for sophomore year
74% got a degree within 4 years

## AFTER GRADUATION

56% pursued further study (35% arts and sciences, 10% law, 3% engineering)
4 Fulbright scholars

## WHAT YOU WILL PAY

Tuition and fees $12,384
Room and board $5150
45% receive need-based financial aid averaging $12,019
25% receive non-need financial aid averaging $3830

# TUFTS UNIVERSITY

Medford, Massachusetts • Suburban setting • Private • Independent • Coed

Tufts is located on a residential campus and enrolls students from 50 states and more than 60 countries. Undergraduate colleges in liberal arts and engineering and 7 graduate schools are available. Over 40 departmental majors and 16 interdisciplinary programs in liberal arts and professional degree programs in chemical, civil and environmental, electrical, mechanical, and interdisciplinary engineering programs prepare students for leadership. Typically, 40% of Tufts students pursue study abroad. Students enjoy the advantages of Boston, an active campus, and the accessibility of faculty members for whom research and scholarship are balanced by a commitment to teaching.

##  Academics

Tufts offers a core academic program; fewer than half of graduate courses are open to undergraduates. It awards bachelor's, master's, doctoral, and first professional **degrees**. Challenging opportunities include advanced placement, self-designed majors, tutorials, an honors program, a senior project, Phi Beta Kappa, and Sigma Xi. Special programs include internships, summer session for credit, off-campus study, study abroad, and Army, Naval, and Air Force ROTC.

The most popular **majors** include English and biology/biological sciences. A complete listing of majors at Tufts appears in the Majors Index beginning on page 380.

The **faculty** at Tufts has 552 full-time graduate and undergraduate teachers, 99% with terminal degrees. 99% of the faculty serve as student advisers. The student-faculty ratio is 13:1, and the average class size in required courses is 25.

##  Computers on Campus

Students are not required to have a computer. Student rooms are linked to a campus network. 254 **computers** available in the computer center, computer labs, CAD lab, the library, the student center, and dormitories provide access to the main academic computer, off-campus computing facilities, e-mail, and on-line services. Staffed computer lab on campus provides training in the use of computers and software.

The 8 **libraries** have 803,000 books, 967,000 microform titles, and 4,793 subscriptions. They are connected to 1 national **on-line** catalog.

##  Campus Life

There are 130 active **organizations** on campus, including a drama/theater group and student-run newspaper and radio station. 15% of eligible men and 4% of eligible women are members of 11 national **fraternities** and 4 national **sororities**. Student **safety services** include security lighting, call boxes to campus police, late night transport/escort service, 24-hour emergency telephone alarm devices, 24-hour patrols by trained security personnel, and electronically operated dormitory entrances.

Tufts is a member of the NCAA (Division III). **Intercollegiate sports** include baseball (m), basketball (m, w), crew (m, w), cross-country running (m, w), field hockey (w), football (m), golf (m), ice hockey (m), lacrosse (m, w), sailing (m, w), soccer (m, w), softball (w), squash (m, w), swimming and diving (m, w), tennis (m, w), track and field (m, w), volleyball (w).

##  Applying

Tufts requires an essay, a high school transcript, 1 recommendation, SAT I or ACT, and 3 SAT II Subject Tests (including SAT II: Writing Test). It recommends 3 years of high school math and science, 3 years of high school foreign language, and an interview. Early and deferred entrance are possible, with a 1/1 deadline and 2/1 for financial aid. **Contact:** Mr. David D. Cuttino, Dean of Undergraduate Admissions, Bendetson Hall, Medford, MA 02155, 617-627-3170; fax 617-627-3860.

### GETTING IN LAST YEAR
7,880 applied
45% were accepted
33% enrolled (1,170)
62% from top tenth of their h.s. class
44% had SAT verbal scores over 600
82% had SAT math scores over 600
3% had SAT verbal scores over 700
28% had SAT math scores over 700
22 National Merit Scholars

### THE STUDENT BODY
Total 8,042, of whom 4,550
    are undergraduates

From 51 states and territories,
    60 other countries
27% from Massachusetts
53% women, 47% men
4% African Americans
4% Hispanics
13% Asian Americans
8% international students

### AFTER FRESHMAN YEAR
99% returned for sophomore year
90% got a degree within 4 years

### AFTER GRADUATION
35% pursued further study (12% law, 10% business, 10% medicine)
137 corporations, 16 government agencies recruited on campus
10 Fulbright scholars

### WHAT YOU WILL PAY
Tuition and fees $20,204
Room and board $5968
39% receive need-based financial aid averaging $11,650
Non-need financial aid averages $750

# TULANE UNIVERSITY

New Orleans, Louisiana • Urban setting • Private • Independent • Coed

▶ Tulane University is known widely for its emphasis on undergraduate teaching and its accomplishments in research. With 5,000 full-time undergraduate students in 5 undergraduate divisions, Tulane gives each student the personal attention and teaching excellence for which small colleges are known, while providing access to the interdisciplinary and research resources of a major research university. The average class size is 25, and over 90% of these classes are taught by faculty members. Tulane is ranked among the nation's top 10 universities for its students' record of receiving prestigious international fellowships, including Rhodes, Marshall, Luce, and Watson fellowships.

 ## Academics

Tulane offers a core academic program; fewer than half of graduate courses are open to undergraduates. It awards associate, bachelor's, master's, doctoral, and first professional **degrees**. Challenging opportunities include advanced placement, accelerated degree programs, self-designed majors, an honors program, Phi Beta Kappa, and Sigma Xi. Special programs include internships, summer session for credit, off-campus study, study abroad, and Army, Naval, and Air Force ROTC.

The most popular **majors** include biology/biological sciences, English, and psychology. A complete listing of majors at Tulane appears in the Majors Index beginning on page 380.

The **faculty** at Tulane has 926 full-time graduate and undergraduate teachers, 98% with terminal degrees. The student-faculty ratio is 12:1, and the average class size in required courses is 25.

 ## Computers on Campus

Students are not required to have a computer. Student rooms are linked to a campus network. 350 **computers** available in the computer center, computer labs, the learning resource center, academic buildings, classrooms, the library, the student center, and dormitories provide access to the main academic computer, e-mail, and on-line services. Staffed computer lab on campus provides training in the use of computers and software.

The 7 **libraries** have 2 million books, 2.3 million microform titles, and 15,112 subscriptions.

 ## Campus Life

There are 200 active **organizations** on campus, including a drama/theater group and student-run newspaper and radio station. 32% of eligible men and 35% of eligible women are members of 16 national **fraternities** and 8 national **sororities**. Student **safety services** include late night transport/escort service, 24-hour emergency telephone alarm devices, 24-hour patrols by trained security personnel, student patrols, and electronically operated dormitory entrances.

Tulane is a member of the NCAA (Division I). **Intercollegiate sports** (some offering scholarships) include baseball (m), basketball (m, w), cross-country running (m, w), football (m), golf (m, w), tennis (m, w), track and field (m, w), volleyball (w).

 ## Applying

Tulane requires an essay, a high school transcript, 1 recommendation, and SAT I or ACT. It recommends 3 years of high school math and science, 3 years of high school foreign language, and SAT II Subject Tests. Early, deferred, and midyear entrance are possible, with a 1/15 deadline and continuous processing to 2/1 for financial aid. **Contact:** Mr. Richard Whiteside, Dean of Admission and Enrollment Management, 316 Gibson Hall, New Orleans, LA 70118-5669, 504-865-5731 or toll-free 800-873-9283; fax 504-862-8715.

### GETTING IN LAST YEAR

7,961 applied
73% were accepted
21% enrolled (1,245)
42% from top tenth of their h.s. class
35% had SAT verbal scores over 600
61% had SAT math scores over 600
6% had SAT verbal scores over 700
17% had SAT math scores over 700
18 National Merit Scholars

### THE STUDENT BODY

Total 11,362, of whom 6,498
  are undergraduates
From 52 states and territories,
  90 other countries

20% from Louisiana
50% women, 50% men
10% African Americans
1% Native Americans
6% Hispanics
4% Asian Americans
4% international students

### AFTER FRESHMAN YEAR

85% returned for sophomore year
71% got a degree within 4 years
72% got a degree within 5 years

### AFTER GRADUATION

57% pursued further study (22% arts and
  sciences, 16% law, 9% medicine)
139 corporations, 25 government agencies,
  40 nonprofit organizations recruited on
  campus
1 Marshall, 5 Fulbright scholars

### WHAT YOU WILL PAY

Tuition and fees $19,550
Room and board $5950
46% receive need-based financial aid
  averaging $12,060
29% receive non-need financial aid averaging
  $18,220

# UNION COLLEGE

Schenectady, New York • Suburban setting • Private • Independent • Coed

▶ Union College, one of the oldest colleges in America, is located in the small city of Schenectady, about 3 hours north of New York City. Its distinctive curriculum combines the traditional liberal arts with engineering study. Three basic tenets undergird a Union education: commitments to lifelong learning, the liberal arts, and a close working relationship between students and faculty. People from many different backgrounds come to Union, attracted by these values and the opportunities they imply: small classes, excellent access to superb facilities, a caring and committed faculty, and an academic program of depth and diversity.

 **Academics**

Union College offers a core academic program; more than half of graduate courses are open to undergraduates. It awards bachelor's, master's, and doctoral **degrees**. Challenging opportunities include advanced placement, accelerated degree programs, self-designed majors, tutorials, a senior project, Phi Beta Kappa, and Sigma Xi. Special programs include summer session for credit, off-campus study, study abroad, and Army, Naval, and Air Force ROTC.

The most popular **majors** include psychology, biology/biological sciences, and economics. A complete listing of majors at Union College appears in the Majors Index beginning on page 380.

The **faculty** at Union College has 171 full-time undergraduate teachers, 96% with terminal degrees. 100% of the faculty serve as student advisers. The student-faculty ratio is 11:1.

 **Computers on Campus**

Students are not required to have a computer. Student rooms are linked to a campus network. 175 **computers** available in the computer center, computer labs, academic buildings, classrooms, the library, and the student center provide access to the main academic computer, off-campus computing facilities, and e-mail. Staffed computer lab on campus (open 24 hours a day) provides training in the use of computers and software.

The **library** has 496,337 books, 31,171 microform titles, and 1,954 subscriptions. It is connected to 4 national **on-line** catalogs.

 **Campus Life**

There are 100 active **organizations** on campus, including a drama/theater group and student-run newspaper and radio station. 40% of students participate in student government elections. 45% of eligible men and 25% of eligible women are members of 15 national **fraternities**, 4 national **sororities**, and 1 coed fraternity. Student **safety services** include late night transport/escort service, 24-hour emergency telephone alarm devices, 24-hour patrols by trained security personnel, student patrols, and electronically operated dormitory entrances.

Union College is a member of the NCAA (Division III). **Intercollegiate sports** include baseball (m), basketball (m, w), crew (m, w), cross-country running (m, w), fencing (m), field hockey (w), football (m), ice hockey (m), lacrosse (m, w), rugby (m, w), skiing (cross-country) (m, w), skiing (downhill) (m, w), soccer (m, w), softball (w), swimming and diving (m, w), tennis (m, w), track and field (m, w), volleyball (w).

 **Applying**

Union College requires an essay, a high school transcript, 2 recommendations, 3 SAT II Subject Tests (including SAT II: Writing Test) or ACT, and in some cases 3 years of high school math and science. It recommends 2 years of high school foreign language and an interview. Early and deferred entrance are possible, with a 2/1 deadline and a 2/1 priority date for financial aid. **Contact:** Mr. Daniel Lundquist, Vice President for Admissions and Financial Aid, Becker Hall, Schenectady, NY 12308-2311, 518-388-6112; fax 518-388-6800.

---

### GETTING IN LAST YEAR
3,440 applied
53% were accepted
30% enrolled (543)
46% from top tenth of their h.s. class

### THE STUDENT BODY
Total 2,374, of whom 2,092
    are undergraduates
From 37 states and territories,
    12 other countries
52% from New York

46% women, 54% men
3% African Americans
0% Native Americans
3% Hispanics
6% Asian Americans
2% international students

### AFTER FRESHMAN YEAR
95% returned for sophomore year
80% got a degree within 4 years
87% got a degree within 5 years
88% got a degree within 6 years

### AFTER GRADUATION
37% pursued further study (15% arts and
    sciences, 10% law, 9% medicine)
55 corporations, 7 government agencies, 14
    nonprofit organizations recruited on campus

### WHAT YOU WILL PAY
Tuition and fees $18,922
Room and board $6204
57% receive need-based financial aid
    averaging $11,620

---

# UNION UNIVERSITY

Jackson, Tennessee • Small-town setting • Private • Independent-Religious • Coed

---

▶ Union University, located between Memphis and Nashville in the growing community of Jackson, Tennessee, offers a full liberal arts curriculum in more than 40 fields of study. A student-faculty ratio of 13:1 guarantees individual attention to student needs, and most majors offer senior seminars to promote research and exchange of ideas. As a Christian university, Union inspires its graduates to pursue goals that stretch higher than the corporate ladder reaches. Union's goal is to bring out the very best in each student, both inside and out of the classroom.

##  Academics

Union offers a liberal arts curriculum and core academic program; a few graduate courses are open to undergraduates. It awards bachelor's and master's **degrees**. Challenging opportunities include advanced placement, accelerated degree programs, self-designed majors, an honors program, and a senior project. Special programs include internships, summer session for credit, and off-campus study.

The most popular **majors** include nursing, education, and business. A complete listing of majors at Union appears in the Majors Index beginning on page 380.

The **faculty** at Union has 99 full-time graduate and undergraduate teachers, 42% with terminal degrees. The student-faculty ratio is 13:1, and the average class size in required courses is 31.

## 🖥 Computers on Campus

Students are not required to have a computer. 140 **computers** available in the computer center, computer labs, classrooms, the library, and dormitories provide access to the main academic computer. Staffed computer lab on campus provides training in the use of computers and software.

The **library** has 115,848 books, 53,206 microform titles, and 1,112 subscriptions. It is connected to 5 national **on-line** catalogs.

##  Campus Life

There are 45 active **organizations** on campus, including a drama/theater group and student-run newspaper and radio station. 26% of eligible men and 27% of eligible women are members of 3 national **fraternities** and 3 national **sororities**. Student **safety services** include 24-hour patrols by trained security personnel.

Union is a member of the NAIA. **Intercollegiate sports** (some offering scholarships) include baseball (m), basketball (m, w), golf (m), softball (w), tennis (m, w).

## ✎ Applying

Union requires a high school transcript, SAT I or ACT, a minimum high school GPA of 2.0, and in some cases an essay, 3 years of high school math and science, some high school foreign language, recommendations, and an interview. Early and midyear entrance are possible, with rolling admissions and continuous processing to 5/15 for financial aid. **Contact:** Mr. Carroll Griffin, Director of Admissions, Highway 45 Bypass North, Jackson, TN 38305, 901-661-5000 or toll-free 800-33 UNION; fax 901-661-5177.

---

**GETTING IN LAST YEAR**
914 applied
84% were accepted
57% enrolled (434)
31% had ACT scores over 26
6% had ACT scores over 30

**THE STUDENT BODY**
Total 2,036, of whom 1,926
 are undergraduates
From 33 states and territories,
 9 other countries

77% from Tennessee
63% women, 37% men
6% African Americans
0% Native Americans
0% Hispanics
0% Asian Americans
1% international students

**AFTER FRESHMAN YEAR**
93% returned for sophomore year

**AFTER GRADUATION**
40% pursued further study
70% had job offers within 3 months

**WHAT YOU WILL PAY**
Tuition and fees $6430
Room and board $2630
Non-need financial aid averages $1200

---

# UNITED STATES AIR FORCE ACADEMY

Colorado Springs, Colorado • Suburban setting • Public • Federally supported • Coed

The Air Force Academy challenge requires a well-rounded academic, physical, and leadership background. Cadets must accept discipline, be competitive, and have a desire to serve others with a sense of duty and morality. Applicants should prepare early to meet the admissions requirements, competition, and demands they will face at the Academy.

 **Academics**

USAFA offers a core academic program. It awards bachelor's **degrees**. Challenging opportunities include advanced placement, self-designed majors, tutorials, an honors program, and a senior project. Special programs include internships, summer session for credit, off-campus study, and study abroad.

A complete listing of majors at USAFA appears in the Majors Index beginning on page 380.

The **faculty** at USAFA has 517 full-time teachers. 75% of the faculty serve as student advisers. The student-faculty ratio is 8:1, and the average class size in required courses is 15.

 **Computers on Campus**

Students are required to have a computer. PCs are provided. 4,500 **computers** available in the computer center, computer labs, the library, and student rooms.

The 3 **libraries** have 653,000 books, 543,000 microform titles, and 3,555 subscriptions. They are connected to 9 national **on-line** catalogs.

 **Campus Life**

There are 70 active **organizations** on campus, including a drama/theater group and student-run radio station. Student **safety services** include late night transport/escort service, 24-hour emergency telephone alarm devices, and 24-hour patrols by trained security personnel.

USAFA is a member of the NCAA (Division I-Men; Division II-Women). **Intercollegiate sports** include baseball (m), basketball (m, w), bowling (m, w), cross-country running (m, w), equestrian sports (m, w), fencing (m, w), football (m), golf (m), gymnastics (m, w), ice hockey (m), lacrosse (m), racquetball (m, w), riflery (m, w), rugby (m, w), skiing (cross-country) (m, w), skiing (downhill) (m, w), soccer (m, w), softball (w), squash (m), swimming and diving (m, w), tennis (m, w), track and field (m, w), volleyball (m, w), water polo (m), weight lifting (m), wrestling (m).

 **Applying**

USAFA requires an essay, a high school transcript, an interview, authorized nomination, and SAT I or ACT. It recommends 4 years of high school math and science, 2 years of high school foreign language, and SAT II Subject Tests. Early entrance is possible, with a 1/31 deadline. **Contact:** Lt. Col. Danny L. Moore, Director of Selections, USAF Academy, CO 80840-5025, 719-472-2520.

### GETTING IN LAST YEAR
8,836 applied
20% were accepted
71% enrolled (1,294)
73% from top tenth of their h.s. class
3.8 average high school GPA
32% had SAT verbal scores over 600
87% had SAT math scores over 600
2% had SAT verbal scores over 700
33% had SAT math scores over 700
194 class presidents
155 valedictorians

### THE STUDENT BODY
4,000 undergraduates
From 55 states and territories, 18 other countries
5% from Colorado
16% women, 84% men
6% African Americans
1% Native Americans
7% Hispanics
4% Asian Americans
1% international students

### AFTER FRESHMAN YEAR
76% returned for sophomore year

### AFTER GRADUATION
3% pursued further study (2% medicine)
1 Rhodes scholar

### WHAT YOU WILL PAY
Comprehensive fee $0

# UNITED STATES COAST GUARD ACADEMY

New London, Connecticut • Suburban setting • Public • Federally supported • Coed

The United States Coast Guard Academy, located halfway between New York City and Boston on Connecticut's shoreline, is committed to the development of professional career Coast Guard officers. Not only as an academic institution, but also as a multimissioned training facility for today's officer, the Academy provides solid academic studies, hands-on leadership experiences, and military training necessary to be successful in the world's premier maritime service. Whether it is rescuing a stranded mariner or enforcing maritime laws, the U.S. Coast Guard can be found in all corners of the world, supporting and shaping national policy every day.

##  Academics

USCGA offers an engineering curriculum and core academic program. It awards bachelor's **degrees**. Challenging opportunities include tutorials, an honors program, and a senior project. Special programs include summer session for credit, off-campus study, and study abroad.

The most popular **majors** include marine engineering, business, and marine sciences. A complete listing of majors at USCGA appears in the Majors Index beginning on page 380.

The **faculty** at USCGA has 113 full-time teachers, 30% with terminal degrees. 81% of the faculty serve as student advisers. The student-faculty ratio is 12:1, and the average class size in required courses is 23.

##  Computers on Campus

Students are required to have a computer. Purchase options are available. Student rooms are linked to a campus network.

120 **computers** available in the computer center, computer labs, engineering, science, math, computer science departments, the library, dormitories, and student rooms provide access to the main academic computer, off-campus computing facilities, and e-mail. Staffed computer lab on campus provides training in the use of computers and software.

The **library** has 150,000 books, 61,000 microform titles, and 1,690 subscriptions. It is connected to 2 national **on-line** catalogs.

##  Campus Life

Active **organizations** on campus include drama/theater group and student-run newspaper. Student **safety services** include 24-hour emergency telephone alarm devices and 24-hour patrols by trained security personnel.

USCGA is a member of the NCAA (Division III). **Intercollegiate sports** include baseball (m), basketball (m, w), bowling (m, w), crew (m, w), cross-country running (m, w), football (m), ice hockey (m), lacrosse (m), riflery (m, w), rugby (m), sailing (m, w), soccer (m, w), softball (w), swimming and diving (m), tennis (m), track and field (m, w), volleyball (m, w), wrestling (m).

##  Applying

USCGA requires an essay, a high school transcript, 3 years of high school math, 3 recommendations, SAT I or ACT, and in some cases an interview. It recommends 3 years of high school science. 12/15 deadline. **Contact:** Capt. R. W. Thorne, Director of Admissions, 15 Mohegan Avenue, New London, CT 06320-4195, 203-444-8500; fax 203-444-8289.

---

### GETTING IN LAST YEAR
2,038 applied
23% were accepted
57% enrolled (266)
66% from top tenth of their h.s. class
25% had SAT verbal scores over 600
75% had SAT math scores over 600
2% had SAT verbal scores over 700
22% had SAT math scores over 700
19 class presidents
21 valedictorians

### THE STUDENT BODY
906 undergraduates
From 50 states and territories,
  9 other countries
7% from Connecticut
20% women, 80% men
4% African Americans
1% Native Americans
6% Hispanics
7% Asian Americans
2% international students

### AFTER FRESHMAN YEAR
75% returned for sophomore year
61% got a degree within 4 years
62% got a degree within 5 years

### WHAT YOU WILL PAY
Comprehensive fee $0

# UNITED STATES MERCHANT MARINE ACADEMY

Kings Point, New York • Suburban setting • Public • Federally supported • Coed

The United States Merchant Marine Academy is a 4-year federal service academy dedicated to educating and training young men and women as officers in America's merchant marine and U.S. Naval Reserve and as future leaders of the maritime and transportation industries. The Academy, in Kings Point, Long Island, offers accredited programs in marine transportation and engineering leading to a BS degree, a U.S. merchant marine officer's license, and a Naval Reserve commission. Students spend two 6-month periods at sea aboard U.S. cargo ships as part of their training. There are about 980 men and women at the Academy.

## Academics

United States Merchant Marine Academy offers a maritime and intermodal transportation curriculum and core academic program. It awards bachelor's **degrees**. An honors program is a challenging opportunity. Special programs include cooperative education, internships, and study abroad.

A complete listing of majors at United States Merchant Marine Academy appears in the Majors Index beginning on page 380.

The **faculty** at United States Merchant Marine Academy has 74 full-time teachers, 85% with terminal degrees. The student-faculty ratio is 11:1, and the average class size in required courses is 26.

## Computers on Campus

Students are required to have a computer. Student rooms are linked to a campus network. 1,200 **computers** available in the computer center, independent study labs,

classrooms, the library, and dormitories provide access to e-mail and engineering and economic applications. Staffed computer lab on campus provides training in the use of computers and software.

The **library** has 232,576 books, 161,576 microform titles, and 985 subscriptions. It is connected to 5 national **on-line** catalogs.

## Campus Life

There are 45 active **organizations** on campus, including a drama/theater group and student-run newspaper. 100% of eligible men and 100% of eligible women are members of Ethnic Culture Club. Student **safety services** include 24-hour patrols by trained security personnel.

United States Merchant Marine Academy is a member of the NCAA (Division III). **Intercollegiate sports** include baseball (m), basketball (m), crew (m, w), cross-country running (m, w), football (m), golf (m, w), ice hockey (m), lacrosse (m), riflery (m, w), rugby (m), sailing (m, w), soccer (m), softball (w), swimming and diving (m, w), tennis (m, w), track and field (m, w), volleyball (m, w), water polo (m), wrestling (m).

## Applying

United States Merchant Marine Academy requires an essay, a high school transcript, 3 years of high school math, 1 recommendation, SAT I or ACT, and in some cases SAT II Subject Tests. It recommends 3 years of high school science, 2 years of high school foreign language, and a campus interview. 3/1 deadline and continuous processing to 3/15 for financial aid. **Contact:** Capt. James M. Skinner, USMS, Director of Admissions, Wiley Hall, Kings Point, NY 11024, 516-773-5391 or toll-free 800-732-6267 (out-of-state); fax 516-773-5390.

---

### GETTING IN LAST YEAR
875 applied
45% were accepted
70% enrolled (275)
34% from top tenth of their h.s. class
27% had SAT verbal scores over 600
45% had SAT math scores over 600
6% had SAT verbal scores over 700
5% had SAT math scores over 700

### THE STUDENT BODY
980 undergraduates
From 53 states and territories,
   6 other countries

14% from New York
10% women, 90% men
1% African Americans
1% Native Americans
4% Hispanics
4% Asian Americans
4% international students

### AFTER FRESHMAN YEAR
80% returned for sophomore year
56% got a degree within 4 years
69% got a degree within 5 years

### AFTER GRADUATION
2% pursued further study (1% business, 1% engineering)
87% had job offers within 3 months
19 corporations, 9 government agencies recruited on campus

### WHAT YOU WILL PAY
Comprehensive fee $0

# UNITED STATES MILITARY ACADEMY

West Point, New York • Small-town setting • Public • Federally supported • Coed

West Point is both a challenge and triumph of will, but it rewards young men and women with a wealth of academic, leadership, and life experiences, providing a foundation for success as an officer in the U.S. Army. An officer must be flexible, resilient, and talented enough to lead in a Persian Gulf conflict or a lifesaving mission in Somalia. West Point is tough and cadets must persevere to succeed. As stated by Cadet Missy Werner from North Dakota, "If I had to go through plebe year 20 times I would, because the person I have become is so much better than the person who came in here."

##  Academics

West Point U.S. Military Academy offers a leaders of character for the nation curriculum and core academic program. It awards bachelor's **degrees**. Challenging opportunities include tutorials and an honors program. Special programs include summer session for credit, off-campus study, and study abroad.

The most popular **majors** include mechanical engineering, civil engineering, and history. A complete listing of majors at West Point U.S. Military Academy appears in the Majors Index beginning on page 380.

The **faculty** at West Point U.S. Military Academy has 491 full-time teachers, 29% with terminal degrees. 51% of the faculty serve as student advisers. The student-faculty ratio is 8:1, and the average class size in required courses is 16.

##  Computers on Campus

Students are required to have a computer. PCs are provided. 5,500 **computers** available in the computer center, computer labs, the research center, the learning resource center, classrooms, the library, dormitories, and student rooms provide access to the main academic computer, e-mail, and on-line services. Staffed computer lab on campus

(open 24 hours a day) provides training in the use of computers and software.

The 2 **libraries** have 429,580 books, 1,223 microform titles, and 2,000 subscriptions. They are connected to 2 national **on-line** catalogs.

##  Campus Life

There are 114 active **organizations** on campus, including a drama/theater group and student-run radio station. Student **safety services** include 24-hour emergency telephone alarm devices and 24-hour patrols by trained security personnel.

West Point U.S. Military Academy is a member of the NCAA (Division I). **Intercollegiate sports** include baseball (m), basketball (m, w), bowling (m, w), crew (m, w), cross-country running (m, w), equestrian sports (m, w), fencing (m, w), football (m), golf (m), gymnastics (m), ice hockey (m), lacrosse (m, w), racquetball (m, w), riflery (m, w), rugby (m), sailing (m, w), skiing (cross-country) (m, w), skiing (downhill) (m, w), soccer (m, w), softball (w), squash (m, w), swimming and diving (m, w), tennis (m, w), track and field (m, w), volleyball (m, w), water polo (m), weight lifting (m, w), wrestling (m).

##  Applying

West Point U.S. Military Academy requires an essay, a high school transcript, 4 recommendations, authorized nomination, medical and physical aptitude exams, proof of age (between 17 and 21 at matriculation), proof of U.S. citizenship (except students nominated by agreement between U.S. and another country), unmarried, not pregnant, no legal obligation to support a child, and SAT I or ACT. It recommends 4 years of high school math, 3 years of high school science, 2 years of high school foreign language, and an interview. Early action is possible, with a 3/21 deadline. **Contact:** Col. Pierce A. Rushton, Director of Admissions, 606 Thayer Road, West Point, NY 10996, 914-938-4041.

---

### GETTING IN LAST YEAR

13,003 applied
12% were accepted
71% enrolled (1,147)
60% from top tenth of their h.s. class
28% had SAT verbal scores over 600
82% had SAT math scores over 600
90% had ACT scores over 26
4% had SAT verbal scores over 700
21% had SAT math scores over 700
42% had ACT scores over 30
222 National Merit Scholars
74 valedictorians

### THE STUDENT BODY

4,095 undergraduates
From 52 states and territories,
   19 other countries
12% women, 88% men
7% African Americans
1% Native Americans
4% Hispanics
5% Asian Americans
1% international students

### AFTER FRESHMAN YEAR

92% returned for sophomore year
81% got a degree within 4 years
82% got a degree within 5 years

### AFTER GRADUATION

2% pursued further study (2% medicine)
1 Rhodes, 1 Marshall scholar

### WHAT YOU WILL PAY

Comprehensive fee $0

---

# UNITED STATES NAVAL ACADEMY

Annapolis, Maryland • Small-town setting • Public • Federally supported • Coed

 **Academics**

Naval Academy offers a leadership-intensive curriculum and core academic program. It awards bachelor's **degrees**. Challenging opportunities include advanced placement, an honors program, and Sigma Xi. Special programs include summer session for credit and study abroad.

The most popular **majors** include political science/government, aerospace engineering, and oceanography. A complete listing of majors at Naval Academy appears in the Majors Index beginning on page 380.

The **faculty** at Naval Academy has 650 full-time teachers. The average class size in required courses is 18.

 **Computers on Campus**

Students are required to have a computer. PCs are provided. Student rooms are linked to a campus network. 6,100 **computers** available in the computer center, the library, and dormitories provide access to the main academic computer, off-campus computing facilities, e-mail, and on-line services. Staffed computer lab on campus provides training in the use of computers and software.

The **library** has 750,000 books and 2,100 subscriptions.

 **Campus Life**

Active **organizations** on campus include drama/theater group and student-run radio station. Student **safety services** include front gate security, 24-hour emergency telephone alarm devices, 24-hour patrols by trained security personnel, and student patrols.

Naval Academy is a member of the NCAA (Division I). **Intercollegiate sports** include baseball (m), basketball (m, w), crew (m, w), cross-country running (m, w), football (m), golf (m), gymnastics (m), ice hockey (m), lacrosse (m), riflery (m), rugby (m), sailing (m, w), soccer (m, w), squash (m), swimming and diving (m, w), tennis (m), track and field (m, w), volleyball (w), water polo (m), wrestling (m).

**Applying**

Naval Academy requires an essay, a high school transcript, 2 recommendations, authorized nomination, SAT I or ACT, and a minimum high school GPA of 2.0. It recommends 4 years of high school math and science, some high school foreign language, and an interview. 3/20 deadline. **Contact:** Capt. John W. Renard, Retd., Dean of Admissions, 117 Decatur Road, Annapolis, MD 21402-5000, 410-293-4336 or toll-free 800-638-9156; fax 410-293-4348.

---

**GETTING IN LAST YEAR**

12,831 applied
12% were accepted
77% enrolled (1,150)
61% from top tenth of their h.s. class
51% had SAT verbal scores over 600
64% had SAT math scores over 600
3% had SAT verbal scores over 700
7% had SAT math scores over 700

**THE STUDENT BODY**

4,216 undergraduates
From 54 states and territories,
  20 other countries
2% from Maryland
14% women, 86% men
8% African Americans
1% Native Americans
7% Hispanics
5% Asian Americans
1% international students

**AFTER FRESHMAN YEAR**

86% returned for sophomore year
75% got a degree within 4 years

**AFTER GRADUATION**

1% pursued further study (1% medicine)

**WHAT YOU WILL PAY**

Comprehensive fee $0

# UNIVERSITY AT ALBANY, STATE UNIVERSITY OF NEW YORK

Albany, New York • Suburban setting • Public • State-supported • Coed

Founded in 1848, the University at Albany is the flagship campus of the State University of New York. Located in the capital of New York State, the University is respected for its diversified curriculum, its commitment to undergraduate scholarship, and the ability of its faculty and staff to personalize the educational process. The University offers more than 75 majors in humanities, fine arts, social and behavioral sciences, science, mathematics, the School of Business, the Rockefeller College of Public Affairs, and the School of Social Welfare. The University is the home of the New York State Writers Institute.

##  Academics

University at Albany offers a general education curriculum and core academic program; fewer than half of graduate courses are open to undergraduates. It awards bachelor's, master's, and doctoral **degrees**. Challenging opportunities include advanced placement, self-designed majors, tutorials, Freshmen Honors College, an honors program, a senior project, Phi Beta Kappa, and Sigma Xi. Special programs include internships, summer session for credit, off-campus study, study abroad, and Army, Naval, and Air Force ROTC.

The most popular **majors** include psychology, English, and business. A complete listing of majors at University at Albany appears in the Majors Index beginning on page 380.

The **faculty** at University at Albany has 692 full-time graduate and undergraduate teachers, 96% with terminal degrees. The student-faculty ratio is 16:1.

##  Computers on Campus

Students are not required to have a computer. Student rooms are linked to a campus network. 500 **computers** available in the computer center, computer labs, the research center, the learning resource center, special user rooms, classrooms, the library, and dormitories provide access to the main academic computer, off-campus computing facilities, e-mail, and on-line services. Staffed computer lab on campus provides training in the use of computers and software.

The **library** has 1.8 million books, 2.6 million microform titles, and 7,000 subscriptions.

##  Campus Life

There are 160 active **organizations** on campus, including a drama/theater group and student-run newspaper and radio station. 20% of eligible men and 15% of eligible women are members of 15 national **fraternities**, 5 national **sororities**, 5 local fraternities, and 6 local sororities. Student **safety services** include late night transport/escort service, 24-hour emergency telephone alarm devices, 24-hour patrols by trained security personnel, and electronically operated dormitory entrances.

University at Albany is a member of the NCAA (Division III). **Intercollegiate sports** include baseball (m), basketball (m, w), crew (m, w), cross-country running (m, w), football (m), gymnastics (m, w), lacrosse (m), rugby (m, w), soccer (m, w), swimming and diving (m, w), tennis (m, w), track and field (m, w), volleyball (w).

##  Applying

University at Albany requires a high school transcript, SAT I or ACT, and in some cases 3 years of high school math and science and portfolio, audition. It recommends an essay, 3 years of high school math and science, and some high school foreign language. Early, deferred, and midyear entrance are possible, with rolling admissions and continuous processing to 3/15 for financial aid. **Contact:** Dr. Michelleen Treadwell, Director of Admissions, 1400 Washington Avenue, Albany, NY 12222-0001, 518-442-5435.

---

### GETTING IN LAST YEAR
13,377 applied
72% were accepted
22% enrolled (2,100)
14% from top tenth of their h.s. class
9% had SAT verbal scores over 600
38% had SAT math scores over 600
1% had SAT verbal scores over 700
5% had SAT math scores over 700

### THE STUDENT BODY
Total 14,798, of whom 10,466 are undergraduates

From 23 states and territories, 29 other countries
97% from New York
48% women, 52% men
9% African Americans
1% Native Americans
7% Hispanics
8% Asian Americans
1% international students

### AFTER FRESHMAN YEAR
90% returned for sophomore year

### AFTER GRADUATION
45% pursued further study

### WHAT YOU WILL PAY
Resident tuition and fees $2936
Nonresident tuition and fees $6836
Room and board $4543
Need-based financial aid averages $1700
Non-need financial aid averages $2760

# UNIVERSITY OF ALABAMA IN HUNTSVILLE

Huntsville, Alabama • Urban setting • Public • State-supported • Coed

Huntsville, one of America's fastest growing small cities, a nationally known center for research and development, and a highly desirable place to live, creates unique opportunities for students and graduates to help support themselves through interesting part-time employment. Some take traditional jobs on campus or in the community, others work on innovative and creative research grants and contracts, while others take advantage of the University's excellent co-op program with local business, industry, and government. Students are encouraged to consider the special advantages that UAH and Huntsville have to offer.

 **Academics**

UAH offers an interdisciplinary curriculum and core academic program; fewer than half of graduate courses are open to undergraduates. It awards bachelor's, master's, and doctoral **degrees**. Challenging opportunities include advanced placement, an honors program, and Sigma Xi. Special programs include cooperative education, internships, summer session for credit, off-campus study, and Army and Air Force ROTC.

The most popular **majors** include electrical engineering, nursing, and management information systems. A complete listing of majors at UAH appears in the Majors Index beginning on page 380.

The **faculty** at UAH has 291 full-time graduate and undergraduate teachers, 88% with terminal degrees. The student-faculty ratio is 12:1, and the average class size in required courses is 25.

 **Computers on Campus**

Students are not required to have a computer. Student rooms are linked to a campus network. 250 **computers**

available in the computer center, computer labs, the library, and the student center provide access to the main academic computer, off-campus computing facilities, e-mail, and on-line services. Staffed computer lab on campus provides training in the use of computers and software.

The **library** has 426,344 books, 413,909 microform titles, and 3,105 subscriptions. It is connected to 5 national **on-line** catalogs.

 **Campus Life**

There are 50 active **organizations** on campus, including a drama/theater group and student-run newspaper. 10% of eligible men and 12% of eligible women are members of 5 national **fraternities**, 5 national **sororities**, and social clubs. Student **safety services** include late night transport/escort service, 24-hour emergency telephone alarm devices, 24-hour patrols by trained security personnel, and electronically operated dormitory entrances.

UAH is a member of the NCAA (Division II). **Intercollegiate sports** (some offering scholarships) include basketball (m, w), cross-country running (m, w), ice hockey (m), soccer (m), tennis (m, w), volleyball (w).

 **Applying**

UAH requires a high school transcript, SAT I or ACT, and in some cases a campus interview. It recommends 3 years of high school math and science and some high school foreign language. Early, deferred, and midyear entrance are possible, with an 8/15 deadline and continuous processing to 4/1 for financial aid. **Contact:** Ms. Sabrina Williams, Assistant Registrar/Admissions, University Center 119, Huntsville, AL 35899, 205-895-6070 or toll-free 800-UAH-CALL (in-state); fax 205-895-6754.

---

**GETTING IN LAST YEAR**
1,365 applied
69% were accepted
54% enrolled (506)
23% from top tenth of their h.s. class
3.28 average high school GPA
15% had SAT verbal scores over 600
30% had SAT math scores over 600
28% had ACT scores over 26
2% had SAT verbal scores over 700
8% had SAT math scores over 700
7% had ACT scores over 30
5 National Merit Scholars

**THE STUDENT BODY**
Total 7,531, of whom 5,512
   are undergraduates

From 50 states and territories,
   46 other countries
80% from Alabama
49% women, 51% men
10% African Americans
1% Native Americans
2% Hispanics
4% Asian Americans
3% international students

**AFTER FRESHMAN YEAR**
65% returned for sophomore year

**AFTER GRADUATION**
65% had job offers within 3 months
1 Rhodes, 3 Fulbright scholars

**WHAT YOU WILL PAY**
Resident tuition and fees $2168
Nonresident tuition and fees $4336
Room and board $3500
27% receive need-based financial aid
   averaging $1000
11% receive non-need financial aid averaging
   $1800

# UNIVERSITY OF ARIZONA

Tucson, Arizona • Urban setting • Public • State-supported • Coed

---

▶ Surrounded by mountains and the dramatic beauty of the Sonoran desert, the University of Arizona offers a top-drawer education in a resort-like setting. Some of the nation's highest-ranked departments make their homes here. Tucson's clear skies provide an ideal setting for one of the country's best astronomy programs. Anthropology, nursing, management information systems, and creative writing are also nationally ranked. The University balances a strong research component with an emphasis on teaching—faculty rolls include Nobel- and Pulitzer-prize holders.

## Academics

U of A offers a core academic program; fewer than half of graduate courses are open to undergraduates. It awards bachelor's, master's, doctoral, and first professional **degrees**. Challenging opportunities include advanced placement, self-designed majors, tutorials, Freshmen Honors College, an honors program, a senior project, Phi Beta Kappa, and Sigma Xi. Special programs include cooperative education, internships, summer session for credit, study abroad, and Army, Naval, and Air Force ROTC.

A complete listing of majors at U of A appears in the Majors Index beginning on page 380.

The **faculty** at U of A has 1,489 full-time undergraduate teachers, 95% with terminal degrees. The student-faculty ratio is 16:1, and the average class size in required courses is 30.

## Computers on Campus

Students are not required to have a computer. **Computers** available in the computer center, computer labs, the research center, the learning resource center, classrooms, the library, dormitories, and student rooms.

The 6 **libraries** have 4.1 million books, 4.6 million microform titles, and 24,052 subscriptions.

## Campus Life

Active **organizations** on campus include drama/theater group and student-run newspaper and radio station. 13% of eligible men and 13% of eligible women are members of 27 national **fraternities** and 18 national **sororities**. Student **safety services** include late night transport/escort service and 24-hour patrols by trained security personnel.

U of A is a member of the NCAA (Division I). **Intercollegiate sports** (some offering scholarships) include baseball (m), basketball (m, w), cross-country running (m, w), football (m), golf (m, w), gymnastics (w), ice hockey (m), lacrosse (m), rugby (m), soccer (m, w), softball (w), swimming and diving (m, w), tennis (m, w), track and field (m, w), volleyball (m, w).

## Applying

U of A requires a high school transcript, 3 years of high school math, SAT I or ACT, and in some cases 3 years of high school science, recommendations, an interview, and a minimum high school GPA of 3.0. It recommends 3 years of high school science and some high school foreign language. Early, deferred, and midyear entrance are possible, with a 4/1 deadline and continuous processing to 3/1 for financial aid. **Contact:** Mr. Loyd Bell, Director of Admissions, Nugent Building, Tucson, AZ 85721, 602-621-3237; fax 602-621-9799.

---

### GETTING IN LAST YEAR

15,433 applied
85% were accepted
34% enrolled (4,481)
30% from top tenth of their h.s. class
3.25 average high school GPA
8% had SAT verbal scores over 600
28% had SAT math scores over 600
30% had ACT scores over 26
1% had SAT verbal scores over 700
5% had SAT math scores over 700
8% had ACT scores over 30
51 National Merit Scholars

### THE STUDENT BODY

Total 35,306, of whom 26,468 are undergraduates

From 52 states and territories, 79 other countries
70% from Arizona
50% women, 50% men
2% African Americans
2% Native Americans
14% Hispanics
5% Asian Americans
3% international students

### AFTER FRESHMAN YEAR

75% returned for sophomore year
19% got a degree within 4 years
45% got a degree within 5 years
51% got a degree within 6 years

### AFTER GRADUATION

244 corporations recruited on campus
4 Fulbright scholars

### WHAT YOU WILL PAY

Resident tuition and fees $1894
Nonresident tuition and fees $7500
Room and board $4230
50% receive need-based financial aid averaging $1388
16% receive non-need financial aid averaging $2011

---

# UNIVERSITY OF CALIFORNIA, BERKELEY

Berkeley, California • Urban setting • Public • State-supported • Coed

Berkeley is widely recognized as one of the best universities in the world. Its rich culture and ethnic diversity help to produce the wide range of opinion and perspective essential to a great university. *U.S. News & World Report* recently ranked Cal the best public university in the nation. A seminar program ensures that freshmen can take small classes taught by distinguished scholars. Undergraduates also undertake research, publishing the results in *Cal Science*. More students who earn bachelor's degrees at Berkeley complete PhDs than graduates of any other university in the country.

 **Academics**

Cal offers a core academic program. It awards bachelor's, master's, doctoral, and first professional **degrees**. Challenging opportunities include advanced placement, accelerated degree programs, self-designed majors, tutorials, an honors program, Phi Beta Kappa, and Sigma Xi. Special programs include cooperative education, internships, summer session for credit, off-campus study, study abroad, and Army, Naval, and Air Force ROTC.

The most popular **majors** include English, molecular biology, and political science/government. A complete listing of majors at Cal appears in the Majors Index beginning on page 380.

The **faculty** at Cal has 1,787 graduate and undergraduate teachers, 95% with terminal degrees. The student-faculty ratio is 16:1.

 **Computers on Campus**

Students are not required to have a computer. Student rooms are linked to a campus network. **Computers** available in the computer center, computer labs, the learning resource center, academic departments, classrooms, the library, the student center, dormitories, and student rooms provide access to the main academic computer, e-mail, and on-line services. Staffed computer lab on campus provides training in the use of computers and software.

The **library** has 8 million books and 89,750 subscriptions.

 **Campus Life**

There are 350 active **organizations** on campus, including a drama/theater group and student-run newspaper and radio station. 14% of eligible men and 13% of eligible women are members of 41 national **fraternities** and 15 national **sororities**. Student **safety services** include Office of Emergency Preparedness, late night transport/escort service, 24-hour emergency telephone alarm devices, 24-hour patrols by trained security personnel, and electronically operated dormitory entrances.

Cal is a member of the NCAA (Division I). **Intercollegiate sports** (some offering scholarships) include baseball (m), basketball (m, w), crew (m, w), cross-country running (m, w), field hockey (w), football (m), golf (m, w), gymnastics (m, w), rugby (m), skiing (downhill) (m, w), soccer (m, w), softball (w), squash (m, w), swimming and diving (m, w), tennis (m, w), track and field (m, w), volleyball (m, w), water polo (m).

 **Applying**

Cal requires an essay, a high school transcript, 3 years of high school math, 2 years of high school foreign language, minimum 3.3 high school GPA, minimum 2.4 college GPA for transfer students, SAT I or ACT, and 3 SAT II Subject Tests (including SAT II: Writing Test). It recommends 4 years of high school math, 3 years of high school science, and 3 years of high school foreign language. Early entrance is possible, with an 11/30 deadline and continuous processing to 3/2 for financial aid. **Contact:** Office of Undergraduate Admission, 110 Sproul Hall, # 5800, Berkeley, CA 94720, 510-642-3175; fax 510-642-7333.

---

**GETTING IN LAST YEAR**
20,820 applied
40% were accepted
40% enrolled (3,344)
96% from top tenth of their h.s. class
3.84 average high school GPA
43% had SAT verbal scores over 600
78% had SAT math scores over 600
9% had SAT verbal scores over 700
44% had SAT math scores over 700

**THE STUDENT BODY**
Total 29,634, of whom 21,138
 are undergraduates
From 53 states and territories,
 100 other countries
88% from California
48% women, 52% men
6% African Americans
1% Native Americans
14% Hispanics
39% Asian Americans
4% international students

**AFTER FRESHMAN YEAR**
93% returned for sophomore year
73% got a degree within 5 years

**WHAT YOU WILL PAY**
Resident tuition and fees $4623
Nonresident tuition and fees $12,322
Room and board $6246

# UNIVERSITY OF CALIFORNIA, DAVIS

Davis, California • Suburban setting • Public • State-supported • Coed

## Academics

UC Davis offers an interdisciplinary education curriculum based on specialization in the major and core academic program; fewer than half of graduate courses are open to undergraduates. It awards bachelor's, master's, doctoral, and first professional **degrees**. Challenging opportunities include advanced placement, self-designed majors, tutorials, Freshmen Honors College, an honors program, a senior project, Phi Beta Kappa, and Sigma Xi. Special programs include internships, summer session for credit, study abroad, and Army and Air Force ROTC.

The most popular **majors** include psychology and biology/biological sciences. A complete listing of majors at UC Davis appears in the Majors Index beginning on page 380.

The **faculty** at UC Davis has 1,369 full-time graduate and undergraduate teachers, 98% with terminal degrees. The student-faculty ratio is 19:1.

## Computers on Campus

Students are not required to have a computer. 600 **computers** available in the computer center, computer labs, various locations on campus, classrooms, the library, and dormitories provide access to the main academic computer, off-campus computing facilities, e-mail, on-line services, and specialized software packages. Staffed computer lab on campus.

The 6 **libraries** have 2.7 million books, 3.3 million microform titles, and 49,098 subscriptions. They are connected to 5 national **on-line** catalogs.

## Campus Life

There are 316 active **organizations** on campus, including a drama/theater group and student-run newspaper and radio station. 10% of students participate in student government elections. 10% of eligible men and 9% of eligible women are members of 26 national **fraternities**, 15 national **sororities**, and 3 state fraternities and 4 state sororities. Student **safety services** include rape prevention programs, late night transport/escort service, 24-hour emergency telephone alarm devices, 24-hour patrols by trained security personnel, student patrols, and electronically operated dormitory entrances.

UC Davis is a member of the NCAA (Division II). **Intercollegiate sports** include baseball (m), basketball (m, w), cross-country running (m, w), football (m), golf (m), gymnastics (w), soccer (m, w), softball (w), swimming and diving (m, w), tennis (m, w), track and field (m, w), volleyball (m, w), water polo (m), wrestling (m).

## Applying

UC Davis requires an essay, a high school transcript, 3 years of high school math, 2 years of high school foreign language, SAT I or ACT, and 3 SAT II Subject Tests (including SAT II: Writing Test). It recommends 4 years of high school math, 3 years of high school science, and 3 years of high school foreign language. Deferred and midyear entrance are possible, with an 11/30 deadline and continuous processing to 3/2 for financial aid. **Contact:** Dr. Gary Tudor, Director of Undergraduate Admissions, Davis, CA 95616, 916-752-2971.

### GETTING IN LAST YEAR

16,812 applied
70% were accepted
27% enrolled (3,222)
3.69 average high school GPA
13% had SAT verbal scores over 600
47% had SAT math scores over 600
36% had ACT scores over 26
1% had SAT verbal scores over 700
11% had SAT math scores over 700
8% had ACT scores over 30
22 National Merit Scholars

### THE STUDENT BODY

Total 22,442, of whom 17,273 are undergraduates
From 45 states and territories, 33 other countries
96% from California
51% women, 49% men
4% African Americans
1% Native Americans
11% Hispanics
29% Asian Americans
1% international students

### AFTER GRADUATION

40% pursued further study (13% arts and sciences, 4% law, 4% medicine)
4 Fulbright scholars

### WHAT YOU WILL PAY

Resident tuition and fees $4099
Nonresident tuition and fees $11,798
Room and board $5285
46% receive need-based financial aid averaging $1427
16% receive non-need financial aid averaging $1017

# UNIVERSITY OF CALIFORNIA, IRVINE

Irvine, California • Suburban setting • Public • State-supported • Coed

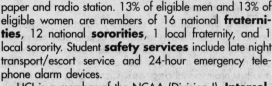

## Academics

UCI offers a core academic program. It awards bachelor's, master's, and doctoral **degrees**. Challenging opportunities include advanced placement, accelerated degree programs, an honors program, Phi Beta Kappa, and Sigma Xi. Special programs include internships, summer session for credit, off-campus study, study abroad, and Army and Air Force ROTC.

The most popular **majors** include biology/biological sciences, economics, and English. A complete listing of majors at UCI appears in the Majors Index beginning on page 380.

The **faculty** at UCI has 811 graduate and undergraduate teachers, 99% with terminal degrees. The student-faculty ratio is 19:1.

## Computers on Campus

Students are not required to have a computer. 500 **computers** available in the computer center, computer labs, the library, and the student center. Staffed computer lab on campus (open 24 hours a day).

The 6 **libraries** have 1.5 million books, 1.8 million microform titles, and 19,500 subscriptions.

## Campus Life

There are 222 active **organizations** on campus, including a drama/theater group and student-run news-

paper and radio station. 13% of eligible men and 13% of eligible women are members of 16 national **fraternities**, 12 national **sororities**, 1 local fraternity, and 1 local sorority. Student **safety services** include late night transport/escort service and 24-hour emergency telephone alarm devices.

UCI is a member of the NCAA (Division I). **Intercollegiate sports** (some offering scholarships) include basketball (m, w), crew (m, w), cross-country running (m, w), golf (m), sailing (m, w), soccer (m, w), swimming and diving (m, w), tennis (m, w), track and field (w), volleyball (m, w), water polo (m).

## Applying

UCI requires an essay, a high school transcript, 3 years of high school math, 2 years of high school foreign language, 2 years of lab science, SAT I or ACT, and 3 SAT II Subject Tests (including SAT II: Writing Test). It recommends 3 years of high school science. Early and deferred entrance are possible, with an 11/30 deadline and continuous processing to 3/2 for financial aid. **Contact:** Ms. Susan Wilbur, Director of Admissions, 260 Administration Building, Irvine, CA 92717-1425, 714-824-6703.

### GETTING IN LAST YEAR

15,757 applied
73% were accepted
24% enrolled (2,781)
85% from top tenth of their h.s. class

### THE STUDENT BODY

Total 17,092, of whom 13,597
  are undergraduates
From 37 states and territories,
  41 other countries

97% from California
53% women, 47% men
3% African Americans
1% Native Americans
13% Hispanics
50% Asian Americans
2% international students

### AFTER FRESHMAN YEAR

93% returned for sophomore year
70% got a degree within 5 years

### WHAT YOU WILL PAY

Resident tuition and fees $4331
Nonresident tuition and fees $12,032
Room and board $5185
Need-based financial aid averages $1630
Non-need financial aid averages $1038

# UNIVERSITY OF CALIFORNIA, LOS ANGELES

Los Angeles, California • Urban setting • Public • State-supported • Coed

 **Academics**

UCLA offers a core academic program. It awards bachelor's, master's, doctoral, and first professional **degrees**. Challenging opportunities include advanced placement, self-designed majors, an honors program, Phi Beta Kappa, and Sigma Xi. Special programs include internships, summer session for credit, off-campus study, study abroad, and Army, Naval, and Air Force ROTC.

The most popular **majors** include biology/biological sciences, psychology, and economics. A complete listing of majors at UCLA appears in the Majors Index beginning on page 380.

The **faculty** at UCLA has 3,210 graduate and undergraduate teachers. The student-faculty ratio is 17:1.

 **Computers on Campus**

Students are not required to have a computer. **Computers** available in the computer center, the library, the student center, and dormitories. Staffed computer lab on campus.

The 15 **libraries** have 6.3 million books, 5.8 million microform titles, and 96,003 subscriptions.

 **Campus Life**

Active **organizations** on campus include drama/theater group and student-run newspaper and radio

station. 13% of eligible men and 12% of eligible women are members of 31 national **fraternities**, 17 national **sororities**, 1 local fraternity, and 3 local sororities. Student **safety services** include late night transport/escort service.

UCLA is a member of the NCAA (Division I). **Intercollegiate sports** (some offering scholarships) include baseball (m), basketball (m, w), cross-country running (m, w), football (m), golf (m, w), gymnastics (m, w), soccer (m), softball (w), swimming and diving (m, w), tennis (m, w), track and field (m, w), volleyball (m, w), water polo (m).

 **Applying**

UCLA requires an essay, a high school transcript, 3 years of high school math, 2 years of high school foreign language, SAT I or ACT, and 3 SAT II Subject Tests. It recommends 3 years of high school science. Early entrance is possible, with an 11/30 deadline and continuous processing to 3/2 for financial aid. **Contact:** Dr. Rae Lee Siporin, Director of Undergraduate Admissions, 405 Hilgard Avenue, Los Angeles, CA 90024-1301, 310-825-3101.

---

**GETTING IN LAST YEAR**

23,406 applied
50% were accepted
34% enrolled (3,995)
3.9 average high school GPA
20% had SAT verbal scores over 600
61% had SAT math scores over 600
2% had SAT verbal scores over 700
22% had SAT math scores over 700
73 National Merit Scholars

**THE STUDENT BODY**

Total 35,110, of whom 23,619
  are undergraduates

From 50 states and territories,
  100 other countries
94% from California
50% women, 50% men
6% African Americans
1% Native Americans
17% Hispanics
35% Asian Americans
3% international students

**AFTER FRESHMAN YEAR**

94% returned for sophomore year

**AFTER GRADUATION**

820 corporations, 27 government agencies, 5
  nonprofit organizations recruited on campus
23 Fulbright scholars

**WHAT YOU WILL PAY**

Resident tuition and fees $3894
Nonresident tuition and fees $11,593
Room and board $4607
Need-based financial aid averages $1787
Non-need financial aid averages $1500

# UNIVERSITY OF CALIFORNIA, RIVERSIDE

Riverside, California • Suburban setting • Public • State-supported • Coed

University of California, Riverside, is one of the 8 general campuses of the University of California, the finest public university in the world. It is a major research institution of 8,600 students with a strong commitment to undergraduate education. Ninety-eight percent of the faculty hold doctorates, classes are small, and freshmen complete their bachelor's degrees in an average of 4.1 years. Extensive undergraduate research and academic internship opportunities exist and placement rates to law, medical, business, and Ph.D. programs are excellent. Ample on-campus housing and financial aid are available and support services and campus life activities are extensive.

## Academics

UCR offers a core academic program; more than half of graduate courses are open to undergraduates. It awards bachelor's, master's, and doctoral **degrees**. Challenging opportunities include advanced placement, accelerated degree programs, self-designed majors, tutorials, Freshmen Honors College, an honors program, a senior project, Phi Beta Kappa, and Sigma Xi. Special programs include cooperative education, internships, summer session for credit, study abroad, and Army and Air Force ROTC.

The most popular **majors** include business, biology/biological sciences, and psychology. A complete listing of majors at UCR appears in the Majors Index beginning on page 380.

The **faculty** at UCR has 513 full-time graduate and undergraduate teachers, 98% with terminal degrees. 50% of the faculty serve as student advisers. The student-faculty ratio is 14:1, and the average class size in required courses is 22.

## Computers on Campus

Students are not required to have a computer. 190 **computers** available in the computer center, computer labs, various locations on campus, the library, the student center, and dormitories provide access to the main academic computer, off-campus computing facilities, e-mail, and on-line services. Staffed computer lab on campus provides training in the use of computers and software.

The 5 **libraries** have 1.7 million books and 13,621 subscriptions. They are connected to 6 national **on-line** catalogs.

## Campus Life

There are 136 active **organizations** on campus, including a drama/theater group and student-run newspaper and radio station. 12% of eligible men and 13% of eligible women are members of 11 national **fraternities**, 9 national **sororities**, 3 local fraternities, 3 local sororities, and 2 coed fraternities. Student **safety services** include late night transport/escort service, 24-hour emergency telephone alarm devices, 24-hour patrols by trained security personnel, student patrols, and electronically operated dormitory entrances.

UCR is a member of the NCAA (Division II). **Intercollegiate sports** (some offering scholarships) include baseball (m), basketball (m, w), cross-country running (m, w), softball (w), tennis (m, w), track and field (m, w), volleyball (w), water polo (m).

## Applying

UCR requires an essay, a high school transcript, 3 years of high school math, 2 years of high school foreign language, SAT I or ACT, 3 SAT II Subject Tests (including SAT II: Writing Test), and a minimum high school GPA of 2.0. It recommends 3 years of high school science. Early and midyear entrance are possible, with an 11/30 deadline and continuous processing to 3/2 for financial aid. **Contact:** Ms. Laurie Nelson, Associate Admissions Officer, 900 University Avenue, Riverside, CA 92521-0102, 909-787-3411.

---

### GETTING IN LAST YEAR
9,756 applied
78% were accepted
19% enrolled (1,465)
70% from top tenth of their h.s. class
3.63 average high school GPA
7% had SAT verbal scores over 600
28% had SAT math scores over 600
19% had ACT scores over 26
1% had SAT verbal scores over 700
8% had SAT math scores over 700
5% had ACT scores over 30

### THE STUDENT BODY
Total 8,591, of whom 7,218
  are undergraduates

From 19 states and territories,
  11 other countries
97% from California
52% women, 48% men
5% African Americans
1% Native Americans
17% Hispanics
37% Asian Americans
1% international students

### AFTER FRESHMAN YEAR
89% returned for sophomore year
43% got a degree within 4 years
60% got a degree within 5 years
64% got a degree within 6 years

### AFTER GRADUATION
31% pursued further study
47 corporations, 5 government agencies, 2
  nonprofit organizations recruited on campus
1 Fulbright scholar

### WHAT YOU WILL PAY
Resident tuition and fees $4093
Nonresident tuition and fees $11,792
Room and board $5430

# UNIVERSITY OF CALIFORNIA, SAN DIEGO

La Jolla, California • Suburban setting • Public • State-supported • Coed

The 5 colleges that comprise UCSD—Revelle, John Muir, Thurgood Marshall, Earl Warren, and Eleanor Roosevelt—are modeled on the Cambridge and Oxford systems found in Great Britain. This idea provides for a small college setting within the context of a large university. Each college has its own educational philosophy and traditions, its own set of general education (GE) requirements, and its own academic and student affairs staffs. When applying to UCSD, students select a college that best matches their personal interests and career goals to the way they prefer to learn. It is important to note that students may pursue any UCSD major through any of the 5 colleges.

 ## Academics

UCSD offers a core academic program. It awards bachelor's, master's, and doctoral **degrees**. Challenging opportunities include advanced placement, accelerated degree programs, self-designed majors, Freshmen Honors College, an honors program, a senior project, and Phi Beta Kappa. Special programs include internships, summer session for credit, off-campus study, and study abroad.

The most popular **majors** include biology/biological sciences, psychology, and political science/government. A complete listing of majors at UCSD appears in the Majors Index beginning on page 380.

The **faculty** at UCSD has 1,170 full-time graduate and undergraduate teachers, 95% with terminal degrees. The student-faculty ratio is 19:1.

## Computers on Campus

Students are not required to have a computer. Student rooms are linked to a campus network. 700 **computers** available in the computer center, each academic college, the library, and the student center.

The 7 **libraries** have 2.2 million books, 2 million microform titles, and 24,414 subscriptions.

## Campus Life

Active **organizations** on campus include drama/theater group and student-run newspaper and radio station. 10% of eligible men and 10% of eligible women are members of 14 national **fraternities** and 8 national **sororities**. Student **safety services** include crime prevention programs and late night transport/escort service.

UCSD is a member of the NCAA (Division III). **Intercollegiate sports** include baseball (m), basketball (m, w), crew (m, w), cross-country running (m, w), fencing (m, w), golf (m, w), soccer (m, w), softball (w), swimming and diving (m, w), tennis (m, w), track and field (m, w), volleyball (m, w), water polo (m, w).

## Applying

UCSD requires an essay, a high school transcript, 3 years of high school math, 2 years of high school foreign language, SAT I or ACT, and 3 SAT II Subject Tests (including SAT II: Writing Test). It recommends 3 years of high school science. Early entrance is possible, with an 11/30 deadline and continuous processing to 5/1 for financial aid. **Contact:** Mr. Tim Johnston, Acting Director, Student Outreach and Recruitment, Student Outreach and Recruitment (SOAR), Box 0337, La Jolla, CA 92093-5003, 619-534-4831.

---

### GETTING IN LAST YEAR
20,011 applied
64% were accepted
22% enrolled (2,863)
95% from top tenth of their h.s. class
3.8 average high school GPA
11% had SAT verbal scores over 600
52% had SAT math scores over 600
1% had SAT verbal scores over 700
14% had SAT math scores over 700

### THE STUDENT BODY
Total 17,776, of whom 14,320
   are undergraduates
96% from California
49% women, 51% men
3% African Americans
1% Native Americans
12% Hispanics
24% Asian Americans
1% international students

### AFTER FRESHMAN YEAR
92% returned for sophomore year

### AFTER GRADUATION
35% pursued further study
7 Fulbright scholars

### WHAT YOU WILL PAY
Resident tuition and fees $3988
Nonresident tuition and fees $11,687
Room and board $6607
42% receive need-based financial aid
   averaging $4453
Non-need financial aid averages $1292

# UNIVERSITY OF CALIFORNIA, SANTA BARBARA

Santa Barbara, California • Suburban setting • Public • State-supported • Coed

The University of California, Santa Barbara, is one of the few residential public university campuses in the state, which gives its students the opportunity to learn from renowned scholars in a setting that fosters personal interaction. Just 50 years old, UC Santa Barbara has become one of the top 50 research campuses in the country, having gained prominence in fields ranging from physics and engineering to religious studies and music. When a new professional School of Environmental Science and Management admitted its first students in fall 1994, the University began to play a pivotal role in training the environmental problem-solvers of the future.

 **Academics**

UCSB offers a core academic program. It awards bachelor's, master's, and doctoral **degrees**. Challenging opportunities include advanced placement, accelerated degree programs, self-designed majors, Freshmen Honors College, an honors program, a senior project, Phi Beta Kappa, and Sigma Xi. Special programs include cooperative education, internships, summer session for credit, study abroad, and Army ROTC.

A complete listing of majors at UCSB appears in the Majors Index beginning on page 380.

The **faculty** at UCSB has 655 full-time graduate and undergraduate teachers, 100% with terminal degrees. The student-faculty ratio is 19:1.

 **Computers on Campus**

Students are not required to have a computer. 2,000 **computers** available in the computer center, departmental labs, the library, and dormitories provide access to e-mail and on-line services. Staffed computer lab on campus provides training in the use of computers and software.

The **library** has 2.2 million books and 24,325 subscriptions.

 **Campus Life**

There are 250 active **organizations** on campus, including a drama/theater group and student-run newspaper and radio station. 15% of eligible men and 16% of eligible women are members of 18 national **fraternities**, 14 national **sororities**, 3 local fraternities, and 4 local sororities. Student **safety services** include late night transport/escort service and 24-hour emergency telephone alarm devices.

UCSB is a member of the NCAA (Division I). **Intercollegiate sports** (some offering scholarships) include baseball (m), basketball (m, w), bowling (m, w), crew (m, w), cross-country running (m, w), fencing (m, w), golf (m, w), gymnastics (m, w), lacrosse (m, w), rugby (m), sailing (m, w), skiing (downhill) (m, w), soccer (m, w), softball (w), swimming and diving (m, w), tennis (m, w), track and field (m, w), volleyball (m, w), water polo (m, w).

 **Applying**

UCSB requires an essay, a high school transcript, 3 years of high school math, 2 years of high school foreign language, 4 years of high school English, 1 year of high school U.S. history, SAT I or ACT, 3 SAT II Subject Tests (including SAT II: Writing Test), and in some cases an interview. It recommends 3 years of high school science. Early and midyear entrance are possible, with an 11/30 deadline and continuous processing to 3/2 for financial aid. **Contact:** Mr. William Villa, Director of Admissions/Relations with Schools, 1234 Cheadle Hall, Santa Barbara, CA 93106, 805-893-2485.

**GETTING IN LAST YEAR**
17,060 applied
83% were accepted
20% enrolled (2,881)
3.45 average high school GPA
5% had SAT verbal scores over 600
30% had SAT math scores over 600
1% had SAT verbal scores over 700
5% had SAT math scores over 700

**THE STUDENT BODY**
Total 17,834, of whom 15,525
  are undergraduates

From 46 states and territories,
  49 other countries
95% from California
52% women, 48% men
3% African Americans
1% Native Americans
12% Hispanics
17% Asian Americans
2% international students

**AFTER FRESHMAN YEAR**
85% returned for sophomore year
36% got a degree within 4 years

64% got a degree within 5 years
69% got a degree within 6 years

**WHAT YOU WILL PAY**
Resident tuition and fees $4098
Nonresident tuition and fees $11,797
Room and board $5901
Need-based financial aid averages $2974
Non-need financial aid averages $3528

# UNIVERSITY OF CALIFORNIA, SANTA CRUZ

Santa Cruz, California • Small-town setting • Public • State-supported • Coed

## Academics

UCSC offers a core academic program. It awards bachelor's, master's, and doctoral **degrees**. Challenging opportunities include advanced placement, self-designed majors, a senior project, Phi Beta Kappa, and Sigma Xi. Special programs include internships, summer session for credit, off-campus study, and study abroad.

The most popular **majors** include biology/biological sciences, psychology, and literature. A complete listing of majors at UCSC appears in the Majors Index beginning on page 380.

The **faculty** at UCSC has 400 full-time graduate and undergraduate teachers, 98% with terminal degrees. The student-faculty ratio is 19:1.

## Computers on Campus

Students are not required to have a computer. 200 **computers** available in the computer center, each academic college, and the student center provide access to the main academic computer, off-campus computing facilities, e-mail, and on-line services. Staffed computer lab on campus (open 24 hours a day) provides training in the use of computers and software.

The 10 **libraries** have 1 million books, 548,215 microform titles, and 10,004 subscriptions.

## Campus Life

Active **organizations** on campus include drama/theater group and student-run newspaper and radio station. 25% of students participate in student government elections. Student **safety services** include evening maingate security, late night transport/escort service, 24-hour emergency telephone alarm devices, and 24-hour patrols by trained security personnel.

UCSC is a member of the NCAA (Division III). **Intercollegiate sports** include basketball (m, w), fencing (m, w), lacrosse (m, w), rugby (m), sailing (m, w), soccer (m), swimming and diving (m, w), tennis (m, w), volleyball (m, w), water polo (m, w).

## Applying

UCSC requires an essay, a high school transcript, 3 years of high school math, 2 years of high school foreign language, SAT I or ACT, and 3 SAT II Subject Tests (including SAT II: Writing Test). It recommends 3 years of high school science. 11/30 deadline and continuous processing to 3/2 for financial aid. **Contact:** Mr. C. James Quann, Associate Vice Chancellor of Enrollment Management, Admissions Office, Cook House, Santa Cruz, CA 95064, 408-459-4008; fax 408-459-4452.

---

### GETTING IN LAST YEAR
10,950 applied
80% were accepted
20% enrolled (1,788)
94% from top tenth of their h.s. class
24% had SAT verbal scores over 600
35% had SAT math scores over 600
3% had SAT verbal scores over 700
5% had SAT math scores over 700

### THE STUDENT BODY
Total 10,117, of whom 9,099
  are undergraduates

From 48 states and territories,
  36 other countries
96% from California
59% women, 41% men
3% African Americans
1% Native Americans
15% Hispanics
15% Asian Americans
2% international students

### AFTER FRESHMAN YEAR
85% returned for sophomore year
41% got a degree within 4 years

62% got a degree within 5 years
67% got a degree within 6 years

### AFTER GRADUATION
50% pursued further study
8 Fulbright scholars

### WHAT YOU WILL PAY
Resident tuition and fees $4390
Nonresident tuition and fees $12,088
Room and board $5064
Need-based financial aid averages $7200
Non-need financial aid averages $2817

# UNIVERSITY OF CHICAGO

Chicago, Illinois • Urban setting • Private • Independent • Coed

▶ The College of the University of Chicago is the liberal arts college at the heart of one of the world's great research centers, where 63 Nobel prize winners have studied, researched, or taught. The College offers the Common Core, the country's oldest and most extensive general education curriculum.

## Academics

Chicago offers a liberal education curriculum and core academic program; more than half of graduate courses are open to undergraduates. It awards bachelor's, master's, doctoral, and first professional **degrees**. Challenging opportunities include advanced placement, accelerated degree programs, self-designed majors, tutorials, a senior project, Phi Beta Kappa, and Sigma Xi. Special programs include internships, summer session for credit, off-campus study, study abroad, and Army and Air Force ROTC.

The most popular **majors** include economics, biology/biological sciences, and English. A complete listing of majors at Chicago appears in the Majors Index beginning on page 380.

The **faculty** at Chicago has 1,232 graduate and undergraduate teachers, 100% with terminal degrees. The student-faculty ratio is 6:1, and the average class size in required courses is 25.

## Computers on Campus

Students are not required to have a computer. Student rooms are linked to a campus network. 1,000 **computers** available in the computer center, computer labs, the research center, the learning resource center, classroom buildings, classrooms, the library, dormitories, and student rooms provide access to the main academic computer, off-campus computing facilities, e-mail, and on-line services. Staffed computer lab on campus provides training in the use of software.

The 9 **libraries** have 5.7 million books, 2 million microform titles, and 47,000 subscriptions. They are connected to 7 national **on-line** catalogs.

## Campus Life

There are 150 active **organizations** on campus, including a drama/theater group and student-run newspaper and radio station. 14% of eligible men and 5% of eligible women are members of 9 national **fraternities** and 2 national **sororities**. Student **safety services** include late night transport/escort service, 24-hour emergency telephone alarm devices, 24-hour patrols by trained security personnel, and electronically operated dormitory entrances.

Chicago is a member of the NCAA (Division III). **Intercollegiate sports** include baseball (m), basketball (m, w), cross-country running (m, w), fencing (m), football (m), soccer (m, w), softball (w), swimming and diving (m, w), tennis (m, w), track and field (m, w), volleyball (w), wrestling (m).

## Applying

Chicago requires an essay, a high school transcript, 3 recommendations, and SAT I or ACT. It recommends 4 years of high school math and science, 3 years of high school foreign language, and an interview. Early and deferred entrance are possible, with a 1/15 deadline and a 2/1 priority date for financial aid. **Contact:** Mr. Theodore O'Neill, Dean of Admissions, 1116 East 59th Street, Chicago, IL 60637-1513, 312-702-8650; fax 312-702-4199.

### GETTING IN LAST YEAR
6,262 applied
50% were accepted
29% enrolled (924)
75% from top tenth of their h.s. class
65% had SAT verbal scores over 600
85% had SAT math scores over 600
85% had ACT scores over 26
18% had SAT verbal scores over 700
41% had SAT math scores over 700
49% had ACT scores over 30
146 National Merit Scholars

### THE STUDENT BODY
Total 11,427, of whom 3,447 are undergraduates

From 52 states and territories, 43 other countries
26% from Illinois
44% women, 56% men
4% African Americans
0% Native Americans
4% Hispanics
26% Asian Americans
4% international students

### AFTER FRESHMAN YEAR
91% returned for sophomore year
70% got a degree within 4 years
79% got a degree within 5 years
81% got a degree within 6 years

### AFTER GRADUATION
35% pursued further study (17% arts and sciences, 8% law, 7% medicine)
30% had job offers within 3 months
70 corporations, 6 government agencies, 15 nonprofit organizations recruited on campus
2 Rhodes, 14 Fulbright scholars

### WHAT YOU WILL PAY
Tuition and fees $19,236
Room and board $6380
Need-based financial aid averages $10,416
Non-need financial aid averages $9671

# UNIVERSITY OF COLORADO AT BOULDER

Boulder, Colorado • Urban setting • Public • State-supported • Coed

The University of Colorado at Boulder, a major research and teaching university, is located in one of the most spectacular environments in the country at the foot of the Rocky Mountains. Ranking 11th among all public universities in federally funded research, the University offers tremendous academic diversity, with faculty committed to bringing their research into the classroom. Students may participate in honors programs, an undergraduate research program, and several residential programs.

 **Academics**

CU-Boulder offers a research and teaching-oriented curriculum and no core academic program; fewer than half of graduate courses are open to undergraduates. It awards bachelor's, master's, doctoral, and first professional **degrees**. Challenging opportunities include advanced placement, accelerated degree programs, self-designed majors, tutorials, Freshmen Honors College, an honors program, a senior project, Phi Beta Kappa, and Sigma Xi. Special programs include cooperative education, internships, summer session for credit, off-campus study, study abroad, and Army, Naval, and Air Force ROTC.

The most popular **majors** include psychology, English, and marketing/retailing/merchandising. A complete listing of majors at CU-Boulder appears in the Majors Index beginning on page 380.

The **faculty** at CU-Boulder has 1,019 full-time graduate and undergraduate teachers, 99% with terminal degrees. The student-faculty ratio is 22:1, and the average class size in required courses is 50.

 **Computers on Campus**

Students are not required to have a computer. Student rooms are linked to a campus network. 1,300 **computers** available in the computer center, computer labs, the research center, the learning resource center, classroom buildings, classrooms, the library, the student center, and dormitories provide access to the main academic computer, off-campus computing facilities, e-mail, and on-line services. Staffed computer lab on campus (open 24 hours a day) provides training in the use of computers and software.

The 7 **libraries** have 2.5 million books and 28,440 subscriptions. They are connected to 300 national **on-line** catalogs.

 **Campus Life**

There are 351 active **organizations** on campus, including a drama/theater group and student-run newspaper and radio station. 15% of eligible men and 15% of eligible women are members of 22 national **fraternities**, 13 national **sororities**, and 1 local sorority. Student **safety services** include university police department, late night transport/escort service, 24-hour emergency telephone alarm devices, 24-hour patrols by trained security personnel, and student patrols.

CU-Boulder is a member of the NCAA (Division I). **Intercollegiate sports** (some offering scholarships) include baseball (m), basketball (m, w), cross-country running (m, w), fencing (m, w), field hockey (w), football (m), golf (m, w), ice hockey (m), lacrosse (m, w), rugby (m, w), skiing (cross-country) (m, w), skiing (downhill) (m, w), soccer (m, w), softball (w), swimming and diving (m, w), tennis (m, w), track and field (m, w), volleyball (w), water polo (m, w), weight lifting (m, w), wrestling (m).

 **Applying**

CU-Boulder requires a high school transcript, 3 years of high school math and science, 2 years of high school foreign language, SAT I or ACT, a minimum high school GPA of 2.0, and in some cases 4 years of high school math and 3 years of high school foreign language. It recommends an essay, recommendations, and a minimum high school GPA of 3.0. Early, deferred, and midyear entrance are possible, with a 2/15 deadline and continuous processing to 4/1 for financial aid. **Contact:** Admissions Counselor, Campus Box 30, Boulder, CO 80309-0030, 303-492-6301; fax 303-492-7115.

## GETTING IN LAST YEAR
14,085 applied
76% were accepted
34% enrolled (3,603)
28% from top tenth of their h.s. class
12% had SAT verbal scores over 600
42% had SAT math scores over 600
44% had ACT scores over 26
1% had SAT verbal scores over 700
9% had SAT math scores over 700
10% had ACT scores over 30

## THE STUDENT BODY
Total 24,548, of whom 19,745
   are undergraduates

From 52 states and territories,
   65 other countries
67% from Colorado
47% women, 53% men
2% African Americans
1% Native Americans
6% Hispanics
6% Asian Americans
3% international students

## AFTER FRESHMAN YEAR
80% returned for sophomore year
34% got a degree within 4 years
60% got a degree within 5 years
66% got a degree within 6 years

## AFTER GRADUATION
28% pursued further study
200 corporations, 50 government agencies, 46
   nonprofit organizations recruited on campus
4 Fulbright scholars

## WHAT YOU WILL PAY
Resident tuition and fees $2700
Nonresident tuition and fees $13,264
Room and board $3964
69% receive need-based financial aid
   averaging $1416
Non-need financial aid averages $1600

# UNIVERSITY OF CONNECTICUT

Storrs, Connecticut • Rural setting • Public • State-supported • Coed

---

▶ UConn provides an academic and social environment that develops the skills students need in order to be successful. Its programs enhance students' independence, sense of responsibility, initiative, and the desire to take an active role in their undergraduate experience and a leading role in all aspects of their education. The process of making choices, asking questions, and solving problems prepares students for the competition, shifting terrain, and expectations of graduate school or the demands of a global, competitive economy. UConn's academic and social offerings reflect the growing links between cultures and countries and emphasize the sophisticated skills needed by citizens in the global marketplace.

 **Academics**

UCONN offers a liberal education curriculum through professional training and core academic program; fewer than half of graduate courses are open to undergraduates. It awards associate, bachelor's, master's, doctoral, and first professional **degrees**. Challenging opportunities include advanced placement, accelerated degree programs, self-designed majors, an honors program, Phi Beta Kappa, and Sigma Xi. Special programs include cooperative education, internships, summer session for credit, off-campus study, study abroad, and Army and Air Force ROTC.

The most popular **majors** include English, human development, and political science/government. A complete listing of majors at UCONN appears in the Majors Index beginning on page 380.

The **faculty** at UCONN has 1,117 full-time graduate and undergraduate teachers, 87% with terminal degrees. The student-faculty ratio is 17:1.

 **Computers on Campus**

Students are not required to have a computer. Student rooms are linked to a campus network. 1,800 **computers** available in the computer center, departmental labs, the library, the student center, and dormitories provide access to the main academic computer, e-mail, and on-line services. Staffed computer lab on campus provides training in the use of computers and software.

The 4 **libraries** have 1.9 million books, 2.8 million microform titles, and 9,589 subscriptions. They are connected to 12 national **on-line** catalogs.

 **Campus Life**

Active **organizations** on campus include drama/theater group and student-run newspaper and radio station. 10% of eligible men and 10% of eligible women are members of 16 national **fraternities** and 9 national **sororities**. Student **safety services** include late night transport/escort service and 24-hour emergency telephone alarm devices.

UCONN is a member of the NCAA (Division I). **Intercollegiate sports** (some offering scholarships) include baseball (m), basketball (m, w), cross-country running (m, w), field hockey (w), football (m), golf (m), ice hockey (m), soccer (m, w), softball (w), swimming and diving (m, w), tennis (m, w), track and field (m, w), volleyball (w).

 **Applying**

UCONN requires an essay, a high school transcript, 3 years of high school math, 2 years of high school foreign language, SAT I, and in some cases 3 years of high school science. It recommends recommendations. Early, deferred, and midyear entrance are possible, with a 4/1 deadline and continuous processing to 3/1 for financial aid. **Contact:** Dr. Ann L. Huckenbeck, Director of Admissions, 28 North Eagleville Road, U-88, Storrs, CT 06269, 203-486-3137; fax 203-486-1909.

---

**GETTING IN LAST YEAR**
9,467 applied
69% were accepted
29% enrolled (1,897)
21% from top tenth of their h.s. class
8% had SAT verbal scores over 600
31% had SAT math scores over 600
1% had SAT verbal scores over 700
5% had SAT math scores over 700
12 valedictorians

**THE STUDENT BODY**
Total 15,626, of whom 10,907
   are undergraduates

88% from Connecticut
50% women, 50% men
4% African Americans
1% Native Americans
3% Hispanics
6% Asian Americans
1% international students

**AFTER FRESHMAN YEAR**
87% returned for sophomore year
34% got a degree within 4 years
62% got a degree within 5 years
68% got a degree within 6 years

**AFTER GRADUATION**
15% pursued further study
3 Fulbright scholars

**WHAT YOU WILL PAY**
Resident tuition and fees $4712
Nonresident tuition and fees $12,544
Room and board $5072
39% receive need-based financial aid
   averaging $2577
9% receive non-need financial aid averaging
   $4358

---

# UNIVERSITY OF DALLAS

Irving, Texas • Suburban setting • Private • Independent-Religious • Coed

▶ The University of Dallas, the Catholic university for independent thinkers, is where debate and discourse are a way of life. The professors guide students in an environment of intellectual inquiry that engages the imagination. UD's distinctive and comprehensive core curriculum emphasizes the use of original texts. Reading great books, sharing a common body of knowledge with other students, and discussing ideas are important parts of a student's education. UD's classical education comes to life on its Rome campus, where nearly 85% of sophomores spend a semester exploring the cities, works of art, and historic landmarks that they have studied in their core courses.

## 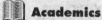 Academics

UD offers an ancient and modern Western civilization curriculum and core academic program; fewer than half of graduate courses are open to undergraduates. It awards bachelor's, master's, and doctoral **degrees**. Challenging opportunities include advanced placement, accelerated degree programs, self-designed majors, tutorials, a senior project, and Phi Beta Kappa. Special programs include internships, summer session for credit, off-campus study, study abroad, and Army and Air Force ROTC.

The most popular **majors** include biology/biological sciences, political science/government, and English. A complete listing of majors at UD appears in the Majors Index beginning on page 380.

The **faculty** at UD has 108 full-time graduate and undergraduate teachers, 95% with terminal degrees. 77% of the faculty serve as student advisers. The student-faculty ratio is 14:1, and the average class size in required courses is 20.

##  Computers on Campus

Students are not required to have a computer. 70 **computers** available in science buildings and the library provide access to the main academic computer. Staffed computer lab on campus provides training in the use of computers and software.

The **library** has 288,566 books, 75,416 microform titles, and 1,022 subscriptions. It is connected to 1 national **on-line** catalog.

##  Campus Life

There are 43 active **organizations** on campus, including a drama/theater group and student-run newspaper. Student **safety services** include late night transport/escort service, 24-hour emergency telephone alarm devices, 24-hour patrols by trained security personnel, and electronically operated dormitory entrances.

UD is a member of the NAIA. **Intercollegiate sports** include basketball (m, w), golf (m), tennis (m, w), volleyball (w).

##  Applying

UD requires an essay, a high school transcript, 1 recommendation, SAT I or ACT, and in some cases a campus interview. It recommends 3 years of high school math and science, 2 years of high school foreign language, and an interview. Early, deferred, and midyear entrance are possible, with a 2/1 deadline and continuous processing to 3/1 for financial aid. **Contact:** Ms. Darbie Ann Dallman, Director of Admissions and Financial Aid, 1845 East Northgate Drive, Irving, TX 75062-4799, 214-721-5266; fax 214-721-5017.

---

### GETTING IN LAST YEAR
696 applied
86% were accepted
42% enrolled (249)
42% from top tenth of their h.s. class
30% had SAT verbal scores over 600
43% had SAT math scores over 600
54% had ACT scores over 26
5% had SAT verbal scores over 700
8% had SAT math scores over 700
22% had ACT scores over 30
9 National Merit Scholars

### THE STUDENT BODY
Total 2,737, of whom 1,103
   are undergraduates

From 47 states and territories,
   22 other countries
61% from Texas
54% women, 46% men
1% African Americans
1% Native Americans
13% Hispanics
10% Asian Americans
3% international students

### AFTER FRESHMAN YEAR
81% returned for sophomore year

### AFTER GRADUATION
50% pursued further study (23% arts and
   sciences, 10% business, 10% medicine)
6 corporations, 1 government agency, 4
   nonprofit organizations recruited on campus
2 Fulbright scholars

### WHAT YOU WILL PAY
Tuition and fees $10,840
Room and board $4830
90% receive need-based financial aid
   averaging $2414
20% receive non-need financial aid averaging
   $3186

# UNIVERSITY OF DELAWARE

Newark, Delaware • Small-town setting • Public • State-related • Coed

▶ Delaware has had a longstanding commitment to undergraduate teaching and research. Delaware's graduation rate, one of the highest among the 50 major public universities, is further evidence of this commitment. Some of the nation's brightest students enroll in the University Honors Program. The enrollment of approximately 15,000 undergraduates is ideal for high-achieving students seeking the diversity and richness of opportunity of a large university and the qualities and spirit of a small, personal campus. A major advantage of the campus location is its proximity to Washington, Philadelphia, and New York.

 ## Academics

Delaware offers an interdisciplinary curriculum and core academic program; all graduate courses are open to undergraduates. It awards associate, bachelor's, master's, and doctoral **degrees**. Challenging opportunities include advanced placement, accelerated degree programs, self-designed majors, tutorials, an honors program, a senior project, Phi Beta Kappa, and Sigma Xi. Special programs include cooperative education, internships, summer session for credit, off-campus study, study abroad, and Army and Air Force ROTC.

The most popular **majors** include English, psychology, and elementary education. A complete listing of majors at Delaware appears in the Majors Index beginning on page 380.

The **faculty** at Delaware has 973 full-time graduate and undergraduate teachers, 87% with terminal degrees. The student-faculty ratio is 15:1, and the average class size in required courses is 35.

 ## Computers on Campus

Students are not required to have a computer. Student rooms are linked to a campus network. 700 **computers** available in the computer center, computer labs, 26 sites throughout campus, the library, the student center, dormitories, and student rooms provide access to the main academic computer, e-mail, and on-line services. Staffed computer lab on campus provides training in the use of computers and software.

The 4 **libraries** have 2.1 million books, 2.4 million microform titles, and 20,000 subscriptions.

 ## Campus Life

There are 150 active **organizations** on campus, including a drama/theater group and student-run newspaper and radio station. 16% of eligible men and 16% of eligible women are members of 25 national **fraternities** and 15 national **sororities**. Student **safety services** include late night transport/escort service, 24-hour emergency telephone alarm devices, 24-hour patrols by trained security personnel, student patrols, and electronically operated dormitory entrances.

Delaware is a member of the NCAA (Division I). **Intercollegiate sports** (some offering scholarships) include baseball (m), basketball (m, w), crew (m, w), cross-country running (m, w), field hockey (w), football (m), golf (m), ice hockey (m), lacrosse (m, w), rugby (m, w), soccer (m, w), softball (w), swimming and diving (m, w), tennis (m, w), track and field (m, w), volleyball (w).

 ## Applying

Delaware requires a high school transcript, 2 years of high school foreign language, SAT I, and in some cases an essay and 1 recommendation. It recommends SAT II Subject Tests. Early, deferred, and midyear entrance are possible, with a 3/1 deadline and continuous processing to 3/15 for financial aid. **Contact:** Dr. Bruce Walker, Associate Provost, Admissions and Student Financial Aid, 116 Hullihen Hall, South College Avenue, Newark, DE 19716, 302-831-8123; fax 302-831-6905.

---

**GETTING IN LAST YEAR**
13,464 applied
73% were accepted
30% enrolled (2,993)
24% from top tenth of their h.s. class
3.2 average high school GPA
32 National Merit Scholars
24 valedictorians

**THE STUDENT BODY**
Total 18,080, of whom 14,870 are undergraduates
From 50 states and territories, 85 other countries
42% from Delaware
57% women, 43% men

5% African Americans
1% Native Americans
1% Hispanics
3% Asian Americans
1% international students

**AFTER FRESHMAN YEAR**
85% returned for sophomore year
50% got a degree within 4 years
65% got a degree within 5 years
70% got a degree within 6 years

**AFTER GRADUATION**
20% pursued further study (9% arts and sciences, 4% law, 3% business)

92% had job offers within 3 months
300 corporations, 25 government agencies, 200 nonprofit organizations recruited on campus
1 Fulbright scholar

**WHAT YOU WILL PAY**
Resident tuition and fees $4100
Nonresident tuition and fees $10,630
Room and board $4230
50% receive need-based financial aid averaging $3850
12% receive non-need financial aid averaging $5000

# UNIVERSITY OF DENVER

Denver, Colorado • Suburban setting • Private • Independent • Coed

 **Academics**

DU offers an interdisciplinary curriculum and core academic program; more than half of graduate courses are open to undergraduates. It awards bachelor's, master's, doctoral, and first professional **degrees**. Challenging opportunities include advanced placement, accelerated degree programs, self-designed majors, tutorials, Freshmen Honors College, an honors program, a senior project, Phi Beta Kappa, and Sigma Xi. Special programs include cooperative education, internships, summer session for credit, study abroad, and Army and Air Force ROTC.

The most popular **majors** include accounting, communication, and psychology. A complete listing of majors at DU appears in the Majors Index beginning on page 380.

The **faculty** at DU has 378 full-time graduate and undergraduate teachers, 91% with terminal degrees. 75% of the faculty serve as student advisers. The student-faculty ratio is 13:1, and the average class size in required courses is 25.

 **Computers on Campus**

Students are not required to have a computer. Student rooms are linked to a campus network. 400 **computers** available in the computer center, computer labs, classrooms, the library, and dormitories provide access to e-mail, on-line services, and campus-wide information system. Staffed computer lab on campus provides training in the use of computers and software.

The **library** has 1.8 million books, 879,528 microform titles, and 5,102 subscriptions. It is connected to 3 national **on-line** catalogs.

 **Campus Life**

There are 80 active **organizations** on campus, including a drama/theater group and student-run newspaper and radio station. 62% of eligible men and 34% of eligible women are members of 9 national **fraternities** and 5 national **sororities**. Student **safety services** include 24-hour locked dormitory entrances, late night transport/escort service, 24-hour emergency telephone alarm devices, 24-hour patrols by trained security personnel, and electronically operated dormitory entrances.

DU is a member of the NCAA (Division II). **Intercollegiate sports** (some offering scholarships) include baseball (m), basketball (m, w), football (m), golf (m), gymnastics (w), ice hockey (m), lacrosse (m, w), rugby (m), skiing (cross-country) (m, w), skiing (downhill) (m, w), soccer (m, w), swimming and diving (m, w), tennis (m, w), volleyball (m, w).

 **Applying**

DU requires an essay, a high school transcript, 2 recommendations, activity sheet, SAT I or ACT, and in some cases 3 years of high school math and science. It recommends 3 years of high school math and science, 2 years of high school foreign language, and an interview. Early, deferred, and midyear entrance are possible, with rolling admissions and continuous processing to 2/19 for financial aid. **Contact:** Ms. Susan Hunt, Director of Admission Counseling, 2199 South University Boulevard, Denver, CO 80208, 303-871-2036 or toll-free 800-525-9495 (out-of-state); fax 303-871-3301.

---

**GETTING IN LAST YEAR**
2,569 applied
81% were accepted
27% enrolled (565)
37% from top tenth of their h.s. class
3.1 average high school GPA
7% had SAT verbal scores over 600
29% had SAT math scores over 600
36% had ACT scores over 26
0% had SAT verbal scores over 700
4% had SAT math scores over 700
7% had ACT scores over 30

**THE STUDENT BODY**
Total 8,522, of whom 2,739
   are undergraduates

From 52 states and territories,
   71 other countries
40% from Colorado
51% women, 49% men
1% African Americans
1% Native Americans
7% Hispanics
5% Asian Americans
11% international students

**AFTER FRESHMAN YEAR**
83% returned for sophomore year
58% got a degree within 4 years
66% got a degree within 5 years
67% got a degree within 6 years

**AFTER GRADUATION**
72 corporations, 2 government agencies, 2
   nonprofit organizations recruited on campus

**WHAT YOU WILL PAY**
Tuition and fees $15,300
Room and board $4695
51% receive need-based financial aid
   averaging $6758
7% receive non-need financial aid averaging
   $8104

# UNIVERSITY OF DETROIT MERCY

Detroit, Michigan • Urban setting • Private • Independent-Religious • Coed

University of Detroit Mercy is Michigan's largest, most comprehensive Catholic university, offering a value-oriented, person-centered education. Small class size and a faculty-student ratio of 1:14 ensure that students will receive individual support and one-on-one interaction with professors. Undergraduate, graduate, and professional degrees are available in over 60 academic fields. A nationally recognized Cooperative Education Program enables students to acquire on-the-job experience with prominent national and international employers. Located in a dynamic urban area, UDM offers unlimited opportunities for enrichment and enjoyment.

##  Academics

U of D Mercy offers a core academic program; fewer than half of graduate courses are open to undergraduates. It awards associate, bachelor's, master's, doctoral, and first professional **degrees**. Challenging opportunities include advanced placement, accelerated degree programs, self-designed majors, tutorials, an honors program, and a senior project. Special programs include cooperative education, internships, summer session for credit, off-campus study, study abroad, and Army ROTC.

The most popular **majors** include nursing, engineering (general), and architecture. A complete listing of majors at U of D Mercy appears in the Majors Index beginning on page 380.

The **faculty** at U of D Mercy has 283 full-time graduate and undergraduate teachers, 81% with terminal degrees. The student-faculty ratio is 14:1, and the average class size in required courses is 25.

##  Computers on Campus

Students are not required to have a computer. 200 **computers** available in the computer center, computer labs, classrooms, the library, and the student center.

The 5 **libraries** have 645,039 books, 88,650 microform titles, and 5,505 subscriptions. They are connected to 3 national **on-line** catalogs.

##  Campus Life

Active **organizations** on campus include drama/theater group and student-run newspaper and radio station. 22% of eligible men and 13% of eligible women are members of 7 national **fraternities**, 7 local fraternities, and 3 local **sororities**. Student **safety services** include late night transport/escort service.

U of D Mercy is a member of the NCAA (Division I). **Intercollegiate sports** (some offering scholarships) include baseball (m), basketball (m, w), cross-country running (m, w), fencing (m, w), golf (m, w), riflery (m, w), soccer (m, w), softball (w), tennis (m), track and field (m, w).

##  Applying

U of D Mercy requires a high school transcript, SAT I or ACT, and in some cases 3 years of high school math and science, some high school foreign language, 1 recommendation, and an interview. It recommends recommendations. Early and deferred entrance are possible, with an 8/15 deadline and continuous processing to 4/1 for financial aid. **Contact:** Dr. Robert Johnson, Dean of Enrollment Management, PO Box 19900, Detroit, MI 48219-0900, 313-993-1245.

---

**GETTING IN LAST YEAR**

1,504 applied
75% were accepted
47% enrolled (535)
24% from top tenth of their h.s. class
2.98 average high school GPA
7% had SAT verbal scores over 600
26% had SAT math scores over 600
23% had ACT scores over 26
0% had SAT verbal scores over 700
4% had SAT math scores over 700
3% had ACT scores over 30

**THE STUDENT BODY**

Total 7,461, of whom 4,465 are undergraduates
From 31 states and territories, 32 other countries
92% from Michigan
65% women, 35% men
40% African Americans
1% Native Americans
2% Hispanics
2% Asian Americans
3% international students

**AFTER FRESHMAN YEAR**

81% returned for sophomore year

**AFTER GRADUATION**

20% pursued further study (6% business, 4% engineering, 3% arts and sciences)
58 corporations, 7 government agencies, 5 nonprofit organizations recruited on campus

**WHAT YOU WILL PAY**

Tuition and fees $11,230
Room and board $3822

# UNIVERSITY OF EVANSVILLE

Evansville, Indiana • Suburban setting • Private • Independent-Religious • Coed

▶ Discover the difference! The University of Evansville seeks students whose expectations know no boundaries. The private, liberal arts and sciences University is an appropriate size for learning with over 80 major areas of study. Nearly 3,000 undergraduates from 48 states and more than 40 countries are usually in classes of 25 or fewer, giving them the opportunity to enjoy stimulating debate and discussion. Outside the classroom, Evansville's students enjoy Division I athletics as well as more than 100 social and academic organizations. Students also have the opportunity to strengthen their understanding of a different culture at Evansville's campus at Harlaxton College in Grantham, England.

 **Academics**

University of Evansville offers a world cultures curriculum and core academic program. It awards associate, bachelor's, and master's **degrees**. Challenging opportunities include advanced placement, tutorials, Freshmen Honors College, and an honors program. Special programs include cooperative education, internships, summer session for credit, and study abroad.

The most popular **majors** include accounting, electrical engineering, and elementary education. A complete listing of majors at University of Evansville appears in the Majors Index beginning on page 380.

The **faculty** at University of Evansville has 171 full-time graduate and undergraduate teachers, 83% with terminal degrees. 60% of the faculty serve as student advisers. The student-faculty ratio is 13:1, and the average class size in required courses is 20.

 **Computers on Campus**

Students are not required to have a computer. 100 **computers** available in computer labs, classrooms, and the library. Staffed computer lab on campus provides training use of computers and software.

The **library** has 238,631 books, 317,014 microfor titles, and 1,168 subscriptions.

 **Campus Life**

There are 124 active **organizations** on campus, including a drama/theater group and student-run newspaper and radio station. 30% of eligible men and 20% of eligible women are members of 5 national **fraternities** and 4 national **sororities**. Student **safety services** include late night transport/escort service, 24-hour emergency telephone alarm devices, and 24-hour patrols by trained security personnel.

University of Evansville is a member of the NCAA (Division I). **Intercollegiate sports** (some offering scholarships) include baseball (m), basketball (m, w), cross-country running (m, w), football (m), golf (m), soccer (m, w), softball (w), swimming and diving (m, w), tennis (m, w), volleyball (w).

 **Applying**

University of Evansville requires an essay, a high school transcript, 1 recommendation, SAT I or ACT, and in some cases 3 years of high school math and science and a campus interview. It recommends 3 years of high school math and science, 2 years of high school foreign language, and a campus interview. Early, deferred, and midyear entrance are possible, with a 2/15 deadline and continuous processing to 3/1 for financial aid. **Contact:** Ms. Elizabeth Lyon, Director of Undergraduate Admission, 1800 Lincoln Avenue, Evansville, IN 47722-0002, 812-479-2468 or toll-free 800-992-5877 (in-state), 800-423-8633 (out-of-state); fax 812-479-2320.

---

**GETTING IN LAST YEAR**
2,338 applied
90% were accepted
36% enrolled (752)
34% from top tenth of their h.s. class
17% had SAT verbal scores over 600
23% had SAT math scores over 600
52% had ACT scores over 26
2% had SAT verbal scores over 700
4% had SAT math scores over 700
13% had ACT scores over 30
1 National Merit Scholar

**THE STUDENT BODY**
Total 3,162, of whom 2,849
    are undergraduates

From 47 states and territories,
    48 other countries
55% from Indiana
57% women, 43% men
3% African Americans
0% Native Americans
1% Hispanics
1% Asian Americans
5% international students

**AFTER FRESHMAN YEAR**
85% returned for sophomore year
57% got a degree within 4 years

60% got a degree within 5 years

**AFTER GRADUATION**
12% pursued further study (4% arts and
    sciences, 2% business, 2% medicine)
22 corporations, 3 government agencies, 95
    nonprofit organizations recruited on campus
1 Fulbright scholar

**WHAT YOU WILL PAY**
Tuition and fees $11,800
Room and board $3790
Need-based financial aid averages $4239
Non-need financial aid averages $4697

# OF FLORIDA

ban setting • Public • State-supported • Coed

...universities, UF participates ...holars and students that ...ed people to address the ...blic land-grant research ...000 students from all 50 states and over 100 countries. As one of the most comprehensive institutions in the United States, it encompasses virtually all academic and professional disciplines. It is the oldest and largest university in Florida and a member of the prestigious American Association of Universities. UF's faculty and staff are dedicated to the common pursuit of the University's mission of teaching, research, and service.

## Academics

UF offers a diverse, interdisciplinary curriculum and core academic program; more than half of graduate courses are open to undergraduates. It awards bachelor's, master's, doctoral, and first professional **degrees**. Challenging opportunities include advanced placement, accelerated degree programs, self-designed majors, tutorials, an honors program, a senior project, Phi Beta Kappa, and Sigma Xi. Special programs include cooperative education, internships, summer session for credit, off-campus study, study abroad, and Army, Naval, and Air Force ROTC.

The most popular **majors** include psychology, finance/banking, and English. A complete listing of majors at UF appears in the Majors Index beginning on page 380.

The **faculty** at UF has 2,920 full-time graduate and undergraduate teachers, 97% with terminal degrees. 86% of the faculty serve as student advisers. The student-faculty ratio is 17:1.

## Computers on Campus

Students are not required to have a computer. 612 **computers** available in the computer center, computer labs, the research center, labs, classrooms, the library, the student center, and dormitories provide access to the main academic computer and e-mail. Staffed computer lab on campus (open 24 hours a day) provides training in the use of computers and software.

The 16 **libraries** have 3 million books and 24,191 subscriptions. They are connected to 4 national **on-line** catalogs.

## Campus Life

There are 420 active **organizations** on campus, including a drama/theater group and student-run newspaper and radio station. 15% of eligible men and 15% of eligible women are members of 28 national **fraternities** and 18 national **sororities**. Student **safety services** include late night transport/escort service, 24-hour emergency telephone alarm devices, 24-hour patrols by trained security personnel, student patrols, and electronically operated dormitory entrances.

UF is a member of the NCAA (Division I). **Intercollegiate sports** (some offering scholarships) include baseball (m), basketball (m, w), cross-country running (m, w), football (m), golf (m, w), gymnastics (w), swimming and diving (m, w), tennis (m, w), track and field (m, w), volleyball (w).

## Applying

UF requires a high school transcript, 3 years of high school math and science, 2 years of high school foreign language, and SAT I or ACT. Early and midyear entrance are possible, with a 2/1 deadline and continuous processing to 4/15 for financial aid. **Contact:** Admissions Office, 201 Criser Hall, Gainesville, FL 32611-8140, 904-392-1365.

**GETTING IN LAST YEAR**
12,571 applied
64% were accepted
41% enrolled (3,258)
50% from top tenth of their h.s. class
20% had SAT verbal scores over 600
59% had SAT math scores over 600
61% had ACT scores over 26
2% had SAT verbal scores over 700
16% had SAT math scores over 700
16% had ACT scores over 30
135 National Merit Scholars

**THE STUDENT BODY**
Total 38,277, of whom 28,479
 are undergraduates

From 52 states and territories,
 114 other countries
92% from Florida
53% women, 47% men
6% African Americans
9% Hispanics
6% Asian Americans

**AFTER FRESHMAN YEAR**
90% returned for sophomore year
32% got a degree within 4 years
58% got a degree within 5 years
64% got a degree within 6 years

**AFTER GRADUATION**
400 corporations, 35 government agencies,
 50 nonprofit organizations recruited on
 campus
6 Fulbright scholars

**WHAT YOU WILL PAY**
Resident tuition and fees $1820
Nonresident tuition and fees $7090
Room and board $4180
36% receive need-based financial aid
 averaging $1450
37% receive non-need financial aid averaging
 $1450

# UNIVERSITY OF GEORGIA

Athens, Georgia • Suburban setting • Public • State-supported • Coed

Academic excellence at the University of Georgia has taken a significant leap forward in the past decade. Although the University's fall 1994 freshman class was one fourth larger than 10 years ago, the average SAT score was 83 points higher, and 1 out of 5 freshmen had SAT scores in the top 90th percentile nationally. The Honors Program, one of the oldest and largest in the nation, provides a strengthened liberal arts foundation for undergraduates with many honors course alternatives for core classes and the opportunity for faculty-guided individual research and progress into graduate-level work.

##  Academics

UGA offers a core academic program; fewer than half of graduate courses are open to undergraduates. It awards associate, bachelor's, master's, doctoral, and first professional **degrees**. Challenging opportunities include advanced placement, accelerated degree programs, self-designed majors, an honors program, a senior project, Phi Beta Kappa, and Sigma Xi. Special programs include cooperative education, internships, summer session for credit, off-campus study, study abroad, and Army and Air Force ROTC.

The most popular **majors** include English, accounting, and political science/government. A complete listing of majors at UGA appears in the Majors Index beginning on page 380.

The **faculty** at UGA has 1,787 full-time graduate and undergraduate teachers, 94% with terminal degrees. The average class size in required courses is 33.

##  Computers on Campus

Students are not required to have a computer. Student rooms are linked to a campus network. 800 **computers** available in the computer center, computer labs, the research center, various campus facilities, the library, the student center, and dormitories provide access to the main academic computer, off-campus computing facilities, e-mail, and on-line services. Staffed computer lab on campus (open 24 hours a day) provides training in the use of computers and software.

The 3 **libraries** have 3 million books and 47,993 subscriptions. They are connected to 3 national **on-line** catalogs.

##  Campus Life

There are 400 active **organizations** on campus, including a drama/theater group and student-run newspaper and radio station. 19% of eligible men and 23% of eligible women are members of 24 national **fraternities** and 22 national **sororities**. Student **safety services** include late night transport/escort service, 24-hour emergency telephone alarm devices, 24-hour patrols by trained security personnel, and electronically operated dormitory entrances.

UGA is a member of the NCAA (Division I). **Intercollegiate sports** (some offering scholarships) include baseball (m), basketball (m, w), cross-country running (m, w), football (m), golf (m, w), gymnastics (w), soccer (m, w), swimming and diving (m, w), tennis (m, w), track and field (m, w), volleyball (m, w).

##  Applying

UGA requires a high school transcript, 3 years of high school math and science, 2 years of high school foreign language, and SAT I or ACT. Early, deferred, and midyear entrance are possible, with a 2/1 deadline and continuous processing to 3/1 for financial aid. **Contact:** Dr. John Albright, Associate Director of Admissions, Terrell Hall, Athens, GA 30602 .

---

### GETTING IN LAST YEAR
12,382 applied
64% were accepted
45% enrolled (3,555)
43% from top tenth of their h.s. class
3.39 average high school GPA
15% had SAT verbal scores over 600
35% had SAT math scores over 600
2% had SAT verbal scores over 700
6% had SAT math scores over 700
29 National Merit Scholars

### THE STUDENT BODY
Total 29,469, of whom 22,832
   are undergraduates

From 52 states and territories,
   115 other countries
84% from Georgia
54% women, 46% men
6% African Americans
1% Native Americans
1% Hispanics
2% Asian Americans
2% international students

### AFTER FRESHMAN YEAR
83% returned for sophomore year
31% got a degree within 4 years
57% got a degree within 5 years
62% got a degree within 6 years

### AFTER GRADUATION
446 corporations, 21 government agencies,
   18 nonprofit organizations recruited on
   campus
2 Fulbright scholars

### WHAT YOU WILL PAY
Resident tuition and fees $2352
Nonresident tuition and fees $6150
Room and board $3600
Need-based financial aid averages $900
Non-need financial aid averages $1400

---

# UNIVERSITY OF ILLINOIS AT URBANA-CHAMPAIGN

Champaign, Illinois • Small-town setting • Public • State-supported • Coed

▶ University of Illinois students say the quality of majors, academic reputation, and quality of the faculty are their most important reasons for choosing the University. The array of top-notch academic choices, including the nation's third-best engineering school (after Stanford and MIT) and number one accountancy program, combine with social and recreational opportunities plus competitive tuition (consistently in *Money* magazine's top 20 best buys) to make Illinois the right choice for highly motivated students who are after a first-class college experience.

 **Academics**

U of I offers a core academic program; fewer than half of graduate courses are open to undergraduates. It awards bachelor's, master's, doctoral, and first professional **degrees**. Challenging opportunities include advanced placement, accelerated degree programs, self-designed majors, tutorials, an honors program, a senior project, Phi Beta Kappa, and Sigma Xi. Special programs include cooperative education, internships, summer session for credit, off-campus study, study abroad, and Army, Naval, and Air Force ROTC.

The most popular **majors** include biology/biological sciences, psychology, and electrical engineering. A complete listing of majors at U of I appears in the Majors Index beginning on page 380.

The **faculty** at U of I has 1,932 full-time graduate and undergraduate teachers, 94% with terminal degrees. The student-faculty ratio is 13:1, and the average class size in required courses is 28.

## 🖥 Computers on Campus

Students are not required to have a computer. Student rooms are linked to a campus network. 3,000 **computers** available in the computer center, computer labs, labs, the library, the student center, and dormitories provide access to e-mail and on-line services. Staffed computer lab on campus (open 24 hours a day) provides training in the use of computers and software.

The 40 **libraries** have 8.5 million books and 91,000 subscriptions. They are connected to 19 national **on-line** catalogs.

 **Campus Life**

There are 617 active **organizations** on campus, including a drama/theater group and student-run newspaper and radio station. 15% of students participate in student government elections. 21% of eligible men and 26% of eligible women are members of 53 national **fraternities**, 25 national **sororities**, 3 local fraternities, and 2 local sororities. Student **safety services** include late night transport/escort service, 24-hour emergency telephone alarm devices, 24-hour patrols by trained security personnel, student patrols, and electronically operated dormitory entrances.

U of I is a member of the NCAA (Division I). **Intercollegiate sports** (some offering scholarships) include baseball (m), basketball (m, w), cross-country running (m, w), football (m), golf (m, w), gymnastics (m, w), swimming and diving (w), tennis (m, w), track and field (m, w), volleyball (w), wrestling (m).

## 📖 Applying

U of I requires a high school transcript, 3 years of high school math, 2 years of high school foreign language, SAT I or ACT, and in some cases an essay, an interview, and audition, statement of professional interest. Early and deferred entrance are possible, with a 1/1 deadline and continuous processing to 3/15 for financial aid. **Contact:** Ms. Tammy Bouseman, Assistant Director of Admissions, 10 Henry Administration Building, Urbana, IL 61820-5711, 217-333-0302.

---

### GETTING IN LAST YEAR
15,616 applied
76% were accepted
48% enrolled (5,734)
50% from top tenth of their h.s. class
41 National Merit Scholars

### THE STUDENT BODY
Total 36,191, of whom 26,348
  are undergraduates
From 50 states and territories,
  56 other countries
92% from Illinois
43% women, 57% men

7% African Americans
1% Native Americans
5% Hispanics
13% Asian Americans
2% international students

### AFTER FRESHMAN YEAR
91% returned for sophomore year
55% got a degree within 4 years
76% got a degree within 5 years
79% got a degree within 6 years

### AFTER GRADUATION
42% pursued further study
10 Fulbright scholars

### WHAT YOU WILL PAY
Resident tuition and fees $3680
Nonresident tuition and fees $8480
Room and board $4260
50% receive need-based financial aid
  averaging $1040
50% receive non-need financial aid averaging
  $1189

# THE UNIVERSITY OF IOWA

Iowa City, Iowa • Small-town setting • Public • State-supported • Coed

Iowa offers strong undergraduate programs in diverse areas, such as the health sciences, traditional liberal arts, and preprofessional programs. Undergraduates are exposed to outstanding opportunities and facilities, from the world-renowned Writer's Workshop to the top-ranked College of Medicine and University of Iowa Hospitals and Clinics, the largest university-owned teaching hospital in the United States. Popular undergraduate areas of study include business administration, engineering, communications, English, psychology, and premedical studies.

##  Academics

Iowa offers a liberal arts curriculum and core academic program; fewer than half of graduate courses are open to undergraduates. It awards bachelor's, master's, doctoral, and first professional **degrees**. Challenging opportunities include advanced placement, accelerated degree programs, self-designed majors, tutorials, an honors program, a senior project, Phi Beta Kappa, and Sigma Xi. Special programs include cooperative education, internships, summer session for credit, off-campus study, study abroad, and Army and Air Force ROTC.

The most popular **majors** include business, communication, and engineering (general). A complete listing of majors at Iowa appears in the Majors Index beginning on page 380.

The **faculty** at Iowa has 1,753 full-time graduate and undergraduate teachers, 99% with terminal degrees. The student-faculty ratio is 15:1, and the average class size in required courses is 21.

##  Computers on Campus

Students are not required to have a computer. 1,137 **computers** available in the computer center, computer labs, classroom buildings, classrooms, the library, the student center, and dormitories provide access to the main academic computer and e-mail. Staffed computer lab on campus (open 24 hours a day) provides training in the use of computers and software.

The **library** has 3.5 million books and 40,009 subscriptions. It is connected to 16 national **on-line** catalogs.

##  Campus Life

There are 337 active **organizations** on campus, including a drama/theater group and student-run newspaper and radio station. 14% of eligible men and 15% of eligible women are members of 25 national **fraternities** and 19 national **sororities**. Student **safety services** include late night transport/escort service, 24-hour emergency telephone alarm devices, and 24-hour patrols by trained security personnel.

Iowa is a member of the NCAA (Division I). **Intercollegiate sports** (some offering scholarships) include badminton (m, w), baseball (m), basketball (m, w), bowling (m, w), crew (m, w), cross-country running (m, w), field hockey (w), football (m), golf (m, w), gymnastics (m, w), ice hockey (m, w), lacrosse (m, w), rugby (m, w), sailing (m, w), soccer (m), softball (w), swimming and diving (m, w), table tennis (m, w), tennis (m, w), track and field (m, w), volleyball (m, w), wrestling (m).

##  Applying

Iowa requires a high school transcript, 3 years of high school math and science, 2 years of high school foreign language, and SAT I or ACT. It recommends a campus interview. Early, deferred, and midyear entrance are possible, with a 5/15 deadline and continuous processing to 1/1 for financial aid. **Contact:** Mr. Michael Barron, Director of Admissions, Calvin Hall, Iowa City, IA 52242, 319-335-3847 or toll-free 800-553-4692; fax 319-335-1535.

---

### GETTING IN LAST YEAR
9,548 applied
86% were accepted
41% enrolled (3,367)
22% from top tenth of their h.s. class
3.4 average high school GPA
37% had ACT scores over 26
9% had ACT scores over 30
23 National Merit Scholars
117 valedictorians

### THE STUDENT BODY
Total 26,932, of whom 18,219
  are undergraduates

From 52 states and territories,
  78 other countries
71% from Iowa
52% women, 48% men
2% African Americans
1% Native Americans
2% Hispanics
4% Asian Americans
3% international students

### AFTER FRESHMAN YEAR
85% returned for sophomore year
30% got a degree within 4 years
54% got a degree within 5 years

### AFTER GRADUATION
293 corporations, 13 government agencies, 4
  nonprofit organizations recruited on campus
6 Fulbright scholars

### WHAT YOU WILL PAY
Resident tuition and fees $2455
Nonresident tuition and fees $8313
Room and board $3468
75% receive need-based financial aid
  averaging $1590
Non-need financial aid averages $1704

---

# UNIVERSITY OF KANSAS

Lawrence, Kansas • Suburban setting • Public • State-supported • Coed

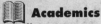 **Academics**

KU offers a core academic program; fewer than half of graduate courses are open to undergraduates. It awards bachelor's, master's, doctoral, and first professional **degrees** (The University of Kansas is a single institution with academic programs and facilities at two primary locations: Lawrence and Kansas City. Undergraduate, graduate, and professional education are the principal missions of the Lawrence campus, with medicine and related health professional education the focus of the Kansas City campus). Challenging opportunities include advanced placement, self-designed majors, tutorials, an honors program, a senior project, Phi Beta Kappa, and Sigma Xi. Special programs include cooperative education, internships, summer session for credit, study abroad, and Army, Naval, and Air Force ROTC.

The most popular **majors** include journalism, business, and psychology. A complete listing of majors at KU appears in the Majors Index beginning on page 380.

The **faculty** at KU has 1,661 full-time graduate and undergraduate teachers, 96% with terminal degrees. The student-faculty ratio is 16:1, and the average class size in required courses is 30.

 **Computers on Campus**

Students are not required to have a computer. 550 **computers** available in the computer center, computer labs, classrooms, the library, and dormitories provide access to the main academic computer, e-mail, and on-line services. Staffed computer lab on campus (open 24 hours a day) provides training in the use of computers and software.

The 12 **libraries** have 3.3 million books, 2.8 million microform titles, and 33,051 subscriptions. They are connected to 18 national **on-line** catalogs.

 **Campus Life**

There are 300 active **organizations** on campus, including a drama/theater group and student-run newspaper and radio station. 21% of eligible men and 23% of eligible women are members of 27 national **fraternities** and 18 national **sororities**. Student **safety services** include late night transport/escort service, 24-hour emergency telephone alarm devices, 24-hour patrols by trained security personnel, and electronically operated dormitory entrances.

KU is a member of the NCAA (Division I). **Intercollegiate sports** (some offering scholarships) include baseball (m), basketball (m, w), crew (m, w), cross-country running (m, w), fencing (m, w), football (m), golf (m, w), ice hockey (m), lacrosse (m, w), racquetball (m, w), rugby (m, w), soccer (m, w), softball (w), swimming and diving (m, w), tennis (m, w), track and field (m, w), volleyball (m, w), wrestling (m).

 **Applying**

KU requires a high school transcript, SAT I or ACT, and in some cases a minimum high school GPA of 3.0. It recommends 3 years of high school math and science and some high school foreign language. Early and midyear entrance are possible, with a 4/1 deadline, 2/1 deadline for nonresidents and continuous processing to 3/1 for financial aid. **Contact:** Ms. Deborah Castrop, Director of Admissions, 126 Strong Hall, Lawrence, KS 66045-1910, 913-864-3911.

---

**GETTING IN LAST YEAR**

8,029 applied
70% were accepted
58% enrolled (3,278)
32% had ACT scores over 26
9% had ACT scores over 30
42 National Merit Scholars

**THE STUDENT BODY**

Total 28,046, of whom 18,804 are undergraduates

From 54 states and territories, 113 other countries
69% from Kansas
50% women, 50% men
3% African Americans
1% Native Americans
2% Hispanics
3% Asian Americans
6% international students

**AFTER FRESHMAN YEAR**

80% returned for sophomore year
25% got a degree within 4 years
49% got a degree within 5 years
55% got a degree within 6 years

**WHAT YOU WILL PAY**

Resident tuition and fees $2038
Nonresident tuition and fees $7382
Room and board $3384
Need-based financial aid averages $689
Non-need financial aid averages $900

---

# UNIVERSITY OF MARYLAND COLLEGE PARK

College Park, Maryland • Suburban setting • Public • State-supported • Coed

Students at Maryland discover many realities. They learn the foundations of a discipline, rigors of research, responsibilities of independence, and common ground of personality and culture. The University's contribution is measured in intellectual challenge, in the degree of commitment and support offered by the faculty, and in the fair measure of a student's performance. The facilities and equipment support academic quality, and the University's connection to the resources of the Baltimore-Washington area supports career development and research opportunities. The faculty provides advice that guides but does not limit, instruction that illuminates and inspires, and experience that strengthens confidence and builds skills.

## Academics

UMCP offers a core academic program. It awards bachelor's, master's, and doctoral **degrees**. Challenging opportunities include advanced placement, accelerated degree programs, self-designed majors, tutorials, an honors program, a senior project, Phi Beta Kappa, and Sigma Xi. Special programs include cooperative education, internships, summer session for credit, off-campus study, study abroad, and Naval and Air Force ROTC.

The most popular **majors** include political science/government, computer science, and electrical engineering. A complete listing of majors at UMCP appears in the Majors Index beginning on page 380.

The **faculty** at UMCP has 1,196 full-time graduate and undergraduate teachers, 97% with terminal degrees. The student-faculty ratio is 13:1, and the average class size in required courses is 28.

## Computers on Campus

Students are not required to have a computer. Student rooms are linked to a campus network. 1,500 **computers** available in the computer center, computer labs, academic buildings, the library, and dormitories. Staffed computer lab on campus (open 24 hours a day) provides training in the use of computers and software.

The 6 **libraries** have 2.2 million books and 19,433 subscriptions.

## Campus Life

There are 300 active **organizations** on campus, including a drama/theater group and student-run newspaper and radio station. 12% of eligible men and 15% of eligible women are members of 27 national **fraternities** and 19 national **sororities**. Student **safety services** include campus police, late night transport/escort service, 24-hour emergency telephone alarm devices, student patrols, and electronically operated dormitory entrances.

UMCP is a member of the NCAA (Division I). **Intercollegiate sports** (some offering scholarships) include baseball (m), basketball (m, w), cross-country running (m, w), field hockey (w), football (m), golf (m), gymnastics (w), lacrosse (m, w), soccer (m, w), softball (w), swimming and diving (m, w), tennis (m, w), track and field (m, w), volleyball (w), wrestling (m).

## Applying

UMCP requires a high school transcript, 3 years of high school math, 2 years of high school foreign language, SAT I or ACT, and in some cases an essay, recommendations, and a campus interview. It recommends 3 years of high school science. Early and midyear entrance are possible, with a 4/30 deadline and continuous processing to 2/15 for financial aid. **Contact:** Dr. Linda Clement, Director of Admissions, 130 Mitchell Building, College Park, MD 20742, 301-314-8385 or toll-free 800-422-5867.

---

### GETTING IN LAST YEAR
14,697 applied
72% were accepted
37% enrolled (3,839)
24% from top tenth of their h.s. class
3.21 average high school GPA
15% had SAT verbal scores over 600
46% had SAT math scores over 600
2% had SAT verbal scores over 700
10% had SAT math scores over 700
30 National Merit Scholars

### THE STUDENT BODY
Total 32,493, of whom 23,724
  are undergraduates

From 46 states and territories,
  68 other countries
75% from Maryland
47% women, 53% men
12% African Americans
1% Native Americans
4% Hispanics
14% Asian Americans
3% international students

### AFTER FRESHMAN YEAR
83% returned for sophomore year
24% got a degree within 4 years
52% got a degree within 5 years
60% got a degree within 6 years

### AFTER GRADUATION
31% pursued further study (12% arts and
  sciences, 12% dentistry, 4% business)
307 corporations, 113 government agencies,
  38 nonprofit organizations recruited on
  campus
4 Fulbright scholars

### WHAT YOU WILL PAY
Resident tuition and fees $3480
Nonresident tuition and fees $9284
Room and board $5146
Need-based financial aid averages $1320
Non-need financial aid averages $3146

# UNIVERSITY OF MASSACHUSETTS AMHERST

Amherst, Massachusetts • Small-town setting • Public • State-supported • Coed

The operative word for students at UMass Amherst is "choice." More than 80 academic majors, the largest library at a public school in the Northeast, and 3,800 courses per semester provide for almost limitless academic exploration. The Honors Program gives students the opportunity to work more closely with faculty. Through the Five College Consortium, students can choose classes at Amherst, Hampshire, Mount Holyoke, and Smith colleges at no extra charge. And the campus enjoys a friendly New England college-town setting.

##  Academics

UMass Amherst offers an interdisciplinary curriculum and core academic program; all graduate courses are open to undergraduates. It awards associate, bachelor's, master's, and doctoral **degrees**. Challenging opportunities include advanced placement, self-designed majors, tutorials, an honors program, a senior project, Phi Beta Kappa, and Sigma Xi. Special programs include cooperative education, internships, summer session for credit, off-campus study, study abroad, and Army and Air Force ROTC.

The most popular **majors** include psychology, English, and hotel and restaurant management. A complete listing of majors at UMass Amherst appears in the Majors Index beginning on page 380.

The **faculty** at UMass Amherst has 1,174 full-time graduate and undergraduate teachers, 96% with terminal degrees. The student-faculty ratio is 17:1, and the average class size in required courses is 66.

##  Computers on Campus

Students are not required to have a computer. Student rooms are linked to a campus network. 1,000 **computers** available in computer labs, academic buildings, the library, and dormitories provide access to the main academic computer, off-campus computing facilities, e-mail, and on-line services. Staffed computer lab on campus.

The 4 **libraries** have 2.6 million books, 2.1 million microform titles, and 15,312 subscriptions. They are connected to 8 national **on-line** catalogs.

##  Campus Life

There are 177 active **organizations** on campus, including a drama/theater group and student-run newspaper and radio station. 25% of students participate in student government elections. 8% of eligible men and 6% of eligible women are members of 21 national **fraternities**, 12 national **sororities**, 1 local fraternity, and 1 local sorority. Student **safety services** include locked dormitories at night and during weekends, late night transport/escort service, 24-hour emergency telephone alarm devices, 24-hour patrols by trained security personnel, and electronically operated dormitory entrances.

UMass Amherst is a member of the NCAA (Division I). **Intercollegiate sports** (some offering scholarships) include baseball (m), basketball (m, w), cross-country running (m, w), equestrian sports (m, w), field hockey (w), football (m), gymnastics (m, w), ice hockey (m), lacrosse (m, w), skiing (cross-country) (m, w), skiing (downhill) (m, w), soccer (m, w), softball (w), swimming and diving (m, w), tennis (m, w), track and field (m, w), volleyball (w), water polo (m).

##  Applying

UMass Amherst requires an essay, a high school transcript, 3 years of high school math, 2 years of high school foreign language, SAT I or ACT, and in some cases 3 years of high school science. It recommends recommendations and SAT II Subject Tests. Early, deferred, and midyear entrance are possible, with a 2/15 deadline and continuous processing to 3/1 for financial aid. **Contact:** Ms. Arlene Cash, Director of Undergraduate Admissions, Box 30120, Amherst, MA 01003-0120, 413-545-0222.

---

### GETTING IN LAST YEAR
16,052 applied
85% were accepted
29% enrolled (3,913)
12% from top tenth of their h.s. class
3.0 average high school GPA
7% had SAT verbal scores over 600
24% had SAT math scores over 600
1% had SAT verbal scores over 700
4% had SAT math scores over 700

### THE STUDENT BODY
Total 22,332, of whom 17,422
    are undergraduates

From 51 states and territories,
    78 other countries
75% from Massachusetts
48% women, 52% men
4% African Americans
1% Native Americans
4% Hispanics
6% Asian Americans
3% international students

### AFTER FRESHMAN YEAR
77% returned for sophomore year
47% got a degree within 4 years
64% got a degree within 5 years
67% got a degree within 6 years

### AFTER GRADUATION
39% pursued further study (20% arts and
    sciences, 6% business, 3% law)
500 corporations, 250 government agencies,
    80 nonprofit organizations recruited on
    campus
2 Fulbright scholars

### WHAT YOU WILL PAY
Resident tuition and fees $5467
Nonresident tuition and fees $11,813
Room and board $4028
Need-based financial aid averages $1500
Non-need financial aid averages $2000

# UNIVERSITY OF MIAMI

Coral Gables, Florida • Suburban setting • Private • Independent • Coed

The University of Miami is moderate in size for a major research university (8,000 undergraduates) but comprehensive with 130 majors. UM features the intimacy of a small school by virtue of its residential college system, where students live with a faculty master and associate masters. Three fourths of all undergraduate classes have 25 or fewer students. Study-abroad programs are available in 22 countries and 51 universities. The location of the University in suburban Coral Gables is just a Metrorail ride away from booming Metropolitan Miami—a city of the 21st century—and offers students a magnificent array of cultural and career opportunities.

 **Academics**

UM offers a general education curriculum and core academic program. It awards bachelor's, master's, doctoral, and first professional **degrees**. Challenging opportunities include advanced placement, accelerated degree programs, self-designed majors, tutorials, an honors program, a senior project, Phi Beta Kappa, and Sigma Xi. Special programs include internships, summer session for credit, study abroad, and Army and Air Force ROTC.

The most popular **majors** include psychology, biology/biological sciences, and finance/banking. A complete listing of majors at UM appears in the Majors Index beginning on page 380.

The **faculty** at UM has 956 full-time graduate and undergraduate teachers, 95% with terminal degrees. The student-faculty ratio is 7:1.

 **Computers on Campus**

Students are not required to have a computer. 2,000 **computers** available in the computer center, computer labs, the research center, the learning resource center, academic departments, classrooms, the library, the student center, and dormitories provide access to the main academic computer, off-campus computing facilities, e-mail, and on-line services. Staffed computer lab on campus (open 24 hours a day).

The 3 **libraries** have 2 million books, 3 million microform titles, and 19,025 subscriptions. They are connected to 4 national **on-line** catalogs.

 **Campus Life**

There are 200 active **organizations** on campus, including a drama/theater group and student-run newspaper and radio station. 10% of students participate in student government elections. 15% of eligible men and 13% of eligible women are members of 15 national **fraternities** and 10 national **sororities**. Student **safety services** include crime prevention workshops, late night transport/escort service, 24-hour emergency telephone alarm devices, 24-hour patrols by trained security personnel, student patrols, and electronically operated dormitory entrances.

UM is a member of the NCAA (Division I). **Intercollegiate sports** (some offering scholarships) include baseball (m), basketball (m, w), crew (m, w), cross-country running (m, w), football (m), golf (w), swimming and diving (m, w), tennis (m, w), track and field (m, w).

 **Applying**

UM requires an essay, a high school transcript, 1 recommendation, SAT I or ACT, and in some cases SAT II Subject Tests. It recommends 3 years of high school math and science, some high school foreign language, and an interview. Early, deferred, and midyear entrance are possible, with a 3/1 deadline and continuous processing to 2/15 for financial aid. **Contact:** Mr. Edward M. Gillis, Associate Dean of Enrollments, PO Box 248025, Coral Gables, FL 33124, 305-284-4323.

## GETTING IN LAST YEAR

9,044 applied
59% were accepted
29% enrolled (1,553)
43% from top tenth of their h.s. class
15% had SAT verbal scores over 600
39% had SAT math scores over 600
44% had ACT scores over 26
2% had SAT verbal scores over 700
9% had SAT math scores over 700
13% had ACT scores over 30
10 National Merit Scholars
28 valedictorians

## THE STUDENT BODY

Total 13,410, of whom 8,046 are undergraduates
From 51 states and territories, 108 other countries
49% from Florida
49% women, 51% men
9% African Americans
1% Native Americans
25% Hispanics
4% Asian Americans
10% international students

## AFTER GRADUATION

136 corporations, 18 government agencies, 2 nonprofit organizations recruited on campus
2 Fulbright scholars

## WHAT YOU WILL PAY

Tuition and fees $17,700
Room and board $6852

# UNIVERSITY OF MICHIGAN

Ann Arbor, Michigan • Suburban setting • Public • State-supported • Coed

▶ The University of Michigan is an arena for excitement and diversity. With over 3,500 microcomputer terminals, Michigan is always at the forefront of technology, offering students exemplary resources. The Undergraduate Research Opportunity Program gives first- and second-year students the experience of working closely with faculty in areas ranging from archaeology to genetics.

 **Academics**

Michigan offers no core academic program; more than half of graduate courses are open to undergraduates. It awards bachelor's, master's, doctoral, and first professional **degrees**. Challenging opportunities include advanced placement, accelerated degree programs, self-designed majors, tutorials, an honors program, a senior project, Phi Beta Kappa, and Sigma Xi. Special programs include cooperative education, internships, summer session for credit, off-campus study, study abroad, and Army, Naval, and Air Force ROTC.

The most popular **majors** include psychology, mechanical engineering, and English. A complete listing of majors at Michigan appears in the Majors Index beginning on page 380.

The **faculty** at Michigan has 2,717 full-time graduate and undergraduate teachers, 95% with terminal degrees. The student-faculty ratio is 12:1, and the average class size in required courses is 28.

 **Computers on Campus**

Students are not required to have a computer. Student rooms are linked to a campus network. 3,500 **computers** available in the computer center, computer labs, the learning resource center, academic buildings, the library, the student center, dormitories, and student rooms provide access to the main academic computer, off-campus computing facili-

ties, e-mail, and on-line services. Staffed computer lab on campus (open 24 hours a day) provides training in the use of computers and software.

The 18 **libraries** have 6.6 million books, 5.1 million microform titles, and 70,336 subscriptions. They are connected to 12 national **on-line** catalogs.

 **Campus Life**

There are 400 active **organizations** on campus, including a drama/theater group and student-run newspaper and radio station. 22% of eligible men and 22% of eligible women are members of 37 national **fraternities**, 22 national **sororities**, 2 local fraternities, and 1 local sorority. Student **safety services** include late night transport/escort service, 24-hour emergency telephone alarm devices, 24-hour patrols by trained security personnel, and electronically operated dormitory entrances.

Michigan is a member of the NCAA (Division I). **Intercollegiate sports** (some offering scholarships) include baseball (m), basketball (m, w), cross-country running (m, w), field hockey (w), football (m), golf (m, w), gymnastics (m, w), ice hockey (m), softball (w), swimming and diving (m, w), tennis (m, w), track and field (m, w), volleyball (w), wrestling (m).

**Applying**

Michigan requires an essay, a high school transcript, SAT I or ACT, and in some cases 3 years of high school math, recommendations, and an interview. It recommends 3 years of high school science and some high school foreign language. Early, deferred, and midyear entrance are possible, with a 2/1 deadline and continuous processing to 2/1 for financial aid. **Contact:** Mr. Ted Spencer, Director of Undergraduate Admissions, 515 East Jefferson, Ann Arbor, MI 48109-1316, 313-764-7433; fax 313-936-0740.

---

**GETTING IN LAST YEAR**
19,393 applied
68% were accepted
37% enrolled (4,891)
65% from top tenth of their h.s. class
3.6 average high school GPA
27% had SAT verbal scores over 600
71% had SAT math scores over 600
70% had ACT scores over 26
3% had SAT verbal scores over 700
27% had SAT math scores over 700
28% had ACT scores over 30
59 National Merit Scholars

**THE STUDENT BODY**
Total 36,543, of whom 23,238
  are undergraduates

From 52 states and territories,
  74 other countries
67% from Michigan
48% women, 52% men
8% African Americans
1% Native Americans
5% Hispanics
11% Asian Americans
3% international students

**AFTER FRESHMAN YEAR**
94% returned for sophomore year
63% got a degree within 4 years
83% got a degree within 5 years
85% got a degree within 6 years

**AFTER GRADUATION**
307 corporations, 16 government agencies,
  39 nonprofit organizations recruited on
  campus
13 Fulbright scholars

**WHAT YOU WILL PAY**
Resident tuition and fees $5215
Nonresident tuition and fees $15,907
Room and board $4659
38% receive need-based financial aid
  averaging $3300
8% receive non-need financial aid averaging
  $2400

# UNIVERSITY OF MICHIGAN–DEARBORN

Dearborn, Michigan • Suburban setting • Public • State-supported • Coed

 Since its founding 35 years ago, the University of Michigan–Dearborn has been distinguished by its commitment to provide outstanding educational opportunities to nearly 8,000 of the most academically qualified students in southeastern Michigan. While many UM-Dearborn students work full- or part-time, many others elect to participate in internships and co-op placements that provide an opportunity for them to combine practical on-the-job experience with the University of Michigan tradition of scholarship and excellence. It is understandable why new UM-Dearborn students have identified academic reputation and excellent jobs after graduation as the 2 primary reasons for enrolling at UM-Dearborn.

## Academics

UM-D offers a core academic program. It awards bachelor's and master's **degrees**. Challenging opportunities include accelerated degree programs, self-designed majors, and an honors program. Special programs include cooperative education, internships, summer session for credit, off-campus study, study abroad, and Army, Naval, and Air Force ROTC.

The most popular **majors** include mechanical engineering, electrical engineering, and psychology. A complete listing of majors at UM-D appears in the Majors Index beginning on page 380.

The **faculty** at UM-D has 203 full-time undergraduate teachers, 84% with terminal degrees. The student-faculty ratio is 21:1.

 **Computers on Campus**

Students are not required to have a computer. 350 **computers** available in the computer center, computer labs, and engineering and writing labs. Staffed computer lab on campus provides training in the use of computers and software.

The **library** has 299,792 books, 432,298 microform titles, and 1,169 subscriptions.

 **Campus Life**

Active **organizations** on campus include drama/theater group and student-run newspaper and radio station. 6% of eligible men and 5% of eligible women are members of 8 national **fraternities** and 4 national **sororities**. Student **safety services** include late night transport/escort service, 24-hour emergency telephone alarm devices, and 24-hour patrols by trained security personnel.

UM-D is a member of the NAIA. **Intercollegiate sports** (some offering scholarships) include basketball (m, w), volleyball (w).

 **Applying**

UM-D requires a high school transcript, SAT I or ACT, and in some cases recommendations and an interview. It recommends 3 years of high school math and science and some high school foreign language. Early entrance is possible, with rolling admissions and continuous processing to 4/1 for financial aid. **Contact:** Ms. Carol S. Mack, Director of Admissions, 4901 Evergreen Road, Dearborn, MI 48128-1491, 313-593-5100.

---

**GETTING IN LAST YEAR**
1,881 applied
74% were accepted
52% enrolled (715)
37% from top tenth of their h.s. class
3.24 average high school GPA
10% had SAT verbal scores over 600
28% had SAT math scores over 600
22% had ACT scores over 26
0% had SAT verbal scores over 700
7% had SAT math scores over 700
2% had ACT scores over 30

**THE STUDENT BODY**
Total 7,453, of whom 6,232 are undergraduates
From 7 states and territories
99% from Michigan
53% women, 47% men
7% African Americans
1% Native Americans
2% Hispanics
4% Asian Americans

**AFTER FRESHMAN YEAR**
82% returned for sophomore year

**AFTER GRADUATION**
105 corporations recruited on campus

**WHAT YOU WILL PAY**
Resident tuition and fees $3540
Nonresident tuition and fees $10,884
Need-based financial aid averages $715
Non-need financial aid averages $1092

# UNIVERSITY OF MINNESOTA, MORRIS

Morris, Minnesota • Small-town setting • Public • State-supported • Coed

The University of Minnesota, Morris, is in the forefront of the nation's small, undergraduate liberal arts colleges. It has become known for a select student body, intellectual excitement and rigor, innovative curriculum, and concern for the participatory quality of student life. The Morris campus promotes close faculty-student interaction, particularly in the popular Undergraduate Research Opportunities Program (UROP) and the Morris Academic Partners (junior-year mentorships). Both activities provide grants for students as well as opportunities for research collaboration with faculty.

 ## Academics

UMM offers a core academic program. It awards bachelor's **degrees**. Challenging opportunities include advanced placement, accelerated degree programs, self-designed majors, an honors program, and a senior project. Special programs include internships, summer session for credit, off-campus study, and study abroad.

The most popular **majors** include English, education, and biology/biological sciences. A complete listing of majors at UMM appears in the Majors Index beginning on page 380.

The **faculty** at UMM has 128 full-time teachers. The student-faculty ratio is 15:1.

 ## Computers on Campus

Students are not required to have a computer. 140 **computers** available in the computer center, computer labs, the research center, the learning resource center, science building, the library, the student center, and dormitories.

The **library** has 152,000 books and 880 subscriptions.

 ## Campus Life

Active **organizations** on campus include drama/theater group and student-run newspaper and radio station. 1% of eligible men and 1% of eligible women are members of 3 national **fraternities** and 2 local **sororities**. Student **safety services** include late night transport/escort service and 24-hour patrols by trained security personnel.

UMM is a member of the NAIA. **Intercollegiate sports** include baseball (m), basketball (m, w), football (m), golf (m, w), softball (w), tennis (m, w), track and field (m, w), volleyball (w), wrestling (m).

 ## Applying

UMM requires a high school transcript, 3 years of high school math and science, 2 years of high school foreign language, ACT, and in some cases an essay. It recommends recommendations and an interview. Early and deferred entrance are possible, with a 3/15 deadline and continuous processing to 4/1 for financial aid. **Contact:** Mr. Robert J. Vikander, Director of Admissions and Financial Aid, Behmler Hall, Morris, MN 56267, 612-589-6035 or toll-free 800-992-8863; fax 612-589-1673.

### GETTING IN LAST YEAR

1,458 applied
60% were accepted
67% enrolled (588)
54% from top tenth of their h.s. class
27% had SAT verbal scores over 600
50% had SAT math scores over 600
52% had ACT scores over 26
5% had SAT verbal scores over 700
18% had SAT math scores over 700
11% had ACT scores over 30
21 National Merit Scholars

### THE STUDENT BODY

1,933 undergraduates
From 22 states and territories,
 11 other countries
79% from Minnesota
55% women, 45% men
4% African Americans
3% Native Americans
1% Hispanics
4% Asian Americans
1% international students

### AFTER FRESHMAN YEAR

89% returned for sophomore year

### AFTER GRADUATION

24% pursued further study (11% arts and sciences, 4% business, 2% engineering)
12 corporations, 10 government agencies, 6 nonprofit organizations recruited on campus

### WHAT YOU WILL PAY

Resident tuition and fees $3888
Nonresident tuition and fees $10,725
Room and board $3246
Need-based financial aid averages $1123
Non-need financial aid averages $1404

# UNIVERSITY OF MINNESOTA, TWIN CITIES CAMPUS

Minneapolis, Minnesota • Urban setting • Public • State-supported • Coed

On this beautiful Big Ten campus in the heart of the Twin Cities of Minneapolis and St. Paul, the hallmarks are quality and opportunity. The quality of a U of M–Twin Cities education is a matter of record. And so are the opportunities—nearly 200 undergraduate and 180 graduate and professional degree programs, many nationally ranked; an Undergraduate Research Opportunities Program that is a national model; one of the largest study-abroad programs in the country; the fifteenth-largest university library system in the country; extraordinary opportunities for internships, employment, and personal enrichment in the culturally rich and thriving Twin Cities area; and more than 400 student organizations.

 **Academics**

U of M offers a diversified core curriculum and core academic program; more than half of graduate courses are open to undergraduates. It awards bachelor's, master's, doctoral, and first professional **degrees**. Challenging opportunities include advanced placement, accelerated degree programs, self-designed majors, tutorials, Freshmen Honors College, an honors program, a senior project, Phi Beta Kappa, and Sigma Xi. Special programs include cooperative education, internships, summer session for credit, off-campus study, study abroad, and Army, Naval, and Air Force ROTC.

The most popular **majors** include mechanical engineering, electrical engineering, and psychology. A complete listing of majors at U of M appears in the Majors Index beginning on page 380.

The **faculty** at U of M has 2,663 full-time graduate and undergraduate teachers, 91% with terminal degrees. The student-faculty ratio is 15:1.

 **Computers on Campus**

Students are not required to have a computer. 20,000 **computers** available in the computer center, computer labs, the learning resource center, the library, the student center, and dormitories.

The 18 **libraries** have 5 million books and 52,018 subscriptions. They are connected to 4 national **on-line** catalogs.

 **Campus Life**

Active **organizations** on campus include a drama/theater group and student-run newspaper and radio station. 3% of eligible men and 3% of eligible women are members of 27 national **fraternities**, 15 national **sororities**, and 2 local sororities. Student **safety services** include victim assistance programs, safety/security orientation, security lighting, late night transport/escort service, 24-hour emergency telephone alarm devices, 24-hour patrols by trained security personnel, student patrols, and electronically operated dormitory entrances.

U of M is a member of the NCAA (Division I). **Intercollegiate sports** (some offering scholarships) include baseball (m), basketball (m, w), cross-country running (m, w), football (m), golf (m, w), gymnastics (m, w), ice hockey (m), swimming and diving (m, w), tennis (m, w), track and field (m, w), volleyball (w), wrestling (m).

 **Applying**

U of M requires a high school transcript, 3 years of high school math and science, 2 years of high school foreign language, ACT, and in some cases SAT I and a minimum high school GPA of 3.0. It recommends a minimum high school GPA of 2.0. Early, deferred, and midyear entrance are possible, with rolling admissions and continuous processing to 4/30 for financial aid. **Contact:** Dr. Wayne Sigler, Director of Admissions, 240 Williamson, Minneapolis, MN 55455-0213, 612-625-2006 or toll-free 800-752-1000; fax 612-626-1693.

| GETTING IN LAST YEAR | THE STUDENT BODY | |
|---|---|---|
| 11,703 applied | Total 36,699, of whom 23,238 | 8% Asian Americans |
| 56% were accepted | are undergraduates | 2% international students |
| 55% enrolled (3,645) | From 55 states and territories, | |
| 28% from top tenth of their h.s. class | 85 other countries | **AFTER FRESHMAN YEAR** |
| 16% had SAT verbal scores over 600 | 76% from Minnesota | 79% returned for sophomore year |
| 47% had SAT math scores over 600 | 49% women, 51% men | |
| 37% had ACT scores over 26 | 3% African Americans | **WHAT YOU WILL PAY** |
| 2% had SAT verbal scores over 700 | 1% Native Americans | Resident tuition and fees $3826 |
| 14% had SAT math scores over 700 | 2% Hispanics | Nonresident tuition and fees $9621 |
| 9% had ACT scores over 30 | | Room and board $3774 |
| 136 valedictorians | | |

# UNIVERSITY OF MISSOURI–COLUMBIA

Columbia, Missouri • Small-town setting • Public • State-supported • Coed

 **Academics**

MU offers a core academic program. It awards bachelor's, master's, doctoral, and first professional **degrees**. Challenging opportunities include advanced placement, accelerated degree programs, self-designed majors, tutorials, Freshmen Honors College, an honors program, a senior project, Phi Beta Kappa, and Sigma Xi. Special programs include cooperative education, internships, summer session for credit, off-campus study, study abroad, and Army, Naval, and Air Force ROTC.

The most popular **majors** include business, journalism, and psychology. A complete listing of majors at MU appears in the Majors Index beginning on page 380.

The **faculty** at MU has 1,512 full-time undergraduate teachers, 87% with terminal degrees. The student-faculty ratio is 19:1.

 **Campus Life**

There are 404 active **organizations** on campus, including a drama/theater group and student-run newspaper and radio station. 11% of students participate in student government elections. 25% of eligible men and 25% of eligible women are members of 33 national **fraternities** and 19 national **sororities**. Student **safety services** include late night transport/escort service, 24-hour emergency telephone alarm devices, and electronically operated dormitory entrances.

MU is a member of the NCAA (Division I). **Intercollegiate sports** (some offering scholarships) include baseball (m), basketball (m, w), cross-country running (m, w), football (m), golf (m, w), gymnastics (w), softball (w), swimming and diving (m, w), tennis (m, w), track and field (m, w), volleyball (w), wrestling (m).

 **Computers on Campus**

Students are not required to have a computer. Student rooms are linked to a campus network. 800 **computers** available in the computer center, computer labs, classrooms, the library, the student center, and dormitories provide access to e-mail and on-line services. Staffed computer lab on campus (open 24 hours a day) provides training in the use of computers and software.

The 11 **libraries** have 2.6 million books, 5.1 million microform titles, and 22,973 subscriptions. They are connected to 200 national **on-line** catalogs.

**Applying**

MU requires a high school transcript, 3 years of high school math, and ACT. It recommends 3 years of high school science and 2 years of high school foreign language. Early, deferred, and midyear entrance are possible, with a 5/1 deadline and a 3/1 priority date for financial aid. **Contact:** Ms. Georgeanne Porter, Director of Undergraduate Admissions, 130 Jesse Hall, Columbia, MO 65211, 314-882-7786 or toll-free 800-225-6075 (in-state); fax 314-882-7887.

**GETTING IN LAST YEAR**
7,880 applied
90% were accepted
51% enrolled (3,635)
31% from top tenth of their h.s. class
41% had ACT scores over 26
15% had ACT scores over 30
21 National Merit Scholars

**THE STUDENT BODY**
Total 22,136, of whom 16,436
   are undergraduates
From 50 states and territories,
   117 other countries

84% from Missouri
52% women, 48% men
5% African Americans
1% Native Americans
1% Hispanics
2% Asian Americans
7% international students

**AFTER FRESHMAN YEAR**
82% returned for sophomore year
30% got a degree within 4 years
55% got a degree within 5 years
59% got a degree within 6 years

**AFTER GRADUATION**
475 corporations recruited on campus
6 Fulbright scholars

**WHAT YOU WILL PAY**
Resident tuition and fees $3765
Nonresident tuition and fees $10,785
Room and board $3645
Need-based financial aid averages $991
Non-need financial aid averages $2137

# UNIVERSITY OF MISSOURI–KANSAS CITY

Kansas City, Missouri • Urban setting • Public • State-supported • Coed

## Academics

UMKC offers a core academic program; fewer than half of graduate courses are open to undergraduates. It awards bachelor's, master's, doctoral, and first professional **degrees**. Challenging opportunities include advanced placement, accelerated degree programs, self-designed majors, an honors program, and a senior project. Special programs include cooperative education, internships, summer session for credit, off-campus study, study abroad, and Army ROTC.

The most popular **majors** include biology/biological sciences, liberal arts/general studies, and business. A complete listing of majors at UMKC appears in the Majors Index beginning on page 380.

The **faculty** at UMKC has 546 full-time undergraduate teachers, 75% with terminal degrees.

## Computers on Campus

Students are not required to have a computer. Student rooms are linked to a campus network. 400 **computers** available in the computer center, computer labs, the research center, the learning resource center, classrooms, the library, the student center, and dormitories provide access to the main academic computer, off-campus computing facilities, e-mail, and on-line services. Staffed computer lab on campus provides training in the use of computers and software.

The 4 **libraries** have 942,116 books, 515,778 microform titles, and 8,764 subscriptions. They are connected to 8 national **on-line** catalogs.

## Campus Life

There are 75 active **organizations** on campus, including a drama/theater group and student-run newspaper. 5% of eligible men and 4% of eligible women are members of 4 national **fraternities**, 3 national **sororities**, and 1 local sorority. Student **safety services** include late night transport/escort service, 24-hour emergency telephone alarm devices, and 24-hour patrols by trained security personnel.

UMKC is a member of the NCAA (Division I). **Intercollegiate sports** (some offering scholarships) include basketball (m, w), cross-country running (m, w), golf (m, w), riflery (m, w), soccer (m), softball (w), tennis (m, w), track and field (m, w), volleyball (w).

## Applying

UMKC requires a high school transcript, 3 years of high school math, 4 years of high school English, 2 years each of science and social science, 1 year of fine arts, and ACT. Early, deferred, and midyear entrance are possible, with rolling admissions and continuous processing to 3/15 for financial aid. **Contact:** Mr. Mel Tyer, Director of Admissions, 5100 Rockhill Road, Kansas City, MO 64110-2499, 816-235-1111; fax 816-235-1717.

---

### GETTING IN LAST YEAR
1,765 applied
61% were accepted
49% enrolled (526)
37% from top tenth of their h.s. class
43% had ACT scores over 26
16% had ACT scores over 30

### THE STUDENT BODY
Total 9,962, of whom 5,319
  are undergraduates
From 43 states and territories,
  63 other countries

75% from Missouri
53% women, 47% men
8% African Americans
1% Native Americans
3% Hispanics
4% Asian Americans
7% international students

### AFTER FRESHMAN YEAR
66% returned for sophomore year
12% got a degree within 4 years
26% got a degree within 5 years
39% got a degree within 6 years

### AFTER GRADUATION
180 corporations, 35 government agencies,
  20 nonprofit organizations recruited on
  campus

### WHAT YOU WILL PAY
Resident tuition and fees $3534
Nonresident tuition and fees $9561
Room and board $3690
Need-based financial aid averages $1080
Non-need financial aid averages $2368

# UNIVERSITY OF MISSOURI–ROLLA

Rolla, Missouri • Small-town setting • Public • State-supported • Coed

The University of Missouri–Rolla has a curriculum with outstanding liberal arts to produce graduates able to meet the complex challenges of a changing world. Leaders learn from leaders. Rolla faculty members are renowned scholars and researchers as well as teachers who care about their students. Opportunities abound in undergraduate research and cooperative learning. Sophisticated laboratory and computer facilities complement the small classes. A student body with outstanding credentials excels in the classroom, and many student organizations augment the social side of campus life. Outstanding career opportunities complete the educational experience.

 ## Academics

UMR offers a core academic program; more than half of graduate courses are open to undergraduates. It awards bachelor's, master's, and doctoral **degrees**. Challenging opportunities include advanced placement, tutorials, an honors program, a senior project, and Sigma Xi. Special programs include cooperative education, summer session for credit, off-campus study, study abroad, and Army and Air Force ROTC.

The most popular **majors** include mechanical engineering, electrical engineering, and civil engineering. A complete listing of majors at UMR appears in the Majors Index beginning on page 380.

The **faculty** at UMR has 304 full-time graduate and undergraduate teachers, 94% with terminal degrees. The student-faculty ratio is 14:1, and the average class size in required courses is 26.

 ## Computers on Campus

Students are not required to have a computer. Student rooms are linked to a campus network. 600 **computers** available in the computer center, computer labs, the learning resource center, classrooms, the library, and dormitories provide access to the main academic computer, off-campus computing facilities, e-mail, and on-line services. Staffed computer lab on campus (open 24 hours a day) provides training in the use of computers and software.

The **library** has 450,619 books, 481,882 microform titles, and 1,405 subscriptions. It is connected to 3 national **on-line** catalogs.

 ## Campus Life

There are 138 active **organizations** on campus, including a drama/theater group and student-run newspaper and radio station. 28% of eligible men and 20% of eligible women are members of 21 national **fraternities** and 5 national **sororities**. Student **safety services** include Pro Active Crime Prevention Programs, late night transport/escort service, 24-hour emergency telephone alarm devices, 24-hour patrols by trained security personnel, student patrols, and electronically operated dormitory entrances.

UMR is a member of the NCAA (Division II). **Intercollegiate sports** (some offering scholarships) include baseball (m), basketball (m, w), cross-country running (m, w), football (m), golf (m), soccer (m, w), softball (w), swimming and diving (m), tennis (m), track and field (m, w).

 ## Applying

UMR requires a high school transcript, 3 years of high school math, and SAT I or ACT. It recommends 3 years of high school science and some high school foreign language. Early, deferred, and midyear entrance are possible, with a 7/1 deadline and continuous processing to 3/1 for financial aid. **Contact:** Mr. Dave Allen, Director of Admissions and Financial Aid, 102 Parker Hall, Rolla, MO 65401-0249, 314-341-4164.

---

### GETTING IN LAST YEAR
2,135 applied
94% were accepted
41% enrolled (822)
46% from top tenth of their h.s. class
23% had SAT verbal scores over 600
72% had SAT math scores over 600
72% had ACT scores over 26
3% had SAT verbal scores over 700
25% had SAT math scores over 700
37% had ACT scores over 30
15 National Merit Scholars

### THE STUDENT BODY
Total 5,472, of whom 4,438
  are undergraduates

From 43 states and territories,
  27 other countries
78% from Missouri
24% women, 76% men
4% African Americans
1% Native Americans
1% Hispanics
3% Asian Americans
3% international students

### AFTER FRESHMAN YEAR
79% returned for sophomore year
9% got a degree within 4 years
37% got a degree within 5 years
49% got a degree within 6 years

### AFTER GRADUATION
250 corporations, 12 government agencies, 2
  nonprofit organizations recruited on campus

### WHAT YOU WILL PAY
Resident tuition and fees $3577
Nonresident tuition and fees $9604
Room and board $3600
51% receive non-need financial aid averaging
  $2594

# UNIVERSITY OF NEW HAMPSHIRE

Durham, New Hampshire • Small-town setting • Public • State-supported • Coed

---

▶ UNH offers an excellent education at a reasonable cost to students with a broad range of interests. Over 100 majors, 2,000 courses, and 100 student clubs and organizations are offered. Programs that provide valuable experience include the honors program, undergraduate research, internships, study abroad, and national exchange. UNH's location also caters to a wide range of interests. The campus itself is in a small-town setting surrounded by woods and farms; within 20 minutes is the Atlantic coastline, and just over an hour away are the White Mountains, Boston, Massachusetts, and Portland, Maine.

 **Academics**

UNH offers an interdisciplinary curriculum and core academic program; fewer than half of graduate courses are open to undergraduates. It awards associate, bachelor's, master's, and doctoral **degrees**. Challenging opportunities include advanced placement, accelerated degree programs, self-designed majors, tutorials, an honors program, a senior project, Phi Beta Kappa, and Sigma Xi. Special programs include internships, summer session for credit, off-campus study, study abroad, and Army and Air Force ROTC.

The most popular **majors** include business, English, and communication. A complete listing of majors at UNH appears in the Majors Index beginning on page 380.

The **faculty** at UNH has 641 full-time graduate and undergraduate teachers, 91% with terminal degrees. 100% of the faculty serve as student advisers. The student-faculty ratio is 18:1, and the average class size in required courses is 25.

 **Computers on Campus**

Students are not required to have a computer. Student rooms are linked to a campus network. 200 **computers** available in the computer center, computer labs, classrooms, and the student center provide access to the main academic computer, off-campus computing facilities, e-mail, and on-line services. Staffed computer lab on campus.

The 6 **libraries** have 1 million books, 714,199 microform titles, and 6,500 subscriptions.

 **Campus Life**

There are 100 active **organizations** on campus, including a drama/theater group and student-run newspaper and radio station. 35% of students participate in student government elections. 10% of eligible men and 10% of eligible women are members of 9 national **fraternities**, 6 national **sororities**, and 1 local fraternity. Student **safety services** include late night transport/escort service, 24-hour emergency telephone alarm devices, 24-hour patrols by trained security personnel, student patrols, and electronically operated dormitory entrances.

UNH is a member of the NCAA (Division I). **Intercollegiate sports** (some offering scholarships) include badminton (m, w), baseball (m), basketball (m, w), crew (m), cross-country running (m, w), equestrian sports (m, w), fencing (m, w), field hockey (w), football (m), golf (m, w), gymnastics (w), ice hockey (m, w), lacrosse (m, w), rugby (m, w), sailing (m, w), skiing (cross-country) (m, w), skiing (downhill) (m, w), soccer (m, w), squash (m, w), swimming and diving (m, w), tennis (m), track and field (m, w), volleyball (m, w).

 **Applying**

UNH requires an essay, a high school transcript, 4 years of high school math, 1 recommendation, and SAT I or ACT. It recommends 4 years of high school science, 3 years of high school foreign language, a campus interview, and SAT II Subject Tests. Early, deferred, and midyear entrance are possible, with a 2/1 deadline and continuous processing to 3/1 for financial aid. **Contact:** Mr. David Kraus, Director of Admissions, Grant House, Durham, NH 03824, 603-862-1360.

---

**GETTING IN LAST YEAR**
9,731 applied
77% were accepted
33% enrolled (2,478)
25% from top tenth of their h.s. class
3.0 average high school GPA
5% had SAT verbal scores over 600
24% had SAT math scores over 600
0% had SAT verbal scores over 700
3% had SAT math scores over 700

**THE STUDENT BODY**
Total 12,518, of whom 10,896
    are undergraduates
From 49 states and territories,
    30 other countries

60% from New Hampshire
57% women, 43% men
1% African Americans
1% Native Americans
1% Hispanics
2% Asian Americans
1% international students

**AFTER FRESHMAN YEAR**
83% returned for sophomore year
50% got a degree within 4 years
69% got a degree within 5 years
74% got a degree within 6 years

**AFTER GRADUATION**
160 corporations, 5 government agencies, 6
    nonprofit organizations recruited on campus
2 Fulbright scholars

**WHAT YOU WILL PAY**
Resident tuition and fees $4559
Nonresident tuition and fees $12,879
Room and board $4038
59% receive need-based financial aid
    averaging $3603
31% receive non-need financial aid averaging
    $5393

---

# UNIVERSITY OF NORTH CAROLINA AT ASHEVILLE

Asheville, North Carolina • Suburban setting • Public • State-supported • Coed

## Academics

UNCA offers a liberal arts curriculum and core academic program. It awards bachelor's and master's **degrees**. Challenging opportunities include advanced placement, accelerated degree programs, self-designed majors, an honors program, a senior project, and Sigma Xi. Special programs include internships, summer session for credit, off-campus study, and study abroad.

The most popular **majors** include business, psychology, and sociology. A complete listing of majors at UNCA appears in the Majors Index beginning on page 380.

The **faculty** at UNCA has 146 full-time graduate and undergraduate teachers, 85% with terminal degrees. 100% of the faculty serve as student advisers. The student-faculty ratio is 13:1, and the average class size in required courses is 21.

## Computers on Campus

Students are not required to have a computer. Student rooms are linked to a campus network. 400 **computers** available in the computer center, computer labs, classroom buildings, the library, and dormitories provide access to the main academic computer, off-campus computing facilities, e-mail, and on-line services. Staffed computer lab on campus provides training in the use of computers and software.

The 2 **libraries** have 223,618 books, 50,000 microform titles, and 2,106 subscriptions. They are connected to 4 national **on-line** catalogs.

## Campus Life

There are 70 active **organizations** on campus, including a drama/theater group and student-run newspaper. 8% of eligible men and 6% of eligible women are members of 3 national **fraternities**, 2 national **sororities**, 1 local fraternity, and 1 local sorority. Student **safety services** include late night transport/escort service, 24-hour patrols by trained security personnel, and electronically operated dormitory entrances.

UNCA is a member of the NCAA (Division I). **Intercollegiate sports** (some offering scholarships) include baseball (m), basketball (m, w), cross-country running (m, w), soccer (m), softball (w), tennis (m, w), track and field (m, w), volleyball (w).

## Applying

UNCA requires a high school transcript, 3 years of high school math and science, 4 years of high school English, 2 years of high school social studies, SAT I or ACT, and in some cases recommendations and an interview. It recommends an essay, 2 years of high school foreign language, SAT II Subject Tests, and a minimum high school GPA of 3.0. Early, deferred, and midyear entrance are possible, with a 7/1 deadline and continuous processing to 3/1 for financial aid. **Contact:** Mr. John White, Director of Admissions, University Heights, Asheville, NC 28804-3299, 704-251-6481.

### GETTING IN LAST YEAR
1,820 applied
60% were accepted
37% enrolled (398)
30% from top tenth of their h.s. class
3.42 average high school GPA
12% had SAT verbal scores over 600
28% had SAT math scores over 600
23% had ACT scores over 26
1% had SAT verbal scores over 700
3% had SAT math scores over 700
0% had ACT scores over 30
6 National Merit Scholars
5 valedictorians

### THE STUDENT BODY
Total 3,195, of whom 3,155
  are undergraduates

From 37 states and territories,
  18 other countries
90% from North Carolina
55% women, 45% men
4% African Americans
0% Native Americans
1% Hispanics
1% Asian Americans
1% international students

### AFTER FRESHMAN YEAR
80% returned for sophomore year
16% got a degree within 4 years
35% got a degree within 5 years
42% got a degree within 6 years

### AFTER GRADUATION
10 corporations, 1 government agency, 8
  nonprofit organizations recruited on campus
1 Fulbright scholar

### WHAT YOU WILL PAY
Resident tuition and fees $1588
Nonresident tuition and fees $7320
Room and board $3240
24% receive need-based financial aid
  averaging $1415
Non-need financial aid averages $1865

# UNIVERSITY OF NORTH CAROLINA AT CHAPEL HILL

Chapel Hill, North Carolina • Small-town setting • Public • State-supported • Coed

The University of North Carolina at Chapel Hill was the first state university to open its doors and the nation's only public university to award degrees in the 18th century. The University was chartered in 1789, and the cornerstone for the first state university building, Old East, was laid in 1793. Now part of the 16-campus UNC System, Carolina has earned a worldwide reputation for vital teaching, cutting-edge research, and distinguished public service. Among the nation's most comprehensive institutions, units include schools of business, education, journalism and mass communication, law, information and library science, and social work, along with dentistry, medicine, nursing, pharmacy, and public health.

 ## Academics

UNC at Chapel Hill offers a core academic program. It awards bachelor's, master's, doctoral, and first professional **degrees**. Challenging opportunities include advanced placement, accelerated degree programs, self-designed majors, an honors program, Phi Beta Kappa, and Sigma Xi. Special programs include internships, summer session for credit, off-campus study, study abroad, and Army, Naval, and Air Force ROTC.

The most popular **majors** include biology/biological sciences, business, and political science/government. A complete listing of majors at UNC at Chapel Hill appears in the Majors Index beginning on page 380.

The **faculty** at UNC at Chapel Hill has 2,297 graduate and undergraduate teachers, 94% with terminal degrees. The student-faculty ratio is 15:1, and the average class size in required courses is 35.

 ## Computers on Campus

Students are not required to have a computer. 460 **computers** available in the computer center, the library,

the student center, and dormitories provide access to off-campus computing facilities and e-mail. Staffed computer lab on campus provides training in the use of computers and software.

The 4 **libraries** have 3.9 million books, 3.4 million microform titles, and 39,044 subscriptions.

 ## Campus Life

There are 300 active **organizations** on campus, including a drama/theater group and student-run newspaper and radio station. 20% of eligible men and 20% of eligible women are members of 29 national **fraternities** and 15 national **sororities**. Student **safety services** include late night transport/escort service, 24-hour emergency telephone alarm devices, 24-hour patrols by trained security personnel, and electronically operated dormitory entrances.

UNC at Chapel Hill is a member of the NCAA (Division I). **Intercollegiate sports** include baseball (m), basketball (m, w), cross-country running (m, w), fencing (m, w), field hockey (w), football (m), golf (m, w), gymnastics (w), lacrosse (m), soccer (m, w), softball (w), swimming and diving (m, w), tennis (m, w), track and field (m, w), volleyball (m, w), wrestling (m).

 ## Applying

UNC at Chapel Hill requires a high school transcript, 3 years of high school math and science, 2 years of high school foreign language, 4 years of high school English, 2 years of high school social studies, and SAT I or ACT. Early action is possible, with a 1/15 deadline and continuous processing to 3/1 for financial aid. **Contact:** Dr. James Walters, Associate Provost/Director of Undergraduate Admissions, CB #2200, Jackson Hall, Chapel Hill, NC 27599, 919-966-3621.

---

### GETTING IN LAST YEAR

15,113 applied
41% were accepted
57% enrolled (3,497)
72% from top tenth of their h.s. class
24% had SAT verbal scores over 600
53% had SAT math scores over 600
4% had SAT verbal scores over 700
15% had SAT math scores over 700
248 class presidents
246 valedictorians

### THE STUDENT BODY

Total 24,463, of whom 15,895 are undergraduates

From 53 states and territories, 55 other countries
81% from North Carolina
60% women, 40% men
10% African Americans
1% Native Americans
1% Hispanics
5% Asian Americans
1% international students

### AFTER FRESHMAN YEAR

93% returned for sophomore year
65% got a degree within 4 years

83% got a degree within 5 years
85% got a degree within 6 years

### WHAT YOU WILL PAY

Resident tuition and fees $1569
Nonresident tuition and fees $9095
Room and board $4200
Need-based financial aid averages $1895
Non-need financial aid averages $3000

# UNIVERSITY OF NOTRE DAME

Notre Dame, Indiana • Suburban setting • Private • Independent-Religious • Coed

---

Notre Dame is a Catholic university that attracts students from all states and many other countries. The unique Freshman Year of Studies program, dynamic faculty, supportive residence hall system, and new state-of-the-art classroom building are special features. Community service, music, drama, and recreational sports are major aspects of student life. Most varsity sports attain national rankings or win conference championships each year.

 **Academics**

Notre Dame offers a liberal arts core curriculum and core academic program; fewer than half of graduate courses are open to undergraduates. It awards bachelor's, master's, doctoral, and first professional **degrees**. Challenging opportunities include advanced placement, accelerated degree programs, tutorials, Freshmen Honors College, an honors program, a senior project, Phi Beta Kappa, and Sigma Xi. Special programs include summer session for credit, off-campus study, study abroad, and Army, Naval, and Air Force ROTC.

The most popular **majors** include accounting and political science/government. A complete listing of majors at Notre Dame appears in the Majors Index beginning on page 380.

The **faculty** at Notre Dame has 647 full-time graduate and undergraduate teachers, 96% with terminal degrees. 50% of the faculty serve as student advisers. The student-faculty ratio is 12:1, and the average class size in required courses is 33.

 **Computers on Campus**

Students are not required to have a computer. Student rooms are linked to a campus network. 455 **computers** available in the computer center, various academic departments, the library, and the student center provide access to the main academic computer and on-line services. Staffed computer lab on campus (open 24 hours a day) provides training in the use of computers and software.

The 9 **libraries** have 2.1 million books, 2.5 million microform titles, and 20,500 subscriptions. They are connected to 3 national **on-line** catalogs.

 **Campus Life**

There are 200 active **organizations** on campus, including a drama/theater group and student-run newspaper and radio station. No national or local **fraternities** or **sororities**. Student **safety services** include late night transport/escort service, 24-hour emergency telephone alarm devices, 24-hour patrols by trained security personnel, and electronically operated dormitory entrances.

Notre Dame is a member of the NCAA (Division I). **Intercollegiate sports** (some offering scholarships) include baseball (m), basketball (m, w), crew (m, w), cross-country running (m, w), equestrian sports (m, w), fencing (m, w), football (m), golf (m, w), gymnastics (m, w), ice hockey (m), lacrosse (m, w), rugby (m), sailing (m, w), skiing (downhill) (m, w), soccer (m, w), softball (w), swimming and diving (m, w), tennis (m, w), track and field (m, w), volleyball (m, w), water polo (m).

 **Applying**

Notre Dame requires an essay, a high school transcript, 3 years of high school science, 2 years of high school foreign language, 1 recommendation, SAT I or ACT, and in some cases 4 years of high school math. It recommends 4 years of high school math and SAT II Subject Tests. Early and deferred entrance are possible, with a 1/6 deadline and continuous processing to 2/28 for financial aid. **Contact:** Mr. Kevin M. Rooney, Director of Admissions, 113 Main Building, Notre Dame, IN 46556, 219-631-7505.

---

### GETTING IN LAST YEAR
9,300 applied
42% were accepted
48% enrolled (1,880)
79% from top tenth of their h.s. class
39% had SAT verbal scores over 600
77% had SAT math scores over 600
75% had ACT scores over 26
5% had SAT verbal scores over 700
29% had SAT math scores over 700
45% had ACT scores over 30
45 National Merit Scholars
250 class presidents
238 valedictorians

### THE STUDENT BODY
Total 10,000, of whom 7,600
  are undergraduates

From 52 states and territories,
  35 other countries
9% from Indiana
43% women, 57% men
4% African Americans
1% Native Americans
6% Hispanics
4% Asian Americans
2% international students

### AFTER FRESHMAN YEAR
97% returned for sophomore year
92% got a degree within 4 years
93% got a degree within 5 years

### AFTER GRADUATION
32% pursued further study (11% arts and
  sciences, 9% law, 8% medicine)
84% had job offers within 3 months
280 corporations, 5 government agencies, 50
  nonprofit organizations recruited on campus
11 Fulbright scholars

### WHAT YOU WILL PAY
Tuition and fees $17,210
Room and board $4400
60% receive need-based financial aid
  averaging $7100
Non-need financial aid averages $13,000

---

# UNIVERSITY OF OKLAHOMA

Norman, Oklahoma • Suburban setting • Public • State-supported • Coed

The University of Oklahoma is a modern-day academic powerhouse that is enhanced by Sooner pride and tradition. Oklahoma University has attracted its share of outstanding students. In fact, OU now has the highest ratio of National Merit Scholars of all the comprehensive public universities in America. OU provides an excellent undergraduate experience. The faculty are not content just teaching established knowledge. Most OU professors are involved in research—in the discovery and creation of *new* knowledge. They are leaders in their fields . . . scholars on the cutting edge who have more to offer in the classroom. OU provides the major college experience in a private college atmosphere.

 ## Academics

OU offers a core academic program; more than half of graduate courses are open to undergraduates. It awards bachelor's, master's, doctoral, and first professional **degrees**. Challenging opportunities include advanced placement, accelerated degree programs, self-designed majors, tutorials, an honors program, a senior project, Phi Beta Kappa, and Sigma Xi. Special programs include cooperative education, internships, summer session for credit, off-campus study, study abroad, and Army, Naval, and Air Force ROTC.

The most popular **majors** include accounting, management information systems, and psychology. A complete listing of majors at OU appears in the Majors Index beginning on page 380.

The **faculty** at OU has 834 full-time graduate and undergraduate teachers, 83% with terminal degrees.

 ## Computers on Campus

Students are not required to have a computer. 600 **computers** available in the computer center, computer labs, the research center, academic units, classrooms, the library, and dormitories provide access to the main academic computer, off-campus computing facilities, e-mail, and on-line services. Staffed computer lab on campus (open 24 hours a day) provides training in the use of computers and software.

The 8 **libraries** have 2.5 million books, 3.4 million microform titles, and 17,400 subscriptions. They are connected to 5 national **on-line** catalogs.

 ## Campus Life

There are 213 active **organizations** on campus, including a drama/theater group and student-run newspaper. 20% of students participate in student government elections. 18% of eligible men and 18% of eligible women are members of 22 national **fraternities** and 15 national **sororities**. Student **safety services** include crime prevention programs, late night transport/escort service, 24-hour emergency telephone alarm devices, 24-hour patrols by trained security personnel, and student patrols.

OU is a member of the NCAA (Division I). **Intercollegiate sports** (some offering scholarships) include baseball (m), basketball (m, w), cross-country running (m, w), football (m), golf (m, w), gymnastics (m, w), softball (w), tennis (m, w), track and field (m, w), volleyball (w), wrestling (m).

 ## Applying

OU requires a high school transcript, 3 years of high school math, 2 years of history (including one year of American history), 2 years of high school lab science, 4 units of high school English, SAT I or ACT, and a minimum high school GPA of 3.0. It recommends some high school foreign language. Early and midyear entrance are possible, with rolling admissions and continuous processing to 7/1 for financial aid. **Contact:** Ms. Leslie Baumert, Director, Prospective Student Services, 407 West Boyd, Norman, OK 73019, 405-325-2151 or toll-free 800-234-6868; fax 405-325-7478.

---

**GETTING IN LAST YEAR**
4,969 applied
86% were accepted
58% enrolled (2,464)
30% from top tenth of their h.s. class
34% had ACT scores over 26
13% had ACT scores over 30
160 National Merit Scholars

**THE STUDENT BODY**
Total 19,683, of whom 15,088
  are undergraduates
From 50 states and territories,
  84 other countries

79% from Oklahoma
45% women, 55% men
7% African Americans
6% Native Americans
3% Hispanics
5% Asian Americans
7% international students

**AFTER FRESHMAN YEAR**
78% returned for sophomore year
16% got a degree within 4 years
36% got a degree within 5 years
41% got a degree within 6 years

**AFTER GRADUATION**
200 corporations recruited on campus
1 Fulbright scholar

**WHAT YOU WILL PAY**
Resident tuition and fees $1870
Nonresident tuition and fees $5110
Room and board $3526
43% receive need-based financial aid
  averaging $896
31% receive non-need financial aid averaging
  $2363

# UNIVERSITY OF PENNSYLVANIA

Philadelphia, Pennsylvania • Urban setting • Private • Independent • Coed

The University of Pennsylvania was founded over 250 years ago by Benjamin Franklin. Based upon his ideas, Penn was the first college to instruct students in the sciences, economics, modern languages, public law, and applied mathematics. It opened the nation's first medical school in 1765 and, in 1779, became the nation's first university. Today, Penn has 4 undergraduate schools and 12 graduate and professional schools.

 ## Academics

Penn offers a core academic program; fewer than half of graduate courses are open to undergraduates. It awards associate, bachelor's, master's, doctoral, and first professional **degrees**. Challenging opportunities include advanced placement, accelerated degree programs, self-designed majors, tutorials, an honors program, a senior project, Phi Beta Kappa, and Sigma Xi. Special programs include internships, summer session for credit, off-campus study, study abroad, and Army, Naval, and Air Force ROTC.

The most popular **majors** include finance/banking, history, and English. A complete listing of majors at Penn appears in the Majors Index beginning on page 380.

The **faculty** at Penn has 2,132 full-time graduate and undergraduate teachers, 95% with terminal degrees. The student-faculty ratio is 5:1.

 ## Computers on Campus

Students are not required to have a computer. Student rooms are linked to a campus network. 555 **computers** available in the computer center, computer labs, the research center, classroom buildings, classrooms, the library, the student center, and dormitories provide access to the main academic computer, off-campus computing facilities, and e-mail. Staffed computer lab on campus (open 24 hours a day).

The 14 **libraries** have 4.2 million books and 33,384 subscriptions. They are connected to 11 national **on-line** catalogs.

 ## Campus Life

There are 306 active **organizations** on campus, including a drama/theater group and student-run newspaper and radio station. 30% of eligible men and 30% of eligible women are members of 29 national **fraternities** and 14 national **sororities**. Student **safety services** include late night transport/escort service, 24-hour emergency telephone alarm devices, 24-hour patrols by trained security personnel, and student patrols.

Penn is a member of the NCAA (Division I). **Intercollegiate sports** include baseball (m), basketball (m, w), crew (m, w), cross-country running (m, w), fencing (m, w), field hockey (w), football (m), golf (m), gymnastics (w), lacrosse (m, w), soccer (m, w), softball (w), squash (m, w), swimming and diving (m, w), tennis (m, w), track and field (m, w), volleyball (w), wrestling (m).

 ## Applying

Penn requires an essay, a high school transcript, 2 recommendations, SAT I or ACT, and 3 SAT II Subject Tests (including SAT II: Writing Test). It recommends 3 years of high school math and science, 3 years of high school foreign language, and an interview. Early and deferred entrance are possible, with a 1/1 deadline and a 2/15 priority date for financial aid. **Contact:** Mr. Willis J. Stetson Jr., Dean of Admissions, 1 College Hall, Levy Park, Philadelphia, PA 19104, 215-898-7507.

---

**GETTING IN LAST YEAR**
13,739 applied
36% were accepted
47% enrolled (2,346)
85% from top tenth of their h.s. class
56% had SAT verbal scores over 600
87% had SAT math scores over 600
10% had SAT verbal scores over 700
45% had SAT math scores over 700
71 class presidents

**THE STUDENT BODY**
Total 22,720, of whom 11,300 are undergraduates

21% from Pennsylvania
47% women, 53% men
6% African Americans
1% Native Americans
4% Hispanics
16% Asian Americans
8% international students

**AFTER FRESHMAN YEAR**
95% returned for sophomore year
79% got a degree within 4 years
85% got a degree within 5 years
88% got a degree within 6 years

**AFTER GRADUATION**
30% pursued further study (9% law, 9% medicine, 4% arts and sciences)
60% had job offers within 3 months
360 corporations, 10 government agencies, 20 nonprofit organizations recruited on campus
8 Fulbright scholars

**WHAT YOU WILL PAY**
Tuition and fees $18,856
Room and board $7270
41% receive need-based financial aid averaging $12,032

# UNIVERSITY OF PITTSBURGH

Pittsburgh, Pennsylvania • Urban setting • Public • State-related • Coed

▶ The University of Pittsburgh offers students a tremendous array of academic, cocurricular, and extracurricular opportunities, which students combine to creatively define their own levels of challenge and innovation. University of Pittsburgh students pursue self-designed, double, or triple majors; internships; teaching and research assistantships; dual degrees; and study-abroad opportunities. Through the University Honors College, academically motivated students also participate in small, in-depth honors courses and pursue the prestigious Bachelor of Philosophy degree. Many win national and international scholarships. The University awards 4-year merit scholarships, including some covering full tuition, room, and board, to freshmen.

 **Academics**

Pitt offers a core academic program. It awards bachelor's, master's, doctoral, and first professional **degrees**. Challenging opportunities include advanced placement, self-designed majors, an honors program, a senior project, Phi Beta Kappa, and Sigma Xi. Special programs include cooperative education, internships, summer session for credit, off-campus study, study abroad, and Army, Naval, and Air Force ROTC.

The most popular **majors** include psychology, business, and communication. A complete listing of majors at Pitt appears in the Majors Index beginning on page 380.

The **faculty** at Pitt has 2,836 full-time graduate and undergraduate teachers, 90% with terminal degrees. The student-faculty ratio is 15:1.

 **Computers on Campus**

Students are not required to have a computer. 600 **computers** available in the computer center, computer labs, the library, and dormitories provide access to the main academic computer, e-mail, and on-line services. Staffed computer lab on campus provides training in the use of computers and software.

The 24 **libraries** have 3.2 million books, 3.1 million microform titles, and 23,380 subscriptions. They are connected to 2,500 national **on-line** catalogs.

 **Campus Life**

There are 340 active **organizations** on campus, including a drama/theater group and student-run newspaper and radio station. 11% of eligible men and 8% of eligible women are members of 21 national **fraternities** and 15 national **sororities**. Student **safety services** include on-call van transportation, late night transport/escort service, 24-hour emergency telephone alarm devices, 24-hour patrols by trained security personnel, and electronically operated dormitory entrances.

Pitt is a member of the NCAA (Division I). **Intercollegiate sports** (some offering scholarships) include baseball (m), basketball (m, w), cross-country running (m, w), football (m), gymnastics (m, w), soccer (m), swimming and diving (m, w), tennis (m, w), track and field (m, w), volleyball (w), wrestling (m).

 **Applying**

Pitt requires a high school transcript and SAT I or ACT. It recommends an essay, 3 years of high school math and science, 3 years of high school foreign language, recommendations, and an interview. Early, deferred, and midyear entrance are possible, with rolling admissions and continuous processing to 3/1 for financial aid. **Contact:** Dr. Betsy A. Porter, Director, Admissions and Financial Aid, Bruce Hall, Second Floor, Pittsburgh, PA 15260-0001, 412-624-7488; fax 412-648-8815.

---

### GETTING IN LAST YEAR
7,709 applied
68% were accepted
38% enrolled (2,016)
27% from top tenth of their h.s. class
9% had SAT verbal scores over 600
24% had SAT math scores over 600
1% had SAT verbal scores over 700
4% had SAT math scores over 700

### THE STUDENT BODY
Total 26,328, of whom 16,721
  are undergraduates

From 46 states and territories,
  52 other countries
90% from Pennsylvania
51% women, 49% men
9% African Americans
1% Native Americans
1% Hispanics
3% Asian Americans
1% international students

### AFTER FRESHMAN YEAR
86% returned for sophomore year

### AFTER GRADUATION
65% had job offers within 3 months
190 corporations, 4 government agencies
  recruited on campus
8 Fulbright scholars

### WHAT YOU WILL PAY
Resident tuition and fees $5416
Nonresident tuition and fees $11,240
Room and board $4560
Need-based financial aid averages $606

# UNIVERSITY OF PITTSBURGH AT JOHNSTOWN

Johnstown, Pennsylvania • Suburban setting • Public • State-related • Coed

At the University of Pittsburgh at Johnstown, learning isn't limited to the boundaries of the campus. There is a variety of opportunities to learn more about the world around us. The Semester-at-Sea allows students to pursue course work while they travel the world on an ocean liner. Students can spend a term in the nation's capital through the Washington Semester. An International Studies Certificate provides an international perspective for any major or degree. And the President's Scholars Program identifies students who show extra intellectual potential, provides special advising and registration provisions, and rewards accomplishments with scholarship assistance.

 **Academics**

Pitt-Johnstown offers a comprehensive curriculum and core academic program. It awards associate and bachelor's **degrees**. Challenging opportunities include advanced placement, accelerated degree programs, self-designed majors, and a senior project. Special programs include internships, summer session for credit, off-campus study, and study abroad.

The most popular **majors** include business economics, elementary education, and biology/biological sciences. A complete listing of majors at Pitt-Johnstown appears in the Majors Index beginning on page 380.

The **faculty** at Pitt-Johnstown has 145 full-time teachers, 68% with terminal degrees. 89% of the faculty serve as student advisers. The student-faculty ratio is 20:1, and the average class size in required courses is 25.

 **Computers on Campus**

Students are not required to have a computer. 171 **computers** available in the computer center, computer labs, and the library provide access to e-mail. Staffed computer lab on campus provides training in the use of computers and software.

The **library** has 132,412 books, 17,209 microform titles, and 651 subscriptions.

 **Campus Life**

There are 70 active **organizations** on campus, including a drama/theater group and student-run newspaper and radio station. 15% of eligible men and 16% of eligible women are members of 4 national **fraternities**, 4 national **sororities**, 1 local fraternity, and 1 local sorority. Student **safety services** include late night transport/escort service and 24-hour patrols by trained security personnel.

Pitt-Johnstown is a member of the NCAA (Division II). **Intercollegiate sports** (some offering scholarships) include baseball (m), basketball (m, w), cross-country running (w), soccer (m), track and field (w), volleyball (w), wrestling (m).

 **Applying**

Pitt-Johnstown requires an essay, a high school transcript, 2 years of high school foreign language, 2 years of high school science, SAT I or ACT, a minimum high school GPA of 2.0, and in some cases a campus interview. It recommends 3 years of high school math. Early, deferred, and midyear entrance are possible, with rolling admissions and continuous processing to 4/1 for financial aid. **Contact:** Mr. James F. Gyure, Director of Admissions, 133 Biddle Hall, Johnstown, PA 15904-2990, 814-269-7050 or toll-free 800-765-4875; fax 814-269-7044.

---

**GETTING IN LAST YEAR**
1,713 applied
80% were accepted
52% enrolled (716)
24% from top tenth of their h.s. class
3.0 average high school GPA
7 valedictorians

**THE STUDENT BODY**
3,138 undergraduates
From 11 states and territories,
  1 other country

98% from Pennsylvania
50% women, 50% men
2% African Americans
1% Native Americans
1% Hispanics
1% Asian Americans
1% international students

**AFTER FRESHMAN YEAR**
77% returned for sophomore year
60% got a degree within 6 years

**WHAT YOU WILL PAY**
Resident tuition and fees $5432
Nonresident tuition and fees $11,256
Room and board $4086
82% receive need-based financial aid
  averaging $705
31% receive non-need financial aid averaging
  $2858

# UNIVERSITY OF PUGET SOUND

Tacoma, Washington • Suburban setting • Private • Independent • Coed

▶ Fundamental to the Puget Sound education is the commitment to the liberal arts and sciences. The University offers a challenging liberal arts and sciences education with 60 academic major options and 4 highly regarded professional schools. Students receive a broad-based, balanced education. Puget Sound is proud of the national recognition it has received for its programs, including Prelude and Passages (orientation program), the Honors Program in the Classics, the Business Leadership Program, and the Pacific Rim Study Program. Puget Sound students engage an academic program with high levels of challenge and support on a campus enhanced by the natural beauty of the Pacific Northwest.

 ## Academics

Puget Sound offers a liberal arts curriculum and core academic program; a few graduate courses are open to undergraduates. It awards bachelor's and master's **degrees**. Challenging opportunities include advanced placement, tutorials, an honors program, a senior project, and Phi Beta Kappa. Special programs include cooperative education, internships, summer session for credit, study abroad, and Army ROTC.

The most popular **majors** include business, English, and political science/government. A complete listing of majors at Puget Sound appears in the Majors Index beginning on page 380.

The **faculty** at Puget Sound has 210 full-time undergraduate teachers, 86% with terminal degrees. 100% of the faculty serve as student advisers. The student-faculty ratio is 13:1, and the average class size in required courses is 29.

 ## Computers on Campus

Students are not required to have a computer. 136 **computers** available in the computer center, computer labs, the learning resource center, the library, and dormitories provide access to the main academic computer, off-campus computing facilities, e-mail, and on-line services. Staffed computer lab on campus (open 24 hours a day) provides training in the use of computers and software.

The **library** has 363,205 books and 1,957 subscriptions. It is connected to 51 national **on-line** catalogs.

 ## Campus Life

There are 38 active **organizations** on campus, including a drama/theater group and student-run newspaper and radio station. 30% of students participate in student government elections. 33% of eligible men and 33% of eligible women are members of 6 national **fraternities** and 6 national **sororities**. Student **safety services** include 24-hour locked residences, late night transport/escort service, 24-hour emergency telephone alarm devices, 24-hour patrols by trained security personnel, student patrols, and electronically operated dormitory entrances.

Puget Sound is a member of the NAIA. **Intercollegiate sports** (some offering scholarships) include baseball (m), basketball (m, w), crew (m, w), cross-country running (m, w), football (m), golf (m, w), lacrosse (m, w), sailing (m, w), skiing (downhill) (m, w), soccer (m, w), softball (w), swimming and diving (m, w), tennis (m, w), track and field (m, w), volleyball (w).

 ## Applying

Puget Sound requires an essay, a high school transcript, 2 recommendations, and SAT I or ACT. It recommends 4 years of high school math and science, 2 years of high school foreign language, an interview, and a minimum high school GPA of 3.0. Early, deferred, and midyear entrance are possible, with a 2/1 deadline and continuous processing to 2/1 for financial aid. **Contact:** Dr. George H. Mills, Dean of Admission, 1500 North Warner Street, Tacoma, WA 98416-0005, 206-756-3211; fax 206-756-3500.

---

### GETTING IN LAST YEAR
4,287 applied
76% were accepted
21% enrolled (695)
43% from top tenth of their h.s. class
3.54 average high school GPA
20% had SAT verbal scores over 600
41% had SAT math scores over 600
50% had ACT scores over 26
3% had SAT verbal scores over 700
9% had SAT math scores over 700
11% had ACT scores over 30
24 National Merit Scholars

### THE STUDENT BODY
Total 3,163, of whom 2,841
  are undergraduates

From 42 states and territories,
  16 other countries
48% from Washington
60% women, 40% men
2% African Americans
1% Native Americans
2% Hispanics
10% Asian Americans
1% international students

### AFTER FRESHMAN YEAR
86% returned for sophomore year
51% got a degree within 4 years
64% got a degree within 5 years
67% got a degree within 6 years

### AFTER GRADUATION
25% pursued further study (18% arts and
  sciences, 4% business, 3% law)
32 corporations, 1 government agency, 1
  nonprofit organization recruited on campus
1 Fulbright scholar

### WHAT YOU WILL PAY
Tuition and fees $16,370
Room and board $4500
65% receive need-based financial aid
  averaging $5538
35% receive non-need financial aid averaging
  $4557

---

# UNIVERSITY OF REDLANDS

Redlands, California • Small-town setting • Private • Independent • Coed

## Academics

Redlands offers a liberal arts curriculum and core academic program; fewer than half of graduate courses are open to undergraduates. It awards bachelor's and master's **degrees**. Challenging opportunities include advanced placement, self-designed majors, tutorials, Freshmen Honors College, an honors program, a senior project, and Phi Beta Kappa. Special programs include internships, off-campus study, study abroad, and Army and Air Force ROTC.

The most popular **majors** include liberal arts/general studies, social science, and business. A complete listing of majors at Redlands appears in the Majors Index beginning on page 380.

The **faculty** at Redlands has 106 full-time under-graduate teachers, 88% with terminal degrees. The student-faculty ratio is 13:1, and the average class size in required courses is 17.

##  Computers on Campus

Students are not required to have a computer. 150 **computers** available in the computer center, computer labs, various academic departments, and classrooms provide access to the main academic computer, e-mail, and on-line services. Staffed computer lab on campus provides training in the use of computers and software.

The **library** has 225,000 books, 45,000 microform titles, and 1,623 subscriptions.

##  Campus Life

There are 60 active **organizations** on campus, including a drama/theater group and student-run newspaper and radio station. 60% of students participate in student govern-ment elections. 14% of eligible men and 16% of eligible women are members of 6 local **fraternities** and 4 local **sororities**. Student **safety services** include safety whistles, late night transport/escort service, 24-hour emergency telephone alarm devices, 24-hour patrols by trained security personnel, student patrols, and electronically operated dormi-tory entrances.

Redlands is a member of the NCAA (Division III). **Intercollegiate sports** include baseball (m), basket-ball (m, w), cross-country running (m, w), football (m), golf (m, w), soccer (m, w), softball (w), swimming and diving (m, w), tennis (m, w), track and field (m, w), volleyball (w), water polo (m, w).

## Applying

Redlands requires an essay, a high school transcript, 2 recommendations, SAT I or ACT, and in some cases 3 years of high school science. It recommends 3 years of high school math, some high school foreign language, an interview, and a minimum high school GPA of 3.0. Early, deferred, and midyear entrance are possible, with a 3/1 deadline and continuous processing to 2/15 for financial aid. **Contact:** Mr. Paul Driscoll, Dean of Admissions, 1200 East Colton Avenue, Redlands, CA 92373-0999, 909-335-4074; fax 909-335-4089.

---

### GETTING IN LAST YEAR
1,393 applied
79% were accepted
29% enrolled (317)
3.47 average high school GPA
5 National Merit Scholars
8 class presidents

### THE STUDENT BODY
Total 3,950, of whom 1,508
 are undergraduates
From 45 states and territories,
 35 other countries

60% from California
51% women, 49% men
2% African Americans
1% Native Americans
11% Hispanics
9% Asian Americans
7% international students

### AFTER FRESHMAN YEAR
77% returned for sophomore year
55% got a degree within 4 years

59% got a degree within 5 years
60% got a degree within 6 years

### AFTER GRADUATION
30% pursued further study

### WHAT YOU WILL PAY
Tuition and fees $16,755
Room and board $6205

---

# UNIVERSITY OF RICHMOND

Richmond, Virginia • Suburban setting • Private • Independent-Religious • Coed

> Students who attend Richmond find a rigorous intellectual experience that prepares them for the best graduate schools and the most challenging occupations in our society. Richmond's campus—350 acres of stately pines, rolling hills, and a magnificent lake—is located 6 miles from the capital of Virginia. Many of Richmond's top students are rewarded with merit-based scholarships, which range from one-half tuition to a full scholarship covering all expenses for 4 years. Student scholars benefit from an average class size of 20, ample opportunities in undergraduate research, and no graduate assistants.

##  Academics

University of Richmond offers a liberal arts curriculum and core academic program; fewer than half of graduate courses are open to undergraduates. It awards associate, bachelor's, master's, and first professional **degrees**. Challenging opportunities include advanced placement, accelerated degree programs, self-designed majors, tutorials, an honors program, a senior project, Phi Beta Kappa, and Sigma Xi. Special programs include internships, summer session for credit, off-campus study, study abroad, and Army ROTC.

The most popular **majors** include business, English, and history. A complete listing of majors at University of Richmond appears in the Majors Index beginning on page 380.

The **faculty** at University of Richmond has 271 full-time graduate and undergraduate teachers, 96% with terminal degrees. The student-faculty ratio is 12:1, and the average class size in required courses is 20.

##  Computers on Campus

Students are not required to have a computer. Student rooms are linked to a campus network. 500 **computers** available in the computer center, computer labs, the learn-ing resource center, classrooms, and the library provide access to the main academic computer, off-campus computing facilities, e-mail, and on-line services. Staffed computer lab on campus.

The 4 **libraries** have 559,291 books, 54,811 microform titles, and 6,827 subscriptions. They are connected to 9 national **on-line** catalogs.

##  Campus Life

There are 174 active **organizations** on campus, including a drama/theater group and student-run newspaper and radio station. 51% of eligible men and 61% of eligible women are members of 11 national **fraternities** and 8 national **sororities**. Student **safety services** include late night transport/escort service, 24-hour emergency telephone alarm devices, 24-hour patrols by trained security personnel, and electronically operated dormitory entrances.

University of Richmond is a member of the NCAA (Division I). **Intercollegiate sports** (some offering scholarships) include baseball (m), basketball (m, w), crew (m, w), cross-country running (m, w), equestrian sports (w), field hockey (w), football (m), golf (m), lacrosse (m, w), rugby (m), soccer (m, w), swimming and diving (m, w), tennis (m, w), track and field (m, w), volleyball (w), water polo (m, w).

##  Applying

University of Richmond requires an essay, a high school transcript, 3 years of high school math, 1 recommendation, SAT I or ACT, 3 SAT II Subject Tests (including SAT II: Writing Test), and a minimum high school GPA of 2.0. It recommends 3 years of high school science and 2 years of high school foreign language. Early and deferred entrance are possible, with a 2/1 deadline and a 2/25 priority date for financial aid. **Contact:** Ms. Pamela Spence, Dean of Admissions, Sarah Brunet Hall, Richmond Way, Richmond, VA 23173, 804-289-8640; fax 804-287-6003.

---

**GETTING IN LAST YEAR**
5,437 applied
55% were accepted
27% enrolled (822)
44% from top tenth of their h.s. class
29% had SAT verbal scores over 600
72% had SAT math scores over 600
75% had ACT scores over 26
5% had SAT verbal scores over 700
18% had SAT math scores over 700
20% had ACT scores over 30
29 National Merit Scholars
44 valedictorians

**THE STUDENT BODY**
Total 4,315, of whom 3,467
  are undergraduates

From 45 states and territories,
  34 other countries
20% from Virginia
50% women, 50% men
4% African Americans
1% Native Americans
1% Hispanics
3% Asian Americans
2% international students

**AFTER FRESHMAN YEAR**
92% returned for sophomore year
80% got a degree within 4 years
83% got a degree within 5 years
84% got a degree within 6 years

**AFTER GRADUATION**
31% pursued further study (18% arts and
  sciences, 7% law, 6% medicine)
63% had job offers within 3 months
173 corporations, 46 government agencies
  recruited on campus
1 Fulbright scholar

**WHAT YOU WILL PAY**
Tuition and fees $14,500
Room and board $3285
24% receive need-based financial aid
  averaging $5975
33% receive non-need financial aid averaging
  $7800

---

# UNIVERSITY OF ROCHESTER

Rochester, New York • Suburban setting • Private • Independent • Coed

Founded in 1850, the University of Rochester is one of the leading private universities in the country. Programs are available in 7 divisions, including Arts and Sciences, Engineering, Nursing, Education, Business, Medicine, and the Eastman School of Music. Special undergraduate opportunities include Freshman Ventures, Take Five, management certificate, Rochester Early Medical Scholars, University Day, and study abroad.

## Academics

U of R offers a core academic program; more than half of graduate courses are open to undergraduates. It awards bachelor's, master's, and doctoral **degrees**. Challenging opportunities include advanced placement, self-designed majors, an honors program, Phi Beta Kappa, and Sigma Xi. Special programs include internships, summer session for credit, off-campus study, study abroad, and Army, Naval, and Air Force ROTC.

The most popular **majors** include psychology, economics, and biology/biological sciences. A complete listing of majors at U of R appears in the Majors Index beginning on page 380.

The **faculty** at U of R has 1,231 full-time graduate and undergraduate teachers, 99% with terminal degrees. The student-faculty ratio is 12:1.

## Computers on Campus

Students are not required to have a computer. 265 **computers** available in the computer center, academic buildings, various locations on campus, the library, and dormitories provide access to the main academic computer and on-line services.

The **library** has 2.8 million books and 13,309 subscriptions. It is connected to 10 national **on-line** catalogs.

## Campus Life

Active **organizations** on campus include drama/theater group and student-run newspaper and radio station. 24% of students participate in student government elections. 24% of eligible men and 19% of eligible women are members of 16 national **fraternities** and 10 national **sororities**. Student **safety services** include late night transport/escort service, 24-hour emergency telephone alarm devices, 24-hour patrols by trained security personnel, and electronically operated dormitory entrances.

U of R is a member of the NCAA (Division III). **Intercollegiate sports** include baseball (m), basketball (m, w), crew (m, w), cross-country running (m, w), equestrian sports (m, w), field hockey (w), football (m), golf (m, w), ice hockey (m), lacrosse (m, w), rugby (m), skiing (cross-country) (m, w), skiing (downhill) (m, w), soccer (m, w), softball (w), squash (m, w), swimming and diving (m, w), tennis (m, w), track and field (m, w), volleyball (m, w).

## Applying

U of R requires an essay, a high school transcript, 1 recommendation, SAT I or ACT, and in some cases audition, portfolio. It recommends 3 years of high school math and science, 2 years of high school foreign language, an interview, and SAT II Subject Tests. Early, deferred, and midyear entrance are possible, with a 1/15 deadline and continuous processing to 2/1 for financial aid. **Contact:** Mr. Wayne A. Locust, Director of Admissions, Meliora Hall, Intercampus Drive, Rochester, NY 14627-0001, 716-275-3221; fax 716-461-4595.

### GETTING IN LAST YEAR
9,133 applied
63% were accepted
22% enrolled (1,246)
49% from top tenth of their h.s. class
21% had SAT verbal scores over 600
58% had SAT math scores over 600
61% had ACT scores over 26
3% had SAT verbal scores over 700
15% had SAT math scores over 700
17% had ACT scores over 30
17 National Merit Scholars

### THE STUDENT BODY
Total 8,336, of whom 5,222
   are undergraduates

From 52 states and territories,
   75 other countries
42% from New York
49% women, 51% men
7% African Americans
4% Hispanics
10% Asian Americans
11% international students

### AFTER FRESHMAN YEAR
94% returned for sophomore year
65% got a degree within 4 years
73% got a degree within 5 years
75% got a degree within 6 years

### AFTER GRADUATION
35% pursued further study (16% arts and
   sciences, 8% medicine, 6% law)
87 corporations recruited on campus
4 Fulbright scholars

### WHAT YOU WILL PAY
Tuition and fees $18,260
Room and board $6583
Need-based financial aid averages $10,000
Non-need financial aid averages $5000

# UNIVERSITY OF SCRANTON

Scranton, Pennsylvania • Urban setting • Private • Independent-Religious • Coed

The Jesuit tradition at the University of Scranton focuses on care for the whole person (cura personalis). In an educational context, this means preparation not only for a career but also for life. Over the last 5 years, an average of 95% of graduates have been working or attending graduate school full-time within 6 months of graduation. This year 35 graduates entered medical school, 40 entered law school, and 4 were named Fulbright Scholars.

## Academics

Scranton offers a flexible liberal arts curriculum and core academic program; fewer than half of graduate courses are open to undergraduates. It awards associate, bachelor's, and master's **degrees**. Challenging opportunities include advanced placement, accelerated degree programs, self-designed majors, tutorials, Freshmen Honors College, an honors program, a senior project, and Sigma Xi. Special programs include internships, summer session for credit, off-campus study, and Army and Air Force ROTC.

The most popular **majors** include biology/biological sciences, accounting, and communication. A complete listing of majors at Scranton appears in the Majors Index beginning on page 380.

The **faculty** at Scranton has 246 full-time graduate and undergraduate teachers, 83% with terminal degrees. 60% of the faculty serve as student advisers. The student-faculty ratio is 14:1, and the average class size in required courses is 20.

## Computers on Campus

Students are not required to have a computer. Student rooms are linked to a campus network. 321 **computers** available in the computer center, computer labs, the research center, the learning resource center, various academic departments, classrooms, the library, the student center, dormitories, and student rooms provide access to the main academic computer, off-campus computing facilities, e-mail, and on-line services. Staffed computer lab on campus provides training in the use of computers and software.

The **library** has 328,081 books, 306,095 microform titles, and 2,153 subscriptions. It is connected to 5 national **on-line** catalogs.

## Campus Life

There are 80 active **organizations** on campus, including a drama/theater group and student-run newspaper and radio station. Student **safety services** include late night transport/escort service, 24-hour emergency telephone alarm devices, 24-hour patrols by trained security personnel, student patrols, and electronically operated dormitory entrances.

Scranton is a member of the NCAA (Division III). **Intercollegiate sports** include baseball (m), basketball (m, w), bowling (m, w), crew (m, w), cross-country running (m, w), equestrian sports (m, w), field hockey (w), golf (m), ice hockey (m), lacrosse (m, w), rugby (m, w), skiing (downhill) (m, w), soccer (m, w), softball (w), swimming and diving (m, w), tennis (m, w), track and field (m, w), volleyball (m, w), wrestling (m).

## Applying

Scranton requires a high school transcript, 3 years of high school math, 2 years of high school foreign language, 2 recommendations, SAT I or ACT, and in some cases 3 years of high school science. It recommends a campus interview. Early, deferred, and midyear entrance are possible, with a 3/1 deadline and continuous processing to 2/15 for financial aid. **Contact:** Rev. Bernard R. McIlhenny, SJ, Dean of Admissions, Room 406, Saint Thomas Hall, Scranton, PA 18510-4622, 717-941-7540; fax 717-941-6369.

---

### GETTING IN LAST YEAR
4,838 applied
62% were accepted
32% enrolled (956)
31% from top tenth of their h.s. class
3.0 average high school GPA
9% had SAT verbal scores over 600
28% had SAT math scores over 600
1% had SAT verbal scores over 700
3% had SAT math scores over 700
3 National Merit Scholars
33 class presidents
22 valedictorians

### THE STUDENT BODY
Total 4,946, of whom 4,215
   are undergraduates

From 24 states and territories,
   21 other countries
48% from Pennsylvania
54% women, 46% men
1% African Americans
0% Native Americans
2% Hispanics
2% Asian Americans
2% international students

### AFTER FRESHMAN YEAR
90% returned for sophomore year
69% got a degree within 4 years
83% got a degree within 5 years

### AFTER GRADUATION
25% pursued further study (10% arts and
   sciences, 5% law, 5% medicine)
55 corporations, 4 government agencies, 1
   nonprofit organization recruited on campus
4 Fulbright scholars

### WHAT YOU WILL PAY
Tuition and fees $12,424
Room and board $5786
80% receive need-based financial aid
   averaging $3327
20% receive non-need financial aid averaging
   $4023

# UNIVERSITY OF SOUTHERN CALIFORNIA

Los Angeles, California • Urban setting • Private • Independent • Coed

▶ As one of the country's leading private research universities, USC provides outstanding teachers, excellent facilities, and an incredible array of academic offerings, including honors programs and undergraduate research opportunities. With a student-faculty ratio of 14:1 and small classes, students work with world-acclaimed professors in every discipline as participants, not spectators. USC offers over 170 undergraduate majors in the College of Letters, Arts and Sciences and 15 professional schools. Over 450 possible combinations are available for double majors, dual majors, and major-minor programs.

 ## Academics

USC offers an interdisciplinary curriculum and core academic program; fewer than half of graduate courses are open to undergraduates. It awards bachelor's, master's, doctoral, and first professional **degrees**. Challenging opportunities include advanced placement, accelerated degree programs, self-designed majors, tutorials, Freshmen Honors College, an honors program, a senior project, Phi Beta Kappa, and Sigma Xi. Special programs include cooperative education, internships, summer session for credit, off-campus study, study abroad, and Army, Naval, and Air Force ROTC.

The most popular **majors** include business, communication, and political science/government. A complete listing of majors at USC appears in the Majors Index beginning on page 380.

The **faculty** at USC has 1,634 full-time graduate and undergraduate teachers, 94% with terminal degrees. The student-faculty ratio is 14:1, and the average class size in required courses is 26.

 ## Computers on Campus

Students are not required to have a computer. 5,000 **computers** available in the computer center, computer labs, classrooms, the library, and the student center provide access to the main academic computer, off-campus computing facilities, e-mail, and on-line services. Staffed computer lab on campus (open 24 hours a day) provides training in the use of computers and software.

The 19 **libraries** have 3.2 million books, 1.5 million microform titles, and 18,000 subscriptions.

 ## Campus Life

There are 450 active **organizations** on campus, including a drama/theater group and student-run newspaper and radio station. 18% of eligible men and 20% of eligible women are members of 26 national **fraternities** and 12 national **sororities**. Student **safety services** include late night transport/escort service, 24-hour emergency telephone alarm devices, 24-hour patrols by trained security personnel, student patrols, and electronically operated dormitory entrances.

USC is a member of the NCAA (Division I). **Intercollegiate sports** (some offering scholarships) include baseball (m), basketball (m, w), crew (w), cross-country running (w), football (m), golf (m, w), sailing (m, w), soccer (w), swimming and diving (m, w), tennis (m, w), track and field (m, w), volleyball (m, w), water polo (m).

 ## Applying

USC requires an essay, a high school transcript, SAT I or ACT, and in some cases recommendations. It recommends 3 years of high school math and science, 2 years of high school foreign language, recommendations, an interview, and SAT II Subject Tests. Early, deferred, and midyear entrance are possible, with a 2/1 deadline and continuous processing to 2/1 for financial aid. **Contact:** Mr. Duncan Murdoch, Director of Admissions, 700 Childs Way, Los Angeles, CA 90089-0911, 213-740-8775; fax 213-740-6364.

---

**GETTING IN LAST YEAR**
11,712 applied
72% were accepted
29% enrolled (2,407)
43% from top tenth of their h.s. class
3.53 average high school GPA
80 National Merit Scholars

**THE STUDENT BODY**
Total 27,864, of whom 14,918 are undergraduates
From 52 states and territories, 110 other countries

66% from California
46% women, 54% men
7% African Americans
1% Native Americans
14% Hispanics
22% Asian Americans
9% international students

**AFTER FRESHMAN YEAR**
90% returned for sophomore year

**AFTER GRADUATION**
390 corporations, 15 government agencies, 5 nonprofit organizations recruited on campus
4 Fulbright scholars

**WHAT YOU WILL PAY**
Tuition and fees $17,560
Room and board $6482
61% receive need-based financial aid averaging $13,988
10% receive non-need financial aid averaging $6898

# UNIVERSITY OF TENNESSEE, KNOXVILLE

Knoxville, Tennessee • Urban setting • Public • State-supported • Coed

The University of Tennessee, Knoxville, is committed to the development of individuals and society through the cultivation of the human mind and spirit. Its mission is accomplished through teaching, scholarship, artistic creation, public service, and professional practice. Opportunity abounds with over 100 academic majors and 300 clubs and organizations. In honors classes, outstanding faculty teach small groups of talented and highly motivated students, including more than 100 National Merit Scholars. The educational experience is enhanced by impressive facilities, including one of the nation's most technologically advanced libraries, a dynamic theater facility, and modern robotics and image laboratories.

 **Academics**

UT Knoxville offers a comprehensive curriculum and no core academic program; fewer than half of graduate courses are open to undergraduates. It awards bachelor's, master's, doctoral, and first professional **degrees**. Challenging opportunities include advanced placement, accelerated degree programs, self-designed majors, tutorials, an honors program, a senior project, Phi Beta Kappa, and Sigma Xi. Special programs include cooperative education, internships, summer session for credit, off-campus study, study abroad, and Army and Air Force ROTC.

The most popular **majors** include psychology, accounting, and business. A complete listing of majors at UT Knoxville appears in the Majors Index beginning on page 380.

The **faculty** at UT Knoxville has 1,152 full-time graduate and undergraduate teachers, 86% with terminal degrees. 85% of the faculty serve as student advisers. The student-faculty ratio is 17:1, and the average class size in required courses is 30.

 **Computers on Campus**

Students are not required to have a computer. 1,500 **computers** available in the computer center, classrooms, the library, the student center, and dormitories.

The 7 **libraries** have 2.1 million books, 1.9 million microform titles, and 14,406 subscriptions. They are connected to 4 national **on-line** catalogs.

 **Campus Life**

There are 300 active **organizations** on campus, including a drama/theater group and student-run newspaper and radio station. 16% of eligible men and 16% of eligible women are members of 26 national **fraternities** and 19 national **sororities**. Student **safety services** include late night transport/escort service, 24-hour emergency telephone alarm devices, and 24-hour patrols by trained security personnel.

UT Knoxville is a member of the NCAA (Division I). **Intercollegiate sports** (some offering scholarships) include baseball (m), basketball (m, w), crew (w), cross-country running (m, w), football (m), golf (m, w), softball (w), swimming and diving (m, w), tennis (m, w), track and field (m, w), volleyball (w).

 **Applying**

UT Knoxville requires a high school transcript, 3 years of high school math, 2 years of high school foreign language, SAT I or ACT, a minimum high school GPA of 2.0, and in some cases an essay, recommendations, and an interview. Early, deferred, and midyear entrance are possible, with a 7/1 deadline and continuous processing to 2/15 for financial aid. **Contact:** Dr. Gordon Stanley, Director of Admissions, 320 Student Services Building, Knoxville, TN 37996, 615-974-2184 or toll-free 800-221-8657 (in-state).

---

### GETTING IN LAST YEAR
7,027 applied
74% were accepted
56% enrolled (2,912)
27% from top tenth of their h.s. class
3.17 average high school GPA
11% had SAT verbal scores over 600
26% had SAT math scores over 600
26% had ACT scores over 26
2% had SAT verbal scores over 700
4% had SAT math scores over 700
6% had ACT scores over 30

### THE STUDENT BODY
Total 25,890, of whom 18,986
  are undergraduates
From 49 states and territories,
  69 other countries
85% from Tennessee
49% women, 51% men
5% African Americans
1% Native Americans
1% Hispanics
2% Asian Americans
2% international students

### AFTER FRESHMAN YEAR
78% returned for sophomore year
23% got a degree within 6 years

### WHAT YOU WILL PAY
Resident tuition and fees $2052
Nonresident tuition and fees $5986
Room and board $3398
Need-based financial aid averages $1200
Non-need financial aid averages $1200

# UNIVERSITY OF TEXAS AT AUSTIN

Austin, Texas • Urban setting • Public • State-supported • Coed

In the 111 years of its existence, UT has grown from a small, 40-acre, one-building campus into an internationally recognized institution. With its current enrollment of just under 48,000 students, the University offers more than 250 graduate and undergraduate degree programs in virtually all major academic disciplines. Approximately 50 honors programs are available to undergraduates in the humanities, the sciences, communication, and business. The University of Texas at Austin extends well beyond the boundaries of the main campus, incorporating research centers around Austin and across the state that keep the University at the forefront of study.

 ## Academics

UT Austin offers a core academic program. It awards bachelor's, master's, and doctoral **degrees**. Challenging opportunities include advanced placement, accelerated degree programs, self-designed majors, an honors program, Phi Beta Kappa, and Sigma Xi. Special programs include cooperative education, internships, summer session for credit, study abroad, and Army, Naval, and Air Force ROTC.

The **faculty** at UT Austin has 2,194 full-time graduate and undergraduate teachers, 91% with terminal degrees. The student-faculty ratio is 19:1.

 ## Computers on Campus

Students are not required to have a computer. Student rooms are linked to a campus network. 500 **computers** available in the computer center, computer labs, classrooms, the library, the student center, and dormitories provide access to the main academic computer, off-campus computing facili-

ties, e-mail, and on-line services. Staffed computer lab on campus (open 24 hours a day) provides training in the use of computers and software.

The 19 **libraries** have 6.8 million books and 51,338 subscriptions.

 ## Campus Life

There are 697 active **organizations** on campus, including a drama/theater group and student-run newspaper and radio station. 11% of eligible men and 13% of eligible women are members of 34 national **fraternities** and 20 national **sororities**. Student **safety services** include late night transport/escort service, 24-hour emergency telephone alarm devices, 24-hour patrols by trained security personnel, student patrols, and electronically operated dormitory entrances.

UT Austin is a member of the NCAA (Division I). **Intercollegiate sports** (some offering scholarships) include baseball (m), basketball (m, w), cross-country running (m, w), football (m), golf (m, w), soccer (w), softball (w), swimming and diving (m, w), tennis (m, w), track and field (m, w), volleyball (w).

 ## Applying

UT Austin requires a high school transcript, 3 years of high school math, 2 years of high school foreign language, SAT I or ACT, and in some cases an essay and SAT II: Writing Test. It recommends 3 years of high school science. Early and midyear entrance are possible, with a 2/1 deadline and continuous processing to 4/1 for financial aid. **Contact:** Ms. Shirley F. Binder, Director of Admissions, Red River and Martin Luther King Blvd., Austin, TX 78712, 512-475-7399.

---

### GETTING IN LAST YEAR

14,320 applied
66% were accepted
59% enrolled (5,547)
46% from top tenth of their h.s. class
22% had SAT verbal scores over 600
55% had SAT math scores over 600
51% had ACT scores over 26
3% had SAT verbal scores over 700
17% had SAT math scores over 700
14% had ACT scores over 30
244 National Merit Scholars

### THE STUDENT BODY

Total 47,957, of whom 34,746
  are undergraduates
From 52 states and territories,
  115 other countries
91% from Texas
48% women, 52% men
4% African Americans
1% Native Americans
15% Hispanics
11% Asian Americans
4% international students

### AFTER FRESHMAN YEAR

86% returned for sophomore year
31% got a degree within 4 years
57% got a degree within 5 years
63% got a degree within 6 years

### WHAT YOU WILL PAY

Resident tuition and fees $1815
Nonresident tuition and fees $6105
Room and board $3528
Need-based financial aid averages $2200
Non-need financial aid averages $2800

---

# UNIVERSITY OF THE SOUTH

Sewanee, Tennessee • Small-town setting • Private • Independent-Religious • Coed

The University of the South (Sewanee) is consistently ranked among the top tier of national liberal arts institutions. Sewanee is committed to an academic curriculum that focuses on the liberal arts. The campus is located on 10,000 acres atop Tennessee's Cumberland Plateau between Chattanooga and Nashville. Sewanee has an impressive record of academic achievement: 22 Rhodes scholars, 18 NCAA Postgraduate Scholarship recipients, and 91% of undergraduates who apply to medical and dental schools are accepted.

 ## Academics

Sewanee offers a liberal arts curriculum and core academic program; fewer than half of graduate courses are open to undergraduates. It awards bachelor's, master's, doctoral, and first professional **degrees**. Challenging opportunities include advanced placement, accelerated degree programs, self-designed majors, tutorials, an honors program, a senior project, Phi Beta Kappa, and Sigma Xi. Special programs include internships, summer session for credit, and study abroad.

The most popular **majors** include history, English, and art/fine arts. A complete listing of majors at Sewanee appears in the Majors Index beginning on page 380.

The **faculty** at Sewanee has 108 full-time graduate and undergraduate teachers, 95% with terminal degrees. 100% of the faculty serve as student advisers. The student-faculty ratio is 11:1, and the average class size in required courses is 19.

 ## Computers on Campus

Students are not required to have a computer. Student rooms are linked to a campus network. 110 **computers** available in the computer center, computer labs, various academic locations, classrooms, and the library provide access to the main academic computer, off-campus computing facilities, e-mail, and on-line services. Staffed computer lab on campus (open 24 hours a day) provides training in the use of computers and software.

The **library** has 443,463 books, 239,078 microform titles, and 3,994 subscriptions. It is connected to 3 national **on-line** catalogs.

 ## Campus Life

There are 110 active **organizations** on campus, including a drama/theater group and student-run newspaper and radio station. 62% of eligible men and 65% of eligible women are members of 11 national **fraternities** and 7 local **sororities**. Student **safety services** include security lighting, late night transport/escort service, 24-hour emergency telephone alarm devices, and 24-hour patrols by trained security personnel.

Sewanee is a member of the NCAA (Division III). **Intercollegiate sports** include baseball (m), basketball (m, w), crew (m, w), cross-country running (m, w), equestrian sports (m, w), fencing (m, w), field hockey (w), football (m), golf (m, w), lacrosse (m, w), rugby (m, w), skiing (cross-country) (m, w), skiing (downhill) (m, w), soccer (m, w), swimming and diving (m, w), tennis (m, w), track and field (m, w), volleyball (w).

 ## Applying

Sewanee requires an essay, a high school transcript, 3 years of high school math, 2 years of high school foreign language, 2 recommendations, and SAT I or ACT. It recommends 3 years of high school science, a campus interview, and SAT II Subject Tests. Early, deferred, and midyear entrance are possible, with a 2/1 deadline and continuous processing to 3/1 for financial aid. **Contact:** Mr. Robert M. Hedrick, Director of Admission, 735 University Avenue, Sewanee, TN 37383-1000, 615-598-1238 or toll-free 800-522-2234; fax 615-598-1667.

## GETTING IN LAST YEAR
1,684 applied
68% were accepted
32% enrolled (371)
54% from top tenth of their h.s. class
3.33 average high school GPA
31% had SAT verbal scores over 600
54% had SAT math scores over 600
90% had ACT scores over 26
5% had SAT verbal scores over 700
11% had SAT math scores over 700
20% had ACT scores over 30
27 National Merit Scholars

## THE STUDENT BODY
Total 1,298, of whom 1,213
   are undergraduates

From 43 states and territories,
   15 other countries
18% from Tennessee
50% women, 50% men
3% African Americans
0% Native Americans
1% Hispanics
1% Asian Americans
2% international students

## AFTER FRESHMAN YEAR
97% returned for sophomore year
79% got a degree within 4 years
80% got a degree within 5 years
81% got a degree within 6 years

## AFTER GRADUATION
38% pursued further study (12% arts and
   sciences, 8% law, 5% business)
57% had job offers within 3 months
35 corporations, 5 government agencies, 15
   nonprofit organizations recruited on campus

## WHAT YOU WILL PAY
Tuition and fees $15,525
Room and board $4080
42% receive need-based financial aid
   averaging $10,700
14% receive non-need financial aid averaging
   $5200

# UNIVERSITY OF TULSA

Tulsa, Oklahoma • Urban setting • Private • Independent-Religious • Coed

 ## Academics

TU offers a liberal arts curriculum and core academic program; fewer than half of graduate courses are open to undergraduates. It awards bachelor's, master's, doctoral, and first professional **degrees**. Challenging opportunities include advanced placement, self-designed majors, an honors program, a senior project, Phi Beta Kappa, and Sigma Xi. Special programs include internships, summer session for credit, and study abroad.

The most popular **majors** include accounting, psychology, and communication. A complete listing of majors at TU appears in the Majors Index beginning on page 380.

The **faculty** at TU has 331 full-time graduate and undergraduate teachers, 96% with terminal degrees. 100% of the faculty serve as student advisers. The student-faculty ratio is 12:1, and the average class size in required courses is 30.

 ## Campus Life

There are 140 active **organizations** on campus, including a drama/theater group and student-run newspaper and radio station. 21% of eligible men and 19% of eligible women are members of 7 national **fraternities** and 7 national **sororities**. Student **safety services** include late night transport/escort service, 24-hour emergency telephone alarm devices, 24-hour patrols by trained security personnel, and electronically operated dormitory entrances.

TU is a member of the NCAA (Division I). **Intercollegiate sports** (some offering scholarships) include basketball (m), cross-country running (m, w), football (m), golf (m, w), soccer (m, w), softball (w), tennis (m, w), track and field (m, w), volleyball (w).

 ## Computers on Campus

Students are not required to have a computer. Student rooms are linked to a campus network. 250 **computers** available in the computer center, computer labs, classrooms, the library, and dormitories provide access to the main academic computer, off-campus computing facilities, e-mail, and on-line services. Staffed computer lab on campus (open 24 hours a day) provides training in the use of computers and software.

The 3 **libraries** have 1.3 million books, 2.4 million microform titles, and 3,430 subscriptions. They are connected to 5 national **on-line** catalogs.

 ## Applying

TU requires a high school transcript, 1 recommendation, SAT I or ACT, and a minimum high school GPA of 2.0. It recommends an essay, 3 years of high school math and science, 2 years of high school foreign language, an interview, and a minimum high school GPA of 3.0. Early, deferred, and midyear entrance are possible, with rolling admissions and continuous processing for financial aid.
**Contact:** Mr. John C. Corso, Assoc. Vice President for Administration/Dean of Admission, Tulsa, OK 74104-3126, 918-631-2307 or toll-free 800-331-3050; fax 918-631-3172.

### GETTING IN LAST YEAR

1,756 applied
86% were accepted
38% enrolled (568)
39% from top tenth of their h.s. class
3.5 average high school GPA
26% had SAT verbal scores over 600
40% had SAT math scores over 600
39% had ACT scores over 26
3% had SAT verbal scores over 700
11% had SAT math scores over 700
12% had ACT scores over 30
13 National Merit Scholars

### THE STUDENT BODY

Total 4,573, of whom 3,162
  are undergraduates
From 52 states and territories,
  60 other countries
60% from Oklahoma
54% women, 46% men
6% African Americans
5% Native Americans
2% Hispanics
3% Asian Americans
10% international students

### AFTER FRESHMAN YEAR

80% returned for sophomore year

### AFTER GRADUATION

200 corporations, 20 government agencies, 2
  nonprofit organizations recruited on campus
1 Fulbright scholar

### WHAT YOU WILL PAY

Tuition and fees $11,750
Room and board $4160
73% receive need-based financial aid
  averaging $6450
45% receive non-need financial aid averaging
  $2000

# UNIVERSITY OF UTAH

Salt Lake City, Utah • Urban setting • Public • State-supported • Coed

## Academics

U of U offers a liberal arts and professional curriculum and core academic program; a few graduate courses are open to undergraduates. It awards bachelor's, master's, doctoral, and first professional **degrees**. Challenging opportunities include advanced placement, accelerated degree programs, self-designed majors, tutorials, an honors program, Phi Beta Kappa, and Sigma Xi. Special programs include cooperative education, internships, summer session for credit, off-campus study, study abroad, and Army, Naval, and Air Force ROTC.

The most popular **majors** include psychology, political science/government, and accounting. A complete listing of majors at U of U appears in the Majors Index beginning on page 380.

The **faculty** at U of U has 1,430 full-time graduate and undergraduate teachers, 93% with terminal degrees. 20% of the faculty serve as student advisers. The student-faculty ratio is 21:1, and the average class size in required courses is 45.

## Campus Life

Active **organizations** on campus include drama/theater group and student-run newspaper and radio station. 12% of students participate in student government elections. 6% of eligible men and 6% of eligible women are members of 9 national **fraternities**, 7 national **sororities**, 1 local fraternity, and 1 local sorority. Student **safety services** include late night transport/escort service, 24-hour emergency telephone alarm devices, 24-hour patrols by trained security personnel, student patrols, and electronically operated dormitory entrances.

U of U is a member of the NCAA (Division I). **Intercollegiate sports** (some offering scholarships) include baseball (m), basketball (m, w), bowling (m, w), cross-country running (m, w), football (m), golf (m), gymnastics (w), ice hockey (m), racquetball (m, w), rugby (m), skiing (cross-country) (m, w), skiing (downhill) (m, w), soccer (m, w), softball (w), swimming and diving (m, w), table tennis (m, w), tennis (m, w), track and field (m, w), volleyball (w).

## Computers on Campus

Students are not required to have a computer. Student rooms are linked to a campus network. 800 **computers** available in the computer center, computer labs, the research center, the learning resource center, several academic departments, the library, the student center, and dormitories provide access to the main academic computer, off-campus computing facilities, e-mail, and on-line services. Staffed computer lab on campus provides training in the use of computers and software.

The 3 **libraries** have 2.3 million books, 3.1 million microform titles, and 21,807 subscriptions.

## Applying

U of U requires a high school transcript, 2 years of high school foreign language, SAT I or ACT, and a minimum high school GPA of 2.0. It recommends 3 years of high school math and science and a minimum high school GPA of 3.0. Early, deferred, and midyear entrance are possible, with a 7/1 deadline and continuous processing to 3/1 for financial aid. **Contact:** Mrs. Pat Goldsmith, Director of High School Services, 250 South Student Services Building, Salt Lake City, UT 84112, 801-581-8761 or toll-free 800-444-8638; fax 801-585-3034.

### GETTING IN LAST YEAR
6,004 applied
91% were accepted
46% enrolled (2,498)
27% from top tenth of their h.s. class
3.39 average high school GPA
14% had SAT verbal scores over 600
34% had SAT math scores over 600
34% had ACT scores over 26
1% had SAT verbal scores over 700
9% had SAT math scores over 700
11% had ACT scores over 30
37 National Merit Scholars
30 class presidents
40 valedictorians

### THE STUDENT BODY
Total 25,226, of whom 20,278 are undergraduates

From 55 states and territories, 106 other countries
90% from Utah
45% women, 55% men
1% African Americans
1% Native Americans
3% Hispanics
3% Asian Americans
6% international students

### AFTER FRESHMAN YEAR
62% returned for sophomore year
17% got a degree within 4 years
31% got a degree within 5 years
42% got a degree within 6 years

### AFTER GRADUATION
27% pursued further study
80% had job offers within 3 months
240 corporations, 47 government agencies, 5 nonprofit organizations recruited on campus
2 Fulbright scholars

### WHAT YOU WILL PAY
Resident tuition and fees $2298
Nonresident tuition and fees $6795
Room and board $4570
48% receive need-based financial aid averaging $868
12% receive non-need financial aid averaging $1563

# UNIVERSITY OF VERMONT

Burlington, Vermont • Small-town setting • Public • State-supported • Coed

▶ The University of Vermont is distinctive among state universities for its unusual balance of students—at least half are from outside Vermont. UVM's mission focuses on teaching undergraduates, including offering students a unique opportunity to work with faculty on research projects. All undergraduates receive a liberal education through the College of Arts and Sciences.

 ## Academics

UVM offers a liberal arts and professional curriculum and no core academic program; more than half of graduate courses are open to undergraduates. It awards associate, bachelor's, master's, doctoral, and first professional **degrees**. Challenging opportunities include advanced placement, self-designed majors, an honors program, Phi Beta Kappa, and Sigma Xi. Special programs include cooperative education, internships, summer session for credit, study abroad, and Army and Air Force ROTC.

The most popular **majors** include political science/government, business, and psychology. A complete listing of majors at UVM appears in the Majors Index beginning on page 380.

The **faculty** at UVM has 867 full-time graduate and undergraduate teachers, 87% with terminal degrees. 60% of the faculty serve as student advisers. The student-faculty ratio is 13:1.

 ## Computers on Campus

Students are not required to have a computer. 500 **computers** available in the computer center, computer labs, engineering and business administration buildings, the library, the student center, and dormitories provide access to the main academic computer, off-campus computing facilities, e-mail, and on-line services. Staffed computer lab on campus.

The 4 **libraries** have 2.17 million books, 212,000 microform titles, and 17,300 subscriptions. They are connected to 2 national **on-line** catalogs.

 ## Campus Life

There are 100 active **organizations** on campus, including a drama/theater group and student-run newspaper and radio station. 7% of eligible men and 7% of eligible women are members of 13 national **fraternities**, 6 national **sororities**, and 2 local fraternities. Student **safety services** include late night transport/escort service and 24-hour patrols by trained security personnel.

UVM is a member of the NCAA (Division I). **Intercollegiate sports** (some offering scholarships) include baseball (m), basketball (m, w), crew (m, w), cross-country running (m, w), fencing (m, w), field hockey (w), golf (m), gymnastics (m, w), ice hockey (m, w), lacrosse (m, w), rugby (m, w), skiing (cross-country) (m, w), skiing (downhill) (m, w), soccer (m, w), softball (w), swimming and diving (m, w), tennis (m, w), track and field (m, w), volleyball (m, w), wrestling (m).

 ## Applying

UVM requires an essay, a high school transcript, 3 years of high school math, 2 years of high school foreign language, and SAT I or ACT. It recommends 2 recommendations and an interview. Early, deferred, and midyear entrance are possible, with a 2/1 deadline and continuous processing to 3/1 for financial aid. **Contact:** Ms. Carol Hogan, Director of Admissions, Clement House, 194 South Prospect Street, Burlington, VT 05401-3596, 802-656-3370; fax 802-656-8611.

---

### GETTING IN LAST YEAR
7,750 applied
80% were accepted
28% enrolled (1,732)
16% from top tenth of their h.s. class
8% had SAT verbal scores over 600
31% had SAT math scores over 600
1% had SAT verbal scores over 700
5% had SAT math scores over 700

### THE STUDENT BODY
Total 9,072, of whom 7,496
  are undergraduates
From 48 states and territories,
  29 other countries

43% from Vermont
53% women, 47% men
1% African Americans
1% Native Americans
1% Hispanics
2% Asian Americans
1% international students

### AFTER FRESHMAN YEAR
83% returned for sophomore year
56% got a degree within 4 years
73% got a degree within 5 years
76% got a degree within 6 years

### AFTER GRADUATION
16% pursued further study
54% had job offers within 3 months
120 corporations, 12 government agencies,
  19 nonprofit organizations recruited on
  campus

### WHAT YOU WILL PAY
Resident tuition and fees $6652
Nonresident tuition and fees $15,954
Room and board $4514
Need-based financial aid averages $4110
Non-need financial aid averages $7715

# UNIVERSITY OF VIRGINIA

Charlottesville, Virginia • Suburban setting • Public • State-supported • Coed

Established in 1825, the University of Virginia today continues to be influenced by the spirit of its founder, Thomas Jefferson. His powerful convictions—the idea that the University exists to train young people for public affairs and that the liberal arts constitute the foundation for any education—continue to inspire the students and faculty and to guide the development of its programs. Mr. Jefferson's vision of the University as a community where scholars and students work closely together remains paramount. Deemed a "public ivy" and consistently rated as one of the best institutions in the country, the University has achieved national stature for teaching, research, and public service.

 ## Academics

UVA offers no core academic program; more than half of graduate courses are open to undergraduates. It awards bachelor's, master's, doctoral, and first professional **degrees**. Challenging opportunities include advanced placement, accelerated degree programs, self-designed majors, tutorials, an honors program, a senior project, Phi Beta Kappa, and Sigma Xi. Special programs include internships, summer session for credit, study abroad, and Army, Naval, and Air Force ROTC.

The most popular **majors** include business, English, and psychology. A complete listing of majors at UVA appears in the Majors Index beginning on page 380.

The **faculty** at UVA has 1,760 full-time graduate and undergraduate teachers, 90% with terminal degrees. 100% of the faculty serve as student advisers. The student-faculty ratio is 14:1, and the average class size in required courses is 33.

 ## Computers on Campus

Students are not required to have a computer. Student rooms are linked to a campus network. 939 **computers** available in the computer center, computer labs, the library, and dormitories provide access to the main academic computer, off-campus computing facilities, e-mail, and on-line services. Staffed computer lab on campus (open 24 hours a day) provides training in the use of computers and software.

The 16 **libraries** have 4 million books and 38,192 subscriptions.

 ## Campus Life

There are 300 active **organizations** on campus, including a drama/theater group and student-run newspaper and radio station. 28% of eligible men and 30% of eligible women are members of 38 national **fraternities**, 22 national **sororities**, and 1 local fraternity. Student **safety services** include late night transport/escort service, 24-hour emergency telephone alarm devices, 24-hour patrols by trained security personnel, and electronically operated dormitory entrances.

UVA is a member of the NCAA (Division I). **Intercollegiate sports** (some offering scholarships) include baseball (m), basketball (m, w), crew (w), cross-country running (m, w), field hockey (w), football (m), golf (m), lacrosse (m, w), soccer (m, w), softball (w), swimming and diving (m, w), tennis (m, w), track and field (m, w), volleyball (w), wrestling (m).

 ## Applying

UVA requires an essay, a high school transcript, 4 years of high school math, 2 years of high school foreign language, 1 recommendation, SAT I, and 3 SAT II Subject Tests (including SAT II: Writing Test). It recommends 3 years of high school science. Early entrance and early decision are possible, with a 1/2 deadline and continuous processing to 3/1 for financial aid. **Contact:** Mr. John A. Blackburn, Dean of Admission, PO Box 9017, Charlottesville, VA 22906, 804-982-3200; fax 804-924-3587.

---

### GETTING IN LAST YEAR
14,921 applied
38% were accepted
48% enrolled (2,761)
76% from top tenth of their h.s. class
40% had SAT verbal scores over 600
74% had SAT math scores over 600
6% had SAT verbal scores over 700
30% had SAT math scores over 700
175 valedictorians

### THE STUDENT BODY
Total 17,704, of whom 11,502
    are undergraduates
From 48 states and territories,
    53 other countries

66% from Virginia
53% women, 47% men
11% African Americans
0% Native Americans
2% Hispanics
10% Asian Americans
2% international students

### AFTER FRESHMAN YEAR
96% returned for sophomore year
80% got a degree within 4 years
90% got a degree within 5 years
91% got a degree within 6 years

### AFTER GRADUATION
400 corporations, 30 government agencies,
    15 nonprofit organizations recruited on
    campus
1 Rhodes, 1 Fulbright scholar

### WHAT YOU WILL PAY
Resident tuition and fees $4484
Nonresident tuition and fees $13,056
Room and board $4000
32% receive need-based financial aid
    averaging $5750

# UNIVERSITY OF WASHINGTON

Seattle, Washington • Urban setting • Public • State-supported • Coed

## Academics

UW offers a core academic program; fewer than half of graduate courses are open to undergraduates. It awards bachelor's, master's, doctoral, and first professional **degrees**. Challenging opportunities include advanced placement, accelerated degree programs, self-designed majors, an honors program, a senior project, Phi Beta Kappa, and Sigma Xi. Special programs include cooperative education, internships, summer session for credit, study abroad, and Army, Naval, and Air Force ROTC.

A complete listing of majors at UW appears in the Majors Index beginning on page 380.

The **faculty** at UW has 3,604 graduate and undergraduate teachers, 99% with terminal degrees. The student-faculty ratio is 9:1.

## Computers on Campus

Students are not required to have a computer. **Computers** available in the computer center, computer labs, the research center, the learning resource center, academic departments, classrooms, the library, the student center, dormitories, and student rooms provide access to the main academic computer and e-mail. Staffed computer lab on campus (open 24 hours a day) provides training in the use of computers and software.

The 22 **libraries** have 5.3 million books.

## Campus Life

Active **organizations** on campus include drama/theater group and student-run newspaper and radio station. 18% of eligible men and 14% of eligible women are members of 32 national **fraternities** and 18 national **sororities**. Student **safety services** include late night transport/escort service, 24-hour emergency telephone alarm devices, 24-hour patrols by trained security personnel, and electronically operated dormitory entrances.

UW is a member of the NCAA (Division I). **Intercollegiate sports** (some offering scholarships) include baseball (m), basketball (m, w), crew (m, w), cross-country running (m, w), football (m), golf (m, w), gymnastics (w), soccer (m, w), softball (w), swimming and diving (m, w), tennis (m, w), track and field (m, w), volleyball (w), wrestling (m).

## Applying

UW requires a high school transcript, 3 years of high school math, 2 years of high school foreign language, and SAT I or ACT. Early and midyear entrance are possible, with a 2/1 deadline and a 2/28 priority date for financial aid. **Contact:** Ms. Stephanie Preston, Assistant Director of Admissions, 1410 Northeast Campus Parkway, Seattle, WA 98195, 206-543-9686; fax 206-685-3655.

### GETTING IN LAST YEAR

12,076 applied
61% were accepted
48% enrolled (3,489)
40% from top tenth of their h.s. class
19% had SAT verbal scores over 600
48% had SAT math scores over 600
39% had ACT scores over 26
3% had SAT verbal scores over 700
13% had SAT math scores over 700
10% had ACT scores over 30
22 National Merit Scholars

### THE STUDENT BODY

Total 33,719, of whom 24,592
  are undergraduates
From 52 states and territories,
  56 other countries
90% from Washington
51% women, 49% men
4% African Americans
1% Native Americans
4% Hispanics
20% Asian Americans
2% international students

### AFTER FRESHMAN YEAR

92% returned for sophomore year

### AFTER GRADUATION

190 corporations, 115 government agencies,
  15 nonprofit organizations recruited on
  campus
8 Fulbright scholars

### WHAT YOU WILL PAY

Resident tuition and fees $2907
Nonresident tuition and fees $8199
Room and board $4944
Need-based financial aid averages $4379

# UNIVERSITY OF WISCONSIN–MADISON

Madison, Wisconsin • Urban setting • Public • State-supported • Coed

---

At Wisconsin, "the largest small school in the country," world-class undergraduate learning opportunities are provided by a faculty that has been placed in the top ten nationally by every scholarly college and university ranking done this century. Close contact to this faculty is ensured because over 85% of all classes include fewer than 30 students. Rich honors programs provide students with the opportunity to engage in original research with faculty mentors dedicated to making the resources of one of the world's great teaching and research universities available to all undergraduate scholars.

##  Academics

Wisconsin offers no core academic program; more than half of graduate courses are open to undergraduates. It awards bachelor's, master's, doctoral, and first professional **degrees**. Challenging opportunities include advanced placement, accelerated degree programs, self-designed majors, tutorials, Freshmen Honors College, an honors program, a senior project, Phi Beta Kappa, and Sigma Xi. Special programs include cooperative education, internships, summer session for credit, study abroad, and Army, Naval, and Air Force ROTC.

The most popular **majors** include political science/government, mechanical engineering, and history. A complete listing of majors at Wisconsin appears in the Majors Index beginning on page 380.

The **faculty** at Wisconsin has 2,245 full-time undergraduate teachers, 96% with terminal degrees. 40% of the faculty serve as student advisers. The student-faculty ratio is 12:1, and the average class size in required courses is 35.

##  Computers on Campus

Students are not required to have a computer. Student rooms are linked to a campus network. 2,700 **computers** available in the computer center, computer labs, the research center, the learning resource center, the library, the student center, and dormitories provide access to the main academic computer, e-mail, and on-line services. Staffed computer lab on campus provides training in the use of computers and software.

The 28 **libraries** have 5.3 million books, 2 million microform titles, and 55,300 subscriptions.

##  Campus Life

There are 900 active **organizations** on campus, including a drama/theater group and student-run newspaper and radio station. 15% of eligible men and 15% of eligible women are members of 27 national **fraternities**, 10 national **sororities**, and 10 eating clubs, social clubs. Student **safety services** include late night transport/escort service, 24-hour emergency telephone alarm devices, 24-hour patrols by trained security personnel, and electronically operated dormitory entrances.

Wisconsin is a member of the NCAA (Division I). **Intercollegiate sports** (some offering scholarships) include basketball (m, w), crew (m, w), cross-country running (m, w), football (m), golf (m, w), ice hockey (m, w), rugby (m), sailing (m), soccer (m, w), softball (w), swimming and diving (m, w), tennis (m, w), track and field (m, w), volleyball (m, w), wrestling (m).

##  Applying

Wisconsin requires a high school transcript, 3 years of high school math, 2 years of high school foreign language, SAT I or ACT, and in some cases recommendations. It recommends an essay and 3 years of high school science. Early, deferred, and midyear entrance are possible, with a 2/1 deadline and continuous processing to 3/1 for financial aid. **Contact:** Office of Admissions, 140 Peterson Office Building, 750 University Avenue, Madison, WI 53706-1490, 608-262-3961; fax 608-262-1429.

---

### GETTING IN LAST YEAR
15,293 applied
69% were accepted
44% enrolled (4,681)
41% from top tenth of their h.s. class
3.42 average high school GPA
24% had SAT verbal scores over 600
55% had SAT math scores over 600
57% had ACT scores over 26
4% had SAT verbal scores over 700
16% had SAT math scores over 700
18% had ACT scores over 30

### THE STUDENT BODY
Total 38,139, of whom 26,207
  are undergraduates
From 53 states and territories,
  76 other countries
64% from Wisconsin
50% women, 50% men
4% African Americans
1% Native Americans
4% Hispanics
5% Asian Americans
4% international students

### AFTER FRESHMAN YEAR
95% returned for sophomore year
71% got a degree within 4 years
77% got a degree within 5 years
85% got a degree within 6 years

### WHAT YOU WILL PAY
Resident tuition and fees $2737
Nonresident tuition and fees $9096
Room and board $2925
Need-based financial aid averages $840
Non-need financial aid averages $1619

# URSINUS COLLEGE

Collegeville, Pennsylvania • Suburban setting • Private • Independent-Religious • Coed

Ursinus, celebrating its 125th anniversary, is a small, residential college located in Collegeville, 30 minutes from Philadelphia, offering the safety and beauty of a small town and access to a vibrant metropolitan community. The main objective of Ursinus's traditional liberal arts curriculum is to prepare students for the professions. Most graduates go on to earn advanced-level degrees through professional or graduate course work, particularly in the areas of science, medicine, and law. Ursinus is committed to a policy of both need-based and merit-based financial aid and awards Ursinus College Merit Scholarships to students who have demonstrated academic and extracurricular leadership.

## Academics

Ursinus offers an interdisciplinary curriculum and core academic program. It awards bachelor's **degrees**. Challenging opportunities include advanced placement, accelerated degree programs, self-designed majors, tutorials, an honors program, a senior project, Phi Beta Kappa, and Sigma Xi. Special programs include internships, summer session for credit, off-campus study, and study abroad.

A complete listing of majors at Ursinus appears in the Majors Index beginning on page 380.

The **faculty** at Ursinus has 95 full-time teachers, 81% with terminal degrees. 100% of the faculty serve as student advisers. The student-faculty ratio is 12:1, and the average class size in required courses is 20.

## Computers on Campus

Students are not required to have a computer. 150 **computers** available in the computer center, computer labs, the research center, academic buildings, classrooms, the library, and dormitories provide access to the main academic computer, off-campus computing facilities, e-mail, and on-line services. Staffed computer lab on campus provides training in the use of computers and software.

The **library** has 185,000 books, 155,000 microform titles, and 900 subscriptions.

## Campus Life

There are 75 active **organizations** on campus, including a drama/theater group and student-run newspaper and radio station. 55% of eligible men and 50% of eligible women are members of 1 national **fraternity**, 8 local fraternities, and 5 local **sororities**. Student **safety services** include late night transport/escort service and 24-hour patrols by trained security personnel.

Ursinus is a member of the NCAA (Division III). **Intercollegiate sports** include baseball (m), basketball (m, w), cross-country running (m, w), field hockey (w), football (m), golf (m, w), gymnastics (w), lacrosse (m, w), soccer (m), softball (w), swimming and diving (m, w), tennis (m, w), track and field (m, w), volleyball (w), wrestling (m).

## Applying

Ursinus requires an essay, a high school transcript, 3 years of high school math, 2 years of high school foreign language, 3 recommendations, SAT I or ACT, and in some cases 3 years of high school science. It recommends a campus interview and 3 SAT II Subject Tests. Early, deferred, and midyear entrance are possible, with a 2/15 deadline and continuous processing to 2/15 for financial aid. **Contact:** Mr. Richard G. Di Feliciantonio, Director of Admissions and Enrollment, Main Street, Collegeville, PA 19426-1000, 610-409-3200 ext. 2224; fax 610-489-0627.

---

**GETTING IN LAST YEAR**
1,466 applied
77% were accepted
28% enrolled (314)
38% from top tenth of their h.s. class.
9% had SAT verbal scores over 600
36% had SAT math scores over 600
1% had SAT verbal scores over 700
5% had SAT math scores over 700

**THE STUDENT BODY**
1,163 undergraduates
From 20 states and territories,
  11 other countries

68% from Pennsylvania
52% women, 48% men
4% African Americans
0% Native Americans
2% Hispanics
4% Asian Americans
3% international students

**AFTER FRESHMAN YEAR**
92% returned for sophomore year
71% got a degree within 4 years
73% got a degree within 5 years

**AFTER GRADUATION**
21% pursued further study (11% arts and
  sciences, 5% medicine, 2% dentistry)
30 corporations, 2 government agencies, 5
  nonprofit organizations recruited on campus

**WHAT YOU WILL PAY**
Tuition and fees $15,070
Room and board $5160
80% receive need-based financial aid
  averaging $7212
12% receive non-need financial aid averaging
  $5000

# UTICA COLLEGE OF SYRACUSE UNIVERSITY

Utica, New York • Suburban setting • Private • Independent • Coed

At Utica College students find the small classes, excellent advising, and personal attention of a small liberal arts college, but they enjoy the broad curriculum and diverse student body of a large university. And, upon graduation, Utica College students receive the internationally recognized Syracuse University degree. Utica College students choose among 5 academic divisions and 35 majors in both the liberal arts/science and professional career programs. Prospective students who visit the campus for an interview and tour notice the friendly, warm atmosphere. Personal attention to each student is the hallmark of Utica College.

##  Academics

Utica College offers a core academic program. It awards bachelor's **degrees**. Challenging opportunities include advanced placement, accelerated degree programs, and an honors program. Special programs include cooperative education, internships, summer session for credit, off-campus study, study abroad, and Army and Air Force ROTC.

The most popular **majors** include business, criminal justice, and occupational therapy. A complete listing of majors at Utica College appears in the Majors Index beginning on page 380.

The **faculty** at Utica College has 111 full-time teachers, 87% with terminal degrees. 100% of the faculty serve as student advisers. The student-faculty ratio is 15:1, and the average class size in required courses is 18.

##  Computers on Campus

Students are not required to have a computer. 144 **computers** available in the computer center, classroom buildings,

the library, and dormitories. Staffed computer lab on campus provides training in the use of computers and software.

The **library** has 165,624 books, 355 microform titles, and 1,038 subscriptions.

##  Campus Life

There are 61 active **organizations** on campus, including a drama/theater group and student-run newspaper and radio station. 18% of eligible men and 4% of eligible women are members of 7 national **fraternities**, 4 national **sororities**, 2 local fraternities, and 3 local sororities. Student **safety services** include late night transport/escort service, 24-hour emergency telephone alarm devices, 24-hour patrols by trained security personnel, and electronically operated dormitory entrances.

Utica College is a member of the NCAA (Division III). **Intercollegiate sports** include baseball (m), basketball (m, w), cross-country running (m, w), golf (m), lacrosse (m), soccer (m, w), softball (w), swimming and diving (m, w), tennis (m, w), volleyball (m).

##  Applying

Utica College requires a high school transcript, and in some cases SAT I. It recommends an essay, 3 years of high school math and science, some high school foreign language, recommendations, an interview, and SAT I or ACT. Early, deferred, and midyear entrance are possible, with rolling admissions and continuous processing to 2/15 for financial aid. **Contact:** Ms. Leslie North, Director of Admissions, 1600 Burrstone Road, Hubbard Hall, Utica, NY 13502-4892, 315-792-3006 or toll-free 800-782-8884; fax 315-792-3292.

---

**GETTING IN LAST YEAR**
1,118 applied
83% were accepted
26% enrolled (246)
15% from top tenth of their h.s. class
9% had SAT verbal scores over 600
20% had SAT math scores over 600
30% had ACT scores over 26
0% had SAT verbal scores over 700
0% had SAT math scores over 700
0% had ACT scores over 30

**THE STUDENT BODY**
1,841 undergraduates
From 26 states and territories,
  13 other countries
70% from New York
58% women, 42% men
8% African Americans
1% Native Americans
4% Hispanics
1% Asian Americans
2% international students

**AFTER FRESHMAN YEAR**
72% returned for sophomore year
47% got a degree within 6 years

**AFTER GRADUATION**
13% pursued further study (3% business, 3% medicine, 1% arts and sciences)

**WHAT YOU WILL PAY**
Tuition and fees $12,770
Room and board $4924

# VALPARAISO UNIVERSITY

Valparaiso, Indiana • Small-town setting • Private • Independent-Religious • Coed

Valparaiso, a Lutheran university, is the school of choice for those who seek excellence in education. *U.S. News & World Report* rates Valparaiso the number one regional university in the Midwest, and a "Best Buy." More than 70% of entering freshmen placed in the upper fifth of their high school class and nearly half ranked in the top tenth. VU ranks in the upper 10% of the nation's schools for enrollment of National Merit Scholars. Nearby Chicago provides opportunities for academic study, the arts, and entertainment.

##  Academics

Valpo offers a liberal arts curriculum and core academic program; fewer than half of graduate courses are open to undergraduates. It awards associate, bachelor's, master's, and first professional **degrees**. Challenging opportunities include advanced placement, accelerated degree programs, self-designed majors, Freshmen Honors College, an honors program, and a senior project. Special programs include cooperative education, internships, summer session for credit, off-campus study, and study abroad.

The most popular **majors** include nursing, business, and elementary education. A complete listing of majors at Valpo appears in the Majors Index beginning on page 380.

The **faculty** at Valpo has 249 full-time graduate and undergraduate teachers, 80% with terminal degrees. 43% of the faculty serve as student advisers. The student-faculty ratio is 14:1, and the average class size in required courses is 20.

##  Computers on Campus

Students are not required to have a computer. Student rooms are linked to a campus network. 350 **computers**

available in the computer center, computer labs, classrooms, the library, dormitories, and student rooms provide access to the main academic computer, off-campus computing facilities, e-mail, and on-line services. Staffed computer lab on campus.

The 2 **libraries** have 259,830 books, 180,000 microform titles, and 1,560 subscriptions. They are connected to 4 national **on-line** catalogs.

##  Campus Life

There are 150 active **organizations** on campus, including a drama/theater group and student-run newspaper and radio station. 42% of eligible men and 39% of eligible women are members of 12 national **fraternities** and 8 local **sororities**. Student **safety services** include late night transport/escort service, 24-hour emergency telephone alarm devices, 24-hour patrols by trained security personnel, and electronically operated dormitory entrances.

Valpo is a member of the NCAA (Division I). **Intercollegiate sports** (some offering scholarships) include baseball (m), basketball (m, w), cross-country running (m, w), football (m), soccer (m, w), softball (w), swimming and diving (m, w), tennis (m, w), volleyball (w), wrestling (m).

##  Applying

Valpo requires a high school transcript, SAT I or ACT, and in some cases 3 years of high school math and science and a campus interview. It recommends an essay, 3 years of high school math and science, 2 years of high school foreign language, and recommendations. Early, deferred, and midyear entrance are possible, with rolling admissions and continuous processing to 3/1 for financial aid. **Contact:** Ms. Karen Foust, Director of Admissions, Kretzmann Hall, Valparaiso, IN 46383-6493, 219-464-5011 or toll-free 800-348-2611 (out-of-state); fax 219-464-5381.

### GETTING IN LAST YEAR

2,435 applied
82% were accepted
28% enrolled (553)
35% from top tenth of their h.s. class
15% had SAT verbal scores over 600
36% had SAT math scores over 600
49% had ACT scores over 26
4% had SAT verbal scores over 700
9% had SAT math scores over 700
17% had ACT scores over 30
11 National Merit Scholars
36 valedictorians

### THE STUDENT BODY

Total 3,480, of whom 2,698 are undergraduates
From 43 states and territories, 43 other countries
43% from Indiana
57% women, 43% men
4% African Americans
1% Native Americans
2% Hispanics
2% Asian Americans
2% international students

### AFTER FRESHMAN YEAR

88% returned for sophomore year

### AFTER GRADUATION

25% pursued further study (10% arts and sciences, 4% law, 2% medicine)
46 corporations, 3 government agencies, 1 nonprofit organization recruited on campus

### WHAT YOU WILL PAY

Tuition and fees $12,250
Room and board $3260
80% receive need-based financial aid averaging $2400
25% receive non-need financial aid averaging $2650

# VANDERBILT UNIVERSITY

Nashville, Tennessee • Urban setting • Private • Independent • Coed

 Vanderbilt University, a national research university of distinction, has been honored repeatedly for its exceptional undergraduate advising system. Generous financial aid programs support the University's commitment to making a Vanderbilt education affordable for all qualified students. Other distinctions include the Summer Undergraduate Research Program, in which students collaborate with faculty on original research.

##  Academics

Vanderbilt offers an interdisciplinary curriculum and core academic program. It awards bachelor's, master's, doctoral, and first professional **degrees**. Challenging opportunities include advanced placement, accelerated degree programs, self-designed majors, tutorials, an honors program, a senior project, Phi Beta Kappa, and Sigma Xi. Special programs include internships, summer session for credit, off-campus study, study abroad, and Army, Naval, and Air Force ROTC.

The most popular **majors** include human development, psychology, and English. A complete listing of majors at Vanderbilt appears in the Majors Index beginning on page 380.

The **faculty** at Vanderbilt has 1,650 full-time graduate and undergraduate teachers, 98% with terminal degrees. The student-faculty ratio is 8:1, and the average class size in required courses is 20.

##  Computers on Campus

Students are not required to have a computer. 400 **computers** available in the computer center, computer labs, the learning resource center, labs, classrooms, the library, and dormitories provide access to the main academic computer, off-campus computing facilities, e-mail, on-line services, and productivity and educational software. Staffed computer lab on campus provides training in the use of computers and software.

The 8 **libraries** have 2.1 million books, 155,145 microform titles, and 16,009 subscriptions. They are connected to 6 national **on-line** catalogs.

##  Campus Life

Active **organizations** on campus include drama/theater group and student-run newspaper and radio station. 38% of eligible men and 50% of eligible women are members of 17 national **fraternities** and 12 national **sororities**. Student **safety services** include late night transport/escort service, 24-hour emergency telephone alarm devices, 24-hour patrols by trained security personnel, student patrols, and electronically operated dormitory entrances.

Vanderbilt is a member of the NCAA (Division I). **Intercollegiate sports** (some offering scholarships) include baseball (m), basketball (m, w), crew (m, w), cross-country running (m, w), equestrian sports (m, w), fencing (m, w), football (m), golf (m, w), ice hockey (m), lacrosse (m, w), riflery (m, w), rugby (m, w), sailing (m, w), skiing (downhill) (m, w), soccer (m, w), squash (m, w), table tennis (m), tennis (m, w), volleyball (m), water polo (m), weight lifting (m).

## Applying

Vanderbilt requires an essay, a high school transcript, 3 years of high school math, 2 recommendations, SAT I or ACT, 3 SAT II Subject Tests (including SAT II: Writing Test), and in some cases 3 years of high school science and some high school foreign language. Early and deferred entrance are possible, with a 1/15 deadline and continuous processing to 2/15 for financial aid. **Contact:** Dr. Neill Sanders, Dean of Undergraduate Admissions, 401 24th Avenue, South, Nashville, TN 37240-1001, 615-322-2561.

### GETTING IN LAST YEAR
- 8,400 applied
- 58% were accepted
- 30% enrolled (1,481)
- 78% from top tenth of their h.s. class
- 35% had SAT verbal scores over 600
- 78% had SAT math scores over 600
- 81% had ACT scores over 26
- 5% had SAT verbal scores over 700
- 25% had SAT math scores over 700
- 34% had ACT scores over 30
- 105 National Merit Scholars
- 12 class presidents
- 121 valedictorians

### THE STUDENT BODY
Total 10,088, of whom 5,805 are undergraduates

From 54 states and territories, 47 other countries
- 13% from Tennessee
- 47% women, 53% men
- 4% African Americans
- 0% Native Americans
- 2% Hispanics
- 5% Asian Americans
- 2% international students

### AFTER FRESHMAN YEAR
- 91% returned for sophomore year
- 73% got a degree within 4 years
- 81% got a degree within 5 years

### AFTER GRADUATION
- 49% pursued further study (22% arts and sciences, 13% law, 7% medicine)
- 136 corporations, 54 government agencies, 53 nonprofit organizations recruited on campus
- 1 Fulbright scholar

### WHAT YOU WILL PAY
Tuition and fees $18,403
Room and board $6341
34% receive need-based financial aid averaging $7198
Non-need financial aid averages $7115

# VASSAR COLLEGE

Poughkeepsie, New York • Suburban setting • Private • Independent • Coed

Since its founding in 1861, Vassar has held a place in the forefront of liberal arts education. Today, it seeks students who value learning and who want to take charge of their own education. Vassar offers a rigorous program that is both diverse and coherent; students learn with the support of a dedicated and distinguished faculty, most of whom live on the school's 1,000-acre Hudson Valley campus. The nearby cities of Poughkeepsie and New York offer opportunities for education and entertainment; Vassar also offers a vital extracurricular program, including varsity sports and widespread participation in drama, dance, music, and writing.

 **Academics**

Vassar offers no core academic program. It awards bachelor's and master's **degrees**. Challenging opportunities include advanced placement, accelerated degree programs, self-designed majors, a senior project, Phi Beta Kappa, and Sigma Xi. Special programs include internships, off-campus study, and study abroad.

The most popular **majors** include English, political science/government, and psychology. A complete listing of majors at Vassar appears in the Majors Index beginning on page 380.

The **faculty** at Vassar has 208 full-time undergraduate teachers, 95% with terminal degrees. 100% of the faculty serve as student advisers. The student-faculty ratio is 11:1, and the average class size in required courses is 19.

 **Computers on Campus**

Students are not required to have a computer. Student rooms are linked to a campus network. 295 **computers** available in the computer center, academic buildings, the library, and dormitories. Staffed computer lab on campus (open 24 hours a day) provides training in the use of computers and software.

The **library** has 750,000 books, 350,000 microform titles, and 3,900 subscriptions.

 **Campus Life**

Active **organizations** on campus include drama/theater group and student-run newspaper and radio station. Student **safety services** include late night transport/escort service, 24-hour emergency telephone alarm devices, 24-hour patrols by trained security personnel, student patrols, and electronically operated dormitory entrances.

Vassar is a member of the NCAA (Division III). **Intercollegiate sports** include baseball (m), basketball (m, w), crew (m, w), cross-country running (m, w), fencing (m, w), field hockey (w), golf (m, w), lacrosse (m, w), rugby (m, w), sailing (m, w), soccer (m, w), squash (m, w), swimming and diving (m, w), tennis (m, w), volleyball (m, w).

 **Applying**

Vassar requires an essay, a high school transcript, 2 recommendations, SAT I or ACT, and 3 SAT II Subject Tests. It recommends 3 years of high school math and science, 3 years of high school foreign language, and an interview. Early and deferred entrance are possible, with a 1/15 deadline and 1/15 for financial aid. **Contact:** Mr. Thomas Matos, Director of Admissions, Raymond Avenue, Poughkeepsie, NY 12601, 914-437-7300; fax 914-437-7063.

## GETTING IN LAST YEAR
3,760 applied
50% were accepted
32% enrolled (606)
58% from top tenth of their h.s. class
52% had SAT verbal scores over 600
69% had SAT math scores over 600
4% had SAT verbal scores over 700
15% had SAT math scores over 700
22 class presidents
22 valedictorians

## THE STUDENT BODY
2,312 undergraduates
From 51 states and territories,
   30 other countries
30% from New York
62% women, 38% men
6% African Americans
1% Native Americans
5% Hispanics
9% Asian Americans
3% international students

## AFTER FRESHMAN YEAR
91% returned for sophomore year
82% got a degree within 4 years
90% got a degree within 5 years
91% got a degree within 6 years

## AFTER GRADUATION
25% pursued further study (14% arts and
   sciences, 7% law, 5% medicine)
8 corporations, 3 government agencies, 6
   nonprofit organizations recruited on campus
1 Fulbright scholar

## WHAT YOU WILL PAY
Tuition and fees $19,220
Room and board $5950
56% receive need-based financial aid
   averaging $11,942

# VILLANOVA UNIVERSITY

Villanova, Pennsylvania • Suburban setting • Private • Independent-Religious • Coed

---

Villanova seeks to enroll academically talented and diverse individuals through a comprehensive scholarship program. In 1994 Villanova offered 235 full and partial merit-based scholarships totaling $2.5 million. Full tuition Presidential Scholarships are awarded to selected students who have a minimum score of 1350 on the SAT, rank in the top 5% of their high school class, and submit their application for admission by December 15.

 **Academics**

Villanova offers an interdisciplinary curriculum and core academic program; fewer than half of graduate courses are open to undergraduates. It awards associate, bachelor's, master's, doctoral, and first professional **degrees**. Challenging opportunities include advanced placement, accelerated degree programs, tutorials, an honors program, a senior project, Phi Beta Kappa, and Sigma Xi. Special programs include internships, summer session for credit, off-campus study, study abroad, and Army, Naval, and Air Force ROTC.

The most popular **majors** include political science/government, communication, and business. A complete listing of majors at Villanova appears in the Majors Index beginning on page 380.

The **faculty** at Villanova has 478 full-time undergraduate teachers, 90% with terminal degrees. The student-faculty ratio is 12:1, and the average class size in required courses is 23.

 **Computers on Campus**

Students are not required to have a computer. Student rooms are linked to a campus network. 400 **computers** available in the computer center, computer labs, the research center, the learning resource center, departmental labs, and classrooms provide access to the main academic computer, off-campus computing facilities, e-mail, and on-line services. Staffed computer lab on campus (open 24 hours a day).

The 2 **libraries** have 642,800 books, 1,456 microform titles, and 2,826 subscriptions. They are connected to 5 national **on-line** catalogs.

 **Campus Life**

Active **organizations** on campus include drama/theater group and student-run newspaper and radio station. 33% of students participate in student government elections. 29% of eligible men and 48% of eligible women are members of 14 national **fraternities** and 8 national **sororities**. Student **safety services** include late night transport/escort service, 24-hour emergency telephone alarm devices, 24-hour patrols by trained security personnel, and electronically operated dormitory entrances.

Villanova is a member of the NCAA (Division I). **Intercollegiate sports** (some offering scholarships) include baseball (m), basketball (m, w), crew (m, w), cross-country running (m, w), field hockey (w), football (m), golf (m), ice hockey (m), lacrosse (m, w), rugby (m), sailing (m, w), soccer (m, w), softball (w), swimming and diving (m, w), tennis (m, w), track and field (m, w), volleyball (m, w), water polo (m), weight lifting (m, w).

 **Applying**

Villanova requires an essay, a high school transcript, 3 years of high school math and science, SAT I or ACT, and in some cases 4 years of high school math, 2 years of high school foreign language, and 2 SAT II Subject Tests. It recommends recommendations. Early and deferred entrance are possible, with a 1/15 deadline and continuous processing to 2/15 for financial aid. **Contact:** Mr. Stephen Merritt, Director of Admissions, Austin Hall, Villanova, PA 19085-1699, 610-519-4000 or toll-free 800-338-7927; fax 610-519-6450.

---

### GETTING IN LAST YEAR
8,233 applied
72% were accepted
28% enrolled (1,642)
32% from top tenth of their h.s. class
15% had SAT verbal scores over 600
47% had SAT math scores over 600
2% had SAT verbal scores over 700
9% had SAT math scores over 700
5 National Merit Scholars
23 valedictorians

### THE STUDENT BODY
Total 10,760, of whom 6,857
   are undergraduates
From 48 states and territories,
   22 other countries
31% from Pennsylvania
49% women, 51% men
2% African Americans
1% Native Americans
2% Hispanics
3% Asian Americans
9% international students

### AFTER FRESHMAN YEAR
93% returned for sophomore year

### AFTER GRADUATION
21% pursued further study (10% arts and
   sciences, 5% law, 3% medicine)
215 corporations, 13 government agencies, 3
   nonprofit organizations recruited on campus
1 Rhodes, 1 Fulbright scholar

### WHAT YOU WILL PAY
Tuition and fees $15,790
Room and board $6850
52% receive need-based financial aid
   averaging $7305
19% receive non-need financial aid averaging
   $12,679

# VIRGINIA POLYTECHNIC INSTITUTE AND STATE UNIVERSITY

Blacksburg, Virginia • Small-town setting • Public • State-supported • Coed

> Virginia Tech ranks in the top 20 nationally in the enrollment of National Merit and National Achievement scholars and students with Advanced Placement (AP) credit. It also offers more degree programs than any other university in the state.

## Academics

Virginia Tech offers a liberal arts and sciences curriculum and core academic program. It awards associate, bachelor's, master's, and doctoral **degrees**. Challenging opportunities include advanced placement, accelerated degree programs, tutorials, an honors program, a senior project, Phi Beta Kappa, and Sigma Xi. Special programs include cooperative education, internships, summer session for credit, study abroad, and Army, Naval, and Air Force ROTC.

The most popular **majors** include electrical engineering, finance/banking, and mechanical engineering. A complete listing of majors at Virginia Tech appears in the Majors Index beginning on page 380.

The **faculty** at Virginia Tech has 1,466 full-time graduate and undergraduate teachers, 87% with terminal degrees. The student-faculty ratio is 18:1.

## Computers on Campus

Student rooms are linked to a campus network. 2,000 **computers** available in computer labs, academic buildings, the library, and dormitories provide access to e-mail and on-line services. Staffed computer lab on campus provides training in the use of computers and software.

The 4 **libraries** have 1.8 million books, 5.7 million microform titles, and 20,380 subscriptions. They are connected to 9 national **on-line** catalogs.

## Campus Life

There are 437 active **organizations** on campus, including a drama/theater group and student-run newspaper and radio station. 13% of eligible men and 22% of eligible women are members of 33 national **fraternities**, 16 national **sororities**, and 1 local fraternity. Student **safety services** include late night transport/escort service, 24-hour emergency telephone alarm devices, 24-hour patrols by trained security personnel, and student patrols.

Virginia Tech is a member of the NCAA (Division I). **Intercollegiate sports** (some offering scholarships) include baseball (m), basketball (m, w), bowling (m, w), crew (m, w), cross-country running (m, w), equestrian sports (m, w), fencing (m, w), field hockey (m, w), football (m), golf (m), gymnastics (m, w), lacrosse (m, w), rugby (m, w), soccer (m, w), swimming and diving (m, w), tennis (m, w), track and field (m, w), volleyball (m, w), weight lifting (m, w), wrestling (m).

## Applying

Virginia Tech requires a high school transcript, 3 years of high school math, SAT I or ACT, 2 SAT II Subject Tests (including SAT II: Writing Test), and in some cases 4 years of high school math and 3 years of high school science. It recommends 3 years of high school science, 2 years of high school foreign language, and a minimum high school GPA of 3.0. Early, deferred, and midyear entrance are possible, with a 2/1 deadline and a 2/15 priority date for financial aid. **Contact:** Office of Undergraduate Admissions, 104 Burruss Hall, Blacksburg, VA 24061-0202, 703-231-6267; fax 703-231-3242.

---

### GETTING IN LAST YEAR
14,925 applied
78% were accepted
37% enrolled (4,296)
29% from top tenth of their h.s. class
10% had SAT verbal scores over 600
40% had SAT math scores over 600
5% had SAT verbal scores over 700
8% had SAT math scores over 700
56 National Merit Scholars

### THE STUDENT BODY
Total 25,842, of whom 19,229
   are undergraduates
From 50 states and territories,
   58 other countries
79% from Virginia
41% women, 59% men
5% African Americans
0% Native Americans
2% Hispanics
7% Asian Americans
1% international students

### AFTER FRESHMAN YEAR
89% returned for sophomore year

### AFTER GRADUATION
337 corporations, 16 government agencies, 5
   nonprofit organizations recruited on campus
1 Fulbright scholar

### WHAT YOU WILL PAY
Resident tuition and fees $3951
Nonresident tuition and fees $10,404
Room and board $3002
65% receive need-based financial aid
   averaging $1614
40% receive non-need financial aid averaging
   $2100

# WABASH COLLEGE

Crawfordsville, Indiana • Small-town setting • Private • Independent • Men

As a college for men, Wabash helps students achieve their full potential—intellectually, athletically, emotionally, and artistically. Wabash prepares students for leadership in an ever-changing world. The College helps them learn to think clearly and openly and to explore a variety of interests. Independence and responsibility are emphasized and defined by the Gentlemen's Rule, which calls on students to conduct themselves as gentlemen at all times. With the guidance of professors who are accessible, a support staff that cares, and a nationwide network of alumni willing to offer assistance and encouragement, Wabash men frequently surpass even their own expectations.

## Academics

Wabash offers an interdisciplinary curriculum and core academic program. It awards bachelor's **degrees**. Challenging opportunities include advanced placement, accelerated degree programs, self-designed majors, tutorials, Phi Beta Kappa, and Sigma Xi. Off-campus study is a special program.

The most popular **majors** include psychology, biology/biological sciences, and English. A complete listing of majors at Wabash appears in the Majors Index beginning on page 380.

The **faculty** at Wabash has 79 full-time teachers, 95% with terminal degrees. 100% of the faculty serve as student advisers. The student-faculty ratio is 10:1, and the average class size in required courses is 13.

## Computers on Campus

Students are not required to have a computer. 125 **computers** available in the computer center, computer labs, the learning resource center, classrooms, and the library provide access to the main academic computer, off-campus computing facilities, and e-mail. Staffed computer lab on campus (open 24 hours a day) provides training in the use of computers and software.

The **library** has 250,092 books, 8,431 microform titles, and 866 subscriptions. It is connected to 4 national **on-line** catalogs.

## Campus Life

There are 30 active **organizations** on campus, including a drama/theater group and student-run newspaper. 65% of students participate in student government elections. 75% of eligible undergraduates are members of 10 national **fraternities**. Student **safety services** include 24-hour emergency telephone alarm devices.

Wabash is a member of the NCAA (Division III). **Intercollegiate sports** include baseball, basketball, crew, cross-country running, football, golf, ice hockey, rugby, sailing, soccer, swimming and diving, tennis, track and field, water polo, wrestling.

## Applying

Wabash requires an essay, a high school transcript, 3 years of high school math, 1 recommendation, and SAT I or ACT. It recommends 3 years of high school science, 2 years of high school foreign language, an interview, and minimum 2.7 high school GPA. Early, deferred, and midyear entrance are possible, with a 12/1 deadline and continuous processing to 3/1 for financial aid. **Contact:** Mr. Gregory Birk, Director of Admissions, 502 West Wabash Avenue, Crawfordsville, IN 47933-0352, 317-364-4253 or toll-free 800-345-5385 (in-state).

---

### GETTING IN LAST YEAR
798 applied
78% were accepted
39% enrolled (240)
44% from top tenth of their h.s. class
3.51 average high school GPA
22% had SAT verbal scores over 600
57% had SAT math scores over 600
2% had SAT verbal scores over 700
19% had SAT math scores over 700
12 National Merit Scholars
7 valedictorians

### THE STUDENT BODY
803 undergraduates
From 33 states and territories,
    24 other countries
74% from Indiana
100% men
5% African Americans
1% Native Americans
3% Hispanics
4% Asian Americans
5% international students

### AFTER FRESHMAN YEAR
81% returned for sophomore year
69% got a degree within 4 years
70% got a degree within 5 years
71% got a degree within 6 years

### AFTER GRADUATION
45% pursued further study (12% medicine,
    10% arts and sciences, 10% law)
19 corporations recruited on campus

### WHAT YOU WILL PAY
Tuition and fees $13,175
Room and board $4125
93% receive need-based financial aid
    averaging $10,005
48% receive non-need financial aid averaging
    $8143

# **W**AKE FOREST UNIVERSITY

Winston-Salem, North Carolina • Suburban setting • Private • Independent • Coed

## Academics

Wake Forest offers a classical liberal arts curriculum and core academic program; a few graduate courses are open to undergraduates. It awards bachelor's, master's, doctoral, and first professional **degrees**. Challenging opportunities include advanced placement, accelerated degree programs, self-designed majors, an honors program, a senior project, Phi Beta Kappa, and Sigma Xi. Special programs include internships, summer session for credit, off-campus study, study abroad, and Army ROTC.

The most popular **majors** include biology/biological sciences, business, and history. A complete listing of majors at Wake Forest appears in the Majors Index beginning on page 380.

The **faculty** at Wake Forest has 976 full-time graduate and undergraduate teachers, 90% with terminal degrees. 80% of the faculty serve as student advisers. The student-faculty ratio is 13:1, and the average class size in required courses is 35.

## Computers on Campus

Students are not required to have a computer. Student rooms are linked to a campus network. 161 **computers** available in the computer center, computer labs, classrooms, the library, the student center, and dormitories provide access to the main academic computer, off-campus computing facilities, e-mail, and on-line services. Staffed computer lab on campus provides training in the use of computers and software.

The 3 **libraries** have 1.2 million books, 334,379 microform titles, and 16,808 subscriptions. They are connected to 6 national **on-line** catalogs.

## Campus Life

There are 100 active **organizations** on campus, including a drama/theater group and student-run newspaper and radio station. 42% of eligible men and 51% of eligible women are members of 15 national **fraternities** and 10 national **sororities**. Student **safety services** include late night transport/escort service.

Wake Forest is a member of the NCAA (Division I). **Intercollegiate sports** (some offering scholarships) include baseball (m), basketball (m, w), cross-country running (m, w), equestrian sports (m, w), field hockey (w), football (m), golf (m, w), ice hockey (m), lacrosse (m, w), soccer (m, w), tennis (m, w), track and field (m, w).

## Applying

Wake Forest requires an essay, a high school transcript, 3 years of high school math, 2 years of high school foreign language, 1 recommendation, and SAT I. It recommends 3 years of high school science and 3 SAT II Subject Tests. Early and deferred entrance are possible, with a 1/15 deadline and continuous processing to 3/1 for financial aid. **Contact:** Mr. William G. Starling, Director of Admissions, PO Box 7305, Winston-Salem, NC 27109, 910-759-5201.

---

### GETTING IN LAST YEAR

5,923 applied
44% were accepted
36% enrolled (948)
66% from top tenth of their h.s. class
37% had SAT verbal scores over 600
75% had SAT math scores over 600
5% had SAT verbal scores over 700
21% had SAT math scores over 700
24 National Merit Scholars
65 class presidents
67 valedictorians

### THE STUDENT BODY

Total 5,748, of whom 3,620
  are undergraduates
From 49 states and territories,
  25 other countries
32% from North Carolina
48% women, 52% men
7% African Americans
1% Native Americans
1% Hispanics
2% Asian Americans
1% international students

### AFTER FRESHMAN YEAR

93% returned for sophomore year
74% got a degree within 4 years
85% got a degree within 5 years
86% got a degree within 6 years

### AFTER GRADUATION

32% pursued further study (16% arts and
  sciences, 6% law, 6% medicine)
140 corporations, 25 nonprofit organizations
  recruited on campus
1 Fulbright scholar

### WHAT YOU WILL PAY

Tuition and fees $13,850
Room and board $4265
26% receive need-based financial aid
  averaging $5797
37% receive non-need financial aid averaging
  $8062

# WARTBURG COLLEGE

Waverly, Iowa • Small-town setting • Private • Independent-Religious • Coed

---

Wartburg College affirms the role of faith and values in preparing students for lives of leadership and service. It challenges students to accept responsibility and assume leadership in addressing issues facing their communities and the world. The Institute for Leadership Education provides academic course work, mentoring relationships, and practical experience to help students develop leadership skills. The College's Global and Multicultural Program offers cultural immersions for one month, a term, or an entire year in settings throughout the world. Campus life is enriched by the presence and participation of international students from more than 20 countries.

## Academics

Wartburg offers an interdisciplinary curriculum and core academic program. It awards bachelor's **degrees**. Challenging opportunities include advanced placement, accelerated degree programs, self-designed majors, tutorials, and a senior project. Special programs include internships, summer session for credit, off-campus study, and study abroad.

The most popular **majors** include business, education, and biology/biological sciences. A complete listing of majors at Wartburg appears in the Majors Index beginning on page 380.

The **faculty** at Wartburg has 91 full-time teachers, 84% with terminal degrees. 100% of the faculty serve as student advisers. The student-faculty ratio is 14:1, and the average class size in required courses is 26.

## Computers on Campus

Students are not required to have a computer. 125 **computers** available in the computer center, computer labs, the learning resource center, science building, business center, writing, journalism labs, classrooms, and the library provide access to the main academic computer, off-campus computing facilities, and e-mail. Staffed computer lab on campus (open 24 hours a day) provides training in the use of computers and software.

The **library** has 145,130 books, 6,300 microform titles, and 744 subscriptions. It is connected to 1 national **on-line** catalog.

## Campus Life

There are 74 active **organizations** on campus, including a drama/theater group and student-run newspaper and radio station. 70% of students participate in student government elections. Student **safety services** include late night transport/escort service, 24-hour patrols by trained security personnel, and electronically operated dormitory entrances.

Wartburg is a member of the NCAA (Division III). **Intercollegiate sports** include baseball (m), basketball (m, w), cross-country running (m, w), football (m), golf (m, w), soccer (m, w), softball (w), tennis (m, w), track and field (m, w), volleyball (w), wrestling (m).

## Applying

Wartburg requires a high school transcript, recommendations, SAT I or ACT, and in some cases an interview. It recommends 3 years of high school math and science, 2 years of high school foreign language, and an interview. Deferred and midyear entrance are possible, with rolling admissions and continuous processing to 3/1 for financial aid. **Contact:** Mr. John Olsen, Director of Admissions, 222 Ninth Street, NW, Waverly, IA 50677-1033, 319-352-8264 or toll-free 800-772-2085; fax 319-352-8514.

---

### GETTING IN LAST YEAR
1,187 applied
93% were accepted
30% enrolled (327)
41% from top tenth of their h.s. class
3.4 average high school GPA
15% had SAT verbal scores over 600
53% had SAT math scores over 600
40% had ACT scores over 26
4% had SAT verbal scores over 700
14% had SAT math scores over 700
7% had ACT scores over 30

### THE STUDENT BODY
1,405 undergraduates
From 30 states and territories,
   20 other countries
74% from Iowa
57% women, 43% men
5% African Americans
0% Native Americans
1% Hispanics
1% Asian Americans
4% international students

### AFTER FRESHMAN YEAR
80% returned for sophomore year
49% got a degree within 4 years
58% got a degree within 5 years
60% got a degree within 6 years

### AFTER GRADUATION
19% pursued further study
34 corporations, 3 government agencies, 1
   nonprofit organization recruited on campus

### WHAT YOU WILL PAY
Tuition and fees $11,720
Room and board $3610
82% receive need-based financial aid
   averaging $2177
16% receive non-need financial aid averaging
   $3515

---

# WASHINGTON AND JEFFERSON COLLEGE

Washington, Pennsylvania • Small-town setting • Private • Independent • Coed

Washington and Jefferson College, located 30 miles south of Pittsburgh, is the eleventh-oldest college in the United States. Since 1781, the College has actively pursued a course of academic excellence through attention to individual needs. This personalized approach to education distinguishes Washington and Jefferson from other colleges. Nationally recognized programs in prelaw and prehealth, averaging over 90% placement, and a strong and varied liberal arts curriculum offer endless opportunities for the bright, creative, and motivated student. An involved faculty, superior academic programs, and an inquisitive student body combine to continue the rich tradition of achievement.

 **Academics**

W & J offers an interdisciplinary curriculum and core academic program. It awards bachelor's **degrees**. Challenging opportunities include advanced placement, accelerated degree programs, self-designed majors, tutorials, an honors program, and Phi Beta Kappa. Special programs include internships, summer session for credit, off-campus study, study abroad, and Army ROTC.

A complete listing of majors at W & J appears in the Majors Index beginning on page 380.

The **faculty** at W & J has 86 full-time teachers, 92% with terminal degrees. The student-faculty ratio is 11:1, and the average class size in required courses is 20.

 **Computers on Campus**

Students are not required to have a computer. 200 **computers** available in the computer center, computer labs, classrooms, the library, and the student center provide access to the main academic computer and e-mail. Staffed computer lab on campus provides training in the use of computers and software.

The **library** has 195,000 books, 5,400 microform titles, and 715 subscriptions. It is connected to 1 national **on-line** catalog.

 **Campus Life**

There are 87 active **organizations** on campus, including a drama/theater group and student-run newspaper and radio station. 53% of eligible men and 67% of eligible women are members of 10 national **fraternities** and 4 national **sororities**. Student **safety services** include late night transport/escort service, 24-hour emergency telephone alarm devices, 24-hour patrols by trained security personnel, and electronically operated dormitory entrances.

W & J is a member of the NCAA (Division III). **Intercollegiate sports** include baseball (m), basketball (m, w), cross-country running (m, w), football (m), golf (m), lacrosse (m), soccer (m, w), softball (w), swimming and diving (m, w), tennis (m, w), track and field (m, w), volleyball (w), wrestling (m).

 **Applying**

W & J requires a high school transcript, 3 years of high school math and science, 2 years of high school foreign language, SAT I or ACT, and 3 SAT II Subject Tests (including SAT II: Writing Test). It recommends an essay, recommendations, and an interview. Early, deferred, and midyear entrance are possible, with a 3/1 deadline and continuous processing to 3/15 for financial aid. **Contact:** Mr. Thomas P. O'Connor, Director of Admissions, 60 South Lincoln Street, Washington, PA 15301-4801, 412-223-6025; fax 412-223-5271.

---

**GETTING IN LAST YEAR**
1,360 applied
84% were accepted
27% enrolled (307)
31% from top tenth of their h.s. class
8% had SAT verbal scores over 600
26% had SAT math scores over 600
1% had SAT verbal scores over 700
5% had SAT math scores over 700

**THE STUDENT BODY**
1,104 undergraduates
From 30 states and territories,
 6 other countries
70% from Pennsylvania
45% women, 55% men
5% African Americans
1% Native Americans
1% Hispanics
2% Asian Americans
1% international students

**AFTER FRESHMAN YEAR**
85% returned for sophomore year
73% got a degree within 4 years

**AFTER GRADUATION**
45% pursued further study (18% medicine,
 17% law, 5% business)
60 corporations recruited on campus

**WHAT YOU WILL PAY**
Tuition and fees $16,540
Room and board $4005
Need-based financial aid averages $8750
Non-need financial aid averages $5060

# Washington and Lee University

Lexington, Virginia • Small-town setting • Private • Independent • Coed

Washington and Lee continues in its traditional mold of educational excellence and unparalleled value per educational dollar. The University is ensuring its future financial strength through a capital campaign targeted to raise an additional $127 million by 1995. The goals of the campaign include a strengthened endowment for educational programs and faculty support, increased revenues for both need-based and non-need-based financial assistance to students, and expansion and improvement of campus facilities. Truly, Washington and Lee adheres to its Latin motto, *Non In Cautus Futuri*—Not Unmindful of the Future.

## Academics

W & L offers a liberal arts curriculum and core academic program; a few graduate courses are open to undergraduates. It awards bachelor's and first professional **degrees**. Challenging opportunities include advanced placement, accelerated degree programs, self-designed majors, tutorials, an honors program, a senior project, and Phi Beta Kappa. Special programs include internships, off-campus study, and study abroad.

The most popular **majors** include history, economics, and business. A complete listing of majors at W & L appears in the Majors Index beginning on page 380.

The **faculty** at W & L has 166 full-time graduate and undergraduate teachers, 94% with terminal degrees. 92% of the faculty serve as student advisers. The student-faculty ratio is 11:1, and the average class size in required courses is 15.

## Computers on Campus

Students are not required to have a computer. Student rooms are linked to a campus network. 195 **computers** available in the computer center, computer labs, academic buildings, upperclass residence hall, classrooms, the library, and dormitories provide access to the main academic computer, e-mail, and on-line services. Staffed computer lab on campus (open 24 hours a day).

The 2 **libraries** have 445,552 books, 120,000 microform titles, and 1,600 subscriptions. They are connected to 5 national **on-line** catalogs.

## Campus Life

Active **organizations** on campus include drama/theater group and student-run newspaper and radio station. 80% of eligible men and 65% of eligible women are members of 16 national **fraternities** and 4 national **sororities**. Student **safety services** include late night transport/escort service, 24-hour emergency telephone alarm devices, and 24-hour patrols by trained security personnel.

W & L is a member of the NCAA (Division III). **Intercollegiate sports** include baseball (m), basketball (m, w), cross-country running (m, w), fencing (m, w), field hockey (w), football (m), golf (m), ice hockey (m, w), lacrosse (m, w), rugby (m), soccer (m, w), softball (w), swimming and diving (m, w), tennis (m, w), track and field (m, w), volleyball (m, w), water polo (m), wrestling (m).

## Applying

W & L requires an essay, a high school transcript, 3 years of high school math, 2 years of high school foreign language, 3 recommendations, ACT or SAT I and 3 unrelated SAT II Subject Tests (including SAT II: Writing Test). It recommends 3 years of high school science and an interview. Early and deferred entrance are possible, with a 1/15 deadline and a 2/1 priority date for financial aid. **Contact:** Mr. William M. Hartog, Dean of Admissions and Financial Aid, Gilliam Admissions House, Lexington, VA 24450, 703-463-8710.

---

### GETTING IN LAST YEAR
3,620 applied
29% were accepted
42% enrolled (443)
76% from top tenth of their h.s. class
63% had SAT verbal scores over 600
89% had SAT math scores over 600
7% had SAT verbal scores over 700
32% had SAT math scores over 700
31 National Merit Scholars
35 class presidents
37 valedictorians

### THE STUDENT BODY
Total 1,990, of whom 1,619 are undergraduates

From 50 states and territories, 18 other countries
12% from Virginia
40% women, 60% men
3% African Americans
0% Native Americans
1% Hispanics
1% Asian Americans
2% international students

### AFTER FRESHMAN YEAR
92% returned for sophomore year
86% got a degree within 4 years
88% got a degree within 5 years
89% got a degree within 6 years

### AFTER GRADUATION
25% pursued further study (9% arts and sciences, 7% law, 5% medicine)
47% had job offers within 3 months
46 corporations, 3 government agencies, 2 nonprofit organizations recruited on campus
2 Fulbright scholars

### WHAT YOU WILL PAY
Tuition and fees $13,885
Room and board $4310
35% receive need-based financial aid averaging $8085
15% receive non-need financial aid averaging $6895

# WASHINGTON COLLEGE

Chestertown, Maryland • Small-town setting • Private • Independent • Coed

Washington College brings illustrious and provocative speakers to campus to meet with its students and faculty. Visitors have included presidents from George Washington to FDR, Truman, and Eisenhower; poet laureates Rita Dove and Richard Wilbur; journalists Carl Rowan and Bob Woodward; Nobel Prize-winning author Toni Morrison; Supreme Court justice Sandra Day O'Connor; and philosopher Mortimer Adler. Off-campus study opportunities in Europe and summer internships around the world add a global dimension to the lives of Washington's students. For those unable to travel abroad, the Internet offers easy access to individuals and data in more than 110 countries.

##  Academics

WC offers a core academic program. It awards bachelor's and master's **degrees**. Challenging opportunities include advanced placement, self-designed majors, tutorials, and a senior project. Special programs include internships, off-campus study, and study abroad.

The most popular **majors** include English, psychology, and business. A complete listing of majors at WC appears in the Majors Index beginning on page 380.

The **faculty** at WC has 65 full-time undergraduate teachers, 95% with terminal degrees. 89% of the faculty serve as student advisers. The student-faculty ratio is 12:1, and the average class size in required courses is 17.

##  Computers on Campus

Students are not required to have a computer. Student rooms are linked to a campus network. 80 **computers** available in the computer center, computer labs, study center, the library, and dormitories provide access to the main academic computer, off-campus computing facilities, e-mail, and on-line services. Staffed computer lab on campus.

The **library** has 206,506 books, 172,686 microform titles, and 807 subscriptions. It is connected to 3 national **on-line** catalogs.

##  Campus Life

There are 50 active **organizations** on campus, including a drama/theater group and student-run newspaper. 25% of eligible men and 25% of eligible women are members of 3 national **fraternities** and 3 national **sororities**. Student **safety services** include late night transport/escort service, 24-hour emergency telephone alarm devices, and 24-hour patrols by trained security personnel.

WC is a member of the NCAA (Division III). **Intercollegiate sports** include baseball (m), basketball (m, w), crew (m, w), field hockey (w), ice hockey (m), lacrosse (m, w), rugby (m), sailing (m, w), soccer (m, w), softball (w), swimming and diving (m, w), tennis (m, w), volleyball (w).

##  Applying

WC requires an essay, a high school transcript, 3 years of high school math, 2 years of high school foreign language, 2 recommendations, and SAT I. It recommends 3 years of high school science and an interview. Early, deferred, and midyear entrance are possible, with a 2/15 deadline and continuous processing to 2/15 for financial aid. **Contact:** Mr. Kevin Coveney, Vice President for Admissions, 300 Washington Avenue, Chestertown, MD 21620-1197, 410-778-7700 or toll-free 800-422-1782; fax 410-778-7287.

### GETTING IN LAST YEAR

1,074 applied
80% were accepted
27% enrolled (236)
39% from top tenth of their h.s. class
3.17 average high school GPA
12% had SAT verbal scores over 600
27% had SAT math scores over 600
3% had SAT verbal scores over 700
5% had SAT math scores over 700
13 valedictorians

### THE STUDENT BODY

Total 888, of whom 840
   are undergraduates

From 35 states and territories,
   20 other countries
49% from Maryland
56% women, 44% men
6% African Americans
0% Native Americans
2% Hispanics
3% Asian Americans
6% international students

### AFTER FRESHMAN YEAR

81% returned for sophomore year
60% got a degree within 4 years
65% got a degree within 5 years
67% got a degree within 6 years

### AFTER GRADUATION

30% pursued further study (20% arts and sciences, 4% law, 2% business)
1 Fulbright scholar

### WHAT YOU WILL PAY

Tuition and fees $15,276
Room and board $5318
60% receive need-based financial aid averaging $7779
20% receive non-need financial aid averaging $8527

# WASHINGTON UNIVERSITY

St. Louis, Missouri • Suburban setting • Private • Independent • Coed

> Learning across disciplines is a way of life at Washington University. Students enrolled in one of the undergraduate schools—Architecture, Art, Arts and Sciences, Business, and Engineering and Applied Science—are able to enroll in courses offered by any of the others. Challenged by the talented faculty, students relish the give-and-take that occurs in the classroom and benefit from trading ideas with bright and curious classmates.

## Academics

Washington offers an interdisciplinary curriculum and core academic program; all graduate courses are open to undergraduates. It awards bachelor's, master's, doctoral, and first professional **degrees**. Challenging opportunities include advanced placement, accelerated degree programs, self-designed majors, tutorials, Phi Beta Kappa, and Sigma Xi. Special programs include cooperative education, internships, summer session for credit, off-campus study, study abroad, and Army and Air Force ROTC.

The most popular **majors** include engineering (general), business, and psychology. A complete listing of majors at Washington appears in the Majors Index beginning on page 380.

The **faculty** at Washington has 1,966 full-time graduate and undergraduate teachers, 99% with terminal degrees. 90% of the faculty serve as student advisers. The student-faculty ratio is 6:1, and the average class size in required courses is 21.

## Computers on Campus

Students are not required to have a computer. Student rooms are linked to a campus network. 2,500 **computers** available in the computer center, computer labs, the research center, classrooms, the library, and dormitories provide access to off-campus computing facilities, e-mail, and on-line services. Staffed computer lab on campus (open 24 hours a day) provides training in the use of computers and software.

The 14 **libraries** have 3 million books and 18,590 subscriptions.

## Campus Life

There are 170 active **organizations** on campus, including a drama/theater group and student-run newspaper and radio station. 24% of students participate in student government elections. 27% of eligible men and 33% of eligible women are members of 11 national **fraternities** and 6 national **sororities**. Student **safety services** include late night transport/escort service, 24-hour emergency telephone alarm devices, 24-hour patrols by trained security personnel, and electronically operated dormitory entrances.

Washington is a member of the NCAA (Division III). **Intercollegiate sports** include baseball (m), basketball (m, w), crew (m, w), cross-country running (m, w), football (m), ice hockey (m), lacrosse (m), soccer (m, w), swimming and diving (m, w), tennis (m, w), track and field (m, w), volleyball (m, w).

## Applying

Washington requires an essay, a high school transcript, 1 recommendation, and SAT I or ACT. It recommends 3 years of high school math and science, 2 years of high school foreign language, and a minimum high school GPA of 3.0. Early, deferred, and midyear entrance are possible, with a 1/15 deadline and 2/15 for financial aid. **Contact:** Mr. Harold Wingood, Dean of Admissions, Campus Box 1089, 1 Brookings Drive, St. Louis, MO 63130-4899, 314-935-6000 or toll-free 800-638-0700; fax 314-935-4290.

---

### GETTING IN LAST YEAR
7,693 applied
65% were accepted
25% enrolled (1,257)
63% from top tenth of their h.s. class
38% had SAT verbal scores over 600
79% had SAT math scores over 600
4% had SAT verbal scores over 700
32% had SAT math scores over 700
49 National Merit Scholars
23 class presidents
66 valedictorians

### THE STUDENT BODY
Total 11,655, of whom 5,082
  are undergraduates

From 50 states and territories,
  70 other countries
16% from Missouri
47% women, 53% men
6% African Americans
1% Native Americans
2% Hispanics
12% Asian Americans
4% international students

### AFTER FRESHMAN YEAR
94% returned for sophomore year
76% got a degree within 4 years
85% got a degree within 5 years
86% got a degree within 6 years

### AFTER GRADUATION
35% pursued further study
164 corporations, 2 government agencies, 24
  nonprofit organizations recruited on campus
5 Fulbright scholars

### WHAT YOU WILL PAY
Tuition and fees $18,800
Room and board $5843
45% receive need-based financial aid
  averaging $10,000
8% receive non-need financial aid averaging
  $10,000

---

# WEBB INSTITUTE

Glen Cove, New York • Suburban setting • Private • Independent • Primarily men

 **Academics**[1]

Webb Institute offers a core academic program. It awards bachelor's **degrees**. A senior project is a challenging opportunity. Special programs include cooperative education, internships, and study abroad.

A complete listing of majors at Webb Institute appears in the Majors Index beginning on page 380.

The **faculty** at Webb Institute has 9 full-time teachers, 44% with terminal degrees. 78% of the faculty serve as student advisers. The student-faculty ratio is 6:1, and the average class size in required courses is 19.

 **Computers on Campus**

Students are not required to have a computer. 28 **computers** available in the computer center, classrooms, and dormitories provide access to e-mail. Staffed computer lab on campus (open 24 hours a day) provides training in the use of computers and software.

The **library** has 49,294 books, 1,664 microform titles, and 250 subscriptions. It is connected to 1 national **on-line** catalog.

 **Campus Life**

84% of students participate in student government elections. **Intercollegiate sports** include basketball (m, w), sailing (m, w), soccer (m, w), tennis (m, w).

 **Applying**

Webb Institute requires a high school transcript, 2 recommendations, an interview, SAT I, and 3 SAT II Subject Tests (including SAT II: Writing Test). Early decision is possible, with a 2/15 deadline and continuous processing to 7/1 for financial aid. **Contact:** Mr. William G. Murray, Director of Admissions, Crescent Beach Road, Glen Cove, NY 11542-1398, 516-671-2213.

---

### GETTING IN LAST YEAR
89 applied
36% were accepted
75% enrolled (24)
75% from top tenth of their h.s. class
3.4 average high school GPA
54% had SAT verbal scores over 600
100% had SAT math scores over 600
0% had SAT verbal scores over 700
54% had SAT math scores over 700

### THE STUDENT BODY
75 undergraduates
From 17 states and territories
25% from New York
19% women, 81% men
1% African Americans
0% Native Americans
0% Hispanics
4% Asian Americans
0% international students

### AFTER FRESHMAN YEAR
72% returned for sophomore year
67% got a degree within 4 years
71% got a degree within 5 years

### AFTER GRADUATION
22% pursued further study (11% engineering, 5% business)
95% had job offers within 3 months
4 corporations, 1 government agency recruited on campus

### WHAT YOU WILL PAY
Tuition and fees $0
Room and board $5250
9% receive non-need financial aid averaging $1200

# WELLESLEY COLLEGE

Wellesley, Massachusetts • Suburban setting • Private • Independent • Women

 ## Academics

Wellesley offers a core academic program. It awards bachelor's **degrees** (double bachelor's with Massachusetts Institute of Technology). Challenging opportunities include advanced placement, accelerated degree programs, self-designed majors, an honors program, Phi Beta Kappa, and Sigma Xi. Special programs include internships, off-campus study, study abroad, and Army, Naval, and Air Force ROTC.

The most popular **majors** include political science/government, economics, and English. A complete listing of majors at Wellesley appears in the Majors Index beginning on page 380.

The **faculty** at Wellesley has 243 full-time teachers, 97% with terminal degrees. The student-faculty ratio is 10:1, and the average class size in required courses is 20.

 ## Computers on Campus

Students are not required to have a computer. Student rooms are linked to a campus network. 200 **computers** available in the computer center, computer labs, the research center, the learning resource center, science center, social science building, classrooms, the library, and dormitories. Staffed computer lab on campus (open 24 hours a day) provides training in the use of computers and software.

The 4 **libraries** have 704,404 books, 75,098 microform titles, and 2,399 subscriptions. They are connected to 5 national **on-line** catalogs.

 ## Campus Life

There are 140 active **organizations** on campus, including a drama/theater group and student-run newspaper and radio station. Student **safety services** include late night transport/escort service, 24-hour emergency telephone alarm devices, 24-hour patrols by trained security personnel, and electronically operated dormitory entrances.

Wellesley is a member of the NCAA (Division III). **Intercollegiate sports** include basketball, crew, cross-country running, fencing, field hockey, lacrosse, rugby, sailing, skiing (downhill), soccer, softball, squash, swimming and diving, tennis, track and field, volleyball.

 ## Applying

Wellesley requires an essay, a high school transcript, 3 recommendations, SAT I or ACT, and 3 SAT II Subject Tests (including SAT II: Writing Test). It recommends 3 years of high school math and science, some high school foreign language, and an interview. Early and deferred entrance are possible, with a 1/15 deadline and 1/15 for financial aid. **Contact:** Ms. Janet Lavin, Dean of Admission, 240 Green Hall, Wellesley, MA 02181, 617-283-2270; fax 617-283-3678.

### GETTING IN LAST YEAR
3,385 applied
38% were accepted
44% enrolled (570)
83% from top tenth of their h.s. class
68% had SAT verbal scores over 600
77% had SAT math scores over 600
13% had SAT verbal scores over 700
24% had SAT math scores over 700

### THE STUDENT BODY
2,288 undergraduates
From 53 states and territories,
  62 other countries
22% from Massachusetts
100% women
6% African Americans
1% Native Americans
5% Hispanics
25% Asian Americans
6% international students

### AFTER FRESHMAN YEAR
95% returned for sophomore year

### AFTER GRADUATION
33% pursued further study (16% arts and
  sciences, 7% medicine, 4% law)
75 corporations, 4 government agencies, 4
  nonprofit organizations recruited on campus
2 Rhodes, 3 Fulbright scholars

### WHAT YOU WILL PAY
Tuition and fees $18,705
Room and board $6155
55% receive need-based financial aid
  averaging $11,803

# WELLS COLLEGE

Aurora, New York • Rural setting • Private • Independent • Women

Wells College believes the 21st century will be a time of unprecedented opportunity for women. Those women who are prepared for leadership roles will have a distinct advantage. Wells students are being prepared to become the 21st-century leaders in a variety of fields: business, government, the arts, science, medicine, and education. The classroom experience and the cocurricular experience are both documented by transcripts that students will present to prospective employers and graduate schools. The Women's Leadership Institute and a focus on leadership issues in the classroom and in student life give Wells women the 21st-century advantage.

##  Academics

Wells offers a liberal arts curriculum and core academic program. It awards bachelor's **degrees**. Challenging opportunities include advanced placement, accelerated degree programs, self-designed majors, tutorials, a senior project, and Phi Beta Kappa. Special programs include internships, off-campus study, study abroad, and Army and Air Force ROTC.

The most popular **majors** include psychology, English, and biology/biological sciences. A complete listing of majors at Wells appears in the Majors Index beginning on page 380.

The **faculty** at Wells has 48 full-time teachers, 96% with terminal degrees. 100% of the faculty serve as student advisers. The student-faculty ratio is 8:1, and the average class size in required courses is 12.

##  Computers on Campus

Students are not required to have a computer. 60 **computers** available in the computer center, computer labs, Zabriskie Hall of Science, Morgan Hall, Macmillan Hall, and the library provide access to e-mail and on-line services. Staffed computer lab on campus (open 24 hours a day).

The 5 **libraries** have 242,451 books, 10,434 microform titles, and 472 subscriptions.

## Campus Life

There are 35 active **organizations** on campus, including a drama/theater group and student-run newspaper. 95% of students participate in student government elections. Student **safety services** include late night transport/escort service and 24-hour patrols by trained security personnel.

Wells is a member of the NCAA (Division III). **Intercollegiate sports** include field hockey, lacrosse, soccer, swimming and diving, tennis.

##  Applying

Wells requires an essay, a high school transcript, 2 recommendations, and SAT I or ACT. It recommends 3 years of high school math and science, 3 years of high school foreign language, an interview, and SAT II Subject Tests. Early and deferred entrance are possible, with a 3/1 deadline and continuous processing to 4/1 for financial aid. **Contact:** Ms. Susan Raith Sloan, Director of Admissions, Route 90, Aurora, NY 13026, 315-364-3264 or toll-free 800-952-9355; fax 315-364-3362.

---

### GETTING IN LAST YEAR

328 applied
86% were accepted
33% enrolled (94)
38% from top tenth of their h.s. class
3.0 average high school GPA
21% had SAT verbal scores over 600
13% had SAT math scores over 600
26% had ACT scores over 26
1% had SAT verbal scores over 700
0% had SAT math scores over 700
6% had ACT scores over 30

### THE STUDENT BODY

425 undergraduates
From 32 states and territories,
  4 other countries
64% from New York
100% women
5% African Americans
1% Native Americans
4% Hispanics
7% Asian Americans
2% international students

### AFTER FRESHMAN YEAR

74% returned for sophomore year
62% got a degree within 4 years
66% got a degree within 5 years

### AFTER GRADUATION

30% pursued further study (13% arts and
  sciences, 4% law, 1% business)

### WHAT YOU WILL PAY

Tuition and fees $15,200
Room and board $5550
80% receive need-based financial aid
  averaging $7900

# WESLEYAN UNIVERSITY

Middletown, Connecticut • Small-town setting • Private • Independent • Coed

---

For more than 160 years, Wesleyan University has championed the values of a liberal education in the arts and sciences. It seeks to train minds and open hearts and asks students to contribute to the good of society and to the world. About 30% of the 2,862 undergraduates are members of minority groups, while 12% are the first members of their families to attend college. Wesleyan is committed to meeting the full demonstrated financial need of all students.

## Academics

Wesleyan offers an interdisciplinary liberal arts and sciences curriculum and no core academic program; all graduate courses are open to undergraduates. It awards bachelor's, master's, and doctoral **degrees**. Challenging opportunities include advanced placement, accelerated degree programs, self-designed majors, tutorials, an honors program, a senior project, Phi Beta Kappa, and Sigma Xi. Special programs include cooperative education, internships, off-campus study, study abroad, and Army, Naval, and Air Force ROTC.

The most popular **majors** include English, political science/government, and American studies. A complete listing of majors at Wesleyan appears in the Majors Index beginning on page 380.

The **faculty** at Wesleyan has 278 full-time graduate and undergraduate teachers, 95% with terminal degrees. The student-faculty ratio is 11:1.

## Computers on Campus

Students are not required to have a computer. Student rooms are linked to a campus network. 250 **computers** available in the computer center, computer labs, the research center, and the library provide access to the main academic computer, off-campus computing facilities, and e-mail. Staffed computer lab on campus (open 24 hours a day) provides training in the use of computers and software.

The 4 **libraries** have 1.2 million books, 228,000 microform titles, and 3,166 subscriptions.

## Campus Life

There are 150 active **organizations** on campus, including a drama/theater group and student-run newspaper and radio station. 8% of eligible men and 2% of eligible women are members of 6 national **fraternities**, 3 national **sororities**, 2 local fraternities, and 6 eating clubs. Student **safety services** include late night transport/escort service, 24-hour patrols by trained security personnel, and student patrols.

Wesleyan is a member of the NCAA (Division III). **Intercollegiate sports** include baseball (m), basketball (m, w), crew (m, w), cross-country running (m, w), equestrian sports (m, w), field hockey (w), football (m), golf (m), ice hockey (m, w), lacrosse (m, w), rugby (m, w), sailing (m, w), skiing (cross-country) (m, w), skiing (downhill) (m, w), soccer (m, w), squash (m, w), swimming and diving (m, w), tennis (m, w), track and field (m, w), volleyball (m, w), water polo (m, w), wrestling (m).

## Applying

Wesleyan requires an essay, a high school transcript, 3 recommendations, SAT I or ACT, and 3 SAT II Subject Tests (including SAT II: Writing Test). It recommends 4 years of high school math and science, 4 years of high school foreign language, and an interview. Early and deferred entrance are possible, with a 1/15 deadline and 2/1 for financial aid. **Contact:** Ms. Barbara-Jan Wilson, Dean of Admissions and Financial Aid, High Street, Middletown, CT 06459-0260, 203-347-9411 ext. 2427; fax 203-685-3001.

---

### GETTING IN LAST YEAR
5,482 applied
36% were accepted
37% enrolled (727)
67% from top tenth of their h.s. class
56% had SAT verbal scores over 600
74% had SAT math scores over 600
8% had SAT verbal scores over 700
29% had SAT math scores over 700
68 National Merit Scholars
27 class presidents
39 valedictorians

### THE STUDENT BODY
Total 3,424, of whom 2,862
 are undergraduates
From 51 states and territories,
 22 other countries
9% from Connecticut
51% women, 49% men
10% African Americans
1% Native Americans
8% Hispanics
11% Asian Americans
4% international students

### AFTER FRESHMAN YEAR
93% returned for sophomore year

### AFTER GRADUATION
18% pursued further study (8% arts and sciences, 4% medicine, 3% law)
36 corporations, 7 government agencies, 18 nonprofit organizations recruited on campus
1 Marshall, 2 Fulbright scholars

### WHAT YOU WILL PAY
Tuition and fees $19,790
Room and board $5250
41% receive need-based financial aid averaging $15,733

---

# WHEATON COLLEGE

Wheaton, Illinois • Suburban setting • Private • Independent-Religious • Coed

Convinced that "all truth is God's truth," Wheaton College actively pursues the integration of biblical Christianity and rigorous study in the liberal arts with the goal of serving Christ in the world. Wheaton's national reputation rests upon a dedicated faculty known for its outstanding teaching and scholarship and a student body committed to academic achievement, leadership, and Christian service. Wheaton typically ranks in the top 1 percent of all colleges and universities in the percentage of its freshman class who are National Merit Scholars.

 **Academics**

Wheaton offers a liberal arts curriculum and core academic program; more than half of graduate courses are open to undergraduates. It awards bachelor's, master's, and doctoral **degrees**. Challenging opportunities include advanced placement, self-designed majors, and a senior project. Special programs include internships, summer session for credit, off-campus study, study abroad, and Army ROTC.

The most popular **majors** include literature, biblical studies, and business economics. A complete listing of majors at Wheaton appears in the Majors Index beginning on page 380.

The **faculty** at Wheaton has 160 full-time graduate and undergraduate teachers, 88% with terminal degrees. 95% of the faculty serve as student advisers. The student-faculty ratio is 15:1, and the average class size in required courses is 28.

 **Computers on Campus**

Students are not required to have a computer. 94 **computers** available in computer labs provide access to the main academic computer, off-campus computing facilities, and e-mail. Staffed computer lab on campus provides training in the use of computers and software.

The 2 **libraries** have 497,708 books, 335,932 microform titles, and 2,256 subscriptions. They are connected to 3 national **on-line** catalogs.

 **Campus Life**

There are 69 active **organizations** on campus, including a drama/theater group and student-run newspaper and radio station. 50% of students participate in student government elections. Student **safety services** include late night transport/escort service and 24-hour patrols by trained security personnel.

Wheaton is a member of the NCAA (Division III). **Intercollegiate sports** include baseball (m), basketball (m, w), crew (m, w), cross-country running (m, w), equestrian sports (w), football (m), golf (m), ice hockey (m), lacrosse (m, w), soccer (m, w), softball (w), swimming and diving (m, w), tennis (m, w), track and field (m, w), volleyball (m, w), wrestling (m).

 **Applying**

Wheaton requires an essay, a high school transcript, 2 recommendations, an interview, and SAT I or ACT. It recommends 3 years of high school math and science, 2 years of high school foreign language, and SAT II Subject Tests. Early and deferred entrance are possible, with a 2/1 deadline and continuous processing to 3/15 for financial aid. **Contact:** Mr. Dan Crabtree, Director of Admissions, 501 East College Avenue, Wheaton, IL 60187-5571, 708-752-5011 or toll-free 800-222-2419 (out-of-state).

## GETTING IN LAST YEAR
1,617 applied
59% were accepted
58% enrolled (553)
58% from top tenth of their h.s. class
3.61 average high school GPA
46% had SAT verbal scores over 600
64% had SAT math scores over 600
85% had ACT scores over 26
8% had SAT verbal scores over 700
20% had SAT math scores over 700
43% had ACT scores over 30
39 National Merit Scholars

## THE STUDENT BODY
Total 2,642, of whom 2,296
  are undergraduates
From 51 states and territories
19% from Illinois
52% women, 48% men
2% African Americans
1% Native Americans
2% Hispanics
6% Asian Americans
1% international students

## AFTER FRESHMAN YEAR
93% returned for sophomore year
72% got a degree within 4 years
83% got a degree within 5 years
84% got a degree within 6 years

## AFTER GRADUATION
28 corporations, 3 government agencies, 48 nonprofit organizations recruited on campus

## WHAT YOU WILL PAY
Tuition and fees $11,480
Room and board $4200
54% receive need-based financial aid
  averaging $5253
15% receive non-need financial aid averaging
  $768

# WHITMAN COLLEGE

Walla Walla, Washington • Small-town setting • Private • Independent • Coed

Whitman combines the educational values of the best liberal arts colleges of the East with the outdoor vigor of the Pacific Northwest. An active student-faculty research program, required senior projects, and comprehensive examinations challenge students in all areas of the arts and sciences. Over 75% of graduates pursue advanced degrees in areas such as law, business, medicine, and education; 35% participate in study-abroad programs around the world. Over 80% of students receive merit and/or need-based assistance, ranging from $500 to $19,500 per year, which is supported by generous alumni and a sizable endowment of $160 million.

 ## Academics

Whitman College offers an antiquity or modernity curriculum and core academic program. It awards bachelor's **degrees**. Challenging opportunities include advanced placement, accelerated degree programs, tutorials, an honors program, a senior project, Phi Beta Kappa, and Sigma Xi. Special programs include internships, off-campus study, and study abroad.

The most popular **majors** include English, political science/government, and economics. A complete listing of majors at Whitman College appears in the Majors Index beginning on page 380.

The **faculty** at Whitman College has 93 full-time teachers, 94% with terminal degrees. 90% of the faculty serve as student advisers. The student-faculty ratio is 11:1.

 ## Computers on Campus

Students are not required to have a computer. Student rooms are linked to a campus network. 100 **computers** available in computer labs, the learning resource center,

academic buildings, and the library provide access to e-mail. Staffed computer lab on campus provides training in the use of computers and software.

The 2 **libraries** have 252,290 books, 13,000 microform titles, and 2,000 subscriptions. They are connected to 3 national **on-line** catalogs.

 ## Campus Life

There are 35 active **organizations** on campus, including a drama/theater group and student-run newspaper and radio station. 50% of students participate in student government elections. 33% of eligible men and 39% of eligible women are members of 4 national **fraternities**, 6 national **sororities**, and 1 local sorority. Student **safety services** include late night transport/escort service, 24-hour emergency telephone alarm devices, 24-hour patrols by trained security personnel, student patrols, and electronically operated dormitory entrances.

Whitman College is a member of the NAIA. **Intercollegiate sports** include baseball (m), basketball (m, w), cross-country running (m, w), golf (m, w), skiing (cross-country) (m, w), skiing (downhill) (m, w), soccer (m, w), swimming and diving (m, w), tennis (m, w), track and field (m, w), volleyball (w).

 ## Applying

Whitman College requires an essay, a high school transcript, 1 recommendation, and SAT I or ACT. It recommends 3 years of high school math and science, 2 years of high school foreign language, and an interview. Early, deferred, and midyear entrance are possible, with a 2/15 deadline and 2/15 for financial aid. **Contact:** Mr. Chris Ellertson, Acting Director of Admission, Walla Walla, WA 99362-2083, 509-527-5176; fax 509-527-4967.

---

### GETTING IN LAST YEAR

2,013 applied
52% were accepted
35% enrolled (370)
55% from top tenth of their h.s. class
3.78 average high school GPA
32% had SAT verbal scores over 600
61% had SAT math scores over 600
5% had SAT verbal scores over 700
18% had SAT math scores over 700
16 National Merit Scholars
43 valedictorians

### THE STUDENT BODY

1,295 undergraduates
From 39 states and territories,
  27 other countries
46% from Washington
52% women, 48% men
1% African Americans
1% Native Americans
3% Hispanics
7% Asian Americans
2% international students

### AFTER FRESHMAN YEAR

93% returned for sophomore year
64% got a degree within 4 years
73% got a degree within 5 years
77% got a degree within 6 years

### AFTER GRADUATION

20% pursued further study (9% arts and
  sciences, 6% law, 3% medicine)
10 corporations, 3 government agencies, 11
  nonprofit organizations recruited on campus
1 Fulbright scholar

### WHAT YOU WILL PAY

Tuition and fees $16,820
Room and board $4900
63% receive need-based financial aid
  averaging $9093
21% receive non-need financial aid averaging
  $3904

# WHITTIER COLLEGE

Whittier, California • Suburban setting • Private • Independent • Coed

> Whittier College is a place where students can make a point in a heated class discussion, research a paper they and their professor will present together, and prepare a senior project that seems to tie together almost everything they have learned. At Whittier, students feel more intellectually alive than ever before.

## Academics

Whittier offers an individualized liberal arts curriculum and core academic program; a few graduate courses are open to undergraduates. It awards bachelor's, master's, and first professional **degrees**. Challenging opportunities include accelerated degree programs, self-designed majors, tutorials, an honors program, and a senior project. Special programs include internships, summer session for credit, study abroad, and Army and Air Force ROTC.

The most popular **majors** include business, English, and biology/biological sciences. A complete listing of majors at Whittier appears in the Majors Index beginning on page 380.

The **faculty** at Whittier has 88 full-time undergraduate teachers, 90% with terminal degrees. 100% of the faculty serve as student advisers. The student-faculty ratio is 15:1, and the average class size in required courses is 20.

## Computers on Campus

Students are not required to have a computer. Student rooms are linked to a campus network. 81 **computers** available in the computer center, computer labs, writing center, academic departments, the library, dormitories, and student rooms provide access to e-mail. Staffed computer lab on campus provides training in the use of computers and software.

The 2 **libraries** have 416,005 books, 55,869 microform titles, and 1,357 subscriptions. They are connected to 1 national **on-line** catalog.

## Campus Life

There are 39 active **organizations** on campus, including a drama/theater group and student-run newspaper and radio station. 33% of students participate in student government elections. 17% of eligible men and 24% of eligible women are members of 4 local **fraternities** and 5 local **sororities**. Student **safety services** include late night transport/escort service, 24-hour patrols by trained security personnel, and electronically operated dormitory entrances.

Whittier is a member of the NCAA (Division III). **Intercollegiate sports** include baseball (m), basketball (m, w), cross-country running (m, w), football (m), golf (m), lacrosse (m), soccer (m, w), softball (w), swimming and diving (m, w), tennis (m, w), track and field (m, w), volleyball (w), water polo (m, w).

## Applying

Whittier requires an essay, a high school transcript, 2 recommendations, and SAT I or ACT. It recommends 3 years of high school math and science, 2 years of high school foreign language, an interview, and SAT II Subject Tests. Early, deferred, and midyear entrance are possible, with rolling admissions and continuous processing to 2/15 for financial aid. **Contact:** Mr. Doug Locker, Director of School Relations, 13406 East Philadelphia Street, Whittier, CA 90608-0634, 310-907-4238.

---

### GETTING IN LAST YEAR

1,712 applied
71% were accepted
29% enrolled (347)
31% from top tenth of their h.s. class
3.0 average high school GPA
7% had SAT verbal scores over 600
16% had SAT math scores over 600
25% had ACT scores over 26
1% had SAT verbal scores over 700
2% had SAT math scores over 700
8% had ACT scores over 30
7 valedictorians

### THE STUDENT BODY

Total 2,182, of whom 1,302
   are undergraduates
From 32 states and territories,
   18 other countries
71% from California
57% women, 43% men
4% African Americans
2% Native Americans
27% Hispanics
9% Asian Americans
3% international students

### AFTER FRESHMAN YEAR

74% returned for sophomore year
45% got a degree within 4 years
54% got a degree within 5 years
56% got a degree within 6 years

### AFTER GRADUATION

28% pursued further study (4% arts and
   sciences, 3% law, 3% medicine)
11 corporations, 2 government agencies, 4
   nonprofit organizations recruited on campus

### WHAT YOU WILL PAY

Tuition and fees $17,187
Room and board $5813
67% receive need-based financial aid
   averaging $4671
11% receive non-need financial aid averaging
   $8133

---

# WILLAMETTE UNIVERSITY

Salem, Oregon • Urban setting • Private • Independent-Religious • Coed

 **Academics**

Williamette offers a traditional liberal arts and interdisciplinary curriculum and core academic program; a few graduate courses are open to undergraduates. It awards bachelor's, master's, and first professional **degrees**. Challenging opportunities include advanced placement, accelerated degree programs, self-designed majors, tutorials, and a senior project. Special programs include internships, off-campus study, study abroad, and Air Force ROTC.

The most popular **majors** include economics, psychology, and biology/biological sciences. A complete listing of majors at Williamette appears in the Majors Index beginning on page 380.

The **faculty** at Williamette has 150 full-time graduate and undergraduate teachers, 90% with terminal degrees. 100% of the faculty serve as student advisers. The student-faculty ratio is 14:1, and the average class size in required courses is 16.

 **Computers on Campus**

Students are not required to have a computer. Student rooms are linked to a campus network. 200 **computers** available in the computer center, computer labs, science center, classrooms, the library, the student center, and dormitories provide access to the main academic computer, off-campus computing facilities, e-mail, and on-line services. Staffed computer lab on campus (open 24 hours a day) provides training in the use of computers and software.

The 3 **libraries** have 241,344 books, 7,353 microform titles, and 1,433 subscriptions.

 **Campus Life**

There are 90 active **organizations** on campus, including a drama/theater group and student-run newspaper. 75% of students participate in student government elections. 31% of eligible men and 23% of eligible women are members of 6 national **fraternities** and 3 national **sororities**. Student **safety services** include late night transport/escort service, 24-hour emergency telephone alarm devices, 24-hour patrols by trained security personnel, student patrols, and electronically operated dormitory entrances.

Williamette is a member of the NCAA (Division III) and NAIA. **Intercollegiate sports** include baseball (m), basketball (m, w), crew (m, w), cross-country running (m, w), football (m), golf (m, w), lacrosse (m), rugby (m, w), soccer (m, w), softball (w), swimming and diving (m, w), tennis (m, w), track and field (m, w), volleyball (w), water polo (m, w).

 **Applying**

Williamette requires an essay, a high school transcript, 3 years of high school math and science, 3 years of high school foreign language, 1 recommendation, SAT I or ACT, a minimum high school GPA of 3.0, and in some cases an interview. It recommends an interview. Early, deferred, and midyear entrance are possible, with a 2/1 deadline and continuous processing to 2/1 for financial aid. **Contact:** Mr. James M. Sumner, Dean of Admissions, 900 State Street, Salem, OR 97301-3931, 503-370-6303; fax 503-375-5363.

## GETTING IN LAST YEAR

1,660 applied
85% were accepted
34% enrolled (474)
45% from top tenth of their h.s. class
3.64 average high school GPA
20% had SAT verbal scores over 600
44% had SAT math scores over 600
75% had ACT scores over 26
3% had SAT verbal scores over 700
7% had SAT math scores over 700
15% had ACT scores over 30
10 National Merit Scholars
16 class presidents
39 valedictorians

## THE STUDENT BODY

Total 2,519, of whom 1,701 are undergraduates
From 38 states and territories, 23 other countries
45% from Oregon
56% women, 44% men
1% African Americans
1% Native Americans
3% Hispanics
7% Asian Americans
5% international students

## AFTER FRESHMAN YEAR

89% returned for sophomore year
65% got a degree within 4 years
71% got a degree within 5 years
72% got a degree within 6 years

## AFTER GRADUATION

35% pursued further study (10% arts and sciences, 3% law, 3% medicine)
12 corporations recruited on campus
1 Fulbright scholar

## WHAT YOU WILL PAY

Tuition and fees $16,490
Room and board $4800
65% receive need-based financial aid averaging $5950
10% receive non-need financial aid averaging $4000

# WILLIAM JEWELL COLLEGE

Liberty, Missouri • Small-town setting • Private • Independent-Religious • Coed

William Jewell College has long been recognized as the "Campus of Achievement." Through curricular and cocurricular activities, plus the College's metropolitan locale, students can engage in the life of the College and community rather than sit on the sidelines. An excellent teaching faculty administers such innovative curricular programs as Foundations for the Future, a general education honors program, and the Oxbridge Tutorial Honors Alternative, an American adaptation of the educational methods of the great English universities Oxford and Cambridge. Graduates discover they build confidence and are prepared for the rigors of postgraduate challenges. William Jewell graduates are leaders.

## Academics

William Jewell offers a core academic program. It awards bachelor's **degrees**. Challenging opportunities include advanced placement, accelerated degree programs, self-designed majors, tutorials, Freshmen Honors College, an honors program, and a senior project. Special programs include cooperative education, internships, summer session for credit, off-campus study, and study abroad.

The most popular **majors** include business, nursing, and elementary education. A complete listing of majors at William Jewell appears in the Majors Index beginning on page 380.

The **faculty** at William Jewell has 90 full-time teachers, 72% with terminal degrees. 94% of the faculty serve as student advisers. The student-faculty ratio is 13:1, and the average class size in required courses is 21.

## Computers on Campus

Students are not required to have a computer. 90 **computers** available in the computer center, computer labs, the learning resource center, academic departments, classrooms, the library, and the student center.

The 2 **libraries** have 218,500 books, 145,208 microform titles, and 868 subscriptions. They are connected to 5 national **on-line** catalogs.

## Campus Life

There are 20 active **organizations** on campus, including a drama/theater group and student-run newspaper and radio station. 50% of students participate in student government elections. 45% of eligible men and 55% of eligible women are members of 4 national **fraternities** and 4 national **sororities**. Student **safety services** include late night transport/escort service, 24-hour emergency telephone alarm devices, 24-hour patrols by trained security personnel, and electronically operated dormitory entrances.

William Jewell is a member of the NAIA. **Intercollegiate sports** (some offering scholarships) include baseball (m), basketball (m, w), cross-country running (m, w), football (m), golf (m), soccer (m), softball (w), tennis (m, w), track and field (m, w), volleyball (w).

## Applying

William Jewell requires an essay, a high school transcript, 2 recommendations, and SAT I or ACT. It recommends 4 years of high school math and science, 2 years of high school foreign language, and an interview. Early, deferred, and midyear entrance are possible, with rolling admissions and continuous processing to 3/15 for financial aid. **Contact:** Mr. Vic Davolt, Interim Director of Admission, 500 College Hill, Liberty, MO 64068-1843, 816-781-7700 ext. 5137 or toll-free 800-753-7009; fax 816-781-3164.

### GETTING IN LAST YEAR
742 applied
86% were accepted
50% enrolled (319)
28% from top tenth of their h.s. class
3.46 average high school GPA
14% had SAT verbal scores over 600
27% had SAT math scores over 600
41% had ACT scores over 26
2% had SAT verbal scores over 700
7% had SAT math scores over 700
12% had ACT scores over 30
1 National Merit Scholar

### THE STUDENT BODY
1,322 undergraduates
From 34 states and territories,
    14 other countries
74% from Missouri
57% women, 43% men
3% African Americans
1% Native Americans
1% Hispanics
1% Asian Americans
2% international students

### AFTER FRESHMAN YEAR
86% returned for sophomore year
45% got a degree within 4 years
55% got a degree within 5 years
58% got a degree within 6 years

### AFTER GRADUATION
29% pursued further study (16% arts and
    sciences, 4% business, 3% law)
31 corporations, 10 government agencies, 5
    nonprofit organizations recruited on campus

### WHAT YOU WILL PAY
Tuition and fees $10,060
Room and board $2970
66% receive need-based financial aid
    averaging $1425
31% receive non-need financial aid averaging
    $3400

# WILLIAMS COLLEGE

Williamstown, Massachusetts • Small-town setting • Private • Independent • Coed

Williams is a community of learning where students and faculty are active and responsible partners. The College emphasizes the continuities between curriculum and extracurricular life, formal education and the lifelong quest for understanding, and commitment to excellence in teaching and support for artistic endeavor and scholarly research. Williams admits students without regard to financial need and provides financial assistance to meet 100% of demonstrated need. The College is dedicated to being a multicultural community in order to enrich the exchange of ideas, to anticipate the diverse world in which its graduates function, and to enhance the educational environment for all its members.

##  Academics

Williams offers a liberal arts curriculum and core academic program; fewer than half of graduate courses are open to undergraduates. It awards bachelor's and master's **degrees**. Challenging opportunities include advanced placement, accelerated degree programs, self-designed majors, tutorials, an honors program, a senior project, Phi Beta Kappa, and Sigma Xi. Special programs include internships, off-campus study, and study abroad.

The most popular **majors** include English, history, and economics. A complete listing of majors at Williams appears in the Majors Index beginning on page 380.

The **faculty** at Williams has 229 full-time undergraduate teachers, 95% with terminal degrees. The student-faculty ratio is 11:1, and the average class size in required courses is 18.

##  Computers on Campus

Students are not required to have a computer. Student rooms are linked to a campus network. 150 **computers** available in the computer center, computer labs, academic buildings, and the library provide access to the main academic computer, off-campus computing facilities, e-mail, and on-line services. Staffed computer lab on campus provides training in the use of computers and software.

The 8 **libraries** have 732,320 books, 387,530 microform titles, and 2,651 subscriptions. They are connected to 7 national **on-line** catalogs.

##  Campus Life

There are 115 active **organizations** on campus, including a drama/theater group and student-run newspaper and radio station. Student **safety services** include late night transport/escort service, 24-hour emergency telephone alarm devices, 24-hour patrols by trained security personnel, student patrols, and electronically operated dormitory entrances.

Williams is a member of the NCAA (Division III). **Intercollegiate sports** include baseball (m), basketball (m, w), crew (m, w), cross-country running (m, w), equestrian sports (m, w), field hockey (w), football (m), golf (m, w), ice hockey (m, w), lacrosse (m, w), rugby (m, w), sailing (m, w), skiing (cross-country) (m, w), skiing (downhill) (m, w), soccer (m, w), softball (w), squash (m, w), swimming and diving (m, w), tennis (m, w), track and field (m, w), volleyball (m, w), water polo (m, w), wrestling (m).

##  Applying

Williams requires an essay, a high school transcript, 4 years of high school math, 4 years of high school foreign language, 2 recommendations, SAT I or ACT, and 3 SAT II Subject Tests. It recommends 3 years of high school science and an interview. Early, deferred, and midyear entrance are possible, with a 1/1 deadline and 2/1 for financial aid. **Contact:** Mr. Philip F. Smith, Dean of Admission, 988 Main Street, Williamstown, MA 01267, 413-597-2211.

---

### GETTING IN LAST YEAR
4,674 applied
27% were accepted
40% enrolled (498)
81% from top tenth of their h.s. class
73% had SAT verbal scores over 600
87% had SAT math scores over 600
89% had ACT scores over 26
31% had SAT verbal scores over 700
51% had SAT math scores over 700
64% had ACT scores over 30
47 National Merit Scholars

### THE STUDENT BODY
Total 2,126, of whom 2,069
  are undergraduates

From 52 states and territories,
  42 other countries
11% from Massachusetts
50% women, 50% men
7% African Americans
1% Native Americans
7% Hispanics
11% Asian Americans
3% international students

### AFTER FRESHMAN YEAR
95% returned for sophomore year
87% got a degree within 4 years
93% got a degree within 5 years
94% got a degree within 6 years

### AFTER GRADUATION
23% pursued further study (12% arts and
  sciences, 5% law, 4% medicine)
60 corporations, 1 government agency, 25
  nonprofit organizations recruited on campus
1 Marshall scholar

### WHAT YOU WILL PAY
Tuition and fees $19,771
Room and board $5790
50% receive need-based financial aid
  averaging $12,800

# WILLIAM SMITH COLLEGE

*Coordinate with Hobart College*

Geneva, New York • Small-town setting • Private • Independent • Women

Hobart and William Smith Colleges together offer the best features of conventionally coeducational colleges: all classes and many residences are coed and students share all campus facilities and social activities. At the same time, each College maintains its own student government, athletic program, and dean's office. Through this coordinate-college system, men and women have equal opportunities for leadership and visibility. Small classes, a dedicated faculty, and extensive opportunities for independent study and off-campus study contribute to a climate that is academically rigorous and strongly supportive. Students balance academics with involvement in over 60 clubs and athletics ranging from intramurals to intercollegiate varsity competition.

 **Academics**

William Smith offers an interdisciplinary curriculum and core academic program. It awards bachelor's **degrees**. Challenging opportunities include advanced placement, accelerated degree programs, self-designed majors, tutorials, an honors program, a senior project, and Phi Beta Kappa. Special programs include internships, off-campus study, and study abroad.

The most popular **majors** include English, psychology, and biology/biological sciences. A complete listing of majors at William Smith appears in the Majors Index beginning on page 380.

The **faculty** at William Smith has 142 full-time teachers, 98% with terminal degrees. 95% of the faculty serve as student advisers. The student-faculty ratio is 13:1, and the average class size in required courses is 20.

 **Computers on Campus**

Students are not required to have a computer. Student rooms are linked to a campus network. 146 **computers** available in the computer center, computer labs, the research center, the learning resource center, honors room, classrooms, and the library provide access to the main academic computer, off-campus computing facilities, e-mail, and on-line services. Staffed computer lab on campus provides training in the use of computers and software.

The 2 **libraries** have 312,000 books, 42,000 microform titles, and 1,860 subscriptions. They are connected to 3 national **on-line** catalogs.

 **Campus Life**

There are 60 active **organizations** on campus, including a drama/theater group and student-run newspaper and radio station. Student **safety services** include late night transport/escort service, 24-hour emergency telephone alarm devices, and 24-hour patrols by trained security personnel.

William Smith is a member of the NCAA (Division III). **Intercollegiate sports** include basketball, crew, cross-country running, field hockey, ice hockey, lacrosse, sailing, skiing (downhill), soccer, swimming and diving, tennis.

 **Applying**

William Smith requires an essay, a high school transcript, 3 years of high school math, 2 years of high school foreign language, 2 recommendations, and SAT I or ACT. It recommends 3 years of high school science, an interview, and SAT II Subject Tests. Early and deferred entrance are possible, with a 2/15 deadline and a 2/15 priority date for financial aid. **Contact:** Ms. Mara O'Laughlin, Director of Admissions, 629 South Main Street, Geneva, NY 14456, 315-781-3472 or toll-free 800-245-0100; fax 315-781-3471.

## GETTING IN LAST YEAR

1,423 applied
80% were accepted
25% enrolled (288)
31% from top tenth of their h.s. class
11% had SAT verbal scores over 600
24% had SAT math scores over 600
32% had ACT scores over 26
1% had SAT verbal scores over 700
2% had SAT math scores over 700
10% had ACT scores over 30

## THE STUDENT BODY

889 undergraduates
From 41 states and territories,
  24 other countries

49% from New York
100% women
4% African Americans
1% Native Americans
4% Hispanics
2% Asian Americans
3% international students

## AFTER FRESHMAN YEAR

95% returned for sophomore year
81% got a degree within 4 years
82% got a degree within 5 years
84% got a degree within 6 years

## AFTER GRADUATION

24% pursued further study (17% arts and
  sciences, 4% law, 2% medicine)
98 corporations, 23 government agencies,
  108 nonprofit organizations recruited on
  campus

## WHAT YOU WILL PAY

Tuition and fees $19,480
Room and board $5841
58% receive need-based financial aid
  averaging $12,345
1% receive non-need financial aid averaging
  $10,000

# WITTENBERG UNIVERSITY

Springfield, Ohio • Suburban setting • Private • Independent-Religious • Coed

Wittenberg University, with a 2,200-student enrollment, offering opportunities found at far larger universities—a geographically diverse student population, a "picture-book" campus, and excellent facilities—has been catapulted onto the national college stage, yet a strong sense of community remains. At Wittenberg, education is multifaceted, carrying a fundamental purpose to harmonize the intellectual, spiritual, aesthetic, social, and physical qualities that characterize wholeness of person. Through personal attention from an outstanding, supportive, and approachable faculty and staff, a challenging curriculum, and valuable experiences outside the classroom, Wittenberg students develop the skills not only for a successful career but also for a meaningful life.

 **Academics**

Wittenberg University offers an interdisciplinary curriculum and core academic program. It awards bachelor's **degrees**. Challenging opportunities include advanced placement, accelerated degree programs, self-designed majors, tutorials, Freshmen Honors College, an honors program, a senior project, Phi Beta Kappa, and Sigma Xi. Special programs include internships, summer session for credit, off-campus study, study abroad, and Army and Air Force ROTC.

The most popular **majors** include business, biology/biological sciences, and English. A complete listing of majors at Wittenberg University appears in the Majors Index beginning on page 380.

The **faculty** at Wittenberg University has 142 full-time teachers, 97% with terminal degrees. 100% of the faculty serve as student advisers. The student-faculty ratio is 13:1, and the average class size in required courses is 25.

 **Computers on Campus**

Students are not required to have a computer. Student rooms are linked to a campus network. 125 **computers** available in the computer center, computer labs, the learn-ing resource center, classrooms, the library, dormitories, and student rooms provide access to the main academic computer, off-campus computing facilities, e-mail, and on-line services. Staffed computer lab on campus provides training in the use of computers and software.

The 2 **libraries** have 350,000 books, 58,248 microform titles, and 1,200 subscriptions. They are connected to 2 national **on-line** catalogs.

 **Campus Life**

There are 100 active **organizations** on campus, including a drama/theater group and student-run newspaper and radio station. 25% of students participate in student government elections. 25% of eligible men and 42% of eligible women are members of 6 national **fraternities** and 8 national **sororities**. Student **safety services** include late night transport/escort service, 24-hour emergency telephone alarm devices, 24-hour patrols by trained security personnel, and electronically operated dormitory entrances.

Wittenberg University is a member of the NCAA (Division III). **Intercollegiate sports** include baseball (m), basketball (m, w), cross-country running (m, w), field hockey (w), football (m), golf (m, w), ice hockey (m), lacrosse (m, w), rugby (m, w), soccer (m, w), softball (w), swimming and diving (m, w), tennis (m, w), track and field (m, w), volleyball (m, w).

 **Applying**

Wittenberg University requires an essay, a high school transcript, 3 years of high school math and science, 3 years of high school foreign language, 1 recommendation, SAT I or ACT, and in some cases an interview. It recommends an interview and SAT II Subject Tests. Early, deferred, and midyear entrance are possible, with a 3/15 deadline and continuous processing to 3/15 for financial aid. **Contact:** Mr. Kenneth G. Benne, Dean of Admissions, Ward Street at North Wittenberg Avenue, Springfield, OH 45501-0720, 513-327-6314 or toll-free 800-677-7558; fax 513-327-6340.

## GETTING IN LAST YEAR

2,075 applied
88% were accepted
32% enrolled (580)
42% from top tenth of their h.s. class
3.5 average high school GPA
6 National Merit Scholars
25 valedictorians

## THE STUDENT BODY

2,160 undergraduates
From 44 states and territories,
   34 other countries

54% from Ohio
54% women, 46% men
7% African Americans
1% Native Americans
2% Hispanics
3% Asian Americans
6% international students

## AFTER FRESHMAN YEAR

86% returned for sophomore year
66% got a degree within 4 years
72% got a degree within 5 years
74% got a degree within 6 years

## AFTER GRADUATION

21% pursued further study

## WHAT YOU WILL PAY

Tuition and fees $16,770
Room and board $4404
68% receive need-based financial aid
   averaging $9500
15% receive non-need financial aid averaging
   $4500

# WOFFORD COLLEGE

Spartanburg, South Carolina • Urban setting • Private • Independent-Religious • Coed

Wofford takes pride in recognizing and encouraging student initiative. Recent independent study projects have included a January Interim at Mother Teresa's Home for Dying Destitutes and computer research at California's Lawrence Livermore Laboratory. Students also enjoy many group opportunities for professional internships and international study. In its residence life and recreational programs, Wofford also treats students as young adults. There are only a few basic rules at Wofford, and most of them are administered through a student judicial commission. More than 60 organizations are active on campus, ranging from Phi Beta Kappa to 11 social fraternities and sororities.

## Academics

Wofford College offers a core academic program. It awards bachelor's **degrees**. Challenging opportunities include advanced placement, accelerated degree programs, self-designed majors, tutorials, and Phi Beta Kappa. Special programs include cooperative education, internships, summer session for credit, off-campus study, study abroad, and Army ROTC.

The most popular **majors** include biology/biological sciences, business economics, and English. A complete listing of majors at Wofford College appears in the Majors Index beginning on page 380.

The **faculty** at Wofford College has 70 full-time teachers, 91% with terminal degrees. 92% of the faculty serve as student advisers. The student-faculty ratio is 14:1.

## Computers on Campus

Students are not required to have a computer. 118 **computers** available in the computer center, all academic buildings, classrooms, and the library provide access to the main academic computer, e-mail, and on-line services. Staffed computer lab on campus.

The **library** has 165,676 books, 60,354 microform titles, and 641 subscriptions.

## Campus Life

Active **organizations** on campus include a drama/theater group and student-run newspaper. 75% of students participate in student government elections. 50% of eligible men and 58% of eligible women are members of 8 national **fraternities** and 3 national **sororities**. Student **safety services** include late night transport/escort service, 24-hour emergency telephone alarm devices, 24-hour patrols by trained security personnel, and electronically operated dormitory entrances.

Wofford College is a member of the NCAA (Division II). **Intercollegiate sports** (some offering scholarships) include baseball (m), basketball (m, w), cross-country running (m, w), fencing (m, w), football (m), golf (m, w), riflery (m, w), soccer (m, w), tennis (m, w), track and field (w), volleyball (w).

## Applying

Wofford College requires an essay, a high school transcript, and SAT I or ACT. It recommends 3 years of high school math and science, some high school foreign language, recommendations, an interview, and SAT II Subject Tests. Early, deferred, and midyear entrance are possible, with a 2/1 deadline and continuous processing to 3/15 for financial aid. **Contact:** Mr. Charles H. Gray Jr., Director of Admissions, 429 North Church Street, Spartanburg, SC 29303-3663, 803-597-4130; fax 803-597-4219.

---

### GETTING IN LAST YEAR
1,108 applied
82% were accepted
34% enrolled (310)
47% from top tenth of their h.s. class
22% had SAT verbal scores over 600
40% had SAT math scores over 600
3% had SAT verbal scores over 700
6% had SAT math scores over 700
25 valedictorians

### THE STUDENT BODY
1,106 undergraduates
From 32 states and territories,
  7 other countries
67% from South Carolina
41% women, 59% men
7% African Americans
0% Native Americans
1% Hispanics
2% Asian Americans
1% international students

### AFTER FRESHMAN YEAR
92% returned for sophomore year
72% got a degree within 4 years
76% got a degree within 5 years

### AFTER GRADUATION
38% pursued further study (17% arts and
  sciences, 7% law, 5% medicine)

### WHAT YOU WILL PAY
Tuition and fees $12,680
Room and board $4150
51% receive need-based financial aid
  averaging $6125

# Worcester Polytechnic Institute

Worcester, Massachusetts • Suburban setting • Private • Independent • Coed

WPI's facilities and faculty are outstanding, the extracurricular and athletic programs are excellent, and the campus setting is attractive. However, it is the academic program—the way in which each student, individually, is able to reach his or her goals—that provides the margin of difference. The WPI Plan involves in-depth project-research work not only in a student's major field but also in the humanities and the linkage between technology and social issues. Approximately one third of the students do one of these projects overseas or in Washington, DC, and more than 200 outside agencies and corporations sponsor projects.

## Academics

WPI offers a hands-on, project-oriented curriculum and no core academic program. It awards bachelor's, master's, and doctoral **degrees**. Challenging opportunities include advanced placement, accelerated degree programs, self-designed majors, a senior project, and Sigma Xi. Special programs include cooperative education, summer session for credit, off-campus study, study abroad, and Army, Naval, and Air Force ROTC.

The most popular **majors** include mechanical engineering, electrical engineering, and civil engineering. A complete listing of majors at WPI appears in the Majors Index beginning on page 380.

The **faculty** at WPI has 203 full-time undergraduate teachers, 95% with terminal degrees. The student-faculty ratio is 12:1.

## Computers on Campus

Students are not required to have a computer. Student rooms are linked to a campus network. 770 **computers** available in the computer center, computer labs, and the library provide access to the main academic computer, off-campus computing facilities, e-mail, and on-line services. Staffed computer lab on campus (open 24 hours a day) provides training in the use of computers and software.

The **library** has 300,000 books, 785,000 microform titles, and 1,400 subscriptions.

## Campus Life

Active **organizations** on campus include drama/theater group and student-run newspaper and radio station. 35% of eligible men and 40% of eligible women are members of 12 national **fraternities** and 2 national **sororities**. Student **safety services** include late night transport/escort service, 24-hour emergency telephone alarm devices, 24-hour patrols by trained security personnel, and student patrols.

WPI is a member of the NCAA (Division III). **Intercollegiate sports** include baseball (m), basketball (m, w), bowling (m, w), crew (m, w), cross-country running (m, w), fencing (m, w), field hockey (w), football (m), golf (m), ice hockey (m), lacrosse (m, w), riflery (m), rugby (m, w), sailing (m, w), skiing (downhill) (m, w), soccer (m, w), softball (w), swimming and diving (m, w), tennis (m, w), track and field (m, w), volleyball (m, w), water polo (m, w), wrestling (m).

## Applying

WPI requires a high school transcript, 4 years of high school math, 2 recommendations, SAT I or ACT, and 3 SAT II Subject Tests (including SAT II: Writing Test). It recommends an essay, 3 years of high school science, and an interview. Early and deferred entrance are possible, with a 2/15 deadline and 3/1 for financial aid. **Contact:** Mr. Robert G. Voss, Executive Director of Admissions and Financial Aid, 100 Institute Road, Worcester, MA 01609-2247, 508-831-5286; fax 508-831-5753.

### GETTING IN LAST YEAR

2,539 applied
86% were accepted
32% enrolled (697)
46% from top tenth of their h.s. class
18% had SAT verbal scores over 600
77% had SAT math scores over 600
95% had ACT scores over 26
1% had SAT verbal scores over 700
28% had SAT math scores over 700
50% had ACT scores over 30
11 National Merit Scholars

### THE STUDENT BODY

Total 3,794, of whom 2,781 are undergraduates
From 52 states and territories, 60 other countries
47% from Massachusetts
19% women, 81% men
1% African Americans
1% Native Americans
1% Hispanics
6% Asian Americans
7% international students

### AFTER FRESHMAN YEAR

94% returned for sophomore year

### AFTER GRADUATION

22% pursued further study (11% engineering, 5% arts and sciences, 3% business)
109 corporations, 12 government agencies recruited on campus

### WHAT YOU WILL PAY

Tuition and fees $16,060
Room and board $5370
75% receive need-based financial aid averaging $7000

# YALE UNIVERSITY

New Haven, Connecticut • Urban setting • Private • Independent • Coed

Students and faculty at Yale are excited by the thought-provoking discussions they find in classes, dining halls, and dormitory rooms. Yale is committed to undergraduate teaching, and every professor at Yale College teaches undergraduate classes. Yale's most distinctive feature is its residential college system, in which each student belongs to an intimate community that is a microcosm of the larger Yale community. In the colleges, academic life merges with other interests, and the result is an environment in which students come to know and respect one another as colleagues and friends. Yale College is a center for arts and athletics, music and drama, religion, politics, and community service.

##  Academics

Yale offers a liberal arts curriculum and core academic program. It awards bachelor's, master's, doctoral, and first professional **degrees**. Challenging opportunities include advanced placement, accelerated degree programs, self-designed majors, tutorials, an honors program, a senior project, Phi Beta Kappa, and Sigma Xi. Special programs include summer session for credit, study abroad, and Army and Air Force ROTC.

The most popular **majors** include history, English, and biology/biological sciences. A complete listing of majors at Yale appears in the Majors Index beginning on page 380.

The **faculty** at Yale has 2,782 graduate and undergraduate teachers, 96% with terminal degrees. 100% of the faculty serve as student advisers. The student-faculty ratio is 6:1.

##  Computers on Campus

Students are not required to have a computer. Student rooms are linked to a campus network. 250 **computers** available in the computer center, computer labs, classrooms, the library, and dormitories provide access to e-mail and on-line services. Staffed computer lab on campus.

The 21 **libraries** have 10.2 million books and 54,601 subscriptions.

##  Campus Life

There are 300 active **organizations** on campus, including a drama/theater group and student-run newspaper and radio station. Student **safety services** include late night transport/escort service, 24-hour emergency telephone alarm devices, 24-hour patrols by trained security personnel, and electronically operated dormitory entrances.

Yale is a member of the NCAA (Division I). **Intercollegiate sports** include baseball (m), basketball (m, w), crew (m, w), cross-country running (m, w), fencing (m, w), field hockey (w), football (m), golf (m, w), gymnastics (w), ice hockey (m, w), lacrosse (m, w), soccer (m, w), softball (w), squash (m, w), swimming and diving (m, w), tennis (m, w), track and field (m, w), volleyball (w).

##  Applying

Yale requires an essay, a high school transcript, 3 recommendations, SAT I or ACT, and 3 SAT II Subject Tests. It recommends 3 years of high school math and science, some high school foreign language, and an interview. Early and deferred entrance are possible, with a 12/31 deadline and 2/1 for financial aid. **Contact:** Admissions Counselor, PO Box 208234, New Haven, CT 06520, 203-432-1900; fax 203-432-7329.

---

### GETTING IN LAST YEAR
12,991 applied
19% were accepted
53% enrolled (1,308)
95% from top tenth of their h.s. class
80% had SAT verbal scores over 600
92% had SAT math scores over 600
36% had SAT verbal scores over 700
59% had SAT math scores over 700

### THE STUDENT BODY
Total 10,964, of whom 5,261
  are undergraduates
From 55 states and territories,
  51 other countries
10% from Connecticut
47% women, 53% men
10% African Americans
1% Native Americans
7% Hispanics
17% Asian Americans
4% international students

### AFTER FRESHMAN YEAR
99% returned for sophomore year

### AFTER GRADUATION
33% pursued further study (14% arts and
  sciences, 9% medicine, 8% law)
1 Rhodes, 3 Marshall, 26 Fulbright scholars

### WHAT YOU WILL PAY
Tuition and fees $19,840
Room and board $6510
44% receive need-based financial aid
  averaging $11,984

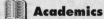

# YESHIVA UNIVERSITY

New York, New York • Urban setting • Private • Independent • Coed

## Academics

YU offers a liberal arts and business curriculum joined with Jewish studies programs and core academic program; fewer than half of graduate courses are open to undergraduates. It awards bachelor's, master's, doctoral, and first professional **degrees** (Yeshiva College and Stern College for Women are coordinate undergraduate colleges of arts and sciences for men and women, respectively. Sy Syms School of Business offers programs at both campuses). Challenging opportunities include advanced placement, self-designed majors, tutorials, an honors program, and a senior project. Special programs include internships, summer session for credit, off-campus study, and study abroad.

The most popular **majors** include economics, psychology, and accounting. A complete listing of majors at YU appears in the Majors Index beginning on page 380.

The **faculty** at YU has 736 full-time graduate and undergraduate teachers, 94% with terminal degrees. 6% of the faculty serve as student advisers. The student-faculty ratio is 9:1.

## Computers on Campus

Students are not required to have a computer. 125 **computers** available in the computer center, computer labs, labs, and the library provide access to the main academic computer and e-mail. Staffed computer lab on campus.

The 7 **libraries** have 995,312 books, 79,432 microform titles, and 9,760 subscriptions.

## Campus Life

Active **organizations** on campus include drama/theater group and student-run newspaper and radio station. 60% of students participate in student government elections. Student **safety services** include late night transport/escort service, 24-hour emergency telephone alarm devices, and 24-hour patrols by trained security personnel.

YU is a member of the NCAA (Division III). **Intercollegiate sports** include basketball (m, w), cross-country running (m), fencing (m), golf (m), tennis (m, w), track and field (m), volleyball (m), wrestling (m).

## Applying

YU requires a high school transcript, 2 years of high school foreign language, 2 recommendations, an interview, and SAT I or ACT. It recommends an essay and SAT II Subject Tests. Early, deferred, and midyear entrance are possible, with a 2/15 deadline and continuous processing to 4/15 for financial aid. **Contact:** Mr. Michael Kranzler, Associate Director of Admissions, 500 West 185th Street, New York, NY 10033-3201, 212-960-5400 ext. 277; fax 212-960-0043.

### GETTING IN LAST YEAR

1,465 applied
80% were accepted
69% enrolled (810)
3.4 average high school GPA
48% had SAT verbal scores over 600
62% had SAT math scores over 600
24% had SAT verbal scores over 700
9% had SAT math scores over 700
3 National Merit Scholars

### THE STUDENT BODY

Total 5,205, of whom 2,154
   are undergraduates
From 31 states and territories,
   21 other countries
57% from New York
47% women, 53% men
5% international students

### AFTER FRESHMAN YEAR

83% returned for sophomore year

### AFTER GRADUATION

89% had job offers within 3 months
60 corporations, 5 government agencies, 5 nonprofit organizations recruited on campus

### WHAT YOU WILL PAY

Tuition and fees $12,914
Room and board $4192
75% receive need-based financial aid averaging $3343
25% receive non-need financial aid averaging $4100

# DESCRIPTIONS OF COMPETITIVE ARTS COLLEGES AND CONSERVATORIES

The listings below show the autonomous colleges specializing in art and/or music that have highly selective application/acceptance ratios.

## Art Center College of Design
Pasadena, California 91103

Founded 1930; suburban setting; independent; coed; awards B, M.

**Enrollment** 1,164 total; 1,089 undergraduates (219 freshmen).
**Faculty** 427 total; 59 full-time; student-faculty ratio is 5:1.
**Expenses (1995–96)** Tuition: $14,400.
**Majors** Advertising, art/fine arts, commercial art, environmental design, film studies, graphic arts, illustration, industrial design, painting/drawing, photography.
**Applying** Required: high school transcript, essay, portfolio. Recommended: Minimum 3.0 high school GPA, some foreign language, interview. SAT I or ACT required for some.
**Application deadlines** Rolling, 3/1 priority date for financial aid.
**Contact** Ms. Kit Baron, Vice President of Student Services, 818-396-2373.

## Boston Conservatory
Boston, Massachusetts 02215

Founded 1867; urban setting; independent; coed; awards B, M.

Enrollment 414 total; 301 undergraduates (72 freshmen).
**Faculty** 165 total; 35 full-time.
**Expenses (1994–95)** Comprehensive fee of $18,795 includes tuition ($12,300), room and board ($6100), and mandatory fees ($395).
**Majors** Dance, music, music education, opera, piano/organ, stringed instruments, theater arts/drama, voice, wind and percussion instruments.
**Applying** Required: essay, high school transcript, 3 recommendations, audition. Recommended: 3 years of high school math and science, some high school foreign language, SAT I or ACT. Interview, SAT I or ACT required for some.
**Application deadlines** Rolling, 3/15 priority date for financial aid.
**Contact** Mr. Richard Wallace, Director of Enrollment, 617-536-6340 Ext. 16.
**From the College** Founded in 1867, The Boston Conservatory is the oldest independent performing arts college in the United States. The mission of the institution is the preparation of literate artists and teachers, within a nurturing individually focused environment, for careers in the performing arts. Faculty is representative of Boston's world-famous performing ensembles in music, dance, and theater, as well as internationally recognized solo artists. Students receive maximum personalized instruction through small classes and extensive one-on-one teaching/coaching. Students are housed in converted Boston town houses adjacent to the Conservatory that offer family-style living. The school is located in a cultural section of Boston near the Museum and Symphony Hall.

## California Institute of the Arts
Valencia, California 91355

Founded 1961; suburban setting; independent; coed; awards B, M.

**Enrollment** 1051 total; 659 undergraduates (97 freshmen).
**Faculty** 212 total; student-faculty ratio is 8:1.
**Expenses (1995–96)** Comprehensive fee of $21,225 includes tuition ($15,450), mandatory fees ($75), and room and board ($5700).
**Majors** Art/fine arts, commercial art, computer graphics, dance, film studies, graphic arts, illustration, jazz, music, photography, piano/organ, sculpture, stringed instruments, studio art, theater arts/drama, voice.
**Applying** Required: essay, high school transcript, portfolio or audition. Interview, recommendations, test scores required for some.
**Application deadlines** 2/1, 3/1 priority date for financial aid.
**Contact** Mr. Kenneth Young, Director of Admissions, 805-255-1050 Ext. 7863.

## Cleveland Institute of Music
Cleveland, Ohio 44106

Founded 1920; urban setting; independent; coed; awards B, M, D.

**Enrollment** 335 total; 206 undergraduates (55 freshmen).
**Faculty** 107 total; 29 full-time; student-faculty ratio is 10:1.
**Expenses (1994–95)** Comprehensive fee of $19,477 includes tuition ($13,650), mandatory fees ($1122), and room and board ($4705).
**Majors** Audio engineering, music, music education, piano/organ, stringed instruments, voice, wind and percussion instruments.
**Applying** Required: essay, high school transcript, 2 recommendations, audition, SAT I or ACT. Recommended:

3 years of high school math and science, some high school foreign language, interview.
**Application deadlines** 1/15, 3/1 priority date for financial aid.
**Contact** Mr. William Fay, Director of Admissions, 216-795-3107.
**From the College** Ranked as one of the foremost schools of music in the United States, CIM's curriculum is based upon solid, traditional musical values while incorporating liberal arts instruction and new technologies that equip students to meet the challenges of the 21st century. Graduates are admitted routinely to leading graduate schools, are winners of major competitions, and occupy important performance and teaching positions throughout the world.

## Corcoran School of Art
**Washington, District of Columbia 20006**

Founded 1890; urban setting; independent; coed; awards B.

**Enrollment** 315 total all undergraduates 82 freshmen).
**Faculty** 80 total; 35 full-time; student-faculty ratio is 10:1.
**Expenses (1994–95)** Tuition: $10,980. Room only: $4150.
**Majors** Applied art, art/fine arts, ceramic art and design, commercial art, graphic arts, painting/drawing, photography, printmaking, sculpture, studio art.
**Applying** Required: high school transcript, portfolio, minimum 2.0 high school GPA. Recommended: SAT I or ACT, letters of recommendation, campus interview.
**Application deadlines** Rolling, 3/15 priority date for financial aid.
**Contact** Mr. Mark Sistek, Director of Admissions, 202-628-9484 Ext. 700.

## The Curtis Institute of Music
**Philadelphia, Pennsylvania 19103**

Founded 1924; urban setting; independent; coed; awards B, M.

**Enrollment** 156 total; 140 undergraduates (36 freshmen).
**Faculty** 84 total; 2 full-time.
**Expenses (1994–95)** Tuition: $0. Mandatory fees: $600.
**Majors** Music, piano/organ, stringed instruments, voice, wind and percussion instruments.
**Applying** Required: high school transcript, recommendations, audition, SAT I. Recommended: 3 years of high school math and science, some high school foreign language. TSWE required for some.
**Application deadlines** 1/15, 6/1 for financial aid.
**Contact** Ms. Judi L. Gattone, Admissions and Financial Aid Officer, 215-893-5262.

## Fashion Institute of Technology
**New York, New York 10001**

Founded 1944; urban setting; state and locally supported; coed; awards A, B, M.

**Enrollment** 8,422 total; 8,370 undergraduates (1,732 freshmen).
**Faculty** 931 total; 181 full-time; student-faculty ratio is 14:1.
**Expenses (1994–95)** State resident tuition: $2100. Nonresident tuition: $5050. Mandatory fees: $210. Room and board: $4800.
**Majors** Advertising, applied art, art/fine arts, commercial art, communications, fashion design and technology, fashion merchandising, illustration, industrial administration, interior design, jewelry and metalsmithing, management engineering, marketing/retailing/merchandising, photography, textile arts, textiles and clothing.
**Applying** Required: essay, high school transcript, portfolio for art and design majors; SAT I required for some.
**Application deadlines** Rolling, 3/15 priority date for financial aid.
**Contact** Mr. Jim Pidgeon, Director of Admissions, 212-760-7675.
**From the College** The Fashion Institute of Technology is a specialized college of SUNY and is located near the corporate and business centers of major companies in fashion and apparel design and manufacture, textiles, advertising, photography, jewelry, and interior design and decoration. Students come from all parts of the United States and 60 other countries to study art, design, business, or technology. The college offers a 2-year AAS degree or a 4-year BS or BFA. All programs are structured to provide a practical approach in the major, a core curriculum in liberal arts, and an opportunity to learn through co-op and internships.

## Juilliard School
**New York, New York 10023**

Founded 1905; urban setting; independent; coed; awards B, M, D.

**Enrollment** 825 total; 483 undergraduates (90 freshmen).
**Faculty** 234 total; 184 full-time; student-faculty ratio is 4:1.
**Expenses (1994–95)** Comprehensive fee of $19,100 includes tuition ($12,200), mandatory fees ($600), and room and board ($6300).
**Majors** Dance, music, opera, piano/organ, stringed instruments, theater arts/drama, voice, wind and percussion instruments.
**Applying** Required: high school transcript, audition. Essay required for some.
**Application deadlines** 1/8, 2/15 priority date for financial aid.
**Contact** Ms. Mary K. Gray, Director of Admissions, 212-799-5000 Ext. 223.

## Manhattan School of Music
### New York, New York 10027

Founded 1917; urban setting; independent; coed; awards B, M, D.

**Enrollment** 921 total; 408 undergraduates (73 freshmen).
**Faculty** 250 total; student-faculty ratio is 11:1.
**Expenses (1994–95)** Tuition: $12,500. Mandatory fees: $530. Room only: $4160.
**Majors** Jazz, music, piano/organ, stringed instruments, voice, wind and percussion instruments.
**Applying** Required: high school transcript, essay, minimum 2.0 GPA, audition. Recommended: SAT I or ACT, 3 years of high school math and science, some high school foreign language, recommendations, interview, minimum 3.0 GPA.
**Application deadlines** 4/1, 4/15 priority date for financial aid.
**Contact** Ms. Carolyn Disnew, Director of Admission, 212-749-2802 Ext. 2.
**From the College** By selecting MSM, students choose to work with faculty members who are performers with international reputations who choose to be with exceptional students from around the world in an environment of intensity, genuine friendliness, and cooperation. With extensive performance opportunities in New York—the heart of music in America—and the chance to freelance and develop professional contacts, students undergo remarkable changes: they begin to function as professional musicians while still in school. This powerful convergence gives MSM students the best chance to go as far as their talent, intelligence, and courage can take them.

## Mannes College of Music
### New York, New York 10024

Founded 1916; urban setting; independent; coed; awards B, M.

**Enrollment** 5,813 university (New School for Social Research) total; 267 unit total; 154 undergraduates (21 freshmen).
**Faculty** 216 total; 15 full-time; student-faculty ratio is 5:1.
**Expenses (1994–95)** Tuition ($12,750), mandatory fees ($225), and room only ($5500).
**Majors** Jazz, music, opera, piano/organ, stringed instruments, voice, wind and percussion instruments.
**Applying** Required: high school transcript, 1 recommendation, audition. Recommended: 3 years of high school math and science, campus interview.
**Application deadlines** 7/15, 7/15 priority date for financial aid.
**Contact** Ms. Marilyn Groves, Director of Admissions and Registration, 212-580-0210 Ext. 46.
**From the College** Founded in 1916 by David and Clara Damrosch Mannes, who were then world renowned as a violin-piano duo, the Mannes College of Music is recognized—nationally and internationally—as among the finest professional music conservatories. As such, its primary focus is on the training of outstanding young musicians who are preparing for professional careers in performance, unlike college and university music departments, which more often prepare students for careers in fields other than performance. Mannes is also distinguished by a relatively small enrollment that permits the close and supportive environment of a craft shop.

## Maryland Institute, College of Art
### Baltimore, Maryland 21217

Founded 1826; urban setting; independent; coed; awards B, M.

**Enrollment** 906 total; 814 undergraduates (187 freshmen).
**Faculty** 136 total; 66 full-time; student-faculty ratio is 11:1.
**Expenses (1995–96)** Comprehensive fee of $19,430 includes tuition ($13,850), room and board ($5440), and mandatory fees ($140).
**Majors** Applied art, art education, art/fine arts, ceramic art and design, commercial art, graphic arts, illustration, interior design, painting/drawing, photography, printmaking, sculpture, studio art, textile arts.
**Applying** Required: high school transcript, essay, portfolio, SAT I or ACT. Recommended: interview, 2 recommendations.
**Application deadlines** Rolling, 11/15 for early decision, 3/1 priority date for financial aid.
**Contact** Ms. Theresa M. Lynch-Bedoya, Dean of Admissions, 410-225-2294.
**From the College** The Maryland Institute, College of Art, founded in 1826, is the nation's oldest degree-granting art college. Its curriculum integrates the study of liberal arts ideas and theory into a concentrated studio experience. It blends a belief in a firm grounding in the artistic and academic disciplines with a respect for the individual voice. Students are encouraged to take risks, break new ground, and make connections between words, images, and ideas. The Institute addresses its students' personal as well as professional and artistic growth. The Institute's urban campus, new housing designed especially for artists, student life programs, and on-site career services reflect its philosophy.

## Massachusetts College of Art
### Boston, Massachusetts 02115

Founded 1873; urban setting; state-supported; coed; awards B, M.

**Enrollment** 1,367 total; 1,279 undergraduates (264 freshmen).
**Faculty** 86 total; 66 full-time; student-faculty ratio is 14:1.
**Expenses (1994–95)** State resident tuition: $1463. Nonresident tuition: $6422. Mandatory fees: $2520. Room and board: $5839.
**Majors** Applied art, architecture, art education, art/fine arts, art history, ceramic art and design, commercial art, computer graphics, fashion design and technology, film

and video, graphic arts, illustration, industrial design, jewelry and metalsmithing, painting/drawing, photography, printmaking, sculpture, studio art, textile arts.
**Applying** Required: essay, high school transcript, 3 years of high school math and science, 2 years of high school foreign language, portfolio, SAT I. Recommended: recommendations, campus interview.
**Application deadlines** 12/1 for early decision, 4/1, 5/1 priority date for financial aid.
**Contact** Ms. Kay Ransdell, Director of Admissions, 617-232-1555 Ext. 235.
**From the College** Unique among institutions of higher education, Massachusetts College of Art is a state-assisted, free-standing college of art, design, and art education. Rigorous, innovative, and multicultural, the curriculum is supplemented by a schedule of exhibitions and visiting artists, cross-registration options, and programs of study abroad. Newly renovated, state-of-the-art facilities meet advanced health and safety standards and offer students extraordinary art-making opportunities. The student body represents a variety of experiences and backgrounds and includes citizens of 60 countries and many states. The College is located in the heart of Boston's cultural area, adjacent to major museums and other colleges.

## New England Conservatory of Music
**Boston, Massachusetts 02115**

Founded 1867; urban setting; independent; coed; awards B, M, D.

**Enrollment** 774 total; 386 undergraduates (75 freshmen).
**Faculty** 191 total; 55 full-time.
**Expenses (1994–95)** Comprehensive fee of $22,700 includes tuition ($15,300), room and board ($7300), and mandatory fees ($100).
**Majors** Jazz, music, music education, music history, opera, piano/organ, stringed instruments, voice, wind and percussion instruments.
**Applying** Required: essay, high school transcript, 1 recommendation, audition, SAT I or ACT.
**Application deadlines** 1/15, 3/1 priority date for financial aid.
**Contact** Ms. Colleen Flannery, Admission Counselor, 617-262-1120 Ext. 430.

## New York School of Interior Design
**New York, New York 10021**

Founded 1916; urban setting; independent; coed; awards A, B.

**Enrollment** 399 total all undergraduates (38 freshmen).
**Faculty** 108 total; 3 full-time; student-faculty ratio is 18:1.
**Expenses (1994–95)** Tuition: $11,040. Mandatory fees: $50.
**Major** Interior design.
**Applying** Required: essay, high school transcript, 3 years of high school math, 2 recommendations, SAT I or ACT.

Recommended: interview. Interview required for some.
**Application deadlines** Rolling, 8/1 priority date for financial aid.
**Contact** Ms. Jessica Aguayo, Admissions Assistant, 212-472-1500 or toll-free 800-336-9743.
**From the College** Manhattan, with its world-famous museums, showrooms, and architectural landmarks, is home to the New York School of Interior Design (NYSID). NYSID was the first and only single-major college in the United States dedicated solely to the study of interior design, a tradition that continues today. Because of its reputation in the design industry, many NYSID graduates have gone on to find work in the best design and architectural firms in New York City and around the world. The Bachelor of Fine Arts degree is a FIDER-accredited program.

## North Carolina School of the Arts
**Winston-Salem, North Carolina 27117-2189**

Founded 1963; urban setting; state-supported; coed; awards B, M.

**Enrollment** 613 total; 552 undergraduates (244 freshmen).
**Faculty** 109 total; 73 full-time; student-faculty ratio is 7:1.
**Expenses (1994–95)** State resident tuition: $1233. Nonresident tuition: $8640. Mandatory fees: $766. Room and board: $3600.
**Majors** Dance, film and video production, film studies, music, theater arts/drama.
**Applying** Required: high school transcript, 3 years of high school math and science, 2 recommendations, audition, SAT I or ACT. Recommended: 2 years of high school foreign language. Essay, interview required for some.
**Application deadlines** Rolling, 3/15 priority date for financial aid.
**Contact** Ms. Carol J. Palm, Director of Admissions, 919-770-3290.
**From the College** The School of the Arts was the first state-supported residential arts school of its kind in the nation, established in 1963. This accredited school became part of the 16-campus University of North Carolina in 1972. Five individual schools—Dance, Design and Production, Drama, Filmmaking, and Music—make up the School of the Arts. Because the School's mission is to train students for professional careers in the performing arts, performance is an integral part of training. The School's diverse enrollment offers the student the opportunity to live and work in a close and supportive environment with artists in other fields, from different backgrounds, and from different areas of the world.

## Otis College of Art and Design
**Los Angeles, California 90057**

Founded 1918; urban setting; independent; coed; awards B, M.

**Enrollment** 714 total; 694 undergraduates (192 freshmen).
**Faculty** 235 total; 24 full-time; student-faculty ratio is 4:1.

**Expenses (1994–95)** Tuition ($13,140), mandatory fees ($720), and room only ($2700).

**Majors** Applied art, art/fine arts, ceramic art and design, commercial art, environmental design, fashion design and technology, graphic arts, illustration, interior design, painting/drawing, photography, sculpture, studio art.

**Applying** Required: high school transcript, portfolio, 4 assigned art exercises. Recommended: recommendations. Essay, interview, SAT I or ACT required for some.

**Application deadlines** Rolling, 3/1 priority date for financial aid.

**Contact** Mr. Michael Fuller, Director of Admissions, 213-251-0504.

## Parsons School of Design, New School for Social Research
**New York, New York 10011**

Founded 1896; urban setting; independent; coed; awards A, B, M.

**Enrollment** 5,813 university total; 1,912 unit total; 1,773 undergraduates (341 freshmen).

**Faculty** 413 total; 17 full-time; student-faculty ratio is 14:1.

**Expenses (1994–95)** Comprehensive fee of $22,600 includes tuition ($15,030), mandatory fees ($150), and room and board ($7420).

**Majors** Art education, art/fine arts, ceramic art and design, commercial art, environmental design, fashion design and technology, fashion merchandising, graphic arts, illustration, industrial design, interior design, jewelry and metalsmithing, painting/drawing, photography, sculpture, textile arts.

**Applying** Required: high school transcript, campus interview, portfolio, at-home examination, SAT I or ACT. Recommended: essay, recommendations. Essay, recommendations required for some.

**Application deadlines** Rolling, 4/1 priority date for financial aid.

**Contact** Ms. Nadine M. Bourgeois, Director of Admissions, 212-229-8910 or toll-free 800-252-0852.

**From the College** For nearly 100 years, Parsons graduates have soared to positions of leadership in art, design, and marketing. Heads of their own companies and top executives in major firms, their accomplishments have won them prestige, industry awards, and brand-name status. Ideas taught at Parsons educate students in what makes one design solution good, another better, and a third best. Parsons also looks to the future. A new Fashion Design Computing Center, Foundation Year Computing Lab, and AUTOCAD Interior Design and Environmental Design Lab complement Parsons' existing Computer Design Center and make Parsons one of the most technologically advanced design schools in America.

## Rhode Island School of Design
**Providence, Rhode Island 02903**

Founded 1877; urban setting; independent; coed; awards B, M.

**Enrollment** 2,011 total; 1,848 undergraduates (375 freshmen).

**Faculty** 302 total; 122 full-time; student-faculty ratio is 12:1.

**Expenses (1994–95)** Comprehensive fee of $23,446 includes tuition ($16,684), mandatory fees ($90), and room and board ($6672).

**Majors** Architecture, art/fine arts, ceramic art and design, fashion design and technology, film studies, graphic arts, illustration, industrial design, interior design, jewelry and metalsmithing, landscape architecture/design, painting/drawing, photography, printmaking, sculpture, textile arts, textiles and clothing.

**Applying** Required: essay, high school transcript, portfolio, drawing assignments, SAT I or ACT. Recommended: 3 recommendations. 3 years of high school math required for some.

**Application deadlines** 1/21, 12/15 for early action, 2/15 priority date for financial aid.

**Contact** Mr. Edward Newhall, Director of Admissions, 401-454-6300.

**From the College** Rhode Island School of Design has been successfully educating aspiring artists and designers for fulfilling lives and careers in the visual arts for more than 117 years. Widely recognized today by professional artists and designers, educators, and comparative college guides as one of the leading colleges for the visual arts, RISD offers an unsurpassed environment to challenge students' ideas and perfect their talents. The combination of a faculty of 300 artists, the student body of 1,980 drawn from around the country and 50 nations around the world, and the campus of 40 buildings housing extensive studios and numerous specialized art-making facilities creates an environment that will encourage and support students' goals.

## Rutgers, The State University of New Jersey, Mason Gross School of the Arts
**New Brunswick, New Jersey 08903**

Founded 1976; small-town setting; state-supported; coed; awards B, M, D.

**Enrollment** 47,697 university total; 647 unit total; 418 undergraduates (97 freshmen).

**Faculty** 77 full-time; student-faculty ratio is 11:1.

**Expenses (1994–95)** State resident tuition: $3640. Nonresident tuition: $7410. Mandatory fees: range from $971 to $1045, according to college affiliation. Room and board: $4748.

**Majors** Art/fine arts, ceramic art and design, dance, film studies, graphic arts, jazz, music, music education, painting/drawing, photography, printmaking, sculpture, theater arts/drama.

**Applying** Required: high school transcript, 3 years of high school math, audition or portfolio or interview, SAT I or ACT. Recommended: 4 years of high school math, 2 years of high school foreign language. 3 SAT II Subject Tests required for some.

**Application deadlines** 1/15, 3/1 priority date for financial aid.

**Contact** Dr. Elizabeth Mitchell, Assistant Vice President for University Undergraduate Admissions, 908-445-3770.

**From the College** Mason Gross School of the Arts is designed for students who aspire to professional careers in the creative and performing arts. MGSA's well-equipped arts facilities include a new comprehensive visual arts center in downtown New Brunswick, 5 theaters, a scene shop, prop-building and costume design shops, a sculpture studio, numerous art galleries, an 800-seat concert hall, an electronic studio based on the Synclavier II, recital halls, and 4 large dance studios. The School is committed to maintaining high standards in the arts through the quality of its programs, faculty, and facilities and is dedicated to encouraging creativity, originality, and professionalism in its students.

## San Francisco Conservatory of Music
### San Francisco, California 94122

Founded 1917; urban setting; independent; coed; awards B, M.

**Enrollment** 273 total; 151 undergraduates (11 freshmen).
**Faculty** 65 total; 24 full-time; student-faculty ratio is 7:1.
**Expenses (1994–95)** Tuition: $13,000. Mandatory fees: $250.
**Majors** Music, opera, piano/organ, stringed instruments, voice, wind and percussion instruments.
**Applying** Required: high school transcript, 2 recommendations, audition, SAT I or ACT. Recommended: some high school foreign language.
**Application deadlines** 3/1, 4/1 priority date for financial aid.
**Contact** Ms. Joan Gordon, Admissions Officer, 415-759-3431.

## Savannah College of Art and Design
### Savannah, Georgia 31401

Founded 1978; urban setting; independent; coed; awards B, M.

**Enrollment** 2,488 total; 2,206 undergraduates (483 freshmen).
**Faculty** 143 total; 113 full-time; student-faculty ratio is 16:1.
**Expenses (1995–96)** Comprehensive fee of $16,550 includes tuition ($10,800) and room and board ($5750).

**Majors** Applied art, architecture, art/fine arts, art history, computer graphics, fashion design and technology, film and video production, graphic arts, historic preservation, illustration, interior design, jewelry and metalsmithing, painting/drawing, photography, textile arts.

**Applying** Required: high school transcript, 3 recommendations, SAT I or ACT. Recommended: 3 years high school math, interview. 3 years high school math required for some.

**Application deadlines** Rolling, 4/1 priority date for financial aid.

**Contact** Mrs. May Poetter, Vice President of Admissions, 912-238-2483.

**From the College** The goal of Savannah College of Art and Design is to nurture and cultivate the special qualities of each student through an interesting curriculum, in an inspiring environment, and under the leadership of involved professors. The College exists for the purpose of preparing talented students for careers in the arts. Classes are student-centered, with the first priority being the student's success in school and beyond. To adapt the words of John Ruskin, this College is where "the hand, the head, and the heart go together." It is the best living, learning, and creative environment for the student of art, architecture, or design.

## Westminster Choir College, The School of Music of Rider College
### Princeton, New Jersey 08540

Founded 1926; small-town setting; independent; coed; awards B, M.

**Enrollment** 320 total; 234 undergraduates (74 freshmen).
**Faculty** 60 total; 40 full-time; student-faculty ratio is 7:1.
**Expenses (1994–95)** Comprehensive fee of $19,310 includes tuition ($13,250), room and board ($5820), and mandatory fees ($240).
**Majors** Liberal arts/general studies, music, music education, piano/organ, sacred music, voice.
**Applying** Required: essay, high school transcript, 3 recommendations, audition, music test, SAT I or ACT. Recommended: 3 years high school math and science, 2 years of high school foreign language, interview, minimum 2.0 high school GPA.
**Application deadlines** Rolling, 3/1 priority date for financial aid.
**Contact** Mr. Mark R. Costello, Assistant Director of Admissions, 609-921-7144 Ext. 103 or toll-free 800-96-CHOIR.
**From the College** Carnegie Hall, The Academy of Music, Avery Fisher Hall, the Kennedy Center—these are the major stages and concert halls where Westminster students sing. They also perform with major orchestras including the New York Philharmonic, the Philadelphia Orchestra, and the New Jersey Symphony Orchestra. These are only a few of the many musical opportunities available at Westminster Choir College, The School of Music of Rider University. Whether a student's musical dream is to be a performer, a music educator, a church musician, or a composer, Westminster's distinctive programs help young singers, organists, composers, and pianists live their dreams.

## Agnes Scott College
Anthropology, art/fine arts, art history, biblical studies, biology/biological sciences, chemistry, classics, creative writing, economics, English, French, German, Greek, history, international relations, Latin, literature, mathematics, music, philosophy, physics, political science/government, psychobiology, psychology, religious studies, sociology, Spanish, theater arts/drama.

## Albert A. List College, Jewish Theological Seminary of America
Biblical studies, history, Judaic studies, literature, museum studies, music, philosophy, religious studies.

## Albertson College
Accounting, anthropology, art/fine arts, biology/biological sciences, business administration/commerce/management, chemistry, computer science, economics, elementary education, English, French, German, history, (pre)law sequence, mathematics, (pre)medicine sequence, music, philosophy, physical education, physical fitness/exercise science, physics, political science/government, psychology, religious studies, science education, secondary education, sociology, Spanish, sports administration, theater arts/drama.

## Albion College
American studies, anthropology, art/fine arts, biology/biological sciences, business administration/commerce/management, chemistry, communication, economics, English, French, geology, German, history, international studies, mathematics, modern languages, music, philosophy, physical education, physics, political science/government, psychology, religious studies, sociology, Spanish, theater arts/drama.

## Albright College
Accounting, American studies, biochemistry, biology/biological sciences, business administration/commerce/management, chemistry, child care/child and family studies, computer science, (pre)dentistry sequence, economics, elementary education, English, environmental sciences, fashion design and technology, fashion merchandising, finance/banking, forestry, French, history, human ecology, interdisciplinary studies, international business, (pre)law sequence, marketing/retailing/merchandising, mathematics, medical technology, (pre)medicine sequence, natural resource management, philosophy, political science/government, psychobiology, psychology, religious studies, secondary education, Spanish, textiles and clothing, theater arts/drama, (pre)veterinary medicine sequence.

## Alfred University
Accounting, applied art, art education, art/fine arts, art therapy, bilingual/bicultural education, biology/biological sciences, biomedical technologies, business administration/commerce/management, business economics, business education, ceramic art and design, ceramic engineering, ceramic sciences, chemistry, clinical psychology, commercial art, communication, computer information systems, computer science, criminal justice, (pre)dentistry sequence, earth science, ecology, economics, education, electrical engineering, elementary education, English, environmental sciences, experimental psychology, finance/banking, forestry, French, geology, German, gerontology, graphic arts, health services administration, history, interdisciplinary studies, international business, (pre)law sequence, liberal arts/general studies, literature, marketing/retailing/

merchandising, mathematics, mechanical engineering, medical laboratory technology, (pre)medicine sequence, modern languages, painting/drawing, philosophy, photography, physics, political science/government, printmaking, psychology, public administration, science, science education, sculpture, secondary education, sociology, Spanish, studio art, theater arts/drama, (pre)veterinary medicine sequence.

## Allegheny College
Anthropology, art/fine arts, art history, biochemistry, biology/biological sciences, chemistry, classics, communication, computer science, (pre)dentistry sequence, economics, education, elementary education, English, environmental sciences, environmental studies, French, geology, German, Greek, history, international studies, Latin, (pre)law sequence, marine sciences, mathematics, (pre)medicine sequence, modern languages, music, philosophy, physics, political science/government, psychology, religious studies, Russian, secondary education, sociology, Spanish, speech/rhetoric/public address/debate, studio art, theater arts/drama, (pre)veterinary medicine sequence, women's studies.

## Alma College
Accounting, art education, art/fine arts, athletic training, biochemistry, biology/biological sciences, business administration/commerce/management, chemistry, communication, computer information systems, computer science, dance, (pre)dentistry sequence, early childhood education, ecology, economics, education, elementary education, English, finance/banking, forestry, French, German, gerontology, health science, history, humanities, international business, journalism, (pre)law sequence, liberal arts/general studies, literature, marketing/retailing/merchandising, mathematics, medical illustration, (pre)medicine sequence, modern languages, music, music education, occupational therapy, painting/drawing, philosophy, physical fitness/exercise science, physics, political science/government, psychology, recreation and leisure services, religious studies, retail management, science, secondary education, social science, sociology, Spanish, sports medicine, stringed instruments, teaching English as a second language, theater arts/drama, (pre)veterinary medicine sequence, voice, wind and percussion instruments, women's studies.

## American University
Accounting, American studies, anthropology, applied art, applied mathematics, art/fine arts, art history, audio engineering, biology/biological sciences, broadcasting, business administration/commerce/management, chemistry, communication, computer information systems, computer science, criminal justice, criminology, early childhood education, ecology, economics, education, elementary education, English, environmental studies, European studies, film and video production, film studies, finance/banking, French, German, Germanic languages and literature, graphic arts, history, interdisciplinary studies, international business, international economics, international relations, international studies, Japanese, journalism, Judaic studies, labor and industrial relations, Latin American studies, (pre)law sequence, legal studies, liberal arts/general studies, literature, management information systems, marketing/retailing/merchandising, mathematics, (pre)medicine sequence, modern languages, music, Near and Middle Eastern studies, peace studies, philosophy, physics, political science/government, psychology, public administration, public affairs and policy studies, public relations, radio and television studies, real estate, religious studies, Russian,

Russian and Slavic studies, science, social science, sociology, Spanish, special education, statistics, studio art, theater arts/drama, urban studies.

## Amherst College

American studies, anthropology, art/fine arts, Asian/Oriental studies, astronomy, biology/biological sciences, black/African-American studies, chemistry, classics, computer science, dance, economics, English, European studies, French, geology, German, Greek, history, interdisciplinary studies, Latin, legal studies, mathematics, music, neurosciences, philosophy, physics, political science/government, psychology, religious studies, Romance languages, Russian, sociology, Spanish, theater arts/drama, women's studies.

## Art Center College of Design

Advertising, art/fine arts, commercial art, environmental design, film studies, graphic arts, illustration, industrial design, painting/drawing, photography.

## Auburn University

Accounting, adult and continuing education, aerospace engineering, agricultural business, agricultural economics, agricultural education, agricultural engineering, agricultural sciences, agronomy/soil and crop sciences, animal sciences, anthropology, applied art, applied mathematics, architecture, art/fine arts, aviation administration, biochemistry, biology/biological sciences, biomedical sciences, botany/plant sciences, broadcasting, business administration/commerce/management, business economics, business education, chemical engineering, chemistry, child care/child and family studies, child psychology/child development, civil engineering, commercial art, communication, computer engineering, computer science, construction management, corrections, criminal justice, dairy sciences, (pre)dentistry sequence, dietetics, early childhood education, earth science, East European and Soviet studies, economics, education, electrical engineering, elementary education, engineering (general), English, entomology, environmental design, environmental sciences, family and consumer studies, fashion merchandising, finance/banking, fish and game management, food sciences, forest engineering, forestry, forest technology, French, geography, geological engineering, geology, German, graphic arts, health education, health services administration, history, home economics, home economics education, horticulture, hotel and restaurant management, human resources, industrial arts, industrial design, industrial engineering, interior design, international business, journalism, laboratory technologies, landscape architecture/design, Latin American studies, law enforcement/police sciences, (pre)law sequence, management information systems, marine biology, marketing/retailing/merchandising, materials engineering, mathematics, mechanical engineering, medical laboratory technology, medical technology, (pre)medicine sequence, microbiology, middle school education, molecular biology, music, music education, nursing, nutrition, ornamental horticulture, pest control technology, pharmacy/pharmaceutical sciences, philosophy, physical education, physical fitness/exercise science, physics, piano/organ, political science/government, poultry sciences, psychology, public administration, public relations, radio and television studies, recreation and leisure services, rehabilitation therapy, religious studies, science education, secondary education, social work, sociology, Spanish, special education, speech pathology and audiology, speech/rhetoric/public address/debate, speech therapy, studio art, textile arts, textile engineering, textiles and clothing, theater arts/drama, transportation technologies, (pre)veterinary medicine sequence, vocational education, wildlife management, wood sciences, zoology.

## Augustana College (IL)

Accounting, anthropology, art education, art/fine arts, art history, Asian/Oriental studies, athletic training, biology/biological sciences, black/African-American studies, business administration/commerce/management, chemistry, classics, communication, computer science, creative writing, cytotechnology, (pre)dentistry sequence, earth science, East Asian studies, economics, education, elementary education, engineering physics, English, environmental studies, finance/banking, French, geography, geology, German, Greek, history, international business, Japanese, jazz, journalism, Latin, Latin American studies, (pre)law sequence, liberal arts/general studies, literature, marketing/retailing/merchandising, mathematics, medical technology, (pre)medicine sequence, music, music education, occupational therapy, philosophy, physical education, physics, piano/organ, political science/government, psychology, public administration, religious studies, sacred music, Scandinavian languages/studies, secondary education, social work, sociology, Spanish, speech pathology and audiology, speech/rhetoric/public address/debate, speech therapy, stringed instruments, studio art, theater arts/drama, (pre)veterinary medicine sequence, voice, wind and percussion instruments.

## Augustana College (SD)

Accounting, art education, aviation administration, biochemistry, biology/biological sciences, biophysics, business administration/commerce/management, chemistry, communication, computer science, (pre)dentistry sequence, early childhood education, ecology, economics, education, elementary education, English, French, geography, German, health services administration, history, international studies, journalism, (pre)law sequence, liberal arts/general studies, management information systems, mathematics, medical technology, (pre)medicine sequence, music, music education, nursing, philosophy, physical education, physical fitness/exercise science, physics, political science/government, psychology, religious studies, Romance languages, secondary education, social work, sociology, special education, speech pathology and audiology, theater arts/drama, (pre)veterinary medicine sequence.

## Austin College

American studies, art/fine arts, biology/biological sciences, business administration/commerce/management, chemistry, classics, communication, (pre)dentistry sequence, economics, English, French, German, history, interdisciplinary studies, international studies, Latin, Latin American studies, (pre)law sequence, mathematics, (pre)medicine sequence, music, philosophy, physical education, physics, political science/government, psychology, religious studies, sociology, Spanish, speech/rhetoric/public address/debate.

## Babson College

Accounting, American studies, business administration/commerce/management, communication, economics, finance/banking, international business, management information systems, marketing/retailing/merchandising, operations research.

## Baldwin-Wallace College

Accounting, art education, art/fine arts, art history, arts administration, athletic training, biology/biological sciences, broadcasting, business administration/commerce/management, business education, chemistry, communication, computer information systems, computer science, criminal justice, dance, (pre)dentistry sequence, economics, education, elementary education, engineering sciences, English, environmental sciences, finance/banking, French, geology, German, health education, history, home economics, home economics education, human services, interdisciplinary studies, international studies, Japanese, (pre)law sequence, marketing/retailing/merchandising, mathematics, medical technology, (pre)medicine sequence, middle school education, music, music business, music education, music history, music therapy, philosophy, physical education, physics, piano/organ, political science/government, psychology, religious studies, science education, secondary education, sociology, Spanish, special education, speech pathology and audiology, sports administration, stringed instruments, studio art, theater arts/drama, (pre)veterinary medicine sequence, voice, wind and percussion instruments.

## Bard College
Adult and continuing education, American studies, anthropology, archaeology, art/fine arts, art history, Asian/Oriental studies, biology/biological sciences, chemistry, Chinese, city/community/regional planning, classics, comparative literature, creative writing, dance, (pre)dentistry sequence, East European and Soviet studies, ecology, economics, English, environmental sciences, environmental studies, ethnic studies, European studies, film and video production, film studies, French, German, Germanic languages and literature, Greek, history, history of science, humanities, interdisciplinary studies, international economics, international studies, Italian, jazz, Latin, (pre)law sequence, literature, mathematics, (pre)medicine sequence, medieval studies, modern languages, music, music history, natural sciences, painting/drawing, philosophy, photography, physical sciences, physics, political science/government, psychology, religious studies, Romance languages, Russian, Russian and Slavic studies, science, sculpture, social science, sociology, Spanish, studio art, theater arts/drama, (pre)veterinary medicine sequence, voice.

## Barnard College
African studies, American studies, anthropology, applied mathematics, architecture, art history, Asian/Oriental studies, astronomy, biochemistry, biology/biological sciences, black/African-American studies, chemistry, classics, comparative literature, computer science, dance, East Asian studies, East European and Soviet studies, economics, education, English, environmental sciences, European studies, French, German, Germanic languages and literature, history, interdisciplinary studies, Italian, Latin, Latin American studies, mathematics, (pre)medicine sequence, medieval studies, music, Near and Middle Eastern studies, philosophy, physics, political science/government, psychobiology, psychology, religious studies, Russian, Russian and Slavic studies, Slavic languages, sociology, South Asian studies, Spanish, statistics, theater arts/drama, urban studies, women's studies.

## Bates College
African studies, American studies, anthropology, art/fine arts, biochemistry, biology/biological sciences, chemistry, classics, East Asian studies, economics, English, French, geology, German, history, interdisciplinary studies, mathematics, medieval studies, music, philosophy, physics, political science/government, psychology, religious studies, Russian, sociology, Spanish, speech/rhetoric/public address/debate, theater arts/drama, women's studies.

## Baylor University
Accounting, African studies, American studies, anthropology, applied art, archaeology, architecture, art education, art/fine arts, art history, Asian/Oriental studies, aviation technology, biblical languages, biology/biological sciences, broadcasting, business administration/commerce/management, business economics, business education, chemistry, child care/child and family studies, child psychology/child development, classics, commercial art, communication, computer engineering, computer information systems, computer programming, computer science, (pre)dentistry sequence, dietetics, early childhood

education, earth science, ecology, economics, education, electrical engineering, elementary education, engineering (general), English, environmental sciences, environmental studies, fashion design and technology, fashion merchandising, finance/banking, forestry, French, geology, geophysics, German, Greek, health education, health science, history, home economics, home economics education, human resources, insurance, interdisciplinary studies, interior design, international business, international studies, journalism, Latin, Latin American studies, (pre)law sequence, management information systems, marketing/retailing/merchandising, mathematics, mechanical engineering, medical technology, (pre)medicine sequence, museum studies, music, music education, music history, neurosciences, nursing, operations research, optometry, philosophy, physical education, physical fitness/exercise science, physical sciences, physics, piano/organ, political science/government, psychology, public administration, reading education, real estate, recreation and leisure services, religious studies, Russian, Russian and Slavic studies, sacred music, science, science education, secondary education, social work, sociology, Spanish, special education, speech pathology and audiology, speech/rhetoric/public address/debate, speech therapy, stringed instruments, studio art, technical writing, telecommunications, theater arts/drama, urban studies, voice, wind and percussion instruments.

## Bellarmine College
Accounting, actuarial science, art education, art/fine arts, biology/biological sciences, business administration/commerce/management, chemistry, communication, computer engineering, computer information systems, computer science, (pre)dentistry sequence, economics, education, elementary education, English, history, jazz, (pre)law sequence, mathematics, (pre)medicine sequence, middle school education, music, music education, nursing, philosophy, political science/government, psychology, science education, secondary education, sociology, special education, studio art, theology, (pre)veterinary medicine sequence.

## Belmont University
Accounting, advertising, applied mathematics, art education, art/fine arts, behavioral sciences, biblical languages, biblical studies, bilingual/bicultural education, biochemistry, biology/biological sciences, broadcasting, business administration/commerce/management, business economics, business education, chemistry, child psychology/child development, communication, computer information systems, computer management, computer programming, computer science, criminal justice, early childhood education, economics, education, elementary education, engineering sciences, English, finance/banking, Greek, guidance and counseling, health education, health services administration, history, hospitality services, hotel and restaurant management, international business, journalism, (pre)law sequence, marketing/retailing/merchandising, mathematics, medical technology, (pre)medicine sequence, ministries, music, music business, music education, music history, nursing, pastoral studies, pharmacology, philosophy, physical education, physics, piano/organ, political science/government, psychology, radio and television studies, reading education, recreation and leisure services, retail management, sacred music, science, secretarial studies/office management, social work, sociology, Spanish, special education, speech/rhetoric/public address/debate, studio art, theater arts/drama, (pre)veterinary medicine sequence, voice, Western civilization and culture.

## Beloit College
Anthropology, art education, art/fine arts, art history, Asian/Oriental studies, biochemistry, biology/biological sciences, business administration/commerce/management, cell biology, chemistry, classics, communication, comparative literature, computer science,

creative writing, (pre)dentistry sequence, economics, education, elementary education, English, environmental biology, environmental sciences, European studies, French, geology, German, history, interdisciplinary studies, international relations, journalism, Latin American studies, (pre)law sequence, literature, mathematics, (pre)medicine sequence, modern languages, molecular biology, museum studies, music, music education, philosophy, physics, political science/government, psychology, religious studies, Romance languages, Russian, Russian and Slavic studies, science education, secondary education, sociology, Spanish, studio art, theater arts/drama, women's studies.

## Bennington College
Anthropology, architecture, art/fine arts, art history, biochemistry, biology/biological sciences, ceramic art and design, chemistry, child psychology/child development, Chinese, comparative literature, computer science, creative writing, dance, early childhood education, ecology, economics, English, environmental biology, environmental sciences, French, German, Greek, history, interdisciplinary studies, international studies, jazz, Latin, (pre)law sequence, liberal arts/general studies, literature, mathematics, (pre)medicine sequence, modern languages, music, music history, natural sciences, painting/drawing, philosophy, photography, physics, piano/organ, political science/government, printmaking, psychology, science, sculpture, sociology, Spanish, stringed instruments, studio art, theater arts/drama, (pre)veterinary medicine sequence, voice.

## Berry College
Accounting, animal sciences, applied art, art education, art/fine arts, behavioral sciences, biochemistry, biology/biological sciences, business administration/commerce/management, business economics, chemistry, communication, computer science, consumer services, (pre)dentistry sequence, early childhood education, economics, education, elementary education, English, family and consumer studies, family services, fashion merchandising, finance/banking, food services management, French, German, health education, history, home economics, home economics education, horticulture, hotel and restaurant management, interdisciplinary studies, international studies, (pre)law sequence, marketing/retailing/merchandising, mathematics, (pre)medicine sequence, middle school education, music, music business, music education, philosophy, physical education, physics, piano/organ, political science/government, psychology, religious studies, science education, secondary education, social science, sociology, Spanish, speech/rhetoric/public address/debate, sports administration, studio art, theater arts/drama, (pre)veterinary medicine sequence, voice.

## Bethel College (MN)
Accounting, adult and continuing education, art education, art/fine arts, art history, athletic training, biblical studies, biology/biological sciences, business administration/commerce/management, chemistry, child care/child and family studies, communication, computer science, creative writing, (pre)dentistry sequence, early childhood education, economics, education, elementary education, English, finance/banking, health education, history, international relations, international studies, (pre)law sequence, literature, management information systems, mathematics, (pre)medicine sequence, ministries, molecular biology, music, music education, nursing, philosophy, physical education, physics, political science/government, psychology, sacred music, science education, secondary education, social work, Spanish, speech/rhetoric/public address/debate, studio art, theater arts/drama, theology, (pre)veterinary medicine sequence.

## Birmingham-Southern College
Accounting, art education, art/fine arts, art history, biology/biological sciences, business administration/commerce/management, chemistry, computer science, dance, (pre)dentistry sequence, early childhood education, economics, education, elementary education, English, French, German, graphic arts, history, human resources, interdisciplinary studies, (pre)law sequence, mathematics, (pre)medicine sequence, music, music education, music history, nursing, philosophy, physics, piano/organ, political science/government, psychology, religious studies, sculpture, secondary education, sociology, Spanish, studio art, theater arts/drama, voice.

## Boston College
Accounting, American studies, art history, biochemistry, biology/biological sciences, business administration/commerce/management, chemistry, classics, communication, computer information systems, computer science, (pre)dentistry sequence, early childhood education, economics, education, elementary education, English, environmental sciences, finance/banking, French, geology, geophysics, German, Germanic languages and literature, Greek, Hispanic studies, history, human development, human resources, interdisciplinary studies, Italian, Latin, (pre)law sequence, linguistics, management information systems, marketing/retailing/merchandising, mathematics, (pre)medicine sequence, music, nursing, operations research, philosophy, physics, political science/government, psychology, Romance languages, Russian, Russian and Slavic studies, science, secondary education, Slavic languages, sociology, Spanish, special education, studio art, theater arts/drama, theology.

## Boston Conservatory
Dance, music, music education, opera, piano/organ, stringed instruments, theater arts/drama, voice, wind and percussion instruments.

## Boston University
Accounting, advertising, aerospace engineering, African studies, American studies, anthropology, archaeology, art education, art/fine arts, art history, astronomy, astrophysics, athletic training, bilingual/bicultural education, biochemistry, biology/biological sciences, biomedical engineering, biomedical technologies, biotechnology, broadcasting, business administration/commerce/management, chemistry, classics, communication, comparative literature, computer engineering, computer information systems, computer science, (pre)dentistry sequence, early childhood education, earth science, East Asian studies, East European and Soviet studies, economics, education, electrical engineering, elementary education, engineering (general), engineering management, English, environmental sciences, environmental studies, film studies, finance/banking, food services management, French, geography, geology, German, Germanic languages and literature, graphic arts, Greek, health education, health science, Hispanic studies, history, hospitality services, hotel and restaurant management, interdisciplinary studies, international relations, international studies, Italian, journalism, Latin, Latin American studies, (pre)law sequence, liberal arts/general studies, linguistics, literature, management information systems, manufacturing engineering, marine biology, marine sciences, marketing/retailing/merchandising, mathematics, mechanical engineering, medical assistant technologies, medical technology, (pre)medicine sequence, mental health/rehabilitation counseling, modern languages, molecular biology, music, music education, music history, occupational therapy, opera, operations research, painting/drawing, paralegal studies, philosophy, photography, physical education, physical fitness/exercise science, physical therapy, physics, physiology, piano/organ, planetary and space sciences, political science/government, psychology, public

relations, recreation and leisure services, rehabilitation therapy, religious studies, Russian, Russian and Slavic studies, sacred music, science education, sculpture, secondary education, social science, social work, sociology, Spanish, special education, speech pathology and audiology, speech therapy, sports medicine, statistics, stringed instruments, studio art, systems engineering, teaching English as a second language, theater arts/drama, urban studies, voice, wind and percussion instruments.

## Bowdoin College

African studies, American studies, anthropology, archaeology, art/fine arts, art history, Asian/Oriental studies, biochemistry, biology/ biological sciences, black/African-American studies, chemistry, Chinese, classics, computer science, dance, ecology, economics, English, environmental studies, European studies, film studies, French, geology, German, history, interdisciplinary studies, Italian, Japanese, Latin American studies, mathematics, (pre)medicine sequence, music, neurosciences, philosophy, physics, political science/government, psychobiology, psychology, religious studies, Romance languages, Russian, sociology, Spanish, studio art, theater arts/drama.

## Bradley University

Accounting, advertising, applied art, art education, art/fine arts, art history, biochemistry, biology/biological sciences, biotechnology, broadcasting, business administration/commerce/management, business economics, ceramic art and design, chemistry, civil engineering, communication, computer engineering, computer information systems, computer programming, computer science, construction engineering, construction management, criminal justice, (pre)dentistry sequence, dietetics, early childhood education, ecology, economics, education, electrical engineering, electrical engineering technology, elementary education, engineering physics, English, environmental biology, environmental sciences, fashion merchandising, film studies, finance/banking, French, geology, German, graphic arts, history, home economics, industrial engineering, interior design, international business, international studies, jewelry and metalsmithing, journalism, law enforcement/police sciences, (pre)law sequence, liberal arts/general studies, management information systems, manufacturing engineering, manufacturing technology, marketing/retailing/ merchandising, mathematics, mechanical engineering, mechanical engineering technology, medical technology, (pre)medicine sequence, music, music education, nursing, nutrition, painting/drawing, philosophy, photography, physical therapy, physics, piano/organ, political science/government, psychology, radio and television studies, religious studies, sculpture, secondary education, social work, sociology, Spanish, special education, stringed instruments, studio art, theater arts/drama, (pre)veterinary medicine sequence, voice, wind and percussion instruments.

## Brandeis University

African studies, American studies, anthropology, archaeology, art/fine arts, art history, biochemistry, biology/biological sciences, biophysics, black/African-American studies, chemistry, classics, cognitive science, comparative literature, computer science, creative writing, economics, engineering physics, English, European studies, French, German, Germanic languages and literature, Greek, history, history of philosophy, international economics, Italian, Judaic studies, Latin, Latin American studies, linguistics, literature, mathematics, music, music history, Near and Middle Eastern studies, neurosciences, philosophy, physics, political science/government, psychology, Russian, Russian and Slavic studies, science, sociology, Spanish, studio art, theater arts/drama.

## Brigham Young University

Accounting, actuarial science, advertising, aerospace sciences, agricultural business, agricultural economics, agricultural sciences, agronomy/soil and crop sciences, American studies, animal sciences, anthropology, applied art, art education, art/fine arts, art history, Asian/Oriental studies, astronomy, athletic training, biblical languages, bilingual/bicultural education, biochemistry, biology/biological sciences, biophysics, biotechnology, botany/plant sciences, broadcasting, business administration/commerce/management, business economics, business education, Canadian studies, cartography, ceramic art and design, chemical engineering, chemistry, child care/child and family studies, child psychology/child development, Chinese, civil engineering, classics, communication, community services, comparative literature, computer engineering, computer information systems, computer science, conservation, construction management, dance, (pre)dentistry sequence, dietetics, drafting and design, early childhood education, earth science, East Asian studies, ecology, economics, education, electrical and electronics technologies, electrical engineering, electrical engineering technology, electronics engineering technology, elementary education, engineering (general), engineering and applied sciences, engineering technology, English, entomology, European studies, family and consumer studies, family services, farm and ranch management, fashion design and technology, fashion merchandising, film studies, finance/banking, food sciences, food services management, French, geography, geological engineering, geology, German, Germanic languages and literature, graphic arts, Greek, health education, health science, history, home economics, home economics education, horticulture, human development, humanities, illustration, industrial administration, industrial arts, industrial design, information science, interior design, international business, international relations, Italian, Japanese, journalism, Latin, Latin American studies, (pre)law sequence, linguistics, literature, management information systems, manufacturing engineering, manufacturing technology, marketing/retailing/ merchandising, mathematics, mechanical engineering, (pre)medicine sequence, Mexican-American/Chicano studies, microbiology, middle school education, military science, molecular biology, music, music education, Near and Middle Eastern studies, nursing, nutrition, ornamental horticulture, painting/drawing, parks management, philosophy, photography, physical education, physical fitness/exercise science, physical sciences, physical therapy, physics, piano/organ, political science/government, Portuguese, printing technologies, printmaking, psychology, public affairs and policy studies, public relations, radio and television studies, range management, recreational facilities management, recreation and leisure services, recreation therapy, retail management, Russian, science education, sculpture, secondary education, social science, social work, sociology, Southeast Asian studies, Spanish, special education, speech pathology and audiology, sports administration, statistics, studio art, textiles and clothing, theater arts/drama, tourism and travel, (pre)veterinary medicine sequence, vocational education, voice, wildlife biology, wildlife management, zoology.

## Brown University

American studies, anthropology, applied mathematics, art/fine arts, art history, Asian/Oriental studies, behavioral sciences, biochemistry, biology/biological sciences, biomedical engineering, biomedical sciences, biophysics, black/African-American studies, chemical engineering, chemistry, Chinese, civil engineering, classics, cognitive science, comparative literature, computer engineering, computer science, creative writing, dance, East Asian studies, ecology, economics, education, electrical engineering, engineering (general), engineering sciences, English, environmental sciences, environmental studies, film and video production, film studies, French, geochemistry, geology, geophysics, German, Germanic languages and literature, Greek, Hispanic studies, history, international relations, international studies, Italian, Judaic studies, Latin, Latin American studies, linguistics, literature, marine biology, materials engineering, mathematics, mechanical engineering, medieval studies, modern languages, molecular biology, music, Near and Middle Eastern studies, neurosciences, philosophy, physics, political science/government, Portuguese, psychology, religious studies, Russian, Russian and Slavic studies, Slavic languages, sociology, South Asian studies, Spanish, studio art, theater arts/drama, urban studies, women's studies.

## Bryn Mawr College

African studies, American studies, anthropology, archaeology, art/fine arts, art history, Asian/Oriental studies, astronomy, behavioral sciences, biochemistry, biology/biological sciences, black/African-American studies, chemistry, classics, comparative literature, computer science, East Asian studies, economics, English, French, geology, German, Greek, Hispanic studies, history, international economics, Italian, Latin, Latin American studies, mathematics, music, neurosciences, philosophy, physics, political science/government, psychology, religious studies, Romance languages, Russian, Russian and Slavic studies, sociology, Spanish, urban studies, women's studies.

## Bucknell University

Accounting, animal sciences, anthropology, art/fine arts, art history, biochemistry, biology/biological sciences, business administration/commerce/management, cell biology, chemical engineering, chemistry, child psychology/child development, civil engineering, classics, computer engineering, computer science, (pre)dentistry sequence, early childhood education, economics, education, electrical engineering, elementary education, engineering management, English, environmental sciences, experimental psychology, French, geography, geology, German, history, international studies, Japanese, Latin American studies, mathematics, mechanical engineering, (pre)medicine sequence, modern languages, music, music education, music history, philosophy, physics, piano/organ, political science/government, psychology, religious studies, Russian, secondary education, sociology, Spanish, statistics, studio art, theater arts/drama, (pre)veterinary medicine sequence, voice, women's studies.

## Buena Vista College

Accounting, art education, art/fine arts, arts administration, athletic training, biology/biological sciences, business administration/commerce/management, business economics, business education, chemistry, communication, computer information systems, computer science, criminal justice, (pre)dentistry sequence, economics, education, elementary education, English, finance/banking, history, international business, (pre)law sequence, liberal arts/general studies, management information systems, marketing/retailing/merchandising, mathematics, (pre)medicine sequence, modern languages, music, music education, natural sciences, philosophy, physical education, physics, political science/government, psychology, public relations, radio and television studies, science, science education, secondary education, social science, social work, Spanish, special education, speech/rhetoric/public address/debate, theater arts/drama, (pre)veterinary medicine sequence.

## Butler University

Accounting, actuarial science, arts administration, biology/biological sciences, broadcasting, business administration/commerce/management, business economics, chemistry, communication, computer science, dance, (pre)dentistry sequence, early childhood education, economics, education, elementary education, English, finance/banking, French, German, Greek, history, international business, international

studies, journalism, Latin, (pre)law sequence, marketing/retailing/merchandising, mathematics, medical technology, (pre)medicine sequence, modern languages, music, music business, music education, pharmacy/pharmaceutical sciences, philosophy, physical education, physics, piano/organ, political science/government, psychology, radio and television studies, religious studies, Romance languages, secondary education, social science, sociology, Spanish, special education, speech pathology and audiology, speech/rhetoric/public address/debate, stringed instruments, telecommunications, theater arts/drama, (pre)veterinary medicine sequence, voice, wind and percussion instruments.

## California Institute of Technology

Aerospace engineering, applied mathematics, astronomy, astrophysics, biochemistry, biology/biological sciences, cell biology, chemical engineering, chemistry, civil engineering, computer science, economics, electrical engineering, engineering and applied sciences, engineering physics, environmental engineering, geology, geophysics, history, literature, materials sciences, mathematics, mechanical engineering, molecular biology, nuclear physics, physical sciences, physics, planetary and space sciences, social science.

## California Institute of the Arts

Art/fine arts, commercial art, computer graphics, dance, film studies, graphic arts, illustration, jazz, music, photography, piano/organ, sculpture, stringed instruments, studio art, theater arts/drama, voice.

## Calvin College

Accounting, art education, art/fine arts, art history, athletic training, biblical studies, bilingual/bicultural education, biochemistry, biology/biological sciences, business administration/commerce/management, business economics, chemistry, civil engineering, classics, communication, computer science, criminal justice, (pre)dentistry sequence, economics, education, electrical engineering, elementary education, engineering (general), English, environmental sciences, European studies, film studies, French, geography, geology, German, Germanic languages and literature, Greek, history, humanities, interdisciplinary studies, Japanese, journalism, Latin, (pre)law sequence, liberal arts/general studies, linguistics, literature, mathematics, mechanical engineering, medical technology, (pre)medicine sequence, music, music education, music history, natural sciences, nursing, occupational therapy, philosophy, physical education, physical fitness/exercise science, physical sciences, physics, political science/government, psychology, recreation and leisure services, religious education, religious studies, sacred music, science, science education, secondary education, social science, social work, sociology, Spanish, special education, speech pathology and audiology, speech/rhetoric/public address/debate, sports medicine, studio art, telecommunications, theater arts/drama, theology, (pre)veterinary medicine sequence, voice.

## Carleton College

Anthropology, art history, Asian/Oriental studies, biology/biological sciences, chemistry, classics, computer science, ecology, economics, English, French, geology, German, Greek, history, Latin, Latin American studies, (pre)law sequence, mathematics, (pre)medicine sequence, music, philosophy, physics, political science/government, psychology, religious studies, Romance languages, Russian, Russian and Slavic studies, sociology, Spanish, studio art, women's studies.

## Carnegie Mellon University

Accounting, applied art, applied mathematics, architecture, art/fine arts, behavioral sciences, biochemistry, bioengineering, biology/biological sciences, biomedical engineering, biomedical sciences, biophysics, business administration/commerce/management, business economics, cell biology, ceramic art and design, chemical engineering, chemistry, child psychology/child development, city/community/regional planning, civil engineering, clinical psychology, commercial art, communication, comparative literature, computer engineering, computer information systems, computer management, computer programming, computer science, creative writing, (pre)dentistry sequence, economics, electrical engineering, electronics engineering, engineering (general), engineering and applied sciences, engineering design, engineering management, engineering mechanics, engineering sciences, English, environmental engineering, environmental sciences, European studies, experimental psychology, finance/banking, French, genetics, German, Germanic languages and literature, graphic arts, Hispanic studies, history, humanities, illustration, industrial administration, industrial design, information science, jewelry and metalsmithing, journalism, labor and industrial relations, (pre)law sequence, liberal arts/general studies, linguistics, literature, management information systems, manufacturing engineering, marketing/retailing/merchandising, materials engineering, materials sciences, mathematics, mechanical engineering, (pre)medicine sequence, metallurgical engineering, metallurgy, microbiology, modern languages, molecular biology, music, music education, opera, operations research, painting/drawing, philosophy, physics, piano/organ, political science/government, polymer science, printing technologies, psychology, public administration, public affairs and policy studies, publishing, robotics, sculpture, social science, sociology, Spanish, speech/rhetoric/public address/debate, statistics, stringed instruments, studio art, systems engineering, systems science, technical writing, technology and public affairs, textile arts, theater arts/drama, toxicology, urban studies, (pre)veterinary medicine sequence, voice, Western civilization and culture, wind and percussion instruments.

## Carroll College (MT)

Accounting, biology/biological sciences, business administration/commerce/management, business economics, chemistry, communication, computer engineering, (pre)dentistry sequence, education, elementary education, engineering (general), English, finance/banking, French, history, international relations, Latin, (pre)law sequence, liberal arts/general studies, mathematics, medical records services, medical technology, (pre)medicine sequence, nursing, occupational therapy, philosophy, physical education, political science/government, psychology, public administration, public relations, religious education, religious studies, science education, secondary education, social science, social work, sociology, Spanish, speech/rhetoric/public address/debate, sports administration, teaching English as a second language, technical writing, theater arts/drama, theology, (pre)veterinary medicine sequence.

## Case Western Reserve University

Accounting, aerospace engineering, American studies, anthropology, applied mathematics, art education, art history, Asian/Oriental studies, astronomy, audio engineering, biochemistry, biology/biological sciences, biomedical engineering, business administration/commerce/management, chemical engineering, chemistry, civil engineering, classics, communication, comparative literature, computer engineering, computer science, (pre)dentistry sequence, dietetics, earth science, economics, electrical engineering, engineering (general), English, environmental sciences, finance/banking, fluid and thermal sciences, French, geology, German, gerontology, Greek, history, history of science, industrial engineering, international studies, Latin, (pre)law sequence, literature, management information systems, materials engineering, materials sciences, mathematics, mechanical engineering, medical technology, (pre)medicine sequence, music, music education, natural sciences, nursing, nutrition, operations research, philosophy,

physics, political science/government, polymer science, psychology, religious studies, sociology, Spanish, speech pathology and audiology, statistics, systems engineering, theater arts/drama, (pre)veterinary medicine sequence.

## Catholic University of America

Accounting, American studies, anthropology, architectural engineering, architecture, art education, art/fine arts, art history, biochemistry, biology/biological sciences, biomedical engineering, business administration/commerce/management, chemistry, civil engineering, classics, communication, computer engineering, computer science, construction engineering, early childhood education, economics, education, electrical engineering, elementary education, engineering (general), English, finance/banking, French, German, Greek, history, human resources, interdisciplinary studies, international economics, international studies, Italian, Latin, mathematics, mechanical engineering, medical technology, (pre)medicine sequence, medieval studies, modern languages, music, music education, music history, nursing, peace studies, philosophy, physics, piano/organ, political science/government, psychology, religious studies, Romance languages, secondary education, social work, sociology, Spanish, studio art, theater arts/drama, (pre)veterinary medicine sequence, voice, wind and percussion instruments.

## Cedarville College

Accounting, American studies, athletic training, behavioral sciences, biblical studies, biology/biological sciences, broadcasting, business administration/commerce/management, business economics, business education, chemistry, communication, computer information systems, criminal justice, (pre)dentistry sequence, early childhood education, economics, education, electrical engineering, elementary education, English, environmental biology, finance/banking, health education, history, international business, international economics, international studies, (pre)law sequence, marketing/retailing/merchandising, mathematics, mechanical engineering, medical technology, (pre)medicine sequence, music, music education, nursing, pastoral studies, philosophy, physical education, political science/government, psychology, public administration, radio and television studies, sacred music, science, science education, secondary education, secretarial studies/office management, social science, social work, sociology, Spanish, special education, speech/rhetoric/public address/debate, technical writing, theater arts/drama, theology, (pre)veterinary medicine sequence, voice.

## Centenary College of Louisiana

Accounting, art education, art/fine arts, arts administration, biblical studies, biochemistry, biology/biological sciences, biophysics, business administration/commerce/management, business economics, chemistry, communication, computer science, dance, (pre)dentistry sequence, early childhood education, earth science, economics, education, elementary education, engineering and applied sciences, English, environmental sciences, environmental studies, French, geology, German, health education, health science, history, interdisciplinary studies, (pre)law sequence, liberal arts/general studies, literature, mathematics, (pre)medicine sequence, middle school education, military science, music, music education, occupational therapy, painting/drawing, philosophy, physical education, physical sciences, physical therapy, physics, piano/organ, political science/government, psychology, religious education, religious studies, sacred music, science education, secondary education, social science, sociology, Spanish, speech pathology and audiology, speech/rhetoric/public address/debate, stringed instruments, studio art, theater arts/drama, (pre)veterinary medicine sequence, voice, wind and percussion instruments.

## Central College (IA)

Accounting, art education, art/fine arts, biology/biological sciences, business administration/commerce/management, chemistry, communication, computer science, (pre)dentistry sequence, economics, education, elementary education, English, environmental sciences, environmental studies, European studies, French, German, history, international business, international studies, Latin American studies, (pre)law sequence, liberal arts/general studies, linguistics, mathematics, (pre)medicine sequence, music, music education, philosophy, physical education, physics, political science/government, psychology, recreation and leisure services, religious studies, secondary education, sociology, Spanish, systems science, theater arts/drama, urban studies, (pre)veterinary medicine sequence.

## Centre College

Anthropology, art/fine arts, art history, biochemistry, biology/biological sciences, chemistry, computer science, (pre)dentistry sequence, economics, elementary education, English, French, German, history, international relations, (pre)law sequence, mathematics, (pre)medicine sequence, molecular biology, music, philosophy, physics, political science/government, psychobiology, psychology, religious studies, secondary education, sociology, Spanish, theater arts/drama.

## Christendom College

Classics, French, history, literature, philosophy, political science/government, theology.

## Christian Brothers University

Accounting, biology/biological sciences, business administration/commerce/management, business economics, chemical engineering, chemistry, civil engineering, communication, computer information systems, computer science, construction engineering, (pre)dentistry sequence, economics, education, electrical engineering, elementary education, engineering physics, English, finance/banking, history, humanities, (pre)law sequence, marketing/retailing/merchandising, mathematics, mechanical engineering, medical technology, (pre)medicine sequence, natural sciences, physics, psychology, secondary education, telecommunications, theater arts/drama.

## Claremont McKenna College

Accounting, American studies, art/fine arts, Asian/Oriental studies, biochemistry, biology/biological sciences, biophysics, black/African-American studies, chemistry, Chinese, classics, computer science, (pre)dentistry sequence, economics, engineering management, English, environmental sciences, environmental studies, European studies, film studies, French, German, Greek, history, international business, international economics, international relations, international studies, Italian, Japanese, Latin, Latin American studies, (pre)law sequence, legal studies, literature, management engineering, mathematics, (pre)medicine sequence, Mexican-American/Chicano studies, modern languages, music, philosophy, physics, political science/government, psychobiology, psychology, religious studies, Russian, Spanish, theater arts/drama, women's studies.

## Clarkson University

Accounting, aerospace engineering, applied mathematics, biochemistry, biology/biological sciences, business administration/commerce/management, business economics, cell biology, chemical engineering, chemistry, civil engineering, computer engineering, computer information systems, computer management, computer science, economics, electrical engineering, engineering (general), engineering management, engineering sciences, environmental engineering, environmental health sciences, finance/banking, history, humanities, industrial engineering, interdisciplinary studies, (pre)law sequence, liberal arts/general studies, management engineering, management information systems, manufacturing engineering, marketing/retailing/merchandising, materials engineering, mathematics, mechanical engineering, (pre)medicine sequence, microbiology, occupational safety and health, operations research, physics, political science/government, psychology, social science, surveying engineering, technical writing, toxicology.

## Clark University

Art/fine arts, art history, biochemistry, biology/biological sciences, business administration/commerce/management, chemistry, classics, communication, comparative literature, computer science, (pre)dentistry sequence, earth science, ecology, economics, education, elementary education, engineering (general), English, environmental sciences, environmental studies, ethnic studies, film studies, French, geography, German, Germanic languages and literature, graphic arts, history, interdisciplinary studies, international relations, international studies, Judaic studies, (pre)law sequence, literature, mathematics, (pre)medicine sequence, middle school education, modern languages, molecular biology, music, natural resource management, neurosciences, philosophy, physics, political science/government, psychology, Romance languages, secondary education, sociology, Spanish, studio art, theater arts/drama, (pre)veterinary medicine sequence.

## Clemson University

Accounting, agricultural business, agricultural economics, agricultural education, agricultural engineering, agricultural sciences, agronomy/soil and crop sciences, animal sciences, applied mathematics, architecture, art/fine arts, biochemistry, biology/biological sciences, botany/plant sciences, business administration/commerce/management, ceramic engineering, chemical engineering, chemistry, city/community/regional planning, civil engineering, communication, computer information systems, computer science, construction management, dairy sciences, early childhood education, earth science, economics, education, electrical engineering, elementary education, engineering (general), English, entomology, finance/banking, food sciences, forestry, French, geology, German, graphic arts, health science, history, horticulture, industrial arts, industrial engineering, international business, landscape architecture/design, (pre)law sequence, liberal arts/general studies, marketing/retailing/merchandising, mathematics, mechanical engineering, medical technology, (pre)medicine sequence, microbiology, modern languages, nursing, occupational safety and health, ornamental horticulture, parks management, philosophy, physics, political science/government, poultry sciences, psychology, reading education, recreation and leisure services, science education, secondary education, sociology, Spanish, special education, textiles and clothing, tourism and travel, (pre)veterinary medicine sequence, vocational education, wildlife biology, wildlife management, wood sciences.

## Cleveland Institute of Music

Audio engineering, music, music education, piano/organ, stringed instruments, voice, wind and percussion instruments.

## Coe College

Accounting, American studies, art education, art/fine arts, Asian/Oriental studies, biology/biological sciences, black/African-American studies, business administration/commerce/management, chemistry, classics, computer science, (pre)dentistry sequence, economics, education, elementary education, English, environmental studies, French, German, history, interdisciplinary studies, (pre)law sequence, liberal arts/general studies, literature, mathematics, medical technology, (pre)medicine sequence, music, music education, nursing, philosophy, physical education, physical sciences, physics, political science/government, psychology, religious studies, science, science education, secondary education, sociology, Spanish, studio art, theater arts/drama, (pre)veterinary medicine sequence.

## Colby College

American studies, anthropology, art/fine arts, art history, biochemistry, biology/biological sciences, business administration/commerce/ management, chemistry, classics, computer science, East Asian studies, economics, English, environmental sciences, French, geology, German, history, international studies, mathematics, music, philosophy, physics, political science/government, psychology, religious studies, Russian and Slavic studies, sociology, Spanish, theater arts/drama.

## Colgate University

African studies, anthropology, art/fine arts, art history, Asian/Oriental studies, astronomy, astrophysics, biochemistry, biology/biological sciences, black/African-American studies, chemistry, Chinese, classics, computer science, East Asian studies, economics, education, English, French, geography, geology, German, Greek, history, humanities, international relations, Japanese, Latin, Latin American studies, mathematics, molecular biology, music, Native American studies, natural sciences, neurosciences, peace studies, philosophy, physical sciences, physics, political science/government, psychology, religious studies, Romance languages, Russian, Russian and Slavic studies, social science, sociology, Spanish, women's studies.

## College of Insurance

Actuarial science, business administration/commerce/management, finance/banking, insurance.

## College of Saint Benedict

Accounting, art education, art/fine arts, art history, biology/biological sciences, business administration/commerce/management, chemistry, classics, communication, computer science, (pre)dentistry sequence, dietetics, economics, education, elementary education, English, forestry, French, German, Greek, history, humanities, Latin, (pre)law sequence, liberal arts/general studies, mathematics, medical technology, (pre)medicine sequence, medieval studies, ministries, music, music education, natural sciences, nursing, nutrition, occupational therapy, peace studies, pharmacy/pharmaceutical sciences, philosophy, physical therapy, physics, political science/government, psychology, religious education, religious studies, sacred music, secondary education, social science, social work, sociology, Spanish, studio art, theater arts/drama, theology, (pre)veterinary medicine sequence.

## College of St. Scholastica

Accounting, behavioral sciences, bilingual/bicultural education, biology/biological sciences, business administration/commerce/ management, chemistry, communication, computer information systems, (pre)dentistry sequence, dietetics, early childhood education, education, elementary education, English, family and consumer studies, fashion merchandising, food services management, health science, health services administration, history, home economics, home economics education, humanities, interdisciplinary studies, international business, (pre)law sequence, liberal arts/general studies, mathematics, medical records services, medical technology, (pre)medicine sequence, ministries, music, music education, natural sciences, nursing, occupational therapy, pastoral studies, physical fitness/exercise science, physical therapy, piano/organ, psychology, religious education, religious studies, science education, secondary education, social work, sociology, sports administration, (pre)veterinary medicine sequence.

## College of the Holy Cross

Accounting, anthropology, art/fine arts, art history, Asian/Oriental studies, biology/biological sciences, black/African-American studies, chemistry, classics, computer science, (pre)dentistry sequence, economics, English, environmental studies, European studies, French, German, gerontology, history, international studies, Italian, Latin American studies, (pre)law sequence, mathematics, (pre)medicine sequence, modern languages, music, Near and Middle Eastern studies, peace studies, philosophy, physics, political science/government, psychobiology, psychology, religious studies, Russian, sociology, Spanish, studio art, theater arts/drama, (pre)veterinary medicine sequence, women's studies.

## College of William and Mary

American studies, anthropology, art/fine arts, art history, biology/ biological sciences, business administration/commerce/management, chemistry, classics, comparative literature, computer science, East Asian studies, economics, English, environmental sciences, European studies, French, geology, German, Greek, history, interdisciplinary studies, international studies, Latin, Latin American studies, linguistics, mathematics, modern languages, music, philosophy, physical fitness/ exercise science, physics, political science/government, psychology, public affairs and policy studies, religious studies, Russian and Slavic studies, sociology, Spanish, speech/rhetoric/public address/debate, theater arts/drama, urban studies.

## The College of Wooster

African studies, art/fine arts, art history, Asian/Oriental studies, biology/biological sciences, black/African-American studies, business economics, chemistry, classics, communication, comparative literature, computer science, (pre)dentistry sequence, economics, English, European studies, French, geology, German, Greek, history, international studies, Latin, Latin American studies, (pre)law sequence, mathematics, (pre)medicine sequence, music, music education, music history, music therapy, Near and Middle Eastern studies, philosophy, physics, political science/government, psychology, religious studies, Russian, sociology, South Asian studies, Spanish, speech pathology and audiology, speech/rhetoric/public address/debate, studio art, theater arts/drama, urban studies, (pre)veterinary medicine sequence, voice.

## The Colorado College

Anthropology, art/fine arts, art history, biochemistry, biology/ biological sciences, chemistry, classics, comparative literature, creative writing, dance, (pre)dentistry sequence, economics, English, environmental sciences, environmental studies, French, geology, German, history, interdisciplinary studies, international economics, international studies, (pre)law sequence, liberal arts/general studies, mathematics, (pre)medicine sequence, music, peace studies, philosophy, physics, political science/government, psychology, religious studies, Romance languages, Russian, sociology, Spanish, theater arts/drama, (pre)veterinary medicine sequence, women's studies.

## Colorado School of Mines

Chemical engineering, chemistry, civil engineering, computer science, economics, electrical engineering, engineering (general), engineering and applied sciences, engineering physics, engineering sciences, geological engineering, geophysical engineering, materials sciences, mathematics, mechanical engineering, metallurgical engineering, mining and mineral engineering, petroleum/natural gas engineering, physics.

## Colorado State University

Accounting, actuarial science, agricultural business, agricultural economics, agricultural education, agricultural engineering, agricultural sciences, agronomy/soil and crop sciences, American studies, animal sciences, anthropology, applied mathematics, art education, art/fine arts, art history, biochemistry, biology/biological sciences, botany/plant sciences, business administration/commerce/management, ceramic art and design, chemical engineering, chemistry, child care/child and family studies, civil engineering, computer engineering, computer information systems, computer science, construction management, consumer services, creative writing, dance, (pre)dentistry sequence, dietetics, economics, electrical engineering, engineering physics, engineering sciences, English, entomology, environmental engineering, environmental health sciences, equestrian studies, family and consumer studies, farm and ranch management, fashion merchandising, finance/banking, fish and game management, food sciences, forestry, French, geology, German, graphic arts, history, home economics, home economics education, horticulture, hotel and restaurant management, human development, humanities, industrial arts, interior design, jewelry and metalsmithing, journalism, landscape architecture/design, (pre)law sequence, liberal arts/general studies, manufacturing technology, marketing/retailing/merchandising, mathematics, mechanical engineering, (pre)medicine sequence, microbiology, music, music education, music therapy, natural resource management, nutrition, occupational therapy, painting/drawing, parks management, philosophy, photography, physical education, physical fitness/exercise science, physical sciences, physics, political science/government, printmaking, psychology, public relations, range management, real estate, recreation and leisure services, sculpture, social science, social work, sociology, soil conservation, Spanish, speech/rhetoric/public address/debate, statistics, studio art, textiles and clothing, theater arts/drama, (pre)veterinary medicine sequence, vocational education, water resources, wildlife biology, zoology.

## Colorado Technical College

Business administration/commerce/management, computer engineering, computer science, electrical engineering, electronics engineering technology, management information systems, telecommunications.

## Columbia College (NY)

African studies, anthropology, archaeology, architecture, art/fine arts, art history, astronomy, astrophysics, biochemistry, biology/biological sciences, biophysics, black/African-American studies, chemistry, classics, comparative literature, computer science, dance, East Asian studies, East European and Soviet studies, economics, English, environmental sciences, film studies, French, geochemistry, geology, geophysics, German, Germanic languages and literature, Greek, Hispanic studies, history, interdisciplinary studies, Italian, Latin, Latin American studies, mathematics, medieval studies, music, Near and Middle Eastern studies, philosophy, physics, political science/government, psychology, religious studies, Russian, Russian and Slavic studies, sociology, Spanish, statistics, theater arts/drama, urban studies, Western civilization and culture, women's studies.

## Columbia University, School of Engineering and Applied Science

Applied mathematics, bioengineering, chemical engineering, civil engineering, computer engineering, computer science, electrical engineering, engineering mechanics, environmental engineering, industrial engineering, materials sciences, mechanical engineering, metallurgical engineering, metallurgy, mining and mineral engineering, operations research, physics.

## Concordia College (Moorhead, MN)

Accounting, advertising, art education, art/fine arts, art history, biology/biological sciences, broadcasting, business administration/commerce/management, business economics, business education, chemistry, child care/child and family studies, classics, communication, computer science, creative writing, criminal justice, (pre)dentistry sequence, dietetics, economics, education, elementary education, English, environmental studies, family and consumer studies, French, German, health education, health services administration, history, home economics, home economics education, humanities, international business, international relations, journalism, Latin, (pre)law sequence, mathematics, medical technology, (pre)medicine sequence, music, music education, nursing, nutrition, philosophy, physical education, physics, piano/organ, political science/government, psychology, radio and television studies, recreation and leisure services, religious studies, Russian and Slavic studies, Scandinavian languages/studies, science education, secondary education, secretarial studies/office management, social work, sociology, Spanish, speech/rhetoric/public address/debate, studio art, textiles and clothing, theater arts/drama, (pre)veterinary medicine sequence, voice, wind and percussion instruments.

## Connecticut College

Anthropology, art/fine arts, art history, Asian/Oriental studies, biochemistry, biology/biological sciences, botany/plant sciences, chemistry, child psychology/child development, Chinese, classics, dance, economics, English, European studies, French, German, Hispanic studies, history, human ecology, interdisciplinary studies, international studies, Italian, Japanese, marine biology, mathematics, medieval studies, music, musical instrument technology, philosophy, physics, political science/government, psychology, religious studies, Russian, Russian and Slavic studies, sociology, studio art, theater arts/drama, urban studies, zoology.

## Cooper Union for the Advancement of Science and Art

Architecture, art/fine arts, chemical engineering, civil engineering, electrical engineering, engineering (general), graphic arts, mechanical engineering.

## The Corcoran School of Art

Applied art, art/fine arts, ceramic art and design, commercial art, graphic arts, painting/drawing, photography, printmaking, sculpture, studio art.

## Cornell College

Anthropology, architecture, art education, art/fine arts, art history, behavioral sciences, biochemistry, biology/biological sciences, business administration/commerce/management, business economics, business education, chemistry, classics, computer science, (pre)dentistry sequence, ecology, economics, education, elementary education, English, environmental sciences, environmental studies, ethnic studies, French, geology, German, history, interdisciplinary studies, international business, international relations, international studies, Latin American studies, (pre)law sequence, liberal arts/general studies, mathematics, medical technology, (pre)medicine sequence, medieval studies, modern languages, molecular biology, music, music education, philosophy, physical education, physics, political science/government, psychology, religious studies, Russian, Russian and Slavic studies, secondary education, sociology, Spanish, speech/rhetoric/public address/debate, studio art, theater arts/drama, (pre)veterinary medicine sequence, women's studies.

## Cornell University

African studies, agricultural business, agricultural economics, agricultural education, agricultural engineering, agricultural sciences, agricultural technologies, agronomy/soil and crop sciences, American studies, anatomy, animal sciences, anthropology, applied art, archaeology, architectural technologies, architecture, art/fine arts, art history, Asian/Oriental studies, astronomy, atmospheric sciences, behavioral sciences, biochemistry, bioengineering, biology/biological sciences, biometrics, black/African-American studies, botany/plant sciences, business administration/commerce/management, cell biology, chemical engineering, chemistry, child care/child and family studies, child psychology/child development, Chinese, city/community/regional planning, civil engineering, classics, communication, community services, comparative literature, computer information systems, computer science, consumer services, creative writing, dairy sciences, dance, dietetics, East Asian studies, East European and Soviet studies, ecology, economics, education, electrical engineering, engineering (general), engineering physics, engineering sciences, English, entomology, environmental design, environmental engineering, environmental sciences, European studies, family and consumer studies, family services, farm and ranch management, food sciences, food services management, French, genetics, geological engineering, geology, German, Germanic languages and literature, Greek, Hebrew, Hispanic studies, history, history of science, home economics education, horticulture, hotel and restaurant management, human development, human ecology, human services, industrial engineering, interdisciplinary studies, international studies, Italian, Japanese, Judaic studies, labor and industrial relations, labor studies, landscape architecture/design, Latin, Latin American studies, (pre)law sequence, liberal arts/general studies, linguistics, marine sciences, materials engineering, materials sciences, mathematics, mechanical engineering, (pre)medicine sequence, medieval studies, meteorology, microbiology, modern languages, molecular biology, music, Native American studies, natural resource management, Near and Middle Eastern studies, neurosciences, nutrition, operations research, ornamental horticulture, painting/drawing, pest control technology, philosophy, photography, physics, physiology, political science/government, poultry sciences, psychology, public affairs and policy studies, religious studies, Romance languages, Russian, Russian and Slavic studies, sculpture, Slavic languages, social work, sociobiology, sociology, Southeast Asian studies, Spanish, statistics, textile arts, textiles and clothing, theater arts/drama, urban studies, (pre)veterinary medicine sequence, women's studies, zoology.

## Creighton University

Accounting, American studies, art/fine arts, atmospheric sciences, biology/biological sciences, business economics, chemistry, classics, communication, computer science, economics, education, elementary education, English, environmental sciences, finance/banking, French, German, Greek, history, international business, journalism, Latin, management information systems, marketing/retailing/merchandising, mathematics, ministries, modern languages, music, nursing, occupational therapy, pharmacy/pharmaceutical sciences, philosophy, physical fitness/exercise science, physical therapy, physics, political science/government, psychology, social work, sociology, Spanish, speech/rhetoric/public address/debate, theater arts/drama, theology.

## The Curtis Institute of Music

Music, piano/organ, stringed instruments, voice, wind and percussion instruments.

## Dartmouth College

Anthropology, applied art, archaeology, art/fine arts, art history, Asian/Oriental studies, biochemistry, biology/biological sciences, black/African-American studies, chemistry, classics, cognitive science, comparative literature, computer science, earth science, economics, education, engineering (general), engineering sciences, English, environmental sciences, film studies, French, geography, German, Hispanic studies, history, Italian, linguistics, mathematics, (pre)medicine sequence, music, Native American studies, philosophy, physics, political science/government, psychology, religious studies, Romance languages, Russian, sociology, Spanish, studio art, theater arts/drama, women's studies.

## David Lipscomb University

Accounting, American studies, applied mathematics, art/fine arts, athletic training, biblical languages, biblical studies, biochemistry, biology/biological sciences, business administration/commerce/management, business economics, chemistry, commercial art, communication, computer information systems, computer science, (pre)dentistry sequence, dietetics, education, elementary education, engineering sciences, English, family and consumer studies, fashion merchandising, finance/banking, food services management, French, German, health education, history, home economics, (pre)law sequence, liberal arts/general studies, marketing/retailing/merchandising, mathematics, (pre)medicine sequence, middle school education, ministries, music, music education, nursing, philosophy, physical education, physical fitness/exercise science, physics, piano/organ, political science/government, psychology, public administration, public relations, secondary education, social work, Spanish, speech/rhetoric/public address/debate, stringed instruments, studio art, theology, urban studies, (pre)veterinary medicine sequence, voice, wind and percussion instruments.

## Davidson College

Anthropology, art/fine arts, art history, biology/biological sciences, chemistry, classics, economics, English, French, German, history, mathematics, music, philosophy, physics, political science/government, psychology, religious studies, sociology, Spanish, studio art, theater arts/drama.

## Deep Springs College

Liberal arts/general studies.

## Denison University

Anthropology, art/fine arts, art history, biochemistry, biology/biological sciences, black/African-American studies, chemistry, classics, communication, computer science, creative writing, dance, East Asian studies, economics, English, environmental sciences, environmental studies, film studies, French, geology, German, history, international studies, Latin American studies, mathematics, music, music education, philosophy, physical education, physics, political science/government, psychology, religious studies, sociology, Spanish, speech/rhetoric/public address/debate, studio art, theater arts/drama, women's studies.

## DePaul University

Accounting, actuarial science, adult and continuing education, advertising, American studies, anthropology, applied art, applied mathematics, art history, arts administration, audio engineering, biochemistry, biology/biological sciences, black/African-American studies, business administration/commerce/management, business economics, chemistry, city/community/regional planning, commercial art, communication, comparative literature, computer graphics, computer information systems, computer programming, computer science, computer technologies, creative writing, criminal justice, (pre)dentistry sequence, early childhood education, ecology, economics, education, electrical and electronics technologies, elementary education, English, environmental sciences, finance/banking, French, geography, German, graphic arts, guidance and counseling, history, human development, human resources, information science, interdisciplinary studies, international business, international relations, international studies, Italian, Japanese, jazz, Judaic studies, Latin American studies, (pre)law sequence, legal studies, linguistics, literature, management information systems, marketing/retailing/merchandising, mathematics, medical laboratory technology, (pre)medicine sequence, military science, modern languages, music, music business, music education, nursing, operations research, painting/drawing, philosophy, physical education, physics, piano/organ, political science/government, psychology, religious education, religious studies, sculpture, secondary education, social science, sociology, Spanish, statistics, stringed instruments, studio art, theater arts/drama, tourism and travel, urban studies, (pre)veterinary medicine sequence, voice, wind and percussion instruments, women's studies.

## DePauw University
Anthropology, art history, Asian/Oriental studies, biology/biological sciences, chemistry, classics, communication, computer science, earth science, East Asian studies, economics, elementary education, English, French, geography, geology, German, Greek, history, interdisciplinary studies, Latin, literature, mathematics, medical technology, music, music business, music education, philosophy, physical education, physics, piano/organ, political science/government, psychology, religious studies, Romance languages, Russian and Slavic studies, sociology, Spanish, studio art, voice, women's studies.

## Dickinson College
American studies, anthropology, art/fine arts, biology/biological sciences, chemistry, computer science, East Asian studies, economics, English, environmental sciences, environmental studies, French, geology, German, Greek, history, international studies, Italian, Judaic studies, Latin, mathematics, music, philosophy, physics, political science/government, psychology, public affairs and policy studies, religious studies, Russian, Russian and Slavic studies, sociology, Spanish, theater arts/drama.

## Drake University
Accounting, actuarial science, advertising, applied art, art education, art/fine arts, art history, Asian/Oriental studies, astronomy, biology/biological sciences, broadcasting, business administration/commerce/management, business education, chemistry, clinical psychology, commercial art, communication, computer information systems, computer science, (pre)dentistry sequence, earth science, economics, education, educational administration, elementary education, English, environmental sciences, experimental psychology, finance/banking, French, geography, German, gerontology, graphic arts, history, insurance, interior design, international business, international relations, journalism, Latin American studies, (pre)law sequence, literature, marine sciences, marketing/retailing/merchandising, mathematics, medical technology, (pre)medicine sequence, military science, music, music business, music education, nursing, painting/drawing, pharmacy/pharmaceutical sciences, philosophy, physical sciences, physics, piano/organ, political science/government, printmaking, psychology, public relations, radio and television studies, religious studies, sacred music, science, science education, sculpture, secondary education, social science, sociology, Spanish, speech/rhetoric/public address/debate, stringed instruments, studio art, theater arts/drama, (pre)veterinary medicine sequence, voice, wind and percussion instruments, women's studies.

## Drew University
American studies, anthropology, applied mathematics, art/fine arts, art history, behavioral sciences, biochemistry, biology/biological sciences, chemistry, classics, computer science, economics, English, French, German, history, Italian, liberal arts/general studies, mathematics, music, philosophy, physics, political science/government, psychobiology, psychology, religious studies, Russian, Russian and Slavic studies, sociology, Spanish, studio art, theater arts/drama.

## Drury College
Accounting, architecture, art education, art/fine arts, art history, behavioral sciences, biology/biological sciences, business administration/commerce/management, chemistry, communication, criminal justice, (pre)dentistry sequence, economics, education, elementary education, English, French, German, history, (pre)law sequence, mathematics, medical technology, (pre)medicine sequence, music, music education, nursing, philosophy, physical education, physics, political science/government, psychology, religious studies, secondary education, sociology, Spanish, special education, studio art, theater arts/drama, (pre)veterinary medicine sequence.

## Duke University
Anatomy, anthropology, art/fine arts, art history, biology/biological sciences, biomedical engineering, black/African-American studies, chemistry, civil engineering, classics, computer science, East European and Soviet studies, economics, electrical engineering, English, environmental sciences, European studies, French, geology, Germanic languages and literature, Greek, history, international studies, Italian, Latin, Latin American studies, literature, materials sciences, mathematics, mechanical engineering, medieval studies, music, philosophy, physics, political science/government, psychology, public affairs and policy studies, religious studies, Russian, Russian and Slavic studies, Slavic languages, sociology, Spanish, theater arts/drama, women's studies.

## Earlham College
African studies, anthropology, art/fine arts, astronomy, biology/biological sciences, black/African-American studies, chemistry, classics, computer science, East Asian studies, economics, education, elementary education, English, environmental studies, French, geology, German, history, human development, international studies, Japanese, Judaic studies, (pre)law sequence, legal studies, literature, mathematics, (pre)medicine sequence, museum studies, music, peace studies, philosophy, physics, political science/government, psychology, religious studies, secondary education, sociology, Spanish, theater arts/drama, (pre)veterinary medicine sequence, women's studies.

## Eckerd College
American studies, anthropology, art/fine arts, biology/biological sciences, business administration/commerce/management, chemistry, comparative literature, computer science, creative writing, (pre)dentistry sequence, ecology, economics, English, environmental studies, French, German, history, human development, humanities, interdisciplinary studies, international business, international relations, international studies, (pre)law sequence, literature, marine sciences, mathematics, medical technology, (pre)medicine sequence, modern languages, music, philosophy, physics, political science/government, psychology, religious studies, Russian, sociology, Spanish, theater arts/drama, (pre)veterinary medicine sequence, women's studies.

## Elizabethtown College
Accounting, actuarial science, anthropology, applied mathematics, art/fine arts, biochemistry, biology/biological sciences, broadcasting, business administration/commerce/management, business economics,

chemistry, child psychology/child development, communication, computer engineering, computer information systems, computer science, cytotechnology, (pre)dentistry sequence, early childhood education, economics, education, elementary education, engineering (general), engineering physics, English, environmental sciences, finance/banking, forestry, French, German, history, industrial engineering, international business, international studies, (pre)law sequence, literature, management information systems, marketing/retailing/merchandising, mathematics, medical technology, (pre)medicine sequence, modern languages, music, music education, music therapy, nursing, occupational therapy, peace studies, philosophy, physical therapy, physics, political science/government, psychology, public administration, public relations, radio and television studies, religious studies, science, science education, secondary education, social science, social work, sociology, Spanish, statistics, theater arts/drama, toxicology, (pre)veterinary medicine sequence.

## Emory University
Accounting, African studies, anthropology, art history, biology/biological sciences, biomedical sciences, black/African-American studies, business administration/commerce/management, business economics, chemistry, classics, comparative literature, computer science, creative writing, East European and Soviet studies, economics, education, elementary education, English, film studies, finance/banking, French, Germanic languages and literature, Greek, history, human ecology, international studies, Italian, Judaic studies, Latin, Latin American studies, liberal arts/general studies, literature, marketing/retailing/merchandising, mathematics, medieval studies, music, nursing, philosophy, physics, political science/government, psychology, religious studies, Russian, secondary education, sociology, Spanish, theater arts/drama, women's studies.

## Eugene Lang College, New School for Social Research
Anthropology, creative writing, economics, education, English, history, humanities, interdisciplinary studies, international studies, liberal arts/general studies, literature, music history, philosophy, political science/government, psychology, religious studies, science, social science, sociology, theater arts/drama, urban studies, women's studies.

## Fairfield University
Accounting, American studies, art/fine arts, biology/biological sciences, business administration/commerce/management, chemistry, clinical psychology, communication, computer information systems, computer science, economics, English, finance/banking, French, German, history, international studies, management information systems, marketing/retailing/merchandising, mathematics, modern languages, music history, nursing, philosophy, physics, political science/government, psychology, religious studies, secondary education, sociology, Spanish.

## Fashion Institute of Technology
Advertising, applied art, commercial art, fashion design and technology, fashion merchandising, illustration, industrial administration, industrial design, interior design, management engineering, manufacturing technology, marketing/retailing/merchandising, textile arts, textiles and clothing.

## Fisk University
Accounting, art/fine arts, biology/biological sciences, business administration/commerce/management, chemistry, economics, English, finance/banking, French, health services administration, history, mathematics, music, music education, philosophy, physics, political

science/government, psychology, public administration, religious studies, sociology, Spanish, speech/rhetoric/public address/debate, theater arts/drama.

## Florida Institute of Technology
Accounting, aerospace engineering, aerospace sciences, applied mathematics, astronomy, astrophysics, aviation administration, behavioral sciences, biochemistry, biology/biological sciences, business administration/commerce/management, cell biology, chemical engineering, chemistry, civil engineering, clinical psychology, communication, computer engineering, computer programming, computer science, data processing, (pre)dentistry sequence, economics, education, electrical engineering, environmental biology, environmental engineering, environmental sciences, finance/banking, flight training, hospitality services, hotel and restaurant management, humanities, (pre)law sequence, liberal arts/general studies, marine biology, marine engineering, marketing/retailing/merchandising, mathematics, mechanical engineering, (pre)medicine sequence, molecular biology, naval architecture, ocean engineering, oceanography, physics, planetary and space sciences, psychology, science education, secondary education, technical writing, (pre)veterinary medicine sequence.

## Florida State University
Accounting, advertising, American studies, anthropology, applied mathematics, archaeology, art education, art/fine arts, art history, art therapy, Asian/Oriental studies, bilingual/bicultural education, biochemistry, biology/biological sciences, botany/plant sciences, broadcasting, business administration/commerce/management, cell biology, chemical engineering, chemistry, child psychology/child development, civil engineering, classics, clinical psychology, communication, comparative literature, computer engineering, computer science, corrections, creative writing, criminal justice, criminology, dance, (pre)dentistry sequence, dietetics, early childhood education, East Asian studies, East European and Soviet studies, ecology, economics, education, electrical engineering, electronics engineering, elementary education, English, environmental engineering, environmental sciences, evolutionary biology, experimental psychology, family and consumer studies, family services, fashion design and technology, fashion merchandising, film and video production, film studies, finance/banking, food sciences, food services management, French, genetics, geography, geology, German, graphic arts, Greek, health education, history, home economics, home economics education, hotel and restaurant management, humanities, human resources, industrial engineering, insurance, interior design, international business, international relations, Italian, Latin, Latin American studies, law enforcement/police sciences, (pre)law sequence, linguistics, literature, management information systems, marine biology, marketing/retailing/merchandising, mathematics, mechanical engineering, (pre)medicine sequence, meteorology, molecular biology, music, music education, music history, music therapy, neurosciences, nursing, nutrition, painting/drawing, parks management, philosophy, photography, physical education, physics, physiology, piano/organ, political science/government, printmaking, psychology, public relations, radio and television studies, reading education, real estate, recreation and leisure services, rehabilitation therapy, religious studies, Russian, Russian and Slavic studies, science education, sculpture, secondary education, Slavic languages, social science, social work, sociology, Spanish, special education, speech pathology and audiology, speech/rhetoric/public address/debate, statistics, stringed instruments, studio art, systems engineering, textile arts, textiles and clothing, theater arts/drama, urban studies, (pre)veterinary medicine sequence, voice, wind and percussion instruments, zoology.

## Fordham University
Accounting, African studies, American studies, anthropology, art/fine arts, art history, bilingual/bicultural education, biology/biological sciences, black/African-American studies, broadcasting, business administration/commerce/management, business economics, chemistry, classics, communication, comparative literature, computer information systems, computer management, computer science, creative writing, criminal justice, (pre)dentistry sequence, East European and Soviet studies, economics, education, elementary education, English, film studies, finance/banking, French, German, Germanic languages and literature, graphic arts, Greek, Hispanic studies, history, information science, interdisciplinary studies, international business, international relations, international studies, Italian, journalism, Latin, Latin American studies, (pre)law sequence, liberal arts/general studies, literature, management information systems, marketing/retailing/merchandising, mathematics, medical technology, (pre)medicine sequence, medieval studies, modern languages, music history, natural sciences, Near and Middle Eastern studies, peace studies, philosophy, photography, physical sciences, physics, political science/government, psychology, public administration, radio and television studies, religious studies, Romance languages, Russian, Russian and Slavic studies, science, science education, secondary education, social science, sociology, Spanish, studio art, theater arts/drama, theology, urban studies, (pre)veterinary medicine sequence, women's studies.

## Franklin and Marshall College
Accounting, American studies, anthropology, art/fine arts, art history, biology/biological sciences, business administration/commerce/management, chemistry, classics, economics, English, French, geology, German, Greek, history, interdisciplinary studies, Latin, mathematics, music, neurosciences, philosophy, physics, political science/government, psychobiology, psychology, religious studies, sociology, Spanish, theater arts/drama.

## Furman University
Accounting, art/fine arts, Asian/Oriental studies, biology/biological sciences, business administration/commerce/management, chemistry, computer science, economics, education, English, French, geology, German, Greek, history, Latin, mathematics, music, music education, music history, philosophy, physical fitness/exercise science, physics, political science/government, psychology, religious studies, sacred music, sociology, Spanish, theater arts/drama, urban studies.

## Georgetown College
Accounting, American studies, art/fine arts, biology/biological sciences, business administration/commerce/management, chemistry, communication, computer information systems, computer science, (pre)dentistry sequence, early childhood education, ecology, education, elementary education, English, environmental sciences, European studies, finance/banking, French, German, history, international business, management information systems, marketing/retailing/merchandising, mathematics, medical technology, (pre)medicine sequence, music, music education, nursing, philosophy, physical education, physics, piano/organ, political science/government, psychology, recreation and leisure services, religious studies, secondary education, sociology, Spanish, speech/rhetoric/public address/debate, theater arts/drama, voice.

## Georgetown University
Accounting, American studies, Arabic, art/fine arts, biology/biological sciences, business administration/commerce/management, chemistry, Chinese, classics, computer science, (pre)dentistry sequence, economics, English, finance/banking, French, German, history, interdisciplinary studies, international business, international

economics, international relations, Italian, Japanese, liberal arts/general studies, linguistics, marketing/retailing/merchandising, mathematics, (pre)medicine sequence, nursing, philosophy, physics, political science/government, Portuguese, psychology, religious studies, Russian, sociology, Spanish.

## The George Washington University
Accounting, anthropology, applied mathematics, archaeology, art/fine arts, art history, Asian/Oriental studies, biology/biological sciences, business administration/commerce/management, business economics, chemistry, Chinese, civil engineering, classics, communication, computer engineering, computer science, criminal justice, dance, (pre)dentistry sequence, East Asian studies, ecology, economics, electrical engineering, emergency medical technology, English, environmental engineering, environmental sciences, European studies, finance/banking, French, geography, geology, Germanic languages and literature, history, human services, information science, interdisciplinary studies, international business, international studies, journalism, Judaic studies, Latin American studies, (pre)law sequence, liberal arts/general studies, management information systems, marketing/retailing/merchandising, mathematics, mechanical engineering, medical technology, (pre)medicine sequence, music, Near and Middle Eastern studies, operations research, philosophy, photography, physical fitness/exercise science, physician's assistant studies, physics, political science/government, psychology, public affairs and policy studies, radio and television studies, radiological sciences, recreation and leisure services, religious studies, Russian and Slavic studies, sociology, Spanish, speech pathology and audiology, speech/rhetoric/public address/debate, statistics, studio art, systems engineering, theater arts/drama.

## Georgia Institute of Technology
Aerospace engineering, applied mathematics, architecture, atmospheric sciences, biochemistry, biology/biological sciences, business administration/commerce/management, ceramic engineering, chemical engineering, chemistry, civil engineering, computer engineering, computer information systems, computer science, construction management, construction technologies, earth science, economics, electrical engineering, engineering mechanics, engineering sciences, health science, history of science, industrial design, industrial engineering, international studies, literature, materials engineering, mathematics, mechanical engineering, nuclear engineering, operations research, physics, polymer science, psychology, systems engineering, technology and public affairs, textile engineering, textiles and clothing.

## Georgia Southern University
Accounting, anthropology, art education, art/fine arts, athletic training, biology/biological sciences, broadcasting, business administration/commerce/management, business economics, business education, business machine technologies, chemistry, child care/child and family studies, civil engineering technology, communication, computer information systems, computer science, construction technologies, criminal justice, (pre)dentistry sequence, early childhood education, economics, education, electrical engineering technology, elementary education, engineering technology, English, family and consumer studies, fashion design and technology, fashion merchandising, finance/banking, food services management, French, geology, German, health education, health science, history, home economics, home economics education, hotel and restaurant management, industrial arts, industrial engineering technology, information science, interior design, journalism, law enforcement/police sciences, (pre)law sequence, liberal arts/general studies, management information systems, manufacturing technology, marketing/retailing/merchandising, mathematics, mechanical engineering technology,

medical technology, (pre)medicine sequence, middle school education, music, music education, nursing, nutrition, physical education, physical fitness/exercise science, physics, political science/government, printing technologies, psychology, reading education, recreation and leisure services, science education, secondary education, social science, sociology, Spanish, special education, sports administration, textiles and clothing, (pre)veterinary medicine sequence.

## Gettysburg College
Accounting, anthropology, art/fine arts, art history, biochemistry, biology/biological sciences, business administration/commerce/management, chemistry, classics, computer science, (pre)dentistry sequence, economics, education, elementary education, English, environmental studies, French, German, Greek, history, international business, international economics, international relations, international studies, Latin, Latin American studies, (pre)law sequence, liberal arts/general studies, literature, marine biology, mathematics, (pre)medicine sequence, modern languages, music, music education, philosophy, physical education, physics, political science/government, psychology, religious studies, Romance languages, science, science education, secondary education, social science, sociology, South Asian studies, Spanish, studio art, theater arts/drama, (pre)veterinary medicine sequence, Western civilization and culture, women's studies.

## GMI Engineering & Management Institute
Accounting, applied mathematics, business administration/commerce/management, computer engineering, computer information systems, computer science, electrical engineering, engineering physics, environmental sciences, industrial administration, industrial engineering, management information systems, manufacturing engineering, marketing/retailing/merchandising, mechanical engineering, statistics, systems engineering.

## Goshen College
Accounting, art education, art/fine arts, art therapy, biblical studies, bilingual/bicultural education, biology/biological sciences, broadcasting, business administration/commerce/management, business education, chemistry, child care/child and family studies, communication, computer information systems, computer science, (pre)dentistry sequence, dietetics, early childhood education, economics, education, elementary education, English, family services, German, Hispanic studies, history, journalism, (pre)law sequence, liberal arts/general studies, mathematics, (pre)medicine sequence, music, music education, natural sciences, nursing, nutrition, physical education, physical sciences, physics, political science/government, psychology, religious studies, science education, secondary education, social work, sociology, Spanish, teaching English as a second language, theater arts/drama, (pre)veterinary medicine sequence.

## Goucher College
American studies, anthropology, applied art, applied mathematics, art education, art/fine arts, art history, arts administration, behavioral sciences, biochemistry, biology/biological sciences, biomedical sciences, black/African-American studies, business administration/commerce/management, business economics, cell biology, chemistry, cognitive science, communication, computer programming, computer science, creative writing, dance, dance therapy, (pre)dentistry sequence, early childhood education, economics, education, elementary education, English, environmental biology, European studies, evolutionary biology, experimental psychology, French, German, historic preservation, history, interdisciplinary studies, international relations, international studies, Latin American studies, (pre)law sequence, liberal arts/general studies, marine biology, mathematics, (pre)medicine sequence, microbiology, modern

languages, molecular biology, music, music history, philosophy, physics, political science/government, psychology, public affairs and policy studies, radio and television studies, religious studies, Romance languages, Russian, Russian and Slavic studies, science, science education, secondary education, social science, social work, sociology, Spanish, special education, studio art, theater arts/drama, (pre)veterinary medicine sequence, voice, wind and percussion instruments, women's studies.

## Grinnell College
American studies, anthropology, art/fine arts, biology/biological sciences, black/African-American studies, chemistry, Chinese, classics, computer science, (pre)dentistry sequence, economics, English, environmental studies, European studies, French, German, history, interdisciplinary studies, Latin American studies, (pre)law sequence, linguistics, mathematics, (pre)medicine sequence, music, philosophy, physical sciences, physics, political science/government, psychology, religious studies, Russian, Russian and Slavic studies, science, sociology, Spanish, technology and public affairs, theater arts/drama, (pre)veterinary medicine sequence, women's studies.

## Grove City College
Accounting, biochemistry, biology/biological sciences, business administration/commerce/management, business economics, chemistry, communication, computer management, (pre)dentistry sequence, economics, electrical engineering, elementary education, English, finance/banking, French, history, industrial administration, international studies, (pre)law sequence, literature, marketing/retailing/merchandising, mathematics, mechanical engineering, (pre)medicine sequence, ministries, modern languages, molecular biology, music business, music education, philosophy, physics, political science/government, psychology, religious studies, secondary education, Spanish, (pre)veterinary medicine sequence.

## Guilford College
Accounting, anthropology, art/fine arts, biology/biological sciences, business administration/commerce/management, chemistry, criminal justice, (pre)dentistry sequence, early childhood education, economics, education, elementary education, English, French, geology, German, history, humanities, international studies, (pre)law sequence, liberal arts/general studies, mathematics, (pre)medicine sequence, music, philosophy, physical education, physician's assistant studies, physics, political science/government, psychology, religious studies, secondary education, sociology, Spanish, sports administration, sports medicine, theater arts/drama, (pre)veterinary medicine sequence.

## Gustavus Adolphus College
Accounting, American studies, anthropology, art education, art/fine arts, arts administration, athletic training, biochemistry, biology/biological sciences, business administration/commerce/management, business economics, chemistry, classics, communication, computer science, criminal justice, dance, (pre)dentistry sequence, economics, education, elementary education, English, French, geography, geology, German, health education, history, interdisciplinary studies, international business, Latin American studies, (pre)law sequence, mathematics, (pre)medicine sequence, music, music education, nursing, occupational therapy, philosophy, physical education, physical therapy, physics, political science/government, psychology, religious studies, Russian, Russian and Slavic studies, sacred music, Scandinavian languages/studies, secondary education, social science, sociology, Spanish, speech/rhetoric/public address/debate, theater arts/drama, (pre)veterinary medicine sequence.

## Hamilton College

African studies, American studies, anthropology, art/fine arts, art history, Asian/Oriental studies, biochemistry, biology/biological sciences, chemistry, classics, comparative literature, computer science, creative writing, dance, East Asian studies, economics, English, French, geology, German, Greek, history, international studies, Latin, linguistics, literature, mathematics, modern languages, molecular biology, music, Near and Middle Eastern studies, philosophy, physics, political science/government, psychobiology, psychology, public affairs and policy studies, religious studies, Russian and Slavic studies, sociology, Spanish, studio art, theater arts/drama, Western civilization and culture, women's studies.

## Hamline University

Anthropology, art/fine arts, art history, Asian/Oriental studies, biology/biological sciences, business administration/commerce/management, chemistry, communication, (pre)dentistry sequence, East Asian studies, East European and Soviet studies, economics, education, elementary education, English, environmental sciences, environmental studies, European studies, French, German, health education, history, international business, international economics, international studies, Judaic studies, Latin American studies, (pre)law sequence, legal studies, mathematics, medical technology, (pre)medicine sequence, music, music education, occupational therapy, paralegal studies, philosophy, physical education, physical fitness/exercise science, physical therapy, physics, political science/government, psychology, public administration, religious studies, Russian and Slavic studies, science education, secondary education, social science, sociology, Spanish, studio art, theater arts/drama, urban studies, (pre)veterinary medicine sequence, women's studies.

## Hampden-Sydney College

Biochemistry, biology/biological sciences, biophysics, business economics, chemistry, classics, computer science, economics, English, French, German, Greek, history, humanities, Latin, mathematics, philosophy, physics, political science/government, psychology, religious studies, Spanish.

## Hampshire College

African studies, agricultural sciences, American studies, animal sciences, anthropology, applied mathematics, archaeology, architecture, art/fine arts, art history, Asian/Oriental studies, astronomy, behavioral sciences, biochemistry, biology/biological sciences, black/African-American studies, botany/plant sciences, Canadian studies, cell biology, chemistry, child care/child and family studies, child psychology/child development, cognitive science, communication, community services, comparative literature, computer graphics, computer science, conservation, creative writing, dance, early childhood education, earth science, East Asian studies, East European and Soviet studies, ecology, economics, education, elementary education, English, environmental biology, environmental design, environmental health sciences, environmental sciences, environmental studies, ethnic studies, European studies, family and consumer studies, film and video production, film studies, genetics, geography, geology, health science, Hispanic studies, history, history of philosophy, history of science, human development, humanities, information science, interdisciplinary studies, international business, international economics, international relations, international studies, Islamic studies, jazz, journalism, Judaic studies, labor and industrial relations, labor studies, Latin American studies, legal studies, liberal arts/general studies, linguistics, literature, marine biology, marine sciences, mathematics, (pre)medicine sequence, medieval studies, Mexican-American/Chicano studies, microbiology, molecular biology, music, music history, Native American studies, natural sciences, Near

and Middle Eastern studies, neurosciences, nutrition, painting/drawing, peace studies, philosophy, photography, physical fitness/exercise science, physical sciences, physics, physiology, political science/government, psychobiology, psychology, public affairs and policy studies, public health, radio and television studies, religious studies, Russian and Slavic studies, science, sculpture, secondary education, social science, sociology, solar technologies, South Asian studies, Southeast Asian studies, statistics, studio art, telecommunications, theater arts/drama, urban studies, (pre)veterinary medicine sequence, women's studies.

## Harding University

Accounting, advertising, American studies, art education, art/fine arts, art history, biblical languages, biblical studies, biochemistry, biology/biological sciences, business administration/commerce/management, business education, chemistry, communication, computer information systems, computer programming, computer science, data processing, (pre)dentistry sequence, dietetics, early childhood education, economics, education, elementary education, English, fashion merchandising, finance/banking, food marketing, food services management, French, history, home economics, home economics education, interior design, international studies, journalism, (pre)law sequence, marketing/retailing/merchandising, mathematics, (pre)medicine sequence, modern languages, music, music education, nursing, painting/drawing, physical education, physics, piano/organ, political science/government, psychology, public administration, public relations, radio and television studies, religious education, religious studies, science, science education, secondary education, social science, social work, sociology, Spanish, special education, speech pathology and audiology, speech/rhetoric/public address/debate, sports administration, stringed instruments, systems science, theater arts/drama, theology, (pre)veterinary medicine sequence, voice.

## Harvard University

African languages, African studies, American studies, anthropology, applied mathematics, Arabic, archaeology, art/fine arts, art history, Asian/Oriental studies, astronomy, astrophysics, biblical languages, biochemistry, bioengineering, biology/biological sciences, biomedical engineering, biophysics, black/African-American studies, cell biology, chemistry, Chinese, classics, comparative literature, computer science, earth science, East Asian studies, East European and Soviet studies, ecology, economics, electronics engineering, engineering (general), engineering and applied sciences, engineering physics, engineering sciences, English, environmental design, environmental engineering, environmental sciences, environmental studies, ethnic studies, European studies, folklore, French, geology, geophysics, German, Germanic languages and literature, Greek, Hebrew, Hispanic studies, history, history of philosophy, history of science, humanities, information science, interdisciplinary studies, Italian, Japanese, Judaic studies, Latin, linguistics, literature, materials engineering, mathematics, mechanical engineering, medieval studies, modern languages, molecular biology, music, music history, Near and Middle Eastern studies, neurosciences, philosophy, physical sciences, physics, planetary and space sciences, political science/government, Portuguese, psychology, religious studies, Romance languages, Russian, Russian and Slavic studies, Scandinavian languages/studies, science, Slavic languages, social science, sociology, South Asian studies, Southeast Asian studies, Spanish, statistics, systems engineering, urban studies, Western civilization and culture, women's studies.

## Harvey Mudd College

Biology/biological sciences, chemistry, computer science, engineering (general), mathematics, physics.

## Haverford College

African studies, anthropology, archaeology, art/fine arts, art history, astronomy, biochemistry, biology/biological sciences, biophysics, chemistry, classics, comparative literature, computer science, East Asian studies, economics, English, French, geology, German, Greek, history, international studies, Italian, Latin, Latin American studies, (pre)law sequence, mathematics, (pre)medicine sequence, music, peace studies, philosophy, physics, political science/government, psychology, religious studies, Russian, sociology, Spanish, urban studies, (pre)veterinary medicine sequence, women's studies.

## Hendrix College

Accounting, American studies, art/fine arts, biology/biological sciences, business economics, chemistry, communication, (pre)dentistry sequence, economics, education, elementary education, English, French, German, history, humanities, international business, international studies, (pre)law sequence, mathematics, (pre)medicine sequence, music, philosophy, physical education, physics, political science/government, psychology, religious studies, sociology, Spanish, theater arts/drama, (pre)veterinary medicine sequence.

## Hillsdale College

Accounting, American studies, art/fine arts, biology/biological sciences, business administration/commerce/management, chemistry, classics, comparative literature, early childhood education, economics, education, elementary education, English, European studies, finance/banking, French, German, history, interdisciplinary studies, international business, marketing/retailing/merchandising, mathematics, (pre)medicine sequence, music, philosophy, physical education, physics, political science/government, psychology, religious studies, secondary education, sociology, Spanish, speech/rhetoric/public address/debate, theater arts/drama.

## Hiram College

Art history, biology/biological sciences, business administration/commerce/management, chemistry, classics, communication, computer science, (pre)dentistry sequence, economics, elementary education, English, French, German, history, international business, international economics, (pre)law sequence, mathematics, (pre)medicine sequence, music, philosophy, physics, political science/government, psychobiology, psychology, religious studies, secondary education, social science, sociology, Spanish, studio art, theater arts/drama, (pre)veterinary medicine sequence.

## Hobart College

American studies, anthropology, architecture, art/fine arts, art history, Asian/Oriental studies, biochemistry, biology/biological sciences, black/African-American studies, chemistry, Chinese, classics, comparative literature, computer science, dance, (pre)dentistry sequence, economics, English, environmental sciences, environmental studies, French, geology, German, Greek, history, Japanese, Judaic studies, Latin, (pre)law sequence, mathematics, (pre)medicine sequence, medieval studies, modern languages, music, philosophy, physics, political science/government, psychology, religious studies, Russian, Russian and Slavic studies, sociology, Spanish, studio art, theater arts/drama, urban studies, (pre)veterinary medicine sequence, women's studies.

## Hofstra University

Accounting, aerospace engineering, African studies, American studies, anthropology, applied art, art education, art/fine arts, art history, Asian/Oriental studies, athletic training, biochemistry, biology/biological sciences, biomedical engineering, black/African-American studies, botany/plant sciences, broadcasting, business administration/

commerce/management, business economics, business education, ceramic art and design, chemistry, civil engineering, classics, communication, computer engineering, computer information systems, computer management, computer science, creative writing, dance, (pre)dentistry sequence, earth science, economics, education, electrical engineering, elementary education, engineering (general), engineering mechanics, engineering sciences, English, environmental engineering, environmental sciences, film and video production, film studies, finance/banking, French, geography, geology, German, Germanic languages and literature, Greek, health education, health services administration, Hebrew, history, humanities, industrial engineering, interdisciplinary studies, international business, Italian, jewelry and metalsmithing, journalism, Judaic studies, Latin, (pre)law sequence, liberal arts/general studies, marketing/retailing/merchandising, mathematics, mechanical engineering, (pre)medicine sequence, modern languages, music, music business, music education, music history, natural sciences, painting/drawing, philosophy, photography, physical education, physical fitness/exercise science, physics, political science/government, psychology, radio and television studies, Romance languages, Russian, science, science education, sculpture, secondary education, social science, sociology, Spanish, speech pathology and audiology, speech/rhetoric/public address/debate, speech therapy, studio art, theater arts/drama, (pre)veterinary medicine sequence, voice.

## Hope College

Accounting, art education, art/fine arts, art history, biochemistry, biology/biological sciences, business administration/commerce/management, chemistry, classics, communication, computer science, dance, dance therapy, (pre)dentistry sequence, economics, education, elementary education, engineering physics, English, environmental sciences, French, geochemistry, geology, geophysics, German, history, humanities, interdisciplinary studies, international studies, Latin, mathematics, medical technology, (pre)medicine sequence, music, music education, nursing, philosophy, physical education, physics, political science/government, psychology, religious education, religious studies, science education, secondary education, social work, sociology, Spanish, special education, sports medicine, studio art, theater arts/drama, (pre)veterinary medicine sequence.

## Houghton College

Accounting, art education, art/fine arts, biblical studies, biology/biological sciences, business administration/commerce/management, chemistry, communication, creative writing, (pre)dentistry sequence, early childhood education, education, elementary education, English, French, history, humanities, international studies, (pre)law sequence, literature, mathematics, medical laboratory technology, medical technology, (pre)medicine sequence, ministries, music, music education, natural sciences, pastoral studies, philosophy, physical education, physical sciences, physics, piano/organ, political science/government, psychology, recreation and leisure services, religious education, religious studies, sacred music, science, science education, secondary education, social science, sociology, Spanish, stringed instruments, (pre)veterinary medicine sequence, voice, wind and percussion instruments.

## Illinois College

Accounting, art/fine arts, biology/biological sciences, business administration/commerce/management, business economics, chemistry, communication, computer information systems, computer science, cytotechnology, (pre)dentistry sequence, economics, education, elementary education, English, finance/banking, French, German, history, interdisciplinary studies, international studies, (pre)law sequence, liberal arts/general studies, management information systems, mathematics, medical technology, (pre)medicine sequence, music, occupational therapy, philosophy, physical education, physics, political science/government, psychology, religious studies, secondary education, sociology, Spanish, speech/rhetoric/public address/debate, theater arts/drama, (pre)veterinary medicine sequence.

## Illinois Institute of Technology

Accounting, aerospace engineering, applied mathematics, architecture, biology/biological sciences, business administration/commerce/management, chemical engineering, chemistry, civil engineering, computer engineering, computer science, electrical engineering, English, finance/banking, history, (pre)law sequence, management information systems, manufacturing technology, mathematics, mechanical engineering, (pre)medicine sequence, metallurgical engineering, philosophy, physics, political science/government, psychology, sociology.

## Illinois Wesleyan University

Accounting, applied art, art/fine arts, art history, arts administration, biology/biological sciences, business administration/commerce/management, chemistry, computer science, (pre)dentistry sequence, economics, education, elementary education, English, European studies, French, German, graphic arts, history, insurance, interdisciplinary studies, international business, international studies, Latin American studies, (pre)law sequence, liberal arts/general studies, mathematics, medical technology, (pre)medicine sequence, music, music business, music education, nursing, painting/drawing, philosophy, physics, piano/organ, political science/government, psychology, religious studies, sacred music, science education, secondary education, sociology, Spanish, stringed instruments, studio art, theater arts/drama, (pre)veterinary medicine sequence, voice, wind and percussion instruments.

## Iowa State University of Science and Technology

Accounting, advertising, aerospace engineering, agricultural business, agricultural education, agricultural engineering, agricultural sciences, agricultural technologies, agronomy/soil and crop sciences, animal sciences, anthropology, applied art, architecture, art/fine arts, biochemistry, biology/biological sciences, biophysics, botany/plant sciences, broadcasting, business administration/commerce/management, ceramic engineering, chemical engineering, chemistry, child care/child and family studies, child psychology/child development, city/community/regional planning, civil engineering, communication, community services, computer engineering, computer science, construction engineering, consumer services, dairy sciences, (pre)dentistry sequence, dietetics, early childhood education, earth science, ecology, economics, education, electrical engineering, elementary education, engineering (general), engineering sciences, English, entomology, environmental studies, family and consumer studies, family services, farm and ranch management, fashion design and technology, fashion merchandising, finance/banking, fish and game management, food sciences, food services management, food services technology, forestry, French, genetics, geology, German, graphic arts, health education, history, home economics, home economics education, horticulture, hotel and restaurant management, industrial engineering, interdisciplinary studies, interior design, international studies, journalism, landscape architecture/design, (pre)law sequence, liberal arts/general studies, linguistics, management information systems, marketing/retailing/merchandising, mathematics, mechanical engineering, medical illustration, (pre)medicine sequence, metallurgical engineering, meteorology, microbiology, music, music education, natural sciences, naval sciences, nutrition, ornamental horticulture, philosophy, physical education,

physics, political science/government, psychology, public administration, religious studies, Russian, secondary education, social work, sociology, Spanish, speech/rhetoric/public address/debate, statistics, textiles and clothing, theater arts/drama, transportation technologies, (pre)veterinary medicine sequence, vocational education, wildlife biology, zoology.

## James Madison University

Accounting, anthropology, art/fine arts, art history, biology/biological sciences, business administration/commerce/management, business economics, business education, chemistry, communication, computer information systems, computer science, dance, (pre)dentistry sequence, dietetics, early childhood education, economics, elementary education, English, finance/banking, French, geography, geology, German, health science, history, industrial administration, international business, international studies, (pre)law sequence, liberal arts/general studies, library science, marketing/retailing/merchandising, mathematics, medical technology, (pre)medicine sequence, modern languages, music, nursing, philosophy, physical education, physics, political science/government, psychology, public administration, religious studies, Russian, secretarial studies/office management, social science, social work, sociology, Spanish, special education, speech pathology and audiology, theater arts/drama, (pre)veterinary medicine sequence.

## John Carroll University

Accounting, art history, Asian/Oriental studies, biology/biological sciences, business administration/commerce/management, chemistry, classics, communication, computer science, (pre)dentistry sequence, early childhood education, East Asian studies, economics, education, electrical engineering, elementary education, engineering physics, English, environmental studies, finance/banking, French, German, gerontology, Greek, history, humanities, interdisciplinary studies, international economics, international studies, Judaic studies, Latin, (pre)law sequence, literature, marketing/retailing/merchandising, mathematics, (pre)medicine sequence, neurosciences, philosophy, physical education, physics, political science/government, psychology, public administration, religious education, religious studies, science, secondary education, sociology, Spanish, special education, (pre)veterinary medicine sequence.

## Johns Hopkins University

Anthropology, art history, astronomy, astrophysics, behavioral sciences, biology/biological sciences, biomedical engineering, biophysics, chemical engineering, chemistry, civil engineering, classics, cognitive science, computer engineering, computer science, creative writing, earth science, economics, electrical engineering, engineering (general), engineering mechanics, English, environmental engineering, environmental sciences, French, geography, German, Hispanic studies, history, history of science, humanities, international studies, Italian, Latin American studies, liberal arts/general studies, materials engineering, materials sciences, mathematics, mechanical engineering, music, natural sciences, Near and Middle Eastern studies, philosophy, physics, planetary and space sciences, political science/government, psychology, social science, sociology, Spanish.

## Juilliard School

Dance, music, opera, piano/organ, stringed instruments, theater arts/drama, voice, wind and percussion instruments.

## Juniata College

Accounting, American studies, anthropology, applied mathematics, art/fine arts, art history, arts administration, behavioral sciences, biochemistry, biology/biological sciences, botany/plant sciences, business administration/commerce/management, business economics, chemistry, communication, computer science, cytotechnology, (pre)dentistry sequence, drug and alcohol/substance abuse counseling, early childhood education, earth science, East European and Soviet studies, ecology, economics, education, elementary education, engineering (general), engineering sciences, English, environmental biology, environmental sciences, European studies, experimental psychology, finance/banking, French, genetics, geology, German, health science, history, humanities, human resources, interdisciplinary studies, international business, international relations, international studies, journalism, labor and industrial relations, (pre)law sequence, liberal arts/general studies, literature, management information systems, marine biology, marine sciences, marketing/retailing/merchandising, mathematics, medical technology, (pre)medicine sequence, microbiology, molecular biology, music, natural sciences, peace studies, philosophy, physics, political science/government, psychology, public administration, public relations, radiological technology, religious studies, Russian, science, science education, secondary education, social science, social work, sociology, Spanish, speech/rhetoric/public address/debate, studio art, (pre)veterinary medicine sequence, voice, Western civilization and culture, wildlife biology.

## Kalamazoo College
African studies, anthropology, art/fine arts, art history, biology/biological sciences, black/African-American studies, business administration/commerce/management, business economics, chemistry, Chinese, classics, computer science, (pre)dentistry sequence, economics, English, environmental sciences, European studies, French, German, Greek, health science, history, human development, human resources, human services, international business, international economics, international studies, Italian, Japanese, Latin, (pre)law sequence, literature, mathematics, (pre)medicine sequence, modern languages, music, philosophy, physics, political science/government, psychology, public affairs and policy studies, religious studies, Romance languages, Russian, secondary education, sociology, Spanish, studio art, theater arts/drama, women's studies.

## Kentucky Wesleyan College
Accounting, art education, art/fine arts, biology/biological sciences, business administration/commerce/management, chemistry, communication, computer science, criminal justice, (pre)dentistry sequence, elementary education, English, history, human resources, (pre)law sequence, mathematics, medical technology, (pre)medicine sequence, middle school education, modern languages, music, music education, nursing, philosophy, physical education, physics, political science/government, psychology, radio and television studies, religious studies, secondary education, social science, sociology, speech/rhetoric/public address/debate, telecommunications, theater arts/drama, (pre)veterinary medicine sequence.

## Kenyon College
American studies, anthropology, art/fine arts, art history, Asian/Oriental studies, biology/biological sciences, black/African-American studies, chemistry, classics, computer science, creative writing, dance, (pre)dentistry sequence, economics, English, environmental studies, French, German, Greek, history, humanities, interdisciplinary studies, international studies, Latin, (pre)law sequence, literature, mathematics, (pre)medicine sequence, modern languages, music, natural sciences, philosophy, physics, political science/government, psychology, religious studies, Romance languages, sociology, Spanish, studio art, theater arts/drama, (pre)veterinary medicine sequence, women's studies.

## Knox College
American studies, anthropology, art/fine arts, art history, biochemistry, biology/biological sciences, black/African-American studies, chemistry, classics, computer science, creative writing, (pre)dentistry sequence, economics, education, elementary education, English, environmental studies, French, German, history, international relations, literature, mathematics, (pre)medicine sequence, modern languages, music, philosophy, physics, political science/government, psychology, religious studies, Russian, Russian and Slavic studies, secondary education, sociology, Spanish, studio art, theater arts/drama, (pre)veterinary medicine sequence, women's studies.

## Lafayette College
American studies, anthropology, art/fine arts, art history, biochemistry, biology/biological sciences, business economics, chemical engineering, chemistry, civil engineering, computer science, economics, electrical engineering, engineering (general), English, environmental engineering, French, geology, German, history, international studies, mathematics, mechanical engineering, music, music history, philosophy, physics, political science/government, psychology, religious studies, Russian and Slavic studies, sociology, Spanish, studio art.

## Lake Forest College
African studies, American studies, anthropology, art history, Asian/Oriental studies, biology/biological sciences, business economics, chemistry, city/community/regional planning, comparative literature, computer science, (pre)dentistry sequence, economics, education, elementary education, English, environmental sciences, European studies, finance/banking, French, German, history, international relations, international studies, Latin American studies, (pre)law sequence, mathematics, (pre)medicine sequence, music, Near and Middle Eastern studies, philosophy, physics, political science/government, psychology, public administration, secondary education, sociology, Spanish, studio art, urban studies, (pre)veterinary medicine sequence, women's studies.

## La Salle University
Accounting, applied mathematics, art education, art/fine arts, art history, biochemistry, biology/biological sciences, broadcasting, business administration/commerce/management, business economics, business education, chemistry, classics, communication, computer information systems, computer programming, computer science, creative writing, criminal justice, (pre)dentistry sequence, early childhood education, earth science, economics, education, elementary education, English, environmental sciences, film studies, finance/banking, French, geology, German, Germanic languages and literature, Greek, health services administration, history, human resources, information science, international business, international studies, Italian, journalism, labor and industrial relations, labor studies, Latin, (pre)law sequence, liberal arts/general studies, literature, management information systems, marketing/retailing/merchandising, mathematics, (pre)medicine sequence, modern languages, music, music history, nursing, philosophy, physics, political science/government, psychology, public administration, radio and television studies, religious education, religious studies, retail management, Russian, Russian and Slavic studies, science education, secondary education, social science, social work, sociology, Spanish, special education, speech/rhetoric/public address/debate, theology, (pre)veterinary medicine sequence, women's studies.

## Lawrence University
Anthropology, art history, biology/biological sciences, chemistry, classics, cognitive science, computer science, (pre)dentistry sequence, East Asian studies, ecology, economics, English, environmental

sciences, French, geology, German, history, international economics, international studies, (pre)law sequence, linguistics, mathematics, (pre)medicine sequence, music, music education, neurosciences, philosophy, physics, piano/organ, political science/government, psychology, religious studies, Russian, Russian and Slavic studies, secondary education, Slavic languages, Spanish, stringed instruments, studio art, theater arts/drama, (pre)veterinary medicine sequence, voice, wind and percussion instruments, women's studies.

## Lehigh University

Accounting, American studies, anthropology, applied mathematics, architecture, art/fine arts, behavioral sciences, biochemistry, biology/biological sciences, business administration/commerce/management, business economics, chemical engineering, chemistry, civil engineering, classics, cognitive science, computer engineering, computer science, (pre)dentistry sequence, East Asian studies, economics, electrical engineering, engineering and applied sciences, engineering mechanics, engineering physics, English, environmental sciences, finance/banking, French, geology, geophysics, German, history, industrial engineering, international business, international relations, journalism, (pre)law sequence, marketing/retailing/merchandising, materials engineering, mathematics, mechanical engineering, (pre)medicine sequence, metallurgy, modern languages, molecular biology, music, natural sciences, neurosciences, philosophy, physics, political science/government, psychology, religious studies, Russian and Slavic studies, social science, sociology, Spanish, statistics, technical writing, theater arts/drama, urban studies, (pre)veterinary medicine sequence.

## Le Moyne College

Accounting, actuarial science, biology/biological sciences, business administration/commerce/management, business education, chemistry, communication, computer science, criminal justice, (pre)dentistry sequence, economics, education, elementary education, English, finance/banking, French, history, human resources, international business, international studies, labor and industrial relations, (pre)law sequence, marketing/retailing/merchandising, mathematics, (pre)medicine sequence, modern languages, operations research, philosophy, physics, political science/government, psychology, religious studies, science, science education, secondary education, sociology, Spanish, special education, statistics, teaching English as a second language, urban studies, (pre)veterinary medicine sequence.

## LeTourneau University

Accounting, aircraft and missile maintenance, aviation technology, biblical studies, biology/biological sciences, business administration/commerce/management, chemistry, computer engineering, computer science, computer technologies, (pre)dentistry sequence, electrical engineering, electrical engineering technology, engineering (general), engineering technology, English, flight training, history, industrial administration, (pre)law sequence, marketing/retailing/merchandising, mathematics, mechanical engineering, mechanical engineering technology, (pre)medicine sequence, ministries, natural sciences, physical education, psychology, public administration, religious studies, sports administration, (pre)veterinary medicine sequence, welding engineering, welding technology.

## Lewis & Clark College

Anthropology, art/fine arts, biochemistry, biology/biological sciences, business administration/commerce/management, chemistry, communication, computer science, (pre)dentistry sequence, East Asian studies, economics, English, French, German, Hispanic studies, history, international studies, (pre)law sequence, mathematics, (pre)medicine sequence, modern languages, music, philosophy, physics, political

science/government, psychology, religious studies, sociology, Spanish, theater arts/drama, (pre)veterinary medicine sequence.

## Linfield College

Accounting, anthropology, art education, art/fine arts, arts administration, biology/biological sciences, botany/plant sciences, business administration/commerce/management, chemistry, child psychology/child development, communication, computer science, creative writing, (pre)dentistry sequence, early childhood education, earth science, ecology, economics, education, elementary education, English, finance/banking, French, German, health education, history, humanities, information science, international business, Japanese, journalism, (pre)law sequence, liberal arts/general studies, mathematics, medical technology, (pre)medicine sequence, modern languages, music, music education, natural sciences, nursing, philosophy, physical education, physics, political science/government, psychology, public relations, radio and television studies, religious studies, science, science education, secondary education, sociology, Spanish, studio art, systems science, theater arts/drama, (pre)veterinary medicine sequence.

## Louisiana State University and Agricultural and Mechanical College

Accounting, advertising, agricultural business, agricultural economics, agricultural education, agricultural engineering, agronomy/soil and crop sciences, animal sciences, anthropology, architecture, art/fine arts, biochemistry, botany/plant sciences, broadcasting, business administration/commerce/management, business education, ceramic art and design, chemical engineering, chemistry, child care/child and family studies, civil engineering, communication, computer engineering, computer science, construction technologies, consumer services, dairy sciences, (pre)dentistry sequence, dietetics, economics, electrical engineering, elementary education, English, environmental sciences, family services, fashion merchandising, finance/banking, fish and game management, food sciences, forestry, French, geography, geology, German, graphic arts, history, home economics education, horticulture, industrial arts, industrial engineering, industrial engineering technology, interior design, international economics, journalism, landscape architecture/design, Latin, (pre)law sequence, liberal arts/general studies, literature, marketing/retailing/merchandising, mathematics, mechanical engineering, (pre)medicine sequence, microbiology, music, music education, nutrition, operations research, painting/drawing, petroleum/natural gas engineering, philosophy, physical education, physics, piano/organ, political science/government, printmaking, psychology, religious studies, Russian and Slavic studies, sculpture, sociology, Spanish, speech pathology and audiology, speech/rhetoric/public address/debate, studio art, textiles and clothing, theater arts/drama, (pre)veterinary medicine sequence, vocational education, voice, wildlife management, zoology.

## Loyola College

Accounting, advertising, art/fine arts, art history, biology/biological sciences, business administration/commerce/management, business economics, chemistry, classics, communication, computer engineering, computer science, creative writing, (pre)dentistry sequence, economics, education, electrical engineering, elementary education, engineering (general), engineering sciences, English, finance/banking, French, German, history, interdisciplinary studies, international business, journalism, Latin, (pre)law sequence, management information systems, marketing/retailing/merchandising, mathematics, (pre)medicine sequence, military science, ministries, modern languages, music, pastoral studies, philosophy, photography, physics, political science/government, psychology, public relations, secondary education, sociology, Spanish, speech pathology and audiology, studio art, theater arts/drama, theology, (pre)veterinary medicine sequence.

## Loyola University Chicago
Accounting, anthropology, art/fine arts, biology/biological sciences, business administration/commerce/management, business economics, chemistry, classics, communication, computer information systems, computer science, criminal justice, (pre)dentistry sequence, economics, elementary education, English, finance/banking, French, German, Greek, history, Italian, Latin, (pre)law sequence, linguistics, management information systems, marketing/retailing/merchandising, mathematics, (pre)medicine sequence, music, nursing, philosophy, physics, political science/government, psychology, social work, sociology, Spanish, special education, speech/rhetoric/public address/debate, statistics, theater arts/drama, theology, (pre)veterinary medicine sequence.

## Luther College
Accounting, African studies, anthropology, art education, art/fine arts, arts administration, biology/biological sciences, black/African-American studies, business administration/commerce/management, chemistry, classics, communication, computer science, cytotechnology, dance, (pre)dentistry sequence, economics, education, elementary education, engineering sciences, English, environmental biology, French, German, Greek, health education, Hebrew, history, interdisciplinary studies, international business, international studies, Latin, Latin American studies, (pre)law sequence, management information systems, marine biology, mathematics, medical technology, (pre)medicine sequence, modern languages, museum studies, music, music business, music education, nursing, philosophy, physical education, physics, political science/government, psychobiology, psychology, religious studies, Scandinavian languages/studies, secondary education, social work, sociology, Spanish, special education, speech pathology and audiology, speech/rhetoric/public address/debate, sports administration, sports medicine, statistics, theater arts/drama, (pre)veterinary medicine sequence.

## Lyon College
Art/fine arts, biology/biological sciences, chemistry, economics, English, history, mathematics, music, philosophy, political science/government, psychology, religious studies, theater arts/drama.

## Macalester College
Anthropology, art history, biology/biological sciences, chemistry, classics, communication, computer science, East Asian studies, economics, English, environmental studies, French, geography, geology, German, Greek, history, humanities, international studies, Latin, Latin American studies, linguistics, mathematics, music, philosophy, physics, political science/government, psychology, religious studies, Russian, Russian and Slavic studies, social science, sociology, Spanish, studio art, theater arts/drama, urban studies, women's studies.

## Manhattan School of Music
Jazz, music, piano/organ, stringed instruments, voice, wind and percussion instruments.

## Mannes College of Music, New School for Social Research
Jazz, music, opera, piano/organ, stringed instruments, voice, wind and percussion instruments.

## Marietta College
Accounting, adult and continuing education, advertising, art/fine arts, athletic training, biochemistry, biology/biological sciences, business administration/commerce/management, chemistry, communication, computer information systems, computer science, (pre)dentistry sequence, economics, education, elementary education, engineering (general), English, environmental sciences, French, geology, history, human resources, industrial engineering, international business, journalism, (pre)law sequence, liberal arts/general studies, marketing/retailing/merchandising, mathematics, (pre)medicine sequence, modern languages, music, petroleum/natural gas engineering, philosophy, physics, political science/government, psychology, public relations, radio and television studies, religious studies, secondary education, Spanish, speech/rhetoric/public address/debate, sports medicine, studio art, theater arts/drama, (pre)veterinary medicine sequence.

## Marlboro College
African studies, American studies, anthropology, applied mathematics, art/fine arts, art history, Asian/Oriental studies, astronomy, astrophysics, behavioral sciences, biblical studies, biochemistry, biology/biological sciences, botany/plant sciences, cell biology, ceramic art and design, chemistry, child psychology/child development, classics, comparative literature, computer science, conservation, creative writing, dance, (pre)dentistry sequence, earth science, East Asian studies, East European and Soviet studies, ecology, economics, energy management technologies, English, environmental biology, environmental design, environmental education, environmental sciences, ethnic studies, European studies, experimental psychology, film studies, folklore, forestry, French, German, Greek, history, history of philosophy, human ecology, humanities, interdisciplinary studies, international economics, international studies, Italian, jazz, Latin, Latin American studies, (pre)law sequence, linguistics, literature, marine biology, mathematics, (pre)medicine sequence, medieval studies, microbiology, modern languages, molecular biology, music, music history, natural sciences, painting/drawing, peace studies, philosophy, photography, physical sciences, physics, piano/organ, planetary and space sciences, political science/government, Portuguese, psychology, religious studies, Romance languages, Russian, Russian and Slavic studies, sacred music, Scandinavian languages/studies, sculpture, social science, social work, sociology, solar technologies, Spanish, stringed instruments, studio art, theater arts/drama, (pre)veterinary medicine sequence, voice, wind and percussion instruments, women's studies, wood sciences.

## Marquette University
Accounting, advertising, anthropology, biochemistry, biology/biological sciences, biomedical engineering, broadcasting, business administration/commerce/management, business economics, chemistry, civil engineering, classics, communication, computer engineering, computer science, criminal justice, criminology, dental services, (pre)dentistry sequence, economics, education, electrical engineering, electronics engineering, elementary education, engineering (general), English, environmental engineering, finance/banking, French, German, history, human development, humanities, human resources, industrial engineering, interdisciplinary studies, international business, international relations, journalism, (pre)law sequence, management information systems, marketing/retailing/merchandising, mathematics, mechanical engineering, medical laboratory technology, (pre)medicine sequence, middle school education, molecular biology, natural sciences, nursing, philosophy, physics, political science/government, psychology, public relations, secondary education, social science, social work, sociology, Spanish,

speech pathology and audiology, speech/rhetoric/public address/ debate, statistics, theater arts/drama, theology.

## Maryland Institute, College of Art

Applied art, art education, art/fine arts, ceramic art and design, commercial art, graphic arts, illustration, interior design, painting/ drawing, photography, printmaking, sculpture, studio art, textile arts.

## Maryville University of Saint Louis

Accounting, actuarial science, art education, art/fine arts, biology/ biological sciences, business administration/commerce/management, chemistry, communication, computer information systems, early childhood education, education, elementary education, English, health services administration, history, humanities, interior design, (pre)law sequence, liberal arts/general studies, management information systems, marketing/retailing/merchandising, mathematics, medical technology, (pre)medicine sequence, middle school education, music, music therapy, nursing, philosophy, physical therapy, political science/ government, psychology, religious studies, science, science education, secondary education, sociology, studio art.

## Mary Washington College

American studies, art/fine arts, art history, biology/biological sciences, business administration/commerce/management, chemistry, classics, computer science, dance, (pre)dentistry sequence, economics, elementary education, English, environmental sciences, French, geography, geology, German, historic preservation, history, interdisciplinary studies, international studies, Latin, (pre)law sequence, liberal arts/general studies, mathematics, (pre)medicine sequence, modern languages, music, music education, philosophy, physics, political science/government, psychology, religious studies, secondary education, sociology, Spanish, studio art, theater arts/drama, (pre)veterinary medicine sequence.

## Massachusetts College of Art

Applied art, architecture, art education, art/fine arts, art history, ceramic art and design, commercial art, computer graphics, fashion design and technology, film and video production, graphic arts, illustration, industrial design, jewelry and metalsmithing, painting/ drawing, photography, printmaking, sculpture, studio art, textile arts.

## Massachusetts Institute of Technology

Aerospace engineering, aerospace sciences, American studies, anthropology, applied mathematics, archaeology, architectural engineering, architecture, art history, astronomy, astrophysics, atmospheric sciences, bacteriology, biochemistry, bioengineering, biology/biological sciences, biomedical engineering, biophysics, business administration/commerce/management, business economics, cell biology, ceramic engineering, chemical engineering, chemistry, city/community/regional planning, civil engineering, cognitive science, communication, computer engineering, computer information systems, computer programming, computer science, construction engineering, construction management, creative writing, (pre)dentistry sequence, earth science, economics, electrical engineering, electronics engineering, engineering (general), engineering and applied sciences, engineering design, engineering management, engineering physics, environmental design, environmental engineering, environmental health sciences, environmental sciences, fluid and thermal sciences, French, genetics, geochemistry, geological engineering, geology, geophysical engineering, geophysics, German, health science, history, history of science, humanities, information science, interdisciplinary studies, international studies, Latin American studies, (pre)law sequence, liberal arts/general studies, linguistics, literature, management engineering, management information systems, manufacturing engineering,

manufacturing technology, marine biology, marine engineering, materials engineering, materials sciences, mathematics, mechanical engineering, (pre)medicine sequence, medieval studies, metallurgical engineering, metallurgical technology, metallurgy, meteorology, microbiology, mining and mineral engineering, molecular biology, music, naval architecture, naval sciences, neurosciences, nuclear engineering, nuclear physics, ocean engineering, pharmacy/ pharmaceutical sciences, philosophy, photography, physical sciences, physics, physiology, planetary and space sciences, plastics engineering, political science/government, polymer science, psychology, robotics, Russian, Russian and Slavic studies, science, Spanish, statistics, systems science, technology and public affairs, theater arts/drama, transportation engineering, urban studies, (pre)veterinary medicine sequence, women's studies.

## Messiah College

Accounting, art/fine arts, art history, behavioral sciences, biblical studies, business administration/commerce/management, chemistry, civil engineering technology, clinical psychology, communication, computer information systems, computer science, dietetics, early childhood education, education, elementary education, engineering (general), English, experimental psychology, family services, French, geography, German, history, humanities, human resources, journalism, (pre)law sequence, liberal arts/general studies, marketing/retailing/ merchandising, mathematics, medical technology, (pre)medicine sequence, modern languages, music, music education, natural sciences, nursing, pastoral studies, physical education, physics, psychology, radio and television studies, recreation and leisure services, religious education, religious studies, secondary education, social science, social work, sociology, Spanish, speech/rhetoric/public address/debate, sports medicine, stringed instruments, theater arts/ drama, theology, (pre)veterinary medicine sequence, voice.

## Miami University

Accounting, American studies, anthropology, architecture, art education, art/fine arts, art history, athletic training, biology/biological sciences, black/African-American studies, botany/plant sciences, broadcasting, business administration/commerce/management, business economics, chemistry, child care/child and family studies, classics, communication, computer science, creative writing, criminal justice, (pre)dentistry sequence, dietetics, early childhood education, earth science, economics, education, elementary education, engineering management, engineering physics, English, environmental design, family and consumer studies, finance/banking, French, geography, geology, German, Greek, health education, history, home economics, home economics education, human resources, interdisciplinary studies, interior design, international relations, international studies, journalism, Latin, (pre)law sequence, linguistics, management information systems, manufacturing engineering, marketing/retailing/merchandising, mathematics, medical technology, (pre)medicine sequence, microbiology, music, music education, nursing, operations research, paper and pulp sciences, philosophy, physical education, physical fitness/exercise science, physics, political science/government, psychology, public administration, public relations, purchasing/inventory management, religious studies, Russian, science education, secondary education, social work, sociology, Spanish, special education, speech pathology and audiology, speech/rhetoric/public address/debate, speech therapy, sports administration, sports medicine, statistics, studio art, systems science, theater arts/drama, urban studies, zoology.

## Michigan State University

Accounting, advertising, agricultural education, agricultural engineering, agricultural sciences, agronomy/soil and crop sciences,

American studies, animal sciences, anthropology, art education, art/fine arts, art history, Asian/Oriental studies, astrophysics, biochemistry, biology/biological sciences, biotechnology, botany/plant sciences, business administration/commerce/management, chemical engineering, chemistry, child psychology/child development, city/community/regional planning, civil engineering, communication, community services, computer engineering, computer science, construction management, criminal justice, (pre)dentistry sequence, dietetics, early childhood education, earth science, East Asian studies, economics, education, electrical engineering, elementary education, engineering mechanics, engineering technology, English, entomology, environmental studies, family and consumer studies, family services, fashion design and technology, fashion merchandising, finance/banking, fish and game management, food sciences, food services management, forestry, French, geography, geology, German, history, home economics, home economics education, horticulture, hotel and restaurant management, humanities, human resources, interdisciplinary studies, interior design, international relations, journalism, laboratory technologies, landscape architecture/design, Latin, (pre)law sequence, linguistics, manufacturing technology, marketing/retailing/merchandising, materials engineering, materials sciences, mathematics, mechanical engineering, medical technology, (pre)medicine sequence, microbiology, music, music education, music therapy, natural resource management, nursing, nutrition, parks management, philosophy, physical education, physical fitness/exercise science, physical sciences, physics, physiology, political science/government, psychology, public administration, public affairs and policy studies, purchasing/inventory management, recreational facilities management, religious studies, Russian, science education, secondary education, social science, social work, sociology, Spanish, speech pathology and audiology, statistics, stringed instruments, studio art, telecommunications, theater arts/drama, (pre)veterinary medicine sequence, veterinary technology, voice, wildlife management, women's studies, zoology.

## Michigan Technological University
Accounting, applied mathematics, biochemistry, bioengineering, biology/biological sciences, biomedical engineering, biotechnology, business administration/commerce/management, business economics, chemical engineering, chemistry, civil engineering, computer engineering, computer information systems, computer programming, computer science, construction engineering, (pre)dentistry sequence, earth science, ecology, economics, electrical engineering, electrical engineering technology, engineering (general), engineering management, engineering mechanics, engineering physics, engineering technology, English, environmental engineering, finance/banking, forestry, geological engineering, geology, geophysics, history, liberal arts/general studies, management information systems, manufacturing engineering, marketing/retailing/merchandising, materials engineering, mathematics, mechanical engineering, mechanical engineering technology, medical technology, (pre)medicine sequence, metallurgical engineering, microbiology, mining and mineral engineering, physical sciences, physics, science education, secondary education, social science, statistics, surveying technology, technical writing, (pre)veterinary medicine sequence, wood sciences.

## Middlebury College
American studies, anthropology, art/fine arts, art history, Asian/Oriental studies, biochemistry, biology/biological sciences, chemistry, Chinese, classics, computer science, dance, (pre)dentistry sequence, East Asian studies, East European and Soviet studies, ecology, economics, education, elementary education, English, film studies, French, geography, geology, German, history, humanities, international economics, international studies, Italian, Japanese, (pre)law sequence, liberal arts/general studies, literature, mathematics, (pre)medicine

sequence, modern languages, molecular biology, music, natural sciences, painting/drawing, philosophy, physical sciences, physics, political science/government, psychology, religious studies, Romance languages, Russian, Russian and Slavic studies, science, secondary education, social science, sociology, Southeast Asian studies, Spanish, studio art, theater arts/drama, (pre)veterinary medicine sequence, women's studies.

## Millikin University
Accounting, American studies, art education, art/fine arts, arts administration, art therapy, athletic training, behavioral sciences, biology/biological sciences, business administration/commerce/management, business economics, chemistry, commercial art, communication, computer graphics, computer management, computer science, creative writing, (pre)dentistry sequence, economics, education, elementary education, English, environmental sciences, experimental psychology, finance/banking, French, German, history, human resources, human services, interdisciplinary studies, international business, international studies, (pre)law sequence, liberal arts/general studies, literature, management information systems, marketing/retailing/merchandising, mathematics, (pre)medicine sequence, modern languages, music, music business, music education, nursing, philosophy, physical education, physics, political science/government, psychology, religious studies, sacred music, science, science education, secondary education, social science, social work, sociology, Spanish, studio art, theater arts/drama, (pre)veterinary medicine sequence, voice.

## Millsaps College
Accounting, art/fine arts, biology/biological sciences, business administration/commerce/management, chemistry, classics, computer science, economics, education, elementary education, English, French, geology, Greek, history, Latin, mathematics, music, music education, philosophy, physics, piano/organ, political science/government, psychology, religious studies, sacred music, sociology, Spanish, theater arts/drama, voice.

## Mills College
American studies, anthropology, art/fine arts, art history, biochemistry, biology/biological sciences, business economics, chemistry, child psychology/child development, communication, comparative literature, computer science, creative writing, dance, early childhood education, economics, education, elementary education, English, environmental sciences, ethnic studies, French, Germanic languages and literature, Hispanic studies, history, interdisciplinary studies, international studies, liberal arts/general studies, mathematics, (pre)medicine sequence, music, philosophy, political, legal, and economic analysis, psychology, social science, sociology, statistics, studio art, theater arts/drama, women's studies.

## Milwaukee School of Engineering
Architectural engineering, biomedical engineering, business administration/commerce/management, communication equipment technology, computer engineering, electrical engineering, electrical engineering technology, industrial engineering, manufacturing technology, mechanical engineering, mechanical engineering technology, technical writing.

## Monmouth College (IL)
Accounting, art/fine arts, biology/biological sciences, business administration/commerce/management, chemistry, classics, communication, computer science, economics, education, elementary education, English, environmental sciences, Greek, history, humanities, Latin, liberal arts/general studies, mathematics, military science,

modern languages, music, natural sciences, philosophy, physical education, physics, political science/government, psychology, religious studies, secondary education, sociology, Spanish, special education, speech/rhetoric/public address/debate, theater arts/drama.

## Morehouse College

Accounting, actuarial science, architecture, art/fine arts, biology/biological sciences, business administration/commerce/management, chemistry, computer science, (pre)dentistry sequence, economics, education, engineering (general), English, finance/banking, French, German, history, insurance, interdisciplinary studies, international studies, (pre)law sequence, marketing/retailing/merchandising, mathematics, (pre)medicine sequence, music, philosophy, physical education, physics, political science/government, psychology, real estate, religious studies, sociology, Spanish, theater arts/drama, urban studies.

## Mount Holyoke College

American studies, anthropology, art history, Asian/Oriental studies, astronomy, biochemistry, biology/biological sciences, black/African-American studies, chemistry, classics, computer science, dance, economics, education, English, environmental studies, European studies, French, geography, geology, German, Greek, history, international studies, Italian, Judaic studies, Latin, Latin American studies, mathematics, medieval studies, music, philosophy, physics, political science/government, psychobiology, psychology, religious studies, Romance languages, Russian, Russian and Slavic studies, sociology, Spanish, statistics, studio art, theater arts/drama, women's studies.

## Mount Union College

Accounting, American studies, art education, art/fine arts, Asian/Oriental studies, astronomy, biology/biological sciences, business administration/commerce/management, chemistry, communication, computer information systems, computer science, cytotechnology, (pre)dentistry sequence, economics, education, elementary education, English, French, geology, health education, history, information science, interdisciplinary studies, international business, international economics, Japanese, (pre)law sequence, liberal arts/general studies, mathematics, medical technology, (pre)medicine sequence, music, music education, philosophy, physical education, physics, political science/government, psychology, religious studies, secondary education, sociology, Spanish, special education, sports administration, sports medicine, theater arts/drama.

## Muhlenberg College

Accounting, American studies, art/fine arts, art history, biochemistry, biology/biological sciences, business administration/commerce/management, chemistry, classics, communication, computer information systems, computer science, dance, (pre)dentistry sequence, economics, elementary education, English, environmental studies, French, German, Greek, history, human resources, information science, international economics, international studies, Latin, (pre)law sequence, mathematics, (pre)medicine sequence, ministries, music, natural sciences, philosophy, physical sciences, physics, political science/government, psychology, religious studies, Russian and Slavic studies, secondary education, social science, social work, sociology, Spanish, studio art, theater arts/drama, (pre)veterinary medicine sequence.

## Nebraska Wesleyan University

Art/fine arts, biology/biological sciences, business administration/commerce/management, chemistry, communication, computer information systems, computer science, economics, elementary education, English, French, German, history, interdisciplinary studies,

international studies, mathematics, middle school education, music, music education, nursing, paralegal studies, philosophy, physical education, physical fitness/exercise science, physics, political science/government, psychobiology, psychology, religious studies, science education, social work, sociology, Spanish, special education, sports administration, theater arts/drama.

## New College of the University of South Florida

Anthropology, art/fine arts, art history, behavioral sciences, biology/biological sciences, cell biology, ceramic art and design, chemistry, child psychology/child development, classics, comparative literature, ecology, economics, environmental biology, environmental studies, European studies, evolutionary biology, experimental psychology, French, genetics, German, Germanic languages and literature, Greek, history, history of philosophy, interdisciplinary studies, international relations, Latin, (pre)law sequence, liberal arts/general studies, literature, marine biology, marine sciences, mathematics, (pre)medicine sequence, medieval studies, modern languages, molecular biology, music, music history, natural sciences, painting/drawing, philosophy, physics, political science/government, psychology, public affairs and policy studies, religious studies, Russian, sculpture, social science, sociology, Spanish, studio art.

## New England Conservatory of Music

Jazz, music, music education, music history, opera, piano/organ, stringed instruments, voice, wind and percussion instruments.

## New Jersey Institute of Technology

Actuarial science, applied mathematics, architecture, business administration/commerce/management, chemical engineering, chemistry, civil engineering, civil engineering technology, computer engineering, computer science, (pre)dentistry sequence, electrical engineering, electrical engineering technology, engineering (general), engineering and applied sciences, engineering sciences, engineering technology, environmental sciences, industrial engineering, information science, interdisciplinary studies, (pre)law sequence, manufacturing engineering, manufacturing technology, materials engineering, materials sciences, mechanical engineering, mechanical engineering technology, (pre)medicine sequence, physics, statistics, surveying technology, technology and public affairs.

## New Mexico Institute of Mining and Technology

Applied mathematics, astrophysics, atmospheric sciences, behavioral sciences, biology/biological sciences, business administration/commerce/management, chemical engineering, chemistry, computer programming, computer science, (pre)dentistry sequence, electrical engineering, electronics engineering, engineering (general), engineering mechanics, engineering sciences, environmental biology, environmental engineering, environmental sciences, experimental psychology, geochemistry, geological engineering, geology, geophysics, interdisciplinary studies, liberal arts/general studies, materials engineering, mathematics, medical technology, (pre)medicine sequence, metallurgical engineering, mining and mineral engineering, petroleum/natural gas engineering, physics, psychology, science, science education, technical writing, (pre)veterinary medicine sequence.

## New York School of Interior Design

Interior design.

## New York University

Accounting, actuarial science, adult and continuing education, anthropology, applied mathematics, art education, art/fine arts, art history, Asian/Oriental studies, audio engineering, behavioral sciences, biochemistry, biology/biological sciences, broadcasting, business administration/commerce/management, business economics, chemical engineering, chemistry, child psychology/child development, city/community/regional planning, civil engineering, classics, communication, comparative literature, computer information systems, computer science, dance, (pre)dentistry sequence, dietetics, early childhood education, East Asian studies, economics, education, electrical engineering, elementary education, engineering (general), engineering physics, English, European studies, film and video production, film studies, finance/banking, food sciences, food services management, French, German, Germanic languages and literature, Greek, Hebrew, Hispanic studies, history, hotel and restaurant management, humanities, information science, interdisciplinary studies, international business, international relations, Islamic studies, Italian, jazz, journalism, Judaic studies, Latin, Latin American studies, (pre)law sequence, liberal arts/general studies, linguistics, literature, marketing/retailing/merchandising, materials engineering, mathematics, mechanical engineering, (pre)medicine sequence, medieval studies, middle school education, modern languages, music, music business, music education, music history, natural sciences, Near and Middle Eastern studies, nursing, nutrition, opera, operations research, painting/drawing, philosophy, photography, physical therapy, physics, piano/organ, political science/government, Portuguese, radio and television studies, rehabilitation therapy, religious studies, retail management, Romance languages, Russian, Russian and Slavic studies, science education, sculpture, secondary education, Slavic languages, social science, social work, sociology, Spanish, special education, speech pathology and audiology, statistics, studio art, theater arts/drama, urban studies, (pre)veterinary medicine sequence, voice, wind and percussion instruments, women's studies.

## North Carolina School of the Arts

Dance, film and video production, film studies, music, theater arts/drama.

## North Carolina State University

Accounting, aerospace engineering, African studies, agricultural business, agricultural economics, agricultural education, agricultural engineering, agricultural sciences, agronomy/soil and crop sciences, animal sciences, anthropology, applied mathematics, architecture, biochemistry, biology/biological sciences, botany/plant sciences, business administration/commerce/management, chemical engineering, chemistry, civil engineering, communication, comparative literature, computer engineering, computer science, conservation, construction engineering, construction management, criminal justice, (pre)dentistry sequence, economics, education, electrical engineering, English, entomology, environmental design, environmental engineering, environmental sciences, film studies, fish and game management, food sciences, forestry, French, geology, geophysics, German, history, horticulture, humanities, human resources, industrial design, industrial engineering, interdisciplinary studies, Japanese, journalism, landscape architecture/design, liberal arts/general studies, linguistics, marketing/retailing/merchandising, materials engineering, mathematics, mechanical engineering, medical technology, (pre)medicine sequence, meteorology, microbiology, natural resource management, nuclear engineering, nutrition, ornamental horticulture, paper and pulp sciences, parks management, philosophy, physical education, physics, political science/government, poultry sciences, psychology, public affairs and policy studies, recreational facilities management, Russian and Slavic studies, science education, secondary education, social

science, social work, sociology, Spanish, speech therapy, statistics, technical writing, textile engineering, textiles and clothing, tourism and travel, (pre)veterinary medicine sequence, vocational education, wildlife biology, women's studies, wood sciences, zoology.

## North Central College

Accounting, actuarial science, anthropology, art education, art/fine arts, athletic training, biochemistry, biology/biological sciences, broadcasting, business administration/commerce/management, business education, chemistry, classics, communication, computer information systems, computer science, (pre)dentistry sequence, early childhood education, economics, education, elementary education, English, finance/banking, French, German, graphic arts, Greek, health education, history, humanities, international business, international relations, Japanese, Latin, (pre)law sequence, liberal arts/general studies, literature, management information systems, marketing/retailing/merchandising, mathematics, (pre)medicine sequence, modern languages, music, natural sciences, philosophy, physical education, physical fitness/exercise science, physics, piano/organ, political science/government, psychology, public relations, reading education, religious studies, science education, secondary education, social science, sociology, Spanish, speech/rhetoric/public address/debate, sports medicine, theater arts/drama, (pre)veterinary medicine sequence, voice.

## Northeast Missouri State University

Accounting, agricultural economics, agricultural sciences, agronomy/soil and crop sciences, animal sciences, applied art, art/fine arts, art history, biology/biological sciences, business administration/commerce/management, chemistry, commercial art, communication, computer science, criminal justice, (pre)dentistry sequence, economics, English, equestrian studies, finance/banking, French, German, graphic arts, health science, history, journalism, law enforcement/police sciences, (pre)law sequence, mathematics, (pre)medicine sequence, music, nursing, philosophy, physical fitness/exercise science, physics, piano/organ, political science/government, psychology, public health, religious studies, Russian, sociology, Spanish, speech pathology and audiology, speech/rhetoric/public address/debate, studio art, theater arts/drama, (pre)veterinary medicine sequence, voice.

## Northwestern College (IA)

Accounting, art/fine arts, biology/biological sciences, business administration/commerce/management, business education, chemistry, communication, computer science, economics, education, elementary education, English, environmental sciences, French, history, humanities, mathematics, medical technology, music, music education, philosophy, physical education, political science/government, psychology, recreation and leisure services, religious studies, secondary education, social work, sociology, Spanish, theater arts/drama, theology.

## Northwestern University

American studies, anthropology, applied mathematics, art/fine arts, art history, Asian/Oriental studies, astronomy, astrophysics, behavioral sciences, biochemistry, bioengineering, biology/biological sciences, biomedical engineering, black/African-American studies, broadcasting, cell biology, chemical engineering, chemistry, child psychology/child development, city/community/regional planning, civil engineering, classics, cognitive science, communication, comparative literature, computer engineering, computer science, dance, (pre)dentistry sequence, economics, education, electrical engineering, engineering (general), engineering and applied sciences, engineering sciences, English, environmental engineering, environmental sciences, ethnic studies, film studies, French, geology, German, Germanic languages and literature, Greek, Hispanic studies, history, human development, humanities, industrial engineering, interdisciplinary studies, Italian, journalism, Latin, Latin American studies, linguistics, literature, manufacturing engineering, materials engineering, materials sciences, mathematics, mechanical engineering, (pre)medicine sequence, microbiology, modern languages, molecular biology, music, music education, music history, natural sciences, neurosciences, opera, philosophy, physics, piano/organ, political science/government, Portuguese, psychology, radio and television studies, religious studies, Romance languages, Russian, Russian and Slavic studies, sacred music, science education, secondary education, Slavic languages, social science, sociology, Spanish, speech pathology and audiology, speech/rhetoric/public address/debate, speech therapy, statistics, stringed instruments, studio art, theater arts/drama, urban studies, voice, wind and percussion instruments, women's studies.

## Oberlin College

Anthropology, archaeology, art/fine arts, art history, biochemistry, biology/biological sciences, black/African-American studies, chemistry, classics, comparative literature, computer science, creative writing, dance, East Asian studies, ecology, economics, English, environmental studies, French, geology, German, Greek, history, jazz, Judaic studies, Latin, Latin American studies, legal studies, mathematics, music, music education, music history, Near and Middle Eastern studies, neurosciences, philosophy, physics, piano/organ, political science/government, psychobiology, psychology, religious studies, Romance languages, Russian, Russian and Slavic studies, sociology, Spanish, stringed instruments, studio art, theater arts/drama, voice, wind and percussion instruments, women's studies.

## Occidental College

American studies, anthropology, art/fine arts, art history, Asian/Oriental studies, behavioral sciences, biochemistry, biology/biological sciences, chemistry, Chinese, classics, cognitive science, comparative literature, (pre)dentistry sequence, East Asian studies, East European and Soviet studies, economics, English, environmental sciences, film studies, French, geology, geophysics, German, Germanic languages and literature, Hispanic studies, history, interdisciplinary studies, international studies, Japanese, Latin American studies, (pre)law sequence, literature, marine biology, mathematics, (pre)medicine sequence, modern languages, molecular biology, music, music education, music history, neurosciences, painting/drawing, philosophy, physical fitness/exercise science, physical sciences, physics, political science/government, psychobiology, psychology, public affairs and policy studies, religious studies, Romance languages, Russian, sculpture, sociology, Spanish, studio art, theater arts/drama, (pre)veterinary medicine sequence, women's studies.

## Oglethorpe University

Accounting, American studies, art/fine arts, biology/biological sciences, business administration/commerce/management, business economics, chemistry, communication, computer science, creative writing, (pre)dentistry sequence, early childhood education, economics, education, elementary education, English, history, interdisciplinary studies, international studies, (pre)law sequence, liberal arts/general studies, mathematics, medical technology, (pre)medicine sequence, middle school education, philosophy, physics, political science/government, psychology, science, secondary education, social work, sociology, urban studies, (pre)veterinary medicine sequence.

## Ohio Northern University

Accounting, art education, art/fine arts, biochemistry, biology/biological sciences, broadcasting, business administration/commerce/management, ceramic art and design, chemistry, civil engineering, communication, computer science, criminal justice, (pre)dentistry

sequence, economics, electrical engineering, elementary education, English, environmental studies, finance/banking, French, graphic arts, health education, history, industrial arts, industrial engineering technology, international studies, (pre)law sequence, marketing/retailing/merchandising, mathematics, mechanical engineering, medical technology, (pre)medicine sequence, music, music education, painting/drawing, pharmacy/pharmaceutical sciences, philosophy, physical education, physics, political science/government, printmaking, psychology, public relations, religious studies, sculpture, sociology, Spanish, special education, speech/rhetoric/public address/debate, sports administration, sports medicine, theater arts/drama, (pre)veterinary medicine sequence.

## Ohio State University

Accounting, actuarial science, aerospace engineering, African studies, agricultural business, agricultural economics, agricultural education, agricultural engineering, agronomy/soil and crop sciences, animal sciences, anthropology, Arabic, architectural engineering, architecture, art education, art/fine arts, art history, Asian/Oriental studies, astronomy, audio engineering, aviation administration, aviation technology, behavioral sciences, biochemistry, biology/biological sciences, black/African-American studies, botany/plant sciences, business administration/commerce/management, business economics, business education, cell biology, ceramic engineering, chemical engineering, chemistry, child care/child and family studies, child psychology/child development, Chinese, civil engineering, classics, cognitive science, communication, computer engineering, computer information systems, computer programming, computer science, consumer services, criminal justice, criminology, dairy sciences, dance, dental services, (pre)dentistry sequence, dietetics, early childhood education, earth science, East Asian studies, East European and Soviet studies, ecology, economics, education, electrical engineering, elementary education, engineering (general), engineering physics, English, entomology, environmental biology, environmental education, environmental sciences, ethnic studies, European studies, experimental psychology, family and consumer studies, family services, fashion merchandising, film studies, finance/banking, fish and game management, flight training, food marketing, food sciences, food services management, forestry, French, genetics, geography, geology, German, gerontology, Greek, health education, Hebrew, history, home economics, home economics education, horticulture, hospitality services, hotel and restaurant management, human development, human ecology, humanities, human resources, illustration, industrial engineering, information science, insurance, interdisciplinary studies, interior design, international business, international economics, international studies, Islamic studies, Italian, Japanese, jazz, journalism, Judaic studies, labor and industrial relations, landscape architecture/design, land use management and reclamation, linguistics, marketing/retailing/merchandising, materials engineering, materials sciences, mathematics, mechanical engineering, medical illustration, medical records services, medical technology, (pre)medicine sequence, medieval studies, metallurgical engineering, microbiology, music, music education, music history, natural resource management, Near and Middle Eastern studies, nursing, nutrition, occupational therapy, parks management, pharmacy/pharmaceutical sciences, philosophy, physical education, physical therapy, physics, piano/organ, political science/government, Portuguese, poultry sciences, psychology, public relations, radiological technology, reading education, real estate, recreation and leisure services, religious studies, respiratory therapy, Russian, Russian and Slavic studies, science education, secondary education, Slavic languages, social work, sociology, South Asian studies, Southeast Asian studies, Spanish, special education, speech pathology and audiology, statistics, stringed instruments, surveying engineering, systems engineering, technical writing, textiles and clothing, theater arts/drama, transportation engineering, transportation technologies, (pre)veterinary medicine sequence, vocational education, voice, welding engineering, wildlife management, wind and percussion instruments, women's studies, zoology.

## Ohio University
Accounting, advertising, African studies, agricultural business, anthropology, applied art, applied mathematics, art education, art/fine arts, art history, Asian/Oriental studies, athletic training, aviation administration, biochemistry, biology/biological sciences, biomedical sciences, black/African-American studies, botany/plant sciences, broadcasting, business administration/commerce/management, business economics, business education, cartography, cell biology, ceramic art and design, chemical engineering, chemistry, child care/child and family studies, civil engineering, classics, commercial art, communication, communication equipment technology, community services, computer engineering, computer information systems, computer science, creative writing, criminal justice, criminology, dance, (pre)dentistry sequence, dietetics, early childhood education, ecology, economics, education, educational media, electrical engineering, elementary education, English, environmental biology, environmental health sciences, environmental studies, European studies, family services, fashion merchandising, film studies, finance/banking, food services management, forensic sciences, French, geography, geology, German, graphic arts, health education, health services administration, history, home economics, home economics education, human resources, industrial arts, industrial engineering, international business, international studies, journalism, labor and industrial relations, Latin, Latin American studies, (pre)law sequence, liberal arts/general studies, linguistics, literature, management information systems, marine biology, marketing/retailing/merchandising, mathematics, mechanical engineering, (pre)medicine sequence, microbiology, mining and mineral engineering, music, music education, music history, music therapy, nursing, nutrition, occupational safety and health, painting/drawing, philosophy, photography, physical education, physical fitness/exercise science, physics, physiology, piano/organ, political science/government, printmaking, psychology, public administration, public relations, radio and television studies, reading education, recreation and leisure services, recreation therapy, sculpture, secondary education, social work, sociology, Southeast Asian studies, Spanish, special education, speech pathology and audiology, speech/rhetoric/public address/debate, speech therapy, stringed instruments, studio art, systems engineering, telecommunications, theater arts/drama, (pre)veterinary medicine sequence, voice, water resources, wildlife biology, wildlife management, wind and percussion instruments, zoology.

## Ohio Wesleyan University
Accounting, anthropology, art education, art/fine arts, art history, art therapy, astronomy, bacteriology, biology/biological sciences, black/African-American studies, botany/plant sciences, broadcasting, business administration/commerce/management, chemistry, classics, computer science, creative writing, (pre)dentistry sequence, earth science, economics, education, elementary education, engineering sciences, English, environmental sciences, ethnic studies, French, genetics, geography, geology, German, health education, history, humanities, international business, international studies, journalism, (pre)law sequence, literature, mathematics, (pre)medicine sequence, medieval studies, music, music education, philosophy, physical education, physics, political science/government, psychology, public administration, religious studies, secondary education, sociology, Spanish, statistics, studio art, theater arts/drama, urban studies, (pre)veterinary medicine sequence, women's studies, zoology.

## Oklahoma State University
Accounting, advertising, aerospace engineering, aerospace sciences, agricultural business, agricultural economics, agricultural education, agricultural engineering, agricultural sciences, agronomy/soil and crop sciences, animal sciences, architectural engineering, architecture, art education, art/fine arts, aviation administration, aviation technology, biochemistry, biology/biological sciences, biotechnology, botany/plant sciences, broadcasting, business administration/commerce/management, business economics, business education, cell biology, chemical engineering, chemistry, child care/child and family studies, child psychology/child development, civil engineering, communication, community services, computer engineering, computer information systems, computer management, computer programming, computer science, computer technologies, construction management, construction technologies, consumer services, dietetics, drafting and design, early childhood education, ecology, economics, education, electrical and electronics technologies, electrical engineering, electronics engineering technology, elementary education, engineering (general), engineering technology, English, entomology, family and consumer studies, family services, farm and ranch management, fashion design and technology, fashion merchandising, finance/banking, fire protection engineering, fish and game management, flight training, forestry, French, geography, geology, German, gerontology, graphic arts, health education, health science, history, home economics, home economics education, horticulture, hotel and restaurant management, human resources, industrial arts, industrial engineering, industrial engineering technology, information science, interior design, international business, journalism, laboratory technologies, landscape architecture/design, (pre)law sequence, management information systems, manufacturing technology, marketing/retailing/merchandising, marriage and family counseling, mathematics, mechanical design technology, mechanical engineering, mechanical engineering technology, medical technology, (pre)medicine sequence, microbiology, middle school education, military science, music, music education, nutrition, petroleum technology, philosophy, physical education, physical sciences, physics, physiology, political science/government, psychology, public relations, radio and television studies, range management, recreation and leisure services, Russian, safety and security technologies, science education, secondary education, social science, social work, sociology, Spanish, special education, speech pathology and audiology, speech/rhetoric/public address/debate, statistics, studio art, technical writing, textiles and clothing, theater arts/drama, (pre)veterinary medicine sequence, vocational education, wildlife management, zoology.

## Otis College of Art and Design
Applied art, art/fine arts, ceramic art and design, commercial art, environmental design, fashion design and technology, graphic arts, illustration, interior design, painting/drawing, photography, sculpture, studio art.

## Pacific Lutheran University
Accounting, anthropology, art education, art/fine arts, art history, biblical studies, biochemistry, biology/biological sciences, broadcasting, business administration/commerce/management, chemistry, classics, communication, computer engineering, computer science, (pre)dentistry sequence, early childhood education, earth science, ecology, economics, education, electrical engineering, elementary education, engineering physics, engineering sciences, English, finance/banking, French, geology, German, history, international business, international studies, jazz, journalism, (pre)law sequence, legal studies, literature, management information systems, marketing/retailing/merchandising, mathematics, medical technology, (pre)medicine sequence, modern languages, music, music education, nursing, philosophy, physical education, physical fitness/exercise

science, physics, piano/organ, political science/government, psychology, public relations, publishing, radio and television studies, reading education, recreational facilities management, recreation and leisure services, recreation therapy, religious studies, sacred music, Scandinavian languages/studies, science education, secondary education, social work, sociology, Spanish, special education, speech/rhetoric/public address/debate, sports administration, sports medicine, stringed instruments, studio art, theater arts/drama, (pre)veterinary medicine sequence, voice.

## Parsons School of Design, New School for Social Research

Art education, art/fine arts, ceramic art and design, commercial art, environmental design, fashion design and technology, graphic arts, illustration, industrial design, interior design, jewelry and metalsmithing, painting/drawing, photography, sculpture, textile arts.

## Pennsylvania State University University Park Campus

Accounting, actuarial science, advertising, aerospace engineering, African studies, agricultural business, agricultural economics, agricultural education, agricultural engineering, agricultural sciences, agronomy/soil and crop sciences, American studies, animal sciences, anthropology, architectural engineering, architecture, art education, art/fine arts, art history, astronomy, astrophysics, biochemistry, biology/biological sciences, black/African-American studies, botany/plant sciences, broadcasting, business administration/commerce/management, cell biology, ceramic engineering, chemical engineering, chemistry, child care/child and family studies, civil engineering, classics, communication, comparative literature, computer engineering, computer science, criminal justice, dairy sciences, early childhood education, earth science, East Asian studies, ecology, economics, education, educational media, electrical engineering, elementary education, engineering (general), engineering sciences, English, entomology, family and consumer studies, film and video production, finance/banking, fish and game management, food sciences, forestry, forest technology, French, geography, German, health education, health services administration, history, horticulture, hotel and restaurant management, human development, industrial engineering, insurance, interdisciplinary studies, international business, international studies, Italian, journalism, labor and industrial relations, landscape architecture/design, landscaping/grounds maintenance, Latin American studies, law enforcement/police sciences, (pre)law sequence, liberal arts/general studies, linguistics, marketing/retailing/merchandising, materials engineering, materials sciences, mathematics, mechanical engineering, (pre)medicine sequence, medieval studies, meteorology, microbiology, mining and mineral engineering, molecular biology, music, music education, nuclear engineering, nursing, nutrition, operations research, parks management, petroleum/natural gas engineering, philosophy, physical fitness/exercise science, physics, political science/government, poultry sciences, psychology, real estate, recreation and leisure services, rehabilitation therapy, religious studies, Russian, science, secondary education, social work, sociology, Spanish, special education, speech/rhetoric/public address/debate, theater arts/drama, vocational education, wildlife management, women's studies, wood sciences.

## Pepperdine University (Malibu)

Accounting, advertising, American studies, art/fine arts, Asian/Oriental studies, biology/biological sciences, broadcasting, business administration/commerce/management, chemistry, communication, computer science, creative writing, (pre)dentistry sequence, economics, education, elementary education, English, French, German, history, humanities, interdisciplinary studies, international studies, journalism,

(pre)law sequence, liberal arts/general studies, literature, mathematics, (pre)medicine sequence, music, music education, natural sciences, nutrition, philosophy, physical education, political science/government, psychology, public relations, recreation and leisure services, religious education, religious studies, secondary education, social science, sociology, Spanish, speech/rhetoric/public address/debate, sports medicine, telecommunications, theater arts/drama.

## Pitzer College

American studies, anthropology, art/fine arts, Asian/Oriental studies, biology/biological sciences, chemistry, classics, economics, English, environmental sciences, European studies, film studies, folklore, French, German, history, international studies, Latin American studies, linguistics, mathematics, Mexican-American/Chicano studies, music, natural sciences, philosophy, physics, political science/government, psychobiology, psychology, religious studies, social science, sociology, Spanish, theater arts/drama, women's studies.

## Polytechnic University, Brooklyn Campus

Actuarial science, aerospace engineering, chemical engineering, chemistry, civil engineering, computer engineering, computer information systems, computer science, electrical engineering, environmental engineering, environmental sciences, humanities, journalism, mathematics, mechanical engineering, physics, social science, technical writing.

## Polytechnic University, Farmingdale Campus

Aerospace engineering, chemical engineering, civil engineering, computer engineering, computer science, electrical engineering, environmental engineering, environmental sciences, mechanical engineering.

## Pomona College

American studies, anthropology, art/fine arts, art history, Asian/Oriental studies, astronomy, biochemistry, biology/biological sciences, black/African-American studies, cell biology, chemistry, Chinese, classics, computer science, dance, East Asian studies, ecology, economics, English, environmental studies, film studies, French, geology, German, Germanic languages and literature, Hispanic studies, history, humanities, interdisciplinary studies, international relations, international studies, Japanese, liberal arts/general studies, linguistics, literature, mathematics, (pre)medicine sequence, Mexican-American/Chicano studies, microbiology, modern languages, molecular biology, music, philosophy, physics, political science/government, psychology, public affairs and policy studies, religious studies, Romance languages, Russian, sociology, Spanish, studio art, theater arts/drama, women's studies.

## Presbyterian College

Accounting, art/fine arts, biology/biological sciences, business administration/commerce/management, chemistry, (pre)dentistry sequence, economics, education, elementary education, English, French, German, history, (pre)law sequence, mathematics, (pre)medicine sequence, modern languages, music, music education, philosophy, physics, political science/government, psychology, religious studies, social science, sociology, Spanish, special education, theater arts/drama, (pre)veterinary medicine sequence.

## Princeton University

Aerospace engineering, African studies, American studies, anthropology, applied mathematics, archaeology, architectural engineering, architecture, art/fine arts, art history, astrophysics, bioengineering, biology/biological sciences, black/African-American studies, chemical engineering, chemistry, civil engineering, classics, cognitive science, comparative literature, computer science, creative writing, East Asian studies, ecology, economics, electrical engineering, energy management technologies, engineering and applied sciences, engineering management, engineering physics, English, environmental engineering, environmental sciences, European studies, evolutionary biology, geological engineering, geology, geophysics, Germanic languages and literature, history, humanities, international studies, Latin American studies, linguistics, management engineering, mathematics, mechanical engineering, molecular biology, music, Near and Middle Eastern studies, philosophy, physics, political science/government, psychology, public affairs and policy studies, religious studies, robotics, Romance languages, Russian and Slavic studies, Slavic languages, sociology, statistics, theater arts/drama, transportation engineering, women's studies.

## Providence College
Accounting, American studies, art/fine arts, art history, biology/biological sciences, business administration/commerce/management, business economics, chemistry, computer science, economics, education, elementary education, English, finance/banking, French, health services administration, history, humanities, instrumentation technology, Italian, Latin American studies, liberal arts/general studies, marketing/retailing/merchandising, mathematics, modern languages, music, painting/drawing, philosophy, photography, political science/government, psychology, secondary education, social science, social work, sociology, Spanish, special education, studio art, systems science, theater arts/drama, theology.

## Purdue University (West Lafayette)
Accounting, actuarial science, advertising, aerospace engineering, agricultural business, agricultural economics, agricultural education, agricultural engineering, agricultural sciences, agricultural technologies, agronomy/soil and crop sciences, aircraft and missile maintenance, air traffic control, American studies, animal sciences, anthropology, applied mathematics, art education, art/fine arts, art history, athletic training, atmospheric sciences, aviation administration, aviation technology, biochemistry, bioengineering, biology/biological sciences, biomedical engineering, biomedical sciences, black/African-American studies, botany/plant sciences, business administration/commerce/management, business economics, cell biology, ceramic art and design, chemical engineering, chemistry, child care/child and family studies, child psychology/child development, civil engineering, clinical psychology, commercial art, communication, community services, comparative literature, computer engineering, computer programming, computer science, computer technologies, conservation, construction engineering, construction management, construction technologies, consumer services, creative writing, criminal justice, criminology, (pre)dentistry sequence, dietetics, drafting and design, early childhood education, earth science, ecology, economics, education, educational media, electrical engineering, electrical engineering technology, elementary education, engineering (general), engineering management, engineering sciences, engineering technology, English, entomology, environmental biology, environmental engineering, environmental health sciences, environmental sciences, evolutionary biology, family and consumer studies, farm and ranch management, fashion design and technology, fashion merchandising, film studies, finance/banking, fish and game management, flight training, food marketing, food sciences, food services management, forestry, forest technology, French, genetics, geochemistry, geological engineering, geology, geophysics, German, Germanic languages and literature, graphic arts, guidance and counseling, health education, health science, history, home economics, home economics education, horticulture, hospitality services, hotel and restaurant management, human resources, illustration, industrial administration, industrial arts,

industrial design, industrial engineering, industrial engineering technology, interdisciplinary studies, interior design, journalism, landscape architecture/design, landscaping/grounds maintenance, (pre)law sequence, linguistics, management engineering, management information systems, manufacturing engineering, manufacturing technology, marketing/retailing/merchandising, materials engineering, materials sciences, mathematics, mechanical engineering, mechanical engineering technology, medical technology, (pre)medicine sequence, medieval studies, metallurgical engineering, meteorology, microbiology, middle school education, molecular biology, natural resource management, neurosciences, nuclear engineering, nuclear physics, nursing, nutrition, occupational safety and health, ocean engineering, operations research, painting/drawing, paleontology, parks management, pharmacology, pharmacy/pharmaceutical sciences, philosophy, photography, physical education, physical fitness/exercise science, physical sciences, physics, physiology, political science/government, poultry sciences, psychology, public relations, radio and television studies, radiological sciences, range management, reading education, recreational facilities management, recreation and leisure services, religious studies, retail management, robotics, Russian, science, science education, secondary education, social science, sociology, soil conservation, Spanish, special education, speech pathology and audiology, speech therapy, sports medicine, statistics, surveying engineering, systems engineering, technical writing, telecommunications, theater arts/drama, tourism and travel, transportation engineering, (pre)veterinary medicine sequence, veterinary sciences, vocational education, water resources, wildlife biology, wildlife management, wood sciences.

## Quincy University
Accounting, art education, art/fine arts, art history, arts administration, athletic training, biology/biological sciences, business administration/commerce/management, chemistry, communication, computer information systems, computer science, criminal justice, (pre)dentistry sequence, elementary education, English, finance/banking, history, humanities, human resources, interdisciplinary studies, international studies, (pre)law sequence, liberal arts/general studies, marketing/retailing/merchandising, mathematics, medical technology, (pre)medicine sequence, music, music business, music education, peace studies, philosophy, physical education, political science/government, psychology, radio and television studies, religious education, secondary education, social work, sociology, special education, sports administration, studio art, theology, (pre)veterinary medicine sequence.

## Randolph-Macon Woman's College
Anthropology, art/fine arts, art history, biology/biological sciences, business economics, chemistry, classics, communication, creative writing, dance, economics, English, French, German, Germanic languages and literature, Greek, history, international relations, Latin, literature, mathematics, museum studies, music, music history, philosophy, physics, political science/government, psychology, religious studies, Russian and Slavic studies, sociology, Spanish, studio art, theater arts/drama, voice.

## Reed College
American studies, anthropology, art/fine arts, art history, biochemistry, biology/biological sciences, biophysics, chemistry, Chinese, classics, dance, economics, English, French, German, Germanic languages and literature, history, international studies, linguistics, literature, mathematics, medieval studies, music, philosophy, physics, political science/government, psychology, religious studies, Russian, sociology, Spanish, studio art, theater arts/drama.

## Rensselaer Polytechnic Institute

Accounting, aerospace engineering, applied mathematics, architectural engineering, architecture, astrophysics, biochemistry, biology/ biological sciences, biomedical engineering, biomedical sciences, biophysics, business administration/commerce/management, cell biology, ceramic engineering, chemical engineering, chemistry, civil engineering, communication, computer engineering, computer graphics, computer management, computer programming, computer science, (pre)dentistry sequence, ecology, economics, electrical engineering, electronics engineering, engineering (general), engineering and applied sciences, engineering management, engineering physics, engineering sciences, environmental biology, environmental engineering, environmental sciences, environmental studies, finance/banking, French, genetics, geochemistry, geological engineering, geology, geophysics, German, industrial engineering, interdisciplinary studies, international business, (pre)law sequence, management engineering, management information systems, manufacturing engineering, materials engineering, mathematics, mechanical engineering, (pre)medicine sequence, metallurgy, microbiology, military science, molecular biology, music, natural sciences, naval sciences, nuclear engineering, nuclear physics, optics, philosophy, physical sciences, physics, physiology, planetary and space sciences, polymer science, psychology, robotics, science, science education, systems engineering, technical writing, technology and public affairs.

## Rhode Island School of Design

Architecture, art/fine arts, ceramic art and design, fashion design and technology, film studies, graphic arts, illustration, industrial design, interior design, jewelry and metalsmithing, landscape architecture/ design, painting/drawing, photography, printmaking, sculpture, textile arts, textiles and clothing.

## Rhodes College

Anthropology, art/fine arts, art history, biochemistry, biology/ biological sciences, business administration/commerce/management, chemistry, classics, computer science, economics, English, French, German, Greek, history, interdisciplinary studies, international business, international economics, international studies, Latin, Latin American studies, mathematics, museum studies, music, philosophy, physics, political science/government, psychology, religious studies, Russian, Russian and Slavic studies, sociology, Spanish, studio art, theater arts/drama, urban studies.

## Rice University

Anthropology, architecture, art/fine arts, art history, Asian/Oriental studies, behavioral sciences, biochemistry, biology/biological sciences, business administration/commerce/management, chemical engineering, chemistry, civil engineering, classics, computer engineering, computer science, ecology, economics, electrical engineering, English, environmental engineering, evolutionary biology, French, geology, geophysics, German, history, linguistics, materials sciences, mathematics, mechanical engineering, music, neurosciences, philosophy, physical education, physics, political science/government, psychology, public affairs and policy studies, religious studies, Russian and Slavic studies, sociology, Spanish, statistics.

## Ripon College

Anthropology, art/fine arts, behavioral sciences, biochemistry, biology/biological sciences, business administration/commerce/ management, chemistry, computer science, (pre)dentistry sequence, economics, education, elementary education, English, French, German, history, interdisciplinary studies, (pre)law sequence, literature, mathematics, (pre)medicine sequence, modern languages, music, music

education, natural sciences, philosophy, physical education, physical sciences, physics, political science/government, psychobiology, psychology, Romance languages, science, secondary education, sociology, Spanish, speech/rhetoric/public address/debate, theater arts/drama, (pre)veterinary medicine sequence.

## Rochester Institute of Technology

Accounting, advertising, aerospace engineering, applied art, applied mathematics, art/fine arts, biochemistry, biology/biological sciences, biomedical sciences, biomedical technologies, biotechnology, business administration/commerce/management, ceramic art and design, chemistry, civil engineering technology, commercial art, communication, computer engineering, computer graphics, computer information systems, computer programming, computer science, computer technologies, criminal justice, (pre)dentistry sequence, dietetics, ecology, economics, electrical and electronics technologies, electrical engineering, electrical engineering technology, engineering (general), engineering technology, environmental engineering, environmental sciences, film and video production, finance/banking, food marketing, food services management, genetics, graphic arts, hotel and restaurant management, illustration, industrial design, industrial engineering, information science, interdisciplinary studies, interior design, international business, jewelry and metalsmithing, law enforcement/police sciences, (pre)law sequence, management information systems, manufacturing engineering, manufacturing technology, marketing/retailing/merchandising, mathematics, mechanical engineering, mechanical engineering technology, medical illustration, medical technology, (pre)medicine sequence, nuclear medical technology, nutrition, painting/drawing, photography, physician's assistant studies, physics, polymer science, printing technologies, printmaking, publishing, science, social work, statistics, studio art, telecommunications, textile arts, tourism and travel, (pre)veterinary medicine sequence.

## Rockhurst College

Accounting, biology/biological sciences, business administration/ commerce/management, business economics, chemistry, communication, computer information systems, computer science, cytotechnology, (pre)dentistry sequence, economics, education, elementary education, English, finance/banking, French, health science, history, humanities, human resources, human services, international studies, labor and industrial relations, (pre)law sequence, liberal arts/general studies, marketing/retailing/merchandising, mathematics, medical technology, (pre)medicine sequence, nursing, occupational therapy, philosophy, physical therapy, physics, political science/government, psychology, religious studies, science education, secondary education, sociology, Spanish, theater arts/drama, theology, (pre)veterinary medicine sequence.

## Rollins College

Anthropology, art/fine arts, art history, biology/biological sciences, chemistry, classics, computer science, (pre)dentistry sequence, economics, education, elementary education, English, environmental sciences, French, German, history, interdisciplinary studies, international studies, Latin American studies, (pre)law sequence, mathematics, (pre)medicine sequence, music, music history, philosophy, physics, political science/government, psychology, religious studies, sociology, Spanish, studio art, theater arts/drama, (pre)veterinary medicine sequence.

## Rose-Hulman Institute of Technology

Chemical engineering, chemistry, civil engineering, computer engineering, computer science, economics, electrical engineering, mathematics, mechanical engineering, optics, physics.

## Rutgers, The State University of New Jersey, College of Engineering

Aerospace engineering, agricultural engineering, biomedical engineering, ceramic engineering, chemical engineering, civil engineering, computer engineering, electrical engineering, engineering and applied sciences, industrial engineering, mechanical engineering.

## Rutgers, The State University of New Jersey, College of Pharmacy

Pharmacy/pharmaceutical sciences.

## Rutgers, The State University of New Jersey, Cook College

Agricultural economics, agricultural education, agricultural engineering, agricultural sciences, agronomy/soil and crop sciences, animal sciences, atmospheric sciences, biochemistry, biology/biological sciences, biomedical sciences, biotechnology, botany/plant sciences, business economics, cell biology, chemistry, chemistry, foods, and nutrition, communication, computer science, conservation, (pre)dentistry sequence, dietetics, earth science, ecology, education, entomology, environmental and business economics, environmental design, environmental education, environmental health sciences, environmental sciences, fish and game management, food sciences, forestry, genetics, geography, geology, health, physical education, and sports studies, horticulture, human ecology, interdisciplinary studies, international studies, journalism, landscape architecture/design, (pre)law sequence, (pre)medicine sequence, meteorology, microbiology, natural resource management, nutrition, oceanography, physical education, physical fitness/exercise science, physiology, public health, radiological sciences, recreation and leisure services, sports administration, (pre)veterinary medicine sequence, vocational education, water resources, wildlife management.

## Rutgers, The State University of New Jersey, Douglass College

Accounting, African studies, American studies, anthropology, art/fine arts, art history, Asian/Oriental studies, atmospheric sciences, biochemistry, biology/biological sciences, biomedical sciences, biometrics, biotechnology, botany/plant sciences, business administration/commerce/management, cell biology, chemistry, chemistry, foods, and nutrition, Chinese, classics, communication, comparative literature, computer science, dance, East European and Soviet studies, ecology, economics, education, English, evolutionary biology, finance/banking, food sciences, French, genetics, geography, geology, German, Greek, health, physical education, and sports studies, Hispanic studies, history, human ecology, interdisciplinary studies, Italian, journalism, Judaic studies, labor studies, Latin, Latin American studies, (pre)law sequence, linguistics, management information systems, marketing/retailing/merchandising, mathematics, medical technology, (pre)medicine sequence, medieval studies, microbiology, molecular biology, music, Near and Middle Eastern studies, nutrition, philosophy, physical education, physical fitness/exercise science, physics, physiology, political science/government, Portuguese, psychology, public health, recreation and leisure services, religious studies, Russian, Russian and Slavic studies, sociology, Spanish, sports administration, statistics, theater arts/drama, urban studies, women's studies.

## Rutgers, The State University of New Jersey, Mason Gross School of the Arts

Art/fine arts, ceramic art and design, dance, film studies, graphic arts, jazz, music, music education, painting/drawing, photography, printmaking, sculpture, theater arts/drama.

## Rutgers, The State University of New Jersey, Rutgers College

Accounting, African studies, American studies, anthropology, art/fine arts, art history, Asian/Oriental studies, biochemistry, biology/biological sciences, biomedical sciences, biometrics, black/African-American studies, botany/plant sciences, business administration/commerce/management, cell biology, chemistry, chemistry, foods, and nutrition, Chinese, classics, communication, comparative literature, computer science, criminal justice, dance, (pre)dentistry sequence, East European and Soviet studies, ecology, economics, education, English, evolutionary biology, finance/banking, French, genetics, geography, geology, German, Greek, health, physical education, and sports studies, Hispanic studies, history, interdisciplinary studies, Italian, journalism, Judaic studies, labor studies, Latin, Latin American studies, (pre)law sequence, linguistics, management information systems, marketing/retailing/merchandising, mathematics, (pre)medicine sequence, medieval studies, microbiology, molecular biology, music, Near and Middle Eastern studies, philosophy, physical education, physical fitness/exercise science, physics, physiology, political science/government, Portuguese, psychology, public health, recreation and leisure services, religious studies, Russian, Russian and Slavic studies, sociology, Spanish, sports administration, statistics, theater arts/drama, urban studies, women's studies.

## St. John's College (MD)

Interdisciplinary studies, liberal arts/general studies, Western civilization and culture.

## St. John's College (NM)

Liberal arts/general studies.

## Saint John's University (MN)

Accounting, art education, art/fine arts, art history, biology/biological sciences, business administration/commerce/management, chemistry, classics, communication, computer science, (pre)dentistry sequence, dietetics, economics, education, elementary education, English, forestry, French, German, Greek, history, humanities, Latin, (pre)law sequence, mathematics, medical technology, (pre)medicine sequence, medieval studies, ministries, music, music education, natural sciences, nursing, nutrition, occupational therapy, peace studies, philosophy, physical therapy, physics, political science/government, psychology, religious education, religious studies, sacred music, secondary education, social science, social work, sociology, Spanish, studio art, theater arts/drama, theology, (pre)veterinary medicine sequence.

## Saint Joseph's University

Accounting, art/fine arts, biology/biological sciences, business administration/commerce/management, chemistry, classics, computer science, criminal justice, (pre)dentistry sequence, economics, education, elementary education, English, finance/banking, food marketing, French, German, health services administration, history, humanities, human services, international business, international relations, labor studies, (pre)law sequence, management information systems, marketing/retailing/merchandising, mathematics, (pre)medicine sequence, modern languages, philosophy, physics, political science/government, psychology, public administration, secondary education, social science, sociology, Spanish, theology.

## St. Lawrence University

Anthropology, art/fine arts, Asian/Oriental studies, biology/biological sciences, biophysics, Canadian studies, chemistry, computer science, creative writing, ecology, economics, English, environmental sciences, French, geology, geophysics, German, history, literature, mathematics, modern languages, music, philosophy, physical education, physics, political science/government, psychology, recreation and leisure services, religious studies, Romance languages, sociology, Spanish, theater arts/drama.

## St. Louis College of Pharmacy

Pharmacy/pharmaceutical sciences.

## Saint Louis University

Accounting, aerospace engineering, aircraft and missile maintenance, American studies, art/fine arts, atmospheric sciences, aviation administration, aviation technology, biology/biological sciences, business administration/commerce/management, business economics, chemistry, classics, communication, community services, computer science, criminal justice, (pre)dentistry sequence, early childhood education, earth science, economics, education, electrical engineering, elementary education, engineering physics, English, finance/banking, flight training, French, geology, geophysics, German, Greek, history, humanities, information science, international business, labor and industrial relations, Latin, (pre)law sequence, management information systems, marketing/retailing/merchandising, mathematics, medical laboratory technology, medical records services, medical technology, (pre)medicine sequence, meteorology, middle school education, modern languages, nuclear medical technology, nursing, occupational therapy, philosophy, physical therapy, physician's assistant studies, physics, political science/government, Portuguese, psychology, religious studies, Russian, secondary education, social work, sociology, Spanish, special education, speech pathology and audiology, speech therapy, theology, tourism and travel, transportation technologies, urban studies, (pre)veterinary medicine sequence.

## Saint Mary's College (IN)

Accounting, anthropology, art education, art/fine arts, biology/biological sciences, business administration/commerce/management, chemistry, communication, creative writing, economics, elementary education, English, finance/banking, French, history, humanities, international business, literature, marketing/retailing/merchandising, mathematics, music, music education, nursing, philosophy, piano/organ, political science/government, psychology, religious studies, social work, sociology, Spanish, theater arts/drama, voice.

## Saint Mary's College of California

Accounting, anthropology, art education, art/fine arts, art history, biology/biological sciences, business administration/commerce/management, chemistry, communication, dance, (pre)dentistry sequence, economics, education, engineering (general), English, French, German, Greek, health education, history, Latin, (pre)law sequence, liberal arts/general studies, mathematics, (pre)medicine sequence, modern languages, music, philosophy, physical education, physics, political science/government, psychology, religious studies, secondary education, sociology, Spanish, theater arts/drama, theology, (pre)veterinary medicine sequence.

## St. Mary's College of Maryland

Anthropology, art/fine arts, biology/biological sciences, chemistry, economics, English, history, human development, mathematics, modern languages, music, natural sciences, philosophy, physics, political science/government, psychology, public affairs and policy studies, sociology, theater arts/drama.

## St. Norbert College

Accounting, anthropology, applied art, art education, art/fine arts, biology/biological sciences, business administration/commerce/management, chemistry, communication, computer information

systems, computer science, (pre)dentistry sequence, early childhood education, ecology, economics, education, elementary education, English, environmental sciences, French, geology, German, graphic arts, history, humanities, international business, international economics, international studies, (pre)law sequence, management information systems, mathematics, medical technology, (pre)medicine sequence, middle school education, music, music education, natural sciences, philosophy, physics, political science/government, psychology, religious education, religious studies, secondary education, social science, sociology, Spanish, theater arts/drama, (pre)veterinary medicine sequence.

## St. Olaf College

American studies, art education, art/fine arts, art history, Asian/Oriental studies, biology/biological sciences, black/African-American studies, chemistry, classics, computer science, dance, (pre)dentistry sequence, East Asian studies, East European and Soviet studies, economics, education, elementary education, English, ethnic studies, French, German, Greek, health science, Hispanic studies, history, home economics education, Latin, (pre)law sequence, literature, mathematics, (pre)medicine sequence, medieval studies, music, music education, nursing, philosophy, physical education, physics, piano/organ, political science/government, psychology, religious studies, Russian, Russian and Slavic studies, sacred music, Scandinavian languages/studies, secondary education, social work, sociology, Spanish, speech/rhetoric/public address/debate, stringed instruments, theater arts/drama, urban studies, (pre)veterinary medicine sequence, voice, Western civilization and culture, wind and percussion instruments, women's studies.

## Samford University

Accounting, adult and continuing education, art education, art/fine arts, athletic training, biology/biological sciences, business administration/commerce/management, chemistry, commercial art, communication, community services, computer information systems, computer science, cytotechnology, (pre)dentistry sequence, early childhood education, education, educational administration, elementary education, engineering physics, English, environmental sciences, family and consumer studies, fashion merchandising, food services management, French, geography, German, graphic arts, health education, history, home economics, home economics education, human resources, interior design, international business, journalism, (pre)law sequence, liberal arts/general studies, literature, mathematics, medical records services, medical technology, (pre)medicine sequence, ministries, music, music education, nursing, nutrition, occupational therapy, painting/drawing, paralegal studies, pastoral studies, pharmacy/pharmaceutical sciences, physical education, physician's assistant studies, physics, piano/organ, political science/government, psychology, public administration, public affairs and policy studies, radiological technology, recreation and leisure services, religious education, religious studies, sacred music, science education, secondary education, sociology, Spanish, speech/rhetoric/public address/debate, sports medicine, stringed instruments, theater arts/drama, (pre)veterinary medicine sequence, voice.

## San Francisco Conservatory of Music

Music, opera, piano/organ, stringed instruments, voice, wind and percussion instruments.

## Santa Clara University

Accounting, anthropology, art/fine arts, biology/biological sciences, business administration/commerce/management, business economics, chemistry, civil engineering, classics, communication, computer engineering, computer information systems, computer science, (pre)dentistry sequence, economics, education, electrical engineering, engineering (general), engineering physics, English, finance/banking, French, German, history, humanities, information science, interdisciplinary studies, international business, Italian, (pre)law sequence, liberal arts/general studies, marketing/retailing/merchandising, mathematics, mechanical engineering, (pre)medicine sequence, modern languages, music, philosophy, physics, political science/government, psychology, religious studies, retail management, science, sociology, Spanish, theater arts/drama, (pre)veterinary medicine sequence.

## Sarah Lawrence College
American studies, anthropology, art/fine arts, art history, Asian/Oriental studies, biology/biological sciences, black/African-American studies, ceramic art and design, chemistry, child psychology/child development, classics, comparative literature, computer science, creative writing, dance, (pre)dentistry sequence, early childhood education, East European and Soviet studies, ecology, economics, English, European studies, film studies, French, geology, German, Greek, history, human development, humanities, interdisciplinary studies, international studies, Italian, Latin, (pre)law sequence, liberal arts/general studies, literature, marine biology, mathematics, (pre)medicine sequence, modern languages, music, music history, natural sciences, painting/drawing, philosophy, photography, physics, piano/organ, political science/government, psychology, public affairs and policy studies, religious studies, Romance languages, Russian, science, sculpture, social science, sociology, Spanish, stringed instruments, studio art, theater arts/drama, voice, wind and percussion instruments, women's studies.

## Savannah College of Art and Design
Applied art, architecture, art/fine arts, art history, computer graphics, fashion design and technology, film and video production, graphic arts, historic preservation, illustration, interior design, jewelry and metalsmithing, painting/drawing, photography, textile arts.

## Scripps College
Accounting, American studies, anthropology, art/fine arts, art history, Asian/Oriental studies, astronomy, biochemistry, biology/biological sciences, black/African-American studies, chemistry, Chinese, classics, comparative literature, computer science, dance, East Asian studies, ecology, economics, engineering (general), English, environmental studies, ethnic studies, European studies, film studies, folklore, French, geography, geology, German, Germanic languages and literature, Hispanic studies, history, humanities, interdisciplinary studies, international relations, international studies, Italian, Japanese, Latin, Latin American studies, legal studies, linguistics, literature, mathematics, Mexican-American/Chicano studies, modern languages, music, philosophy, photography, physics, political science/government, psychobiology, psychology, religious studies, Russian, sociology, South Asian studies, Southeast Asian studies, Spanish, studio art, theater arts/drama, women's studies.

## Shepherd College
Accounting, applied art, applied mathematics, art education, art/fine arts, athletic training, biochemistry, biology/biological sciences, botany/plant sciences, broadcasting, business administration/commerce/management, business economics, business education, chemistry, child care/child and family studies, commercial art, communication, computer information systems, computer management, computer programming, computer science, data processing, (pre)dentistry sequence, early childhood education, earth science, economics, education, elementary education, English, European studies, fashion merchandising, finance/banking, food services

management, graphic arts, health education, history, home economics, home economics education, hotel and restaurant management, international studies, (pre)law sequence, library science, literature, management information systems, marketing/retailing/merchandising, mathematics, (pre)medicine sequence, middle school education, molecular biology, music, music education, music history, nursing, painting/drawing, photography, physical education, physical fitness/exercise science, physical sciences, piano/organ, political science/government, printmaking, psychology, public administration, recreational facilities management, recreation and leisure services, recreation therapy, science, science education, secondary education, secretarial studies/office management, social work, sociology, sports administration, studio art, textiles and clothing, theater arts/drama, (pre)veterinary medicine sequence, voice, Western civilization and culture, wind and percussion instruments, zoology.

## Siena College
Accounting, American studies, biology/biological sciences, business economics, chemistry, classics, computer science, (pre)dentistry sequence, economics, English, finance/banking, French, history, marketing/retailing/merchandising, mathematics, (pre)medicine sequence, philosophy, physics, political science/government, psychology, religious studies, secondary education, social work, sociology, Spanish.

## Simon's Rock College of Bard
American studies, art/fine arts, ecology, English, environmental sciences, French, literature, (pre)medicine sequence, natural sciences, social science, Spanish, statistics.

## Simpson College (IA)
Accounting, advertising, art education, art/fine arts, arts administration, athletic training, biology/biological sciences, business administration/commerce/management, chemistry, commercial art, communication, computer information systems, computer management, computer science, corrections, criminal justice, (pre)dentistry sequence, early childhood education, economics, education, elementary education, English, environmental biology, French, German, history, international business, international relations, (pre)law sequence, mathematics, medical technology, (pre)medicine sequence, music, music education, philosophy, physical education, physical therapy, political science/government, psychology, religious studies, science, secondary education, social science, sociology, Spanish, sports administration, theater arts/drama, (pre)veterinary medicine sequence.

## Skidmore College
American studies, anthropology, art/fine arts, art history, biochemistry, biology/biological sciences, business administration/commerce/management, business economics, chemistry, classics, computer science, creative writing, dance, (pre)dentistry sequence, economics, elementary education, English, French, geology, German, history, literature, mathematics, (pre)medicine sequence, music, philosophy, physical education, physics, political science/government, psychology, social work, sociology, Spanish, studio art, theater arts/drama, (pre)veterinary medicine sequence.

## Smith College
American studies, anthropology, architecture, art/fine arts, art history, astronomy, biochemistry, biology/biological sciences, black/African-American studies, chemistry, classics, comparative literature, computer science, dance, economics, education, English, French, geology, German, Germanic languages and literature, Greek, history, interdisciplinary studies, Italian, Latin, Latin American studies, mathematics, medieval studies, music, Near and Middle Eastern

studies, philosophy, physics, political science/government, Portuguese, psychology, religious studies, Russian, Russian and Slavic studies, sociology, Spanish, studio art, theater arts/drama, women's studies.

## South Dakota School of Mines and Technology
Chemical engineering, chemistry, civil engineering, computer engineering, computer science, electrical engineering, geological engineering, geology, industrial engineering, interdisciplinary studies, mathematics, mechanical engineering, metallurgical engineering, mining and mineral engineering, physics.

## Southern Methodist University
Accounting, advertising, African studies, anthropology, applied mathematics, archaeology, art/fine arts, art history, behavioral sciences, biochemistry, bioengineering, biology/biological sciences, biomedical engineering, black/African-American studies, broadcasting, business administration/commerce/management, business economics, chemistry, communication, computer engineering, computer science, creative writing, dance, (pre)dentistry sequence, earth science, economics, electrical engineering, English, environmental sciences, ethnic studies, European studies, film studies, finance/banking, French, geology, geophysics, German, Germanic languages and literature, history, humanities, international business, international studies, journalism, Latin American studies, (pre)law sequence, literature, management information systems, marketing/retailing/merchandising, mathematics, mechanical engineering, (pre)medicine sequence, Mexican-American/Chicano studies, modern languages, music, music education, music history, music therapy, philosophy, physics, piano/organ, political science/government, psychology, public relations, radio and television studies, real estate, religious studies, Russian, Russian and Slavic studies, social science, sociology, Spanish, statistics, stringed instruments, studio art, theater arts/drama, voice, wind and percussion instruments.

## Southwestern University
Accounting, American studies, animal sciences, art education, art/fine arts, art history, biology/biological sciences, business administration/commerce/management, chemistry, communication, computer science, economics, English, experimental psychology, French, German, history, international studies, literature, mathematics, modern languages, music, music education, music history, philosophy, physical education, physics, piano/organ, political science/government, psychology, religious studies, sacred music, social science, sociology, Spanish, studio art, theater arts/drama, (pre)veterinary medicine sequence, women's studies.

## Spelman College
Art/fine arts, biochemistry, biology/biological sciences, chemistry, child psychology/child development, computer science, economics, engineering (general), English, French, history, mathematics, music, natural sciences, philosophy, physics, political science/government, psychology, religious studies, sociology, Spanish, theater arts/drama.

## Stanford University
Aerospace sciences, African studies, American studies, anthropology, art/fine arts, art history, Asian/Oriental studies, biology/biological sciences, black/African-American studies, chemical engineering, chemistry, Chinese, civil engineering, classics, communication, comparative literature, computer engineering, computer science, earth science, East Asian studies, economics, electrical engineering, engineering (general), English, environmental sciences, European studies, French, geology, geophysics, German, history, humanities, industrial design, industrial engineering, interdisciplinary studies,

international relations, Italian, Japanese, journalism, Latin American studies, linguistics, materials engineering, materials sciences, mathematics, mechanical engineering, medieval studies, microbiology, music, music history, petroleum/natural gas engineering, philosophy, physics, political science/government, Portuguese, psychology, public affairs and policy studies, religious studies, Russian, Slavic languages, sociology, Spanish, statistics, studio art, theater arts/drama, urban studies, women's studies.

## State University of New York at Binghamton
Accounting, African studies, American studies, anthropology, Arabic, art/fine arts, art history, biochemistry, biology/biological sciences, black/African-American studies, business administration/commerce/management, chemistry, classics, comparative literature, computer information systems, computer science, creative writing, (pre)dentistry sequence, East Asian studies, ecology, economics, electrical engineering, English, environmental studies, film studies, French, geography, geology, geophysics, German, Germanic languages and literature, Hebrew, history, interdisciplinary studies, Italian, Judaic studies, Latin American studies, (pre)law sequence, liberal arts/general studies, literature, mathematics, mechanical engineering, (pre)medicine sequence, medieval studies, music, Near and Middle Eastern studies, nursing, painting/drawing, philosophy, physics, political science/government, psychobiology, psychology, Romance languages, social science, sociology, Spanish, studio art, theater arts/drama, (pre)veterinary medicine sequence.

## State University of New York at Buffalo
Accounting, aerospace engineering, American studies, anthropology, architecture, art education, art/fine arts, art history, biochemistry, biology/biological sciences, biophysics, black/African-American studies, business administration/commerce/management, cell biology, chemical engineering, chemistry, civil engineering, classics, communication, computer science, dance, (pre)dentistry sequence, early childhood education, ecology, economics, electrical engineering, engineering (general), engineering physics, engineering sciences, English, environmental biology, environmental design, film studies, French, geography, geology, German, gerontology, health science, history, human services, industrial engineering, interdisciplinary studies, international studies, Italian, Judaic studies, (pre)law sequence, legal studies, linguistics, mathematics, mechanical engineering, medical technology, (pre)medicine sequence, modern languages, molecular biology, music, music education, Native American studies, nuclear medical technology, nursing, occupational therapy, painting/drawing, pharmacology, pharmacy/pharmaceutical sciences, philosophy, photography, physical fitness/exercise science, physical therapy, physics, political science/government, psychology, public affairs and policy studies, radio and television studies, religious studies, Russian, science education, secondary education, social science, sociology, Spanish, speech pathology and audiology, statistics, studio art, theater arts/drama, urban studies, (pre)veterinary medicine sequence, women's studies.

## State University of New York College at Geneseo
Accounting, American studies, anthropology, applied art, art/fine arts, art history, biochemistry, biology/biological sciences, biophysics, black/African-American studies, broadcasting, business administration/commerce/management, chemistry, communication, comparative literature, computer science, (pre)dentistry sequence, early childhood education, economics, education, elementary education, English, French, geochemistry, geography, geology, geophysics, history, (pre)law sequence, mathematics, medical technology, (pre)medicine sequence, music, natural sciences, philosophy, physics,

political science/government, psychology, radio and television studies, sociology, Spanish, special education, speech pathology and audiology, speech/rhetoric/public address/debate, speech therapy, studio art, theater arts/drama, (pre)veterinary medicine sequence.

## State University of New York College of Environmental Science and Forestry

Biochemistry, biology/biological sciences, botany/plant sciences, chemistry, (pre)dentistry sequence, ecology, entomology, environmental biology, environmental design, environmental education, environmental engineering, environmental sciences, fish and game management, forest engineering, forestry, landscape architecture/design, land use management and reclamation, (pre)law sequence, (pre)medicine sequence, molecular biology, natural resource management, paper and pulp sciences, polymer science, science education, (pre)veterinary medicine sequence, wildlife biology, wildlife management, wood sciences, zoology.

## State University of New York Maritime College

Business administration/commerce/management, electrical engineering, humanities, marine engineering, maritime sciences, mechanical engineering, meteorology, naval architecture, naval sciences, oceanography.

## Stetson University

Accounting, American studies, art/fine arts, biology/biological sciences, business administration/commerce/management, business economics, chemistry, communication, computer science, (pre)dentistry sequence, economics, education, elementary education, English, finance/banking, French, geography, German, history, humanities, Latin American studies, (pre)law sequence, marketing/retailing/merchandising, mathematics, medical technology, (pre)medicine sequence, music, music education, philosophy, physical education, physics, piano/organ, political science/government, psychology, religious studies, Russian and Slavic studies, sacred music, social science, sociology, Spanish, speech/rhetoric/public address/debate, theater arts/drama, urban studies, (pre)veterinary medicine sequence, voice.

## Stevens Institute of Technology

Applied mathematics, biochemistry, biology/biological sciences, chemical engineering, chemistry, civil engineering, computer engineering, computer information systems, computer science, construction engineering, construction management, (pre)dentistry sequence, electrical engineering, engineering (general), engineering and applied sciences, engineering management, engineering physics, engineering sciences, English, environmental engineering, geological engineering, history, history of science, humanities, (pre)law sequence, liberal arts/general studies, management engineering, management information systems, manufacturing engineering, marine engineering, materials engineering, materials sciences, mathematics, mechanical engineering, (pre)medicine sequence, metallurgical engineering, metallurgy, nuclear engineering, ocean engineering, optics, philosophy, physics, plastics engineering, polymer science, robotics, science, statistics, systems science, technology and public affairs, telecommunications, transportation engineering, water resources.

## Swarthmore College

Anthropology, art/fine arts, art history, Asian/Oriental studies, astronomy, astrophysics, biochemistry, biology/biological sciences, black/African-American studies, chemistry, civil engineering, classics, computer engineering, economics, education, electrical engineering, engineering (general), English, environmental sciences, environmental

studies, French, German, Greek, history, international relations, international studies, Latin, linguistics, literature, mathematics, mechanical engineering, medieval studies, music, peace studies, philosophy, physics, political science/government, psychobiology, psychology, public affairs and policy studies, religious studies, Russian, sociology, Spanish, theater arts/drama, women's studies.

## Sweet Briar College

American studies, anthropology, art history, biochemistry, biology/biological sciences, chemistry, classics, computer science, creative writing, dance, ecology, economics, English, European studies, French, German, Greek, Hispanic studies, history, interdisciplinary studies, international studies, Italian, Latin, mathematics, modern languages, music, philosophy, physics, political science/government, psychology, religious studies, sociology, Spanish, studio art, theater arts/drama.

## Syracuse University

Accounting, advertising, aerospace engineering, American studies, anthropology, applied art, architecture, art education, art/fine arts, art history, behavioral sciences, bilingual/bicultural education, bioengineering, biology/biological sciences, black/African-American studies, broadcasting, business administration/commerce/management, ceramic art and design, chemical engineering, chemistry, child care/child and family studies, civil engineering, classics, communication, comparative literature, computer engineering, computer graphics, computer information systems, computer science, consumer services, (pre)dentistry sequence, dietetics, early childhood education, economics, education, electrical engineering, elementary education, engineering physics, English, environmental design, environmental engineering, family services, fashion design and technology, film studies, finance/banking, food services management, French, geography, geology, German, gerontology, health education, history, human development, human resources, illustration, industrial design, information science, interdisciplinary studies, interior design, international relations, Italian, jewelry and metalsmithing, journalism, labor and industrial relations, Latin American studies, (pre)law sequence, linguistics, management information systems, manufacturing engineering, marketing/retailing/merchandising, mathematics, mechanical engineering, (pre)medicine sequence, medieval studies, modern languages, music, music business, music education, natural sciences, nursing, nutrition, painting/drawing, philosophy, photography, physical education, physics, piano/organ, political science/government, printmaking, psychology, public affairs and policy studies, public relations, radio and television studies, rehabilitation therapy, religious studies, retail management, Romance languages, Russian, Russian and Slavic studies, science education, sculpture, secondary education, social science, social work, sociology, Spanish, special education, speech pathology and audiology, speech/rhetoric/public address/debate, statistics, stringed instruments, studio art, telecommunications, textile arts, textiles and clothing, theater arts/drama, (pre)veterinary medicine sequence, voice, wind and percussion instruments, women's studies.

## Taylor University

Accounting, art education, art/fine arts, athletic training, biblical languages, biblical studies, biology/biological sciences, broadcasting, business administration/commerce/management, chemistry, communication, computer information systems, computer programming, computer science, creative writing, (pre)dentistry sequence, economics, education, elementary education, English, environmental biology, environmental sciences, French, graphic arts, history, international business, international economics, international studies, journalism, (pre)law sequence, liberal arts/general studies, literature, mathematics, medical laboratory technology, medical technology, (pre)medicine sequence, middle school education, ministries, music, music education, natural sciences, philosophy, physical education, physics, political science/government, psychology, recreation and leisure services, religious education, religious studies, sacred music, science education, secondary education, social science, social work, sociology, Spanish, speech/rhetoric/public address/debate, theater arts/drama, theology, (pre)veterinary medicine sequence, voice.

## Texas A&M University (College Station)

Accounting, aerospace engineering, agricultural business, agricultural economics, agricultural education, agricultural engineering, agronomy/soil and crop sciences, animal sciences, anthropology, applied mathematics, architecture, bilingual/bicultural education, biochemistry, bioengineering, biology/biological sciences, biomedical sciences, biophysics, botany/plant sciences, business administration/commerce/management, chemical engineering, chemistry, civil engineering, communication, computer engineering, computer science, construction management, dairy sciences, economics, educational administration, electrical engineering, elementary education, engineering technology, English, entomology, environmental design, finance/banking, fish and game management, food sciences, forestry, French, genetics, geography, geology, geophysics, German, health education, history, horticulture, industrial administration, industrial engineering, interdisciplinary studies, Italian, journalism, landscape architecture/design, management information systems, marine biology, marine sciences, maritime sciences, marketing/retailing/merchandising, mathematics, mechanical engineering, meteorology, microbiology, mining and mineral engineering, nuclear engineering, nutrition, ocean engineering, ornamental horticulture, parks management, petroleum/natural gas engineering, philosophy, physical education, physics, political science/government, poultry sciences, psychology, range management, recreation and leisure services, safety and security technologies, sociology, soil conservation, Spanish, speech/rhetoric/public address/debate, theater arts/drama, tourism and travel, wildlife management, zoology.

## Texas Christian University

Accounting, advertising, applied art, art education, art/fine arts, art history, astrophysics, biochemistry, biology/biological sciences, broadcasting, business administration/commerce/management, chemistry, commercial art, communication, computer science, criminal justice, dance, (pre)dentistry sequence, dietetics, economics, education, engineering (general), English, environmental sciences, fashion design and technology, fashion merchandising, film studies, finance/banking, French, geology, history, interior design, journalism, Latin American studies, (pre)law sequence, liberal arts/general studies, marketing/retailing/merchandising, mathematics, medical technology, (pre)medicine sequence, modern languages, music, music education, music history, neurosciences, nursing, nutrition, painting/drawing, philosophy, physical education, physical fitness/exercise science, physics, piano/organ, political science/government, psychology, public relations, radio and television studies, reading education, real estate, religious studies, sacred music, social work, sociology, Spanish, special education, speech pathology and audiology, speech/rhetoric/public address/debate, stringed instruments, studio art, theater arts/drama, (pre)veterinary medicine sequence, voice, wind and percussion instruments.

## Thomas Aquinas College

Interdisciplinary studies, liberal arts/general studies, Western civilization and culture.

## Transylvania University

Anthropology, art education, art/fine arts, biology/biological sciences, business administration/commerce/management, chemistry, computer science, economics, education, elementary education, English, French, history, mathematics, music, music education, philosophy, physical education, physical fitness/exercise science, physics, political science/government, psychology, religious studies, secondary education, sociology, Spanish, studio art, theater arts/drama.

## Trenton State College

Accounting, art education, art/fine arts, art therapy, biology/biological sciences, business administration/commerce/management, business economics, chemistry, commercial art, communication, computer graphics, computer science, criminal justice, early childhood education, economics, education, elementary education, engineering sciences, English, finance/banking, graphic arts, health education, history, interior design, international business, journalism, (pre)law sequence, marketing/retailing/merchandising, mathematics, (pre)medicine sequence, music, music education, nursing, philosophy, physical education, physical fitness/exercise science, physics, political science/government, psychology, public administration, radio and television studies, secondary education, sociology, special education, statistics, (pre)veterinary medicine sequence.

## Trinity College (CT)

American studies, art/fine arts, art history, Asian/Oriental studies, biochemistry, biology/biological sciences, biomedical engineering, black/African-American studies, chemistry, classics, comparative literature, computer science, dance, East European and Soviet studies, ecology, economics, education, electrical engineering, engineering (general), English, French, German, Greek, history, international relations, Italian, Judaic studies, Latin, Latin American studies, literature, mathematics, mechanical engineering, modern languages, music, neurosciences, philosophy, physical sciences, physics, political science/government, psychology, public affairs and policy studies, religious studies, Romance languages, Russian, Russian and Slavic studies, sociology, Spanish, studio art, theater arts/drama, women's studies.

## Trinity University

Accounting, American studies, anthropology, art/fine arts, art history, Asian/Oriental studies, biochemistry, biology/biological sciences, business administration/commerce/management, business economics, chemistry, classics, communication, computer science, (pre)dentistry sequence, earth science, economics, education, engineering (general), engineering sciences, English, European studies, French, geology, German, history, interdisciplinary studies, international studies, journalism, (pre)law sequence, mathematics, (pre)medicine sequence, music, philosophy, physics, political science/government, psychology, religious studies, Russian, sociology, Spanish, speech/rhetoric/public address/debate, studio art, theater arts/drama, urban studies, (pre)veterinary medicine sequence.

## Tufts University

American studies, anthropology, archaeology, architectural engineering, art/fine arts, art history, Asian/Oriental studies, astronomy, behavioral sciences, biology/biological sciences, black/African-American studies, chemical engineering, chemistry, child care/child and family studies, child psychology/child development, Chinese, civil engineering, classics, computer engineering, computer science, early childhood education, ecology, economics, electrical engineering, elementary education, engineering and applied sciences, engineering design, engineering physics, engineering sciences, English, environmental engineering, environmental sciences, experimental psychology, French, geology, geophysical engineering, German, Greek, history, international relations, international studies, Latin, manufacturing engineering, mathematics, mechanical engineering, mental health/rehabilitation counseling, music, philosophy, physics, political science/government, psychology, public health, Romance languages, Russian, Russian and Slavic studies, secondary education, sociobiology, sociology, Southeast Asian studies, Spanish, special education, theater arts/drama, urban studies, women's studies.

## Tulane University
American studies, anthropology, architecture, art/fine arts, art history, Asian/Oriental studies, biochemistry, biology/biological sciences, biomedical engineering, business administration/commerce/management, chemical engineering, chemistry, civil engineering, classics, cognitive science, communication, computer engineering, computer information systems, computer science, earth science, ecology, economics, electrical engineering, English, environmental engineering, environmental studies, French, geology, German, Germanic languages and literature, Greek, history, international relations, Italian, Judaic studies, Latin, Latin American studies, liberal arts/general studies, linguistics, mathematics, mechanical engineering, medieval studies, music, philosophy, physical fitness/exercise science, physics, political science/government, Portuguese, psychology, public affairs and policy studies, Russian, Russian and Slavic studies, sociology, Spanish, sports administration, studio art, theater arts/drama, women's studies.

## Union College (NY)
American studies, anthropology, art/fine arts, biology/biological sciences, business economics, chemistry, civil engineering, classics, computer science, East Asian studies, East European and Soviet studies, economics, electrical engineering, English, environmental studies, geology, history, humanities, interdisciplinary studies, Latin American studies, mathematics, mechanical engineering, (pre)medicine sequence, modern languages, philosophy, physics, political science/government, psychology, science, social science, sociology, women's studies.

## Union University
Accounting, art education, art/fine arts, biology/biological sciences, business administration/commerce/management, business economics, business education, chemistry, communication, computer information systems, computer science, data processing, dental services, (pre)dentistry sequence, early childhood education, economics, education, elementary education, English, finance/banking, French, Greek, health education, history, interdisciplinary studies, journalism, (pre)law sequence, marine biology, marketing/retailing/merchandising, mathematics, medical technology, (pre)medicine sequence, music, music education, nursing, philosophy, physical education, psychology, radio and television studies, religious studies, sacred music, science, science education, secondary education, social work, sociology, Spanish, telecommunications, theology, (pre)veterinary medicine sequence, voice.

## United States Air Force Academy
Aerospace engineering, aerospace sciences, behavioral sciences, biochemistry, biology/biological sciences, business administration/commerce/management, chemistry, civil engineering, computer science, economics, electrical engineering, engineering (general), engineering mechanics, engineering sciences, English, environmental engineering, geography, history, humanities, legal studies, materials sciences, mathematics, mechanical engineering, meteorology, modern languages, operations research, philosophy, physics, planetary and space sciences, political science/government, science, social science.

## United States Coast Guard Academy
Business administration/commerce/management, civil engineering, electrical engineering, marine engineering, marine sciences, mathematics, mechanical engineering, naval architecture, political science/government.

## United States Merchant Marine Academy
Marine engineering, maritime sciences.

## United States Military Academy
Aerospace engineering, American studies, applied mathematics, Arabic, automotive engineering, behavioral sciences, biology/biological sciences, business administration/commerce/management, chemical engineering, chemistry, Chinese, civil engineering, computer engineering, computer information systems, computer science, East Asian studies, East European and Soviet studies, economics, electrical engineering, engineering and applied sciences, engineering management, engineering physics, English, environmental engineering, environmental sciences, environmental studies, European studies, French, geography, German, history, humanities, interdisciplinary studies, international studies, Latin American studies, (pre)law sequence, literature, management engineering, mathematics, mechanical engineering, (pre)medicine sequence, military science, modern languages, Near and Middle Eastern studies, nuclear engineering, operations research, philosophy, physical sciences, physics, political science/government, Portuguese, psychology, public affairs and policy studies, Russian, science, social science, sociology, Spanish, systems engineering.

## United States Naval Academy
Aerospace engineering, chemistry, computer science, economics, electrical engineering, engineering (general), engineering and applied sciences, English, history, marine engineering, mathematics, mechanical engineering, naval architecture, ocean engineering, oceanography, physics, political science/government, systems engineering.

## University at Albany, State University of New York
Accounting, African studies, anthropology, applied mathematics, art/fine arts, art history, Asian/Oriental studies, atmospheric sciences, biochemistry, biology/biological sciences, black/African-American studies, business administration/commerce/management, chemistry, Chinese, classics, communication, computer science, criminal justice, earth science, East Asian studies, East European and Soviet studies, economics, education, English, French, geography, geology, German, Greek, Hispanic studies, history, information science, interdisciplinary studies, Italian, Japanese, Judaic studies, Latin, Latin American studies, linguistics, management information systems, mathematics, medical technology, medieval studies, meteorology, molecular biology, music, philosophy, physical education, physics, political science/government, psychology, public affairs and policy studies, religious studies, Romance languages, Russian, Russian and Slavic studies, secondary education, Slavic languages, social work, sociology, Spanish, speech/rhetoric/public address/debate, studio art, theater arts/drama, urban studies, women's studies.

## University of Alabama in Huntsville
Accounting, art/fine arts, biology/biological sciences, business administration/commerce/management, business economics, chemical engineering, chemistry, civil engineering, communication, computer engineering, computer science, education, electrical engineering, English, finance/banking, French, German, history, industrial engineering, international business, management information systems,

marketing/retailing/merchandising, mathematics, mechanical engineering, music, music education, nursing, optics, philosophy, physics, political science/government, psychology, purchasing/inventory management, Russian and Slavic studies, sociology, Spanish, systems engineering.

## University of Arizona

Accounting, aerospace engineering, agricultural economics, agricultural education, agricultural engineering, agricultural technologies, agronomy/soil and crop sciences, animal sciences, anthropology, architecture, art education, art/fine arts, art history, Asian/Oriental studies, astronomy, atmospheric sciences, biochemistry, biology/biological sciences, black/African-American studies, botany/plant sciences, broadcasting, business administration/commerce/management, business economics, cell biology, chemical engineering, chemistry, child care/child and family studies, child psychology/child development, city/community/regional planning, civil engineering, classics, communication, computer engineering, computer information systems, computer science, consumer services, creative writing, criminal justice, dance, early childhood education, earth science, East Asian studies, East European and Soviet studies, ecology, economics, education, electrical engineering, elementary education, energy management technologies, engineering physics, English, entomology, environmental sciences, evolutionary biology, family and consumer studies, farm and ranch management, fashion merchandising, finance/banking, fish and game management, food sciences, food services management, French, geography, geological engineering, geology, German, Greek, health education, health services administration, history, home economics, home economics education, horticulture, human ecology, humanities, human resources, human services, industrial engineering, information science, interdisciplinary studies, interior design, Italian, jazz, Judaic studies, Latin, Latin American studies, liberal arts/general studies, linguistics, management information systems, marine biology, marketing/retailing/merchandising, materials engineering, materials sciences, mathematics, mechanical engineering, medical technology, metallurgical engineering, Mexican-American/Chicano studies, microbiology, mining and mineral engineering, molecular biology, music, music education, music history, Native American studies, natural resource management, Near and Middle Eastern studies, nuclear engineering, nursing, nutrition, occupational safety and health, optics, parks management, pharmacy/pharmaceutical sciences, philosophy, photography, physical fitness/exercise science, physics, piano/organ, planetary and space sciences, political science/government, Portuguese, psychology, public administration, radio and television studies, range management, real estate, recreation and leisure services, rehabilitation therapy, religious studies, Romance languages, Russian, Russian and Slavic studies, secondary education, social science, sociology, Spanish, speech pathology and audiology, speech/rhetoric/public address/debate, stringed instruments, studio art, systems engineering, textiles and clothing, theater arts/drama, urban studies, (pre)veterinary medicine sequence, veterinary sciences, voice, water resources, wildlife management, wind and percussion instruments, women's studies.

## University of California, Berkeley

American studies, anthropology, applied mathematics, architecture, art/fine arts, art history, Asian/Oriental studies, astrophysics, bioengineering, biology/biological sciences, black/African-American studies, botany/plant sciences, business administration/commerce/management, cell biology, chemical engineering, chemistry, Chinese, civil engineering, cognitive science, communication, comparative literature, computer engineering, computer science, conservation, dance, dietetics, earth science, East Asian studies, ecology, economics,

electrical engineering, engineering physics, engineering sciences, English, entomology, environmental sciences, ethnic studies, film studies, food sciences, forestry, forest technology, French, geography, geology, geophysical engineering, geophysics, German, Greek, history, humanities, industrial engineering, interdisciplinary studies, Italian, Japanese, landscape architecture/design, Latin, Latin American studies, legal studies, linguistics, literature, manufacturing engineering, materials sciences, mathematics, mechanical engineering, Mexican-American/Chicano studies, mining and mineral engineering, molecular biology, music, Native American studies, naval architecture, Near and Middle Eastern studies, nuclear engineering, nutrition, optometry, paleontology, peace studies, petroleum/natural gas engineering, philosophy, physical education, physical sciences, physics, political science/government, psychology, religious studies, Russian and Slavic studies, Scandinavian languages/studies, Slavic languages, social science, social work, sociology, soil conservation, South Asian studies, Southeast Asian studies, Spanish, speech/rhetoric/public address/debate, statistics, theater arts/drama, women's studies.

## University of California, Davis

Aerospace engineering, agricultural business, agricultural economics, agricultural education, agricultural engineering, agricultural sciences, agronomy/soil and crop sciences, American studies, animal sciences, anthropology, applied art, art/fine arts, art history, Asian/Oriental studies, atmospheric sciences, bacteriology, behavioral sciences, biochemistry, bioengineering, biology/biological sciences, black/African-American studies, botany/plant sciences, chemical engineering, chemistry, child psychology/child development, Chinese, civil engineering, classics, comparative literature, computer engineering, computer science, dietetics, early childhood education, East Asian studies, ecology, economics, electrical engineering, engineering and applied sciences, English, entomology, environmental biology, environmental design, environmental sciences, environmental studies, ethnic studies, family and consumer studies, farm and ranch management, fish and game management, food sciences, food services management, French, genetics, geography, geology, German, graphic arts, Greek, history, human development, interdisciplinary studies, interior design, international relations, Italian, Japanese, landscape architecture/design, Latin, linguistics, materials engineering, materials sciences, mathematics, mechanical engineering, medieval studies, Mexican-American/Chicano studies, microbiology, military science, music, music history, Native American studies, natural resource management, nutrition, philosophy, physical education, physics, physiology, political science/government, polymer science, poultry sciences, psychology, public affairs and policy studies, range management, religious studies, Russian, sociology, soil conservation, Spanish, speech/rhetoric/public address/debate, statistics, studio art, textile arts, textiles and clothing, theater arts/drama, toxicology, water resources, wildlife biology, women's studies, zoology.

## University of California, Irvine

Anthropology, art/fine arts, art history, biology/biological sciences, business administration/commerce/management, chemistry, civil engineering, classics, comparative literature, computer science, dance, ecology, economics, electrical engineering, engineering (general), English, ethnic studies, film studies, French, geography, German, history, human ecology, humanities, information science, linguistics, literature, mathematics, mechanical engineering, music, philosophy, physics, political science/government, psychology, Russian, social science, sociology, Spanish, studio art, theater arts/drama.

## University of California, Los Angeles

Aerospace engineering, African languages, African studies, anthropology, applied art, applied mathematics, Arabic, art/fine arts, art history, Asian/Oriental studies, astronomy, astrophysics, atmospheric sciences, biochemistry, biology/biological sciences, black/African-American studies, business economics, cell biology, chemical engineering, chemistry, Chinese, civil engineering, classics, cognitive science, communication, computer engineering, computer science, dance, earth science, East Asian studies, economics, electrical engineering, engineering (general), engineering and applied sciences, English, environmental studies, film studies, French, geochemistry, geography, geological engineering, geology, geophysical engineering, geophysics, German, Greek, Hebrew, history, international economics, international studies, Italian, Japanese, Judaic studies, Latin, Latin American studies, linguistics, materials engineering, materials sciences, mathematics, mechanical engineering, Mexican-American/Chicano studies, microbiology, music, music education, music history, natural resource management, Near and Middle Eastern studies, neurosciences, nursing, philosophy, physical fitness/exercise science, physics, physiology, planetary and space sciences, political science/government, Portuguese, psychobiology, psychology, radio and television studies, religious studies, Russian, Russian and Slavic studies, Scandinavian languages/studies, Slavic languages, sociology, Spanish, systems science, theater arts/drama, Western civilization and culture, women's studies.

## University of California, Riverside

Agronomy/soil and crop sciences, anthropology, art/fine arts, art history, Asian/Oriental studies, biochemistry, biology/biological sciences, biomedical sciences, botany/plant sciences, business administration/commerce/management, business economics, chemical engineering, chemistry, classics, comparative literature, computer science, creative writing, dance, economics, electrical engineering, English, entomology, environmental engineering, environmental sciences, ethnic studies, French, geography, geology, geophysics, German, history, human development, humanities, Latin American studies, (pre)law sequence, liberal arts/general studies, linguistics, mathematics, modern languages, music, philosophy, physical sciences, physics, political science/government, psychobiology, psychology, public administration, religious studies, Russian and Slavic studies, social science, sociology, Spanish, statistics, studio art, theater arts/drama, women's studies.

## University of California, San Diego

Aerospace engineering, anthropology, applied mathematics, art/fine arts, art history, Asian/Oriental studies, biochemistry, bioengineering, biology/biological sciences, biophysics, cell biology, chemical engineering, chemistry, Chinese, classics, cognitive science, communication, computer engineering, computer science, creative writing, earth science, ecology, economics, electrical engineering, engineering (general), engineering and applied sciences, engineering physics, engineering sciences, English, environmental sciences, ethnic studies, evolutionary biology, experimental psychology, film studies, French, German, Germanic languages and literature, history, information science, interdisciplinary studies, international studies, Italian, Judaic studies, linguistics, literature, mathematics, mechanical engineering, microbiology, molecular biology, music, music history, philosophy, photography, physics, physiology, political science/government, psychology, religious studies, Russian, sociology, Spanish, studio art, systems engineering, theater arts/drama, urban studies, women's studies.

## University of California, Santa Barbara

Accounting, anthropology, archaeology, art/fine arts, art history, Asian/Oriental studies, biochemistry, biology/biological sciences, biomedical sciences, black/African-American studies, botany/plant sciences, business economics, cell biology, chemical engineering,

chemistry, Chinese, classics, communication, comparative literature, computer science, creative writing, criminal justice, dance, ecology, economics, electrical engineering, English, environmental studies, evolutionary biology, film studies, French, geochemistry, geography, geology, geophysics, Germanic languages and literature, Greek, history, interdisciplinary studies, international relations, Italian, Japanese, Latin, Latin American studies, legal studies, linguistics, marine biology, mathematics, mechanical engineering, medieval studies, Mexican-American/Chicano studies, microbiology, molecular biology, music, nuclear engineering, operations research, painting/drawing, pharmacology, philosophy, physics, physiology, piano/organ, political science/government, Portuguese, psychobiology, psychology, public affairs and policy studies, religious studies, sculpture, Slavic languages, sociology, Spanish, statistics, studio art, theater arts/drama, voice, water resources, women's studies, zoology.

## University of California, Santa Cruz

American studies, anthropology, applied mathematics, art/fine arts, art history, biochemistry, biology/biological sciences, botany/plant sciences, business economics, cell biology, chemistry, classics, clinical psychology, comparative literature, computer engineering, computer science, creative writing, dance, earth science, East Asian studies, ecology, economics, English, environmental sciences, ethnic studies, evolutionary biology, experimental psychology, film and video production, film studies, French, geology, geophysics, German, Greek, history, information science, Italian, Japanese, Latin American studies, legal studies, linguistics, literature, marine biology, mathematics, medieval studies, molecular biology, music, natural resource management, painting/drawing, peace studies, philosophy, photography, physics, political science/government, printmaking, psychobiology, psychology, religious studies, Russian, Russian and Slavic studies, sculpture, sociology, South Asian studies, Southeast Asian studies, Spanish, studio art, theater arts/drama, Western civilization and culture, women's studies.

## University of Chicago

African studies, American studies, anthropology, applied mathematics, Arabic, art/fine arts, art history, Asian/Oriental studies, behavioral sciences, biblical languages, biochemistry, biology/biological sciences, black/African-American studies, chemistry, Chinese, classics, computer science, creative writing, East Asian studies, East European and Soviet studies, economics, English, environmental studies, French, geography, geophysics, German, Germanic languages and literature, Greek, history, history of science, humanities, interdisciplinary studies, Italian, Japanese, Judaic studies, Latin, Latin American studies, liberal arts/general studies, linguistics, mathematics, medieval studies, modern languages, music, music history, Near and Middle Eastern studies, philosophy, physics, political science/government, psychology, public affairs and policy studies, religious studies, Romance languages, Russian, Russian and Slavic studies, Slavic languages, social science, sociology, South Asian studies, Southeast Asian studies, Spanish, statistics, studio art.

## University of Colorado at Boulder

Accounting, advertising, aerospace engineering, American studies, anthropology, applied mathematics, architectural engineering, architecture, art education, art/fine arts, art history, Asian/Oriental studies, biochemistry, biology/biological sciences, broadcasting, business administration/commerce/management, cell biology, chemical engineering, chemistry, Chinese, civil engineering, classics, communication, computer engineering, computer information systems, computer science, conservation, dance, (pre)dentistry sequence, East Asian studies, East European and Soviet studies, ecology, economics, education, electrical engineering, engineering physics, English, environmental biology, environmental design, environmental engineering, environmental sciences, environmental studies, ethnic studies, film studies, finance/banking, French, geography, geology, Germanic languages and literature, history, humanities, interdisciplinary studies, international studies, Italian, Japanese, journalism, Latin, Latin American studies, linguistics, management information systems, marketing/retailing/merchandising, mathematics, mechanical engineering, (pre)medicine sequence, microbiology, molecular biology, music, music education, music history, philosophy, physical fitness/exercise science, physics, political science/government, psychology, religious studies, Russian and Slavic studies, sociology, Spanish, speech pathology and audiology, studio art, theater arts/drama, women's studies.

## University of Connecticut (Storrs)
Accounting, actuarial science, agricultural economics, agricultural education, agricultural sciences, agronomy/soil and crop sciences, animal sciences, anthropology, applied mathematics, art/fine arts, art history, biology/biological sciences, biophysics, business administration/commerce/management, ceramic art and design, chemical engineering, chemistry, civil engineering, classics, communication, computer engineering, cytotechnology, dietetics, East European and Soviet studies, economics, electrical engineering, elementary education, English, family and consumer studies, finance/banking, French, geography, geology, geophysics, German, graphic arts, health services administration, history, horticulture, human development, insurance, interdisciplinary studies, Islamic studies, Italian, journalism, landscape architecture/design, Latin American studies, linguistics, management information systems, marketing/retailing/merchandising, mathematics, mechanical engineering, medical laboratory technology, medical technology, molecular biology, music, music education, natural resource management, nursing, nutrition, painting/drawing, pharmacy/pharmaceutical sciences, philosophy, photography, physical education, physical fitness/exercise science, physical therapy, physics, physiology, political science/government, Portuguese, printmaking, psychology, real estate, recreation and leisure services, Russian, sculpture, secondary education, sociology, Spanish, special education, statistics, theater arts/drama, urban studies, women's studies.

## University of Dallas
Art education, art/fine arts, art history, biochemistry, biology/biological sciences, chemistry, classics, (pre)dentistry sequence, economics, education, elementary education, English, French, German, history, (pre)law sequence, mathematics, (pre)medicine sequence, philosophy, physics, political science/government, psychology, secondary education, Spanish, theater arts/drama, theology.

## University of Delaware
Accounting, agricultural business, agricultural economics, agricultural education, agricultural engineering, agricultural sciences, agronomy/soil and crop sciences, animal sciences, anthropology, applied art, art/fine arts, art history, astronomy, athletic training, bilingual/bicultural education, biochemistry, biology/biological sciences, biotechnology, black/African-American studies, botany/plant sciences, business administration/commerce/management, business economics, chemical engineering, chemistry, child care/child and family studies, child psychology/child development, civil engineering, cognitive science, communication, community services, comparative literature, computer science, criminal justice, (pre)dentistry sequence, dietetics, early childhood education, East Asian studies, ecology, economics, education, electrical engineering, elementary education, English, entomology, environmental engineering, environmental engineering technology, environmental sciences, European studies, family and

consumer studies, family services, fashion design and technology, fashion merchandising, film studies, finance/banking, food marketing, food sciences, French, geography, geology, geophysical engineering, geophysics, German, Germanic languages and literature, graphic arts, health education, historic preservation, history, home economics, horticulture, hotel and restaurant management, human development, information science, international business, international studies, Italian, jazz, journalism, Judaic studies, Latin, Latin American studies, (pre)law sequence, legal studies, liberal arts/general studies, linguistics, management information systems, marketing/retailing/merchandising, mathematics, mechanical engineering, medical technology, (pre)medicine sequence, medieval studies, music, music education, nursing, nutrition, ocean engineering, ornamental horticulture, paleontology, parks management, philosophy, physical education, physical fitness/exercise science, physics, piano/organ, political science/government, psychology, public administration, recreational facilities management, religious studies, Russian, science education, secondary education, sociology, soil conservation, Spanish, special education, statistics, technical writing, textiles and clothing, theater arts/drama, transportation engineering, (pre)veterinary medicine sequence, voice, wildlife management, women's studies.

## University of Denver
Accounting, animal sciences, anthropology, art/fine arts, art history, biochemistry, biology/biological sciences, business administration/commerce/management, business economics, chemistry, classics, communication, comparative literature, computer science, construction management, creative writing, (pre)dentistry sequence, economics, electrical engineering, engineering (general), English, environmental sciences, finance/banking, French, geography, German, graphic arts, Greek, history, hotel and restaurant management, interdisciplinary studies, international business, international studies, Italian, Japanese, jazz, journalism, Latin, Latin American studies, (pre)law sequence, marketing/retailing/merchandising, mathematics, mechanical engineering, (pre)medicine sequence, music, music business, music education, natural sciences, philosophy, physics, political science/government, psychology, public affairs and policy studies, real estate, religious studies, Russian, science, social science, sociology, Spanish, statistics, studio art, theater arts/drama, (pre)veterinary medicine sequence, women's studies.

## University of Detroit Mercy
Accounting, architecture, behavioral sciences, biochemistry, biology/biological sciences, broadcasting, business administration/commerce/management, chemical engineering, chemistry, child psychology/child development, civil engineering, classics, communication, computer engineering, computer information systems, computer programming, computer science, computer technologies, criminal justice, dental services, (pre)dentistry sequence, drug and alcohol/substance abuse counseling, early childhood education, economics, education, electrical engineering, elementary education, engineering (general), English, finance/banking, health education, health services administration, history, hotel and restaurant management, humanities, human resources, human services, industrial administration, information science, international business, journalism, labor and industrial relations, (pre)law sequence, legal studies, management information systems, marketing/retailing/merchandising, mathematics, mechanical engineering, (pre)medicine sequence, nursing, philosophy, physical education, plastics engineering, plastics technology, political science/government, polymer science, psychology, public administration, public relations, radio and television studies, religious studies, science education, secondary education, social work, sociology, Spanish, special education, sports medicine, systems engineering, theater arts/drama.

## University of Evansville

Accounting, advertising, anthropology, archaeology, art education, art/fine arts, art history, arts administration, biology/biological sciences, business administration/commerce/management, business economics, ceramic art and design, chemistry, civil engineering, communication, computer engineering, computer science, creative writing, criminal justice, (pre)dentistry sequence, economics, education, electrical engineering, elementary education, engineering management, English, environmental studies, finance/banking, French, German, graphic arts, history, international business, international studies, journalism, (pre)law sequence, legal studies, liberal arts/general studies, literature, marketing/retailing/merchandising, mathematics, mechanical engineering, medical technology, (pre)medicine sequence, music, music business, music education, music therapy, nursing, painting/drawing, philosophy, physical education, physical fitness/exercise science, physical therapy, physics, political science/government, psychobiology, psychology, public relations, religious studies, science education, sculpture, secondary education, sociology, Spanish, special education, telecommunications, theater arts/drama, (pre)veterinary medicine sequence.

## University of Florida

Accounting, advertising, aerospace engineering, agricultural business, agricultural economics, agricultural education, agricultural engineering, agronomy/soil and crop sciences, American studies, animal sciences, anthropology, architecture, art education, art/fine arts, art history, Asian/Oriental studies, astronomy, botany/plant sciences, business administration/commerce/management, chemical engineering, chemistry, civil engineering, classics, computer engineering, computer science, conservation, construction management, criminal justice, dairy sciences, East Asian studies, ecology, economics, electrical engineering, elementary education, engineering sciences, English, entomology, environmental engineering, finance/banking, food sciences, forestry, French, geography, geology, German, graphic arts, health education, health science, history, horticulture, industrial engineering, insurance, interdisciplinary studies, interior design, journalism, Judaic studies, landscape architecture/design, linguistics, management information systems, marketing/retailing/merchandising, materials engineering, mathematics, mechanical engineering, microbiology, music, music education, music history, natural resource management, nuclear engineering, nursing, nutrition, occupational therapy, pharmacy/pharmaceutical sciences, philosophy, photography, physical education, physical therapy, physician's assistant studies, physics, political science/government, Portuguese, poultry sciences, psychology, public relations, real estate, recreation and leisure services, religious studies, Russian, sociology, soil conservation, Spanish, special education, speech pathology and audiology, statistics, studio art, surveying engineering, telecommunications, theater arts/drama, zoology.

## University of Georgia

Accounting, advertising, agricultural business, agricultural economics, agricultural education, agricultural engineering, agricultural sciences, agricultural technologies, agronomy/soil and crop sciences, animal sciences, anthropology, applied art, art education, art/fine arts, art history, astronomy, biochemistry, biology/biological sciences, black/African-American studies, botany/plant sciences, broadcasting, business administration/commerce/management, business education, chemistry, child care/child and family studies, child psychology/child development, Chinese, classics, communication, comparative literature, computer science, criminal justice, dairy sciences, dance, (pre)dentistry sequence, dietetics, early childhood education, economics, education, elementary education, English, entomology, environmental health sciences, family and consumer studies, fashion merchandising, film studies, finance/banking, fish and game management, food sciences,

food services management, forestry, forest technology, French, genetics, geography, geology, German, Germanic languages and literature, graphic arts, Greek, health education, history, home economics, home economics education, horticulture, hotel and restaurant management, human resources, industrial arts, insurance, interdisciplinary studies, interior design, international business, international studies, Italian, Japanese, journalism, labor and industrial relations, landscape architecture/design, landscaping/grounds maintenance, Latin, Latin American studies, (pre)law sequence, linguistics, literature, management information systems, marketing/retailing/merchandising, mathematics, medical technology, (pre)medicine sequence, medieval studies, microbiology, middle school education, music, music education, music history, music therapy, nursing, nutrition, operations research, optometry, painting/drawing, pest control technology, pharmacy/pharmaceutical sciences, philosophy, photography, physical education, physical fitness/exercise science, physics, piano/organ, political science/government, poultry sciences, psychology, public relations, publishing, radio and television studies, reading education, real estate, recreation and leisure services, religious studies, Romance languages, Russian, science education, sculpture, secondary education, Slavic languages, social science, social work, sociology, Spanish, special education, speech pathology and audiology, speech/rhetoric/public address/debate, statistics, stringed instruments, studio art, telecommunications, textiles and clothing, theater arts/drama, theology, (pre)veterinary medicine sequence, vocational education, voice, water resources, wildlife biology, wind and percussion instruments, zoology.

## University of Illinois at Urbana-Champaign

Accounting, actuarial science, advertising, aerospace engineering, agricultural business, agricultural economics, agricultural education, agricultural engineering, agricultural sciences, agronomy/soil and crop sciences, aircraft and missile maintenance, American studies, anatomy, animal sciences, anthropology, architecture, art education, art/fine arts, art history, Asian/Oriental studies, astronomy, biochemistry, bioengineering, biology/biological sciences, biophysics, botany/plant sciences, broadcasting, business administration/commerce/management, business education, cell biology, ceramic engineering, chemical engineering, chemistry, child care/child and family studies, city/community/regional planning, civil engineering, classics, communication, comparative literature, computer engineering, computer science, consumer services, dairy sciences, dance, dietetics, early childhood education, East European and Soviet studies, ecology, economics, education, electrical engineering, elementary education, engineering (general), engineering mechanics, engineering physics, English, entomology, family and consumer studies, fashion design and technology, finance/banking, food sciences, food services management, forestry, French, genetics, geography, geology, German, Germanic languages and literature, gerontology, graphic arts, Greek, health education, health services administration, history, history of science, home economics, home economics education, horticulture, hotel and restaurant management, human development, humanities, human resources, industrial design, industrial engineering, interdisciplinary studies, interior design, Italian, journalism, landscape architecture/design, Latin, Latin American studies, (pre)law sequence, liberal arts/general studies, linguistics, literature, management information systems, manufacturing engineering, marketing/retailing/merchandising, materials engineering, materials sciences, mathematics, mechanical engineering, medieval studies, metallurgical engineering, microbiology, music, musical instrument technology, music education, music history, nuclear engineering, nutrition, ornamental horticulture, painting/drawing, parks management, philosophy, photography, physical education, physics, physiology, piano/organ, political science/government, polymer science, Portuguese, psychology, real estate, recreation and leisure services, religious studies, Russian, Russian and Slavic studies, science education, sculpture, secondary education, social science, sociology, soil conservation, Spanish, special education, speech pathology and audiology, speech/rhetoric/public address/debate, statistics, stringed instruments, textiles and clothing, theater arts/drama, urban studies, (pre)veterinary medicine sequence, vocational education, voice, wind and percussion instruments.

## The University of Iowa

Accounting, actuarial science, advertising, African studies, American studies, anthropology, art education, art/fine arts, art history, Asian/Oriental studies, astronomy, athletic training, biochemistry, biology/biological sciences, biomedical engineering, black/African-American studies, botany/plant sciences, broadcasting, business administration/commerce/management, business economics, ceramic art and design, chemical engineering, chemistry, child psychology/child development, Chinese, civil engineering, classics, clinical psychology, communication, comparative literature, computer engineering, computer science, creative writing, dance, (pre)dentistry sequence, earth science, East European and Soviet studies, economics, education, electrical engineering, elementary education, engineering (general), English, environmental engineering, environmental studies, experimental psychology, film and video production, film studies, finance/banking, French, geography, geology, German, Greek, health education, history, humanities, human resources, industrial engineering, interdisciplinary studies, international business, international studies, Italian, Japanese, jazz, jewelry and metalsmithing, journalism, labor and industrial relations, Latin, Latin American studies, (pre)law sequence, liberal arts/general studies, linguistics, literature, management engineering, marketing/retailing/merchandising, materials engineering, mathematics, mechanical engineering, medical technology, (pre)medicine sequence, microbiology, museum studies, music, music education, music history, music therapy, Native American studies, Near and Middle Eastern studies, nuclear medical technology, nursing, opera, painting/drawing, pharmacy/pharmaceutical sciences, philosophy, photography, physical education, physical fitness/exercise science, physics, piano/organ, political science/government, Portuguese, printmaking, psychology, public relations, radio and television studies, recreational facilities management, recreation and leisure services, recreation therapy, religious studies, Russian, science education, sculpture, secondary education, social science, social work, sociology, Spanish, speech pathology and audiology, speech/rhetoric/public address/debate, speech therapy, sports administration, sports medicine, statistics, stringed instruments, studio art, theater arts/drama, urban studies, (pre)veterinary medicine sequence, voice, wind and percussion instruments, women's studies, zoology.

## University of Kansas

Accounting, advertising, aerospace engineering, African studies, American studies, anthropology, applied art, archaeology, architectural engineering, architecture, art education, art/fine arts, art history, Asian/Oriental studies, astronomy, biochemistry, biology/biological sciences, black/African-American studies, broadcasting, business administration/commerce/management, ceramic art and design, chemical engineering, chemistry, child care/child and family studies, child psychology/child development, Chinese, civil engineering, classics, commercial art, computer engineering, computer science, cytotechnology, dance, (pre)dentistry sequence, early childhood education, East Asian studies, East European and Soviet studies, economics, electrical engineering, elementary education, engineering physics, English, environmental studies, film studies, French, genetics, geography, geology, German, Germanic languages and literature, graphic arts, health education, history, human development, humanities, industrial design, interior design, Japanese, jewelry and

metalsmithing, journalism, Latin American studies, (pre)law sequence, liberal arts/general studies, linguistics, mathematics, mechanical engineering, medical records services, medical technology, (pre)medicine sequence, microbiology, music, music education, music history, music therapy, nursing, occupational therapy, painting/drawing, petroleum/natural gas engineering, pharmacy/pharmaceutical sciences, philosophy, physical education, physical fitness/exercise science, physics, physiology, piano/organ, political science/government, psychology, radio and television studies, radiological technology, religious studies, respiratory therapy, Russian, Russian and Slavic studies, science education, sculpture, secondary education, Slavic languages, social work, sociology, Spanish, speech pathology and audiology, speech/rhetoric/public address/debate, stringed instruments, studio art, textile arts, theater arts/drama, voice, wind and percussion instruments, women's studies.

## University of Maryland College Park

Accounting, advertising, aerospace engineering, agricultural business, agricultural economics, agricultural education, agricultural engineering, agricultural sciences, agronomy/soil and crop sciences, American studies, animal sciences, anthropology, architecture, art education, art/fine arts, art history, astronomy, biochemistry, biology/biological sciences, black/African-American studies, botany/plant sciences, broadcasting, business administration/commerce/management, business education, cartography, chemical engineering, chemistry, child care/child and family studies, Chinese, city/community/regional planning, civil engineering, classics, community services, computer science, conservation, consumer services, criminal justice, criminology, dairy sciences, dance, (pre)dentistry sequence, dietetics, early childhood education, East Asian studies, economics, education, educational administration, electrical engineering, elementary education, engineering (general), English, entomology, family and consumer studies, fashion design and technology, fashion merchandising, finance/banking, fire protection engineering, fire science, food sciences, French, geography, geology, German, Germanic languages and literature, health education, history, home economics, home economics education, horticulture, human ecology, industrial arts, interior design, Italian, Japanese, journalism, Judaic studies, labor and industrial relations, landscape architecture/design, Latin, law enforcement/police sciences, (pre)law sequence, liberal arts/general studies, linguistics, marketing/retailing/merchandising, mathematics, mechanical engineering, (pre)medicine sequence, microbiology, music, music education, music history, natural resource management, nuclear engineering, nutrition, philosophy, physical education, physical fitness/exercise science, physical sciences, physics, political science/government, Portuguese, poultry sciences, psychology, public relations, Romance languages, Russian, Russian and Slavic studies, science education, secondary education, secretarial studies/office management, Slavic languages, sociology, soil conservation, Spanish, special education, speech pathology and audiology, speech/rhetoric/public address/debate, speech therapy, statistics, studio art, textiles and clothing, theater arts/drama, transportation technologies, urban studies, (pre)veterinary medicine sequence, vocational education, wildlife management, zoology.

## University of Massachusetts Amherst

Accounting, agricultural economics, agronomy/soil and crop sciences, animal sciences, anthropology, art education, art/fine arts, art history, astronomy, biochemistry, biology/biological sciences, black/African-American studies, botany/plant sciences, business administration/commerce/management, chemical engineering, chemistry, Chinese, civil engineering, classics, communication, comparative literature, computer engineering, computer science, dance, (pre)dentistry sequence, drafting and design, East European and Soviet studies, economics, education, electrical engineering, English, entomology, environmental design, environmental sciences, fashion merchandising, finance/banking, food sciences, forestry, French, geography, geology, German, history, home economics, hotel and restaurant management, industrial engineering, interdisciplinary studies, Italian, Japanese, journalism, Judaic studies, landscape architecture/design, (pre)law sequence, legal studies, liberal arts/general studies, linguistics, marketing/retailing/merchandising, mathematics, mechanical engineering, medical technology, (pre)medicine sequence, microbiology, music, natural resource management, Near and Middle Eastern studies, nursing, nutrition, philosophy, physical fitness/exercise science, physics, political science/government, Portuguese, psychology, Russian, science, sociology, Spanish, speech pathology and audiology, sports administration, studio art, theater arts/drama, (pre)veterinary medicine sequence, wildlife biology, women's studies, wood sciences.

## University of Miami

Accounting, actuarial science, advertising, aerospace engineering, African studies, American studies, anthropology, applied mathematics, architectural engineering, architecture, art education, art/fine arts, art history, astronomy, audio engineering, biochemistry, biology/biological sciences, biomedical engineering, black/African-American studies, broadcasting, business administration/commerce/management, ceramic art and design, chemistry, civil engineering, communication, computer engineering, computer information systems, computer science, criminology, cytotechnology, (pre)dentistry sequence, economics, electrical engineering, electronics engineering, elementary education, engineering sciences, English, environmental engineering, environmental health sciences, environmental sciences, film and video production, film studies, finance/banking, French, geography, geology, German, graphic arts, health science, health services administration, history, human services, illustration, industrial administration, industrial engineering, insurance, international business, international studies, jazz, journalism, Judaic studies, landscape architecture/design, Latin American studies, (pre)law sequence, legal studies, liberal arts/general studies, manufacturing engineering, marine biology, marine sciences, marketing/retailing/merchandising, mathematics, mechanical engineering, medical technology, (pre)medicine sequence, meteorology, microbiology, music, music business, music education, music therapy, nuclear engineering, nuclear medical technology, nursing, ocean engineering, oceanography, painting/drawing, philosophy, photography, physical therapy, physics, piano/organ, political science/government, printmaking, psychobiology, psychology, public affairs and policy studies, public relations, radio and television studies, radiological technology, real estate, religious studies, science education, secondary education, sociology, Spanish, special education, speech/rhetoric/public address/debate, statistics, stringed instruments, studio art, systems science, telecommunications, theater arts/drama, transportation engineering, voice, wildlife management, wind and percussion instruments, women's studies.

## University of Michigan (Ann Arbor)

Accounting, aerospace engineering, African studies, American studies, anthropology, applied art, applied mathematics, Arabic, archaeology, architecture, art education, art history, Asian/Oriental studies, astronomy, atmospheric sciences, biblical studies, biochemistry, biology/biological sciences, biomedical sciences, biometrics, biophysics, black/African-American studies, botany/plant sciences, business administration/commerce/management, cell biology, ceramic art and design, chemical engineering, chemistry, Chinese, civil engineering, classics, communication, comparative literature, computer engineering, computer information systems, computer science, creative writing, dance, dental services, (pre)dentistry sequence, ecology,

economics, education, electrical engineering, elementary education, engineering (general), engineering physics, engineering sciences, English, environmental design, environmental education, environmental engineering, environmental sciences, environmental studies, European studies, film studies, fish and game management, French, geography, German, graphic arts, Greek, Hebrew, Hispanic studies, history, humanities, industrial design, industrial engineering, interdisciplinary studies, interior design, international studies, Islamic studies, Italian, Japanese, jazz, jewelry and metalsmithing, journalism, Judaic studies, landscape architecture/design, Latin, Latin American studies, liberal arts/general studies, linguistics, literature, marine engineering, materials engineering, materials sciences, mathematics, mechanical engineering, (pre)medicine sequence, medieval studies, metallurgical engineering, meteorology, Mexican-American/Chicano studies, microbiology, molecular biology, music, music education, music history, natural resource management, naval architecture, Near and Middle Eastern studies, nuclear engineering, nursing, nutrition, oceanography, painting/drawing, pharmacy/pharmaceutical sciences, philosophy, photography, physical education, physical fitness/exercise science, physics, piano/organ, political science/government, printmaking, psychology, religious studies, Romance languages, Russian, Russian and Slavic studies, sacred music, Scandinavian languages/studies, sculpture, secondary education, social science, sociology, Spanish, special education, speech pathology and audiology, speech/rhetoric/public address/debate, sports administration, statistics, stringed instruments, textile arts, theater arts/drama, voice, wildlife biology, wind and percussion instruments, women's studies, zoology.

## University of Michigan–Dearborn

American studies, anthropology, art education, art history, arts administration, behavioral sciences, bilingual/bicultural education, biochemistry, biology/biological sciences, business administration/commerce/management, chemistry, child care/child and family studies, child psychology/child development, communication equipment technology, comparative literature, computer information systems, computer science, early childhood education, economics, education, electrical engineering, elementary education, engineering (general), English, environmental sciences, environmental studies, finance/banking, French, German, health services administration, Hispanic studies, history, humanities, industrial engineering, information science, interdisciplinary studies, international studies, liberal arts/general studies, manufacturing engineering, marketing/retailing/merchandising, mathematics, mechanical engineering, medieval studies, microbiology, middle school education, music, music history, natural sciences, philosophy, physical sciences, physics, political science/government, psychology, public administration, science, science education, secondary education, social science, sociology, Spanish, speech/rhetoric/public address/debate, women's studies.

## University of Minnesota, Morris

Art history, biology/biological sciences, business economics, chemistry, communication, computer science, (pre)dentistry sequence, economics, education, elementary education, English, European studies, French, geology, German, history, human services, Latin American studies, (pre)law sequence, mathematics, (pre)medicine sequence, music, philosophy, physics, political science/government, psychology, secondary education, social science, sociology, Spanish, speech/rhetoric/public address/debate, studio art, theater arts/drama, (pre)veterinary medicine sequence.

## University of Minnesota, Twin Cities Campus

Accounting, actuarial science, aerospace engineering, African studies, agricultural business, agricultural education, agricultural engineering, agricultural sciences, agronomy/soil and crop sciences, American studies, animal sciences, anthropology, applied art, architecture, art/fine arts, art history, astronomy, astrophysics, biochemistry, biology/biological sciences, black/African-American studies, botany/plant sciences, business administration/commerce/management, business education, cell biology, chemical engineering, chemistry, child psychology/child development, Chinese, civil engineering, classics, communication, comparative literature, computer science, criminology, dance, dental services, (pre)dentistry sequence, early childhood education, East Asian studies, ecology, economics, education, electrical engineering, elementary education, engineering (general), engineering and applied sciences, English, environmental design, environmental studies, film studies, fish and game management, food sciences, forestry, forest technology, French, funeral service, genetics, geography, geological engineering, geology, geophysics, German, Greek, Hebrew, Hispanic studies, history, home economics, home economics education, human development, humanities, interdisciplinary studies, interior design, international relations, Italian, Japanese, journalism, Judaic studies, landscape architecture/design, Latin, Latin American studies, (pre)law sequence, linguistics, marketing/retailing/merchandising, materials engineering, materials sciences, mathematics, mechanical engineering, medical technology, (pre)medicine sequence, Mexican-American/Chicano studies, microbiology, modern languages, music, music education, music therapy, Native American studies, natural resource management, Near and Middle Eastern studies, nursing, nutrition, occupational therapy, parks management, pharmacy/pharmaceutical sciences, philosophy, physical education, physical fitness/exercise science, physical therapy, physics, physiology, political science/government, Portuguese, psychology, recreational facilities management, recreation and leisure services, religious studies, Russian, Russian and Slavic studies, Scandinavian languages/studies, secondary education, social science, sociology, South Asian studies, Spanish, speech pathology and audiology, speech therapy, statistics, technical writing, textiles and clothing, theater arts/drama, urban studies, (pre)veterinary medicine sequence, vocational education, wildlife management, women's studies.

## University of Missouri–Columbia

Accounting, advertising, agricultural economics, agricultural education, agricultural engineering, agricultural sciences, agricultural technologies, agronomy/soil and crop sciences, animal sciences, anthropology, archaeology, art education, art/fine arts, art history, atmospheric sciences, behavioral sciences, biochemistry, biology/biological sciences, broadcasting, business administration/commerce/management, business economics, business education, chemical engineering, chemistry, child care/child and family studies, child psychology/child development, civil engineering, classics, communication, computer engineering, computer science, cytotechnology, (pre)dentistry sequence, dietetics, early childhood education, economics, education, electrical engineering, elementary education, English, environmental design, family and consumer studies, fashion merchandising, finance/banking, fish and game management, food sciences, forestry, French, geography, geology, German, guidance and counseling, health education, history, home economics education, horticulture, hotel and restaurant management, human development, industrial arts, industrial engineering, insurance, interdisciplinary studies, interior design, international business, international studies, journalism, liberal arts/general studies, marketing/retailing/merchandising, mathematics, mechanical engineering, medical laboratory technology, (pre)medicine sequence, microbiology, music, music education, nuclear medical technology, nursing, nutrition, occupational therapy, parks management, philosophy, photography, physical therapy, physics, political science/government, psychology, publishing, radio and television studies,

radiological sciences, reading education, real estate, recreation and leisure services, religious studies, respiratory therapy, Romance languages, Russian, Russian and Slavic studies, science education, secondary education, social work, sociology, South Asian studies, Spanish, special education, speech pathology and audiology, speech/rhetoric/public address/debate, speech therapy, statistics, textiles and clothing, theater arts/drama, tourism and travel, (pre)veterinary medicine sequence, vocational education.

## University of Missouri–Kansas City

Accounting, American studies, art/fine arts, art history, biology/biological sciences, business administration/commerce/management, chemistry, civil engineering, communication, computer science, criminal justice, dance, dental services, earth science, economics, education, electrical engineering, elementary education, English, French, geography, geology, German, history, interdisciplinary studies, Judaic studies, liberal arts/general studies, mathematics, mechanical engineering, medical technology, music, music education, music therapy, nursing, pharmacy/pharmaceutical sciences, philosophy, physical education, physics, piano/organ, political science/government, psychology, secondary education, sociology, Spanish, stringed instruments, studio art, theater arts/drama, urban studies, voice, wind and percussion instruments.

## University of Missouri–Rolla

Aerospace engineering, applied mathematics, biochemistry, biology/biological sciences, ceramic engineering, chemical engineering, chemistry, civil engineering, computer science, (pre)dentistry sequence, economics, electrical engineering, engineering management, English, geological engineering, geology, geophysics, history, (pre)law sequence, management information systems, mechanical engineering, (pre)medicine sequence, metallurgical engineering, mining and mineral engineering, nuclear engineering, nursing, petroleum/natural gas engineering, philosophy, physics, polymer science, psychology.

## University of New Hampshire (Durham)

Accounting, adult and continuing education, agricultural business, agricultural sciences, agronomy/soil and crop sciences, American studies, animal sciences, anthropology, art education, art/fine arts, art history, athletic training, biochemistry, biology/biological sciences, biomedical technologies, botany/plant sciences, business administration/commerce/management, cell biology, chemical engineering, chemistry, child care/child and family studies, city/community/regional planning, civil engineering, classics, communication, computer engineering, computer science, conservation, dairy sciences, dance, dietetics, earth science, ecology, economics, electrical engineering, electrical engineering technology, engineering technology, English, environmental engineering, environmental sciences, equestrian studies, evolutionary biology, family and consumer studies, forestry, French, geography, geology, German, Greek, health services administration, history, home economics, horticulture, hotel and restaurant management, humanities, interdisciplinary studies, international studies, journalism, Latin, linguistics, literature, marine biology, marine sciences, mathematics, mechanical engineering, mechanical engineering technology, medical laboratory technology, (pre)medicine sequence, microbiology, modern languages, molecular biology, music, music education, music history, natural resource management, natural sciences, nursing, nutrition, occupational therapy, parks management, philosophy, physical education, physics, piano/organ, political science/government, psychology, recreation and leisure services, recreation therapy, Romance languages, Russian, science, science education, social work, sociology, soil conservation, Spanish, special education, speech pathology and audiology, speech therapy, sports administration, sports medicine, statistics, stringed instruments, studio art, theater arts/drama, tourism and travel, (pre)veterinary medicine sequence, vocational education, voice, water resources, wildlife biology, wildlife management, wind and percussion instruments, women's studies, zoology.

## University of North Carolina at Asheville

Accounting, actuarial science, applied mathematics, art/fine arts, atmospheric sciences, biology/biological sciences, business administration/commerce/management, chemistry, classics, communication, computer information systems, computer science, economics, education, English, environmental sciences, finance/banking, French, German, Greek, health services administration, history, Latin, literature, marketing/retailing/merchandising, mathematics, music, philosophy, physics, political science/government, psychology, sociology, Spanish, statistics, theater arts/drama.

## University of North Carolina at Chapel Hill

Actuarial science, advertising, African studies, American studies, anthropology, applied mathematics, archaeology, art education, art/fine arts, art history, Asian/Oriental studies, astronomy, biology/biological sciences, black/African-American studies, business administration/commerce/management, chemistry, city/community/regional planning, classics, communication, comparative literature, criminal justice, dental services, (pre)dentistry sequence, early childhood education, East Asian studies, economics, education, elementary education, engineering and applied sciences, English, environmental engineering, environmental sciences, film studies, folklore, French, geography, geology, German, Greek, health education, health services administration, history, industrial administration, interdisciplinary studies, international studies, Italian, journalism, Latin American studies, (pre)law sequence, linguistics, mathematics, medical technology, (pre)medicine sequence, middle school education, music, music education, naval sciences, nursing, nutrition, operations research, peace studies, pharmacy/pharmaceutical sciences, philosophy, physical education, physics, political science/government, Portuguese, psychology, public administration, public affairs and policy studies, public health, public relations, radio and television studies, radiological sciences, reading education, recreation and leisure services, religious studies, Russian, Russian and Slavic studies, science, secondary education, social science, sociology, Spanish, speech/rhetoric/public address/debate, statistics, studio art, theater arts/drama, urban studies, women's studies.

## University of Notre Dame

Accounting, aerospace engineering, American studies, anthropology, architecture, art/fine arts, art history, biochemistry, biology/biological sciences, black/African-American studies, business administration/commerce/management, business economics, chemical engineering, chemistry, civil engineering, classics, communication, computer engineering, computer science, (pre)dentistry sequence, earth science, economics, electrical engineering, engineering (general), engineering sciences, English, environmental engineering, environmental sciences, film and video production, finance/banking, French, geology, German, Germanic languages and literature, Greek, history, humanities, interdisciplinary studies, international relations, international studies, Italian, Japanese, Latin, Latin American studies, liberal arts/general studies, literature, management information systems, marketing/retailing/merchandising, mathematics, mechanical engineering, (pre)medicine sequence, medieval studies, microbiology, modern languages, music, painting/drawing, peace studies, philosophy, photography, physics, political science/government, psychology,

Romance languages, Russian, science education, sculpture, secondary education, sociology, Spanish, studio art, theater arts/drama, theology, Western civilization and culture.

## University of Oklahoma

Accounting, advertising, aerospace engineering, African studies, anthropology, architectural engineering, architecture, art/fine arts, art history, Asian/Oriental studies, astronomy, astrophysics, biochemistry, botany/plant sciences, broadcasting, business administration/commerce/management, business economics, ceramic art and design, chemical engineering, chemistry, civil engineering, classics, communication, computer engineering, computer science, construction technologies, creative writing, dance, (pre)dentistry sequence, early childhood education, earth science, economics, education, electrical engineering, elementary education, engineering (general), engineering physics, English, environmental design, environmental engineering, environmental sciences, European studies, film and video production, film studies, finance/banking, French, geography, geological engineering, geology, geophysics, German, history, industrial engineering, interior design, international business, jewelry and metalsmithing, journalism, laboratory technologies, land use management and reclamation, Latin American studies, (pre)law sequence, liberal arts/general studies, linguistics, management information systems, marketing/retailing/merchandising, mathematics, mechanical engineering, (pre)medicine sequence, meteorology, microbiology, music, music education, music history, Native American studies, painting/drawing, petroleum/natural gas engineering, petroleum technology, philosophy, photography, physical education, physics, piano/organ, political science/government, printmaking, psychology, public administration, public affairs and policy studies, public relations, radio and television studies, real estate, religious studies, Russian, Russian and Slavic studies, science education, sculpture, secondary education, social work, sociology, Spanish, special education, stringed instruments, studio art, theater arts/drama, (pre)veterinary medicine sequence, voice, wind and percussion instruments, women's studies, zoology.

## University of Pennsylvania

Accounting, actuarial science, adult and continuing education, African languages, African studies, American studies, anthropology, applied art, Arabic, archaeology, art/fine arts, art history, Asian/Oriental studies, astronomy, astrophysics, behavioral sciences, biochemistry, bioengineering, biology/biological sciences, biomedical engineering, biophysics, black/African-American studies, botany/plant sciences, business administration/commerce/management, chemical engineering, chemistry, child psychology/child development, Chinese, city/community/regional planning, civil engineering, communication, comparative literature, computer engineering, computer programming, computer science, creative writing, (pre)dentistry sequence, early childhood education, East Asian studies, East European and Soviet studies, ecology, economics, education, electrical engineering, electrical engineering technology, elementary education, engineering (general), engineering and applied sciences, English, environmental design, environmental sciences, ethnic studies, European studies, finance/banking, folklore, French, geology, German, Germanic languages and literature, Greek, Hebrew, Hispanic studies, history, history of science, insurance, interdisciplinary studies, international business, international economics, international relations, international studies, Italian, Japanese, Judaic studies, labor and industrial relations, Latin, Latin American studies, (pre)law sequence, legal studies, liberal arts/general studies, linguistics, literature, marketing/retailing/merchandising, materials engineering, materials sciences, mathematics, mechanical engineering, mechanical engineering technology, (pre)medicine sequence, microbiology, military science, modern languages, molecular biology, music, music history, natural sciences, naval sciences, Near and Middle Eastern studies, nursing, painting/drawing, peace studies, philosophy, physics, political science/government, Portuguese, psychobiology, psychology, real estate, religious studies, robotics, Romance languages, Russian, Russian and Slavic studies, Scandinavian languages/studies, secondary education, Slavic languages, social work, sociology, South Asian studies, Southeast Asian studies, Spanish, statistics, systems engineering, systems science, theater arts/drama, transportation engineering, urban studies, (pre)veterinary medicine sequence, women's studies.

## University of Pittsburgh
Accounting, anthropology, applied mathematics, architectural technologies, art/fine arts, astronomy, biology/biological sciences, black/African-American studies, business administration/commerce/management, business education, chemical engineering, chemistry, child care/child and family studies, child psychology/child development, Chinese, civil engineering, classics, communication, computer science, criminal justice, dietetics, ecology, economics, electrical engineering, engineering physics, English, film studies, French, geology, German, health education, history, history of philosophy, humanities, industrial engineering, information science, Italian, Japanese, legal studies, liberal arts/general studies, linguistics, literature, materials engineering, materials sciences, mathematics, mechanical engineering, medical records services, medical technology, metallurgical engineering, microbiology, molecular biology, music, natural sciences, neurosciences, nursing, nutrition, occupational therapy, pharmacy/pharmaceutical sciences, philosophy, physical education, physics, political science/government, psychology, public administration, religious studies, Russian, Slavic languages, social science, social work, sociology, Spanish, speech/rhetoric/public address/debate, statistics, studio art, theater arts/drama, urban studies, vocational education.

## University of Pittsburgh at Johnstown
Accounting, American studies, biology/biological sciences, business administration/commerce/management, business economics, chemistry, civil engineering technology, communication, computer science, creative writing, (pre)dentistry sequence, ecology, economics, education, electrical engineering technology, elementary education, engineering technology, English, finance/banking, geography, geology, history, humanities, journalism, (pre)law sequence, literature, mathematics, mechanical engineering technology, medical technology, (pre)medicine sequence, natural sciences, political science/government, psychology, science education, secondary education, social science, sociology, theater arts/drama, (pre)veterinary medicine sequence.

## University of Puget Sound
Accounting, art/fine arts, art history, Asian/Oriental studies, biology/biological sciences, business administration/commerce/management, chemistry, communication, computer science, (pre)dentistry sequence, economics, English, finance/banking, French, geology, German, history, international business, international economics, (pre)law sequence, mathematics, (pre)medicine sequence, music, music business, music education, natural sciences, occupational therapy, philosophy, physical education, physics, political science/government, psychology, public administration, religious studies, sociology, Spanish, sports medicine, theater arts/drama, (pre)veterinary medicine sequence.

## University of Redlands
Accounting, anthropology, applied mathematics, art/fine arts, art history, Asian/Oriental studies, behavioral sciences, biology/biological sciences, business administration/commerce/management, ceramic art and design, chemistry, computer science, creative writing, economics,

education, elementary education, English, environmental sciences, environmental studies, ethnic studies, French, German, history, humanities, international relations, (pre)law sequence, liberal arts/general studies, literature, mathematics, (pre)medicine sequence, modern languages, music, music education, music history, philosophy, physics, piano/organ, political science/government, psychology, religious studies, secondary education, social science, sociology, Spanish, speech pathology and audiology, speech therapy, stringed instruments, studio art, technical writing, voice, wind and percussion instruments, women's studies.

## University of Richmond
Accounting, American studies, art education, art/fine arts, art history, biology/biological sciences, business administration/commerce/management, business economics, chemistry, classics, computer science, criminal justice, early childhood education, East Asian studies, economics, education, elementary education, English, European studies, finance/banking, French, German, Greek, health education, health science, history, interdisciplinary studies, international business, international studies, journalism, Latin, Latin American studies, management information systems, marketing/retailing/merchandising, mathematics, middle school education, military science, music, music education, music history, philosophy, physical education, physics, piano/organ, political science/government, psychology, religious studies, Russian and Slavic studies, secondary education, sociology, Spanish, speech/rhetoric/public address/debate, stringed instruments, studio art, theater arts/drama, urban studies, voice, wind and percussion instruments, women's studies.

## University of Rochester
Anthropology, applied mathematics, art history, astronomy, biochemistry, biology/biological sciences, cell biology, chemical engineering, chemistry, classics, cognitive science, computer science, earth science, economics, electrical engineering, engineering and applied sciences, engineering sciences, English, environmental sciences, environmental studies, evolutionary biology, film studies, French, genetics, geology, German, health science, history, interdisciplinary studies, Japanese, linguistics, mathematics, mechanical engineering, microbiology, music, music education, music history, natural sciences, neurosciences, nursing, optics, philosophy, physics, political science/government, psychology, religious studies, Russian, science, Spanish, statistics, studio art, women's studies.

## University of Scranton
Accounting, advertising, biochemistry, biology/biological sciences, biophysics, broadcasting, business administration/commerce/management, business economics, chemistry, classics, communication, computer engineering, computer information systems, computer science, criminal justice, (pre)dentistry sequence, economics, education, electronics engineering, elementary education, English, environmental sciences, film and video production, finance/banking, French, German, gerontology, Greek, health services administration, history, human services, international business, international studies, journalism, Latin, (pre)law sequence, marketing/retailing/merchandising, mathematics, medical technology, (pre)medicine sequence, modern languages, neurosciences, nursing, occupational therapy, philosophy, physical therapy, physics, political science/government, psychology, public administration, radio and television studies, religious studies, Romance languages, secondary education, sociology, Spanish, theology, (pre)veterinary medicine sequence.

## University of Southern California
Accounting, aerospace engineering, American studies, anthropology, architecture, art/fine arts, art history, astronomy, audio engineering,

biology/biological sciences, biomedical engineering, black/
African-American studies, broadcasting, business administration/
commerce/management, chemical engineering, chemistry, city/
community/regional planning, civil engineering, classics,
communication, comparative literature, computer engineering,
computer science, creative writing, dental services, East Asian studies,
economics, education, electrical engineering, English, environmental
engineering, environmental studies, ethnic studies, film and video
production, film studies, French, geography, geology, German,
gerontology, Greek, history, history of philosophy, industrial
engineering, interdisciplinary studies, international relations, Italian,
jazz, journalism, Judaic studies, Latin, linguistics, mathematics,
mechanical engineering, Mexican-American/Chicano studies,
molecular biology, music, music education, nursing, occupational
therapy, petroleum/natural gas engineering, philosophy, photography,
physical fitness/exercise science, physical sciences, physician's
assistant studies, physics, piano/organ, political science/government,
polymer science, psychobiology, psychology, public administration,
public affairs and policy studies, public relations, radio and television
studies, religious studies, Russian, safety and security technologies,
sociology, Spanish, stringed instruments, studio art, systems
engineering, theater arts/drama, voice, water resources, wind and
percussion instruments, women's studies.

## University of Tennessee, Knoxville
Accounting, adult and continuing education, advertising, aerospace
engineering, agricultural business, agricultural economics, agricultural
education, agricultural engineering, agricultural sciences, agronomy/
soil and crop sciences, American studies, animal sciences,
anthropology, applied art, applied mathematics, archaeology,
architecture, art education, art/fine arts, art history, Asian/Oriental
studies, astronomy, behavioral sciences, biochemistry, biology/
biological sciences, biomedical engineering, black/African-American
studies, botany/plant sciences, broadcasting, business administration/
commerce/management, business economics, business education, cell
biology, ceramic art and design, chemical engineering, chemistry, child
care/child and family studies, child psychology/child development,
city/community/regional planning, civil engineering, classics,
communication, comparative literature, computer engineering,
computer science, creative writing, criminal justice, cytotechnology,
dance, (pre)dentistry sequence, dietetics, early childhood education,
East Asian studies, East European and Soviet studies, ecology,
economics, education, electrical engineering, elementary education,
engineering and applied sciences, engineering mechanics, engineering
physics, engineering sciences, English, environmental sciences, family
and consumer studies, fashion merchandising, film studies, finance/
banking, fish and game management, food sciences, forestry, French,
geography, geology, German, graphic arts, Greek, health education,
history, home economics education, horticulture, hotel and restaurant
management, human ecology, humanities, human services, illustration,
industrial engineering, interdisciplinary studies, interior design,
international business, Italian, jazz, journalism, landscape architecture/
design, Latin, Latin American studies, liberal arts/general studies,
linguistics, literature, marketing/retailing/merchandising, materials
engineering, mathematics, mechanical engineering, medical laboratory
technology, medical records services, medical technology,
(pre)medicine sequence, medieval studies, metallurgical engineering,
metallurgy, microbiology, music, music education, music history, natural
sciences, nuclear engineering, nursing, nutrition, ornamental
horticulture, painting/drawing, philosophy, physical education,
physical fitness/exercise science, physics, piano/organ, political
science/government, psychology, public administration, public health,
public relations, recreation and leisure services, religious studies, retail
management, Romance languages, Russian, Russian and Slavic

studies, sacred music, science, science education, sculpture, secondary
education, Slavic languages, social science, social work, sociology,
Spanish, special education, speech pathology and audiology, speech/
rhetoric/public address/debate, sports administration, statistics,
stringed instruments, studio art, textiles and clothing, theater arts/
drama, urban studies, (pre)veterinary medicine sequence, vocational
education, voice, wildlife management, wind and percussion
instruments, women's studies, zoology.

## University of Texas at Austin
Accounting, advertising, aerospace engineering, African languages,
African studies, American studies, anthropology, applied art,
archaeology, architectural engineering, architecture, art education,
art/fine arts, art history, Asian/Oriental studies, astronomy, bilingual/
bicultural education, biochemistry, biology/biological sciences,
black/African-American studies, botany/plant sciences, broadcasting,
business administration/commerce/management, chemical
engineering, chemistry, child psychology/child development, civil
engineering, classics, communication, computer science, dance,
(pre)dentistry sequence, dietetics, East European and Soviet studies,
ecology, economics, education, electrical engineering, elementary
education, English, ethnic studies, European studies, evolutionary
biology, fashion design and technology, fashion merchandising, film
studies, finance/banking, French, geography, geology, geophysics,
German, Greek, Hebrew, history, home economics, humanities,
interdisciplinary studies, interior design, international business,
international studies, Italian, Japanese, journalism, Latin, Latin
American studies, (pre)law sequence, liberal arts/general studies,
linguistics, management information systems, marketing/retailing/
merchandising, mathematics, mechanical engineering, medical
technology, (pre)medicine sequence, Mexican-American/Chicano
studies, microbiology, molecular biology, music, music education, Near
and Middle Eastern studies, nursing, nutrition, painting/drawing,
petroleum/natural gas engineering, pharmacy/pharmaceutical
sciences, philosophy, photography, physical education, physics,
political science/government, Portuguese, psychology, public relations,
radio and television studies, reading education, Russian, Russian and
Slavic studies, Scandinavian languages/studies, Slavic languages,
social work, sociology, Spanish, special education, speech pathology
and audiology, studio art, textiles and clothing, theater arts/drama,
(pre)veterinary medicine sequence, zoology.

## University of the South
American studies, anthropology, applied art, art/fine arts, art history,
Asian/Oriental studies, biology/biological sciences, chemistry, classics,
comparative literature, computer science, economics, English,
environmental sciences, European studies, forestry, French, geology,
German, Greek, history, international studies, Latin, literature,
mathematics, medieval studies, music, music history, natural resource
management, painting/drawing, philosophy, physics, political science/
government, psychology, religious studies, Russian, Russian and Slavic
studies, social science, Spanish, studio art, theater arts/drama.

## University of Tulsa
Accounting, advertising, anthropology, applied mathematics, art
education, art/fine arts, art history, athletic training, biochemistry,
biology/biological sciences, broadcasting, business administration/
commerce/management, cell biology, ceramic art and design,
chemical engineering, chemistry, commercial art, communication,
comparative literature, computer information systems, computer
science, (pre)dentistry sequence, earth science, ecology, economics,
education, electrical engineering, elementary education, engineering
physics, English, environmental biology, environmental studies,
finance/banking, French, geological engineering, geology, geophysics,

German, health education, health science, history, international studies, journalism, (pre)law sequence, literature, management information systems, marketing/retailing/merchandising, mathematics, mechanical engineering, (pre)medicine sequence, music, music education, nursing, painting/drawing, petroleum/natural gas engineering, philosophy, physical sciences, physics, piano/organ, political science/government, printmaking, psychology, public relations, radio and television studies, real estate, religious studies, Russian and Slavic studies, science, science education, sculpture, secondary education, sociology, Spanish, special education, speech pathology and audiology, sports medicine, stringed instruments, studio art, theater arts/drama, (pre)veterinary medicine sequence, voice, wind and percussion instruments.

## University of Utah
Accounting, anthropology, Arabic, architecture, art/fine arts, art history, Asian/Oriental studies, biology/biological sciences, biomedical sciences, broadcasting, business administration/commerce/management, chemical engineering, chemistry, child care/child and family studies, child psychology/child development, Chinese, civil engineering, classics, communication, computer engineering, computer science, dance, economics, electrical engineering, elementary education, English, family and consumer studies, film studies, finance/banking, food sciences, French, geography, geological engineering, geology, geophysics, German, Greek, health education, history, home economics education, journalism, liberal arts/general studies, linguistics, marketing/retailing/merchandising, materials engineering, materials sciences, mathematics, mechanical engineering, medical laboratory technology, metallurgical engineering, meteorology, mining and mineral engineering, music, music education, Near and Middle Eastern studies, nursing, pharmacy/pharmaceutical sciences, philosophy, physical education, physical therapy, physics, political science/government, psychology, public relations, radio and television studies, recreation and leisure services, Russian, secondary education, social science, sociology, Spanish, speech pathology and audiology, speech/rhetoric/public address/debate, theater arts/drama, urban studies.

## University of Vermont
Accounting, agricultural economics, agricultural sciences, agricultural technologies, agronomy/soil and crop sciences, animal sciences, anthropology, applied mathematics, art education, art/fine arts, art history, Asian/Oriental studies, biochemistry, biology/biological sciences, botany/plant sciences, business administration/commerce/management, Canadian studies, chemistry, child care/child and family studies, child psychology/child development, civil engineering, classics, computer science, consumer services, dairy sciences, (pre)dentistry sequence, dietetics, early childhood education, East European and Soviet studies, ecology, economics, education, electrical engineering, elementary education, engineering (general), engineering management, English, environmental biology, environmental education, environmental sciences, environmental studies, European studies, family and consumer studies, fashion design and technology, fashion merchandising, finance/banking, fish and game management, food sciences, forestry, French, geography, geology, German, Greek, health education, history, home economics, home economics education, horticulture, human development, industrial arts, Latin, Latin American studies, (pre)law sequence, marine biology, marketing/retailing/merchandising, mathematics, mechanical engineering, medical technology, (pre)medicine sequence, microbiology, modern languages, molecular biology, music, music education, music history, natural resource management, nursing, nutrition, parks management, philosophy, physical education, physical therapy, physics, political science/government, psychology, reading education, recreational facilities management, recreation and leisure services, religious studies,

Romance languages, Russian, Russian and Slavic studies, science education, secondary education, social work, sociology, soil conservation, Spanish, special education, speech pathology and audiology, speech therapy, statistics, studio art, textiles and clothing, theater arts/drama, (pre)veterinary medicine sequence, vocational education, water resources, wildlife biology, wildlife management, zoology.

## University of Virginia
Aerospace engineering, anthropology, applied mathematics, architecture, astronomy, biology/biological sciences, black/African-American studies, business administration/commerce/management, chemical engineering, chemistry, city/community/regional planning, civil engineering, classics, comparative literature, computer science, economics, electrical engineering, engineering sciences, English, environmental sciences, ethnic studies, French, German, history, interdisciplinary studies, international studies, Italian, mathematics, mechanical engineering, music, nursing, philosophy, physical education, physics, political science/government, psychology, religious studies, Slavic languages, sociology, Spanish, speech pathology and audiology, studio art, systems engineering, theater arts/drama.

## University of Washington
Accounting, advertising, aerospace engineering, anthropology, Arabic, architecture, art/fine arts, art history, Asian/Oriental studies, astronomy, atmospheric sciences, audio engineering, biochemistry, biology/biological sciences, black/African-American studies, botany/plant sciences, broadcasting, business administration/commerce/management, business economics, Canadian studies, cell biology, ceramic art and design, ceramic engineering, chemical engineering, chemistry, Chinese, city/community/regional planning, civil engineering, classics, communication, comparative literature, computer engineering, computer information systems, computer science, construction management, creative writing, criminal justice, dance, dental services, (pre)dentistry sequence, East Asian studies, East European and Soviet studies, ecology, economics, education, electrical engineering, elementary education, engineering (general), English, environmental engineering, environmental health sciences, ethnic studies, finance/banking, forest engineering, forestry, French, geography, geology, German, Germanic languages and literature, graphic arts, Greek, health services administration, Hebrew, history, history of science, human resources, industrial design, industrial engineering, interdisciplinary studies, international business, international studies, Italian, Japanese, journalism, Judaic studies, landscape architecture/design, Latin, Latin American studies, liberal arts/general studies, linguistics, management information systems, marketing/retailing/merchandising, materials engineering, mathematics, mechanical engineering, medical technology, (pre)medicine sequence, metallurgical engineering, Mexican-American/Chicano studies, microbiology, molecular biology, music, music education, music history, Native American studies, Near and Middle Eastern studies, nursing, occupational therapy, ocean engineering, oceanography, painting/drawing, paper and pulp sciences, peace studies, pharmacy/pharmaceutical sciences, philosophy, photography, physical therapy, physics, piano/organ, political science/government, Portuguese, psychology, religious studies, Romance languages, Russian, Russian and Slavic studies, Scandinavian languages/studies, sculpture, secondary education, Slavic languages, social work, sociology, South Asian studies, Spanish, speech pathology and audiology, statistics, stringed instruments, studio art, technical writing, theater arts/drama, (pre)veterinary medicine sequence, voice, wildlife management, women's studies, wood sciences, zoology.

## University of Wisconsin–Madison

Accounting, actuarial science, advertising, African languages, African studies, agricultural business, agricultural economics, agricultural education, agricultural engineering, agricultural sciences, agronomy/soil and crop sciences, American studies, animal sciences, anthropology, applied art, applied mathematics, art education, art/fine arts, art history, Asian/Oriental studies, astronomy, bacteriology, biochemistry, biology/biological sciences, black/African-American studies, botany/plant sciences, broadcasting, business administration/commerce/management, cartography, cell biology, chemical engineering, chemistry, child care/child and family studies, child psychology/child development, Chinese, civil engineering, classics, communication, comparative literature, computer engineering, computer science, construction management, consumer services, dairy sciences, dietetics, early childhood education, earth science, economics, electrical engineering, elementary education, engineering and applied sciences, engineering mechanics, engineering physics, English, entomology, environmental engineering, experimental psychology, family and consumer studies, farm and ranch management, fashion merchandising, finance/banking, food sciences, forestry, French, genetics, geography, geology, geophysics, German, Greek, Hebrew, Hispanic studies, history, history of science, home economics, home economics education, horticulture, industrial engineering, insurance, interior design, international studies, Italian, Japanese, journalism, labor and industrial relations, landscape architecture/design, Latin, Latin American studies, linguistics, mathematics, mechanical engineering, medical technology, metallurgical engineering, mining and mineral engineering, molecular biology, music, music education, natural resource management, nuclear engineering, nursing, nutrition, occupational therapy, pharmacology, pharmacy/pharmaceutical sciences, philosophy, physical education, physician's assistant studies, physics, political science/government, Portuguese, poultry sciences, psychology, public relations, radio and television studies, real estate, recreation and leisure services, Russian, Scandinavian languages/studies, science education, secondary education, Slavic languages, social science, social work, sociology, Southeast Asian studies, Spanish, special education, speech therapy, statistics, surveying engineering, textiles and clothing, theater arts/drama, toxicology, urban studies, water resources, wildlife management, women's studies, zoology.

## Ursinus College

Accounting, anthropology, applied mathematics, art/fine arts, athletic training, biology/biological sciences, business administration/commerce/management, chemistry, classics, communication, computer science, creative writing, (pre)dentistry sequence, East Asian studies, ecology, economics, education, English, French, German, Greek, health education, health science, history, international relations, international studies, Japanese, Latin, (pre)law sequence, liberal arts/general studies, mathematics, (pre)medicine sequence, modern languages, music, philosophy, physical education, physical therapy, physics, political science/government, psychology, religious studies, Romance languages, secondary education, sociology, South Asian studies, Spanish, sports medicine, (pre)veterinary medicine sequence.

## Utica College of Syracuse University

Accounting, actuarial science, anthropology, art/fine arts, biology/biological sciences, business administration/commerce/management, business economics, chemistry, child psychology/child development, communication, computer science, construction management, corrections, criminal justice, (pre)dentistry sequence, economics, English, gerontology, history, human development, international business, international studies, journalism, law enforcement/police sciences, (pre)law sequence, liberal arts/general studies, mathematics,

(pre)medicine sequence, nursing, occupational therapy, philosophy, physical therapy, physics, political science/government, psychology, public relations, recreation therapy, secondary education, social science, sociology, speech/rhetoric/public address/debate, theater arts/drama, (pre)veterinary medicine sequence.

## Valparaiso University

Accounting, American studies, art education, art/fine arts, art history, Asian/Oriental studies, astronomy, athletic training, behavioral sciences, biblical languages, biblical studies, biochemistry, biology/biological sciences, biomedical sciences, broadcasting, business administration/commerce/management, chemistry, city/community/regional planning, civil engineering, classics, communication, computer engineering, computer information systems, computer science, criminal justice, (pre)dentistry sequence, East Asian studies, economics, education, electrical engineering, elementary education, engineering (general), engineering sciences, English, finance/banking, French, geography, geology, German, Greek, health science, history, humanities, human resources, interdisciplinary studies, international economics, journalism, land use management and reclamation, Latin, (pre)law sequence, liberal arts/general studies, literature, marketing/retailing/merchandising, mathematics, mechanical engineering, medical technology, (pre)medicine sequence, meteorology, modern languages, music, music business, music education, music history, natural sciences, nursing, philosophy, physical education, physics, piano/organ, political science/government, psychology, public relations, radio and television studies, reading education, religious studies, Romance languages, sacred music, science education, secondary education, social science, social work, sociology, Spanish, special education, stringed instruments, studio art, theater arts/drama, theology, (pre)veterinary medicine sequence, voice, wind and percussion instruments.

## Vanderbilt University

African studies, American studies, anthropology, art/fine arts, astronomy, biology/biological sciences, biomedical engineering, black/African-American studies, chemical engineering, chemistry, civil engineering, classics, cognitive science, communication, computer engineering, computer science, early childhood education, East Asian studies, East European and Soviet studies, ecology, economics, education, electrical engineering, elementary education, engineering (general), engineering sciences, English, European studies, French, geology, German, history, human development, interdisciplinary studies, Latin American studies, mathematics, mechanical engineering, molecular biology, music, philosophy, physics, piano/organ, political science/government, Portuguese, psychology, religious studies, Russian, secondary education, sociology, Spanish, special education, stringed instruments, theater arts/drama, urban studies, voice, wind and percussion instruments.

## Vassar College

African studies, American studies, anthropology, art/fine arts, art history, Asian/Oriental studies, astronomy, biochemistry, biology/biological sciences, chemistry, classics, cognitive science, computer science, economics, elementary education, English, film studies, French, geography, geology, German, Greek, Hispanic studies, history, interdisciplinary studies, international studies, Italian, Latin, Latin American studies, mathematics, medieval studies, music, philosophy, physics, political science/government, psychobiology, psychology, religious studies, Russian, sociology, studio art, technology and public affairs, theater arts/drama, urban studies, women's studies.

## Villanova University
Accounting, art history, astronomy, astrophysics, biochemistry, biology/biological sciences, business administration/commerce/management, business economics, chemical engineering, chemistry, civil engineering, classics, communication, computer engineering, computer science, criminal justice, (pre)dentistry sequence, economics, education, electrical engineering, elementary education, English, environmental education, finance/banking, French, geography, German, history, humanities, human services, interdisciplinary studies, international business, (pre)law sequence, liberal arts/general studies, marketing/retailing/merchandising, mathematics, mechanical engineering, (pre)medicine sequence, meteorology, military science, natural sciences, naval sciences, nursing, philosophy, physics, political science/government, psychology, religious studies, secondary education, sociology, Spanish, special education, (pre)veterinary medicine sequence.

## Virginia Polytechnic Institute and State University
Accounting, aerospace engineering, agricultural economics, agricultural education, agricultural engineering, agronomy/soil and crop sciences, animal sciences, architecture, art/fine arts, art history, biochemistry, biology/biological sciences, black/African-American studies, broadcasting, business administration/commerce/management, business economics, business education, chemical engineering, chemistry, child care/child and family studies, civil engineering, classics, communication, computer engineering, computer science, construction management, dairy sciences, (pre)dentistry sequence, dietetics, early childhood education, economics, education, electrical engineering, elementary education, engineering sciences, English, environmental sciences, family and consumer studies, farm and ranch management, fashion design and technology, fashion merchandising, finance/banking, fish and game management, food sciences, forestry, French, geography, geology, geophysics, German, health education, history, home economics, home economics education, horticulture, hotel and restaurant management, human development, human resources, human services, industrial design, industrial engineering, interior design, international studies, journalism, landscape architecture/design, (pre)law sequence, liberal arts/general studies, management information systems, marketing/retailing/merchandising, materials engineering, mathematics, mechanical engineering, medical technology, (pre)medicine sequence, medieval studies, mining and mineral engineering, music, music education, music history, nutrition, ocean engineering, operations research, parks management, philosophy, physical education, physical fitness/exercise science, physics, political science/government, poultry sciences, psychology, public administration, public relations, religious studies, Russian and Slavic studies, science education, secondary education, sociology, Spanish, speech/rhetoric/public address/debate, sports administration, statistics, studio art, textiles and clothing, theater arts/drama, tourism and travel, urban studies, (pre)veterinary medicine sequence, vocational education, wildlife management, women's studies, wood sciences.

## Wabash College
Art/fine arts, biology/biological sciences, chemistry, classics, economics, English, French, German, Greek, history, Latin, (pre)law sequence, mathematics, (pre)medicine sequence, music, philosophy, physics, political science/government, psychology, religious studies, Spanish, speech/rhetoric/public address/debate, theater arts/drama, (pre)veterinary medicine sequence.

## Wake Forest University
Accounting, anthropology, art history, biology/biological sciences, business administration/commerce/management, chemistry, classics,

communication, computer science, economics, education, elementary education, English, French, German, Greek, health science, history, Latin, (pre)law sequence, mathematics, (pre)medicine sequence, middle school education, music, philosophy, physical education, physician's assistant studies, physics, political science/government, psychology, religious studies, Russian, sociology, Spanish, speech/rhetoric/public address/debate, studio art, theater arts/drama.

## Wartburg College
Accounting, art education, art/fine arts, arts administration, biology/biological sciences, broadcasting, business administration/commerce/management, chemistry, communication, computer information systems, computer science, early childhood education, economics, education, elementary education, engineering (general), English, finance/banking, French, German, health science, history, international business, journalism, law enforcement/police sciences, liberal arts/general studies, marketing/retailing/merchandising, mathematics, medical technology, music, music education, music therapy, occupational therapy, philosophy, physical education, physical fitness/exercise science, physics, political science/government, psychology, public health, public relations, religious education, religious studies, secondary education, social work, sociology, Spanish.

## Washington and Jefferson College
Accounting, art education, art history, biology/biological sciences, business administration/commerce/management, chemistry, (pre)dentistry sequence, economics, education, English, French, German, history, (pre)law sequence, mathematics, medical technology, (pre)medicine sequence, philosophy, physics, political science/government, psychology, secondary education, sociology, Spanish, (pre)veterinary medicine sequence.

## Washington and Lee University
Accounting, anthropology, art/fine arts, art history, biology/biological sciences, business administration/commerce/management, chemical engineering, chemistry, classics, cognitive science, communication, computer science, (pre)dentistry sequence, East Asian studies, economics, engineering physics, English, environmental sciences, forestry, French, geology, geophysics, Germanic languages and literature, history, interdisciplinary studies, journalism, (pre)law sequence, marine biology, mathematics, (pre)medicine sequence, medieval studies, music, natural sciences, neurosciences, philosophy, physics, political science/government, psychology, public affairs and policy studies, religious studies, Romance languages, Russian and Slavic studies, sociology, Spanish, studio art, theater arts/drama, (pre)veterinary medicine sequence.

## Washington College
American studies, art/fine arts, biology/biological sciences, business administration/commerce/management, chemistry, (pre)dentistry sequence, economics, English, French, German, history, humanities, international studies, Latin American studies, (pre)law sequence, mathematics, (pre)medicine sequence, music, philosophy, physics, political science/government, psychology, sociology, Spanish, theater arts/drama, (pre)veterinary medicine sequence.

## Washington University
Accounting, African studies, anthropology, applied art, applied mathematics, Arabic, archaeology, architectural technologies, architecture, art/fine arts, art history, Asian/Oriental studies, biochemistry, biology/biological sciences, black/African-American studies, business administration/commerce/management, business economics, ceramic art and design, chemical engineering, chemistry, Chinese, civil engineering, classics, commercial art, comparative

literature, computer engineering, computer information systems, computer science, creative writing, (pre)dentistry sequence, earth science, East Asian studies, economics, education, electrical engineering, elementary education, engineering (general), engineering and applied sciences, engineering physics, engineering sciences, English, environmental studies, ethnic studies, European studies, fashion design and technology, finance/banking, French, German, Germanic languages and literature, graphic arts, Greek, Hebrew, history, illustration, interdisciplinary studies, international business, international studies, Islamic studies, Italian, Japanese, jewelry and metalsmithing, Judaic studies, Latin, Latin American studies, (pre)law sequence, liberal arts/general studies, linguistics, literature, marketing/retailing/ merchandising, mathematics, mechanical engineering, (pre)medicine sequence, medieval studies, modern languages, music, natural sciences, Near and Middle Eastern studies, painting/drawing, philosophy, photography, physical sciences, physics, planetary and space sciences, political science/government, printmaking, psychology, religious studies, Romance languages, Russian, sculpture, secondary education, Spanish, studio art, systems engineering, systems science, technology and public affairs, theater arts/drama, urban studies, (pre)veterinary medicine sequence, women's studies.

## Webb Institute
Marine engineering, naval architecture.

## Wellesley College
African studies, American studies, anthropology, archaeology, architecture, art/fine arts, art history, astronomy, biochemistry, biology/biological sciences, black/African-American studies, chemistry, Chinese, classics, cognitive science, computer science, East Asian studies, economics, English, European studies, French, geology, German, Greek, history, international relations, Italian, Japanese, Judaic studies, Latin, Latin American studies, linguistics, mathematics, (pre)medicine sequence, medieval studies, music, peace studies, philosophy, physics, political science/government, psychobiology, psychology, religious studies, Russian, Russian and Slavic studies, sociology, Spanish, studio art, theater arts/drama, women's studies.

## Wells College
American studies, art/fine arts, art history, biology/biological sciences, chemistry, computer science, dance, (pre)dentistry sequence, economics, elementary education, engineering (general), English, environmental studies, French, German, history, international studies, Italian, (pre)law sequence, mathematics, (pre)medicine sequence, music, political science/government, psychology, public affairs and policy studies, religious studies, Russian, secondary education, sociology, Spanish, studio art, theater arts/drama, (pre)veterinary medicine sequence, women's studies.

## Wesleyan University
African studies, American studies, anthropology, art/fine arts, art history, Asian/Oriental studies, astronomy, behavioral sciences, biochemistry, biology/biological sciences, black/African-American studies, chemistry, Chinese, classics, computer science, dance, earth science, East Asian studies, East European and Soviet studies, ecology, economics, English, environmental sciences, film studies, French, German, Germanic languages and literature, Greek, history, humanities, interdisciplinary studies, Italian, Japanese, Latin American studies, liberal arts/general studies, mathematics, medieval studies, molecular biology, music, neurosciences, philosophy, physics, political science/government, psychobiology, psychology, religious studies, Romance languages, Russian, Russian and Slavic studies, social science, sociology, Spanish, studio art, technology and public affairs, theater arts/drama, women's studies.

## Westminster Choir College of Rider University
Liberal arts/general studies, music, music education, piano/organ, sacred music, voice.

## Wheaton College (IL)
Archaeology, art education, art/fine arts, art history, biblical languages, biblical studies, biology/biological sciences, business economics, chemistry, communication, computer science, economics, elementary education, engineering (general), environmental sciences, French, geology, German, history, interdisciplinary studies, journalism, literature, mathematics, music, music business, music education, music history, nursing, philosophy, physical education, physics, piano/organ, political science/government, psychology, religious education, religious studies, sociology, Spanish, speech/rhetoric/public address/debate, stringed instruments, studio art, theater arts/drama, voice, wind and percussion instruments.

## Whitman College
Anthropology, art/fine arts, art history, biology/biological sciences, chemistry, computer science, economics, English, environmental studies, French, geology, German, history, literature, mathematics, music, philosophy, physics, political science/government, psychology, sociology, Spanish, theater arts/drama.

## Whittier College
Anthropology, applied art, art/fine arts, athletic training, biochemistry, biology/biological sciences, business administration/commerce/ management, chemistry, child psychology/child development, (pre)dentistry sequence, early childhood education, economics, education, elementary education, English, French, geology, history, international studies, Latin American studies, (pre)law sequence, liberal arts/general studies, literature, mathematics, (pre)medicine sequence, modern languages, music, philosophy, physical education, physical sciences, physics, political science/government, psychology, religious studies, Romance languages, secondary education, social science, social work, sociology, Spanish, speech pathology and audiology, theater arts/drama, urban studies, (pre)veterinary medicine sequence.

## Willamette University
American studies, art/fine arts, art history, Asian/Oriental studies, biology/biological sciences, business economics, chemistry, computer science, (pre)dentistry sequence, East European and Soviet studies, economics, English, environmental sciences, European studies, French, German, Hispanic studies, history, humanities, international studies, (pre)law sequence, literature, mathematics, (pre)medicine sequence, music, music education, music therapy, philosophy, physical education, physics, political science/government, psychology, religious studies, Russian and Slavic studies, sociology, Spanish, speech/rhetoric/public address/debate, studio art, theater arts/drama, (pre)veterinary medicine sequence.

## William Jewell College
Accounting, art/fine arts, biology/biological sciences, business administration/commerce/management, chemistry, communication, computer science, data processing, (pre)dentistry sequence, economics, education, elementary education, English, French, German, history, international business, international relations, (pre)law sequence, mathematics, medical technology, (pre)medicine sequence, music, music education, nursing, philosophy, physics, political science/ government, psychology, public relations, religious studies, secondary education, sociology, Spanish, (pre)veterinary medicine sequence.

## Williams College

American studies, anthropology, art history, Asian/Oriental studies, astronomy, astrophysics, biology/biological sciences, chemistry, classics, computer science, economics, English, French, geology, German, history, literature, mathematics, music, philosophy, physics, political science/government, psychology, religious studies, Russian, sociology, Spanish, studio art, theater arts/drama.

## William Smith College

American studies, anthropology, architecture, art/fine arts, art history, Asian/Oriental studies, biochemistry, biology/biological sciences, black/African-American studies, chemistry, Chinese, classics, comparative literature, computer science, dance, (pre)dentistry sequence, economics, English, environmental sciences, environmental studies, French, geology, German, Greek, history, interdisciplinary studies, Japanese, Judaic studies, Latin, (pre)law sequence, mathematics, (pre)medicine sequence, medieval studies, modern languages, music, philosophy, physics, political science/government, psychology, religious studies, Russian, Russian and Slavic studies, sociology, Spanish, studio art, theater arts/drama, urban studies, (pre)veterinary medicine sequence, women's studies.

## Wittenberg University

Accounting, American studies, art education, art/fine arts, art history, Asian/Oriental studies, behavioral sciences, biochemistry, biology/biological sciences, business administration/commerce/management, business economics, cartography, ceramic art and design, chemistry, child psychology/child development, comparative literature, computer science, creative writing, (pre)dentistry sequence, earth science, East Asian studies, East European and Soviet studies, economics, education, elementary education, English, environmental studies, finance/banking, French, geography, geology, German, graphic arts, history, humanities, interdisciplinary studies, international business, international studies, (pre)law sequence, liberal arts/general studies, literature, marine biology, marketing/retailing/merchandising, mathematics, (pre)medicine sequence, microbiology, middle school education, ministries, modern languages, music, music education, natural sciences, painting/drawing, philosophy, physical sciences, physics, piano/organ, political science/government, psychology, religious studies, Russian and Slavic studies, science, science education, sculpture, secondary education, social science, sociology, Spanish, special education, studio art, theater arts/drama, theology, urban studies, (pre)veterinary medicine sequence, voice.

## Wofford College

Accounting, art history, biology/biological sciences, business economics, chemistry, computer science, (pre)dentistry sequence, economics, English, finance/banking, French, German, history, humanities, international studies, (pre)law sequence, mathematics, (pre)medicine sequence, philosophy, physics, political science/government, psychology, religious studies, sociology, Spanish, (pre)veterinary medicine sequence.

## Worcester Polytechnic Institute

Actuarial science, aerospace engineering, applied mathematics, biochemistry, bioengineering, biology/biological sciences, biomedical engineering, biomedical sciences, biotechnology, business administration/commerce/management, cell biology, chemical engineering, chemistry, city/community/regional planning, civil engineering, computer engineering, computer information systems, computer management, computer science, construction engineering, construction management, (pre)dentistry sequence, economics, electrical engineering, electronics engineering, engineering (general), engineering and applied sciences, engineering design, engineering management, engineering mechanics, engineering physics, engineering sciences, environmental engineering, environmental sciences, fire protection engineering, fluid and thermal sciences, genetics, geophysical engineering, history of science, humanities, industrial engineering, information science, interdisciplinary studies, (pre)law sequence, management engineering, manufacturing engineering, materials engineering, materials sciences, mathematics, mechanical engineering, (pre)medicine sequence, metallurgical engineering, metallurgy, microbiology, molecular biology, music, natural sciences, nuclear engineering, nuclear physics, operations research, optics, physics, science, statistics, systems engineering, technical writing, technology and public affairs, transportation engineering, (pre)veterinary medicine sequence.

## Yale University

African studies, American studies, anthropology, applied mathematics, archaeology, architecture, art/fine arts, art history, Asian/Oriental studies, astronomy, biochemistry, biology/biological sciences, biophysics, black/African-American studies, chemical engineering, chemistry, Chinese, classics, comparative literature, computer science, East Asian studies, East European and Soviet studies, ecology, economics, electrical engineering, engineering mechanics, engineering sciences, English, European studies, film studies, French, geology, geophysics, German, Greek, history, history of science, humanities, interdisciplinary studies, Italian, Japanese, Judaic studies, Latin, Latin American studies, linguistics, literature, mathematics, mechanical engineering, music, Near and Middle Eastern studies, philosophy, physics, political science/government, psychology, religious studies, Russian, Russian and Slavic studies, sociology, Spanish, theater arts/drama, women's studies.

## Yeshiva University

Accounting, biology/biological sciences, business administration/commerce/management, chemistry, classics, communication, computer science, (pre)dentistry sequence, early childhood education, economics, education, elementary education, English, finance/banking, French, Hebrew, history, interdisciplinary studies, Judaic studies, (pre)law sequence, management information systems, marketing/retailing/merchandising, mathematics, (pre)medicine sequence, music, philosophy, physics, political science/government, psychology, sociology, speech pathology and audiology, speech/rhetoric/public address/debate, theater arts/drama.

# COMPETITIVE COLLEGES INDEXES

The indexes that follow show which of the competitive colleges share certain characteristics in which students are very often interested. To get in-depth information on any of the colleges in these indexes, turn back to the individual college listings in the Comparative Descriptions section.

## Colleges Costing $7000 or Less

| | |
|---|---|
| Deep Springs College | $0‡ |
| United States Air Force Academy | $0 |
| United States Coast Guard Academy | $0‡ |
| United States Merchant Marine Academy | $0 |
| United States Military Academy | $0‡ |
| United States Naval Academy | $0‡ |
| Texas A&M University (College Station) | $3952† |
| University of North Carolina at Asheville | $4828† |
| Georgia Southern University | $5082††‡ |
| North Carolina State University | $5124† |
| Oklahoma State University | $5187† |
| Webb Institute | $5250 |
| New Mexico Institute of Mining and Technology | $5284† |
| Cooper Union for the Advancement of Science and Art | $5288*‡ |
| University of Texas at Austin | $5343† |
| University of Oklahoma | $5396† |
| University of Kansas | $5422† |
| University of Tennessee, Knoxville | $5450† |
| University of Wisconsin–Madison | $5662† |
| University of Alabama in Huntsville | $5668† |
| New College of the University of South Florida | $5747† |
| University of North Carolina at Chapel Hill | $5769† |
| Shepherd College | $5884† |
| Brigham Young University | $5920 |
| The University of Iowa | $5923† |
| University of Georgia | $5952† |
| Louisiana State University and Agricultural and Mechanical College | $5955† |
| Iowa State University of Science and Technology | $5960††‡ |
| University of Florida | $6000† |
| Florida State University | $6083† |
| University of Arizona | $6124† |
| Northeast Missouri State University | $6138† |
| University of Colorado at Boulder | $6664† |
| Clemson University | $6830† |
| South Dakota School of Mines and Technology | $6840† |
| University of Utah | $6868† |
| Colorado State University | $6889† |
| Auburn University | $6948*† |
| Virginia Polytechnic Institute and State University | $6953† |
| Purdue University (West Lafayette) | $6984† |

*Full room and board not available; estimated cost figured in.
†Cost for in-state students.
‡Figures are for 1995–96.

## Colleges Reporting 50% or More Need-Based Financial Aid Recipients

| | |
|---|---|
| Hiram College | 95% |
| Wabash College | 93% |
| Clarkson University | 90% |
| Fordham University | 90% |
| Georgetown College | 90% |
| University of Dallas | 90% |
| Simpson College (IA) | 87% |
| Houghton College | 86% |
| College of St. Scholastica | 85% |
| Carroll College (MT) | 83% |
| Millikin University | 82% |
| Thomas Aquinas College | 82% |
| University of Pittsburgh at Johnstown | 82% |
| Wartburg College | 82% |
| Augustana College (IL) | 81% |
| Central College (IA) | 81% |
| Quincy University | 81% |
| Belmont University | 80% |
| La Salle University | 80% |
| Marietta College | 80% |
| Stevens Institute of Technology | 80% |
| University of Scranton | 80% |
| Ursinus College | 80% |
| Valparaiso University | 80% |
| Wells College | 80% |
| Knox College | 79% |
| Bennington College | 78% |
| Mills College | 78% |
| Nebraska Wesleyan University | 78% |
| LeTourneau University | 77% |
| Hamline University | 76% |
| Allegheny College | 75% |
| Coe College | 75% |
| Harvey Mudd College | 75% |
| Linfield College | 75% |
| Loyola University Chicago | 75% |
| Marlboro College | 75% |
| Northwestern College (IA) | 75% |
| Ripon College | 75% |
| The University of Iowa | 75% |
| Worcester Polytechnic Institute | 75% |
| Yeshiva University | 75% |
| Alma College | 74% |
| Baldwin-Wallace College | 74% |
| Albright College | 73% |
| Florida Institute of Technology | 73% |
| University of Tulsa | 73% |
| College of Saint Benedict | 72% |
| Concordia College (Moorhead, MN) | 72% |
| Illinois College | 72% |
| Lyon College | 72% |
| Ohio Northern University | 72% |
| Bellarmine College | 70% |
| Colorado School of Mines | 70% |
| Hofstra University | 70% |
| Le Moyne College | 70% |
| Macalester College | 70% |
| Saint John's University (MN) | 70% |
| Beloit College | 69% |
| Christian Brothers University | 69% |
| Goshen College | 69% |
| Pacific Lutheran University | 69% |
| University of Colorado at Boulder | 69% |
| Agnes Scott College | 68% |
| Bard College | 68% |
| Eugene Lang College, New School for Social Research | 68% |
| Grinnell College | 68% |
| Gustavus Adolphus College | 68% |
| Luther College | 68% |
| Simon's Rock College of Bard | 68% |
| Wittenberg University | 68% |
| Albertson College | 67% |
| Eckerd College | 67% |
| Lake Forest College | 67% |
| University of Miami | 67% |
| Whittier College | 67% |
| Monmouth College (IL) | 6? |
| New York University | |
| St. Lawrence University | |
| William Jewell College | |

| | | | |
|---|---|---|---|
| California Institute of Technology | 65% | Centre College | 55% |
| Calvin College | 65% | Drake University | 55% |
| Colgate University | 65% | Drew University | 55% |
| Earlham College | 65% | Hamilton College | 55% |
| Furman University | 65% | Hampshire College | 55% |
| Illinois Wesleyan University | 65% | Lafayette College | 55% |
| New College of the University of South Florida | 65% | Lewis & Clark College | 55% |
| Oglethorpe University | 65% | Ohio Wesleyan University | 55% |
| St. John's College (NM) | 65% | Rutgers, The State University of New Jersey, Rutgers | |
| St. Norbert College | 65% | College | 55% |
| State University of New York College at Geneseo | 65% | St. John's College (MD) | 55% |
| University of Puget Sound | 65% | Saint Mary's College of California | 55% |
| Virginia Polytechnic Institute and State University | 65% | Wellesley College | 55% |
| Willamette University | 65% | Bates College | 54% |
| Occidental College | 64% | Brandeis University | 54% |
| Providence College | 64% | Connecticut College | 54% |
| Santa Clara University | 64% | Kalamazoo College | 54% |
| Austin College | 63% | Massachusetts Institute of Technology | 54% |
| Clark University | 63% | Pomona College | 54% |
| College of the Holy Cross | 63% | Randolph-Macon Woman's College | 54% |
| Dickinson College | 63% | Wheaton College (IL) | 54% |
| Kentucky Wesleyan College | 63% | Columbia College (NY) | 53% |
| Whitman College | 63% | Creighton University | 53% |
| Rutgers, The State University of New Jersey, College of | | Pepperdine University (Malibu) | 53% |
| Pharmacy | 62% | Purdue University (West Lafayette) | 53% |
| St. Olaf College | 62% | Rutgers, The State University of New Jersey, College of | |
| Iowa State University of Science and Technology | 61% | Engineering | 53% |
| Siena College | 61% | Boston University | 52% |
| Southwestern University | 61% | Cedarville College | 52% |
| University of Southern California | 61% | Christendom College | 52% |
| Barnard College | 60% | Colorado State University | 52% |
| Birmingham-Southern College | 60% | Guilford College | 52% |
| Bucknell University | 60% | Lehigh University | 52% |
| Columbia University, School of Engineering and Applied | | Oberlin College | 52% |
| Science | 60% | Sarah Lawrence College | 52% |
| Elizabethtown College | 60% | Villanova University | 52% |
| Harding University | 60% | Franklin and Marshall College | 51% |
| Hillsdale College | 60% | Gettysburg College | 51% |
| Hope College | 60% | New Jersey Institute of Technology | 51% |
| Northwestern University | 60% | University of California, Berkeley | 51% |
| Rochester Institute of Technology | 60% | University of California, Riverside | 51% |
| State University of New York at Buffalo | 60% | University of Denver | 51% |
| Syracuse University | 60% | Wofford College | 51% |
| University of Notre Dame | 60% | Albert A. List College, Jewish Theological Seminary of | |
| University of Redlands | 60% | America | 50% |
| Washington College | 60% | The Colorado College | 50% |
| Albion College | 59% | Scripps College | 50% |
| Carleton College | 59% | University of Arizona | 50% |
| Stetson University | 59% | University of Delaware | 50% |
| University of New Hampshire (Durham) | 59% | University of Illinois at Urbana-Champaign | 50% |
| Catholic University of America | 58% | Williams College | 50% |
| Hobart College | 58% | | |
| Illinois Institute of Technology | 58% | | |
| Millsaps College | 58% | **Colleges Reporting 20% or More** | |
| William Smith College | 58% | **Non-Need-Based Financial Aid Recipients** | |
| Carnegie Mellon University | 57% | Oglethorpe University | 82% |
| ⸱⸱⸱Western Reserve University | 57% | Nebraska Wesleyan University | 79% |
| ⸱⸱⸱Kenna College | 57% | Presbyterian College | 78% |
| | 57% | Goshen College | 76% |
| ⸱⸱⸱s and Technology | 56% | Augustana College (IL) | 71% |
| | 56% | Carroll College (MT) | 71% |
| | 56% | Case Western Reserve University | 70% |
| | 56% | Quincy University | 68% |
| | 55% | Colorado Technical College | 60% |
| | | Illinois College | 60% |

433

| | |
|---|---|
| Northeast Missouri State University | 59% |
| Kentucky Wesleyan College | 51% |
| University of Missouri–Rolla | 51% |
| St. Mary's College of Maryland | 50% |
| University of Illinois at Urbana-Champaign | 50% |
| Catholic University of America | 48% |
| Maryville University of Saint Louis | 48% |
| Wabash College | 48% |
| Agnes Scott College | 46% |
| Centre College | 46% |
| Pepperdine University (Malibu) | 46% |
| Texas Christian University | 46% |
| Allegheny College | 45% |
| Kalamazoo College | 45% |
| University of Tulsa | 45% |
| Butler University | 44% |
| Transylvania University | 42% |
| DePauw University | 40% |
| Goucher College | 40% |
| Virginia Polytechnic Institute and State University | 40% |
| Shepherd College | 39% |
| Monmouth College (IL) | 37% |
| New Mexico Institute of Mining and Technology | 37% |
| University of Florida | 37% |
| Wake Forest University | 37% |
| Hiram College | 36% |
| Illinois Institute of Technology | 36% |
| Trenton State College | 36% |
| Harding University | 35% |
| Louisiana State University and Agricultural and Mechanical College | 35% |
| Rice University | 35% |
| University of Puget Sound | 35% |
| Centenary College of Louisiana | 34% |
| Creighton University | 33% |
| Drake University | 33% |
| Grove City College | 33% |
| Rutgers, The State University of New Jersey, College of Pharmacy | 33% |
| University of Richmond | 33% |
| Bradley University | 32% |
| Elizabethtown College | 32% |
| Ohio Northern University | 32% |
| Southern Methodist University | 32% |
| Christian Brothers University | 31% |
| Michigan Technological University | 31% |
| University of New Hampshire (Durham) | 31% |
| University of Oklahoma | 31% |
| University of Pittsburgh at Johnstown | 31% |
| William Jewell College | 31% |
| Bellarmine College | 30% |
| Birmingham-Southern College | 30% |
| Davidson College | 30% |
| Stetson University | 30% |
| Tulane University | 29% |
| College of William and Mary | 28% |
| Miami University | 28% |
| Austin College | 27% |
| Carnegie Mellon University | 27% |
| The George Washington University | 27% |
| Hampden-Sydney College | 27% |
| Rutgers, The State University of New Jersey, College of Engineering | 27% |

| | |
|---|---|
| Rutgers, The State University of New Jersey, Rutgers College | 27% |
| St. Norbert College | 27% |
| Sweet Briar College | 27% |
| Auburn University | 26% |
| Hope College | 26% |
| Rutgers, The State University of New Jersey, Douglass College | 26% |
| Alma College | 25% |
| Calvin College | 25% |
| Rhodes College | 25% |
| Trinity University | 25% |
| Valparaiso University | 25% |
| Yeshiva University | 25% |
| Christendom College | 24% |
| Denison University | 24% |
| Guilford College | 24% |
| James Madison University | 24% |
| Le Moyne College | 24% |
| Lyon College | 24% |
| Bennington College | 23% |
| Wofford College | 23% |
| Albion College | 22% |
| Cedarville College | 22% |
| College of St. Scholastica | 22% |
| Colorado State University | 22% |
| Millsaps College | 22% |
| Rutgers, The State University of New Jersey, Cook College | 22% |
| South Dakota School of Mines and Technology | 22% |
| Ohio Wesleyan University | 21% |
| Whitman College | 21% |
| Illinois Wesleyan University | 20% |
| Northwestern College (IA) | 20% |
| Rochester Institute of Technology | 20% |
| Rollins College | 20% |
| University of Dallas | 20% |
| University of Scranton | 20% |
| Washington College | 20% |

## Ten Largest Colleges

| | |
|---|---|
| Ohio State University | 49,542 |
| University of Texas at Austin | 47,957 |
| Texas A&M University (College Station) | 42,018 |
| Michigan State University | 40,254 |
| Pennsylvania State University University Park Campus | 38,294 |
| University of Florida | 38,277 |
| University of Wisconsin–Madison | 38,139 |
| University of Minnesota, Twin Cities Campus | 36,699 |
| University of Michigan (Ann Arbor) | 36,543 |
| University of Illinois at Urbana-Champaign | 36,191 |

## Ten Smallest Colleges

| | |
|---|---|
| Deep Springs College | 26 |
| Webb Institute | 75 |
| Christendom College | 173 |
| Thomas Aquinas College | 221 |
| Marlboro College | 270 |
| Simon's Rock College of Bard | 318 |
| Eugene Lang College, New School for Social Research | 363 |
| Wells College | 425 |
| Bennington College | 458 |
| Albert A. List College, Jewish Theological Seminary of America | 476 |

## Colleges Accepting Fewer than Half of Their Applicants

Amherst College
Bard College
Barnard College
Bates College
Boston College
Bowdoin College
Brown University
California Institute of Technology
Claremont McKenna College
Colby College
College of the Holy Cross
College of William and Mary
Columbia College (NY)
Columbia University, School of Engineering and Applied
    Science
Connecticut College
Cooper Union for the Advancement of Science and Art
Cornell University
Dartmouth College
Davidson College
Deep Springs College
Duke University
Emory University
Fisk University
Georgetown University
Grove City College
Harvard University
Harvey Mudd College
Haverford College
Johns Hopkins University
Lyon College
Massachusetts Institute of Technology
Middlebury College
New College of the University of South Florida
Northwestern University
Pomona College
Princeton University
Rice University
Rutgers, The State University of New Jersey, College of
    Pharmacy
Rutgers, The State University of New Jersey, Rutgers
    College
Spelman College
Stanford University
State University of New York at Binghamton
State University of New York College of Environmental
    Science and Forestry
Swarthmore College
Trenton State College
Tufts University
United States Air Force Academy
United States Coast Guard Academy
United States Merchant Marine Academy
United States Military Academy
United States Naval Academy
University of California, Berkeley
University of North Carolina at Chapel Hill
University of Notre Dame
University of Pennsylvania
University of Virginia
Wake Forest University
Washington and Lee University

Webb Institute
Wellesley College
Wesleyan University
Williams College
Yale University

## Colleges Requiring All Students to Take a Computer Course

Augustana College (SD)
Babson College
Bradley University
Butler University
California Institute of Technology
Clarkson University
College of Insurance
Colorado School of Mines
Colorado Technical College
Columbia University, School of Engineering and Applied
    Science
Fisk University
Florida Institute of Technology
GMI Engineering & Management Institute
Goucher College
Hamline University
Harding University
Harvey Mudd College
Illinois Institute of Technology
James Madison University
Juniata College
Kentucky Wesleyan College
La Salle University
LeTourneau University
Michigan Technological University
Milwaukee School of Engineering
Mount Union College
Nebraska Wesleyan University
New Jersey Institute of Technology
New Mexico Institute of Mining and Technology
Northeast Missouri State University
Ohio Northern University
Polytechnic University, Brooklyn Campus
Polytechnic University, Farmingdale Campus
Rose-Hulman Institute of Technology
Rutgers, The State University of New Jersey, College of
    Engineering
Rutgers, The State University of New Jersey, Cook
    College
Scripps College
Shepherd College
Simon's Rock College of Bard
South Dakota School of Mines and Technology
Spelman College
State University of New York Maritime College
Stevens Institute of Technology
Taylor University
Texas A&M University (College Station)
Trinity University
United States Air Force Academy
United States Coast Guard Academy
United States Merchant Marine Academy
United States Military Academy
United States Naval Academy
University of Connecticut (Storrs)
University of Denver

University of Detroit Mercy
University of Minnesota, Morris
University of Missouri–Rolla
Webb Institute

## Single-Sex Colleges

Agnes Scott College                                                W
Barnard College                                                    W
Bryn Mawr College                                                  W
College of Saint Benedict                                          W
Deep Springs College                                               M
Hampden-Sydney College                                             M
Hobart College                                                     M
Mills College                                                      W
Morehouse College                                                  M
Mount Holyoke College                                              W
Randolph-Macon Woman's College                                     W
Rutgers, The State University of New Jersey, Douglass
   College                                                         W
Saint John's University (MN)                                       M
Saint Mary's College (IN)                                          W
Scripps College                                                    W
Smith College                                                      W
Spelman College                                                    W
Sweet Briar College                                                W
Wabash College                                                     M
Wellesley College                                                  W
Wells College                                                      W
William Smith College                                              W

## Predominantly African-American Colleges

Fisk University
Morehouse College
Spelman College

## Colleges with Religious Affiliation

### Baptist
Baylor University
Belmont University
Bethel College (MN)
Cedarville College
Georgetown College
Linfield College
Samford University
Union University
University of Richmond
William Jewell College

### Brethren
Elizabethtown College
Messiah College

### Christian Church (Disciples of Christ)
Hiram College
Texas Christian University
Transylvania University

### Churches of Christ
David Lipscomb University
Harding University
Pepperdine University (Malibu)

### Episcopal
Hobart College
University of the South

### Friends
Earlham College
Guilford College

### Interdenominational
Illinois College

### Jewish
Albert A. List College, Jewish Theological Seminary of
   America

### Latter-day Saints (Mormon)
Brigham Young University

### Lutheran
Augustana College (IL)
Augustana College (SD)
Concordia College (Moorhead, MN)
Gustavus Adolphus College
Luther College
Muhlenberg College
Pacific Lutheran University
St. Olaf College
Valparaiso University
Wartburg College
Wittenberg University

### Mennonite
Goshen College

### Methodist
Albion College
Albright College
Allegheny College
American University
Baldwin-Wallace College
Birmingham-Southern College
Centenary College of Louisiana
Cornell College
DePauw University
Drew University
Duke University
Emory University
Hamline University
Hendrix College
Kentucky Wesleyan College
Millsaps College
Mount Union College
Nebraska Wesleyan University
North Central College
Ohio Northern University
Ohio Wesleyan University
Randolph-Macon Woman's College
Simpson College (IA)
Southern Methodist University
Southwestern University
University of Evansville
Willamette University
Wofford College

### Nondenominational
LeTourneau University
Wheaton College (IL)

### Presbyterian
Agnes Scott College
Alma College
Austin College
Buena Vista College

Coe College
The College of Wooster
Davidson College
Eckerd College
Grove City College
Hampden-Sydney College
Lafayette College
Lyon College
Macalester College
Millikin University
Monmouth College (IL)
Presbyterian College
Rhodes College
Trinity University
University of Tulsa

**Reformed Churches**
Calvin College
Central College (IA)
Hope College
Northwestern College (IA)

**Roman Catholic**
Bellarmine College
Boston College
Carroll College (MT)
Catholic University of America
Christendom College
Christian Brothers University
College of Saint Benedict
College of St. Scholastica
College of the Holy Cross
Creighton University
DePaul University
Fairfield University
Fordham University
Georgetown University
John Carroll University
La Salle University
Le Moyne College
Loyola College
Loyola University Chicago
Marquette University
Providence College
Quincy University
Rockhurst College
Saint John's University (MN)
Saint Joseph's University
Saint Louis University
Saint Mary's College (IN)
Saint Mary's College of California
St. Norbert College
Santa Clara University
Siena College
Thomas Aquinas College
University of Dallas
University of Detroit Mercy
University of Notre Dame
University of Scranton
Villanova University

**United Church of Christ**
Fisk University
Ursinus College

**Wesleyan**
Houghton College

**Public Colleges**
Auburn University
Clemson University
College of William and Mary
Colorado School of Mines
Colorado State University
Florida State University
Georgia Institute of Technology
Georgia Southern University
Iowa State University of Science and Technology
James Madison University
Louisiana State University and Agricultural and
    Mechanical College
Mary Washington College
Miami University
Michigan State University
Michigan Technological University
New College of the University of South Florida
New Jersey Institute of Technology
New Mexico Institute of Mining and Technology
North Carolina State University
Northeast Missouri State University
Ohio State University
Ohio University
Oklahoma State University
Pennsylvania State University University Park Campus
Purdue University (West Lafayette)
Rutgers, The State University of New Jersey, College of
    Engineering
Rutgers, The State University of New Jersey, College of
    Pharmacy
Rutgers, The State University of New Jersey, Cook
    College
Rutgers, The State University of New Jersey, Douglass
    College
Rutgers, The State University of New Jersey, Rutgers
    College
St. Mary's College of Maryland
Shepherd College
South Dakota School of Mines and Technology
State University of New York at Binghamton
State University of New York at Buffalo
State University of New York College at Geneseo
State University of New York College of Environmental
    Science and Forestry
State University of New York Maritime College
Texas A&M University (College Station)
Trenton State College
United States Air Force Academy
United States Coast Guard Academy
United States Merchant Marine Academy
United States Military Academy
United States Naval Academy
University at Albany, State University of New York
University of Alabama in Huntsville
University of Arizona
University of California, Berkeley
University of California, Davis
University of California, Irvine
University of California, Los Angeles
University of California, Riverside
University of California, San Diego
University of California, Santa Barbara
University of California, Santa Cruz

University of Colorado at Boulder
University of Connecticut (Storrs)
University of Delaware
University of Florida
University of Georgia
University of Illinois at Urbana-Champaign
The University of Iowa
University of Kansas
University of Maryland College Park
University of Massachusetts Amherst
University of Michigan (Ann Arbor)
University of Michigan–Dearborn
University of Minnesota, Morris
University of Minnesota, Twin Cities Campus
University of Missouri–Columbia
University of Missouri–Kansas City
University of Missouri–Rolla
University of New Hampshire (Durham)
University of North Carolina at Asheville
University of North Carolina at Chapel Hill
University of Oklahoma
University of Pittsburgh
University of Pittsburgh at Johnstown
University of Tennessee, Knoxville
University of Texas at Austin
University of Utah
University of Vermont
University of Virginia
University of Washington
University of Wisconsin–Madison
Virginia Polytechnic Institute and State University

## Colleges Reporting 70% or More Students Completing a Degree

| | |
|---|---|
| Colby College | 97% |
| Harvard University | 97% |
| Duke University | 95% |
| Princeton University | 94% |
| College of the Holy Cross | 93% |
| University of Notre Dame | 93% |
| Williams College | 93% |
| Brown University | 92% |
| Emory University | 92% |
| Haverford College | 92% |
| Providence College | 92% |
| Stanford University | 91% |
| Cornell University | 90% |
| University of Virginia | 90% |
| Vassar College | 90% |
| Carleton College | 89% |
| Massachusetts Institute of Technology | 89% |
| Pomona College | 89% |
| Bates College | 88% |
| Bucknell University | 88% |
| Colgate University | 88% |
| Connecticut College | 88% |
| Washington and Lee University | 88% |
| Hamilton College | 87% |
| Kenyon College | 87% |
| Union College (NY) | 87% |
| Davidson College | 86% |
| Dickinson College | 86% |
| Johns Hopkins University | 86% |
| Lafayette College | 86% |

| | |
|---|---|
| Smith College | 86% |
| Barnard College | 85% |
| Rice University | 85% |
| University of Pennsylvania | 85% |
| Wake Forest University | 85% |
| Washington University | 85% |
| Babson College | 84% |
| Bryn Mawr College | 84% |
| Lehigh University | 83% |
| University of Michigan (Ann Arbor) | 83% |
| University of North Carolina at Chapel Hill | 83% |
| University of Richmond | 83% |
| University of Scranton | 83% |
| Wheaton College (IL) | 83% |
| Grinnell College | 82% |
| Harvey Mudd College | 82% |
| Presbyterian College | 82% |
| United States Military Academy | 82% |
| William Smith College | 82% |
| Claremont McKenna College | 81% |
| Furman University | 81% |
| St. Olaf College | 81% |
| Santa Clara University | 81% |
| Vanderbilt University | 81% |
| Gettysburg College | 80% |
| James Madison University | 80% |
| Juniata College | 80% |
| Pitzer College | 80% |
| University of the South | 80% |
| Brandeis University | 79% |
| The Colorado College | 79% |
| Grove City College | 79% |
| St. Lawrence University | 79% |
| Siena College | 79% |
| University of Chicago | 79% |
| Bard College | 78% |
| DePauw University | 78% |
| Fordham University | 78% |
| Hobart College | 78% |
| Le Moyne College | 78% |
| Saint Mary's College (IN) | 78% |
| State University of New York at Binghamton | 78% |
| Denison University | 77% |
| Franklin and Marshall College | 77% |
| Gustavus Adolphus College | 77% |
| Miami University | 77% |
| University of Wisconsin–Madison | 77% |
| Hillsdale College | 76% |
| Macalester College | 76% |
| Skidmore College | 76% |
| State University of New York College at Geneseo | 76% |
| University of Illinois at Urbana-Champaign | 76% |
| Wofford College | 76% |
| Catholic University of America | 75% |
| Illinois Wesleyan University | 75% |
| John Carroll University | 75% |
| Marquette University | 75% |
| Rollins College | 75% |
| Saint Joseph's University | 75% |
| Sarah Lawrence College | 75% |
| Lawrence University | 74% |
| Luther College | 74% |
| St. Norbert College | 74% |
| Allegheny College | 73% |

| | | | |
|---|---|---|---|
| Augustana College (IL) | 73% | Tulane University | 72% |
| Cooper Union for the Advancement of Science and Art | 73% | Wittenberg University | 72% |
| Hiram College | 73% | Earlham College | 71% |
| Knox College | 73% | Hampden-Sydney College | 71% |
| Mary Washington College | 73% | New York University | 71% |
| Southwestern University | 73% | Ohio Wesleyan University | 71% |
| University of California, Berkeley | 73% | St. John's College (NM) | 71% |
| University of Rochester | 73% | Webb Institute | 71% |
| University of Vermont | 73% | Willamette University | 71% |
| Ursinus College | 73% | Albright College | 70% |
| Whitman College | 73% | Birmingham-Southern College | 70% |
| Alma College | 72% | Lewis & Clark College | 70% |
| Clarkson University | 72% | Taylor University | 70% |
| Drew University | 72% | University of California, Irvine | 70% |
| Spelman College | 72% | Wabash College | 70% |
| Thomas Aquinas College | 72% | | |

# Geographical Index of Colleges

| | | | | |
|---|---|---|---|---|

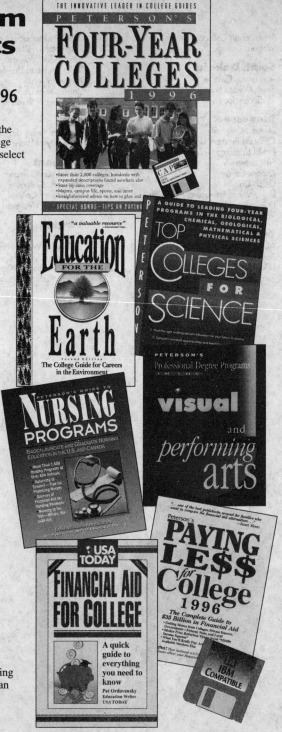
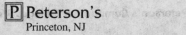